MW00994217

MUSICAL MATHEMATICS

ON THE ART AND SCIENCE OF ACOUSTIC INSTRUMENTS

MUSICAL MATHEMATICS

ON THE ART AND SCIENCE OF ACOUSTIC INSTRUMENTS

Text and Illustrations

by Cris Forster

CHRONICLE BOOKS
SAN FRANCISCO

Copyright © 2010 by Cristiano M.L. Forster

All Rights Reserved. No part of this book may be reproduced in any form without written permission from the publisher.

Library of Congress Cataloging-in-Publication Data available.

ISBN: 978-0-8118-7407-6

Manufactured in the United States.

All royalties from the sale of this book go directly to the Chrysalis Foundation, a public 501(c)3 nonprofit arts and education foundation.

www.chrysalis-foundation.org

Photo Credits:
Will Gullette, Plates 1–12, 14–16.
Norman Seeff, Plate 13.

10 9 8 7 6 5 4 3 2 1

Chronicle Books LLC
680 Second Street
San Francisco, California 94107

www.chroniclebooks.com

In Memory of Page Smith

my enduring teacher

And to Douglas Monsour

our constant friend

I would like to thank the following individuals and foundations for their generous contributions in support of the writing, designing, and typesetting of this work:

Peter Boyer and Terry Gamble-Boyer
The family of Jackson Vanfleet Brown
Thomas Driscoll and Nancy Quinn
Marie-Louise Forster
David Holloway
Jack Jensen and Cathleen O'Brien
James and Deborah Knapp
Ariano Lembi, Aidan and Yuko Fruth-Lembi
Douglas and Jeanne Monsour
Tim O'Shea and Peggy Arent
Fay and Edith Strange
Charles and Helene Wright

Ayrshire Foundation
Chrysalis Foundation

The jewel that we find, we stoop and take't,
Because we see it; but what we do not see
We tread upon, and never think of it.

W. Shakespeare

CONTENTS

CHAPTER 12   ORIGINAL INSTRUMENTS   788

Stringed Instruments:

Percussion Instruments:

Friction Instrument:

Wind Instruments:

CHAPTER 13   BUILDING A LITTLE CANON   834

Foreword

I met Cris Forster more than thirty years ago. Shortly thereafter, I saw him perform *Song of Myself*, his setting of Walt Whitman poems from *Leaves of Grass*. His delivery was moving and effective. Several of the poems were accompanied by his playing on unique instruments — one an elegant box with many steel strings and moveable bridges, a bit like a koto in concept; the other had a big wheel with strings like spokes from offset hubs, and he rotated the wheel as he played and intoned the poetry. I was fascinated.

Since that time, Cris has built several more instruments of his own design. Each shows exquisite care in conception and impeccable craftsmanship in execution. And of course, they are a delight to hear. Part of what makes them sound so good is his deep understanding of how acoustic musical instruments work, and part is due to his skill in working the materials to his exacting standards.

But another important aspect of their sound, and indeed one of the main reasons Cris could not settle for standard instruments, is that his music uses scales and harmonies that are not found in the standard Western system of intonation (with each octave divided into twelve equal semitones, called equal temperament). Rather, his music employs older notions of consonance, which reach back as far as ancient Greek music and to other cultures across the globe, based on what is called just intonation. Here, the musical intervals that make up the scales and chords are those that occur naturally in the harmonic series of overtones, in stretched flexible strings, and in organ pipes, for example.

In just intonation, the octave is necessarily divided into unequal parts. In comparison to equal temperament, the harmonies of just intonation have been described as smoother, sweeter, and/or more powerful. Many theorists consider just intonation to be the standard of comparison for consonant intervals. There has been a resurgence of interest in just intonation since the latter part of the twentieth century, spurred by such pioneers as Harry Partch and Lou Harrison. Even so, the community of just intonation composers remains comparatively quite small, and the subset of those who employ only acoustic instruments is much smaller still. I know of no other living composer who has created such a large and varied ensemble of high-quality just intoned acoustical instruments, and a body of music for them, as Cris Forster.

Doing what he has done is not easy, far from it. The long process of developing his instruments has required endless experimentation and careful measurement, as well as intense study of the literature on acoustics of musical instruments. In this way Cris has developed deep and rich knowledge of how to design and build instruments that really work. Also, in the service of his composing, Cris has studied the history of intonation practices, not only in the Western tradition, but around the world.

This book is his generous offering of all that hard-earned knowledge, presented as clearly as he can make it, for all of you who have an interest in acoustic musical instrument design and/or musical scales over time and space. The unifying theme is how mathematics applies to music, in both the acoustics of resonant instruments and the analysis of musical scales. The emphasis throughout is to show how to use these mathematical tools, without requiring any background in higher mathematics; all that is required is the ability to do arithmetic on a pocket calculator, and to follow Cris' clear step-by-step instructions and examples. Any more advanced mathematical tools required, such as logarithms, are carefully explained with many illustrative examples.

The first part of the book contains practical information on how to design and build musical instruments, starting from first principles of vibrating sound sources of various kinds. The ideas are explained clearly and thoroughly. Many beautiful figures have been carefully conceived to illuminate the concepts. And when Cris gives, say, formulas for designing flutes, it's not just something he read in a book somewhere (though he has carefully studied many books); rather, you can be sure it is something he has tried out: he knows it works from direct experience. While some of this information can be found (albeit in a less accessible form) in other books on musical acoustics, other information appears nowhere else. For example, Cris developed a method for tuning the overtones of marimba bars that results in a powerful, unique tone not found in commercial instruments. Step-by-step instructions are given for applying this technique (see Chapter 6). Another innovation is Cris' introduction of a new unit of mass, the "mica," that greatly simplifies calculations using lengths measured in inches. And throughout Cris gives careful explanations, in terms of physical principles, that make sense based on one's physical intuition and experience.

The latter part of the book surveys the development of musical notions of consonance and scale construction. Chapter 10 traces Western ideas about intonation, from Pythagoras finding number in harmony, through "meantone" and then "well-temperament" in the time of J.S. Bach, up to modern equal temperament. The changing notions of which intervals were considered consonant when, and by whom, make a fascinating story. Chapter 11 looks at the largely independent (though sometimes parallel) development of musical scales and tunings in various Eastern cultures, including China, India, and Indonesia, as well as Persian, Arabian, and Turkish musical traditions. As far as possible, Cris relies on original sources, to which he brings his own analysis and explication. To find all of these varied scales compared and contrasted in a single work is unique in my experience.

The book concludes with two short chapters on specific original instruments. One introduces the innovative instruments Cris has designed and built for his music. Included are many details of construction and materials, and also scores of his work that demonstrate his notation for the instruments. The last chapter encourages the reader (with explicit plans) to build a simple stringed instrument (a "canon") with completely adjustable tuning, to directly explore the tunings discussed in the book. In this way, the reader can follow in the tradition of Ptolemy, of learning about music through direct experimentation, as has Cris Forster.

David R. Canright, Ph.D.
Del Rey Oaks, California
January 2010

Introduction and Acknowledgments

In simplest terms, human beings identify musical instruments by two aural characteristics: a particular kind of sound or timbre, and a particular kind of scale or tuning. To most listeners, these two aspects of musical sound do not vary. However, unlike the constants of nature — such as gravitational acceleration on earth, or the speed of sound in air — which we cannot change, the constants of music — such as string, percussion, and wind instruments — are subject to change. A creative investigation into musical sound inevitably leads to the subject of musical mathematics, and to a reexamination of the meaning of variables.

The first chapter entitled "Mica Mass" addresses an exceptionally thorny subject: the derivation of a unit of mass based on an inch constant for acceleration. This unit is intended for builders who measure wood, metal, and synthetic materials in inches. For example, with the mica unit, builders of string instruments can calculate tension in pounds-force, or lbf, without first converting the diameter of a string from inches to feet. Similarly, builders of tuned bar percussion instruments who know the modulus of elasticity of a given material in pounds-force per square inch, or lbf/in^2, need only the mass density in $mica/in^3$ to calculate the speed of sound in the material in inches per second; a simple substitution of this value into another equation gives the mode frequencies of uncut bars.

Chapters 2–4 explore many physical, mathematical, and musical aspects of strings. In Chapter 3, I distinguish between four different types of ratios: ancient length ratios, modern length ratios, frequency ratios, and interval ratios. Knowledge of these ratios is essential to Chapters 10 and 11. Many writers are unaware of the crucial distinction between ancient length ratios and frequency ratios. Consequently, when they attempt to define arithmetic and harmonic divisions of musical intervals based on frequency ratios, the results are diametrically opposed to those based on ancient length ratios. Such confusion leads to anachronisms, and renders the works of theorists like Ptolemy, Al-Fārābī, Ibn Sīnā, and Zarlino incomprehensible.

Chapter 5 investigates the mechanical interactions between piano strings and soundboards, and explains why the large physical dimensions of modern pianos are not conducive to explorations of alternate tuning systems.

Chapters 6 and 7 discuss the theory and practice of tuning marimba bars and resonators. The latter chapter is essential to Chapter 8, which examines a sequence of equations for the placement of tone holes on concert flutes and simple flutes.

Chapter 9 covers logarithms, and the modern cent unit. This chapter serves as an introduction to calculating scales and tunings discussed in Chapters 10 and 11.

In summary, this book is divided into three parts. (1) In Chapters 1–9, I primarily examine various vibrating systems found in musical instruments; I also focus on how builders can customize their work by understanding the functions of variables in mathematical equations. (2) In Chapter 10, I discuss scale theories and tuning practices in ancient Greece, and during the Renaissance and Enlightenment in Europe. Some modern interpretations of these theories are explained as well. In Chapter 11, I describe scale theories and tuning practices in Chinese, Indonesian, and Indian music, and in Arabian, Persian, and Turkish music. For Chapters 10 and 11, I consistently studied original texts in modern translations. I also translated passages in treatises by Ptolemy, Al-Kindī, the Ikhwān al-Ṣafā, Ibn Sīnā, Stifel, and Zarlino from German into English; and in collaboration with two contributors, I participated in translating portions of works by Al-Fārābī, Ibn Sīnā, Ṣafī Al-Dīn, and Al-Jurjānī from French into English. These translations reveal that all the abovementioned theorists employ the language of ancient length ratios. (3) Finally, Chapters 12 and 13 recount musical instruments I have built and rebuilt since 1975.

I would like to acknowledge the assistance and encouragement I received from Dr. David R. Canright, associate professor of mathematics at the Naval Postgraduate School in Monterey,

California. David's unique understanding of mathematics, physics, and music provided the foundation for many conversations throughout the ten years I spent writing this book. His mastery of differential equations enabled me to better understand dispersion in strings, and simple harmonic motion of air particles in resonators. In Section 4.6, David's equation for the effective length of stiff strings is central to the study of inharmonicity; and in Section 6.7, David's figure, which shows the effects of two restoring forces on the geometry of bar elements, sheds new light on the physics of vibrating bars. Furthermore, David's plots of compression and rarefaction pulses inspired numerous figures in Chapter 7. Finally, we also had extensive discussions on Newton's laws. I am very grateful to David for his patience and contributions.

Heartfelt thanks go to my wife, Heidi Forster. Heidi studied, corrected, and edited myriad versions of the manuscript. Also, in partnership with the highly competent assistance of professional translator Cheryl M. Buskirk, Hcidi did most of thc work translating extensive passages from *La Musique Arabe* into English. To achieve this accomplishment, she mastered the often intricate verbal language of ratios. Heidi also assisted me in transcribing the Indonesian and Persian musical scores in Chapter 11, and transposed the traditional piano score of "The Letter" in Chapter 12. Furthermore, she rendered invaluable services during all phases of book production by acting as my liaison with the editorial staff at Chronicle Books. Finally, when the writing became formidable, she became my sparring partner and helped me through the difficult process of restoring my focus. I am very thankful to Heidi for all her love, friendship, and support.

I would also like to express my appreciation to Dr. John H. Chalmers. Since 1976, John has generously shared his vast knowledge of scale theory with me. His mathematical methods and techniques have enabled me to better understand many historical texts, especially those of the ancient Greeks. And John's scholarly book *Divisions of the Tetrachord* has furthered my appreciation for world tunings.

I am very grateful to Lawrence Saunders, M.A. in ethnomusicology, for reading Chapters 3, 9, 10, and 11, and for suggesting several technical improvements.

Finally, I would like to thank Will Gullette for his twelve masterful color plates of the Original Instruments and String Winder, plus three additional plates. Will's skill and tenacity have illuminated this book in ways that words cannot convey.

Cris Forster
San Francisco, California
January 2010

TONE NOTATION

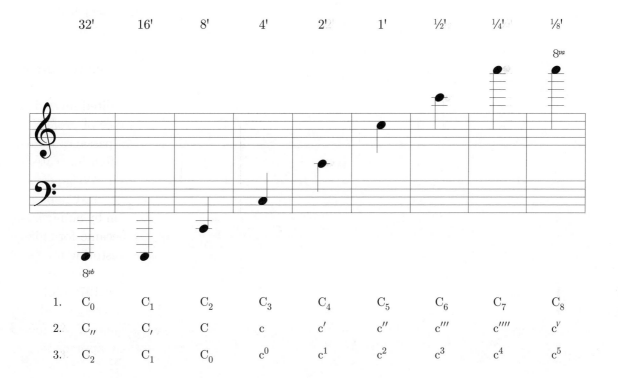

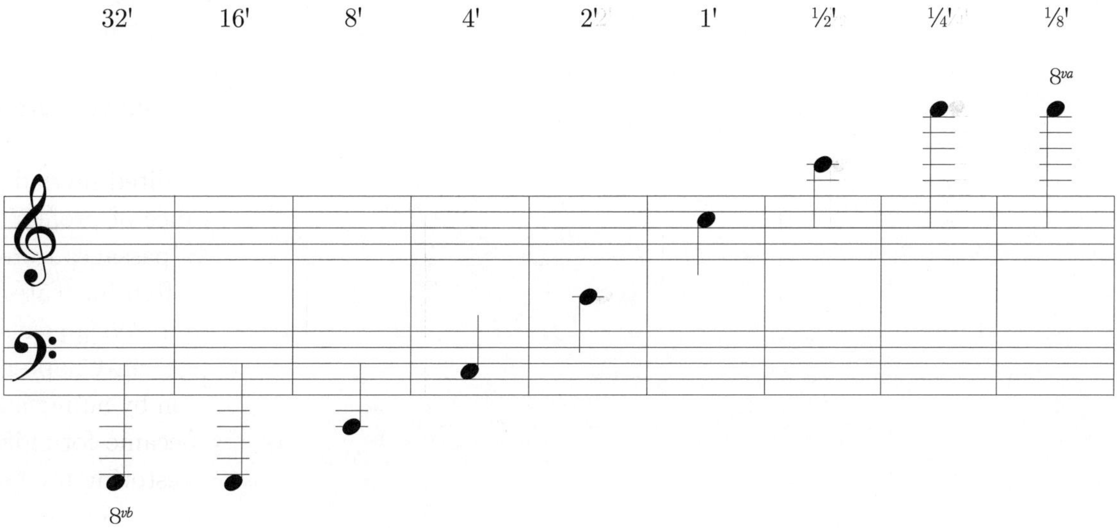

1.	C_0	C_1	C_2	C_3	C_4	C_5	C_6	C_7	C_8
2.	$C_{\prime\prime}$	$C_{\prime}$	C	c	c'	c''	c'''	c''''	c^V
3.	C_2	C_1	C_0	c^0	c^1	c^2	c^3	c^4	c^5

1. American System, used throughout this text.
2. Helmholtz System.
3. German System.

LIST OF SYMBOLS

Latin

12-TET	12-tone equal temperament
a	Acceleration; in/s^2
a.l.r.	Ancient length ratio; dimensionless
B	Bending stiffness of bar; lbf·in^2, or mica·in^3/s^2
B'	Bending stiffness of plate; lbf·in, or mica·in^2/s^2
B_A	Adiabatic bulk modulus; psi, lbf/in^2, or mica/(in·s^2)
B_I	Isothermal bulk modulus; psi, lbf/in^2, or mica/(in·s^2)
b	Width; in
C_n	Mode cent; dimensionless
¢	Cent, 1/100 of a "semitone," or 1/1200 of an "octave"; dimensionless
$\bar{¢}$	Coefficient of inharmonicity of string; cent
c_B	Bending wave speed; in/s
c_L	Longitudinal wave speed, or speed of sound; in/s
c_T	Transverse wave speed; in/s
c.d.	Common difference of an arithmetic progression; dimensionless
c.r.	Common ratio of a geometric progression; dimensionless
cps	Cycle per second; 1/s
D	Outside diameter; in
D_i	Inside diameter of wound string; in
D_m	Middle diameter of wound string; in
D_o	Outside diameter of wound string; in
D_w	Wrap wire diameter of wound string; in
d	Inside diameter, or distance; in
E	Young's modulus of elasticity; psi, lbf/in^2, or mica/(in·s^2)
F	Frequency; cps
F_c	Critical frequency; cps
F_n	Resonant frequency; cps
$\bar{F}_n$	Inharmonic mode frequency of string; cps
f	Force; lbf, or mica·in/s^2
f.r.	Frequency ratio; dimensionless
g	Gravitational acceleration; 386.0886 in/s^2
h	Height, or thickness; in
I	Area moment of inertia; in^4
i.r.	Interval ratio; dimensionless
J	Stiffness parameter of string; dimensionless
K	Radius of gyration; in
k	Spring constant; lbf/in, or mica/s^2
L	Length; in, cm, or mm
ℓ_M	Multiple loop length of string; in
ℓ_S	Single loop length of string; in
l.r.	Length ratio; dimensionless
lbf	Pounds-force; mica·in/s^2
lbm	Pounds-mass; 0.00259008 mica

$M/u.a.$	Mass per unit area; mica/in^2, or lbf·s^2/in^3
$M/u.l.$	Mass per unit length; mica/in, or lbf·s^2/in^2
m	Mass; mica, or lbf·s^2/in
n	Mode number, or harmonic number; any positive integer
P	Pressure; psi, lbf/in^2, or mica/(in·s^2)
p	Excess acoustic pressure; psi, lbf/in^2, or mica/(in·s^2)
psi	Pounds-force per square inch; lbf/in^2, or mica/(in·s^2)
q	Bar parameter; dimensionless
R	Ideal gas constant; in·lbf/(mica·°R), or in^2/(s^2·°R)
r	Radius; in
S	Surface area; in^2
SHM	Simple harmonic motion
T	Tension; lbf, or mica·in/s^2
T_{A}	Absolute temperature; dimensionless
t	Time; s
U	Volume velocity; in^3/s
u	Particle velocity; in/s
V	Volume; in^3
v	Phase velocity; in/s
W	Weight density, or weight per unit volume; lbf/in^3, or mica/(in^2·s^2)
w	Weight; lbf, or mica·in/s^2
Y_{A}	Acoustic admittance; in^4·s/mica
Z_{A}	Acoustic impedance; mica/(in^4·s)
Z_{r}	Acoustic impedance of room; mica/(in^4·s)
Z_{t}	Acoustic impedance of tube; mica/(in^4·s)
Z_{M}	Mechanical impedance; mica/s
Z_{b}	Mechanical impedance of soundboard; mica/s
Z_{p}	Mechanical impedance of plate; mica/s
Z_{s}	Mechanical impedance of string; mica/s
Z_{R}	Radiation impedance; mica/s
Z_{a}	Radiation impedance of air; mica/s
z	Specific acoustic impedance; mica/(in^2·s)
z_{a}	Characteristic impedance of air; 0.00153 mica/(in^2·s)

Greek

$\mathit{\Delta}$	Correction coefficient, or end correction coefficient; dimensionless
$\Delta\ell$	Correction, or end correction; in, cm, or mm
δ	Departure of tempered ratio from just ratio; cent
γ	Ratio of specific heat; dimensionless
θ	Angle; degree
κ	Conductivity; in
$\mathit{\Lambda}$	Bridged canon string length; in
$\mathit{\Lambda}_{\mathrm{A}}$	Arithmetic mean string length; in
$\mathit{\Lambda}_{\mathrm{G}}$	Geometric mean string length; in
$\mathit{\Lambda}_{\mathrm{H}}$	Harmonic mean string length; in

λ	Wavelength; in
λ_{B}	Bending wavelength; in
λ_{L}	Longitudinal wavelength; in
λ_{T}	Transverse wavelength; in
μ	Poisson's ratio; dimensionless
Π	Fretted guitar string length; mm
π	Pi; ≈ 3.1416
ρ	Mass density, or mass per unit volume; mica/in^3, or lbf·s^2/in^4
τ	Period, or second per cycle; s

1 / MICA MASS

There is nothing obvious about the subject of mass. For thousands of years mass remained undefined until Isaac Newton (1642–1727) published his *Principia Mathematica* in 1687. The mass density of a material as signified by the lowercase of the Greek letter *rho* (ρ) appears in all acoustic frequency equations and in many other equations as well. Unfortunately, the concept of mass persists in a shroud of unnecessary complexity and confusion. This is especially true for those who measure distances in inches. Unlike the metric system, which has two consistent mass-distance standards (the kilogram-meter combination and the gram-centimeter combination), the English system has only one consistent mass-distance standard: the slug-foot combination. Not only is the latter standard totally inadequate for musical instrument builders, but countless scientists and engineers who use inches have acknowledged the need for a second English mass unit. (See Note 19.) Although no one has named such a unit, many designers and engineers do their calculations as though it exists. This practice is completely unacceptable. Reason tells us that a measurement in inches should be just as admissible as a measurement in meters, centimeters, or feet. And yet, when someone substitutes inch measurements into an equation that also requires a mass density value, they cannot calculate the equation without a specialized understanding for an undefined and unnamed mass unit. To dispense with this practice, the following chapter defines and names a new unit of mass called *mica*. Throughout this book we will use a consistent mica-inch standard (see Equation 1.15) designed to make frequency and other related calculations easily manageable.

Readers not interested in the subject of mass may simply disregard this chapter. If all your distance measurements are in inches, turn to Appendix C or E, find the mass density of a material in the mica/in^3 column, substitute this value for ρ into the equation, and calculate the result. This chapter is for those interested in gaining a fundamental understanding of mass. In Part I, we will discuss principles of force, mass, and acceleration, and in Part II, mica mass definitions, mica unit derivations, and sample calculations. Although some of this material may seem inappropriate to discussions on the acoustics of musical instruments, readers with a thorough understanding of mass will avoid many conceptual and computational errors.

Part I

PRINCIPLES OF FORCE, MASS, AND ACCELERATION

~ 1.1 ~

All musical systems such as strings, bars, membranes, plates, and columns of air vibrate because they have (1) an elastic property called a restoring force, and (2) an inertial property called a mass. When we pluck a string, or strike a marimba bar, we apply an initial force to the object that accelerates it from stillness to motion. Our applied force causes a displacement, or a small distortion of the object's original shape. Because the string has tension, and because the bar has stiffness, a restoring force responds to this displacement and returns the object to its equilibrium position. (Gently displace and release a telephone cord, and note how this force restores the cord to the equilibrium position. Now try the same experiment with a piece of paper or a ruler.) However, because the string and the bar each have a mass, the motion of the object continues beyond this position. Mass causes the object to overshoot the equilibrium position, which in turn causes another distortion and a subsequent reactivation of the restoring force, etc. To understand in greater detail how force and mass interact to produce musical vibrations,[1] we turn to Newton's first law of motion.

According to Newton's first law, (1) an object at rest remains at rest, and in the absence of friction, (2) an object in motion remains in motion, unless acted on by a force. This law states that all objects have inertia; that is, all objects have a resistance to a change in either the *magnitude* or the *direction* of motion. (1) An object without motion will not move unless a force acts to cause motion. (2) An object in motion will not speed up, slow down, stop, or change direction unless a force acts to cause such changes. Newton quantified this inertial property of matter and called it the *mass* (m) of an object. Therefore, an object's mass is a measure of its inertia.

Refer now to Figure 1.1 and consider the motion of a slowly vibrating rubber cord. If we pluck such a cord (or any musical instrument string), it will snap back to its equilibrium position, but it will not simply stop there. (a) As we displace the cord upward, tension (the *elastic property* of the cord) acts as a restoring force (f) that pulls the cord in a downward direction. (b) After we release the cord and as it moves toward the equilibrium position, its particle velocity[2] (u) increases while the restoring force decreases.[3] During this time, tension is acting in a downward direction and the cord is moving downward. (c) Upon reaching the equilibrium position, the cord has maximum velocity for the instant that the restoring force = 0, and therefore the cord's acceleration = 0. According to Newton's first law, the cord continues to move past this position because the cord's mass (the *inertial property* of the cord) will not stop moving, or change direction, unless a force acts to cause such changes.[4] (d) Once through the equilibrium position, the restoring force reverses direction. Consequently, the velocity decreases because the restoring force is working in the opposite direction of the cord's motion. During this time, tension acts in an upward direction as the cord moves downward. (e) At a critical moment when the restoring force is at a maximum, the cord comes to rest and, for an instant, the velocity is zero. (f) Immediately after this moment, the cord reverses its direction and returns to the equilibrium position. Once again, the cord's velocity increases while the restoring force decreases. During this time, tension is acting in an upward direction and the cord is moving upward. (g) After the cord passes through the equilibrium position, (h) the restoring force again reverses direction, and the cord's velocity decreases. (i) When the restoring force is at a maximum, the cord comes to rest. This position marks the beginning of the next cycle.

1.2

Before we proceed, let us first distinguish between the *vertical* particle velocity of a string, and the *horizontal* transverse speed of waves in a string.[5] As transverse waves travel horizontally in the string, each particle of the string moves vertically up and down; that is, each particle moves at right angles to the direction of wave propagation. Furthermore, the vertical motion of musical instrument strings is also due to the principle of superposition. Superposition occurs when two transverse waves traveling horizontally in opposite directions combine and produce a third wave that vibrates in a vertical direction. Such waves are called standing waves.[6] (See Sections 3.1 and 3.3.) The purpose of Figure 1.1 is to illustrate the function of tension and mass in the motion of transverse standing waves. Since the existence of transverse standing waves in strings depends on the presence of transverse traveling waves, it follows that particle velocity calculations depend on transverse wave speed calculations. Moreover, particle motion also occurs in a longitudinal direction, in which case particle velocity calculations depend on longitudinal wave speed calculations. (See Chapter 7.) This is especially true for waves in gases like the surrounding air. In general, particle velocities depend on transverse wave speeds (c_T) in strings and solids, or on longitudinal wave speeds (c_L) also in solids,

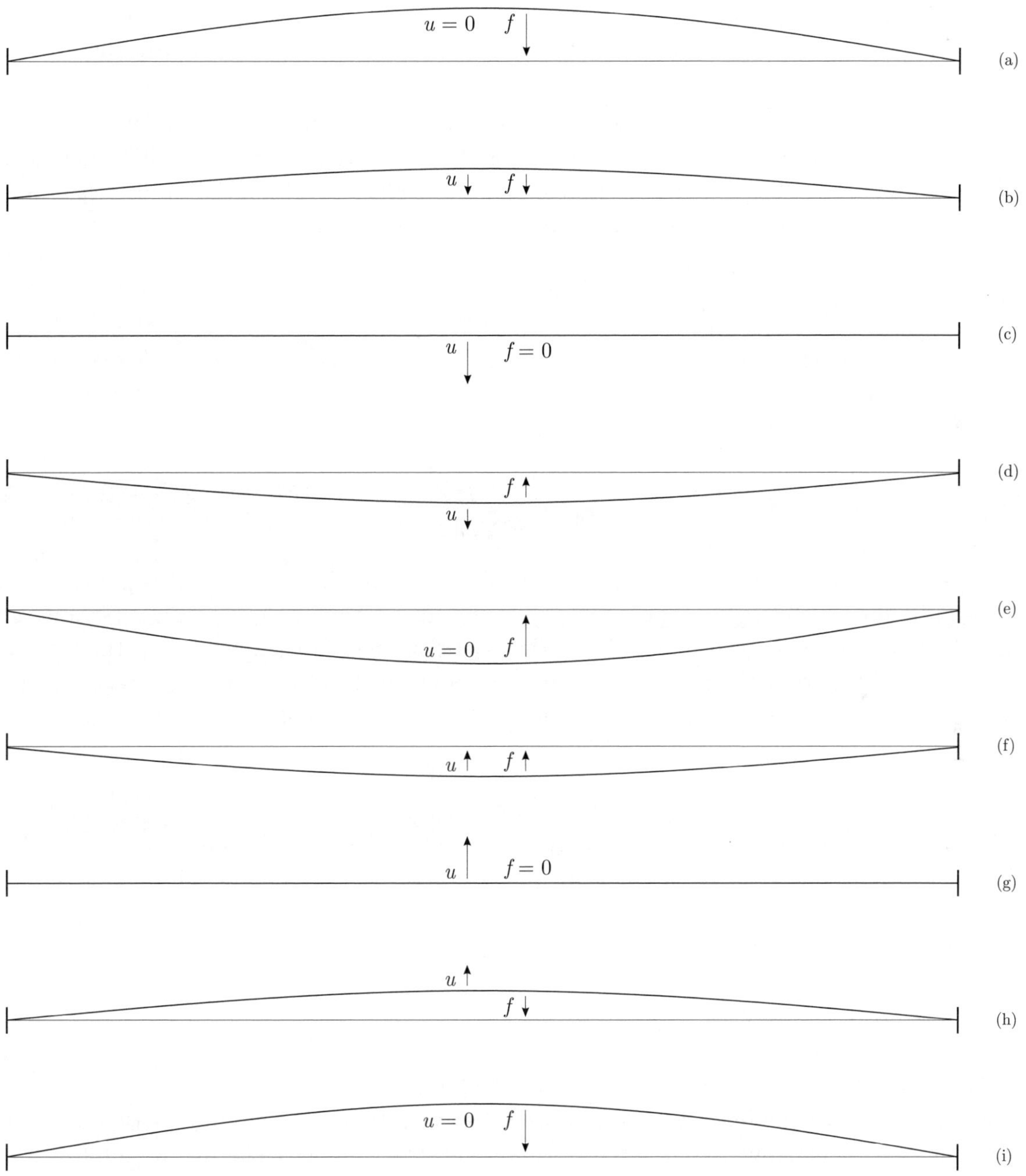

Figure 1.1 Particle velocity and restoring force of a flexible cord vibrating in the first mode of vibration. The lengths of the arrows indicate the relative magnitudes of the particle velocity (u), and the restoring force (f). When the cord moves in the same direction as the restoring force, frames (b) and (f), the velocity of the cord increases. When the cord moves in the opposite direction of the restoring force, frames (d) and (h), the velocity of the cord decreases.

and in fluids (liquids or gases). Therefore, it is in the context of transverse and longitudinal wave speed calculations that we encounter the elastic and the inertial properties of a given medium:

$$c_{\mathrm{T}} \text{ (or) } c_{\mathrm{L}} = \sqrt{\frac{\text{elastic property}}{\text{inertial property}}}$$

For strings, the elastic property is tension; for solids, the elastic property is Young's modulus of elasticity; and for liquids or gases, the elastic property is the adiabatic bulk modulus (see Section 7.2). For strings, the inertial property is the mass per unit length (see Section 1.12). And for solids, liquids, and gases, the inertial property is the mass density, or the mass per unit volume (see Section 1.13).

Particle velocity calculations concern scientists and engineers. In contrast, frequency equations concern instrument builders, tuners, and musicians. Since all frequency calculations include wave speed calculations, solutions to such equations require the elastic and inertial properties of a given vibrating medium. For flexible strings the frequency equation states

$$F_{\mathrm{n}} = \frac{c_{\mathrm{T}}}{\lambda_{\mathrm{n}}} \tag{1.1}$$

where F_{n} is the frequency of a given harmonic or mode of vibration, in cycles per second, or cps; c_{T} is the transverse wave speed, in inches per second; and λ_{n} is the wavelength of a given mode, in inches. The c_{T} variable represents the following subequation:

$$c_{\mathrm{T}} = \sqrt{\frac{T}{M/u.l.}} \tag{1.2}$$

where T is the tension of the string, in pounds-force, or lbf; and $M/u.l.$ is the mass per unit length, in mica/in. In flexible strings, as opposed to stiff strings (see Chapter 4), the transverse wave speed is a *constant.* To determine c_{T} we must know the elastic property, or the tension of the string, and we must know the inertial property, or the mass per unit length of the string. In Section 1.12, we will return to the T and $M/u.l.$ variables and use Equation 1.2 for a sample string calculation.

1.3

At this point in the discussion, the reader may wonder what the new mica mass unit means. Before we discuss this unit, and the conventional slug mass unit, let us examine the nature of acceleration.

Whenever we look at the speedometer of a moving car, we are reminded of the concept of velocity. Velocity is the rate at which distance changes per unit of time:

$$\text{velocity} = \frac{\text{distance}}{\text{time}} \quad \text{(as in)} \quad \frac{\text{meters}}{\text{second}}, \frac{\text{feet}}{\text{second}}, \frac{\text{inches}}{\text{second}}$$

For example, a typical velocity of a moving car is 15.0 miles/hour.

Although all of us experience acceleration whenever we set a parked car into motion, the units of acceleration are less familiar. Acceleration is the rate at which velocity changes per unit of time:

$$\text{acceleration} = \frac{\text{velocity}}{\text{time}} \quad \text{(as in)} \quad \frac{\text{m/s}}{\text{second}}, \frac{\text{ft/s}}{\text{second}}, \frac{\text{in/s}}{\text{second}}$$

Consider what happens when you accelerate a car from a parked position. As you press down on the gas pedal or accelerator, and as long as you continue to accelerate, the velocity of the car changes. Acceleration causes the needle of the speedometer to indicate a continuous increase in velocity. The moment you stop accelerating, and give the engine just enough gas to overcome mechanical friction and air resistance, the speedometer needle stops moving, and the car proceeds with a constant velocity.

For example, suppose a car has an acceleration of 22.0 ft/s/s, pronounced "22.0 feet per second per second." If at the start the velocity = 0, and the car has uniform acceleration (a), then the following equation gives the velocity (v) of the car at the end of each second:

$$v = at \tag{1.3}$$

where t is time, in seconds. Therefore, after 2.0 seconds the car's velocity is

$$v = \left(\frac{\frac{22.0 \text{ ft}}{\text{s}}}{\cancel{\text{s}}} \right) (2.0 \, \cancel{\text{s}}) = 44.0 \text{ ft/s} = 30.0 \text{ mi/hr}$$

Now consider what happens when you push a stalled car by applying a force in the form of muscular effort. On a level road, it is possible to increase the velocity of a car from 0 in/s to 9.0 in/s in 1.0 second. Such a force gives the car an acceleration of 9.0 inches per second per second. If you continue to push with the same amount of force, that is, if the car continues to move with uniform acceleration, then at the end of five seconds it will have a velocity of

$$v = \left(\frac{\frac{9.0 \text{ in}}{\text{s}}}{\cancel{\text{s}}} \right) (5.0 \, \cancel{\text{s}}) = 45.0 \text{ in/s} = 2.56 \text{ mi/hr}$$

If you now stop pushing, and apply just enough force to overcome mechanical friction and air resistance, then the acceleration of the car becomes zero, and the car continues to move with constant velocity: 45.0 in/s, or 2.56 mi/hr.

Intuition and experience tell us that if we double the force, or if we push twice as hard, then the acceleration doubles. In this case, if we double the force, the acceleration would increase to 18.0 inches per second per second; then at the end of 5.0 seconds the car would have a velocity of 90.0 in/s, or 5.12 mi/hr. Newton's second law of motion confirms that this is true; according to this law, a force that acts on an object is the product of the object's mass and the object's acceleration:

$$f = ma \tag{1.4}$$

For a given mass, force is directly proportional to acceleration:

$$f \propto a$$

As the force increases, the acceleration increases as well. Doubling the force doubles the acceleration, and halving the force halves the acceleration. In the event that the force acting on the object is zero, $f = 0$, then the acceleration of the object is zero, $a = 0$. Consequently, the object is (1) at rest, or (2) in motion with a constant and maximum velocity. Note that this is precisely what Newton's first law states: An object will not change the magnitude or direction of its motion unless acted on by a force.

Equation 1.4 also states that for a given acceleration, force is directly proportional to mass:

$$f \propto m$$

As the mass increases, the force increases as well. Doubling the mass requires doubling the force, and halving the mass requires halving the force. Therefore, if a second car has twice the mass of the first car, then we must push twice as hard to achieve the original acceleration of 9.0 inches per second per second.

If we solve Equation 1.4 for mass, Newton's second law shows that mass is a measure of an object's resistance to acceleration,

$$m = \frac{f}{a} \tag{1.5}$$

because mass is inversely proportional to acceleration:

$$m \propto \frac{1}{a}$$

As the mass increases, the acceleration decreases. Equation 1.5 defines mass as the ratio of force to acceleration. This is an extremely important equation because it allows us to calculate the mass of a given object. If we apply a known force to an object, and measure its acceleration, then the object's mass equals f divided by a.

Finally, if we solve Equation 1.4 for acceleration, Newton's second law shows that

$$a = \frac{f}{m} \tag{1.6}$$

Equation 1.6 summarizes two previous observations, namely, that force and acceleration are directly proportional, and that mass and acceleration are inversely proportional.

1.4

Objects that fall freely to the ground do *not* descend with a constant velocity. Because of the force of gravity, dropped objects fall with gravitational acceleration (g). On earth, values for g vary (1) with the density of the earth because the earth's mass is not uniform, (2) with location because the earth is not a perfect sphere, and (3) with elevation because the strength of any gravitational field decreases with distance. At sea level, 45°N. latitude, the local value of g is approximately 9.81 meters per second per second, or 32.17 feet per second per second, or 386.09 inches per second per second. To avoid repeating the time unit, we may simply write 9.81 m/s^2, 32.17 ft/s^2, and 386.09 in/s^2. The following dimensional analysis shows the derivation of the latter unit of acceleration:

$$a = \frac{\text{velocity}}{\text{time}} = \frac{\text{in/s}}{\text{s}} = \frac{\text{in}}{\text{s}} \div \frac{\text{s}}{1} = \frac{\text{in}}{\text{s}} \times \frac{1}{\text{s}} = \frac{\text{in}}{\text{s}^2} = \text{in/s}^2$$

which is pronounced "inches per second squared." Other values for g range from 32.09 ft/s^2 at the equator, to 32.26 ft/s^2 at the North Pole.[7] Consequently, g varies by about 0.53 percent over the surface of the earth, and only by about 0.25 percent between the equator and 45°N. latitude.[8]

Near the surface of the earth, all objects have weight (w). Weight is a force due to gravitational acceleration. Refer to Newton's second law, substitute g for a, and note that Equation 1.4 not only defines force, but also weight. Since

$$f = ma$$

it follows that

$$w = mg \tag{1.7}$$

At any given location, the force of gravity pulls on all objects with the same acceleration. Neglecting air resistance, for every second that an object falls to the ground, it increases its velocity by another 9.81 m/s, 32.17 ft/s, or 386.09 in/s over its previous velocity. According to Equation

1.3, the velocity of an object in free fall is

$$v = gt$$

Therefore, if a dropped object begins its descent from a position at rest, then after 2.0 seconds the object's velocity is

$$v = \left(\frac{32.17\ \text{ft}}{\text{s}^{\cancel{2}\,1}}\right)(2.0\ \cancel{\text{s}}) = 64.34\ \text{ft/s} = 43.87\ \text{mi/hr}$$

1.5

Equation 1.7 reminds us that all objects on earth have both a mass and a weight. Measuring objects in units of mass and units of weight requires widening our previous definition of force. We know that force causes acceleration. We now add a second attribute: Force causes distortion. Sitting on the hood of a car may cause the sheet metal to bend. Our weight is the force that distorts the metal. Under certain conditions, applying a force may cause an object to lengthen. For example, when we pull on a coiled metal spring it stretches to a longer length. When we release the spring, it returns to its original length. If we pull on the spring with greater force, it stretches farther. The ability to respond to force, and to recover from force, means that a spring is an ideal tool for measuring incremental differences in force by observing incremental differences in length (distortion).

Imagine that a spring scale like the one shown in Figure 1.2 hangs from your ceiling. The scale is equipped with a metal frame and a pointer set to zero. Pick up a cube of platinum[9] labeled 1.0 pound-mass,[10] attach it to the scale, release the cube, and observe the pointer. The cube and pointer descend as the spring stretches and lengthens. This distortion of the spring is due to the force of gravity pulling vertically down on the cube. When the pointer stops moving, take a pencil and mark on the metal frame 1.0 pound-force.

Now imagine you are sitting in a spacecraft on the moon. The same calibrated scale hangs from the cabin ceiling. Pick up the same cube, attach it to the scale, release the cube, and observe the

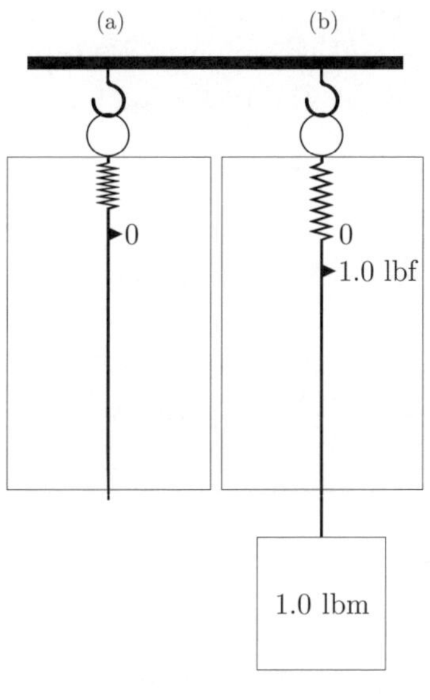

Figure 1.2 Spring scale before and after calibration. (a) The scale shows 0 lbf before calibration. (b) The scale shows 1.0 lbf for 1.0 lbm after calibration.

pointer. When compared to the 1.0 pound-force mark inscribed on earth, the pointer descends only about ⅙ the distance below zero. Why? The value of g on the moon is 1.67 m/s^2, or 5.48 ft/s^2, approximately ⅙ of the acceleration on earth. Since weight is a force (Equation 1.7), and since force is directly proportional to acceleration (Equation 1.4), it follows that the weight of an object on the moon is much less than on earth.

The force of gravity (f_g) on an object is the same as the object's weight:

$$f_g = mg \tag{1.8}$$

Note that the force of gravity, or the weight of an object, is a *relative and extrinsic* property. It changes with the gravitational field strength of a celestial body. In deep space, far removed from any gravitational field, g = zero, and therefore w or $f_g = 0$. However, even in deep space, $m \neq 0$. Consequently, the question remains, "What is mass?"

Simply stated, mass is quantity of matter. It is the number of fundamental atomic particles contained in an object. Unless we physically alter the size of an object, mass is a *constant and intrinsic* property. Unlike force and acceleration, mass never changes. Furthermore, Newton's first law states that mass is the inertial property of an object that determines its resistance to a change in its motion. Combine these two definitions and note that since mass describes a constant quantity of matter and a resistance to acceleration, then an object's response to a force must be the same wherever the object is located. For example, if we transport the stalled car mentioned in Section 1.3 to the moon, the car's mass does not change and, therefore, the amount of force required to accelerate the car is the same as on earth. When viewed from this perspective, Equation 1.5 states that the ratio of force to acceleration is a constant called *mass.*

To measure an object's resistance to acceleration, we need a spring scale to measure force, a stopwatch to measure time, a tape measure to measure length, and a frictionless surface. This kind of surface is important because it eliminates the possibility of a hidden force like friction contributing to the object's resistance. Because we will conduct the following test in a horizontal plane, the experiment does *not* involve the force of gravity. Gravity only pulls in a vertical or inclined plane. Therefore, imagine conducting this experiment anywhere in the universe: on earth, on the moon, or in deep space. As shown in Figure 1.3, take the same calibrated scale down from the ceiling and attach it to the same platinum cube. Make a line on the frictionless surface to indicate the starting location of the cube. With the scale held horizontally to the surface, pull on the 1.0 lbm so that the pointer on the scale indicates 1.0 lbf, and continue to sustain this amount of force for exactly 1.0 second. After 1.0 second has passed, mark the new position of the cube, and measure the distance it traveled from the starting line.

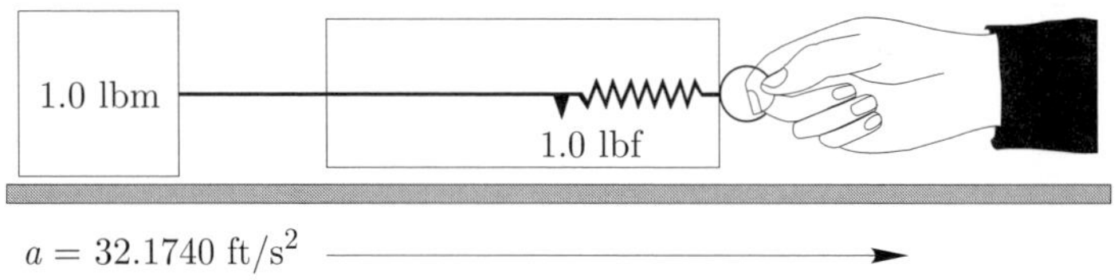

Figure 1.3 The acceleration of a 1.0 lbm on a frictionless surface. Under ideal conditions of weightlessness, as in a spacecraft far removed from any gravitational field, a mass would "float" above the surface as shown in the illustration. This would result in no friction and yield very precise measurements. The experiment demonstrates that a force of 1.0 lbf gives a mass of 1.0 lbm an acceleration of 32.1740 ft/s^2.

The distance is 16.0870 ft exactly. We are now able to calculate the cube's acceleration. If at the start the velocity = 0, and the cube had uniform acceleration, then the following equation gives the distance (d) traveled:

$$d = \frac{1}{2}at^2 \tag{1.9}$$

Solve Equation 1.9 for a,

$$a = \frac{2d}{t^2} \tag{1.10}$$

and note that the cube's acceleration was

$$a = \frac{2(16.0870 \text{ ft})}{1.0 \text{ s}^2} = 32.1740 \text{ ft/s}^2$$

This experiment demonstrates that a force of 1.0 lbf gives a mass of 1.0 lbm an acceleration of 32.1740 ft/s^2. If we attach two 1-lbm cubes to the scale, Newton's second law predicts that 2.0 lbm requires 2.0 lbf to achieve the same acceleration.

1.6

The *English Engineering System*,[11] which is widely used in the United States, measures force in pounds-force, mass in pounds-mass, and acceleration in feet per second squared. Unfortunately, this system constitutes an *inconsistent* set of units. Although the results of the previous experiment are correct, we cannot substitute these findings into Equation 1.4 and compute a consistent solution. Since

$$f = ma$$

the following substitutions give an inconsistent result simply because $1 \times 32.1740 \neq 1$:

$$f = (1.0 \text{ lbm})(32.1740 \text{ ft/s}^2) = 1.0 \text{ lbf}$$

Engineers who use this system include in their calculations a conversion factor called a gravitational constant (g_c), which makes equations containing lbm and lbf dimensionally consistent.[12]

The *English Gravitational System*,[13] also widely used in the United States, constitutes a *consistent* (or coherent) set of units that eliminates the use of the g_c conversion factor. In a consistent system, the product or quotient of any two base units gives the base unit of the resultant quantity. For example, when we divide *unit length* (1.0 inch) by *unit time* (1.0 second) the quotient is a combination of base units called *unit velocity* (1.0 in/s). In the context of the present discussion, engineers who use the *English Gravitational System* retain the same unit of force (1.0 lbf), but use a different unit of mass called the *slug*.[14] To understand the functional value of the slug mass unit, let us first reexamine the inconsistent system and calculate the following equivalent unit of force:

$$f = (1.0 \text{ lbm})(32.1740 \text{ ft/s}^2) = 32.1740 \text{ lbm·ft/s}^2 = 1.0 \text{ lbf}$$

This equivalent force unit suggests many *mass-acceleration* combinations. For example, suppose we observe that a mass of 32.1740 lbm moves on a frictionless surface with an acceleration of 1.0 ft/s^2. What is the acting force? According to Equation 1.4, it is the identical force calculated in the preceding equation:

$$f = (32.1740 \text{ lbm})(1.0 \text{ ft/s}^2) = 32.1740 \text{ lbm·ft/s}^2 = 1.0 \text{ lbf}$$

We conclude, therefore, that a force of 1.0 lbf gives a mass of 32.1740 lbm an acceleration of 1.0 ft/s^2. To verify the accuracy of this calculation, refer to Figure 1.4 and repeat the previous experiment, only this time replace the 1-lbm cube with a larger mass equal to 32.1740 cubes; in other words, we will now accelerate 32.1740 lbm. Again, attach the same calibrated scale to the larger cube and mark the location on the surface. Hold the scale horizontally to the surface and pull on the cube so that the pointer indicates 1.0 lbf for exactly 1.0 second. After 1.0 second has passed, mark the new position of the cube and measure the distance it traveled from the starting line. The distance is 0.5 ft exactly. Substitute the result into Equation 1.10 and calculate the acceleration:

$$a = \frac{2(0.5 \text{ ft})}{1.0 \text{ s}^2} = 1.0 \text{ ft/s}^2$$

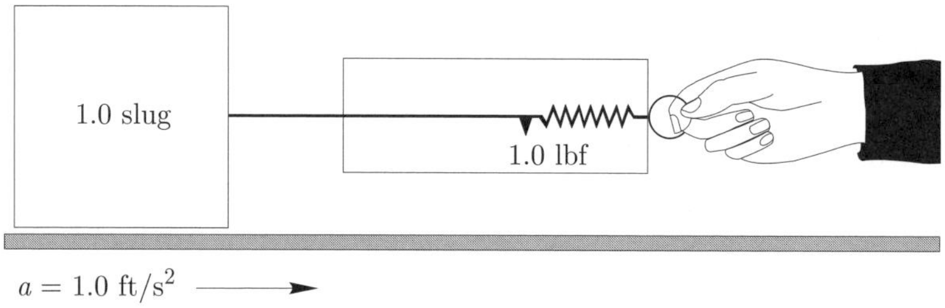

Figure 1.4 The acceleration of a 1-slug mass on a frictionless surface. The experiment demonstrates that a unit force of 1.0 lbf gives a unit mass of 1.0 slug a unit acceleration of 1.0 ft/s^2.

Since 32.1740 lbm = 1.0 slug, the experiment demonstrates that a unit force of 1.0 lbf gives a unit mass of 1.0 slug a unit acceleration of 1.0 ft/s^2. Substitute these findings directly into Equation 1.4 and note that the solution describes a system of units that is by definition mathematically consistent:

$$f = (1.0 \text{ slug})(1.0 \text{ ft/s}^2) = \boxed{1.0 \text{ slug·ft/s}^2} = 1.0 \text{ lbf}$$

Unit mass times unit acceleration equals unit force.

The next step is to measure the gravitational force, or the weight of a 1-slug mass. However, before we proceed, let us review two earlier experiments. Recall that the first vertical experiment demonstrated that gravity pulls on 1.0 lbm with 1.0 lbf. Recall also that the first horizontal experiment demonstrated that 1.0 lbf causes a 1.0 lbm to accelerate at 32.1740 ft/s^2. Consequently, we conclude that (1) a mass of 1.0 lbm must have a gravitational acceleration of 32.1740 ft/s^2 to produce a weight of 1.0 lbf, and (2) a mass of 1.0 lbm must have an acceleration of 32.1740 ft/s^2 to produce a force of 1.0 lbf. This means that the original calibration of the scale took place at a particular location on earth where g equals 32.1740 ft/s^2. Remember, the spring will not stretch, and the pointer will not descend and indicate 1.0 lbf for 1.0 lbm, unless g has this exact value.

Therefore, to measure the weight of 1.0 slug, hang the scale from the ceiling, attach the larger mass, release it, and watch as gravity pulls with an acceleration of 32.1740 ft/s^2. According to

Equation 1.7, the standard weight (see Section 1.8) of 1.0 slug has the value

$$w_S = (1.0 \text{ slug})(32.1740 \text{ ft/s}^2) = 32.1740 \text{ slugs·ft/s}^2 = 32.1740 \text{ lbf}$$

~ 1.7 ~

In summary of Sections 1.3–1.6, it is important to distinguish between two different kinds of force: the mechanically controlled force of a spring and the natural gravitational force of a celestial body. According to Equation 1.6, the ratio of a mechanical force to mass is a *variable:*

$$a = \frac{f}{m}$$

The amount of force applied to a mass depends on the operator of the spring. When we pull different masses with a constant force (and note that as the mass increases, the acceleration decreases), our intent is to define a consistent system of units. Given a constant force of 1.0 lbf, we find that a mass of 1.0 slug has a slower acceleration, and therefore travels a shorter total distance in 1.0 second than a mass of 1.0 lbm. If we want a constant acceleration for both masses, then we must either increase the force on the larger mass, or decrease the force on the smaller mass.

However, according to Equation 1.8, the ratio of *weight to mass*, or the ratio of the *force of gravity to mass*, is a *local constant:*

$$g = \frac{w}{m} \quad \text{(or)} \quad g = \frac{f_g}{m}$$

Unlike a mechanical spring that the operator controls to pull different masses with a constant force, it is the nature of gravity to pull on a large mass with greater gravitational force than a small mass. For example, a rock has a larger mass than a feather. Since gravity exerts a proportionately greater force on a larger mass than a smaller mass, we find that a rock weighs more than a feather. However, a greater gravitational force does not mean that a rock falls with greater gravitational acceleration. Newton's first law states than an object with a large mass has a greater resistance to acceleration. The rock's greater gravitational force is, therefore, offset by its greater inertia. Consequently, when we eliminate air resistance by pumping air out of a glass chamber, we observe that a feather falls with the same gravitational acceleration as a rock. When released simultaneously, both hit the bottom of the chamber at the same time. Therefore, the ratio of weight to mass for a rock is the same as the ratio of weight to mass for a feather, namely, the value of local g. With respect to our vertical scale experiments, the ratio of 1.0 lbf to 1.0 lbm is the same as the ratio of 32.1740 lbf to 1.0 slug, namely, 32.1740 ft/s^2:

$$g = \frac{32.1740 \text{ lbf}}{1.0 \text{ slug}} = 32.1740 \text{ ft/s}^2$$

~ 1.8 ~

The value of g in Sections 1.4 and 1.6 is a deliberate choice. In 1901, the International Commission of Weights and Measures[15] agreed that the *standard unit of force* is the weight of a *standard unit of mass* located in a gravitational field where *standard gravity* (g_0) equals 9.80665 m/s^2, or 32.1740 ft/s^2;

the former acceleration converts to 386.0886 in/s^2. Since g is not a global constant, the international community found it necessary to define units of force by specifying this standard value for gravitational acceleration. Therefore, whenever a technical publication gives the standard weight (w_S) of an object in lbf,[16] we conclude that the engineers calculated the weight with g_0 functioning as a multiplier on the right side of Equation 1.7:

$$w_S = mg_0 \tag{1.11}$$

For example, a technical journal reports that a car has a standard weight of 3000.0 lbf. Suppose you live near the equator. What is the car's local weight (w_L)? First, solve Equation 1.11 for mass:

$$m = \frac{w_S}{g_0} \tag{1.12}$$

Next, substitute the values of w_S and g_0 into Equation 1.12 and calculate the car's mass in slugs:

$$m = \frac{3000.0 \text{ lbf}}{32.1740 \text{ ft/s}^2} = 93.24 \text{ slugs}$$

Finally, substitute this mass and the value of local gravity (g_L) at the equator (see Section 1.4) into Equation 1.7 and calculate the local weight:

$$w_L = (93.24 \text{ slug})(32.09 \text{ ft/s}^2) = 2992.1 \text{ lbf}$$

(To facilitate dimensional analysis, units on unsolved sides of equations are not pluralized; here one does not write 93.24 slugs.)

If an engineer measures an object in slug mass units instead of pounds-force units, and publishes these results directly, then Equation 1.12 represents an unnecessary step. This is a rare occurrence.[17] Most English engineering tables are organized in pounds-force units. However, since in the inconsistent *English Engineering System* (see Section 1.6) an object's standard weight in lbf is numerically equal to the object's mass in lbm,

$$w_S = x \text{ lbm} \times g_0 = x \text{ lbf} \tag{1.13}$$

or in this case,

$$w_S = (3000.0 \text{ lbm})(32.1740 \text{ ft/s}^2) = 3000.0 \text{ lbf}$$

there is a convenient method that allows direct conversion from lbm to slugs. We have already established that 32.1740 lbm = 1.0 slug. Therefore, the conversion factor

$$\frac{32.1740 \text{ lbm}}{1.0 \text{ slug}}$$

makes it possible to convert slugs to lbm. Remember, in a conversion factor the unwanted unit always cancels out of the denominator.[18] For example, convert 15.0 slugs to lbm:

$$(15.0 \text{ \sout{slug}})\left(\frac{32.1740 \text{ lbm}}{1.0 \text{ \sout{slug}}}\right) = 482.61 \text{ lbm}$$

The inverse of the slug-to-lbm conversion factor results in the lbm-to-slug conversion factor:

$$\frac{1.0 \text{ slug}}{32.1740 \text{ lbm}}$$

Use this conversion factor to convert directly from lbm to slugs. For example, according to Equation 1.13, a car with a listed standard weight of 3000.0 lbf also has a mass of 3000.0 lbm. The following conversion from 3000.0 lbm to slugs gives the same result as a previous calculation:

$$(3000.0\ \cancel{\text{lbm}})\left(\frac{1.0\ \text{slug}}{32.1740\ \cancel{\text{lbm}}}\right) = 93.24\ \text{slugs}$$

~ 1.9 ~

For engineers who design canals and build bridges, measurements in foot and slug units work very well. This is decidedly not the case for designers and builders of musical instruments. In the United States, it is far more likely that a designer-builder measures strings, bars, or columns of air in inches. Furthermore, consider the following items, all manufactured in inch dimensions:

Threaded fasteners, machine parts, and tooling components
Metal plates, bars, rods, and tubes
Steel, copper, brass, and bronze wires
Pulleys, sprockets, and bearings
Precision measuring instruments
Lathe and milling machine cutters
Drills, reamers, taps, and dies
Arbors, chucks, and collets
Lumber and construction supplies
Thousands of hand tools

In light of this overwhelming evidence, it seems almost inconceivable that an English mass unit based on a unit acceleration of 1.0 in/s^2 has never received a mathematical definition or an official name.

A fundamental rule of mathematics states that all units in an equation must be consistent with one another. If, for example, string lengths and diameters are in inches, then the slug mass unit based on a unit acceleration of 1.0 ft/s^2 cannot be used in the same equation. Therefore, to work and measure all day in inches, and then to convert hundreds of measurements into feet constitutes an exercise in error-inducing futility at best, and an incredible waste of time and energy at worst.

Moreover, the unit *pounds-force per square inch*, or psi, is the most widely used English unit for pressure. Almost all technical tables list Young's modulus of elasticity for solids, and the adiabatic bulk modulus for fluids in psi units. Engineers who measure in feet must use the conversion factor

$$\left(\frac{12.0\ \text{in}}{1.0\ \text{ft}}\right)^2$$

to convert pounds-force per square inch to pounds-force per square foot. With length measurements in inches, and a mass unit based on a unit acceleration of 1.0 in/s^2, such conversions are not necessary. For example, simply insert a given psi value for E or B_A directly into a longitudinal wave speed equation, and calculate c_L in in/s. (See Equations 1.24 and 1.25, and Section 7.2.)

Finally, in the Notes, ten major scientific works either list or use the value of standard gravity $g_0 = 386.0886$ in/s^2 in equations that require the following *undefined* and *unnamed* unit of mass:[19]

$$\frac{w_S}{386.0886\ \text{in/s}^2} = ? \qquad (1.14)$$

Part II

MICA MASS DEFINITIONS, MICA UNIT DERIVATIONS, AND SAMPLE CALCULATIONS

1.10

Mica is an acronym for **M**ass (unit based on the) **I**nch **C**onstant (for) **A**cceleration. To understand the functional value of the mica mass unit, repeat the last experiment one last time, and replace the 1-slug cube with a larger cube equal to 386.0886 lbm cubes; in other words, we will now accelerate 386.0886 lbm. On the frictionless surface, pull horizontally on the larger cube with 1.0 lbf for 1.0 second. The distance this cube traveled from the starting line is 0.5 in. exactly. Substitute the result into Equation 1.10 and calculate the acceleration:

$$a = \frac{2(0.5 \text{ in})}{1.0 \text{ s}^2} = 1.0 \text{ in/s}^2$$

Since 386.0886 lbm = 1.0 mica, this experiment demonstrates that a *unit force* of 1.0 lbf gives a *unit mass* of 1.0 mica a *unit acceleration* of 1.0 in/s^2. Substitute these findings directly into Equation 1.4 and note that the solution describes a system of units that is by definition mathematically *consistent:*[20]

$$f = (1.0 \text{ mica})(1.0 \text{ in/s}^2) = \boxed{1.0 \text{ mica·in/s}^2} = 1.0 \text{ lbf} \qquad (1.15)$$

Again, unit mass times unit acceleration equals unit force. According to Equation 1.11, the standard weight of 1.0 mica has the value

$$w_S = (1.0 \text{ mica})(386.0886 \text{ in/s}^2) = 386.0886 \text{ micas·in/s}^2 = 386.0886 \text{ lbf}$$

And in response to Equation 1.14,

$$m = \frac{386.0886 \text{ lbf}}{386.0886 \text{ in/s}^2} = 1.0 \text{ mica}$$

Finally, since 386.0886 lbm = 1.0 mica, the following conversion factor makes it possible to convert mica to lbm:

$$\frac{386.0886 \text{ lbm}}{1.0 \text{ mica}}$$

The inverse of the mica-to-lbm conversion factor results in the lbm-to-mica conversion factor:

$$\frac{1.0 \text{ mica}}{386.0886 \text{ lbm}}$$

In summary, notice that the numerical value of the 386.0886 lbm/mica conversion factor represents a physical quantity that does not depend on g. Refer to the inconsistent system of units described in Section 1.6 and calculate the following equivalent unit of force:

$$f = (1.0 \text{ lbm})(386.0886 \text{ in/s}^2) = 386.0886 \text{ lbm·in/s}^2 = 1.0 \text{ lbf}$$

As before, this equivalent force unit suggests the following possibility. If we observe that a mass of 386.0886 lbm moves on a frictionless surface with an acceleration of 1.0 in/s^2, then the acting force must be 1.0 lbf, or the identical force calculated in the preceding equation:

$$f = (386.0886 \text{ lbm})(1.0 \text{ in/s}^2) = 386.0886 \text{ lbm·in/s}^2 = 1.0 \text{ lbf}$$

Figure 1.5 illustrates the significance of this equation in graphic detail. In contrast to Figure 1.2, Figures 1.3, 1.4, and 1.5 illustrate acceleration in a horizontal direction to emphasize that the calibrations of these scales do not depend on gravitational acceleration. In other words, it is possible to invert the logic of the preceding experiment and compute the same result. That is, when a unit mass of 1.0 mica achieves a unit acceleration of 1.0 in/s^2, the pointer of an uncalibrated scale indicates a unit force of 1.0 lbf. This is in complete agreement with Newton's second law of motion and serves as the foundation for a consistent system of units. Therefore, the experiment explains the functional value of the mica: a **m**ass unit based on the *one **i**nch per second squared* **c**onstant for unit **a**cceleration.

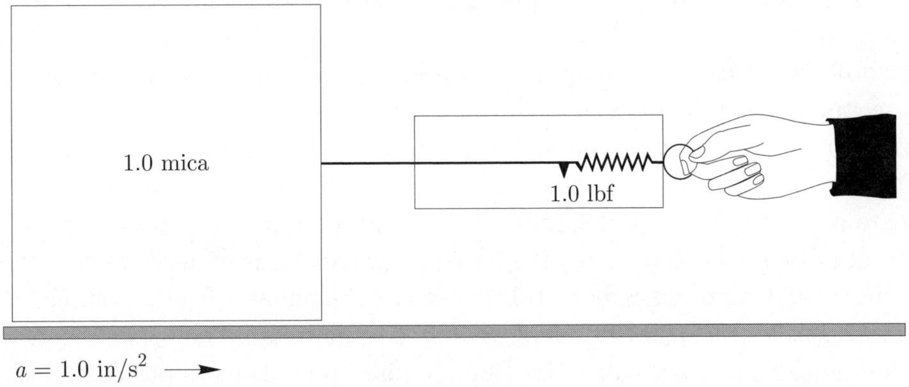

Figure 1.5 The acceleration of a 1-mica mass on a frictionless surface. This experiment enables us to locate the value of unit force on a previously uncalibrated scale. When we give a unit mass of 1.0 mica a unit acceleration of 1.0 in/s^2, the pointer of the spring scale indicates a unit force of 1.0 lbf.

With unit mass in mica, unit acceleration in in/s^2, and unit force in lbf, we have a consistent system of units suitable for the precise and demanding task of musical instrument construction in the United States.

∾ 1.11 ∾

In this text, force in pound-force is defined as mass in mica times acceleration in inch per second squared,

$$f \text{ (lbf)} \equiv m \text{ (mica)} \times a \text{ (in/s}^2\text{)} \tag{1.16}$$

and mass in mica is defined as force in pound-force divided by acceleration in inch per second squared:

$$m \text{ (mica)} \equiv \frac{f \text{ (lbf)}}{a \text{ (in/s}^2\text{)}} \tag{1.17}$$

Similarly, standard weight in pound-force is defined as mass in mica times standard gravity in inch per second squared,

$$w_S \text{ (lbf)} \equiv m \text{ (mica)} \times g_0 \text{ (in/s}^2\text{)} \tag{1.18}$$

and mass in mica is defined as standard weight in pound-force divided by standard gravity in inch per second squared:

$$m \text{ (mica)} \equiv \frac{w_S \text{ (lbf)}}{g_0 \text{ (in/s}^2\text{)}} \tag{1.19}$$

According to Equation 1.19, a car with a standard weight of 3000.0 lbf has a mass of 7.770 micas. Neglecting air resistance and mechanical friction, the muscular effort required to push this stalled car (see Section 1.3) with an acceleration of 9.0 in/s^2 is

$$f = (7.770 \text{ mica})(9.0 \text{ in/s}^2) = 69.93 \text{ lbf}$$

To experience such a force, place a bathroom scale against a wall and push on the scale until the pointer indicates 70 lbf.

Composite objects like cars and computers have simple weights. However, uniform materials like steel, glass, or copper have weight densities. In the English system, engineers identify uniform materials by a specific quantity known as the *weight per unit volume* (W), or simply *weight density.* For solids, the quantity *per unit volume* refers to a cube of material. The most frequently cited weight density units are pounds-force per cubic foot (lbf/ft^3) and pounds-force per cubic inch (lbf/in^3).

For reasons discussed in Sections 1.1–1.2, all frequency equations require an inertial property, or a mass unit. Scientists and engineers refer to this quantity as the mass per unit volume, or simply mass density. Again, for solids, this quantity refers to a cube of material. The most frequently cited mass density units are pounds-mass per cubic foot (lbm/ft^3) and pounds-mass per cubic inch (lbm/in^3).

Regrettably, the typical dimensional listing for a material

Density:

lb/in^3

does not distinguish between mass and weight. If "density" means mass density, the listing should state lbm/in^3; if "density" means weight density, it should state lbf/in^3. However, since we cannot substitute lbm/in^3 for ρ in an equation, we must either (1) convert lbm/in^3 to mica/in^3, or (2) use lbf/in^3 to calculate mica/in^3. The former operation requires multiplication, and the latter, division. Unless the reader understands these differences exactly and can accurately determine a mica/in^3 quantity, even the simplest frequency calculation will end in failure and, thereby, discourage further investigation. There is no logical reason why anything so simple and crucial as figuring a mica/in^3 quantity should remain mathematically undefined and shrouded in confusion.

The reason why this deplorable listing persists is due to the inconsistent *English Engineering System.* Refer to Equation 1.13 and note that for a given material the mass density is numerically equal to the weight density:

$$x \text{ lbm/in}^3 \text{ is numerically equal to } x \text{ lbf/in}^3$$

For steel,

$$0.283 \text{ lbm/in}^3 \text{ is numerically equal to } 0.283 \text{ lbf/in}^3$$

Since the number 0.283 quantifies both the pound-mass and the pound-force of a one-inch cube of steel, most authors and publishers do not make a distinction and simply write 0.283 lb/in^3.

However, if 0.283 lbm/in^3 appears in a text or an equation, we know immediately that a dimensionally consistent operation requires a *conversion to* mica/in^3. Similarly, if 0.283 lbf/in^3 appears, we know that a dimensionally consistent operation requires a *solution for* mica/in^3. When someone states, "0.283 lb/in^3 divided by 386.09 in/s^2 equals 0.00073299 mica/in^3," the operation is incorrect if they assume that 0.283 lb/in^3 represents 0.283 lbm/in^3. Since

$$w = mg$$

it follows that

$$m = \frac{w}{g}$$

In this text, calculate the mass density for steel in mica/in^3 in two different ways. (1) Use the lbm-to-mica conversion factor mentioned in Section 1.10 and convert lbm/in^3 to mica/in^3:

$$\rho = (0.283\ \cancel{\text{lbm}}/\text{in}^3)\left(\frac{1.0\ \text{mica}}{386.0886\ \cancel{\text{lbm}}}\right) = 0.00073299\ \text{mica/in}^3$$

(2) Rewrite Equation 1.19 to define mass density,

$$\rho \equiv \frac{W}{g_0} \tag{1.20}$$

and then use lbf/in^3 to calculate mica/in^3:

$$\rho = \frac{0.283\ \text{lbf/in}^3}{386.0886\ \text{in/s}^2} = 0.00073299\ \text{mica/in}^3$$

(When quantities equal less than one, dimensions are not pluralized; here one does not write 0.00073299 micas/in^3.)[21]

The following dimensional analysis shows the derivation of the mica/in^3 unit. According to Equation 1.18, lbf = mica·in/s^2. Consequently, lbf/in^3 is equivalent to

$$\frac{\text{mica} \times \text{in}}{\text{s}^2} \div \frac{\text{in}^3}{1} =$$

$$\frac{\text{mica} \times \text{in}}{\text{s}^2} \times \frac{1}{\text{in}^3} =$$

$$\frac{\text{mica} \times \cancel{\text{in}}}{\text{s}^2} \times \frac{1}{\text{in}^{\cancel{3}2}} = \frac{\text{mica}}{\text{in}^2 \times \text{s}^2}$$

This result divided by acceleration in in/s^2 becomes

$$\frac{\text{mica}}{\text{in}^2 \times \text{s}^2} \div \frac{\text{in}}{\text{s}^2} =$$

$$\frac{\text{mica}}{\text{in}^2 \times \text{s}^2} \times \frac{\text{s}^2}{\text{in}} =$$

$$\frac{\text{mica}}{\text{in}^2 \times \cancel{\text{s}^2}} \times \frac{\cancel{\text{s}^2}}{\text{in}} = \frac{\text{mica}}{\text{in}^3}$$

(To simplify future calculations, we will approximate the lbm-to-mica conversion ratio and use 1.0 mica/386.09 lbm. Also, to help speed calculations, consult Appendix C for the mica mass densities of 12 string making materials, and Appendix E for the mica mass densities of 15 bar making materials.)

1.12

When a tuner turns a tuning pin and adjusts the frequency of a string, the physical consequences are either an increase or a decrease in the string's tension. Refer to Figure 1.6 and note that similar changes in tension occur if a set of dumbbells hangs from the end of a string, and we either increase or decrease the mass of the suspended weight. Therefore, if we hang a weight called pounds-force from a string, the weight defines the tension of the string. Tension and weight have identical definitions; in this text,

$$T\ (\text{lbf})\ \ {\scriptstyle(\text{or})}\ \ w\ (\text{lbf}) \equiv m\ (\text{mica}) \times g_0\ (\text{in/s}^2) \tag{1.21}$$

Again, to simplify future calculations, we will approximate g_0 and use the value $g = 386.09$ in/s^2.

The following dimensional analysis shows how $T = \text{mica·in/s}^2$ is derived. Consider these dimensions of a typical C_4 (middle C) piano string:

$D = 0.039$ in.
$r = 0.0195$ in.
$L = 26.50$ in.
$F = 261.63$ cps

where D is the diameter of the string, in inches; r is the radius of the string, in inches; L is the overall length of the string, in inches; and F is the string's fundamental frequency, in cps. (See Appendix A.) For a detailed discussion on string frequency and string tension equations refer to Chapter 2. In the interim, use the following equation to calculate tension:

$$T = F^2 L^2 D^2 \pi \rho \qquad \text{(Eq. 2.10)}$$

where ρ is the mass density for steel, in mica/in^3; and π is the constant 3.1416. For clarity, perform this calculation in two steps: first the numbers,

$$(261.63)^2(26.5)^2(0.039)^2(3.1416)(0.00073299) = 168.36$$

and now the units,

$$\frac{1}{\text{s}^2} \times \frac{\cancel{\text{in}^2}}{1} \times \frac{\text{in}^{\cancel{2}\,1}}{1} \times \frac{\text{mica}}{\cancel{\text{in}^3}} = \frac{\text{mica·in}}{\text{s}^2}$$

(*Cycles*, as in cycles per second, and π are dimensionless entities that do not appear in this analysis.) Note that tension is the force mentioned in Section 1.1, or the elastic property mentioned in Section 1.2, which restores a vibrating string to its equilibrium position.

Also included in Figure 1.6 is a reference to mass, or the inertial property that causes the string to overshoot its equilibrium position. (See Sections 1.1–1.2.) Account for this variable by considering either the string's mass per unit length, or the string's total mass. The *M/u.l.* variable is due to Equation 1.2. Scientists prefer to write frequency equations with a transverse or longitudinal wave speed subequation. According to Equation 1.2, a calculation for the speed of transverse waves in flexible strings requires a *M/u.l.* variable. However, since the total mass of the string causes periodic vibrations, we now break with convention and offer an alternate frequency equation that includes a variable for m. First, consider the traditional version of Equation 1.1 in full detail,[22]

$$F_{\text{n}} = \frac{c_{\text{T}}}{\lambda_{\text{n}}} = \frac{\sqrt{\dfrac{T}{M/u.l.}}}{\dfrac{2L}{n}} = \frac{n}{2L}\sqrt{\frac{T}{\pi r^2 \rho}} \tag{1.22}$$

and now the unconventional version of Equation 1.1, which accounts for the string's total mass,

$$F_{\text{n}} = \frac{\sqrt{\dfrac{T}{mL}}}{\dfrac{2}{n}} = \frac{n}{2}\sqrt{\frac{T}{(\pi r^2 \rho L)L}} \tag{1.23}$$

where n is the mode number, any positive integer; and m is the total mass of the string, in micas. Equations 1.22 and 1.23 give identical results.

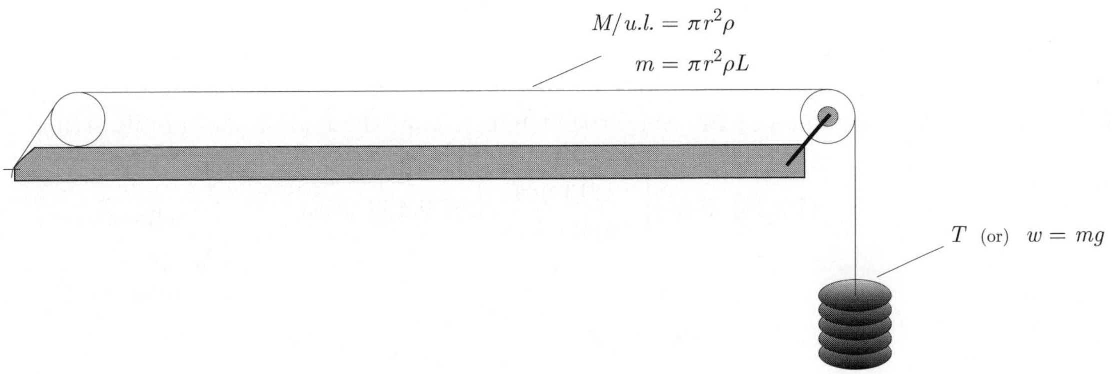

Figure 1.6 Tuned string with a calibrated weight. Turning a tuning pin and increasing the tension of a string has the same effect as increasing the mass of the weight hanging from the string's end. Tension measured in pounds-force acts as the restoring force that returns a vibrating string to its equilibrium position. Since the frequency of a string is directly proportional to the square root of the tension, as the tension increases, the frequency increases as well. (See Section 2.6.)

Since future discussions depend on wave speed calculations, we continue with a solution to Equation 1.2. Use the following equation (see Sections 2.3–2.4) to calculate the mass per unit length:

$$M/u.l. = \pi r^2 \rho$$

Again, first compute the numbers,

$$3.1416(0.0195)^2(0.00073299) = 0.0000008756$$

and now the units,

$$\frac{\cancel{\text{in}^2}}{1} \times \frac{\text{mica}}{\text{in}^{\cancel{3}\,1}} = \frac{\text{mica}}{\text{in}}$$

Finally, refer to Equation 1.2 and calculate the speed of transverse traveling waves in the string:

$$c_{\mathrm{T}} = \sqrt{\frac{168.36 \text{ lbf}}{0.0000008756 \text{ mica/in}}} = 13{,}866.49 \text{ in/s}$$

The following dimensional analysis shows the derivation of the velocity unit. First divide the equivalent force unit by the mass per unit length unit, and then take the square root of the quotient:

$$\frac{\text{mica} \times \text{in}}{\text{s}^2} \div \frac{\text{mica}}{\text{in}} =$$

$$\frac{\text{mica} \times \text{in}}{\text{s}^2} \times \frac{\text{in}}{\text{mica}} =$$

$$\frac{\cancel{\text{mica}} \times \text{in}}{\text{s}^2} \times \frac{\text{in}}{\cancel{\text{mica}}} = \frac{\text{in}^2}{\text{s}^2}$$

$$\sqrt{\frac{\text{in}^2}{\text{s}^2}} = \frac{\text{in}}{\text{s}}$$

To conclude an earlier discussion, suppose you are inside a spacecraft on the moon, and on your workbench is the same string-testing device illustrated in Figure 1.6. What is the frequency of the string? First, calculate the mass of the weight that hangs from the end of the sample string:

$$(168.36 \ \cancel{\text{lbm}})\left(\frac{1.0 \text{ mica}}{386.09 \ \cancel{\text{lbm}}}\right) = 0.436 \text{ mica}$$

(or)

$$\frac{168.36 \text{ lbf}}{386.09 \text{ in/s}^2} = 0.436 \text{ mica}$$

Next, convert lunar gravitational acceleration from ft/s^2 to in/s^2,

$$(5.48 \ \cancel{\text{ft}}/\text{s}^2)\left(\frac{12.0 \text{ in}}{1.0 \ \cancel{\text{ft}}}\right) = 65.76 \text{ in/s}^2$$

and calculate the lunar weight that hangs from the string:

$$w = (0.436 \text{ mica})(65.76 \text{ in/s}^2) = 28.67 \text{ lbf}$$

Since we are interested in the string's fundamental frequency, or the frequency of the first mode of vibration, substitute the number 1 for the mode number n into Equation 1.22. Then substitute into the same equation the string's vibrating length, the weight of the 0.436 mica mass as the tension variable, and the previously calculated mass per unit length. Finally, calculate the string's lunar fundamental frequency:

$$F_1 = \frac{1}{2(26.5 \text{ in})}\sqrt{\frac{28.67 \text{ lbf}}{0.0000008756 \text{ mica/in}}} = 107.97 \text{ cps}$$

When compared to the string's frequency on earth, the fundamental decreased from C_4 down to about A_2, a drop of approximately one "octave and a minor third." However, if we had originally adjusted the tension of this string on a musical instrument equipped with tuning pins instead of calibrated weights, then the string's fundamental frequency on the moon would be the same as on earth. There are two reasons for this consistency. First, the tension of the string stretched between two pins is not subject to the relative and extrinsic property of gravitational force, or weight. Second, the total mass of the string is a constant and intrinsic property not subject to change.

1.13

One of the notable advantages of the mica unit is that it greatly simplifies longitudinal wave speed calculations. Since sound waves propagate through solids and fluids as longitudinal traveling waves, or alternating regions of compression and rarefaction, we find that frequency equations for many kinds of vibrating systems include a longitudinal wave speed subequation.[23] Musical instrument builders encounter these subequations when they calculate the transverse mode frequencies of bars, rods, and tubes (see Equations 6.1 and 6.15); and the longitudinal mode frequencies of tube resonators and columns of air (see Equation 7.2). Use Equation 1.24 to obtain the speed of longitudinal traveling waves or the speed of sound in solids,

$$c_{\mathrm{L}} = \sqrt{\frac{E}{\rho}} \tag{1.24}$$

where E is Young's modulus of elasticity, in psi; and ρ is the mass density of a material, in mica/in^3. And use Equation 1.25 to obtain the speed of sound in fluids,[24]

$$c_{\mathrm{L}} = \sqrt{\frac{B_{\mathrm{A}}}{\rho}} \tag{1.25}$$

where B_{A} is the adiabatic bulk modulus, in psi; and ρ is the mass density of a liquid or gas, in mica/in^3.

The modulus of elasticity of a solid and the adiabatic bulk modulus of a fluid are measures of the compressibility of a given medium. In Equations 1.24 and 1.25, the modulus refers to the elastic property that restores the medium to its equilibrium position, and the mass density, to the inertial property that causes the medium to stay in motion.

For example, consider a high-quality Honduras rosewood bar where $E =$ 3,200,000 psi, and $W =$ 0.0382 lbf/in^3. Refer to Equation 6.2 and note that this equation for the fundamental frequency of transverse vibrations in a free-free bar requires a solution for Equation 1.24. First, calculate the mica mass density:

$$\rho = (0.0382\ \cancel{\text{lbm}}/\text{in}^3)\left(\frac{1.0\ \text{mica}}{386.09\ \cancel{\text{lbm}}}\right) = 0.00009894\ \text{mica/in}^3$$

(or)

$$\rho = \frac{0.0382\ \text{lbf/in}^3}{386.09\ \text{in/s}^2} = 0.00009894\ \text{mica/in}^3$$

Next, substitute the values for E and ρ into Equation 1.24 and calculate the speed of sound, or the speed of longitudinal waves in Honduras rosewood:

$$c_{\mathrm{L}} = \sqrt{\frac{3{,}200{,}000\ \text{psi}}{0.00009894\ \text{mica/in}^3}} = 179{,}841.1\ \text{in/s}$$

The following dimensional analysis shows the derivation of the velocity unit. Pressure (P), or unit force per unit area, is here defined as pounds-force per square inch, or simply psi:

$$P\ (\text{psi}) \equiv \frac{\textit{force}\ (\text{lbf})}{\textit{area}\ (\text{in}^2)} \tag{1.26}$$

According to Equation 1.18, lbf = mica·in/s^2. Therefore, lbf/in^2 is equivalent to

$$\frac{\text{mica} \times \text{in}}{\text{s}^2} \div \frac{\text{in}^2}{1} =$$

$$\frac{\text{mica} \times \text{in}}{\text{s}^2} \times \frac{1}{\text{in}^2} =$$

$$\frac{\text{mica} \times \cancel{\text{in}}}{\text{s}^2} \times \frac{1}{\text{in}^{\cancel{2}1}} = \frac{\text{mica}}{\text{in} \times \text{s}^2}$$

To calculate the velocity unit, first divide this pressure unit by the mass density unit, and then take the square root of the quotient:

$$\frac{\text{mica}}{\text{in} \times \text{s}^2} \div \frac{\text{mica}}{\text{in}^3} =$$

$$\frac{\text{mica}}{\text{in} \times \text{s}^2} \times \frac{\text{in}^3}{\text{mica}} =$$

$$\frac{\cancel{\text{mica}}}{\cancel{\text{in}} \times \text{s}^2} \times \frac{\text{in}^{\cancel{3}2}}{\cancel{\text{mica}}} = \frac{\text{in}^2}{\text{s}^2}$$

$$\sqrt{\frac{\text{in}^2}{\text{s}^2}} = \frac{\text{in}}{\text{s}}$$

Now consider a calculation for the speed of sound in air. Because many tables give the physical properties of materials in metric units, we will use this opportunity to introduce a conversion technique between two different consistent systems of units.

The adiabatic bulk modulus for a gas like the surrounding air equals the product of the ratio of specific heat (γ) times the barometric pressure:[25]

$$B_{\text{A}} = \gamma P$$

For air at 1 standard atmosphere of pressure (sea level),[26] $P = 14.696$ psi, and $\gamma = 1.402$. At this pressure and a temperature of 68°F (20°C), $\rho = 1.21$ kg/m^3. First, determine the adiabatic bulk modulus: $B_{\text{A}} = 1.402 \times 14.696$ psi $= 20.604$ psi. Next, define a conversion factor. Since 0.000036127 lbm/in^3 = 1.0 kg/m^3, and 1.0 mica/in^3 = 386.09 lbm/in^3, calculate the following conversion factor to convert kg/m^3 to mica/in^3:

$$\left(\frac{0.000036127\ \cancel{\text{lbm/in}^3}}{1.0\ \text{kg/m}^3}\right)\left(\frac{1.0\ \text{mica/in}^3}{386.09\ \cancel{\text{lbm/in}^3}}\right) = \frac{0.00000009357\ \text{mica/in}^3}{1.0\ \text{kg/m}^3}$$

Therefore, the mass density of air is

$$\rho = (1.21\ \cancel{\text{kg/m}^3})\left(\frac{0.00000009357\ \text{mica/in}^3}{1.0\ \cancel{\text{kg/m}^3}}\right) = 0.000000113\ \text{mica/in}^3$$

Now substitute these values for B_A and ρ into Equation 1.25 and calculate the speed of sound in air:

$$c_L = \sqrt{\frac{20.604\ \text{psi}}{0.000000113\ \text{mica/in}^3}} = 13{,}503.20\ \text{in/s}$$

Most physics texts[27] give the speed of sound in air at 343 m/s, which is closer to 13,503.94 in/s, or 13,504 in/s. For a complete set of conversion factors from metric units to the units used in this text, see Appendix B.

~ 1.14 ~

Many scientific calculators and mathematical computer applications contain unit conversion programs that allow conversions between standard units and user defined units. Although mica and mica/in^3 do not appear as standard units, one may easily define them with three existing units: lbf, second, and inch. Note that the following definitions for m and ρ make any kind of mica and mica/in^3 conversion possible:

$$m \equiv \frac{w}{g} = \frac{\text{lbf}}{\frac{\text{in}}{\text{s}^2}} = \frac{\text{lbf}}{1} \div \frac{\text{in}}{\text{s}^2} = \frac{\text{lbf}}{1} \times \frac{\text{s}^2}{\text{in}} = \frac{\text{lbf} \times \text{s}^2}{\text{in}} = \text{mica}$$

$$\rho \equiv \frac{W}{g} = \frac{\frac{\text{lbf}}{\text{in}^3}}{\frac{\text{in}}{\text{s}^2}} = \frac{\text{lbf}}{\text{in}^3} \div \frac{\text{in}}{\text{s}^2} = \frac{\text{lbf}}{\text{in}^3} \times \frac{\text{s}^2}{\text{in}} = \frac{\text{lbf} \times \text{s}^2}{\text{in}^4} = \text{mica/in}^3$$

For example, to convert from mica to lbm, instruct the program to make a conversion from lbf·s^2/in units to lbm units. Or, to convert from kg/m^3 to mica/in^3, instruct the program to make a conversion from kg/m^3 units to lbf·s^2/in^4 units. Furthermore, in many advanced computer applications like *Mathematica* and *Mathcad*, the following definition:

mica := PoundForce × Second^2/Inch (*Mathematica*)

$$\text{mica} := \frac{\text{lbf} \times \text{s}^2}{\text{in}} \qquad (\textit{Mathcad})$$

enables the operator to simply substitute the term *mica* — as in $\rho \equiv \text{mica/in}^3$ — into all dimensionally consistent calculations. This renders the following obscure mass density notation[28] obsolete:

$$\rho \equiv \frac{\text{lbf} \times \text{s}^2}{\text{in}^4}$$

Finally, note that the conversion factors in Appendix B serve a double function. For example, to convert kilograms to micas, multiply kilograms by the factor 0.00571. Conversely, to convert micas to kilograms, simply divide micas by the same factor, 0.00571.[29]

Notes

1. Scientists refer to the cyclical motion of vibrating objects as *simple harmonic motion.* See Sections 3.2 and 7.1.

2. For more information on particle velocity, see Sections 5.2–5.3, 7.1, and 7.5.

3. The velocity of the cord increases as long as the restoring force acts.

4. The motion eventually stops because of friction.

5. Norton, M.P. (1989). *Fundamentals of Noise and Vibration Analysis for Engineers*, pp. 10–13. Cambridge University Press, Cambridge, Massachusetts.

6. Transverse standing waves occur only in solids. Longitudinal standing waves occur in solids, liquids, and gasses.

7. Halliday, D., and Resnick, R. (1970). *Fundamentals of Physics*, 2nd ed., p. 253. John Wiley & Sons, New York, 1981.

8. Bray, A., Barbato, G., and Levi, R. (1990). *Theory and Practice of Force Measurement*, p. 76. Academic Press, San Diego, California.

   The authors list 13 values for g throughout the United States between approximately 25°N. latitude and 50°N. latitude. Many other locations around the world are included as well.

9. Platinum has a very high mass density of 21,450.0 kg/m^3, or 0.77493 lbm/in^3, or 0.002007 mica/in^3. A 7.92759 inch cube, with a volume of 498.22 in^3, has a mass of 1.0 mica and a weight of 386.0886 lbf.

10. Jerrard, H.G., and McNeill, D.B. (1963). *Dictionary of Scientific Units*, 6th ed., p. 127. Chapman and Hall, London, England, 1992.

    This is an excellent reference on the historical evolution of units like the pound-mass, and on the creation of units like the slug.

11. Lindeburg, M.R. (1990). *Engineer-in-Training Reference Manual*, 8th ed., p. **1**-2. Professional Publications, Inc., Belmont, California, 1992.

12. *Ibid.*

    The gravitational constant has the value 32.1740 lbm·ft/lbf·s^2.

13. *Ibid.*, pp. **1**-3 – **1**-4.

14. *Dictionary of Scientific Units*, p. 152.

    "The [slug] unit is reputed to have been invented by John Perry in 1890 but the name was not used until 1902. The name is no doubt associated with slow progress of the slug."

15. *Ibid.*, p. 5.

16. Klein, H.A. (1974). *The Science of Measurement*, p. 203. Dover Publications, Inc., New York, 1988.

17. *Engineer-in-Training Reference Manual*, p. **A**-31.

The author gives many mass density values of water in slugs/ft^3.

18. A conversion factor is a unity fraction, or a fraction equivalent to 1. For example, the conversion factor 1.0 ft/12.0 in = 12.0 in/12.0 in = 1, or 12.0 in/1.0 ft = 1.0 ft/1.0 ft = 1. To make a conversion, choose a unity fraction that cancels the unwanted units out of the denominator and leaves the desired units in the numerator. So, to convert from inches to feet, use 1.0 ft/12.0 in. Conversely, to convert from feet to inches, use 12.0 in/1.0 ft.

19. (A) Den Hartog, J.P. (1934). *Mechanical Vibrations*, pp. 34–35. Dover Publications, Inc., New York, 1985.

(B) Den Hartog, J.P. (1948). *Mechanics*, p. 177, 184. Dover Publications, Inc., New York, 1984.

(C) Zebrowski, E., Jr. (1979). *Fundamentals of Physical Measurement*, p. 262. Duxbury Press, Belmont, California.

(D) Fogiel, M., Editor (1980). *The Strength of Materials & Mechanics of Solids Problem Solver*, p. 168, 703. Research and Education Association, Piscataway, New Jersey, 1990.

(E) Oberg, E., Jones, F.D., Horton, H.L., and Ryffel, H.H. (1914). *Machinery's Handbook*, 24th ed., p. 94. Industrial Press Inc., New York, 1992.

(F) Lindeburg, M.R. (1988). *Engineering Unit Conversions*, 2nd ed., p. 62. Professional Publications, Inc., Belmont, California, 1990.

(G) Blevins, R.D. (1979). *Formulas for Natural Frequency and Mode Shape*, Reprint, p. 10. Krieger Publishing Company, Malabar, Florida, 1993.

(H) Rao, S.S. (1986). *Mechanical Vibrations*, 2nd ed., pp. xx–xxiv, 702–703. Addison-Wesley Publishing Company, Reading, Massachusetts, 1990.

At the beginning of the book, the author devotes five pages to a set of English units in the i.p.s. (inch, pound-force, second) system of units. At the end of the book, the author gives in/s^2 as unit acceleration, and refers to the entire system as a "Consistent set of units."

(I) Thomson, W.T. (1972). *Theory of Vibration with Application*, 4th ed., p. 2. Prentice Hall, Englewood Cliffs, New Jersey, 1993.

(J) Weaver, W., Jr., Timoshenko, S.P., and Young, D.H., *Vibration Problems in Engineering*, 5th ed., p. 555. John Wiley and Sons, New York, 1990.

In Table A.3, the authors list the mass densities of five construction materials in lbf·s^2/in^4 units. Refer to Section 1.14 and note that lbf·s^2/in^4 is equivalent to mica/in^3.

20. It is important to understand the distinction between 1.0 mica and 1.0 mica·in/s^2. The former is a unit of mass, and the latter is a unit of force. 1.0 mica has a weight of 386.0886 lbf, whereas 1.0 mica·in/s^2 is equivalent to 1.0 lbf.

21. Since mass per unit length and mass density quantities expressed as mica/in and mica/in^3, respectively, are always less than one, the latter two dimensions are not pluralized. Consequently, dimensions such as micas/in and micas/in^3 do not appear in this text.

22. See Section 3.6.

23. See Section 7.2 for longitudinal wave speed calculations in fluids.

24. Towne, D.H. (1967). *Wave Phenomena*, p. 27. Dover Publications, Inc., New York, 1988.

25. Sears, F.W., Zemansky, M.W., and Young, H.D. *University Physics*, 7th ed., p. 489. Addison-Wesley Publishing Company, Reading, Massachusetts, 1988.

26. Gray, D.E., Editor (1957). *American Institute of Physics Handbook*, 3rd ed., p. **3**-69. McGraw-Hill Book Company, New York, 1972.

This reference lists the standard ICAO atmosphere at 1.01325×10^5 newtons/meter^2, which is equivalent to 14.69595 psi.

27. Kinsler, L.E., and Frey, A.R. (1950). *Fundamentals of Acoustics*, 2nd ed., p. 503. John Wiley & Sons, Inc., New York, 1962.

28. *Vibration Problems in Engineering*, p. 555.

29. If in the future the scientific community agrees to accept the mica unit as a standard unit of mass, I would like to suggest the abbreviation "mc" for all mica mass specifications and calculations.

2 / PLAIN STRING AND WOUND STRING CALCULATIONS

In Western music, strings constitute the primary source of musical sound. This is a remarkable fact because instrument builders encounter serious structural problems when they attempt to tune strings over a wide range of frequencies. The laws of vibrating strings clearly demonstrate the difficulties involved in building stringed instruments with a range of six or more "octaves." Despite these obstacles, piano and harp builders persevered and eventually solved the range problem by overwinding plain strings with copper, bronze, and silver wire. Wound strings replace the need for extremely long plain strings. Furthermore, because of their rich tone, wound strings are also found on narrow range instruments like violins and guitars. To help distinguish between these two different kinds of strings and their respective calculations, this chapter is divided into two parts. Part I covers plain strings, and Part II, wound strings. In both parts, discussions center on mass per unit length, string length, and tension calculations. Finally, we will also consider constructive and destructive aspects of the force of tension.

Part I

PLAIN STRINGS

2.1

The most commonly cited frequency equation for plain and wound strings is

$$F_n = \frac{n}{2L}\sqrt{\frac{T}{M/u.l.}}$$

where F_n is the frequency of a given harmonic or mode of vibration, in cycles per second; n is the mode number, any positive integer; L is the overall length of a flexible string, in inches; T is the tension, in pounds-force (lbf); and $M/u.l.$ is the mass per unit length, in mica per inch. (For a definition of the mica mass unit, see Section 1.10.) Since this chapter focuses primarily on the fundamental frequencies of strings, we now rewrite this equation to read

$$F_1 = \frac{1}{2L}\sqrt{\frac{T}{M/u.l.}} \tag{2.1}$$

where F_1 is the frequency of the first harmonic or the first mode of vibration, in cps.

The $M/u.l.$ variable in Equation 2.1 does not consist of a simple measurable quantity. Rather, it expresses the ratio of a mass to a unit length. For plain strings, mass per unit length calculations are straightforward, but for wound strings, they are complicated. In either case, the mass per unit length ratio deserves special consideration because it appears in several equations. Looking ahead, we find the $M/u.l.$ variable in equations for calculating the transverse wave speed[1] (c_T), the dimensionless stiffness parameter[2] (J), and the characteristic mechanical impedance[3] (Z_s) of plain strings.

~ 2.2 ~

Two equations enable us to calculate the $M/u.l.$ variable of plain strings. The first equation states

$$M/u.l. = \frac{m}{L} \tag{2.2}$$

where m is the total mass of the string, in micas.[4] Equation 2.2 requires a highly accurate scale. Suppose such a scale indicates that a plain string with a length of 19.25 inches has a weight of 0.006178 lbf, and therefore a mass of 0.006178 lbm.[5] Turn to Appendix B, find the lbm-to-mica conversion factor, and make the following conversion:

$$(0.006178 \text{ ~~lbm~~})\left(\frac{1.0 \text{ mica}}{386.09 \text{ ~~lbm~~}}\right) = 0.000016002 \text{ mica}$$

Now substitute the values for m and L into Equation 2.2 and calculate the string's mass per unit length:

$$M/u.l. = \frac{0.000016002 \text{ mica}}{19.25 \text{ in}} = 0.0000008313 \text{ mica/in}$$

Although this technique is mathematically valid, it is not very practical. Given thousands of material-and-length combinations, the empirical method of weighing and measuring individual string samples is extremely time consuming and expensive. When faced with many stringing possibilities, musical instrument builders have good reason to do all their mass per unit length calculations on paper.

~ 2.3 ~

The second $M/u.l.$ equation[6] for plain strings states

$$M/u.l. = \pi r^2 \rho \tag{2.3}$$

where r is the radius of the string, in inches; and ρ is the mass density, or the mass per unit volume of the stringing material, in mica per cubic inch.[7] Notice that Equation 2.3 takes into account the radius, or the diameter of the string. However, if we examine this equation more closely, it seems inappropriate that πr^2, the equation for the area of a two-dimensional plane figure (a circle), should appear in an equation designed to calculate the mass per unit length of a three-dimensional solid (a cylinder). Before we explain the reason for this apparent contradiction in the context of Equation 2.3, let us reconsider Equation 2.2.

A plain string has the geometric shape of a cylinder. Placing a string on a scale gives the cylinder's total mass. As an alternative, the following equation allows us to simply calculate the mass of a cylinder:

$$m_{\text{cylinder}} = V\rho \tag{2.4}$$

where m is the total mass of the cylinder, in micas; and V is the volume of the cylinder, in cubic inches. The volume of a cylinder is given by

$$V = \pi r^2 h \tag{2.5}$$

where r is the radius of the cylinder, in inches; and h is the height or length of the cylinder, also in inches. Suppose now that the previously mentioned sample is a 0.038 in. diameter plain steel string. Substitute the values for r and L into Equation 2.5 and calculate the volume of the string or cylinder:

$$V = 3.1416(0.019\text{ in})^2(19.25\text{ in}) = 0.0218318\text{ in}^3$$

Next, turn to Appendix C, and find the mass density of spring steel. Substitute the values for V and ρ into Equation 2.4 and calculate the total mass of the string or cylinder:

$$m = (0.0218318\ \cancel{\text{in}^3})\left(\frac{0.00073299\text{ mica}}{\cancel{\text{in}^3}}\right) = 0.000016002\text{ mica}$$

Finally, refer to Equation 2.2 and recalculate the mass per unit length:

$$M/u.l. = \frac{0.000016002\text{ mica}}{19.25\text{ in}} = 0.0000008313\text{ mica/in}$$

~ 2.4 ~

Unlike Equation 2.2, Equation 2.3 does not include a variable for either the height of a cylinder or the vibrating string length. We conclude, therefore, that the equation does not represent the string as a solid object. To correct this deficiency, consider the following three-dimensional interpretation of Equation 2.3. In this text, the $M/u.l.$ variable represents the cylindrical mass of a 1-inch string segment. According to Equation 2.4, cylindrical mass calculations include a volume variable. In fulfillment of this requirement, we may rewrite Equation 2.3 to state

$$M/u.l. = V/u.l. \times \rho \tag{2.6}$$

where $V/u.l.$ is volume per unit length, or the cylindrical volume of a 1-inch string segment, in cubic inches per inch. Define $V/u.l.$ with the following equation:

$$V/u.l. \equiv \frac{\pi r^2 h}{1.0\text{ in}} \tag{2.7}$$

If we now substitute the $V/u.l.$ ratio and the mass density ratio into Equation 2.6, the result is a three-dimensional interpretation of Equation 2.3:

$$M/u.l. = \frac{\pi r^2 h}{1.0\text{ in}} \times \frac{\text{mica}}{\text{in}^3} \tag{2.8}$$

By definition, volume per unit length refers to volume per inch. Therefore, as depicted in Figure 2.1, the h variable in Equation 2.7 must also equal one inch. The inclusion of a unit length variable in the numerator, and a unit length constant in the denominator, seems redundant. Notice, however, that the units of Equation 2.7 give a solution that accurately describes the three-dimensional

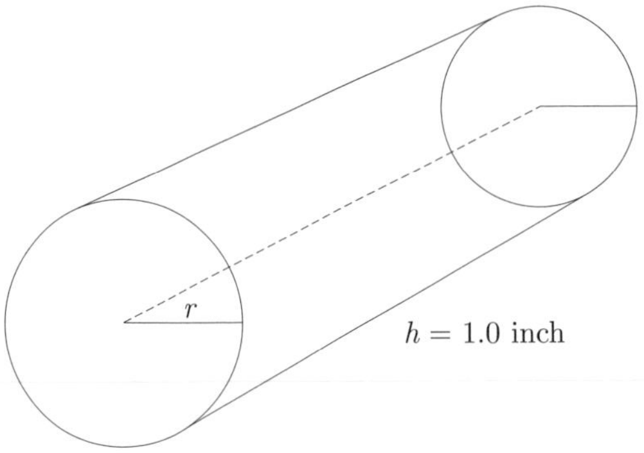

Figure 2.1 A unit length of string. According to Equation 2.8, the $M/u.l.$ equation for plain strings requires the cylindrical volume of a 1-inch string segment.

geometry of the string:

$$V/u.l. = \frac{3.1416(0.019 \text{ in})^2(1.0 \text{ in})}{1.0 \text{ in}} = \frac{0.0011341 \text{ in}^3}{\text{in}}$$

Finally, substitute this result and the mass density for spring steel into Equation 2.8 and calculate the mass per unit length of the sample string:

$$M/u.l. = \left(\frac{0.0011341 \cancel{\text{in}^3}}{\text{in}}\right)\left(\frac{0.00073299 \text{ mica}}{\cancel{\text{in}^3}}\right) = 0.0000008313 \text{ mica/in}$$

Equation 2.3 is conceptually misleading because the area of a circle does not dimensionally describe the volume of a cylinder. However, if we first cancel *unit length* out of the numerator and the denominator of Equation 2.7 and then substitute the result into Equation 2.3, the solution for $M/u.l.$ will be dimensionally and numerically identical:

$$\frac{\pi r^2 \cancel{1.0 \text{ in}}}{\cancel{1.0 \text{ in}}} = \pi r^2$$

$$3.1416(0.019 \text{ in})^2 = 0.0011341 \text{ in}^2$$

$$M/u.l. = (0.0011341 \cancel{\text{in}^2})\left(\frac{0.00073299 \text{ mica}}{\text{in}^{\cancel{3}\,1}}\right) = 0.0000008313 \text{ mica/in}$$

~ 2.5 ~

Mass per unit length calculations for plain strings are easy because a straight solid wire has only a single geometric shape. In Part II, we will discover that wound strings are more complicated because they consist of two geometric shapes. In Section 2.10, we will discuss a wound sample string made from steel, nylon, and bronze. As before, the steel core wire is in the shape of a solid cylinder. However, the inner nylon fiber bedding and the outer bronze wrap wire are in the shape of tubes, or hollow cylinders. This added complication further demonstrates the need for a three-dimensional understanding of strings. Otherwise, the language used to describe strings, and the simplified algebraic equation used to measure strings do not give a consistent interpretation of the $M/u.l.$ variable. Therefore, whether we seek the mass per unit length of a solid or a hollow cylinder, we must think of strings as three-dimensional objects and recognize the significance of the canceled units in the $M/u.l.$ equation.

2.6

In addition to fundamental frequency calculations, a successful stringing design depends on tension, length, and diameter calculations. We may solve Equation 2.1 for these variables, but first we must transform this equation three times and change the r^2 variable into a diameter[8] (D) variable:

$$F_1 = \frac{1}{2L}\sqrt{\frac{T}{M/u.l.}} = \frac{1}{2L}\sqrt{\frac{T}{\pi r^2 \rho}} = \frac{1}{2rL}\sqrt{\frac{T}{\pi\rho}} = \frac{1}{DL}\sqrt{\frac{T}{\pi\rho}} \tag{2.9}$$

Now solve Equation 2.9 for T, L, and D:

$$T = F^2 L^2 D^2 \pi\rho \tag{2.10}$$

$$L = \frac{1}{FD}\sqrt{\frac{T}{\pi\rho}} \tag{2.11}$$

$$D = \frac{1}{FL}\sqrt{\frac{T}{\pi\rho}} \tag{2.12}$$

where F is the fundamental frequency of the string, in cps. With these solutions in mind, let us examine the nature of vibrating strings in greater detail. Equation 2.9 expresses the four cardinal laws of vibrating strings.[9]

(1) The frequency of a string is directly proportional to the square root of the tension:

$$F \propto \sqrt{T}$$

As the tension increases, the frequency increases and *vice versa.*

(2) The frequency of a string is inversely proportional to the square root of the mass density of the stringing material:

$$F \propto \sqrt{\frac{1}{\rho}}$$

As the mass density of the stringing material decreases, the frequency increases and *vice versa.*

(3) The frequency of a string is inversely proportional to the diameter:

$$F \propto \frac{1}{D}$$

As the diameter decreases, the frequency increases and *vice versa.*

(4) The frequency of a string is inversely proportional to the length:

$$F \propto \frac{1}{L}$$

As the length decreases, the frequency increases and *vice versa.*

For example, with all other variables held constant, we may increase a string's fundamental frequency by an "octave," ratio 2⁄1, in four different ways. (1) Multiply the tension by the frequency ratio squared:

$$\frac{1}{DL}\sqrt{\frac{T(2)^2}{\pi\rho}} = 2F_1$$

(2) Divide the mass density by the frequency ratio squared:

$$\frac{1}{DL}\sqrt{\frac{T}{\pi(\rho/2^2)}} = 2F_1$$

(3) Divide the diameter by the frequency ratio:

$$\frac{1}{L(D/2)}\sqrt{\frac{T}{\pi\rho}} = 2F_1$$

(4) Divide the length by the frequency ratio:

$$\frac{1}{D(L/2)}\sqrt{\frac{T}{\pi\rho}} = 2F_1$$

Most of these adjustments are meant for theoretical consideration because significant changes in T, ρ, and D will not yield practical results. For example, to achieve an "octave" by (1) quadrupling a string's tension, (2) decreasing a string's mass density to a quarter of the original density, or (3) halving a string's diameter will only end in breaking the string. Strings break if the tension is too high, if the stringing material does not have a high tensile strength,[10] or if the strings are too thin. (Turn to Appendix C and notice a rough correlation between high density and high tensile strength; gut is a notable exception.) For these reasons, changes in L represent the most efficient means by which to alter the frequencies of strings. This accounts for the fingerboards of guitars and violins, and the graduated string lengths of pianos and harps.

2.7

Designing strings for pianos and harps requires a great deal of thought and experience. The simple technique of halving string lengths to produce ascending "octaves," and doubling string lengths to produce descending "octaves" works only over a limited range of frequencies. A simple curve best illustrates the problems associated with stringing large musical instruments. Figure 2.2(a) shows a plot of the equation

$$y = \frac{1}{x} \tag{2.13}$$

Equation 2.13 expresses the relation "y is inversely proportional to x":

$$y \propto \frac{1}{x}$$

As x increases, y decreases and *vice versa*. According to Equation 2.11, we may substitute L for y and F for x, and define the relation "L is inversely proportional to F":

$$L \propto \frac{1}{F}$$

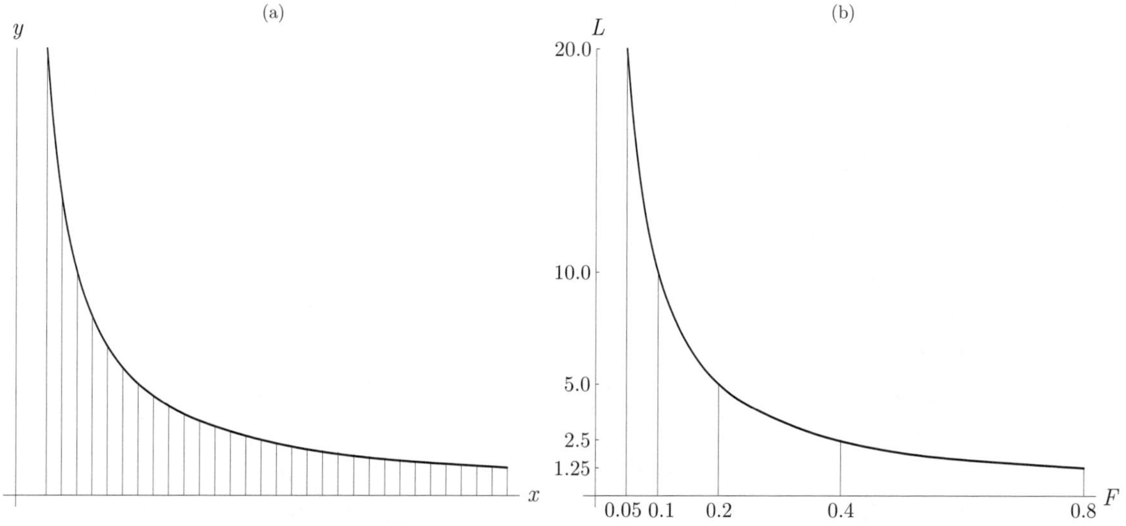

Figure 2.2 The plots $y = 1/x$ and $L = 1/F$. (a) This plot shows the origin of the characteristic shapes of many different kinds of musical instruments. (b) The same plot shows a representation of five isolated strings that span an interval of four "octaves." As "frequency" values increase by a factor of 2 from left to right on the x-axis, "string length" values decrease by a factor of 2 on the y-axis.

Figure 2.2(b) illustrates this inverse proportionality between length and frequency. As "frequency" values increase by the ratio $^2\!/\!_1$ from left to right along the x-axis, "string length" values decrease by the ratio $^2\!/\!_1$ along the y-axis.

Variations of this graceful curve determine the basic shapes of many different kinds of musical instruments. Among stringed instruments, we see a representation of the curve in the familiar shapes of harpsichords, grand pianos, and harps. Among wind instruments, we see an outline of the curve in the graduated lengths of organ pipes and pan pipes. And among percussion instruments, a similar outline appears due to the changing lengths of marimba bars and resonators.

A reading of Figure 2.2(b) from right to left shows how uniform decreases in F produce rapid increases in L. The steep angle of the curve near the y-axis illustrates why builders of large stringed instruments cannot simply utilize a 2:1 stringing ratio without incurring major structural problems. Consider, for example, a grand piano that spans seven "octaves" between lowest C_1 and highest C_8. The latter note has a typical string length of about two inches. If piano builders used a 2:1 stringing ratio and doubled the string length for each descending "octave," C_1 would have a length of

$$(2.0 \text{ in})(2)^7 = 256.0 \text{ in} = 21.33 \text{ ft}$$

This bass string length is too long and completely unmanageable.

Surprisingly, the 2:1 stringing ratio produces the exact opposite problem when we reverse the direction and consider string lengths in the treble section. For example, in quality pianos the optimum string length for middle C_4 is approximately 26.5 inches. If piano builders used a 2:1 stringing ratio and halved the string length for each ascending "octave," C_8 would have a length of

$$26.5 \text{ in} \div (2)^4 = 1.66 \text{ in}$$

There are two reasons why this length is too short. (1) Short strings have small total masses. Unless a vibrating string has a relatively large mass,[11] mechanical friction from the soundboard and steel plate, and ambient friction from the surrounding air will quickly dampen the string's motion and bring it to rest. Therefore, the predicted length for C_8 is too short to produce a sustained tone. (2) Short strings tend to be stiff and sound very inharmonic. Since J is inversely proportional to L^2,[12] or since the dimensionless stiffness parameter increases as the string length decreases, the predicted length is also too short to produce a quality tone.

Instrument builders resolve these difficulties by manipulating both the lengths and the diameters of strings. On the one hand, piano and harp[13] builders employ a *stringing scale* that generates longer strings in the treble and shorter strings in the bass. On the other hand, they vary the diameters of strings and install thin strings in the treble and thick strings in the bass. For example, to give strings a longer length in the treble section, piano builders use a stringing scale of 1.88 : 1. This gives C_8 a length[14] of

$$26.5 \text{ in} \div (1.88)^4 = 2.12 \text{ in}$$

However, Equation 2.10 states that T is directly proportional to L^2 and D^2. Therefore, to avoid increases in tension from longer strings, builders must decrease the diameters of the treble strings. Average piano string diameters vary from about 0.040 in. for C_4 to 0.030 in. for C_8.

Unfortunately, the 1.88 : 1 stringing scale does not solve the problem of extremely long bass strings. Given an optimum length of 26.5 inches for C_4, the stringing scale gives C_1 a length of

$$(26.5 \text{ in})(1.88)^3 = 176.08 \text{ in} = 14.67 \text{ ft}$$

This is a definite improvement over the earlier C_1 calculation of 21.33 ft, but the longest grand piano strings are "only" about 6.5 feet long, or less than half the length of the preceding calculation. To achieve low frequencies with relatively short strings, piano builders must increase the diameters (or increase the mass per unit length) of all bass strings. According to Equation 2.9, diameter and frequency are inversely proportional: as D increases, F decreases. However, since J is directly proportional to D^4,[15] or since the dimensionless stiffness parameter increases as the string diameter increases, thick strings tend to be stiff and sound very inharmonic. In response to these conflicting requirements, piano bass string makers wind copper wire over plain steel strings. Like the coils of a spring, the copper wrap wire is flexible and bends easily with the vibratory motion of the steel core wire. Consequently, wound strings have the required mass but not the stiffness and poor tone quality of comparable solid steel strings.

Finally, a general stringing scale for bass strings does not exist. From the smallest spinets to the largest concert grands, every manufacturer uses a different scale depending on the size and quality of the instrument.

2.8

We close this discussion on plain strings with tension calculations. Builders of traditional or original stringed instruments recognize the importance of this subject because tension is both a constructive and a destructive force. If there is not enough tension, strings will not produce sound.[16] If there is too much tension, strings and instruments alike will not endure and simply break apart.

Suppose you have a newly built canon[17] that needs 48 identical steel strings. After inspecting the instrument, you decide that it can safely withstand 4000.0 pounds of force. You are certain that 6000.0 pounds-force would destroy it. Given the following string dimensions:

$D = 0.024$ in.
$L = 39.37$ in.
$F = 196.0$ cps

three important questions come to mind. Will the instrument support the total force from a full set of strings? Will the strings endure the produced tension? Will the strings give a good tone? In response to the first question, substitute the above-mentioned string dimensions into Equation 2.10 and calculate the tension[18] of the proposed string:

$$T = (196.0 \text{ cps})^2(39.37 \text{ in})^2(0.024 \text{ in})^2(3.1416)(0.00073299 \text{ mica/in}^3) = 78.98 \text{ lbf}$$

Or, utilize Equation 2.14 and calculate the tension with a *M/u.l.* variable:

$$T = 2^2(196.0 \text{ cps})^2(39.37 \text{ in})^2(0.0000003316 \text{ mica/in}) = 78.98 \text{ lbf}$$

Now, to compute the total force, multiply the number of strings by this tension: 48×78.98 lbf = 3791.02 lbf. This result confirms that the combined tension from all the strings is well below the maximum limit and that the instrument will last.

In response to the second and third questions, we begin with the general observation that most strings are tensioned between 40% and 65% of their *break strength*, or the amount of force required to break the string. (See Appendix D.) If the tension falls too much below the lower limit, the strings are too loose and will sound weak. If the tension rises too much above the upper limit, the strings are too tight and will break prematurely. Beyond these mechanical requirements, builders choose a suitable tension based on the string's tone quality (or timbre), and the feel of the string under the hands, pick, or bow. In general, strings with high tension have a stronger and more brilliant tone,[19] but they also demand greater muscular effort from the performer. A harp[20] would be very difficult to play if its strings had the same tension as piano strings.

To calculate a string's break strength, we must know the *tensile strength* of the stringing material. Tensile strength refers to the maximum tension a material can withstand without tearing. Engineers measure this property in units of force per unit cross-sectional area, or pounds-force per square inch, or psi. For spring steel, tensile strength values range between 300,000–400,000 psi. (See Appendix C.) In other words, a 1.0 in. × 1.0 in. square steel bar requires an average tension of 350,000 lbf to tear it apart. Use this value to obtain the break strength of the proposed string. First, find the string's cross-sectional surface area:

$$S = \pi r^2$$
$$S = 3.1416(0.012 \text{ in})^2 = 0.00045 \text{ in}^2$$

Now, to calculate the string's break strength, multiply the surface area by the tensile strength of spring steel:

$$\text{Break Strength} = (0.00045 \cancel{\text{in}^2})\left(\frac{350{,}000 \text{ lbf}}{\cancel{\text{in}^2}}\right) = 157.5 \text{ lbf}$$

Finally, determine what percentage 78.98 lbf is of 157.5 lbf. Divide the smaller number by the larger, and multiply the quotient by 100:

$$100\left(\frac{78.98 \cancel{\text{lbf}}}{157.5 \cancel{\text{lbf}}}\right) = 50.15$$

A string tensioned at 50.15% of its break strength is well within the desired range. We conclude, therefore, that this string will last and give a good tone.[21]

Part II

WOUND STRINGS

2.9

We turn now to mass per unit length and tension calculations for wound strings. Note that the weighing technique described in Section 2.2 works equally well for plain and wound strings. However, for reasons already described, mass per unit length calculations are best accomplished without precision scales.

Before we start with a detailed technical analysis, let us first compare plain and wound strings. Plain strings consist of a single material in the shape of a smooth solid cylinder. In contrast, wound strings consist of (1) two or more materials,[22] (2) a coiled outer surface that requires special consideration, and (3) solid and hollow cylindrical shapes. For these three reasons, we must expand our previous description of the plain string $M/u.l.$ variable and consider a wound string $M/u.l.$ variable that consists of a *complex composite* of different materials and different geometric shapes. In this context, the diameter variable in Equations 2.9–2.12 has no meaning because the smooth surface of a solid cylinder is geometrically different from the coiled surface of a wound string. Therefore, return now to Equation 2.1 and consider the following solutions for T, L, and $M/u.l.$:

$$T = 2^2F^2L^2(M/u.l.) \tag{2.14}$$

$$L = \frac{1}{2F}\sqrt{\frac{T}{M/u.l.}} \tag{2.15}$$

$$M/u.l. = \frac{T}{2^2F^2L^2} \tag{2.16}$$

Since our goal is to use Equation 2.14 for wound strings, we will now develop a method for calculating *composite* $M/u.l.$ variables.

2.10

Suppose we would like to determine the tension of a wound string made from three different materials: a steel core wire, an interior nylon fiber bedding, and an exterior phosphor bronze wrap wire. (The nylon fibers provide a soft bedding that prevents the wrap wire from buzzing against the core wire when the string is vibrating.) Figure 2.3(a) illustrates a longitudinal cross-section of the string. Unlike the straight smooth surfaces of the steel core and the nylon fibers, the bronze wrap wire resembles the coiled surface of a spring. Between the coils of the bronze winding, note the presence of air pockets devoid of any wrap material. Figure 2.3(b) illustrates a detailed cross-sectional view of one bronze coil and four air pockets. These pockets indicate that the outer winding does not consist of a solid continuous material. In this case, the winding is a combination of bronze and air. Since the amount of air locked inside the winding is very small, we will exclude the mass density of air from all mass per unit length calculations. (The air outside the winding is not a part of the string and, therefore, not a factor.) However, we cannot use the standard mass density of bronze in wound string mass per unit length calculations because ρ for metals only represents the mass per unit volume of solid materials, not partially hollow materials. Therefore, to accurately calculate the mass per unit length of the bronze wrap, first determine the percentage[23] of the winding that is solid material, and then modify the mass density of bronze according to this percentage.

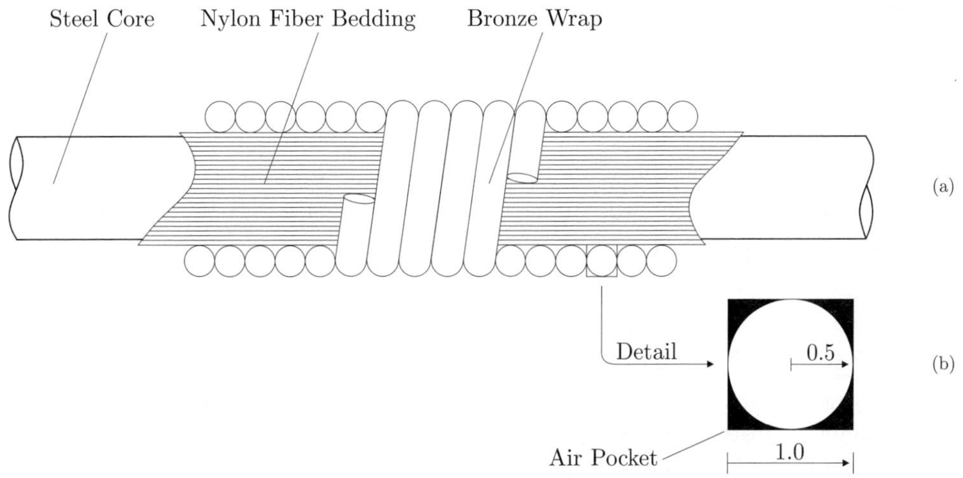

Figure 2.3 The longitudinal cross-section of a wound string. (a) This figure shows the structure of a wound string made from three different stringing materials. Note the air pockets between adjacent coils of the outer winding. (b) This detailed figure shows the cross-sectional surface area of a bronze coil and four air pockets.

Refer to Figure 2.3(b) and note that the square represents the cross-sectional surface area of the *space* between adjacent coils; it has a value of $(1.0)^2 = 1.0$ square unit. The inscribed circle represents the cross-sectional surface area of a coil; it has a value of πr^2, or $3.1416 \times (0.5)^2 = 0.7854$ square units. Since $1.0 - 0.7854 = 0.2146$, we conclude that the coil occupies 78.54% of the space, and the air, 21.46%. Turn to Appendix C, find ρ for phosphor bronze (CDA 510), and multiply 0.7854×0.00082883 mica/in^3 $= 0.00065096$ mica/in^3. In Section 2.12, we will use this modified mass density value for bronze to calculate the mass per unit length of the outer winding.

~ 2.11 ~

The next step requires us to analyze the geometric structure of the wound sample string. Consider two small tubes, one larger in diameter than the other, fitted tightly together like a telescope joint and slipped over your finger. The finger represents the steel core, and it is always in the shape of a solid cylinder. The tubes represent the inner nylon fiber bedding and the outer bronze wrap, and they are always in the shape of hollow cylinders. Given this design, we must carry out four separate calculations. First, determine the mass per unit length of one solid steel cylinder, one hollow nylon cylinder, and one hollow bronze cylinder, and then add these results together. The grand total equals the composite $M/u.l.$ of this particular wound string.

According to Equations 2.3 and 2.6, mass per unit length calculations are possible with either a two-dimensional surface area equation, or a three-dimensional volume per unit length equation. Although the latter method gives a more accurate interpretation of string geometry, we will use a two-dimensional approach because area equations are less complicated than $V/u.l.$ equations. Since this wound string consists of three different stringing materials and two different geometric shapes, it is important to keep mass per unit length calculations as simple as possible. Note, however, that the principle of a three-dimensional approach (see Section 2.4, Equation 2.8) applies equally well to solid and hollow cylinders. Anyone who prefers this method should include a unit length variable in the numerator and a unit length constant in the denominator of Equation 2.21. This will give the volume per unit length of a hollow cylinder, in cubic inches per inch.

In its simplest and most general form, the mass per unit length equation states

$$M/u.l. = S\rho \tag{2.17}$$

where S is the cross-sectional surface area of the stringing material, in square inches. Figure 2.1 shows that for a solid cylinder, S represents the surface area of a *circle*. In contrast, Figure 2.4 shows that for a hollow cylinder, S represents the surface area of a *ring*. By definition, a ring consists of the area between two concentric circles. Since a ring has two circles, it also has two diameters: a large diameter (D) for the outer circle, and a small diameter (d) for the inner circle. To determine the surface area of a ring, we must subtract the area of the small inner circle from the area of the large outer circle. Such calculations are easily accomplished with the standard equation for the area of a circle. However, there is a better and more direct way. Since it is common practice to give wire thicknesses in diameter dimensions, consider the following equation designed for calculating the surface area of a circle with a diameter variable:

$$\text{Area of Circle} = \pi r^2 = \pi\left(\frac{D}{2}\right)^2 = \pi\frac{D^2}{4} = 0.7854D^2 \tag{2.18}$$

Now adjust this equation to calculate the surface area of a ring with two diameter variables:

$$\text{Area of Ring} = 0.7854(D^2 - d^2) \tag{2.19}$$

Finally, substitute Equation 2.18 into Equation 2.17 and define a $M/u.l.$ equation for a solid cylinder:

$$M/u.l. \text{ of Solid Cylinder} = 0.7854D^2\rho \tag{2.20}$$

Similarly, substitute Equation 2.19 into Equation 2.17 and define a $M/u.l.$ equation for a hollow cylinder:

$$M/u.l. \text{ of Hollow Cylinder} = 0.7854(D^2 - d^2)\rho \tag{2.21}$$

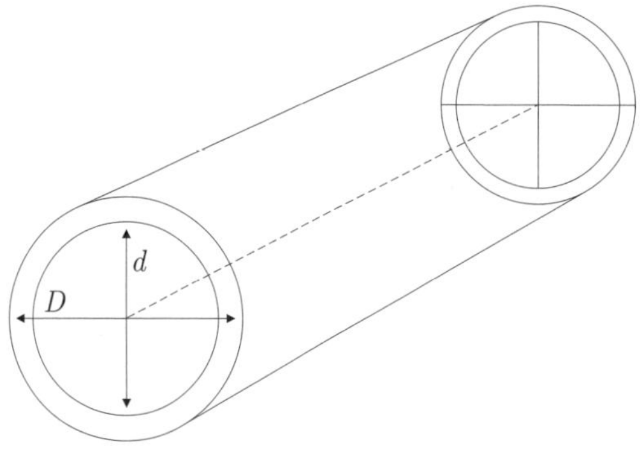

Figure 2.4 A tube or hollow cylinder. The cross-section of a hollow cylinder is in the shape of a ring. All rings have a large outer diameter (D), and a small inner diameter (d).

2.12

The inclusion of three different stringing materials results in the formation of three diameters. Figure 2.5 illustrates a transverse cross-section of the string and how these materials are distributed. The inside diameter (D_i) includes only the cross-section of the steel core; the middle diameter (D_m) includes the cross-section from the steel core to the nylon fibers; the outside diameter (D_o) includes the entire cross-section from the steel core to the bronze wrap.

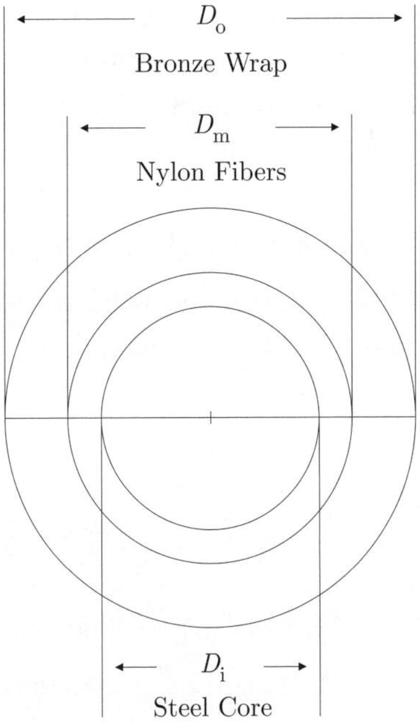

Figure 2.5 The transverse cross-section of a wound string. The inclusion of three different stringing materials results in the formation of three diameters. A calculation for the *composite M/u.l.* of this particular string will require the surface areas of one circle and two rings.

Before we start with mass per unit length calculations, one unique problem remains. It is not possible to physically measure the soft nylon fibers that make up the string's D_m dimension. Therefore, we must obtain the middle diameter indirectly. Consider the following wound string, designed for the Bass Canon in Plate 3:

D_o = 0.044 in.
D_i = 0.022 in.
D_w = 0.007 in.
L = 47.244 in.
F = 98.0 cps

The wrap wire diameter (D_w) expands the unwrapped diameter of a string by twice its own diameter. Therefore, according to Equation 2.22, calculate D_m in two steps; first multiply D_w by two, and then subtract this product from D_o:

$$D_m = D_o - 2D_w \tag{2.22}$$

$$D_m = 0.044 \text{ in} - 2(0.007 \text{ in}) = 0.030 \text{ in}$$

We are ready now to determine the surface areas of one circle and two rings. Substitute the appropriate D_i, D_m, and D_o dimensions into Equations 2.18 and 2.19, and calculate the steel core circle area, the small nylon ring area, and the large bronze ring area:

$$\begin{aligned}\text{Steel Core Circle Area} &= 0.7854(0.022\text{ in})^2 = 0.00038\text{ in}^2\\ \text{Small Nylon Ring Area} &= 0.7854(0.030^2\text{ in}^2 - 0.022^2\text{ in}^2) = 0.00033\text{ in}^2\\ \text{Large Bronze Ring Area} &= 0.7854(0.044^2\text{ in}^2 - 0.030^2\text{ in}^2) = 0.00081\text{ in}^2\end{aligned}$$

Next, substitute the correct surface area and mass density combinations into Equation 2.17 and calculate the mass per unit length of the steel core, the nylon fibers, and the bronze wrap. (See Appendix C for the mass density of nylon.) Remember, the mass density for bronze was modified (see Section 2.10) from 0.00082882 mica/in^3 to 0.00065096 mica/in^3.

$$\begin{aligned}M/u.l.\text{ of Steel Core} &= (0.00038\text{ in}^2)(0.00073299\text{ mica/in}^3) = 0.00000028\text{ mica/in}\\ M/u.l.\text{ of Nylon Fibers} &= (0.00033\text{ in}^2)(0.00010101\text{ mica/in}^3) = 0.00000003\text{ mica/in}\\ M/u.l.\text{ of Bronze Wrap} &= (0.00081\text{ in}^2)(0.00065096\text{ mica/in}^3) = 0.00000053\text{ mica/in}\end{aligned}$$

Now add these separate results together for a grand total composite $M/u.l.$ of 0.00000084 mica/in. Finally, substitute the above-mentioned string variables and this $M/u.l.$ variable into Equation 2.14 and compute the tension:

$$\begin{aligned}T &= 2^2(98.0\text{ cps})^2(47.244\text{ in})^2(0.00000084\text{ mica/in})\\ T &= 4(9604.0\text{ cps}^2)(2232.0\text{ in}^2)(0.00000084\text{ mica/in})\\ T &= 72.0\text{ lbf, or }72.0\text{ micas}\cdot\text{in/s}^2\end{aligned}$$

Since the wrap wire contributes nothing to the break strength of the core wire, note that the break strength of the 0.022 in. core wire equals 133.0 lbf. We conclude, therefore, that this wound string is tensioned at 54% of its break strength. (See Section 2.8.)

2.13

The preceding wound string required special considerations. Piano strings are less complicated because they consist of only two different stringing materials: a steel core wire and a copper wrap wire. Simply measure the D_i and D_o dimensions of a given bass string, substitute these measurements into Equations 2.20 and 2.21, and calculate the mass per unit length of one solid steel cylinder and one hollow copper cylinder. Due to the coiled surface of the winding, modify the mass density of copper (CDA 110) by multiplying 0.7854×0.00083660 mica/in^3 = 0.00065707 mica/in^3.

For example, consider the following G_2 bass string dimensions taken from a quality console piano:

D_o = 0.082 in.
D_i = 0.040 in.
L = 36.38 in. (This is the length of the copper winding.)
F = 98.0 cps (See Appendix A.)

Therefore,

$$M/u.l. \text{ of Solid Steel Cylinder} =$$
$$0.7854(0.040\text{ in})^2(0.00073299\text{ mica/in}^3) = 0.00000092\text{ mica/in}$$

$$M/u.l. \text{ of Hollow Copper Cylinder} =$$
$$0.7854(0.082^2\text{ in}^2 - 0.040^2\text{ in}^2)(0.00065707\text{ mica/in}^3) = 0.00000264\text{ mica/in}$$

Now add these separate results together for a grand total composite $M/u.l.$ of 0.00000356 mica/in. Finally, substitute the above-mentioned string variables and this $M/u.l.$ variable into Equation 2.14 and compute the tension:

$$T = 2^2(98.0\text{ cps})^2(36.38\text{ in})^2(0.00000356\text{ mica/in})$$
$$T = 4(9604.0\text{ cps}^2)(1323.5\text{ in}^2)(0.00000356\text{ mica/in})$$
$$T = 181.0\text{ lbf, or } 181.0\text{ micas}\cdot\text{in/s}^2$$

For conventional steel core and copper wound bass piano strings, Equation 2.23 combines the former sequence of calculations into a convenient formula:

$$T = 2^2F^2L^2\left[0.7854(D_\text{i})^2(0.00073299) + 0.7854(D_\text{o}^{\,2} - D_\text{i}^{\,2})(0.00065707)\right] \tag{2.23}$$

Notes

1. See Equation 3.11.

2. See Equation 4.7.

3. See Equation 5.2.

4. See Section 1.12.

5. Remember, according to Equation 1.13, an object's standard weight in lbf is numerically equal to the object's mass in lbm.

6. (A) Rossing, T.D. (1989). *The Science of Sound*, 2nd ed., p. 56. Addison-Wesley Publishing Co., Inc., Reading, Massachusetts, 1990.

   (B) Wood, A.B. (1930). *A Textbook of Sound*, p. 88. The Macmillan Company, New York, 1937.

   Scientists also use the terms *line density* and *linear density* for *mass per unit length.*

7. See Equation 1.20.

8. Oberg, E., Jones, F.D., Horton, H.L., and Ryffel, H.H. (1914). *Machinery's Handbook*, 24th ed., pp. 359–360. Industrial Press Inc., New York, 1992.

   In the United States, most wire diameters are listed in fractional or decimal parts of an inch.

9. (A) Crew, H., and De Salvio, A., Translators (1914). *Dialogues Concerning Two New Sciences*, by Galileo Galilei, pp. 100–103. Dover Publications, Inc., New York.

The first edition of this work was printed in 1637 and published in 1638.

(B) Chapman, R.E., Translator (1957). *Harmonie universelle: The Books on Instruments*, by Marin Mersenne, pp. 176–180. Martinus Nijhoff, The Hague, Netherlands.

The first edition of this work was published in 1636.

Galileo Galilei (1564–1642) and Marin Mersenne (1588–1648) independently discovered the quantitative relationship between the frequency of a vibrating string and its length, diameter, density, and tension.

10. The tensile strength of a wire varies with the *temper* and *diameter* of the material. For metal wires, a high classification is called spring and hard tempered, and a low classification, soft tempered. Steel music wire has a spring-tempered classification, which means that it can withstand a maximum amount of force. Also, thin metal strings, nylon strings, and gut strings have a higher tensile strength than thick strings. The drawing process through smaller and smaller dies creates a greater alignment of molecules that results in greater elasticity and strength. (See Appendix D.)

11. See Section 1.1 on Newton's first law of motion.

12. See Equation 4.6.

13. Campbell, M., and Greated, C. (1987). *The Musician's Guide to Acoustics*, p. 230. Schirmer Books, New York, 1988.

The authors cite a harp stringing scale of 1.72 : 1.

14. See Table 4.1.

15. See Equation 4.6.

16. See Section 5.14.

17. See Section 3.11.

18. For a dimensional analysis of Equation 2.10, see Equation 1.21.

19. The characteristic mechanical impedance of strings (Z_s) is directly proportional to tension: as the tension increases, the string impedance increases as well. (See Equation 5.2.) As Z_s increases, so does the transfer of energy from the string to the soundboard. This results in a stronger sound. (See Sections 5.1–5.6.)

20. *The Musician's Guide to Acoustics*, p. 231.

21. According to Equations 1.22 and 3.11, the speed of transverse waves in the string is

$$c_T = \sqrt{\frac{T}{M/u.l.}} = \sqrt{\frac{78.98 \text{ lbf}}{0.0000003316 \text{ mica/in}}} = 15{,}433.03 \text{ in/s}$$

Since this speed exceeds the speed of longitudinal sound waves in the air ($c_L = 13{,}504$ in/s), the string radiates sound.

22. Notable exceptions are guitar and harp bass strings with a core and wrap made of nylon.

23. Fenner, K. *On the Calculation of the Tension of Wound Strings*, 2nd ed. pp. 8–9. Verlag Das Musikinstrument, Frankfurt, Germany, 1976.

3 / FLEXIBLE STRINGS

Perfectly flexible strings do not exist. All strings must exhibit a minimum amount of stiffness; otherwise, they could not resist the force of tension. However, from a mathematical perspective the study of ideal strings is important because some strings have a tendency to behave as though they were perfectly flexible. This is especially true for strings that are long, thin, and very flexible. Such strings tend to produce higher mode frequencies that are near perfect integer multiples of a fundamental frequency. The physical presence of such "harmonics," and the mathematical language used to describe them, have greatly influenced our thoughts, ideas, and opinions about music. Since the 6th century B.C., when Pythagoras discovered the relationship between vibrating string lengths and musical intervals, countless experiments have been conducted and hundreds of treatises have been written to explain the nature of vibrating strings and the art of tuning to ratios. Although much of this knowledge has great value, it is in the spirit of firsthand experience that we begin our analysis in Part I by focusing on traveling waves, standing waves, and simple harmonic motion in strings. We then continue in Part II with period and frequency equations of waves in strings; in Part III, with length, frequency, and interval ratios of the harmonic series and on canon strings; in Part IV, with length, frequency, and interval ratios of non-harmonic tones, also on canon strings; and in Part V, with the musical, mathematical, and linguistic origins of length ratios.

Part I

TRANSVERSE TRAVELING AND STANDING WAVES, AND SIMPLE HARMONIC MOTION IN STRINGS

~ 3.1 ~

When we snap a rubber cord with a single rapid up-and-down motion of the hand, a *pulse* in the shape of a crest will begin to travel along the cord. Two such rapid motions of the hand in quick succession produce a *sine wave* in the shape of a crest and a trough. By definition, a wave (or one complete oscillation) consists of a positive (upward) displacement and a negative (downward) displacement of the cord. In contrast, a pulse (or one-half oscillation) is a simpler kind of wave because it consists only of a single positive or negative displacement. For this reason, we will begin the discussion on waves in strings by examining pulses in cords because they are easier to observe and illustrate.

Figure 3.1(a) shows the motion of a pulse as a crest. As it advances, individual particles of the cord move in an upward transverse direction at the leading edge of the pulse, and in a downward transverse direction at the trailing edge. For a pulse as a trough, Figure 3.1(b) shows that the cord particles move downward at the leading edge and upward at the trailing edge. Note carefully that in both examples the cord moves vertically up and down as the pulse travels horizontally from left to

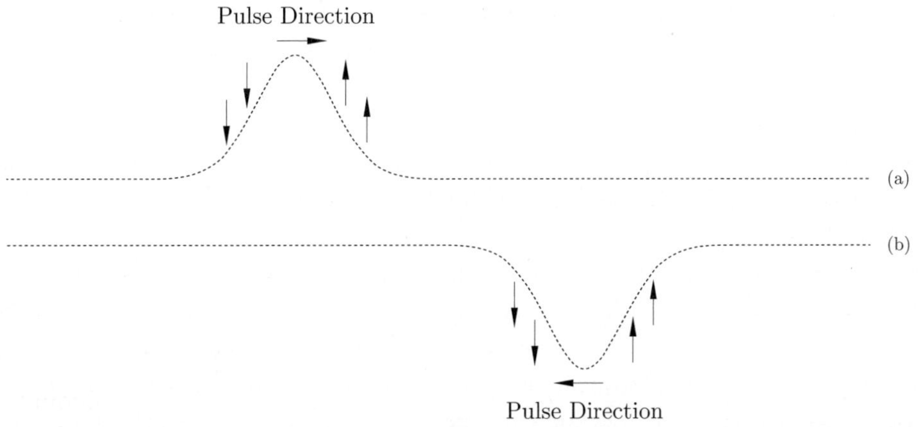

Figure 3.1 Vertical particle motion of a cord. (a) As a traveling pulse in the shape of a crest moves from left to right, vertical arrows indicate an initial upward motion followed by a downward motion of particles in the cord. (b) As a traveling pulse in the shape of a trough moves from right to left, vertical arrows indicate an initial downward motion followed by an upward motion of particles in the cord.

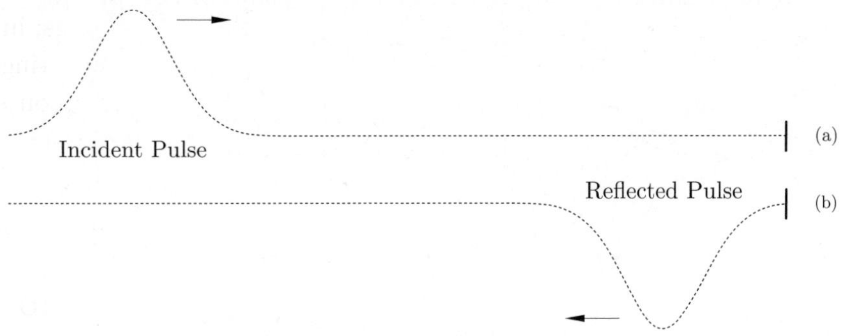

Figure 3.2 Reflection of a pulse. (a) An incident pulse in the shape of a crest travels from left to right. (b) After reflecting from a rigid support, the same pulse in the shape of a trough travels from right to left.

right, or from right to left. This kind of disturbance is called a transverse traveling pulse because the direction of particle motion is perpendicular to the direction of pulse propagation.[1] (See Figure 3.5.)

If we now tie one end of the cord to a rigid support and then give it a single snap, the pulse will travel to the fixed end, reflect, and return to the hand. As shown in Figure 3.2, notice that a reflected pulse reverses not only its direction of motion but also its position. In other words, an *incident* pulse moving from left to right in the shape of a crest becomes a *reflected* pulse moving from right to left in the shape of a trough.

Consider now the case of a musical instrument string fixed at both ends. The act of plucking, striking, or bowing such a string in its central region will send many transverse sine waves traveling toward both ends of the string. As a result, some waves will reflect sooner than others. When incident and reflected waves are simultaneously present in a given medium, they are by definition traveling in opposite directions. Consequently, the waves will collide. At the moment of collision, two possibilities arise: (1) either two crests or two troughs will meet while moving on the same side of the string, or (2) a crest and a trough will meet while moving on opposite sides of the string. In either case, we find that when two sine waves or two pulses collide, they move through each other and emerge from the collision without changing their original shapes.[2]

To observe the sequence of events before, during, and after a collision, refer to Figures 3.3 and 3.4. Here dashed lines illustrate a pulse moving from left to right, dotted lines, a pulse moving from right to left, and solid lines, the cord. In frames (a) and (i), the dashed and dotted pulse lines are

Similar Pulses Before and After the Collision in Figure 3.3

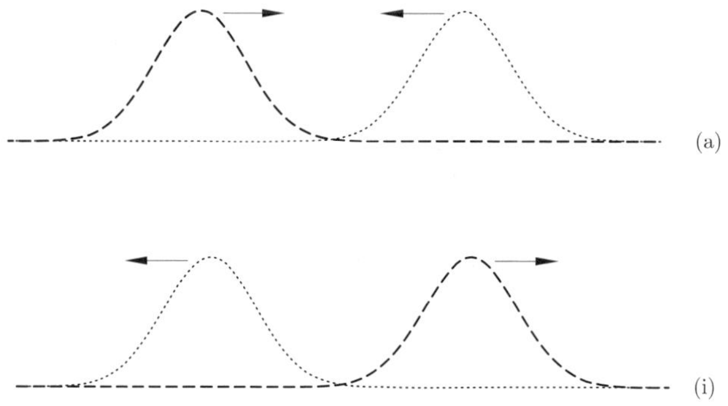

Opposite Pulses Before and After the Collision in Figure 3.4

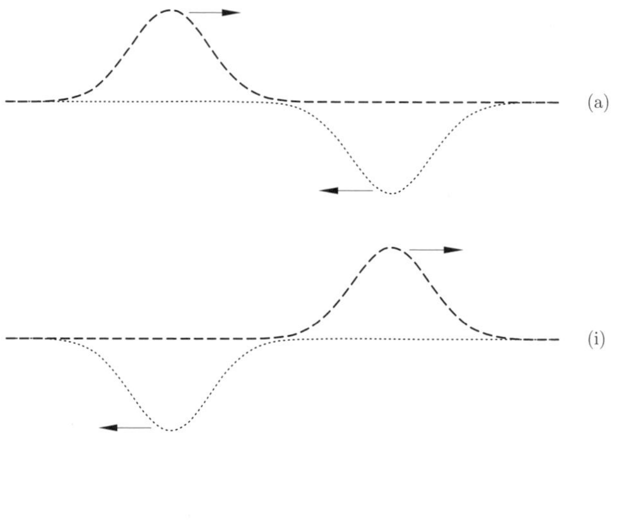

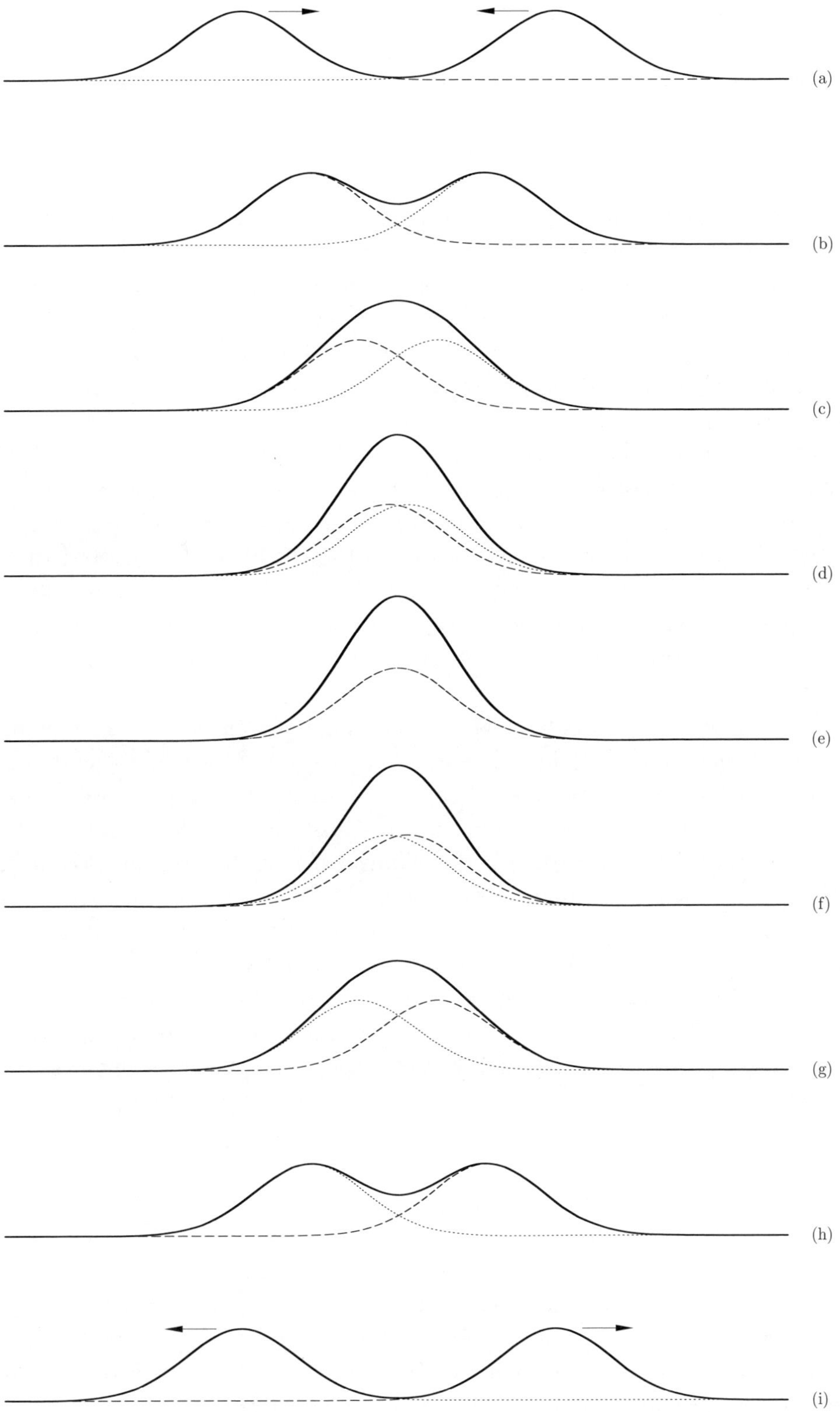

Figure 3.3 Two crests (dashed and dotted lines) with identical amplitudes traveling in opposite directions. When they meet in frame (e), the displacement of the cord (solid line) equals the sum of the amplitudes of the individual pulses. Here the crests combine to produce an amplitude in the cord that is exactly two times greater than each individual pulse. This state of maximum displacement is called constructive interference.

not visible because at these moments, the pulses and the cord have the same shape. To indicate the position of the pulses, the following two illustrations show frames (a) and (i) of Figures 3.3 and 3.4 without the cord lines. Also, in frames (a)–(i) all dashed and dotted pulse lines have only symbolic significance. They show the advancing positions of the pulses relative to the changing shape of the cord. To view the actual net effect of the two pulses, always follow the solid line that represents the cord.

In Figures 3.3 and 3.4, the shape and motion of the cord illustrate the *principle of superposition:* the cord's displacement at any given time equals the sum of the displacements of the incident and reflected pulses. In a larger context, the principle of superposition describes the process whereby two *traveling waves* combine and produce a third wave called a *standing wave.* (See Section 3.3.) Superposition applies not only to transverse waves traveling in solids like strings, soundboards, and marimba bars, but also to longitudinal waves traveling in gases like the air columns of flutes, organ pipes, and resonators.[3]

The effects of superposition are called *interference.* In Figure 3.3, frames (b)–(h) illustrate seven sequential and varying states of interference when two pulses in the shape of *crests* superpose while traveling in opposite directions. The most important image in Figure 3.3 is frame (e), which shows a moment when two crests occupy the same space in the cord. At that instant, the amplitude of the cord represents the sum of the amplitudes of the separate pulses. Because the amplitudes of both crests are identical, and because the crests are displacing the cord in the same direction, they reinforce each other and produce an amplitude exactly two times greater than the individual pulses. Now, turn Figure 3.3 upside down and note that this illustration also shows seven sequential and varying states of interference when two pulses in the shape of *troughs* superpose while traveling in opposite directions. Again, because the amplitudes of both troughs are identical and displacing the cord in the same direction, the amplitude of the cord in frame (e) is exactly two times greater than the individual pulses. When two crests coincide, the pulses are in phase and produce maximum displacement of the cord in the positive direction. Conversely, when two troughs coincide, the pulses are also in phase and produce maximum displacement of the cord in the negative direction. In either case, this state of reinforcement or maximum displacement is called *constructive interference.* In Section 3.3, we will find that varying states of interference in a direction toward constructive interference lead to the formation of antinodes, or regions of maximum motion in the string.

Turn now to Figure 3.4, where frames (b)–(h) illustrate seven sequential and varying states of interference when two pulses — one in the shape of a crest, and the other in the shape of a trough — superpose while traveling in opposite directions. Again, the most important image is frame (e), which shows a moment when a crest and trough occupy the same space in the cord. At that instant, the amplitude of the cord represents the sum of the amplitudes of the separate pulses. Because the amplitudes of the crest and trough are identical, and because the crest and trough are displacing the cord in opposite directions, they cancel each other out and produce a displacement of the cord exactly equal to zero. In frame (e), the cord appears in a state of equilibrium, or as though no transverse traveling waves were present. However, note carefully, that in a state of dynamic equilibrium the cord is moving and not at rest. We conclude, therefore, that when the amplitudes of crests and troughs coincide, the pulses are out of phase and produce no displacement of the cord. This state of cancellation or zero displacement is called *destructive interference.*

In Figure 3.4, each frame also indicates a center point in the cord that does *not* move. Because the magnitudes of the opposing pulses are identical, there exists a counterbalancing of forces at the location of this point. Although the positions of the pulses are continuously changing, the vertical displacement of the cord at the center point is constant and equals zero. In Section 3.3, we will find that varying states of interference in a direction toward destructive interference lead to the formation of nodes, or points of minimum motion in the string.

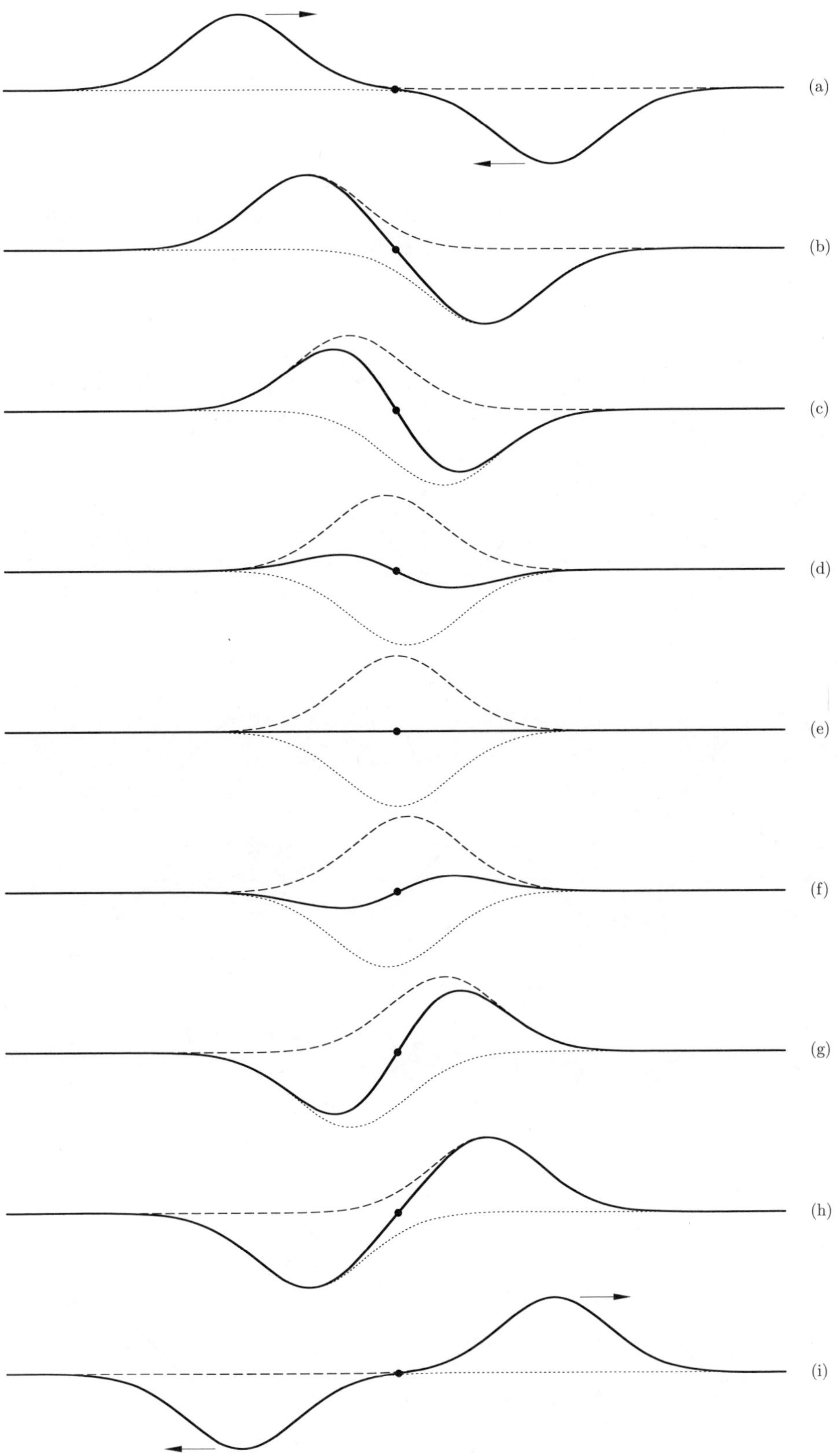

Figure 3.4 A crest and trough (dashed and dotted lines) with identical amplitudes traveling in opposite directions. When they meet in frame (e), the displacement of the cord (solid line) equals the sum of the amplitudes of the individual pulses. Here the crest and trough produce a displacement in the cord that is exactly equal to zero. This state of no displacement is called destructive interference.

~ 3.2 ~

The single most important motion associated with the vibrations of all acoustic musical instruments is called *simple harmonic motion.* SHM describes the periodic motion of a particle in a solid, liquid, or gas as it vibrates in a linear direction about its equilibrium position. To observe SHM, refer to Figure 3.5 and note that when we move the left end of the rubber cord in a repetitive vertical motion, transverse traveling waves begin moving down the length of the cord from left to right. Such a continuous succession of waves, which disturbs the cord at regular time intervals, is called

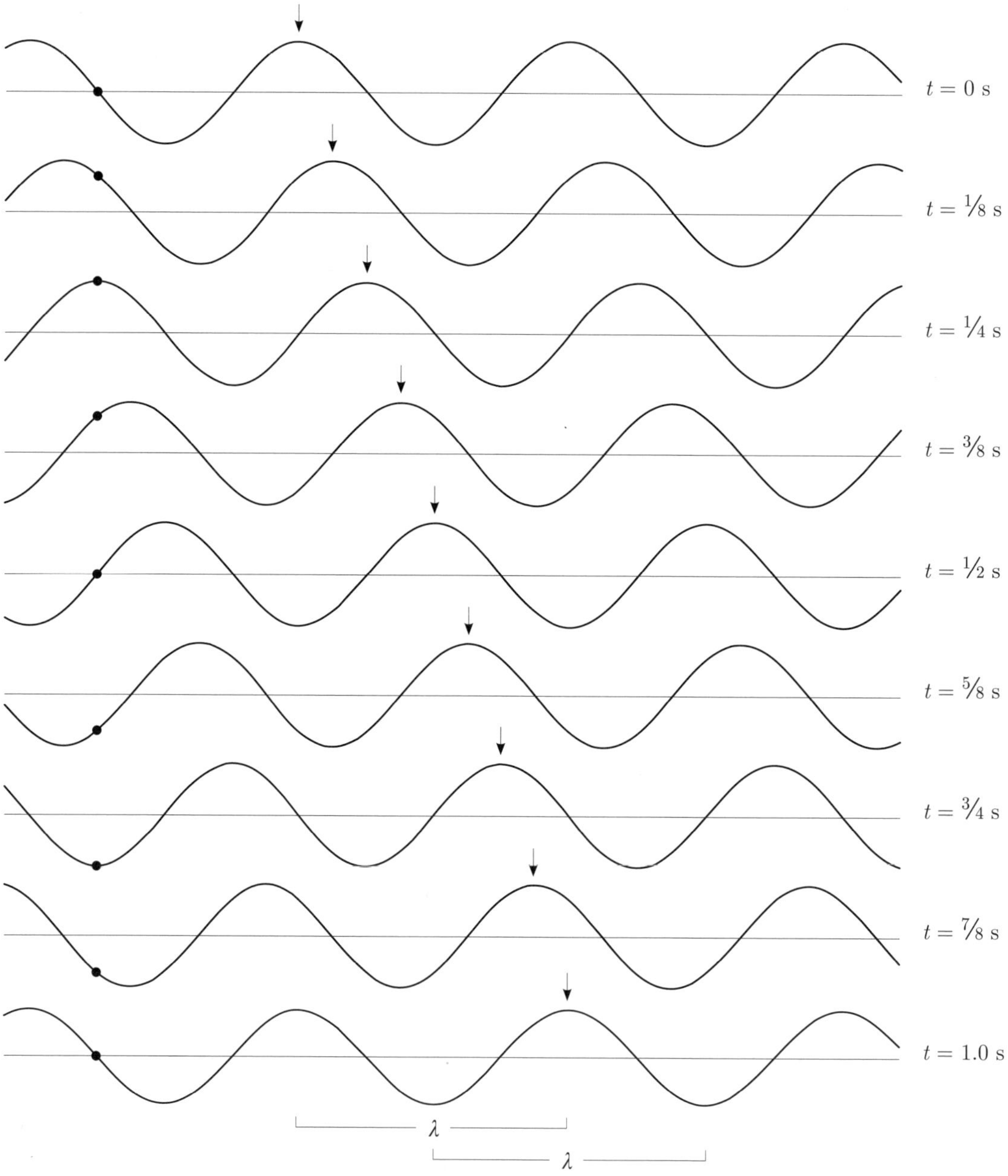

Figure 3.5 The wave train of a transverse traveling wave in a cord. Dots indicate the vertical motion of a particle in the cord, and arrows indicate the horizontal motion of a wave in the cord. The particle undergoes simple harmonic motion in the vertical direction, but does not advance with the wave that travels in the horizontal direction.

a *waveform*, or a *wave train*. The positions of the arrows indicate that in one second, the crest and trough of a wave advances the distance of one wavelength (λ) to the right. (See Section 3.4.) Furthermore, the position of a dot in each frame illustrates that a displaced particle in the cord undergoes simple harmonic motion. A close examination of SHM shows that when $t = 0$ s, the marked particle in Figure 3.5 is passing through the equilibrium position. At this location, the particle has maximum velocity. When $t = 1/8$ s, the particle is moving in the positive direction, and at $t = 1/4$ s, it reaches maximum positive displacement. Here the velocity = 0. When $t = 3/8$ s, the particle is now moving in the negative direction. At $t = 1/2$ s, the particle again passes through the equilibrium position. When $t = 5/8$ s, the particle continues its movement in the negative direction, and at $t = 3/4$ s, it reaches maximum negative displacement. Here again, the velocity = 0. Finally, when $t = 7/8$ s, the particle is now moving again in the positive direction, and at $t = 1.0$ s, it returns to the same position as in the first frame. This position marks the beginning of the next cycle.

We may also view this motion by looking straight down onto the page. Imagine the nine dots in the pathway of a pendulum bob as it swings back and forth between the top and the bottom of the page. Note, therefore, that only the mechanical energy associated with the disturbance travels in the direction of wave propagation. The particles of the medium do not travel but simply oscillate about their respective equilibrium positions. This kind of disturbance is called a transverse traveling wave because the direction of particle motion is *perpendicular* to the direction of wave propagation.

3.3

Let us now examine the movement of a string fixed at both ends. In Figure 3.6, dashed and dotted lines represent two traveling waves with identical frequencies and amplitudes propagating in opposite directions. To clarify this motion, note two vertical arrows: one points to the crest of a dashed wave that travels from left to right, and the other, to the trough of a dotted wave that travels from right to left. The solid line again illustrates the resulting displacement of the string. At the beginning of the sequence when $t = 0$ s, in the middle when $t = 1/2$ s, and at the end when $t = 1.0$ s, there is only one dashed-dotted line. At these moments, the superposition of traveling waves results in constructive interference. Here the string achieves maximum displacement, as in Figure 3.3, frame (e). When $t = 1/4$ s and $3/4$ s, the superposition of traveling waves results in destructive interference. Here the string is in dynamic equilibrium and has no displacement, as in Figure 3.4, frame (e). When $t = 1/8$ s, $3/8$ s, $5/8$ s, and $7/8$ s, the frames show varying states of interference between the superposing traveling waves.

Also, consider the motion of the traveling waves with respect to their wavelengths. (See Section 3.4.) When $t = 1/8$ s, the dashed wave has propagated one-eighth wavelength to the right, and the dotted wave, one-eighth wavelength to the left. When $t = 1/4$ s, the waves have traveled one-quarter wavelength to the right and to the left. Here the waves are out of phase and the string is in a state of dynamic equilibrium. When $t = 1/2$ s, the waves have traveled one-half wavelength to the right and to the left. The waves are in phase again, but compared to the beginning, the displacement of the string is now reversed: crests have become troughs, and troughs have become crests. Finally, when $t = 1.0$ s, the waves have traveled one wavelength to the right and to the left. Now the displacement of the string is the same as in the beginning.

This analysis illustrates the principle of superposition in strings: two transverse traveling waves that propagate horizontally in opposite directions combine to produce a third wave that vibrates in the vertical direction. The profile of the string advances neither to the left nor to the right. Instead, each particle of the string vibrates up and down in SHM. Waves that vibrate, or do not propagate, are called *standing waves*.

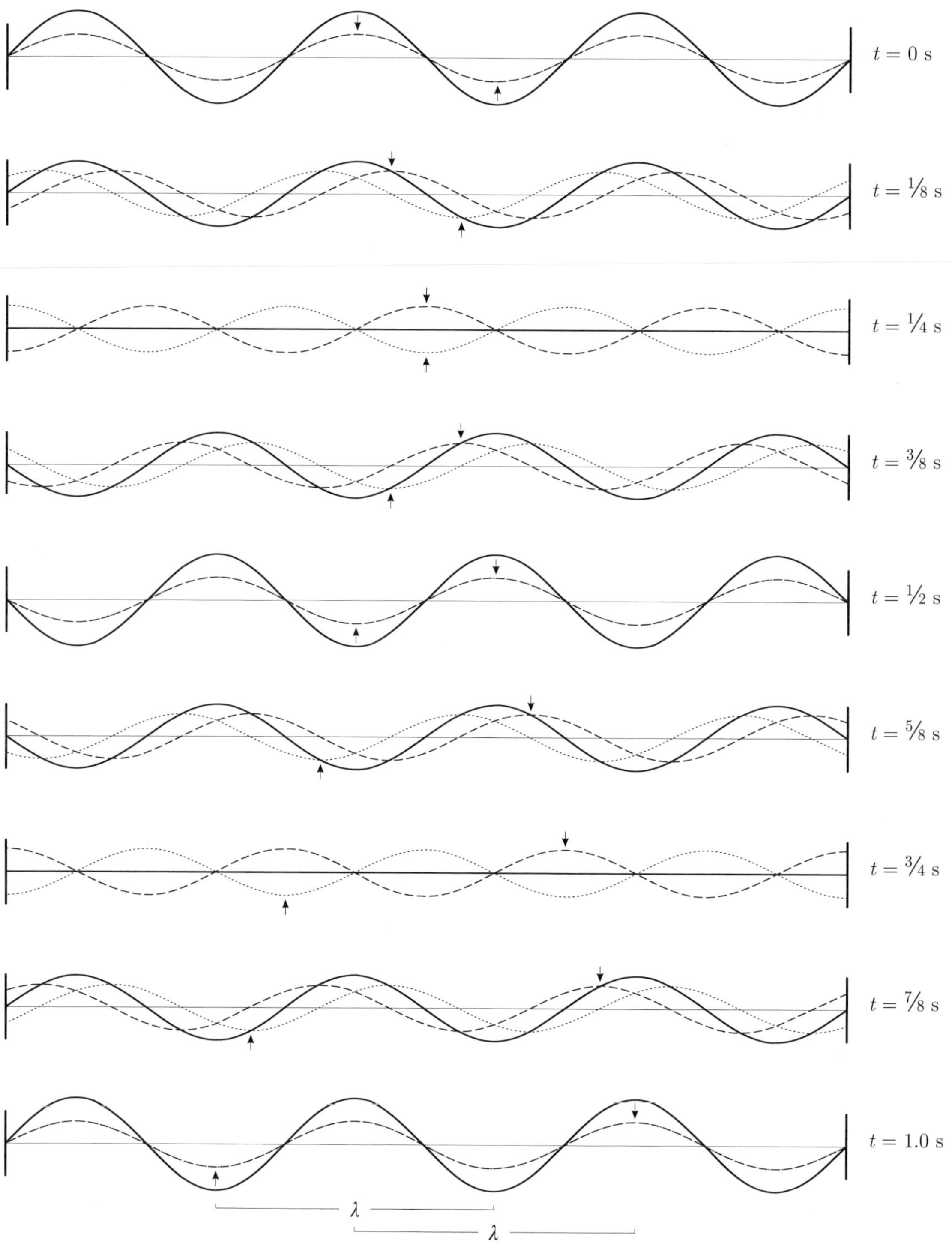

Figure 3.6 Transverse traveling waves and a transverse standing wave in a string fixed at both ends. The superposition of two transverse waves (dashed and dotted lines) that travel or propagate horizontally in opposite directions produces a standing wave (solid line) that vibrates up and down in the vertical direction.

Figure 3.7 shows the standing wave profile of the string in Figure 3.6. Here the thick and dashed lines represent the shape of the string at $t = 0$ s, ½ s, 1.0 s, and the thin lines, the shape of the string at $t =$ ⅛ s, ¼ s, ⅜ s, and ⅝ s, ¾ s, ⅞ s. If we were to replace the string with a slowly vibrating rubber cord, our eyes would be able to see the oscillating profile formed by the thick and dashed lines. However, we would not be able to detect the presence of traveling waves at any speed.

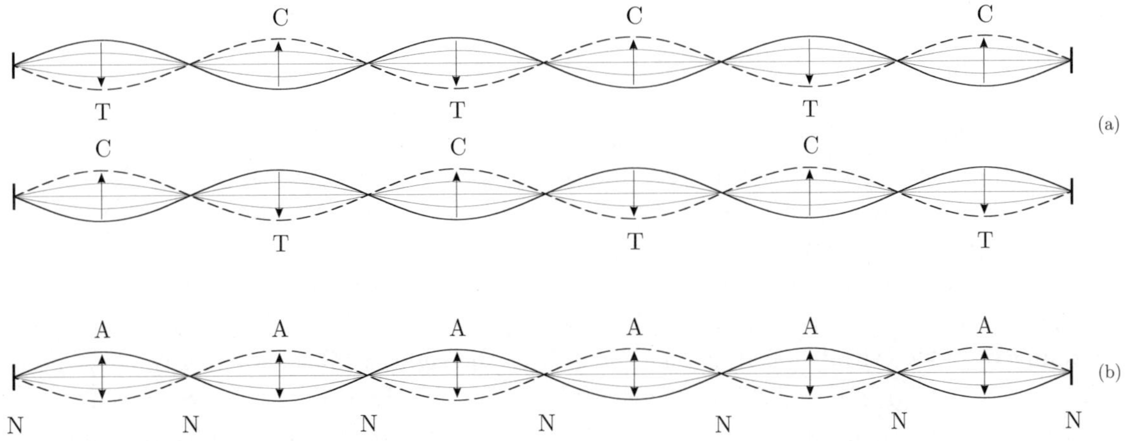

Figure 3.7 Transverse standing wave profile of the string in Figure 3.6. (a) This figure shows the alternating displacements of crests (C) and troughs (T), and arrows indicate the vertical direction of motion of the crests and troughs immediately after $t = 0$ s and $t =$ ½ s. (b) Double-headed arrows indicate the vertical direction of vibrating crests and troughs, defined here by an alternating pattern of nodes (N) and antinodes (A). Standing waves do not propagate to the left or right, but simply vibrate in place.

Figure 3.7(a) shows the alternating displacements of crests (C) and troughs (T) of the transverse standing wave, and arrows indicate the vertical direction of motion of the crests and troughs immediately after $t = 0$ s and $t =$ ½ s. And in Figure 3.7(b), double-headed arrows indicate the vertical direction of vibrating crests and troughs, defined here by an alternating pattern of nodes (N) and antinodes (A). Crests and troughs occur halfway between two adjacent nodes. At the inner nodes, or points of minimum motion, the string pivots up and down in opposite directions, very much like a teeter-totter pivots up and down on a motionless point called the fulcrum. Two outer nodes also exist at the fixed ends of the string. (See Section 3.5.) In contrast, at the crests and troughs, points of maximum motion are called antinodes.

With respect to size, nodes do not change because they occur where the sum of the displacements of the two traveling waves always equals zero. Therefore, nodes occur during varying states of interference, including constructive interference when the string exhibits maximum positive and maximum negative displacement. However, regarding size, antinodes are subject to change because they occur where the sum of the displacements always equals either a positive or a negative value. Therefore, antinodes also occur during varying states of interference, and most notably during constructive interference, when the displacements at the crests and troughs have maximum positive and maximum negative values, respectively. Now, let us assume that nodes and antinodes are interdependent, or that one cannot exist without the other. Then in a state of destructive interference — or when the string has no displacement and is in a state of dynamic equilibrium — there are no antinodes and, consequently, there are no nodes present in the string. We conclude, therefore, that the superposition of traveling waves causes the formation of nodes and antinodes; or that varying states of interference — either in a direction toward constructive interference, or in a direction toward destructive interference — cause nodes and antinodes. Finally, note carefully, only standing waves have nodes and antinodes, and only standing waves produce periodic or musical sound.

Part II

PERIOD AND FREQUENCY EQUATIONS OF WAVES IN STRINGS

~ 3.4 ~

As discussed in Section 3.3 and illustrated in Figure 3.6, at the end of one second, or one cycle, a linear measurement shows that the traveling waves have propagated the precise distance of one wavelength.[4] By definition, a wavelength is the distance between two crests, two troughs, or any two successive points that have identical displacements in a repeating wave shape. (See Figures 3.5 and 3.10.) In other words, a wavelength spans the distance in a wave after which the pattern of displacement repeats itself. We conclude, therefore, that after one second the arrow that points to the traveling wave's crest advanced one wavelength to the right, while the arrow that points to the traveling wave's trough advanced one wavelength to the left. During the same time interval, the standing wave in the string oscillated through one complete cycle: from crest to trough, and back to crest. The amount of time that a traveling wave requires to propagate past a given reference point — or the time a standing wave requires for one complete vibration — is called the period,

$$\tau = \frac{\lambda}{c_{\mathrm{T}}} \tag{3.1}$$

where τ is the period, in seconds per cycle; λ is the wavelength, in inches per cycle; and c_{T} is the transverse wave speed, in inches per second. Equation 3.1 expresses the familiar ratio

$$\text{time} = \frac{\text{distance}}{\text{speed}} \tag{3.2}$$

If we now substitute the appropriate units into Equation 3.1, a dimensional analysis shows that $\tau =$ seconds per cycle:

$$\tau = \frac{\lambda}{c_{\mathrm{T}}} = \frac{\dfrac{\text{inches}}{\text{cycle}}}{\dfrac{\text{inches}}{\text{second}}} = \frac{\cancel{\text{inches}}}{\text{cycle}} \times \frac{\text{second}}{\cancel{\text{inches}}} = \frac{\text{second}}{\text{cycle}}$$

Cycles are dimensionless quantities.

Figure 3.8 shows a wave train designed to illustrate the calculation of a period. Imagine you are standing at a railroad crossing with a stopwatch in your hand. A train passes where all the boxcars are linked together without gaps between cars. All cars are identical in length and each car represents one wavelength. Now, start the watch just as the beginning of a wave moves past a given reference point, and stop the watch as the end of the wave moves past the same point. The recorded time equals the period, in either seconds per boxcar, seconds per wave, or seconds per cycle.

Although the period is an important quantity for scientists and engineers, it is the inverse of τ, or the frequency (F) that concerns instrument builders, tuners, and musicians:

$$\frac{1}{\tau} = F$$

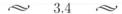

The number of traveling waves that propagate past an imaginary reference point in a horizontal direction in one second — or the number of standing waves that vibrate in the vertical direction in one second — is called a frequency. To calculate F in flexible strings, we must know (1) the transverse wave speed of the traveling wave, and (2) the wavelength of either the traveling wave or the standing wave. The ratio of these two physical quantities determines frequency:

$$F = \frac{c_{\mathrm{T}}}{\lambda} \tag{3.3}$$

Equation 3.3 expresses the less familiar ratio

$$\text{frequency} = \frac{\text{speed}}{\text{distance}} \tag{3.4}$$

If we substitute the appropriate units into Equation 3.3, a dimensional analysis shows that $F =$ cycles per second:

$$F = \frac{c_{\mathrm{T}}}{\lambda} = \frac{\frac{\text{inches}}{\text{second}}}{\frac{\text{inches}}{\text{cycle}}} = \frac{\cancel{\text{inches}}}{\text{second}} \times \frac{\text{cycle}}{\cancel{\text{inches}}} = \frac{\text{cycle}}{\text{second}}$$

Figure 3.9 shows the same wave train, this time designed to illustrate the calculation of a frequency. Again, start the stopwatch just as the beginning of a wave moves past a given reference point, and then stop the watch after exactly one second has elapsed. Now, count the number of boxcars or waves that moved past the point. This number equals the frequency, in either boxcars per second, waves per second, or cycles per second.

Before we close this section on wavelengths and frequencies, one theoretical problem regarding the λ variable in Equations 3.1 and 3.3 still needs some clarification. Due to the high speeds of traveling waves in strings, there is no practical method to measure the lengths of such waves. However, in Figure 3.6, notice from the vertical alignment of crests and troughs in the first and last frames that the wavelength of the standing wave and the wavelengths of the constituent traveling waves are identical. Since the λ variable with respect to standing waves depends on the physical length of the string (see Section 3.5), wavelength calculations for either kind of wave turn out to be simple and straightforward.

3.5

Before we proceed with detailed wavelength calculations, let us first examine some of the vibrational characteristics of stretched strings. Since the standing wave represents the actual shape of a vibrating string, all wavelength calculations require string length dimensions. (We assume for a moment that F is an unknown variable and that Equation 3.3, in the form $\lambda = c_{\mathrm{T}}/F$, does not provide a solution.) For all flexible strings, the vibrating length equals the overall measured length (L) from one fixed end to the other. As discussed in Section 3.3, points along the length of a vibrating string that exhibit minimum displacement or minimum motion are called nodes, from the Latin *nodus* (lit. *knot*). Conversely, points that exhibit maximum displacement or maximum motion halfway between two adjacent nodes are called antinodes. Nodes also exist at the motionless fixed ends of a string. However, we should make one important distinction here between the end nodes and the nodes in a string's inner region. When traveling waves reflect at the rigid supports, they reverse their position and direction of motion. In other words, a reflection of elastic wave energy takes place at the end nodes. In contrast, traveling waves at the inner nodes do not reverse their

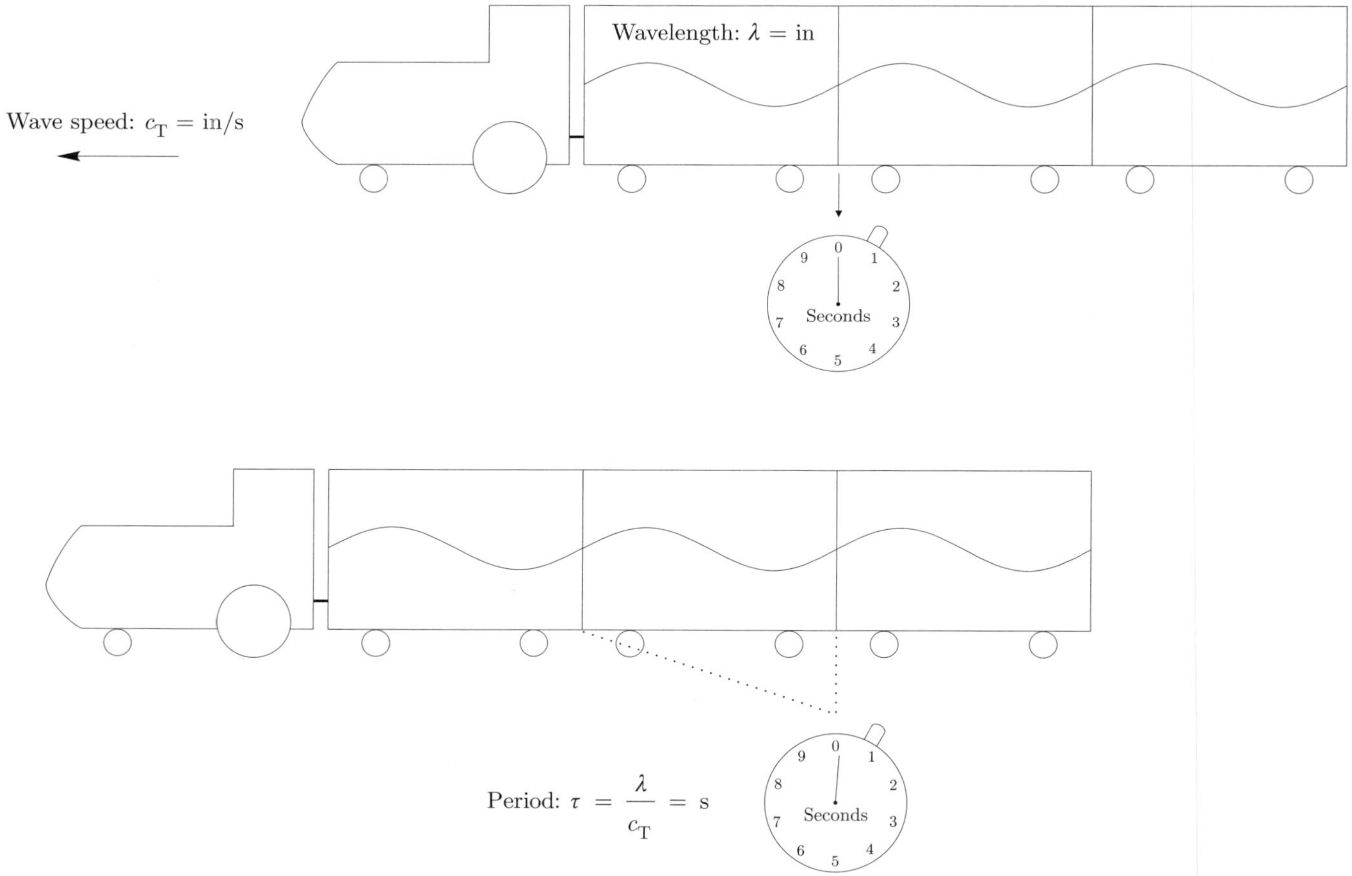

Figure 3.8 A wave train designed to illustrate the calculation of a period. For a given wavelength, the time required for one traveling wave to move past a given reference point (vertical arrow) is a function of speed. The period of a traveling wave typically consists of a very small fraction of a second per cycle. For the fundamental mode of vibration, the sample string described in Section 3.6 has the dimensions $\lambda_1 = 94.488$ in. and $c_T = 9258.2$ in/s; consequently, $\tau = 0.0102$ s. For the wave train, the stopwatch shows a period of some small fraction of a second per cycle.

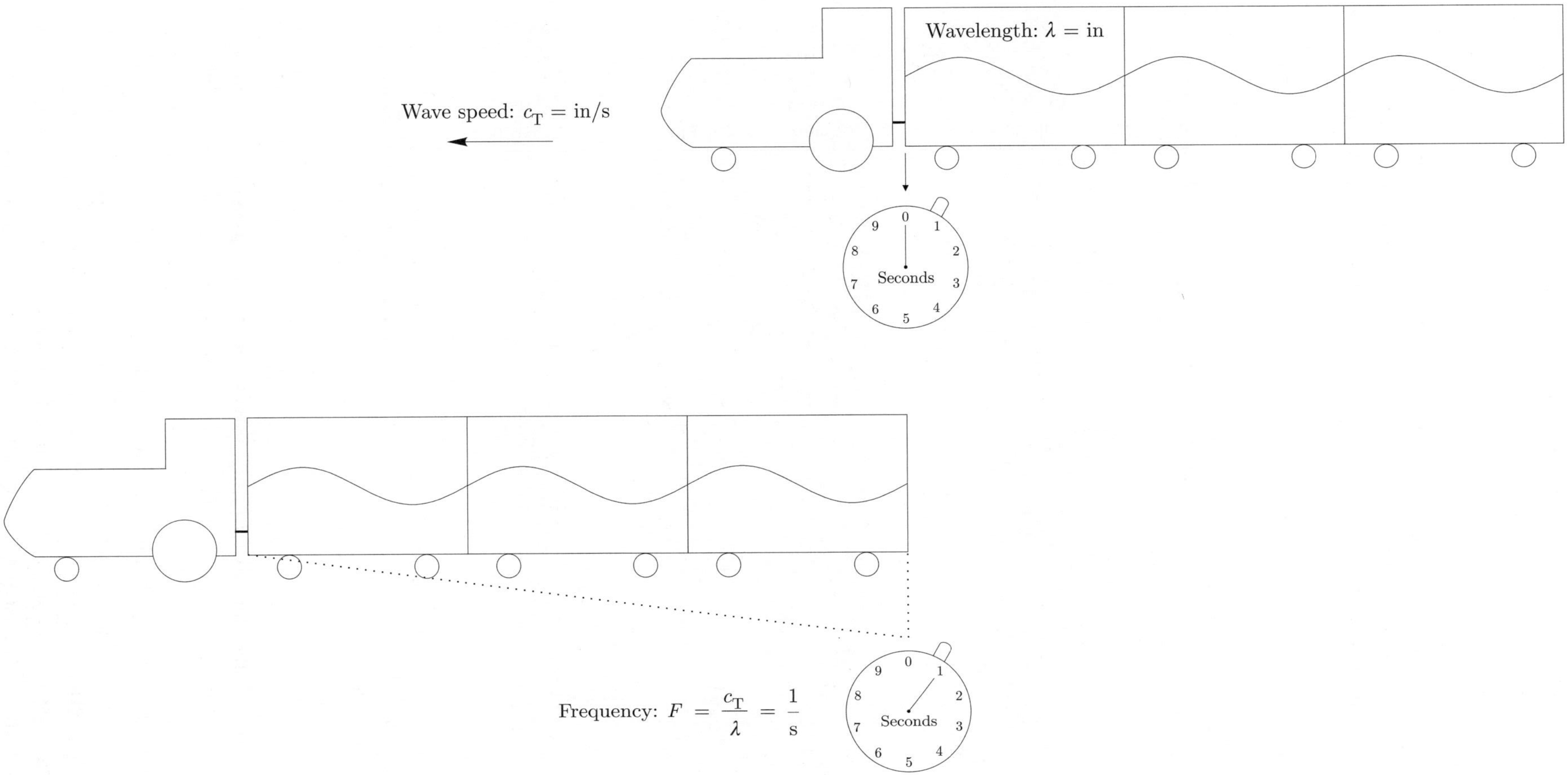

Figure 3.9 A wave train designed to illustrate the calculation of a frequency. For a given wave speed, the number of traveling waves that move past a given reference point (vertical arrow) in one second is a function of wavelength. The frequency of a traveling wave produced by a vibrating string typically consists of a large number of cycles per second. For the fundamental mode of vibration, the sample string described in Section 3.6 has the dimensions $\lambda_1 = 94.488$ in. and $c_T = 9258.2$ in/s; consequently, $F_1 = 98.0$ cps. For the wave train, the stopwatch indicates a frequency of 3 cycles per second.

position or their direction. Consequently, the superposition of traveling waves causes elastic wave energy to pass through the inner nodes. As a result, the inner nodes are not absolutely at rest, but exhibit small amounts of motion.[5]

Figure 3.10 illustrates the first six standing wave patterns or modes of vibration of a flexible string. The word "mode" refers to the simplest physical patterns, shapes, or forms a vibrating system is capable of producing. When we pluck, strike, or bow a string, the disturbance sends numerous standing waves with varying wavelengths, frequencies, and amplitudes through the string.

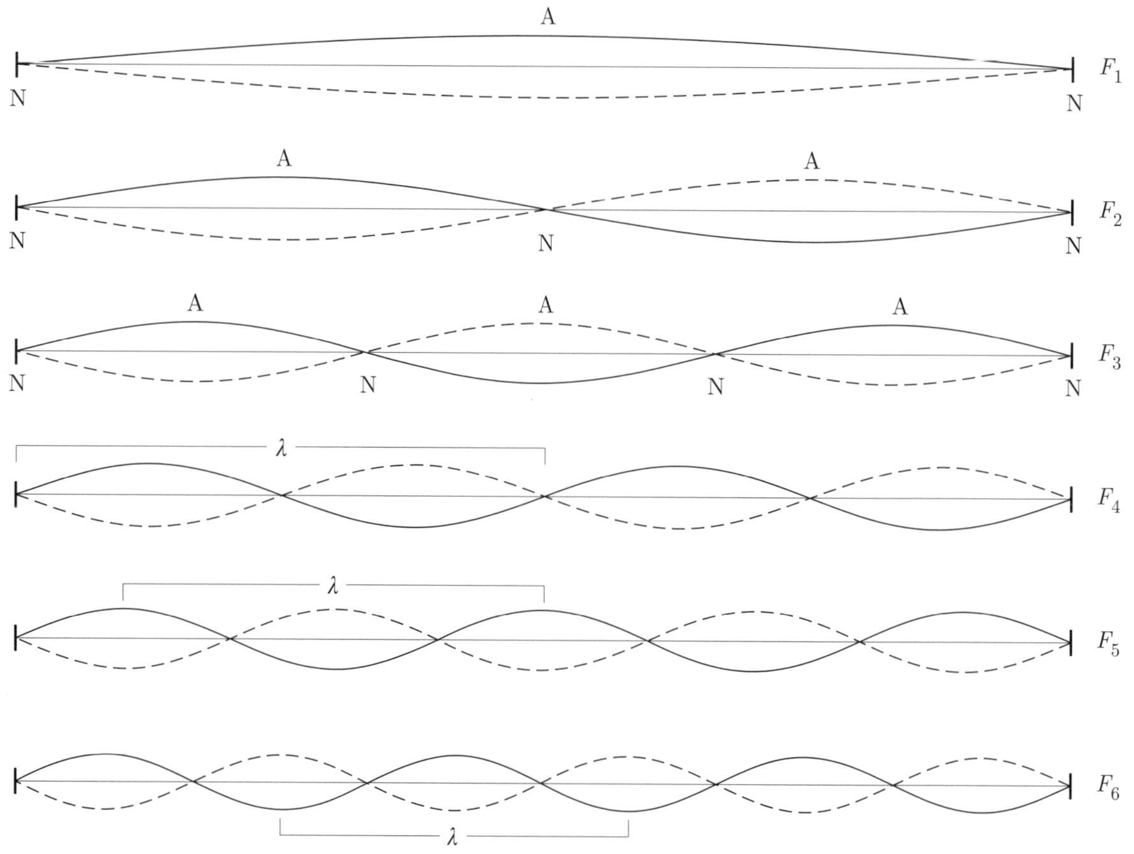

Figure 3.10 The standing waves of the first six modes of vibration of a flexible string. Vibrating strings bend and subdivide into an integer number of equidistant sections called loops. A loop has two nodes (N), one at either end, and one antinode (A) in the middle. A wavelength (λ) consists of the combined length of two loops.

Because of the boundary conditions, not all traveling waves superpose into standing waves. Only those standing waves emerge that have zero displacement at the string's fixed ends. With several different superposing standing waves simultaneously present in the string, the string's vibrating shape changes rapidly and is therefore difficult to illustrate. However, it is possible to shake a rubber cord by hand, or to vibrate a string with an electrically driven tuning fork, and to view the individual standing wave patterns that cause the string's continuously changing shape.

Since several standing waves exist in the string simultaneously, the sound emanating from a freely vibrating string contains all the frequencies produced by the constituent standing waves. To account for all these mode frequencies, we must rewrite Equation 3.3 to read

$$F_{\text{n}} = \frac{c_{\text{T}}}{\lambda_{\text{n}}} \tag{3.5}$$

where F_{n} is the mode frequency, in cps; and λ_{n} is the mode wavelength, in inches. In Figure 3.10, notice that due to the boundary conditions of two fixed ends, a vibrating string bends into an integer number of equidistant parts called loops. Each loop has two nodes and one antinode. The mode number indicates the total integer number of loops in a given mode. For the first mode (F_1), the string bends in the shape of one loop. Here the outer two nodes are the string's two fixed ends. For the second mode (F_2), the string subdivides into two loops; here one inner node divides the string into two equal parts. For the third mode (F_3), the string subdivides into three loops; here two inner nodes divide the string into three equal parts.

Part III

LENGTH, FREQUENCY, AND INTERVAL RATIOS OF THE HARMONIC SERIES ON CANON STRINGS

3.6

As the string continues to subdivide into shorter loops, a simple pattern begins to emerge. For the first mode, the string vibrates in the shape of a single loop; since a single loop spans the entire length of the whole string, the ratio of one loop to the whole string is $^1/_1$. For the second mode, the string subdivides into 2 equal parts; since a single loop spans 1 of those parts, one loop of the second mode occupies one-half of the whole string. Therefore, the ratio of one loop to the mode number of loops is $^1/_2$. Similarly, for the third mode, the string subdivides into 3 equal parts; since a single loop spans 1 of those parts, one loop of the third mode occupies one-third of the whole string. Therefore, the ratio of one loop to the mode number of loops is $^1/_3$.

In this text, the ratio of the length of one loop of a higher mode of vibration to the length of the total number of n loops is defined as a length ratio (*l.r.*):

$$l.r. \equiv \frac{1}{n} \tag{3.6}$$

And the ratio of a single loop length (ℓ_{S}) to the whole string length is defined as a length ratio as well:

$$l.r. \equiv \frac{\ell_{\text{S}}}{L} \tag{3.7}$$

Because these two ratios express the same relation, they form a proportion. By definition, a proportion is a statement that two ratios are equal. The proportion

$$\frac{a}{b} = \frac{c}{d}$$

states that "a is to b as c is to d." In this context, the following proportion states that a single loop length is to the whole string length as the length of one loop is to the length of the total mode number of loops:

$$\frac{\ell_S}{L} = \frac{1}{n} \tag{3.8}$$

Now, to calculate a single loop length, solve Equation 3.8 for ℓ_S:[6]

$$\ell_S = \frac{L}{n} \tag{3.9}$$

For a sample string, where $L = 47.244$ inches (1200.0 mm), the loop lengths of the first, second, and third modes are

$$\ell_{S_1} = \frac{47.244 \text{ in}}{1} = 47.244 \text{ in}$$
$$\ell_{S_2} = \frac{47.244 \text{ in}}{2} = 23.622 \text{ in}$$
$$\ell_{S_3} = \frac{47.244 \text{ in}}{3} = 15.748 \text{ in}$$

Furthermore, since a mode wavelength consists of any two successive points in the wave that have identical displacements (see Section 3.4), Figure 3.10 shows that a wavelength consists of the combined length of two loops. Therefore, a wavelength calculation requires that we multiply Equation 3.9 by two:

$$\lambda_n = \frac{2L}{n} \tag{3.10}$$

Consequently, the wavelengths of the first, second, and third modes are

$$\lambda_1 = \frac{2(47.244 \text{ in})}{1} = 94.488 \text{ in}$$
$$\lambda_2 = \frac{2(47.244 \text{ in})}{2} = 47.244 \text{ in}$$
$$\lambda_3 = \frac{2(47.244 \text{ in})}{3} = 31.496 \text{ in}$$

We turn now to the numerator of Equation 3.3, the transverse wave speed. Under ideal conditions, the speed of traveling waves in perfectly flexible strings is a constant because it depends exclusively on two physical properties of the string: mass per unit length and tension. Once stringing materials and string diameters have been selected, and the strings are tuned, the mass per unit length and the tension are not subject to change. Whether the string is one mile or one inch long, the wave speed for all mode frequencies and all mode wavelengths remains constant. To calculate the transverse wave speed, use the following equation:

$$c_T = \sqrt{\frac{T}{M/u.l.}} \tag{3.11}$$

where T is the tension, in pounds-force (lbf); and $M/u.l.$ is the mass per unit length, in mica per inch. (For a definition of the mica mass unit, see Section 1.10.) Now substitute Subequations 3.10

and 3.11 into Equation 3.5 and rewrite the mode frequency equation in full detail,

$$F_n = \frac{c_T}{\lambda_n} = \frac{\sqrt{\dfrac{T}{M/u.l.}}}{\dfrac{2L}{n}} \tag{3.12}$$

where n is called the mode number, any positive integer.

To utilize Equation 3.12, consider a bass canon equipped with identical wound strings. All strings are made with a steel core wire, an inner nylon fiber bedding, and an outer bronze wrap wire (see Sections 2.10–2.12), and have the following sample string dimensions:

D_o = 0.080 in.
D_i = 0.028 in.
D_w = 0.020 in.
L = 47.244 in. (1200.0 mm)
F = 65.0 cps
$M/u.l.$ = 0.00000297 mica/in
T = 112.0 lbf, or 112.0 micas·in/s^2 (See Equations 1.21 and 2.10.)

Substitute the tension and the mass per unit length into Equation 3.11 and determine the transverse wave speed:

$$c_T = \sqrt{\frac{112.0 \text{ mica·in/s}^2}{0.00000297 \text{ mica/in}}} = 6140.9 \text{ in/s}$$

Now, substitute this result, the string length dimension, and the mode numbers into Equation 3.12, and calculate the frequencies of the first three modes:

$$F_1 = \frac{6140.9 \text{ in/s}}{\dfrac{2(47.244 \text{ in})}{1}} = \frac{6140.9 \text{ in/s}}{94.488 \text{ in}} = 65.0 \text{ cps} = C_2$$

$$F_2 = \frac{6140.9 \text{ in/s}}{\dfrac{2(47.244 \text{ in})}{2}} = \frac{6140.9 \text{ in/s}}{47.244 \text{ in}} = 130.0 \text{ cps} = C_3$$

$$F_3 = \frac{6140.9 \text{ in/s}}{\dfrac{2(47.244 \text{ in})}{3}} = \frac{6140.9 \text{ in/s}}{31.496 \text{ in}} = 195.0 \text{ cps} = G_3$$

In summary of Section 3.6, we conclude that the mode frequencies of perfectly flexible strings are inversely proportional to the mode wavelengths:[7]

$$F_n \propto \frac{1}{\lambda_n} \propto \frac{1}{\dfrac{2L}{n}}$$

As the mode wavelengths decrease, the mode frequencies increase. Furthermore, an inspection of the previous mode frequency calculations shows that Equation 3.12 includes *two constants:* the transverse wave speed and the wavelength of the first mode of vibration. For the first mode, the string does not subdivide into equal parts but vibrates in the shape of a single loop. As a result, the fundamental wavelength

$$\lambda_1 = \frac{2L}{1}$$

appears as a constant in all mode frequency calculations. Therefore, to calculate the fundamental frequency of the sample string, simply divide the wave speed constant by the wavelength constant:

$$F_1 = \frac{6140.9 \text{ in/s}}{94.488 \text{ in}} = 65.0 \text{ cps}$$

~ 3.7 ~

For all other mode frequency calculations, length ratio $1/n$ is the only remaining variable in Equation 3.12. To understand the mathematical significance of this ratio, consider Equation 3.13, which shows four transformations of Equation 3.12:

$$F_\text{n} = \frac{c_\text{T}}{\lambda_\text{n}} = \frac{c_\text{T}}{\frac{2L}{n}} = \frac{\frac{c_\text{T}}{2L}}{\frac{1}{n}} = \frac{F_1}{\frac{1}{n}} = F_1 n \tag{3.13}$$

In the first transformation, length ratio $1/n$ functions as a multiplier of L; according to Equation 3.9, as the mode number increases, the single loop length decreases. The second transformation places the fundamental wavelength constant ($2L$) into the numerator; therefore, according to the third transformation, length ratio $1/n$ now functions as the divisor of F_1. Finally, the fourth transformation places the inverse of length ratio $1/n$ into the numerator, which means that $n/1$ now functions as the multiplier of F_1. The last transformation states that the frequencies of the higher modes are *integer multiples* of the fundamental frequency.[8] For the first mode, the string vibrates as a whole expressed by length ratio $1/1$; since the first mode vibrates at the same rate as the whole string, $F_1 = F_1 \times 1/1$. For the second mode, the string subdivides into two equal parts expressed by length ratio $1/2$; since the second mode vibrates 2 times faster than the whole string, $F_2 = F_1 \times 2/1$. Similarly, for the third mode, the string subdivides into three equal parts expressed by length ratio $1/3$; since the third mode vibrates 3 times faster than the whole string, $F_3 = F_1 \times 3/1$.

In this text, the ratio of the rate of vibration of a higher mode loop to the rate of vibration of the whole string is defined as a frequency ratio (*f.r.*):

$$f.r. \equiv \frac{n}{1} \tag{3.14}$$

Furthermore, the ratio of a higher mode frequency to the fundamental mode frequency is defined as a frequency ratio as well:

$$f.r. \equiv \frac{F_\text{n}}{F_1} \tag{3.15}$$

Therefore, according to Equation 3.13, we may also calculate the first three mode frequencies of the sample string in the following manner:

$$F_1 = \frac{65.0 \text{ cps}}{\frac{1}{1}} = (65.0 \text{ cps})(1) = 65.0 \text{ cps} = \text{C}_2$$

$$F_2 = \frac{65.0 \text{ cps}}{\frac{1}{2}} = (65.0 \text{ cps})(2) = 130.0 \text{ cps} = \text{C}_3$$

$$F_3 = \frac{65.0 \text{ cps}}{\frac{1}{3}} = (65.0 \text{ cps})(3) = 195.0 \text{ cps} = \text{G}_3$$

Equation 3.13 describes the inverse proportionality between length ratio $1/n$ and frequency ratio $n/1$. These transformations indicate that we may invert the length ratio of a given mode shape to identify the corresponding frequency ratio. Throughout this book, and especially in Chapters 10 and 11 on the subject of canon and lute string divisions, an arrow that points from a modern length ratio to a frequency ratio signifies such an inversion. Furthermore, in Section 3.11, I used the notation (l.r. $1/3 \rightarrow$ f.r. $3/1$) and (l.r. $1/4 \rightarrow$ f.r. $4/1$) to identify the inverse proportionality between modern length ratios and frequency ratios in the tuning of canon strings with moveable bridges. In Sections 3.13–3.14, this notation applies equally well to length ratio x/n and frequency ratio n/x.

Finally, Figure 3.11 shows the inverse proportionality between the length ratios and frequency ratios of the first three modes of the previously calculated sample string. Substitute the appropriate values from this figure into Equations 3.7 and 3.15, respectively, and for the variables C_2, C_3, and G_3, calculate length ratios $1/1$, $1/2$, $1/3$, and frequency ratios $1/1$, $2/1$, $3/1$.

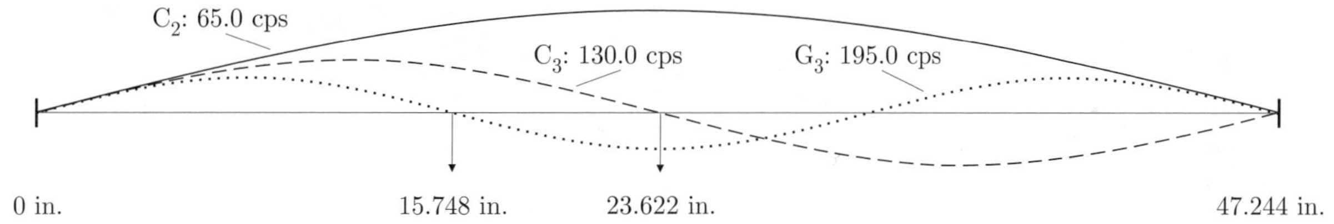

Figure 3.11 Loop lengths and frequencies of the first three modes of the sample string. A substitution of these values into Equations 3.7 and 3.15, respectively, demonstrates the inverse proportionality between length ratios and frequency ratios.

~ 3.8 ~

Whenever a vibrating system produces mode frequencies that are integer multiples of a fundamental frequency, we call such frequencies *harmonics*.[9] Therefore, all the mode frequencies of perfectly flexible strings are called harmonics because the quotient of any frequency ratio $n/1$ is a positive integer. A simplified version of Equation 3.13 states

$$\text{Harmonic Frequencies:} \quad F_n = F_1 n \tag{3.16}$$

A perfectly flexible vibrating string subdivides into a theoretically infinite number of equidistant integer parts,[10] and therefore produces a theoretically infinite number of harmonic frequencies.

Each part that represents 1, $1/2$, $1/3$, $1/4$, $1/5$, $1/6$, . . . of the string's whole length produces a harmonic frequency 1, $2/1$, $3/1$, $4/1$, $5/1$, $6/1$, . . . times the string's fundamental frequency. In mathematics, the former sequence of length ratios is called a *harmonic progression*, and in acoustics, the latter sequence of frequency ratios is called the *harmonic series*. To understand the musical significance of the harmonic series, Figure 3.12 shows the first sixteen harmonics of two perfectly flexible strings. The first series belongs to a string tuned to C_2 (65.0 cps), and the second series, to a string tuned to G_2 (97.5 cps). Arrows pointing upward indicate harmonics that sound considerably higher, and arrows pointing downward indicate harmonics that sound considerably lower than the notated frequencies of the conventional piano scale tuned in 12-tone equal temperament. With the exception of the 2nd, 4th, 8th, and 16th harmonics, all the other harmonics also sound either higher or lower than the tones of the Western scale. For the marked harmonics, the differences are distinctly noticeable, and for the unmarked harmonics, the differences vary from subtle to obvious. (See Section 9.3.)

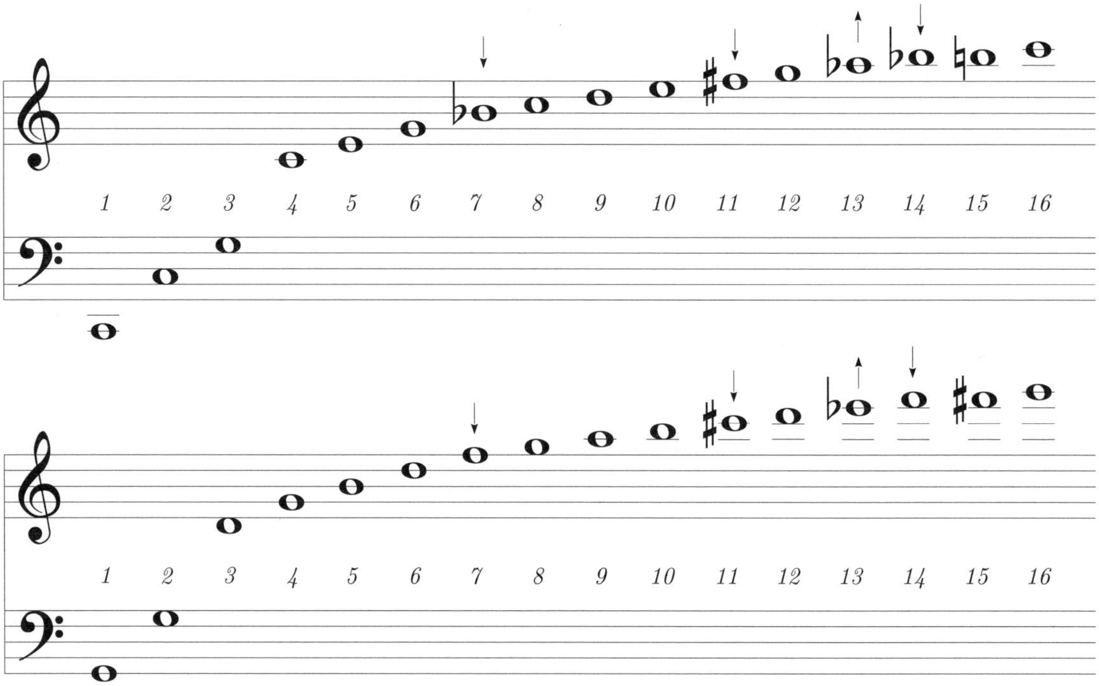

Figure 3.12 The first sixteen harmonics of two different harmonic series. The first series begins on C_2, and the second series begins on G_2. Arrows pointing upward or downward indicate harmonics that sound considerably higher or lower than the tones of the conventional piano scale tuned in 12-tone equal temperament.

~ 3.9 ~

We turn now to the formidable task of describing key elements of the harmonic series in greater detail. The naming of intervals between harmonics is fraught with difficulty because conventional musical terminology has its roots in music theory, and not in mathematics and acoustics. For example, a "fifth" in music simply means the fifth tone in a scale. It does not represent a ratio, as in the length ratio $1/5$; consequently, a "fifth" does not refer to frequency ratio $5/1$. The lack of mathematical precision in the description and naming of musical tones and intervals leads to a deplorable confusion of words and ideas. To mitigate these problems, the following discussion will attempt to straddle the gap between these two worlds. Eventually, however, in later chapters on musical ratios, cents, and tuning, we must jettison convention and work only with numbers. Just as some words fail to describe the immense experiences of color, so other words fail to describe the vast experiences of sounds. Stated bluntly, the rich mathematical complexity of the harmonic series defies all attempts at meaningful *verbal* nomenclature.

3.10

String harmonics are difficult to hear because the amplitudes of the upper harmonics are weak, and because high frequencies place many harmonics beyond the audible range of human ears.[11] However, for strings tuned to low frequencies, careful listening confirms that the tonal distance between the first and second harmonics sounds like an interval called the "octave" in Western music. (See Figure 3.12.) Similarly, the interval between the first and third harmonics sounds like a "twelfth," or "one octave and a fifth"; the interval between the first and fourth harmonics sounds like a "double-octave"; the interval between the first and fifth harmonics sounds like "two octaves and a major third"; the interval between the first and sixth harmonics sounds like "two octaves and a fifth," and so on for the harmonics in the "double-octave," "triple-octave," and higher "multiple-octave" regions.

To investigate the nature of vibrating strings, and to make the frequencies and intervals of the harmonic series clearly audible, musicians and mathematicians have for thousands of years built simple instruments with long strings and moveable bridges. When such an instrument has only one string, it is called a monochord, and when it has two or more strings, it is called a polychord, sonometer, or canon. In Greek, the word *kanon* means (1) a straight rule or rod, as in measuring instrument, and (2) a general rule or principle, as in code of law.[12] The purpose of all these instruments is to use moveable bridges to divide strings into carefully measured length ratios, which in turn makes it possible to identify the corresponding frequency ratios and interval ratios. By placing the bridge underneath a string, and allowing it to push up against the string, the bridge prevents the string from vibrating across its entire length. The function of the bridge is, therefore, to change the string's length and, thereby, change the string's frequency. (See Sections 11.52 and 12.2–12.3; Chapter 13; and Plates 2, 3, and 12.)

This method of decreasing the length and increasing the frequency of a string is very similar to the action of the left-hand fingers of guitar or violin players. Minor differences are (1) that the fingers push down against a fretted or fretless fingerboard; and (2) that due to varying finger widths, only one section of a stopped guitar or violin string represents an exact length ratio. The string, therefore, produces only one predictable frequency. On a monochord or canon, however, both sections of a divided string may under favorable conditions generate very accurate frequencies. To achieve close results, the bridge must not be too high; otherwise, it will increase the string's deflection, which in turn increases the downward force that the string exerts on the bridge. This secondary vertical force effectively increases the tension of the string and causes it to sound sharp. Hence, the length ratio-to-frequency ratio relation no longer applies. In addition, a string must not be too short. When one moves a bridge closer to either end of the string, the angle of deflection of the string between nut and bridge increases. As this angle increases, the downward force increases as well. Consequently, this vertical force has a greater sharpening effect on short strings than on long strings. Now, if the bridge has a sharp point, and if the string is long, thin, and very flexible, then the sections on both sides of the bridge will produce highly accurate frequencies. Since we may place a bridge nearly anywhere along the string's length, the mathematical possibilities of exploration and the musical experiences of listening are truly vast.

∼ 3.11 ∼

Suppose you own a canon with six strings. All the strings have the same dimensions as the sample string described in Section 3.6. Let us use this instrument to produce the frequencies of the first six harmonics. Begin by tuning all the open strings to the same fundamental frequency, C_2 at 65.0 cps. (This frequency is the same as the fundamental frequency of the first harmonic series in Figure 3.12.) The strings are now completely identical. Reserve the first open string for the frequency of the first harmonic, or F_1. Now substitute the value for L into Equation 3.9 and make five single loop length calculations. For F_2, calculate $L/2$ and place a bridge at ½ the length of the second string. Simultaneously play the first string and the right section of the second string, and listen to the interval that sounds like an "octave."[13] For F_3, calculate $L/3$ and place a bridge at ⅓ the length of the third string. Simultaneously play the first string and the right section of the third string, and listen to the interval that sounds like a "twelfth," or "one octave and a fifth." For the other three strings, continue to place bridges at ¼, ⅕, and ⅙ the length of the strings, and listen to intervals that sound like a "double-octave," "two octaves and a major third," and "two octaves and a fifth," respectively.

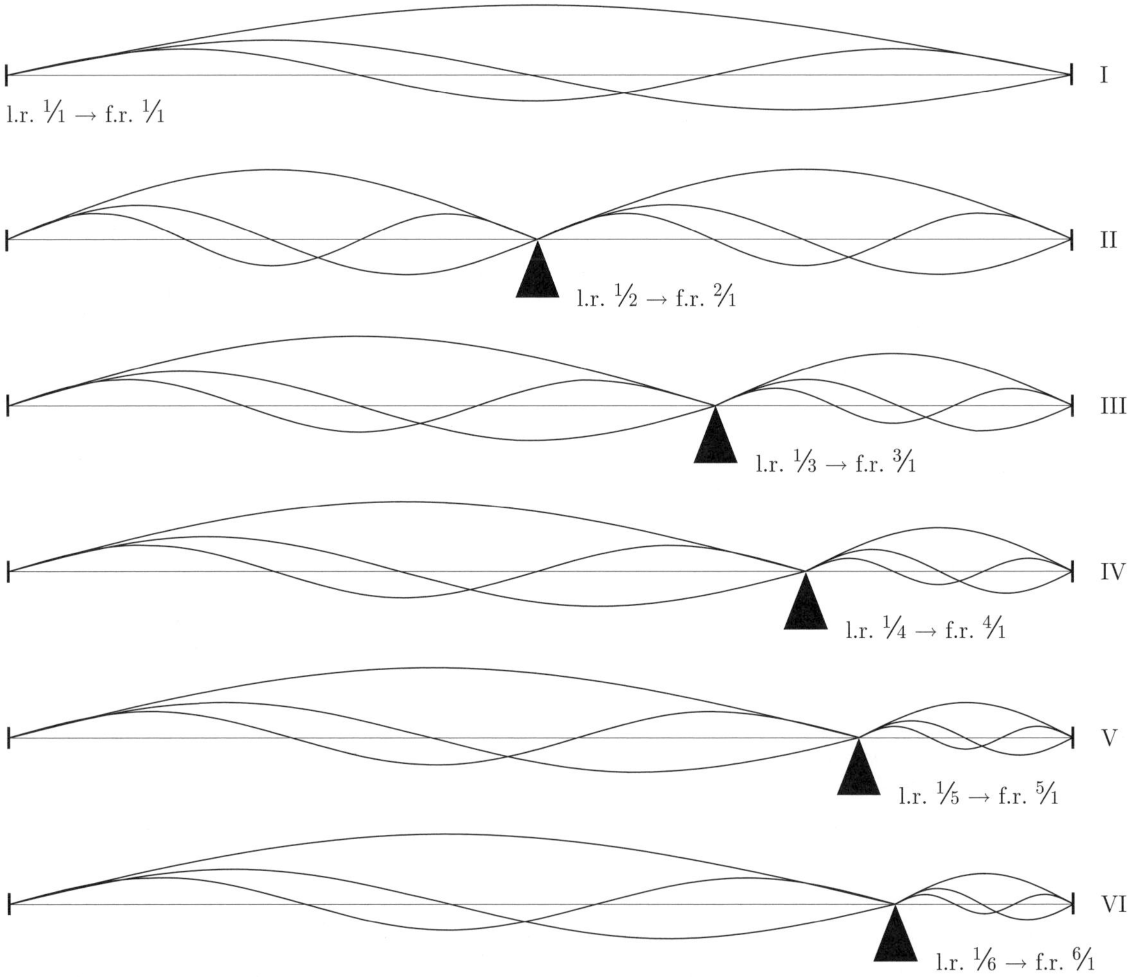

Figure 3.13 Six identical canon strings, five of which are equipped with bridges. The open string and the five string sections on the right sides of the bridges produce the frequency ratios of the first six harmonics. (See Figure 3.14.) The open string and the five string sections on the left sides of the bridges produce frequency ratios proportional to the interval ratios between the first six harmonics. (See Figures 3.15 and 3.17.)

Figure 3.13 shows a stylized representation of these canon strings and bridge arrangements. In this figure, the vibrating string sections and the corresponding frequency ratios appear to the right of the bridges. Notice that the bridge positions mark the locations of the first inner nodes of the standing wave patterns in Figure 3.10. We conclude, therefore, that the respective sections to the right of the bridges vibrate with the same loop lengths and the same frequencies as modes 2, 3, 4, 5, and 6 of the open canon string. However, to emphasize that we should not think of these segments as actual harmonics, Figure 3.13 shows that each string section subdivides into standing waves in the same manner as the open string. The illustration shows the first three modes of vibration of each section. In other words, a string section vibrates in a shape determined by 1, 2, 3, 4, . . . or any higher integer number of loops. Every section, therefore, generates another harmonic series.

Now, substitute length ratio ½ and the fundamental frequency of String I into Equation 3.13 and calculate the frequency of the second harmonic produced by the right (or left) section of String II:

$$F_2 = \frac{F_1}{\frac{1}{2}} = F_1 \times 2 = (65.0 \text{ cps})(2) = 130.0 \text{ cps}$$

Note that a direct substitution of frequency ratio ²⁄₁ and 65.0 cps into Equation 3.16 gives the same result. Similarly, observe that the right section of String III (l.r. ⅓ → f.r. ³⁄₁) produces F_3, or G_3 at 195.0 cps; and the right section of String IV (l.r. ¼ → f.r. ⁴⁄₁) produces F_4, or C_4 at 260.0 cps, etc.

3.12

During the above-mentioned exercise, when we listened to the first and second strings that produce an "octave," and then to the first and third strings that produce "one octave and a fifth," we experienced a third kind of ratio called an *interval ratio.* An interval ratio defines the musical interval between any two given frequency ratios, or between any two given length ratios.[14] Calculate an "octave," or a ²⁄₁ interval ratio between the first harmonic (F_1) and the second harmonic (F_2) by dividing the frequency ratio of the upper harmonic by the frequency ratio of the lower harmonic:

$$\text{Interval Ratio of the "Octave"} = \frac{C_3}{C_2} = \frac{\frac{2}{1}}{\frac{1}{1}} = \frac{2}{\not{1}} \times \frac{\not{1}}{1} = \frac{2}{1}$$

Similar solutions reveal that the frequency ratios of the upper harmonics have dual identities as interval ratios with respect to the first harmonic ¹⁄₁. This dual frequency ratio-interval ratio identity stems from the fact that a division by ¹⁄₁ has no effect on the value of a frequency ratio. We conclude, therefore, that the first harmonic represents a constant, and that all frequency ratios are also interval ratios in relation to the first harmonic.

For a different perspective, consider the musical slide rule discussed in Section 9.14. Here frequency ratio ¹⁄₁ refers to the "tonic," or to the first degree of a scale. In this context, the frequency ratio-interval ratio identity applies to all the other higher scale degrees. For example, frequency ratio ⁴⁄₃, or the "fourth" degree in the Western diatonic scale, refers to a frequency that vibrates 1.33 times faster than frequency ratio ¹⁄₁, or the "tonic." Whether or not we actually play the interval ¹⁄₁–⁴⁄₃ is immaterial. However, when we do play this interval, frequency ratio ⁴⁄₃ becomes interval ratio ⁴⁄₃.

This generality does not apply to the interval ratios between upper sequential harmonics because here ratio ¹⁄₁ is not a factor. Calculate a "fifth," or interval ratio ³⁄₂ between the second harmonic (F_2) and the third harmonic (F_3) by dividing the frequency ratio of the upper harmonic by the frequency ratio of the lower harmonic:

$$\text{Interval Ratio of the “Fifth”} = \frac{G_3}{C_3} = \frac{\frac{3}{1}}{\frac{2}{1}} = \frac{3}{\cancel{1}} \times \frac{\cancel{1}}{2} = \frac{3}{2}$$

In this context, interval ratio $^3\!/_2$ informs us that the third harmonic vibrates 1.5 times faster than the second harmonic. To verify this relation, turn back to Figure 3.11 and observe: 130.0 cps + (130.0 cps ÷ 2) = 195.0 cps.

Finally, also calculate interval ratio $^3\!/_2$ between the second and third harmonics by dividing the length ratio of the larger loop by the length ratio of the smaller loop:

$$\text{Interval Ratio of the “Fifth”} = \frac{C_3}{G_3} = \frac{\frac{1}{2}}{\frac{1}{3}} = \frac{\cancel{1}}{2} \times \frac{3}{\cancel{1}} = \frac{3}{2}$$

Here interval ratio $^3\!/_2$ states that the loop length of the second harmonic is 1.5 times longer than the loop length of the third harmonic. In Figure 3.11, note the following relation: 15.748 in + (15.748 in ÷ 2) = 23.622 in. We conclude, therefore, that because the loop length of the second

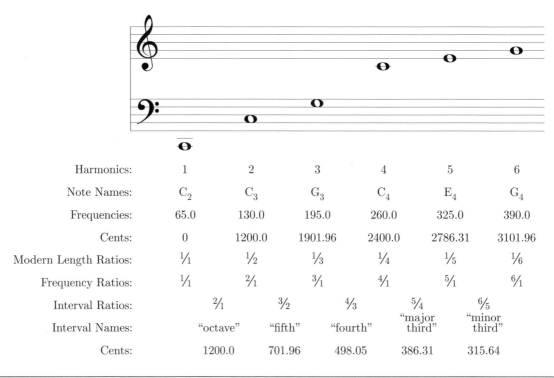

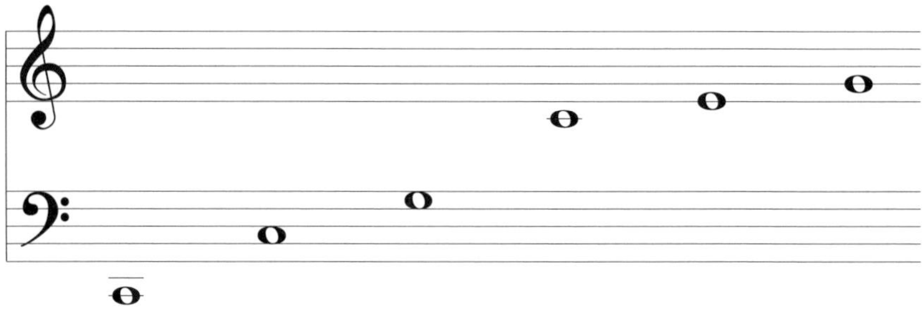

Harmonics:	1		2		3		4		5		6
Note Names:	C_2		C_3		G_3		C_4		E_4		G_4
Frequencies:	65.0		130.0		195.0		260.0		325.0		390.0
Cents:	0		1200.0		1901.96		2400.0		2786.31		3101.96
Modern Length Ratios:	$^1\!/_1$		$^1\!/_2$		$^1\!/_3$		$^1\!/_4$		$^1\!/_5$		$^1\!/_6$
Frequency Ratios:	$^1\!/_1$		$^2\!/_1$		$^3\!/_1$		$^4\!/_1$		$^5\!/_1$		$^6\!/_1$
Interval Ratios:		$^2\!/_1$		$^3\!/_2$		$^4\!/_3$		$^5\!/_4$		$^6\!/_5$	
Interval Names:		“octave”		“fifth”		“fourth”		“major third”		“minor third”	
Cents:		1200.0		701.96		498.05		386.31		315.64	

Figure 3.14 Nine items that describe the first six harmonics as produced by the right sections of the canon strings in Figure 3.13. These items are (1) harmonics: the sequential integer numbers of the harmonics; (2) note names: the letter names and octave numbers of the harmonics in this series that begins on C_2 at 65.0 cps; (3) frequencies: the frequencies in cycles per second of the harmonics; (4) cents: the relative sizes of the upper harmonics, or frequency ratios $^2\!/_1$, $^3\!/_1$, $^4\!/_1$, . . . with respect to first harmonic $^1\!/_1$; (5) modern length ratios: the fractional parts of a canon string that produce the harmonics; (6) frequency ratios: the frequency ratios of the upper harmonics with respect to the first harmonic $^1\!/_1$; (7) interval ratios: the interval ratios between sequential harmonics; (8) interval names: the conventional names for mathematically defined interval ratios; and (9) cents: the relative sizes of the interval ratios.

harmonic is 1.5 times longer than the loop length of the third harmonic, the three loops of the third harmonic vibrate 1.5 times faster than the two loops of the second harmonic. Similarly, because the loop length of the first harmonic (or the fundamental) is 2 times longer than the loop length of the second harmonic, the second harmonic vibrates 2 times faster than the first harmonic.

Figure 3.14 shows the length ratios, frequency ratios, interval ratios, and interval sizes in cents of the first six harmonics as produced by the right sections of the canon strings in Figure 3.13. See Chapter 9, Part III, for a discussion on cent calculations, and Equation 9.21, which I use throughout this book to calculate cents.

Part IV

LENGTH, FREQUENCY, AND INTERVAL RATIOS OF NON-HARMONIC TONES ON CANON STRINGS

3.13

Consider now the frequency ratios of the left sections of Strings III–VI in Figure 3.13. To compute these ratios, we must first calculate the length ratios of these sections. Since we already know the length ratios of the right sections, it is easy to calculate the length ratios of the left sections. Whenever a length ratio on one side of a bridge is known, we call the unknown length ratio on the other side of the bridge the *complementary ratio.* There are two different kinds of complementary ratios. One is the complementary ratio of a single loop length ratio, and the other is the complementary ratio of a multiple loop length ratio. (See Section 3.15 for calculating the complementary ratio of a multiple loop length ratio.) In Figure 3.13, the right string sections are all single loops as evidenced by the number 1 in the numerators of the following length ratios: $\frac{1}{2}$, $\frac{1}{3}$, $\frac{1}{4}$, $\frac{1}{5}$, $\frac{1}{6}$. When a length ratio represents a single loop on one side of the bridge, use Equation 3.17 to calculate the complementary ratio on the other side of the bridge:

$$\text{Complementary Length Ratio of } \frac{1}{n} = \frac{n-1}{n} \tag{3.17}$$

Equation 3.17 requires two steps: (1) subtract 1 from n in the denominator, and (2) substitute this result into the numerator. Therefore, the complementary ratio of single loop length ratio $\frac{1}{2}$ is $\frac{1}{2}$, of $\frac{1}{3}$ is $\frac{2}{3}$, of $\frac{1}{4}$ is $\frac{3}{4}$, of $\frac{1}{5}$ is $\frac{4}{5}$, and of $\frac{1}{6}$ is $\frac{5}{6}$. By definition, when the number 1 does not appear in the numerator of a modern length ratio, such a string length produces a non-harmonic frequency. We conclude, therefore, that the left sections of Strings III–VI do not produce frequencies of the harmonic series.

Turn now to Figure 3.15, which combines the standing wave patterns shown in Figure 3.10 with the canon bridge locations shown in Figure 3.13. For Strings III–VI, the left sides of bridges indicate the spans of two, three, four, and five loops, respectively. For String III, the left side of the bridge stops the string at 2 loops out of a total number of 3 loops; since this distance spans two-thirds of the whole string, the ratio of x loops to n loops is $\frac{2}{3}$. Similarly, for String IV, the left side of the bridge stops the string at 3 loops out of a total number of 4 loops; since this distance spans three-fourths of the whole string, the ratio of x loops to n loops is $\frac{3}{4}$.

In this text, the ratio of the length of two or more x loops of a stopped string to the length of the total number of n loops of the whole string is defined as a length ratio:

$$l.r. \equiv \frac{x}{n} \tag{3.18}$$

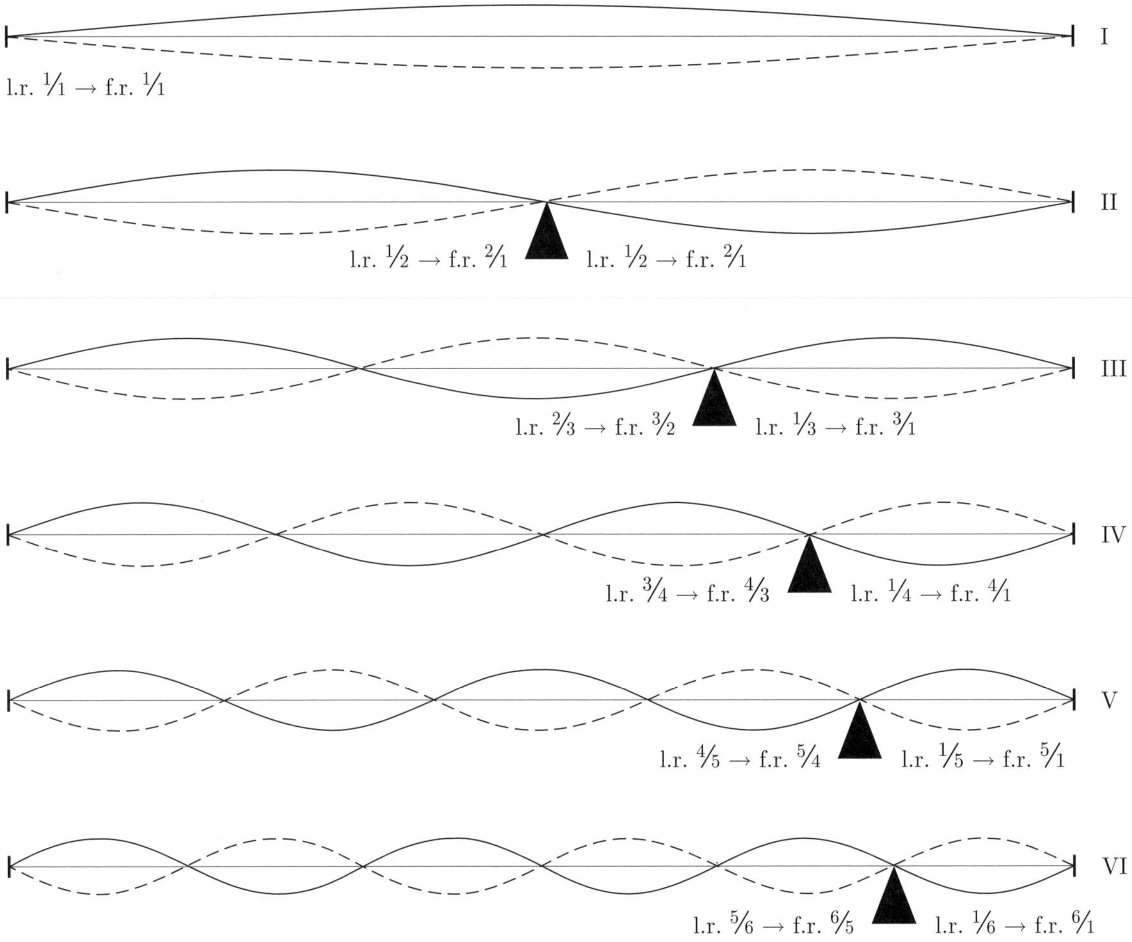

Figure 3.15 Standing wave patterns as shown in Figure 3.10, and bridge locations as shown in Figure 3.13. For Strings II–VI, the left sides of the bridges indicate the spans of one, two, three, four, and five loops, respectively.

And the ratio of a stopped multiple loop length (ℓ_{M}) to the whole string length is defined as a length ratio as well:

$$l.r. \equiv \frac{\ell_{\mathrm{M}}}{L} \tag{3.19}$$

Because these two ratios express the same relation, they form a proportion. The following proportion states that ℓ_{M} is to L as the length of x loops is to the length of the total number of n loops:

$$\frac{\ell_{\mathrm{M}}}{L} = \frac{x}{n} \tag{3.20}$$

To calculate a multiple loop length, solve Equation 3.20 for ℓ_{M}:

$$\ell_{\mathrm{M}} = L\frac{x}{n} \tag{3.21}$$

For the sample string, where $L = 47.244$ inches, the multiple loop lengths of the left sections of Strings III and IV are

$$\ell_{\text{M}} = (47.244 \text{ in})\left(\frac{2}{3}\right) = 31.496 \text{ in}$$

$$\ell_{\text{M}} = (47.244 \text{ in})\left(\frac{3}{4}\right) = 35.433 \text{ in}$$

A wavelength calculation requires that we multiply Equation 3.21 by two. Therefore,

$$\tilde{\lambda} = 2L\frac{x}{n} \tag{3.22}$$

where $\tilde{\lambda}$ is the wavelength of a multiple loop length. Consequently, the wavelengths of the left sections of Strings III and IV are

$$\tilde{\lambda} = 2(47.244 \text{ in})\left(\frac{2}{3}\right) = 62.992 \text{ in}$$

$$\tilde{\lambda} = 2(47.244 \text{ in})\left(\frac{3}{4}\right) = 70.866 \text{ in}$$

Since Equation 3.12 does not include the multiple loop length variable x, we cannot use this equation to calculate the non-harmonic frequencies of the string sections on the left sides of the bridges. To calculate the frequencies of such string sections, change the latter equation by replacing the mode frequency variable F_{n} with a new non-harmonic frequency variable $\tilde{F}$, and the mode wavelength variable λ_{n} with the multiple loop wavelength variable $\tilde{\lambda}$.

$$\tilde{F} = \frac{c_{\text{T}}}{\tilde{\lambda}} = \frac{\sqrt{\dfrac{T}{M/u.l.}}}{\dfrac{2Lx}{n}} \tag{3.23}$$

Transform Equation 3.23 four times:

$$\tilde{F} = \frac{c_{\text{T}}}{\tilde{\lambda}} = \frac{c_{\text{T}}}{\dfrac{2Lx}{n}} = \frac{\dfrac{c_{\text{T}}}{2L}}{\dfrac{x}{n}} = \frac{F_1}{\dfrac{x}{n}} = F_1 \times \frac{n}{x} \tag{3.24}$$

Observe that the fourth transformation places the inverse of length ratio x/n into the numerator, which means that n/x now functions as a multiplier of F_1. In Section 3.7, frequency ratio $n/1$ represents an *integer ratio*, or a positive integer, because when we divide the numerator by the denominator, the value of n does not change. In Equation 3.24, frequency ratio n/x with a denominator greater than 1 is also an integer ratio. However, here a division of the numerator by the denominator results in a conversion into a *decimal ratio*, such as $3/2 = 1.50$, $4/3 = 1.33$, etc.[15] Consequently, the last transformation states that the frequencies of the stopped string lengths on the left sides of the bridges are *decimal multiples* of the fundamental frequency. For String III, the left side of the bridge stops two-thirds of the string expressed by length ratio $2/3$; since this section vibrates 1.50 times faster than the whole string, $\tilde{F} = F_1 \times 3/2$. Similarly, for String IV, the left side is three-fourths of the string, or length ratio $3/4$; since it vibrates 1.33 times faster than the whole string, $\tilde{F} = F_1 \times 4/3$.

In this text, the ratio of the rate of vibration of 2 or more loops of a stopped string to the rate of vibration of the whole string is defined as a frequency ratio:

$$f.r. \equiv \frac{n}{x} \tag{3.25}$$

Furthermore, the ratio of the frequency of such a stopped string to the fundamental frequency of the whole string is defined as a frequency ratio as well:

$$f.r. \equiv \frac{\widetilde{F}}{F_1} \tag{3.26}$$

To verify the inverse proportionality between length ratio $^x\!/\!_n$ and frequency ratio $^n\!/\!_x$, calculate the non-harmonic frequencies of Strings III and IV in four separate steps. In Equation 3.24, (1) substitute the length ratios of Strings III and IV; (2) invert these length ratios to express the corresponding frequency ratios; (3) substitute the fundamental frequency of String I; and (4) multiply the fundamental frequency by the frequency ratios:

$$\frac{F_1}{\frac{2}{3}} = F_1 \times \frac{3}{2} = (65.0 \text{ cps})\left(\frac{3}{2}\right) = 97.50 \text{ cps} = \text{G}_2$$

$$\frac{F_1}{\frac{3}{4}} = F_1 \times \frac{4}{3} = (65.0 \text{ cps})\left(\frac{4}{3}\right) = 86.67 \text{ cps} = \text{F}_2$$

Finally, Figure 3.16 shows the inverse proportionality between length ratios and frequency ratios of the two previously calculated canon strings. Substitute the appropriate values from this figure into Equations 3.19 and 3.26, respectively, and for the variables G_2 and F_2, calculate length ratios $^2\!/\!_3$ and $^3\!/\!_4$, and frequency ratios $^3\!/\!_2$ and $^4\!/\!_3$.

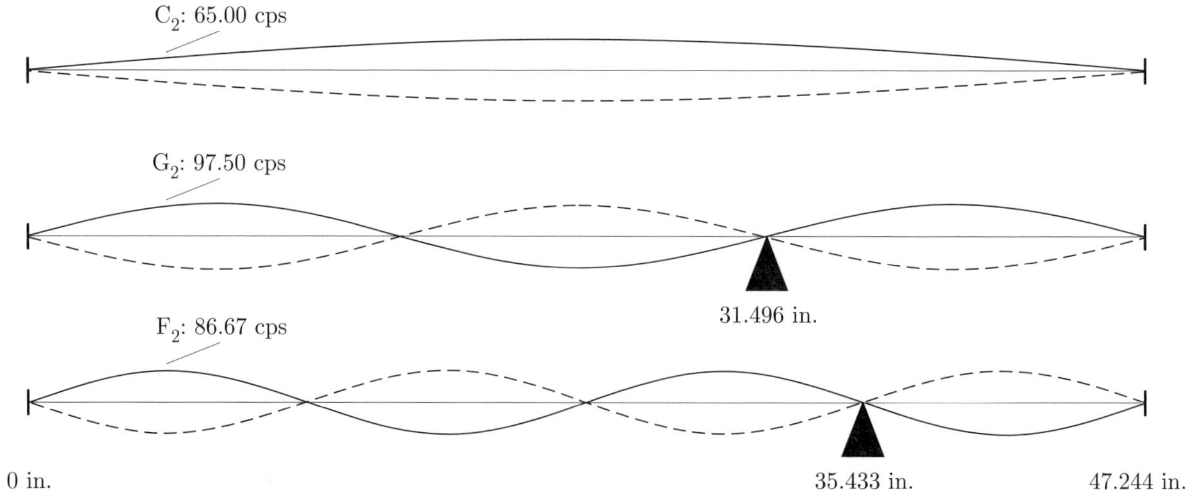

Figure 3.16 Open length and fundamental frequency, and two multiple loop lengths and two non-harmonic frequencies of the sample string. A substitution of these values into Equations 3.19 and 3.26, respectively, demonstrates the inverse proportionality between length ratios and frequency ratios.

In the context of these additional length ratios and frequency ratios, we now expand our previous definitions from

$$\text{Single Loop Length Ratio } \frac{1}{n}, \text{ to Multiple Loop Length Ratio } \frac{x}{n}$$

and from

$$\text{Harmonic Frequency Ratio } \frac{n}{1}, \text{ to Non-harmonic Frequency Ratio } \frac{n}{x}$$

where x and n are positive integers, and x is smaller than n, $(x < n)$. Finally, a simplified version of Equation 3.24 states

$$\text{Non-harmonic Frequencies:} \quad \tilde{F} = F_1 \times \frac{n}{x} \tag{3.27}$$

The question remains, "How do we identify and name frequency ratios n/x?" Let us begin with frequency ratio $3/2$. In Figure 3.14, observe that the interval ratio between the second and third harmonics sounds like a "fifth." Refer to Figure 3.15 and note that if we simultaneously play the right section of String II (l.r. $1/2 \rightarrow$ f.r. $2/1$) and the right section of String III (l.r. $1/3 \rightarrow$ f.r. $3/1$), we will hear this "fifth" between F_2 (or C_3) and F_3 (or G_3). Now, if in Figure 3.15 we simultaneously play String I (l.r. $1/1 \rightarrow$ f.r. $1/1$) and the left section of String III (l.r. $2/3 \rightarrow$ f.r. $3/2$), we will hear a "fifth" above the first string, or between F_1 (or C_2) and $\tilde{F}$ (or G_2). The former "fifth" sounds exactly one "octave" higher than the latter "fifth." The mathematical reason why these intervals are the same is that the length ratios and frequency ratios of both "fifths" form a proportion. (See Section 3.6.) In this case, l.r. $1/2$ of String II is to l.r. $1/3$ of String III as l.r. $1/1$ of String I is to l.r. $2/3$ of String III:

$$\frac{\frac{1}{2}}{\frac{1}{3}} = \frac{\frac{1}{1}}{\frac{2}{3}}$$

Conversely, f.r. $3/1$ of String III is to f.r. $2/1$ of String II as f.r. $3/2$ of String III is to f.r. $1/1$ of String I:

$$\frac{\frac{3}{1}}{\frac{2}{1}} = \frac{\frac{3}{2}}{\frac{1}{1}}$$

Recall that the open string of your canon is tuned to C_2 at 65.0 cps, and that the right string sections produce harmonics F_2–F_6 as shown in Figure 3.14. If we substitute the appropriate frequency ratios for F_2 and F_3, and calculate the resulting interval ratio, then the left side of the latter proportion states

$$\text{Interval Ratio of the "Fifth"} = \frac{G_3}{C_3} = \frac{F_3}{F_2} = \frac{\frac{3}{1}}{\frac{2}{1}} = \frac{3}{\cancel{1}} \times \frac{\cancel{1}}{2} = \frac{3}{2}$$

According to the harmonic series, a "fifth," or a $3/2$ interval constitutes a tonal distance where one frequency vibrates exactly 1.50 times faster than another frequency. Similarly, the right side of the proportion states

$$\text{Interval Ratio of the “Fifth”} = \frac{\mathrm{G}_2}{\mathrm{C}_2} = \frac{\widetilde{F}}{F_1} = \frac{\frac{3}{2}}{\frac{1}{1}} = \frac{3}{2} \times \frac{1}{1} = \frac{3}{2}$$

(Since G_2, on the first line of the bass staff, is a non-harmonic frequency ratio, it does not appear in Figure 3.14.) Because the open string and the left section of String III produce the same interval ratio as between the second and third harmonics, both intervals are called 3⁄2's, or "fifths."

With regard to the remaining left string sections in Figure 3.15, identify and name interval ratios 4⁄3, 5⁄4, and 6⁄5 by examining the intervals between the third and fourth, fourth and fifth, and fifth and sixth harmonics in Figure 3.14. In general, identify any given interval ratio in two separate steps. First, match integers n and x to harmonics n and x. Second, analyze the corresponding interval between these two harmonics. In Figure 3.15, the open string and the left string sections of the bridged strings produce interval ratios that are proportional to the sequential intervals between the first six harmonics in Figure 3.14. Therefore, the 4⁄3 produced by String I and the left section of String IV sounds like a "fourth"; the 5⁄4 produced by String I and the left section of String V sounds like a "major third"; and the 6⁄5 produced by String I and the left section of String VI sounds like a "minor third." When compared to the piano tuned in 12-tone equal temperament, a 4⁄3 sounds slightly lower, a 3⁄2 slightly higher, a 5⁄4 obviously lower, and a 6⁄5 obviously higher than the intervals of the conventional Western scale. (See Section 10.37.)

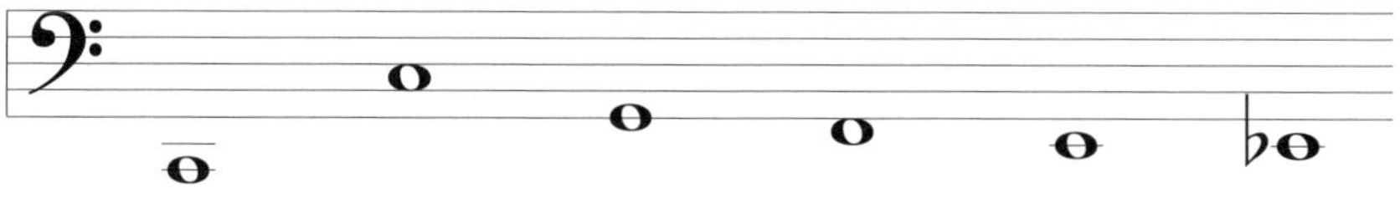

Harmonics:	1	2	none	none	none	none
Note Names:	C_2	C_3	G_2	F_2	E_2	$E\flat_2$
Frequencies:	65.0	130.0	97.5	86.7	81.3	78.0
Cents:	0	1200.0	701.96	498.05	386.31	315.64
Modern Length Ratios:	1⁄1	1⁄2	2⁄3	3⁄4	4⁄5	5⁄6
Frequency Ratios:	1⁄1	2⁄1	3⁄2	4⁄3	5⁄4	6⁄5

Interval Ratios:	2⁄1	4⁄3	9⁄8	16⁄15	25⁄24
Interval Names:	"octave"	"fourth"	"major second"	"minor second"	none
Cents:	1200.0	498.05	203.91	111.73	70.67

Figure 3.17 Nine items that describe the tones produced by the open string and the left sections of the canon strings in Figure 3.15. In Figure 3.14, the ascending sequence of interval ratios 2⁄1, 3⁄2, 4⁄3, 5⁄4, 6⁄5 appears here as the following descending sequence of frequency ratios: 2⁄1, 3⁄2, 4⁄3, 5⁄4, 6⁄5.

Finally, Figure 3.17 shows the length ratios, frequency ratios, intervals ratios, and interval sizes as produced by the open string and the left sections of the canon strings in Figure 3.15. For example, calculate the "major second," or a 9⁄8 interval ratio between the frequency ratios of the left sections of Strings III and IV, in the following manner:

$$\text{Interval Ratio of the “Major Second”} = \frac{\mathrm{G}_2}{\mathrm{F}_2} = \frac{\tilde{F}}{\tilde{F}} = \frac{\frac{3}{2}}{\frac{4}{3}} = \frac{3}{2} \times \frac{3}{4} = \frac{9}{8}$$

3.14

In preparation for discussions in Part V, and in Chapters 10 and 11, we must now take two critical exceptions into consideration because length ratio $^x\!/\!_n$ and frequency ratio $^n\!/\!_x$ do not always appear in other texts as defined in this chapter. In antiquity — *long before the idea of frequency existed* — music theorists wrote length ratios in the form $^n\!/\!_x$, where the open or long string length is in the numerator, and the bridged or short string length is in the denominator. For example, the ancient Greeks notated the “fourth” as length ratio 4/3, because two canon strings, where the open one is 4 units long, and the bridged one is 3 units long, produce such an interval. Consistent with length ratio $^n\!/\!_x$, some modern theorists write frequency ratios in the form $^x\!/\!_n$, where the slow frequency is in the numerator, and the fast frequency is in the denominator. For example, they notate the “fourth” as frequency ratio 3/4, because two frequencies, where one vibrates 0.75 times slower than the other, produce such an interval. Therefore, in the case of l.r. $^n\!/\!_x \rightarrow$ f.r. $^x\!/\!_n$, we identify the “fourth” as a descending interval; that is, we may think of the open and slow vibrating string as producing an interval below the bridged and fast vibrating string.

Figure 3.18(a) shows the standard inverse proportionality of l.r. 3/4 → f.r. 4/3 as an *ascending* interval. Here we assign the open canon string a unity length of 1000.0 mm, and the frequency of C_2 at 65.0 cps. Therefore, if we stop this string with a bridge so that the right section has a length of three-fourths, this shorter section produces the higher frequency of F_2 at 86.67 cps. Conversely, Figure 3.18(b) shows the non-standard inverse proportionality of l.r. 4/3 → f.r. 3/4 as a *descending* interval. Here we assign the right section of the stopped string a unity length of three-thirds, and the frequency of F_2. Therefore, if we remove the bridge, the open string with a length of four-thirds produces the lower frequency of C_2.

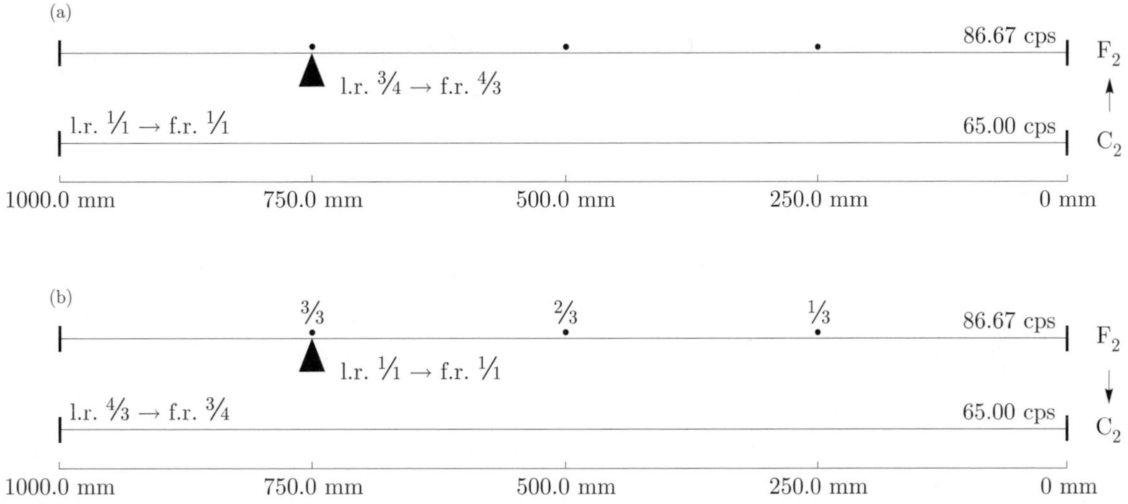

Figure 3.18 Two different interpretations of the musical interval of a “fourth.” (a) The open string and the right section of the bridged string express the ascending interval C_2–F_2 as l.r. 3/4 → f.r. 4/3. (b) The right section of the bridged string and the open string express the descending interval F_2–C_2 as l.r. 4/3 → f.r. 3/4.

Music theorists did not invent these two different kinds of length ratios and frequency ratios to distinguish between ascending and descending intervals. On the contrary: the notation of musical ratios is not standardized. Consequently, a reader must carefully consider the context of a particular discussion to correctly interpret the meaning of a musical ratio. For example, consider the following text from a treatise reputedly written by Euclid (fl. *c.* 300 B.C.) called the *Division of the Canon:*

> Let there be a length of the *kanōn* which is also the length AB of the string, and let it be divided into four equal parts, at C, D and E. Therefore BA, being the lowest, will be the bass note. Now this AB is the epitritic [lit. 1 + ⅓, or 4:3] of CB, so that CB will be concordant with AB at the fourth ***above*** it.[16] (Bold italics, and ratios in brackets mine.)

Here l.r. $\frac{4}{3}$ not only defines AB with a length of four units, and CB with a length of three units, but l.r. $\frac{4}{3}$ also represents an ascending interval. Turn to Figure 3.19 and observe that if we first play AB and then CB, l.r. $\frac{4}{3}$ identifies the "fourth" above the open string. In the context of musical intervals, *ancient length ratio* (a.l.r.) $\frac{4}{3}$ in Figure 3.19 and frequency ratio $\frac{4}{3}$ in Figure 3.18(a) are identical and aurally indistinguishable! However, note carefully that in a.l.r. $\frac{4}{3}$ the larger number (4) defines the lower tone of the open string with the greater length, whereas in f.r. $\frac{4}{3}$ the larger number (4) defines the higher tone of the bridged string with the greater frequency. Therefore, if the open string in Figure 3.19 is tuned to C_2, a.l.r. $\frac{4}{3}$ identifies the interval C_2/F_2, whereas f.r. $\frac{4}{3}$ identifies the interval F_2/C_2. As discussed in Sections 3.18–3.19, when one calculates the arithmetic mean and the harmonic mean of a given musical interval, the *dimensional distinction* between a.l.r. $\frac{n}{x}$ and f.r. $\frac{n}{x}$ yields two diametrically opposed divisions. In my opinion, and contrary to some ancient and most modern interpretations, only arithmetic divisions and harmonic divisions of a.l.r. $\frac{n}{x}$ produce historically authentic and mathematically consistent results. (See Section 10.58.)

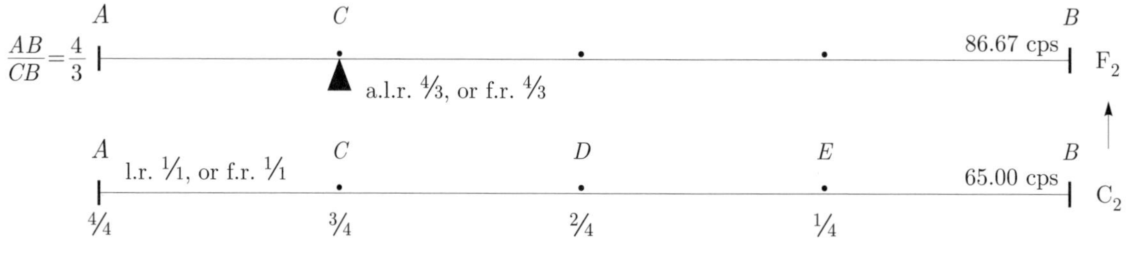

Figure 3.19 An ascending "fourth" expressed as ancient length ratio $\frac{4}{3}$. Throughout Chapters 10 and 11, a given *ancient length ratio* (a.l.r.) represents two length dimensions of a single canon string. In this example, the numerator refers to four aliquot parts, or to the overall length of the open string, and the denominator, to three of these parts, or to the stopped length to the right of the bridge. In Euclid's text, this ratio defines the canon string lengths AB and CB, respectively, and the musical interval of a "fourth" produced by CB ***above*** AB.

In summary of the preceding discussions, we conclude that the "fourth" has four different ratio manifestations:

$$\text{Length ratios of the "fourth"} = \tfrac{3}{4} \text{ or } \tfrac{4}{3}$$

$$\text{Frequency ratios of the "fourth"} = \tfrac{4}{3} \text{ or } \tfrac{3}{4}$$

To diminish the confusion presented by the interchangeability of these ratios, I have limited my calculations of musical tones and intervals to six equations. Because in Chapters 9, 10, and 11 we will encounter *rational* and *irrational* numbers, in the following four equations, ${}^{x}\!/\!_{n}$ and ${}^{n}\!/\!_{x}$ represent both rational and irrational length ratios and frequency ratios, respectively:[17]

$$\text{Ascending Tone, or Decreasing Length: } \Lambda = L \times \frac{x}{n} \tag{3.28}$$

$$\text{Descending Tone, or Increasing Length: } \Lambda = L \div \frac{x}{n} \tag{3.29}$$

$$\text{Ascending Tone, or Increasing Frequency: } F = F_1 \times \frac{n}{x} \tag{3.30}$$

$$\text{Descending Tone, or Decreasing Frequency: } F = F_1 \div \frac{n}{x} \tag{3.31}$$

where ${}^{x}\!/\!_{n}$ represents a rational or an irrational *modern length ratio*[18] that is less than or equal to 1 (${}^{x}\!/\!_{n} \leq 1$); ${}^{n}\!/\!_{x}$ represents a rational or an irrational frequency ratio that is greater than or equal to 1 (${}^{n}\!/\!_{x} \geq 1$); and Λ is the required string length, in inches or millimeters. [I intentionally chose the uppercase of the Greek letter *lambda* (Λ) for the first two equations because it resembles the shape of a triangular canon bridge.] Notice that for these four equations, I exclusively associate modern length ratios with string length calculations, and frequency ratios with frequency calculations. However, note the following two critical exceptions. Most of the discussions in Chapters 10 and 11 on scales and tunings focus on *ancient length ratios* ${}^{n}\!/\!_{x}$ as shown in Figure 3.19, and on frequency ratios ${}^{n}\!/\!_{x}$. Since it is not only convenient but also appropriate to compute string length calculations (1) without inverting ${}^{n}\!/\!_{x}$ as required by Equations 3.28 and 3.29, and (2) without insisting that ${}^{n}\!/\!_{x}$ must be a length ratio, I also use Equations 3.32 and 3.33,

$$\text{Ascending Tone, or Decreasing Length: } \Lambda = L \div \frac{n}{x} \tag{3.32}$$

$$\text{Descending Tone, or Increasing Length: } \Lambda = L \times \frac{n}{x} \tag{3.33}$$

where ${}^{n}\!/\!_{x}$ is either a rational or irrational ancient length ratio or frequency ratio, which is greater than or equal to 1 (${}^{n}\!/\!_{x} \geq 1$).

~ 3.15 ~

The great mathematical and musical beauty of a canon is that it allows us to hear, analyze, and appreciate intervals, scales, and tonal systems not familiar to our civilization. Since a subdividing string has a theoretically infinite number of nodes and antinodes, anywhere we place a bridge (along one-half of the string's length) produces a new frequency. For this reason, I refer to the canon as a "limited form of infinity."

The act of moving a bridge in small increments has a profound influence over our perception of sound. This method enables us to distinguish many frequencies where on first impression there seems to be only one frequency. It also teaches us to understand and appreciate why an instrument or a musical composition from another part of the world sounds the way it does. The endless diversity of musical ratios explains many "strange" phenomena.

Continuous studies and experiments with canon strings further our understanding of musical sounds. We discover that our ears and brain are willing and able participants because human anatomy is not subject to the dictates of learned "correctness." For example, since the tuning of musical instruments in Western civilization does not include frequencies based on prime number 7, refer to Figure 3.20 and consider listening to frequency ratio $7/5$ on the 6-string canon. Refer to the first harmonic series in Figure 3.12 and note that the interval ratio between the fifth and the seventh harmonics sounds like a "tritone." The direction of the arrow above the seventh harmonic indicates that this tone sounds considerably lower than the note of the Western piano scale. Now, invert frequency ratio $7/5$ to obtain length ratio $5/7$. Since $5/7$ is a multiple loop length ratio, use Equation 3.34 to calculate the complementary ratio on the other side of the bridge:

$$\text{Complementary Length Ratio of } \frac{x}{n} = \frac{n-x}{n} \tag{3.34}$$

Equation 3.34 requires two steps: (1) subtract the value of x from n in the denominator, and (2) substitute this result into the numerator. In this case, the complementary ratio of multiple loop length ratio $5/7$ is $2/7$. The inverse of the latter ratio identifies frequency ratio $7/2$. Refer to Figure 3.12 and note that the interval ratio between the second harmonic and the seventh harmonic sounds like "one octave and a minor seventh." Again, the arrow above the seventh harmonic indicates a relatively low sounding tone.

To determine the location of l.r. $5/7$ on the sample string, substitute the string length and length ratio into Equation 3.28 and calculate the following distance from the left end of the string:

$$\Lambda = (1200.0\text{ mm})\left(\frac{5}{7}\right) = 857.14\text{ mm}$$

Finally, tune two open strings (l.r. $1/1 \rightarrow$ f.r. $1/1$) to C_2, place a bridge under one of these strings at 857.14 mm, simultaneously play the open string and the left section of the bridged string (l.r. $5/7 \rightarrow$ f.r. $7/5$), and listen to a "flat tritone" interval between F_1 (or C_2) and $\tilde{F}$ (or $F\sharp_2$). Conversely, simultaneously play the open string and the right section of the bridged string (l.r. $2/7 \rightarrow$ f.r. $7/2$), and listen to a "one octave and a flat minor seventh" interval between F_1 (or C_2) and $\tilde{F}$ (or $B\flat_3$). Finally, if we divide a string into seven equal parts, and then move a bridge to produce frequency ratios $7/1$, $7/2$, $7/3$, $7/4$, $7/5$, and $7/6$, we will experience a set of musical intervals most musicians have never heard. In general, all ratios with prime numbers[19] greater than the number 5, including 7, 11, 13, 17, 19, . . . offer unique listening experiences and a great wealth of new musical resources. This is ironic because the Greek mathematician and astronomer Claudius Ptolemy (*c.* A.D. 100 – *c.* 165), who frequently alludes to canon string calculations in his *Harmonics*, advocated using prime numbers 2 through 11 in the 2nd century A.D.[20]

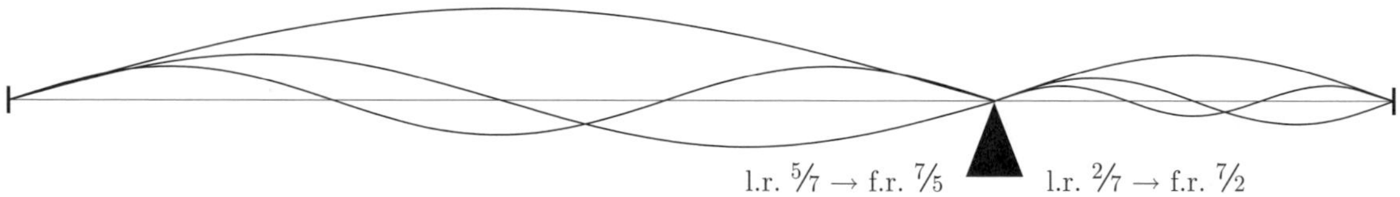

Figure 3.20 Seldom heard consonances: frequency ratios $7/5$ and $7/2$. In the West, most musicians have no experiences listening to musical intervals with primes greater than the number 5.

Part V

MUSICAL, MATHEMATICAL, AND LINGUISTIC ORIGINS OF LENGTH RATIOS

3.16

We may use the preceding example, which describes the tuning process of two unfamiliar frequency ratios, $7/5$ and $7/2$, to analyze the musical, mathematical, and linguistic origins of length ratios. Although aural experiences of sound depend on frequencies, our anatomy does not enable us to quantify rates of vibration from vibrating strings. As such, the frequencies produced while playing musical intervals have always and will always remain incomprehensible quantities. Therefore, if we spontaneously tune two canons strings to an unfamiliar musical interval, we cannot identify the new interval by counting cycles per second and constructing a frequency ratio. To comprehend such an experience, we must measure the corresponding string lengths, and through the construction of a length ratio, identify the unfamiliar interval. Conversely, to intentionally tune two strings to a new musical interval, we cannot locate the required position of a canon bridge by simply listening to frequencies. Instead, we must divide the strings according to a length ratio that determines the frequency ratio we have not yet experienced. In both of these cases, our intellectual ability to comprehend aurally perceived frequency ratios depends on our mathematical ability to measure and compare string lengths.

We may summarize the preceding discussion by referring to Equation 3.3, which states that frequency is a function of wavelength. Before we analyze this statement further, let us first examine modern mathematical notation with respect to the term "function." Typically, a function constitutes a cause-and-effect relation between two variables x and y, where the x-number, chosen randomly or at will, is called the *independent variable*, and the y-number, determined only after the x-number has been selected, is called the *dependent variable.* For example, if we state that the area of circle (y) equals π (3.1416) times the radius (x) squared, then the expression $y = \pi x^2$ defines y *as a function of* x, or the area as a function of the radius. To specify this functional relation, mathematicians replace y with $f(x)$, which reads, "f of x," or stated in full, "the value of the function f at x." Therefore, the previous equation in functional notation states $f(x) = \pi x^2$. This notation informs us that in the functional relation between variables x and y, values of x determine values of y. Now, substitute the radius $x = 2$ into these two equations, and calculate the area y:

$$y = \pi r^2 \qquad f(x) = \pi r^2$$
$$y = \pi(2)^2 \qquad f(2) = \pi(2)^2$$
$$y = 12.566 \qquad f(2) = 12.566$$

In the left column, a sequence of equations simply terminates in a solution for the area y, whereas in the right column, a sequence of equations in functional notation terminates not only in a solution, but indicates the value of radius x that determines area y.

If we solve this equation for x, the expression $x = \sqrt{y/\pi}$ defines x *as a function of* y, or the radius as a function of the area. Therefore, in functional notation: $f(y) = \sqrt{y/\pi}$. Substitute the area $y = 4$ into these two equations, and calculate the radius x:

$$x = \sqrt{y/\pi} \qquad f(y) = \sqrt{y/\pi}$$
$$x = \sqrt{4/\pi} \qquad f(4) = \sqrt{4/\pi}$$
$$x = 1.128 \qquad f(4) = 1.128$$

Now, recall Equation 3.3,

$$F = \frac{c_{\mathrm{T}}}{\lambda}$$

and express F *as a function of* λ:

$$f(\lambda) = \frac{c_{\mathrm{T}}}{\lambda} \tag{3.35}$$

Next, solve Equation 3.3 for λ,

$$\lambda = \frac{c_{\mathrm{T}}}{F}$$

and express λ *as a function of F:*

$$f(F) = \frac{c_{\mathrm{T}}}{F} \tag{3.36}$$

Equation 3.36 expresses a functional relation that is algebraically and scientifically correct: as frequencies increase, wavelengths decrease and *vice versa.* However, since we cannot count rates of vibration from vibrating strings, we cannot substitute values for the independent variable F into this equation. That is, our aural experience of an unfamiliar interval does not enable us to quantify a frequency ratio, which we could then invert to identify the corresponding length ratio.

In contrast, Equation 3.35 essentially describes the musical and mathematical process by which musicians create ascending sequences of tones that result in tuned scales. By shortening the lengths of strings in precise increments, as wavelengths decrease, frequencies increase. This tuning process requires two steps. (1) Our anatomy enables us to measure, quantify, and comprehend all changes in string lengths. (2) The inverse proportionality between length ratios and frequency ratios — l.r. $^{x}\!/_{n} \rightarrow$ f.r. $^{n}\!/_{x}$ — permits us to interpret these length ratios as frequency ratios, which we then identify as musical intervals. This second step is crucial simply because we do not hear wavelengths or string lengths. However, note carefully that we also do not hear f.r. $^{3}\!/_{2}$ as an auditory phenomenon where one frequency vibrates 1.5 times faster than another frequency. Instead, to give meaning to such an aural experience, we define f.r. $^{3}\!/_{2}$ as a musical interval called the "fifth." Although for known musical intervals, we may notate the inverse proportionality between frequency ratios and length ratios — f.r. $^{n}\!/_{x} \rightarrow$ l.r. $^{x}\!/_{n}$ — music as an exploratory science and as a meaningful art principally depends on the knowledge acquired through comprehensible string length measurements and on the construction of length ratios.

Furthermore, in the context of the harmonic series, recall that the superposition of traveling waves causes nodes in strings. These internal obstructions cause decreases in loop lengths, which in turn cause decreases in wavelengths: as wavelengths decrease, mode frequencies increase. From this perspective, Equation 3.35 expresses the natural process by which a string, through a harmonic progression of length ratios 1, $^{1}\!/_{2}$, $^{1}\!/_{3}$, $^{1}\!/_{4}$, $^{1}\!/_{5}$, $^{1}\!/_{6}$, . . . shortens itself![21] We conclude, therefore, that in the scientific relationship between vibrating strings and the internal processes of subdivision, mode frequencies are a function of mode wavelengths; and in the historical relationship between musicians and the mathematics of canon string divisions, frequency ratios are a function of length ratios. Stated differently, for a constant transverse wave speed, length ratios constitute the primary factor in identifying, determining, and controlling frequency ratios.

~   3.17   ~

The Greeks primarily used verbal terms to describe mathematical ratios. Furthermore, due to linguistic complications, the Greeks never employed fractions such as ½, ⅔, ¾, ⁸⁄₉, etc., to identify musical intervals. Instead, the ratios of Greek music always have quotients greater than one. For example, examine Figure 3.21 and observe that the term for the ratio of the "octave" (or *diapason*) is *diplasios*. Since the prefix *di* means *two*, and *plasma* means *something formed*, *diplasios* means *twofold*, or *double*, as in $1 + 1 = \frac{1}{1} \times 2 = \frac{2}{1}$. Therefore, the "octave" is a musical interval produced by a string that is twice as long as another string; hence, l.r. $\frac{2}{1}$. Similarly, the term for the ratio of the "fifth" (or *diapente*) is *hemiolios*. Since the prefix *hemi* means *half*, and *olos* means *whole*, *hemiolios* means *half and whole*: $\frac{1}{2} + 1 = \frac{1}{2} + \frac{2}{2} = \frac{3}{2}$. Therefore, the "fifth" is a musical interval produced by a string that is by a half longer than another string; hence, l.r. $\frac{3}{2}$. The Greek term for the ratio of the "fourth" (or *diatessaron*) is *epitritos*. Since, in a mathematical context, the prefix *epi* describes the operation of addition,[22] and *tritos* means *third*, the term *epitritos* denotes *one-third*

The "octave" expressed as a.l.r. $\frac{2}{1}$. The Greek term *diplasios* means $1 + 1$, or $\frac{1}{1} \times 2 = \frac{2}{1}$.

The "fifth" expressed as a.l.r. $\frac{3}{2}$. The Greek term *hemiolios* means $\frac{1}{2} + 1$, or $\frac{1}{2} + \frac{2}{2} = \frac{3}{2}$.

The "fourth" expressed as a.l.r. $\frac{4}{3}$. The Greek term *epitritos* means $1 + \frac{1}{3}$, or $\frac{3}{3} + \frac{1}{3} = \frac{4}{3}$.

The "whole tone" expressed as a.l.r. $\frac{9}{8}$. The Greek term *epogdoos* means $1 + \frac{1}{8}$, or $\frac{8}{8} + \frac{1}{8} = \frac{9}{8}$.

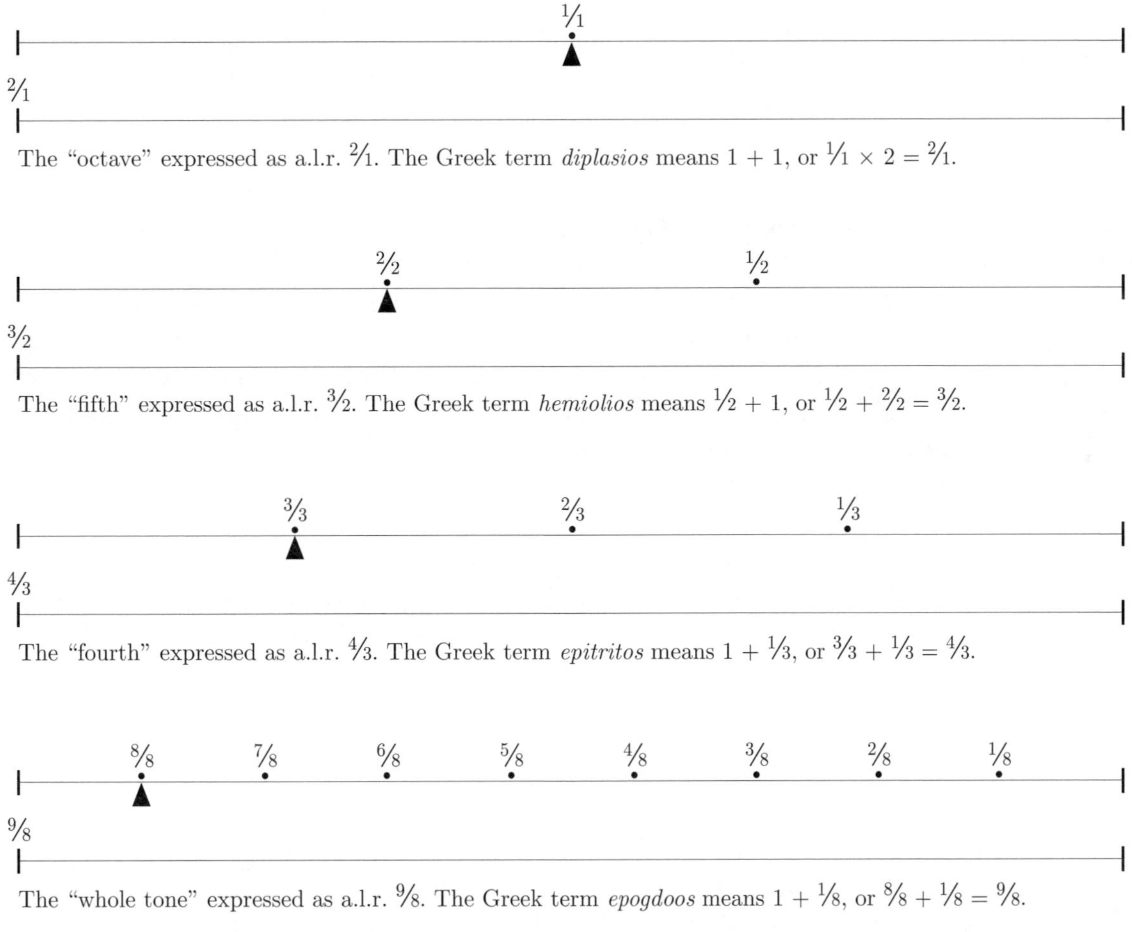

Figure 3.21 A descending "octave," "fifth," "fourth," and "whole tone" expressed as ancient length ratios $\frac{2}{1}$, $\frac{3}{2}$, $\frac{4}{3}$, and $\frac{9}{8}$, respectively. In the *Division of the Canon*, reputedly written by Euclid (fl. *c.* 300 B.C.), the verbal terms *diplasios*, *hemiolios*, *epitritos*, and *epogdoos* refer exclusively and unequivocally to length ratios. As discussed in Section 3.14, these ratios also define ascending musical intervals. For example, if in the first example we define the lower open string as l.r. $\frac{2}{2}$, and the upper bridged string as a.l.r. $\frac{2}{1}$, then the bridged string would sound an ascending "octave"; similarly, if in the second example we define the open string as l.r. $\frac{3}{3}$, and the bridged string as a.l.r. $\frac{3}{2}$, then the string to the right of the bridge would sound an ascending "fifth"; etc.

in addition, and connotes *one and one-third:* $1 + 1/3 = 3/3 + 1/3 = 4/3$. Therefore, the "fourth" is a musical interval produced by a string that is by a third longer than another string; hence, l.r. $4/3$. Similarly, the term for the ratio of the "whole tone" (or *tonon*) is *epogdoos* (or *epiogdoos*), which connotes *one and one-eighth:* $1 + 1/8 = 8/8 + 1/8 = 9/8$. Therefore, the "whole tone" is a musical interval produced by a string that is by an eighth longer than another string; hence, l.r. $9/8$.

In contrast, to notate common ratios whose quotients are less than one, the Greeks inverted these ratios by attaching a prefix *hyp* or *hyph*, from *hypo*, which means *under*, as in the reciprocal of a number, or $1/x$. Therefore, *hypodiplasios* means *half*, or $1 \div 2 = 1/2$; *hyphhemiolios* means *two-thirds*, or $1 \div (1 + 1/2) = 2/3$; *hypepitritos* means *three-fourths*, or $1 \div (1 + 1/3) = 3/4$; and *hypepogdoos* means *eight-ninths*, or $1 \div (1 + 1/8) = 8/9$.[23] These kinds of ratios occurred very rarely in the context of canon string divisions, and were never used to identify musical intervals.

In his translation of Euclid's *Division of the Canon*, André Barbera observes

> If the long version of the *Division of the Canon* originated in the fourth century B.C., it contains the earliest musical division of a canon in Western history.[24]

Because this book was written by a geometrician, all letter ratios and number ratios refer exclusively and unequivocally to the lengths of straight lines, which in turn represent the lengths of canon strings. Indeed, all ancient Greek[25] and Arabian[26] theorists who described the art of tuning from the perspective of practicing musicians, tabulated their tuning data in either string length units, or in length ratios. The author of the *Division of the Canon* specifies *diplasios*, *hemiolios*, *epitritos*, and *epogdoos* in Propositions 6–9, 12–14, and 19–20; the latter two propositions describe the process of tuning a complete diatonic "double-octave" on canon strings.

The oldest extant departures from this practice occurred approximately 400 years later in the *Manual of Harmonics* by the mathematician Nicomachus of Gerasa (b. *c.* A.D. 60) and in a dialog entitled *On Music*, contained in the *Moralia* of the biographer Plutarch (*c.* A.D. 46 – *c.* 120). Before we discuss these exceptions, note that both texts are devoid of the mathematical techniques and procedural methods required to describe a complete tuning on a musical instrument. The writers only assign numeric values to the "octave," "fifth," "fourth," and "whole tone," without integrating these intervals into a mathematical description of a complete scale. Such accounts typically stem from theoreticians who are not practicing musicians, which probably explains why neither Nicomachus nor Plutarch contributed a single original tetrachord division to the history of music.

Nicomachus abandons the concept of length ratios in Chapter 6 of his *Manual of Harmonics.* He begins the discussion by telling a fallacious story in which Pythagoras compares various weights suspended from the ends of strings and, thereby, discovers that the "octave," "fifth," and "fourth" vary directly with tension:

I

> {Pythagoras} found that the string stretched by the greatest weight produced, when compared with that stretched by the smallest, an octave. The weight on one string was **twelve pounds**, while that on the other was **six pounds**. Being therefore in a double ratio [2:1], it produced the octave, the ratio being evidenced by the weights themselves. Again, he found that the string under the greatest tension compared with that next to the string under the least tension (the string stretched by a weight of **eight pounds**), produced a fifth. Hence he discovered that this string was in a hemiolic ratio [3:2] with the string under the greatest tension, the ratio in which the weights also stood to one another. Then he found that the string stretched by the greatest weight, when compared with that which was next to it in

> weight, being under a tension of **nine pounds**, produced a fourth, analogous to the weights. He concluded, therefore, that this string was undoubtedly in an epitritic ratio [4:3] with the string under the greatest tension . . .[27] (Bold text, and text in braces mine. Text in parentheses and ratios in brackets in Levin's translation.)

In short, Nicomachus claims that one may produce these three cardinal consonances of music by tensioning strings according to the following "weight ratios":

$$\text{the ``octave''} = \frac{12\ \cancel{\text{lbs}}}{6\ \cancel{\text{lbs}}} = \frac{2}{1}$$

$$\text{the ``fifth''} = \frac{12\ \cancel{\text{lbs}}}{8\ \cancel{\text{lbs}}} = \frac{3}{2}$$

$$\text{the ``fourth''} = \frac{12\ \cancel{\text{lbs}}}{9\ \cancel{\text{lbs}}} = \frac{4}{3}$$

Nicomachus then assigns the following unspecified quantities to the "tonic," "fourth," "fifth," and "octave" of the standard Greek Dorian Mode between E and $E^{\prime}$:

II

> {Pythagoras} called the note partaking of the number 6, *hypate* {or E}, that of the number 8, *mese* {or A}, this number being in an epitritic proportion with the number 6; that of the number 9, he called *paramese* {or B}, which is higher than *mese* by a whole tone and what is more, stands in a sesquioctave {Latin for 9:8} proportion with it; that of 12, he called *nete* {or $E^{\prime}$}. Filling out the intervening intervals in the diatonic genus with analogous notes, he thus subordinated the octachord to the consonant numbers, the double ratio [2:1], the hemiolic [3:2], the epitritic [4:3], and the difference between them, the sesquioctave [9:8].[28] (Italics, and text in braces mine. Ratios in brackets in Levin's translation.)

If we assume that Nicomachus is conjuring "weight ratios," then

$$\begin{aligned}
\text{the ``fourth''}\ \frac{A}{E} &= \frac{8\ \cancel{\text{lbs}}}{6\ \cancel{\text{lbs}}} = \frac{4}{3}\\
\text{the ``fifth''}\ \frac{B}{E} &= \frac{9\ \cancel{\text{lbs}}}{6\ \cancel{\text{lbs}}} = \frac{3}{2} \qquad \text{(Weight Ratios)}\\
\text{the ``octave''}\ \frac{E^{\prime}}{E} &= \frac{12\ \cancel{\text{lbs}}}{6\ \cancel{\text{lbs}}} = \frac{2}{1}
\end{aligned}$$

Contrary to observable fact, these weight measurements are false because Nicomachus assumed that "the notes," or the aurally perceived frequencies of strings, are directly proportional to tension.

	E	A	B	$E^{\prime}$
Incorrect Tension:	6	8	9	12

As discussed in Section 2.6, the frequency of a string is directly proportional to the square root of tension (T), in pounds-force (lbf). Therefore, with all other variables held constant, to increase the fundamental frequency (F_1) by an "octave," we must increase Nicomachus' tension of 6.0 lbf by the factor $^2\!/_1$ squared. Similarly, to increase F_1 by a "fifth" and by a "fourth," we must increase the tension by the factors $^3\!/_2$ squared and $^4\!/_3$ squared, respectively:

$$\frac{1}{DL}\sqrt{\frac{(6.0\text{ lbf})(2.00)^2}{\pi\rho}} = 2.00F_1 = \text{E}^{\prime}$$

$$\frac{1}{DL}\sqrt{\frac{(6.0\text{ lbf})(1.50)^2}{\pi\rho}} = 1.50F_1 = \text{B}$$

$$\frac{1}{DL}\sqrt{\frac{(6.0\text{ lbf})(1.33)^2}{\pi\rho}} = 1.33F_1 = \text{A}$$

Therefore, the correct weights for these frequencies are

	E	A	B	E'
Correct Tension:	6.00	10.61	13.50	24.00

Nicomachus continues his numeric analysis of vibrating strings in Chapter 10, where he correctly concludes that frequency is inversely proportional to length. He begins the discussion by comparing functional differences in magnitude between the numeric values assigned to "weight ratios" and those assigned to length ratios:

> . . . measurements based on the lengths . . . of strings . . . are seen to be inverse to measurements that are based on tension, [since] in . . . [the latter] case [1] the smaller the term, the lower the pitch, and the greater the term, the higher the pitch. [However], in the former case, there is an inverse proportion in that [2] the smaller the term, the higher is the pitch, while the greater the term, the lower is the pitch.[29] (Text and numbers in brackets mine.)

Observation 1 is true because lesser tension or a smaller term produces a lower tone, and greater tension or a larger term produces a higher tone. Furthermore, Observation 2 is also true because a shorter length or a smaller term produces a higher tone, and a longer length or a greater term produces a lower tone. Nicomachus then gives the following highly accurate description:

III

> If, therefore, one takes a long string that is kept under one and the same tension . . . — the string having been stopped by a bridge . . . at its very center so that the vibration caused by the plucking of the string may not progress beyond the half-way point — he will find the interval of an octave, the sound of half {*hemiseias*} the string compared with that of the whole string being in a greater proportion, that is, in a duple {2:1} proportion, a result ***exactly inverse*** to the reciprocal data of the length. And if one keeps the vibration down to a third of the string . . . the sound from two thirds {*dimoirou*} of the string will necessarily be in a hemiolic [3:2] relation to that of the sound from the whole string, or ***inversely proportional*** to the length of the string. And if one sections off a fourth part of the string . . . the sound from three parts of the string will be in an epitritic [4:3] relation

to that of the whole string, or ***inversely proportional*** to the length of the string.[30] (Bold italics, and ratio in braces mine. Italics in braces in Nicomachus' original text. Ratios in brackets in Levin's translation.)

Refer to Equation 2.9 and observe that the frequency of a string is inversely proportional to length. Therefore, with all other variables held constant, to increase F_1 by an "octave," we must decrease a string length by the factor $^2\!/_1$. Similarly, to increase F_1 by a "fifth" and by a "fourth," we must decrease the length by the factors $^3\!/_2$ and $^4\!/_3$, respectively. If we utilize Nicomachus' numeric values to quantify string lengths, then

$$\frac{1}{D(12.0\text{ in}/2.00)}\sqrt{\frac{T}{\pi\rho}} = \frac{1}{D(6.0\text{ in})}\sqrt{\frac{T}{\pi\rho}} = 2.00F_1 = \text{E}^{|}$$

$$\frac{1}{D(12.0\text{ in}/1.50)}\sqrt{\frac{T}{\pi\rho}} = \frac{1}{D(8.0\text{ in})}\sqrt{\frac{T}{\pi\rho}} = 1.50F_1 = \text{B}$$

$$\frac{1}{D(12.0\text{ in}/1.33)}\sqrt{\frac{T}{\pi\rho}} = \frac{1}{D(9.0\text{ in})}\sqrt{\frac{T}{\pi\rho}} = 1.33F_1 = \text{A}$$

Although mathematicians in the 1st century A.D. had no scientific methods to determine the exact frequencies of strings, Nicomachus' conclusions regarding rates of vibration are correct. He accurately observes that "the sound" from $^1\!/_2$ of a string vibrates $^2\!/_1$ times faster, from $^2\!/_3$ of a string vibrates $^3\!/_2$ times faster, and from $^3\!/_4$ of a string vibrates $^4\!/_3$ times faster than the whole length of the string. Therefore, if we utilize Nicomachus' numeric values to quantify string vibrations (or modern frequencies, in cycles per second), then

$$\text{the "fourth"}\quad \frac{\text{A}}{\text{E}} = \frac{8\ \cancel{\text{vib}}}{6\ \cancel{\text{vib}}} = \frac{4}{3}$$

$$\text{the "fifth"}\quad \frac{\text{B}}{\text{E}} = \frac{9\ \cancel{\text{vib}}}{6\ \cancel{\text{vib}}} = \frac{3}{2} \qquad \text{(Vibration Ratios)}$$

$$\text{the "octave"}\quad \frac{\text{E}^{|}}{\text{E}} = \frac{12\ \cancel{\text{vib}}}{6\ \cancel{\text{vib}}} = \frac{2}{1}$$

Note that for these musical intervals, "weight ratios" and "vibration ratios" are identical with respect to the numeric values of the numerators and denominators. Since "weight ratios" represent *incorrect* quantities, and "vibration ratios" represent *correct* quantities, we will avoid "weight ratios" in all future calculations. In other words, when Nicomachus and Plutarch refer to unspecified quantities such as 6, 8, 9, and 12, we will assume they mean vibration numbers that are equivalent to modern frequencies, such as 6.0 cps, 8.0 cps, 9.0 cps, and 12.0 cps. However, because "vibration ratios" are also problematic, we will only work with frequency ratios.

Finally, if we express these intervals according to the previously calculated string lengths, then

$$\text{the "fourth"}\quad \frac{\text{E}}{\text{A}} = \frac{12\ \cancel{\text{in}}}{9\ \cancel{\text{in}}} = \frac{4}{3}$$

$$\text{the "fifth"}\quad \frac{\text{E}}{\text{B}} = \frac{12\ \cancel{\text{in}}}{8\ \cancel{\text{in}}} = \frac{3}{2} \qquad \text{(Length Ratios)}$$

$$\text{the "octave"}\quad \frac{\text{E}}{\text{E}^{|}} = \frac{12\ \cancel{\text{in}}}{6\ \cancel{\text{in}}} = \frac{2}{1}$$

Of the Greek treatises on music that have survived, Quotes I and II represent the first occurrences where the terms *diplasios*, *hemiolios*, *epitritos*, and *epogdoos* do not refer to ancient length ratios, but to "weight ratios," or to numerically identical "vibration ratios." Consequently, whereas in the former case music theorists assign larger numbers to lower tones, in the latter case, they assign larger numbers to higher tones. In Sections 3.18–3.19, we will discuss how these two different quantifications of musical intervals affect the division of the "octave"; and in Section 3.20, we will examine several reasons why — throughout the history of music — creative theorists and musicians never mention weight numbers or vibration numbers in their descriptions and discussions of tetrachord divisions and scale constructions.

3.18

Before we compare crucial differences between ancient length ratios and frequency ratios, let us first discuss several basic concepts of formal scale construction. A scale consists of a progression of tones expressed as a sequence of numbers in a definite order. The numbers contained in such a sequence are called *terms.* The Greeks defined three fundamental number sequences through the identification of three different *means:* the arithmetic mean, the harmonic mean, and the geometric mean. A mean represents an intermediate value, or several intermediate values, between two outer terms called the *extremes.* Consequently, in an arithmetic progression, in a harmonic progression, or in a geometric progression, a mean expresses a value that is larger than the small extreme, and smaller than the large extreme. In a musical context, a mean represents the division of a large interval into two or more smaller intervals. For the rest of this chapter, we will focus exclusively on Greek definitions of the arithmetic and harmonic means. See Chapter 9, Part I, and Chapter 10, Part III, for detailed discussions on geometric mean calculations.

The oldest extant Greek text that defines the three means of music is preserved in a fragment by Archytas (fl. *c.* 400 B.C.). Like Euclid after him, Archytas was a famous geometrician, who also wrote extensively on sound and music. Unfortunately, none of his works have survived intact. According to Ptolemy, Archytas calculated three different tetrachord divisions in string length units, which means that Archytas used length ratios to identify the musical intervals of his scales.[31] Again, this is perfectly consistent with the work of a geometrician. We may calculate the three means with the following modern equations:

$$\text{Arithmetic mean} = \frac{a_1 + a_2 + a_3 + \ldots + a_n}{n} \tag{3.37}$$

$$\text{Harmonic mean} = \frac{n}{\dfrac{1}{a_1} + \dfrac{1}{a_2} + \dfrac{1}{a_3} + \ldots + \dfrac{1}{a_n}} \tag{3.38}$$

$$\text{Geometric mean} = \sqrt[n]{a_1 \times a_2 \times a_3 \times \ldots \times a_n} \tag{3.39}$$

When there are only two variables these equations simplify to

$$\text{Arithmetic mean} = \frac{a + c}{2} \tag{3.37A}$$

$$\text{Harmonic mean} = \frac{2ac}{a + c} \tag{3.38A}$$

$$\text{Geometric mean} = \sqrt{ac} \tag{3.39A}$$

Archytas describes these three means in the following manner:

> There are three means in music. One is arithmetic, the second geometric, the third subcontrary, which they call 'harmonic'.
>
> [1] There is an **arithmetic mean** when there are three terms, proportional in that they exceed one another in the following way: ***the second exceeds the third*** by the same amount as that by which the first exceeds the second. In this proportion it turns out that the interval between the **greater terms** is less, and that between the **lesser terms** is greater.
>
> [2] There is a **geometric mean** when they are such that as the first is to the second, so is the second to the third. With these the interval made by the greater terms is equal to that made by the lesser.
>
> [3] There is a subcontrary mean, which we call '**harmonic**', when they are such that the part of the third by which ***the middle term exceeds the third*** is the same as the part of the first by which the first exceeds the second. In this proportion the interval between the **greater terms** is greater, and that between the **lesser terms** is less.[32] (Bold italics, bold text, and numbers in brackets mine.)

Because Archytas did not explicitly state whether the "greater terms" and "lesser terms" represent length numbers or vibration numbers, these definitions are completely open to interpretation. However, note carefully that in Definitions 1 and 3, the second or middle term "exceeds the third" term, which means that for the arithmetic mean and the harmonic mean, respectively, Archytas describes two descending sequences of numbers. As we shall see, in the context of musical interval calculations, music theorists primarily associate such progressions with string length measurements, or with the construction of length ratios.

The arithmetic mean refers to the familiar average value of two numbers. On the other hand, the harmonic mean is not so simple. Recall that Archytas' definition specifies, ". . . that the part of the third [term] by which the middle term exceeds the third is the same as the part of the first [term] by which the first exceeds the second." (Text in brackets mine.) Therefore, if the second term exceeds the third term by a given fractional value of the third term, the first term must exceed the second term by the same fractional value of the first term. Or, stated another way, the harmonic mean is smaller than the large extreme by the same fraction that it is larger than the small extreme. For example, since in the progression 12:8:6, the harmonic mean (8) is smaller than the first term (12) by one-third (⅓) of 12, the harmonic mean (8) must be larger than the third term (6) by one-third (⅓) of 6:

$$12 - 12 \times \frac{1}{3} = 8$$

$$8 = 6 + 6 \times \frac{1}{3}$$

To understand how differences in length numbers and vibration numbers yield diametrically opposed interval divisions, begin by considering the arithmetic division of the "octave" according to length numbers. Refer to Equation 3.37A, substitute the values $a = 12.0$ in. and $c = 6.0$ in. into this equation, and calculate the arithmetic mean (Λ_{A}) of the "octave":

$$\Lambda_{\text{A}} = \frac{12.0 \text{ in} + 6.0 \text{ in}}{2} = \frac{18.0 \text{ in}}{2} = 9.0 \text{ in}$$

To compute the musical interval of the bridged canon string at 9.0 in. with respect to the fundamental at 12.0 in., divide the length ratio of the upper interval $^{12}/_{9}$ by the length ratio of the fundamental $^{12}/_{12}$:

$$\text{Lower Arithmetic Interval} = \frac{12.0\text{ in}}{9.0\text{ in}} \div \frac{12.0\text{ in}}{12.0\text{ in}} = \frac{\cancel{12.0\text{ in}}}{9.0\text{ in}} \times \frac{12.0\text{ in}}{\cancel{12.0\text{ in}}} = \frac{12.0\ \cancel{\text{in}}}{9.0\ \cancel{\text{in}}} = \frac{4}{3}$$

And to calculate the musical interval of the bridged string at 9.0 in. with respect to the "octave" at 6.0 in., again divide the length ratio of the upper interval $^{12}/_{6}$ by the length ratio of the lower interval $^{12}/_{9}$:

$$\text{Upper Arithmetic Interval} = \frac{12.0\text{ in}}{6.0\text{ in}} \div \frac{12.0\text{ in}}{9.0\text{ in}} = \frac{\cancel{12.0\text{ in}}}{6.0\text{ in}} \times \frac{9.0\text{ in}}{\cancel{12.0\text{ in}}} = \frac{9.0\ \cancel{\text{in}}}{6.0\ \cancel{\text{in}}} = \frac{3}{2}$$

Refer to Figure 3.22 and observe that we may interpret these interval ratios as the quantities described by Archytas' first definition: the greater terms [$^{12}/_{9}$] identify the lesser arithmetic interval [$^{4}/_{3}$], and the lesser terms [$^{9}/_{6}$] identify the greater arithmetic interval [$^{3}/_{2}$].

The Arithmetic Division of the "Octave" Expressed as Ancient Length Ratio $^{2}/_{1}$

Lengths:	$L =$ 12.0 in.	→	$\Lambda_A =$ 9.0 in.	→	$\Lambda =$ 6.0 in.	→	$L =$ 0 in.
Ancient Length Ratios:	$^{12}/_{12} = {}^{1}/_{1}$		$^{12}/_{9} = {}^{4}/_{3}$		$^{12}/_{6} = {}^{2}/_{1}$		
Latter Denominators:	12	:	9	:	6		
Least Terms:	4	:	3	:	2		
Frequencies:	6.0 cps		8.0 cps		12.0 cps		
Frequency Ratios:	$^{6}/_{6} = {}^{1}/_{1}$		$^{8}/_{6} = {}^{4}/_{3}$		$^{12}/_{6} = {}^{2}/_{1}$		
Latter Numerators:	6	:	8	:	12		
Least Terms:	3	:	4	:	6		

Interval Ratio Notation: The longer length for Λ_A, and the higher frequency for F, appear in the numerator.

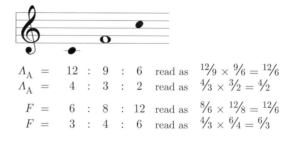

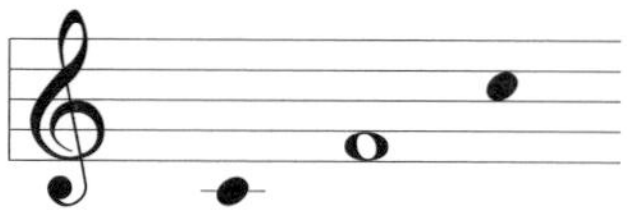

Λ_A	=	12	: 9	:	6	read as	$^{12}/_{9} \times {}^{9}/_{6} = {}^{12}/_{6}$
Λ_A	=	4	: 3	:	2	read as	$^{4}/_{3} \times {}^{3}/_{2} = {}^{4}/_{2}$
F	=	6	: 8	:	12	read as	$^{8}/_{6} \times {}^{12}/_{8} = {}^{12}/_{6}$
F	=	3	: 4	:	6	read as	$^{4}/_{3} \times {}^{6}/_{4} = {}^{6}/_{3}$

Figure 3.22 Arithmetic division of the "octave" expressed as length ratio $^{2}/_{1}$. On this canon string, the "octave" is defined by 12.0 in. and 6.0 in. lengths, and the arithmetic mean, by a 9.0 in. length.

However, before we continue, consider a harmonic division of the "octave" according to vibration numbers. Refer to Equation 3.38A, substitute the values $a = 6.0$ cps and $c = 12.0$ cps into this equation, and calculate the harmonic mean (F_H) of the "octave":

$$F_{\mathrm{H}} = \frac{2(6.0 \text{ cps})(12.0 \text{ cps})}{6.0 \text{ cps} + 12.0 \text{ cps}} = \frac{144.0 \text{ cps}^{\not{2}}}{18.0 \not{\text{cps}}} = 8.0 \text{ cps}$$

Again, examine Figure 3.22 and note that length numbers in arithmetic progression (12.0 in., 9.0 in., and 6.0 in.) produce vibration numbers in harmonic progression (6.0 cps, 8.0 cps, and 12.0 cps). Consequently, with respect to the latter vibration numbers, we may equally well interpret these frequencies as producing interval ratios described by Archytas' third definition: the greater terms [12/8] identify the greater harmonic interval [3/2], and the lesser terms [8/6] identify the lesser harmonic interval [4/3].

So, although I describe Figure 3.22 as the arithmetic division of the "octave" expressed as length ratio 2/1, most scholars of ancient Greek music interpret Figure 3.22 as the harmonic division of the "octave" expressed as frequency ratio 2/1.

Next, consider a harmonic division of the "octave" according to length numbers. Refer to Equation 3.38A, substitute the values $a = 12.0$ in. and $c = 6.0$ in. into this equation, and calculate the harmonic mean (Λ_{H}) of the "octave":

$$\Lambda_{\mathrm{H}} = \frac{2(12.0 \text{ in})(6.0 \text{ in})}{12.0 \text{ in} + 6.0 \text{ in}} = \frac{144.0 \text{ in}^{\not{2}}}{18.0 \not{\text{in}}} = 8.0 \text{ in}$$

Now, to compute the musical interval of the bridged canon string at 8.0 in. with respect to the fundamental frequency, divide

$$\text{Lower Harmonic Interval} = \frac{12.0 \text{ in}}{8.0 \text{ in}} \div \frac{12.0 \text{ in}}{12.0 \text{ in}} = \frac{\not{12.0 \text{ in}}}{8.0 \text{ in}} \times \frac{12.0 \text{ in}}{\not{12.0 \text{ in}}} = \frac{12.0 \not{\text{in}}}{8.0 \not{\text{in}}} = \frac{3}{2}$$

Similarly, to compute the musical interval of the bridged string at 8.0 in. with respect to the "octave" at 6.0 in., divide

$$\text{Upper Harmonic Interval} = \frac{12.0 \text{ in}}{6.0 \text{ in}} \div \frac{12.0 \text{ in}}{8.0 \text{ in}} = \frac{\not{12.0 \text{ in}}}{6.0 \text{ in}} \times \frac{8.0 \text{ in}}{\not{12.0 \text{ in}}} = \frac{8.0 \not{\text{in}}}{6.0 \not{\text{in}}} = \frac{4}{3}$$

Refer to Figure 3.23 and observe that we may interpret these interval ratios as the quantities described by Archytas' third definition: the greater terms [12/8] identify the greater harmonic interval [3/2], and the lesser terms [8/6] identify the lesser harmonic interval [4/3].

However, before we continue, consider an arithmetic division of the "octave" according to vibration numbers. Refer to Equation 3.37A, substitute the values $a = 6.0$ cps and $c = 12.0$ cps into this equation, and calculate the arithmetic mean (F_{A}) of the "octave":

$$F_{\mathrm{A}} = \frac{6.0 \text{ cps} + 12.0 \text{ cps}}{2} = \frac{18.0 \text{ cps}}{2} = 9.0 \text{ cps}$$

Again, turn to Figure 3.23 and observe that length numbers in harmonic progression (12.0 in., 8.0 in., and 6.0 in.) produce vibration numbers in arithmetic progression (6.0 cps, 9.0 cps, 12.0 cps). Consequently, with respect to the latter vibration numbers, we may equally well interpret these frequency ratios as producing interval ratios described by Archytas' first definition: the greater terms [12/9] identify the lesser arithmetic interval [4/3], and the lesser terms [9/6] identify the greater arithmetic interval [3/2].

So, although I describe Figure 3.23 as the harmonic division of the "octave" expressed as length ratio 2/1, most scholars of ancient Greek music interpret Figure 3.23 as the arithmetic division of the "octave" expressed as frequency ratio 2/1.

The Harmonic Division of the "Octave" Expressed as Length Ratio $\frac{2}{1}$

Lengths:	$L =$ 12.0 in. →		$\Lambda_H =$ 8.0 in. →	$\Lambda =$ 6.0 in. →	$L =$ 0 in.
Ancient Length Ratios:	$\frac{12}{12} = \frac{1}{1}$		$\frac{12}{8} = \frac{3}{2}$	$\frac{12}{6} = \frac{2}{1}$	
Latter Denominators:	12	:	8 :	6	
Least Terms:	6	:	4 :	3	

Frequencies:	6.0 cps		9.0 cps	12.0 cps	
Frequency Ratios:	$\frac{6}{6} = \frac{1}{1}$		$\frac{9}{6} = \frac{3}{2}$	$\frac{12}{6} = \frac{2}{1}$	
Latter Numerators:	6	:	9 :	12	
Least Terms:	2	:	3 :	4	

Interval Ratio Notation: The longer length for Λ_H, and the higher frequency for F, appear in the numerator.

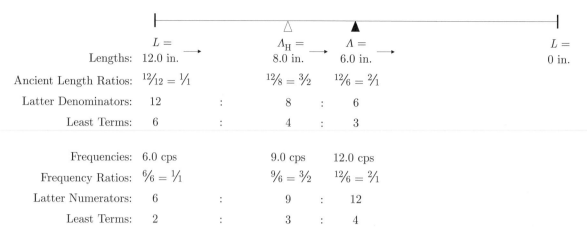

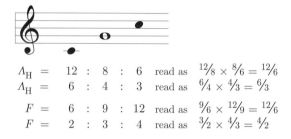

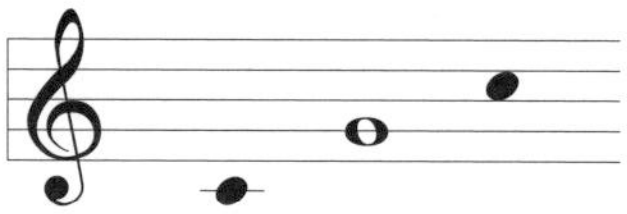

Λ_H = 12 : 8 : 6 read as $\frac{12}{8} \times \frac{8}{6} = \frac{12}{6}$
Λ_H = 6 : 4 : 3 read as $\frac{6}{4} \times \frac{4}{3} = \frac{6}{3}$

F = 6 : 9 : 12 read as $\frac{9}{6} \times \frac{12}{9} = \frac{12}{6}$
F = 2 : 3 : 4 read as $\frac{3}{2} \times \frac{4}{3} = \frac{4}{2}$

Figure 3.23 Harmonic division of the "octave" expressed as length ratio $\frac{2}{1}$. On this canon string, the "octave" is defined by 12.0 in. and 6.0 in. lengths, and the harmonic mean, by an 8.0 in. length.

However, to confirm the historic authenticity of my interpretations as shown in Figures 3.22 and 3.23, see Section 10.8, Quote I, and Section 10.16, Quote II, for Ptolemy's descriptions of the arithmetic and harmonic divisions of the "octave" on canon strings.

In Figure 3.22, notice that we may express interval ratios $\frac{4}{3}$ and $\frac{3}{2}$ with respect to string lengths, and interval ratios $\frac{4}{3}$ and $\frac{6}{4}$ [$\frac{3}{2}$] with respect to frequencies, in shorthand notation 4:3:2. Similarly, in Figure 3.23 we may express interval ratios $\frac{6}{4}$ [$\frac{3}{2}$] and $\frac{4}{3}$ with respect to string lengths, and interval ratios $\frac{3}{2}$ and $\frac{4}{3}$ with respect to frequencies, in shorthand notation 2:3:4. Now, observe carefully that the integers of the latter two sequences are identical. To distinguish between intervals based on string lengths on the one hand, and frequencies on the other, music theorists (who understand this crucial difference) use two different methods of notation. Length ratios appear in descending numerical order; here the first integer represents the overall length of an open string. Consequently, one writes interval ratios according to string length calculations as 4:3:2, 6:4:3, etc. In contrast, frequency ratios appear in ascending numerical order; here the first integer represents the fundamental frequency of an open string. Consequently, one writes interval ratios according to frequency calculations as 2:3:4, 3:4:6, etc.

Finally, as discussed in Chapter 10, Part VI, the arithmetic division of strings plays an extremely important role in determining the *minor tonality*, and the harmonic division, in determining the *major tonality* of Western music. Furthermore, although the musical intervals in Figures 3.22 and 3.23 are notated in ascending order, music theorists have also described the arithmetic and harmonic divisions of musical intervals in descending order. For example, in Sections 10.62–10.64 we will examine the work of Jean-Philippe Rameau (1683–1764), who investigated a so-called *subharmonic series*, where musical intervals appear in reverse order from the harmonic series. Even though Rameau eventually conceded that such a phenomenon does not exist in nature, he nevertheless used a purely mathematical construction of the subharmonic series to define the minor tonality. Note, therefore, that the subject of interval notation is extremely complex, and that we must be constantly aware of the mathematical context in which a musical description of interval ratios occurs.

3.19

As dimensionless entities, ancient length ratios and modern frequency ratios are indistinguishable. For example, it makes no difference if a theorist specifies a.l.r. 4/3 or f.r. 4/3 because both ratios represent the "fourth." Crucial differences occur only in the context of interval divisions! Figure 3.24 shows that the arithmetic division of the "octave" expressed as a length ratio yields a "fourth" as the lower interval, and a "fifth" as the upper interval; whereas the harmonic division yields a "fifth" as the lower interval, and a "fourth" as the upper interval. In contrast, an arithmetic division of the "octave" expressed as a frequency ratio yields a "fifth" as the lower interval, and a "fourth" as the upper interval; whereas the harmonic division yields a "fourth" as the lower interval, and a "fifth" as the upper interval.

(a)

	12.0 in		9.0 in		8.0 in		6.0 in
	E		A		B		E′
Λ_A:	**E**	4/3	**A**		3/2		**E′**
Λ_H:	**E**		3/2		**B**	4/3	**E′**

(b)

	6.0 cps		8.0 cps		9.0 cps		12.0 cps
	E		A		B		E′
F_A:	**E**		3/2		**B**	4/3	**E′**
F_H:	**E**	4/3	**A**		3/2		**E′**

Figure 3.24 Two different divisions of the "octave." (a) The arithmetic and harmonic divisions of the "octave" expressed as a.l.r. 12/6 yield diametrically opposed distributions of intervals when compared to (b) the arithmetic and harmonic divisions of the "octave" expressed as f.r. 12/6.

We may also find evidence of the use of length ratios in Plato (427–347 B.C.). Although Plato mentions Philolaus (fl. *c.* 420 B.C.) on two occasions in a dialog entitled *Phaedo*,[33] he does not acknowledge the scientific and musical accomplishments of this renowned philosopher. (See Section 10.10.) Consequently, he plagiarizes Philolaus' famous diatonic tetrachord: 256/243, 9/8, 9/8 in a dialog entitled *Timaeus*. In commentaries by Nicomachus and Plutarch, both writers discuss the following passage from the *Timaeus*, which describes how God created the soul of the universe by dividing its divine "mixture" into several sequences of numerically defined musical intervals:[34]

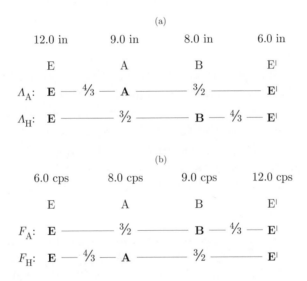

> And {God} proceeded to divide after this manner. First of all, he ***took away one part*** of the whole [1], and then he separated a second part which was double the first [2], and then he took away a third part which

> was half as much again as the second and three times as much as the first [3], and then he took a fourth part which was twice as much as the second [4], and a fifth part which was three times the third [9], and a sixth part which was eight times the first [8], and a seventh part which was twenty-seven times the first [27]. After this he filled up the double intervals [that is, between 1, 2, 4, 8] and the triple [that is, between 1, 3, 9, 27], ***cutting off yet other portions*** from the mixture and placing them in the intervals, so that in each interval there were two kinds of means, the one {**harmonic**} exceeding and exceeded by equal parts of its extremes, the other {**arithmetic**} being that kind of mean which exceeds and is exceeded by an equal number. Where there were intervals of $\frac{3}{2}$ and of $\frac{4}{3}$ and of $\frac{9}{8}$, made by the connecting terms in the former intervals, he filled up all the intervals of $\frac{4}{3}$ with the interval of $\frac{9}{8}$, leaving a fraction over, and the interval which this fraction expressed was in the ratio of 256 to 243. And thus the whole mixture out of which he cut these portions was all exhausted by him.[35] (Bold italics, and text in braces mine. Text and numbers in brackets in Jowett's translation.)

If it were not for the cosmic "mixture," it would be difficult to imagine how the process of taking parts, cutting portions, and quantifying mathematical intervals depicts anything but the work of a master musician at a canon. I am particularly intrigued by the verbs *to take* and *to cut*, which also occur in Euclid's canon tuning description.[36] However, because Plato does not explicitly state whether his ratios express length numbers or vibration numbers, this passage (like Archytas' fragment) is completely open to interpretation. Of course, neither Nicomachus nor Plutarch allude to Plato's obvious references to canon tuning techniques. So, it is not surprising that both authors suppressed the *mathematical* possibility that the "intervals of $\frac{3}{2}$ and $\frac{4}{3}$" could have originated from harmonic and arithmetic divisions of the "octave" expressed as length ratio $\frac{12}{6}$. Approximately 500 years after Plato wrote the *Timaeus*, Nicomachus and Plutarch attempted to eliminate length ratios in favor of frequency ratios because they undoubtedly believed that the concrete reality of geometry interfered with developments in "pure" mathematics. In Chapter 8, Nicomachus gives the following interpretation:

> **Explanation of the references to harmonics in the *Timaeus***
>
> . . . Plato expressed himself as follows: "so that within each interval there are two means, the one superior and inferior to the extremes by the same fraction, the other by the same number. He (the Demiurge) filled up the distance between the hemiolic interval [3:2] and the epitritic [4:3] with the remaining interval of the sesquioctave [9:8]."
>
> For the double interval is as 12 is to 6, but there are two means, 9 and 8. The number 8, however, in the harmonic proportion is midway between 6 and 12, being greater than 6 by one third of 6 (that is, 2), and being less than 12 by one third of 12 (that is, 4). ...
>
> The other mean, 9, which is fixed at the *paramese* degree {or B}, is observed to be at the arithmetic mean between the extremes, being less than 12 and greater than 6 by the same number (3).[37] (Italics, and text in braces mine. Text in parentheses and ratios in brackets in Levin's translation.)

Refer to Figure 3.24 and note that because Nicomachus identifies abstract number 9 as an arithmetic mean that represents the tone B, he interprets Plato's division of the "octave" expressed as frequency ratio $\frac{12}{6}$.

Finally, here is Plutarch's explanation:

> So Plato, wishing to show in terms of the science of harmonics the harmony of the four elements in the soul [represented by the numbers 6, 8, 9, and 12] . . . presents in each interval two means of the soul, in accordance with the ratio of music. For it so happens that in music the consonance of the octave has two mean intervals. ... Now the consonance of the octave is seen to be in the duple ratio; and this ratio, expressed in numbers, is illustrated by six and twelve . . . Six then and twelve being the extremes, the *hypate* {or E} . . . is represented by the number six, the *nete* {or E'} . . . by the number twelve. ... . . . it is evident that the *mese* {or A} will be represented by the number 8, the *paramese* {or B} by the number nine.[38] (Italics, and text in braces mine. Text and numbers in brackets in Einarson's translation.)

Again, since Plutarch equates the tone A with abstract number 8, and tone B with abstract number 9, the former number represents the harmonic division, and the latter number represents the arithmetic division of the "octave" expressed as frequency ratio $^{12}/_{6}$.

3.20

Many ancient writers avoid dimensional descriptions of quantities such as 6, 8, 9, and 12, because a specific reference to a "weight ratio" or "vibration ratio" would have compelled them to define a new kind of complicated "length ratio." For example, in Section 3.17, Quote III, Nicomachus states that the *sound* of the "fifth" — or the frequency ratio of the "fifth" — is in a *hemiolic* [$^{3}/_{2}$] relation with the whole string; consequently, the *length* of the "fifth" must be in a *dimoiros* [$^{2}/_{3}$] relation with the whole string.[39] In his next example, the *sound* of the "fourth" — or the frequency ratio of the "fourth" — is in an *epitritic* [$^{4}/_{3}$] relation with the whole string; consequently, the *length* of the "fourth" must be in a *hypepitritic* [$^{3}/_{4}$] relation with the whole string. Here already, Nicomachus fails to identify the complicated fraction that describes three-fourths of the string. Instead, he simply compares four parts to three parts and, thereby, equates ancient length ratio $^{4}/_{3}$ with frequency ratio $^{4}/_{3}$.

The introduction of weight numbers and vibration numbers instigated a double standard whereby music theorists silently interpreted ancient length ratios as "weight ratios" or "vibration ratios." Since ancient length ratio $^{n}/_{x}$ is indistinguishable from Nicomachus' "vibration ratio," a switch from a.l.r. $^{n}/_{x}$ to f.r. $^{n}/_{x}$ incurs no numeric changes, and a switch in the opposite direction from f.r. $^{n}/_{x}$ to a.l.r. $^{n}/_{x}$ also incurs no numeric changes. However, all readers of ancient texts, and of most interpretations of ancient texts, must remain vigilant with respect to interval divisions. Confusion, mistakes, and anachronisms will inevitably occur if a reader fails to recognize whether a particular writer is describing the division of a.l.r. $^{n}/_{x}$, or of f.r. $^{n}/_{x}$.

Creative theorist-musicians like Euclid (fl. *c.* 300 B.C.), Ssu-ma Ch'ien (*c.* 145 B.C. – *c.* 87 B.C.), Ptolemy (*c.* A.D. 100 – *c.* 165), Al-Kindī (d. *c.* 874), Al-Fārābī (d. *c.* 950), Ibn Sīnā (980–1037), Ṣafī Al-Dīn (d. 1294), Ramis (*c.* 1440 – *c.* 1500), Rāmāmātya (fl. *c.* 1550), Zarlino (1517–1590), and Nārāyaṇa and Ahobala (fl. *c.* 1670) reject or simply ignore "weight ratios" and "vibration ratios." The inclusion of such ratios would have hopelessly confused their monumental achievements. In Chapters 10 and 11, we will examine detailed tuning descriptions by all these writers who — within the realm of human experience — based their work on the premise that frequency ratios are a function of length ratios.

Notes

1. See Figure 5.1.

2. Newton, R.E.I. (1990). *Wave Physics*, Chapter 4. Edward Arnold, A division of Hodder & Stoughton, London, England.

   This book contains many excellent photographs of superposing wave pulses in springs.

3. (A) Fishbane, P.M., Gasiorowicz, S., and Thornton, S.T. (1993). *Physics for Scientists and Engineers*, Chapter 15. Prentice-Hall, Englewood Cliffs, New Jersey.

   (B) Sears, F.W., Zemansky, M.W., and Young, H.D. *University Physics*, 7th ed., Chapter 22. Addison-Wesley Publishing Company, Reading, Massachusetts, 1988.

4. In most scientific texts, the lowercase of the Greek letter *lambda* (λ) represents wavelength.

5. (A) Morse, P.M., and Ingard, K.U. (1968). *Theoretical Acoustics*, p. 119. Princeton University Press, Princeton, New Jersey, 1986.

   (B) Wood, A.B. (1930). *A Textbook of Sound*, p. 89. The Macmillan Company, New York, 1937.

6. If we solve Equation 3.8 for string length,

$$L = \frac{\ell_S}{\frac{1}{n}} = \ell_S \times n$$

   note the following two conditions: (1) a flexible string bends into an integer number of equidistant loops; and (2) a flexible string has a length that equals an integer multiple of single loop lengths. Turn to Figure 6.1 and note that a vibrating bar free at both ends meets the first condition, but not the second condition.

7. Also, the mode frequencies of *stiff* strings are inversely proportional to the *effective* mode wavelengths, and directly proportional to the *effective* mode wave speeds. See Chapter 4.

8. Consider the following equalities:

$$F_n = \frac{c_T}{\lambda_n} = \frac{c_T}{\frac{2L}{n}} = \frac{c_T}{2L} \times n = \frac{n}{2L}\sqrt{\frac{T}{M/u.l.}}$$

   The last two equations illustrate how abstract algebraic notation often obscures the origin of physical phenomena. Although these two equations appear most often in standard texts, they do not immediately suggest how a string, while subdividing into shorter wavelengths, produces progressively higher mode frequencies. This obfuscation arises from the fact that for the last two equations n no longer appears in the denominator as a divisor of L. Instead, the mode number n now resides in the numerator as a multiplier of F_1. As a result, the inverse proportionality between mode wavelengths and mode frequencies disappears.

9. Therefore, the mode frequencies of stiff strings are *not* harmonics. (See Section 4.11.)

10. All strings must be stiff to resist tension. It is the stiffness of a string that prevents it from actually subdividing into an infinite number of sections.

11. When a string is sufficiently long, thin, and very flexible, the first sixteen "harmonics" come very close to sounding like perfect harmonics.

12. (A) Liddell, H.G., and Scott, R. (1843). *A Greek-English Lexicon*, p. 875. The Clarendon Press, Oxford, England, 1992.

(B) Barker, A., Translator (1989). *Greek Musical Writings, Volume 2*, Chapter 11. Cambridge University Press, Cambridge, Massachusetts.

See Sections 10.8 and 10.19 for discussions on Ptolemy's ancient Greek canon.

(C) D'Erlanger, R., Bakkouch, 'A.'A., and Al-Sanūsī, M., Translators (Vol. 1, 1930; Vol. 2, 1935; Vol. 3, 1938; Vol. 4, 1939; Vol. 5, 1949; Vol. 6, 1959). *La Musique Arabe, Volume 3.* Librairie Orientaliste Paul Geuthner, Paris, France.

See Section 11.52 for a discussion on Al-Jurjānī's ancient Arabian canon.

13. Anyone who attempts to tune two identical $^2/_1$'s (or "octaves") on a single string soon discovers that the ears locate the center of the string far more accurately than the eyes.

14. See Section 3.18 for examples on how to divide *ancient length ratios* $^n/_1$ and $^n/_x$, where the long string length is in the numerator and the short string length is in the denominator; such as $^3/_1$, $^3/_2$, $^4/_3$, $^5/_2$, etc. Also, note the discussion in Section 10.4.

15. Note that a decimal ratio may be either a rational number (i.e., a terminating or a repeating decimal), or an irrational number (i.e., a non-repeating decimal). (See Section 10.2.) In the context of (1) naturally subdividing strings, and (2) dividing canon strings into equal sections, a decimal ratio always represents a rational number, or a number expressed as the quotient of two positive integers.

16. *Greek Musical Writings, Volume 2*, p. 205.

17. With respect to approximating an irrational number as the quotient of two positive integers $^n/_x$, simply round the irrational number to x-number of decimal places, remove the decimal point, and divide by 1 and x-number of zeros. For example, $\sqrt{2} = 1.4142135624...$ Now, write a rational approximation of this irrational number as the quotient of the following two integers:

$$\frac{14{,}142{,}135{,}624}{10{,}000{,}000{,}000} = 1.4142135624$$

Also, see Sections 9.8–9.9 and 10.2 for discussions on rational and irrational numbers.

18. See Sections 10.9 and 10.24–10.26 for examples of length ratios expressed as irrational decimal ratios.

19. See Section 10.1.

20. *Greek Musical Writings, Volume 2*, Chapter 11.

21. See Section 10.58.

22. *A Greek-English Lexicon*, p. 623.

23. (A) D'Ooge, M.L., Translator (1926). *Nicomachus of Gerasa: Introduction to Arithmetic*, p. 299. The Macmillan Company, New York.

(B) *A Greek-English Lexicon*, p. 1857.

24. (A) Barbera, A., Translator (1991). *The Euclidean Division of the Canon: Greek and Latin Sources*, p. 60. University of Nebraska Press, Lincoln, Nebraska.

The long version includes the text that spans pp. 170–185, which describes the tuning of a diatonic "double-octave." See Section 10.11 for a complete analysis and discussion of this tuning.

(B) *Greek Musical Writings, Volume 2*, pp. 205–207.

In Barker's translation, the long version includes Propositions 19 and 20.

25. See Chapter 10, Part II.

26. See Chapter 11, Part IV.

27. Levin, F.R., Translator (1994). *The Manual of Harmonics, of Nicomachus the Pythagorean*, p. 84. Phanes Press, Grand Rapids, Michigan.

28. *Ibid.*, p. 85.

See Figure 10.10, which shows the Greek note names *hypate*, *mese*, *paramese*, and *nete* in the context of a "double-octave" scale known as the Greater Perfect System.

29. *Ibid.*, p. 141.

30. (A) *The Manual of Harmonics*, p. 141.

(B) Jan, K. von, Editor (1895). *Musici Scriptores Graeci*, p. 254. Lipsiae, in aedibus B.G. Teubneri.

This work includes the Greek text of Nicomachus' *Manual of Harmonics.*

In contrast to a previous discussion in this section on Greek terms for ratios whose quotients are less than one, Nicomachus uses *hemiseias* from *hemisus*, lit. *half;* and *dimoirou* from *dimoiros*, lit. *two-thirds.*

(C) Zanoncelli, L., Translator (1990). *La Manualistica Musicale Greca*, p. 164, 166. Angelo Guerini e Associati, Milan, Italy.

This book gives the Greek text of Nicomachus' *Manual of Harmonics* as it appears in Jan's *Musici Scriptores Graeci*, and it includes a modern Italian translation.

31. (A) Diels, H. (1903). *Die Fragmente der Vorsokratiker, Griechisch und Deutsch, Volume 1*, p. 428. Weidmannsche Verlagsbuchhandlung, Berlin, Germany, 1951.

Diels identifies Archytas' description of three tetrachord divisions as authentic fragment A16. This page gives Archytas' fragment as it appears in Ptolemy's original Greek text.

(B) Burkert, W. (1962). *Lore and Science in Ancient Pythagoreanism*, pp. 379–380, Footnote 47. Translated by E.L. Minar, Jr. Harvard University Press, Cambridge, Massachusetts, 1972.

In Footnote 47, Burkert agrees with Diels that A16 is an authentic fragment. On p. 380, Burkert states, ". . . Archytas apparently assigned the smaller number to the high tone and the larger to the low."

(C) Düring, I., Translator (1934). *Ptolemaios und Porphyrios über die Musik*, pp. 46–47. Georg Olms Verlag, Hildesheim, Germany, 1987.

(D) *Greek Musical Writings, Volume 2*, pp. 43–44, and p. 304.

32. *Greek Musical Writings, Volume 2*, p. 42.

33. Hamilton, E., and Cairns, H., Editors (1963). *The Collected Dialogues of Plato*, p. 44. The *Phaedo* translated by H. Tredennick. Random House, Inc., New York, 1966.

34. *Greek Musical Writings, Volume 2*, pp. 59–60, Footnote 17.

Barker gives a complete analysis of these sequences.

35. (A) *The Collected Dialogues of Plato*, pp. 1165–1166.

(B) *Greek Musical Writings, Volume 2*, pp. 59–60.

36. See Section 10.11.

37. *The Manual of Harmonics*, p. 107.

38. Einarson, B., Translator (1967). *On Music*, by Plutarch, pp. 401–403. In *Plutarch's Moralia, Volume 14*. Harvard University Press, Cambridge, Massachusetts.

39. See Note 30.

4 / INHARMONIC STRINGS

In Chapter 3, we used Equation 3.13 to calculate the frequencies of string harmonics as exact integer multiples of the fundamental frequency. Further discussions focused on the mathematical structure of the harmonic series and the subsequent organization of musical ratios. Although integer ratios (see Section 3.13) are important to scales and tuning, a detailed examination of vibrating strings reveals that exact integer harmonics do not exist. When we multiply a given fundamental frequency by a sequence of integers, the result is a series of resonant frequencies that is only theoretically correct. On any given string, a true harmonic series could only occur if the string were perfectly flexible. Since all strings exhibit varying degrees of *stiffness*, the flexible string model no longer applies. Stiffness causes the modes to vibrate at frequencies considerably higher than suggested by Equation 3.13. For this reason, we call the sharp mode frequencies of stiff strings *inharmonic mode frequencies* ($\bar{F}_{\mathrm{n}}$), a term that refers to *non*-integer multiples of the fundamental frequency.

This chapter consists of three parts. In Part I, we will consider equations for stiffness in plain strings; in Part II, equations for calculating coefficients of inharmonicity in cents; and in Part III, equations for stiffness in wound strings.

Part I

DETAILED EQUATIONS FOR STIFFNESS IN PLAIN STRINGS

4.1

The language used to describe vibrating strings and other kinds of vibrating systems is of special interest to this discussion. Figure 3.10 shows the first six *modes of vibration* of a flexible string, and Figure 4.1 shows the first four modes of a stiff string. The term *mode* refers to the simplest physical patterns, shapes, or forms a vibrating system is capable of producing. The frequency associated with a given mode shape is called the resonant frequency, the natural frequency, or the mode frequency of the system. Within this context, the noun or adjective *mode* does *not* define a particular kind of pattern or frequency, so that a mode frequency may be either harmonic or inharmonic.

Regarding perfectly flexible strings, however, we consistently call the mode frequencies *harmonics*. This term (as in "second harmonic") has a strict definition: it includes only those frequencies that are integer multiples of the fundamental frequency. Mode frequencies of stiff strings are, therefore, not included. When describing stiff strings, we should not refer to the frequency of the "second harmonic" if we mean the "second inharmonic." Since the latter term sounds contrived, we will use the word *mode* (as in "frequency of the second mode," or "second mode frequency") to correctly identify a noninteger or inharmonic frequency.

4.2

To understand why the inharmonic mode frequencies of stiff strings sound higher than the harmonic mode frequencies of flexible strings, recall that for ideal strings,

$$F_n = \frac{c_T}{\lambda_n} \tag{4.1}$$

where F_n is the mode frequency, in cps; c_T is the transverse wave speed, in inches per second; and λ_n is the mode wavelength, in inches. Note that the numerator of this equation requires only one transverse wave speed, which indicates that in flexible strings c_T is constant. This is decidedly *not* the case for stiff strings. The influence of stiffness significantly alters both the mode wave speeds and the mode wavelengths of vibrating strings. Therefore, to calculate the inharmonic mode frequencies of stiff strings we must now rewrite Equation 4.1 to state

$$\bar{F}_n = \frac{c_{n\ eff}}{\lambda_{n\ eff}} \tag{4.2}$$

where $c_{n\ eff}$ is the effective mode wave speed; and $\lambda_{n\ eff}$ is the effective mode wavelength.

In comparison to flexible strings, the mode wave speeds in stiff strings are not constant. Instead, stiffness causes the effective wave speeds to *increase* with each higher mode of vibration. Consequently, no two modes have the same wave speed. Furthermore, in stiff strings the effective vibrating length (L_{eff}) is *shorter* than the measured length of the string. Since for flexible strings, $\lambda_n = 2L/n$, we find that for stiff strings,

$$\lambda_{n\ eff} = \frac{2L_{eff}}{n} \tag{4.3}$$

Solutions to Equation 4.2 require detailed analyses of the physical properties of strings. A simpler method consists of a purely mathematical approach. This equation states

$$\bar{F}_n = nF\sqrt{1 + 2J(n^2 - 1)} \tag{4.4}$$

where $\bar{F}_n$ is the inharmonic mode frequency *relative* to the fundamental frequency (F); J is the dimensionless stiffness parameter of the string (see Sections 4.3–4.4); and n is the mode number, any positive integer. Equations 4.2 and 4.4 give virtually identical results. In this chapter, we will examine the former equation because it focuses on the mechanical aspects of vibrating strings, and the latter because it offers convenient solutions.

4.3

Mathematicians use a dimensionless stiffness parameter to calculate the influence of stiffness on the mode wave speeds, the mode wavelengths, and the mode frequencies of vibrating strings. It is, therefore, highly appropriate to start the mechanical analysis of stiff strings with two different equations for J. The first equation, by Robert W. Young, includes a tension variable;[1] and the second, by Harvey Fletcher, includes a frequency variable.[2] Young's equation states

$$J = \frac{\pi^2 ESK^2}{2TL^2} \tag{4.5}$$

where E is Young's modulus of elasticity, in pounds-force per square inch, or psi; S is the cross-sectional area of the string, in square inches; K is the radius of gyration, in inches; T is the tension of the string, in pounds-force; and L is the measured length of the string, in inches. Before proceeding, simplify this equation. The variables S and K^2 represent two subequations that include the radius (r) of the string:

$$S = \pi r^2$$

$$K^2 = \left(\frac{r}{2}\right)^2$$

Converting the quantities r^2 and $(r/2)^2$ to diameter (D) dimensions will make the equation easier to use. Since $r = D/2$,

$$S = \pi r^2 = \pi \frac{D^2}{4}$$

$$K^2 = \left(\frac{r}{2}\right)^2 = \frac{r^2}{4} = \frac{\frac{D^2}{4}}{4} = \frac{D^2}{16}$$

Now substitute, collect and simplify:

$$J = \frac{\pi^2 E \pi D^2 D^2}{(2)(4)(16)TL^2}$$

$$\boxed{J = \frac{\pi^3 ED^4}{128TL^2}} \tag{4.6}$$

Fletcher's equation states

$$J = \frac{\pi^2 ESK^2}{8F^2L^4(M/u.l.)} \tag{4.7}$$

where F is the fundamental frequency of the string, in cps; and $M/u.l.$ is the mass per unit length of the string,[3] in mica per inch. (For a definition of the mica mass unit, see Section 1.10.) Again, simplify this equation for practical use. Since $S = \pi r^2$ and $M/u.l. = \pi r^2 \rho$, begin by canceling πr^2 out of the numerator and denominator. This removes S from the equation and leaves only the mass density (ρ) in the denominator. Since we will calculate material-based stringing constants in Section 4.4, move ρ into the numerator as a divisor of E. Finally, as described above, replace K^2 with $D^2/16$. We now have

$$J = \frac{\pi^2 (E/\rho) D^2}{(8)(16)F^2L^4}$$

$$\boxed{J = \frac{\pi^2 (E/\rho) D^2}{128F^2L^4}} \tag{4.8}$$

∾ 4.4 ∾

Before we turn to string calculations, simplify the equations by Young and Fletcher one last time. Since piano strings are made from high-carbon spring steel music wire, E = 30,000,000 psi, and ρ = 0.00073299 mica/in^3. If we combine these material properties with the appropriate numeric constants found in Equations 4.6 and 4.8, it is possible to calculate two different material-based stringing constants.

Steel Constant for Eq. 4.6: $$\frac{(3.1416)^3(30{,}000{,}000)}{128} \approx 7.267 \times 10^6$$

Steel Constant for Eq. 4.8: $$\frac{(3.1416)^2(30{,}000{,}000/0.00073299)}{128} \approx 3.156 \times 10^9$$

To compute a typical value for J, consider the following G_4 sample string dimensions taken from a quality console piano:

$D = 0.038$ in.
$r = 0.019$ in.
$L = 19.25$ in.
$F = 392.00$ cps, G_4 above middle C
$T = 189.343$ lbf, or 189.343 micas·in/s^2 (See Equation 1.21.)

Now, substitute the steel stringing constants and the appropriate string variables into Equations 4.6 and 4.8, and calculate the dimensionless stiffness parameter:[4] for Equation 4.6,

$$J = \frac{7.267 \times 10^6 (0.038)^4}{(189.343)(19.25)^2} = 0.0002160$$

and for Equation 4.8,

$$J = \frac{3.156 \times 10^9 (0.038)^2}{(392.00)^2 (19.25)^4} = 0.0002160$$

For brass, bronze, gut, or nylon string calculations, be sure to change the values of E and ρ.

4.5

We must now examine the influence of stiffness on the length of a vibrating string. In Chapter 3, we observed that a string with perfect flexibility vibrates freely and completely across its entire length. For flexible strings, the measured length equals the actual vibrating length. However, this does not apply to stiff strings. Stiffness inhibits motion. Consequently, for stiff strings the *acoustic or effective* length is slightly shorter than the *geometric or measured* length. With respect to modes of vibration, the effective lengths are of paramount importance because they alone determine the string's effective mode wavelengths.

Figure 4.1 illustrates the dynamic displacement of a stiff string. Notice that the outer loops and, specifically, the outer two nodes at the ends of the string do not resemble the shape of a flexible string. When a string is perfectly flexible it assumes a *rounded* sine wave shape; here all nodes act as dimensionless points where the string pivots up and down as it subdivides into smaller loops.[5] However, when a string is stiff the outer loops assume a *tapered* hyperbolic shape; here the outer two nodes function as motionless end sections of measurable length. Since the string is stiff and rigidly secured at the ends, it cannot immediately lift and drop at the exact locations of the clamping points. Instead, the string vibrates with a length diminished by two motionless sections that constitute its outer two nodes. Consequently, the acoustic or effective vibrating length of a stiff string is shorter than its geometric or measured length.[6] Note, however, that the difference between these two lengths occurs *only* at the outer two nodes. As the string continues to subdivide into three sections, four sections, etc., the inner loops resume the shape of true sine waves, and produce the *same* dimensionless pivot points found in flexible strings.

David R. Canright gives this equation for calculating the effective lengths of stiff strings:[7]

$$L_{\text{eff}} = L\left(1 - \frac{2}{\pi}\sqrt{2J}\right) \tag{4.9}$$

The sample piano string in Section 4.4 has the following effective vibrating length:

$$L_{\text{eff}} = (19.25 \text{ in})\left[1 - \frac{2}{3.1416}\sqrt{2(0.0002160)}\right] = 18.9953 \text{ in}$$

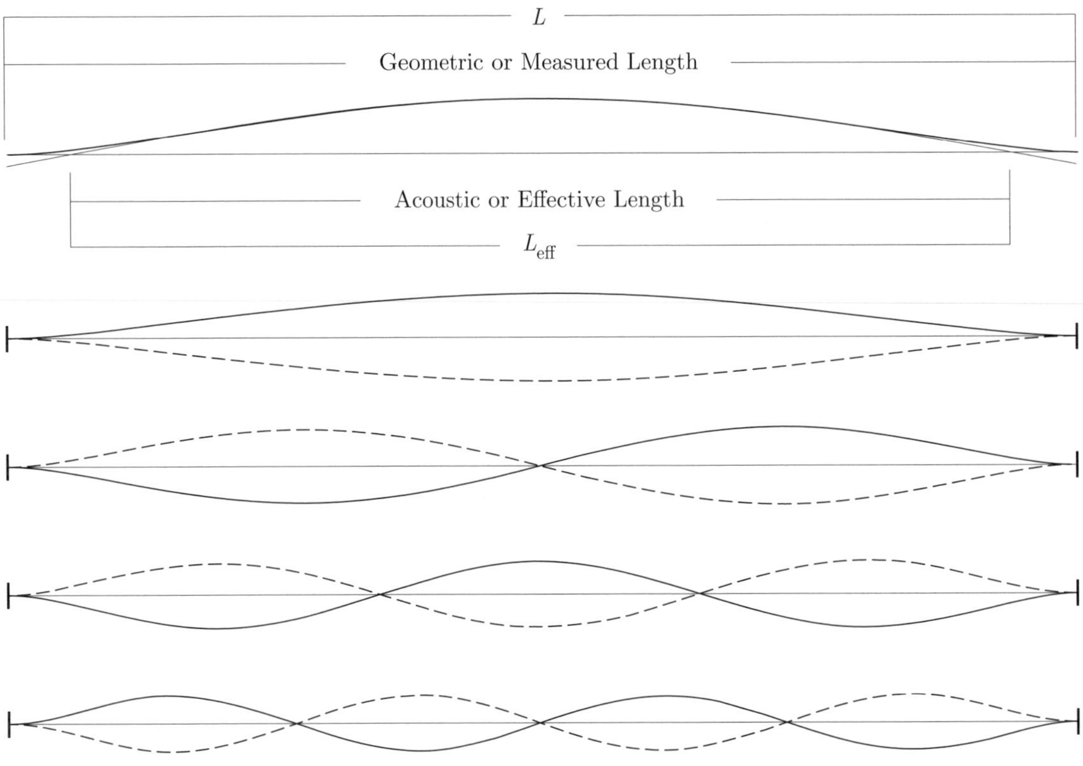

Figure 4.1 The dynamic displacement of a stiff string clamped at both ends. The first two plots illustrate the shape of a stiff string vibrating in the fundamental mode, followed by examples of the second, third, and fourth modes. As the string continues to subdivide into shorter loops, the motionless end sections that constitute the outer two nodes remain basically unchanged. To show the influence of stiffness within the spatial confines of this page, the equations used to generate these plots required an exceptionally high value for the dimensionless stiffness parameter; here $J = 0.20$. Although such a string could never be used on a musical instrument, in this case the benefits of illustration override the need for exact representation.

Therefore, according to Equation 4.3, the effective wavelengths of the first four modes are

$$\lambda_{1\text{ eff}} = \frac{2(18.9953\text{ in})}{1} = 37.9906\text{ in}$$

$$\lambda_{2\text{ eff}} = \frac{2(18.9953\text{ in})}{2} = 18.9953\text{ in}$$

$$\lambda_{3\text{ eff}} = \frac{2(18.9953\text{ in})}{3} = 12.6635\text{ in}$$

$$\lambda_{4\text{ eff}} = \frac{2(18.9953\text{ in})}{4} = 9.4977\text{ in}$$

∼ 4.6 ∼

We begin this discussion on the speed of transverse waves by referring once more to the flexible string model. Here it is important to distinguish between two similar equations:

$$c_{\mathrm{T}} \equiv \sqrt{\frac{T}{M/u.l.}} \tag{4.10}$$

$$c_{\mathrm{T}} = F_{\mathrm{n}}\lambda_{\mathrm{n}} \tag{4.11}$$

Equation 4.10 states that the speed of transverse waves in perfectly flexible strings is "defined as," or is "by definition equal to," the square root of the tension divided by the mass per unit length. Therefore, the transverse wave speed depends exclusively on two physical properties of the string: tension and mass per unit length. Under ideal conditions, c_{T} is a constant because once stringing materials and string diameters have been selected, and the strings are tuned, $M/u.l.$ and T are not subject to change.

Assume that the sample piano string in Section 4.4 is perfectly flexible and calculate the transverse wave speed for the fundamental mode of vibration. Begin by finding the mass per unit length; multiply π by the radius squared r^2, and by the mass per unit volume ρ for steel, in mica per cubic inch,[8] as follows:

$$M/u.l. = 3.1416(0.019 \text{ in})^2(0.00073299 \text{ mica/in}^3) = 0.0000008313 \text{ mica/in}$$

Now substitute mass per unit length and tension into Equation 4.10 and determine the transverse wave speed:

$$c_{\mathrm{T}} = \sqrt{\frac{189.343 \text{ mica·in/s}^2}{0.0000008313 \text{ mica/in}}} = 15{,}092.0 \text{ in/s}$$

Since we are describing a perfectly flexible string, its length is not a determining factor. Whether the string is one mile or one inch long, the transverse wave speed remains constant.

Equation 4.11 states that the speed of transverse waves in perfectly flexible strings simply equals the fundamental frequency times the fundamental wavelength, or the mode frequency times the mode wavelength. The variables on the right side of Equation 4.11 represent the following sub-equations:

$$F_{\mathrm{n}} = nF \tag{4.12}$$

$$\lambda_{\mathrm{n}} = \frac{2L}{n} \tag{4.13}$$

Since we may substitute an infinite number of values for variables F, L, and n, Equation 4.11 does not express a "definition," or an "identity." This equation simply suggests many possible solutions. Physically shortening a string will change the fundamental wavelength and the fundamental frequency; and a string subdividing into shorter loops will change mode wavelengths and mode frequencies. However, in either case, c_{T} remains unchanged because the transverse wave speed in flexible strings does *not* depend on the properties of the wave: frequency and wavelength.

To illustrate this point, substitute Equations 4.12 and 4.13 into Equation 4.11,

$$c_{\mathrm{T}} = (nF)\left(\frac{2L}{n}\right) \tag{4.14}$$

and then substitute the sample piano string dimensions listed in Section 4.4 into Equation 4.14. The fundamental frequency $F_1 = 392.0$ cps, and the measured string length $L = 19.25$ in. For the first mode, the string vibrates across its entire length in the shape of a single loop. If this were a perfectly flexible string, the wavelength of the fundamental mode $\lambda_1 = 2(19.25 \text{ in}) \div 1 = 38.5$ in. Therefore, the transverse wave speed for the fundamental mode $c_1 = 1(392.0 \text{ cps}) \times 38.5 \text{ in.} = 15{,}092.0$ in/s. For the second mode, the string subdivides into two loops, and the wavelength $\lambda_2 = 2(19.25 \text{ in.}) \div 2 = 19.25$ in. Consequently, the transverse wave speed for the second mode $c_2 = 2(392.0 \text{ cps}) \times 19.25 \text{ in.} = 15{,}092.0$ in/s, again the same speed. The wave speed does not or cannot change because the mode number n, which functions both as multiplier and as divisor in Equation 4.14, cancels out. We conclude, therefore, that c_T in perfectly flexible strings is constant for all wavelengths, whether the string subdivides internally into shorter wavelengths, or is physically shortened by external means. In the latter case, stopping the string in the center produces $F_2 = 784.0$ cps, and $\lambda_2 = 19.25$ in. Again, the transverse wave speed does not change because it depends exclusively on tension and mass per unit length.

4.7

If we compare ideal strings to real strings, we find that the speed of transverse waves in stiff strings is *not* constant. According to Equation 4.10, for a perfectly flexible string, tension is the only restoring force that returns a curved vibrating string to its straight equilibrium position. However, when a string is not perfectly flexible, a second restoring force due to stiffness functions together with tension in returning the string to a motionless state. Unlike tension, however, stiffness is a dynamic force that increases continuously, even *after* a string is tuned.

Examine the influence of stiffness by noting the force required to bend a loose string (or steel ruler). The stiffness of a string increases significantly with (1) stringing materials (compare bending a steel string to a nylon string); (2) string diameter (compare bending a thick string to a thin string); (3) string length (compare bending a short string to a long string); and (4) the mode shape. To experience the last condition, bend a string into two sections, then three sections, four sections, etc., and note that the restoring force due to stiffness increases significantly with each additional section.

Applying these observations to the discussion in Section 4.2, we also find that the speed of transverse waves increases with stiffness. Hold the string (or ruler) in your hand, bend it, and then quickly let go. Note the speed of the string as it returns to a state of equilibrium. (1) A steel string, (2) a thick string, or (3) a short string returns with greater speed than a nylon string, a thin string, or a long string, respectively. (4) With regard to the mode shape, bend the string into two sections, and let go; then bend it into three sections, and let go; etc. Note the speed as it returns to a state of equilibrium. As you bend the string into progressively shorter sections and then release it, the speed of the string increases significantly with each additional section.

4.8

Of these four physical states, conditions (3) and (4) are especially important. As stiff strings get physically shorter and the fundamental wavelengths decrease, and as strings subdivide into a greater number of sections or loops and the mode wavelengths decrease, the transverse wave speeds increase. In both cases, we find that the speed of transverse waves is inversely proportional to wavelength:

$$c_T \propto \frac{1}{\lambda_n}$$

As λ_n decreases, c_T increases. This variation of wave speed with wavelength is a phenomenon known as *dispersion*. Hence the classical definition: Any medium in which the speed of a wave depends on wavelength (or frequency) is said to possess the property of dispersion.

Looking back to Section 4.2 and ahead to Section 4.10, we find Equations 4.2 and 4.15 consistent with these observations. The latter equation states that the effective mode wave speeds of a stiff string are directly proportional to the square root of the dimensionless stiffness parameter and to the square of the mode number. The following series of relations indicate how these variables produce the sharp inharmonic mode frequencies associated with all stiff strings:

$$\bar{F}_{\text{n}} \propto c_{\text{n eff}} \propto \sqrt{J} \qquad \text{(Eqs. 4.2, 4.15)}$$

$$\bar{F}_{\text{n}} \propto c_{\text{n eff}} \propto n^2 \qquad \text{(Eqs. 4.2, 4.15)}$$

Refer back to Equations 4.6 and 4.8, and note that J is inversely proportional to L^2 or L^4:

$$J \propto \frac{1}{L^2} \qquad \text{(Eq. 4.6)}$$

$$J \propto \frac{1}{L^4} \qquad \text{(Eq. 4.8)}$$

As strings get physically shorter and L decreases (or as λ_1 decreases), J increases and, therefore, $c_{\text{n eff}}$ increases directly with $\sqrt{J}$. Here the *static* and *controllable* length determines the dispersive or inharmonic quality of the string. However, increases in $c_{\text{n eff}}$ also occur as strings subdivide into an increasingly greater number of shorter loops. In this context, the mode number represents the loop count of a given mode. For the fundamental or first mode of vibration, the string produces one loop; and for the second, third, and fourth modes, it produces two, three, and four loops, respectively. Consequently, as the curvature of the string increases (or as λ_{n} decreases), the effective mode wave speed increases directly with n^2. Here the *dynamic* and *uncontrollable* increases in mode number determine the dispersive or inharmonic quality of the higher modes of vibration.

~ 4.9 ~

To understand stiffness from a mechanical point of view, return once more to the flexible string model; first solve Equation 4.11 for F_{n} and then substitute Equation 4.10 for c_{T}. Note that in flexible strings, the square root of tension, wave speed, and frequency are all directly proportional to each other:

$$F_{\text{n}} = \frac{c_{\text{T}}}{\lambda_{\text{n}}} = \frac{\sqrt{\dfrac{T}{M/u.l.}}}{\lambda_{\text{n}}}$$

Increases in the restoring force produce increases in wave speed, which in turn produce increases in the harmonic mode frequencies. With respect to stiff strings, tension and stiffness function together as a composite restoring force. However, unlike tension, stiffness does not depend exclusively on the manipulation of a tuning pin. It increases automatically and uncontrollably, either as strings get physically shorter, or as they subdivide into an increasingly greater number of shorter loops. Consequently, under the dynamic influence of stiffness, the composite restoring force of a string is *not* constant, but increases with each succeeding mode of vibration, so that every mode generates an increasingly faster effective wave speed. The resulting rise (1) in the inharmonic mode frequencies and, therefore, (2) in the uncontrollable beat rates of the higher modes, severely restricts the tuning possibilities of pianos. (See Section 5.21.)

~ 4.10 ~

Since we have calculated the effective mode wavelengths of the first four modes, we must also compute a matching set of effective mode wave speeds. However, before we proceed with these calculations, recall that for the effective vibrating length, Equation 4.9 requires the measured length, which equals the length of the string if it were perfectly flexible. In other words, by applying the square root of the dimensionless stiffness parameter to the long measured length, it is possible to determine the short effective length. Calculating the wave speeds of stiff strings requires a similar approach. Consider the following equation used to find the effective mode wave speeds:

$$c_{\text{n eff}} = c_{\text{ref}}\sqrt{1 + 2Jn^2} \tag{4.15}$$

Here the reference speed (c_{ref}) represents the transverse wave speed if the shorter effective vibrating length of the string were perfectly flexible. Once again, to determine the property of a stiff string, we apply the square root of the dimensionless stiffness parameter to the property of a flexible string. Within this context, note that c_{ref} is a constant. Any string considered perfectly flexible has only one transverse wave speed. (See Section 4.6.)

To calculate the effective wave speeds, solve Equation 4.15 for the reference speed:

$$c_{\text{ref}} = \frac{c_{\text{n eff}}}{\sqrt{1 + 2Jn^2}} \tag{4.16}$$

Refer to Equation 4.2 and note that the effective wave speed of the tuned fundamental mode *also* has the following solution: if

$$F_1 = \frac{c_{\text{1 eff}}}{\lambda_{\text{1 eff}}}$$

then

$$c_{\text{1 eff}} = F_1 \lambda_{\text{1 eff}} \tag{4.17}$$

Now determine the effective wave speed of the fundamental. Substitute the known values for frequency and effective wavelength into Equation 4.17:

$$c_{\text{1 eff}} = (392.0 \text{ cps})(37.9906 \text{ in}) = 14{,}892.3 \text{ in/s}$$

Since these calculations concern the first mode of vibration, return to Equation 4.16 and substitute the number one for the mode number n. This equation now reads

$$c_{\text{ref}} = \frac{c_{\text{1 eff}}}{\sqrt{1 + 2J(1)^2}} \tag{4.18}$$

Finally, substitute the values for $c_{\text{1 eff}}$ and J into Equation 4.18 to obtain the reference speed:

$$c_{\text{ref}} = \frac{14{,}892.3 \text{ in/s}}{1.0002160} = 14{,}889.1 \text{ in/s}$$

Therefore, according to Equation 4.15, the effective mode wave speeds of the first four modes of the sample piano string are

$$c_{1\text{ eff}} = 14{,}889.1 \text{ in/s}\sqrt{1 + 2(0.0002160)(1)^2} = 14{,}892.3 \text{ in/s}$$

$$c_{2\text{ eff}} = 14{,}889.1 \text{ in/s}\sqrt{1 + 2(0.0002160)(2)^2} = 14{,}902.0 \text{ in/s}$$

$$c_{3\text{ eff}} = 14{,}889.1 \text{ in/s}\sqrt{1 + 2(0.0002160)(3)^2} = 14{,}918.0 \text{ in/s}$$

$$c_{4\text{ eff}} = 14{,}889.1 \text{ in/s}\sqrt{1 + 2(0.0002160)(4)^2} = 14{,}940.5 \text{ in/s}$$

4.11

Now substitute $c_{1-4\text{ eff}}$ and $\lambda_{1-4\text{ eff}}$ into Equation 4.2 and calculate the inharmonic mode frequencies ($\overline{F}_{1-4}$) of the sample string:

$$\overline{F}_1 = \frac{14{,}892.3 \text{ in/s}}{37.9906 \text{ in}} = 392.00 \text{ cps}$$

$$\overline{F}_2 = \frac{14{,}902.0 \text{ in/s}}{18.9953 \text{ in}} = 784.51 \text{ cps}$$

$$\overline{F}_3 = \frac{14{,}918.0 \text{ in/s}}{12.6635 \text{ in}} = 1178.03 \text{ cps}$$

$$\overline{F}_4 = \frac{14{,}940.5 \text{ in/s}}{9.4977 \text{ in}} = 1573.07 \text{ cps}$$

Next, use Equation 4.4 to obtain the inharmonic mode frequencies of the same piano string:

$$\overline{F}_1 = 1(392.00 \text{ cps})\sqrt{1 + 2(0.0002160)(1^2 - 1)} = 392.00 \text{ cps}$$

$$\overline{F}_2 = 2(392.00 \text{ cps})\sqrt{1 + 2(0.0002160)(2^2 - 1)} = 784.51 \text{ cps}$$

$$\overline{F}_3 = 3(392.00 \text{ cps})\sqrt{1 + 2(0.0002160)(3^2 - 1)} = 1178.03 \text{ cps}$$

$$\overline{F}_4 = 4(392.00 \text{ cps})\sqrt{1 + 2(0.0002160)(4^2 - 1)} = 1573.07 \text{ cps}$$

A comparison of these results to the previous set of frequencies, when carried out to *three* decimal places, reveals only insignificant discrepancies.

4.12

One of the interesting and practical facts to emerge from the mechanical analysis concerns the tension requirements of stiff strings. Since there are *two* restoring forces acting in the string, it would seem that stiff strings require less tension than flexible strings. To calculate the actual amount of tension on the sample piano string, remember that the reference speed is the speed of transverse waves if the string were perfectly flexible, or is the transverse wave speed in the absence of stiffness. Therefore, the amount of tension required by c_{ref} determines the actual tension of the string.

To calculate the actual tension of the sample string, substitute the reference speed and the mass per unit length into Equation 4.10 and solve for *T:*

$$c_{\text{ref}} = \sqrt{\frac{T}{M/u.l.}}$$

$$14{,}889.1 \text{ in/s} = \sqrt{\frac{\text{lbf}}{0.0000008313 \text{ mica/in}}}$$

$$(14{,}889.1)^2 \text{ in}^2/\text{s}^2 = \frac{\text{lbf}}{0.0000008313 \text{ mica/in}}$$

$$\left[(14{,}889.1)^2 \text{ in}^2/\text{s}^2\right](0.0000008313 \text{ mica/in}) = \text{lbf}$$

$$= 184.29 \text{ lbf, or } 184.29 \text{ micas·in/s}^2$$

Compared to the flexible string tension of 189.34 lbf in Section 4.4, the stiff string has 5.05 lbf less tension. My own tests show that the sample string requires 185.20 lbf, a small cumulative discrepancy caused by weighing fourteen individual dumbbell weights.

Part II

EQUATIONS FOR COEFFICIENTS OF INHARMONICITY IN CENTS

~ 4.13 ~

The musical significance of inharmonic frequencies is the subject of Sections 5.21–5.22. As discussed in these two sections, the frequencies of the inharmonic modes affect our perceptions of consonance and dissonance. That is, stiff piano strings produce uncontrollable beat rates that may significantly alter the musical quality of single intervals or entire tunings.

However, in the construction of musical instruments, detailed inharmonic frequency calculations are impractical because they require lengthy beat rate computations. Instead, string designers rely on inharmonic cent calculations to measure the overall inharmonicity of stiff strings. Measurements in cents provide an efficient and exact means by which to compare a wide variety of string dimensions. After many calculations, and after long sessions listening to the mode frequencies of stiff strings, instrument builders organize their findings into cent tables. These tables are then used to establish acceptable and unacceptable levels of inharmonicity.

For such evaluations, we must convert the quantity $1 + J$ into cents. Note that the expression inside the radical of Equation 4.4, and inside the radicals of equations at the end of Section 4.11, functions as a frequency ratio. Therefore, the ratio of the second inharmonic mode frequency (of the actual stiff string) to the second harmonic mode frequency (of the theoretical flexible string) is

$$\frac{\overline{F}_2}{F_2} = \frac{784.51 \text{ cps}}{784.00 \text{ cps}} = \sqrt{1 + 2(0.0002160)(2^2 - 1)} : 1 \approx 1.0006478 : 1$$

Although this frequency ratio accurately describes the second inharmonic mode, it does not represent the string in its fundamental mode of vibration. For a tuned string, there is no distinction between the fundamental frequency of a stiff string ($\overline{F}_1$) and the fundamental frequency of a flexible string (F_1). A frequency ratio for the fundamental mode of vibration simply does not exist.

However, suppose for a moment that the sample piano string is a perfectly flexible string tuned to 392.00 cps. If we were to suddenly impose the condition of stiffness on such a string, the fundamental frequency would increase from F_1 to $F_1 \times \sqrt{1 + 2J(1)^2} = \bar{F}_1$. Due to the influence of stiffness, the ratio between these two frequencies would be

$$\frac{\bar{F}_1}{F_1} = \frac{392.08 \text{ cps}}{392.00 \text{ cps}} = \sqrt{1 + 2(0.0002160)(1)^2} : 1 \approx 1.0002160 : 1$$

Now, notice that the expression $1 + J$ very closely approximates the ratio on the right-hand side of the latter equation. When converted into cents, this quantity provides a useful measurement of the inharmonicity of stiff strings.

~ 4.14 ~

In 12-tone equal temperament, the "semitone" is theoretically divided into one hundred cents (¢); therefore, 1 "semitone" = 100 ¢. Hence, 12 "semitones," or 1 "octave" = 1200 ¢. With logarithms, it is possible to convert any frequency ratio (x) into cents. To make such a conversion,[9] we must substitute a given frequency ratio into Equation 9.18:

$$\log_{1.00057779} x = ¢ \qquad \text{(Eq. 9.18)}$$

With respect to the sample piano string, we would now like to determine how many inharmonic cents ($\bar{¢}$) there are in frequency ratio 1.0002160:

$$\log_{1.00057779} 1.0002160 = \bar{¢}$$

Use the LOG calculator key for the following calculation:

$$\bar{¢} = \frac{\log_{10} 1.0002160}{\log_{10} 1.00057779} = \frac{0.0000938}{0.0002509} = 0.374\ ¢$$

However, it is also possible to convert from base 10 logarithms to base e logarithms, or natural logarithms. Use the LN calculator key, and observe that the result is the same:

$$\bar{¢} = \frac{\log_e 1.0002160}{\log_e 1.00057779} = \frac{0.000215977}{0.000577623} = 0.374\ ¢$$

Note that when one plus J is much less than two, $1 + J \ll 2$, the logarithm of the number to the base e is approximately equal to J:

$$\log_e(1 + J) \approx J$$

For this reason, $\log_e 1.000216 \approx 0.000216$, and $\log_e 1.000578 \approx 0.000578$. Therefore, a cent conversion to the base e does not require us to find $\log_e(1 + J)$. Since in all cent calculations 0.000577623 functions as a constant, we may obtain a very close approximation[10] of $\bar{¢}$ by directly multiplying J by the inverse of 0.000577623, rounded here to zero decimal places:

$$\bar{¢} \approx \frac{0.0002160}{0.000577623} = \left(\frac{1}{0.000577623}\right)(0.0002160)$$

$$= 1731(0.0002160) = 0.374\ ¢$$

To obtain $\overline{¢}$ without this extra step, return to Equations 4.6 and 4.8 and include 1731 as a multiplier in the numerators of both equations:

$$\overline{¢} = \frac{1731\pi^3 ED^4}{128TL^2} \tag{4.19}$$

$$\overline{¢} = \frac{1731\pi^2 (E/\rho) D^2}{128F^2L^4} \tag{4.20}$$

Now, to calculate two logarithmic constants for steel, multiply 1731 by the two steel constants in Section 4.4.

Log Constant for Steel, for Eq. 4.19:

$$1731(7.267 \times 10^6) = 1.258 \times 10^{10}$$

Log Constant for Steel, for Eq. 4.20:

$$1731(3.156 \times 10^9) = 5.463 \times 10^{12}$$

Finally, calculate $\overline{¢}$ for the sample piano string: for Equation 4.19,

$$\overline{¢} = \frac{1.258 \times 10^{10}(0.038)^4}{(189.34)(19.25)^2} = 0.374\ ¢$$

and for Equation 4.20,

$$\overline{¢} = \frac{5.463 \times 10^{12}(0.038)^2}{(392.00)^2(19.25)^4} = 0.374\ ¢$$

The cent value $\overline{¢}$ is called the *coefficient of inharmonicity* of the string. A coefficient is a number (a *constant*) used to multiply another number (a *variable*). So, once calculated for a particular string, $\overline{¢}$ does not change. Regarding a string's higher modes of vibration, the following equation gives the mode cents (C_n) *relative* to the first or fundamental mode of vibration:

$$C_n = \overline{¢}(n^2 - 1) \tag{4.21}$$

Therefore, the mode cents of the first four modes of the sample string are

For G_4: $C_1 = 0.374(1^2 - 1) = 0.000\ ¢$

For G_5: $C_2 = 0.374(2^2 - 1) = 1.122\ ¢$

For D_6: $C_3 = 0.374(3^2 - 1) = 2.992\ ¢$

For G_6: $C_4 = 0.374(4^2 - 1) = 5.610\ ¢$

4.15

The coefficients of inharmonicity enable us to compare proportional changes in inharmonicity, from one string to the next, over the entire range of a musical instrument. Inharmonic cent calculations also provide important historical information on the development of instrument construction and tuning practice. Large instruments with relatively thick strings like harpsichords, pianos, and harps are particularly susceptible to the effects of inharmonicity. If the designer or builder does not attempt to control and minimize the values of $\overline{¢}$, a very poor overall timbre will result, and a fine tuning will be impossible to achieve.

We may analyze the rate of inharmonicity without disturbing the strings of an instrument. Anyone contemplating restringing or retuning a fine instrument should undertake such an analysis before removing the old strings. Identifying the rate of inharmonicity and staying close within the range is very important. On the other hand, it is also possible to accomplish significant improvements on poorly strung instruments, especially if the builder neglected to include inharmonicity calculations in the original design. Undesirable tone quality is, therefore, not necessarily a reflection of inferior construction. However, remember that there are physical limits in restringing an instrument with the intent to reduce inharmonicity. Although J and $\overline{¢}$ will always decrease as T increases, the total tension of the new strings should *never* exceed the total tension of the old strings. Otherwise, the instrument could fly apart and cause serious bodily injury. Finally, music wire *break strength* calculations must be considered as well. (See Section 2.8.) The finest and most subtle stringing is not going to work if the strings are too loose or too tight.

Table 4.1

DIMENSIONLESS STIFFNESS PARAMETERS
and
COEFFICIENTS OF INHARMONICITY

Average Piano String Values

	F cps	L in.	D in.	T lbf	J	$\overline{¢}$
G_3	196.00	31.125	0.041	144.06	0.0001471	0.255
C_4	261.63	26.500	0.039	168.36	0.0001422	0.246
G_4	392.00	19.250	0.038	189.34	0.0002160	0.374
C_5	523.25	14.875	0.037	190.98	0.0003223	0.558
G_5	784.00	9.875	0.036	178.88	0.0006997	1.211
C_6	1046.50	7.500	0.036	183.85	0.0011803	2.043
G_6	1568.00	5.250	0.034	180.39	0.0019532	3.381
C_7	2093.00	4.000	0.034	186.58	0.0032531	5.631
G_7	3136.00	2.750	0.032	175.37	0.0057455	9.946
C_8	4186.00	2.125	0.031	175.10	0.0084879	14.693
(1)	(2)	(3)	(4)	(5)	(6)	(7)

Table 4.1 gives average steel piano string values for J and $\overline{¢}$, calculated with Equations 4.8 and 4.20, respectively. Harpsichord strings in general have approximately 1/10 the inharmonicity of piano strings.[11] (See Section 5.7.) Therefore, to estimate average harpsichord string values for J and $\overline{¢}$, simply move the decimal points of the numbers in Columns 6 and 7 one place to the left.

4.16

In Table 4.1, Column 2 lists the 12-tone equal tempered frequencies of four "octaves" between G_3 and G_7, and four "octaves" between C_4 and C_8. (See Appendix A.) The table shows all "octaves" as multiples of the frequency ratio 2:1. However, when compared to actual tuned "octaves," these frequencies are only theoretically correct. Due to the effects of inharmonicity, one frequently finds *stretched* "octaves" tuned more than 30 ¢ sharp in the treble, and more than 30 ¢ flat in the bass.[12] In practice, one tunes "octaves" by matching the upper fundamentals to the second mode frequencies of the lower fundamentals. So, a piano tuner tunes C_5 to the second mode of C_4, C_6 to the second mode of C_5, etc. (See Section 5.18.) Due to the influence of stiffness, the frequencies of the second modes are *not* exact multiples of two. Therefore, tuning "octaves" to the second inharmonic modes of stiff strings results in a series of frequencies that departs at a significant rate from the ideal 2:1 standard.

For the rest of this section, we will concentrate on the span between C_4 and C_8. A piano tuner normally tunes C_4 by listening to a tuning fork. In this case, the second inharmonic mode of another string is not a determining factor. However, after the process of tuning C_5, C_6, C_7, and C_8 to the second inharmonic modes of C_4, C_5, C_6, and C_7, respectively, these "octaves" will vibrate at frequencies considerably higher (sharper) than indicated by the $\frac{2}{1}$ ratio. Consequently, the values for J above C_4 in Table 4.1 no longer apply. Recall that in Equation 4.8, F is inversely proportional to J: as F increases, J decreases. For this reason, the following sequence of calculations includes values for J that are slightly less than those in Table 4.1. To help keep the present discussion focused on the subject of tuning, recalculations for J as determined by the inharmonic frequencies of the sharp "octaves" are here left to the reader.

To measure the cumulative effects of inharmonicity on the tuning of piano "octaves," refer to Equation 4.4 and calculate the second inharmonic mode frequency of C_4, which also represents the fundamental frequency of C_5. Next, substitute the inharmonic frequency of C_5 and the new value for J into the same equation and calculate C_6. Repeat these substitutions and calculations for C_7 and C_8:

$$\overline{F}_2 \text{ for } C_4 = 2(261.63 \text{ cps})\sqrt{1 + 2(0.0001422)(2^2 - 1)} = 523.48 \text{ cps} = C_5$$

$$\overline{F}_2 \text{ for } C_5 = 2(523.48 \text{ cps})\sqrt{1 + 2(0.0003220)(2^2 - 1)} = 1047.97 \text{ cps} = C_6$$

$$\overline{F}_2 \text{ for } C_6 = 2(1047.97 \text{ cps})\sqrt{1 + 2(0.0011770)(2^2 - 1)} = 2103.33 \text{ cps} = C_7$$

$$\overline{F}_2 \text{ for } C_7 = 2(2103.33 \text{ cps})\sqrt{1 + 2(0.0032212)(2^2 - 1)} = 4247.12 \text{ cps} = C_8$$

We may now organize the theoretical "octave" frequencies and the actual "octave" frequencies into frequency ratios, and convert the results into cents. Such an analysis will illustrate how far sharp a typical piano tuning has shifted due to the influence of stiff strings:

$$\text{For } C_5\text{:} \quad \frac{523.48 \text{ cps}}{523.25 \text{ cps}} = 1.0004396 = 0.76\ ¢$$

$$\text{For } C_6\text{:} \quad \frac{1047.97 \text{ cps}}{1046.50 \text{ cps}} = 1.0014047 = 2.43\ ¢$$

$$\text{For } C_7\text{:} \quad \frac{2103.33 \text{ cps}}{2093.00 \text{ cps}} = 1.0049355 = 8.52\ ¢$$

$$\text{For } C_8\text{:} \quad \frac{4247.12 \text{ cps}}{4186.00 \text{ cps}} = 1.0146011 = 25.10\ ¢$$

4.17

The reason piano tuners tune the bass flat is that the direction of the tuning process changes. The bass "octaves" are tuned downward from the center of the keyboard. For example, notice what happens when we tune C_4 to C_5 by adjusting the second mode of C_4 to the fundamental frequency of C_5. First, tune C_5 with a tuning fork to the exact 12-tone equal tempered frequency 523.25 cps. Then lower the second inharmonic mode of C_4 from 523.48 cps to 523.25 cps. Consequently, the fundamental frequency of C_4 drops and the tuning goes flat.

The higher mode frequencies of bass strings are particularly important because the fundamental frequencies of wound strings are very difficult and often impossible to hear. For example, the tuner tunes G_2 by matching the sixth mode of G_2 to the third mode of G_3. The common mode frequency (or the coincident harmonic) is D_5. Because the sixth inharmonic mode of G_2 has a higher frequency than the third inharmonic mode of G_3, the tuner lowers the sixth mode to match the third mode. Consequently, the fundamental frequency of G_2 goes flat.

Part III

GENERAL EQUATIONS FOR STIFFNESS IN WOUND STRINGS

4.18

In his paper, Fletcher also gives a detailed account for calculating the inharmonicity of wound bass strings.[13] Fletcher states there is "fair agreement" between his observed and calculated values. There are three principal reasons why wound strings defy exact inharmonic analysis. First, the precise mass of a wound string is difficult to predict. During the winding process, the wrap wire is under tension and begins to stretch, which causes slight irregularities in the finished diameter of the string. Second, the actual amount of wrap wire distributed around the core depends on the string winding machine and operator control. A string maker may wind the coils with varying degrees of compression, from very tight on some strings, to less compact on others. Third, soon after the winding operation, the coiled wire crystallizes (hardens) into place. This stiffening process occurs at an unpredictable rate. For these reasons, the most accurate way to measure the inharmonic mode frequencies of wound strings is to test each string with an electronic tuning device.

However, we may obtain fairly accurate results by solving Equation 4.7 for wound strings. This requires a special set of calculations with respect to the mass per unit length variable in the denominator. Note that wound piano strings (and many violin, guitar, and harp strings as well) consist of two different kinds of materials. Moreover, unlike the smooth surface of the inner steel core wire, the coiled (or ribbed) surface of the outer copper winding is not smooth. Between adjacent coils of the winding, there are small areas devoid of any wrap wire material. (See Section 2.10.) Equation 4.22 represents an algebraically streamlined version of Equation 4.7, and it contains a *M/u.l.* variable for two different materials and accounts for the mass density of the coiled surface of the winding.[14] Although not immediately obvious, the variables S and K^2 are also a part of this equation. Therefore, the following equation gives the dimensionless stiffness parameter of a wound string:

$$J = \frac{\pi^2 E_{\text{in}}\, D_{\text{i}}^{\,4}}{32F^2L^4\left[(\pi\rho_{\text{out}}\, D_{\text{o}}^{\,2}) + (4\rho_{\text{in}}\, D_{\text{i}}^{2}) - (\pi\rho_{\text{out}}\, D_{\text{i}}^{2})\right]} \tag{4.22}$$

where E_{in} is Young's modulus of the *inside core wire material*, in psi; ρ_{in} is the density of the *inside core wire material*, in mica per cubic inch; ρ_{out} is the density of the *outside wrap wire material*, in mica per cubic inch; D_i is the inside or the core wire diameter, in inches; D_o is the outside diameter of the whole string, in inches; and L is the length of the *wrapped* section of the string, in inches. If the string has two layers of wrap, then L is the shorter double-wound length.

Before we proceed, simplify this equation. Since the inside core wire material for wound piano strings is high-carbon spring steel music wire, $E_{in} = 30{,}000{,}000$ psi. Combine this material constant with the numeric constants found in Equation 4.22 and calculate the material-based stringing constant.

$$\text{Steel Constant for Eq. 4.22:} \quad \frac{(3.1416)^2(30{,}000{,}000)}{32} \approx 9.253 \times 10^6$$

To compute a typical value for J, consider the following G_2 string dimensions taken from the same quality console piano:

$D_i = 0.040$ in.
$D_o = 0.082$ in.
$F = 98.00$ cps
$L = 36.375$ in.

Next, substitute the steel stringing constant, the density of the steel core wire, the *unmodified* density of the copper wrap wire ($\rho_{in} = 0.00073299$ mica/in^3 and $\rho_{out} = 0.00083660$ mica/in^3, respectively), and the string variables into Equation 4.22, and calculate the dimensionless stiffness parameter:

$$J = \frac{9.253 \times 10^6(0.040)^4}{(98.00)^2(36.375)^4(0.00001767 + 0.00000469 - 0.00000421)} = 0.00007762$$

Substitute this J into Equation 4.4 and calculate the inharmonic mode frequencies for the first six modes of the G_2 string:

$$\begin{aligned} \overline{F}_1 &= 98.0 \text{ cps} \\ \overline{F}_2 &= 196.0 \text{ cps} \\ \overline{F}_3 &= 294.2 \text{ cps} \\ \overline{F}_4 &= 392.5 \text{ cps} \\ \overline{F}_5 &= 490.9 \text{ cps} \\ \overline{F}_6 &= 589.6 \text{ cps} \end{aligned}$$

Refer to Table 4.1, calculate the third inharmonic mode of the G_3 string, and note that this mode vibrates at 588.7 cps. Therefore, the sixth mode of the G_2 string vibrates approximately 1.0 cps faster than the third mode of G_3. Since the bass "octaves" are tuned downward from the center of the keyboard, we can only tune these two inharmonic modes to the same frequency (or coincident harmonic) by lowering the fundamental frequency of the G_2 string. Consequently, the tuning of the bass string goes flat.

4.19

Now, by including 1731 as a multiplier in the numerator of Equation 4.22, the following equation gives the coefficient of inharmonicity of a wound string:

$$\bar{\text{¢}} = \frac{1731\pi^2 E_{\text{in}}\, D_{\text{i}}^{\,4}}{32F^2L^4\left[(\pi\rho_{\text{out}}\, D_{\text{o}}^{\,2}) + (4\rho_{\text{in}}\, D_{\text{i}}^{\,2}) - (\pi\rho_{\text{out}}\, D_{\text{i}}^{\,2})\right]} \qquad (4.23)$$

To compute a logarithmic constant for steel (see Section 4.14), multiply 1731 by the steel constant in Section 4.18.

Log Constant for Steel, for Eq. 4.23:

$$1731(9.253 \times 10^6) = 1.602 \times 10^{10}$$

Finally, the most efficient way to calculate $\bar{\text{¢}}$ for the wound sample piano string would be as follows:

$$\bar{\text{¢}} = \frac{1.602 \times 10^{10}(0.040)^4}{(98.00)^2(36.375)^4(0.00001767 + 0.00000469 - 0.00000421)} = 0.134\ \text{¢}$$

Now compare 0.134 ¢ of the G_2 wound string to 0.255 ¢ of the G_3 plain string, and to 0.374 ¢ of the G_4 plain string. Since $\bar{\text{¢}}$ is inversely proportional to L^4, notice that the rate of inharmonicity has significantly increased due to shorter strings. From a design perspective, changes in string length have a much greater effect on inharmonicity than changes in diameter. Therefore, musical instruments with long strings (large harpsichords, large harps, and grand pianos) have the best tone quality and are much easier to tune. In the treble section, as strings get progressively shorter, instrument builders control inharmonicity by using thin strings. Under all circumstances, ideal strings are always both long and thin because these two properties provide maximum flexibility.

Notes

1. Young, R.W. (1952). Inharmonicity of plain wire piano strings. *Journal of the Acoustical Society of America* **24**, No. 3, pp. 267–272.

   Equation 4.5 is a slightly altered version of Young's Equation 7 on p. 268.

2. Fletcher, H. (1964). Normal vibration frequencies of a stiff piano string. *Journal of the Acoustical Society of America* **36**, No. 1, pp. 203–209.

   Equation 4.7 is a slightly altered version of Fletcher's Equation 27 on p. 205.

   Regarding inharmonic mode frequency calculations *relative* to the fundamental frequency, one must replace n^2 in Young's Equation 6, and in Fletcher's Equation 24, with $(n^2 - 1)$. Under these conditions, Young's equation, Fletcher's equation, and Equation 4.4 produce identical results. On p. 269, Young discusses relative inharmonicity in the context of mode cent calculations. (See Equation 4.21.)

3. See Sections 1.12 and 2.3–2.4.

4. The following analysis shows why the stiffness parameter is a dimensionless or unitless quantity. In this text, Young's modulus of elasticity, in pounds-force per square inch (or psi), is defined as mica/(in·s²). (See Section 1.13.) Therefore, in Equation 4.6 the numerator has the units

$$\frac{\text{mica}}{\cancel{\text{in}} \times \text{s}^2} \times \frac{\text{in}^{\cancel{4}\,3}}{1} = \frac{\text{mica} \times \text{in}^3}{\text{s}^2}$$

Also, in this text, tension, in pounds-force (or lbf), is defined as mica·in/s^2. (See Sections 1.11–1.12.) Therefore, in Equation 4.6 the denominator has the units

$$\frac{\text{mica} \times \text{in}}{\text{s}^2} \times \frac{\text{in}^2}{1} = \frac{\text{mica} \times \text{in}^3}{\text{s}^2}$$

Since the numerator and denominator are identical, they cancel out of the equation.

Regarding Equation 4.8, first divide E by the mass density ρ, in mica/in^3; or simply multiply E by the inverse, in^3/mica:

$$\frac{\cancel{\text{mica}}}{\cancel{\text{in}} \times \text{s}^2} \times \frac{\text{in}^{\cancel{3}2}}{\cancel{\text{mica}}} = \frac{\text{in}^2}{\text{s}^2}$$

Therefore, the numerator in this equation has the units

$$\frac{\text{in}^2}{\text{s}^2} \times \frac{\text{in}^2}{1} = \frac{\text{in}^4}{\text{s}^2}$$

Next, the denominator of this equation has the units

$$\frac{1}{\text{s}^2} \times \frac{\text{in}^4}{1} = \frac{\text{in}^4}{\text{s}^2}$$

Again, since the numerator and denominator are identical, they cancel out of the equation.

5. To better understand the pivoting motion of subdividing strings, turn to Figure 3.7(b). Here a series of double-headed arrows indicates the vertical vibrations of adjacent loops of a transverse standing wave. The string produces such vibrations as it pivots in opposite directions at the locations of nodes. To demonstrate this movement, hold a pencil between your thumb and forefinger and wiggle it up and down; the changing position of the pencil represents the vibration of the string, and the motionless point between the two fingers, the node.

6. Although a highly complex mathematical analysis shows that the effective length of the string increases asymptotically by a very small amount with each succeeding mode of vibration, we will assume for the practical purposes of this discussion that L_{eff} remains constant. As the string subdivides into a greater number of loops, the internal restoring force due to stiffness increases. Consequently, this force begins to push with greater intensity against the ends of the string, an action that slightly decreases the motionless end sections and, therefore, increases L_{eff}. However, since no amount of internal restoring force will ever enable the string to vibrate across its entire length, portions at the ends of the string will always remain unyielding and without motion.

7. Unpublished correspondence, 1992.

8. See Equation 1.20.

9. See Section 9.9.

10. *JASA* **24**, 1952, p. 268.

"The fractional error in δ (or $\bar{\cancel{c}}$) resulting from the approximations is less than one percent if δ is less than 35 cents."

11. Goodway, M., and Odell, J.S. (1987). *The Historical Harpsichord, Volume Two: The Metallurgy of 17th– and 18th–Century Music Wire*, p. 97. Pendragon Press, Stuyvesant, New York.

The authors list several coefficients of inharmonicity for iron harpsichord strings. Based on the ancient $A_4 = 415.00$ cps standard, C_4, C_5, and C_6 were tuned to 246.76 cps, 493.52 cps, and 987.04 cps, respectively. The corresponding values for $\overline{¢}$ are: 0.014 ¢, 0.044 ¢, and 0.149 ¢, respectively.

12. Schuck, O.H., and Young, R.W. (1943). Observations on the vibrations of piano strings. *Journal of the Acoustical Society of America* **15**, No. 1, pp. 1–11.

13. *JASA* **36**, 1964, pp. 208–209.

14. As discussed in Section 2.13, due to the coiled surface of the winding, the modified mass density of copper is 0.7854×0.00083660 mica/in^3 = 0.00065707 mica/in^3. However, since Equation 4.22 accounts for the latter density, do *not* use the modified value in this equation.

5 / PIANO STRINGS VS. CANON STRINGS

The problems associated with inharmonic piano strings are far more severe than stretched "octaves" tuned 30 ¢ sharp in the treble and 30 ¢ flat in the bass. (See Sections 4.16–4.17.) Stiff strings constitute a primary source of harmonic and melodic dissonance. For this reason, no piano builder has ever intentionally increased the inharmonicity of an instrument by installing thick strings. On the contrary, all builders design their instruments with the thinnest strings possible. Even so, conventional piano strings do not encourage musical exploration and, therefore, do not advance the development of acoustic music. Most piano tuning experiments end in failure. Unless the builder understands the nature of inharmonically induced dissonance, and attempts to restring a piano with thin strings, the authentic rendition of a scale — based on the intervals of the harmonic series — remains in doubt. All scales and tunings benefit from flexible strings. Such strings are ideal because they produce truer harmonics and, thereby, minimize the obliterating effects of excessive inharmonicity.

If inharmonicity is not just an obscure technical subject, then the *musical* question arises: "Why are the dimensionless stiffness parameters (J), or the coefficients of inharmonicity ($\bar{¢}$), of typical piano strings so high?" (See Table 4.1.) In a word, the answer is "Power!" Since the early 18th century when Bartolomeo Cristofori (1655–1730) built his first *gravicembalo col piano e forte*, or *harpsichord with soft and loud*, the primary goal of all builders consisted of a single-minded determination to make the grand piano as loud as humanly possible. At the beginning of the 20th century, this process came to an inevitable end. To understand why instrument builders could not make the piano any "grander," we must discuss three fundamental concepts of the physics of stringed instruments: (1) the transfer of energy from strings to soundboard and into the surrounding air; (2) the mechanical wave impedances of strings and soundboards, and the radiation impedance of air; and (3) the phenomenon of dispersion in soundboards. We will explore these subjects in Parts I–IV, and in Part V, examine how piano tuners tune intervals to the beat rates of coincident string harmonics. Finally, in Part VI a mathematical analysis will demonstrate the musical advantages of thin strings and thin soundboards. In short, while thick strings and thick soundboards produce very loud sounds, these heavy mechanical components severely restrict the intonational possibilities of all modern pianos.

Part I

TRANSMISSION AND REFLECTION OF MECHANICAL AND ACOUSTIC ENERGY

5.1

Sound production in a piano may be traced by way of an energy chain that begins when a finger delivers a force of sufficient magnitude to depress a key. The *mechanical energy* resulting from this force is then transferred through the key to the action levers, to the hammer, to the string(s), and finally to the soundboard. Here mechanical energy is transformed and radiated as *acoustic energy* (sound waves) into the surrounding air. From finger to soundboard, every link in this chain is associated with a force, and the amount of energy in the system (how loud or soft the piano sounds at any given time) is directly proportional to the magnitude of these forces.

However, to produce loud sounds, generating large forces is not enough. The amplification of sound is also dependent on an efficient displacement of large amounts of air. A vibrating string or tuning fork radiates only small amounts of sound because the surface area of either object displaces very little air. When the same string or tuning fork contacts a soundboard or table top, and *transfers* its vibrational energy to a larger surface, the radiation of sound increases dramatically. Suddenly, upon contacting a large structure, a faint sound becomes clearly audible from a distance. For pianos, both the initial intensity (how loud or soft the strings will sound) and the ensuing duration (how long or short the strings will continue to vibrate) depend not only on the forces of the energy chain, but also on the critical rate at which vibrational energy is transferred from the strings to the soundboard. Consequently, if the string-to-soundboard proportion is incorrect, no amount of pounding (forcing) will contribute to the desired dynamic range.

5.2

Consider for a moment two extremely different situations that illustrate how a wave either *transmits* most of its energy (with intensity and no duration), or *reflects* most of its energy (with duration and no intensity) at the boundary between the string and the soundboard. In the first example, a string is coupled over a bridge to a very thin wood plate designed to move as though it were a physical extension of the string. A wave traveling on the string would barely notice the boundary, and would transmit most of its energy (without significant reflection) at the bridge. As a result, the plate would respond to this rapid transfer of vibrational energy with a loud (but brief) pitchless

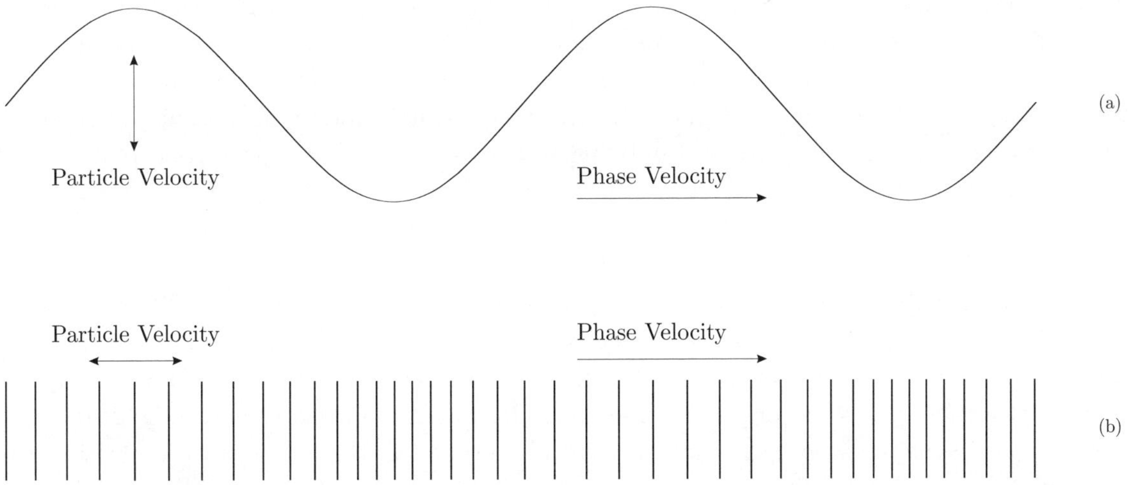

Figure 5.1 Particle and phase velocities in solids and fluids. (a) In solids, the particle velocity (u) is *perpendicular* to the phase velocity (v). In this chapter, the phase velocity refers to the speed of transverse waves in strings (c_T), or the speed of transverse bending waves in soundboards (c_B). (b) In fluids, the particle velocity is *parallel* to the phase velocity. Here the phase velocity refers to the speed of longitudinal sound waves in air (c_L). See Sections 5.14–5.15 for detailed descriptions on the speed (c) of waves. In either case, the particle velocity is associated with the *amplitude*, while the phase velocity is associated with the *frequency* of a wave.

thud. In the second example, a string is coupled over a bridge to a thick steel plate designed not to move with the string. A similar traveling wave would be unable to cross the boundary, and would reflect most of its energy (without significant transmission) at the bridge. Due to a very slow transfer of vibrational energy, there is only a faint (but long-lasting) sound coming directly from the string. We may observe a similar situation by holding a vibrating tuning fork against a concrete wall: very little, if any, amplification takes place, but the fork vibrates for a long time.

Now imagine changing the boundary, and the consequent transfer of energy, by coupling the same string to plates of medium height. In the first case, increasing the height of the thin wood plate also increases the reflection of wave energy at the bridge, which results in a greater duration (but less intensity) of the radiated sound; in the second case, decreasing the height of the thick steel plate increases the transmission of wave energy at the bridge, which results in a greater intensity (but less duration) of the radiated sound. Finally, making the wood plate thick enough, and the steel plate thin enough, reverses the order of the above-mentioned extremes. Therefore, regarding strings and plates, we may conclude the following: (1) rapidly transferred energy is due to a high rate of transmission, which results in great intensity of sound; (2) slowly transferred energy is due to a high rate of reflection, which results in great duration of sound; (3) transmission and reflection are inversely proportional: as one increases, the other decreases.

Part II

MECHANICAL IMPEDANCE AND SOUNDBOARD-TO-STRING IMPEDANCE RATIOS

5.3

All these comparisons suggest that the structural displacement of a vibrating object, also known as the particle velocity,[1] depends on the elastic and inertial properties of the medium, or its stiffness and mass. For example, consider two identical steel strings tuned to the same pitch and coupled to two identically proportioned plates, one made out of wood and the other out of steel. If we pluck both strings equally, thereby ensuring the same driving force, a greater structural displacement or particle velocity results in the wood plate. In other words, it sounds louder. This difference may be confirmed by touching the plates and noticing that when compared to the wood plate, the steel plate barely moves. (To make simple amplitude comparisons, hold a tuning fork against different kinds of solid objects. Generally, a relatively louder sound indicates a greater particle velocity.) We may perform a similar experiment with two identical piano hammers exerting a consistent driving force on two identically proportioned strings made of contrasting materials: the lighter string with less tension would have a greater particle velocity than the heavier string with greater tension.

In general, all wave-carrying media (solids, liquids, and gases) present a complex wave impedance ($\boldsymbol{Z}$ or $\boldsymbol{z}$) to a given driving force, or driving pressure. This quantity measures how difficult it is to produce vibrations in the medium. For solids, like strings and plates, the complex ratio of driving force ($\boldsymbol{f}$) to particle velocity ($\boldsymbol{u}$) defines the complex mechanical (wave) impedance ($\boldsymbol{Z}_{\mathrm{M}}$) of an object:

$$\boldsymbol{Z}_{\mathrm{M}} = \frac{\boldsymbol{f}}{\boldsymbol{u}} \tag{5.1}$$

Now solve Equation 5.1 for $\boldsymbol{u}$:

$$\boldsymbol{u} = \frac{\boldsymbol{f}}{\boldsymbol{Z}_{\mathrm{M}}}$$

The latter equation explains the discussion in the previous paragraph. For a constant driving force, as the mechanical wave impedance increases (switching from wood to steel), the particle velocity decreases. Conversely, as $\boldsymbol{Z}_{\mathrm{M}}$ decreases, $\boldsymbol{u}$ increases.

Figure 5.1(a) illustrates the relationship between transverse particle velocity and transverse phase velocity in solids. Figure 5.1(b) illustrates the relationship between longitudinal particle velocity and longitudinal phase velocity in fluids (either liquids or gases). For more detailed descriptions and illustrations of these two different yet simultaneous forms of motion, see Section 7.1.

~ 5.4 ~

Equation 5.1 is not very practical. Measuring driving forces and particle velocities to determine the complex mechanical impedances of strings and plates is a highly complicated and difficult process. Instead, we may also calculate the complex wave impedance of a driven system by considering the system's resistance and reactance variables. However, in this context, we must carefully distinguish between piano strings and piano soundboards, because the hammer-to-string relation constitutes a free vibration, and the string-to-soundboard relation constitutes a forced vibration. The free vibrations of a piano string are not dependent on a continuous, forced contact with the hammer. On the contrary, the percussive impulse of a piano hammer lasts only from 1 to 4 milliseconds. Consequently, when the hammer (the driving system) leaves the string (the driven system) to vibrate freely upon release, almost all of the energy passes unilaterally from the hammer to the string. Therefore, the string's mechanical impedance is a pure resistance, because there is no reactance, or return of energy from the string back to the hammer. Whenever two systems constitute a free vibration, the wave impedance of the driven system is not a complex wave impedance, because $\boldsymbol{Z}$ or $\boldsymbol{z}$ must include a resistance and a reactance variable. So, for the practical purposes of this discussion, the non-complex mechanical (wave) impedance of a piano string (Z_{s}) equals the string's resistance (R_{s}),

$$Z_{\mathrm{s}} = R_{\mathrm{s}}$$

$$Z_{\mathrm{s}} = \sqrt{T(M/u.l.)} \tag{5.2}$$

where T is the tension (the elastic property) of the string, in pounds-force (lbf); and $M/u.l.$ is mass per unit length (the inertial property) of the string, in mica per inch. (For a definition of the mica mass unit, see Section 1.10.)

The plain steel strings of pianos (and harpsichords) are organized by wire gages into groups that range from 2, 3, 4, . . . up to 10, 11, 12, or more notes per group. On upright pianos near the center of the keyboard (which is also in line with the central area of the soundboard), a 0.040 in. diameter wire commonly spans a group of notes that includes D_4. Other average dimensions for this kind of string are as follows:

$D = 0.040$ in.
$r = 0.020$ in.
$L = 25.00$ in.
$F = 293.67$ cps
$T = 199.0$ lbf, or 199.0 micas·in/s^2 (See Equation 1.21.)

To determine the wave impedance of such a string, first calculate the mass per unit length; multiply π by the radius squared (r^2), and by the mass density (ρ) of steel, in mica per cubic inch,[2] as follows:

$$M/u.l. = 3.1416(0.020 \text{ in})^2(0.00073299 \text{ mica/in}^3) = 0.00000092 \text{ mica/in}$$

Next, substitute the tension and the mass per unit length into Equation 5.2 and compute the wave impedance:

$$Z_s = \sqrt{(199.0 \text{ mica·in/s}^2)(0.00000092 \text{ mica/in})} = 0.0135 \text{ mica/s}$$

5.5

Soundboards, on the other hand, vibrate because they are in continuous, forced contact with the strings. Through this point of contact (the string-soundboard coupling or downbearing at the bridges), transverse standing waves in the vibrating strings exert an oscillating driving force that puts the soundboard into motion. From here, a uniquely different set of bending waves travels through the soundboard. At the outer boundaries of the board, these waves are then reflected and sent back again to the bridges. This reflection of bending waves, determined by the size and shape of the soundboard, results in the formation of transverse standing waves. For the most part, the frequencies of the *driving* string waves (F) and the resonant frequencies of the *driven* soundboard waves (F_n) are not the same: $F \neq F_n$. Consequently, the string waves and the soundboard waves are usually out of phase. That is, the motions of the two vibrating systems are not synchronized. The physical motion of the soundboard, in reaction (or response) to the driving forces of the vibrating strings, continually changes the wave impedance of the board. Depending on the angular position of the soundboard waves with respect to the string waves, the wave impedance in the board's central region can fluctuate more than 500 per cent. Therefore, the mechanical load presented by the soundboard to the strings is *not* a pure resistance. We cannot determine the mechanical wave impedance of the soundboard by considering only the elastic and inertial properties of the board's resistance (R_b).

The vibrational reaction is called the reactance (jX) of the soundboard. To calculate the complex mechanical wave impedance of the soundboard ($\boldsymbol{Z}_b$), the reactance must be added to the resistance. In very general terms, such an equation would read

$$\boldsymbol{Z}_b = R_b + jX$$

To solve for the reactance, one must know the exact frequencies of the driven soundboard waves at any given moment in time. However, there is no equation to solve for these frequencies because the edges of the soundboard (the boundary conditions) defy mathematical analysis. At the boundaries, the soundboard moves and bends in an extremely complicated manner, which yields equally complicated results. Moreover, the 88 locations where the board is excited (the excitation positions) determine which of these unpredictable frequencies are active, an additional complexity that also does not have a mathematical solution.

Klaus Wogram investigated the wave impedance of piano soundboards with sophisticated electronic instruments.[3] His thorough treatment includes many graph printouts. These show the soundboard wave impedance and phase angles changing rapidly (up and down on the y-axes) with respect to the frequencies of an externally applied shaker or driver (from 20 cps to 10,000 cps on the x-axes). Most interesting are the *minimum* wave impedance values on the y-axes, when the jagged impedance curves suddenly plunge downward for a given frequency on the x-axes. These distinct valleys on the curve indicate moments when the frequencies of the driver and the resonant frequencies of the soundboard are the same: $F = F_n$. Therefore, in a state of *resonance*, jX vanishes and the two systems begin vibrating in phase. That is, for a discrete set of frequencies from the driver, the mechanical wave impedance of the soundboard equals the board's resistance:

$$Z_b = R_b$$

At resonance, the soundboard wave impedance stands at a minimum because there is no reflection of waves from the boundaries of the board. In this unidirectional state, the finite board behaves as though it were infinite. To approximate the minimum wave impedance of a soundboard under these limited conditions, we may use an equation cited by L. Cremer, *et al.* for calculating the mechanical wave impedance of thin, isotropic, infinite plates.[4] Wood, as such, is not an isotropic material. It does not have uniform mechanical properties in all directions. For example, Young's modulus of elasticity for spruce is about 20 times greater (more stiff) in a direction with the grain than across it. In response, harpsichord and piano builders have for centuries glued high, narrow ribs across the grain. This technique produces soundboards that are, for all practical purposes, uniformly stiff in both directions.

The wave impedance equation for a thin, isotropic, infinite plate states

$$Z_p = 8\sqrt{B'(M/u.a.)}$$

where B' is the bending stiffness (the elastic property) of the plate; and $M/u.a.$ is the mass per unit area (the inertial property) of the plate. These two quantities have the following values:

$$Z_p = 8\sqrt{\frac{Eh^3}{12(1-\mu^2)}\rho h} \qquad (5.3)$$

For the bending stiffness: E is Young's modulus of elasticity, in pounds-force per square inch, or psi, or mica/(in·s^2);[5] μ is Poisson's ratio, dimensionless; and h is the height of the plate, in inches. For the mass per unit area: ρ is the mass density of a given plate material, in mica/in^3; and h is again the height of the plate. Poisson's ratio for Sitka spruce[6] has a value in the vicinity of $\mu \approx 0.02$. Therefore, the wave impedance of a spruce plate with a standard piano soundboard height of 3⁄8 in. is

$$Z_p = 8\sqrt{\frac{(1{,}600{,}000 \text{ psi})(0.375 \text{ in})^3}{12\left[1-(0.02)^2\right]}(0.00003885 \text{ mica/in}^3)(0.375 \text{ in})} = 2.56 \text{ micas/s}$$

where $B' = 7034.0636$ micas·in^2/s^2, and $M/u.a. = 0.000014569$ mica/in^2.

Turn now to Wogram's data in Figure 5.2(a) and examine the graph for Measuring Point #8. This marks the location where the D_4 strings — tuned to 293.7 cps — cross the treble bridge of an upright piano. Because this area is closest to the flexible center of the soundboard and farthest removed from the difficult boundary conditions, some minimum impedance values resemble the result of the infinite plate, as expressed by Equation 5.3. For example, at approximately 294 cps on the x-axis, the jagged input impedance curve plunges downward and verifies that a soundboard resonant frequency is in sympathetic resonance with the driver. If we read across,[7] the y-axis indicates the impedance $Z_b = 562$ kg/s. We may easily convert this kilogram-second impedance result to the new mica-second impedance unit. Since 2.2 lbm = 1 kg, and 1 mica = 386.09 lbm,[8] use the following conversion factors to convert kilograms to micas:

$$\left(\frac{2.2 \,\cancel{\text{lbm}}}{1.0 \text{ kg}}\right)\left(\frac{1.0 \text{ mica}}{386.09 \,\cancel{\text{lbm}}}\right) = \frac{0.0057 \text{ mica}}{1.0 \text{ kg}}$$

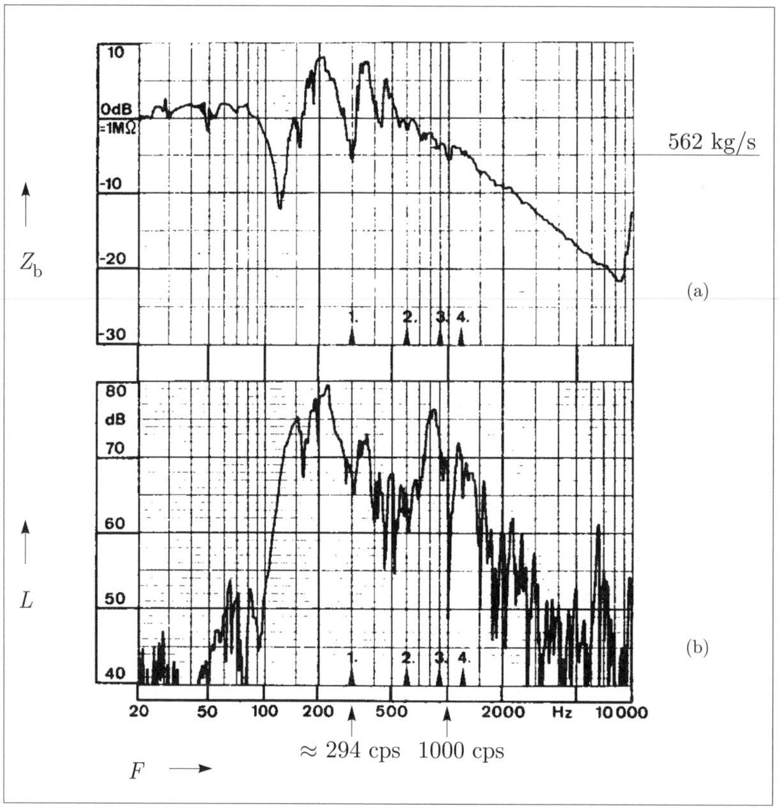

Figure 5.2 Piano soundboard data for Measuring Point #8 (Wogram, 1981). (a) This graph shows a mechanical wave impedance (Z_b) of 562 kg/s for a resonant frequency at approximately 294 cps. (b) As described in Section 5.15, due to the increased speed of bending waves (c_B), the soundboard generates a favored region of acoustic radiation (L) across the entire central frequency range. (Arrowheads along the x-axes indicate the first four mode frequencies of the D_4 strings tuned to 293.7 cps.)

Therefore, the wave impedance of the soundboard in micas/s is

$$Z_b = (562 \cancel{\text{kg}}/\text{s})\left(\frac{0.0057 \text{ mica}}{1.0 \cancel{\text{kg}}}\right) = 3.20 \text{ micas/s}$$

Within this limited context, a comparison of the wave impedance of an infinite spruce plate (2.56 micas/s) and the typical value of a finite soundboard (3.20 micas/s) indicates an increase of 25%. There are two reasons that account for this discrepancy. (1) The ideal plate equation does not include the presence of ribs, bridges, and liners. (The latter are wood strips located on the inside walls of a piano case that hold the outer edges of the soundboard.) These three components have the effect of increasing the stiffness and mass, and therefore also the wave impedance, of all soundboards when compared to flat plates of the same thickness. (2) The wave impedance of a finite soundboard also increases with a rise in the resonant frequencies of the board. Refer to Section 4.7 and notice that the force needed to bend a steel ruler into progressively shorter sections (shorter wavelengths) increases significantly with each additional section. Since shorter wavelengths produce higher frequencies, Equation 5.1 suggests that $\boldsymbol{Z}_{\text{M}}$ increases not only as a function of $\boldsymbol{f}$,

$$\boldsymbol{Z}_{\text{M}} = \frac{\boldsymbol{f}}{\boldsymbol{u}}$$

but as a function of frequency as well.

~ 5.6 ~

We may now combine the results of these calculations and observations to form a soundboard-to-string wave impedance ratio. Refer to Section 5.2 and note that the ratio below describes, in very general terms, the rate at which vibrational energy is transferred from the strings to the soundboard.

$$\text{Piano:} \quad \frac{Z_b}{Z_s} = \frac{3.20}{0.0135} \approx 240 : 1$$

Since at resonance the wave impedance in the central area of the soundboard is typically 240 times greater than the wave impedance of a steel string,[9] we conclude that pianos are built in favor of a *slow transfer* of energy. At the boundary between string and soundboard, the board reflects most of the wave energy, which results in greater duration but less intensity of sound. A multiple stringing design helps alleviate this problem. To increase the volume (or the amount of energy transferred to the soundboard), all the treble notes have three plain steel strings, and most of the bass notes, two or three wound strings. This doubles or triples the amount of force exerted on the soundboard, which causes the board to move with two or three times greater amplitude.

~ 5.7 ~

To understand the historical and musical significance of these calculations, we turn our attention momentarily to the harpsichord. By comparing the wave impedance ratios of harpsichords and pianos, we will understand more thoroughly the motivations of harpsichord and piano builders, and how generations of musicians influenced their work.

Frank Hubbard gives the string lengths and diameters of several northern European harpsichords.[10] An average D_4 (or d') harpsichord string has the following dimensions:

$D = 0.012$ in.
$r = 0.006$ in.
$L = 24.50$ in.
$F = 293.67$ cps (This frequency is based on the modern A-440.0 cps standard.)
$T = 17.00$ lbf, or 17.00 micas·in/s^2

To determine the wave impedance of such a sample string, first find the mass per unit length:

$$M/u.l. = 3.1416(0.006\text{ in})^2(0.00073299\text{ mica/in}^3) = 0.000000083\text{ mica/in}$$

Next, substitute the tension and the mass per unit length into Equation 5.2 and compute the wave impedance:

$$Z_s = \sqrt{(17.00\text{ mica·in/s}^2)(0.000000083\text{ mica/in})} = 0.0012\text{ mica/s}$$

Harpsichord soundboards are typically ⅛ in. thick; they have only one-third the height of piano soundboards. Since electronic data on the wave impedance of harpsichord soundboards are not available, substitute this new height into Equation 5.3 and compute the impedance of a thin, isotropic, infinite spruce plate,

$$Z_p = 8\sqrt{\frac{(1{,}600{,}000\text{ psi})(0.125\text{ in})^3}{12\left[1-(0.02)^2\right]}(0.00003885\text{ mica/in}^3)(0.125\text{ in})} = 0.285\text{ mica/s}$$

where $B' = 260.5209$ micas·in^2/s^2, and $M/u.a. = 0.000004856$ mica/in^2.

We must also account for ribs, bridges, and liners, and for the effects of higher resonant frequencies in finite soundboards. As explained at the end of Section 5.5, add 25% to the wave impedance of the harpsichord soundboard:

$$0.285 \times 0.25 = 0.071$$
$$0.285 \text{ mica/s} + 0.071 \text{ mica/s} = 0.356 \text{ mica/s}$$

Finally, the general soundboard-to-string wave impedance ratio is

$$\text{Harpsichord:} \qquad \frac{Z_{\text{b}}}{Z_{\text{s}}} = \frac{0.356}{0.0012} \approx 300 : 1$$

When we compare this ratio to the piano wave impedance ratio of 240:1 in Section 5.6, a remarkable similarity emerges. Both instruments are designed to produce a sustained singing tone, without sounding too weak in the compromise between duration and intensity of sound. However, a glaring difference does exist if we compare string diameters and inharmonicity. Refer to Section 4.14 and locate the Log Constant for Steel, for Equation 4.20. Substitute this constant and the dimensions of average D_4 piano and harpsichord strings into Equation 4.20 and calculate the coefficients of inharmonicity.

$$\text{Piano String:} \qquad \bar{¢} = \frac{5.463 \times 10^{12}(0.040)^2}{(293.67)^2(25.00)^4} = 0.259\ ¢$$

$$\text{Harpsichord String:} \qquad \bar{¢} = \frac{5.463 \times 10^{12}(0.012)^2}{(293.67)^2(24.50)^4} = 0.025\ ¢$$

Finally, determine the percent change between 0.025 ¢ and 0.259 ¢. Subtract the smaller number from the larger, divide the difference by the smaller number, and multiply the quotient by 100, as in $100[(0.259 - 0.025) \div 0.025] = 936$. We conclude, therefore, that the inharmonicity of the piano string represents an increase of 936% over the inharmonicity of a comparable harpsichord string.

Part III

RADIATION IMPEDANCE AND AIR-TO-SOUNDBOARD IMPEDANCE RATIOS

5.8

Arthur H. Benade reminds us:

> The history of keyboard instrument development from the earliest times reveals an intense though not always conscious interest in reducing inharmonicity.[11]

So, the question naturally comes to mind, "Why was this intense interest in reducing inharmonicity abandoned?"

A response to this question requires that we extend our analysis beyond the mechanical wave impedance of piano strings and soundboards to include the characteristic impedance of air. Like all wave-carrying media, the surrounding air, which connects the soundboard to our ears, has physical properties that are of paramount importance. Among these, the density of air and the speed of sound in the air are most relevant to this discussion. Both constants have remained unchanged for millions of years. Although natural and manmade musical instrument building materials will continue to change in time, the surrounding air represents a common inheritance, and its influence has determined the size and shape of every acoustic instrument the world over. After all, what value does a vibrating string, soundboard, flute, or membrane have if it cannot efficiently radiate its energy through the air? if no one can hear it?

5.9

The primary function of the soundboard is to transform mechanical (string wave) energy into acoustic (sound wave) energy. An understanding for this process of transformation requires that we examine the rate at which the soundboard radiates vibrational energy into the surrounding air. Since the flow of energy from one wave-carrying medium to another immediately suggests the presence of two characteristic impedances, let us now proceed with a definition for the wave impedance of air. Although such a calculation is not too difficult, the *acoustic coupling* between a solid plate and a compressible gas turns out to be far more complicated than the *mechanical coupling* between solid objects, like strings and soundboards. Therefore, it will be helpful to divide the following discussion into three segments. We begin by defining a constant called the characteristic impedance of air, and then proceed by considering a variable called the radiation impedance of air. Finally, we conclude with a very general description of the soundboard-to-air coupling. In Part IV, the discussion continues in greater detail when we examine why the efficiency of sound radiation varies with the speed of bending waves (or the bending wavelength) in soundboards.

The following analysis requires a new approach because the *mechanical* wave impedance of a solid is fundamentally different from the *acoustic* wave impedance of a fluid (either liquid or gas). Reminiscent of Section 5.3 we begin, therefore, by stating that all fluids present a complex wave impedance to a given driving pressure. This quantity measures how difficult it is to produce vibrations in a fluid. The complex ratio of driving pressure ($\boldsymbol{P}$) to particle velocity ($\boldsymbol{u}$) defines the complex specific acoustic (wave) impedance ($\boldsymbol{z}$) of a fluid:

$$\boldsymbol{z} = \frac{\boldsymbol{P}}{\boldsymbol{u}} \tag{5.4}$$

Notice that when compared to Equation 5.1, the concept of a mechanical driving force is no longer applicable. In the former case, we considered a string-to-soundboard coupling at the bridge, and how energy is *transferred through a point of contact* between these two solids. Here, however, we must consider a soundboard-to-air coupling at the surface of the board, and how energy is *radiated over an area of contact* between a solid and a gas. Therefore, it is now appropriate to describe the soundboard as exerting a mechanical driving pressure, or a *force per unit area*, on the surrounding air. Pressure, also known as psi, is here defined as lbf/in^2:

$$P\,(\text{psi}) \equiv \frac{\textit{force}\,(\text{lbf})}{\textit{area}\,(\text{in}^2)}$$

Just like Equation 5.1, Equation 5.4 is not very practical. Measuring pressures and particle velocities is a highly complicated task. However, when a fluid's specific acoustic impedance is a pure resistance (r), and there is *no* reactance (jx), we may calculate z by considering only the fluid's characteristic elastic and inertial properties,

$$z = \sqrt{\rho B_{\text{A}}} \tag{5.4A}$$

where ρ is the mass density (the inertial property) of the fluid, in mica/in^3; and B_A is the adiabatic bulk modulus (the elastic property) of the fluid, in psi. Since B_A is not a convenient quantity (see Section 1.13), most acoustics texts give Equation 5.4A as[12] $z = \rho c$. Before we proceed with this calculation for air, let us first cover some relevant background information.

5.10

Like the string-to-soundboard relation, the soundboard-to-air relation also constitutes a forced vibration: that is, the air vibrates because it is in continuous contact with the board. Over this area of contact, transverse standing waves in the soundboard exert an oscillating driving pressure that puts the air into motion. From here, a uniquely different set of longitudinal sound waves travels through the air. At the walls of the room, these waves are then reflected and sent back again to the soundboard. This reflection of sound waves, determined by the size and shape of the room,[13] results in the formation of longitudinal standing waves. For the most part, the frequencies of the driving soundboard waves, and the resonant frequencies of the driven room waves are not the same: $F \neq F_n$. Consequently, the soundboard waves and the room waves are usually out of phase. The physical motion of the air, in reaction (or response) to the driving pressure of the soundboard, continually changes the wave impedance of the air. (Detailed data is not available.) Therefore, the acoustic load presented by the air on the soundboard is *not* a pure resistance. We cannot determine the complex specific acoustic impedance of air ($\boldsymbol{z}_a$) by considering only the elastic and inertial properties of the air's resistance (r_a). Instead, to calculate the complex wave impedance of the air, a reactance must be added to the resistance. In very general terms, such an equation would read

$$\boldsymbol{z}_a = r_a + jx$$

To solve for the reactance, one must know the exact frequencies of the driven room waves at any given moment in time. However, if we place the piano in an anechoic chamber where the reflection of sound waves is at an absolute minimum (or if we consider a state of *resonance* when the frequencies of the driving soundboard waves and the resonant frequencies of the driven room waves are the same: $F = F_n$), then jx vanishes and the two systems begin vibrating in phase. Under these conditions, with respect to the driving pressure of the soundboard, the non-complex specific acoustic impedance of air equals the air's resistance:

$$z_a = r_a$$

Therefore, the *characteristic impedance* of air (z_a),[14] for progressive plane waves in air, or for standing waves in air where the reactance is zero, has the following value:

$$z_a = \rho c \tag{5.5}$$

where c is the speed of sound, in inches per second. We will use Equation 5.5 with both metric and English units. For air at 68°F (20°C) and 1 atmosphere of pressure (sea level), $\rho = 1.21$ kg/m^3. Refer to Section 1.13 for the derivation of the following conversion factor, and convert the mass density of air from kg/m^3 to mica/in^3:

$$\rho = (1.21\ \cancel{\text{kg/m}^3})\left(\frac{0.00000009357\ \text{mica/in}^3}{1.0\ \cancel{\text{kg/m}^3}}\right) = 0.000000113\ \text{mica/in}^3$$

Next, convert the speed of sound from meters/s to inches/s:

$$c = (343\ \cancel{\text{m}}/\text{s})\left(\frac{39.37\ \text{in}}{1.0\ \cancel{\text{m}}}\right) = 13{,}504\ \text{in/s}$$

Now substitute these values for ρ and c into Equation 5.5 and calculate the characteristic impedance of air:

$$z_a = (0.000000113 \text{ mica/in}^3)(13{,}504 \text{ in/s}) = 0.00153 \text{ mica/(in}^2\text{·s)}$$

Or in metric units,

$$z_a = (1.21 \text{ kg/m}^3)(343 \text{ m/s}) = 415 \text{ kg/(m}^2\text{·s)}$$

≈ 5.11 ≈

We return now to the coupling between the soundboard and the surrounding air. Note that the units of mechanical wave impedance and specific acoustic wave impedance are not compatible. Consequently, any comparison would be meaningless. We may resolve this difficulty by applying the characteristic impedance of air to the entire surface area of the soundboard. By definition, the load of a fluid at the surface of a given driving source is called the *complex radiation impedance* ($\boldsymbol{Z}_R$) of the fluid.[15] A dimensional analysis[16] shows that the *non-complex radiation impedance* of air (Z_a) at the surface of the soundboard belongs dimensionally to the *mechanical impedance* of a vibrating system,

$$Z_a = z_a S \tag{5.6}$$

where S is the two-dimensional surface area of the soundboard, in square inches.

For an average soundboard size, we will use the upright piano dimensions of 1.4 m × 1.0 m mentioned in Wogram's paper; this size also approximates the soundboard area of a 6 ft grand piano and a large harpsichord. This board has the following surface area dimensions in square inches:

$$S = (55 \text{ in})(39 \text{ in}) = 2145 \text{ in}^2$$

which means that

$$Z_a = \left[0.00153 \text{ mica/(in}^2\text{·s)}\right](2145 \text{ in}^2) = 3.28 \text{ micas/s}$$

≈ 5.12 ≈

In conclusion, it is now possible to construct two air-to-soundboard wave impedance ratios.

$$\text{Piano Soundboard:} \quad \frac{Z_a}{Z_b} = \frac{3.28}{3.20} \approx 1:1$$

$$\text{Harpsichord Soundboard:} \quad \frac{Z_a}{Z_b} = \frac{3.28}{0.356} \approx 9:1$$

However, due to the compressibility of air (discussed at length in Part IV), these wave impedance ratios do not provide a highly accurate description of the coupling between the soundboard and the surrounding air. Refer to Section 5.5 and recall that the piano soundboard wave impedance value, 562 kg/s or 3.20 micas/s, was located on a graph in the vicinity of D_4, at 293.7 cps. If we assume that the nearly perfect impedance match of 3.28 : 3.20 accurately describes the coupling between the air and the soundboard, then the most direct and efficient radiation of acoustic energy would have to occur in the middle C, or C_4, frequency range. However, Wogram's paper flatly contradicts this assumption. A separate radiation graph for Measuring Point #8 in Figure 5.2(b), and four others like it, show measurements taken from different treble and bass bridge locations. These graphs confirm (on average) that the radiation of acoustic energy from the soundboard into the surrounding air is equally strong or stronger in the 1000 cps, or C_6, frequency range. Part IV will describe the reasons for this discrepancy in greater detail.

Meanwhile, a very general comparison of the air-to-soundboard wave impedance ratios shows that any soundboard less than 3/8 in. thick is at a clear disadvantage in overcoming the radiation impedance of air at the surface of the board. When viewed from this perspective, we may now explain why instrument builders and musicians gradually abandoned their "intense interest in reducing inharmonicity." (See Section 5.8.)

Although the piano is historically identified with Cristofori's technically brilliant hammer action design (*c.* 1709), his instrument underwent another two hundred years of development before it became capable of producing the full dynamic range from very soft (pianissimo) to very loud (fortissimo). Early builders of the pianoforte were quick to realize that the impact hammer action alone would not produce a powerful sound, nor would increasing the wave impedance of strings. (See Equation 5.2.) Higher string tension, thicker strings (or greater mass per unit length), and double stringing were all tried by Cristofori with little success. Ultimately, full dynamic power required replacing traditional harpsichord strings and traditional harpsichord soundboards. A seemingly insignificant 200% increase in the height of the soundboard from 1/8 in. to 3/8 in., while maintaining a high wave impedance ratio of 240:1, resulted in a 900% increase in string tension (from about 20 lbf to 200 lbf), and due to thicker strings, a 900% increase in inharmonicity (from an average mid-range value of 0.025 ¢ to 0.250 ¢). Such extreme increases in tension called for the structural support of a massive cast-iron frame capable of withstanding approximately 20 tons of force. In short, all the major technical developments of piano construction, including crucial advances in the manufacture of high-tensile-strength steel wire,[17] evolved in direct response to the demanding presence of the radiation impedance of air.

Part IV

DISPERSION, THE SPEED OF BENDING WAVES, AND CRITICAL FREQUENCIES IN SOUNDBOARDS

5.13

We return now to the subject of dispersion, described earlier in conjunction with inharmonic strings. (See Chapter 4.) When compared to strings, soundboards are extremely dispersive. The internal restoring force due to stiffness is the only force that returns a vibrating board to its equilibrium position. Consequently, all the resonant frequencies of a soundboard are exceedingly inharmonic. Since soundboards do not produce any musical vibrations except those received from the strings, these inharmonic resonant frequencies do not significantly affect the tuning of piano strings. However, dispersion does influence how efficiently the board radiates sound. Therefore, we must now reexamine the phenomenon of dispersion from an entirely different perspective.

5.14

A motionless gas like the surrounding air has density and pressure values that are constant and uniform. When the disturbance of a vibrating string displaces the air from its equilibrium position, longitudinal sound waves, or alternating regions of compression and rarefaction, begin propagating through the medium. Due to the presence of these waves, the pressure and density of the air change by rising above normal during compression (positive pressure and high density), and dropping below normal during rarefaction (negative pressure and low density). For a vibrating string, the process of compression takes place in front of the string's leading surface, and the process of rarefaction, behind the string's trailing surface.

Not all vibrations produce sound. The critical difference between the absence and the presence of sound is speed (c), from the Latin *celeritas*. If a disturbance vibrates with a speed considerably less than the speed of longitudinal sound waves in the air (c_L), the air escapes compression and no sound results. For example, if a slack string displaces the air, the compression-rarefaction cycle is practically nonexistent. The air particles are merely pushed forward and sideways, and simply end up filling the empty space behind the string. Like a hand waving in the air, this motion cannot generate even the faintest sound.

However, if we raise the tension of a slack string, sound production starts to occur. Remember, the speed of transverse waves in strings (c_T), also known as the phase velocity, is directly proportional to the square root of the tension:

$$c_T = \sqrt{\frac{T}{M/u.l.}}$$

With greater tension and increased transverse wave speed, the air can no longer escape compression by moving faster than the string. As a result, the vibrating string begins to compress and rarefy the surrounding air, which in turn leads to the production of sound. Although the string does not have a great surface area and will radiate only small amounts of sound, an unmistakable difference is, nevertheless, evident. Now at least a faint sound may be heard.

The same fundamental principle also applies to piano soundboards. When the speed of transverse bending waves in the board (c_B) is less than the speed of sound in air ($c_B < c_L$), the compression of air and the subsequent radiation of sound is low. Conversely, as c_B increases and approaches the speed of sound, the board starts to radiate sound more efficiently. Such variations in the speed of bending waves are directly attributable to the influence of stiffness (or the internal restoring force) of the board. Consider once more the steel ruler example mentioned in Section 4.7 and in this chapter at the end of Section 5.5. Again, hold the ruler in your hand, bend it, and then quickly let go. Note the speed as it returns to a state of equilibrium. Next, bend it into two sections, and let go; then bend it into three sections, and let go. As you bend the ruler into progressively shorter subdivisions, or shorter bending wavelengths (λ_B), and release it, c_B increases significantly with each additional subdivision. From this example, we conclude that the bending wave speed in any stiff object with a substantial internal restoring force (piano soundboards, marimba bars, steel strings, church bells, etc.) is inversely proportional to the bending wavelength:

$$c_B \propto \frac{1}{\lambda_B}$$

As λ_B decreases, c_B increases. This variation of wave speed with wavelength (or frequency) is a phenomenon known as *dispersion.* (See Section 4.8.) Hence the classical definition: Any medium in which the speed of a wave depends on wavelength (or frequency) is said to possess the property of dispersion.[18]

Since shorter wavelengths (or shorter subdivisions) produce higher mode frequencies, it is also possible to relate increases in bending wave speed to a rise in the resonant frequencies (F_n) of the soundboard. Unfortunately, as discussed in Section 5.5, an exact equation for these resonant frequencies does not exist, and for this reason calculating the speed of bending waves in piano soundboards is impossible. However, to approximate the wave speed, we may use an equation cited by Cremer for calculating c_B in thin, isotropic, infinite plates.[19] This equation shows that the bending wave speed is directly proportional to the square root of the resonant frequency:

$$c_{\mathrm{B}} = \sqrt[4]{\frac{B'}{M/u.a.}}\sqrt{2\pi F_{\mathrm{n}}} \tag{5.7}$$

As $\sqrt{F_{\mathrm{n}}}$ increases, c_{B} increases as well.

We conclude, therefore, that in response to higher frequencies generated by the strings, the bending wavelengths of soundboards decrease, while the resonant frequencies increase. Due to stiffness (and the dispersion phenomenon), c_{B} in the board is inversely proportional to λ_{B}, and directly proportional to $\sqrt{F_{\mathrm{n}}}$.[20] Finally, as c_{B} increases with frequency, so does the efficiency of sound radiation.

(Item: The following sections on the radiation of sound will demonstrate that for the practical purposes of this discussion, Equation 5.7 gives reasonably accurate results. Its usefulness is not restricted to homogenous, infinite plates.)

5.15

The radiation efficiency of a piano soundboard is dependent on how well the speed of bending waves matches (or exceeds) the speed of longitudinal sound waves in the air. The match $c_{\mathrm{B}} = c_{\mathrm{L}}$ occurs at the *critical frequency* (F_{c}) of the soundboard.[21] To determine the critical frequency, first substitute the speed of sound into Equation 5.7 and then solve for F_{c}:

$$13{,}504 \text{ in/s} = \sqrt[4]{\frac{B'}{M/u.a.}}\sqrt{2\pi F_{\mathrm{c}}}$$

$$F_{\mathrm{c}} = \frac{\left(13{,}504 \Big/ \sqrt[4]{\frac{B'}{M/u.a.}}\right)^2}{2\pi} \tag{5.8}$$

It is now possible to describe (1) why pianos radiate sound more efficiently in the central frequency range of the instrument, and (2) why pianos sound louder than harpsichords. First, refer to Section 5.5, substitute the ⅜ in. piano soundboard values for B' and $M/u.a.$ into Equation 5.8, and compute the critical frequency. Next, refer to Section 5.7, substitute the ⅛ in. harpsichord soundboard values for B' and $M/u.a.$ into Equation 5.8, and repeat the calculation.

$$\text{Piano Soundboard:} \quad F_{\mathrm{c}} = \frac{\left(13{,}504 \Big/ \sqrt[4]{\frac{7034.0636}{0.000014569}}\right)^2}{2\pi} = 1320.9 \text{ cps}$$

$$\text{Harpsichord Soundboard:} \quad F_{\mathrm{c}} = \frac{\left(13{,}504 \Big/ \sqrt[4]{\frac{260.5209}{0.000004856}}\right)^2}{2\pi} = 3962.4 \text{ cps}$$

Wogram's piano radiation graph for Measuring Point #8 in Figure 5.2(b) is in general agreement with the first result. This graph has two strong radiation peaks (measured in decibels, dB) near 900 cps and 1200 cps on the x-axis. Moreover, the graph also shows how the increased speed of bending waves in the soundboard generates a favored region of acoustic radiation between 150 cps and 1500 cps. (Within this context, neither the peak near 230 cps, nor the deep fissures of the radiation curve in the upper frequency region are of great importance. A combination of strong resonant frequencies in the board causes the peak, and the fissures result from the directional pattern of the soundboard and/or the location of the microphone.)[22]

A reexamination of the impedance graph for Measuring Point #8 in Figure 5.2(a) supports these conclusions fairly well. Notice a small yet distinct valley in the curve at 1000 cps on the x-axis, which indicates that the soundboard is in sympathetic resonance with the driver. (See Section 5.5.) This point on the graph also marks the upper resonant frequency limit, beyond which the board no longer exhibits any sympathetic resonances. Substitute 1000 cps into Equation 5.7 and note that the bending waves at this specified location reach a top speed of about 11,750 in/s, which is slightly slower than the speed of sound in air. Since the last resonant frequency is close to the predicted critical frequency and occurs well within the musical range of the instrument, we conclude that a ⅜ in. thick soundboard radiates sound efficiently.

In contrast, the harpsichord is an inefficient radiator of sound because it does not produce any sympathetic resonances in the critical frequency range near 4000 cps. The highest key on most harpsichords is only C_6, at 1046.5 cps. Moreover, even if a set of harpsichord strings was tuned two "octaves" higher to C_8 (4186.0 cps), the ⅛ in. thick soundboard would not respond with a resonant frequency. The proximity of the rigid liners makes the treble section extremely stiff and incapable of subdividing into progressively shorter wavelengths. Conversely, the slow speed of bending waves in the bass sections of both piano and harpsichord soundboards contributes to poor radiation from these areas. Therefore, only a relatively large surface area accounts for the amplification of sound from the outer regions of the board. Neither section initiates the highly efficient compression-rarefaction cycle that effectively radiates sound beyond the immediate vicinity of the instrument.

5.16

One hundred years ago, the development of the modern piano came to an inevitable end. Although Equation 5.8 suggests that a ½ in. thick soundboard would yield even greater volume, further increases in the height of the board pose serious technical and musical problems. To understand these difficulties consider, for a moment, what kind of strings such a board would require. First, substitute the new value for h into Equation 5.3 and calculate the wave impedance of a ½ in. thick spruce plate:

$$Z_{\text{p}} = 8\sqrt{\frac{(1{,}600{,}000\text{ psi})(0.50\text{ in})^3}{12\left[1-(0.02)^2\right]}(0.00003885\text{ mica/in}^3)(0.50\text{ in})} = 4.55\text{ micas/s}$$

Account for the ribs, bridges, and liners, and add 25% to the wave impedance of the soundboard:

$$4.55 \times 0.25 = 1.14$$
$$4.55\text{ mica/s} + 1.14\text{ mica/s} = 5.69\text{ micas/s}$$

Next, construct a proportion based on the average soundboard-to-string wave impedance ratio of 240:1, and solve for the wave impedance of the required string:

$$\frac{5.69\text{ mica/s}}{Z_{\text{s}}} = \frac{240}{1}$$
$$Z_{\text{s}} \times 240 = 5.69\text{ mica/s} \times 1$$
$$Z_{\text{s}} = \frac{5.69\text{ mica/s}}{240}$$
$$Z_{\text{s}} = 0.0237\text{ mica/s}$$

Finally, refer to Equation 5.2 and determine a tension and mass per unit length combination so that

$$Z_{\text{s}} = \sqrt{T(M/u.l.)} = 0.0237\text{ mica/s}$$

Remember, the new string should have a tension approximately 50% of the break strength of the wire.[23] Otherwise the string will be too loose and sound weak, or too tight and break prematurely. We propose, therefore, a 0.053 in. diameter wire that has a break strength of about 666 lbf. (See Appendix D.) According to the other D_4 string specifications mentioned in Section 5.4, this wire has the following tension:

$$T = (293.67 \text{ cps})^2(25.00 \text{ in})^2(0.053 \text{ in})^2(3.1416)(0.00073299 \text{ mica/in}^3) = 348.66 \text{ lbf}$$

Divide the tension by the break strength, multiply the quotient by 100, and confirm that the string is tensioned at 52% of its break strength. Next, calculate the mass per unit length,

$$M/u.l. = 3.1416(0.0265 \text{ in})^2(0.00073299 \text{ mica/in}^3) = 0.000001617 \text{ mica/in}$$

and note that the string has the required wave impedance:

$$Z_s = \sqrt{(348.66 \text{ mica·in/s}^2)(0.000001617 \text{ mica/in})} = 0.0237 \text{ mica/s}$$

We must now evaluate the technical and musical implications of these numbers. A typical piano has 220 strings, each held at about 200 lbf. Therefore, the total force on a given instrument is roughly 44,000 lbf, or 22 tons. If we multiply 220 strings by the new average tension of about 340 lbf, then a piano with a ½ in. soundboard would have a force of approximately 74,800 lbf, or 37.4 tons. Such a piano would require a cast-iron frame of truly enormous proportions. The largest grand pianos, for example, withstand "only" 26–27 tons of force.

When viewed from a musical perspective, the newly proposed string has the following coefficient of inharmonicity:

$$\bar{\cent} = \frac{5.463 \times 10^{12}(0.053)^2}{(293.67)^2(25.00)^4} = 0.456 \ \cent$$

Compared to the original 0.040 in. diameter string at 0.259 ¢, this rate is 76% higher and completely unacceptable. The worst pianos have better sounding strings. It is possible to argue that a piano with a ½-in.-thick soundboard could be constructed with extra long strings. This would help to reduce inharmonicity. However, any advantage from longer strings quickly disappears because T is directly proportional to L^2. Consequently, with longer strings the total force becomes even greater.

~ 5.17 ~

In summary, let us review the mechanical requirements for a loud piano. First, we need a thick soundboard. There are two principal reasons why a ⅜-in.-thick piano soundboard radiates sound efficiently. (1) A very general air-to-soundboard wave impedance ratio of 3.28 : 3.20 indicates a close match between the radiation impedance of the surrounding air and the mechanical wave impedance of the board. (2) A more detailed analysis shows that the radiation of acoustic energy depends on a critical frequency at which the speed of bending waves in the board matches the speed of sound in air. For a piano soundboard, the critical frequency of approximately 1300 cps occurs well within the musical range of the instrument. Second, we need thick strings. A typical soundboard-to-string wave impedance ratio of 240:1 calls for strings with high tension and high mass per unit length values. Only large diameter wires can fulfill both of these requirements.

Although thick strings coupled to thick soundboards do produce loud sounds, they also pose serious structural and musical problems. Since T and $\bar{\cent}$ are directly proportional to D^2, tension and inharmonicity increase rapidly with large diameter wires. With respect to tension, piano builders reached a *force limit* of approximately 25 tons. With respect to inharmonicity, composers and musicians reached a *tuning limit* called the 12-tone equal tempered scale. Loud, thick strings produce dissonance. The inharmonic mode frequencies of stiff strings cause a dissonant beating phenomenon that piano builders and piano tuners cannot control. Although tempered tunings do not suffer very much from the dissonance of thick strings, the beating phenomenon severely restricts the tuning possibilities of other kinds of scales. As described in Part VI, anyone who attempts to tune a scale based on the intervals of the harmonic series must use thin strings. Thin strings are less loud than thick strings; that is, with small diameter wires the soundboard-to-string wave impedance ratio increases, which means that less energy is transferred from the strings to the soundboard. However, thin strings generate truer harmonics and, therefore, provide greater tuning accuracy.

In Sections 5.18–5.19, we will examine the nature of the beating phenomenon, and how tuners listen to beats when they tune an instrument. In Sections 5.20–5.21, we will discuss how beat rates influence our perceptions of consonance and dissonance, and why thick strings are inherently dissonant. And in Sections 5.22–5.23, we will analyze the musical benefits of thin strings, and propose alternate methods in piano construction.

Before we proceed, consider the popular argument that states, "The lack of being harmonic gives rise to the peculiar quality known as piano quality, namely, the live-ness or warmth."[24] Harvey Fletcher, *et al.* came to this conclusion based on a survey that found most listeners prefer the "warm" timbre of inharmonic strings over the artificially synthesized timbre of pure harmonic strings. This kind of juxtaposition serves only to uphold the status quo. It obscures the central issue of consonance and dissonance, and the related topics of tuning and cultural conditioning. (1) In general, listeners prefer the familiar. Given an equal amount of time (say, 20 or 30 years) and a wide variety of musical experiences, the possibility exists that a jury would reach the opposite conclusion. Under these circumstances, a group of listeners might reject the excessive dissonance of thick piano strings and conclude instead that "warmth" is a musical quality intimately related to and inseparable from tuning, performance, and composition. (Similarly, any foreign language can initially sound remote and obscure; not until we make an effort to speak the language does it begin to resonate in our ears.) (2) Pianos are acoustic instruments that produce acoustic timbres. Using electronically synthesized *non-acoustic* timbres as a measure of comparison creates artificial distinctions by denying degrees of inharmonicity. All real strings are by nature inharmonic. Far more relevant to this debate would be a comparative study based on acoustic pianos built with thinner soundboards and strung with thinner strings.

Part V

METHODS FOR TUNING PIANO INTERVALS TO BEAT RATES OF COINCIDENT STRING HARMONICS

~ 5.18 ~

Stringed instruments like harpsichords and pianos are tuned by listening to beats: a cyclical swelling and receding of sound produced when two strings with *different* frequencies vibrate simultaneously, as illustrated in Figure 5.3. For a given instant after sounding both strings, their motions compress the surrounding air at the same time, which sends an especially strong wave (or loud sound) to our ears. At this moment, we say the strings are vibrating "in phase." However, because one string is moving faster than the other, they quickly begin vibrating "out of phase." Consequently, the strength of the sound wave begins to diminish until it almost disappears. When the sound is at its weakest, the strings are vibrating in "opposite phase"; while one string is compressing air, the other is rarefying it. From here, the volume of the sound wave begins to build until the two strings are again vibrating in phase. The alternating pulse sensation ranging back and forth from strong (plainly audible) to weak (almost inaudible) is called the *beat rate*. It consists of the arithmetic difference between the two frequencies. For example, if two strings are vibrating at 100.0 cps and 102.0 cps, respectively, the beat rate is 2.0 cps. To understand this beating phenomenon a little better, say the word "wow" two times per second, or ten times in five seconds. In stringing the words together, "wow-wow-wow," whisper the first and last "w" in each word. Such cyclical variations in volume (or amplitude) simulate the beat rate (or changes in phase) when two strings vibrate simultaneously at different frequencies.

The human ear can only identify a limited number of beats per second. Tuning a piano to 12-tone equal temperament requires the ability to count and adjust several beat rates ranging from 0.6 cps to 1.1 cps. An experienced tuner also has the skill to accurately recognize the gradually ascending rate 7, 7.5, 8, 8.5, . . . up to 15.5 and 16 cps. Beyond this top limit, the ear loses its analytical power and can only respond to the general "roughness" (dissonance) or "smoothness" (consonance) of an interval. Compared to most intervals found in the central region of the keyboard, these rates are very slow. For example, suppose we tune D_4 as an exact or just "fifth," frequency ratio $3/2$ (see Section 3.12) above G_3 (196.0 cps). D_4 now vibrates at 196.0 cps $\times$ $3/2$ = 294.0 cps, and the beat rate equals 294.0 cps $-$ 196.0 cps = 98.0 cps. Since we cannot count a beat-frequency of this magnitude, and since it is much too fast for general recognition, we ignore the fundamental frequencies and listen instead to the harmonics. Note that the third harmonic of G_3 and the second harmonic of D_4 are (theoretically) identical; that is, $196.0 \times 3 = 294.0 \times 2 = 588.0$ cps, or D_5.

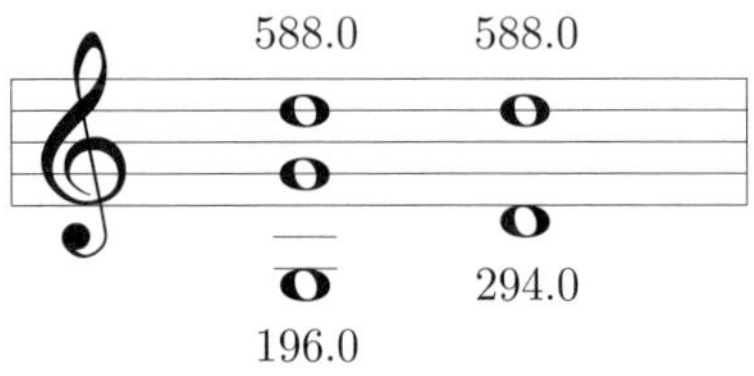

D_5 is called a *coincident harmonic*, a frequency both series have in common. If these two harmonics do not have the same frequency, then the slightest beating produced by their arithmetic difference would mean that the fundamentals are out of tune.

All equal temperaments require a mathematically determined beat rate between coincident harmonics. Suppose we would like to change the former just "fifth" to a tempered "fifth" in 12-tone equal temperament, the conventional piano scale. Since the frequency ratio of the tempered "fifth" is $\sqrt[12]{2}^{7}$ (see Section 9.13), D_4 now vibrates at 196.0 cps $\times$ $\sqrt[12]{2}^{7}$ = 196.0 cps $\times$ 1.4983 = 293.67 cps. Tuning this tempered fundamental frequency requires lowering the second harmonic of D_4 until it produces the following beat rate with the third harmonic of G_3:

$$\begin{aligned} 196.00 \text{ cps} \times 3 &= 588.00 \text{ cps} \\ 293.67 \text{ cps} \times 2 &= \underline{587.34 \text{ cps}} \\ & \quad\;\, 0.66 \text{ cps} \end{aligned}$$

Most tuners count such a slow beat rate in 5-second increments, here equal to about 0.7 cps $\times$ 5.0 s = 3.5 cycles every five seconds.

Before we analyze the beating caused by inharmonic strings, let us make one more comparison. Consider tuning B_3 as a just "major third" and as a tempered "major third" above G_3. Since the frequency ratio of a just "major third" is $5/4$, B_3 vibrates at 196.0 cps $\times$ $5/4$ = 245.0 cps. Tuning a just "major third" requires matching the fourth harmonic of B_3 to the fifth harmonic of G_3 without producing beats. Here the coincident harmonic is 196.0 cps $\times$ 5 = 245.0 cps $\times$ 4 = 980.0 cps, or B_5.

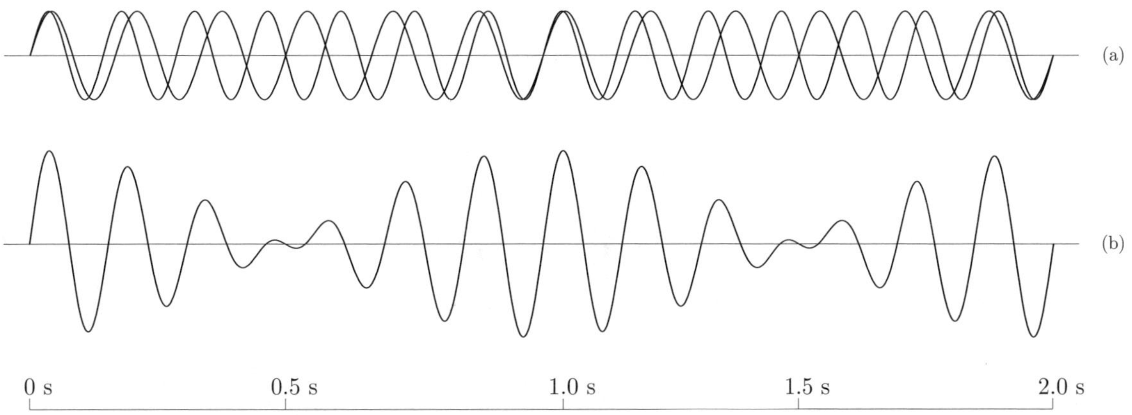

Figure 5.3 A graphic representation of beats. (a) Two waves vibrating separately at 7.0 cps and 6.0 cps, shown over a 2.0-second period. (b) The resulting beat rate (or change in amplitude) when both waves vibrate simultaneously. The rate (produced by the arithmetic difference between the two frequencies) is 1.0 cps. Initially, the two waves are moving in phase; at 0.5 s, in opposite phase; and at 1.0 s, in phase again: this is a strong-weak-strong cycle. A different pattern begins at 0.5 s. Here the two waves are moving in opposite phase; at 1.0 s, in phase; and at 1.5 s, in opposite phase again. This weak-strong-weak cycle is easier to discern, and very much like saying the word "wow." Although these two waves vibrate below the threshold of human hearing (which begins around 20 cps), the illustration shows the beating phenomenon without obscuring the figure with too many waves.

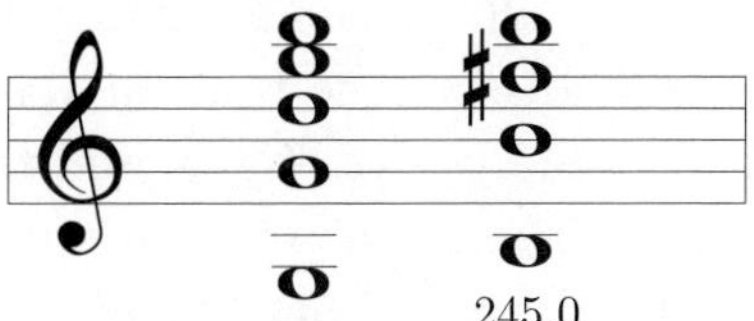

On the other hand, a tempered "major third" has the frequency ratio $\sqrt[12]{2}^4$, so that B_4 now vibrates at 196.0 cps $\times \sqrt[12]{2}^4 = 196.0$ cps $\times$ 1.2599 = 246.94 cps. Unlike the tempered "fifth," piano tuners do not tune this interval by ear because it produces a very fast beat rate between the fourth harmonic of B_3 and the fifth harmonic of G_3:

$$\begin{aligned} 246.94 \text{ cps} \times 4 &= 987.76 \text{ cps} \\ 196.00 \text{ cps} \times 5 &= \underline{980.00 \text{ cps}} \\ & \ \ 7.76 \text{ cps} \end{aligned}$$

Instead, B_3 is tuned downward as a "fourth" from E_4, with a beat rate of approximately 1.1 cps.[25]

~ 5.19 ~

We may ask, "What causes some intervals to sound consonant while others sound dissonant?" This complex question has many acoustical and psychological ramifications. In many cases, however, the beating of the *intermediate harmonics* determines the musical quality of an interval. Because these harmonics reside between coincident harmonics, they cannot be matched and tuned beatless. Consequently, their presence has a critical influence over our perceptions of consonance and dissonance. In general, if the number of intermediate harmonics is relatively small, the interval will tend to sound smooth and consonant; if large, it will sound rough and dissonant.

Consider, for example, the most consonant of all musical intervals, ratio ²⁄₁, also known as the "octave." The following illustration shows two harmonic series spaced one "octave" apart; the lower fundamental is again G_3, at 196.0 cps, and the "octave" is G_4, at 392.0 cps.

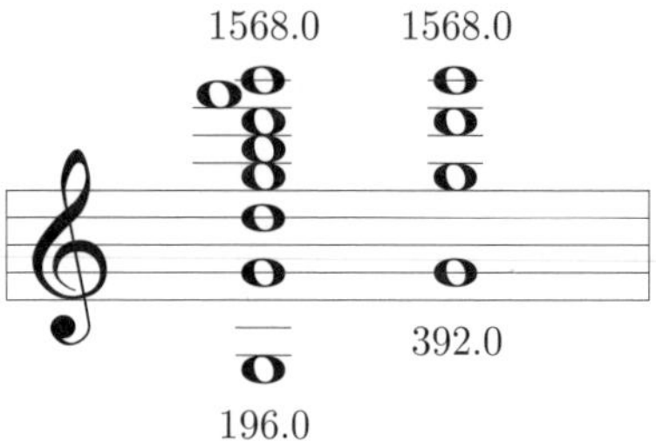

Note from the outline below that the harmonics of the G_4 series match every second harmonic or all the *even* numbers in the G_3 series; that is, the entire G_4 series consists of coincident harmonics.

1	**2**	3	**4**	5	**6**	7	**8**
	1		**2**		**3**		**4**

As a result, both series overlap perfectly, without producing any beats. Notice also the absence of an intermediate harmonic between the fundamental or first harmonic G_3, and the "octave" or second harmonic G_4, just as there is no whole number between 1 and 2. (Remember, in producing harmonics, a string can only subdivide into a whole number of parts.) Furthermore, beginning with D_5 (the third harmonic of G_3), there is only one intermediate harmonic per coincident harmonic. These intermediate harmonics account for all the *odd* numbers in the G_3 series. So, for the "octave," consonance stands at a maximum, while dissonance is at an absolute minimum.

In contrast, a similar and expanded analysis of ³⁄₂, ⁵⁄₄, and the "minor third" ⁶⁄₅ shows that ratios with progressively larger integers incorporate an ever-greater number of intermediate harmonics between coincident harmonics. This results in a complex pattern of staggered harmonic intervals leading to potentially dissonant beat rates. Especially potent are the clusters of "major seconds" (or "whole tones") and "minor seconds" (or "semitones") near the first coincident harmonic. Although the beating of these intervals is very rapid and cannot be counted, a rate up to about 45 cps (in the audible frequency range) leaves a definite impression on the listener. Consider, for instance, the final ⁶⁄₅ ratio example below. The interval between the fifth harmonic of G_3 and the fourth harmonic of $B\flat_3$ beats at $(196.0 \text{ cps} \times 5) - (235.2 \text{ cps} \times 4) = 39.2$ cps. This beat rate, well within the top limit of human perception, renders the "minor third" more dissonant than the "octave," "fifth," or "major third." Without calculating all possible beat combinations, the following illustrations demonstrate the escalating acoustic complexity and musical dissonance of increasingly larger *integer ratios.*[26] Here the underlined coincident harmonics represent the highest two notes in each measure.

1		2		**3**		4		5		**6**		7		8		**9**
	1			**2**			3			**4**			5			**6**

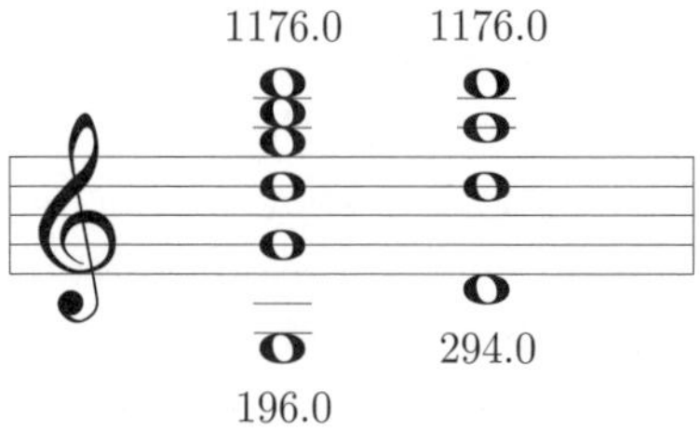

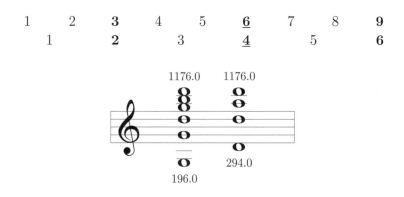

1 2 3 4 5 6 7 8 9 **10**
1 2 3 4 5 6 7 **8**

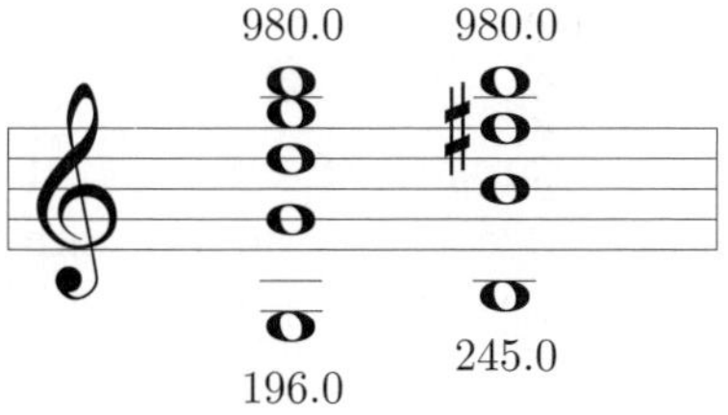

1 2 3 4 5 6 7 8 9 10 11 **12**
1 2 3 4 5 6 7 8 9 **10**

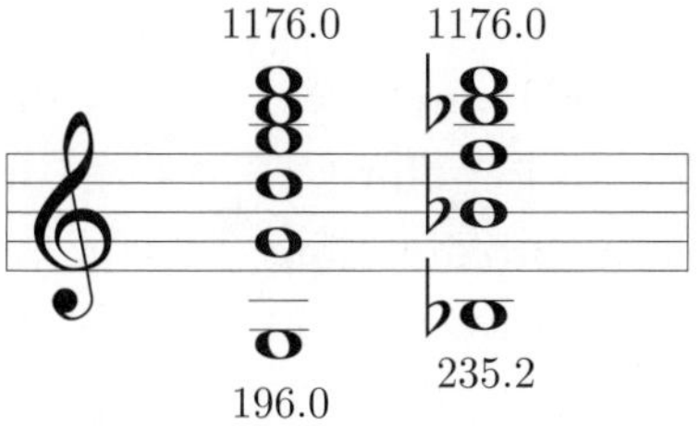

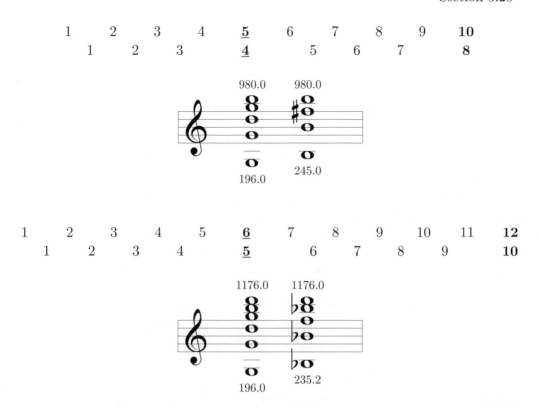

H.F. Cohen discusses how the proponents of 12-tone equal temperament have used this kind of analysis to argue in favor of dissonant thirds.[27] Cohen reasons as follows: "Octaves" require correct tuning because the proportion of coincident harmonics to intermediate harmonics is high. Any mistuning would immediately result in the increased beating of all the numerous coincident harmonics. For example, if the "octave" mentioned at the beginning of this section is tuned to 390.0 cps, the first coincident harmonic ($^2\!/\!_1$) will beat at (196.0 cps × 2) − (390.0 cps × 1) = 2.0 cps. However, the next coincident harmonic ($^4\!/\!_2$) will beat at (196.0 cps × 4) − (390.0 cps × 2) = 4.0 cps, and the following ($^6\!/\!_3$) at (196.0 cps × 6) − (390.0 cps × 3) = 6.0 cps. In the central frequency range, the beat rates of mistuned "octaves" are extremely noticeable and effectively destroy the potential consonance of this ratio. On the other hand, if the proportion of coincident harmonics to intermediate harmonics is low, the opposite holds true. According to Cohen, "In the case of the major third much fewer coinciding notes are present, and therefore much less additional beating will arise from a slight mistuning." That is, in the central frequency range, "major thirds" and "minor thirds" may be tuned to beat from 7 cps to 16 cps because a relatively large number of intermediate harmonics renders these intervals less consonant than the "octave." Cohen concludes, "The fact that the major third can bear much more tempering than the octave follows immediately from the above analysis." Put another way, consonant intervals with small integers demand exact tuning, while dissonant intervals with large integers tolerate mistuning.

5.20

The preceding explanation has a color analogy. Suppose white and black represent consonance and dissonance, respectively. By mixing in a color like red or blue, white would easily distort, whereas black would barely change. Therefore, to preserve the consonance of small ratios, only minor alterations (minimum beats between coincident harmonics) are acceptable. In contrast, the dissonance of large ratios imposes no such restrictions, which leads the proponents of this argument to conclude that the dissonant beating of intermediate harmonics constitutes an acoustic basis for tempered tuning. They believe that ". . . the major third can bear much more tempering than the octave . . ." because it is inherently more dissonant and therefore less susceptible to the effects of mistuning. Stated another way, this theory suggests that a tempered "major third" resembles a just $5/4$, whereas a similarly tempered "octave" does not resemble a just $2/1$.

A great deal has been written about the virtues of tempered tuning. Granted, modulation into all 24 keys requires 12-tone equal temperament. However, a $2/1 \leftrightarrow 5/4$ comparison does not necessarily justify the disparity that exists between just "major thirds" tuned to 0 cps, and tempered "major thirds" tuned to an average 9.0 cps.[28] Although dissonance does intensify with increasingly larger integer ratios, notice that a direct $5/4 \leftrightarrow \sqrt[12]{2}^4$ comparison contradicts the assumption that a $5/4$ ratio constitutes a dissonance. First, consider two rational approximations of the tempered "major third," ratios $223/177$ and $63/50$; note that according to this comparison, a $5/4$ emerges as a true consonance, or as a small integer ratio. The two approximations reveal the intense beating of the intermediate harmonics of all tempered "major thirds." Therefore, a $5/4$ does *not* resemble a $\sqrt[12]{2}^4$. What a $5/4$ can and cannot "bear" belongs to the art of music and perception, not science.

Just "Major Third":	$5/4$	$= 386.31$ ¢
12-TET "Major Third":	$\sqrt[12]{2}^4$	$= 400.00$ ¢
Rational Approximation:	$223/177$	$= 399.95$ ¢
Rational Approximation:	$63/50$	$= 400.11$ ¢

To appreciate the consonance of an accurately tuned $5/4$ ratio requires flexible strings. Stiff strings prohibit just intonation because inharmonicity causes the coincident harmonics not only to sound sharp, but to beat as well. (See Section 5.21.) Moreover, large integer ratios present a special problem because for a given string, the *inharmonic mode frequencies* and the corresponding *mode cents* increase directly with the square of the mode number minus one $(n^2 - 1)$. (See Equations 4.4 and 4.21, respectively.) For this reason, the effects of inharmonicity are more severe on a $5/4$ or $7/6$ ratio than on a $2/1$ or $3/2$ ratio.

The advocates of piano music and 12-tone equal temperament have argued for centuries against the inclusion of prime number 7 in Western music, to say nothing of 11, 13, 17, 19, . . . Without entering this debate, is it not reasonable to suggest that an objective experience of such ratios would further our understanding of sound and music, and diminish the hard division between consonance and dissonance, between white and black?

5.21

Mixtures of white and black result in shades of gray. At the piano, unfortunately, gradations in intonation cannot be appreciated due to the dissonance of stiff strings. Consider, for example, the inharmonic difficulties that occur while tuning a $7/6$ above G_3. Since this ratio is roughly equivalent to a "flat minor third" (see Figure 3.12), we would retune $B\flat_3$ (233.08 cps) to the new frequency 196.0 cps $\times$ $7/6$ $=$ 228.67 cps. Here the coincident harmonic is 196.0 cps $\times$ 7 $=$ 228.67 cps $\times$ 6 $=$ 1372.0 cps, or F_6.

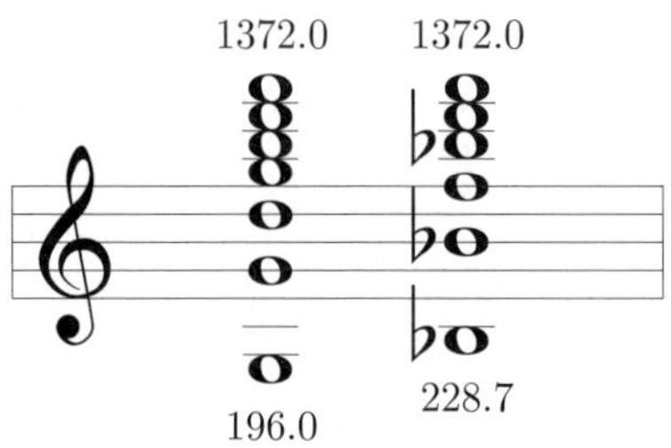

We must now calculate the actual inharmonic frequencies of this coincident harmonic for both strings. Begin by measuring the diameter and length of the appropriate strings. The following are average piano string dimensions:

G_3	$B\flat_3$
$D = 0.041$ in.	$D = 0.040$ in.
$L = 31.125$ in.	$L = 28.750$ in.

Next, refer to Section 4.4 and locate the Steel Constant for Equation 4.8. Now calculate the dimensionless stiffness parameter (J) and the inharmonic mode frequency ($\bar{F}_n$) of each string:

$$J = \frac{3.156 \times 10^9 (0.041)^2}{(196.00)^2 (31.125)^4} = 0.0001471 \qquad (G_3)$$

$$J = \frac{3.156 \times 10^9 (0.040)^2}{(228.67)^2 (28.750)^4} = 0.0001413 \qquad (B\flat_3)$$

$$\bar{F}_7 \text{ for } G_3 = 7(196.00 \text{ cps})\sqrt{1 + 2(0.0001471)(7^2 - 1)} = 1381.65 \text{ cps}$$

$$\bar{F}_6 \text{ for } B\flat_3 = 6(228.67 \text{ cps})\sqrt{1 + 2(0.0001413)(6^2 - 1)} = 1378.79 \text{ cps}$$

Subtract the second mode frequency from the first, and note that these two "coincident" harmonics beat 2.86 cps, or nearly three cycles per second, a considerable dissonance in any tuning system. If these mode frequencies were tuned beatless, either by lowering G_3 or by raising $B\flat_3$, then the interval between the fundamentals — the 7/6 ratio — would be false and would sound more dissonant than it actually is. Note also that these coincident harmonics are not the only source of additional inharmonic beating. The same equations for J and $\bar{F}_n$ apply to all the sharp-sounding intermediate harmonics as well. Finally, the effect of inharmonically induced dissonance is not confined to basic intervals. The most severe test comes from playing chords. Under these conditions, the dissonance associated with inharmonic strings intensifies and the problem develops beyond simple mathematical analysis.

Part VI

MUSICAL ADVANTAGES OF THIN STRINGS AND THIN SOUNDBOARDS

~ 5.22 ~

The solution, however, is simple: Use long, thin strings. On the Harmonic/Melodic Canon in Plate 2, the same 7/6 ratio has a completely different sound and texture. To understand the reasons for this change, consider these canon string dimensions,

G_3	$B\flat_3$
$D = 0.024$ in.	$D = 0.024$ in.
$L = 39.370$ in.	$L = 33.746$ in.

and calculate J and $\bar{F}_n$ again:

$$J = \frac{3.156 \times 10^9 (0.024)^2}{(196.00)^2 (39.370)^4} = 0.0000197 \qquad (G_3)$$

$$J = \frac{3.156 \times 10^9 (0.024)^2}{(228.67)^2 (33.746)^4} = 0.0000268 \qquad (B\flat_3)$$

$$\overline{F}_7 \text{ for } G_3 = 7(196.00 \text{ cps})\sqrt{1 + 2(0.0000197)(7^2 - 1)} = 1373.30 \text{ cps}$$

$$\overline{F}_6 \text{ for } B\flat_3 = 6(228.67 \text{ cps})\sqrt{1 + 2(0.0000268)(6^2 - 1)} = 1373.31 \text{ cps}$$

Because these two mode frequencies are practically identical, they represent a true coincident harmonic. Although less consonant than a 6⁄5 ratio, a 7⁄6 ratio under these favorable conditions does *not* give the impression of a bona fide dissonance. This also applies to the 7⁄5, or "diminished fifth," and the 7⁄4, or "minor seventh," ratios.

When compared to the G_3 piano string, the G_3 canon string has one disadvantage. The mechanical wave impedance of the canon string equals only 0.0051 mica/s. (See Equation 5.2.) Coupling this string to a 3⁄8 in. piano soundboard, where Z_b equals 3.20 micas/s, gives a soundboard-to-string wave impedance ratio of approximately 630:1. Unlike the standard wave impedance ratio of 240:1, this new impedance ratio shows that the canon string transfers its vibrational energy to the soundboard even more slowly. In general, long and thin strings are not very loud. However, as an experiment I once restrung parts of a piano's long bass string section with 0.024 in. wire, and can report that these strings gave a surprisingly full sound.

5.23

All the impedance equations of this chapter, the reflections on the history and development of piano construction, and the final discussion on tuning were designed to exemplify what piano strings can and cannot do. The importance of stringed keyboard instruments is not at issue. Instead, the central question of this discussion concerns the future of acoustic music. For structural reasons and distortion-free tuning, thicker soundboards and thicker strings are unacceptable alternatives for the continuing development of this instrument. When musicians decide that the consonance-dissonance split is too wide and artificial, and that too many musical resources have literally fallen between the cracks of the keyboard, a lighter and more flexible instrument will emerge. Such an instrument would have the following ideal components:

1. A 1⁄4 in. thick soundboard.
2. Plain steel strings with diameters ranging from 0.020 in. up to 0.035 in.
3. Wound strings equally light and flexible.
4. An aircraft alloy aluminum frame. Note that the G_3 canon string has a tension of only 78.9 lbf. If the strings of the new instrument average 100 lbf, the total force is only about 11 tons, or half the force of a typical piano. A lighter frame could handle such a load.
5. Lighter hammers, action parts, and keys.
6. A keyboard with alternating black and white keys that eliminates wasted space between E and F, B and C, and provides a maximum number of keys per 2⁄1, or per "octave."
7. Adjustable bridges allowing the owner to vary string lengths to accommodate custom tunings.
8. A frequency range from G_1 (49.0 cps) to G_6 (1568.0 cps), or to C_7 (2093.0 cps). This would eliminate the upper and lower "octaves," the least used keys of the standard piano. The G_1 string would have the same length as the lowest contemporary A_0 string.

Notes

1. Scientists also use the terms *velocity amplitude* and *vibrational velocity* for *particle velocity.*

2. See Equation 1.20.

3. Wogram, K. (1981). Akustische Untersuchungen an Klavieren. Teil I: Schwingungseigenschaften des Resonanzbodens. *Das Musikinstrument* **24**, pp. 694–702, 776–782, 872–879. English translation: Acoustical research on pianos. Part I: Vibrational characteristics of the soundboard. In *Musical Acoustics: Selected Reprints*, T.D. Rossing, Editor, pp. 85–98. American Association of Physics Teachers, College Park, Maryland, 1988.

4. Cremer, L., Heckl, M., and Ungar, E.E. (1973). *Structure-Borne Sound*, 2nd ed., p. 98, 100, 284, 290, 317. Springer-Verlag, Berlin and New York, 1988.

5. The following dimensional analysis shows the derivation of the bending stiffness unit (mica·in^2/s^2) and the mass per unit area unit (mica/in^2). As part of the bending stiffness, Young's modulus is a pressure unit called *pounds-force per square inch,* or simply psi. This unit commonly appears as lb/in^2. Since *pounds* in this context refers to weight or force (f), writing lbf/in^2 is also correct. Refer to Newton's second law: force = mass × acceleration, and write force as *unit mass* times *unit acceleration:* f = mica·in/s^2. (See Section 1.11.) Therefore, according to the following calculation (see Section 1.13), lbf/in^2 is here equivalent to mica/(in·s^2):

$$\frac{\text{mica} \times \text{in}}{\text{s}^2} \div \frac{\text{in}^2}{1} =$$

$$\frac{\text{mica} \times \text{in}}{\text{s}^2} \times \frac{1}{\text{in}^2} =$$

$$\frac{\text{mica} \times \cancel{\text{in}}}{\text{s}^2} \times \frac{1}{\text{in}^{\cancel{2}\,1}} = \frac{\text{mica}}{\text{in} \times \text{s}^2}$$

To calculate the bending stiffness unit, multiply this psi equivalent by the cubic height of the soundboard in inches:

$$\frac{\text{mica}}{\cancel{\text{in}} \times \text{s}^2} \times \frac{\text{in}^{\cancel{3}\,2}}{1} = \frac{\text{mica} \times \text{in}^2}{\text{s}^2}$$

To calculate the mass per unit area unit, multiply the mass density of the soundboard in mica/in^3 by the height of the soundboard in inches:

$$\frac{\text{mica}}{\text{in}^{\cancel{3}\,2}} \times \frac{\cancel{\text{in}}}{1} = \frac{\text{mica}}{\text{in}^2}$$

Finally, to calculate the mechanical wave impedance unit of Equation 5.3, multiply the bending stiffness unit by the mass per unit area unit, and then take the square root of the product:

$$\frac{\text{mica} \times \cancel{\text{in}^{2}}}{\text{s}^2} \times \frac{\text{mica}}{\cancel{\text{in}^{2}}} = \frac{\text{mica}^2}{\text{s}^2}$$

$$\sqrt{\frac{\text{mica}^2}{\text{s}^2}} = \frac{\text{mica}}{\text{s}}$$

6. (A) *Musical Acoustics, Selected Reprints*, 1988, p. 86.

(B) Fletcher, N.H., and Rossing, T.D. (1991). *The Physics of Musical Instruments*, 2nd ed., p. 721. Springer-Verlag, Berlin and New York, 1998.

7. On p. 88 of *Musical Acoustics: Selected Reprints*, Wogram calls the mechanical impedance unit a *mechanical ohm*, symbolized by the uppercase of the Greek letter *omega* (Ω). He gives the following definition:

$$1.0\ \Omega = 1.0\ \text{g/s}$$

He goes on to explain that at 10,000 cps on the x-axis, most soundboards have an *approximate* impedance value of 160,000 g/s on the y-axis. Since the lowercase of the Greek letter *kappa* (κ) represents the number 1000, we may write 160,000 g/s = 160 kg/s, or 160,000 g/s = 160 kΩ. This value is located on the graph between −15 and −20 on the y-axis, directly below 1 MΩ. Since the uppercase of the Greek letter *mu* (M) represents the number 1,000,000, we may write 1.0 MΩ = 1000.0 kg/s, or 1.0 MΩ = 1000.0 kΩ. From these facts, we conclude that Wogram used a 20 log scale because the value 160 kg/s sits between −15 and −20 on such a scale. Therefore,

$$10^{\frac{-15}{20}} \times 1000.0\ \text{kg/s} = 177.8\ \text{kg/s}$$

$$10^{\frac{-20}{20}} \times 1000.0\ \text{kg/s} = 100.0\ \text{kg/s}$$

The soundboard wave impedance graph for Measuring Point 8 shows that D_4 (294 cps) on the x-axis has a coordinate at −5 on the y-axis. Therefore, the mechanical impedance associated with this sympathetic resonance has the value

$$10^{\frac{-5}{20}} \times 1000.0\ \text{kg/s} = 562.3\ \text{kg/s}$$

8. See Section 1.10.

9. *The Physics of Musical Instruments*, 2nd ed., p. 383.

The authors cite a typical soundboard-to-string wave impedance ratio of 200:1.

10. Hubbard, F. (1965). *Three Centuries of Harpsichord Making*, 4th ed., p. 8, 208, 233. Harvard University Press, Cambridge, Massachusetts, 1972.

On p. 8, Hubbard lists large Ruckers harpsichord string lengths for C_4 (c') and C_5 (c'') at 25.5 in. and 13.5 in., respectively. The approximate change in string length for this "octave" is 1.00 in. per "semitone." This gives the D_4 (d') string a length of 23.50 in. On p. 233, Hubbard also cites the Flemish builder K. Douwes, who lists large harpsichord string lengths for C_4 and C_5 at 28.0 in. and 14.0 in., respectively. Here the approximate change in string length is 1.17 in. per "semitone." This gives the D_4 string a length of 25.67 in. The average length of these two D_4 strings is, therefore, 24.6 in. On p. 208, Hubbard lists string diameters of many different kinds of harpsichords. Typical diameters for a D_4 string range between 0.010 in. and 0.0135 in. An average diameter for the D_4 string is, therefore, 0.012 in.

11. Benade, A.H. (1976). *Fundamentals of Musical Acoustics*, p. 333. Dover Publications, Inc., New York, 1990.

12. Refer to Section 1.13, substitute the appropriate values for air into Equation 5.4A, and note that the result is the same as the solution to Equation 5.5 at the end of Section 5.10:

$$z_a = \sqrt{(0.000000113\ \text{mica/in}^3)(20.604\ \text{psi})} = 0.00153\ \text{mica/(in}^2\cdot\text{s)}$$

13. Kinsler, L.E., and Frey, A.R. (1950). *Fundamentals of Acoustics*, 2nd ed., p. 439. John Wiley & Sons, Inc., New York, 1962.

14. *Ibid.*, pp. 122–123.

15. *Ibid.*, p. 190.

16. Pierce, J.R. (1983). *The Science of Musical Sound*, Appendix D. Scientific American Books, W.H. Freeman and Company, New York.

This is a good introduction to dimensional analysis. The discussion focuses on three fundamental physical quantities: time, mass, and length.

17. Wolfenden, S. (1916). *A Treatise on the Art of Pianoforte Construction*, p. 6. The British Piano Museum Charitable Trust, Brentford, Middlesex, England, 1975.

"It is not too much to say, that the improvements in the tenacity and elasticity of steel wire, made during the last century, have rendered possible the modern piano."

18. In contrast, air is not a dispersive medium. Consequently, all the frequencies of an orchestral chord arrive in our ear canals at the same time. If the air were a dispersive medium, then the high frequencies would arrive ahead of the low frequencies; and if the musical passage were a rapid chord progression, the result would be a grand irregularly syncopated cacophony of sound.

19. Cremer, L. (1981). *The Physics of the Violin*, 2nd ed., p. 287. The MIT Press, Cambridge, Massachusetts, 1984.

20. Ingard, K.U. (1988). *Fundamentals of Waves and Oscillations*, p. 533. Cambridge University Press, Cambridge, Massachusetts, 1990.

Ingard cites both equations that show c_B is inversely proportional to λ_B, and directly proportional to $\sqrt{F_n}$.

21. **(A)** Norton, M.P. (1989). *Fundamentals of Noise and Vibration Analysis for Engineers*, Chapter 3. Cambridge University Press, Cambridge, Massachusetts.

(B) Skudrzyk, E. (1968). *Simple and Complex Vibratory Systems*, Chapter 12. Pennsylvania State University Press, University Park, Pennsylvania, 1981.

(C) Suzuki, H. (1986). Vibration and sound radiation of a piano soundboard. *Journal of the Acoustical Society of America* **80**, No. 6, pp. 1573–1582.

The critical frequency also occurs when the wavelength of bending waves in the board matches the wavelength of longitudinal sound waves in the air ($\lambda_B = \lambda_L$). When viewed from this perspective, the efficiency of sound radiation depends on the modal areas (or surface modes) of the plate or soundboard. The first two sources listed above discuss this subject in plates, and the third, in grand piano soundboards.

(D) *Structure-Borne Sound*, p. 523.

The critical frequency of a soundboard is also given by

$$F_c = \frac{c_L^{\,2}}{2\pi}\sqrt{\frac{M/u.a.}{B'}} = \frac{c_L^{\,2}}{2\pi}\sqrt{\rho h \Big/ \frac{Eh^3}{12(1-\mu^2)}} = \frac{c_L^{\,2}}{2\pi}\sqrt{\frac{12(1-\mu^2)}{Eh^{\cancel{3}2}}\,\rho\cancel{h}} = \frac{c_L^{\,2}}{2\pi}\sqrt{\frac{12(1-\mu^2)}{Eh^2}\,\rho}$$

where c_L is the speed of sound in air.

22. *The Physics of Musical Instruments*, 2nd ed., Chapter 10, Section 9.

23. See Section 2.8.

24. Fletcher, H., Blackham, E.D., and Stratton, R.S. (1962). Quality of piano tones. *Journal of the Acoustical Society of America* **34**, No. 6, pp. 749–761.

25. White, W.B. (1917). *Piano Tuning and Allied Arts*, 5th ed., pp. 88–89. Tuners Supply Company, Boston, Massachusetts, 1972.

26. In this text, an *integer ratio* consists of a numerator x and denominator y, where both x and y are positive integers. Therefore, by definition, integer ratios constitute positive rational numbers. See Section 10.1.

27. Cohen, H.F. (1984). *Quantifying Music*, p. 240. D. Reidel Publishing Company, Dordrecht, Netherlands.

28. At the piano, the tuner tunes the temperament through a series of ascending "fifths" and descending "fourths" between F_3 (174.61 cps) and F_4 (349.23 cps). Upon completion, the lowest "major third" F_3–A_3 should beat 7.0 cps, and the highest "major third" $D\flat_4$–F_4 should beat 11.0 cps. Therefore, the average "major third" beat rate is 9.0 cps.

6 / BARS, RODS, AND TUBES

On first impression, it seems that marimbas, orchestral chimes, mbiras,[1] and harmonicas do not have many common properties. From a mathematical perspective, however, musical instruments made from bars, rods, or tubes fall into two principal groups. The first group consists of bars, rods, or tubes that are free at both ends. All the instruments in the free-free group are percussion instruments such as marimbas, xylophones, vibraphones, celestas, gamelan bars, orchestra bell bars, glockenspiels, bell lyras, orchestral chimes, metal tubes,[2] solid rods,[3] and tuning forks.[4] The second group consists largely of bars and reeds clamped at one end. The instruments in this group are either percussion instruments or wind instruments because some are played with mallets or fingers, whereas others are driven with compressed air. Percussion instruments in the clamped-free group include mbiras, slit drums, music boxes, and jaw's harps; wind instruments include reed organ pipes, accordions, harmonicas, harmoniums, and concertinas.

A mathematical classification is important because it emphasizes the acoustical similarities among different kinds of musical instruments. For example, all the instruments in the free-free group produce identical mode shapes; this also applies to the clamped-free group. Consequently, the principles and techniques used to tune rosewood marimba bars and aluminum tubes are the same; similarly, the tuning techniques of steel mbira keys and brass harmonica reeds are also the same. Because there are more similarities than differences in the frequency equations and mode shapes of the objects belonging to either group, the phrase "bars, rods, and tubes" will appear only when appropriate. Future discussions will primarily focus on free-free bars and clamped-free bars with the understanding that rods and tubes are included as well.

Because of the overall complexity of this subject, and some significant differences between free-free bars and clamped-free bars, this chapter is divided into four parts. Part I examines frequency equations, mode shapes, and restoring forces of free-free bars, and Part II gives a detailed description of free-free bar tuning techniques. Part III examines the frequency equations, mode shapes, and restoring forces of clamped-free bars, and Part IV gives a brief description of clamped-free bar tuning techniques.

Part I

FREQUENCY EQUATIONS, MODE SHAPES, AND RESTORING FORCES OF FREE-FREE BARS

~ 6.1 ~

Stiff strings, soundboards, and bars have one common property: a restoring force due to stiffness. When an object vibrates under the influence of stiffness, two important characteristics come to mind. (1) In strings, stiffness causes increases in the speed of transverse waves (c_{T}), and in soundboards and bars, stiffness causes increases in the speed of transverse bending waves (c_B). (2) As a result of such increases in mode wave speeds, these vibrating systems produce mode frequencies that do not form a harmonic series. We call such frequencies *inharmonic mode frequencies* because they are *not* integer multiples of a fundamental frequency.

The general topic of increasing mode wave speeds falls under the subject known as *dispersion.* This phenomenon received a great deal of attention in Sections 4.8 and 5.14. The reader should read, study, and absorb this material because it is essential for a thorough understanding of vibrating bars. Bars are extremely dispersive; here stiffness acts as the *only* restoring force that returns a vibrating bar to its equilibrium position. However, there exists an important difference between stiff strings and ribbed soundboards on the one hand, and bars on the other. Only in bars are tuners of percussion instruments able to methodically change the restoring force due to stiffness and, thereby, intentionally tune the inharmonic modes to a wide variety of alternate frequencies.

~ 6.2 ~

The frequency equation for a slender, uniform, isotropic bar, rod, or tube free at both ends states[5]

$$F_{\text{n free-free}} = \frac{\pi K\sqrt{E/\rho}}{8}\left(\frac{q_n}{L}\right)^2 \quad \begin{cases} q_1 \approx 3.01124 \approx 3.0112 \\ q_2 \approx 4.99951 \approx 5 \\ q_3 \approx 7.00002 \approx 7 \\ q_4 \approx 8.99999 \approx 9 \\ q_{n>4} \approx 2n+1 \end{cases} \tag{6.1}$$

where F_n is the mode frequency of transverse vibrations, in cps; E is Young's modulus of elasticity of the material, in pounds-force per square inch, or psi; ρ is the mass density, or mass per unit volume of the material, in mica per cubic inch;[6] L is the length of the object, in inches; q_n is a dimensionless bar parameter; and K is the radius of gyration of the object, in inches. In Section 6.7, turn to Table 6.1, find K for bars, and rewrite Equation 6.1 to read

$$F_{\text{n bar}} = \frac{\pi\left(h/\sqrt{12}\right)\sqrt{E/\rho}}{8}\left(\frac{q_n}{L}\right)^2 \tag{6.2}$$

where h is the height or thickness of the bar, in inches.

The dimensionless bar parameter depends on the end conditions of the bar and on the mode of vibration.[7] Although rational approximations $q_2 \approx 5$, $q_3 \approx 7$, . . . seem justified, the exact values of q_n represent irrational numbers.[8] Therefore, none of the higher mode frequencies of free-free bars are true harmonics. (See Equation 3.13.) Instead, all the modes consist of inharmonic frequencies not found in the harmonic series. The following frequency ratios define the relations between the fundamental frequency and the frequencies of the second, third, and fourth modes:

$$F_2 \propto \left(\frac{q_2}{q_1}\right)^2 \approx 2.757$$

$$F_3 \propto \left(\frac{q_3}{q_1}\right)^2 \approx 5.404$$

$$F_4 \propto \left(\frac{q_4}{q_1}\right)^2 \approx 8.933$$

Let us now analyze the musical intervals associated with these frequency ratios. Since 2.757 is greater than 2, but less than 4, the second mode is higher than an "octave," ratio 2/1 [1200.0 ¢], above the fundamental, but lower than a "double-octave," ratio 4/1 [2400.0 ¢].[9] To determine the identity of F_2 in cents, refer to Equation 9.21;[10] that is, multiply the logarithm of 2.757 to the base 10 by the constant 3986.314. Then, to simplify the result, or to identify this interval within the span of the first "octave," subtract 1200.0 ¢:

$$F_2 = \log_{10} 2.757 \times 3986.314 = 1755.7\ ¢$$
$$1755.7\ ¢ - 1200.0\ ¢ = 555.7\ ¢$$

Therefore, F_2 is approximately one "octave" plus a "flat tritone" above the fundamental. By the same method, confirm that F_3 is approximately a "double-octave" plus a "sharp fourth" above the fundamental:

$$F_3 = \log_{10} 5.404 \times 3986.314 = 2920.8\ ¢$$
$$2920.8\ ¢ - 2400.0\ ¢ = 520.8\ ¢$$

A comparison shows that the second and third modes of free-free bars are almost one "octave," or exactly 1165.1 ¢, apart. In Section 6.14, we will discuss the effect this interval has on the tuning of the second and third modes of bass marimba bars.

6.3

Before we calculate the first three mode frequencies of a uniform rosewood bar, let us examine the phenomenon of dispersion in free-free bars. Recall that in Sections 4.7 and 5.14 we demonstrated dispersion by bending and releasing a bar in the shape of a steel ruler. We concluded from this experiment that as you bend a stiff object into progressively shorter sections, or shorter bending wavelengths (λ_B), and then release it, the speed of c_B increases significantly with each additional section. From this example, we conclude that the bending wave speed is inversely proportional to the bending wavelength:

$$c_B \propto \frac{1}{\lambda_B}$$

As λ_B decreases, c_B increases. This dependence of wave speed on wavelength (or frequency) is the hallmark of dispersion. Philip K. Morse and K. Uno Ingard observe, "A bar is sometimes said to be a *dispersing* medium for waves of bending."[11]

Since rapid increases in the speed of bending waves cause the inharmonic mode frequencies of free-free and clamped-free bars, consider an alternate equation that expresses frequency as a function of bending wave speed and bending wavelength variables:

$$F_n = \frac{c_{B_n}}{\lambda_{B_n}} \tag{6.3}$$

Express c_{B_n} as a subequation with a wavelength[12] or frequency[13] variable:

$$c_{B_n} = \frac{2\pi K\sqrt{E/\rho}}{\lambda_{B_n}} \tag{6.4A}$$

$$c_{B_n} = \sqrt{2\pi F_n K\sqrt{E/\rho}} \tag{6.4B}$$

And express λ_{B_n} as a subequation with a wave speed or frequency variable:

$$\lambda_{B_n} = \frac{2\pi K\sqrt{E/\rho}}{c_{B_n}} \tag{6.5A}$$

$$\lambda_{B_n} = 2\pi\sqrt{\frac{K\sqrt{E/\rho}}{2\pi F_n}} \tag{6.5B}$$

Note, however, that we cannot use Equation 6.3 with Equation 6.5B because the mode frequencies are unknown. Consequently, we will use Equation 6.5C, which does *not* require foreknowledge of F_n:

$$\lambda_{B_n} = \frac{4L}{q_n} \tag{6.5C}$$

Now, consider the physical dimensions and material properties of a large, high-quality Honduras rosewood bass marimba bar, where b is the width of the bar:

$h = 1.250$ in. ($1\frac{1}{4}$ in.)
$b = 4.250$ in. ($4\frac{1}{4}$ in.)
$L = 40.4375$ in. ($40\frac{7}{16}$ in.)
$K = h/\sqrt{12} = 0.360844$ in.
$E = 3{,}200{,}000$ psi
$\rho = 0.00009894$ mica/in^3

To use Equation 6.3, first substitute Equation 6.5C into Equation 6.4A and simplify:

$$c_{B_n} = \frac{2\pi K\sqrt{E/\rho}}{\lambda_{B_n}} = \frac{2\pi K\sqrt{E/\rho}}{\frac{4L}{q_n}} = \frac{\not{2}\pi K\sqrt{E/\rho}}{\frac{\not{4}^2 L}{q_n}} = \frac{\pi K\sqrt{E/\rho}}{2L}q_n \tag{6.6}$$

Next, substitute the required bar values and the approximations of q_n into Equation 6.6 and calculate the bending wave speeds for the first three modes of vibration:

$$c_{B_1} = \frac{\pi\,(h/\sqrt{12})\sqrt{E/\rho}}{2L}q_1 = 7590.75 \text{ in/s}$$

$$c_{B_2} = \frac{\pi\,(h/\sqrt{12})\sqrt{E/\rho}}{2L}q_2 = 12{,}604.20 \text{ in/s}$$

$$c_{B_3} = \frac{\pi\,(h/\sqrt{12})\sqrt{E/\rho}}{2L}q_3 = 17{,}645.87 \text{ in/s}$$

Next, substitute the required values into Equation 6.5C and calculate the bending wavelengths for the first three modes of vibration:

$$\lambda_{B_1} = \frac{4L}{q_1} = 53.72 \text{ in}$$

$$\lambda_{B_2} = \frac{4L}{q_2} = 32.35 \text{ in}$$

$$\lambda_{B_3} = \frac{4L}{q_3} = 23.11 \text{ in}$$

Finally, substitute $c_{B_{1-3}}$ and $\lambda_{B_{1-3}}$ into Equation 6.3 and calculate the frequencies of the first three modes:

$$F_1 = \frac{7590.75 \text{ in/s}}{53.72 \text{ in}} = 141.30 \text{ cps}$$

$$F_2 = \frac{12{,}604.20 \text{ in/s}}{32.35 \text{ in}} = 389.62 \text{ cps}$$

$$F_3 = \frac{17{,}645.87 \text{ in/s}}{23.11 \text{ in}} = 763.56 \text{ cps}$$

Except for unavoidable decimal-rounding discrepancies, Equation 6.2 gives identical results.

~ 6.4 ~

An analysis of the preceding calculations shows that we twice divided Equation 6.4A by Equation 6.5C. The first division yielded Equation 6.6, and the second division gave solutions to Equation 6.3. We may simplify these calculations and express two consecutive divisions of a given constant x by a given variable y as a single division by the variable squared:

$$\frac{\frac{x}{y}}{y} = \frac{x}{y} \div \frac{y}{1} = \frac{x}{y} \times \frac{1}{y} = \frac{x}{y^2}$$

Therefore, if we place $(\lambda_{B_n})^2$ directly into the denominator of Equation 6.4A, note that after further simplification, the final equation is identical to Equation 6.1:

$$F_{\text{n free-free}} = \frac{2\pi K\sqrt{E/\rho}}{(\lambda_{B_n})^2} = \frac{2\pi K\sqrt{E/\rho}}{\left(\frac{4L}{q_n}\right)^2} = \frac{\cancel{2}\pi K\sqrt{E/\rho}}{\frac{\cancel{16}^{\,8} L^2}{q_n^{\,2}}} = \frac{\pi K\sqrt{E/\rho}}{8}\left(\frac{q_n}{L}\right)^2$$

Equation 6.1 is an algebraically simplified equation and, therefore, does not convey any direct information about the physical phenomena of increasing bending wave speeds and decreasing bending wavelengths. However, there are two important variables in this equation that indicate the presence of dispersion in free-free bars: $q_n^{\,2}$ and L^2. Before we discuss the significance of these two variables, let us first review some relevant background information discussed in Chapters 3 and 4.

In all musical instruments, the reflection and superposition of traveling waves causes the formation of sound-producing standing waves.[14] Traveling waves and standing waves are uniquely different because only standing waves have nodes and antinodes. In vibrating systems, nodes indicate points of minimum motion, and antinodes, points of maximum motion.[15] Vibrating solids with nodes and antinodes bend and subdivide into a series of regularly spaced sections called loops.[16] A loop consists of two nodes (N) and one antinode (A).[17] In the frequency equations of strings[18] and bars, the mode number [(n) for strings, and (n) for bars] indicates the loop count of a given mode. For the fundamental or the first mode frequency, strings and bars produce one loop; and for the second, third, and fourth mode frequencies, they produce two, three, and four loops, respectively. Note, however, that in Equation 6.1 for bars, the mode number appears only as a subscript, and not as a variable. However, as an alternative, consider Equation 6.7, which includes a mode number variable that gives close mode frequency approximations for free-free bars:

$$F_{\text{n free-free}} \approx \frac{\pi K\sqrt{E/\rho}}{8}\left(\frac{2n+1}{L}\right)^2 \quad \{n = 1, 2, 3, 4, \ldots\} \tag{6.7}$$

A comparison of various frequency equations demonstrates that the values of n and L convey important information about the dispersive nature of a vibrating system. The following examples show that for flexible strings,

$$F_n \propto n \quad \{n = 1, 2, 3, \ldots\} \qquad \text{(Eq. 3.13)}$$

$$F_n \propto \frac{1}{L}$$

for air columns open at both ends (organ pipes and flutes),

$$F_n \propto n \quad \{n = 1, 2, 3, \ldots\} \qquad \text{(Eq. 7.23)}$$

$$F_n \propto \frac{1}{L_o}$$

and for air columns closed at one end (organ pipes and marimba resonators),

$$F_n \propto (2n - 1) \quad \{n = 1, 2, 3, \ldots\} \qquad \text{(Eq. 7.28)}$$

$$F_n \propto \frac{1}{L_c}$$

Therefore, when $F_n \propto$ n and $F_n \propto 1/L$, an equation indicates that dispersion is *not* a factor. In contrast, the following examples show that for stiff strings,

$$\bar{F}_n \propto (n^2 - 1) \quad \{n = 1, 2, 3, \ldots\} \qquad \text{(Eq. 4.4)}$$

$$J \propto \frac{1}{L^2} \qquad \text{(Eq. 4.6)}$$

for free-free bars,

$$F_n \propto (2n + 1)^2 \quad \{n = 1, 2, 3, \ldots\} \qquad \text{(Eq. 6.7)}$$

$$F_n \propto \frac{1}{L^2} \qquad \text{(Eq. 6.1)}$$

and for clamped-free bars (see Section 6.17),

$$F_n \propto (2n - 1)^2 \quad \{n = 1, 2, 3, \ldots\} \qquad \text{(Eq. 6.16)}$$

$$F_n \propto \frac{1}{L^2} \qquad \text{(Eq. 6.15)}$$

Therefore, when $F_n \propto n^2$ and $F_n \propto 1/L^2$, an equation informs us that dispersion *is* a factor. In the former three cases, the vibrating systems do not have a bending stiffness restoring force, and in the latter three cases, they do have a bending stiffness restoring force. The absence or presence of bending stiffness has important consequences on the musical quality of a sound-producing medium.

Equations 6.7 and 6.16 give approximate solutions, because for free-free and clamped-free bars, mode frequencies that are integer multiples of a fundamental frequency do not exist. Solutions to the wave equation of free-free and clamped-free bars require hyperbolic and trigonometric functions that produce noninteger (irrational) numbers.[19] In Equations 6.1 and 6.15, the dimensionless bar parameter represents such numbers. Although q_{n} functions like a mode number, we cannot define it as such because it never has the value of a positive integer.

Notice that in Equations 6.1 and 6.15, q_{n} and L appear as the ratio

$$\left(\frac{q_{\mathrm{n}}}{L}\right)^2$$

This notation indicates that q_{n} has its origin in wavelength calculations. For example, consider the similarity between Equation 3.10 for the transverse wavelengths of flexible strings, and Equation 6.5C for the bending wavelengths of free-free bars. There is one critical difference between these two equations. In the former equation, L/n gives the single loop length of a given string mode, but in the latter equation, L/q_{n} does not give the single loop length of a given bar mode. Again, this difference is due to the fact that q_{n} is not a true mode number.

~ 6.5 ~

We turn now to the standing wave patterns of free-free bars.[20] Figure 6.1 shows the first three mode shapes of a free-free bar. Note that free-free bars like flexible strings bend and subdivide into an integer number of equidistant sections called loops. (See Section 3.5.) However, unlike the fixed ends of strings, the two free ends of bars are not nodes. On the contrary, free-free and clamped-free bars are unique because they exhibit two different kinds of antinodes, or points of great motion and displacement. In this text, we call the inner antinodes located between any two consecutive nodes *bending antinodes* (BA) because they mark the locations of maximum bending in the bar. And we call the outer antinodes located at the free ends *displacement antinodes* (DA) because they mark the locations of maximum displacement in the bar. Figures 6.1 and 6.12 show that for all modes the displacement antinodes have a greater amplitude of vibration than the bending antinodes.

As a bar continues to bend and subdivide into an increasingly greater number of shorter loops and the curvature of the bar increases, the number of bending antinodes increases as well. Pick up a

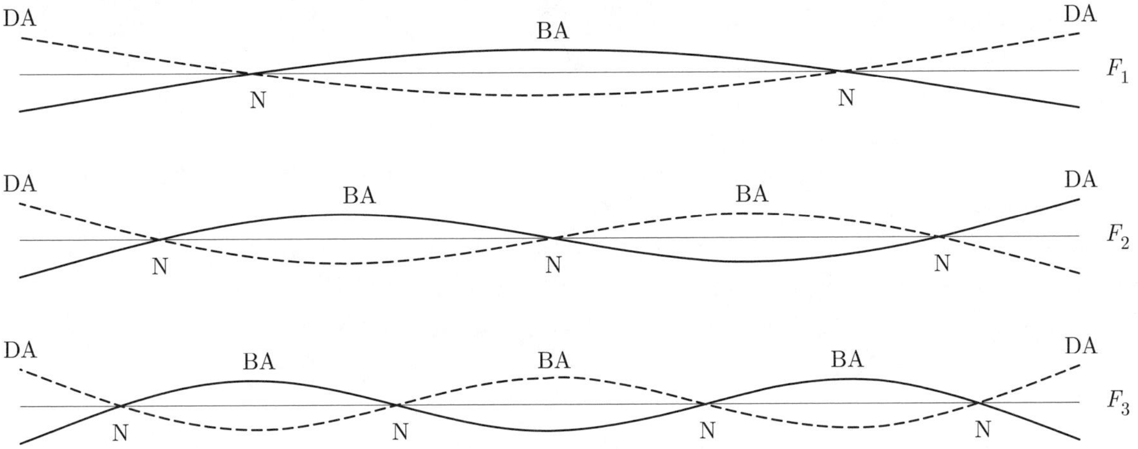

Figure 6.1 The first three modes of vibration of a free-free bar, rod, or tube. Bending antinodes (BA), or points of maximum bending, are located halfway between two consecutive nodes (N), or points of minimum displacement. Displacement antinodes (DA), or points of maximum displacement, are located at the free ends of the bar.

steel ruler, bend it in the shape of a single loop, then two loops, then three loops, etc. Notice that the magnitude of the restoring force that returns the ruler to its straight equilibrium position increases significantly with each additional section. We conclude, therefore, that for vibrating bars an increase in the loop count, or an increase in bending antinodes, produces an increase in restoring force.

6.6

The restoring force that returns a vibrating bar to its equilibrium position consists of two forces: a bending moment (M) that induces rotation about a given point in the bar, and a shear force (V) that induces translation in a direction perpendicular to the bar's horizontal axis.[21] That is, M causes bending motion in a circular direction, and V causes linear motion in a vertical direction.[22] In vibrating bars, these two forces act as a single restoring force.[23] Note, however, that M and V do not appear as variables in frequency Equations 6.1 and 6.15. The reason for this omission is that both forces vary with *space* (or a given location in the bar) and *time* (or a given instant in the period of vibration). Therefore, it is not possible to quantify M and V for use in frequency equations. Since both forces are directly proportional to the bending stiffness (B) of a bar, we may interpret an increase or decrease in B as an increase or decrease in M and V. (See Sections 6.7–6.8.)

The partial differential equation that describes the bending moment states

$$M = -ESK^2 \frac{\partial^2 y}{\partial x^2} \tag{6.8}$$

The first term ESK^2 refers to the elastic property or the bending stiffness of a bar. (See Section 6.7.) It confirms that M is directly proportional to Young's modulus of elasticity of the bar material, to the cross-sectional surface area (S) of the bar, and to the bar's radius of gyration squared. Since $S \propto h$ and $K^2 \propto h^2$ (see Table 6.1), Equation 6.8 is crucial to tuners of bar percussion instruments because it shows that $M \propto h^3$. Consequently, when a tuner decreases h, it causes a decrease in M and, therefore, a reduction in the bar's total restoring force.

The second term $\partial^2 y/\partial x^2$ refers to the curvature and to the length of a bar.[24] In the symbolic language of calculus, this term describes four relations. (1) M is directly proportional to a bar's curvature. As a bar subdivides into shorter wavelengths and produces higher mode frequencies, the curvature of the bar increases, and so M increases as well. (2) M is directly proportional to deflection (y). In the standard x-y coordinate system, the horizontal x-axis coincides with the unbent equilibrium position of the bar, and the vertical y-axis coincides with the direction of bending. Therefore, when a bar bends in a direction perpendicular to its equilibrium position, as the deflection increases, the bending moment increases as well. (3) M and y are functions of x. Mathematicians write $M(x)$ and $y(x)$ to indicate that the bending moment and the deflection, respectively, are not constant but vary along the length of the bar in the x direction; that is, $M(x)$ and $y(x)$ increase and decrease with distance from either end of the bar. (4) A solution to Equation 6.8 for the maximum bending moment in a bar shows that the x^2 term in the denominator represents L^2. Therefore, M_{max} is inversely proportional to the bar's length squared:

$$M_{\text{max}} \propto \frac{1}{L^2}$$

As L^2 decreases, M_{max} increases.

In the context of bar tuning practice, we may summarize the significance of the curvature term by emphasizing two points. (1) $M(x)$ varies in magnitude along the length of a vibrating bar, and (2) because of these variations, there are precise places in a vibrating bar where $M(x)$ has an especially high value. If a tuner knows where M is high and decreases h at such a location, then the consequent reduction in M will result in a very efficient lowering of F_n.

The partial differential equation that describes the shear force states

$$V \equiv -\frac{\partial M}{\partial x} = ESK^2 \frac{\partial^3 y}{\partial x^3} \tag{6.9}$$

The first expression reads, "The shear force is by definition equal to the slope of the bending moment with respect to x." In the specialized language of calculus, this statement indicates that V and M are interdependent: because one force defines the other, one force does not exist without the other force. This means that the magnitude of the bending moment determines the magnitude of the shear force and *vice versa*. Moreover, since $V \propto M \propto h^3$, as h decreases, the bending moment decreases, the shear force decreases and, therefore, the total restoring force of the bar decreases. Finally, the second equality in Equation 6.9 indicates the same proportionalities with respect to $V(x)$ already discussed in the context of $M(x)$, with the exception that the maximum shear force is inversely proportional to the bar's length cubed:

$$V_{max} \propto \frac{1}{L^3}$$

As L^3 decreases, V_{max} increases.

For a graphic representation of $y(x)$, $M(x)$, and $V(x)$, refer to Figure 6.2. It shows the deflection and the spatial distribution of the bending moment and the shear force of a uniform free-free bar in the fundamental mode of vibration.[25] When such a bar bends in the shape of the first mode, M_{max} occurs in the center of the bar, or at the location of the bending antinode. Here the bar makes the greatest bending deflection in the direction of the y-axis. V_{max} occurs to the left and right of the bar's center, or at two locations where the slope of the $M(x)$ curve is the greatest. Notice that the slope of the $M(x)$ curve, or the angle that the $M(x)$ curve makes with the x-axis, is greatest approximately halfway between the left end and the center of the curve, and halfway between the

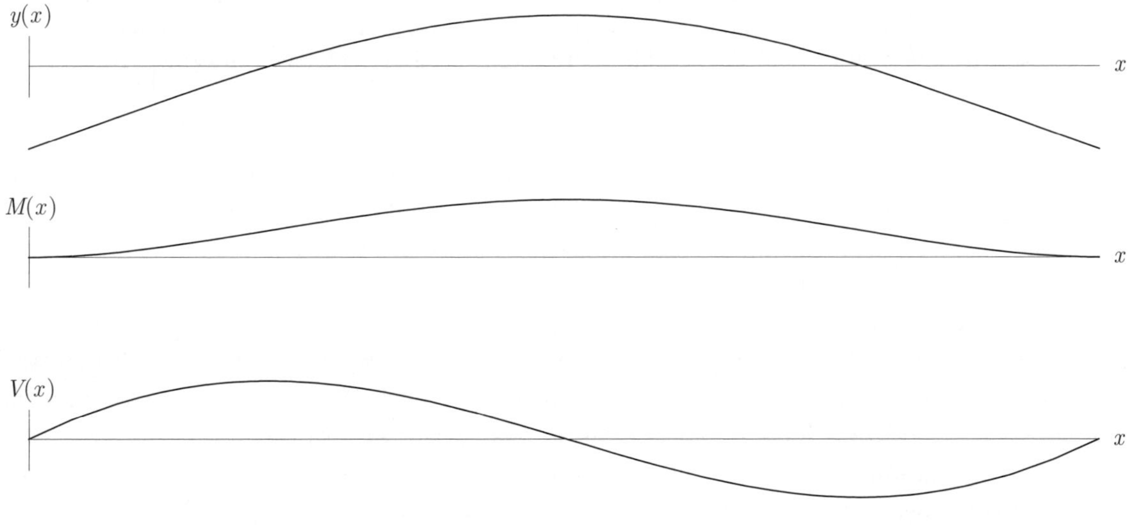

Figure 6.2 The deflection, bending moment, and shear force of a uniform free-free bar in the fundamental mode of vibration. In the center of the bar and at the location of a bending antinode, $M(x)$ has a maximum value, and $V(x) = 0$. At the extreme ends of the bar, $M(x) = 0$ and $V(x) = 0$ because here the bar does not bend and it does not shear.

right end and the center of the curve. In contrast, at the very center of the curve where $M(x)$ has the maximum value, the slope of the $M(x)$ curve is zero (or nonexistent) because at that point the angular direction of the curve is parallel to the x-axis. (Recall from geometry that parallel lines do not form angles.) This marks the location where the $V(x)$ curve crosses the x-axis because at that point $V(x) = 0$. We conclude, therefore, that at all bending antinodes, $M(x)$ has a maximum value, and $V(x) = 0$. Finally, at the extreme ends, $M(x) = 0$ and $V(x) = 0$ because for a free-free bar the ends are not constrained, which means that the ends do not bend, and they do not shear.

David R. Canright contributed Figure 6.3, which shows the longitudinal cross-section of a bent free-free bar in the fundamental mode of vibration, and the effects of the M and V restoring forces on the geometry of the bar elements. In the center of the bar, curved arrows indicate that M has a maximum value in bending the bar elements in a circular direction; and at the nodes of the bar, straight arrows indicate that V has a maximum value in shearing the bar elements in a vertical direction.

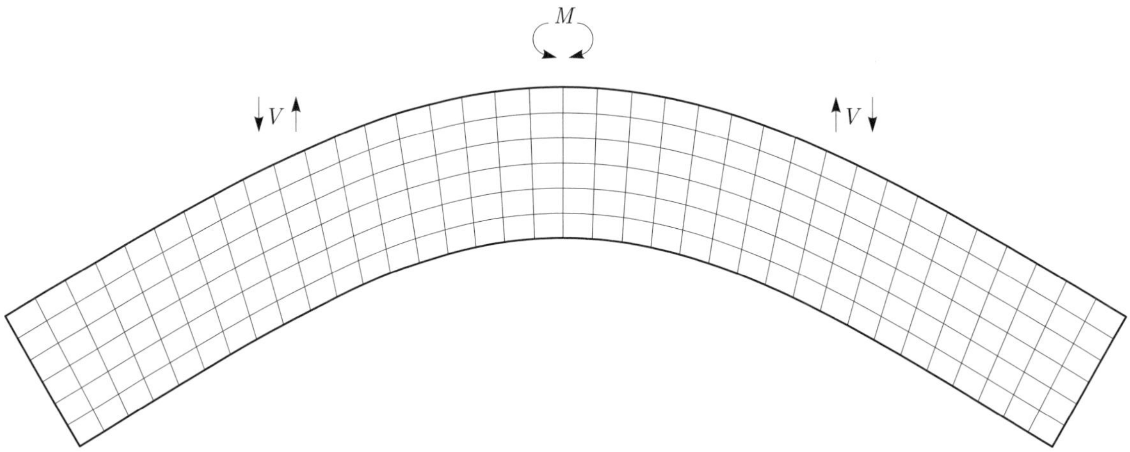

Figure 6.3 The longitudinal cross-section of a bent bar that shows the effects of M and V on the geometry of bar elements. In the center, or at the antinode, M has a maximum value in bending bar elements in a circular direction; and at the nodes, V has a maximum value in shearing bar elements in a vertical direction. For visual clarity, this figure shows a greatly enhanced shearing effect.

Finally, turn to Figure 6.4 for a dynamic representation of changes in M and V as a free-free bar oscillates through one complete cycle. Figure 1.1 illustrates similar changes in the restoring force (f) and particle velocity (u) of a flexible cord. Although Figure 6.4 does not include particle velocity arrows, relative changes in u for bars are exactly the same. However, the M and V restoring force in bars is significantly different. Figure 6.4 represents M with two curved arrows to indicate that M tends to bend and unbend the bar in a circular direction. Figure 6.4 represents V with two straight arrows to indicate that V tends to shear and unshear the bar in a vertical direction. (a) Immediately after we deliver a percussive force that displaces the bar in an upward direction, M and V are at a maximum. At this instant, M acts to unbend the bar and make it straight. At the same instant, V acts to shear the inner portion of the bar (between the two nodes) in an upward direction, and the two outer portions of the bar (between the nodes and the ends) in a downward direction. (b) As the bar moves toward the equilibrium position, its particle velocity increases while M and V — two aspects of a single restoring force — decrease. (c) Upon reaching the equilibrium position, the bar has maximum velocity for the instant that $M = 0$, $V = 0$, and therefore the bar's acceleration $= 0$.

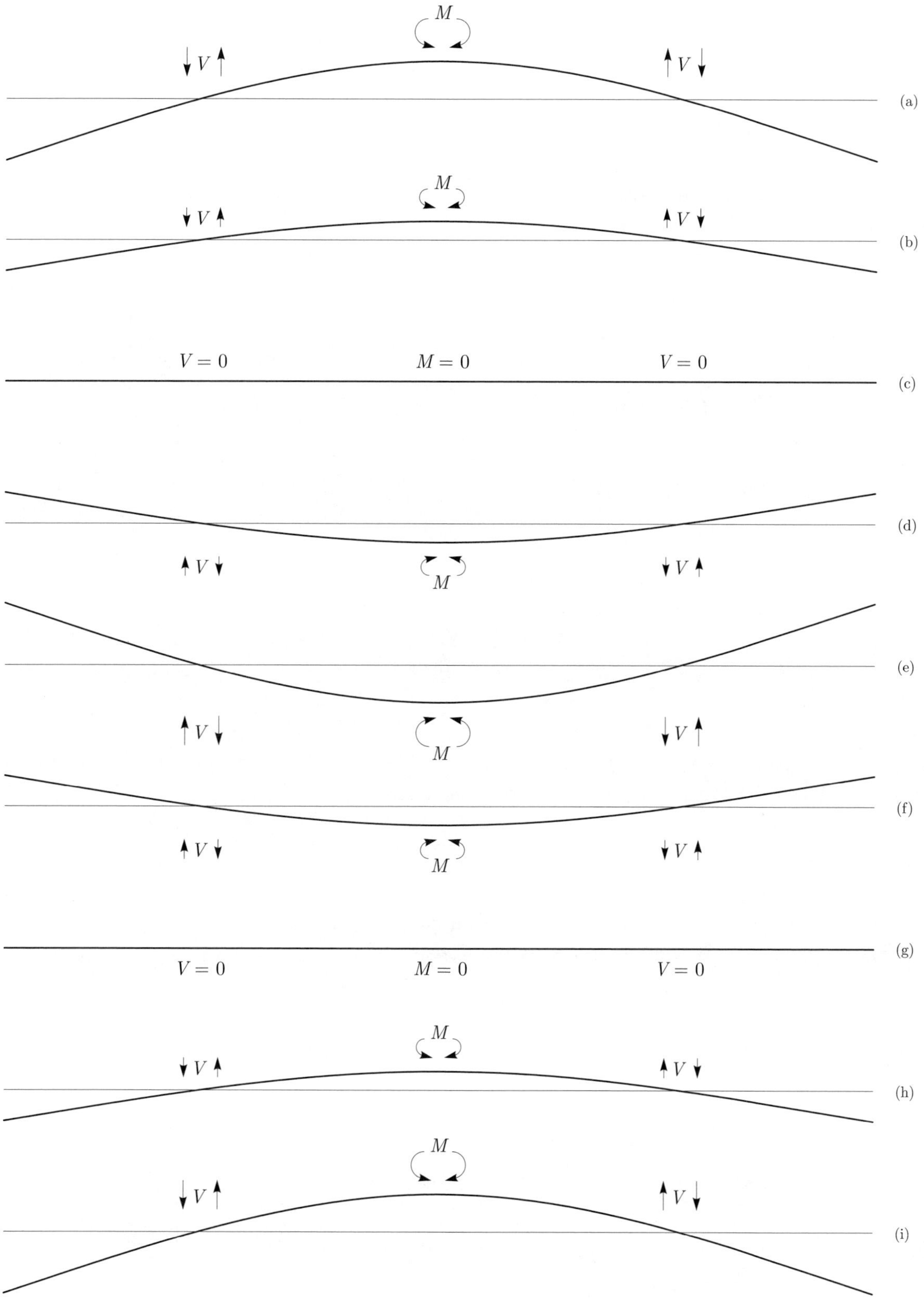

Figure 6.4 Bending moment (M) and shear force (V) of a free-free bar vibrating in the first mode of vibration. The lengths of the arrows indicate the relative magnitudes of the forces, and the direction of the arrows indicate the tendencies of the forces. M and V act as a single restoring force that returns the bar to its equilibrium position.

(See Section 1.1.) Now, according to Newton's first law, the bar continues to move past this position because the bar's mass will not stop moving, or change direction, unless a force acts to cause such changes. (d) Once through the equilibrium position, M and V reverse direction. Consequently, the velocity decreases because the restoring force is working in the opposite direction of the bar's motion. (e) At a critical moment when M and V are again at a maximum, the bar comes to rest, and for that instant, the velocity is zero. (f) Immediately after this moment, the bar reverses direction and returns to the equilibrium position. Once again, the bar's velocity increases while the restoring force decreases. (g) After the bar passes through the equilibrium position, (h) the restoring force again reverses direction, and the bar's velocity decreases. (i) When the restoring force is at a maximum, the bar comes to rest. This position marks the beginning of the next cycle.

~ 6.7 ~

With Equations 6.8 and 6.9 in mind, consider the following alternate frequency equation for a slender, uniform, isotropic bar, rod, or tube free at both ends:

$$F_{\text{n free-free}} = \frac{\pi}{8}\sqrt{\frac{B}{M/u.l.}}\left(\frac{q_{\text{n}}}{L}\right)^2 \tag{6.10}$$

where B is the bending stiffness (the elastic property) of the object, in lbf·in^2; $M/u.l.$ is the mass per unit length (the inertial property) of the object, in mica/in. Here

$$B = EI$$

$$I = SK^2$$

where I is the area moment of inertia of the object, in inches to the fourth power; and S is the cross-sectional surface area of the object, in square inches. Also,

$$M/u.l. = \rho S$$

Table 6.1 lists S, K, K^2, and I for bars, rods, and tubes. Here D is the outside diameter of a rod or tube, and d is the inside diameter of a tube; all dimensions in inches.

In many physics texts the bending stiffness appears as

$$B = ESK^2 \tag{6.11}$$

Refer to Table 6.1, find S and K^2 for bars, and make the required substitutions:

$$B_{\text{bar}} = E(bh)(h^2/12) = \frac{Ebh^3}{12} \tag{6.11A}$$

The following transformations show that the variable h in Equation 6.2 has its origin in B:

$$\sqrt{\frac{B}{M/u.l.}} = \sqrt{\frac{EI}{\rho S}} = \sqrt{\frac{ESK^2}{\rho S}} = \sqrt{\frac{\dfrac{E\cancel{b}\cancel{h}h^2}{12}}{\rho\cancel{b}\cancel{h}}} = \sqrt{\frac{\dfrac{Eh^2}{12}}{\rho}} = \frac{h}{\sqrt{12}}\sqrt{\frac{E}{\rho}} \tag{6.12}$$

Substitute the last transformation into Equation 6.10 and confirm that this equation is identical to Equation 6.2. Therefore, both equations state that F_{n} is directly proportional to h:

$$F_{\text{n}} \propto h$$

As the height of a bar decreases, the mode frequencies decrease as well and *vice versa*. Consequently, if you strike two bars of the same material and length, one bar half as thick as the other, the thin bar sounds an "octave" *lower* than the thick bar. It may seem that the thick bar with twice the mass should vibrate more slowly and sound lower. Indeed, if we had two identical bars and loaded one with clay or some other malleable substance, the bar with the extra mass would sound lower. However, when a larger mass is an integral part of the bar's molecular structure, it not only makes the bar more massive, but it also gives the bar greater bending stiffness. Consequently, the mode frequencies of thick bars always sound higher than thin bars.

Table 6.1

PROPERTIES OF PLANE SECTIONS

Section	Surface Area S	Radius of Gyration K	K^2	Area Moment of Inertia $I = SK^2$
Bar	bh	$\frac{h}{\sqrt{12}}$	$\frac{h^2}{12}$	$\frac{bh^3}{12}$
Rod	$\frac{\pi D^2}{4}$	$\frac{D}{4}$	$\frac{D^2}{16}$	$\frac{\pi D^4}{64}$
Tube	$\frac{\pi(D^2 - d^2)}{4}$	$\frac{\sqrt{D^2 + d^2}}{4}$	$\frac{D^2 + d^2}{16}$	$\frac{\pi(D^4 - d^4)}{64}$

~ 6.8 ~

Finally, we may also calculate $c_{\mathrm{B_n}}$ with a combination of bending stiffness and bending wavelength variables, or bending stiffness and mode frequency variables:[26]

$$c_{\mathrm{B_n}} = \frac{2\pi\sqrt{\frac{B}{M/u.l.}}}{\lambda_{\mathrm{B_n}}} \tag{6.13A}$$

$$c_{\mathrm{B_n}} = \sqrt[4]{\frac{B}{M/u.l.}}\sqrt{2\pi F_{\mathrm{n}}} \tag{6.13B}$$

In summary, note the direct proportionalities in Equations 6.8, 6.11, 6.11A,

$$M \propto B \propto h^3$$

in Equation 6.13A (via Equation 6.12),

$$c_{\mathrm{B_n}} \propto h$$

and again in Equations 6.2 and 6.10:

$$F_n \propto h$$

We conclude, therefore, that the common dependence of these variables on h shows that a reduction in the height of a bar has four simultaneous consequences. If a tuner makes a *uniform reduction* in h along the entire length of a bar, such an action decreases (1) the bending moment, (2) the bending stiffness, (3) the bending wave speeds, and therefore, (4) the mode frequencies of the bar. However, if a tuner makes *local reductions* in h wherever M_{max} occurs, then such actions will cause large decreases in the restoring force of some modes, and small decreases in other modes. That is, by carefully decreasing h at the *bending antinodes* of free-free bars, a tuner is able to adjust and control the restoring force for a select group of mode frequencies. Since in all vibrating systems a reduction in restoring force causes a reduction in mode frequencies, the entire mode tuning process consists of making local reductions in h, which in turn produce decreases in F_n.

Part II

FREE-FREE BAR TUNING TECHNIQUES

6.9

Marimba, xylophone, and vibraphone builders tune their instruments by sawing and sanding material from the undersides of bars. A tuner removes large amounts of material from a bar's central area, and (only when necessary) smaller amounts from the areas near the ends. These two techniques produce opposite effects: the former removal causes a decrease in F_1, while the latter removal causes an increase in F_1. Consider the two bars in Figure 6.5. Both bars consist of the same material and have the same physical dimensions. Bar (a) has an incision in the center, and bar (b) has an identical incision near the end. As a result of removing identical amounts of mass, the frequency of bar (a) decreases, while the frequency of bar (b) increases.

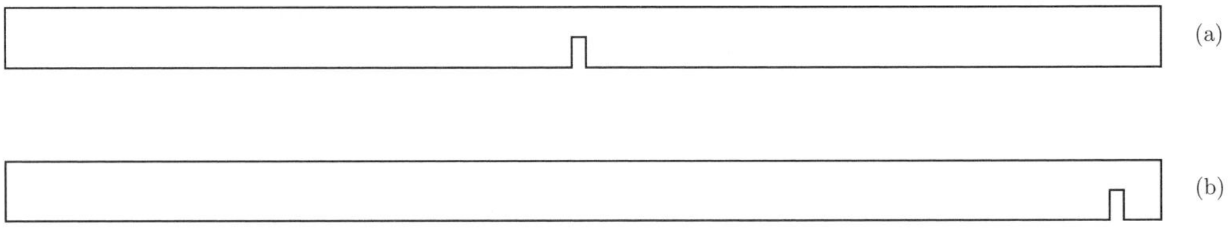

Figure 6.5 Two free-free bars made of the same material and with the same dimensions. (a) An incision in the center of the first bar causes a decrease in F_1. (b) An identical incision near the end of the second bar causes an increase in F_1.

To understand why these two incisions have opposite effects, consider Figure 6.6, which shows the mode shape of a slender bar as it bends in the fundamental mode of vibration. Lines in the center mark the area of one bending antinode, and lines at the ends mark the areas near two displacement antinodes. A removal of material from the central area causes a significant reduction in restoring force, which in turn produces a significant decrease in the fundamental frequency. Similar cuts outside this area also decrease F_1, but this effect gradually diminishes as one makes incisions farther away from the bending area. Near the displacement antinodes, the bending moment and

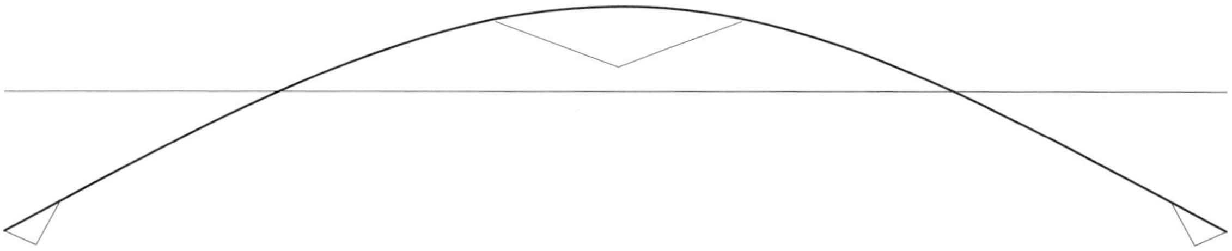

Figure 6.6 Areas of a bent free-free bar that indicate a bending antinode in the center and two displacement antinodes near the ends. A removal of material from the center causes a relatively large reduction in restoring force and a small decrease in mass. Conversely, a removal of material from the ends causes a relatively large reduction in mass and a small decrease in restoring force.

the shear force are very small. Here an identical incision causes an insignificant reduction in restoring force. However, such an incision does produce a noticeable decrease in the bar's mass. Because of less mass (or less inertia), the relatively straight ends of the bar vibrate more rapidly, and the fundamental frequency increases. Note that tuners employ the latter technique sparingly and only to *fine-tune* flat sounding bars.[27] Since a bar bends over its entire length, its response to changes in the restoring force is far more pronounced than to changes in mass. Moreover, a powerful and sustained tone requires great flexibility in the center of the bar and a large mass at the ends. A substantial removal of mass from the ends jeopardizes the production of a sustained musical tone.

6.10

The practice of tuning bars by reducing the restoring force at the bending antinodes is equally effective on the frequencies of the higher modes. To tune these modes we must know the locations of their respective antinodes. Table 6.2 gives the positions of the nodes and antinodes of bars, rods, and tubes free at both ends for the first five modes of vibration. A comparison of Figure 6.1 and Table 6.2 shows an alternating pattern of antinodes at $0.500L$ for all odd-numbered modes, and nodes for all even-numbered modes. This overlapping pattern and the proximity of antinodes throughout the length of a bar means that the removal of material affects numerous modes simultaneously. Isolated changes in mode frequency are therefore not possible. However, since the frequencies of F_4, F_5, F_6, . . . in most bars are extremely high and barely audible, we do not include these modes in the tuning process.

In Section 6.14, we will discuss techniques for tuning the first three modes of bass marimba bars in the G_1–G_3 (49.0–196.0 cps) range. (See Appendix A.) And in Section 6.15, we will discuss similar techniques for the first two modes of treble marimba bars in the G_3–G_5 (196.0–784.0 cps) range. Figure 6.7 illustrates sequential changes in a bass bar as it progresses through the tuning process. Figure 6.7(a) shows the bar with five straight vertical lines that mark the antinode locations of the first three modes, and with three curved lines used to guide the bar through a band saw; (b) shows the bar after cutting three shallow arches on a band saw; and (c) shows the final profile of the same bar after completing the sanding and tuning process. The last figure also shows the bar supported on two pieces of flexible foam that allow the bar to vibrate for the longest possible time.

Figure 6.8 illustrates the reasons for the triple-arch design of a bass marimba bar with three tuned modes. In this figure, the numbers above the horizontal line represent the primary modes affected at the indicated locations, and the numbers below represent the secondary modes also affected. For example, Modes 1 and 3 have an antinode at $0.500L$. This means that a local reduction in the center of the bar will effect both F_1 and F_3. However, recall from Section 6.6 that $M \propto y$. Since the deflection y in the bar's center is much greater for Mode 1 than Mode 3, a local reduction

Table 6.2

NODES AND ANTINODES OF FREE-FREE
BARS, RODS, AND TUBES

First Five Modes of Vibration

Mode 1	Mode 2	Mode 3	Mode 4	Mode 5
0.224 N	0.132 N	0.094 N	0.073 N	0.060 N
0.500 A	0.308 A	0.220 A	0.171 A	0.140 A
0.776 N	0.500 N	0.356 N	0.277 N	0.226 N
	0.692 A	0.500 A	0.389 A	0.318 A
	0.868 N	0.644 N	0.500 N	0.409 N
		0.780 A	0.611 A	0.500 A
		0.906 N	0.723 N	0.591 N
			0.829 A	0.682 A
			0.927 N	0.774 N
				0.860 A
				0.940 N

has a greater effect on decreasing the restoring force of Mode 1 than Mode 3.[28] Therefore, a reduction in h at this antinode location causes a large decrease in F_1, and a small decrease in F_3.

A similar situation exists for Modes 2 and 1 at $0.308L$ and $0.692L$. Because these locations are not too close to the center, and in line with the antinodes of the second mode, a removal of material produces a large decrease in F_2 and a small decrease in F_1. (The effect on F_3 is very small.) The function of the peaks at these two locations is to keep the bar sufficiently stiff. Without these peaks, F_2 would decrease too rapidly and not produce the desired frequency at the end of the tuning process. (See Section 6.14.)

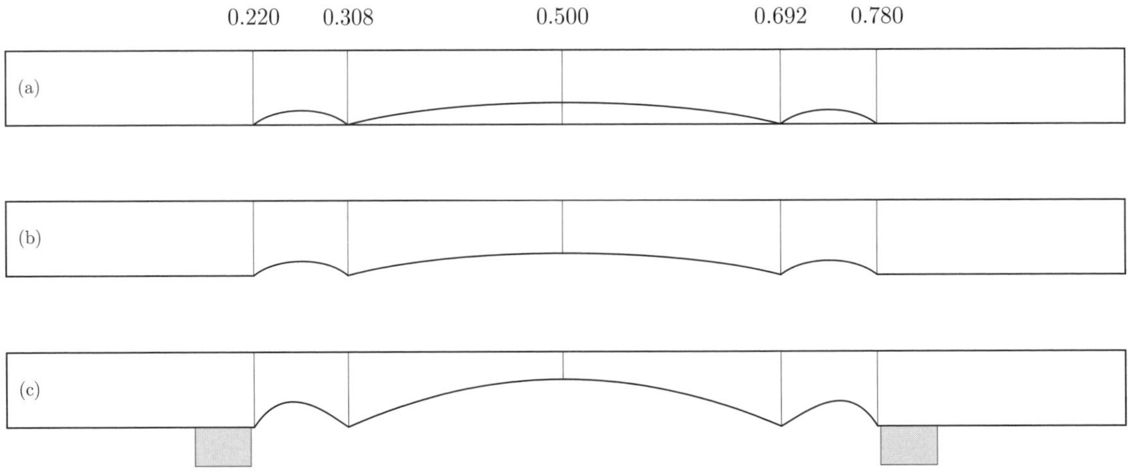

Figure 6.7 A bass marimba bar as it progresses through the tuning process. (a) The bar with antinode locations for the first three modes of vibration, and with guidelines for cutting shallow arches. (b) The bar after cutting out the arched sections on a band saw. (c) The bar after the sanding and tuning process is finished. Two pieces of flexible foam support the bar for a sustained musical tone.

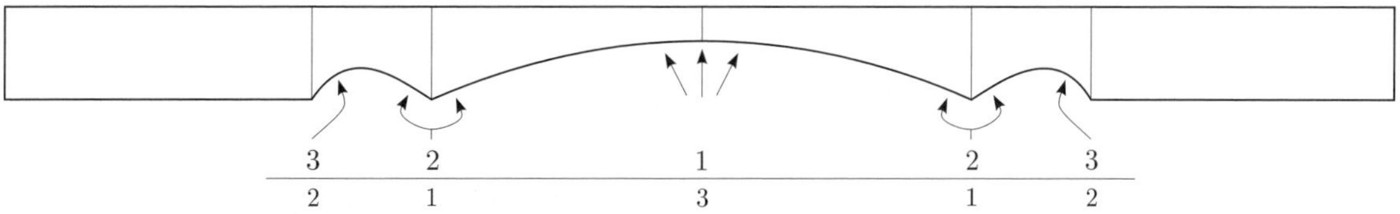

Figure 6.8 Primary and secondary tuning locations for the first three modes of a bass marimba bar. Numbers above the horizontal line represent primary modes, and numbers below represent secondary modes. One cannot change the tuning of a primary mode without simultaneously affecting the tuning of a secondary mode.

Finally, consider the following spatial conflict between bar mounting and mode tuning requirements. The best place for mounting bars, rods, and tubes is at the *nodes* of the first mode of vibration. Since $0.224L$ and $0.776L$ mark the node locations of F_1, and $0.220L$ and $0.780L$ mark the outer antinode locations of F_3, there exists an unavoidable difficulty between tuning and mounting techniques. To effectively tune F_3 without encroaching on the mounting areas, and without sanding too close to the Mode 2 antinodes, one must angle the sander into the outside corners of the outer arches. This explains the asymmetrical appearance of the outer arches.

6.11

Before we consider mode tuning in full detail, let us analyze the frequency calculations of the rosewood bar mentioned in Section 6.3. Note the following differences between theoretical and actual frequencies:

Theoretical Frequencies	Actual Frequencies
$F_1 = 141.30$ cps = C♯$_3$ +34 ¢	$F_1 = 141.01$ cps = C♯$_3$ +30 ¢
$F_2 = 389.62$ cps = G$_4$ −11 ¢	$F_2 = 383.05$ cps = G$_4$ −40 ¢
$F_3 = 763.56$ cps = G$_5$ −46 ¢	$F_3 = 729.38$ cps = F♯$_5$ −25 ¢

Equation 6.2 fairly accurately predicts the frequencies of the first three modes provided that the bar has a slender shape; that is, the bar must be much longer than it is thick. For steel, aluminum, and rosewood bars that are ¼ in. thick and 10–12 in. long, tests show that Mode 2 is typically 2–10 cents flat, and Mode 3, 10–20 cents flat. For bass marimba rosewood bars 1 in. thick and 20–40 in. long, Mode 2 is typically 20–50 cents flat, and Mode 3, 50–100 cents flat. For treble marimba rosewood bars ¾ in. thick and 8–15 in. long, Mode 2 is typically 100–200 cents flat. As the length-to-thickness ratio decreases and bars become less slender, rotary inertia and shear deformation significantly lower the mode frequencies of bars from the predicted frequencies.[29] However, these effects do not alter the basic principles of bar tuning. Whether a bar is thin or thick, tune the modes to the exact proposed frequencies by removing material at the antinode locations.

6.12

In the G$_1$–A$_3$ frequency range, F_2 and F_3 of bars fall well within the span of human hearing. More important, these two modes greatly influence our pitch perception of the fundamental frequency. For example, if we tune F_2 to a "double-octave" plus 25 ¢ above a tuned F_1, then the fundamental will have a tendency to sound sharp even if it is exactly in tune. In this context, the subject of pitch perception should not be confused with the subject of timbre. The former is about tuning, and the latter, about tone color or quality of sound. (See Sections 5.19–5.20.) Since tuners of bar percussion instruments adjust the higher modes to a great variety of frequencies, the art of mode tuning is wide open to interpretation. In short, there are no hard rules that govern the tuning of bars.

Consider, however, the advantages of a tuning that designates Mode 2 as an exact "double-octave" [2400.0 ¢], and Mode 3 as an exact "triple-octave" [3600.0 ¢] above the fundamental frequency, so that $F_2 = 4F_1$ and $F_3 = 8F_1$. Such a mode tuning would give maximum reinforcement and clarification to our pitch perception of the fundamental frequency. All the Honduras rosewood bars of the Bass Marimba in Plate 8 were tuned in this manner. The tuning sequence in Section 6.14 gives the exact method I used to tune the low C_2 bar (64.33 cps) on this instrument. Note that the triple-arch design does *not* impose any arbitrary tuning limits, but provides marimba builders with many possibilities. For example, after tuning F_1, F_2, and F_3 to C_2, C_4, and C_5, respectively, a further removal of material could also produce a G_1, G_3, and $B\flat_4$ tuning. Or, if at the very beginning of the tuning process the removal of material had been carried out in a different manner, many other kinds of tunings would have been possible as well.

6.13

The bar tuning process requires four essential tools. (1) To accurately tune mode frequencies, we must have an electronic tuning device. Because the higher modes have a very short ring-time, only tuners with revolving disks or revolving lights will work. (Tuners with needles or flashing lights will not work.) A good tuner should have an eight "octave" C_1–B_9 (32.70–15,804.28 cps) range, and come equipped with two cent dials: a coarse dial calibrated in 5-cent increments, and a fine dial calibrated in ½-cent increments. The coarse dial should measure 55 cents in the sharp and flat directions, and the fine dial, 8 cents in the sharp and flat directions.

(2) A portable, high-quality 4 in. × 24 in. belt sander is also essential. Rigidly mount the sander on its side so that the belt makes a 90° angle with the top of the workbench. The revolving front roller is where all the work takes place. Hold the bar against the roller and sand out the arches. Note, however, that during the sanding process the bar becomes hot and will sound flat. Heat "softens" the bar and causes a decrease in Young's modulus of elasticity. Since $F_n \propto \sqrt{E}$, as the modulus decreases, the mode frequencies decrease as well. Therefore, let all bars thoroughly cool overnight, and fine-tune the next day.

(3) We also need a collection of hard and soft mallets. To hear F_3, use a hard mallet and hit the bar at $0.500L$, the location of a Mode 3 antinode. Be sure not to touch the bar, because any mass loading will cause a decrease in frequency. (See Section 6.7.) Similarly, to hear F_2, hit the bar with a hard mallet at $0.308L$ (or about ⅓ of the length), the location of a Mode 2 antinode. And to hear F_1, hit the bar with a soft mallet again at $0.500L$, the location of the Mode 1 antinode.

(4) Finally, obtain two long strips of flexible foam, approximately 1 in. wide and 1 in. high. These strips serve as resilient supports for testing the bars during the tuning process. Arrange the strips in a V-pattern so that they can hold a variety of long and short bars. Foam strips make it possible to check the tuning of bars without touching them, and to compare a whole set of bars for tone consistency. The two most important qualities are strength of tone or amplitude, and duration of tone or ring-time.[30] Check for tone consistency only when the bars are stone cold because heat from sanding also produces internal damping, which in turn causes a decrease in both amplitude and ring-time.

6.14

On all bar percussion instruments, the longest and thickest bars give the most powerful and long-lasting tone. However, tuning requirements impose definite limitations on bar dimensions. For bass bars, F_1 of an *uncut* bar must be between a "minor seventh" [1000.0 ¢] and a "major ninth" [1400.0 ¢]

above the proposed fundamental. If F_1 is less than 1000.0 ¢ above the proposed fundamental, then F_1 will arrive at the fundamental tuning *before* F_2 and F_3 reach the "double-octave" and "triple-octave" tunings; or it may also happen that F_2 and F_3 arrive before F_1. It all depends on how the initial process of removing material occurred. Also, if F_1 is more than 1400.0 ¢ above the proposed fundamental, the bar will be too short and will not produce a powerful and long-lasting tone.

Figure 6.9 shows three stages in the process of tuning the C_2 bar analyzed in Sections 6.3 and 6.11. The first group of white notes represents the approximate frequencies of Modes 1–3 of the uncut bar. The second group of black notes represents the approximate mode frequencies after three shallow band saw cuts. The tuning schedule below indicates that F_2 and F_3 are almost an "octave" apart. This is an ideal situation because it shows the required "octave" between F_2 and F_3 a full "major third" [400.0 ¢] above the proposed tuning. All the tuner must do is to maintain the same interval between these two modes while collectively decreasing Modes 1–3. The third group of white notes gives the exact frequencies of F_1, F_2, and F_3 at the end of the tuning process.

The following *Tuning Sequence of the C_2 Bass Marimba Bar* illustrates 18 separate steps required to tune the bar. Each step consists of a cent/frequency table and an analysis/decision procedure. With the exception of Bar 1, the first column below each bar diagram gives decreases in cent values that result from the indicated actions, and the second column, the bar's current mode frequencies in conventional note letter names and cents. Beginning with Bar 3, two different kinds of arrows indicate the action performed on the bar. Long black arrows show areas of large wood removal, and short white arrows show areas of small wood removal. Remember, a removal of material at a particular location in the bar always has a twofold effect. (See Figure 6.8.) Unfortunately, no diagram can illustrate the exact sanding locations, or the exact amount of material removed. However, the analysis/decision procedures, which explain the reasons for these steps, do provide a logical progression of events that a tuner may apply over a wide range of frequencies.

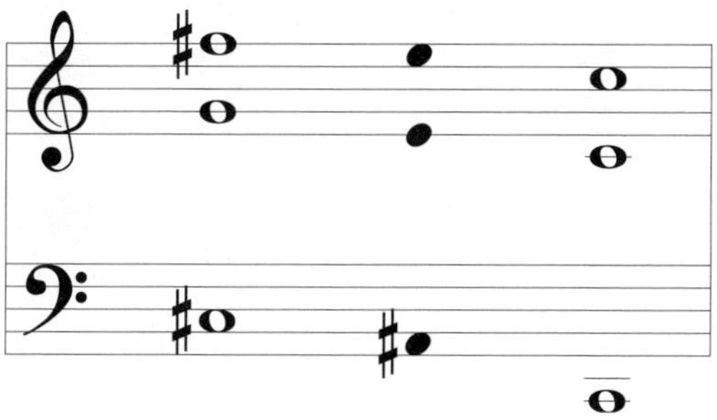

Figure 6.9 The first three modes of a bass marimba bar before, during, after tuning. The first group of notes represents the approximate frequencies of Modes 1–3 before tuning, and the second group, the approximate frequencies after three shallow cuts on the band saw. The third group shows the exact mode frequencies at the end of the tuning process.

TUNING SEQUENCE OF THE C_2 BASS MARIMBA BAR

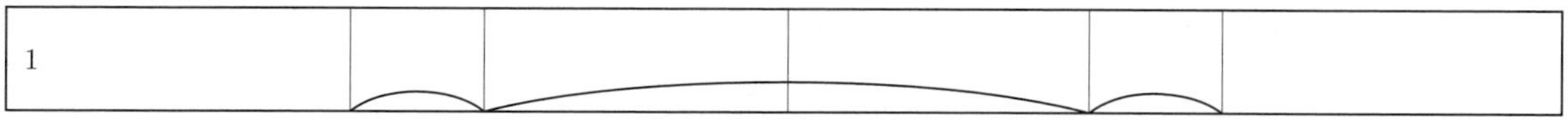

C♯$_3$ +30 ¢
G$_4$ −40 ¢
F♯$_5$ −25 ¢

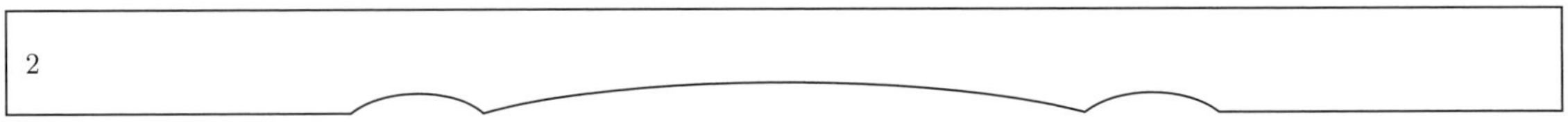

−315 ¢	$A\sharp_2$	+15 ¢
−225 ¢	E_4	+35 ¢
−160 ¢	E_5	+15 ¢

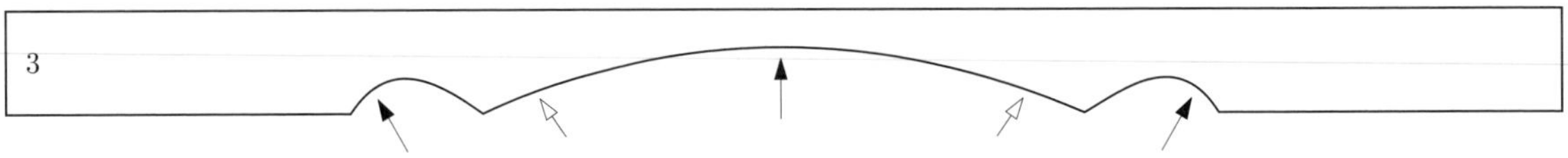

−60 ¢	$A\sharp_2$	−45 ¢
−20 ¢	E_4	+15 ¢
−25 ¢	E_5	−10 ¢

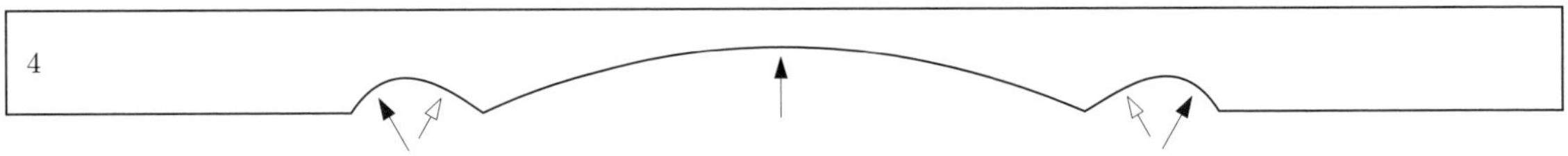

−35	A_2	+20
−15	E_4	0
−20	E_5	−30

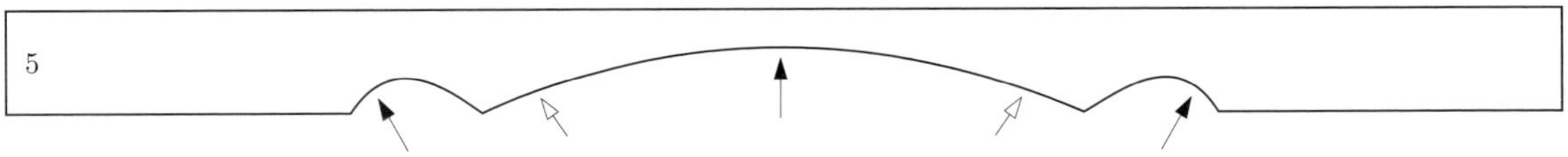

−60	A_2	−40
−15	E_4	−15
−20	E_5	−50

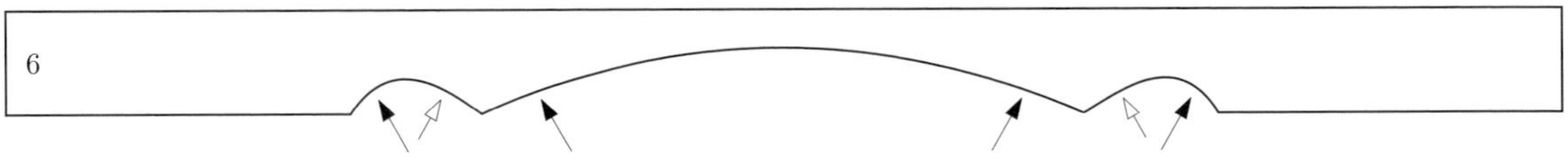

−10	A_2	−50
−50	$D\sharp_4$	+35
−45	$D\sharp_5$	+5

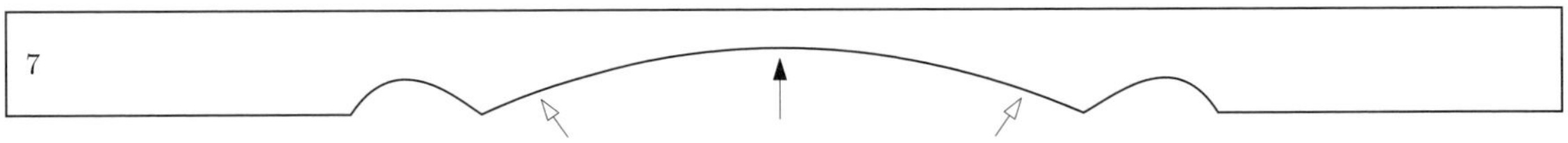

−30	$G\sharp_2$	+20
−15	$D\sharp_4$	+20
−10	$D\sharp_5$	−5

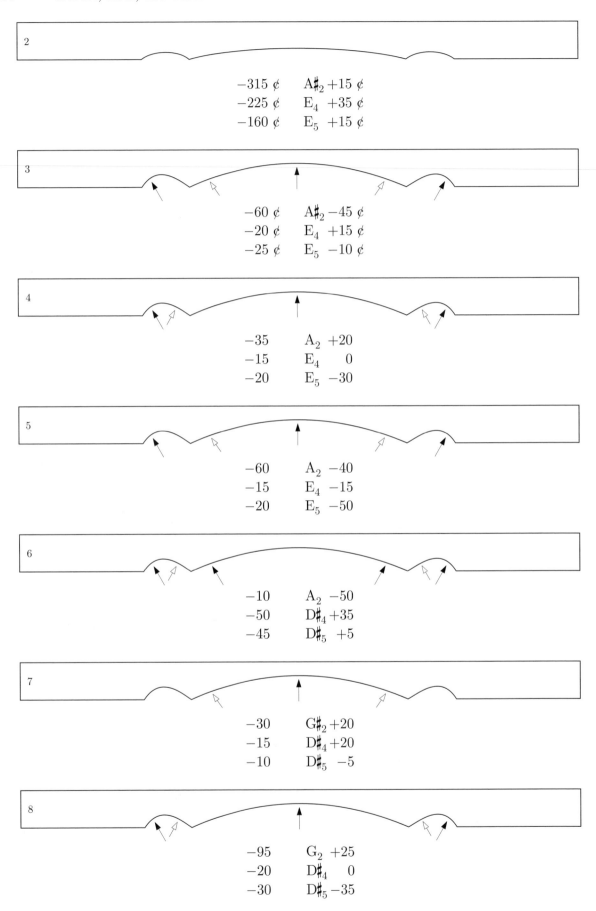

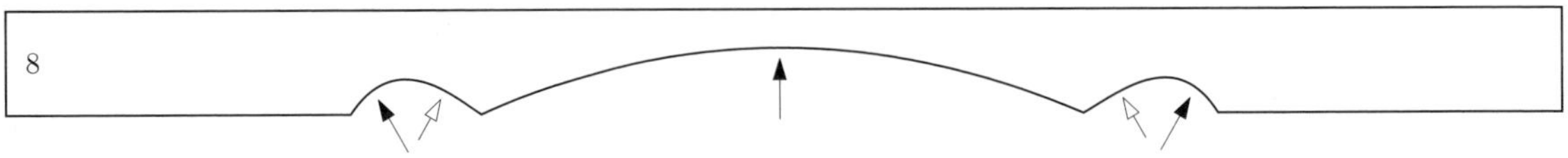

−95	G_2	+25
−20	$D\sharp_4$	0
−30	$D\sharp_5$	−35

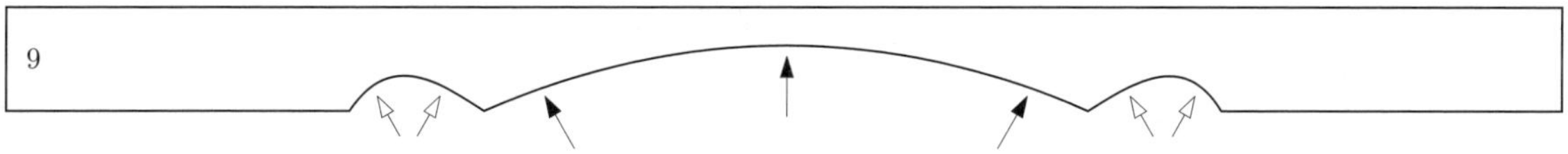

−140	$F\sharp_2$	−15
−50	D_4	+50
−30	D_5	+35

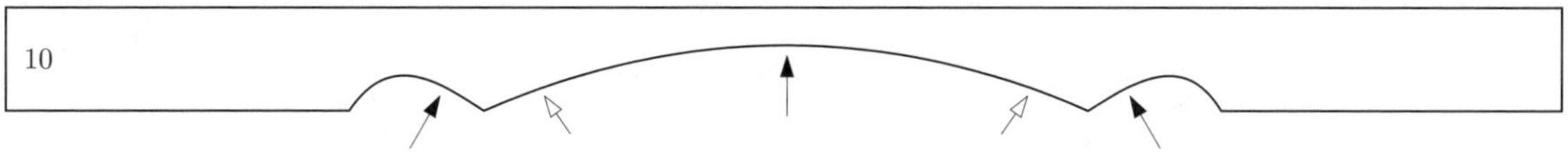

−65	F_2	+20
−30	D_4	+20
−15	D_5	+20

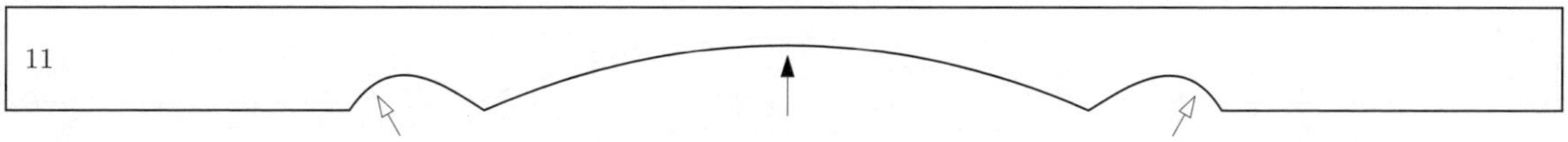

−95	E_2	+25
−10	D_4	+10
−20	D_5	0

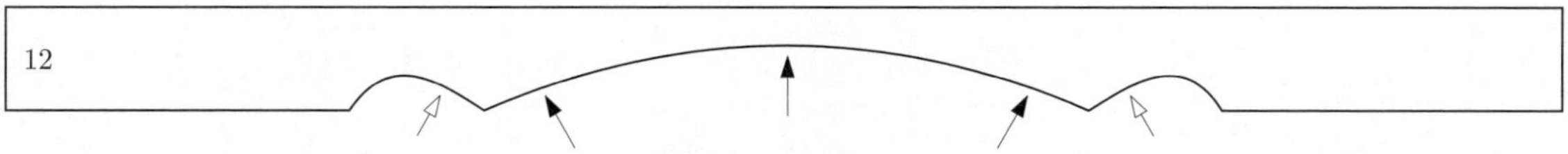

−125	$D\sharp_2$	0
−40	D_4	−30
−15	D_5	−15

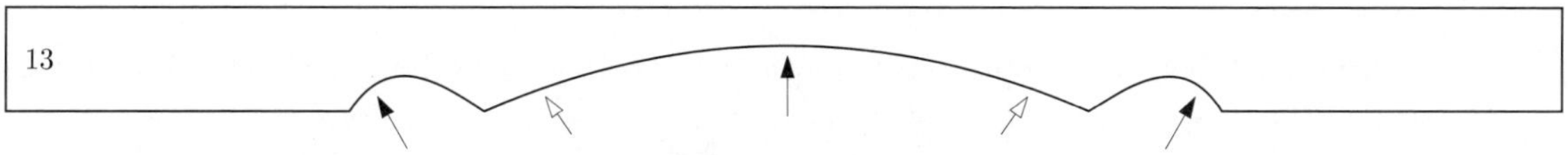

−100	D_2	0
−40	$C\sharp_4$	+30
−55	$C\sharp_5$	+30

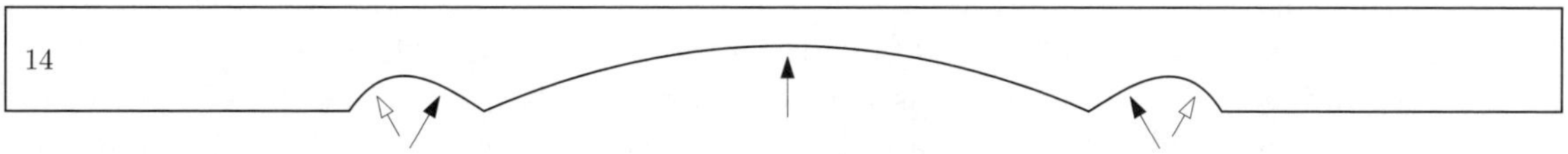

−80	$C\sharp_2$	+20
−40	$C\sharp_4$	−10
−20	$C\sharp_5$	+10

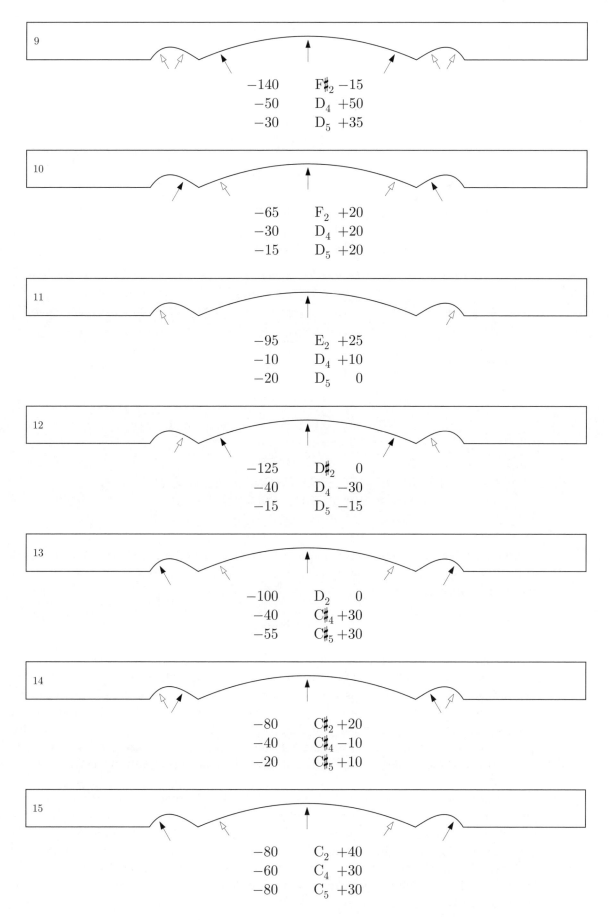

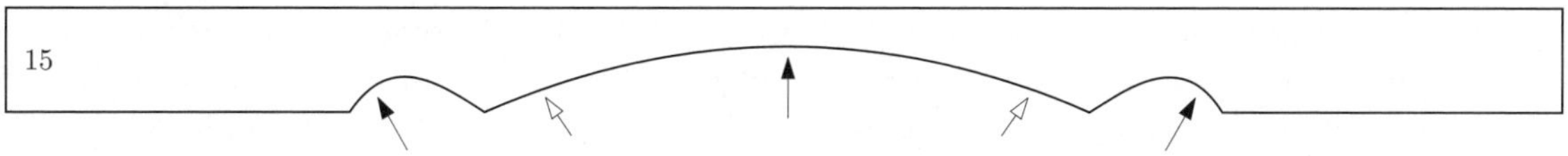

−80	C_2	+40
−60	C_4	+30
−80	C_5	+30

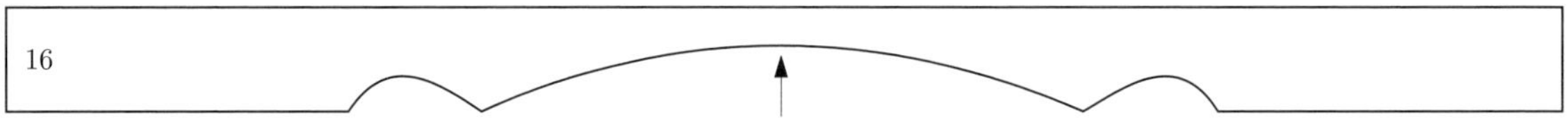

−10 C_2 +30
0 C_4 +30
−2 C_5 +28

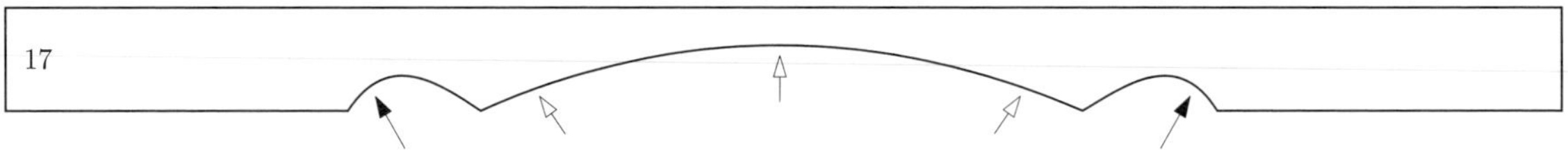

−20 C_2 +10
−20 C_4 +10
−18 C_5 +10

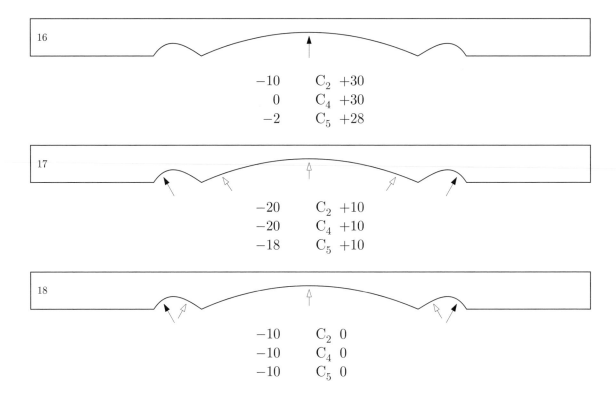

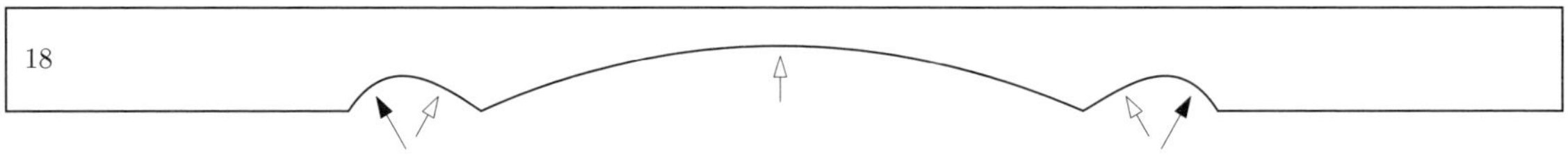

−10 C_2 0
−10 C_4 0
−10 C_5 0

ANALYSIS/DECISION PROCEDURES FOR TUNING THE C_2 BASS MARIMBA BAR

Bar 1 **Analysis:** Given a fundamental frequency between a "minor seventh" and a "ninth" above the proposed fundamental, and given the large dimensions of this uncut bar, attempt a C_2 tuning.

Decision: Cut three shallow arches on the band saw.

Bar 2 **Analysis:** After three initial cuts, F_2 and F_3 are almost one "octave" apart. Both modes are also a full "major third" above the proposed tuning, which is very good. If at the beginning of the tuning process F_2 and F_3 are less than a "minor third" above the final tuning, they will arrive at C_4 and C_5, respectively, *before* the fundamental frequency arrives at C_2, which would ruin the bar. Also, F_1 is a full "minor seventh" above C_2, which is good because it is not too close and not too far from the proposed tuning. With skill and care, all three modes should arrive at their destinations simultaneously.

Decision: Since decreases in F_3 are always difficult and require sanding deep into the outside corners of the outer arches, always make sure in the early stages of the tuning process that Mode 3 is one "octave" or less above Mode 2. If one neglects F_3 and the third mode remains too high, it may be impossible to regain the "octave" interval with F_2. Also, during the early stages of tuning, make large reductions in the central area of the bar so that F_1 comes down rapidly. Finally, make even reductions on *both* sides of the peaks so that F_2 comes down as well.

Bar 3 **A:** F_3 decreased by 25 ¢, F_2 by 20 ¢, and F_1 by 60 ¢. F_3 is one "octave" −25 ¢ above F_2, which is good.

D: Continue to sand at the outer arches to bring F_3 down and maintain the "flat octave" above F_2. Also, continue to sand in the center to bring F_1 down and at the peaks to bring F_2 down.

Bar 4 **A:** Again, a large decrease for F_1, a medium decrease for F_3, and a small decrease for F_2.

D: Same as Bar 3.

Bar 5 **A:** Same as Bar 4. However, F_3 is one "octave" −35 ¢ above F_2, which means that F_2 is now too high.

D: Sand on both sides of the peaks and bring F_2 down, and sand at the outer arches to bring F_3 down.

Bar 6 **A:** A large, medium, and small decrease for F_2, F_3, and F_1, respectively. F_3 is one "octave" −30 ¢ above F_2, which is good.

D: Sand in the center and bring F_1 down, and at the peaks to bring F_2 down.

Bar 7 **A:** A large, medium, and small decrease for F_1, F_2, and F_3, respectively. F_3 is one "octave" −25 ¢ above F_2, which is still acceptable.

D: Sand in the central area for a large decrease in F_1, and make similar decreases at the peaks and at the outer arches to maintain the "flat octave" between F_2 and F_3.

Bar 8 **A:** Almost a semitone decrease for F_1, a medium decrease for F_3, and a small decrease for F_2, which means that F_2 is again too high. (See Bar 5.)

D: Sand in the central area for a large decrease in F_1, and at the peaks for a large decrease in F_2. Continue to work the outer arches so that F_3 does *not* remain too high.

Bar 9 **A:** A large 140 ¢ decrease for F_1, a medium 50 ¢ decrease for F_2, and a small 30 ¢ decrease for F_3. F_3 is one "octave" −15 ¢ above F_2, which is still acceptable, but could be wider.

D: Sand in the center and at the peaks.

Bar 10 **A:** A large, medium, and small decrease for F_1, F_2, and F_3, respectively. Note the perfect "octave" between F_2 and F_3, and the interval of one "octave and a major sixth" between F_1 and F_2. Since the band saw cuts, F_1 has decreased by 495 ¢, F_2 by 215 ¢, and F_3 by 195 ¢.

D: Sand in the central area for another large decrease in F_1, and work on the outer arches for a decrease in F_3.

Bar 11 **A:** Again, almost a semitone decrease for F_1, a medium decrease for F_3, and a small decrease for F_2. Since F_1 is about one "octave and a minor seventh" below F_2, try to widen this interval to about one "octave and a major seventh."

D: Same as Bar 9.

Bar 12 **A:** Two large decreases for F_1 and F_2. Note that F_3 did not decrease very much and is now one "octave" +15 ¢ above F_2. This is *not* good, especially because late in the tuning process, decreases in F_3 are more difficult to achieve.

D: Continue to make heavy reductions in the center and at the outer arches to bring F_1 and F_3 down; make light reductions at the peaks to bring F_2 down as well.

Bar 13 **A:** Two large decreases for F_1 and F_3. Note that F_2 and F_3 are again one "octave" apart. Also, F_1 is two "octaves" −70 ¢ below F_2, and three "octaves" −70 ¢ below F_3.

D: Again, sand in the center to decrease F_1, at the peaks to decrease F_2, and at the outer arches to decrease F_3.

Bar 14 **A:** A large, medium, and small decrease for F_1, F_2, and F_3, respectively. However, F_3 is one "octave" +20 ¢ above F_2, which again is *not* good. For the first time, F_1 and F_2 are almost a "double-octave" apart, and F_1 and F_3, almost a "triple-octave" apart.

D: Make large reductions at the outer arches and in the center to bring F_3 and F_1 down. Make smaller reductions at the peaks to bring F_2 down.

Bar 15 **A:** Large decreases for F_1 and F_3. All three mode frequencies are very close to the final tuning.

D: Sand only in the center to bring F_1 down by 10 ¢.

Bar 16 **A:** F_1 came down by 10 ¢, and F_3 by 2 ¢. A very close alignment at about 30 ¢ sharp of the final tuning.

D: Sand *more* at the outer arches to bring F_3 down, and sand *less* in the center and near the peaks to bring F_1 and F_2 down.

Bar 17 **A:** A perfect alignment 10 ¢ sharp of the final tuning.

D: Same as Bar 16.

Bar 18 **A:** A perfect alignment of the proposed tuning.

D: Let the bar cool overnight, and fine tune the next day.

6.15

We turn now to the mode tuning of treble bars. Figure 6.10 shows a typical tuned treble bar in the G_3–G_5 frequency range. A single line at $0.500L$ again marks the antinode location for Mode 1, and two lines at $0.308L$ and $0.692L$ mark the antinode locations for Mode 2. We do not consider Mode 3 in the tuning of treble bars because this mode is too high and weak to influence our pitch perception of the fundamental. Note two more lines in Figure 6.10 that mark the nodes of Mode 1 at $0.224L$ and $0.776L$. Two black dots in the center of the node lines represent mounting holes that pass through the width of the bar. On traditional marimbas, xylophones, and vibraphones, bars are mounted by passing a cord through these holes. Tests show, however, that a flexible foam mounting imposes the least restriction on the movement of bars, and gives the greatest possible amplitude and ring-time.

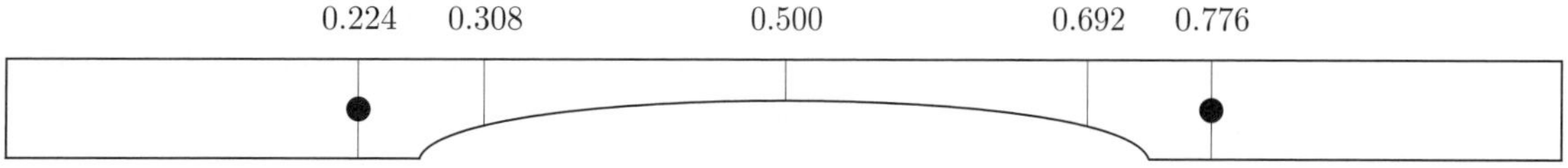

Figure 6.10 Profile of a tuned treble marimba bar. Vertical lines indicate the antinode locations of the first two modes, and the node locations of the first mode. Two black dots in the center of the node lines represent two mounting holes for the bar.

In the G_3–G_5 (196.0–784.0 cps) range, marimba bars have lengths that decrease from 15½ in. to 10½ in., widths that decrease from 2¼ in. to 1½ in., and uniform heights of 13⁄16 in. To produce a powerful and long-lasting tone in this frequency range, F_1 of an *uncut* bar should sound approximately one "octave" plus a "tritone" [1200.0 ¢ + 600.0 ¢ = 1800.0 ¢] above the proposed fundamental. Since F_2 of an uncut bar is about one "octave" plus a "flat tritone" above F_1, Mode 2 of such a bar sounds approximately a "triple-octave" above the tuned fundamental.[31] Suppose we would like to tune a C_4 (261.63 cps) marimba bar. For this pitch, a high-quality Honduras rosewood bar would have the following physical dimensions and material properties:

h = 0.8125 in. (13⁄16 in.)
b = 2.250 in. (2¼ in.)
L = 14.375 in. (14⅜ in.)
$K = h/\sqrt{12} = 0.234549$ in.
E = 3,200,000 psi
ρ = 0.00009894 mica/in^3

Substitute the required values into Equation 6.2 and calculate the theoretical frequencies of the first two modes of vibration: F_1 = 726.85 cps, and F_2 = 2004.05 cps. Again, we propose a tuning that designates Mode 2 as an exact "double-octave" above the tuned fundamental frequency, so that $F_2 = 4F_1$.[32] Figure 6.11 shows the mode frequencies of F_1 and F_2 before and after tuning. The first group of notes represents the approximate frequencies of Modes 1 and 2 of the uncut bar. And the second group gives the exact frequencies of F_1 and F_2 at the end of the tuning process.

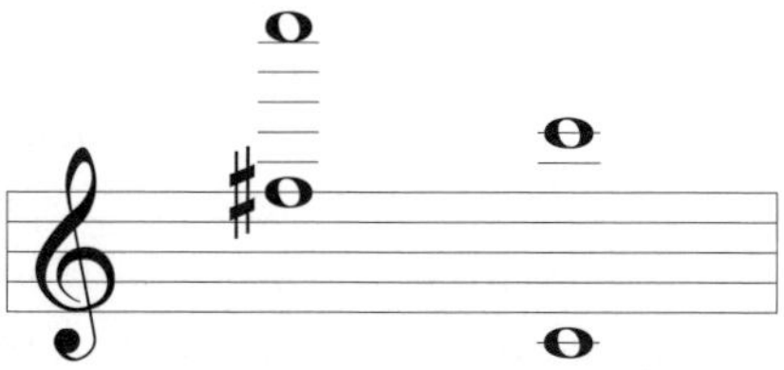

Figure 6.11 The first two modes of a treble bar before and after tuning. The first group of notes represents the approximate frequencies of F_1 and F_2 before tuning, and the second group, the exact mode frequencies at the end of the tuning process.

The mode tuning process of treble bars is essentially the same as bass bars, only much simpler. In this example, we must decrease F_1 of the uncut bar by about one "octave and a tritone," which is easily accomplished. However, we must also decrease F_2 by about one "octave." Recall from the *Analysis/Decision Procedures for Tuning the C_2 Bass Marimba Bar* in Section 6.14 that decreases in the higher mode frequencies are always more difficult to achieve. To decrease F_2 by an "octave," one must angle the sander into the outside corners of the central arch and make deep reductions in the areas halfway between the antinodes of Mode 2 and the nodes of Mode 1. Note, therefore, that the arch of the bar in Figure 6.10 extends well beyond the exact Mode 2 antinode locations at $0.308L$ and $0.692L$.

On the Diamond Marimba in Plate 7, the lowest G_3 bar has a "double-octave" and a "triple-octave" mode tuning. All the bars in the $^{16}\!/\!_{13}$–$^{7}\!/\!_{5}$ (241.2–1097.6 cps) range have "double-octave" mode tunings. The remaining higher bars in the $^{13}\!/\!_{9}$–$^{13}\!/\!_{8}$ (1132.4–2548.0 cps) range have only fundamental frequency tunings.

6.16

Before we analyze clamped-free bars, let us examine the material properties E and ρ in greater detail. On the Bass Marimba, the lowest and highest Honduras rosewood values for E are 2,740,599 psi and 3,561,111 psi, respectively, and the lowest and highest values for ρ are 0.00009638 mica/in^3 and 0.00010555 mica/in^3, respectively. The percent change[33] between the values of E is approximately 30%, and between the values of ρ, approximately 10%. We conclude, therefore, that even on a thoroughly tested musical instrument, variations in E are far more unpredictable than variations in ρ. Refer to Appendix E, and note that on a quality Honduras rosewood marimba, E in most bars should vary between 2,900,000–3,200,000 psi. Given the high cost and rarity of rosewood, the question arises, "How can an instrument builder test for E and determine whether a given stock of material is *acoustically* acceptable?"

In all solids, E is a measure of a material's stiffness or springiness.[34] Metals consist of substances that are isotropic (uniform mechanical properties in all directions) and homogeneous (uniform chemical composition at all locations). For a given metal element or alloy, E and ρ are constants. In contrast, wood is an anisotropic material, which means that E is not constant but changes with the direction of grain.[35] Moreover, tests show that after cutting a clear, straight-grained rosewood bar in half, E frequently varies by 15–20% between the two short bars. There are two chief reasons that account for these variations. (1) Wood is a heterogeneous material, which means that ρ is also not constant but changes with such irregularities as moisture content, grain, gums, resins, growing spaces, and soil deposits. It follows, therefore, that inconsistencies in density cause variations in stiffness. (2) The elastic modulus also decreases with an increase in moisture content.[36] Water saturation causes wood fibers to become soft and pliable. Even small amounts of moisture can have an acoustically noticeable effect on stiffness. Moreover, because water concentrations vary with location, E is not constant in a given log or bar. Tests with a moisture meter show that in kiln-dried rosewood, the moisture content varies by 10–15% at different locations in a bar.

Suppose now that we would like to determine if a stock of Honduras rosewood has suitable values for E and ρ. Such an analysis requires an electronic tuner, a quality scale, and a tape measure. Begin by solving Equation 6.2 for E. First, to simplify this equation for F_1 calculations, compute the following numeric constant:

$$\frac{\pi(1/\sqrt{12})}{8}(q_1)^2 = \frac{3.1416(0.28868)}{8}(3.0112)^2 = 1.0279$$

Place it in the numerator of Equation 6.2:

$$F_1 = \frac{1.0279\,h}{L^2}\sqrt{E/\rho}$$

Next, remove the radical, and square the constant and three variables:

$$F_1^2 = \frac{(1.0279)^2 h^2 E}{L^4 \rho}$$

Now, solve this equation for E,

$$E = \frac{F_1^2 L^4 \rho}{(1.0279)^2 h^2}$$

Finally, calculate the constant and its inverse, and place it in the numerator:

$$E = \frac{0.94645 F_1^2 L^4 \rho}{h^2} \tag{6.14}$$

Consider a kiln-dried rosewood bar with a moisture content of 6%. The bar has the following dimensions: $L = 44\frac{1}{16}$ in., $h = 1\frac{1}{32}$ in., and $b = 4\frac{1}{4}$ in. These dimensions give a volume of 193.12 in^3. Place the bar on a scale, and record the weight at 7.639 lbf. Calculate the weight density (W) by dividing weight by volume:

$$W = \frac{7.639 \text{ lbf}}{193.12 \text{ in}^3} = \frac{0.03956 \text{ lbf}}{\text{in}^3}$$

Next, calculate the mass density by dividing W by the acceleration of gravity in inches per second squared:[37]

$$\rho = \frac{W}{g_0} = \frac{0.03956 \text{ lbf/in}^3}{386.09 \text{ in/s}^2} = 0.00010246 \text{ mica/in}^3$$

According to Appendix E, this bar has the required mass density. Next, find a large soft mallet, turn on the tuner, hit the bar, and record F_1 at F$\sharp_2$ +40 ¢ = 94.66 cps. Finally, substitute the appropriate variables into Equation 6.14 and calculate Young's modulus of elasticity:[38]

$$E = \frac{0.94645(94.66 \text{ cps})^2(44.0625 \text{ in})^4(0.00010246 \text{ mica/in}^3)}{(1.03125 \text{ in})^2} = 3{,}079{,}878.9 \text{ micas/(in}\cdot\text{s}^2)$$

Refer to Equation 1.26 and note a dimensional analysis that shows mica/(in·s^2) is equivalent to lbf/in^2, or psi. We conclude, therefore, that the bar meets the requirements for both E and ρ, and barring any unknown internal defects, has the potential to produce a powerful and long-lasting musical tone. This turned out to be the case, and it is now the 1/1 bar, or G_1 at 49.0 cps, on the Bass Marimba in Plate 8.

Part III

FREQUENCY EQUATIONS, MODE SHAPES, AND RESTORING FORCES OF CLAMPED-FREE BARS

6.17

The frequency equation for a slender, uniform, isotropic bar, rod, or tube clamped at one end and free at the other states[39]

$$F_{\text{n clamped-free}} = \frac{\pi K\sqrt{E/\rho}}{8}\left(\frac{q_{\text{n}}}{L}\right)^2 \quad \left\{\begin{matrix} q_1 \approx 1.19373 \approx 1.1937 \\ q_2 \approx 2.98835 \approx 2.9884 \\ q_3 \approx 5.00049 \approx 5 \\ q_4 \approx 6.99998 \approx 7 \\ q_{\text{n}>4} \approx 2n - 1 \end{matrix}\right\} \tag{6.15}$$

where L is the *vibrating length* (not the overall length) of the object, in inches. The *only* difference between the frequency equation for a free-free and a clamped-free bar is the value of the dimensionless bar parameter. For a complete description of the other variables in Equation 6.15, see Sections 6.2 and 6.7. Subequations for K appear in Section 6.7, Table 6.1.

The following frequency ratios define the relation between the fundamental frequency and the frequencies of the second, third, and fourth modes:

$$F_2 \propto \left(\frac{q_2}{q_1}\right)^2 \approx 6.267$$

$$F_3 \propto \left(\frac{q_3}{q_1}\right)^2 \approx 17.545$$

$$F_4 \propto \left(\frac{q_4}{q_1}\right)^2 \approx 34.388$$

Since 6.267 is greater than 4 but less than 8, the second mode is higher than a 4/1, or a "double-octave" above the fundamental, but lower than an 8/1, or a "triple-octave." The same method used in Section 6.2 shows that F_2 of a clamped-free bar is approximately a "double-octave" [2400.0 ¢] plus a "flat minor sixth" above the fundamental:

$$F_2 = \log_{10} 6.267 \times 3986.314 = 3177.3\ ¢$$
$$3177.3\ ¢ - 2400.0\ ¢ = 777.3\ ¢$$

Also, confirm that F_3 is approximately a "quadruple-octave" [4800.0 ¢] plus a "flat major second" above the fundamental:

$$F_3 = \log_{10} 17.545 \times 3986.314 = 4959.6\ ¢$$
$$4959.6\ ¢ - 4800.0\ ¢ = 159.6\ ¢$$

A comparison of identical objects shows that the fundamental frequency of a free-free object sounds 3203.6 ¢ *higher* than a clamped-free object:

$$\left(\frac{q_{1\ \text{free-free}}}{q_{1\ \text{clamped-free}}}\right)^2 = \left(\frac{3.0112}{1.1937}\right)^2 \approx 6.363$$

$$\log_{10} 6.363 \times 3986.314 = 3203.6\ \text{¢}$$

Finally, note that Equations 6.3–6.5C apply to both free-free and clamped-free bars, and that Equation 6.16 gives close mode frequency approximations for clamped-free bars:

$$F_{\text{n clamped-free}} \approx \frac{\pi K \sqrt{E/\rho}}{8}\left(\frac{2n-1}{L}\right)^2 \qquad \{n = 1, 2, 3, 4, \ldots\} \tag{6.16}$$

~ 6.18 ~

Figure 6.12 shows the first three mode shapes of a clamped-free bar. Again, the inner bending antinodes mark the locations of maximum bending, and the outer displacement antinodes mark the locations of maximum displacement in the bar.

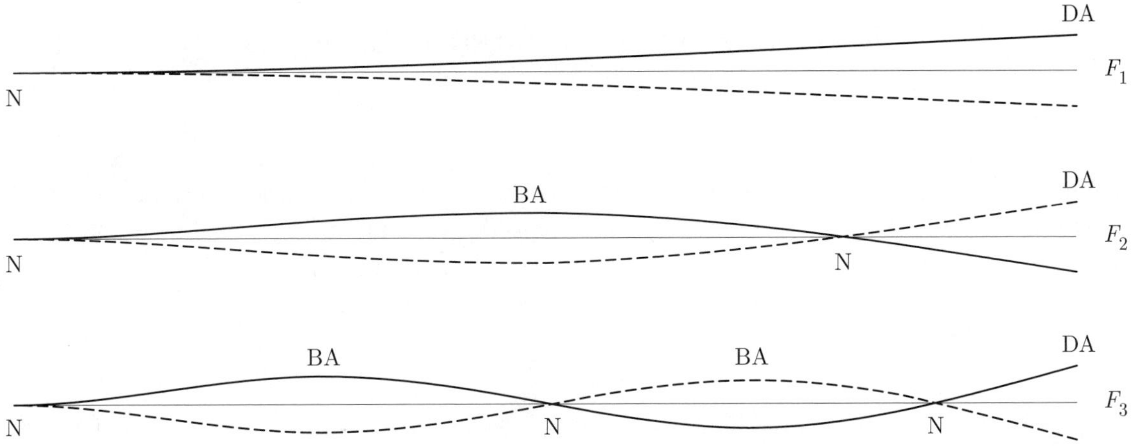

Figure 6.12 The first three modes of vibration of a clamped-free bar, rod, or tube. Bending antinodes (BA), or points of maximum bending, are located approximately halfway between two consecutive nodes (N), or points of minimum displacement. Displacement antinodes (DA), or points of maximum displacement, are located at the free end of the bar.

Figure 6.13 illustrates the deflection and the spatial distribution of the bending moment and the shear force for the first mode of vibration of a uniform clamped-free bar. Note the similarities between Figures 6.2 and 6.13. At the free end and near a displacement antinode, $M(x) = 0$ and $V(x) = 0$ because here the bar does not bend, and it does not shear. However, in stark contrast to free-free bars, M_{max} and V_{max} occur at the clamped end, or at the location of a node. Figures 6.12 and 6.13 show that for the fundamental mode of vibration, a clamped bar does not produce a bending antinode along its vibrating length. Instead, the maximum restoring force for F_1 occurs at the bar's constrained end.

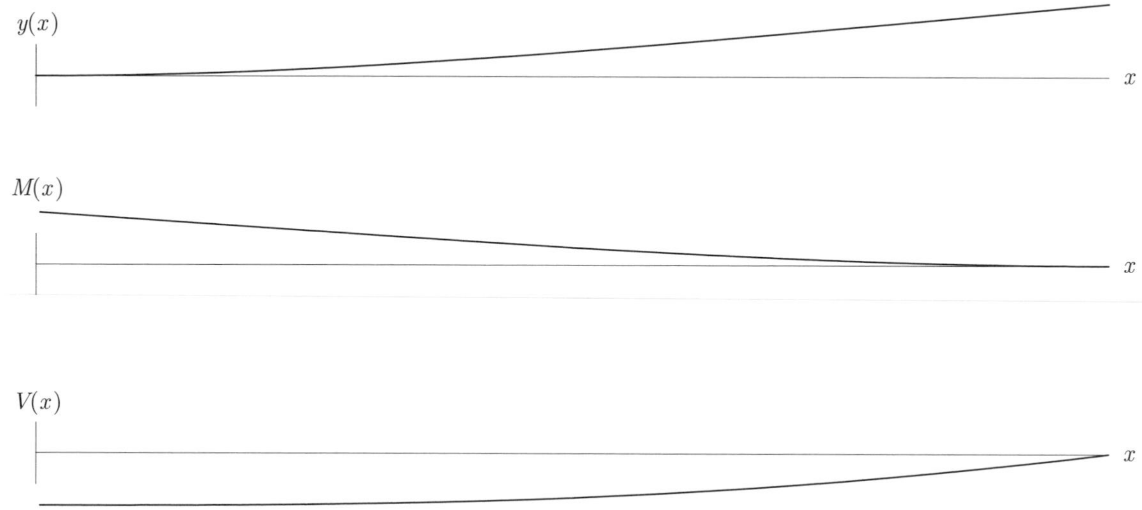

Figure 6.13 The deflection, bending moment, and shear force of a uniform clamped-free bar in the fundamental mode of vibration. At the clamped end and at the location of a node, $M(x)$ and $V(x)$ have maximum values, and at the free end $M(x) = 0$ and $V(x) = 0$.

Part IV

CLAMPED-FREE BAR TUNING TECHNIQUES

6.19

The mathematical principles discussed in Sections 6.6–6.8 and the tuning techniques discussed in Sections 6.9–6.10 apply also to clamped-free bars. Consider the bars in Figure 6.14. Again, both bars consist of the same material and have the same physical dimensions. Bar (a) has an incision near the clamped end, and bar (b) has an identical incision near the free end. As a result of removing identical amounts of mass, the frequency of bar (a) decreases, while the frequency of bar (b) increases.

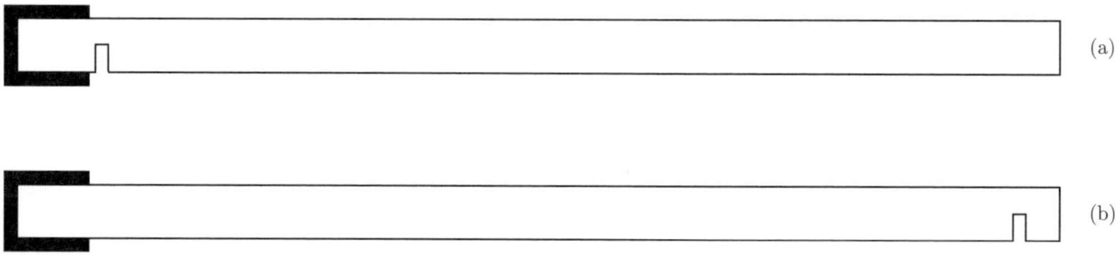

Figure 6.14 Two clamped-free bars made of the same material and with the same dimensions. (a) An incision near the left clamped end causes a decrease in F_1. (b) An identical incision near the right free end causes an increase in F_1.

Figure 6.15 explains the reasons for these opposite effects on a clamped-free bar as it bends in the fundamental mode of vibration. Lines at the clamped end mark the area near the node, and lines at the free end mark the area near the displacement antinode. A removal of material from the node area causes a significant reduction in restoring force, which in turn produces a significant decrease in the fundamental frequency. Similar cuts outside this area also decrease F_1, but this

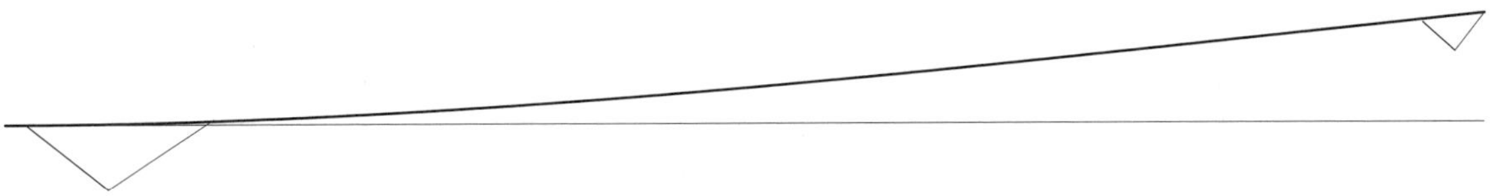

Figure 6.15 Areas of a bent clamped-free bar that indicate a node near the clamped end, and a displacement antinode near the free end. A removal of material near the clamped end causes a relatively large reduction in restoring force and a small decrease in mass. Conversely, a removal of material from the free end causes a relatively large reduction in mass and a small reduction in restoring force.

effect gradually diminishes as one makes incisions farther away from the node. Near the displacement antinode, the bending moment and the shear force are very small. Here an identical incision causes an insignificant reduction in restoring force. However, the effect of such an incision does produce a noticeable decrease in the bar's mass. Because of less mass (or less inertia), the relatively straight end of the bar vibrates more rapidly and the fundamental frequency increases.

~ 6.20 ~

The mode tuning techniques discussed in Part II also apply to clamped-free bars. Here again, we must know the locations of the bending antinodes. Table 6.3 gives the positions of the nodes and antinodes of clamped-free bars, rods, and tubes for the first four modes of vibration as measured from the clamped end. However, on most musical instruments that have clamped-free bars or vibrating reeds, the mode frequencies are too high, the mode amplitudes are too weak, and the mode ring-times are too short to influence our pitch perception of the fundamental frequency. Consequently, most tuners only tune F_1 on clamped-free bars.

To tune the metal reeds of harmoniums, harmonicas, etc., carefully insert a thin piece of cardboard between the reed and the opening of the air chamber. This holds the reed in place and prevents it from bending down into the aperture. With a fine file, remove small amounts of material at the clamped end to lower F_1, or at the free end to raise F_1. Avoid touching the reed because heat will cause it to sound flat. (See Section 6.13.)

Table 6.3

NODES AND ANTINODES OF CLAMPED-FREE BARS, RODS, AND TUBES

First Four Modes of Vibration

Mode 1	Mode 2	Mode 3	Mode 4
0.000 N	0.000 N	0.000 N	0.000 N
	0.471 A	0.291 A	0.208 A
	0.783 N	0.504 N	0.358 N
		0.692 A	0.501 A
		0.868 N	0.644 N
			0.780 A
			0.906 N

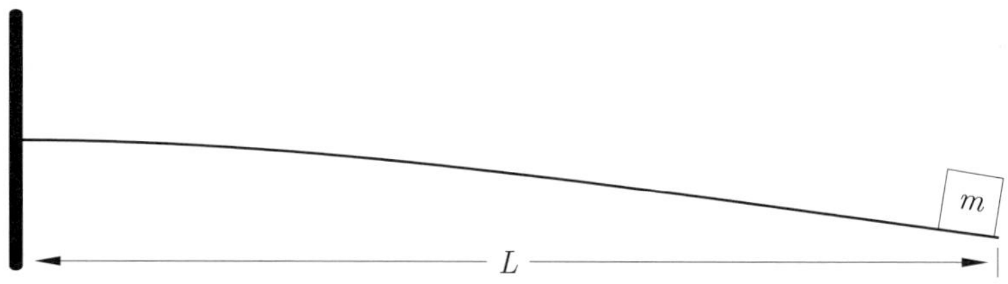

Figure 6.16 A clamped-free bar with a mass (m) attached at the free end. One frequently finds tuned mass-loaded reeds in the bass sections of harmonicas, accordions, and other wind instruments.

One notable difference between bars and reeds is that in the bass sections of harmonicas, accordions, etc., one frequently finds small masses soldered to the free ends of metal reeds. Figure 6.16 shows a clamped-free bar with a mass attached at the free end. In the confined spaces of small musical instruments, one cannot use long reeds to produce low frequencies. Consequently, musical instrument builders developed this tuning technique, which significantly lowers the fundamental frequencies of relatively short reeds. Mass loading does not work very well on percussion instruments because the extra mass on a bar's free end severely dampens vibration. However, this problem does not apply to wind instruments because a continuous flow of compressed air keeps the reeds in motion. The following equation gives the fundamental frequency of a clamped-free bar with a mass at the free end:[40]

$$F_1 = \frac{\sqrt{\dfrac{3ESK^2}{mL^3}}}{2\pi} \tag{6.17}$$

where m is the total mass of the bar or reed, in micas (see Equation 1.19); and L is the vibrating length, in inches.

Notes

1. Berliner, P.F. (1978). *The Soul of Mbira.* University of California Press, Berkeley, California, 1981.

   This instrument also has the unfortunate name "thumb piano."

2. (A) Sadie, S., Editor (1984). *The New Grove Dictionary of Musical Instruments*, Volume 3, p. 670. Macmillan Press Limited, London, England.

   (B) Stiller, A. (1985). *Handbook of Instrumentation*, p. 236. University of California Press, Berkeley, California.

   Both references refer to a tube instrument as a "tubaphone." Among microtonal musicians this instrument is also known as a "tubulong."

3. This instrument is usually made from solid aluminum or steel rods suspended on flexible foam and played with sticks or mallets. One mainly finds it in experimental and improvisational ensembles.

4. (A) Kinsler, L.W., and Frey, A.R. (1950). *Fundamentals of Acoustics*, 2nd ed., pp. 77–78. John Wiley & Sons, Inc., New York, 1962.

(B) Wood, A. (1940). *Acoustics*, pp. 424–425. Dover Publications, Inc., New York, 1966.

Both of these references analyze the motion of a tuning fork as a kind of free-free bar.

5. *Fundamentals of Acoustics*, p. 76.

6. See Equation 1.20.

7. *Fundamentals of Acoustics*, p. 73.

8. See Section 10.2.

9. See Section 3.11.

10. See Section 9.10.

11. Morse, P.M., and Ingard, K.U. (1968). *Theoretical Acoustics*, p. 179. Princeton University Press, Princeton, New Jersey, 1986.

12. Elmore, W.C., and Heald, M.A. (1969). *Physics of Waves*, p. 117. Dover Publications, Inc. New York, 1985.

13. *Fundamentals of Acoustics*, p. 74.

14. See Section 3.3.

15. *Ibid.*

16. See Section 3.5.

17. *Ibid.*

18. For flexible strings, see Equation 3.13; and for stiff strings, see Equation 4.4.

19. *Fundamentals of Acoustics*, pp. 65–78.

20. Blevins, R.D. (1979). *Formulas for Natural Frequency and Mode Shape*, Reprint, pp. 108–109. Krieger Publishing Company, Malabar, Florida, 1993.

The plots in Figures 6.1 and 6.12 were produced with equations given by Blevins.

21. *Fundamentals of Acoustics*, pp. 68–69.

22. Cremer, L., Heckl, M., and Ungar, E.E. (1973). *Structure-Borne Sound*, 2nd ed., pp. 95–101. Springer-Verlag, Berlin and New York, 1988.

The authors give a thorough account of the angular velocity (w_z) associated with the bending moment (M_z), and the vertical velocity (v_y) associated with the shear force (F_y).

23. *Theoretical Acoustics*, p. 177.

24. (A) Nash, W.A. (1957). *Strength of Materials*, 3rd ed., pp. 198–199. Schaum's Outline Series, McGraw-Hill, Inc., New York, 1994.

(B) Thompson, S.P. (1910). *Calculus Made Easy*, 3rd ed., Chapter 22. St. Martin's Press, New York, 1984.

In calculus, the second derivative with respect to x describes the rate of change of slope or the curvature of a function.

25. Fletcher, N.H., and Rossing, T.D. (1991). *The Physics of Musical Instruments*, 2nd ed., p. 628. Springer-Verlag, Berlin and New York, 1998.

This page illustrates the bending moment and shear force of a uniform free-free bar for the first five modes of vibration.

26. *Structure-Borne Sound*, p. 101.

27. The best way to tune a flat-sounding bar is to drill large flat-bottomed holes with a Forstner bit into the underside of a bar near the ends. With the bit mounted in a drill press, a tuner has great control over the cutting process and is able to carefully remove small amounts of material from the bar.

28. The deflection of a bar is also a measure of the bar's amplitude of vibration. A large deflection produces a louder sound than a small deflection. Since F_1 sounds louder than F_3, it follows that F_1 has a greater deflection than F_3.

29. *Formulas for Natural Frequency and Mode Shape*, p. 175, 180.

30. The terms "decay time" and "decay pattern" are often used to describe the duration of a musical sound. Scientists frequently refer to sustained tones as having "slow decay," and brief tones as having "fast decay." Musical instrument builders and musicians, however, tend to describe the former as having a "long ring-time," and the latter as having a "short ring-time." The difference here is one of emphasis and approach. A builder strives to make an instrument that "rings," not one that has "slow decay."

31. See Section 6.2.

32. See Section 6.12.

33. See Section 5.7.

34. Hoadley, R.B. (1980). *Understanding Wood*, pp. 107–109. The Taunton Press, Newtown, Connecticut, 1981.

This is a clear and non-technical description of Young's modulus of elasticity in wood. For more technical definitions, consult any major physics textbook under the subject of elasticity.

35. See Section 5.5.

36. Dunlop, J.I. (1981). Testing of poles by using acoustic pulse method. *Wood Science and Technology* **15**, pp. 301–310.

37. See Equation 1.20.

38. (A) Stauss, H.E., Martin, F.E., and Billington, D.S. (1951). A piezoelectric method for determining Young's modulus and its temperature dependence. *Journal of the Acoustical Society of America* **23**, No. 6, pp. 695–696.

This excellent article compares dynamic vibration tests to static deflection tests for E in metals.

(B) Timoshenko, S.P. (1953). *History of Strength of Materials*, p. 92. Dover Publications, Inc., New York, 1983.

Young's modulus of elasticity is named after Thomas Young (1773–1829). According to Timoshenko, "Young had determined the weight of the modulus of steel from the frequency of vibration of a tuning fork and found it equal to 29×10^6 lb per in^2."

39. *Fundamentals of Acoustics*, p. 74.

40. *Formulas for Natural Frequency and Mode Shape*, p. 52.

7 / ACOUSTIC RESONATORS

Vibrating bars do not radiate sound very efficiently. To amplify the radiation of sound from bars, instrument builders mount tuned acoustic resonators underneath the bars of marimbas, xylophones, and vibraphones.[1] Acoustic resonators fall into two categories. The most common type consists of a straight cylindrical tube made of bamboo, metal, or plastic that is open at the top end and closed on the bottom end. Length and frequency equations for tube resonators are easy to understand, and building a set of such resonators is not very difficult. The other kind of acoustic resonator consists of a regularly or irregularly shaped cavity.[2] On African marimbas and xylophones one frequently finds hollow spherical or tubular gourd resonators, and on central American marimbas, flared pyramidical resonators made of wood.[3] Although the mathematics of cavity resonators are far more complicated than the mathematics of tube resonators, building and tuning such resonators does not require a detailed knowledge of complex equations. Instead, to construct such resonators, all one needs is a basic knowledge of cavity resonator mechanics, coupled with patience, experience, and a little bit of luck.

Since the acoustic principles of these two types of resonators are very different, this chapter consists of two different areas: Parts I–VI cover tube resonators, and Parts VII–VIII cover cavity resonators. Furthermore, because vibrating air columns in narrow tubes constitute the principal sound-producing systems of flutes, Parts I–VI also serve as an essential introduction to Chapter 8. Included in this discussion will be the propagation of longitudinal traveling waves or sound waves in the surrounding air and in tubes, the reflection of longitudinal traveling waves at the open and closed ends of tubes, the acoustic impedances of tubes and rooms, and the formation of pressure and displacement standing waves in tubes. Readers who need immediate access to tube resonator equations should refer to Section 7.11, which cites length and frequency equations for tubes open at both ends (called *open* tubes), and tubes open at one end and closed on the other end (called *closed* tubes). Also, Section 7.12 includes three important practical considerations for anyone interested in building tube resonators.

Part I

SIMPLE HARMONIC MOTION OF LONGITUDINAL TRAVELING WAVES IN AIR

7.1

The single most important motion associated with the vibrations of all acoustic musical instruments is called *simple harmonic motion*. SHM describes the periodic motion of a particle in a solid, liquid, or gas as it vibrates in a linear direction about its equilibrium position. To observe SHM in a string, return for a moment to the slow motions of a flexible cord in Figure 3.5. The positions of the arrows indicate that in one second, every crest and trough advances the distance of one wavelength (λ) to the right. Furthermore, the position of a given dot in each frame illustrates that every displaced particle in the cord undergoes simple harmonic motion. That is, each particle moves in a linear positive direction above its equilibrium position, and in a linear negative direction below its equilibrium position. This kind of disturbance is called a *transverse traveling wave* because the direction of particle motion is *perpendicular* to the direction of wave propagation.[4]

Now, if one plucks a stretched string fixed at both ends, the string's fundamental mode of vibration will produce a transverse standing wave pattern[5] as shown in a sequence of nine string displacements along the left edge of Figure 7.1. Such a disturbance causes a compression of air particles in front of the string's leading surface, and a rarefaction of air particles behind the string's trailing surface. By definition, a compression is an area of positive pressure or high molecular density, and a rarefaction is an area of negative pressure or low molecular density. Again, notice that the positions of the arrows in each frame show that for a frequency of 1.0 cps, every center of compression and rarefaction advances the distance of one wavelength per second to the right. Moreover, the locations of circles around a given air particle indicate that every particle undergoes SHM. A particle near a compression moves in a forward or positive direction to the right, and near a rarefaction, in a backward or negative direction to the left. Therefore, positive pressure causes a propulsion of air particles in the forward direction, and negative pressure causes a suction of air particles in the backward direction. Note again that only the acoustic energy associated with the disturbance travels in the direction of wave propagation.

A close examination of SHM shows that when $t = 0$ s, the marked particle in Figure 7.1 is passing through the equilibrium position. At this location, the particle has maximum velocity. When $t = \frac{1}{8}$ s, the particle is moving in the positive direction, and at $t = \frac{1}{4}$ s, it reaches maximum positive displacement. Here the velocity = 0. When $t = \frac{3}{8}$ s, the particle is now moving in the negative direction. At $t = \frac{1}{2}$ s, the particle again passes through the equilibrium position. Now, observe the following unique feature of a longitudinal traveling wave. When a particle passes through the equilibrium position, and moves in the same direction as the longitudinal wave, it is located at the center of a compression. This occurs when $t = 0$ s, $t = 1.0$ s, $t = 2.0$ s, etc. Conversely, when a particle passes through the equilibrium position, and moves in the opposite direction of the longitudinal wave, it is located at the center of a rarefaction. This occurs when $t = \frac{1}{2}$ s, $t = 1\frac{1}{2}$ s, $t = 2\frac{1}{2}$ s, etc. When $t = \frac{5}{8}$ s, the particle continues its movement in the negative direction, and at $t = \frac{3}{4}$ s, it reaches maximum negative displacement. Here again, the velocity = 0. Finally, when $t = \frac{7}{8}$ s, the particle is now moving again in the positive direction, and at $t = 1.0$ s, it returns to the same position as in the first frame. This position marks the beginning of the next cycle.

We may also view this motion by looking straight down onto the page. Imagine the nine marked particles in the pathway of a pendulum bob as it swings back and forth between the left and right margins of the page. Note, therefore, that only the mechanical energy associated with the disturbance travels in the direction of wave propagation. The particles of the medium do not travel, but simply oscillate about their respective equilibrium positions. This kind of disturbance is called a *longitudinal traveling wave* or *sound wave* because the direction of particle motion is *parallel* to the direction of wave propagation.

Let us now examine a spring-mass system designed to demonstrate simple harmonic motion. Figure 7.2 shows that such a system consists of two distinct parts: a spring or elastic component that restores the system to its equilibrium position, and a mass or inertial component that causes the system to overshoot its equilibrium position.[6] Aspects of these two mechanical or acoustical components belong to *all* vibrating systems. Scientists refer to the spring-mass system as a *lumped system* because both parts exist independently of each other. In contrast, most vibrating systems and musical instruments are called *distributed*[7] or *continuous*[8] systems because a clear physical

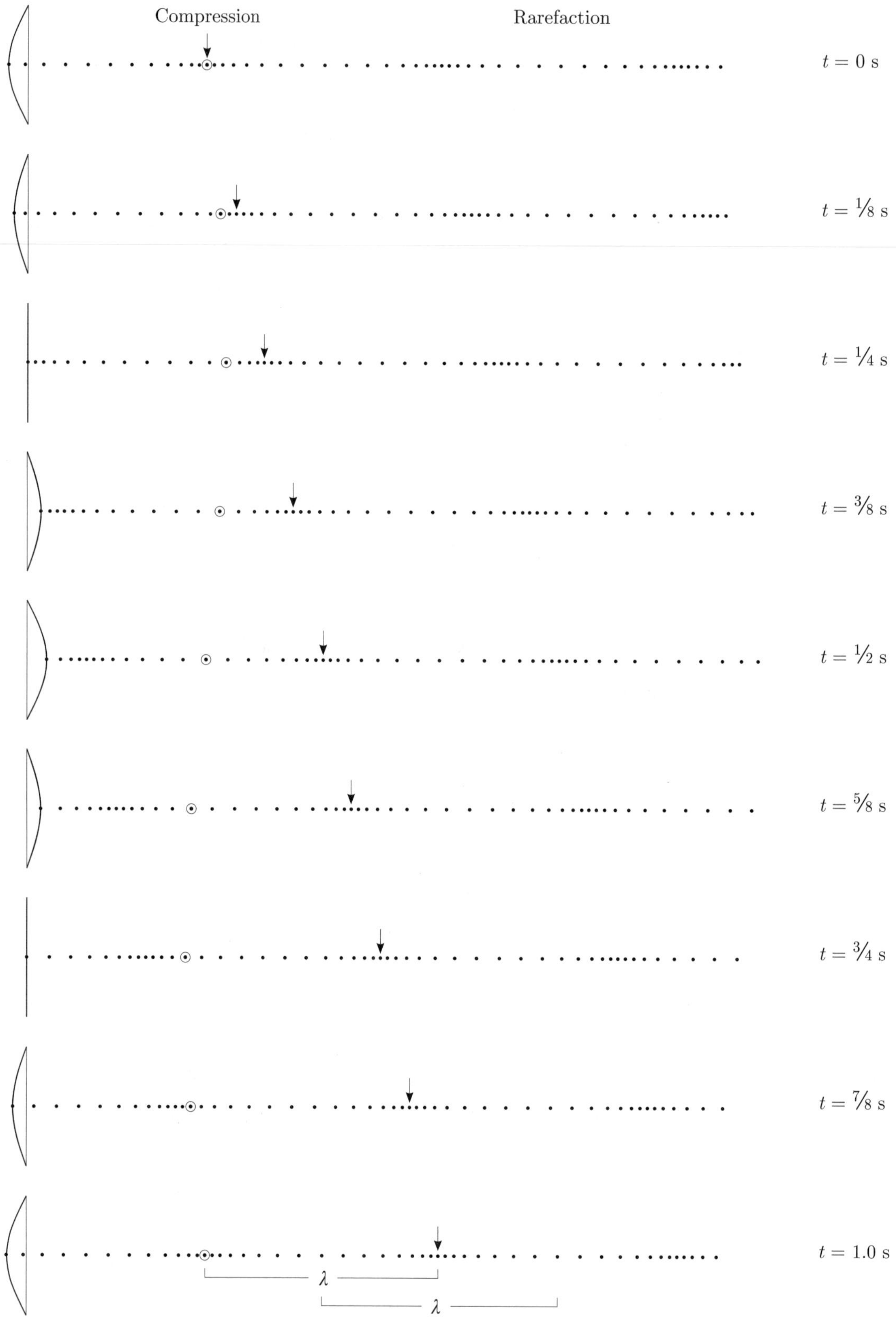

Figure 7.1 A longitudinal traveling wave or sound wave in the air. Circles indicate the horizontal oscillation of a given air particle, and arrows, the horizontal propagation of a sound wave. The particle undergoes simple harmonic motion, but does not advance with the wave that travels in the same direction as the particle.

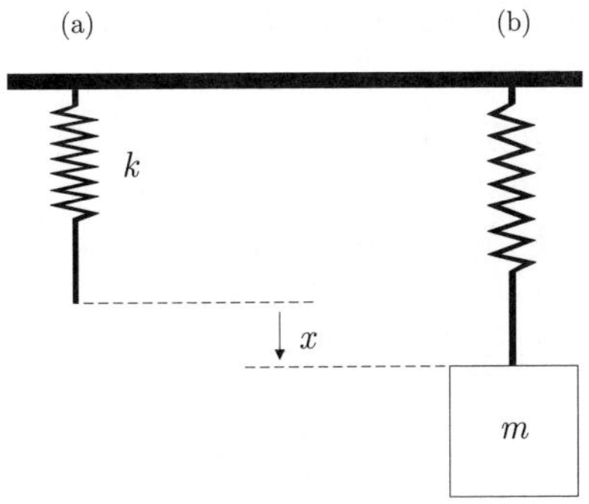

Figure 7.2 A spring-mass system designed to demonstrate simple harmonic motion. (a) The spring constant (k) represents the system's elastic component, and (b) the mass (m), the system's inertial component. The displacement (x) indicates the effect that the weight of the attached mass has on the spring's length.

separation between the elastic and inertial components does not exist. Here it is more difficult to isolate and recognize the function of each part. The purpose of the spring-mass system is to show how a clearly delineated elastic component and a clearly delineated inertial component interact to produce simple harmonic motion.

The following equation gives the natural frequency of the spring-mass system:

$$F = \frac{1}{2\pi}\sqrt{\frac{k}{m}} \tag{7.1}$$

where k is the spring constant,[9] in pounds-force per inch, or lbf/in; and m is the mass, in micas. (For a definition of the mica mass unit, see Section 1.10.) The variable k refers to the stiffness of a spring. A displaced compression spring with a high value for k pushes back harder than one with a low k value; and a displaced extension spring, like the kind seen in Figure 7.2, with a high value for k pulls back harder than one with a low k value. (See Note 50.) Finally, as the term *spring constant* implies, for a given spring the value of k is always the same.

Suppose that a spring-mass system with a very flexible spring[10] hangs from our ceiling and that we would like to predict its frequency of oscillation. Calculate the value of k in three steps. (1) Measure the spring's unstretched length. (2) Attach a weight and calculate the spring's displacement (x). That is, subtract the spring's unstretched length from its stretched length. (3) Divide the weight by the displacement. Consider a weight of 0.325 lbf, and a displacement of 23.5 inches. Then,

$$k = \frac{w}{x} = \frac{0.325 \text{ lbf}}{23.5 \text{ in}} = 0.0138 \text{ lbf/in}$$

Next, according to Equation 1.19, calculate the mass of the attached weight by dividing pounds-force by the acceleration of gravity, in inches per second squared:

$$m = \frac{w}{g} = \frac{0.325 \text{ lbf}}{386.09 \text{ in/s}^2} = 0.00084 \text{ mica}$$

Finally, substitute the values of k and m into Equation 7.1 and calculate the frequency[11] of the system:

$$F = \frac{\sqrt{\dfrac{0.0138 \text{ lbf/in}}{0.00084 \text{ mica}}}}{2\pi} = 0.645 \text{ cps}$$

This system oscillates with simple harmonic motion at a rate of approximately 19.4 cycles per thirty seconds.

Figure 7.2 illustrates simple harmonic motion in the vertical direction. We could also attach the spring to a wall and illustrate simple harmonic motion in a horizontal direction. Such an experiment would give the same frequency.[12] However, rotating the system by 90° poses a serious problem. Equation 7.1 does not account for the damping effects of friction. To accurately operate the oscillator in the horizontal direction, we must provide a frictionless surface for the mass, a formidable task at best.[13]

Finally, note that this system has the same frequency on the moon or any other celestial body. Lunar gravitational acceleration is only 65.76 in/s^2. Consequently, since the lunar weight of the attached mass is much less, the spring's displacement is much less as well. However, because the ratio of weight to displacement is the same on the moon as on earth, the spring constant remains unchanged. Therefore, since k is the same and m is always constant,[14] the frequency of the system does not change.

Part II

EQUATIONS FOR THE SPEED OF LONGITUDINAL WAVES IN SOLIDS, LIQUIDS, AND GASES

7.2

Refer now to Figure 7.3 and consider the propagation of a longitudinal traveling wave or plane sound wave as it enters an undisturbed medium. The vertical lines in this figure represent layers of particles in either a solid, liquid, or gas. (a) The medium is in a state of static equilibrium. (b) Upon applying a very brief percussive force or percussive pressure to the left end of the medium, the particles immediately displace in the positive direction to the right. This causes a compression pulse, or area of high molecular density, to begin traveling through the medium. As the pulse moves in the positive direction, the rate of compression and the particle velocity gradually decrease. (c) The first layer reaches maximum positive displacement. Here the particle velocity = 0, and the restoring force or restoring pressure in the medium is at a maximum. (d) Consequently, the outer layers begin moving in the opposite negative direction to the left. Due to the uneven distribution of particles, a rarefaction pulse, or area of low molecular density, begins traveling in the negative direction to the left. Meanwhile, the original compression pulse continues its advance into the undisturbed medium to the right. (e) The first layer reaches its equilibrium position. Here the particle velocity is at a maximum, and the restoring force or restoring pressure = 0. (f) According to Newton's first law, the medium overshoots the equilibrium position because the medium's mass will not stop moving, or change direction, unless a force acts to cause such changes.[15] As the rarefaction pulse moves in the negative direction, the rate of rarefaction and the particle velocity gradually decrease. (g) The first layer reaches maximum negative displacement, which means the particle velocity = 0, and the restoring force or pressure is at a maximum. (h) As a result, the outer layers reverse their direction once more and begin traveling in the positive direction to the right. This action produces another compression pulse. (i) Here the first layer reaches its equilibrium position for a second time. Provided there is enough energy in the system, and the damping effects of friction are not too great, the medium's inertia will cause the first layer to overshoot its equilibrium position and, thereby, begin a second cycle of simple harmonic motion.

As an example of the ubiquitous presence of longitudinal traveling waves in many different media,[16] consider the following equation[17] that gives the longitudinal mode frequencies (F_n) of

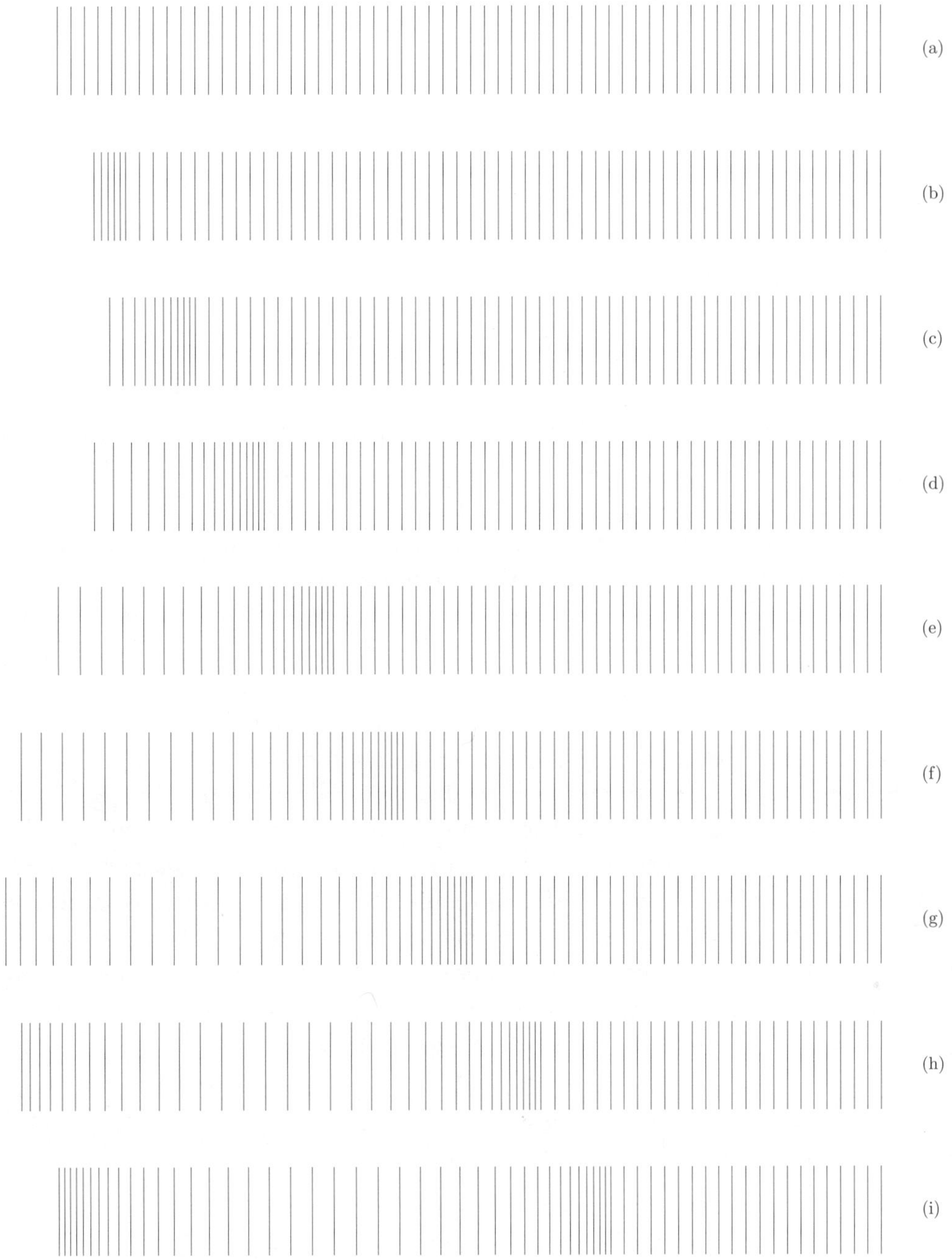

Figure 7.3 A plane sound wave as it enters an undisturbed medium. Vertical lines represent layers of particles in either a solid, liquid, or gas. Each layer performs simple harmonic motion in the horizontal direction, while the wave advances in the positive direction from left to right.

(1) plain strings fixed at both ends, (2) uniform bars, rods, and tubes clamped or free at both ends, and (3) columns of fluids (liquids or gases) in tubes open or closed at both ends:

$$F_{\text{n longitudinal}} = n\frac{c_{\text{L}}}{2L} \tag{7.2}$$

where n is the mode number, any positive integer; c_{L} is the speed of longitudinal traveling waves or the speed of sound in a given medium, in inches per second; and L is the length of the object, in inches.

For solids,

$$c_{\text{L solids}} = \sqrt{\frac{E}{\rho}} \tag{7.3}$$

for liquids,[18]

$$c_{\text{L liquids}} = \sqrt{\frac{\gamma B_{\text{I}}}{\rho}} = \sqrt{\frac{B_{\text{A}}}{\rho}} \tag{7.4}$$

and for gases,[19]

$$c_{\text{L gases}} = \sqrt{\frac{\gamma P}{\rho}} = \sqrt{\frac{B_{\text{A}}}{\rho}} \tag{7.5}$$

where E is Young's modulus of elasticity of a solid, in pounds-force per square inch, or psi; γ is the ratio of specific heats, dimensionless; B_{I} is the isothermal bulk modulus,[20] and B_{A} is the adiabatic bulk modulus of a fluid (liquid or gas), in psi; P is the barometric pressure, in psi; and ρ is the mass density, or mass per cubic volume of the medium, in mica per cubic inch.[21] Appendices F, G, and H list values for the variables that appear in Equations 7.3–7.5.

Equation 7.5 is subject to misinterpretation because it seems to suggest that increases in pressure produce increases in the speed of sound of a gas. This is not the case. For example, if we double the pressure by pumping air into a partially deflated tire, we also double the density of air inside the tire. Since the ratio P/ρ remains unchanged, the speed of sound inside the tire is the same as outside the tire. If we take a tuned instrument into the mountains where there is less atmospheric pressure, its tuning does not change because the density of air at high elevations is also proportionately less. So, the speed of sound near the ocean and in the mountains is constant. However, an instrument does go out of tune due to changes in temperature. A rise in temperature causes gases to expand and decrease in density, while a fall in temperature causes gases to contract and increase in density.[22] Note that thermal expansion or contraction of an *unconfined* gas like the surrounding air produces negligible changes in pressure. Temperature fluctuations in the air have a much greater effect on ρ than on P. Furthermore, the presence of moisture also changes the density of the surrounding air, but when compared to temperature, these effects are minor.[23]

Use Equation 7.6 to calculate the speed of sound in gases as a function of temperature,

$$c_{\text{L gases}} = \sqrt{\gamma R T_{\text{A}}} \tag{7.6}$$

where R is the ideal gas constant, in inch·lbf/(mica·°R); and T_{A} is the absolute temperature of a gas, in Rankine. In the meter-kilogram-second system, $R = 286.7$ Joules/(kg·K) for air,[24] which is equivalent to 286.7 $\text{m}^2/(\text{s}^2\cdot\text{K})$. A conversion shows that in the inch-mica-second system used throughout this book, $R = 246{,}881$ inches·lbf/(mica·°R) for air, which is equivalent to $R = 246{,}881\ \text{in}^2/(\text{s}^2\cdot°\text{R})$. Since $\gamma = 1.402$ for air, compute the following m/s and in/s constants:

$$\sqrt{\gamma R} = \sqrt{1.402(286.7\ \text{m}^2/\text{s}^2)} = 20.05\ \text{m/s}$$

$$\sqrt{\gamma R} = \sqrt{1.402(246{,}881\ \text{in}^2/\text{s}^2)} = 588.33\ \text{in/s}$$

Now rewrite Equation 7.6 to read

$$c_{\text{L gases}} = (20.05\ \text{m/s})\sqrt{T_{\text{A}}} \tag{7.6A}$$

$$c_{\text{L gases}} = (588.33\ \text{in/s})\sqrt{T_{\text{A}}} \tag{7.6B}$$

Use Equation 7.7A to convert Celsius temperature (T_C) to Kelvin,[25]

$$T_A = T_C + 273.15 = \text{K} \tag{7.7A}$$

and Equation 7.7B to convert Fahrenheit temperature (T_F) to Rankine:

$$T_A = T_F + 459.67 = {}^\circ\text{R} \tag{7.7B}$$

Now convert 20°C into K and 68°F into °R, substitute these results into Equations 7.6A and 7.6B, respectively, and calculate the speed of sound in the air as 343.29 m/s and 13,514.57 in/s, respectively. (Most physics texts give the metric value $c_L \approx 343$ m/s; therefore, $c_L \approx 13{,}504$ in/s.) Further calculations show that the speed of sound in the air increases by approximately 0.6 m/s per degree rise on the Celsius scale, or 13.1 in/s per degree rise on the Fahrenheit scale.[26]

Suppose a standard flute open at the mouthpiece and open at the far end has a length of 15.35 inches, and is tuned to A_4 (440.00 cps) at 68°F. What is the flute's frequency when the temperature rises by 18 degrees Fahrenheit? At 86°F, the speed of sound in the air equals 13,743.1 in/s. Substitute the flute's length and this wave speed into Equation 7.2 and calculate the new fundamental frequency:

$$F_{\text{new}} = \frac{13{,}743.1 \text{ in/s}}{2(15.35 \text{ in})} = 447.66 \text{ cps}$$

To determine the magnitude of this frequency shift in cents,[27] multiply the logarithm of the following frequency ratio to the base 10 by the constant 3986.314:

$$\log_{10} \frac{447.66 \text{ cps}}{440.0 \text{ cps}} \times 3986.314 = 29.9 \text{ ¢}$$

We conclude, therefore, that a rise of 18 degrees Fahrenheit causes the flute to sound nearly a third of a semitone sharp, a significant mistuning that an ensemble player must correct before giving a performance with other musicians.

Part III

REFLECTIONS OF LONGITUDINAL TRAVELING WAVES AT THE CLOSED AND OPEN ENDS OF TUBES

7.3

With this background information, let us now focus the discussion on the reflection of longitudinal traveling waves in tubes. Recall that in Chapter 3, we examined the reflection of transverse traveling waves from the fixed ends of strings, and how the principle of superposition leads to the production of transverse standing waves. Musical instrument strings are not very complicated because the fixed ends of strings present only one possibility for the reflection of waves. Upon reflection from the fixed ends, all transverse waves reverse both their direction of travel and their position in the string. A reversal in position (or a phase change) means that crests reflect as troughs, and troughs reflect as crests. In contrast, longitudinal traveling waves in resonators and wind instruments reflect from both the open and closed ends of tubes, with completely different consequences.

To understand the reflection of traveling waves in tubes, we begin with a preliminary examination of Figures 7.4–7.7. In all frames, we may interpret the vertical lines that represent layers of air particles inside the tubes from two different perspectives. (1) When a pulse propagates through the tube, the *locations* of these lines indicate the displacements of air particles from their respective equilibrium positions. (2) In contrast, the *spaces* between these lines indicate the types of pressures that are present in the tube. Narrow spaces represent *compression pulses*, and wide spaces represent *rarefaction pulses*. Note, however, that at the closed end of a tube, Figures 7.4 and 7.5 do not immediately suggest that the displacement of air particles equals zero. For example, refer to Figure 7.4, which shows that a compression pulse reflects as a compression pulse (no phase change) when it reaches the tube's closed end. In frame (e), we see a compression pulse — in this case, a region of maximum positive pressure — at the tube's cap. Here the displacement equals zero because the closed end obstructs the motion of all air particles. To understand why the air particle displacement is zero wherever the positive pressure of a compression is at a maximum, consider the following example. Suppose you pump air into a tire that has a huge hole. The air pressure inside the tire equals zero, while the displacement of air particles through the hole is at a maximum. If you fix the hole and resume pumping, the displacement of air at the repair patch is now zero, while the positive pressure inside the tire begins to rise; this causes the tire to inflate. Similarly, at a point of reflection in the tube where there is maximum compression, there is no particle displacement; and at a point of reflection where there is maximum particle displacement, there is no compression. The latter condition occurs at the open end of a tube. (See Section 7.4.)

Return once more to Figure 7.4 and reconsider in greater detail the reflection of a compression pulse at the closed end of a cylindrical resonator tube. (a) The air inside the resonator is in a state of static equilibrium. (b) Start a region of high pressure (or high air density) by rapidly pushing your hand against the tube's open end. This action compresses the air at the opening, and (c) produces an *incident compression pulse* that travels down the length of the tube. (d) As the incident pulse approaches the tube's closed end, the positive pressure of the pulse gradually increases as the particle displacement decreases. (e) The compression pulse arrives at the closed end. Note that the compressed layers of particles are now more closely crowded together. Here the positive pressure of the compression pulse is at a maximum and has twice the value than at any other location in the tube. (f) As a *reflected compression pulse* travels in the opposite direction back toward the open end, notice that the process of reflection did not change the character (or phase) of the pulse. To understand why the compression pulse remains unchanged, consider a closely spaced set of balls rolling at an oblique angle toward a rigid wall. As the balls reflect from the wall, the relative distances between the balls do not change. In other words, the proximity of the balls, or in this case, the proximity of the air particles, remains unchanged when the reflection occurs at a hard rigid surface. (g) The compression pulse continues to travel back toward the opening, and (h) provided that it does not have the energy required to overshoot the open end, (i) it simply stops at the tube's opening. Consequently, the air inside the resonator regains its previous state of equilibrium.

Refer to Figure 7.5 and note that a similar condition occurs when a rarefaction pulse reflects at the closed end of a tube. (a) The air inside the resonator is in a state of static equilibrium. (b) Start a region of low pressure (or low air density) by rapidly pulling your hand from the tube's open end. This action rarefies the air at the opening, and (c) produces an *incident rarefaction pulse* that travels down the length of the tube. (d) As the incident pulse approaches the tube's closed end, the negative pressure of the pulse gradually increases as the particle displacement decreases. Recall for a moment the previously mentioned tire analogy, only in this case suppose you are using a vacuum pump to suck air out of a tire that has a huge hole. Again, the air pressure inside the tire equals zero, while the displacement of air particles through the hole is at a maximum. If you fix the hole, and continue pumping air out of the tire, the displacement of air at the repair patch is now zero, while the negative pressure inside the tire begins to rise; this causes the tire to collapse. Similarly, at a point of reflection in the tube where there is maximum rarefaction, there is no particle displacement. Conversely, at a point of reflection in the tube where there is maximum particle displacement, there is no rarefaction. (The latter condition occurs at the open end of a tube.) (e) The rarefaction pulse arrives at the closed end. Note that the rarefied layers of particles are now more widely spaced apart. Here the negative pressure of the rarefaction pulse is at a maximum, and the particle displacement equals zero. (f) As a *reflected rarefaction pulse* travels in the opposite direction back toward the open end, notice that the process of reflection did not change the phase of the pulse. To understand why the rarefaction pulse remains unchanged, consider a widely spaced set of balls rolling at an oblique angle toward a rigid wall. As the balls reflect from the wall, the relative distances between the balls do not change. That is, the separation of the balls, or in this case, the separation of the air particles, remains unchanged when the reflection occurs at a hard rigid surface. (g) The rarefaction pulse continues to travel back toward the opening, and (h) provided that it does not have the energy required to overshoot the open end, (i) it simply stops at the tube's opening. Consequently, the air inside the resonator regains its previous state of equilibrium.

7.4

In Section 7.3, we observed that compression and rarefaction pulses reflect from the closed ends of tubes without changes in phase. A similar condition occurs when transverse traveling waves reflect from the loose ends of cords: here crests reflect as crests, and troughs reflect as troughs.[28] However, at the fixed ends of cords, traveling waves undergo a phase reversal in position because crests reflect as troughs, and troughs reflect as crests.[29] Similarly, compression and rarefaction pulses also experience phase reversals when they reflect from the open ends of tubes.

Turn to Figure 7.6 and consider the reflection of a compression pulse at the open end of a cylindrical resonator tube. (a) The air inside the resonator is in a state of static equilibrium. (b) Start a region of high pressure at the closed end by rapidly accelerating the tube in a forward direction, or in a direction toward the tube's open end. This action compresses the air at the closed end, and (c) produces an *incident compression pulse* that travels up the length of the tube. (d) As the incident pulse approaches the tube's open end, the positive pressure of the pulse gradually decreases as the particle displacement through the opening increases. (e) The compression pulse arrives at the open end. Note that for a brief moment the air inside the resonator is in a state of dynamic equilibrium. Here the air particles are moving and not at rest. (f) Because the pulse has inertia, it overshoots the opening and, thereby, propels air out of the tube. This creates a region of negative pressure (or low air density) at the opening, and (g) produces a *reflected rarefaction pulse* that begins to travel in the opposite direction down the length of the tube. (h) Provided that this pulse does not have the energy required to reflect from the closed end as a rarefaction, (i) it simply stops at the tube's cap. Consequently, the air inside the resonator regains its previous state of static equilibrium. In summary, when a compression overshoots the open end of a tube, it undergoes a phase reversal in pressure, which means that the compression reflects back into the tube as a rarefaction.

Finally, refer to Figure 7.7 and consider the reflection of a rarefaction pulse at the open end of a resonator tube. (a) Again, the air inside the resonator is in a state of static equilibrium. (b) Start a region of low pressure at the closed end by rapidly accelerating the tube in a backward direction, or in a direction toward the tube's closed end. This action rarefies the air at the closed end, and (c) produces an *incident rarefaction pulse* that travels up the length of the tube. (d) As the incident pulse approaches the tube's open end, the negative pressure of the pulse gradually decreases as the particle displacement through the opening increases. (e) The rarefaction pulse arrives at the open end. Note that for a brief moment the air inside the resonator is in a state of dynamic equilibrium. (f) Because the pulse has inertia, it overshoots the opening and, thereby, sucks air into the tube. This creates a region of positive pressure (or high air density) at the opening, and (g) produces a *reflected compression pulse* that travels in the opposite direction down the length of the tube.

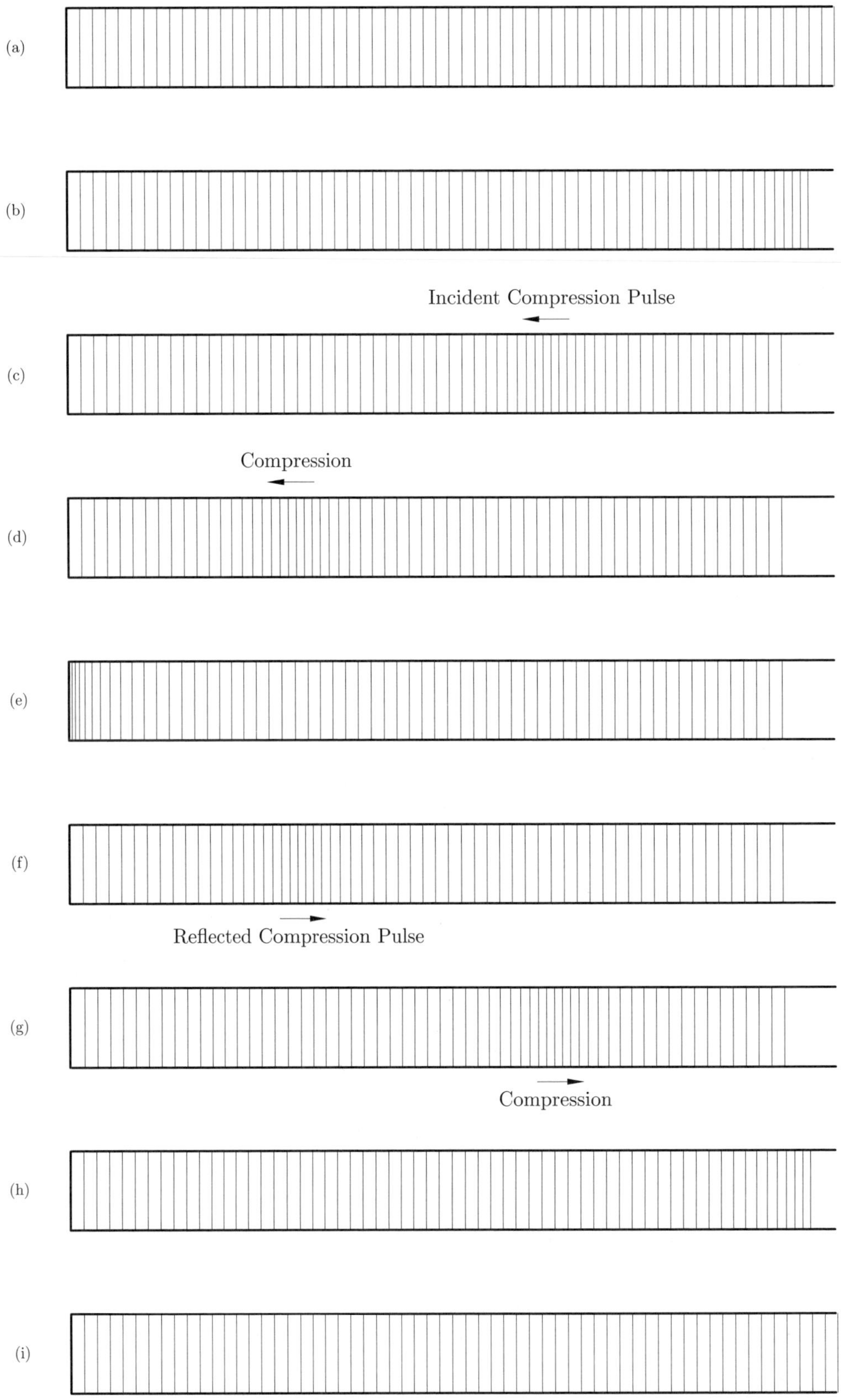

Figure 7.4 At the closed end of a tube, a compression pulse reflects without phase reversal as another compression pulse.

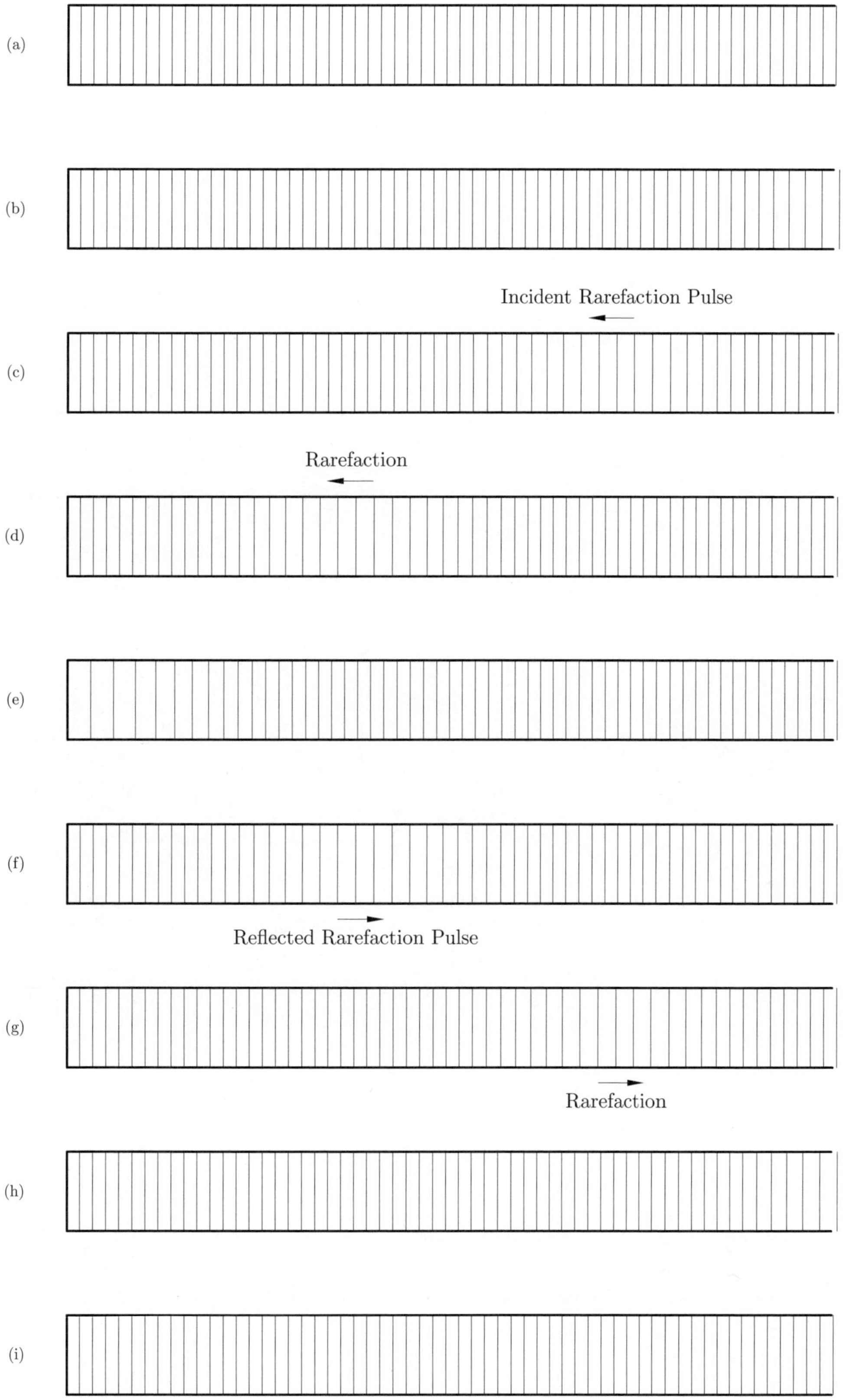

Figure 7.5 At the closed end of a tube, a rarefaction pulse reflects without phase reversal as another rarefaction pulse.

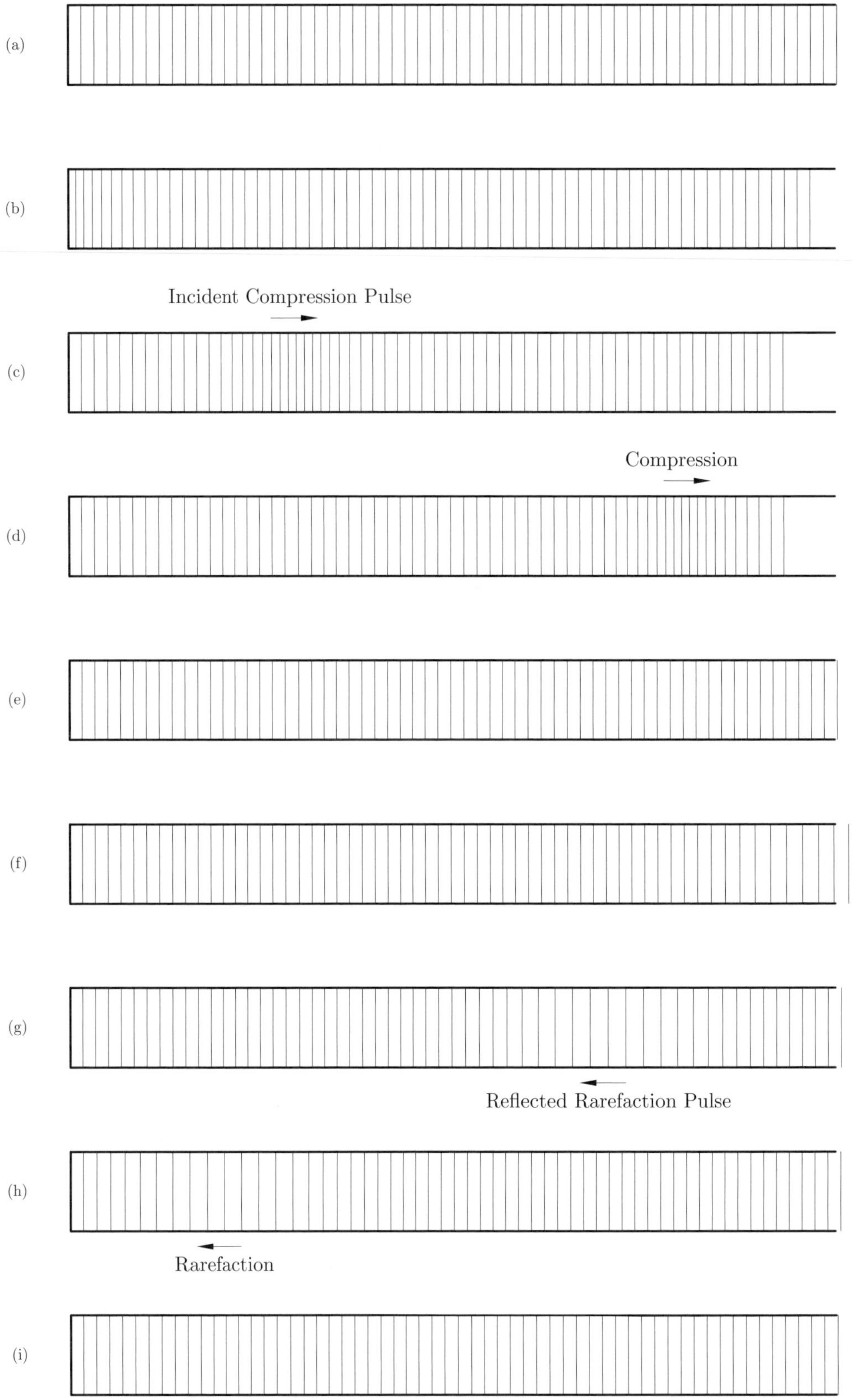

Figure 7.6 At the open end of a tube, a compression pulse reflects with phase reversal as a rarefaction pulse.

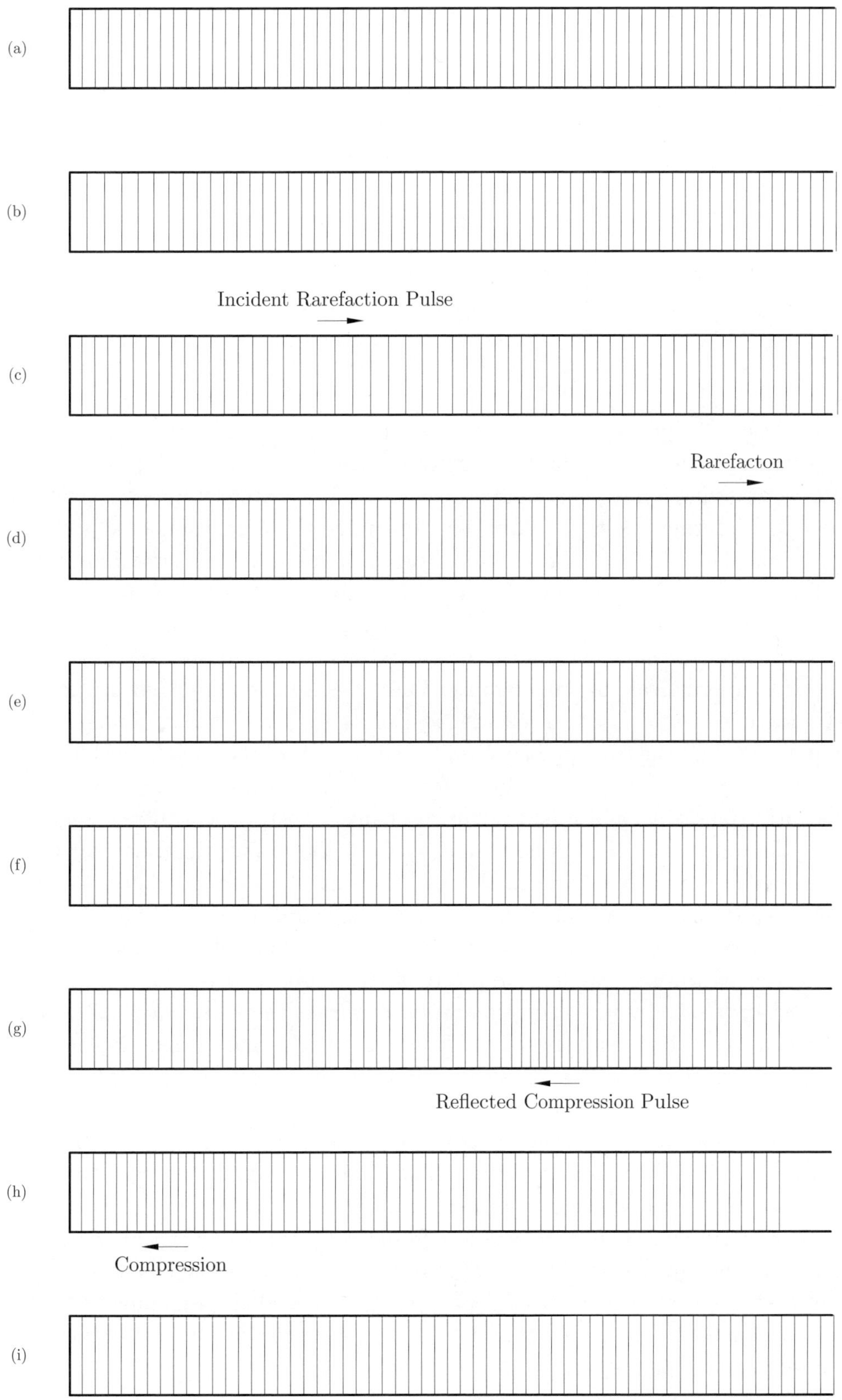

Figure 7.7 At the open end of a tube, a rarefaction pulse reflects with phase reversal as a compression pulse.

(h) Provided that this pulse does not have the energy required to reflect from the closed end as a compression, (i) it simply stops at the tube's cap. Consequently, the air inside the resonator regains its previous state of static equilibrium. In summary, when a rarefaction overshoots the open end of a tube, it undergoes a phase reversal in pressure, which means that the rarefaction reflects back into the tube as a compression.

Part IV

ACOUSTIC IMPEDANCE AND TUBE-TO-ROOM IMPEDANCE RATIO

7.5

The question arises, "Why do waves reflect from the open end of a resonator?" To answer this question, we return to the subject of wave impedance discussed at length in Chapter 5. In short, the reflection or transmission of wave energy depends on the change of impedance at the boundary between any two vibrating systems.[30] Scientists determine the magnitude of this change by calculating a wave impedance ratio. For example, if two systems have the same impedance, the wave impedance ratio is 1:1, which means that a wave originating in the first system barely notices the boundary and transmits most if its energy (without significant reflection) to the second system. Conversely, if the first system cannot cause the second system to vibrate, the impedance of the second system is for all practical purposes infinite. This gives a wave impedance ratio of $1 : \infty$, which means that a wave in the first system reflects most of its energy (without significant transmission) at the boundary between the two systems. Recall that in pianos, the soundboard has two functions: (1) it receives mechanical energy from the strings, and (2) due to its thickness and large surface area, it efficiently transforms and radiates this mechanical energy as acoustic energy into the surrounding air. The rate at which it receives energy from the strings depends on a soundboard-to-string wave impedance ratio (see Section 5.6), and the rate at which it radiates energy into the air depends (in part) on an air-to-soundboard wave impedance ratio (see Section 5.12).

A similar process also occurs when we strike a marimba bar with a mallet. Such a percussive force displaces the bar from its equilibrium position and causes it to vibrate. As the bar vibrates, it transforms mechanical energy into acoustic energy. However, there are two reasons why the bar is not an efficient radiator of acoustic energy. (1) Due to the bar's small size, it displaces very little air; (2) due to the unrestricted flow of air between the bar's upper and lower surfaces, the bar simply "pumps" most of the air back and forth between its top and bottom sides.[31] In contrast, an efficient radiator does not simply move air back and forth, it compresses and rarefies the air. The main function of the resonator is to disrupt the free flow of air around the bar and, thereby, to amplify the bar's radiated energy through a phenomenon called *resonance.* Resonance occurs when a *tuned* resonator receives an oscillating driving pressure from a vibrating bar whose fundamental frequency is the same as the fundamental frequency of the resonator. When resonance occurs, a very efficient compression-rarefaction cycle takes place. As a result, longitudinal standing waves begin vibrating inside the resonator. Some of the acoustic energy generated by these standing waves radiates through the resonator's opening into the surrounding air and, thereby, produces a great amplification of sound.

Longitudinal standing waves in a resonator can only occur if longitudinal traveling waves reflect from both ends of the resonator. At the closed end, the resonator's wave impedance is infinitely large. That is, the cap that closes the resonator does not vibrate in response to a sound wave inside the resonator. Consequently, when longitudinal traveling waves reflect from the cap, a transmission of wave energy does not take place, and there is no radiation of sound from that end of the resonator. At the open end, however, the wave impedance is not infinitely large and some acoustic energy transmits into the surrounding air as clearly audible sound. The amount of energy that *reflects into* the resonator and the amount of energy that *transmits out of* the resonator depend on the size and shape of the resonator, and on the size and shape of the room. Here the room acts as a second resonator with enormously large proportions. Therefore, to describe the rate at which acoustic energy radiates from the open end of a straight cylindrical resonator, we must now calculate a tube-to-room wave impedance ratio.

Recall that Section 5.9 described a soundboard-to-air coupling, and how energy is radiated *over an area of contact* between a solid and a gas. In a tube-to-room coupling, we must consider how energy is radiated *through an area of contact* between two enclosed gases. We begin, therefore, by stating that all enclosed fluids present a complex wave impedance to a given driving pressure. This quantity measures how difficult it is to produce vibrations in a confined fluid (liquid or gas). The complex ratio of driving pressure ($\boldsymbol{P}$) to volume velocity ($\boldsymbol{U}$) defines the complex acoustic (wave) impedance ($\boldsymbol{Z}_{\mathrm{A}}$) of a fluid:

$$\boldsymbol{Z}_{\mathrm{A}} = \frac{\boldsymbol{P}}{\boldsymbol{U}} \tag{7.8}$$

Here

$$U\ (\mathrm{in}^3/\mathrm{s}) \equiv S\ (\mathrm{in}^2) \times u\ (\mathrm{in/s})$$

where S is the cross-sectional area of a given surface, in square inches; and u is the particle velocity of the fluid, in inches per second. This dimensional analysis shows that U represents the volume of air that flows through a surface area per second.

Just like Equations 5.1 and 5.4, Equation 7.8 is not very practical. Measuring driving pressures and volume velocities is a highly complicated and difficult task. However, when the air's acoustic impedance is a pure resistance (R), and there is *no* reactance (jX), we may calculate Z_{A} by considering only the fluid's characteristic impedance (z),[32] and the surface area through which it flows:

$$Z_{\mathrm{A}} = \frac{P}{U} = \frac{P}{uS} = \frac{P/u}{S} = \frac{z}{S} = \frac{\sqrt{\rho B_{\mathrm{A}}}}{S} \tag{7.8A}$$

(See Equation 5.4A.) Furthermore, since B_{A} is not a convenient quantity (see Section 1.13), most acoustics texts give Equation 7.8A as[33]

$$Z_{\mathrm{A}} = \frac{\rho c}{S} \tag{7.9}$$

where c is the speed of sound in the air, in inches per second. Before proceeding with this calculation for the acoustic impedance of air in a tube, let us first cover some relevant background information.

~ 7.6 ~

Section 5.5 described the string-to-soundboard relation as a forced vibration because the strings (the driving system) must be in continuous contact with the soundboard (the driven system), or the soundboard will not vibrate. Similarly, Section 5.10 described the soundboard-to-air relation as a forced vibration because the soundboard (the driving system) must be in continuous contact with the surrounding air (the driven system), or the air will not vibrate. Whenever two vibrating systems constitute a forced vibration, the complex wave impedance ($\boldsymbol{Z}$ or $\boldsymbol{z}$) of the driven system includes a resistance variable (R or r), and a reactance variable (jX or jx). The resistance variable does not depend on the frequency of the driven system, while the reactance variable does depend on the frequency of the driven system. Most often, the frequencies of the *driving system* (F), and the resonant frequencies of the *driven system* (F_{n}) are not the same: $F \neq F_{\text{n}}$, which means that the two systems vibrate out of phase. As a result, the reactance of the driven system varies according to whether the driving system vibrates at a frequency less than the resonant frequency of the driven system: $F < F_{\text{n}}$, or greater than the resonant frequency of the driven system: $F > F_{\text{n}}$. However, when the frequency of the driving system and the resonant frequency of the driven system are the same: $F = F_{\text{n}}$, then the reactance variable vanishes and the two systems vibrate in phase. Under these conditions, we may calculate the wave impedance of the driven system by considering only the resistance variable.

The bar-to-resonator relation also constitutes a forced vibration: that is, the air in the resonator vibrates because it is in continuous contact with the air that surrounds the bar. Recall, however, that on a keyboard percussion instrument, the bar (as the driving system) and the air in the resonator (as the driven system) always vibrate in a state of *resonance* because tuners intentionally tune both systems to the same fundamental frequency. Consequently, the reactance of the driven system vanishes, so that the acoustic impedance of the resonator tube (Z_{t}) equals the tube's resistance (R_{t}):

$$Z_{\text{t}} = R_{\text{t}}$$

Then, according to Equation 7.9,

$$Z_{\text{t}} = \frac{\rho c}{S} \tag{7.9A}$$

Consider now the following inch and centimeter dimensions (see Section 7.12) of the lowest G_3 resonator on the Diamond Marimba in Plate 7:

d = 2.250 in., manufactured inside diameter; or ≈ 5.72 cm
r = 1.125 in., manufactured inside radius; or ≈ 2.86 cm
L = 42.04 cm, cut length; or ≈ 16.55 in.
F = 196.00 cps

To use Equation 7.9A, first calculate the tube's cross-sectional surface area:

$$S = \pi r^2$$
$$S = 3.1416(1.125 \text{ in})^2 = 3.976 \text{ in}^2$$

Next, substitute ρ and c for air,[34] and the surface area into Equation 7.9A and compute the tube's acoustic impedance:

$$Z_{\text{t}} = \frac{(0.000000113 \text{ mica/in}^3)(13{,}504 \text{ in/s})}{3.976 \text{ in}^2} = 0.0003838 \text{ mica/(in}^4\text{·s)}$$

7.7

Like the bar-to-resonator relation, the tube-to-room relation also constitutes a forced vibration: that is, the air in the room vibrates because it is in continuous contact with the air in the tube. Through the cross-sectional surface area of the tube's open end, longitudinal standing waves in the tube exert an oscillating driving pressure that puts the air in the room into motion. From here, longitudinal sound waves travel throughout the room. At the walls of the room these waves are then reflected back again to the tube opening. This reflection of sound waves, determined by the size and shape of the room, results in the formation of longitudinal standing waves. For the most part, the frequencies of the driving tube waves, and the resonant frequencies of the driven room waves are not the same: $F \neq F_{\text{n}}$. Consequently, the tube waves and the room waves are usually out of phase. The physical motion of the room air (in reaction or response to the driving pressure of the tube air) continually changes the wave impedance of the air. Therefore, the acoustic load exerted by the room air on the tube air is *not* a pure resistance. We cannot determine the complex acoustic impedance of the room ($\boldsymbol{Z}_{\text{r}}$) by considering only the elastic and inertial properties of the room's resistance (R_{r}). Instead, to calculate the complex acoustic (wave) impedance of the room, a reactance must be added to the resistance. In very general terms, such an equation would read

$$\boldsymbol{Z}_{\text{r}} = R_{\text{r}} + jX$$

To solve for the reactance, one must know the exact frequencies of the driven room waves at any given moment in time. However, if we place the tube in an anechoic chamber where the reflection of sound waves is at an absolute minimum (or if we consider a state of *resonance* when the frequencies of the driving tube waves and the resonant frequencies of the driven room waves are the same: $F = F_{\text{n}}$), then jX vanishes and the two systems begin vibrating in phase. Therefore, with respect to the driving pressure of the tube, the acoustic impedance of the room equals the room's resistance:

$$Z_{\text{r}} = R_{\text{r}}$$

$$Z_{\text{r}} = \frac{\rho c}{S}$$

For a standard size of 8 feet × 20 feet, a typical room has the following surface area dimensions in square inches:

$$S = (96\text{ in})(240\text{ in}) = 23{,}040\text{ in}^2$$

Given this area, the room's acoustic impedance is

$$Z_{\text{r}} = \frac{(0.000000113\text{ mica/in}^3)(13{,}504\text{ in/s})}{23{,}040.0\text{ in}^2} = 0.000000066\text{ mica/(in}^4\text{·s)}$$

~ 7.8 ~

We may now construct a tube-to-room wave impedance ratio, and describe in very general terms the rate at which vibrational energy is transferred from the tube to the room:

$$\frac{Z_{\text{t}}}{Z_{\text{r}}} = \frac{0.0003838}{0.000000066} \approx 6000 : 1$$

This ratio tells us that for a resonator in the central frequency range, the acoustic impedance of the tube is typically 6000 times greater than the acoustic impedance of the room. Due to a sudden change in wave impedance at the open end of the tube, most of the tube's acoustic energy reflects at the opening and returns into the tube. Consequently, very little acoustic energy radiates through the opening as audible sound. For example, pick up a resonator, strike the closed end with a mallet, and notice that the fundamental frequency of the tube sounds very weak. Note, however, that although the acoustic impedance of the room is extremely small, it is not infinitely small. If the room's acoustic impedance was infinitely small, all the acoustic energy would reflect as though the opening had a cap, and a transfer of acoustic energy would not take place. Under such a hypothetical condition, the tube would not radiate any sound.

Part V

LONGITUDINAL PRESSURE AND DISPLACEMENT STANDING WAVES IN TUBES

7.9

The reflection of longitudinal traveling waves from both the closed and open ends of tubes leads to the formation of longitudinal standing waves inside the tube. In this context, the *principle of superposition* applies not only to transverse traveling waves in strings, but also to longitudinal traveling waves in tubes. However, because waves in tubes are more complex than waves in strings, the reader should study Sections 3.1–3.3. Knowledge of superposition, constructive and destructing interference, and nodes and antinodes is essential for the following discussion.

When we strike a bar mounted over a resonator, the resulting disturbance causes longitudinal traveling waves to enter the resonator through the opening. At the closed end, some of these waves will reflect sooner than others. When incident and reflected waves are simultaneously present in a given medium, they are by definition traveling in opposite directions. Consequently, the waves will collide and superpose. Before we continue, it is important to make a critical distinction. Strings, bars, soundboards, etc. are all solids. When such objects vibrate, their densities do not change. However, when gases vibrate, their densities do change. In an air column, the superposition of traveling waves, or the formation of standing waves, causes pressure fluctuations throughout the tube. Inside the tube, compression — or positive pressure — causes air to become more dense, and rarefaction — or negative pressure — causes air to become less dense than the ambient air outside the tube. It is, therefore, possible to discuss the consequences of superposition in tubes in terms of pressure standing waves and/or displacement standing waves.

Turn to Figure 7.8, which shows 11 infinite air columns or tubes. An infinite tube does not reflect longitudinal traveling waves from its ends, and so does not produce longitudinal standing waves that are audible as resonant frequencies of the tube. The sole purpose of an infinite tube is to demonstrate how propagations of traveling waves result in pressure oscillations or displacement oscillations of standing waves.

Refer to the first nine tubes, which collectively represent a single tube. Beneath each tube notice two longitudinal traveling waves. Dashed arrows show that the upper traveling waves are propagating from right to left, and the lower traveling waves, from left to right. Furthermore, the letter C indicates locations of maximum positive pressure, or compression, and the letter R, locations of maximum negative pressure, or rarefaction. Also, dots above one C and one R in each wave help clarify the motions of the waves. Since longitudinal traveling waves move in the same horizontal plane as longitudinal standing waves, it is not possible to illustrate the interactions of these two kinds of waves inside a single tube. For this reason, I placed the longitudinal standing waves inside the tubes, and the longitudinal traveling waves outside the tubes.

Suppose now that on the right side of the tube a tuning fork is sending traveling waves, or alternating regions of compression and rarefaction, from right to left through the tube; conversely, on the left side a tuning fork is sending traveling waves from left to right through the tube. Because the frequencies and amplitudes of these two waves are identical, and because they are traveling in opposite directions, superposition produces a longitudinal standing wave throughout the tube.

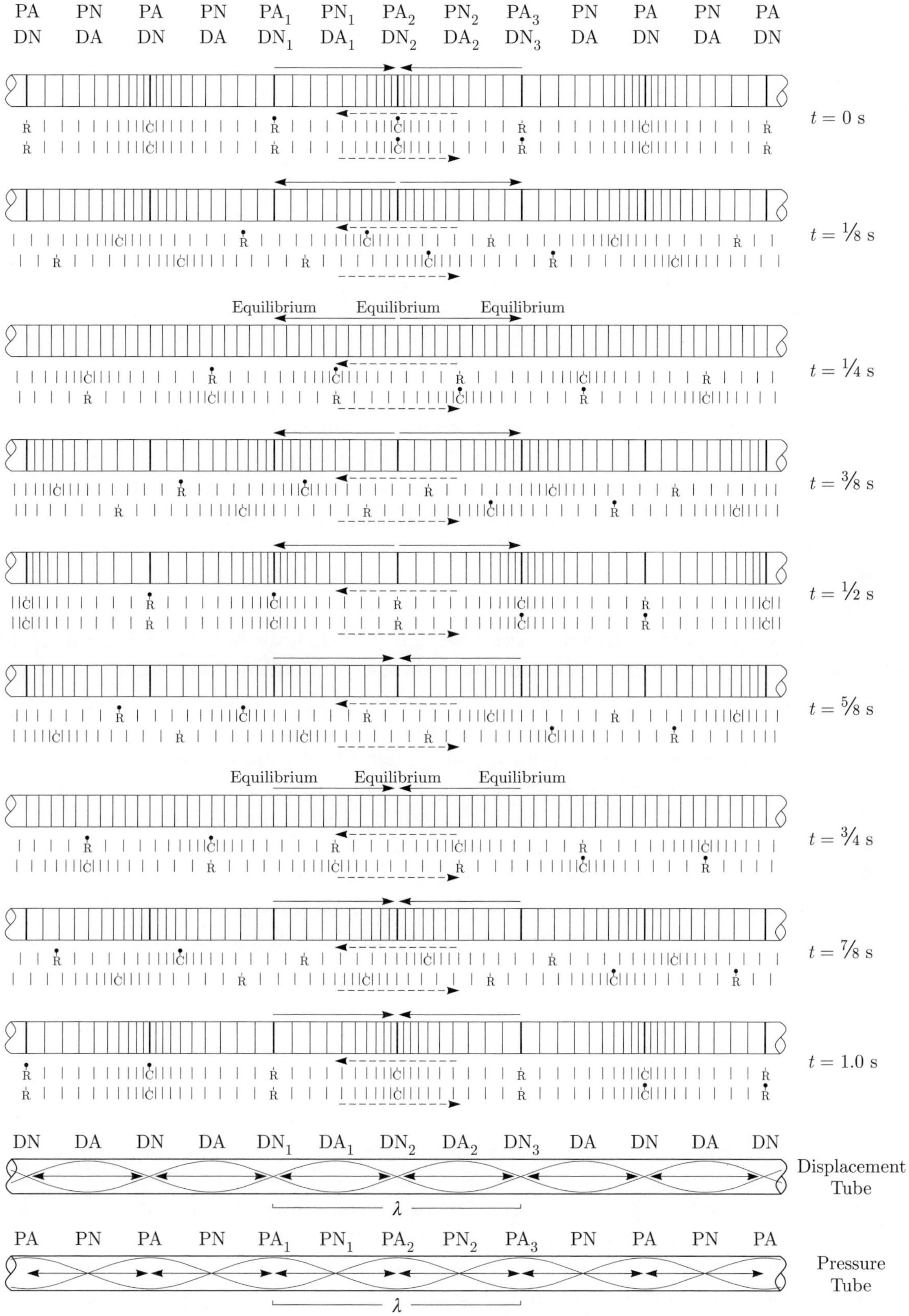

Figure 7.8 Longitudinal traveling waves and longitudinal standing waves in an infinite tube. Vertical lines, which represent layers of air particles, indicate the linear motions of traveling waves (dashed arrows) and the vibrations of standing waves (solid arrows).

Consequently, at any given moment, the pressure of the standing wave equals the *sum* of the pressures of the traveling waves. In Figure 7.8, we will focus on the central area of the tube defined by three pressure antinodes: PA_1, PA_2, and PA_3. At the beginning when $t = 0$ s, in the middle when $t = \frac{1}{2}$ s, and at the end when $t = 1.0$ s, notice that the compressions of the two traveling waves coincide, and that the rarefactions coincide as well. This state of reinforcement — or maximum pressure — results in *constructive interference.* Therefore, at these moments, PA_1, PA_2, and PA_3 indicate that the compressions and rarefactions of the standing wave are exactly two times greater than each of the individual traveling waves. When $t = \frac{1}{4}$ s and $\frac{3}{4}$ s, compressions coincide with rarefactions and *vice versa.* This state of cancellation — or minimum pressure — results in *destructive interference.* At these moments, the air particles in the tube appear in a state of equilibrium, or as though no waves were present. However, note carefully, that in a state of dynamic equilibrium the air particles are moving and not at rest. Finally, when $t = \frac{1}{8}$ s, $\frac{3}{8}$ s, $\frac{5}{8}$ s, and $\frac{7}{8}$ s, the standing wave exhibits intermediate levels of compression and rarefaction.

Before we continue, notice two solid arrows above the central area of each tube. These arrows span the distances between pressure antinodes, shown here by three thick vertical lines. Immediately after $t = 0$ s and $\frac{1}{2}$ s, or immediately after the standing wave has achieved maximum positive or maximum negative pressure, the solid arrows change their directions to indicate a reversal from maximum compression toward maximum rarefaction and *vice versa.* Consequently, the solid arrows demonstrate that the pressure fluctuations of the standing wave are vibrating back and forth within the confines of their pressure antinodes.

Halfway between two adjacent pressure antinodes, locations that exhibit minimum pressure fluctuations are called pressure nodes; in this case, PN_1 and PN_2 show where the pressure of the longitudinal standing wave is almost the same as the ambient air outside the tube. Consequently, at PN_1 and PN_2, the density of air remains virtually unchanged throughout the entire cycle. To help remember what the term *node* means, always think of the "no" in node. In this case, pressure nodes indicate regions of *no* pressure fluctuations. Finally, refer to the tube at the bottom of the figure labeled Pressure Tube. Here sine waves indicate the locations of pressure nodes and antinodes, and double-headed arrows, the horizontal direction of vibrating regions of compression and rarefaction, which, in closed or open resonators, constitute the source of periodic or musical sound.

In Figure 7.8, we may also consider the displacement of air particles from their equilibrium position. (See Section 3.3 for analogous descriptions of displacement in strings.) Again, we will focus on the central area of the tube, this time defined by three displacement nodes: DN_1, DN_2, and DN_3. However, because displacement nodes indicate locations of *no* particle displacement, or *no* particle motion, consider the two displacement antinodes: DA_1 and DA_2. At the beginning when $t = 0$ s, in the middle when $t = \frac{1}{2}$ s, and at the end when $t = 1.0$ s, the displacements of the two traveling waves coincide. This state of reinforcement or maximum displacement results in constructive interference. Therefore, at these moments, DA_1 and DA_2 are locations where the displacement of air particles in the standing wave is exactly two times greater than in each individual traveling wave. Here the air particles are farthest from their equilibrium positions. When $t = \frac{1}{4}$ s and $\frac{3}{4}$ s the displacements of the two traveling waves cancel out, which results in destructive interference. At these moments, the displacement of the standing wave is in a state of dynamic equilibrium. And when t = $\frac{1}{8}$ s, $\frac{3}{8}$ s, $\frac{5}{8}$ s, and $\frac{7}{8}$ s, the standing wave exhibits intermediate levels of displacement. Finally, at the bottom of the figure, refer to the Displacement Tube. In this tube, sine waves indicate the locations of displacement nodes and antinodes, and double-headed arrows, the horizontal direction of vibrating particle displacements, which, in closed or open resonators, produce periodic or musical sound.

Usually, sine waves represent transverse waves, not longitudinal waves. Because it is not possible to graph longitudinal pressure and displacement variations in wave format, mathematicians use sine waves to illustrate such changes. In the Displacement Tube and Pressure Tube, we must interpret the amplitudes of the sine waves as variations in either the displacement or pressure of the longitudinal standing wave. In the Displacement Tube, crests represent maximum displacements in the positive direction, and troughs, maximum displacements in the negative direction. And in the Pressure Tube, crests represent maximum compressions, and troughs, maximum rarefactions. Finally, we may define points of minimum and maximum displacement as an alternating pattern of displacement nodes and displacement antinodes; and points of maximum and minimum pressure fluctuation as an alternating pattern of pressure antinodes and pressure nodes.

In previous sections, we discussed *closed* tubes, or tubes open at one end and closed at the other end. These tubes produce only odd-number harmonics. (See Section 7.10.) Closed resonators exist on all keyboard percussion instruments. Many organs also have ranks of closed cylindrical and closed square flue pipes. Such pipes are closed at the far end and open at the mouth where a jet of air streams past a slit and causes the air column to vibrate. The clarinet also has a tendency to vibrate as though it were a closed tube.[35] Here the air column is open at the far end and closed at the reed, which during playing stays in a closed position most of the time. In addition to closed tubes, we now extend this analysis to include *open* tubes, or tubes open at both ends. Such resonators produce all the even-number and odd-number harmonics of the harmonic series. Many wind instruments, including flutes, recorders, and most organ pipes, have air columns that are open at the mouthpiece, fipple hole, or mouth, respectively, and open at the far end. Chapter 8 discusses simple flute construction.

Refer to Figures 7.9 and 7.10, which show pressure standing waves and displacement standing waves in an open tube for the first three modes of vibration, and to Figures 7.11 and 7.12, which show pressure standing waves and displacement standing waves in a closed tube, also for the first three modes of vibration. In all four figures, the nodes of sine waves indicate the locations where the compressions and rarefactions of standing waves equal zero, or where air particle displacements of standing waves equal zero; and antinodes indicate the locations where the compressions and rarefactions are at a maximum, or where air particle displacements are at a maximum.

Part VI

LENGTH AND FREQUENCY EQUATIONS OF TUBE RESONATORS

~ 7.10 ~

We now turn our attention to length and frequency equations for open and closed resonators. However, the reader should be aware that the equations in this section apply only to ideal tubes; that is, Equations 7.11–7.15 and 7.16–7.19 give only theoretically correct results. Calculations that are more accurate require an additional subequation that accounts for the *end correction* of an open or a closed tube. (See Section 7.11.)

Meanwhile, the following equation gives the mode frequencies of open and closed tubes:

$$F_{\text{n}} = \frac{c_{\text{L}}}{\lambda_{\text{n}}} \tag{7.10}$$

In Section 7.2, we found that at 68°F, $c_{\text{L}} \approx 13{,}504$ in/s. This leaves the mode wavelengths (λ_{n}) as the only remaining variable in Equation 7.10. Recall from Section 3.4 that a wavelength spans the distance in a wave after which the pattern of displacement repeats itself. In the context of longitudinal standing waves, modify this definition to read, "A wavelength spans the distance in a wave after which a pressure pattern repeats itself." For example, when a region of compression of

STANDING WAVES IN OPEN TUBES

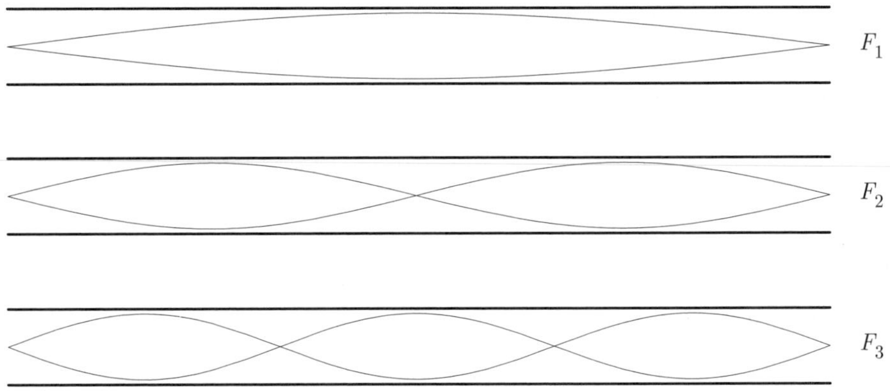

Figure 7.9 Pressure standing wave in an open tube. Nodes at the open ends mark the locations of least pressure change. At all node locations, the pressure and density of air is the same as in the surrounding air.

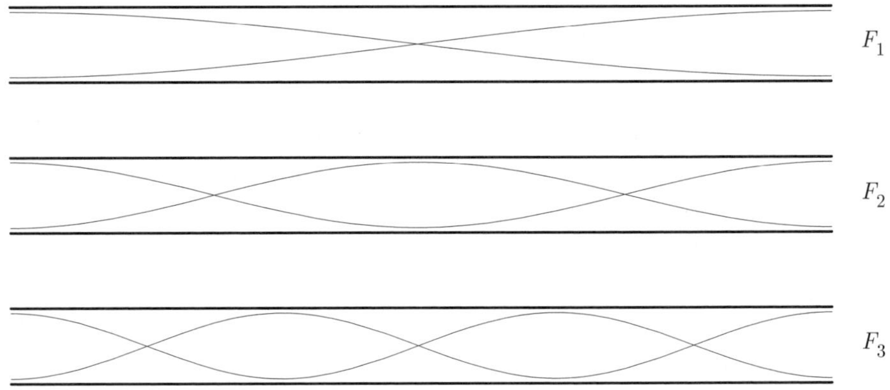

Figure 7.10 Displacement standing wave in an open tube. Antinodes at the open ends mark the locations of greatest particle displacement. At all antinode locations, air particles undergo maximum simple harmonic motion inside the tube.

STANDING WAVES IN CLOSED TUBES

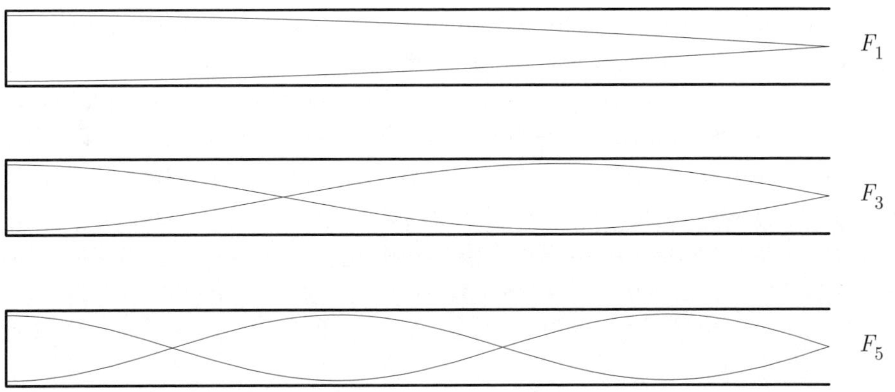

Figure 7.11 Pressure standing wave in a closed tube. Antinodes at the closed ends mark the locations of greatest pressure change. Here the tube's cap acts to maximize the pressure and density of air.

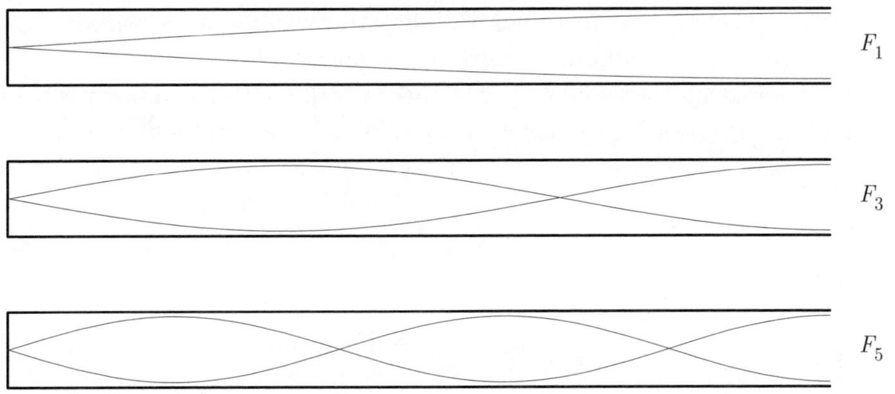

Figure 7.12 Displacement standing wave in a closed tube. Nodes at the closed ends mark the locations of zero particle displacement. Here the tube's cap acts to obstruct the simple harmonic motion of air particles.

a longitudinal traveling wave enters an open tube, it undergoes a phase reversal at the other open end, and reflects as a rarefaction. Upon returning to the first open end, the region of rarefaction also undergoes a phase reversal and reflects as a compression. As a result, all regions of compression or rarefaction travel the length of an open tube *two times* before returning to their original state. In an open tube, this distance equals the length of two loops,[36] or one wavelength. Consequently, the *theoretical* fundamental wavelength of a pressure standing wave inside an open tube equals two times the length of the tube: $\lambda_1 = 2L_o$, or $L_o = \lambda_1/2$. The latter equation explains why open tubes are called half-wavelength resonators. (Section 7.11 shows why the actual fundamental wavelength is always longer than two times the tube length, and why an open tube always sounds a fundamental frequency lower than predicted by Equation 7.12.) Figure 7.9 shows that a mode number of half-wavelengths, or single loops, fits between the ends of the tubes. For the first three modes, the open tube accommodates 1, 2, and 3 half-wavelengths, respectively. Therefore, with respect to the theoretical wavelengths of all higher modes,

$$\lambda_{\text{n theoretical}} = \frac{2L_o}{n} \qquad \{n = 1, 2, 3, 4, \ldots\} \tag{7.11}$$

Substitute this expression into Equation 7.10 and use the following equation to calculate the theoretical mode frequencies of an open tube:

$$F_{\text{n theoretical}} = \frac{c_L}{\lambda_{\text{n theoretical}}} = n\frac{c_L}{2L_o} \tag{7.12}$$

We conclude, therefore, that open tubes (like flexible strings) generate a complete harmonic series that includes both even-number and odd-number harmonics.

Next, consider an equation that solves for the theoretical length of an open tube given a fundamental frequency (F_1). First, solve Equation 7.10 for the fundamental wavelength (λ_1):

$$\lambda_1 = \frac{c_L}{F_1} \tag{7.13}$$

Since we know that

$$\lambda_{\text{1 theoretical}} = 2L_o \tag{7.14}$$

substitute this expression into Equation 7.13,

$$2L_o = \frac{c_L}{F_1}$$

and solve for L_o:

$$L_{\text{o theoretical}} = \frac{c_L}{2F_1} \tag{7.15}$$

A similar but more complicated analysis applies to closed tubes. For example, when a region of compression of a longitudinal traveling wave enters a closed tube, it does *not* change phase at the closed end, but reflects as a compression. Upon returning to the open end, it undergoes a phase reversal and reflects as a rarefaction. At the closed end, it again does *not* change phase but reflects as a rarefaction, and at the open end, it undergoes a second phase reversal and reflects as a compression. As a result, all compressions or rarefactions travel the length of a closed tube *four times* before returning to their original state. In a closed tube, this distance equals the length of two loops, or one wavelength. Consequently, the *theoretical* fundamental wavelength of a pressure standing wave inside a closed tube equals four times the length of the tube: $\lambda_1 = 4L_c$, or $L_c = \lambda_1/4$. The latter equation explains why closed tubes are called quarter-wavelength resonators. (Section 7.11 explains why the actual fundamental wavelength is always longer than four times the tube length, and why a closed tube always sounds a fundamental frequency lower than predicted by Equation 7.17.) Refer to Figure 7.11 and note that only an odd integer number of quarter-wavelengths, or half-loop lengths, fits between the ends of the tubes. For the first three modes, the closed tube only accommodates ¼, ¾, and 5⁄4 wavelengths, respectively. Therefore, with regard to the theoretical wavelength of all higher modes,

$$\lambda_{\text{n theoretical}} = \frac{4L_c}{2n - 1} \qquad \{n = 1, 2, 3, 4, \ldots\} \tag{7.16}$$

Substitute this expression into Equation 7.10 and use the following equation to calculate the theoretical mode frequencies of a closed tube:

$$F_{\text{n theoretical}} = \frac{c_L}{\lambda_{\text{n theoretical}}} = (2n - 1)\frac{c_L}{4L_c} \tag{7.17}$$

We conclude, therefore, that closed tubes generate an incomplete harmonic series that includes only odd-number harmonics. A comparison between Equations 7.12 and 7.17 shows that for a given length, the fundamental frequency of a closed tube sounds exactly one "octave" lower than an open tube.

Now consider an equation that solves for the theoretical length of a closed tube given a fundamental frequency. Since we know that

$$\lambda_{\text{1 theoretical}} = 4L_c \tag{7.18}$$

substitute this expression into Equation 7.13,

$$4L_c = \frac{c_L}{F_1}$$

and solve for L_c:

$$L_{\text{c theoretical}} = \frac{c_L}{4F_1} \tag{7.19}$$

~ 7.11 ~

The discussions in Sections 7.3–7.4 assumed that waves reflect in the same manner from the closed end of a tube as from the open end. This is not the case. The "hard" reflections of waves at a tube's closed end occur at the exact position of the cap, whereas the "soft" reflections of waves at a tube's open end do not occur at a precise location. For the fundamental mode of vibration, Figure 7.13 shows that both the pressure node and the displacement antinode extend a small distance beyond the physical length of the tube. To understand why these reflections take place outside the tube, we return to the subject of impedance. In Section 7.8, we observed that although the wave impedance of the surrounding air is extremely small, it is not infinitely small, which means that a resonator radiates small amounts of energy into the surrounding air. If the wave impedance of the air were infinitely small, then the reflection of waves at the open end would be the same as the reflection at the closed end, and no sound would radiate from the tube. However, because the surrounding

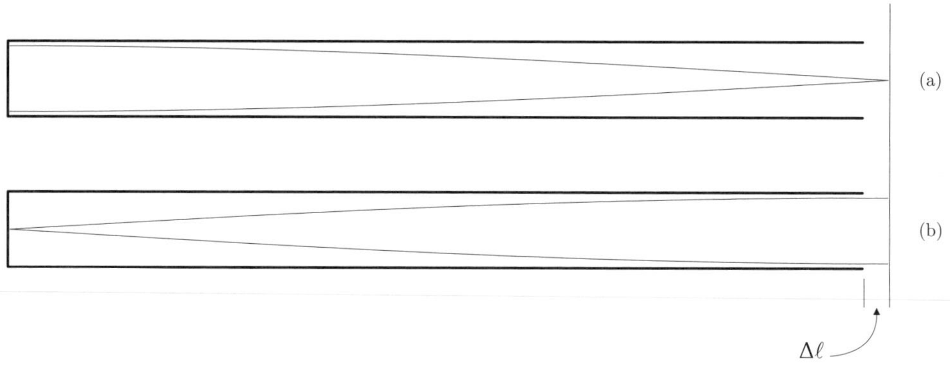

Figure 7.13 The end correction (Δℓ) at a tube's open end. (a) The pressure node, or (b) the displacement antinode for the first mode of vibration occurs outside the tube. Consequently, the effective wavelengths of the pressure standing waves, or the effective wavelengths of the displacement standing waves of either open or closed tubes are slightly longer than given by either Equation 7.11 or 7.16, respectively. (End correction to scale.)

air does not provide a "hard" obstruction at the end of the tube, Figures 7.13(a) and 7.13(b) show that the fundamental pressure wave and the fundamental displacement wave, respectively, not only exist within the tube, but also extend a slight distance beyond the tube. We conclude, therefore, that the tube's *acoustic or effective length* (L_{eff}) is slightly longer than its *geometric or measured length* (L). (See Figure 8.1.) Because of this end correction phenomenon, Equations 7.11 and 7.16, and all other wavelength and frequency equations in Section 7.10, give only approximately correct results.

An exact equation for the end correction of open and closed tubes does not exist because the end correction depends slightly on wavelength.[37] (See Section 7.12.) Tests show that the mode frequencies of open and closed pipes sound *sharp* when compared to the frequencies of exact integer harmonics.[38] The higher modes have relatively shorter wavelengths when compared to the lower modes. Since frequency is inversely proportional to wavelength, as the wavelength decreases, the frequency increases. However, a closer examination of Equation 7.9A reveals that for slender pipes, the end correction also varies directly with the tube diameter. According to this equation, the acoustic wave impedance of a tube is inversely proportional to the diameter squared:

$$Z_{\text{t}} \propto \frac{1}{S} \propto \frac{1}{\pi r^2} \propto \frac{1}{\pi \dfrac{d^2}{4}}$$

As d^2 decreases, Z_{t} increases. For a tube with a very small diameter, the tube-to-room wave impedance ratio is extremely large, and approaches infinity. Therefore, pressure waves in very narrow pipes reflect almost completely at the open end, which means that the end correction is negligibly small. This tells us that the mode frequencies of narrow-scaled pipes constitute almost true harmonics. In contrast, when a tube has a very large diameter, the wave impedance ratio is small, and so the pressure fluctuations extend a considerable distance beyond the tube's open end. Consequently, wide-scaled pipes produce mode frequencies that depart from the frequencies of the harmonic series. However, we must distinguish here between the inharmonic mode frequencies of tubes on the one hand, and those of stiff strings and bars on the other. In air columns dispersion is not a factor;[39] that is, the speed of sound is a constant. For all solids, liquids, and gases, c_{L} does *not* increase with a decrease in wavelength, or an increase in frequency.

A good approximation for the end correction ($\Delta\ell$) of a straight cylindrical tube opening is

$$\Delta\ell = 0.6r = 0.3d \tag{7.20}$$

where r is the inside radius of a tube, in inches; and d is the inside diameter of a tube, also in inches. (Read the uppercase of the Greek letter *delta* Δ as *change in*, so that $\Delta\ell$ represents *change in length*.) This equation applies to slender tubes with a high wavelength-to-diameter ratio. To calculate the acoustic or effective length of an open tube, multiply the end correction by two and then add this extra length to the tube's geometric or measured length:

$$L_{\text{o eff}} = L_{\text{o}} + 2(0.6r) = L_{\text{o}} + 2(0.3d) = L_{\text{o}} + 0.6d \tag{7.21}$$

Equation 7.21 accounts for both ends of an open tube. Now substitute this effective length into Equation 7.11 to determine the actual wavelengths of the higher modes:

$$\lambda_{\text{n actual}} = \frac{2(L_{\text{o}} + 0.6d)}{n} \tag{7.22}$$

Substitute this expression into Equation 7.10 and use the following equation to calculate the actual mode frequencies of a slender open tube:

$$\boxed{F_{\text{n actual}} = \frac{c_{\text{L}}}{\lambda_{\text{n actual}}} = n\frac{c_{\text{L}}}{2(L_{\text{o}} + 0.6d)}} \tag{7.23}$$

Equation 7.23 is not very practical. Builders of musical instruments are primarily interested in length calculations based on a set of fundamental frequencies. To define a length equation, first express Equation 7.22 for the fundamental mode of vibration:

$$\lambda_{\text{1 actual}} = 2(L_{\text{o}} + 0.6d) \tag{7.24}$$

Next, substitute this expression into Equation 7.13,

$$2(L_{\text{o}} + 0.6d) = \frac{c_{\text{L}}}{F_1}$$

and solve for the open tube's speaking length, or cut length ($L_{\text{o cut}}$):

$$\boxed{L_{\text{o cut}} = \frac{c_{\text{L}}}{2F_1} - 0.6d} \tag{7.25}$$

Note that we *add* the end correction in Equation 7.23 to calculate a tube's mode frequencies, and we *subtract* the end correction in Equation 7.25 to calculate a tube's speaking length. Remember, in the final analysis, the end correction has the effect of making the tube longer than its geometric measured length. So, only by cutting the tube intentionally short does it attain the required acoustic length, which in turn produces the desired fundamental frequency.

Finally, the following equation gives the acoustic or effective length of a closed tube:

$$L_{\text{c eff}} = L_{\text{c}} + 0.6r = L_{\text{c}} + 0.3d \tag{7.26}$$

Substitute the effective length into Equation 7.16 to determine the actual wavelengths of the higher modes:

$$\lambda_{\text{n actual}} = \frac{4(L_c + 0.3d)}{2n - 1} \tag{7.27}$$

Substitute this expression into Equation 7.10 and use the following equation to calculate the actual mode frequencies of a slender closed tube:

$$\boxed{F_{\text{n actual}} = \frac{c_L}{\lambda_{\text{n actual}}} = (2\text{n} - 1)\frac{c_L}{4(L_c + 0.3d)}} \tag{7.28}$$

Marimba makers need an equation to calculate the lengths of resonators based on a scale of fundamental frequencies. To define such an equation, first express Equation 7.27 for the fundamental mode of vibration:

$$\lambda_{\text{1 actual}} = 4(L_c + 0.3d) \tag{7.29}$$

Next, substitute this expression into Equation 7.13,

$$4(L_c + 0.3d) = \frac{c_L}{F_1}$$

and solve for the closed tube's speaking length, or cut length $(L_{\text{c cut}})$:

$$\boxed{L_{\text{c cut}} = \frac{c_L}{4F_1} - 0.3d} \tag{7.30}$$

For a closed *square tube*, where a is the internal length of the sides, use this equation:[40]

$$L_{\text{c cut}} = \frac{c_L}{4F_1} - a$$

~ 7.12 ~

In conclusion to Part VI, consider three practical considerations. (1) Section 7.6 lists the G_3 resonator diameter in inches because in the United States, manufacturers produce tube diameters and wall thicknesses in English units. It is important to understand that the resonator dimensions are also given in metric units because one can greatly simplify the job of cutting and sanding resonators by using centimeter units. For example, on a meter rule graduated in centimeters and millimeters, the length 20.6 cm simply consists of 20 centimeters and 6 millimeters. This exact length is very easy to see on the meter rule. The same length of 8.11 inches is very difficult to locate on any English rule. As a practice example, substitute the English and metric units of the G_3 resonator into Equation 7.30 and calculate the speaking length:

$$L_{\text{c cut}} = \frac{13{,}504 \text{ in/s}}{4(196.0 \text{ cps})} - 0.3(2.25 \text{ in}) = 16.55 \text{ in}$$

$$L_{\text{c cut}} = \frac{34{,}300 \text{ cm/s}}{4(196.0 \text{ cps})} - 0.3(5.72 \text{ cm}) = 42.03 \text{ cm}$$

The latter length rounded to 42.0 cm is equivalent to 16.54 in.

(2) With metric calculations in mind, consider now a set of six closed resonators designed to test the accuracy of the end correction coefficient in Equation 7.28. In Table 7.1, Row 1 lists the lengths of these resonators, all of which have an inside diameter of 5.0 cm. Row 2 gives the theoretical frequencies according to Equation 7.28; Row 3, the actual frequencies at 20°C, where $c_{\mathrm{L}} =$ 34,300 cm/s; and Row 4, the differences between Rows 2 and 3.

Table 7.1

THEORETICAL AND ACTUAL FREQUENCIES OF CLOSED RESONATORS

Tube Lengths, (cm)	50	40	30	20	10	5	(1)
Eq. 7.28 results, (cps)	166.50	206.63	272.22	398.84	745.65	1319.23	(2)
Test Data, (cps)	165.28	205.27	270.04	395.41	735.77	1292.11	(3)
Differences, (cps)	1.22	1.36	2.18	3.43	9.88	27.12	(4)

The results in Row 4 are due to changes in end correction. To investigate the reason for these changes, first rewrite Equation 7.28 with an end correction coefficient ($\mathit{\Delta}$), and then solve this equation for $\mathit{\Delta}$. Now, substitute the resonator variables and the Test Data into Equation 7.31, and calculate the coefficients:

$$F_1 = \frac{c_{\mathrm{L}}}{4\left[L_{\mathrm{c}} + \mathit{\Delta}(d)\right]}$$

$$\mathit{\Delta} = \frac{\dfrac{0.25c_{\mathrm{L}}}{F_1} - L_{\mathrm{c}}}{d} \tag{7.31}$$

$$\mathit{\Delta} = \begin{matrix} 0.376 \\ 0.355 \\ 0.351 \\ 0.337 \\ 0.331 \\ 0.327 \end{matrix}$$

We conclude, therefore, that the "actual" solutions of Equations 7.21–7.25 and 7.26–7.30 do not give perfect results because $\mathit{\Delta}$ is inversely proportional to F; as F increases, $\mathit{\Delta}$ decreases.

(3) Finally, remember that the cap of a closed resonator must form an airtight seal with the tube. Any air leakage at the cap will destroy the performance of the resonator because the standing wave inside the tube will no longer have the required wavelength. The resonators on the Diamond Marimba in Plate 7 were made from cast acrylic tubes, and the caps, from cast acrylic sheet. I jointed the caps to the tubes with a clear solvent cement that melts the pieces together. To test the cap joint, I filled the tubes with water and checked for leaks.

Part VII

THEORY OF CAVITY RESONATORS

7.13

Tube resonators and cavity resonators work on completely different principles. Tube resonators are classified as *wavelength resonators*, because for a given speed of sound in air, λ is the principal variable in Equation 7.10. In contrast, we may categorize cavity resonators as *volume resonators*, because the principal variable in Equation 7.37 is the volume of air contained inside a regularly or irregularly shaped cavity. (Note that λ does not appear in this equation.) Although both types of resonators amplify sound equally well, many marimba builders use tube resonators in the treble sections and cavity resonators in the bass sections of their instruments. On bass marimbas, cavity resonators serve a particularly useful function because the long wavelengths associated with low frequencies prohibit the use of tube resonators. For example, the lowest tone on the Bass Marimba in Plate 8 is G_1 at 49.00 cps. According to Equation 7.30, a 4.0 in. diameter closed tube tuned to this frequency requires a cut length of

$$L_{\text{c cut}} = \frac{13{,}504 \text{ in/s}}{4(49.00 \text{ cps})} - 0.3(4.0 \text{ in}) = 67.70 \text{ in} = 5.64 \text{ ft}$$

A bass marimba frame equipped with bar mounting rails and casters would raise the bars of such an instrument more than six feet above the floor. As an alternative, the tuned G_1 cavity resonator of the Bass Marimba has an inside height of only 33½ in., and yet it produces a powerful and sustained tone that is indistinguishable from a comparable tube resonator.

Cavity resonators are often called Helmholtz resonators, in honor of Hermann Helmholtz (1821–1894) who first used them to hear the faint harmonics of strings and organ reeds.[41] Unfortunately, Helmholtz's original frequency equation and many other related equations[42] give reasonably accurate results only *if* the walls of the resonator are absolutely rigid. Many cavity resonators fulfill this requirement. When we blow across the opening of a glass bottle to produce a musical tone, the walls of the bottle do not vibrate in response to changes in air pressure inside the cavity. Tests show there is fair agreement between the theoretical and the actual frequencies of the bottle. However, when the walls of the cavity are not rigid — as in the hollow bodies of violins,[43] guitars, and bass marimba resonators — the actual resonant frequencies are significantly *lower* than the calculated frequencies. Such discrepancies may prompt us to reject Equation 7.37. This would be a mistake. From a theoretical perspective, this equation is important because it accurately describes a cavity resonator as a spring-mass system. A detailed examination shows that Equation 7.37 not only accounts for the basic mechanics of cavity resonators, but also suggests how to tune the natural frequencies of such resonators.

7.14

Figure 7.14(a) shows the cross-section of a typical marimba cavity resonator, and three variables that determine the magnitude of the analogous *air spring-air mass* system illustrated in Figure 7.14(b).[44] I intentionally drew the resonator with thick walls to emphasize the length of the opening, or the length of the neck (L_N). As discussed in Section 7.1, a mechanical spring-mass system consists of two distinct parts: a spring or elastic component, and a mass or inertial component. Figure 7.14(b) indicates that the air inside the cavity functions as an *air spring* (k_1), and the air inside the opening or neck, as an *air mass* (m), which tends to move as a unit, or as a *plug* of air. Figure

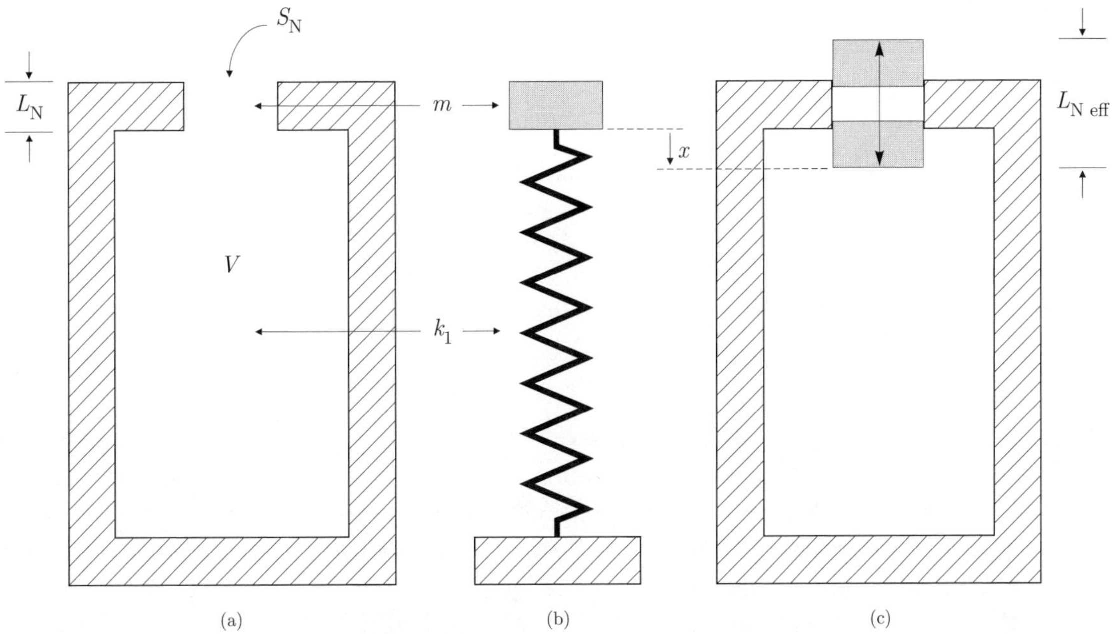

Figure 7.14 Cross-sectional view of a marimba cavity resonator. (a) Three variables determine the magnitude of (b) the analogous *air spring-air mass* system. (c) The effective length of the neck ($L_{N\ eff}$), drawn here to scale, indicates that the *air mass* (m) vibrates a substantial distance beyond the inner and outer boundaries of the neck. The surface area (S_N) of the air mass and the volume (V) of the cavity determine the magnitude of the *air spring* (k_1).

7.14(c) shows the effective length of the neck ($L_{N\ eff}$) to scale, and the displacement (x) of the air mass into the resonator. We will discuss all these variables in full detail in Sections 7.15–7.16.

Consider a bellows at the edge of the opening of a cavity resonator. A burst of air across the opening displaces the air mass inside the opening a considerable distance into the cavity. This causes a decrease in the volume of the cavity, and therefore a corresponding compression of the air inside the cavity. Consequently, the excess pressure inside the cavity rises above the ambient pressure outside the resonator. Immediately after maximum compression, the air inside the cavity undergoes expansion and pushes the air mass in the opening back to its equilibrium position. Now, because the air mass has momentum, it overshoots its equilibrium position and continues to move a considerable distance outside the opening. This causes an increase in the volume of the cavity, and therefore a corresponding rarefaction of the air inside the cavity. Consequently, the pressure inside the cavity drops below the ambient pressure outside the resonator. Negative pressure inside the cavity now sucks the air mass back to its equilibrium position. This marks the beginning of the second cycle.

Unlike the air mass inside the opening, which is moving very rapidly, the air inside the cavity is compressing and expanding very rapidly and, therefore, not moving very much at all. We conclude, therefore, that the rapid vibrations of the air mass in the opening cause the compression and rarefaction of the ambient air outside the resonator, which in turn produce the audible resonant frequency of the resonator. This explains why *after* a burst of air across the opening, the resonator continues to "hum" as its vibration decays.

Figure 7.14(b) indicates that the volume of air inside the resonator cavity functions as an air spring. To experience an air spring, locate a bicycle pump or a plastic syringe,[45] block the open end, slide a plunger into the chamber, release it, and observe that the plunger rebounds as though a spring was pushing on it.

Now, consider a large vibrating bar that is causing periodic pressure fluctuations near the opening of a large cavity resonator. If the fundamental frequency of the vibrating bar and the natural frequency of the air mass-air spring system are identical, then resonance occurs. When a bar and resonator are tuned to the same fundamental frequency, a very efficient compression-rarefaction cycle takes place, which in turn produces a great amplification of sound.

7.15

For an ideal resonator, the theoretical air mass has the value

$$m_{\text{theoretical}} = \rho S_{\text{N}} L_{\text{N}} \tag{7.32}$$

where m is the air mass, in micas; ρ is the mass density of air, in mica/in^3; S_{N} is the cross-sectional area of the neck, in square inches; and L_{N} is the length of the neck, in inches. Because the air mass vibrates as a unit beyond the inner and outer boundaries of the neck, we must apply two end corrections to all cavity resonator openings. (See Section 7.11.) Consequently, the effective length of the neck is considerably longer than the measured length, which means that the actual size of the air mass in the neck is substantially larger than the theoretical size.

Refer to Figure 7.15 and note that most cavity resonator necks have either a duct or a flange opening to the surrounding air. Figure 7.15(a) shows that a common bottle neck has a length that is greater than its inside diameter: $L_{\text{N}} > d$. One often finds this kind of neck on wine bottles and on mufflers. The opening of a neck that extends into open space is called a duct opening. In contrast, Figure 7.15(b) shows another kind of neck that has an inside diameter that is greater than its length: $d > L_{\text{N}}$. Typical examples include a window opening in a wall, and the opening at the top of a bass marimba resonator. The surface that surrounds such an opening is called a flange or baffle. For the bottle, notice that although the neck's outer end has a duct opening, the neck's inner end has a flange opening.

The end correction for a duct opening is the same as for a tube resonator, namely, $\Delta\ell = 0.6r = 0.3d$. On the other hand, the end correction for a flange opening[46] is $\Delta\ell = 0.850r = 0.425d$. To

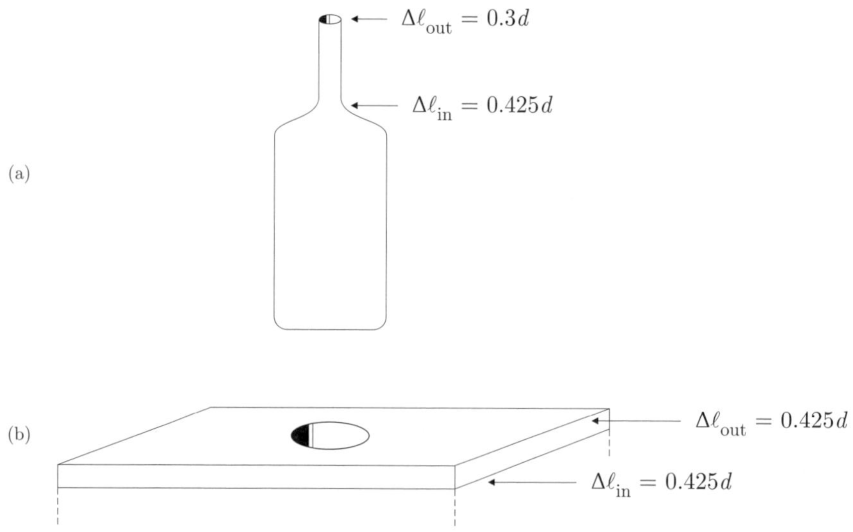

Figure 7.15 Two different kinds of cavity resonator necks and their respective end corrections. (a) The length of the wine bottle neck is greater than its diameter. (b) The diameter of a bass marimba resonator neck is greater than its length.

calculate a neck's effective length, add the two end corrections to the measured length:

$$L_{\mathrm{N\ eff}} = L_{\mathrm{N}} + \Delta\ell_{\mathrm{in}} + \Delta\ell_{\mathrm{out}} \tag{7.33}$$

Consequently, for a wine bottle resonator,

$$L_{\mathrm{N\ eff}} = L_{\mathrm{N}} + 1.45r = L_{\mathrm{N}} + 0.725d$$

and for a bass marimba resonator,

$$L_{\mathrm{N\ eff}} = L_{\mathrm{N}} + 1.7r = L_{\mathrm{N}} + 0.85d \tag{7.34}$$

Finally, the actual air mass inside the neck of a bass marimba resonator is given by

$$m_{\mathrm{actual}} = \rho S_{\mathrm{N}}(L_{\mathrm{N}} + 0.85d) \tag{7.35}$$

When the flange opening is *not circular*, the following equation gives approximate results:[47]

$$m_{\mathrm{actual}} = \rho S_{\mathrm{N}}(L_{\mathrm{N}} + 0.96\sqrt{S_{\mathrm{N}}})$$

In this text, ρ is the mass density of air in mica per cubic inch. At 1 atmosphere of pressure, $\rho = 0.000000113$ mica/in^3. Turn now to Section 7.17, substitute the relevant values of Resonator II into Equations 7.32 and 7.35, and note that the actual air mass exceeds the theoretical air mass by 807%.

~ 7.16 ~

For an ideal cavity resonator with rigid walls, the air spring has the value

$$k_1 = \frac{\rho c_{\mathrm{L}}^2 S_{\mathrm{N}}^2}{V} \tag{7.36}$$

where V is the volume of air in the chamber, in cubic inches; and c_{L} is the speed of sound in the air, in inches per second. To calculate the resonant frequency of a cavity resonator with rigid walls, substitute Equations 7.35 and 7.36 into Equation 7.1:

$$F = \frac{1}{2\pi}\sqrt{\frac{k_1}{m_{\mathrm{actual}}}} = \frac{1}{2\pi}\sqrt{\frac{\frac{\rho c_{\mathrm{L}}^2 S_{\mathrm{N}}^2}{V}}{\rho S_{\mathrm{N}} L_{\mathrm{N\ eff}}}} = \frac{1}{2\pi}\sqrt{\frac{\frac{\cancel{\rho} c_{\mathrm{L}}^2 S_{\mathrm{N}}^{\cancel{2}}}{V}}{\cancel{\rho}\cancel{S_{\mathrm{N}}} L_{\mathrm{N\ eff}}}} = \frac{c_{\mathrm{L}}}{2\pi}\sqrt{\frac{\frac{S_{\mathrm{N}}}{V}}{L_{\mathrm{N\ eff}}}}$$

Two more transformations show that

$$F = \frac{c_{\mathrm{L}}}{2\pi}\sqrt{\frac{S_{\mathrm{N}}}{V L_{\mathrm{N\ eff}}}} = \frac{c_{\mathrm{L}}}{2\pi}\sqrt{\frac{S_{\mathrm{N}}}{V(L_{\mathrm{N}} + 0.85d)}} \tag{7.37}$$

This equation gives reasonably accurate results. It is not a perfect formula because the end correction coefficient is not an absolute number, but decreases as the frequency of the resonator increases.[48] (See Section 7.12.)

Notice that F is directly proportional to the square root of S_{N}:

$$F \propto \sqrt{S_{\mathrm{N}}}$$

That is, as the surface area of the neck increases, the frequency increases as well and *vice versa.* However, according to Equation 7.35, the air mass is also directly proportion to S_N:

$$m_{\text{actual}} \propto S_N$$

It seems paradoxical that an increase in the mass of the system in Figures 7.2 and 7.14 would increase the frequency. To explain why this is *not* the case, note that according to Equation 7.36, k_1 is directly proportional to ${S_N}^2$:

$$k_1 \propto {S_N}^2$$

Recall that in Section 7.1, we referred to k as a spring constant and calculated k for a spring that already exists. However, let us now consider the value of k from a design perspective. For example, the following equation gives the spring constant for a helical compression or extension spring:[49]

$$k_{\text{mechanical spring}} = \frac{Gd^4}{8nD^3}$$

where G is the shear modulus of the spring material, in pounds-force per square inch, or lbf/in^2; d is the diameter of the spring wire, in inches; n is the number of active coils (which is always less than the total number of coils), any integer; and D is the outside diameter of the spring, also in inches. This equation states that an increase in d increases the *mechanical stiffness* of the spring. Similarly, Equation 7.36 informs us that an increase in S_N increases the *acoustical stiffness* of the air spring. Why? Consider two cavity resonators identical in all respects except that Resonator A has a large opening, or a large value for S_N, and Resonator B, a small opening, or a small value for S_N. Now, given identical displacements of the air mass into both resonators, or identical values for x in Figure 7.14, the stiffness of the system of Resonator A will be greater than Resonator B. In other words, for a constant displacement, the excess pressure inside Resonator A is greater than in Resonator B because the air spring pushes back harder on a large surface area than a small surface area.[50] We conclude, therefore, that an increase in S_N has a greater effect on the air spring or elastic component than on the air mass or inertial component of the system.[51] Consequently, as S_N increases, F increases as well.

Also, notice that F is inversely proportional to the square root of V:

$$F \propto \sqrt{\frac{1}{V}}$$

That is, as the volume of the resonator increases, the frequency decreases and *vice versa.* To explain why this is the case, note that according to Equation 7.36, k_1 is inversely proportional to V:

$$k_1 \propto \frac{1}{V}$$

As the volume of the resonator increases, the stiffness of the air spring decreases. Why? Again, consider two cavity resonators identical in all respects except that Resonator A has a large volume, and Resonator B, a small volume. Now, given *identical* values for S_N, and again *identical* displacements of the air mass into both resonators, the stiffness of the system of Resonator A will be less than Resonator B. In other words, for a given displacement, it is more difficult to build up pressure in a large cavity than in a small cavity. Therefore, the excess pressure inside Resonator A is less than Resonator B, which means that the air spring pushes back less hard on the air mass in Resonator A than in Resonator B. Consequently, as V increases, F decreases.

Finally, notice that F is inversely proportional to the square root of L_N:

$$F \propto \sqrt{\frac{1}{L_N}}$$

That is, as the length of the neck increases, the frequency decreases and *vice versa.* To explain why this is the case, note that according to Equation 7.35, m is directly proportional to L_N:

$$m_{\text{actual}} \propto L_N$$

As the length of the neck increases, the mass increases as well. Equations 7.1 and 7.37 both state that as m increases, F decreases.

7.17

Consider two bass marimba cavity resonators with the following *inside* dimensions. According to Equation 7.37, F is the theoretical frequency of each resonator.

Resonator I:

$V = H \times L \times W = 33.625 \text{ in.} \times 23.0 \text{ in.} \times 7.0 \text{ in.} = 5413.625 \text{ in}^3$

$d = 5.0$ in.

$L_N = 0.50$ in.

$F = 59.39$ cps (theoretical)

Resonator II:

$V = H \times L \times W = 32.0 \text{ in.} \times 21.0 \text{ in.} \times 5.0 \text{ in.} = 3360.0 \text{ in}^3$

$d = 4.75$ in.

$L_N = 0.50$ in.

$F = 73.27$ cps (theoretical)

However, the *actual* frequency of Resonator I is 51.47 cps, and the *actual* frequency of Resonator II is 55.64 cps. For Resonator I, the interval between the theoretical and the actual frequencies is approximately two and a half "semitones,"

$$\log_{10} \frac{59.39 \text{ cps}}{51.47 \text{ cps}} \times 3986.314 = 247.8 \text{ ¢}$$

and for Resonator II, the interval is approximately four and three-quarter "semitones":

$$\log_{10} \frac{73.27 \text{ cps}}{55.64 \text{ cps}} \times 3986.314 = 476.5 \text{ ¢}$$

To understand why the actual frequencies are substantially lower than the theoretical frequencies, consider the six walls of a cavity resonator. The top, bottom, front and back walls all have the same width. Because these walls are narrow and rigid, their motion is negligible. However, the large surfaces of the left and right sidewalls are very susceptible to motion. Figure 7.16 shows the greatly magnified displacement of the sidewalls. Positive pressure inside the cavity — due to the compression of air from a vibrating bar — pushes the sidewalls outward. Conversely, negative pressure inside the cavity — due to the rarefaction of air from a vibrating bar — sucks the sidewalls inward. These periodic pressure fluctuations cause the sidewalls to vibrate in and out like a spring. Therefore, we must now include a second air spring (k_2) constant. Imagine a balloon inside the cavity resonator. As we blow up the balloon, the pressure increases as the sidewalls expand outward. In Section 7.16,

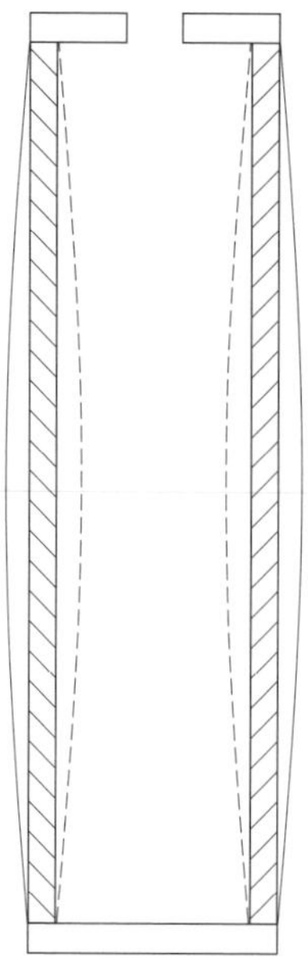

Figure 7.16 The greatly amplified motion of cavity resonator sidewalls. Due to pressure fluctuations from a vibrating bar, both sidewalls vibrate in and out like a spring.

we considered how hard the k_1 air spring inside the cavity pushes back on the air mass inside the opening. Now, we must also consider how hard the k_2 air spring at the sidewalls pushes back on the air mass inside the opening.

Due to the presence of the k_2 air spring, we must modify the simple spring-mass system shown in Figures 7.2 and 7.14, and consider a more complicated model that includes two springs. The stiffness of a composite spring, which includes two springs in series,[52] or two springs in a straight line, is given by

$$k_{\text{composite}} = \frac{k_1 k_2}{k_1 + k_2} \tag{7.38}$$

where the value of $k_{\text{composite}}$ is always less than k_1, and less than k_2. Therefore, in Figure 7.17, a spring-mass system with two springs in series and one mass always vibrates slower than with either single spring.

Equation 7.38 also tells us that as the value of k_2 increases and approaches infinity, $k_2 \rightarrow \infty$, the value of $k_{\text{composite}}$ will equal k_1. Imagine that k_2 is very flexible but gradually becomes stiffer until eventually it ceases to function, and is rigid like the ceiling from which it hangs. As a result, k_2 has an infinitely large value, and $k_{\text{composite}}$ would equal k_1, because k_1 is now the only elastic component of the system.

Since the value of $k_{\text{composite}}$ is always less than k_1, and less than k_2, the actual frequency of a cavity resonator must be lower than the theoretical frequency. For a resonator with given V and L_{N} dimensions, Equation 7.37 tells us that increasing S_{N} is the only method by which we can increase F. However, space limitations underneath marimba bars require that cavity resonators have narrow width dimensions, so large increases in S_{N} are not possible. Furthermore, as discussed in Section 7.18, a relatively small resonator with a reduced volume and, therefore, a higher resonant frequency also is not the answer. Flexible sidewalls seriously deplete a resonator's acoustic energy, which results in low amplitude and weak overall resonance. In short, the only tuning technique that works effectively is to increase the stiffness of the sidewalls.

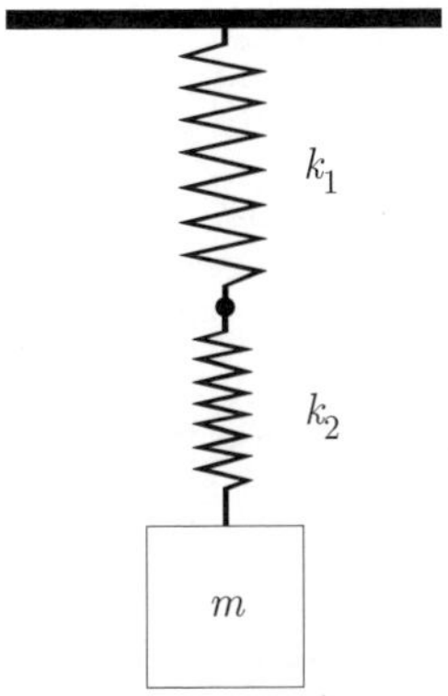

Figure 7.17 A mass-spring system with two springs in series and one mass. This kind of system always vibrates slower than with either single spring.

Part VIII

CAVITY RESONATOR TUNING TECHNIQUES

~ 7.18 ~

Equation 7.39 gives the resonant frequency of a system with two springs in series and one mass, and of a cavity resonator with two springs and one mass:

$$F = \frac{1}{2\pi}\sqrt{\frac{\frac{k_1 k_2}{k_1 + k_2}}{m}} \tag{7.39}$$

This equation states that an increase in k_2 produces an increase in F_1. To achieve such an increase, Figure 7.18 shows six dowels fastened between the sidewalls of a bass marimba cavity resonator. The purpose of these dowels is to stiffen the walls and, thereby, increase the frequency of the resonator. This technique enables one to achieve two important goals. (1) With the correct placement of the dowels — a great deal of patience and a little bit of luck goes a long way here — a marimba builder can change the tuning of a resonator by more than a "minor third," or more than 300 cents. (2) The increased stiffness of the walls also dramatically increases the amplitude of a resonator. Since less wave energy is spent in vibrating the walls, the amplitude of a tuned resonator with dowels is much greater than an untuned resonator without dowels. To understand this process, imagine riding a bicycle that has flexible springs for pedals. Most of the energy supplied by your legs would be lost in compressing and expanding the springs, and very little energy would actually go into turning the front sprocket and driving the chain. Similarly, when a pressure wave encounters a moveable surface, a great deal of the wave energy is lost in bending the surface, instead of compressing and rarefying the air.

Finally, Figure 7.19 gives the *outside* dimensions of two resonators mentioned in Section 7.17 and the exact locations of six tuning dowels per resonator. The distances between dowels are the same for both resonators. Figure 7.19 also shows how each dowel increased the frequency of the

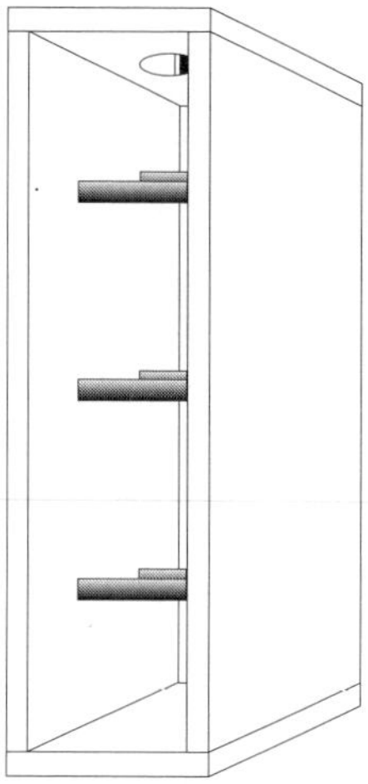

Figure 7.18 Open cavity resonator with six tuning dowels. By stiffening the walls with dowels, a builder can tune the resonant frequency of the resonator to a wide variety of frequencies and also increase the amplitude or acoustic power of the resonator.

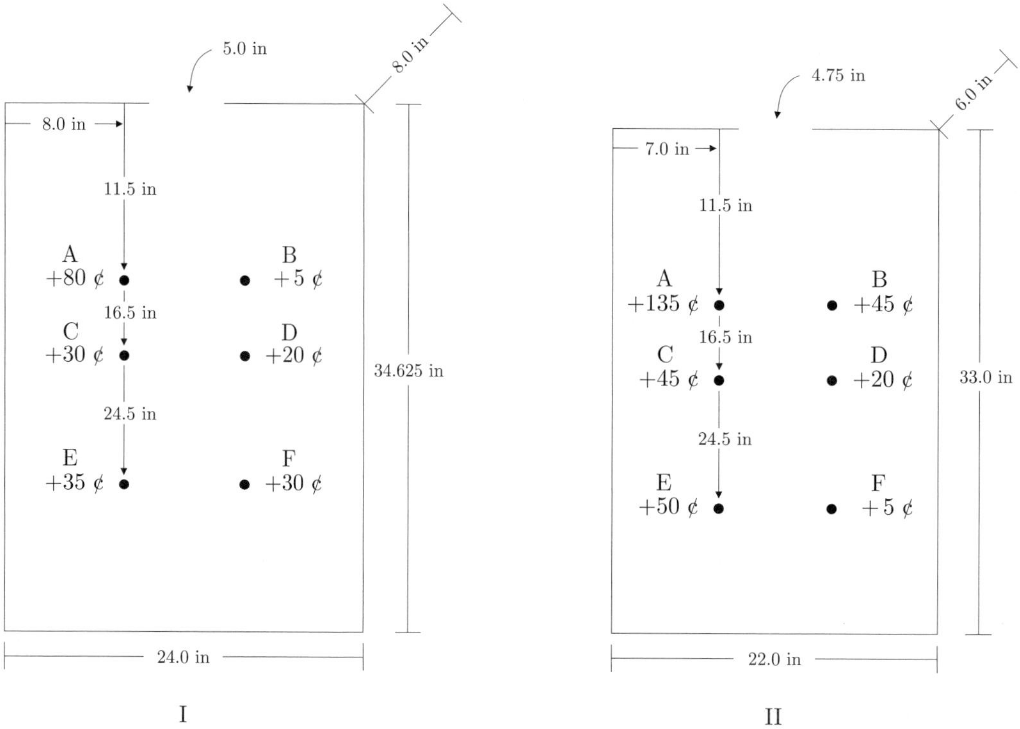

Figure 7.19 Outside dimensions of tuned cavity Resonators I and II. The figure shows how the position of each dowel increased the frequency in cents. Six dowels per resonator increased the frequency of Resonator I by 200 ¢, and of Resonator II by 300 ¢.

resonator in cents. The tuning sequence begins with Dowel A and ends with Dowel F. This particular pattern increased the frequency of Resonator I by 200 ¢, and of Resonator II by 300 ¢. Because the sidewalls of Resonator I are larger and more flexible than Resonator II, Resonator I would require more dowels to achieve the same increase in frequency as Resonator II. Furthermore, it is a good idea to intentionally build large resonators that are about 200–300 cents flat of the desired tuning. The more dowels a resonator requires, the stiffer its walls will be and, consequently, the more powerful its amplitude will be as well.

7.19

Resonator I was an experiment and does not belong to any musical instrument. However, Resonator II is the 4/3, or C_2, cavity resonator of the Bass Marimba in Plate 8. Consider how the tuning dowels of this resonator increased the value of k_2 and F. For air at 1 atmosphere of pressure, $\rho =$ 0.000000113 mica/in^3, and $c_L = 13{,}504$ in/s. (See Appendix H.) Substitute these constants and the dimensions of Resonator II given in Section 7.17 into Equations 7.35 and 7.36, and calculate the air mass and air spring:

$m = 0.000009086$ mica
$k_1 = 1.9$ lbf/in

Next, solve Equation 7.39 for k_2:

$$k_2 = \frac{4\pi^2 F^2 m}{k_1 - 4\pi^2 F^2 m} k_1 \tag{7.40}$$

Substitute the values of k_1, m, and the *actual* (untuned) frequency of 55.64 cps into Equation 7.40 and determine that $k_2 = 2.7$ lbf/in. Let us interpret these findings. Substitute the values of k_1 and k_2 into Equation 7.38 and note that $k_{\text{composite}} = 1.1$ lbf/in. This tells us that it takes a force of 1.1 pounds to displace the air mass inside the opening one inch into the cavity; or it takes a force of 1.1 pounds to compress the $k_{\text{composite}}$ air spring inside the resonator by one inch.

Because the tuning dowels increased the resonant frequency by 300 ¢, we must now calculate the tuned frequency. To increase a frequency by a given number of cents (see Section 9.12), raise the twelve hundredth root of 2

$$\sqrt[1200]{2} \approx 1.00057779$$

to the power of the cent value, and multiply the frequency by the product:

$$(55.64 \text{ cps})(1.00057779)^{300} = 66.17 \text{ cps}$$

Substitute the *tuned* resonator frequency of 66.17 cps into Equation 7.40 and note that now $k_2 =$ 9.1 lbf/in; this represents an increase of 237%. Also, note that $k_{\text{composite}} = 1.6$ lbf/in. Therefore, it now takes a force of 1.6 pounds to displace the air mass inside the opening one inch into the container. In other words, because the tuning dowels increased the value of the k_2 air spring at the sidewalls, as $k_{\text{composite}}$ increases, F increased as well.

Finally, note carefully, that k_2 defines an *acoustical stiffness*, or the stiffness that the k_2 air spring presents to the air mass inside the opening. Therefore, k_2 does *not* define a *mechanical stiffness*, or how hard a sidewall — i.e., a rectangular plate with four clamped sides — pushes back on an externally applied point load at the center of the plate. Given the following *inside* resonator sidewall dimensions and properties of hardwood plywood:

$L = 32.0$ in.
$W = 21.0$ in.
$h = 0.5$ in.
$\mu = 0.3$ (Poisson's ratio)
$E = 2{,}000{,}000$ psi (Young's modulus of elasticity)

we find that the mechanical spring constant $k_{\text{sidewall spring}} \approx 7900$ lbf/in; consequently, it takes a force of approximately 7900 pounds to displace the center of a clamped sidewall plate by one inch.[53]

7.20

Consider several aspects of fine-tuning cavity resonators. In a state of resonance, the resonant frequency of the driving system and the resonant frequency of the driven system are the same: $F = F_n$. When the driving system vibrates at a frequency less than the resonant frequency of the driven system: $F < F_n$, it means that a *stiffness reactance* exists between the two vibrating systems. Conversely, when the driving system vibrates at a frequency greater than the resonant frequency of the driven system: $F > F_n$, it means that a *mass reactance* exists between the two vibrating systems. With respect to the acoustic coupling between a bar and a resonator, a *small* stiffness reactance produces a stronger attack tone (or attack transient), and a shorter decay tone (or decay transient) than in a state of resonance. That is, when a tube resonator or cavity resonator is tuned slightly higher than the frequency of the bar, the amplitude of the bar's attack tone is noticeably greater, and the duration of the decay tone is noticeably shorter, than when both systems vibrate in a state of resonance. Conversely, a *small* mass reactance produces an attack tone with a weaker amplitude, and a decay tone with a longer duration, than when both systems have the same frequency.

To ensure a powerful attack tone for the first five bars on the Bass Marimba, all the cavity resonator frequencies were tuned 30–40 cents sharp of the bar frequencies. For example, the low 4/3 Honduras rosewood bar is tuned to

$$F_{\text{bar}} = C_2 - 2\ ¢ = 65.41 \text{ cps} \div (1.00057779)^2 = 65.33 \text{ cps}$$

which is the same frequency as G_1 at 49.00 cps × 4/3 = 65.33 cps. However, Resonator II is tuned to

$$F_{\text{resonator}} = 65.33 \text{ cps} + 35\ ¢ = (65.33 \text{ cps})(1.00057779)^{35} = 66.66 \text{ cps}$$

In this case, the ratio $F_{\text{bar}}/F_{\text{resonator}} = 0.98$, and indicates a *small* stiffness reactance. Since an acoustic resonator always vibrates with the same frequency as the bar, this slightly mistuned coupling has no effect on pitch perception. However, the amplitude of the bar's attack tone is noticeably stronger and, due to the bar's large mass, the loss in ring-time is not significant. To fine-tune Resonator II from 66.17 cps to 66.66 cps, which represents an increase of 12.8 ¢, I enlarged the resonator opening with a 2-inch drum sander mounted in a hand drill.

Notes

1. The Indonesian *gendèr* also has tube resonators.

2. The Indonesian *saron* (or *gangsa*) and *gambang* have trough resonators, which are designed to amplify several different bars simultaneously. Because trough resonators do not have a specific pitch, they are not as efficient as tube resonators.

3. Stringed instruments such as violins and guitars are designed with hollow bodies that also act as cavity resonators.

4. See Sections 3.1–3.2; and also Figure 5.1.

5. See Figure 3.10.

6. See Section 1.1.

7. Kinsler, L.E., and Frey, A.F. (1950). *Fundamentals of Acoustics*, 2nd ed., p. 196. John Wiley & Sons, Inc., New York, 1962.

8. Newton, R.E.I. (1990). *Wave Physics*, p. 42. Edward Arnold, a division of Hodder & Stoughton, London, England.

9. Den Hartog, J.P. (1934). *Mechanical Vibrations*, p. 33. Dover Publications, Inc., New York, 1985.

   This model of the spring-mass system neglects the mass of the spring. For more accurate calculations, use the following equation from Den Hartog's book, p. 430, which includes a spring mass variable:

$$F = \frac{\sqrt{\dfrac{k}{m + \dfrac{m_{\text{spring}}}{3}}}}{2\pi}$$

10. An excellent mechanical component for this experiment is a helical Slinky spring available from most toy stores.

11. Since lbf is here defined as mica·in/s^2 (see Equation 1.16), the following dimensional analysis shows that lbf/in is equivalent to mica/s^2:

$$\frac{\text{mica} \times \text{in}}{\text{s}^2} \div \frac{\text{in}}{1} =$$

$$\frac{\text{mica} \times \text{in}}{\text{s}^2} \times \frac{1}{\text{in}} =$$

$$\frac{\text{mica} \times \cancel{\text{in}}}{\text{s}^2} \times \frac{1}{\cancel{\text{in}}} = \frac{\text{mica}}{\text{s}^2}$$

12. Lindeburg, M.R. (1990). *Engineer-in-Training Reference Manual*, 8th ed., p. **45**-4. Professional Publications, Inc., Belmont, California, 1992.

13. See Figure 1.3.

14. See Section 1.12.

15. See Section 1.1.

16. To produce longitudinal vibrations in tensioned strings or rigidly mounted rods, rub some rosin into the fingertips of a glove, grab a string or rod with the glove, and pull in a direction parallel to the object. Produce longitudinal vibrations in bars, rods, and solid tubes by striking the vertical end surface with a hard mallet; and in closed acoustic tubes, by striking the cap with a mallet.

17. *Mechanical Vibrations*, p. 431.

18. *Fundamentals of Acoustics*, p. 117.

19. See Section 1.13.

20. For a technical definition of the isothermal bulk modulus and the adiabatic bulk modulus, consult any major physics textbook under the subject of thermodynamics.

21. See Equation 1.20.

22. *Fundamentals of Acoustics*, p. 117.

The following equation gives the mass density of air as a function of temperature:

$$\rho = \frac{P_0}{RT_A}$$

where ρ is the mass density of a gas, in mica per cubic inch; P_0 is the barometric pressure at 1 standard atmosphere, in psi; R is the ideal gas constant, in inch·lbf/(mica·°R), (see Note 24, which gives metric and English values for R); and T_A is the absolute temperature of air, in Kelvin when used with metric units (see Equation 7.7A); or Rankine when used with English units (see Equation 7.7B). In the meter-kilogram-second system, $P_0 = 1.01325 \times 10^5$ newtons/m^2, and in the inch-mica-second system $P_0 = 14.696$ psi (see Section 1.13). A solution to this equation for air at 20°C gives $\rho = 1.21$ kg/m^3, and at 68°F gives $\rho = 0.000000113$ mica/in^3. In contrast, at 30°C, $\rho = 1.17$ kg/m^3, and at 86°F, $\rho = 0.000000109$ mica/in^3. Note, therefore, as T_A increases, ρ decreases; and according to Equation 7.5, as ρ decreases, c_L increases.

23. Wood, A.B. (1930). *A Textbook of Sound*, p. 231. The Macmillan Company, New York, 1937.

24. Pierce, A.D. (1981). *Acoustics*, p. 29. Acoustical Society of America, Woodbury, New York. 1991.

Pierce gives the following derivation of the ideal gas constant R:

$$R = \frac{R_0}{M}$$

$$R_0 = \frac{k}{m}$$

where R_0 is the universal gas constant. Here R_0 equals the Boltzmann constant ($k = 1.380658 \times 10^{-23}$ Joule/Kelvin), divided by the mass corresponding to 1 atomic mass unit ($m = 1.6605402 \times 10^{-27}$ kg); and M is the average molecular weight of the different types of molecules in a gas: for air the number is 29. So, the universal gas constant $R_0 = 8314.5$ Joules/(kg·K), or $R_0 = 7{,}159{,}723$ inches·lbf/(mica·°R), and the ideal gas constant $R = 286.7$ Joules/(kg·K), or $R = 246{,}881$ inches·lbf/(mica·°R).

25. In 1967, the General Conference on Weights and Measures agreed to drop the term "degree" as in "degrees Kelvin," and the "degree" symbol as in °K. For example, in SI nomenclature, it is correct to write a normal room temperature of 20°C as "293.15 kelvins," and to notate it as 293.15 K.

26. The following equations give good approximations of Equations 7.6A and 7.6B, respectively:

$$c_L = 331.37 \text{ m/s} + 0.6T_C$$

$$c_L = 13,045.41 \text{ in/s} + 13.1(T_F - 32°\text{F})$$

where 331.37 m/s is the speed of sound at 0°C, and 13,045.41 in/s is the speed of sound at 32°F.

27. See Section 9.10.

28. *Wave Physics*, p. 86.

29. See Section 3.1.

30. See Sections 5.1–5.2.

31. Askenfelt, A., Editor (1990). *Five Lectures on the Acoustics of the Piano*, p. 17. Royal Swedish Academy of Music No. 64, Stockholm, Sweden.

The free flow of air between opposite sides of a piano soundboard leads to an acoustic short-circuiting effect, which decreases the radiation of sound from the bass section of the board. This principle also explains poor sound radiation of plain bars without resonators.

32. See Sections 5.9–5.10, and Equations 5.4–5.4A.

33. *Fundamentals of Acoustics*, p. 196.

34. See Appendix H.

35. Askill, J. (1979). *Physics of Musical Sound*, p. 131. D. Van Nostrand Company, New York.

"As the reed acts as a node, one would expect the clarinet and saxophone to act like closed pipes with only odd harmonics present. In fact, this is not the case. Although a typical harmonic spectrum for a clarinet shows a strong first and third harmonic with no second harmonic, the fourth, sixth, and eighth harmonics are usually quite strong as well."

36. See Section 3.5.

37. *A Textbook of Sound*, p. 172.

38. (A) Helmholtz, H.L.F., and Ellis A.J., Translator (1885). *On the Sensations of Tone*, p. 93. Dover Publications, Inc., New York, 1954.

(B) Capstick, J.W. (1913). *Sound*, p. 175. Cambridge University Press, London, England, 1932.

39. See Chapters 4 and 5 for discussions on the phenomenon of dispersion.

40. Jones, A.T. (1941). End corrections of organ pipes. *Journal of the Acoustical Society of America* **12**, pp. 387–394.

41. *On the Sensations of Tone*, pp. 43–44, 372–374.

42. Blevins, R.D. (1979). *Formulas for Natural Frequency and Mode Shape*, Reprint, Chapter 13. Krieger Publishing Company, Malabar, Florida, 1993.

43. Campbell, M., and Greated, C. (1987). *The Musician's Guide to Acoustics*, pp. 208–209. Schirmer Books, New York, 1988.

44. *Formulas for Natural Frequency and Mode Shape*, pp. 353–354.

45. Hardware stores carry large plastic syringes as glue-injecting devices.

46. (A) Olson, H.F. (1952). *Music, Physics and Engineering*, 2nd ed., p. 73. Dover Publications, Inc., New York, 1967.

(B) *Fundamentals of Acoustics*, p. 187.

47. (A) Ingard, U. (1953). On the theory and design of acoustic resonators. *Journal of the Acoustical Society of America* **25**, No. 6, pp. 1037–1061.

(B) *Music, Physics and Engineering*, p. 73.

Ingard gives an approximate end correction coefficient of 0.96, and Olson gives 1.0.

48. *Fundamentals of Acoustics*, p. 194.

49. *Mechanical Vibrations*, p. 429.

50. *Fundamentals of Acoustics*, p. 187.

This equation gives the excess pressure (p) inside a cavity resonator,

$$p = \frac{\rho {c_{\mathrm{L}}}^2 S_{\mathrm{N}}}{V} x$$

where x is the displacement of the air mass from its equilibrium position, in inches. Use the following equation to calculate the restoring force of a spring-mass system,

$$f = -kx$$

and this equation to compute the restoring force of a cavity resonator with rigid walls:

$$f = -k_1 x = -\frac{\rho {c_{\mathrm{L}}}^2 {S_{\mathrm{N}}}^2}{V} x$$

where the minus sign has *no* effect on the value of f, but indicates that the force acts — pushes back or pulls back — in the opposite direction of the displacement.

51. See Section 12.16 for a similar discussion on how removing rings of glass from the rim of a brandy snifter has a greater effect on the restoring force than on the mass.

52. *Formulas for Natural Frequency and Mode Shape*, p. 40.

53. Timoshenko, S., and Woinowsky-Krieger, S. (1940). *Theory of Plates and Shells*, 2nd ed., pp. 203–205. McGraw-Hill Book Company, New York, 1959.

8 / SIMPLE FLUTES

Flutes, harps, and drums are the oldest musical instruments created by man. Wind instruments are unique, however, because they alone embody the physical dimensions of scales and tunings. In a work entitled *The Greek Aulos*, Kathleen Schlesinger (1862–1953) attempted to reconstruct Greek music theory by analyzing the remains of ancient reed flutes.[1] It is possible to approach the subject of flute tunings from two different perspectives. We may predict the tuning of an existing instrument by first measuring various flute bore, embouchure hole, and tone hole dimensions, and then substituting these data into a sequence of equations. This method provides convenient solutions when a flute is extremely fragile and cannot be played, or is simply not available for playing. On the other hand, we may realize a given tuning by making a flute according to another sequence of equations. From a mathematical perspective, these two approaches are distinctly different and require separate discussions.

As all experienced flute players know, the intonation of a transverse flute — with either a very simple or a very complex embouchure hole — depends not only on the precision of instrument construction, but also on the performer. The mathematics of flute tubes, embouchure holes, and tone holes does not necessarily produce an accurate sounding instrument. The intonation of a flute is also governed by the strength of the airstream, and by the amount the lips cover the embouchure hole. Because these two variables exist beyond the realm of mathematical predictability, they depend exclusively on the skill of the performer.

Due to the overall complexity of flutes, this chapter is divided into three parts. Part I investigates equations for the placement of tone holes, and Part II, mathematical procedures required to analyze existing flutes. Since Part II is unintelligible without a thorough understanding of Part I, the reader should study this chapter from beginning to end. Finally, Part III gives some suggestions on how to make very inexpensive yet highly accurate simple flutes.

Part I

EQUATIONS FOR THE PLACEMENT OF TONE HOLES ON CONCERT FLUTES AND SIMPLE FLUTES

8.1

In writing this chapter, I am indebted to Cornelis J. Nederveen. In his book entitled *Acoustical Aspects of Woodwind Instruments*,[2] Nederveen carefully defines all the mathematical variables needed for a thorough investigation into woodwind acoustics. Numerous tables of woodwind instrument dimensions are included at the end of the book. Because a full description of flute acoustics requires many different variables, this discussion begins with a list of symbols originally defined by Nederveen. Since most of these symbols appear only in this chapter, they are not included in the List of Symbols at the beginning of this book. Furthermore, the List of Flute Symbols below gives seven symbols that do not appear in Nederveen's book: effective length $L_{B(h)}$ replaces λ_H; effective length $L_{B(e)}$ replaces λ_E; correction $\Delta\ell_E$ replaces $L_{B(e)}$ in the context of flute length calculations; corrections $\Delta\ell_H$ and $\Delta\ell_T$, and length ℓ_T, represent simplifications. Finally, L_A replaces L_S when, in predicting the frequencies of an existing flute, we cannot determine L_S, which represents an *exact* acoustic half-wavelength; in this context, we must calculate L_A, which represents an *approximate* acoustic half-wavelength. In preparation for Chapter 8, the reader should read, study, and absorb Chapter 7. Knowledge of longitudinal pressure waves and end correction terminology is essential for an understanding of flute acoustics.

LIST OF FLUTE SYMBOLS

d_1 Bore diameter at tone hole.

d_0 Bore diameter at embouchure hole.

d_H Tone hole diameter.

d_E Embouchure hole diameter.

S_E Surface area of embouchure hole.

S_0 Surface area of bore at embouchure hole.

ℓ_H Geometric or measured length (or height) of tone hole; that is, (1) the shortest distance of a tone hole chimney on a concert flute with key pads, or (2) the wall thickness of a simple flute without key pads.

L_H Acoustic or effective length of tone hole. (See Note 13.)

$L_{B(h)}$ Acoustic or effective length of bore at tone hole. (Nederveen: λ_H, p. 64.)

ℓ_E Geometric or measured length of embouchure hole.

L_E Acoustic or effective length of embouchure hole. (See Note 13.)

$L_{B(e)}$ Acoustic or effective length of bore at embouchure hole. (Nederveen: λ_E, p. 26.)

Δ Correction coefficient.

$\Delta\ell_E$ Approximate correction at embouchure hole. In principle, the same as $L_{B(e)}$. Although $\Delta\ell_E$ does not have an exact mathematical value, $\Delta\ell_E$ is always greater than $L_{B(e)}$.

$\Delta\ell_H$ Correction at tone hole. (Nederveen: L_X, p. 13; and zL_S, p. 48.)

$\Delta\ell_T$ End correction at open tube end: $0.3d_1$. (Nederveen: ξa, p. 27.)

$\Delta\ell_K$ Correction at key pad. (Nederveen: $\Delta\ell_d$, p. 64.)

h Geometric or measured distance of key pad in the open position above the center of a tone hole.

ℓ_T Geometric or measured length of flute tube from the embouchure hole center to the open tube end.

ℓ_L Geometric or measured length of the flute tube from the embouchure hole center to a tone hole center.

g Interval ratio minus one between two adjacent tones on the flute. In 12-tone equal temperament, $g = \sqrt[12]{2} - 1$. In just intonation, $g = {}^{x}\!/\!_{y} - 1$, where x and y are positive integers whose quotients are greater than one and less than two.

z Dimensionless tone hole parameter.

L_S *Exact* acoustic half-wavelength of Nederveen's *substitution tube*, calculated according to a frequency variable: $L_S = c/(2F)$.

L_A *Approximate* acoustic half-wavelength, calculated according to flute variables: $L_A = \ell_T + \Delta\ell_E + \Delta\ell_T$, or $L_A = \ell_L + \Delta\ell_E + \Delta\ell_H$. (Unfortunately, on p. 47, Nederveen also uses L_S in this context of approximate half-wavelengths.)

L_T $L_T = \ell_T + \Delta\ell_E + \Delta\ell_T$, or $L_T = \ell_L + \Delta\ell_E + \Delta\ell_H$. (This apparent redundancy with respect to the two previous equations for L_A is explained in Section 8.10.)

L_L Approximate length of the flute tube from a tone hole center to the correction at embouchure hole: $L_L = \ell_L + \Delta\ell_E$.

L_R Tube-piece that extends past an open tone hole: $L_R = L_T - L_L$.

Recall that in Section 7.12 we discussed the great convenience of centimeter measurements for cutting resonator lengths. A similar advantage also applies to flute construction. However, because many flute dimensions are much smaller than resonator dimensions, we will use millimeter measurements throughout this chapter. To convert inches to millimeters, multiply inches by 25.40; and to convert millimeters to inches, multiply millimeters by 0.039370.[3]

Finally, we must also define a dimensionally consistent speed of sound (c) *inside* a flute. Heat, water vapor, and carbon dioxide from the player's breath, as well as mechanical boundary layer effects that are frequency sensitive, all affect the value of c.[4] For simplicity, assume an average temperature of 25°C (or 77°F) inside the flute, and not accounting for changes due to frequency,[5] we will therefore use c = 346,000 mm/s in all future calculations.[6]

8.2

We begin this discussion on the mathematics of flute construction by carefully distinguishing between a tube's *invisible* acoustic length and its *visible* geometric length. Figure 8.1 shows that for the fundamental mode of vibration, the acoustic length of a tube open at both ends spans the distance of a half-wavelength. Similarly, Figures 7.13(a) and 7.13(b) show that the acoustic length of a resonator closed at one end spans the distance of a quarter-wavelength. The latter three figures illustrate that a tube's *acoustic or effective length* (L_{eff}) is slightly longer than its *geometric or measured length* (L). In this context, the acoustic length is of paramount importance because it alone determines a tube's fundamental wavelength (λ_1). For a tube open at both ends, $\lambda_1 = 2L_{\text{o eff}}$. (See Equations 7.22 and 7.24.) And for a tube closed at one end, $\lambda_1 = 4L_{\text{c eff}}$. (See Equations 7.27 and 7.29.)

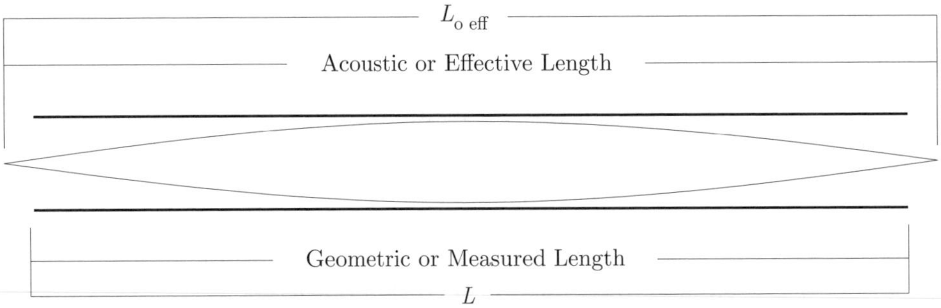

Figure 8.1 The acoustic or effective length, and the geometric or measured length of a tube open at both ends. The reflection of pressure waves occurs a small distance beyond the physical length of the tube. Consequently, the tube's acoustic length is longer than its geometric length. (Not to scale.)

Until now, we have not considered tubes closed at both ends because they serve no practical musical purpose. However, such tubes are fundamentally important because they provide a theoretical basis for flute length calculations. Figure 8.2 shows a tube closed at both ends, also called a closed-closed tube. For a closed-closed tube, the distinction between an acoustic/effective length and a geometric/measured length does *not* exist. Since there are no openings, pressure waves or displacement waves inside the tube do not reflect a small distance beyond the tube's physical length. Instead, all waves reflect precisely at the tube's closed ends. Consequently, end corrections are not a factor,[7] which means that for a tube closed at both ends, $\lambda_1 = 2L_{\text{closed-closed}}$. The equation for the theoretical and actual fundamental frequency (F_1) of a closed-closed tube states

$$F_{1\ \text{closed-closed: theoretical and actual}} = \frac{c}{\lambda_1} = \frac{c}{2L} \tag{8.1}$$

where L is the tube's inner measured length.

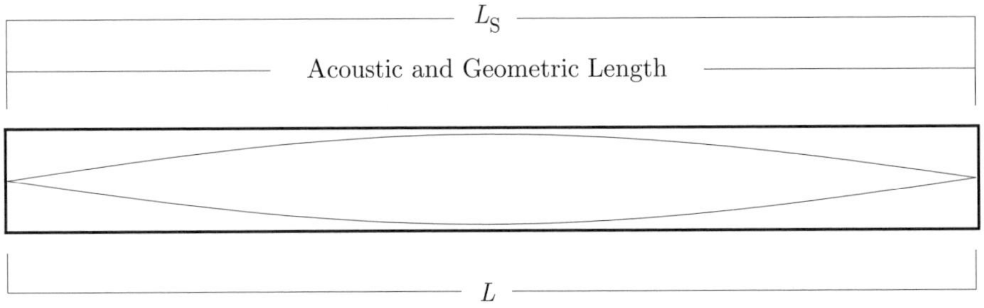

Figure 8.2 For a tube closed at both ends, the acoustic and geometric lengths are identical. Nederveen refers to this tube as a *substitution tube*, and notates its exact acoustic half-wavelength as L_S.

Nederveen refers to a closed-closed tube as a *substitution tube*, and notates its inner geometric length L, or its exact acoustic half-wavelength, as L_S.[8] Since the acoustic and geometric lengths are identical, we now set $L_S = L$. Substitute L_S into Equation 8.1 and solve for the acoustic half-wavelength in the following manner:[9]

$$F = \frac{c}{\lambda}$$

$$F = \frac{c}{2L_S} \tag{8.2A}$$

$$L_S = \frac{c}{2F} \tag{8.2B}$$

A transverse flute consists of a tube open at both ends. The embouchure hole provides the first opening, and the far end of the flute, or an open tone hole, provides the second opening. In Figures 8.3(a), 8.3(b), and 8.3(c), each illustration consists of two sections. The top portion shows a substitution tube closed at both ends, and the bottom portion shows a flute tube open at both ends. Nederveen's substitution tube exemplifies a tube *without* any openings that generates exactly the

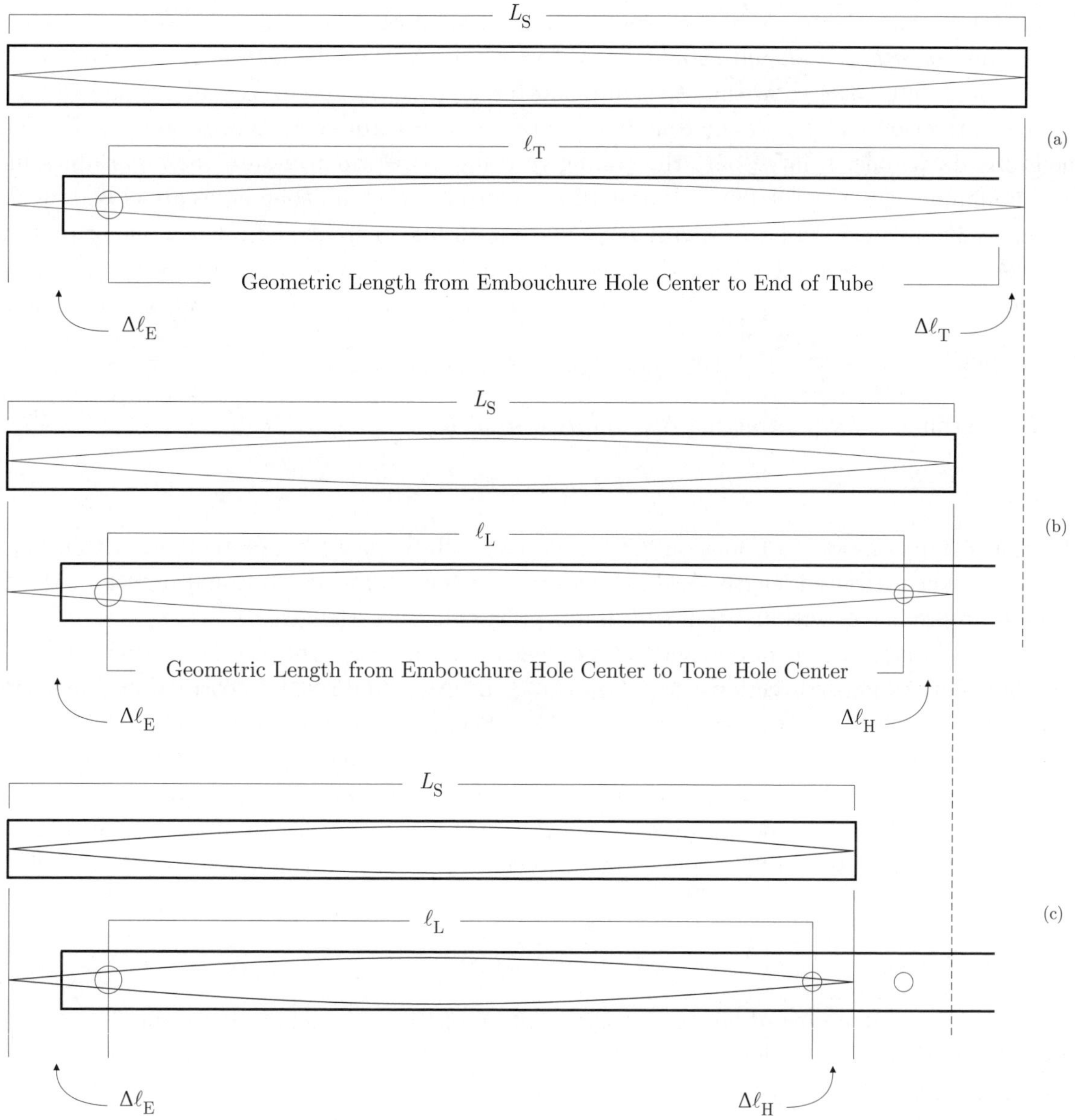

Figure 8.3 Variables and strategies for determining the overall tube length and tone hole locations of flutes. (a) L_S represents the acoustic half-wavelength produced when all tone holes are closed. (b) L_S represents the acoustic half-wavelength when the first tone hole is open. (c) L_S represents the acoustic half-wavelength when the first two tone holes are open. (Not to scale.)

same frequency as a flute tube *with* two openings.[10] Stated another way, L_S represents the acoustic half-wavelength that a flute tube produces when it sounds a given frequency. Therefore, we now write the following condition for the purposes of flute length calculations:

$$L_S \equiv L_{o\ eff}$$

This expression states that the acoustic/geometric length of a substitution tube, or of a tube closed at both ends, is by definition identical to the acoustic/effective length of a tube open at both ends.

Due to the reflection of waves a small distance beyond the flute openings, the geometric/measured length from the embouchure hole center to the open tube end (ℓ_T), and the geometric/measured length from the embouchure hole center to a tone hole center (ℓ_L), are always shorter than L_S. Figure 8.3(a) shows that ℓ_T is shorter than L_S because of an added embouchure correction ($\Delta\ell_E$) at the *top or high end*, and an added end correction ($\Delta\ell_T$) at the *bottom or low end*. Similarly, Figures 8.3(b) and 8.3(c) show that ℓ_L is also shorter than L_S because of $\Delta\ell_E$ at the top end, and a tone hole correction ($\Delta\ell_H$) past the tone hole center at the bottom end. Since the ℓ_T and ℓ_L length dimensions determine in large part the tuning of a flute, we will compute these variables in the following manner. (1) For the flute's lowest tube frequency when all tone holes are closed, evaluate Equation 8.2B and then replace L_S with $L_{S(t)}$; and for all higher frequencies when one or more tone holes are open, again evaluate Equation 8.2B and then replace L_S with $L_{S(h)}$. (2) Next, calculate the corrections $\Delta\ell_E$, $\Delta\ell_T$, and $\Delta\ell_H$. (3) Finally, determine ℓ_T by subtracting $\Delta\ell_E$ and $\Delta\ell_T$ from $L_{S(t)}$,

$$\ell_T = L_{S(t)} - \Delta\ell_E - \Delta\ell_T \tag{8.3}$$

and (4) determine ℓ_L by subtracting $\Delta\ell_E$ and $\Delta\ell_H$ from $L_{S(h)}$:

$$\ell_L = L_{S(h)} - \Delta\ell_E - \Delta\ell_H \tag{8.4}$$

In Section 8.3, a solution to Equation 8.3 for a concert flute with keys predicts ℓ_T within 3.5 mm (0.138 in.) of the measured length. And in Section 8.6, twelve solutions to Equation 8.4 for the same concert flute predict ℓ_L within 1 mm (0.039 in.) of the measured lengths.

Before we continue, it is important to first clear up a semantic problem. In Section 8.1, the List of Symbols defines four corrections: $\Delta\ell_E$, $\Delta\ell_H$, $\Delta\ell_T$, and $\Delta\ell_K$. The last two corrections have simple, straightforward solutions. However, as explained in Sections 8.3 and 8.5, the first two corrections are more complicated because they are derived from proportions. The List of Symbols carefully defines $\Delta\ell_E$ as a "correction at the embouchure hole." It does *not* define $\Delta\ell_E$ as an "embouchure hole correction." The latter definition suggests that $\Delta\ell_E$ is a sole function of the embouchure hole. This is not the case. Section 8.3 explains that $\Delta\ell_E$ has its origins in the following proportion:

$$\frac{S_E}{L_E} = \frac{S_0}{L_{B(e)}}$$

where S_0 is the *surface area of the bore* at the location of the embouchure hole, and $L_{B(e)}$ is the *effective length of the bore* at the location of the embouchure hole. At the end of Section 8.3 we will replace $L_{B(e)}$ with $\Delta\ell_E$. This example demonstrates why it is technically more accurate to call $\Delta\ell_E$ a "correction at the embouchure hole" than to give the impression that $\Delta\ell_E$ is an "embouchure hole correction." However, phrases like "the correction at the embouchure hole" and "the correction at a tone hole" are awkward in the context of a difficult discussion. Therefore, we will continue to use the phrases "embouchure hole correction" and "tone hole correction" even though such expressions do not give exactly correct descriptions.

8.3

We turn our attention now to solutions for $\Delta\ell_T$ and $\Delta\ell_E$. Section 7.11 discussed at length the end correction phenomenon that occurs at the open ends of cylindrical resonators. Since the end correction for a flute tube is the same as for a resonator tube, refer to Equation 7.20, set $\Delta\ell_T = \Delta\ell$, and use this equation for the end correction:

$$\Delta\ell_T = 0.3d_1 \tag{8.5}$$

Unfortunately, an exact equation for the embouchure correction does not exist. $\Delta\ell_E$ depends on the position of the player's lips over the embouchure hole. Increased lip coverage increases $\Delta\ell_E$.[11] This causes an increase in L_S (see Equation 8.20), which in turn decreases the frequencies of the flute. However, Nederveen does give a solution for the minimum theoretical value[12] for the effective length of the bore at the embouchure hole,[13]

$$L_{B(e)} = (\ell_E + d_E)\left(\frac{d_0}{d_E}\right)^2 - 0.45d_0 \tag{8.6}$$

where ℓ_E is the measured length or height of the embouchure hole, in millimeters; d_E is the diameter of the embouchure hole, in millimeters; and d_0 is the diameter of the flute bore at the location of the embouchure hole, also in millimeters.

To understand the origins of Equation 8.6, we must first consider the acoustic admittance (Y_A) of a flute bore or flute hole. This quantity measures the ease with which air flows through a duct. Acoustic admittance is the reciprocal (or opposite) of acoustic impedance:[14]

$$\boldsymbol{Y}_A = \frac{1}{\boldsymbol{Z}_A}$$

As the impedance of a duct increases, the admittance decreases and *vice versa.* A non-complex definition[15] of acoustic impedance is

$$Z_A = \frac{\rho c}{S} = \frac{\rho ck}{\kappa} \tag{8.7}$$

Therefore, a non-complex definition of acoustic admittance is

$$Y_A = \frac{S}{\rho c} = \frac{\kappa}{\rho ck} \tag{8.8}$$

where S is the surface area of the duct, in square millimeters; ρ is the density of air, in kilograms per cubic millimeters; k is the angular wave number,[16] in radians per millimeter; and κ is the conductivity of the hole, in millimeters. Conductivity is the reciprocal (or opposite) of resistance. We define conductivity as the ratio of a duct's surface area divided by its effective length,[17]

$$\kappa = \frac{S}{L_{eff}} = \frac{S}{\ell + \Delta(d)} \tag{8.9}$$

where S is the surface area of a bore or hole, in square millimeters; ℓ is the measured length of a bore or hole, in millimeters; d is the diameter of a bore or hole, also in millimeters; and Δ is the correction coefficient of a bore or hole,[18] dimensionless. Equation 8.9 states that the airflow through a hole is directly proportional to surface area, and inversely proportional to effective length. A wide shallow hole conducts air more efficiently than a narrow deep hole. Note, however, when κ is too large or too small for a given bore, the flute tube is either too long or too short and will not work. Similarly, when κ is too small for a given tone hole, the hole is too narrow and will not work. Equations 8.7 and 8.8 show that Z_A and Y_A are functions of conductivity. For a given bore or hole, the ratio of S to $\ell + \Delta(d)$ must be correct, otherwise the terminating admittance (or terminating impedance) will not cause a reflection of pressure waves from the openings of a bore, nor from the opening of a hole.[19] Without the reflection of pressure waves, there can be no standing waves, and without standing waves, there is no sound.

Consider now the locations on a flute where two admittances (of conductivities κ) are simultaneously present. Such a place exists at the top end of the flute. Here the conductivity of the embouchure hole interacts with the conductivity of the flute bore at the location of the embouchure hole. The flute provides us with the dimensions of the diameter and the length of the embouchure hole, and the diameter of the bore. However, because the effective length of the bore at the location of the embouchure hole remains unknown, we may solve for $L_{B(e)}$ by considering the following proportion. Equation 8.10 states that the surface area of the embouchure hole (S_E) is to the effective length of the embouchure hole (L_E), as the surface area of the main bore at the embouchure hole (S_0) is to $L_{B(e)}$:

$$\left[\frac{S_E}{L_E} = \frac{S_0}{L_{B(e)}}\right] = \left[\frac{\pi\left(\frac{d_E}{2}\right)^2}{\ell_E + \Delta(d_E)} = \frac{\pi\left(\frac{d_0}{2}\right)^2}{L_{B(e)}}\right] \tag{8.10}$$

To solve for $L_{B(e)}$, cross-multiply, divide, cancel, and simplify:

$$L_{B(e)} \times \pi\left(\frac{d_E}{2}\right)^2 = \pi\left(\frac{d_0}{2}\right)^2 \times [\ell_E + \Delta(d_E)]$$

$$L_{B(e)} = \frac{\pi\left(\frac{d_0}{2}\right)^2 [\ell_E + \Delta(d_E)]}{\pi\left(\frac{d_E}{2}\right)^2}$$

$$L_{B(e)} = \frac{\cancel{\pi}\left(\frac{d_0}{\cancel{2}}\right)^2 [\ell_E + \Delta(d_E)]}{\cancel{\pi}\left(\frac{d_E}{\cancel{2}}\right)^2}$$

$$L_{B(e)} = \left(\frac{d_0}{d_E}\right)^2 [\ell_E + \Delta(d_E)] \tag{8.11}$$

Equation 8.10 defines the conductivity of one duct in terms of another duct. The difference between these two ducts is that the left side of Equation 8.10 represents the actual duct of the embouchure hole, whereas the right side of Equation 8.10 represents a fictitious duct associated with the flute bore. This fictitious duct has the same diameter as the bore, and by definition, the same conductivity as the embouchure hole. Figures 8.3(a), 8.3(b), and 8.3(c) show that $L_{B(e)}$ (or $\Delta\ell_E$) of the fictitious duct has the effect of extending the tube beyond the top end of the flute. Equation 8.10 states that the actual and the fictitious ducts must have the same conductivity, otherwise two different admittances would result. If two different admittances existed, then the pressure waves would not reflect from the same location to the left of the bore. We conclude, therefore, that for a given frequency, the combined terminating admittances of the embouchure hole and the bore cause a reflection of pressure waves a moderate distance $L_{B(e)}$ beyond the physical location of the embouchure hole center. Similarly, recall that in Section 7.11, the impedance of a resonator causes a reflection of pressure waves a small distance $\Delta\ell$ beyond the physical length of the tube.

According to Arthur H. Benade,[20] a good estimate for the coefficient of both the inside and outside corrections[21] of an embouchure hole or tone hole is $\mathit{\Delta} = 0.75$. To ensure that the results of Equations 8.6 and 8.11 are very close, we will use a slightly smaller correction coefficient, $\mathit{\Delta} = 0.71$. Consider now the following embouchure and bore dimensions of a typical concert metal flute:

ℓ_E = 4.3 mm. Due to the presence of a lip plate, the length of the embouchure hole is much greater than the thickness of the flute tube; the wall of a typical concert flute is only 0.5 mm thick.

d_E = 11.2 mm. On most concert flutes the embouchure hole is in the shape of an oval and has a diameter of 12.0 mm; here 11.2 mm represents a mean value.[22]

d_0 = 17.4 mm. The embouchure end of a concert flute — also known as the head joint — has a slight taper that decreases the tube's diameter from 19.0 mm at the joint to approximately 16.8 mm at the far upper end of the tube.

A substitution of these values into Equation 8.6 gives $L_{B(e)} = 29.58$ mm, and into Equation 8.11 gives $L_{B(e)} = 29.57$ mm.

Four years after the publication of his book, Nederveen concluded that empirical observations over a wide frequency range indicate $L_{B(e)} \approx 50$ mm.[23] Theobald Boehm[24] (1794–1881), the inventor of the modern concert flute, and Benade give the same approximation. Since the effective length of the bore at the embouchure hole acts as a correction, express the following condition for the purposes of flute length calculations:

$$\Delta\ell_E \equiv L_{B(e)}$$

and assign the value $\Delta\ell_E = 50$ mm. Now, to calculate ℓ_T for a concert flute tuned to middle C (or C_4 at 261.63 cps), first use Equation 8.2B to compute the acoustic length of the substitution tube:

$$L_{S(t)} = \frac{346{,}000 \text{ mm/s}}{2(261.63 \text{ cps})} = 661.2 \text{ mm}$$

Next, substitute a 19.0 mm diameter bore into Equation 8.5 to obtain the end correction:

$$\Delta\ell_T = 0.3(19.0 \text{ mm}) = 5.7 \text{ mm}$$

Finally, substitute the values for $L_{S(t)}$, $\Delta\ell_E$, and $\Delta\ell_T$ into Equation 8.3 to obtain the tube length:

$$\ell_T = 661.2 \text{ mm} - 50 \text{ mm} - 5.7 \text{ mm} = 605.5 \text{ mm}$$

8.4

On the Armstrong Concert Flute (Serial Number 104-25-29992), $\ell_T = 602$ mm, which is 3.5 mm shorter than given by the previous calculation. To account for this shorter length, we must examine the profile of a flute bore in greater detail. While playing the lowest frequency, a flute bore does not have a perfectly smooth surface. Instead, a series of closed tone holes gives the bore an interrupted and irregular profile. Closed tone hole cavities have the effect of enlarging the volume of the bore and perturbing the flow of air through the bore.[25] This causes the flute to sound flat. Furthermore, the viscous and thermal losses associated with a thin boundary layer against the flute's inner surface, and the shape of the tapered head joint at the top end of the flute, also effectively decrease the frequencies of a flute throughout the first "octave" of its three "octave" range. For a Gemeinhardt Concert Flute,[26] which is very similar to the Armstrong Concert Flute, Nederveen shows that these combined corrections cause the flute to sound C_4 between 15–30 cents flat. To help offset these effects, flute makers intentionally shorten ℓ_T by a small amount. According to Equation 8.1, as ℓ_T or L decreases, λ_1 decreases, and so F_1 increases. Although a 3.5 mm shorter length for this flute sounds F_1 only 9.2 ¢ higher, the performer's blowing technique at the embouchure hole corrects any remaining intonational discrepancies.

During the early stages of making a simple flute, mark the location of the embouchure hole 32.0 mm (1¼ in.) from the upper end of the tube; now cut the tube 10.0 mm longer than given by Equation 8.3. Drill the embouchure hole, and place a cork into the tube so that the cork's inner surface sits 17.0 mm to the left of the embouchure hole center. (In concert flutes, 17.0 mm is the standard distance between the embouchure hole center and cork.) Test the frequency of the tube *without* tone holes. Gradually shorten the tube until it gives a frequency about 30 ¢ flat of the fundamental frequency. Stop for now. For the embouchure hole correction use $\Delta\ell_E = 52$ mm (see Section 8.7), and calculate the tone hole locations as specified in Section 8.5. Drill the tone holes with a small diameter drill at first: this causes all the holes to sound flat. Fine-tune the flute by gradually enlarging the tone hole diameters: this raises the frequencies. Intermittently test the lowest frequency of the flute with all tone holes closed. Finally, fine-tune the flute bore by gradually decreasing the length of the tube. As ℓ_T decreases, F_1 increases and comes into tune.

8.5

Our next task is to calculate the tone hole correction. On first impression, Figure 8.3(b) seems to suggest that $\Delta\ell_E$ and $\Delta\ell_H$ represent equivalent quantities. This is not the case. Equations 8.17 and 8.18 show that $\Delta\ell_H$ is a function of the effective length of the bore at the location of a tone hole ($L_{B(h)}$). Unlike $L_{B(e)}$, $L_{B(h)}$ has a predictable value because it does not depend on the technique of the flute player. Analogous to $L_{B(e)}$, $L_{B(h)}$ represents the length of a fictitious duct that has the same diameter as the main tube, and the same conductivity as the tone hole. However, $L_{B(h)}$ alone does not define $\Delta\ell_H$. With respect to $L_{B(e)}$, the flute tube ends near the embouchure hole. But with respect to $L_{B(h)}$, the flute tube does not end near the open tone hole. Instead, pressure waves continue to travel inside the bore beyond the physical location of the open tone hole. For this reason, we must also account for the terminating admittance of the short tube-piece that extends past the open hole. For the first tone hole in Figure 8.3(b), the effective length of this tube-piece spans the distance from the tone hole center to the dashed line. This line marks the end correction at the open end of the tube. Similarly, in the case of two adjacent open holes, the effective length of the tube-piece in Figure 8.3(c) spans the distance from the second tone hole center to the dashed line. Here the line marks the tone hole correction of the first tone hole. We conclude, therefore, that $\Delta\ell_H$ is a function of three admittances. For a given frequency, the combined terminating admittances of the tone hole, the flute bore, and the tube-piece cause the reflection of pressure waves a moderate distance $\Delta\ell_H$ beyond the physical location of the tone hole center.[27]

Before proceeding with detailed calculations, let us first distinguish between flutes with key pads, and those without key pads. A key pad has the effect of decreasing the frequency of a tone hole. Consequently, a tone hole with a key pad sits higher on the bore (or nearer the embouchure hole) than a tone hole without a key pad, which sits lower on the bore (or nearer the flute's open end). For a tone hole with a key pad, the higher position compensates for this flattening effect and, thereby, increases the frequency of the hole. Since most modern concert flutes come equipped with key pads, we continue our analysis of the previously mentioned concert flute.

For a flute with key pads, $\Delta\ell_H$ requires preliminary solutions to Equations 8.2B, 8.12, 8.13, 8.16, and 8.17; and for a flute without key pads, $\Delta\ell_H$ requires solutions to Equations 8.2B, 8.14, 8.16, and 8.17. Nederveen gives the following equation for the effective length of the bore at the location of a tone hole:[28]

$$L_{B(h)} = (\ell_H + d_H + \Delta\ell_K)\left(\frac{d_1}{d_H}\right)^2 - 0.45d_1 \tag{8.12}$$

where ℓ_H is the shortest distance of a tone hole chimney,[29] in millimeters; d_H is the diameter of the tone hole, in millimeters; $\Delta\ell_K$ is the key pad correction, in millimeters; and d_1 is the diameter of the bore, also in millimeters. With the exception of the $\Delta\ell_K$ variable, notice the similarities between Equations 8.6 and 8.12. Nederveen and Benade give[30]

$$\Delta\ell_K = 0.325d_H\left[\left(\frac{d_H}{2h}\right)^{0.39} - 1\right] \tag{8.13}$$

where h is the key pad distance in an open position above the center of the tone hole, in millimeters. Remember, however, that for a simple flute without key pads, we must rewrite Equation 8.12 without the $\Delta\ell_K$ variable:

$$L_{B(h)} = (\ell_H + d_H)\left(\frac{d_1}{d_H}\right)^2 - 0.45d_1 \tag{8.14}$$

Equation 8.14 suggests that the proportion expressed by Equation 8.10 applies not only to embouchure holes, but to tone holes as well. Consequently, Equation 8.15 also gives good results:

$$L_{B(h)} = \left(\frac{d_1}{d_H}\right)^2(\ell_H + 0.71d_H) + \Delta\ell_K \tag{8.15}$$

Consider now the following C$\sharp_4$ tone hole dimensions, key pad and bore dimensions, and key pad correction of the same concert flute:

$\ell_H = 2.0$ mm
$d_H = 15.3$ mm
$h = 3.0$ mm
$d_1 = 19.0$ mm
$\Delta\ell_K = 2.2$ mm

A substitution of these values into Equation 8.12 gives $L_{B(h)} = 21.5$ mm, and into Equation 8.15 gives 22.0 mm.

To determine $\Delta\ell_H$, we must also consider a musical interval or an interval ratio between two adjacent tone holes on the flute. In this context, Nederveen gives the variable[31]

$$g = {}^{x}\!/\!_{y} - 1 \tag{8.16}$$

where ${}^{x}\!/\!_{y}$ is either a rational or irrational interval ratio. For a scale in 12-tone equal temperament,[32] where all the intervals between adjacent tones are constant, g equals the 12th root of 2 minus one:

$$g = \sqrt[12]{2} - 1 = 1.05946 - 1 = 0.05946$$

However, for a scale in just intonation,[33] g is not necessarily a constant. For example, if the first tone hole is a 9⁄8, or a "just major second," then the interval ratio between the lowest frequency of the flute tube and the first hole is a 9⁄8,

$$\frac{9}{8} \div \frac{1}{1} = \frac{9}{8} \times \frac{1}{1} = \frac{9}{8}$$

and so,

$$g = \frac{9}{8} - 1 = 1.125 - 1 = 0.125$$

But if the second tone hole is a 5⁄4, or a "just major third," then the interval ratio between the first hole and the second hole is a 10⁄9,

$$\frac{5}{4} \div \frac{9}{8} = \frac{5}{\not 4} \times \frac{\not 8^{2}}{9} = \frac{10}{9}$$

and so,

$$g = \frac{10}{9} - 1 = 1.111 - 1 = 0.111$$

Nederveen combines variables $L_{B(h)}$, g, and L_S into a dimensionless tone hole parameter:[34]

$$z = \frac{1}{2} g \sqrt{1 + 4\frac{L_{B(h)}}{gL_S}} - \frac{1}{2} g \tag{8.17}$$

According to Equation 8.2B, for the first C♯$_4$ tone hole,

$$L_{S(h)} = \frac{346{,}000 \text{ mm/s}}{2(277.18 \text{ cps})} = 624.1 \text{ mm}$$

so that

$$z = \frac{0.05946}{2} \sqrt{1 + 4\frac{21.5 \text{ mm}}{0.05946(624.1 \text{ mm})}} - \frac{0.05946}{2} = 0.0244$$

Finally, Nederveen gives the tone hole correction[35]

$$\Delta\ell_H = zL_S \tag{8.18}$$

so that

$$\Delta\ell_H \text{ for C}\sharp_4 = 0.0244(624.1 \text{ mm}) = 15.2 \text{ mm}$$

For the location of the C♯$_4$ tone hole, substitute the values for $L_{S(h)}$, $\Delta\ell_E$, and $\Delta\ell_H$ into Equation 8.4 to obtain the tube length:

$$\ell_L = 624.1 \text{ mm} - 50 \text{ mm} - 15.2 \text{ mm} = 559 \text{ mm}$$

This corresponds to the exact location of the first hole on the concert flute.

8.6

Table 8.1, Columns 3–5 list tone hole and key pad dimensions of the Armstrong Concert Flute, and Columns 6–10 list the results of five equations required to compute ℓ_L. Finally, Column 11 gives the calculated tone hole locations, and Column 12 gives the measured tone hole locations, rounded here to the nearest millimeter. With the exception of the C♯$_5$ tone hole, there is very good agreement between calculated and measured locations. The C♯$_5$ hole also serves as a vent or register hole for D_5 and D♯$_5$.[36] Its location is designed to correct the lengthening (or flattening) effect of the tapered head joint.[37] For this reason, the C♯$_5$ hole has a comparatively small diameter and sits 3.5 millimeters higher on the bore than predicted by theory.

Table 8.1

ARMSTRONG CONCERT FLUTE TONE HOLE DIMENSIONS AND LOCATIONS

Scale	F	ℓ_H	d_H	h	$\Delta\ell_K$	$L_{B(h)}$	L_S	z	$\Delta\ell_H$	Calc. ℓ_L	Meas. ℓ_L
C♯$_4$	277.18	2.0	15.3	3.0	2.2	21.5	624.1	0.0244	15.2	559	559
D_4	293.66	2.0	15.3	3.0	2.2	21.5	589.1	0.0255	15.0	524	524
D♯$_4$	311.13	2.0	15.3	3.0	2.2	21.5	556.0	0.0267	14.8	491	491
E_4	329.63	2.0	13.8	2.0	2.8	26.7	524.8	0.0328	17.2	458	457
F_4	349.23	2.0	13.8	2.0	2.8	26.7	495.4	0.0342	16.9	428	427
F♯$_4$	369.99	2.0	13.8	2.0	2.8	26.7	467.6	0.0357	16.7	401	400
G_4	392.00	2.0	13.8	2.0	2.8	26.7	441.3	0.0372	16.4	375	375
G♯$_4$	415.30	2.0	12.8	2.0	2.4	29.3	416.6	0.0415	17.3	349	350
A_4	440.00	2.0	12.8	2.0	2.4	29.3	393.2	0.0432	17.0	326	327
A♯$_4$	466.16	2.0	12.8	2.0	2.4	29.3	371.1	0.0450	16.7	304	304
B_4	493.88	2.0	12.7	2.0	2.3	29.6	350.3	0.0471	16.5	284	283
C_5	523.25	2.0	12.7	2.0	2.3	29.6	330.6	0.0491	16.2	264	264
C♯$_5$	554.37	2.0	7.3	2.0	0.6	58.7	312.1	0.0801	25.0	237	233
(1)	(2)	(3)	(4)	(5)	(6)	(7)	(8)	(9)	(10)	(11)	(12)

8.7

One of the most important relations to emerge from Table 8.1 is that ℓ_L is directly proportional to d_H:

$$\ell_L \propto d_H$$

As the diameter of a tone hole decreases, the distance from the embouchure hole center to a tone hole center decreases as well and *vice versa*. For a given frequency, a small diameter hole sits higher on the bore than a large diameter hole. For example, if we decrease the diameter of the C♯$_4$ hole in Table 8.1 to 14.3 mm, then $\ell_L = 558$ mm, which means that this smaller hole would have a position 1 mm higher on the bore than the existing hole. This is an important consideration for makers of simple keyless flutes. The usefulness of a simple flute depends in large part on the spaces between tone holes, because if the tone holes are too difficult to reach, the instrument is unplayable.

Most simple flutes consist of an embouchure hole and six tone holes. One plays the fundamental by closing all the holes, then six more tones by opening each hole, and finally the eighth tone, or the "octave," by closing all the holes again and overblowing at the embouchure hole.[38] Consider such a flute tuned to G_4 at 392.0 cps. To play a *just intoned* diatonic scale on this instrument requires six tones holes that produce the following six frequency ratios and six interval ratios:[39]

	①	②	③	④	⑤	⑥	
G_4	A_4	B_4	C_5	D_5	E_5	$F\sharp_5$	G_5
1/1	9/8	5/4	4/3	3/2	5/3	15/8	2/1
9/8	10/9	16/15	9/8	10/9	9/8		

Between 15/8 and 2/1, we do not include the last interval, ratio 16/15, because it occurs naturally while overblowing the flute.

Table 8.2(a) lists tone hole dimensions and solutions for a flute tuned to 392.0 cps., where d_1 = 19.0 mm (3/4 in.), ℓ_H = 3.2 mm (1/8 in.), and ℓ_T = 384 mm (15.1 in.). The latter value results when we substitute $\Delta\ell_E$ = 52 mm into Equation 8.3:

$$\ell_T = \frac{346{,}000 \text{ mm/s}}{2(392.0 \text{ cps})} - 52 \text{ mm} - 5.7 \text{ mm} = 384 \text{ mm}$$

The embouchure hole has the following dimensions: d_0 = 19.0 mm, ℓ_E = 3.2 mm, and d_E = 9.5 mm (3/8 in.). Substitute these values into Equation 8.6 and calculate $L_{B(e)}$ = 42.3 mm. Tests show that for such a cylindrical flute with a simple circular embouchure hole, and without a tapered head joint,[40] $\Delta\ell_E$ = 52 mm. This actual correction is typically between 9–10 mm greater than the theoretical correction, and 2.0 mm greater than the empirical correction of a standard concert flute. Such conclusions are based not only on experimental observation, but also on personal preference. Equation 8.4 shows that $\Delta\ell_E$ plays a critical role in determining the locations of all tone holes. That is, as $\Delta\ell_E$ increases, ℓ_L decreases, which means that a higher value for $\Delta\ell_E$ places all the tone holes closer to the top end of the flute. Since ℓ_L is inversely proportional to F (see Section 8.8), as ℓ_L decreases, F increases. Note, however, that the intonation of a tone hole depends not only on location, but also on the strength of a player's airstream, and on the lip coverage of the embouchure hole! A weak airstream and a large lip coverage tend to flatten (or decrease), and a strong airstream and a small lip coverage tend to sharpen (or increase) all the tones of a flute. Consequently, when a series of tone holes sits 2.0 mm higher on the bore, the player is more relaxed because high tone hole locations require less air pressure and allow more lip coverage without the risk of sounding flat. On the other hand, if the player chooses to play loud, or play in the second or third registers, the flute requires greater air pressure and less lip coverage, two conditions that tend to sharpen all the tones. These potentially conflicting relations indicate that there are no hard rules governing $\Delta\ell_E$. The final value of the embouchure correction is (within limits) subject to the discretion of the flute maker.

We return now to Table 8.2(a), where Column 7 gives the frequencies of the tone holes in just intonation. To calculate these frequencies, multiply 392.0 cps by a given frequency ratio. For example, the frequency of $F\sharp_5$ is 392.0 cps × 15/8 = 735.0 cps. (As before, use c = 346,000 mm/s to calculate L_S.) For all holes d_H = 9.5 mm (3/8 in.). Notice that the space between holes ① and ② is 38 mm, and between holes ② and ③ is 17 mm, which constitutes an irregular spacing, but between holes ④ and ⑤ it is 28 mm, and between ⑤ and ⑥ it is 29 mm, which constitutes a regular spacing. The irregular spacing of the first three holes is due in large part to the semitone between B_4 and C_5. If we decrease the diameters of holes ① and ③ to d_H = 6.4 mm (1/4 in.), then ℓ_L for ① = 299 mm, and for ③ = 248 mm, so that both holes would occupy higher locations on the bore. Now the spacing between holes ① and ② would be 24 mm, and between holes ② and ③ would be 27 mm. This is a much more comfortable design. The only drawback for such small diameter holes is that the surface areas are also smaller. According to Equation 8.7, as S decreases, Z_A increases, which means that smaller holes have a higher wave impedance and, therefore, radiate acoustic energy less efficiently than large holes.[41] Consequently, for a given blowing pressure, small holes are not as loud as large holes. This discrepancy between 9.5 mm holes and 6.4 mm holes in the lower part of the bore is rather noticeable. However, Table 8.2(b) shows that if we decrease the diameters of holes ① and ③ from the original 9.5 mm to 7.2 mm (9⁄32 in.), then the space between holes ① and ② is 29 mm, and between holes ② and ③ is 24 mm. Although a 9⁄32 in. hole is only 1⁄32 in. larger than a 1⁄4 in. hole, the difference in amplitude is strikingly perceptible and very similar to the amplitude of a large 3⁄8 in. hole. Note that the new spacing between the lower three holes also represents a well-balanced design. In Plate 11, the flute on the left — or Flute 1 — has the dimensions and tuning of this flute described in Table 8.2(b).

Table 8.2(a)

SIMPLE FLUTE WITH CONSTANT TONE HOLE DIAMETERS

Scale	Ratio	g	ℓ_H	d_H	$L_{B(h)}$	F	L_S	z	$\Delta\ell_H$	ℓ_L
A_4	9⁄8	0.125	3.2	9.5	42.3	441.0	392.3	0.0693	27.2	① = 313
B_4	5⁄4	0.111	3.2	9.5	42.3	490.0	353.1	0.0724	25.6	② = 275
C_5	4⁄3	0.067	3.2	9.5	42.3	522.7	331.0	0.0648	21.4	③ = 258
D_5	3⁄2	0.125	3.2	9.5	42.3	588.0	294.2	0.0853	25.1	④ = 217
E_5	5⁄3	0.111	3.2	9.5	42.3	653.3	264.8	0.0887	23.5	⑤ = 189
$F\sharp_5$	15⁄8	0.125	3.2	9.5	42.3	735.0	235.4	0.0998	23.5	⑥ = 160
(1)	(2)	(3)	(4)	(5)	(6)	(7)	(8)	(9)	(10)	(11)

Table 8.2(b)

SIMPLE FLUTE WITH TWO VARIED TONE HOLE DIAMETERS

Scale	Ratio	g	ℓ_H	d_H	$L_{B(h)}$	F	L_S	z	$\Delta\ell_H$	ℓ_L
A_4	9⁄8	0.125	3.2	7.2	63.9	441.0	392.3	0.0933	36.6	① = 304
B_4	5⁄4	0.111	3.2	9.5	42.3	490.0	353.1	0.0724	25.6	② = 275
C_5	4⁄3	0.067	3.2	7.2	63.9	522.7	331.0	0.0849	28.1	③ = 251
D_5	3⁄2	0.125	3.2	9.5	42.3	588.0	294.2	0.0853	25.1	④ = 217
E_5	5⁄3	0.111	3.2	9.5	42.3	653.3	264.8	0.0887	23.5	⑤ = 189
$F\sharp_5$	15⁄8	0.125	3.2	9.5	42.3	735.0	235.4	0.0998	23.5	⑥ = 160
(1)	(2)	(3)	(4)	(5)	(6)	(7)	(8)	(9)	(10)	(11)

8.8

In conclusion to Part I, let us continue the discussion begun in Section 8.7 and examine the interaction between flute variables in greater detail. A careful examination of the various flute equations indicates the following proportionalities with respect to the ℓ_L:

$$\ell_L \propto \frac{1}{F}$$

$$\ell_L \propto \frac{1}{d_1}$$

$$\ell_L \propto \frac{1}{\ell_H}$$

$$\ell_L \propto d_H$$

In words, ℓ_L is inversely proportional to F, d_1, and ℓ_H. An increase in F, d_1, or ℓ_H produces a decrease in ℓ_L, and so moves a hole to a higher location on the bore. However, an increase in d_H also increases ℓ_L and, therefore, moves a hole to a lower location on the bore. A similar analysis indicates the following proportionalities with respect to F:

$$F \propto \frac{1}{\ell_L}$$

$$F \propto \frac{1}{d_1}$$

$$F \propto \frac{1}{\ell_H}$$

$$F \propto d_H$$

Again in words, F is inversely proportional to ℓ_L, d_1, and ℓ_H, so that increases in these variables produce decreases in F. However, an increase in d_H also increases F, which means that after a flute maker has drilled all the tone holes, subtle increases in hole diameter constitute the most important technique for fine tuning a flute.[42]

Part II

EQUATIONS FOR ANALYZING THE TUNINGS OF EXISTING FLUTES

8.9

A flute constitutes the physical embodiment of a tuning. For this reason, flutes and other wind instruments are unique because they provide tangible evidence about the musical intent of a society, or of an individual maker. In Plate 11, the flute in the middle — or Flute 2 — is a simple Amaranth Flute I made a few years ago. To a traditional Western flute maker this is a rather unusual instrument because all six tone holes have identical diameters, and the spaces between tone hole centers are identical. One frequently finds such flutes among "primitive" instruments throughout the world.[43] The word *primitive* comes from the Latin *primus* (lit. *first*). Given a set of flute tube, embouchure hole, and tone hole dimensions, it is possible to accurately predict the tuning of such an instrument.

Consider the following measurable dimensions of the Amaranth Flute:[44]

d_1 = 17.5 mm; or ≈ 11⁄16 in.
ℓ_H = 2.5 mm; or ≈ 7⁄64 in.
d_H = 10.2 mm; or ≈ 13⁄32 in.
ℓ_T = 394 mm; or ≈ 15½ in.
d_0 = 17.5 mm
ℓ_E = 2.5 mm
d_E = 9.5 mm; or ≈ 3⁄8 in.

ℓ_L
① = 329 mm
② = 296 mm
③ = 263 mm
④ = 230 mm
⑤ = 197 mm
⑥ = 164 mm

Solutions for F require an embouchure hole correction. Substitute the appropriate values into Equation 8.6 and calculate $L_{B(e)} = 32.8$ mm. As discussed in Section 8.7, $\Delta\ell_E$ is approximately 9–10 mm greater than $L_{B(e)}$. We will therefore use $\Delta\ell_E = 42$ mm for the Amaranth Flute.

Before we begin with detailed calculations, let us first establish a basic strategy for analyzing the frequencies of this flute. (1) Determine the *approximate* acoustic half-wavelength of the overall flute tube (L_{A_0}). Similarly, determine six more *approximate* acoustic lengths ($L_{A_{1-6}}$), one length for each open tone hole. (2) Substitute these lengths into Equation 8.2A,

$$F = \frac{c}{2L_A} \tag{8.19}$$

and calculate a total number of seven resonant frequencies.

The flute data enables us to determine the acoustic length of the flute tube. First substitute L_{A_0} into Equation 8.3 and then solve for L_{A_0}:

$$\ell_T = L_{A_0} - \Delta\ell_E - \Delta\ell_T \qquad \text{(Eq. 8.3)}$$

$$L_{A_0} = \ell_T + \Delta\ell_E + \Delta\ell_T \tag{8.20}$$

Next, substitute the appropriate flute values into Equation 8.20 and calculate the approximate acoustic half-wavelength of the flute tube:

$$L_{A_0} = 394 \text{ mm} + 42 \text{ mm} + 5.3 \text{ mm} = 441.3 \text{ mm}$$

Finally, substitute this approximate length into Equation 8.19 and calculate the fundamental frequency of the flute tube:

$$F_0 = \frac{346{,}000 \text{ mm/s}}{2(441.3 \text{ mm})} = 392.0 \text{ cps}$$

Note carefully that Equation 8.2A and Equation 8.19 are not identical. Equation 8.2A gives exact results. Due to the difficulties associated with $\Delta\ell_E$, Equation 8.19 gives approximate results. (See Section 8.7.)

∼ 8.10 ∼

The next step is not so obvious. If we first substitute L_A into Equation 8.4 and then solve for L_A,

$$L_A = \ell_L + \Delta\ell_E + \Delta\ell_H \tag{8.21}$$

observe that we cannot use Equation 8.21 simply because the flute's frequencies are not known. According to Equation 8.18, $\Delta\ell_H$ is a function of z, which, according to Equation 8.17, is a function of L_S, which, according to Equation 8.2B, is a function of F. However, the flute does provide the required data to calculate two variables. (1) From the given dimensions, we may calculate $L_{B(h)}$ for six tone holes. (2) We may also calculate the effective lengths of the short tube-pieces (L_R) below the open tone holes. (See Section 8.5.) With these two variables, it is possible to calculate $L_{A_{1-6}}$ *without* foreknowledge of the flute's frequencies.

Nederveen gives this alternate equation for L_A,[45]

$$L_{A_{1-6}} = L_L + L_{B(h)} \frac{L_T - L_L}{L_T - L_L + L_{B(h)}} \tag{8.22}$$

where

$$L_L = \ell_L + \Delta\ell_E \tag{8.23}$$

and

$$L_T = \ell_T + \Delta\ell_E + \Delta\ell_T \tag{8.24}$$

Refer to Figures 8.4(a) and 8.4(b) and note that

$$L_R = L_T - L_L$$

Because Equations 8.20 and 8.24 are identical, Figure 8.4(a) shows that L_{A_0} and L_{T_1} have identical lengths. Therefore, to calculate L_{A_1}, we now set

$$L_{T_1} = L_{A_0} \tag{8.25}$$

Next, substitute the appropriate flute dimensions into Equations 8.14 and 8.23, and calculate $L_{B(h)} =$ 29.5 mm and $L_{L_1} = 371$ mm, respectively. According to Equation 8.25, $L_{T_1} = 441.3$ mm. (See Section 8.9.) Now, substitute these values into Equation 8.22 to obtain the tube length:

$$L_{A_1} = 371 \text{ mm} + 29.5 \text{ mm} \frac{441.3 \text{ mm} - 371 \text{ mm}}{441.3 \text{ mm} - 371 \text{ mm} + 29.5 \text{ mm}} = 391.8 \text{ mm}$$

Finally, substitute this approximate length into Equation 8.19 and calculate the frequency of the first tone hole:

$$F_{①} = \frac{346{,}000 \text{ mm/s}}{2(391.8 \text{ mm})} = 441.6 \text{ cps}$$

To calculate L_{A_2}, first set

$$L_{T_2} = L_{A_1}$$

and calculate

$$L_{A_2} = 338 \text{ mm} + 29.5 \text{ mm} \frac{391.8 \text{ mm} - 338 \text{ mm}}{391.8 \text{ mm} - 338 \text{ mm} + 29.5 \text{ mm}} = 357.1 \text{ mm}$$

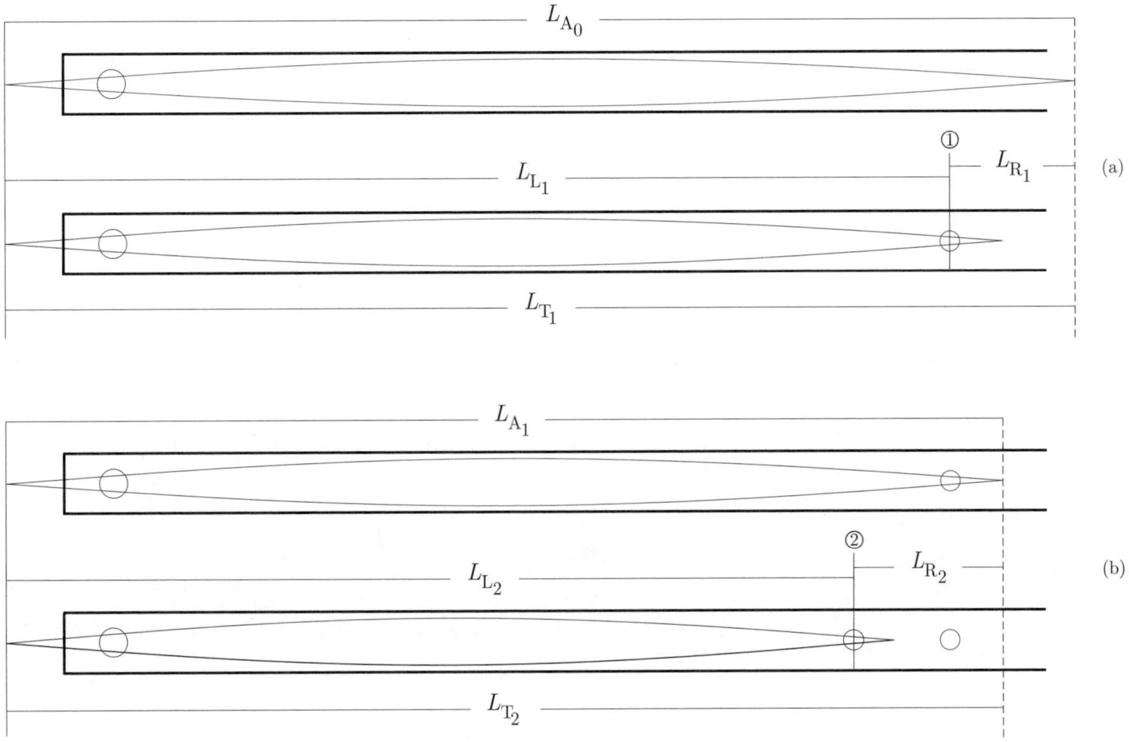

Figure 8.4 Variables and strategies for predicting the frequencies of existing flutes. (a) The length $L_{R_1} = L_{T_1} - L_{L_1}$ defines the effective length of a tube-piece that spans the distance from the first tone hole center to the end correction of the open flute tube, or to the dashed line. (b) The length $L_{R_2} = L_{T_2} - L_{L_2}$ defines the effective length of a tube-piece that spans the distance from the second tone hole center to the tone hole correction of the first hole, or to the dashed line. These effective lengths appear in the numerator and denominator of Equation 8.22. (Not to scale.)

This gives the following frequency for the second tone hole:

$$F_{②} = \frac{346{,}000 \text{ mm/s}}{2(357.1 \text{ mm})} = 484.5 \text{ cps}$$

~ 8.11 ~

Table 8.3, Columns 2–5 give solutions for the length variables of the Amaranth Flute discussed in Sections 8.9–8.10. Column 6 lists the resulting frequencies, and Column 7, the intervals of the tone holes above the tonic in cents. The cent value of the first tone hole was computed in the following manner. Since the fundamental frequency of the flute is G_4 at 392.0 cps, determine the cent interval[46] of tone hole ① by multiplying the logarithm of frequency ratio 441.6 cps/392.0 cps to the base 10 by the constant 3986.314:

$$\log_{10} \frac{441.6 \text{ cps}}{392.0 \text{ cps}} \times 3986.314 = 206.3 \text{ ¢}$$

Because a “whole tone” in 12-tone equal temperament equals 200.0 ¢, this interval is only 6.3 ¢ sharp of A_4 at 440.0 cps. Tone hole ② is moderately sharp of B$\flat_4$, or the “neutral third” of 24-tone equal temperament at 350.0 ¢; tone hole ③ is considerably sharp of C_5, or a “fourth” at 500.0 ¢;

tone hole ④ is considerably sharp of D_5, or a "fifth" at 700.0 ¢; tone hole ⑤ is considerably sharp of E_5, or a "major sixth" at 900.0 ¢; and tone hole ⑥ is moderately sharp of F𝄲$_5$, or the "leading tone" of 24-tone equal temperament at 1150.0 ¢. (See Table 11.52.)

Table 8.3

AMARANTH FLUTE LENGTH VARIABLES, FREQUENCIES, AND SCALE IN CENTS

Tone Hole	L_{L}	$L_{\mathrm{B(h)}}$	L_{T}	L_{A}	F	Scale
One	371	29.5	441.3	391.8	441.6	① = A_4 + 6.3 ¢ = 206.3 ¢
Two	338	29.5	391.8	357.1	484.5	② = B𝄳$_4$ + 16.8 ¢ = 366.8 ¢
Three	305	29.5	357.1	323.8	534.3	③ = C_5 + 36.2 ¢ = 536.2 ¢
Four	272	29.5	323.8	290.8	594.9	④ = D_5 + 22.2 ¢ = 722.2 ¢
Five	239	29.5	290.8	257.8	671.1	⑤ = E_5 + 30.8 ¢ = 930.8 ¢
Six	206	29.5	257.8	224.8	769.6	⑥ = F𝄲$_5$ + 17.9 ¢ = 1167.9 ¢
(1)	(2)	(3)	(4)	(5)	(6)	(7)

Part III

SUGGESTIONS FOR MAKING INEXPENSIVE YET HIGHLY ACCURATE SIMPLE FLUTES

8.12

All the equations in this chapter require that the flute walls are smooth, hard, and cylindrical. One of the finest materials for experimental flute making that meets all these requirements is extruded acrylic tubing. (See Plate 11.) Extruded tubing is manufactured to very close tolerances, and is available in many different diameters. This material is also easy to machine and very inexpensive, which means that mistakes and experiments don't turn into time-consuming and costly affairs. Since all plastics are impervious to moisture, this material is very stable and does not require special care.

Drilling holes into plastic is always difficult because conventional drill bits have a tendency to bind, twist, and crack the plastic as the drill emerges through the material. Plastic supply companies sell specialty drills with custom ground points designed to correct this problem. The point of such a drill is also very sharp, which counteracts the tendency of the drill bit to wander from the layout marks. At low speeds of approximately 600 rpm, these drills generate very little heat, and so eliminate the need for messy lubricants. After drilling with a plastic drill, one may use conventional drill bits in 1/64-inch increments to safely and accurately enlarge a given tone hole.

Anyone interested in making many precision flutes should consider investing in a set of matched V-blocks with clamps. These blocks are specifically designed to hold round stock during drilling and cutting operations. It is very important that the drill bit enters at top dead center of the tubing. Otherwise, the flute will be difficult to play, and will not sound in tune. A set of V-blocks firmly holds the tubing in place, and enables the flute maker to concentrate on the process of drilling holes.

8.13

In closing, consider an experiment designed to demonstrate how the thickness of a flute wall, or the length of a tone hole, affects the timbre of a flute. Purchase a standard length of extruded acrylic tubing with a 19.0 mm (¾ in.) inside diameter and a 3.18 mm (⅛ in.) thick wall, and a length with the same inside diameter and a 1.59 mm (1⁄16 in.) thick wall. For a given tuning, calculate the tone hole locations for the thick tube, and the thin tube. Mark the locations on both tubes and drill the holes. Insert a wine bottle cork at the embouchure end, play the flute, and note that the thin flute has a slightly brighter timbre than the thick flute. Benade explained this change in timbre by defining a tone hole cutoff frequency. This frequency represents the tone above which the terminating admittance of a flute hole no longer produces a reflection of pressure waves. As a result, the tone hole ceases to generate musical sounds. To calculate the cutoff frequency, Benade gives the following equation:[47]

$$F_{\text{cutoff}} = 0.110c\frac{d_{\text{H}}}{d_1}\sqrt{\frac{1}{s(\ell_{\text{H}} + 0.75d_{\text{H}})}} \tag{8.26}$$

where s is half the distance between tone hole centers, in millimeters.

Consider now a simple flute tuned in just intonation to 392.0 cps, as described in Section 8.7. For the thick flute with a 19.0 mm bore, a 3.2 mm wall, and a 9.5 mm diameter embouchure hole, $L_{\text{B(e)}} = 42.3$ mm; so we will use $\Delta\ell_{\text{E}} = 52$ mm. Here $\ell_{\text{T}} = 384$ mm. Tone holes ① and ③ have a 7.2 mm diameter, and all other holes, a 9.5 mm diameter. For the thin flute with a 19.0 mm bore, a 1.6 mm wall, and a 9.5 mm diameter embouchure hole, $L_{\text{B(e)}} = 35.8$ mm; so we will use $\Delta\ell_{\text{E}} = 46$ mm. Here $\ell_{\text{T}} = 390$ mm. The thin flute has the same tone hole diameters as the thick flute. These dimensions give the following values for ℓ_{L}:

	ℓ_{L} 3.2 mm wall	ℓ_{L} 1.6 mm wall
①	304	314
②	275	284
③	251	260
④	217	226
⑤	189	198
⑥	160	168

The average distance between tone holes on the thick flute equals 28.8 mm, so that $s = 14.4$ mm. And the average distance between tone holes on the thin flute equals 29.2 mm, so that $s = 14.6$ mm. Now substitute these values for s, and $d_{\text{H}} = 9.5$ mm into Equation 8.26 and calculate a cutoff frequency of 1560.7 cps for the large tone holes on the thick flute, and a cutoff frequency of 1686.1 cps for the large tone holes on the thin flute. This tells us that the thick flute does *not* produce any harmonics above approximately 1550 cps, and that the thin flute does not produce any harmonics above approximately 1675 cps. Consequently, the thin flute has a slightly brighter timbre than the thick flute.

Throughout this chapter, we have not encountered Young's modulus of elasticity because the flute material as such does not influence the sound quality of a given flute. It is the column of air inside the flute that vibrates, not the flute itself. This statement suggests that a flute made from gold, and an identical flute made from plastic, should have the same timbre. The reason why gold and plastic flutes do not sound alike is primarily due to the level of craftsmanship invested in a given instrument. Professional flutists prefer instruments made from precious metals because they are very durable and highly resistant to tarnishing. Moreover, silver, gold, and platinum are extremely ductile and malleable materials. In the hands of an expert flute maker, these materials can be formed and shaped with a high degree of precision. This is especially true of the tapered head joint and the embouchure hole. As a result, professional concert flutes produce a better tone because they are made from mechanically superior materials and with greater skill.

Notes

1. Schlesinger, K. (1939). *The Greek Aulos*, Plate 12 between pp. 74–75, and Plate 17 between pp. 420–421. Methuen & Co. Ltd., London, England.

2. Nederveen, C.J. (1969). *Acoustical Aspects of Woodwind Instruments.* Frits Knuf, Amsterdam, Netherlands.

3. See Appendix B for a complete list of conversion factors.

4. *Acoustical Aspects of Woodwind Instruments*, pp. 15–17.

5. Coltman, J.W. (1979). Acoustical analysis of the Boehm flute. *Journal of the Acoustical Society of America* **65**, No. 2, pp. 499–506.

6. See Section 7.2.

7. See Section 7.11.

8. (A) *Acoustical Aspects of Woodwind Instruments*, p. 13, pp. 47–48.

   (B) Nederveen, C.J. (1973). Blown, passive and calculated resonance frequencies of the flute. *Acustica* **28**, pp. 13–14.

9. Appendix A lists the frequencies of eight "octaves" in 12-tone equal temperament.

10. In Figures 8.3(a), 8.3(b), and 8.3(c), the *substitution tubes* show *displacement standing waves* with nodes at the ends and an antinode in the center, while the flute tubes show *pressure standing waves* with nodes at the ends and an antinode in the center. Although such inconsistencies may lead to confusion, here the emphasis is on wavelength and visual imagery and not on wave physics. For a given mode of vibration, a displacement standing wave and a pressure standing wave have exactly the same length.

11. Benade, A.H., and French, J.W. (1965). Analysis of the flute head joint. *Journal of the Acoustical Society of America* **37**, No. 4, pp. 679–691.

12. This value assumes no lip coverage at the embouchure hole.

13. *Acoustical Aspects of Woodwind Instruments*, p. 26, 47.

    With the exception of the key pad correction ($\Delta\ell_K$), Equation 38.8 on p. 64 of Nederveen's book (or Equation 7 on p. 14 of Nederveen's article in *Acustica* **28**, 1973) functions as a variable in determining (1) the effective length of the bore at the embouchure hole (as in Equation 8.6 with d_E, ℓ_E, and d_0 variables), and (2) the effective length of the bore at a tone hole (as in Equation 8.14 with d_H, ℓ_H, and d_1 variables). For example, Equation 8.14 is derived in the following manner. On p. 63 of his book,

Nederveen gives the outside correction of a tone hole as

$$\Delta\ell_{\text{out}} = \frac{1}{2} 0.7 d_{\text{H}}$$

Also on p. 63, Nederveen's Equation 38.3 is Benade's solution (see Note 30) for the inside correction of a tone hole. This equation states

$$\Delta\ell_{\text{in}} = \frac{1}{2}\left(1.3 - 0.9\frac{d_{\text{H}}}{d_1}\right) d_{\text{H}}$$

The effective length of a tone hole (L_{H}) is then given by

$$L_{\text{H}} = \ell_{\text{H}} + \Delta\ell_{\text{in}} + \Delta\ell_{\text{out}}$$

To use this equation, first simplify $\Delta\ell_{\text{in}}$ and $\Delta\ell_{\text{out}}$:

$$L_{\text{H}} = \ell_{\text{H}} + \left(0.65 d_{\text{H}} - 0.45\frac{{d_{\text{H}}}^2}{d_1}\right) + 0.35 d_{\text{H}}$$

Now add these two corrections and simplify again:

$$L_{\text{H}} = \ell_{\text{H}} + d_{\text{H}} - 0.45\frac{{d_{\text{H}}}^2}{d_1}$$

Therefore, the equivalent effective length of an embouchure hole (L_{E}) equals

$$L_{\text{E}} = \ell_{\text{E}} + d_{\text{E}} - 0.45\frac{{d_{\text{E}}}^2}{d_0}$$

This latter equation is more accurate than the denominator of Equation 8.9. Refer to Equation 8.11 and note that a substitution of L_{H} and two equivalent tone hole variables into this equation gives the effective length of the bore at a tone hole location:

$$L_{\text{B(h)}} = \left(\frac{d_1}{d_{\text{H}}}\right)^2 L_{\text{H}}$$

$$L_{\text{B(h)}} = \left(\frac{d_1}{d_{\text{H}}}\right)^2 \left(\ell_{\text{H}} + d_{\text{H}} - 0.45\frac{{d_{\text{H}}}^2}{d_1}\right)$$

A simplification of this equation gives Equation 8.14 in Section 8.5:

$$L_{\text{B(h)}} = (\ell_{\text{H}} + d_{\text{H}})\left(\frac{d_1}{d_{\text{H}}}\right)^2 - 0.45 d_1$$

And a similar substitution of L_{E} into Equation 8.11 gives Equation 8.6 in Section 8.3:

$$L_{\text{B(e)}} = (\ell_{\text{E}} + d_{\text{E}})\left(\frac{d_0}{d_{\text{E}}}\right)^2 - 0.45 d_0$$

14. See Chapter 7.

15. See Section 7.5.

16. The angular wave number is given by

$$k = \frac{\omega}{c} = \frac{2\pi F}{c}$$

17. Richardson, E.G. (1929). *The Acoustics of Orchestral Instruments and of the Organ*, p. 49, 148. Edward Arnold & Co., London, England.

18. See Section 7.12.

19. A flute tube three centimeters long has a terminating impedance that is too small for the production of pressure standing waves. In contrast, a tube three meters long has a terminating impedance that is too large for human beings to produce pressure standing waves. Most musicians are not able to deliver the air pressure required for sound production from very long tubes. Furthermore, with respect to tone holes, a very small diameter hole drilled into a flute tube has an extremely large terminating impedance. Pressure standing waves inside the tube vibrate in the region of this tiny hole as though it was not there. Consequently, the presence of such a hole does not change the frequency of the tube.

20. Benade, A.H. (1976). *Fundamentals of Musical Acoustics*, p. 449, 495. Dover Publications, Inc., New York, 1990.

Also, see Equation 8.26.

21. *Acustica* **28**, pp. 12–23.

Nederveen states, "Regarding the outside correction for a hole . . . we observe that the main tube acts as a partial flange to the hole-end, so that we have an end correction in between those for an unflanged end and a fully flanged end."

22. Steinkopf, O. (1983). *Zur Akustik der Blasinstrumente*, p. 19. Moeck Verlag, Celle, Germany.

23. *Acustica* **28**, 1973, p. 16.

24. (A) Boehm, T. (1847). *On the Construction of Flutes, Über den Flötenbau*, p. 55. Frits Knuf Buren, Amsterdam, Netherlands, 1982.

The English version of this essay does not have page numbers. A reference to the 50 mm correction in the English translation appears four pages from the end of the book.

(B) Boehm, T. (1871). *The Flute and Flute-Playing*, p. 42. Dover Publications, Inc., New York, 1964.

Here Boehm gives a slightly longer correction at 51.5 mm.

(C) *Fundamentals of Musical Acoustics*, p. 495.

25. This cavity effect is especially significant on concert metal flutes. Here most tone holes have a small chimney that sits above the curved outer surface of the tube. These chimneys provide a straight airtight closing surface for the key pads.

26. *Acoustical Aspects of Woodwind Instruments*, p. 76.

27. *Ibid.*, p. 48.

28. *Ibid.*, p. 64.

29. See Note 25.

30. (A) *Acoustical Aspects of Woodwind Instruments*, p. 64.

(B) Benade, A.H. (1967). Measured end corrections for woodwind toneholes. *Journal of the Acoustical Society of America* **41**, No. 6, p. 1609.

31. *Ibid.*, p. 48.

32. See Section 9.13.

33. See Section 9.14.

34. *Acoustical Aspects of Woodwind Instruments*, p. 48.

35. *Ibid.*, p. 48, in Figure 32.3.

36. Rossing, T.D. (1989). *The Science of Sound*, 2nd ed., pp. 246–247. Addison-Wesley Publishing Co., Inc., Reading, Massachusetts, 1990.

37. *JASA* **37**, 1965, p. 689.

38. According to Equation 7.12, a tube open at both ends generates a complete harmonic series of both even-number and odd-number harmonics; and according to Equation 7.17, a tube closed at one end generates an incomplete harmonic series of only odd-number harmonics. The act of overblowing a flute — or increasing the blowing pressure — causes these faint harmonics to sound as plainly audible tones. Therefore, the first overblown tone of a flute open at both ends produces the second harmonic, ratio $^2/_1$; and the first overblown tone of a flute closed at the far end produces the third harmonic, ratio $^3/_1$.

39. See Figure 10.15.

40. *JASA* **37**, 1965, p. 688.

41. See Sections 7.5–7.8.

42. *Fundamentals of Musical Acoustics*, pp. 473–480.

Another important fine-tuning technique consists of changing the bore diameter of woodwind instruments at the location of a pressure antinode, or at the location of a displacement antinode for a given mode of vibration. If we expand the bore by lightly sanding the inner surface of the flute tube at the location of a pressure antinode, such an increase in diameter causes a local increase in volume (V), which in turn produces a local decrease in pressure. Refer to Equation 7.36 and note that as V increases, the springiness of the air decreases. We may interpret such a local decrease in the air spring constant as causing a decrease in the potential energy of the vibrating system. When the potential energy of a pressure standing wave decreases, the frequency decreases as well. In contrast, if we constrict the bore by applying several coats of lacquer at the location of a pressure antinode, the frequency of a given mode of vibration increases.

On the other hand, a contraction at the location of a displacement antinode decreases the frequency of a given mode of vibration. A local constriction causes an increase in the inertia — or in the resistance to motion — of the air as it flows through the constriction. However, for a given amplitude of vibration, the same volume of air must flow through the constricted portion of the bore per second of time as through the regular bore. This requires an increase in the particle velocity of the air (u) as it passes through the constriction. We may interpret such an increase in particle velocity as causing an increase in the kinetic energy of the vibrating system. When the kinetic energy of a displacement standing wave increases, the frequency decreases. In contrast, if we expand the bore at the location of a displacement antinode, the frequency of a given mode of vibration increases.

Reminiscent of the discussion in Section 6.10, a pattern of overlapping pressure antinodes and displacement antinodes means that a constriction or expansion anywhere along the length of the bore affects numerous modes simultaneously. Moreover, the physical length of a given constriction or expansion also determines which mode frequencies are affected. For example, on the Armstrong flute the constriction of the head joint taper extends 114 mm to the right of the embouchure hole center. Since the embouchure hole marks the location of a displacement antinode of the first mode of vibration, the constriction flattens the frequencies of the first "octave." Furthermore, according to Figure 7.9, a pressure antinode of the second mode of vibration is located a quarter-wavelength ($0.25\lambda_2$) from either end of an open tube. On the Armstrong flute, the C_5 pressure antinode exists approximately 115.3 mm to the right of the embouchure hole center. That is, $\lambda_2 = c/F_2 = 346{,}000$ mm/s $\div$ 523.25 cps $=$ 661.3 mm, so that 0.25(661.3 mm) $=$ 165.3 mm, and 165.3 mm $-$ 50 mm $=$ 115.3 mm. (To locate the position of the second mode pressure antinode with respect to the embouchure hole center, we must account for the embouchure hole correction and, therefore, subtract 50 mm.) Since the 114 mm constriction extends into the vicinity of this pressure antinode, it also sharpens the frequencies of the second "octave." This sharpening effect on the second register produces tones that are *less flat* than in the first register. According to Nederveen's graph in *Acustica* **28**, 1973, p. 17, the head joint taper causes G_4 at 392.0 cps to sound 51 ¢ flat, which gives a frequency of 380.6 cps, and G_5 at 784.0 cps to sound only 10 ¢ flat, which gives a frequency of 779.5 cps. Note, however, that several factors such as increases in the speed of sound due to the warmth and chemical composition of the player's breath (see Coltman in *JASA* **40**, 1966, pp. 99–107), and increases in the player's blowing pressure at the embouchure hole, act to sharpen and correct the tendencies of these tones to sound flat. The acoustic need for a tapered head joint is discussed at length by Benade and French in *JASA* **37,** 1965, pp. 679–691, and by Benade in *Fundamentals of Musical Acoustics*, pp. 495–497.

43. (A) Baines, A. (1967). *Woodwind Instruments and Their History*, p. 182. Dover Publications, Inc., New York, 1991.

(B) *The Greek Aulos*, Plate 10 between pp. 68–69.

44. Since this simple flute has neither a tapered head joint nor significant tone hole cavities because the fingertips nearly fill the tone holes completely, the perturbation of airflow through the bore is at a minimum. Therefore, we will not assume that ℓ_T is slightly longer than the measured length. (See Section 8.4.)

Amaranth, also called *purpleheart*, is a very dense and stable tropical hardwood.

45. *Acoustical Aspects of Woodwind Instruments*, p. 47.

Nederveen uses L_S on the left side of his Equation 32.14. As discussed in Section 8.1, because this equation gives an *approximate* acoustic half-wavelength, I use the symbol L_A on the left side of Equation 8.22.

46. See Section 9.10.

47. *Fundamentals of Musical Acoustics*, p. 449.

9 / THE GEOMETRIC PROGRESSION, LOGARITHMS, AND CENTS

Cent calculations provide a highly accurate method to measure the relative sizes of musical intervals. Equation 9.21 shows a convenient method for computing cent values on calculators equipped with LOG keys. However, because texts on music theory and musical instrument construction seldom discuss logarithms and cents in full detail, many aspects of this analytical technique remain obscure. Furthermore, technical difficulties often occur because instrument builders, music theorists, and ethnomusicologists utilize different kinds of numerical notation to record their data. For example, suppose a researcher gives an Indonesian 7-tone *pélog* scale in cents, and a flute maker wants to build an instrument in that tuning. This problem raises the inevitable question, "How does one convert cents into decimal ratios?" Or, a piano tuner who wants to increase the pitch of an instrument might ask, "What changes in frequency and, therefore, in string tension will occur if I raise A_4-440.0 cps by 25 ¢?" Answers to these and other related questions require thorough investigations into logarithms and cents. Once achieved, such a study provides a powerful tool for understanding many different tuning systems throughout the world.

In preparation for this chapter, the reader should read, study, and absorb the following topics discussed in Chapter 3: (1) the mathematical structure of the harmonic series, (2) the distinctions between ancient length ratios, modern length ratios, frequency ratios, and interval ratios, and (3) the mathematical methods used in the division of canon strings. In Part I of this chapter we will discuss human perception of the harmonic series as a geometric progression; in Part II, logarithmic processes in mathematics and human hearing; in Part III, the derivation and application of cent calculations; and in Part IV, logarithmic equations for the placement of guitar frets, and for the construction of musical slide rules.

Part I

HUMAN PERCEPTION OF THE HARMONIC SERIES AS A GEOMETRIC PROGRESSION

~ 9.1 ~

We begin this discussion by considering two fundamental mathematical sequences: the arithmetic progression, and the geometric progression. Because these two progressions have profound and far-reaching consequences, we will encounter them in many different contexts.

One may write an arithmetic progression by beginning with a given number a, and then repeatedly *adding* a constant number d. For example, the following sequence:

$$2,\ 5,\ 8,\ 11,\ 14$$

is an arithmetic progression in which $d = 3$. Since d represents a difference between consecutive terms, it is called the *common difference* (c.d.) of an arithmetic progression. A general expression for an arithmetic progressions states

$$a,\ a + d,\ a + 2d,\ a + 3d,\ \ldots$$

One may write a geometric progression by beginning with a given number a, and then repeatedly *multiplying* by a constant number r. For example, the following sequence:

$$2,\ 6,\ 18,\ 54,\ 162$$

is a geometric progression in which $r = 3$. Since r represents a ratio between consecutive terms, it is called the *common ratio* (c.r.) of a geometric progression. A general expression for a geometric progression states

$$a,\ ar,\ ar^2,\ ar^3,\ \ldots$$

Notice that the exponents of a geometric progression form an arithmetic progression, where c.d. = 1. Also, observe that the former arithmetic progression has a uniform increase (3, 3, 3, 3) between terms, while the latter geometric progression has a varied increase (4, 12, 36, 108) between terms.

9.2

A mathematical and a musical examination of Figure 9.1 shows that we may interpret the harmonic series as an arithmetic progression *or* as a geometric progression. The arithmetic progression consists of a simple sequence of harmonics numbered 1, 2, 3, . . . which continues theoretically to infinity. Each harmonic generates a frequency that is an integer multiple of the fundamental frequency. So, if the first harmonic of a flexible string,[1] or an open column of air,[2] produces C_2 at 65.0 cps, then the first five harmonics of this arithmetic progression generate frequencies

65.0 cps, 130.0 cps, 195.0 cps, 260.0 cps, 325.0 cps

65.0 cps 65.0 cps 65.0 cps 65.0 cps

$\frac{2}{1}$ $\frac{3}{2}$ $\frac{4}{3}$ $\frac{5}{4}$

Although the harmonics of this particular arithmetic progression have a common difference, where c.d. = 65.0 cps, the human ear *cannot* identify a recurring interval pattern between the consecutive tones of the harmonic series. Figure 9.1 shows that with increases in frequencies, the intervals between harmonics never repeat, and simply become progressively smaller. Consequently, the harmonic series as an arithmetic progression is musically meaningless!

In contrast, when a sequence of frequencies forms a geometric progression, the human ear *can* identify a recurring interval pattern between tones. The underlined harmonics below constitute such a progression:

$$\underline{\mathbf{1}},\ \underline{\mathbf{2}},\ 3,\ \underline{\mathbf{4}},\ 5,\ 6,\ 7,\ \underline{\mathbf{8}},\ 9,\ 10,\ 11,\ 12,\ 13,\ 14,\ 15,\ \underline{\mathbf{16}},\ 17,\ \ldots \qquad \text{(i)}$$

Upon hearing these five harmonics, musicians recognize four identical musical intervals. Again, if the first harmonic C_2 vibrates at 65.0 cps, then the underlined harmonics of the latter geometric progression generate frequencies

65.0 cps, 130.0 cps, 260.0 cps, 520.0 cps, 1040.0 cps (ii)

65.0 cps 130.0 cps 260.0 cps 520.0 cps

$\frac{2}{1}$ $\frac{2}{1}$ $\frac{2}{1}$ $\frac{2}{1}$

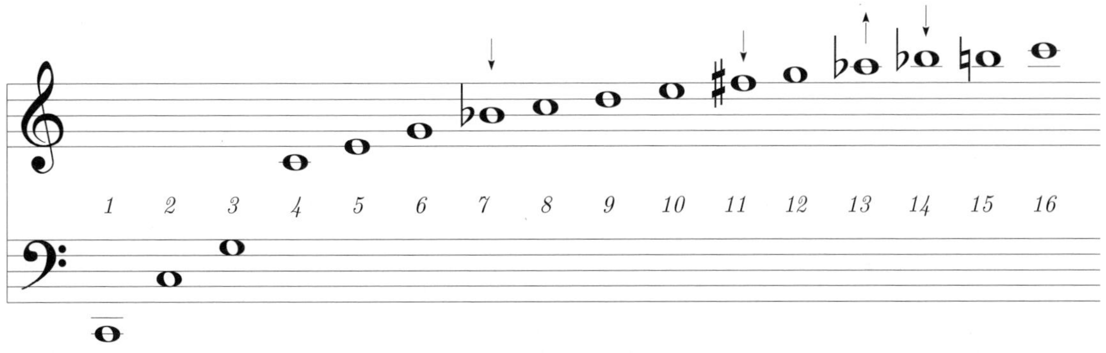

Figure 9.1 The first sixteen harmonics of a harmonic series that begins on C_2 at 65.0 cps. Arrows pointing upward or downward indicate harmonics that sound considerably higher or lower than the tones of the conventional piano scale tuned in 12-tone equal temperament. (See Figure 3.12.)

The harmonics of this geometric progression have a common ratio, where c.r. = $^2/_1$. When musicians perceive that a group of intervals are identical, they assign a common name to all such intervals. In this case, *all* intervals that sound common ratio $^2/_1$ are called "octaves."

Musicians depend on their ability to memorize intervals. For example, if members of a chorus heard an "octave" between 65.0 cps and 130.0 cps played on a piano, they could easily sing the next "octave" between 130.0 cps and 260.0 cps without the piano.

The ability to perceive identical intervals gives human beings the ability to create myriad varieties of music. Consider the following harmonics:

2, 3, 4, 6

Although these tones do *not* form a geometric progression, the ear recognizes a common ratio between the second and third harmonics, and the fourth and sixth harmonics. Based on a fundamental frequency of 65.0 cps, these four harmonics produce frequencies

130.0 cps, 195.0 cps, 260.0 cps, 390.0 cps

65.0 cps 130.0 cps

$^3/_2$ $^3/_2$

Notice common ratio $^3/_2$ between the first two harmonics, and the last two harmonics. Again, musicians perceive that these two intervals are identical and, therefore, assign a common name to all such intervals. In this case, *all* intervals that sound common ratio $^3/_2$ are called "fifths." An examination of Figure 9.1 shows $^3/_2$'s, or "fifths," between harmonics 3–2, 6–4, 9–6, 12–8, and 15–10.

Now that we have established an important mathematical/musical connection between common ratios and identical intervals, let us dispense with the mathematical term *common ratio*, and substitute instead the musical term *interval ratio*. As discussed in Section 3.12, an interval ratio defines the musical interval between any two given frequency ratios, or between any two given length ratios. For instance, in the latter example, calculate the interval of a "fifth," ratio $^3/_2$, by dividing the frequency ratio of the third harmonic by the frequency ratio of the second harmonic:

$$\text{Interval Ratio of the “Fifth”} = \frac{G_3}{C_3} = \frac{\frac{195.0\text{ cps}}{65.0\text{ cps}}}{\frac{130.0\text{ cps}}{65.0\text{ cps}}} = \frac{\frac{3}{1}}{\frac{2}{1}} = \frac{3}{\cancel{1}} \times \frac{\cancel{1}}{2} = \frac{3}{2}$$

9.3

Some readers may ask, "Why is interval ratio $2/1$ called an 'octave', and interval ratio $3/2$ called a 'fifth'?" To answer these questions, consider the organization of the traditional diatonic scale in Western music. Here are two examples of this scale:

$$\text{C, D, E, F, G, A, B, C}^{\text{I}} \qquad \text{(iii)}$$

$$\text{G, A, B, C, D, E, F}\sharp\text{, G}^{\text{I}}$$

Since the interval from C to C^{I}, or from G to G^{I}, includes eight tones, it is called an "octave"; and since the interval from C to G, or from G to D, includes five tones, it is called a "fifth." Although this method of identifying intervals is of some value, the ear does not perceive intervals through an elaborate process of counting tones. Instead, the ear instantaneously recognizes a single musical interval by its signature interval ratio. For this reason, we will often dispense with terms like "octave" and "fifth," and adopt the language of ratios. Readers not familiar with intervals such as a $5/4$ (pronounced "five-four"), or a $16/9$ ("sixteen-nine"), should refer to Figure 9.1. Identify a given interval ratio by analyzing the acoustic distance between the harmonic number in the numerator and the harmonic number in the denominator of the ratio. Such an examination shows that a $5/4$ — the interval from 5 (E_4) to 4 (C_4) — refers to a "major third," and a $16/9$ — the interval from 16 (C_6) to 9 (D_5) — refers to a "minor seventh."

The interval ratios of the harmonic series belong to a tuning system called just intonation. Most instruments in the West are *not* tuned in just intonation, but to a system called 12-tone equal temperament. Just intonation is a system composed of rational numbers.[3] In contrast, 12-tone equal temperament is a system primarily composed of irrational numbers.[4] The only interval these two systems have in common is ratio $2/1$. Therefore, to equate a just intoned $16/9$ with an equal tempered "minor seventh" is technically and musically incorrect. In Section 10.37, we will discuss the differences between the intervals of just intonation and those of 12-TET. For now, we must accept Figure 9.1 as an imperfect yet workable representation of the harmonic series. Note carefully the directions of the arrows above harmonics 7, 11, 13, and 14. Arrows pointing upward or downward indicate harmonics that sound considerably higher or lower than the tones of the conventional piano scale tuned in 12-TET.

9.4

No one knows how the ear recognizes that two intervals are identical. It is a great mystery of human hearing. One of the direct consequences of this phenomenon is the $2/1$ interval limit. To demonstrate this limit, imagine you are listening to two frequency generators tuned to C_3 at 130.0 cps. Now turn the dial of one generator so that the frequency slowly and steadily increases to C_4 at 260.0 cps. As the frequencies increase, a seemingly infinite number of musical intervals fills our ears with sound. In actuality, the most sensitive and highly trained ear hears a maximum of 600 intervals. Since there are 1200 cents to an "octave," and since the finest ear in this frequency range cannot distinguish between two frequencies unless they are at least 2 cents apart, there exists a limit of approximately 600 intervals per "octave." (See Section 9.11.) Now, continue to turn the dial until the generator produces frequency ratio $9/4$. This tone occurs when the frequency increases to D_4 at 292.5 cps; that is, 130.0 cps $\times$ $9/4$ = 292.5 cps. It is impossible to interpret this interval as a completely novel experience, because the earlier increase from C_3 to D_3 one "octave" below sounds very similar to the current increase from C_4 to D_4. Interval ratio $9/8$ between C_3 and D_3 is called a "whole tone," or a "major second." Interval ratio $9/4$ between C_3 and D_4 is called a "major ninth" because it consists of an "octave" plus a "whole tone," as in 8 + 1 = 9. However, due to the $\frac{2}{1}$ interval limit, intervals larger than an "octave" do not have the same distinct identity as intervals smaller than an "octave."

The $\frac{2}{1}$ interval limit is also called an "octave" equivalence phenomenon. An "octave" equivalent is a ratio where, upon dividing the numerator by the denominator, the quotient is greater than 2. To simplify an "octave" equivalent, or to bring an equivalent within the range of ratio $\frac{2}{1}$, multiply the denominator by factors of 2 until the quotient is less than 2, but is greater than 1.[5] Note, therefore, that "octave" equivalents $\frac{8}{3}$, $\frac{9}{4}$, and $\frac{27}{5}$ represent frequency ratios $\frac{4}{3}$, $\frac{9}{8}$, and $\frac{27}{20}$, respectively. The latter intervals are easier to comprehend in the context of modes, scales, and tunings.

References to the $\frac{2}{1}$ interval limit can be found in music throughout the world. Its perception is a universally recognized human trait. For this reason, the "octave" appears as an interval among some of the most dissimilar tuning systems imaginable. At the end of Section 9.3, we noted that scales in just intonation and 12-TET have no intervals in common except interval ratio $\frac{2}{1}$. Musicians of acoustic music who disagree on all aspects of intonation tend to agree that "octave" equivalents do not represent uniquely different tones in a scale or tuning.

Part II

LOGARITHMIC PROCESSES IN MATHEMATICS AND HUMAN HEARING

9.5

Before we return to the interval ratios of the harmonic series, let us first examine some basic mathematical definitions of exponents and logarithms. Logarithmic calculations may be applied to all musical scales and tunings, and in that capacity, provide a great wealth of information.

John Napier (1550–1617), the inventor of logarithms, named his creation after two Greek words: *logos*, ratio, and *arithmos*, number. Napier's "ratio-number" refers to a number mathematicians now call an exponent.[6] Consider the equation

$$x = a^y \tag{9.1}$$

where y is the exponent or power of a number or ratio, and a is a constant. Equation 9.1 is called an *exponential function.* In this equation, the exponent is a number that indicates the operation of repeated multiplication. Therefore, if we know a and y, solutions for x are straightforward and easy. As an example, if $a = 10$ and $y = 1$, then $x = 10$; if $y = 2$, $x = 100$; if $y = 3$, $x = 1{,}000$; and if $y = 4$, $x = 10{,}000$ because

$$\begin{aligned} 10^1 &= 10 \\ 10^2 &= 10 \times 10 = 100 \\ 10^3 &= 10 \times 10 \times 10 = 1{,}000 \\ 10^4 &= 10 \times 10 \times 10 \times 10 = 10{,}000 \end{aligned}$$

Suppose that we switch known and unknown variables and try to solve Equation 9.1 for y:

$$10^y = 10{,}000 \tag{9.2}$$

Equation 9.2 does not have an immediate solution because there are no algebraic techniques that allow us to solve for y in an exponential function. Consequently, we must restate Equation 9.1 as a *logarithmic function:*

$$y = \log_a x \tag{9.3}$$

Equation 9.3 reads, "y is the logarithm of x to the base a." Figure 9.2 shows how Equations 9.1 and 9.3 are related.

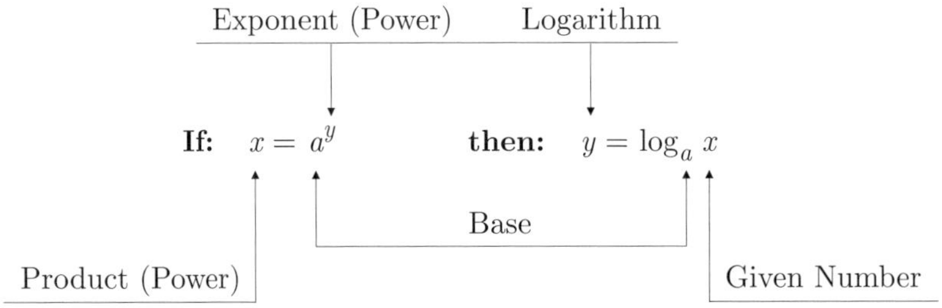

Figure 9.2 The "if — then — " relation between an exponential function and a logarithmic function. The exponent of Equation 9.1 is equivalent to the logarithm of Equation 9.3 and *vice versa.* We may express any exponential equation as a logarithmic equation, and any logarithmic equation as an exponential equation.

Figure 9.2 conveys three important aspects of the exponential-logarithmic relation. (1) Variable x in Equation 9.1 is a product or result, whereas variable x in Equation 9.3 is any given real positive number.[7] (2) The logarithm of Equation 9.3 is the exponent of Equation 9.1 and *vice versa.* That is, the logarithm (y) of a given number (x) to the base a is the exponent to which a must be raised to produce x. For example, since 3 is the logarithm of 1,000 to the base 10, 3 is the exponent to which 10 must be raised to produce 1,000. (3) The word "power" appears twice in Figure 9.2 because it has two different meanings: (i) power is a term that refers to the exponent, and so we read 10^4 as "10 to the fourth power"; (ii) power is also a term that refers to the product, or the result of multiplication, and so we read $10^4 = 10{,}000$ as "the fourth power of 10 is 10,000." Equation 9.1 is equivalent to Equation 9.3 and *vice versa.* The only difference between these two equations is that we solve the former explicitly for x, and the latter, explicitly for y. Return now to the previous problem, and express Equation 9.2 in logarithmic form:

$$y = \log_{10} 10{,}000 \tag{9.4}$$

Equation 9.4 reads, "y is the logarithm of 10,000 to the base 10."

The mathematical techniques for computing logarithms are beyond the scope of this discussion.[8] For any given logarithm, we simply look up the number in a log table, or press the appropriate log keys on a calculator, or type the appropriate log command in a computer math application. There are two different kinds of logarithms. Logarithms to the base 10 ($\log_{10}$) are called *common logarithms* and appear most often in simple calculations, and logarithms to the base e ($\log_e$) are called *natural logarithms* and appear most often in complex calculations. In this chapter, and throughout the entire book, we will work exclusively with common logarithms. However, in Section 4.14, note how natural logarithms simplify cent calculations of $1 + J$, or of all numbers that are much less than two, as in $1 + J \ll 2$.

For common logarithms, press the [LOG] key on a scientific calculator, and for natural logarithms, press the [LN] key, which stands for *logarithmus naturalis*. Equation 9.4 has the following solution:

$$y = \log_{10} 10{,}000 = 4$$

To obtain this result on a standard algebraic calculator, or on a Hewlett-Packard RPN (Reverse Polish Notation) calculator, press six keys:

$$y = 10000 \; \boxed{\text{LOG}} \; \rightarrow \; 4$$

Verify this result. Substitute 4 into Equation 9.2 and calculate $10^4 = 10 \times 10 \times 10 \times 10 = 10{,}000$. Although the latter proof is technically correct, we will find in future calculations that it is more desirable to express exponential equations as logarithmic equations. To accomplish such a transformation, switch the known and unknown variables in Equation 9.4. That is, substitute 4 for y, and x for 10,000:

$$4 = \log_{10} x \tag{9.5}$$

Equation 9.5 reads, "4 is the logarithm of x to the base 10." This equation requires us to find the number x whose logarithm is 4. In Equation 9.5, x is called the antilogarithm[9] of 4. In this case, calculate

$$x = \text{antilog}_{10}\, 4 = 10{,}000$$

by pressing the 4 key, followed by the antilog key:

$$x = 4 \; \boxed{10^x} \; \rightarrow \; 10{,}000$$

These keystrokes give the same result.

$$\text{ALG:} \quad 10 \; \boxed{y^x} \; 4 \; \boxed{=} \; 10{,}000$$

$$\text{RPN:} \quad 10 \; \boxed{\text{Enter}} \; 4 \; \boxed{y^x} \; \rightarrow \; 10{,}000$$

Below is a complete list of the above-mentioned expressions (a^y), the numbers (x), and their logarithms (y) to the base 10.[10] The numbers indicate a geometric progression, where c.r. = 10, and their logarithms, an arithmetic progression, where c.d. = 1.

The Expressions:	10^0,	10^1,	10^2,	10^3,	10^4, . . .
The Numbers:	1,	10,	100,	1000,	10000, . . .
Their Logarithms:	0,	1,	2,	3,	4, . . .

9.6

The first law of exponents states[11]

$$a^m \times a^n = a^{m+n} \tag{9.6}$$

For example, we may multiply $100 \times 1{,}000 = 100{,}000$ in the usual manner, or we may write these two factors in exponential form, and then add the exponents:

$$100 \times 1{,}000 = 10^2 \times 10^3 = 10^{2+3} = 10^5 = 10 \times 10 \times 10 \times 10 \times 10 = 100{,}000$$

In an analogous manner, we may use this method to describe (1) changes in frequency, and (2) the ensuing response of human hearing. Consider the frequency generators first mentioned in Section 9.4, only this time tune both generators to C_2 at 65.0 cps. Slowly turn the dial of one generator until it produces C_3 at 130.0 cps, and then continue to turn the dial until it produces C_4 at 260.0 cps. A mathematical analysis of these increases indicates the process of *multiplying* frequencies. However, an examination of the aural response indicates the process of *adding* "octaves."

Refer to Figure 9.3(a) and note that as the tone changed from 65.0 cps to 130.0 cps along the x-axis, the frequency went up by a factor of 2, and so increased 65.0 cps. Similarly, as the tone changed from 130.0 cps to 260.0 cps, the frequency went up by another factor of 2, but this time increased 130.0 cps. [In Figure 9.3(a), the spaces between vertical lines are to scale and accurately reflect that the latter increase is twice the size of the former increase.] On the other hand, the human ear hears the same changes not by repeatedly multiplying these frequencies by a factor of 2, but by adding the perceived intervals together. The ear recognizes the first interval between 65.0–130.0 cps as an "octave," and the second interval between 130.0–260.0 cps as another "octave." It then adds the first "octave" to the second "octave," and identifies the resulting interval as a "double-octave." In this case, the "double-octave" spans the interval from C_2 to C_4. [In Figure 9.3(a), the spaces between horizontal lines are also to scale and accurately show that all "octaves" are equally spaced apart.]

To demonstrate this additive process of human hearing on a mathematical basis, consider calculating the first "octave" increase in frequency by adding logarithms. First, calculate the logarithm of 65 to the base 10,

$$y = \log_{10} 65$$

$$y = 65 \ \boxed{\text{LOG}} \ \rightarrow \ 1.8129$$

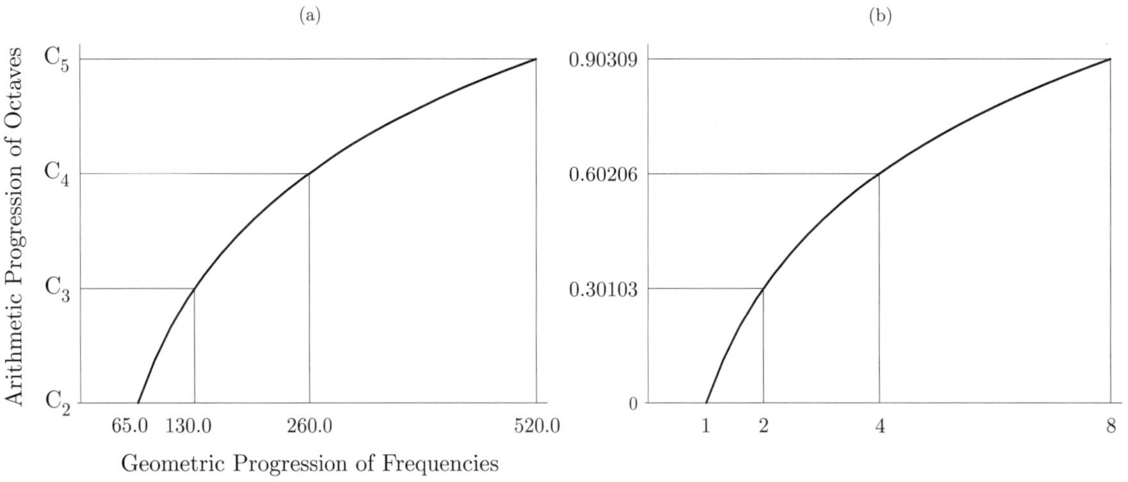

Figure 9.3 Two identical plots. (a) Along the x-axis, this plot shows a geometric progression of frequencies with interval ratio $^2\!/_1$. [See Section 9.2, Progression (ii).] Along the y-axis, the same plot shows that the human ear perceives this sequence of frequencies as an arithmetic progression of "octaves" with a common difference of 1 "octave." (b) The plot of the equation $y = \log_{10} x$. Along the x-axis, this plot shows a geometric progression of numbers, where c.r. = 2, and along the y-axis, an arithmetic progression of logarithms to the base 10, where c.d. = 0.30103.

and the logarithm of 2 to the base 10:

$$y = \log_{10} 2$$

$$y = 2 \;\boxed{\text{LOG}}\; \rightarrow \; 0.30103$$

Next, write 65.0 cps and 2 in exponential form, add the exponents (logarithms), and calculate the resulting increase in frequency by raising 10 to the 2.11394 power:

$$65.0 \text{ cps} \times 2 = 10^{1.81291} \times 10^{0.30103} = 10^{1.81291+0.30103} = 10^{2.11394} = 130.0 \text{ cps}$$

Repeat a similar set of calculations for the frequency of the second "octave":

$$130.0 \text{ cps} \times 2 = 10^{2.11394} \times 10^{0.30103} = 10^{2.11394+0.30103} = 10^{2.41497} = 260.0 \text{ cps}$$

We conclude, therefore, that when the frequency of a tone doubles, the ear hears interval ratio $2/1$, or a "single-octave"; when the frequency quadruples, it hears interval ratio $4/1$, or a "double-octave"; and when the frequency octuples, it hears interval ratio $8/1$, or a "triple-octave." Figure 9.3(a) shows this additive process of human hearing along the y-axis: the interval from C_2 to C_3 equals

1 "octave," or a "single-octave,"

the interval from C_2 to C_4 equals

2 "octaves," or a "double-octave,"

and the interval from C_2 to C_5 equals

3 "octaves," or a "triple-octave."

This arithmetic progression has a common difference of 1 "octave."

Figure 9.3(b) is a plot of the logarithmic function

$$y = \log_{10} x \tag{9.7}$$

In Figure 9.3(b), the numbers on the y-axis are the logarithms to the base 10 of the given numbers on the x-axis. Because exponents are equivalent to logarithms, note the relation between these two sets of numbers:[12]

$$\textbf{If:}\quad \begin{aligned} 10^{0} &= 1 \\ 10^{0.30103} &= 2 \\ 10^{0.60206} &= 4 \\ 10^{0.90309} &= 8 \end{aligned} \qquad \textbf{then:}\quad \begin{aligned} 0 &= \log_{10} 1 \\ 0.30103 &= \log_{10} 2 \\ 0.60206 &= \log_{10} 4 \\ 0.90309 &= \log_{10} 8 \end{aligned}$$

With respect to human hearing, logarithms to the base 10 are not very practical. Nevertheless, let us finish this section with one final example. Suppose that the x-axis of Figure 9.3(b) represents these frequencies: 1.0 cps, 2.0 cps, 4.0 cps, and 8.0 cps. Now consider the question, "If the fundamental frequency of a system vibrates at 1.0 cps, what is the system's frequency three 'octaves' higher?" We may solve this problem in two different ways. (1) Because the frequency ratios of the harmonic series constitute a geometric progression, multiply the fundamental frequency by interval ratio $2/1$ three times:

$$1.0 \text{ cps} \times \frac{2}{1} \times \frac{2}{1} \times \frac{2}{1} = 8.0 \text{ cps}$$

(2) Because human ears perceive sequences of musical intervals as though they constitute an arithmetic progression,[13] add the logarithm of 2 to the base 10 three times,

$$\log_{10} 2 + \log_{10} 2 + \log_{10} 2 = 0.90309$$

and calculate the antilogarithm of the sum 0.90309:

$$\begin{aligned} \log_{10} x &= 0.90309 \\ x &= \text{antilog}_{10}\, 0.90309 \\ x &= 0.90309 \ \boxed{10^x} \ \rightarrow \ 8.0 \end{aligned}$$

The first method represents a mathematical truth, while the second method represents an aural truth. Both methods follow the rules of mathematics. However, the second method is more relevant to musicians because the act of adding logarithms simulates the natural process of adding musical intervals.

9.7

We return now to the harmonic series. Refer to Section 9.2, Progression (i), and consider these "octave" expressions (a^y), the "octave" harmonics (x), and their logarithms (y) to the base 2.

The Expressions:	2^0,	2^1,	2^2,	2^3,	2^4, . . .
The Harmonics:	1,	2,	4,	8,	16, . . .
Their Logarithms:	0,	1,	2,	3,	4, . . .

The "octave" harmonics produce a geometric progression, where c.r. = 2⁄1, and their logarithms, an arithmetic progression, where c.d. = 1. From this, it is apparent that the sixth term in the geometric progression is 32. However, suppose we ask, "What is y in this equation?"

$$2^y = 32 \tag{9.8}$$

First, express Equation 9.8 in logarithmic form:

$$y = \log_2 32 \tag{9.9}$$

Note carefully that Equation 9.9 requires a logarithm to the base 2. Therefore, the next step is not so obvious. Because scientific calculators are not designed with keys that give logarithms to the base 2, we must make a conversion. The equation below shows how to convert from original $\log_a x$ logarithms to new $\log_b x$ logarithms:

$$\log_b x = \frac{\log_a x}{\log_a b}$$

Here we must convert from base 10 logarithms to base 2 logarithms:

$$\log_2 x = \frac{\log_{10} x}{\log_{10} 2} \tag{9.10}$$

To utilize Equation 9.9, substitute 32 into Equation 9.10 and calculate the logarithm of 32 to the base 2:

$$y = \log_2 32 = \frac{\log_{10} 32}{\log_{10} 2} = \frac{1.50515}{0.30103} = 5$$

These keystrokes give the same result on either kind of scientific calculator.

ALG: 32 [LOG] [÷] 2 [LOG] [=] 5

RPN: 32 [LOG] 2 [LOG] [÷] → 5

Verify this solution. Calculate the antilogarithm of 5,

$$\log_2 x = 5$$

$$x = \text{antilog}_2\, 5$$

by raising 2 to the fifth power.

ALG: 2 [y^x] 5 [=] 32

RPN: 2 [Enter] 5 [y^x] → 32

Here we must use the exponent key because scientific calculators are not designed with keys that give antilogarithms to the base 2.

Figure 9.4 is a plot of the equation $y = \log_2 x$. The numbers on the y-axis are the logarithms to the base 2 of the given numbers on the x-axis. Again, observe the crucial relation between exponents and logarithms.

If:	$2^0 = 1$	**then:**	$0 = \log_2 1$
	$2^1 = 2$		$1 = \log_2 2$
	$2^2 = 4$		$2 = \log_2 4$
	$2^3 = 8$		$3 = \log_2 8$

Figures 9.3(b) and 9.4 demonstrate an important mathematical principle: whenever a sequence of logarithms constitutes an arithmetic progression, the numbers form a geometric progression and *vice versa.* However, there is also a significant difference between these two figures. Only Figure 9.4 accurately represents the first three consecutive "octaves" in the harmonic series. For each doubling

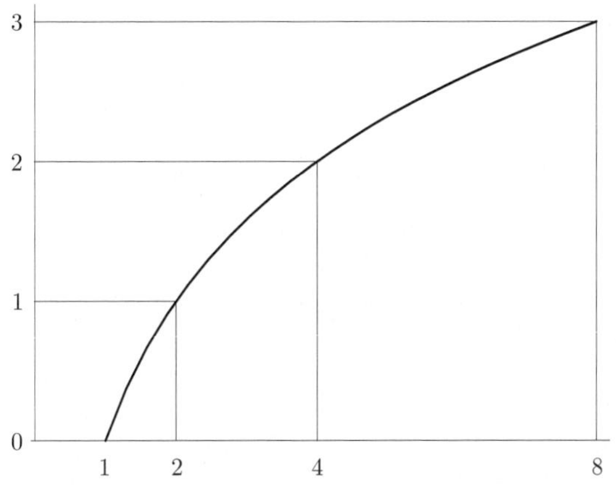

Figure 9.4 The plot of the equation $y = \log_2 x$. Along the x-axis, this plot shows a geometric progression of numbers, where c.r. = 2, and along the y-axis, an arithmetic progression of logarithms to the base 2, where c.d. = 1.

of "frequencies" along the x-axis, there is a corresponding adding of "octaves" along the y-axis. Refer to Figure 9.1 and note that Figure 9.4 correctly shows the 2nd harmonic as one "octave," the 4th harmonic as two "octaves," and the 8th harmonic as three "octaves" above the fundamental.

Recall that in Section 9.4 we discussed the importance of the ²⁄₁ interval limit. Frequency ratio ²⁄₁, or simply 2, plays a crucial role in the tuning of all acoustic instruments. Consider the significance of this ratio by formally calculating the logarithm of frequency ratio ²⁄₁ to the base 2:

$$y = \log_2 \frac{2}{1} = \frac{\log_{10} \frac{2}{1}}{\log_{10} 2} = \frac{0.30103}{0.30103} = 1$$

Since logarithms are exponents, this tells us that whenever the exponent in Equation 9.11 increases arithmetically by 1,

$$2^y = x \tag{9.11}$$

the product x increases geometrically by a factor of 2. In the context of musical intervals, such an increase in y signifies an increase by one "octave" and, therefore, the resulting increase in x signifies an increase by frequency ratio ²⁄₁.

Let us now calculate the frequency ratio of a "triple-octave," or a 2^3, in two different ways. (1) Multiply interval ratio ²⁄₁ three times:

$$\frac{2}{1} \times \frac{2}{1} \times \frac{2}{1} = \frac{8}{1}$$

(2) Simulate the additive process of human hearing. Add the logarithms of 2 to the base 2 three times,

$$\log_2 2 + \log_2 2 + \log_2 2 = 3$$

and calculate the antilogarithm of the sum 3,

$$\log_2 x = 3$$

$$x = \text{antilog}_2\, 3$$

by raising 2 to the third power.

ALG: 2 [y^x] 3 [=] 8

RPN: 2 [Enter] 3 [y^x] → 8

In closing this section, consider Figure 9.5(a), which shows a polar plot of the equation

$$r = 2^{\frac{\theta}{360°}}$$

where r is the length of the radius from the center to a point on the spiral, in any units; and θ is the angle of that radius, in degrees.[14] Here θ includes the angles from 0° to 1440.0°. So, when $\theta = 0°$, $r = 1$ unit;[15] when $\theta = 360.0°$ (revolution #1), $r = 2.0$ units; when $\theta = 720.0°$ (revolution #2), $r = 4.0$ units; when $\theta = 1080.0°$ (revolution #3), $r = 8.0$ units; etc. Mathematicians call this a logarithmic spiral because r increases geometrically per revolution.[16] Here the length of the radius increases by a factor of 2 per revolution. We may interpret Figure 9.5(a) as a representation of the first four "octave" frequencies, or the first four "octave" frequency ratios of the harmonic series.

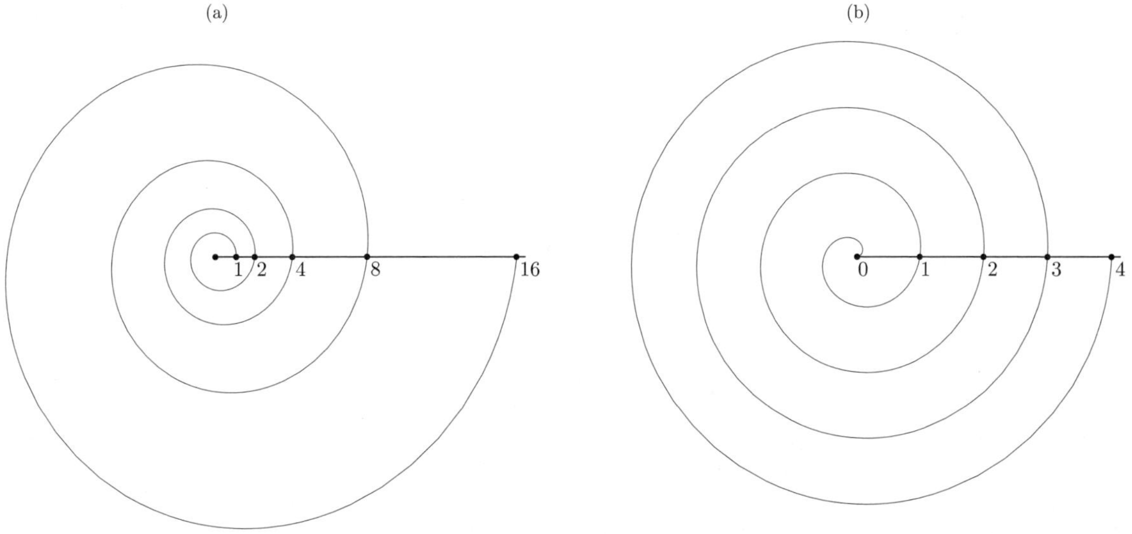

Figure 9.5 Two different mathematical spirals designed to represent the same acoustic event. (a) In a logarithmic spiral, as the radius revolves and expands outward it produces a geometric progression of changing lengths. This spiral represents varied increases of "octave" frequencies. (b) In an Archimedean spiral, the radius produces an arithmetic progression of changing lengths. This spiral represents uniform increases of "octave" intervals.

In contrast, Figure 9.5(b) is called an Archimedean spiral, after the Greek mathematician Archimedes (*c.* 287 B.C. – *c.* 212 B.C.). Figure 9.5(b) shows a polar plot of the equation

$$r = \theta$$

Again, θ includes the angles from 0° to 1440.0°. So, when $\theta = 0°$, $r = 0$ units; when $\theta = 360.0°$ (revolution #1), $r = 360.0$ units; when $\theta = 720.0°$ (revolution #2), $r = 720.0$ units; when $\theta = 1080.0°$ (revolution #3), $r = 1080.0$ units. In an Archimedean spiral, r increases arithmetically per revolution. Here we take every incremental increase of 360.0 units and show it as an increase of 1 unit per revolution. We may interpret Figure 9.5(b) as a representation of the first four "octave" intervals of the harmonic series. Taken together, Figures 9.5(a) and 9.5(b) present two different mathematical images of the same acoustic event. The first spiral represents *varied geometric increases* of "octave" frequencies as produced by a vibrating system, while the second spiral represents *uniform arithmetic increases* of "octave" intervals as heard by human beings.

Part III

DERIVATIONS AND APPLICATIONS OF CENT CALCULATIONS

~ 9.8 ~

The calculator exercises in Sections 9.5–9.7 served as an introduction to logarithms and logarithmic calculations. Unfortunately, these examples do not clearly demonstrate the advantages of working with logarithms in a musical context. To fully appreciate the benefits of logarithmic interval calculations,[17] we must examine the work of Alexander J. Ellis (1814–1890).[18] However, before we consider his important contribution, let us first acquaint ourselves with fractional exponents.

Recall the standard equation that states that the square root of x equals z, because z squared, or z multiplied by itself, equals x:

$$\sqrt{x} = z \text{ because } z^2 = x$$

For example,

$$\sqrt{9} = 3 \text{ because } 3^2 = 9$$

Similarly, recall the equation that states that the yth root of x equals z, because z multiplied by itself y number of times equals x:

$$\sqrt[y]{x} = z \text{ because } z^y = x$$

For example, the 3rd root of 125 equals 5, because 5 raised to the third power equals 125:

$$\sqrt[3]{125} = 5 \text{ because } 5^3 = 125$$

Calculators and computers perform these kinds of calculations with logarithms. To understand this process of computation, consider the following logarithmic solution for the square root of 2. First, remove the conventional radical sign, and write the square root of 2 with a fractional exponent:

$$\sqrt{2} = 2^{\frac{1}{2}}$$

Now define the equation:

$$2^{\frac{1}{2}} = x \tag{9.12}$$

Express Equation 9.12 in logarithmic form:

$$\log_2 x = \frac{1}{2}$$

Show x as a base 2 logarithm in full detail:

$$\frac{\log_{10} x}{\log_{10} 2} = \frac{1}{2} \tag{9.13}$$

Multiply both sides of Equation 9.13 by $\log_{10} 2$:

$$\log_{10} x = \frac{\log_{10} 2}{2} \tag{9.14}$$

Finally, (1) compute the right side of Equation 9.14,

$$\log_{10} x = \frac{0.30103}{2}$$
$$= 0.15051$$

and (2) calculate the antilogarithm of 0.15051:

$$x = \text{antilog}_{10}\, 0.15051$$
$$x = 0.15051 \; \boxed{10^x} \; \rightarrow \; 1.4142$$

Therefore,[19]

$$2^{\frac{1}{2}} \approx 1.4142 \text{ because } (1.4142)^2 \approx 2$$

Ellis' original idea consists of "dividing" a "semitone" into 100 equal parts called "cents" (¢). On the piano, a "semitone" is the musical interval between any two adjacent keys. Since the chromatic scale in traditional Western music has 12 "semitones," there are 1200 ¢ in every "octave." Given such a system of measurement, the question arises, "How does one 'divide' frequency ratio ⅔ into 1200 equal parts?" In this context of frequency ratios, "divide" does *not* mean

$$2 \div 1200 = 0.00167 \tag{9.15}$$

Equation 9.15 states that 0.00167 *added* to itself 1200 times equals 2. The act of repeatedly adding the same number produces an arithmetic progression. In that sense, Equation 9.15 represents an *arithmetic division* of the number 2. However, recall that the frequency ratios of the harmonic series constitute a geometric progression. The principal mathematical operation in a geometric progression is multiplication. Therefore, a "division" of frequency ratio ⅔ into 1200 equal parts requires finding the twelve hundredth root of 2:

$$\sqrt[1200]{2} = x \tag{9.16}$$

Equation 9.16 states that x *multiplied* by itself 1200 times equals 2. In Ellis' system, the number x has the function of a common ratio in a geometric progression. For this reason, Equation 9.16 represents a *geometric division* of the number 2.[20] The following algebraic transformations show how to calculate the twelve hundredth root of 2 with logarithms:

$$\sqrt[1200]{2} = 2^{\frac{1}{1200}}$$

$$2^{\frac{1}{1200}} = x$$

$$\log_2 x = \frac{1}{1200}$$

$$\frac{\log_{10} x}{\log_{10} 2} = \frac{1}{1200}$$

$$\log_{10} x = \frac{\log_{10} 2}{1200}$$

$$\log_{10} x = 0.00025086$$

$$x = \text{antilog}_{10}\, 0.00025086$$

$$x = 0.00025086 \;\boxed{10^x}\; \rightarrow 1.00057779$$

Therefore,

$$2^{\frac{1}{1200}} \approx 1.00057779 \text{ because } (1.00057779)^{1200} \approx 2$$

Refer to Equation 9.16 and compute the same result on a calculator.

ALG: 2 $\boxed{\sqrt[x]{y}}$ 1200 $\boxed{=}$ 1.00057779

RPN: 2 $\boxed{\text{Enter}}$ 1200 $\boxed{\sqrt[x]{y}}$ $\rightarrow$ 1.00057779

~ 9.9 ~

Observe the following relation from the previous calculations.

$$\textbf{If:}\quad (1.00057779)^{1200\,¢} = \frac{2}{1} \qquad \textbf{then:}\quad 1200\,¢ = \log_{1.00057779}\frac{2}{1} \tag{9.17}$$

We conclude, therefore, that cents are the logarithms of frequency ratios to the base $2^{\frac{1}{1200}}$, or simply to the base 1.00057779.

$$\boxed{\textbf{If:}\quad (1.00057779)^{¢} = x \qquad \textbf{then:}\quad ¢ = \log_{1.00057779} x} \tag{9.18}$$

Note that in Equations 9.18–9.25 and 9.28–9.29, x represents a frequency ratio, and not a simple integer. This frequency ratio may be a rational number, as in $2/1 = 2$, $15/8 = 1.875$, etc., or it may be an irrational number, as in $\sqrt[12]{2} \approx 1.0594631$, $\sqrt[31]{2} \approx 1.0226114$, etc. (See Section 10.2.)

Suppose we ask, "How many cents are there in a $3/2$, or in a just 'fifth'?" To answer this question, solve Equation 9.18 for frequency ratio $3/2$:

$$(1.00057779)^{¢} = \frac{3}{2}$$

$$\log_{1.00057779}\frac{3}{2} = ¢$$

$$\frac{\log_{10}\frac{3}{2}}{\log_{10} 1.00057779} = ¢$$

$$\frac{\log_{10} 1.5}{0.00025086} = ¢$$

$$\frac{0.17609126}{0.00025086} = 701.95\,¢$$

Given any frequency ratio x, the third transformation suggests that we may determine any ¢ with Equation 9.19,

$$\frac{\log_{10} x}{0.00025086} = ¢ \tag{9.19}$$

where x is any real positive ratio greater than 1 ($x > 1$).

~ 9.10 ~

Although Equation 9.19 gives accurate results, the constant 0.00025086 is difficult to remember. As an alternative, consider Equation 9.20, where ¢ appears as the numerator of a fractional exponent:

$$2^{\frac{¢}{1200}} = x \tag{9.20}$$

Use this equation to calculate how many cents there are in a $^5\!/_4$, or in a just "major third":

$$2^{\frac{¢}{1200}} = \frac{5}{4}$$

$$\log_2 \frac{5}{4} = \frac{¢}{1200}$$

$$1200 \times \log_2 \frac{5}{4} = ¢$$

$$1200 \times \frac{\log_{10} \frac{5}{4}}{\log_{10} 2} = ¢$$

$$\frac{1200}{\log_{10} 2} \times \log_{10} 1.25 = ¢$$

$$\frac{1200}{0.30103} \times \log_{10} 1.25 = ¢$$

$$3986.314 \times \log_{10} 1.25 = ¢$$

$$3986.314 \times 0.09691001 = 386.31\ ¢$$

Because the constant 3986.314 is easier to remember and gives accurate results, all cent calculations in this book are based on Equation 9.21,

$$\boxed{\log_{10} x \times 3986.314 = ¢} \tag{9.21}$$

where x is any real positive ratio greater than 1 ($x > 1$). Try a $^6\!/_5$, or a just "minor third" cent computation on a calculator.

ALG: 6 [÷] 5 [=] [LOG] [×] 3986.314 [=] 315.64 ¢

RPN: 6 [Enter] 5 [÷] [LOG] 3986.314 [×] → 315.64 ¢

~ 9.11 ~

Consider the advantages of converting frequency ratios into cents. Because cents are logarithms, we may add cents in the same manner in which the ear "adds" musical intervals. To show that a "fifth" plus a "fourth" equals an "octave," add

$$701.95\ ¢ + 498.04\ ¢ = 1200.0\ ¢$$

A *multiplication* of the respective frequency ratios gives the same result in ratio form:

$$\frac{\cancel{3}}{\cancel{2}} \times \frac{\cancel{4}^2}{\cancel{3}} = \frac{2}{1}$$

Of course, we may also subtract cents to simulate how the ear "subtracts" musical intervals. To show that a "fifth" minus a "major third" equals a "minor third," subtract

$$701.95\ ¢ - 386.31\ ¢ = 315.6\ ¢$$

A *division* of the respective frequency ratios gives the same result in ratio form:

$$\frac{3}{2} \div \frac{5}{4} = \frac{3}{\not{2}} \times \frac{\not{4}^{2}}{5} = \frac{6}{5}$$

Cent calculations are most helpful when used to compare the relative sizes of musical intervals. Although decimal ratios[21] also provide a means of comparison, such numbers do not convey any meaningful information about the intonational differences between intervals. For example, in Section 9.3, Sequence (iii), we may interpret the interval between C–E as a tempered "major third," which equals 400.0 ¢, or as a just "major third," interval ratio 5⁄4, which equals 386.3 ¢. A comparison reveals that a tempered "major third" sounds approximately 14 ¢ sharp of a 5⁄4; or a 5⁄4 sounds approximately 14 ¢ flat of a tempered "major third." The finest ear can hear a 2 ¢ difference between two intervals in the central frequency range between F_3 at 174.6 cps and F_4 at 349.2 cps. Therefore, a 14 ¢ difference in this range is not subtle. Most listeners are able to hear the discrepancy between these two intervals. However, a comparison of the decimal ratios of the two intervals

$$\sqrt[12]{2}^{\,4} \approx 1.2599 \qquad \textit{vs.} \qquad \frac{5}{4} = 1.2500$$

shows that the numbers do not convey any detailed information about these intervals other than that the former ratio produces a higher frequency than the latter ratio.

~ 9.12 ~

For builders of stringed instruments the question may arise, "If one raises or lowers a given frequency by a specific number of cents, what will be the frequency of the new tuning?" Suppose you own an instrument that has a string tuned to A-440.0 cps, and you would like to retune this string to a frequency that is 25 ¢ higher. To determine the string's new frequency, one must first convert the cent factor into a decimal ratio. Calculate this decimal ratio in one of two ways. (1) Either use Equation 9.18,

$$(1.00057779)^{¢} = x \tag{9.22}$$

(2) or the inverse of Equation 9.21:

$$10^{\frac{¢}{1200/\log_{10} 2}} = 10^{\frac{¢}{3986.314}} = x \tag{9.23}$$

Both methods give identical results. The decimal ratio of 25 ¢ approximately equals

$$(1.00057779)^{25\ ¢} \approx 1.0145$$

$$10^{\frac{25\ ¢}{3986.314}} \approx 1.0145$$

These keystrokes show how to calculate the latter conversion[22] on either kind of scientific calculator.

ALG: 25 [÷] 3986.314 [=] [10^x] → 1.0145

RPN: 25 [Enter] 3986.314 [÷] [10^x] → 1.0145

Finally, the new frequency equals

$$440.0 \text{ cps} \times 1.0145 = 446.4 \text{ cps}$$

Conversely, to calculate a new frequency that is 25 ¢ lower than the original frequency, divide the original frequency by the decimal ratio of 25 ¢:

$$440.0 \text{ cps} \div 1.0145 = 433.7 \text{ cps}$$

Part IV

LOGARITHMIC EQUATIONS FOR GUITAR FRETS AND MUSICAL SLIDE RULES

9.13

The fret pattern on a guitar fingerboard is perhaps the most familiar exponential-logarithmic design associated with a musical instrument. The mathematical equation used to compute the fret positions requires a separate set of calculations for the irrational frequency ratios of the 12-tone equal tempered scale. As discussed in Sections 10.32–10.33, the Western scale consists of 12 consecutive intervals called "semitones." We compute the frequency ratios of these "semitones" by "dividing" the "octave" into 12 equal parts. Reminiscent of cent calculations, such a *geometric division* of the "octave" requires calculating the twelfth root of 2:

$$\sqrt[12]{2} \approx 1.0594631$$

According to Equation 9.24, raise this constant to the 1st, 2nd, 3rd, . . . , 12th power to compute the frequency ratios of this tempered scale,

$$\sqrt[12]{2}^{\,y} = x \tag{9.24}$$

Table 9.1

IRRATIONAL FREQUENCY RATIOS OF
12-TONE EQUAL TEMPERAMENT

$(1.0594631)^1$	$= 1.0594631$
$(1.0594631)^2$	$= 1.1224621$
$(1.0594631)^3$	$= 1.1892071$
$(1.0594631)^4$	$= 1.2599211$
$(1.0594631)^5$	$= 1.3348399$
$(1.0594631)^6$	$= 1.4142136$
$(1.0594631)^7$	$= 1.4983071$
$(1.0594631)^8$	$= 1.5874011$
$(1.0594631)^9$	$= 1.6817929$
$(1.0594631)^{10}$	$= 1.7817975$
$(1.0594631)^{11}$	$= 1.8877487$
$(1.0594631)^{12}$	$= 2.0000001$

where y represents the arithmetic progression 1, 2, 3, . . . , 12; and x is the irrational frequency ratio of each consecutive degree in the scale. The frequency ratios of 12-TET rounded to seven decimal places appear in Table 9.1.

For fret calculations, use Equation 9.25, which is the same as Equation 3.32,

$$\Pi = \frac{L}{x} \tag{9.25}$$

where L is the length of the guitar string from the bridge on the soundboard to the nut, in millimeters; Π is the position of the fret as measured from the bridge, also in millimeters; and x is either a rational or irrational frequency ratio. [I intentionally chose the uppercase of the Greek letter *pi* (Π) for this equation because the horizontal line of this letter resembles a fret, and the vertical lines, two strings.] Now, to calculate the fret positions on a 12-tone equal tempered guitar, Equation 9.26 states

$$\Pi = \frac{L}{\sqrt[12]{2}^{\,y}} \tag{9.26}$$

It is also possible to compute the fret positions with logarithms. The algebraic transformations below show how to solve Equation 9.26 as a logarithmic equation:

$$\begin{aligned}
\frac{L}{\sqrt[12]{2}^{\,y}} &= \Pi \\
\sqrt[12]{2}^{\,y} &= \frac{L}{\Pi} \\
\log_{1.0594631} L - \log_{1.0594631} \Pi &= y \\
\frac{\log_{10} L - \log_{10} \Pi}{\log_{10} 1.0594631} &= y \\
\log_{10} L - \log_{10} \Pi &= \log_{10} 1.0594631 \times y \\
-\log_{10} \Pi &= -\log_{10} L + (\log_{10} 1.0594631 \times y) \\
\log_{10} \Pi &= \log_{10} L - (\log_{10} 1.0594631 \times y) \\
\Pi &= \text{antilog}_{10}\left[\log_{10} L - (\log_{10} 1.0594631 \times y)\right] \qquad (9.27)
\end{aligned}$$

A general equation for logarithmic fret calculations states

$$\begin{aligned}
\log_{10} \Pi &= \log_{10} L - \log_{10} x \qquad (9.28) \\
\Pi &= \text{antilog}_{10}(\log_{10} L - \log_{10} x)
\end{aligned}$$

In Table 9.2, Equation 9.26 or 9.27 gives the locations to the nearest millimeter of 19 frets on an acoustic 12-tone equal tempered guitar with a string length of 652 mm.

Anyone interested in alternate fret positions must change the *frequency ratio* in Equation 9.25 or 9.28. For example, to calculate the fret position for an $^{11}\!/_{8}$, or a just "flat tritone," substitute the string length and this frequency ratio into Equation 9.25 to obtain the location:

$$\Pi = \frac{652 \text{ mm}}{\frac{11}{8}} = \frac{652 \text{ mm}}{1.3750} = 474 \text{ mm}$$

Table 9.2

GUITAR FRET LOCATIONS FOR A STRING LENGTH OF 652 MM

Fret 1	615 mm
Fret 2	581 mm
Fret 3	548 mm
Fret 4	517 mm
Fret 5	488 mm
Fret 6	461 mm
Fret 7	435 mm
Fret 8	411 mm
Fret 9	388 mm
Fret 10	366 mm
Fret 11	345 mm
Fret 12	326 mm
Fret 13	308 mm
Fret 14	290 mm
Fret 15	274 mm
Fret 16	259 mm
Fret 17	244 mm
Fret 18	231 mm
Fret 19	218 mm

Or, substitute the same variables into Equation 9.28 to obtain the location:

$$\log_{10} \Pi = \log_{10} 652 - \log_{10} 1.375 = 2.67594$$

$$\Pi = \text{antilog}_{10} 2.67594$$

$$\Pi = 2.67594 \ \boxed{10^x} \ \rightarrow \ 474$$

∼ 9.14 ∼

Although the calculator has replaced the slide rule as a practical tool for mathematical calculations, this old-fashioned logarithmic device has one important advantage over the calculator. Like a plot or graph, a slide rule shows a wide range of numerical relationships at a single glance. Furthermore, since it is possible to construct a musical slide rule on the same mathematical principles as a standard slide rule, we may use such a tool to effortlessly calculate countless musical intervals. The knowledge thus gained greatly furthers our understanding of unfamiliar scales and tunings. Therefore, anyone interested in studying new or exotic tunings should seriously consider the advantages of working with a musical slide rule.

In Table 9.3, the top row gives the note names of the Western 12-tone scale between C–C$^{|}$, and the bottom row, the same scale between G–G$^{|}$. The middle row represents an interpretation of 12-TET based on the 5-limit rational frequency ratios of *just intonation.*[23]

Table 9.3

AN INTERPRETATION OF 12-TONE EQUAL TEMPERAMENT BASED ON THE 5-LIMIT RATIONAL FREQUENCY RATIOS OF JUST INTONATION

C	C♯	D	E♭	E	F	F♯	G	A♭	A	B♭	B	C′
1/1	16/15	9/8	6/5	5/4	4/3	45/32	3/2	8/5	5/3	16/9	15/8	2/1
G	G♯	A	B♭	B	C	C♯	D	E♭	E	F	F♯	G′

Now, Figure 9.6 shows a musical slide rule based on the following equation:

$$M = L \log_2 x \tag{9.29}$$

where M is the location of a mark as measured from the left end of the rule, in millimeters; L is the overall length of the rule, also in millimeters; and x is a frequency ratio of any given scale, dimensionless. For a musical slide rule with a length of 100.0 mm, calculate the location of the "semitone" mark by substituting frequency ratio 16/15, and the length of the rule, into Equation 9.29:

$$M_{\text{“semitone”}} = (100.0\text{ mm})\left(\frac{\log_{10}\frac{16}{15}}{\log_{10} 2}\right) = 9.3\text{ mm}$$

Table 9.4 gives the ratio lengths for the remaining frequency ratios in Table 9.3.

Table 9.4

1/1	16/15	9/8	6/5	5/4	4/3	45/32	3/2	8/5	5/3	16/9	15/8	2/1
0	9.3	17.0	26.3	32.2	41.5	49.2	58.5	67.8	73.7	83.0	90.7	100.0

Because these millimeter dimensions represent logarithmic lengths to the base 2, the act of multiplying two ratios is equivalent to adding their ratio lengths. Conversely, the act of dividing two ratios is equivalent to subtracting their ratio lengths.[24] Refer to Table 9.4 and note that when we multiply two ratios, the product equals a ratio that appears above the *sum* of the respective ratio lengths; that is, since 3/2 × 4/3 = 12/6 = 2/1, we find that

$$58.5\text{ mm} + 41.5\text{ mm} = 100.0\text{ mm}$$

Similarly, when we divide two ratios, the quotient equals a ratio that appears above the *difference* of the respective ratio lengths; that is, since 3/2 ÷ 5/4 = 12/10 = 6/5, we find that

$$58.5\text{ mm} - 32.2\text{ mm} = 26.3\text{ mm}$$

In Figure 9.6, an alignment of marks on the upper rule with the middle rule, or an alignment on the lower rule with the middle rule, indicates either the sum of two musical intervals, or the difference of two musical intervals. However, even where there are no alignments, the musical slide rule still conveys important information. As an example, the upper rule shows that the interval between a 4/3 and a 45/32 is smaller than a 16/15, or is less than 111.7 ¢.

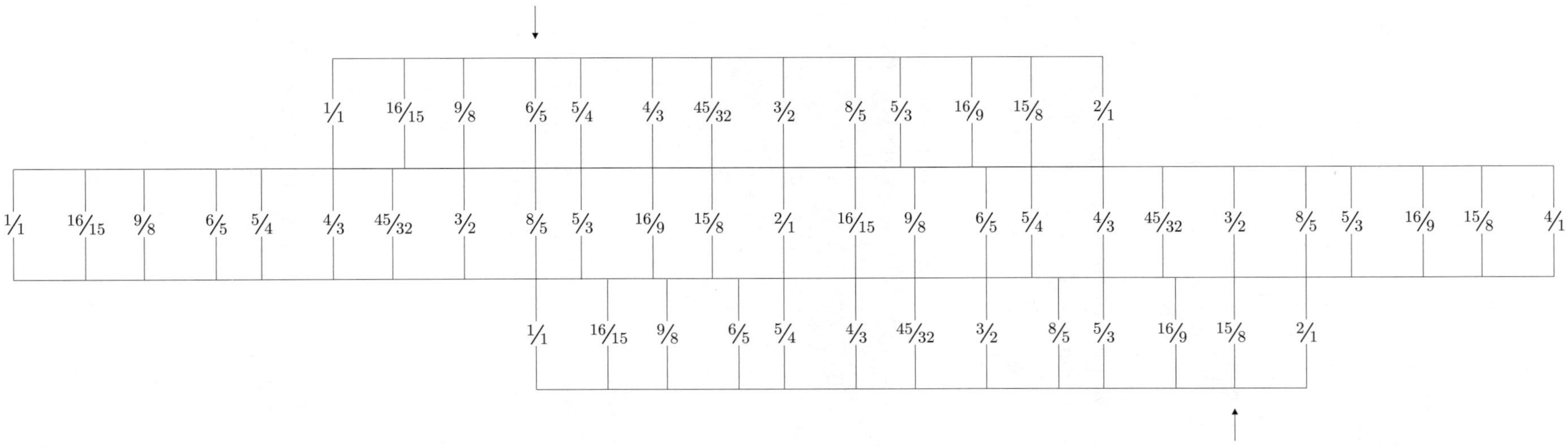

Figure 9.6 A musical slide rule based on the equation $M = L \log_2 x$. With this device, the multiplication and division of ratios is simplified to the mechanical equivalent of adding and subtracting logarithmic ratio lengths.

For this particular design, the upper and lower rules slide against the stationary middle rule. The short sliding rules are identical and span the interval of one 2/1, or one "octave," while the long fixed middle rule spans the interval of two 2/1's, or a "double-octave." Ideally, the ratios of the *second* 2/1 on the middle rule should appear as 32/15, 9/4, 12/5, 5/2, . . . instead of 16/15, 9/8, 6/5, 5/4, . . .[25] The middle rule gives the latter sequence because the ratios of the first 2/1 are more familiar and easier to interpret than the ratios of the second 2/1. As discussed in Section 3.12, the ratios of the middle rule represent *frequency ratios* of a scale that begins on the tonic, ratio 1/1; and the ratios of the upper and lower rules represent *interval ratios* between any two frequency ratios, or between any two scale degrees. For example, the arrow at the upper rule shows interval ratio 6/5, or the interval of a just "minor third" between the "fourth," frequency ratio 4/3, and the "minor sixth," frequency ratio 8/5, of the scale on the middle rule. Similarly, the arrow at the lower rule shows interval ratio 15/8, or the interval of a just "major seventh" between the "minor sixth," frequency ratio 8/5, of the lower "octave," and the "twelfth" (or "fifth"), frequency ratio 3/1 (or 3/2), of the upper "octave" of the scale. We may interpret the arrow at the upper rule in two different ways. A reading in the upward direction from left to right shows that when the ear hears a "fourth" and then "adds" a "minor third," it perceives the "sum" as a "minor sixth":

$$\frac{4}{\cancel{3}} \times \frac{\cancel{6}^{2}}{5} = \frac{8}{5}$$

Conversely, a reading in the downward direction from right to left shows that when the ear hears a "minor sixth" and then "subtracts" a "minor third," it perceives the "difference" as a "fourth":

$$\frac{8}{5} \div \frac{6}{5} = \frac{\cancel{8}^{4}}{\cancel{5}} \times \frac{\cancel{5}}{\cancel{6}^{3}} = \frac{4}{3}$$

Notes

1. For the harmonic series of flexible strings, see Section 3.8.

2. For the harmonic series of open columns of air, see Section 7.10.

3. See Section 10.1

4. See Section 10.2.

5. Observe carefully that "octave" equivalents also occur in a downward direction. For example, in a sequence of four 3/2's that descends *below* 2/1 — 2/1, 4/3, 8/9, 16/27, 32/81 — the last three "octave" equivalents represent frequency ratios 16/9, 32/27, and 128/81, respectively. In this context, to simplify an "octave" equivalent, or to bring it within the range of a 2/1, multiply the numerator by factors of 2 until the quotient is greater than 1, but less than 2.

6. (A) Tropfke, J. (1921). *Geschichte der Elementar-Mathematik, Volume 2*, p. 171. Vereinigung Wissenschaftlicher Verleger, Walter de Gruyter & Co., Berlin and Leipzig, Germany.

The term *exponent* first appears in a work entitled *Arithmetica integra* (1544) by the German mathematician Michael Stifel (1487–1567). Stifel was also the first mathematician to define the four laws of exponents cited in Note 11. In the *Arithmetica integra*, he describes the four laws in the context of the following two rows:

0.	1.	2.	3.	4.	5.	6.	7.	8.
1.	2.	4.	8.	16.	32.	64.	128.	256.

I translated the following description by Stifel from Tropfke's book:

"Addition in the arithmetic row corresponds to multiplication in the geometric [row], likewise subtraction in the former, to division in the latter. Simple multiplication in the arithmetic row becomes multiplication to itself (exponentiation) in the geometric row. Division in the arithmetic row is assigned to the extraction of a root in the geometric row, as dividing in half, to the extraction of a square root." (Text in brackets mine. Text in parentheses in Tropfke's German translation.)

(B) Smith, D.E. (1925). *History of Mathematics, Volume 2,* p. 521. Dover Publications, Inc., New York, 1958.

Smith cites excerpts from Stifel's original Latin text.

(C) Lindley, M. (1987). "Stimmung und Temperatur." In *Geschichte der Musiktheorie, Volume 6,* F. Zaminer, Editor. Wissenschaftliche Buchgesellschaft, Darmstadt, Germany.

On p. 144, Lindley reproduces Stifel's sophisticated limma and comma notation.

Finally, refer to Sections 10.38, 10.43–10.44, 10.46–10.47, and 10.58–10.60 for discussions on Stifel's contributions to the history of music with respect to the *harmonic sequence:* 10, 12, 15, 20, 30, 60, which appears in the works of Zarlino and Rameau.

7. The definition excludes negative numbers.

8. McLeish, J. (1991). *Number,* pp. 171–173. Bloomsbury Publishing Limited, London, England.

McLeish discusses the method used by Napier to calculate logarithms.

9. In Equation 9.3, y is the logarithm of x, and x is the antilogarithm of y.

10. To understand why $10^0 = 1$, refer to Law 2 in Note 11. When the exponents of a given number are *identical,* a simplification shows

$$\frac{a^3}{a^3} = a^{3-3} = a^0$$

However, ordinary division states that when we divide a given number into itself, the quotient equals

$$\frac{a^3}{a^3} = 1$$

Therefore, since both ratios are identical, it follows that $a^0 = 1$, for all finite values of a.

11. There are *four laws of exponents.*

Law 1. $a^m \times a^n = a^{m+n}$

Law 2. $a^m / a^n = a^{m-n}$

Law 3. $(a^m)^n = a^{m \times n}$

Law 4. $\sqrt[n]{a^m} = a^{\frac{m}{n}}$

12. See Note 10.

13. There are *four laws of logarithms.*

$$\text{Law 1.}\quad \log(m \times n) = \log m + \log n$$

$$\text{Law 2.}\quad \log(m\,/\,n) = \log m - \log n$$

$$\text{Law 3.}\quad \log a^{n} = n \log a$$

$$\text{Law 4.}\quad \log \sqrt[n]{a} = \log a^{\frac{1}{n}} = \frac{1}{n}\log a$$

Napier invented logarithms to simplify difficult mathematical calculations. Observe how the following logarithmic operations greatly aid in the computation of numbers.

Law 1. The logarithmic equivalent of multiplying two numbers is to *add* the logarithms of the numbers.

Law 2. The logarithmic equivalent of dividing two numbers is to *subtract* the logarithms of the numbers.

Law 3. The logarithmic equivalent of raising a number to a power is to *multiply* the logarithm of the number by the power.

Law 4. The logarithmic equivalent of extracting a root of a number is to *divide* the logarithm of the number by the root.

Implementations of these laws occur throughout Chapter 9. Note the application of Law 1 at the end of Section 9.6,

$$\log_{10}(2 \times 2 \times 2) = \log_{10} 2 + \log_{10} 2 + \log_{10} 2$$

of Law 2 in the transformations of Equation 9.27,

$$\log_{10}(L\,/\,\Pi) = \log_{10} L - \log_{10} \Pi$$

of Law 3 also in the transformations of Equation 9.27,

$$\log_{10} \sqrt[12]{2}^{\,y} = \log_{10} 1.0594631 \times y$$

and of Law 4 in the transformations of Equation 9.16:

$$\log_{10} \sqrt[1200]{2} = \frac{\log_{10} 2}{1200}$$

14. Readers with a background in trigonometry may prefer to express the angles of this polar plot equation in radians:

$$r = 2^{\frac{\theta}{2\pi}}$$

15. See Note 10.

16. Land, F. (1960). *The Language of Mathematics*, pp. 141–143. Doubleday & Company, Inc., Garden City, New York.

From the common garden snail to the exotic sea-faring nautilus, nature produces many different kinds of shells in the shape of logarithmic spirals. Land gives a detailed mathematical analysis of a nautilus that expands by a factor of 3.2 per revolution.

17. Pikler, A.G. (1966). Logarithmic frequency systems. *Journal of the Acoustical Society of America* **39**, No. 6, pp. 1102–1110.

This paper gives a concise history of logarithmic frequency ratio calculations.

18. Helmholtz, H.L.F., and Ellis, A.J., Translator (1885). *On the Sensations of Tone*, pp. 446–457. Dover Publications, Inc., New York, 1954.

19. The square root of 2 is an irrational number. Therefore, we must use an approximately equal sign ($\approx$) instead of an equal sign ($=$). See Section 10.2.

20. The ancient Greeks did not have logarithms and, therefore, could not apply mathematical methods to compute irrational numbers like $\sqrt{2}$. However, they were able to calculate such numbers with geometry. Greek mathematicians used ruler and compass to construct the *geometric division* of a line; the final result is called a *common ratio*, a *geometric mean*, or a *mean proportional.* In this context, the term *geometric division* refers to a single division as in the square root of two, and *not* to *multiple divisions* as in the twelve hundredth root of two. This explains the origin of the term *geometric progression*, or a progression of ratios that mathematicians could only determine through geometric means. See Section 10.9 and 10.24–10.26.

21. See Section 3.13.

22. We may also convert decimal ratios into ${}^{x}/_{y}$ integer ratios, where the numerator x and the denominator y are both positive integers. If the decimal ratio is a rational number, then the conversion results in an exact ${}^{x}/_{y}$ ratio. If the decimal ratio is an irrational number, then the conversion results in a very close ${}^{x}/_{y}$ approximation. See Section 10.69.

23. See Section 10.37.

24. See Note 13.

25. A multiplication by ratio ${}^{2}/_{1}$ shows that ${}^{16}/_{15} \times {}^{2}/_{1} = {}^{32}/_{15}$, ${}^{9}/_{8} \times {}^{2}/_{1} = {}^{18}/_{8} = {}^{9}/_{4}$, etc.

10 / WESTERN TUNING THEORY AND PRACTICE

Approximately 2500 years ago, the semi-legendary Greek philosopher and mathematician Pythagoras (*c.* 570 B.C. – *c.* 500 B.C.) reputedly discovered the crucial nexus between sound and number. Since that time, numbers in the form of ratios enabled musicians to accurately control the tuning of their instruments, and provided mathematicians with a means to analyze and classify new scales and tunings. The numeration of music presented common ground to musicians and mathematicians, and inspired a rich tradition of cooperation and controversy that lasted well into the 18th century. Unfortunately, for the last two hundred years, a tendency toward specialization in the arts and sciences produced a deep chasm between music and mathematics. Due to the universal standardization of 12-tone equal temperament, and a coexisting lack of development in the construction of new musical instruments, recent generations of musicians have shown very little interest in mathematics. As a result, the history of music in the West since the time of the ancient Greeks consists largely of an innocuous recounting of "music theory." However, since one cannot intelligently discuss music theory without confronting the subject of consonance and dissonance, and since the latter topic has its roots in polemics over scales and tunings, the exclusion of mathematics from music constitutes a deplorable aberration at best. Only a mathematical approach to music brings to full consciousness the possibilities of consonances and dissonances not yet heard. This in essence is the legacy of the Greek mathematician and astronomer Claudius Ptolemy (*c.* A.D. 100 – *c.* 165). In the *Harmonics*, Ptolemy continuously demonstrates to his reader that the ancient synthesis of music and mathematics inculcates an inner capacity for diversity, and encourages verification through experimentation.

The subject of tuning theory and practice is truly vast and could easily fill a half-dozen volumes. To help organize and limit the discussion, this chapter is divided into six parts. Part I analyzes formal mathematical definitions of four different types of numbers; Part II, Greek classifications of musical ratios, tetrachords, scales, and modes; Part III, arithmetic and geometric divisions on canon strings; and Part IV, scales by Philolaus, Euclid, Aristoxenus, and Ptolemy. In Table 10.12, Ptolemy's Catalog of Scales also includes tunings by Archytas, Eratosthenes, and Didymus. The remaining parts focus on two areas in the recent history of Western tuning: Part V covers tempered tunings, and Part VI, just intoned tunings.

Chapters 3 and 9 are indispensable to an understanding of this chapter. As discussed in Chapter 3, the reader should know: (1) the mathematical structure of the harmonic series, (2) the distinctions between ancient length ratios, modern length ratios, frequency ratios, and interval ratios, and (3) the mathematical methods used in the division of canon strings. Furthermore, as discussed in Chapter 9, the reader should also know: (1) the distinction between an arithmetic progression and a geometric progression, (2) the procedure by which the human ear "adds" and "subtracts" musical intervals, and why this is equivalent to the multiplication and division of ratios, and (3) how to convert length ratios and frequency ratios into cents. Furthermore, as discussed in Sections 9.2–9.3, 9.8, and 9.13, the reader should also fully understand the intellectual and mathematical processes that make all equal temperaments, and in particular 12-tone equal temperament, possible. In summary, the intellectual process states that in the context of the harmonic series, the human ear identifies interval patterns according to geometric progressions, and it recognizes a single musical interval by its signature interval ratio. The mathematical process states that geometric progressions, frequency ratios, and interval ratios are governed by operations of multiplication and division. Therefore, with respect to 12-tone equal temperament, a *geometric division* of ratio $^2\!/_1$ into 1200 equal parts requires the extraction of the twelve-hundredth root of 2.

A simple canon with six or more strings and moveable bridges (see Chapter 13) is an essential tool for a musical understanding of this chapter, but not a requirement for intellectual comprehension. Perhaps some day the discussions in this chapter will inspire a reader to build such an instrument.

Part I

DEFINITIONS OF PRIME, COMPOSITE, RATIONAL, AND IRRATIONAL NUMBERS

10.1

The numbers that constitute musical ratios are called real numbers. Real numbers consist of both rational and irrational numbers. A rational number is defined as the quotient of two integers. With respect to scales and tunings, the integers that constitute musical ratios are classified as positive natural numbers, which include all odd numbers, even numbers, and prime numbers. Therefore, by definition, ratios such as $^x\!/_y$, where variables x and y represent positive integers, are called *integer ratios.*

Definition 1. A prime number is an integer whose only divisors are itself and 1. For example, 3 is a prime number because only 3 and 1 divide this number without a remainder. The first ten prime numbers are

$$2, 3, 5, 7, 11, 13, 17, 19, 23, 29, \ldots$$

Note that 1 is not a prime number,[1] and that 2 is the only even prime number.

Definition 2. An integer greater than 1 that is not a prime number is called a composite number. The first ten composite numbers are

$$4, 6, 8, 9, 10, 12, 14, 15, 16, 18, \ldots$$

All composite numbers may be factored into prime numbers. To determine the prime factors of a composite number, divide the number by primes until the result is a prime. For example, the following factorization:

$$\frac{42}{\mathbf{7}} = 6, \ \frac{6}{\mathbf{3}} = \mathbf{2}$$

reveals that composite number 42 is a product of prime numbers $7 \times 3 \times 2$.

A factorization into primes enables one to understand the numerical and musical structure of a ratio. Consider the factorization

$$\frac{4}{\mathbf{2}} = \mathbf{2}$$

which states that composite 4 is a product of primes 2×2. This example tells us that a just ratio with integer 4 has a musical relation to all ratios with prime number 2. Similarly, since

$$\frac{10}{\mathbf{5}} = \mathbf{2}$$

a ratio with integer 10 has a musical relation to all ratios with primes 5 and 2.

Prime numbers disclose important information about the musical character of a given scale. For example, if we can factor all the integers of a scale into prime numbers 2 and 3, we know immediately that ratio $5/4$, or a just "major third," is missing from the scale. Before the Renaissance, music theorists argued vehemently against the integration of prime number 5. Polemics over the inclusion or the exclusion of various prime numbers have occupied musicians and mathematicians for thousands of years. To understand the physical implications of these arguments, consider a canon string divided into 12 equal parts. Place a bridge under the string, and move the bridge only to those locations that one can factor with primes 2 and 3. Such a *prime limit* restricts the bridge to modern length ratios $1/12$, $2/12$, $3/12$, $4/12$, $6/12$, $8/12$, and $9/12$, which in turn produce frequency ratios $12/1$, $6/1$, $4/1$, $3/1$, $2/1$, $3/2$, and $4/3$, respectively. Refer to Figure 3.12 and note, however, that a $12/1$, or a "triple-octave and a fifth," a $6/1$, or a "double-octave and a fifth," a $3/1$, or a "single-octave and a fifth," and a $3/2$, or a "fifth," all have the interval of a "fifth" in common. The fact that the numerators of the first three frequency ratios are all numerically different does little to bring variety to this group of ratios. Similarly, a $4/1$, or a "double-octave," and a $2/1$, or a "single-octave," both have the interval of an "octave" in common. In the entire group, only $4/3$, or the "fourth," has a unique identity. So, due to the influence of two prime numbers, this group of seven ratios produces only three types of distinctly different musical intervals: the "octave," the "fifth," and the "fourth."

Now suppose you would like to hear a just "minor third," or frequency ratio $6/5$. Integer 6 in the numerator has prime factors 2 and 3; no problem. However, integer 5 in the denominator has no prime factors except itself and 1, which means that it is a prime number. Consequently, it is impossible to produce a $6/5$ given the present prime limit of 2 and 3. This example demonstrates the importance of knowing the underlying prime number composition of musical ratios. Since all just intoned scales have prime number limits, knowledge of primes enables us to accurately analyze the harmonic and melodic potential of a particular scale. If we now expand our previous restriction of 3-limit ratios and choose instead 5-limit ratios, we may simply move the bridge to modern length ratio $10/12$, which produces frequency ratio $6/5$. As discussed in Sections 3.7 and 3.11, invert a given modern length ratio to identify the corresponding frequency ratio; in this case, l.r. $5/6 \rightarrow$ f.r. $6/5$. Observe, however, that all frequency ratios beyond 11-limit ratios, such as $13/8$ and $17/9$, are not available due to the inherent limitations of the division of this string into 12 equal parts.

10.2

At the beginning of Section 10.1, we classified all musical ratios as real numbers.[2] We may now categorize all real numbers into two distinctly different groups: rational numbers, and irrational numbers. Before examining irrational numbers, let us first expand our understanding of rational numbers.

The subject of musical mathematics requires numbers in the form of integers and fractions. A rational number may be expressed as a fraction (or ratio) that has a positive integer in the numerator, and a positive integer in the denominator. There are two different kinds of rational numbers. (1) The first type of rational number is called a *terminating decimal* because it has a limited or finite number of decimal places. Examples are the decimal fraction $1 \div 4 = 0.25$, and the mixed decimal[3] or decimal ratio $3 \div 2 = 1.5$. (2) The second type of rational number is called a *repeating decimal.* This kind of number has an infinite number of decimal places with a predictable pattern of repetition. Examples are the decimal fraction $1 \div 3 = 0.333333...$, and the decimal ratio $14 \div 13 = 1.076923...$ To indicate that a number is a repeating decimal, place a bar over the digits that repeat:

$$\frac{1}{17} = 0.\overline{0588235294117647}$$

$$\frac{4}{3} = 1.\overline{3}$$

In contrast, an irrational number cannot be expressed as a ratio of two positive integers because it has an infinite number of *non*-repeating decimal places. For mathematicians, the most famous irrational number is the square root of 2, and for musicians, it is the twelfth root of two:

$$\sqrt{2} \approx 1.4142136$$

$$\sqrt[12]{2} \approx 1.0594631$$

A technically correct notation always requires an approximately equal sign ($\approx$) between the expression and the value of an irrational number because it is impossible to give the exact value of such a number.

To further understand the distinction between rational numbers and irrational numbers, consider an experiment by Galileo Galilei (1564–1642). In 1638, Galileo published a book entitled *Dialogues Concerning Two New Sciences.* The author described this book as containing ". . . results which I consider the most important of all my studies."[4] At the end of the first chapter, Galileo used pendulums to explain the difference between commensurable (measurable or rational) numbers and incommensurable (immeasurable or irrational) numbers.[5] Consider a set of pendulums where the string length ratios are defined by commensurable numbers. Displace these pendulums from their equilibrium positions, release them at the same instant, and note ". . . that after a definite interval of time and after a definite number of vibrations, all the threads, whether three or four, will reach the same terminus at the same instant, and then begin a repetition of the cycle. If however the vibrations of two or more strings are incommensurable . . . they never complete a definite number of vibrations at the same instant . . ."[6] This latter kind of vibration is caused by incommensurable length ratios. In other words, if the string length ratio of two pendulums constitutes an irrational number, the pendulums could theoretically swing back and forth for an infinite amount of time without every vibrating "in phase."[7]

~ 10.3 ~

During the 4th century B.C., the Greeks developed sophisticated geometric techniques for the calculation of irrational numbers. The geometrician Archytas (fl. *c.* 400 B.C.) constructed the cube root of 2 by a complex three-dimensional method of intersecting curves,[8] and the geometrician Euclid (fl. *c.* 300 B.C.) extracted the square roots of real numbers by a simple two-dimensional method of intersecting lines in a semicircle.[9] However, no Greek music theorist ever recorded or advocated the use of irrational numbers in the design of scales and tunings. Despite this fact, the geometric division of musical intervals occupied many Greek theorists and fueled great polemics. We will return to the subject of irrational numbers in Greek music in Sections 10.13–10.18.

Part II

GREEK CLASSIFICATIONS OF RATIOS, TETRACHORDS, SCALES, AND MODES

10.4

The Greeks made significant contributions to the history of music by developing meticulous definitions of ratios and elaborate constructions of scales and tetrachord divisions. Pythagoras and his followers managed to classify all relevant musical ratios into six groups. Nicomachus of Gerasa (b. *c.* A.D. 60) in the *Introduction to Arithmetic*,[10] Theon of Smyrna (fl. *c.* A.D. 100) in *Mathematics Useful for Understanding Plato*,[11] and Boethius (*c.* A.D. 480 – *c.* 524) in *Fundamentals of Music*[12] systematically recorded these groups as (1) *equal* ratios, (2) *multiple* ratios, (3) *epimore* ratios (Latin: *superparticular* ratios), (4) *multiple-epimore* ratios (Latin: *multiple-superparticular* ratios), (5) *epimere* ratios (Latin: *superpartient* ratios), and (6) *multiple-epimere* ratios (Latin: *multiple-superpartient* ratios).

We may represent these ratios with the aid of modern algebraic equations.[13] The *equal* equation

$$\frac{n}{n} \tag{10.1}$$

defines unison ratios $1/1$, $2/2$, $3/3$, etc. In an equal ratio, both terms are the same.

The *multiple* equation

$$\frac{mn}{n} \tag{10.2}$$

has one condition: $m > 1$, which states that m must be greater than one. In a multiple ratio, the larger term contains the smaller term two or more times exactly. For the following values of m and n, Equation 10.2 gives ratios

$$\begin{Bmatrix} m = 2 \\ n = 1 \end{Bmatrix} = \frac{2}{1}$$

$$\begin{Bmatrix} m = 4 \\ n = 2 \end{Bmatrix} = \frac{8}{2}$$

The *epimore* (*superparticular*) equation

$$\frac{n+1}{n} \tag{10.3}$$

has one condition: $n > 1$, which states that n must be greater than one. In an epimore ratio, the larger term contains the smaller term one time, plus one part of the smaller term. Given the following values for n, Equation 10.3 yields ratios

$$\{n = 2\} = \frac{3}{2}$$

$$\{n = 4\} = \frac{5}{4}$$

The *multiple-epimore* (*multiple-superparticular*) equation

$$\frac{mn+1}{m} \tag{10.4}$$

has two conditions: (1) m $>$ 1; (2) $n > 1$, which state that both m and n must be greater than one. In a multiple-epimore ratio, the larger term contains the smaller term two or more times, plus one part of the smaller term. For the following values for m and n, Equation 10.4 gives ratios

$$\begin{Bmatrix} m = 2 \\ n = 2 \end{Bmatrix} = \frac{5}{2}$$

$$\begin{Bmatrix} m = 2 \\ n = 3 \end{Bmatrix} = \frac{7}{2}$$

For ratio $\frac{5}{2}$, the numerator (5) contains the denominator (2) two times, plus one part of 2, or $5 = 2 \times 2 + 1$; and for ratio $\frac{7}{2}$, the numerator (7) contains the denominator (2) three times, plus one part of 2, or $7 = 2 \times 3 + 1$.

The *epimere* (*superpartient*) equation

$$1 + \frac{m}{m + n} \tag{10.5}$$

has two conditions: (1) $m > 1$; (2) $n \neq m \times x$, where x is any positive integer. Condition one states that m must be greater than one. Condition two states that n must not equal an integer multiple of m. Therefore, do not substitute pairs like $\{m = 2,\ n = 2\}$ and $\{m = 2,\ n = 4\}$ into Equation 10.5, otherwise the equation yields epimore ratios. In an epimere ratio, the larger term contains the smaller term one time, plus two or more parts of the smaller term. Given the following values for m and n, Equation 10.5 yields ratios

$$\begin{Bmatrix} m = 2 \\ n = 1 \end{Bmatrix} = \frac{5}{3}$$

$$\begin{Bmatrix} m = 3 \\ n = 1 \end{Bmatrix} = \frac{7}{4}$$

The first example reads[14]

$$1 + \frac{2}{2 + 1} = 1 + \frac{2}{3} = \frac{3}{3} + \frac{2}{3} = \frac{5}{3}$$

The *multiple-epimere* (*multiple-superpartient*) equation

$$p + \frac{m}{m + n} \tag{10.6}$$

has three conditions: (1) $p > 1$; (2) $m > 1$; (3) $n \neq m \times x$. Condition one states that p must be greater than one. Conditions two and three are the same as conditions one and two of Equation 10.5, respectively. Again, do not substitute pairs like $\{m = 2,\ n = 8\}$ and $\{m = 3,\ n = 6\}$ into Equation 10.6, otherwise the equation yields multiple-epimore ratios. In a multiple-epimere ratio, the larger term contains the smaller term two or more times, plus two or more parts of the smaller term. For the following values, Equation 10.6 gives ratios

$$\begin{Bmatrix} p = 2 \\ m = 2 \\ n = 1 \end{Bmatrix} = \frac{8}{3}$$

$$\begin{Bmatrix} p = 3 \\ m = 4 \\ n = 3 \end{Bmatrix} = \frac{25}{7}$$

The second example reads

$$3+\frac{4}{4+3}=3+\frac{4}{7}=\frac{21}{7}+\frac{4}{7}=\frac{25}{7}$$

For $^{8}\!/_{3}$, the numerator (8) contains the denominator (3) two times, plus two parts of 3, or $8 = 3 \times 2 + 2$; and for $^{25}\!/_{7}$, the numerator (25) contains the denominator (7) three times, plus four parts of 7, or $25 = 7 \times 3 + 4$.

The question naturally occurs, "To what do these ratios refer?" Nicomachus states

> Of relative quantity, then, the highest generic divisions are two: equality and inequality; for everything viewed in comparison with another thing is either equal or unequal, and there is no third thing besides these.
>
> Now the equal is seen, when of the things compared one neither exceeds nor falls short in comparison with the other, for example, 100 compared with 100, 10 with 10, 2 with 2, a mina with a mina, a talent with a talent, a cubit with a cubit, and the like, either in bulk, length, weight, or any kind of quantity . . .
>
> The unequal, on the other hand, is split up by ***subdivisions***, and one part of it is the greater, the other the less, which have opposite names and are antithetical to one another in their quantity and relation . . .
>
> Moreover, of the greater, separated by a second subdivision into five species, one kind is the multiple, another the superparticular, another the superpartient, another the multiple superparticular, and another the multiple superpartient.[15] (Bold italics mine.)

And Theon observes

> The ratio of proportion of two terms of the same species is a certain relationship that these terms have to each other . . . such as lengths with lengths, surfaces with surfaces, solids with solids, weights with weights . . .[16]

Note that both explanations of ratios include comparisons of measurable physical objects. Examine Tables 10.1–10.3, which give the Greek names and mathematical constructions of four multiple ratios, eleven epimore ratios, and seven epimere ratios, respectively. (See Section 3.17 for detailed discussions on the linguistic origins of these ratio names.) Observe that in Tables 10.2 and 10.3, formulas $1 + {}^{1}\!/_{x}$ and $1 + {}^{y}\!/_{x}$ reflect the custom of defining ratios based on the practice of subdividing tangible quantities. Furthermore, Greek-English lexicons inform us that epimore ratios also have deep historic roots in finance. For example, a person who lends money expects the borrower to pay back the principal plus interest. Therefore, a loan in *hemiolic* ratio $[1 + {}^{1}\!/_{2}]$ exacts 50% interest, a loan in *epitritic* ratio $[1 + {}^{1}\!/_{3}]$, 33.33% interest, a loan in *epitetartic* ratio $[1 + {}^{1}\!/_{4}]$, 25% interest, etc.

Table 10.1

GREEK TERMS FOR FOUR MULTIPLE RATIOS

diplasios	*double*	Ancient length ratio: $^{2}\!/_{1}$
triplasios	*triple*	Ancient length ratio: $^{3}\!/_{1}$
tetraplasios	*quadruple*	Ancient length ratio: $^{4}\!/_{1}$
pentaplasios	*quintuple*	Ancient length ratio: $^{5}\!/_{1}$

Table 10.2

GREEK TERMS FOR ELEVEN EPIMORE RATIOS

hemiolios	*half and whole*	$1/2 + 1$	Ancient length ratio: $3/2$
epitritos	*one and one-third*	$1 + 1/3$	Ancient length ratio: $4/3$
epitetartos	*one and one-fourth*	$1 + 1/4$	Ancient length ratio: $5/4$
epipemptos	*one and one-fifth*	$1 + 1/5$	Ancient length ratio: $6/5$
ephektos (*epihektos*)	*one and one-sixth*	$1 + 1/6$	Ancient length ratio: $7/6$
epihebdomos	*one and one-seventh*	$1 + 1/7$	Ancient length ratio: $8/7$
epogdoos (*epiogdoos*)	*one and one-eighth*	$1 + 1/8$	Ancient length ratio: $9/8$
epienatos	*one and one-ninth*	$1 + 1/9$	Ancient length ratio: $10/9$
epidekatos	*one and one-tenth*	$1 + 1/10$	Ancient length ratio: $11/10$
epihendekatos	*one and one-eleventh*	$1 + 1/11$	Ancient length ratio: $12/11$
epidodekatos	*one and one-twelfth*	$1 + 1/12$	Ancient length ratio: $13/12$

Table 10.3

GREEK TERMS FOR SEVEN EPIMERE RATIOS

epiditritos	$1 + 2/3$	Ancient length ratio: $5/3$
epitritetartos	$1 + 3/4$	Ancient length ratio: $7/4$
epitetrapemptos	$1 + 4/5$	Ancient length ratio: $9/5$
epipenthektos	$1 + 5/6$	Ancient length ratio: $11/6$
trisepipemptos	$1 + 3/5$	Ancient length ratio: $8/5$
tetrakisephebdomos	$1 + 4/7$	Ancient length ratio: $11/7$
pentakisepenatos	$1 + 5/9$	Ancient length ratio: $14/9$

As discussed in Sections 3.14 and 3.17, the oldest extant Greek text[17] on music that utilizes multiple and epimore ratios to describe the lengths of strings is a treatise entitled *Division of the Canon*, reputedly written by Euclid. In this text, terms such as *diplasios*, *hemiolios*, *epitritos*, and *epogdoos* refer exclusively and unequivocally to the proportional lengths of straight lines, which in turn represent the proportional lengths of canon strings. Furthermore, as discussed in Sections 3.18–3.19, there is no doubt that music theorists originally used such ratio constructions to identify musical intervals expressed as length ratios. To emphasize the historic significance of ancient length ratio n/x — *where the long string length with the larger number of parts is in the numerator, and the short string length with the smaller number of parts is in the denominator* — in Section 10.8 we will analyze a key passage from a work by Claudius Ptolemy entitled the *Harmonics;* and in Section 10.11 we will discuss Euclid's diatonic canon tuning in full detail. Ptolemy accurately recorded the scales of his predecessors in string length units, and computed all his original tetrachord divisions in length ratios. Furthermore, he also described the arithmetic division of the "octave" on a canon string, which produces the same intervals as a calculation for the arithmetic mean of the "octave" in string length units. We conclude, therefore, that the practice of *direct canon string division* provided the Greeks with a system of ratio construction and interval identification that was consistent not only with the original language of ratios, but with the aural experience of musical intervals as well.

10.5

The early Pythagoreans classified small integer ratios $n/1$ and n/x as consonances.[18] Among the most consonant intervals, they included three multiple ratios: the "octave," ratio $2/1$, the "twelfth," ratio $3/1$, and the "double-octave," ratio $4/1$. Next came two less consonant epimore ratios: the "fifth," ratio $3/2$, and the "fourth," ratio $4/3$. All other ratios were considered equally dissonant. Although theorist-musicians like Philolaus (fl. *c.* 420 B.C.), Archytas, and Euclid continued to advance the subject of musical mathematics after Pythagoras' death, later generations of Pythagoreans became recalcitrant in their methods and opinions. A deep-seated number mysticism enveloped these Pythagoreans,[19] and in a dialog entitled the *Republic*, Plato (427–347 B.C.) criticized them for subjecting all aspects of sound to numbers.

> . . . for the numbers they seek are those found in these heard concords [i.e., in these audible consonances], but they do not ascend to generalized problems and the consideration which numbers are inherently concordant [consonant] and which not and why in each case.[20] (Text in brackets mine.)

Five centuries later, Ptolemy also argued against the Pythagoreans because they rejected ratio $8/3$ as a consonance on grounds that it is a multiple-epimere ratio. Ptolemy contends

> This being the postulate of the Pythagoreans concerning the concords {i.e., the consonances}, the octave and a fourth {8:3}, which is quite plainly a concord, is an embarrassment to . . . them. For it is always true of the concord of the octave, . . . that when it is attached to one of the others it keeps the form of the latter unaltered . . . . . . it is to be expected that the same impression comes to the ears from the fourth and an octave as there does from the fourth alone, and that the impression of the fifth and an octave is the same as that of the fifth alone; and that it plainly follows from the fact that {since} the fifth is concordant, that the octave and a fifth {3:1} is concordant too, and from the fact that {since} the fourth is concordant, that the octave and a fourth is concordant too; . . . which accords with what is found by plain perceptual experiment.
>
> Another crucial problem is . . . that they associate the concords only with those epimoric and multiple ratios and not with others — I mean such ratios as the epitetartic [5:4] and the five-times multiple [5:1] . . .[21] (Text and ratios in braces mine. Ratios in brackets in Barker's translation.)

In the first paragraph, Ptolemy reasons that if one increases or decreases a consonant interval by an "octave," such a difference does not change the consonant quality of the interval. Therefore, since the "fifth" is a consonance, the "twelfth" — $3/2 \times 2/1 = 3/1$ — must also be a consonance; and since the "fourth" is a consonance, the so-called "eleventh" — $4/3 \times 2/1 = 8/3$ — must be a consonance as well.

In the second paragraph, Ptolemy also criticizes the Pythagoreans for not classifying the "major third," epimore ratio $5/4$, and the "double-octave and a major third," multiple ratio $5/1$, as consonances. Here, however, Ptolemy's observations are primarily argumentative and not based on reason and observation. In a later chapter, he does not define ratio $5/4$ as a bona fide *symphonic* interval, but gives a definition that implies it is an *emmelic* or melodic interval (see Section 10.19, Quote VIII). Nevertheless, Ptolemy does manage to expose one of the most sensitive nerves in the history of Western music, namely, whether 5-limit ratios should be classified as consonances or dissonances. In the above-mentioned passage, Ptolemy emerges as the first Western theorist to propose a break in the 3-limit barrier of Pythagorean music theory by considering the possibility of including 5-limit ratios as consonances. (Fifteen centuries later, Christiaan Huygens broke the 5-limit barrier and recognized 7-limit ratios as consonances. See Section 10.34.) So, although the original sixfold classification fulfilled an important mathematical function in defining all musical ratios by types, later Pythagorean purists subjected sound to number, and effectively ignored music as a perceptual phenomenon, and as an evolving art. In contrast, Ptolemy developed a sophisticated theory of *relative consonance* based on his experiments with tuned canon strings. In Sections 10.19–10.20, we will examine Ptolemy's numerical analysis of graduated consonance, and investigate his arithmetic divisions of tetrachords on canon strings.

10.6

Before the time of the semi-legendary musician Terpander (b. *c.* 710 B.C.), Greek lyres were built with four strings. Musicians and theorists tuned these strings to tetrachords, or to simple scales that span the interval of a "fourth."[22] According to Ptolemy, Archytas identified three different kinds of tetrachords: the *diatonic genus*, the *chromatic genus*, and the *enharmonic genus*.[23] These three genera also appear in a treatise entitled *The Elements of Harmony* by Aristoxenus (fl. *c.* 300 B.C.).[24] The Greeks regarded the first and fourth tones of a given tetrachord as fixed tones, and always tuned them to ratios $\frac{1}{1}$ and $\frac{4}{3}$, respectively. The second and third tones were considered moveable tones and, therefore, not limited to a specific tuning. Most important, the tuning of the third string, or the interval between the third and fourth tones, characterized the genus of a particular tetrachord. However, for a given genus, musicians did *not* restrict this interval to only one tuning. For the diatonic genus, the interval was tuned to various "major tones," for the chromatic genus, to various "minor thirds," and for the enharmonic genus, to various "major thirds." Figure 10.1 shows a typical tetrachord for each genus. Here circles indicate fixed tones, dots indicate moveable tones, and the characteristic interval of each tetrachord appears in bold typeface. We may think of these tetrachords as occurring between B–E, E–A, and A–D in Greek scale theory.

According to legend, Terpander joined two diatonic tetrachords by a common tone and, thereby, created a heptachord that consists of two *conjunct* tetrachords:

E	F	G	A			
			A	B♭	C	D

Approximately a century later, Pythagoras reputedly joined two diatonic tetrachords by inserting a $\frac{9}{8}$ "tone" between $\frac{4}{3}$ of the lower tetrachord and $\frac{1}{1}$ of the upper tetrachord.[25] The result is an octachord, or a scale comprising two *disjunct* tetrachords:

E	F	G	A	B	C	D	E$^{\prime}$
			$\frac{9}{8}$				

During the next two hundred years, Greek musicians and theoreticians continued to combine disjunct and conjunct tetrachords in the design of more complicated scales. Two famous scales emerged from this process: the larger scale was called the Greater Perfect System, and the smaller scale, the Lesser Perfect System. Of the Greek texts that survived, the first complete description of the GPS may be found in Euclid's *Division of the Canon*.[26] Figure 10.2 shows that the GPS consists of a $\frac{9}{8}$, two conjunct tetrachords, another $\frac{9}{8}$, and two more conjunct tetrachords, or fifteen strings that span the interval of a "double-octave."[27] Figure 10.2 also shows that the LPS consists of a $\frac{9}{8}$, and three conjunct tetrachords, or eleven strings that span the interval of an "octave and a fourth." As in Figure 10.1, circles represent fixed tones, and dots, moveable tones. Finally, note that in the GPS, the standard Greek "octave" occurs between E–E$^{\prime}$.

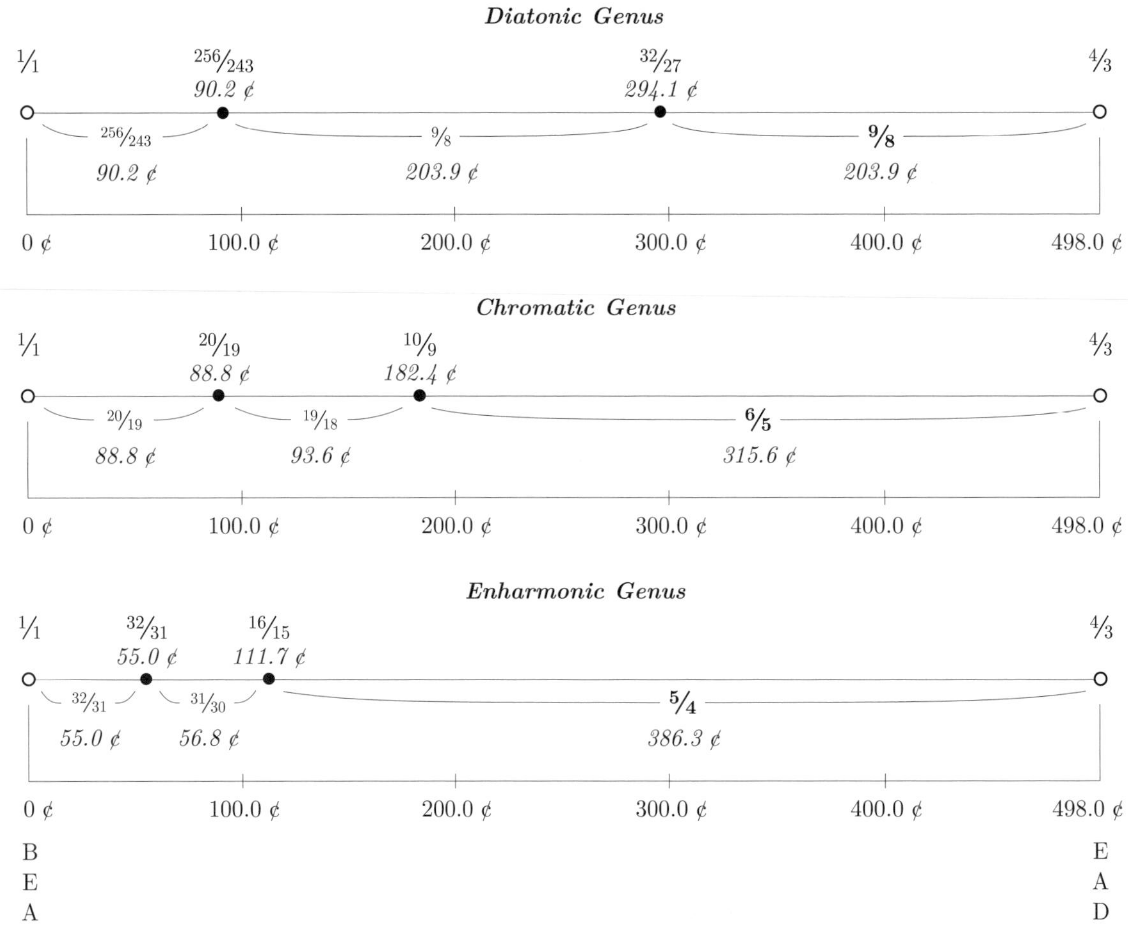

Figure 10.1 Three different genera of Greek music. Although all tetrachords span the interval 1/1–4/3, the characteristic interval between the third and fourth tones gives each genus its unique identity.

The Greeks tuned the tetrachords of the GPS and LPS to either a diatonic, a chromatic, or an enharmonic genus. Figure 10.3 shows three tunings of the GPS based on the tetrachords in Figure 10.1. Since Greek musicians used rational numbers in the tuning of their instruments, the notes in Figure 10.3 are only approximations. The rational frequency ratios of the Greek genera should never be confused with the irrational frequency ratios of the conventional 12-tone equal tempered scale as depicted in Figure 10.3. This discrepancy applies especially to the last genus in Figure 10.1. Note a 32/31 "quarter-tone" interval [55.0 ¢] between the first and second tones, and a 31/30 "quarter-tone" interval [56.8 ¢] between the second and third tones of this enharmonic genus. In the last example of Figure 10.3, the note of the second tone of each tetrachord is marked with a special "quarter-tone sharp" sign: $\overset{4}{\sharp}$. In this context, the sign should read an "approximate quarter-tone sharp," because an equal tempered "quarter-tone" equals 50.0 ¢ exactly. Also in this figure, white notes represent fixed tones, and black notes, moveable tones.

Finally, the Greeks also identified seven *harmoniai* or modes within the GPS. Figure 10.4 lists these modes based on the diatonic genus in Figure 10.1. In ascending order, this diatonic tetrachord consists of the following three intervals: 1/2 "tone," 1 "tone," and 1 "tone." Note carefully that the modes appear here in the *original* Greek order. Due to mistakes by medieval monks, most musicians learn the names of the ecclesiastic modes in a different order. In Section 10.21, we will examine the supreme importance of the diatonic Lydian Mode in Western music theory.

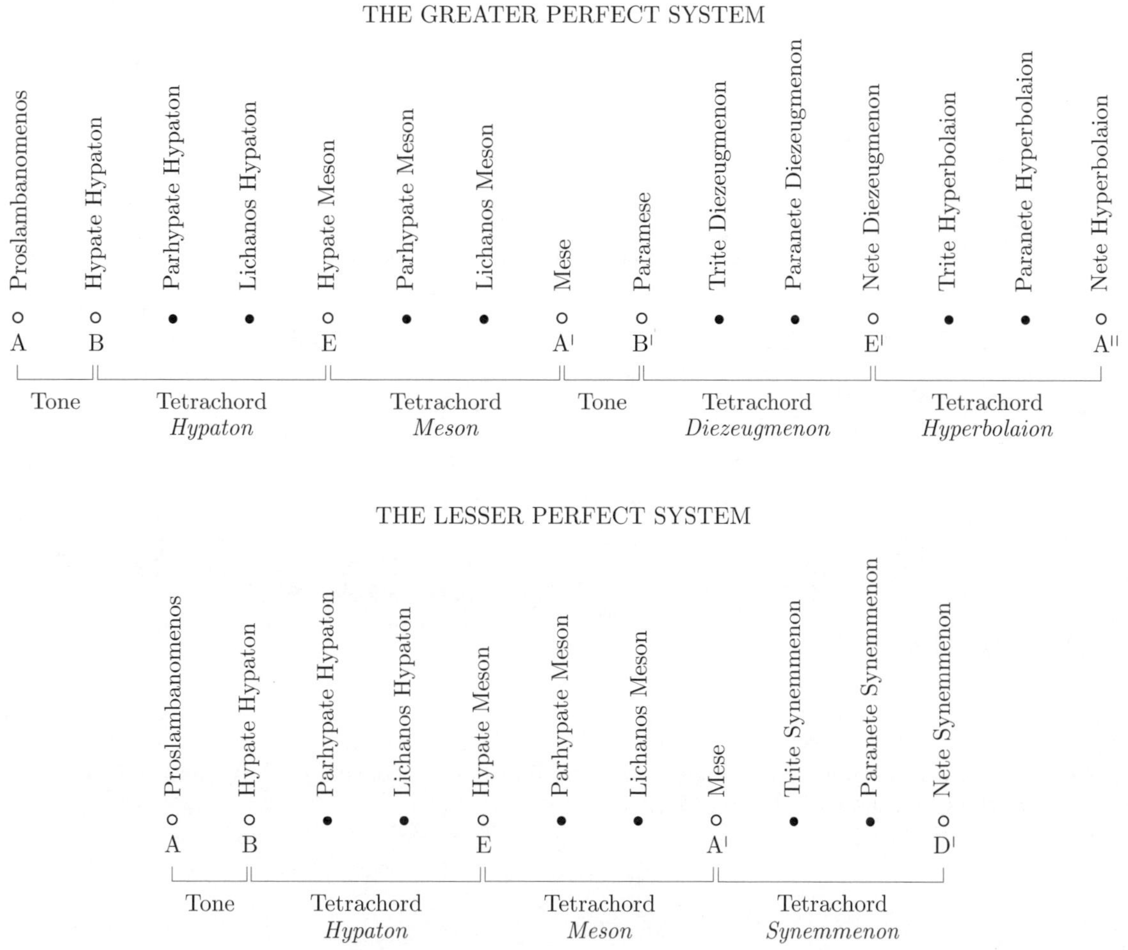

Figure 10.2 Two famous scales of ancient Greece. The Greater Perfect System consists of a "double-octave," or four tetrachords and two "whole tones." The Lesser Perfect System consists of an "octave and a fourth," or three tetrachords and one "whole tone."

Part III

ARITHMETIC AND GEOMETRIC DIVISIONS ON CANON STRINGS

10.7

The history of ancient Greek music is extremely controversial. Because only a few fragments and a handful of books survived, it is very difficult to comment on this subject without expressing an interpretation or a personal opinion. Moreover, Greek writers habitually engaged in biased criticism and innuendo. As a result, many authors did not bother to explain basic theoretical and practical facts. The following discussion does not attempt to resolve unanswerable questions of antiquity. Instead, we will here focus on fundamental elements of Greek music, especially as they pertain to the tuning of the canon.

In Greece, during the 7th century B.C., musicians and mathematicians began arguing over the allowable number of strings on a lyre. Although Terpander had the mental courage to revolutionize Greek music by transforming the original 4-string lyre into a 7-string instrument, he was loath to add an eighth string that would sound an "octave" interval with the first string.[28] The ancient

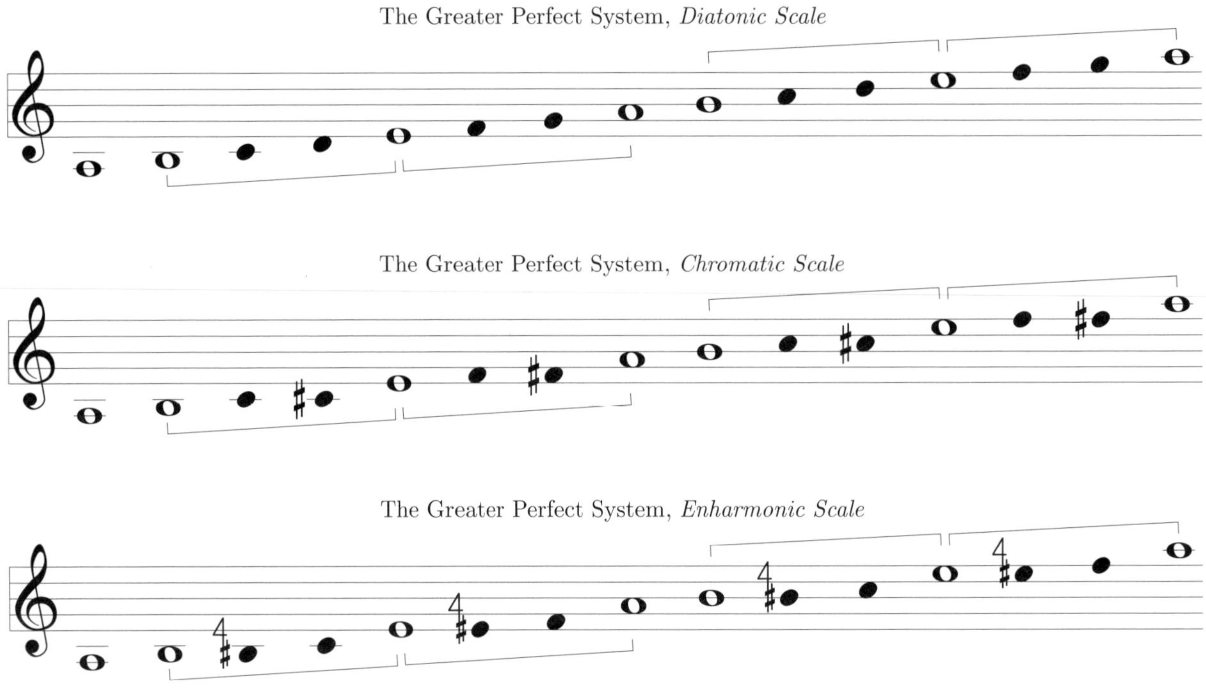

Figure 10.3 Three tunings of the Greater Perfect System. These scales are based on three genera shown in Figure 10.1. However, in Figure 10.3, the tones of the conventional Western scale only approximate the tones shown in Figure 10.1.

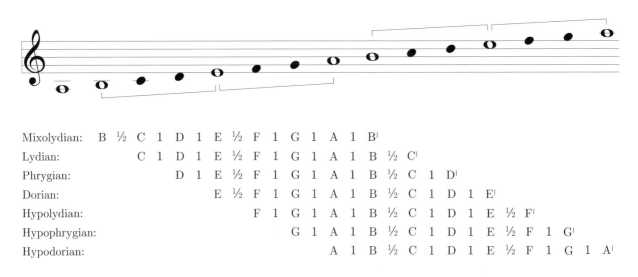

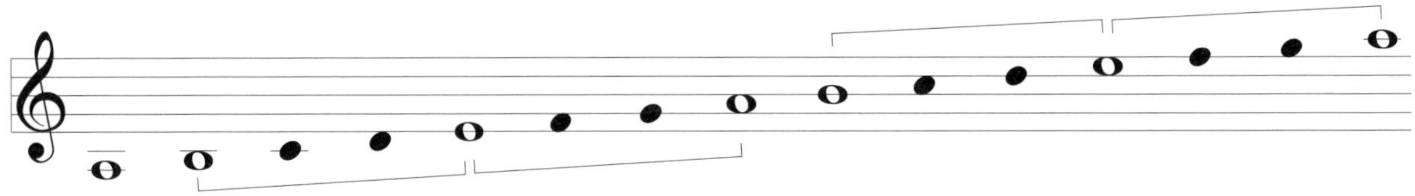

Mixolydian:	B	½	C	1	D	1	E	½	F	1	G	1	A	1	B′												
Lydian:			C	1	D	1	E	½	F	1	G	1	A	1	B	½	C′										
Phrygian:					D	1	E	½	F	1	G	1	A	1	B	½	C	1	D′								
Dorian:							E	½	F	1	G	1	A	1	B	½	C	1	D	1	E′						
Hypolydian:									F	1	G	1	A	1	B	½	C	1	D	1	E	½	F′				
Hypophrygian:											G	1	A	1	B	½	C	1	D	1	E	½	F	1	G′		
Hypodorian:													A	1	B	½	C	1	D	1	E	½	F	1	G	1	A′

Figure 10.4 Seven diatonic *harmoniai* or modes of the Greater Perfect System. The diatonic Lydian Mode has influenced the tuning of instruments in the West since its inception in Greek antiquity.

diatonic tetrachord consisted of the following three ascending intervals:[29] Semitone, Tone, Tone. Terpander's design consisted of two conjunct diatonic tetrachords. The result was a heptachord, or a 7-tone scale that spans the interval of a "minor seventh":

	S	T	T			
E	F	G	A			
			S	T	T	
			A	B♭	C	D

An eighth "octave" string would have destroyed the symmetry of a scale based on the sacred number seven, and it would also have sounded a dissonant B♭–E′ "tritone" interval in the second tetrachord. Consequently, the Argives strictly forbade the inclusion of such a string. However, in his determination to play the E–E′ "octave," Terpander managed to avoid both of these objections by simply removing the B♭ string and attaching the E′ string. The result was a heptachord with an A–C "minor third" gap between the fourth and fifth strings:[30]

E F G A C D E′

The renowned mathematician Nicomachus of Gerasa writes in his *Manual of Harmonics* that Pythagoras not only discovered the mathematical principles of music, but also managed to resolve the inherent imbalance of Terpander's 7-string "octave." Nicomachus informs us that in the original heptachord, Pythagoras tuned B♭ up to B, and then added the eighth "octave" string. This revolutionary design replaced the heptachord with an octachord, or a scale that consists of two disjunct tetrachords.[31] The "whole tone" interval A–B acted as the disjunct between the two tetrachords:

	S	T	T	**T**	S	T	T
E	F	G	A	B	C	D	E′

It is in the context of this new scale that Nicomachus tells the story of Pythagoras' great mathematical discovery:

> The interval of strings comprising a fourth, that of a fifth, and that formed by the union of both, which is called an octave, as well as that of the whole-tone lying between the two tetrachords, was confirmed by Pythagoras to have this ***numerical quantity*** by means of a certain method which he discovered.[32] (Bold italics mine.)

Nicomachus begins his story by telling us that Pythagoras ". . . was deep in thought and seriously considering whether it could be possible to devise some kind of instrumental aid for the ears which would be firm and unerring, such as vision obtains through the compass and the ruler . . ."[33] In other words, human sense-perceptions are imperfect. For example, we need a compass to draw a circle because our eyes do not enable us to produce such a perfect shape. However, note that a compass is not only a drawing tool, but also a precise mathematical instrument. The act of drawing a perfect circle with a compass produces the following ratio:

$$\frac{C}{D} = \pi$$

where C is the circumference of the circle; D is the diameter of the circle; and the lowercase of the Greek letter *pi* (π) represents the ratio 3.1416..., or the ratio of the circumference to the diameter. Therefore, all compasses have both visual and mathematical functions.

Nicomachus suggests that our ears are also incapable of precise numerical analysis. Both eyes and ears need the assistance of mechanical instruments to comprehend and construct exact mathematical comparisons: i.e., ratios. Pythagoras contemplated the possibility of some kind of device because he wanted to measure and verify the following intervalic relationships of his new scale: (1) that the "fourth" E–A plus the "fifth" A–E$^{|}$ equals the "octave" E–E$^{|}$; and (2) that the difference between the "fifth" A–E$^{|}$ and the "fourth" E–A equals the "whole tone," as between A–B.

To understand Pythagoras' problem, imagine a world in which musicians tune their instruments strictly by ear, without any knowledge of the mathematical relationships between tones. Before the time of Pythagoras, instrument builders and musicians had no knowledge of musical ratios. If one performer preferred sharp "fourths," and another preferred flat "fourths," no method existed that enabled musicians to quantify the magnitude of their tuning discrepancies. Lyre players must have encountered serious difficulties in consistently tuning their instruments to a given scale. In those days, players of stringed instruments probably relied on wind instruments to help remind them of difficult or long forgotten tunings.

Nicomachus recounts the legend of Pythagoras as he walked past a blacksmith shop and heard the ringing of hammers during the pounding of iron on an anvil.

> He recognized in these sounds the consonance of the octave, the fifth and the fourth . . . [He] ran into the smithy and found by various experiments that the difference of sound arose from the weight of the hammers, but not from the force of the blows, nor from the shapes of the hammers, nor from the alteration of the iron being forged . . . [He] went home . . . and suspended four strings of the same material and made of an equal number of strands, equal in thickness and of equal torsion [stiffness]. He then attached a weight to the bottom of each string . . . [and] arranged that the lengths of the strings should be exactly equal . . . He found that the string stretched by the greatest weight produced, when compared with that stretched by the smallest, an octave.[34] (Text in brackets mine.)

Nicomachus then describes numerous "weight ratios," which, as discussed in Section 3.17, are false. Despite these errors, Nicomachus' observations are extremely important because they correctly identify weight (or tension) as a *quantifiable variable* in the frequency equation of strings. The universal presence of such variables in other musical instruments did not escape Nicomachus.

> Using this as a standard and as it were an infallible pointer, he extended the test henceforward to various instruments, namely, to the percussion on plates, to auloi and panpipes, to monochords and triangular harps, and the like. And in all of these he found consistent and unchanging, ***the determination by number.***[35] (Bold italics mine.)

The last four words express the essence of Pythagoreanism. They best explain why Pythagoras' discovery has astonished and delighted musicians and mathematicians for centuries. However, equally important to the history of music is the notion that numbers not only determine physical rates of vibration, but the perceived quality of vibration as well. In other words, we judge the consonance and dissonance of musical intervals based on the relative magnitudes of ratios.

Nicomachus continues his discussion by observing that the frequency of a string is inversely proportional to its length. Although musicians and mathematicians in the 1st century A.D. had no method to determine the exact frequencies of strings, Nicomachus' conclusions regarding a string's rate of vibration are correct. He accurately observes that half of a string vibrates in a $^2\!/_1$ relation, and two-thirds vibrates in a $^3\!/_2$ relation, when compared to the vibrations of the whole string.

Nicomachus also describes how one may investigate musical ratios on a monochord or canon equipped with ". . . a long string that is kept under one and the same tension and that lies over a ruler, but is raised far enough above it so as not to touch it . . . the string having been stopped by a bridge . . ."[36] (See Chapter 3, Parts III–V; Sections 11.52 and 12.2–12.3; Chapter 13; and Plates 2, 3, and 12.) This is the instrument Pythagoras needed to confirm the numeric proportions of his new scale, because a canon aids the ears in a similar manner that a compass aids the eyes. The compass produces π, or the ratio that defines the characteristic shape of a circle. In an analogous manner, a measured canon string section produces — in relation to the length of the whole string — a given length ratio, or a ratio that defines the characteristic sound of a musical interval.[37]

10.8

To mathematically verify that the "octave" consists of a "fourth" plus a "fifth," consider the following description by Ptolemy:

I

> Of the homophonic octave in the ratio 2:1, which is constructed from two strings where one is twice as long as the other, one obtains from a division into two equal parts the ratio 3:2 of the fifth, where one string is by a half longer than the other, and 4:3 of the fourth, where one string is by a third longer than the other.[38]

Turn to Figure 3.22, and observe that such a canon tuning technique produces an *arithmetic division* of ancient length ratio $2/1$.

Consider a canon with three identical strings 1000.0 mm long, all tuned to the same frequency. As shown in Figure 10.5(a), divide the third string into four aliquot sections, and place a bridge at two of these sections, or at 500.0 mm, under the first string. Note, therefore, that the third string is *twice* as long as the left or right section of the first string. Ancient length ratio $4/2$ [$2/1$] means that the third string sounds an "octave" below the first string, or that the first string sounds an "octave" above the third string. Next, as shown in Figure 10.5(b), divide the left section of the first string in half, transfer this center point to the second string, and place a bridge at this location. Observe that the right section of the second string has a length of 500.0 mm + (500.0 mm ÷ 2) = 750.0 mm; consequently, the second string is by a *half* longer than the left or the right section of the first string. Ancient length ratio $1 + 1/2$, or $2/2 + 1/2 = 3/2$, means that the second string sounds a "fifth" below the first string, or that the first string sounds a "fifth" above the second string. Finally, Figure 10.5(c) shows that the third string has a length of 750.0 mm + (750.0 mm ÷ 3) = 1000.0 mm; consequently, the third string is by a *third* longer than the right section of the second string. Ancient length ratio $1 + 1/3$, or $3/3 + 1/3 = 4/3$, means that the third string sounds a "fourth" below the second string, or that the second string sounds a "fourth" above the third string.

If we initially tune all three open strings to C_3, then the first string with a bridge at 500.0 mm produces C_4, and the second string with a bridge at 750.0 mm produces F_3. Now, simultaneously play the first and the third strings and listen to the "octave" between C_3–C_4; next, play the first string and the right section of the second string and listen to the "fifth" between F_3–C_4; finally, play the right section of the second string and the third string and listen to the "fourth" between C_3–F_3.

We may also compute an arithmetic division of the left section of the first string by calculating the *arithmetic mean* of the "octave" expressed as ancient length ratio $2/1$, or 1000.0 mm/500.0 mm. Refer to Equation 3.37A, substitute the values $a = 1000.0$ mm and $c = 500.0$ mm into this equation, and calculate the arithmetic mean (Λ_A) of the "octave":

$$\Lambda_A = \frac{1000.0 \text{ mm} + 500.0 \text{ mm}}{2} = 750.0 \text{ mm}$$

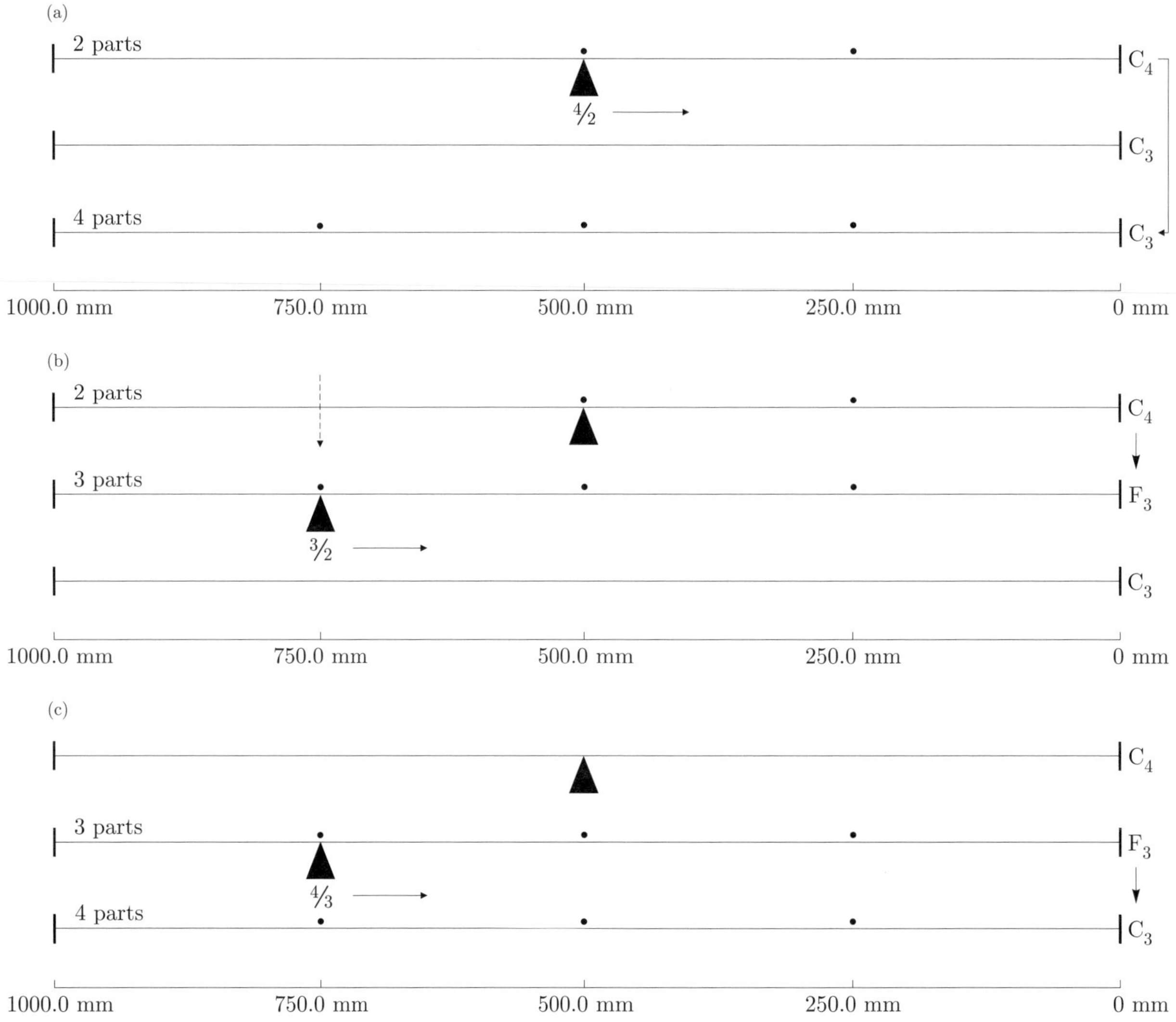

Figure 10.5 The arithmetic division of the "octave" expressed as ancient length ratio $^4\!/_2$ [$^2\!/_1$]. (a) Given three identically tuned canon strings, divide the first string in half, and sound the descending "octave" C_4–C_3. (b) Divide the left section of the first string in half, transfer the center point to the second string, place a bridge at this location, and sound the descending "fifth" C_4–F_3. (c) Finally, play the right section of the second string and the open third string and sound the descending "fourth" F_3–C_3. Note that the arithmetic division of length ratio $^2\!/_1$ into two *equal* subsections yields two *unequal* musical intervals: the upper two strings produce a "fifth" expressed as length ratio $^3\!/_2$, and the lower two strings produce a "fourth" expressed as length ratio $^4\!/_3$.

Next, arrange these three values in a descending sequence of string lengths, 1000.0 mm : 750.0 mm : 500.0 mm, divide all three lengths by the greatest common divisor 250.0 mm, and organize the arithmetic progression 4:3:2. Note carefully that such a progression expresses an ascending sequence of musical intervals; in this case, a lower "fourth," ratio $^4\!/_3$ [498.0 ¢], and an upper "fifth," ratio $^3\!/_2$ [702.0 ¢]. (See Section 3.18.) We conclude, therefore, that the division of a bridged string into two *equal* subsections produces (1) two *unequal* musical intervals; and that this procedure yields (2) the same results as an arithmetic mean calculation of a musical interval expressed as ancient length ratio $^n\!/_x$, where n and x are positive integers, and n is greater than x.

Finally, we may also compute the arithmetic mean of the "octave" in the following manner: multiply the numerator and denominator of $^2\!/_1$ by 2, $^2\!/_1 \times {^2\!/_2} = {^4\!/_2}$, insert the missing integer, and write the arithmetic progression 4:3:2. This technique works equally well for calculating three or more arithmetic means. For example, calculate three arithmetic means of the "fourth"; first multiply, $\frac{4}{3} \times \frac{3}{3} = \frac{12}{9}$, then insert and organize the arithmetic progression 12:11:10:9. Therefore, length ratio $\frac{4}{3}$ consists of the following three ascending intervals: $\frac{12}{11}$, $\frac{11}{10}$, $\frac{10}{9}$.

10.9

We turn our attention now to the *geometric division* of the "octave" expressed as ancient length ratio $\frac{2}{1}$. Such a construction divides the "octave" into two equal "tritone" intervals. The "octave" in 12-tone equal temperament consists of six successive "whole tones." For example, go to a piano, begin on any C, and play the following "whole tone" scale:

C D E F♯ G♯ A♯ C$^{|}$

Observe that F♯ marks the geometric center of the scale, which means that the two musical intervals C–F♯ and F♯–C$^{|}$ are identical. In this case, the interval is called a "tritone" because it consists of three "whole tones."

Before the widespread distribution of logarithms[39] in the middle of the 17th century, geometric divisions of ratios $\frac{2}{1}$, $\frac{5}{4}$, $\frac{9}{8}$, etc. were difficult to compute because such calculations result in irrational numbers. Today we simply press the square root key on a scientific calculator. However, before the invention of computers, mathematicians, music theorists, and instrument builders used ruler and compass, and more complicated mechanical devices,[40] to calculate irrational numbers.

No evidence exists that the Greeks used irrational numbers in the tuning of their instruments. However, because Archytas defined the geometric mean in a musical context,[41] and because a knowledge of irrational numbers is crucial to an understanding of Western tuning theory, let us now examine an ancient construction that results in the geometric division of length ratio $\frac{2}{1}$. Since the Greeks did not have an algebraic method to calculate irrational square roots, they solved this problem by resorting to geometry. Hence the term, *geometric mean.* The geometric method for calculating an irrational square root requires the physical construction of a line called the *mean proportional.*

Euclid's *Elements*, Book VI, Proposition 13, describes a ruler and compass method for the construction of a mean proportional between any two given straight lines.[42] Refer to Figure 10.6 and draw a line AB. Divide this line so that AD is 2 units long, and BD is 1 unit long. Next, draw a semicircle with AB as the diameter. Now, extend a perpendicular from D to the circumference at C. The line CD represents the mean proportional,[43] or the geometric mean of length ratio $\frac{2}{1}$. In the geometric progression AD:CD:BD, the length CD represents the value of the second or middle term. Finally, organize this progression into the following proportion:

$$\frac{\text{AD}}{\text{CD}} = \frac{\text{CD}}{\text{BD}} \tag{10.7}$$

To verify that Equation 10.7 defines a geometric progression of lengths, suppose that AD = 1000.0 mm and BD = 500.0 mm. Place a ruler against the perpendicular, and note that CD = 707.1 mm. Substitute these lengths into Equation 10.7, and calculate — through simple division — the following *common ratio*[44] between terms:

$$\text{Common Ratio} = \frac{1000.0\ \text{mm}}{707.1\ \text{mm}} = \frac{707.1\ \text{mm}}{500.0\ \text{mm}} = 1.4142$$

That is, 500.0 mm × 1.4142 = 707.1 mm, and 707.1 mm × 1.4142 = 1000.0 mm. In modern notation, the common ratio equals the square root of the ratio of the outer two terms:

$$\text{Common Ratio} = \sqrt{\frac{1000.0 \text{ mm}}{500.0 \text{ mm}}} = \sqrt{\frac{2}{1}} \approx 1.4142$$

With a calculator, we may also compute the value of CD without resorting to geometry. Substitute the lengths of AD and BD into Equation 10.7, cross-multiply, and extract the square root of the right side of the equation:

$$\frac{1000.0 \text{ mm}}{\text{CD}} = \frac{\text{CD}}{500.0 \text{ mm}}$$

$$\text{CD}^2 = (1000.0 \text{ mm})(500.0 \text{ mm})$$

$$\text{CD} = \sqrt{(1000.0 \text{ mm})(500.0 \text{ mm})}$$

$$\text{CD} \approx 707.1 \text{ mm}$$

This example explains the origin of Equation 3.39A.

We may also compute a geometric mean directly. Refer to Equation 3.39A, substitute the dimensions $a = 1000.0$ mm and $c = 500.0$ mm into this equation, and calculate the geometric mean ($\mathit{\Lambda}_{\text{G}}$) of the "octave":

$$\mathit{\Lambda}_{\text{G}} = \sqrt{(1000.0 \text{ mm})(500.0 \text{ mm})} \approx 707.1 \text{ mm}$$

Next, arrange these three values in a descending geometric progression of string lengths 1000.0 mm : 707.1 mm : 500.0 mm, divide all three lengths by 500.0 mm, and organize the sequence 2.0 : 1.4142 : 1.0. Note that because the middle value represents the common ratio of a geometric progression (or the square root of the ratio of the outer two terms), this progression expresses an ascending sequence of identical musical intervals; in this case, a low "tritone" followed by a high "tritone," or $^{2.0}/_{1.4142}$ followed by $^{1.4142}/_{1.0}$.

To verify that the square root of 2 produces two identical musical intervals on a set of identically tuned canon strings, substitute the overall string length and this common ratio into Equation

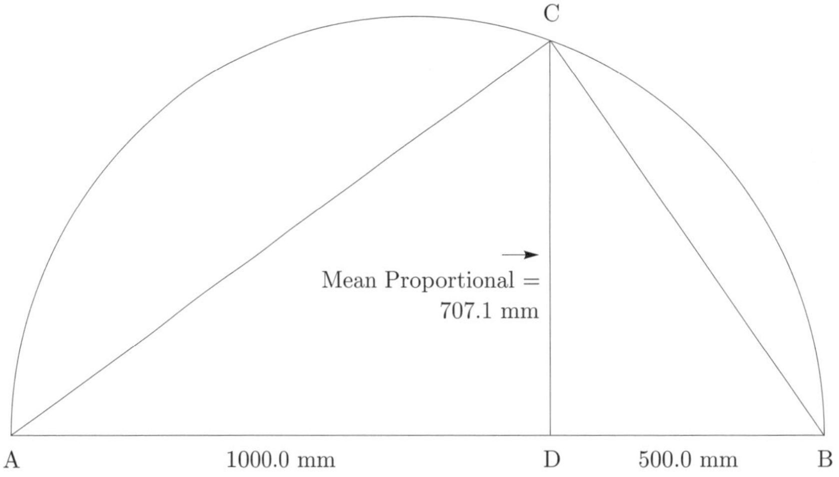

Figure 10.6 Euclid's method for the construction of a mean proportional between any two straight lines. This technique makes possible the calculation of an irrational square root. The geometric progression AD:CD:BD expresses the proportion AD:CD = CD:BD, where CD = $\sqrt{\text{AD} \times \text{BD}}$.

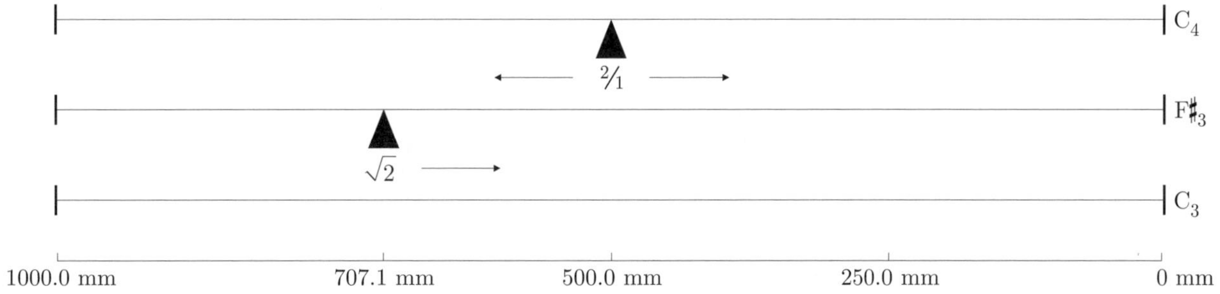

Figure 10.7 The geometric division of the "octave" expressed as ancient length ratio $^2\!/\!_1$. The bridge under the middle string at 707.1 mm represents the geometric mean of the "octave" between C_3–C_4. The division of the left section of the top string into two *unequal* subsections yields two *equal* musical intervals: the open and middle string produce a low "tritone" expressed as length ratio $^{2.0}\!/\!_{1.4142}$, and the middle and top string produce a high "tritone" expressed as length ratio $^{1.4142}\!/\!_{1.0}$.

3.32, and calculate the required length:

$$\Lambda_G = \frac{1000.0 \text{ mm}}{\sqrt{2}} \approx \frac{1000.0 \text{ mm}}{1.4142} = 707.1 \text{ mm}$$

Refer to Figure 10.7, and place a bridge at 707.1 mm from the right end of the middle string. The right section[45] of the middle string now sounds $F\sharp_3$, or the geometric division of the "octave" between C_3–C_4. Now, simultaneously play the open string and the right section of the middle string, and listen to the "tritone" between C_3–$F\sharp_3$; finally, play the right section of the middle string and the top string, and listen to the "tritone" between $F\sharp_3$–C_4. We conclude, therefore, that a geometric division of ancient length ratio $^2\!/\!_1$ has two consequences: (1) it divides the left section of the top string into two *unequal* subsections, and (2) it produces two *equal* musical intervals: a low "tritone" with respect to the open string, length ratio $^1\!/\!_1$, and a high "tritone" with respect to the top string, length ratio $^2\!/\!_1$.

Part IV

PHILOLAUS, EUCLID, ARISTOXENUS, AND PTOLEMY

~ 10.10 ~

Recall from the discussion in Section 10.6 that the first and last tones of a tetrachord are fixed and always sound the interval of a "fourth"; in contrast, the inner two tones are moveable according to the precepts of three different genera. Because the Greeks considered many different kinds of diatonic scales, in the following passage Nicomachus quotes Philolaus — the most venerated Pythagorean of antiquity — as an authority on the tuning of the diatonic tetrachord:

> The magnitude of *harmonia* is *syllaba* and *di'oxeian*. The *di'oxeian* is greater than the *syllaba* in epogdoic ratio. From *hypatē* [E] to *mesē* [A] is a *syllaba*, from *mesē* [A] to *neatē* [or *nete*, E|] is a *di'oxeian*, from *neatē* [E|] to *tritē* [later *paramese*, B] is a *syllaba*, and from *tritē* [B] to *hypatē* [E] is a *di'oxeian*. The interval between *tritē* [B] and *mesē* [A] is epogdoic, the *syllaba* is epitritic [4:3], the *di'oxeian* hemiolic [3:2], and the *dia pasōn* is duple [2:1]. Thus *harmonia* consists of five epogdoics and two dieses; *di'oxeian* is three epogdoics and a diesis, and *syllaba* is two epogdoics and a diesis.[46] (Text and ratios in brackets mine.)

	Hypate Meson	Parhypate Meson	Lichanos Meson	Mese	Trite (later, Paramese)	Trite Diezeugmenon	Paranete Diezeugmenon	Nete Diezeugmenon
	○	●	●	○	○	●	●	○
	E	F	G	A	B	C	D	E^{I}
Ancient Length Ratios, or Frequency Ratios:	$1/1$	$256/243$	$32/27$	$4/3$	$3/2$	$128/81$	$16/9$	$2/1$

Philolaus' Interval Ratios: $256/243$, $9/8$, $9/8$, ($9/8$), $256/243$, $9/8$, $9/8$

Figure 10.8 Philolaus' diatonic disjunct tetrachords as they occur in the standard Greek "octave" between E–E^{I}.

Philolaus spoke a Greek dialect called Doric, which explains his unusual vocabulary.[47] In this passage, Philolaus defines three intervals in ratio form:

$$\textit{Syllaba} = 4/3$$

$$\textit{Di'oxeian} = 3/2$$

$$\textit{Dia Pasōn} = 2/1$$

Two more interval descriptions are consistent with the latter definitions:

$$\textit{Harmonia} = 4/3 \times 3/2 = 2/1$$

$$\textit{Epogdoic Ratio} = 3/2 \div 4/3 = 9/8$$

Refer to Figure 10.1, and note that Philolaus calls the smallest interval of the diatonic genus, ratio $256/243$, a *diesis.*[48] With the exception of Philolaus, all ancient Greek and modern theorists refer to ratio $256/243$ as a *limma* (lit. *remainder*), or the interval that remains after one subtracts two "whole tones" from a "fourth":

$$\text{Two ``Whole Tones''} = \frac{9}{8} \times \frac{9}{8} = \frac{81}{64}$$

$$\text{Philolaus' } \textit{Diesis}\text{, or } \textit{Limma} = \frac{4}{3} \div \frac{81}{64} = \frac{4}{3} \times \frac{64}{81} = \frac{256}{243} = 90.2\ ¢$$

Finally, Philolaus' last sentence states

$$\textit{Harmonia} = \left(\frac{9}{8}\right)^5 \times \left(\frac{256}{243}\right)^2 = \frac{2}{1}$$

$$\textit{Di'oxeian} = \left(\frac{9}{8}\right)^3 \times \frac{256}{243} = \frac{3}{2}$$

$$\textit{Syllaba} = \left(\frac{9}{8}\right)^2 \times \frac{256}{243} = \frac{4}{3}$$

A		B		C		D		E		F		G		A^{I}		B^{I}		C^{I}		D^{I}		E^{I}		F^{I}		G^{I}		A^{II}
	(9/8)		256/243		9/8		9/8		256/243		9/8		9/8		(9/8)		256/243		9/8		9/8		256/243		9/8		9/8	

	E	F	G	A	B	C	D	E^{I}	(Standard Greek E–E^{I} Octave)
Dorian Mode:	1/1	256/243	32/27	4/3	3/2	128/81	16/9	2/1	

	C	D	E	F	G	A	B	C^{I}	(Standard Western C–C^{I} Octave)
Lydian Mode:	1/1	9/8	81/64	4/3	3/2	27/16	243/128	2/1	

Figure 10.9 Philolaus' diatonic scale in the Dorian and Lydian Modes. In Europe, variations of this scale lasted well into the 15th century.

Consider now Philolaus' *harmonia* in the context of the GPS. Begin by distributing five 9/8's and two 256/243's according to his note name descriptions. Figure 10.8 shows that Philolaus' diatonic scale consists of two disjunct tetrachords that span the standard Greek "octave" between E–E^{I}. According to Figure 10.4, Figure 10.8 shows this scale in the Dorian Mode. For a second perspective, refer to Figure 10.9, which illustrates Philolaus' diatonic scale distributed over the entire GPS, and in the context of the Dorian and Lydian Modes.

With respect to the two moveable tones of the lower tetrachord, interval ratio 9/8 that descends from 4/3 requires ancient length ratio $4/3 \div 9/8 = 32/27$; and interval ratio 9/8 that descends from 32/27 requires ratio $32/27 \div 9/8 = 256/243$. To calculate these two locations on the previously mentioned canon, substitute 1000.0 mm and these ratios into Equation 3.32, and make two calculations:

$$\Lambda = \frac{1000.0\text{ mm}}{\frac{32}{27}} = 843.8\text{ mm}$$

$$\Lambda = \frac{1000.0\text{ mm}}{\frac{256}{243}} = 949.2\text{ mm}$$

For the upper tetrachord, make two similar calculations for 16/9 and 128/81.

Finally, observe that in the Dorian Mode, Philolaus' diatonic scale forms a sequence of five descending 3/2's, and in the Lydian Mode, a sequence of five ascending 3/2's. If we simplify "octave" equivalents (see Section 9.4), these progressions emerge.

Dorian Mode: ↓ 2/1 [E], 4/3 [A], 16/9 [D], 32/27 [G], 128/81 [C], 256/243 [F]

Lydian Mode: ↑ 1/1 [C], 3/2 [G], 9/8 [D], 27/16 [A], 81/64 [E], 243/128 [B]

In Europe, variations of this scale lasted well into the 15th century. Why? Because despite its formidable appearance, musicians can quickly and accurately tune this scale by ear; that is, without the aid of a monochord.

Before we examine a tuning sequence for the Lydian Mode (or for the standard Western C–C^{I} "octave" range), let us first calculate the frequencies of the complete 8-tone scale. Suppose C_4 is tuned to 260.0 cps. According to Equation 3.30, the remaining frequencies are

$$D_4 = 260.0 \text{ cps} \times \frac{9}{8} = 292.5 \text{ cps}$$

$$E_4 = 260.0 \text{ cps} \times \frac{81}{64} = 329.1 \text{ cps}$$

$$F_4 = 260.0 \text{ cps} \times \frac{4}{3} = 346.7 \text{ cps}$$

$$G_4 = 260.0 \text{ cps} \times \frac{3}{2} = 390.0 \text{ cps}$$

$$A_4 = 260.0 \text{ cps} \times \frac{27}{16} = 438.8 \text{ cps}$$

$$B_4 = 260.0 \text{ cps} \times \frac{243}{128} = 493.6 \text{ cps}$$

$$C_5 = 260.0 \text{ cps} \times \frac{2}{1} = 520.0 \text{ cps}$$

To achieve these frequencies by ear, first tune F_4, G_4, and C_5 as $4/3$, $3/2$, and $2/1$ above C_4, respectively. Now, tune D_4, A_4, E_4, and B_4 through a sequence of descending "fourths" and ascending "fifths," starting on G_4 at 390.0 cps:

$$D_4 = \frac{390.0 \text{ cps}}{\frac{4}{3}} = 292.5 \text{ cps}$$

$$A_4 = 292.5 \text{ cps} \times \frac{3}{2} = 438.8 \text{ cps}$$

$$E_4 = \frac{438.8 \text{ cps}}{\frac{4}{3}} = 329.1 \text{ cps}$$

$$B_4 = 329.1 \text{ cps} \times \frac{3}{2} = 493.6 \text{ cps}$$

To this day, harpsichord and piano tuners use a similar technique of descending "fourths" and ascending "fifths" in the tuning of their instruments.[49] Undoubtedly, the ancient Greeks also employed such methods in tuning scales on the open strings of lyres, kitharas, and triangular harps.

~ 10.11 ~

The earliest known mathematical description of a systematic canon tuning is contained in a work entitled *Division of the Canon* by Euclid. The last two propositions of this treatise accurately describe the string divisions that produce a 15-tone "double-octave" tuning in the diatonic genus of the GPS. In the following passages, Euclid duplicates the intervals of the lower "octave" between A–A$^{|}$ in the upper "octave" between A$^{|}$–A$^{||}$:

> Proposition 19 *To mark out the kanōn according to the so-called immutable systēma*
>
> Let there be a length of the *kanōn* which is also the length AB of the string, and let it be divided into four equal parts, at C, D and E. Therefore BA,

> being the lowest, will be the bass note. Now this AB is the epitritic [1 + $1/3$, or 4:3] of CB, so that CB will be concordant [consonant] with AB at the fourth above it. And AB is *proslambanomenos* [A]: therefore CB is *diatonos hypatōn* [or *lichanos hypatōn*, D]. Again, since AB is double [2:1] BD, BD will be concordant with AB at the octave, and BD will be *mesē* [A′]. Again, since AB is quadruple [4:1] EB, EB will be *nētē hyperbolaiōn* [A″].
>
> I cut CB in half at F. CB will be double FB, so that CB is concordant with FB at the octave: hence FB is *nētē synēmmenōn* [should read *paranētē diezeugmenōn*, D′]. From DB I subtracted DG, a third part of DB. DB will be the hemiolic [1 + $1/2$, or 3:2] of GB, so that DB will be concordant with GB at the fifth. Therefore GB will be *nētē diezeugmenōn* [E′].
>
> I then constructed GH, equal to GB, so that HB will be concordant with GB at the octave, making HB *hypatē mesōn* [E]. From HB I subtracted HK, a third part of HB. HB will be the hemiolic of KB, so that KB is *paramesē* [B′]. I marked off LK, equal to KB, and LB will be the lower *hypatē* [B]. Thus we shall have found on the *kanōn* all the fixed notes of the immutable *systēma.*
>
> Proposition 20 *It remains to find the moveable notes*
>
> I divided EB into eight parts, and I constructed EM, equal to one of the parts, so that MB is the epogdoic [1 + $1/8$, or 9:8] of EB. Next, I divided MB into eight parts, and constructed NM, equal to one of these parts. Thus NB is a tone lower than BM, and MB is a tone lower than EB, so that NB will be *tritē hyperbolaiōn* [F′], and MB will be *diatonos hyperbolaiōn* [or *paranētē hyperbolaiōn*, G′]. I took a third part of NB and constructed NX, so the XB is the epitritic of NB, and is concordant with it at the fourth below: XB is *tritē diezeugmenōn* [C′]. Again, I took a half of XB and constructed XO, so that OB is concordant at the fifth with XB: therefore OB will be *parhypatē mesōn* [F]. And I constructed OP, equal to XO, so that PB becomes *parhypatē hypatōn* [C]. Finally, I found CR, a fourth part of BC, so that RB becomes *diatonos mesōn* [or *lichanos mesōn*, G].[50] (Text and ratios in brackets mine.)

Euclid's text contains several technical difficulties. (1) His reference to *nete synemmenon*, ratio $8/3$, is incorrect because he also defines *nete diezeugmenon*, ratio $3/1$, and *trite diezeugmenon*, ratio $64/27$. Since *tetrachord synemmenon* and *tetrachord diezeugmenon* do *not* exist in the same tuning system (see Figure 10.2), and since Euclid duplicates the intervals of the lower "octave" in the upper "octave," only the tones of *tetrachord diezeugmenon* are admissible. Hence, we must change *nete synemmenon* to read *paranete diezeugmenon.* (2) In Proposition 19, Euclid summarizes his discussion as a description of *fixed* tones, and in the heading of Proposition 20, he addresses the subject of *moveable* tones. However, in Proposition 19 he defines *lichanos hypaton*, ratio $4/3$, and *paranete diezeugmenon*, ratio $8/3$, which, in the context of the GPS, are *not* fixed tones, but moveable tones. (3) Finally, note carefully that Euclid refers to the third tones of tetrachords *hypaton, meson,* and *hyperbolaion not* as *lichanos, lichanos,* and *paranete*, respectively, but as *diatonos: diatonos hypaton*, ratio $4/3$, *diatonos meson*, ratio $16/9$, and *diatonos hyperbolaion*, ratio $32/9$. Compare the diatonic genus in Figure 10.1 to the distribution of tetrachords in Figure 10.10. Observe that the latter three tones — $4/3$ [D], $16/9$ [G], $32/9$ [G′] — produce the characteristic *diatonic* interval, ratio $9/8$, below the fourth tone of their respective tetrachords. Therefore, Euclid's substitution of the term *diatonos* identifies these tetrachords as belonging to the diatonic genus, that is

$$\text{D} = 3/2 \div 9/8 = 4/3$$
$$\text{G} = 2/1 \div 9/8 = 16/9$$
$$\text{G}^{\text{I}} = 4/1 \div 9/8 = 32/9$$

In Euclid's text, fourteen bridge locations depend on previously calculated results, which means he achieved his scale through a series of interdependent divisions. For example, Euclid states that from *DB* he subtracted *DG*, or a third part of *DB*, where *DB* represents the "octave," ratio $2/1$. Consequently, Figure 10.11(a) shows that on our sample string, *GB* has a length of 500.0 mm − (500.0 mm ÷ 3) = 333.3 mm. This example shows the process of shortening a string section by dividing a previously calculated length into three aliquot (exact) parts and *subtracting* one of those parts; the result is an ascending "fifth," interval ratio $3/2$, from A^{I} to E^{I}. We conclude, therefore, that *DB* is the *hemiolic* [1 + $1/2$] of *GB*, where *DB* has a length of 333.3 mm + (333.3 mm ÷ 2) = 500.0 mm. In contrast, Euclid also states that *MB* is the *epogdoic* [1 + $1/8$] of *EB*, where *EB* represents the "double-octave," ratio $4/1$. Consequently, Figure 10.11(b) shows that *MB* has a length of 250.0 mm + (250.0 mm ÷ 8) = 281.3 mm. This example shows the process of lengthening a string section by dividing a previously calculated length into eight aliquot parts and *adding* one of those parts; the result is a descending "whole tone," interval ratio $9/8$, from A^{II} to G^{I}. Euclid then states that *XB* is the *epitritic* [1 + $1/3$] of *NB*, where *NB* represents the "minor sixth," ratio $256/81$, in the upper "octave." Consequently, Figure 10.11(c) shows that *XB* has a length of 316.4 + (361.4 mm ÷ 3) = 421.9 mm. Again, this example demonstrates the process of lengthening a string section; the result is a descending "fourth," interval ratio $4/3$, from F^{I} to C^{I}. Figure 10.12 illustrates the string divisions in the order described by Euclid. Fourteen proportions in the left column show that Euclid's scale requires only five different length ratios, namely, $4/1$, $2/1$, $3/2$, $4/3$, and $9/8$.

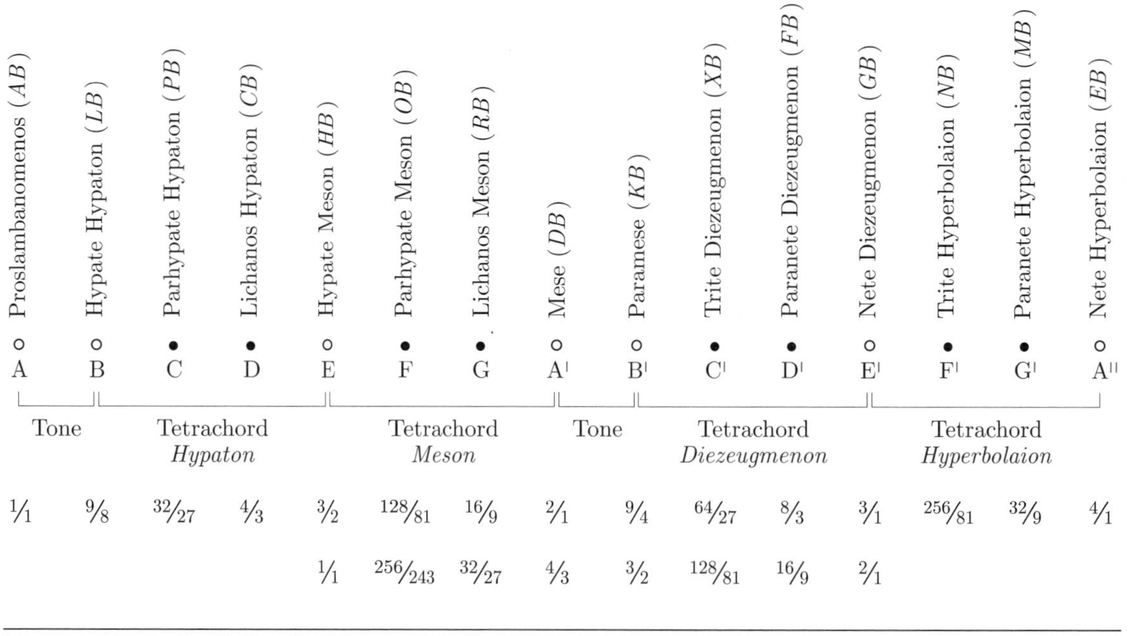

Figure 10.10 Euclid's "double-octave" diatonic scale in the GPS. Refer to Table 10.4 for modern length ratio → frequency ratio calculations in the first row of ratios between A–A^{II}. The second row of ratios between E–E^{I} shows that Euclid's scale consists of an extended version of Philolaus' scale. Letters in parentheses indicate Euclid's canon string sections.

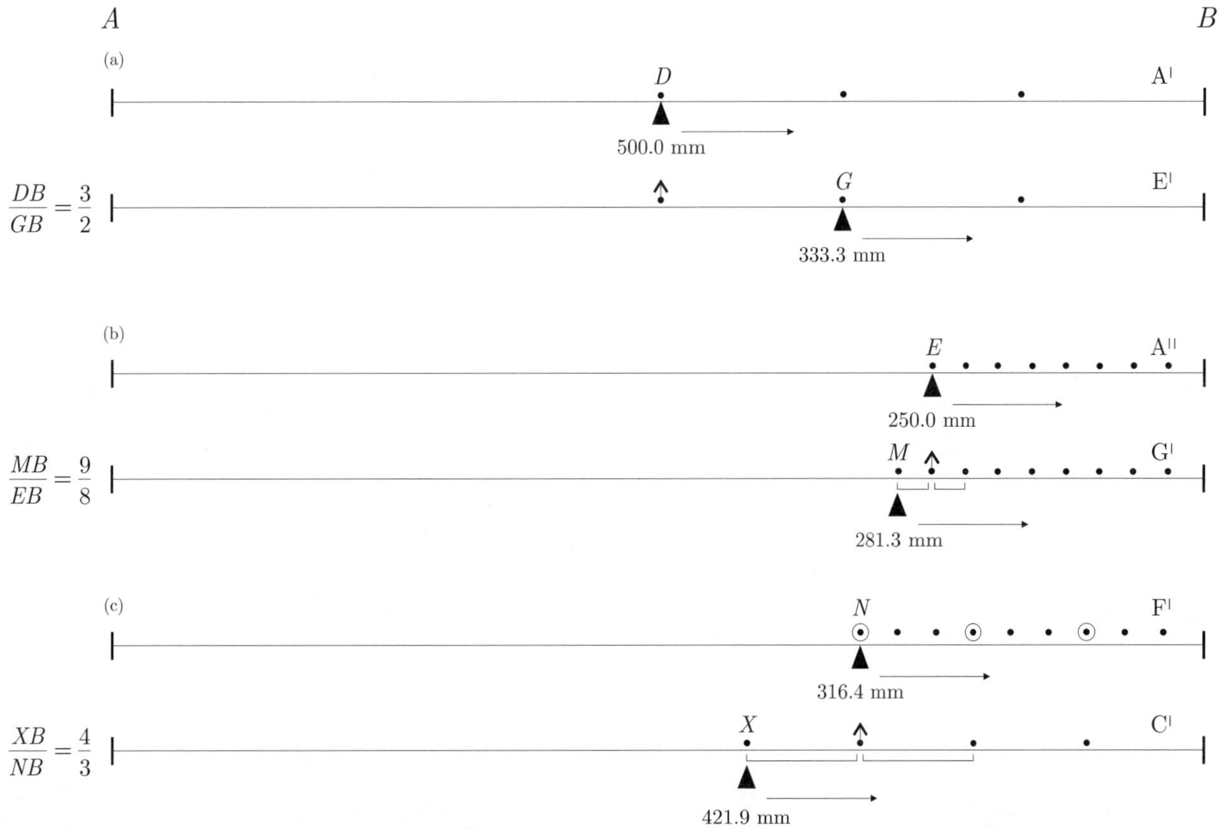

Figure 10.11 Three examples that demonstrate Euclid's canon tuning technique. (a) Euclid tuned the upper "fifth," length *GB*, by dividing the "octave," length *DB*, into three aliquot parts and subtracting one of those parts. (b) He tuned the upper "minor seventh," length *MB*, by dividing the second "octave," length *EB*, into eight aliquot parts and adding one of those parts. (c) Finally, he tuned the upper "minor third," length *XB*, by dividing the upper "minor sixth," length *NB*, into three aliquot parts and adding one of those parts. (Dots with arrows point to previously calculated divisions.)

With respect to length *MB*, ratio $^{32}\!/_9$ in the upper "octave," the utilization of length ratio $^9\!/_8$ is especially noteworthy. Euclid could have produced G| by first tuning D| — a "fifth," ratio $^3\!/_2$ — down from $^4\!/_1$, and then tuning G| — a "fourth," or ratio $^4\!/_3$ — up from $^8\!/_3$:

$$\text{D}^{|} = {}^4\!/_1 \div {}^3\!/_2 = {}^8\!/_3$$

$$\text{G}^{|} = {}^8\!/_3 \times {}^4\!/_3 = {}^{32}\!/_9$$

However, such a procedure would have violated the practice of defining the genus of a given tetrachord by tuning the characteristic interval as an interval that *descends* from the fourth tone to the third tone of the tetrachord. In this case, length ratio $^9\!/_8$ that descends from $^4\!/_1$ to $^{32}\!/_9$ defines the diatonic genus:

$$\text{G}^{|} = {}^4\!/_1 \div {}^9\!/_8 = {}^{32}\!/_9$$

Table 10.4 gives a detailed analysis of the calculations of the ratios below the bridges in Figure 10.12. As described in Section 3.7, I use arrows in this table to indicate the inverse proportionality between modern length ratio $^x\!/_n$ and frequency ratio $^n\!/_x$, or l.r. $^x\!/_n \rightarrow$ f.r. $^n\!/_x$. This technique provides a method of analysis that is universally applicable to all tuning descriptions based on string

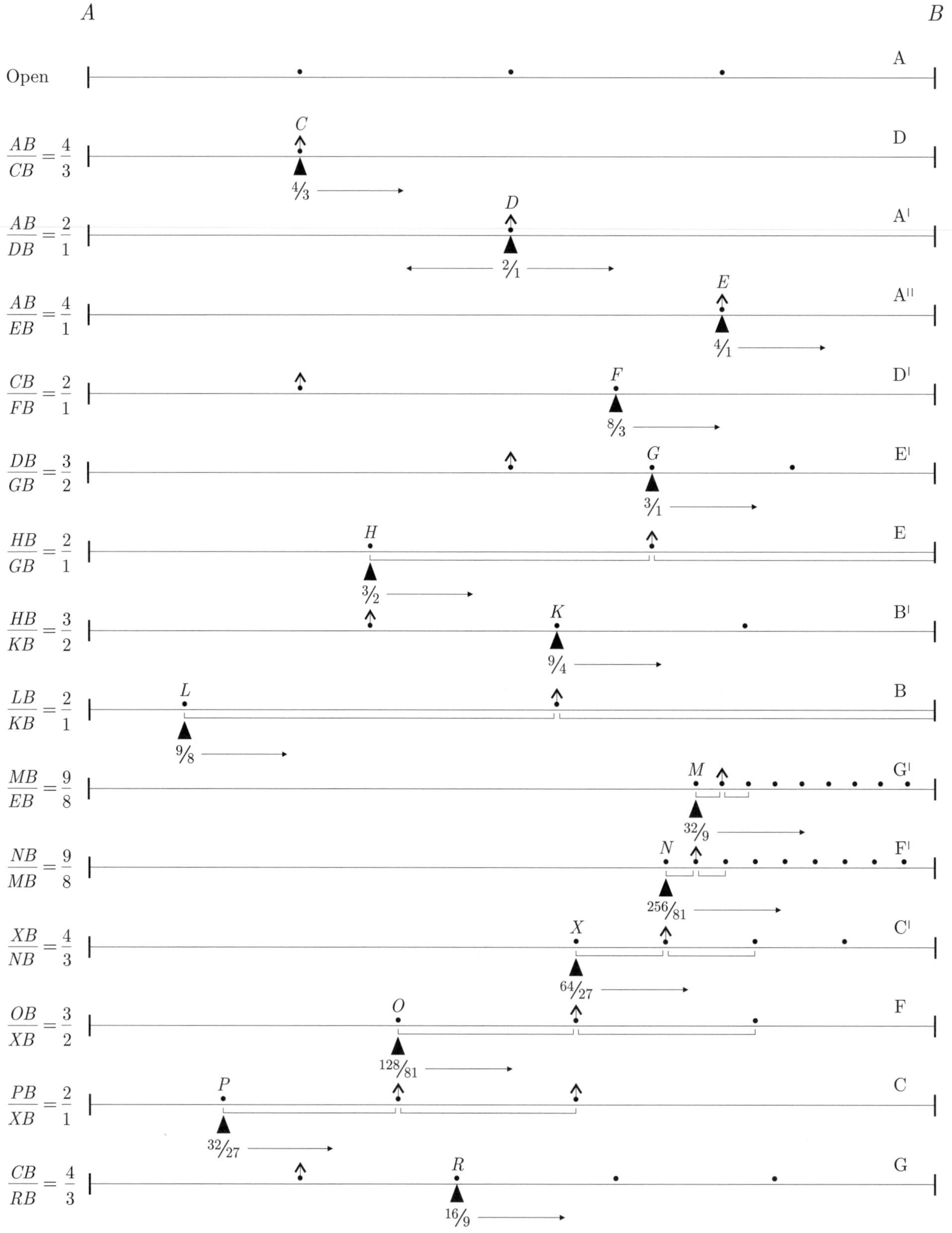

Figure 10.12 Ancient length ratios, or modern frequency ratios of Euclid's "double-octave" canon tuning. Fourteen proportions show that Euclid's scale consists of a series of interdependent string divisions that require only five different length ratios: 4⁄1, 2⁄1, 3⁄2, 4⁄3, and 9⁄8. (Dots with arrows point to previously calculated divisions.)

length divisions. For this reason, tables such as this also appear in Chapter 11 on world tunings. Finally, as discussed in Section 3.20, since ancient length ratio $^{n}/_{x}$ is indistinguishable from frequency ratio $^{n}/_{x}$, Table 10.4 represents an attempt to simplify the language of string division and ratio calculation. Provided we remember that in the writing of most creative theorist-musicians, (1) frequency ratios are a function of length ratios, and that in the context of interval divisions, (2) we must carefully distinguish between ancient length ratio $^{n}/_{x}$ and frequency ratio $^{n}/_{x}$, simplicity of language greatly enhances comprehension.

Table 10.4

MODERN LENGTH RATIO TO FREQUENCY RATIO CALCULATIONS OF EUCLID'S DIATONIC CANON TUNING

Letter *A*, Tone A	$^{1}/_{1}$	Whole string length.
Letter *C*, Tone D	$1 \times {^{3}/_{4}} = {^{3}/_{4}} \rightarrow {^{4}/_{3}}$	Three-quarters of string.
Letter *D*, Tone A^{I}	$1 \times {^{1}/_{2}} = {^{1}/_{2}} \rightarrow {^{2}/_{1}}$	Half of string.
Letter *E*, Tone A^{II}	$1 \times {^{1}/_{4}} = {^{1}/_{4}} \rightarrow {^{4}/_{1}}$	Quarter of string.
Letter *F*, Tone D^{I}	${^{3}/_{4}} \times {^{1}/_{2}} = {^{3}/_{8}} \rightarrow {^{8}/_{3}}$	Half of $^{3}/_{4}$ section.
Letter *G*, Tone E^{I}	${^{1}/_{2}} \times {^{1}/_{3}} = {^{1}/_{6}}$ ${^{1}/_{2}} - {^{1}/_{6}} = {^{3}/_{6}} - {^{1}/_{6}} = {^{2}/_{6}} = {^{1}/_{3}} \rightarrow {^{3}/_{1}}$	Third of $^{1}/_{2}$ section. $^{1}/_{2}$ section minus subsection.
Letter *H*, Tone E	${^{1}/_{3}} \times 2 = {^{2}/_{3}} \rightarrow {^{3}/_{2}}$	Double of $^{1}/_{3}$ section.
Letter *K*, Tone B^{I}	${^{2}/_{3}} \times {^{1}/_{3}} = {^{2}/_{9}}$ ${^{2}/_{3}} - {^{2}/_{9}} = {^{6}/_{9}} - {^{2}/_{9}} = {^{4}/_{9}} \rightarrow {^{9}/_{4}}$	Third of $^{2}/_{3}$ section. $^{2}/_{3}$ section minus subsection.
Letter *L*, Tone B	${^{4}/_{9}} \times 2 = {^{8}/_{9}} \rightarrow {^{9}/_{8}}$	Double of $^{4}/_{9}$ section.
Letter *M*, Tone G^{I}	${^{1}/_{4}} \times {^{1}/_{8}} = {^{1}/_{32}}$ ${^{1}/_{4}} + {^{1}/_{32}} = {^{8}/_{32}} + {^{1}/_{32}} = {^{9}/_{32}} \rightarrow {^{32}/_{9}}$	Eighth of $^{1}/_{4}$ section. $^{1}/_{4}$ section plus subsection.
Letter *N*, Tone F^{I}	${^{9}/_{32}} \times {^{1}/_{8}} = {^{9}/_{256}}$ ${^{9}/_{32}} + {^{9}/_{256}} = {^{72}/_{256}} + {^{9}/_{256}} = {^{81}/_{256}} \rightarrow {^{256}/_{81}}$	Eighth of $^{9}/_{32}$ section. $^{9}/_{32}$ section plus subsection.
Letter *X*, Tone C^{I}	${^{81}/_{256}} \times {^{1}/_{3}} = {^{27}/_{256}}$ ${^{81}/_{256}} + {^{27}/_{256}} = {^{108}/_{256}} = {^{27}/_{64}} \rightarrow {^{64}/_{27}}$	Third of $^{81}/_{256}$ section. $^{81}/_{256}$ section plus subsection.
Letter *O*, Tone F	${^{27}/_{64}} \times {^{1}/_{2}} = {^{27}/_{128}}$ ${^{27}/_{64}} + {^{27}/_{128}} = {^{54}/_{128}} + {^{27}/_{128}} = {^{81}/_{128}} \rightarrow {^{128}/_{81}}$	Half of $^{27}/_{64}$ section. $^{27}/_{64}$ section plus subsection.
Letter *P*, Tone C	${^{81}/_{128}} - {^{27}/_{64}} = {^{81}/_{128}} - {^{54}/_{128}} = {^{27}/_{128}}$ ${^{81}/_{128}} + {^{27}/_{128}} = {^{108}/_{128}} = {^{27}/_{32}} \rightarrow {^{32}/_{27}}$	*OX* section. $^{81}/_{128}$ section plus subsection.
Letter *R*, Tone G	${^{3}/_{4}} \times {^{1}/_{4}} = {^{3}/_{16}}$ ${^{3}/_{4}} - {^{3}/_{16}} = {^{12}/_{16}} - {^{3}/_{16}} = {^{9}/_{16}} \rightarrow {^{16}/_{9}}$	Quarter of $^{3}/_{4}$ section. $^{3}/_{4}$ section minus subsection.

10.12

The most controversial writer on Greek music was Aristoxenus (b. *c.* 360 B.C.). According to C. André Barbera,[51] many crucial words and ideas in Aristoxenus' book entitled *The Elements of Harmony* were originally defined in Euclid's *Elements.* Aristoxenus adopted these Euclidean concepts in direct opposition to Pythagorean extremists who subjected all aspects of sound and music to numbers. A generation earlier, Plato wrote of these Pythagoreans:

> They talk of something they call minims [*πυκνώματα* — *pyknomata* — or condensed tones] and, laying their ears alongside, as if trying to catch a voice from next door, some affirm that they can hear a note between and that this is the least interval and the unit of measurement, while others insist that the strings now render identical sounds, both preferring their ears to their minds.
>
> You, said I, are speaking of the worthies who vex and torture the strings and rack them on the pegs . . .[52] (Text in brackets mine.)

Similarly, Aristoxenus complained of musicians who engage in ". . . the massing of small intervals."[53] However, Aristoxenus also disagreed with Plato when he wrote

> The geometrician makes no use of his faculty of sense-perception. He does not in any degree train his sight to discriminate the straight line, the circle . . . But for the student of musical science accuracy of sense-perception is a fundamental requirement.[54]

Here Aristoxenus expresses the central theme of his treatise, namely, that the ear is the final arbiter of sound. His insistence on the pivotal role of the listener was so adamant, that throughout the entire discourse on the tuning of tetrachords, he gives not a single ratio in numeric form. Aristoxenus refused to quantify his divisions of the tetrachords by means of ratios and, thereby, relegated the tuning of his tetrachords to the discretion of the listener. Consequently, his entire work is completely open to interpretation. The following discussion will examine Aristoxenus from several different perspectives. The final decision as to what it all means is in the hands of the reader.

The single most important question at the core of *The Elements of Harmony* is, "Did Aristoxenus in theory or practice advocate the use of irrational numbers?" Despite all that has been written about Aristoxenus' musical ideas, including important works by R.P. Winnington-Ingram,[55] Malcolm Litchfield,[56] Richard L. Crocker,[57] and John H. Chalmers, Jr.,[58] this question remains unresolved. For Aristoxenus, there exists a very close relationship between geometric space and musical space. For example, Euclid's 23rd Definition states

> Parallel *straight lines are straight lines which, being in the same plane and being produced indefinitely in both directions, do not meet one another in either direction.*[59]

Sir Thomas L. Heath, the translator of this famous work, explains the term *indefinitely* in this way:

> . . . *εἰς ἄπειρον* [*eis apeiron*] . . . [means] "without limit," i.e. "indefinitely." Thus the expression is used of a magnitude being "infinitely divisible," or of a series of terms extending without limit.[60] (Text in brackets mine.)

Four times on three pages, Aristoxenus refers to high and low tones as ". . . distance[s] on the line of pitch . . ."[61] He then gives the following definition:

> An **interval**, on the other hand, is the distance bounded by two notes which have not the same pitch. For, roughly speaking, an interval is a difference between points of pitch, a space potentially admitting notes higher than the lower of the two points of pitch which bound the interval, and lower than the higher of them.[62]

And finally, with respect to the general divisions of tetrachords, Aristoxenus uses the Euclidean concept of ἄπειρους (*apeirous*) to describe the function of the *Lichanos*, or plural *Lichani:* the crucial and defining third tones of the two lower tetrachords of the GPS in Figure 10.2.

> For we must regard the Lichani as infinite in number.[63]

Litchfield analyzes these passages to mean

> Unlike the Pythagorean theorists, Aristoxenus did not use ratios to define the *loci* or positions of the moveable notes within the tetrachord. Instead, he postulated a potentially infinite continuum of musical pitch within which a specific segment represented the fourth.[64]
>
> It is reasonable to assume that he would admit an infinite progress since he compares pitch to a geometric line, and all lines in geometry are potentially infinite.[65]

With these fundamental geometric conceptualizations of sound in mind, Aristoxenus simply concluded

> Here we shall assume that its apparent value is correct [i.e., the value of the Fourth], and that it consists of two and a half tones.[66] (Text in brackets mine.)
>
> A tone is the excess of the Fifth over the Fourth; the Fourth consists of two tones and a half.[67]

He also defined ". . . three genera of melodies; Diatonic, Chromatic, and Enharmonic,"[68] and proceeded to use quarter-, third-, and half-tones to indicate the positions of the inner two moveable tones of the different tetrachords.

~ 10.13 ~

Because Aristoxenus decided that the "fourth" consists of "two and a half tones" exactly, many writers since the Renaissance interpret the reference to a "half-tone" as a geometric or tempered division of the tetrachord. As discussed in Section 10.8, an arithmetic division does *not* divide a given length ratio or frequency ratio into two equal interval ratios, or in this case, a "tone" into two equal "half-tones." Only a geometric division can perform such a feat. (See Section 10.9.) Furthermore, Table 10.5 shows Aristoxenus' *fractional parts* of a "tone" for six different tetrachords.

Cleonides (fl. *c.* A.D. 50), the most important Aristoxenian theorist of antiquity, arbitrarily assigned the "whole tone" 12 *integer parts* and, therefore, the "semitone" 6 parts; consequently, the "fourth," ratio $4/3$, consists of 6 parts + 12 parts + 12 parts = 30 parts.[69] Many theorists prefer to work with these parts. Table 10.6 shows 16 transformations of Aristoxenus' *fractional parts* into Cleonides' *integer parts;* here two intervals at 4.5 parts each are the only noninteger exceptions.

Table 10.5

ARISTOXENUS' TETRACHORDS IN GREEK ASCENDING ORDER

Enharmonic					
	$\frac{1}{4}$	+	$\frac{1}{4}$	+	2
Chromatic					
Soft	$\frac{1}{3}$	+	$\frac{1}{3}$	+	$1\frac{5}{6}$
Hemiolic	$\frac{3}{8}$	+	$\frac{3}{8}$	+	$1\frac{3}{4}$
Tonic	$\frac{1}{2}$	+	$\frac{1}{2}$	+	$1\frac{1}{2}$
Diatonic					
Soft	$\frac{1}{2}$	+	$\frac{3}{4}$	+	$1\frac{1}{4}$
Tense	$\frac{1}{2}$	+	1	+	1

Table 10.6

CLEONIDES' INTEGER PARTS OF ARISTOXENUS' TETRACHORDS

Enharmonic					
	3	+	3	+	24
Chromatic					
Soft	4	+	4	+	22
Hemiolic	4.5	+	4.5	+	21
Tonic	6	+	6	+	18
Diatonic					
Soft	6	+	9	+	15
Tense	6	+	12	+	12

Since the "fourth" equals 498.0 ¢, calculate the cent values of these x-number of parts by solving the following proportion for ¢:

$$\frac{x}{30} = \frac{¢}{498.0\ ¢}$$

$$\frac{x \times 498.0\ ¢}{30} = ¢$$

For example, when $x = 3$ parts, $¢ = 49.8\ ¢$. Therefore, a transformation of Cleonides' parts into cents yields the values in Table 10.7.

Table 10.7

Enharmonic					
	49.8 ¢	+	49.8 ¢	+	398.4 ¢
Chromatic					
Soft	66.4 ¢	+	66.4 ¢	+	365.2 ¢
Hemiolic	74.7 ¢	+	74.7 ¢	+	348.6 ¢
Tonic	99.6 ¢	+	99.6 ¢	+	298.8 ¢
Diatonic					
Soft	99.6 ¢	+	149.4 ¢	+	249.0 ¢
Tense	99.6 ¢	+	199.2 ¢	+	199.2 ¢

In his paper, Litchfield flatly states

> This geometric arrangement, however, cannot be empirically derived, and this is the crux. The only way to reproduce Aristoxenus' tunings in terms of actual pitches (a problem that did not concern him) is to use more sophisticated mathematics than were available to Aristoxenus . . . Using the mathematics available to him, Aristoxenus could never have represented the precise pitches indicated by his various tunings using numerals and ratios . . . Aristoxenus' geometric conception of pitch does not translate to geometric divisions on a string. It is impossible to divide a string into thirty parts so that the sonic intervals are equal.[70]
>
> Aristoxenus' concept is thus revealed as abstract; it could not be aurally demonstrated nor empirically derived.[71]

Litchfield's conclusion is based on the mathematical fact that one needs the thirtieth root of $4/3$,

$$\sqrt[30]{\frac{4}{3}} \approx 1.00964$$

to precisely calculate the Aristoxenian tetrachords. Indeed, if one adopts a strict reading of these tetrachordal divisions, then the Greeks could not have divided a set of canon strings in the manner prescribed by Aristoxenus. To calculate the thirtieth root of $4/3$ requires logarithms, which were unknown to the ancient Greeks. However, as an alternative, consider the possibility of assigning the value $4/3 = 500.0$ ¢. Such a small increase changes the cent values in Table 10.7 to the values in Table 10.8.

Table 10.8

Enharmonic					
	50.00 ¢	+	50.00 ¢	+	400.00 ¢
Chromatic					
Soft	66.67 ¢	+	66.67 ¢	+	366.67 ¢
Hemiolic	75.00 ¢	+	75.00 ¢	+	350.00 ¢
Tonic	100.00 ¢	+	100.00 ¢	+	300.00 ¢
Diatonic					
Soft	100.00 ¢	+	150.00 ¢	+	250.00 ¢
Tense	100.00 ¢	+	200.00 ¢	+	200.00 ¢

Now, since Archytas managed to calculate the cube root of two, and since Euclid provided a means to calculate the square roots of all real numbers — rational and irrational — the Greeks could have performed Aristoxenus' geometric divisions as specified in Table 10.8. Some readers may find this interpretation objectionable. The impossible often seems more logical than the possible. Nevertheless, the following discussion focuses on what the Greeks could have known, as opposed to what they did not know.

With the mathematical solutions provided by Archytas[72] and Euclid,[73] first calculate the four decimal ratios that are equivalent to 100.0 ¢, 50.0 ¢, 25.0 ¢, and 33.3 ¢:

$$\frac{\sqrt[3]{2}}{\sqrt[4]{2}} \approx 1.05946\text{:}\;\; \log_{10} 1.05946 \times 3986.314 \;=\; 100.0\ ¢$$

$$\sqrt{\frac{\sqrt[3]{2}}{\sqrt[4]{2}}} \approx 1.02930\text{:}\;\; \log_{10} 1.02930 \times 3986.314 \;=\; 50.0\ ¢$$

$$\sqrt[4]{\frac{\sqrt[3]{2}}{\sqrt[4]{2}}} \approx 1.01455\text{:}\;\; \log_{10} 1.01455 \times 3986.314 \;=\; 25.0\ ¢$$

$$\sqrt[3]{\frac{\sqrt[3]{2}}{\sqrt[4]{2}}} \approx 1.01944\text{:}\;\; \log_{10} 1.01944 \times 3986.314 \;=\; 33.3\ ¢$$

With these four decimal ratios, we may calculate all the required frequency ratios of the Aristoxenian tetrachords as shown in Table 10.8. The notion that Aristoxenus' tetrachords represent abstract divisions by default is, therefore, not correct.[74] For example, to calculate the frequency ratio and cents that are equivalent to 22 Parts, simply multiply

$$(1.05946)^3 \times (1.01944)^2 \;=\; 1.23588$$

$$\log_{10} 1.23588 \times 3986.314 \;=\; 366.67\ ¢$$

Therefore, according to Equation 3.32, the *Lichanos* of the Soft Chromatic Tetrachord requires a bridge

$$\frac{1000.0 \text{ mm}}{1.23588} = 809.1 \text{ mm}$$

from the right end of the sample string.

∼ 10.14 ∼

In the context of ancient Greek music theory, some readers may object to the cent values in Table 10.8, and to the final extraction of a cube root that results in the value 1.01944. For a different set of computations that do not involve cube root calculations, refer to Table 10.9. Note that the second, third, fourth, and seventh irrational numbers in the upper portion of Column 1 represent iterated (or nested) square root decimal ratios. For example, we may express the fourth irrational as

$$\sqrt{\sqrt{\sqrt{\sqrt{\frac{4}{3}}}}} = \sqrt[16]{\frac{4}{3}} \approx 1.018$$

All other ratios in this column are products of simple multiplication. Column 2 gives the cents of the decimal ratios in Column 1, and Column 3 compares the cent values in Column 2 to those in Table 10.7, rounded here to the nearest cent. The last entry in Column 3 shows a maximum difference of -20 ¢, which is smaller than Aristoxenus' tuning error as described in Section 10.15. Again, the purpose of these calculations is to refute the notion that Aristoxenus' tetrachords represent abstractions by default. Although it is highly unlikely that Aristoxenus used geometric divisions in theory or practice, the calculations in Table 10.9 show that the ancient Greeks could have constructed close approximations of quarter-, third-, and half-tone divisions on their canons. Finally, at the end of Section 10.18 we will discuss Ptolemy's observations that even experienced musicians had difficulties hearing tuning errors smaller than 10–15 ¢ on low-tensioned gut strings.

Table 10.9

Square Roots and Products	Cents	Cent Differences: [Table 10.7] − [Table 10.9, Column 2]
$\sqrt{4/3} \approx 1.155$	249 ¢	
$\sqrt{1.155} \approx 1.075$	125 ¢	
$\sqrt{1.075} \approx 1.037$	63 ¢	66 ¢ − 63 ¢ = 3 ¢
$\sqrt{1.037} \approx 1.018$	31 ¢	
$1.037 \times 1.018 = 1.056$	94 ¢	100 ¢ − 94 ¢ = 6 ¢
$\sqrt{1.056} \approx 1.028$	48 ¢	50 ¢ − 48 ¢ = 2 ¢
$\sqrt{1.028} \approx 1.014$	24 ¢	
$1.028 \times 1.014 = 1.042$	71 ¢	75 ¢ − 71 ¢ = 4 ¢
$1.056 \times 1.028 = 1.086$	143 ¢	149 ¢ − 143 ¢ = 6 ¢
$1.056^2 = 1.115$	188 ¢	199 ¢ − 188 ¢ = 11 ¢
$1.056^2 \times 1.028 = 1.146$	236 ¢	249 ¢ − 236 ¢ = 13 ¢
$1.056^3 = 1.178$	284 ¢	299 ¢ − 284 ¢ = 15 ¢
$1.056^3 \times 1.028 = 1.211$	331 ¢	349 ¢ − 331 ¢ = 18 ¢
$1.056^3 \times 1.037 = 1.221$	346 ¢	365 ¢ − 346 ¢ = 19 ¢
$1.056^4 = 1.244$	378 ¢	398 ¢ − 378 ¢ = 20 ¢
(1)	(2)	(3)

10.15

Ptolemy has been severely criticized for his string length computations of Aristoxenus' tetrachords.[75] Before we analyze these objections in full detail, refer to Table 10.10 for comparisons of arithmetic mean and geometric mean calculations on the sample string. According to these figures, the arithmetic mean of the "octave" expressed as length ratio 2/1 (or 1000.0 mm/500.0 mm) requires a bridge at 750.0 mm, whereas the geometric mean requires a bridge at 707.1 mm. Now, transfer the arithmetic mean of the first calculation into the numerator of the next calculation. Therefore, the

Table 10.10

Arithmetic Mean	Geometric Mean
Of 2/1: $\dfrac{1000.0 \text{ mm} + 500.0 \text{ mm}}{2} = 750.0 \text{ mm}$	Of 2/1: $\sqrt{(1000.0 \text{ mm})(500.0 \text{ mm})} \approx 707.1 \text{ mm}$
Of 4/3: $\dfrac{1000.0 \text{ mm} + 750.0 \text{ mm}}{2} = 875.0 \text{ mm}$	Of 4/3: $\sqrt{(1000.0 \text{ mm})(750.0 \text{ mm})} \approx 866.0 \text{ mm}$
Of 8/7: $\dfrac{1000.0 \text{ mm} + 875.0 \text{ mm}}{2} = 937.5 \text{ mm}$	Of 8/7: $\sqrt{(1000.0 \text{ mm})(875.0 \text{ mm})} \approx 935.4 \text{ mm}$
Of 16/15: $\dfrac{1000.0 \text{ mm} + 937.5 \text{ mm}}{2} = 968.8 \text{ mm}$	Of 16/15: $\sqrt{(1000.0 \text{ mm})(937.5 \text{ mm})} \approx 968.2 \text{ mm}$
Of 32/31: $\dfrac{1000.0 \text{ mm} + 968.8 \text{ mm}}{2} = 984.4 \text{ mm}$	Of 32/31: $\sqrt{(1000.0 \text{ mm})(968.8 \text{ mm})} \approx 984.3 \text{ mm}$

arithmetic mean of the "fourth" expressed as length ratio $\frac{4}{3}$ (or 1000.0 mm/750.0 mm) requires a bridge at 875.0 mm, whereas the geometric mean requires a bridge at 866.0 mm. Table 10.10 shows that for a sequentially decreasing progression of length ratios, the bridge locations of these two different means begin to converge! For example, the arithmetic mean of length ratio $\frac{8}{7}$ requires a bridge at 937.5 mm, and the geometric mean, a bridge at 935.4 mm; here the difference is 2.1 mm. Next, the arithmetic mean of length ratio $\frac{16}{15}$ requires a bridge at 968.8 mm, and the geometric mean, a bridge at 968.2 mm; here the difference is only 0.6 mm. However, because the arithmetic means represent rational numbers, and the geometric means represent irrational numbers, these two sets of numbers can never be identical. Mathematicians refer to values or lines that converge but never meet or intersect as asymptotes. In this case, there are arithmetic-geometric asymptotes for both length ratios and frequency ratios. For example, with respect to ratio $\frac{8}{7}$, the lower interval of the arithmetic mean equals

$$\frac{1000.0 \text{ mm}}{937.5 \text{ mm}} = \frac{16}{15} = 111.7 \text{ ¢}$$

whereas the lower interval of the geometric mean equals

$$\frac{1000.0 \text{ mm}}{935.4 \text{ mm}} \approx 1.0691 = 115.6 \text{ ¢}$$

Most musicians are unable to musically perceive an interval of only 3.9 ¢.

Aristoxenus' definitions regarding small intervals are as follows:

> The voice cannot differentiate, nor can the ear discriminate, any interval smaller than the smallest diesis . . .[76]
>
> The following fractions of a tone occur in melody: the half, called a semitone [or the smallest Diatonic diesis]; the third, called the smallest Chromatic diesis; the quarter, called the smallest Enharmonic diesis. ***No smaller interval than the last exists in melody*** [i.e., in music].[77] (Bold italics, and text in brackets mine.)

Table 10.7 shows that his Enharmonic diesis equals 49.8 ¢. For a writer who based his entire theory of music on sense perception, such a definition for the smallest melodic interval is not only intellectually arbitrary, but musically unsophisticated. Most musicians are able to distinguish two frequencies that produce an interval of 20 ¢. So, two questions naturally arise, "What was the purpose of this definition?" and "What did this definition accomplish?" At the end of Book II, Aristoxenus attempted a proof to show that the "fourth" consists of "two and a half tones."[78] Aristoxenus heard the final interval of this proof as a $\frac{3}{2}$ [702.0 ¢]. However, a ratio analysis shows that this interval is actually a $\frac{262144}{177147}$ [678.5 ¢]. To calculate the discrepancy between these two ratios, divide the former by the latter:

$$\frac{\frac{3}{2}}{\frac{262144}{177147}} = \frac{531441}{524288} = 23.5 \text{ ¢}$$

Furthermore, in Section 10.18 we will examine Ptolemy's proof that the "fourth" does *not* consist of "two and a half tones," but rather, that it is smaller. Recall from Section 10.10 that a "fourth" is composed of two "tones," or a ditone $\frac{81}{64}$, plus a limma, or $\frac{256}{243}$. Ptolemy's calculations prove that the limma represents the small portion, and the *apotome* (lit. *segment*), ratio $\frac{2187}{2048}$, represents the large portion of a "tone," ratio $9/8$. In other words, the limma [90.2 ¢] signifies a "small semitone," and the apotome [113.7 ¢], a "large semitone." To calculate the discrepancy between these two unequal "semitones" divide

$$\frac{\frac{2187}{2048}}{\frac{256}{243}} = \frac{531441}{524288} = 23.5\ ¢$$

Finally, Euclid[79] and Ptolemy[80] also challenged the assumption of the Aristoxenians that the "octave" consists of 6 "whole tones," and proved that it is smaller. In modern notation, the discrepancy equals

$$\frac{\left(\frac{9}{8}\right)^6}{\frac{2}{1}} = \frac{\frac{531441}{262144}}{\frac{2}{1}} = \frac{531441}{524288} = 23.5\ ¢$$

In all three cases, modern theorists refer to this discrepancy as the *comma of Pythagoras.*[81] Because this comma is less than half the size of the Enharmonic diesis, Aristoxenus simply ignored its existence, and never discussed the theoretical or practical significance of small discrepancies.

In Part V, we will examine how the *comma of Didymus* and the comma of Pythagoras played a crucial role in the development and evolution of meantone and equal temperaments. *These small yet significant discrepancies result from divisions with prime numbers.* For example, in the previous calculation we noted that 6 "whole tones" approximate 1 "octave." The mathematical reason for this approximation is that powers of prime factor 3 in the numerator ($3^2 = 9$) divided by prime number 2 in the denominator must, by definition, generate a remainder. In this context, a division of two different prime numbers generates a musical discrepancy, or a comma. Therefore, powers of prime factors 3 and 2 (as in $9/8$, $81/64$, . . .) cannot equal powers of prime factors of 2 and 3 (as in $4/3$, $16/9$, . . .), or powers of prime number 2 (as in $2/1$, $4/1$, . . .). With respect to the latter calculation, $9/8$ to the sixth power only approximates 2. The comma is by definition inevitable.

Aristoxenus managed to avoid these inconvenient by-products of prime number division by advocating quarter-, third-, and half-tone divisions of tonal "space." With fractional parts of tones, Aristoxenus was able to disregard the comma of Pythagoras, and evade an inevitable encounter with irrational numbers. As discussed in Part V, irrational numbers occur when one attempts to geometrically divide a given comma or musical interval into two or more equal parts. However, to seriously consider his abstraction, Aristoxenus was either unable or unwilling to hear this comma. If the former, he was not a musician, and if the latter, he was promulgating a cause. In either case, denial and dismissal of the comma is a fundamental requirement of Aristoxenian music theory. Furthermore, a close examination of the arithmetic-geometric asymptote, and the inherent inaccuracies of the ear with respect to small interval divisions, reveals that both the limitations and inclinations of human hearing work in Aristoxenus' favor. *As frequency ratios decrease, arithmetic divisions sound increasingly like geometric divisions.* [This fact did not escape Vincenzo Galilei, who adopted $18/17$ (99.0 ¢), or the lower interval of the arithmetic division of ancient length ratio $9/8$ (203.9 ¢), as a flat tempered "semitone" on his 12-tone lute. See Section 10.31.] Aristoxenus' fractional parts did not contradict his sense perceptions, because for very small interval ratios, the subtle aural differences between arithmetic divisions and geometric divisions seemed insignificant, or nonexistent. Finally, note that a "half-tone," or an "Exact semitone," exceeds a limma by a half-comma of Pythagoras, or by only 11.73 ¢:

$$\sqrt{\frac{9}{8}} \div \frac{256}{243} = \sqrt{\frac{531441}{524288}} = 11.73\ ¢$$

Therefore, since two "whole tones" plus a limma equal a "fourth,"

$$\frac{81}{64} \times \frac{256}{243} = \frac{4}{3} = 498.0\ ¢$$

we find that Aristoxenus' "two and a half tones" *actually* equal a "fourth" plus a half-comma:

$$\frac{81}{64} \times \sqrt{\frac{9}{8}} = \frac{4}{3} \times \sqrt{\frac{531441}{524288}} = 509.8\ ¢$$

Consequently, it seems Aristoxenus mistakenly heard arithmetic divisions as geometric divisions, and simply decided, in the absence of this half-comma discrepancy, that the "fourth" consists of 2½ "tones" exactly. That is, Aristoxenus either ignored, failed to experience, or failed to comprehend the fact that

$$\frac{81}{64} \times \sqrt{\frac{9}{8}} \neq \frac{4}{3}$$

On the other hand, most interpreters of Aristoxenus' treatise contend that any attempt to analyze the text according to rational ratios constitutes a distortion of the author's original intent. These writers claim that in Aristoxenus' definition

A tone is the excess of the Fifth over the Fourth . . .

all three intervals express fractional parts of tones, so that

Fifth − Fourth = 3½ Tones − 2½ Tones = 1 Tone

If this is the case, and if we are to endow these intervals with musical meaning, then Aristoxenus must have calculated geometric string divisions (i.e., irrational numbers) because no human being is able to tune such a "fifth," "fourth," or "tone" by simply listening to frequency ratios.

~ 10.16 ~

Ptolemy interpreted Aristoxenus' fractional parts of a tone as integer parts of a given string length. In other words, he gave these tetrachords an arithmetic interpretation. In Book II, Chapter 13, Ptolemy introduces the subject of tuning tetrachords on canon strings by defining the arithmetic mean, 90 parts, and the harmonic mean, 80 parts, of the "octave" expressed as ancient length ratio ²⁄₁, or 120 parts/60 parts.[82]

II

> . . . we have divided the string length from a common starting point to the lowest tone of the octave under consideration into 120 parts; the string a fourth higher is 90 [parts], {in *epitritic* ratio}, [4:3]; the string a fifth higher is 80 [parts], {in *hemiolic* ratio}, [3:2]; and the highest string of the octave is 60 [parts], {in *diplasios* ratio}, [2:1]. The moveable tones between them take their numbers in agreement with the ratios of each genus.[83] (Italics in braces, and text and ratios in brackets mine. Text in braces in Ptolemy's original text.)

Turn to Table 10.6 and note that Aristoxenus' Enharmonic Tetrachord requires the following three intervals in ascending order: 3 parts, 3 parts, and 24 parts. Since the first tone of the tetrachord, length ratio $^{1}/_{1}$, is the open string at 120 parts, locate the second tone by subtracting 3 parts from 120 parts; this gives 117 parts, or length ratio $^{120}/_{117} = {}^{40}/_{39} = 43.8$ ¢. Therefore, the interval between the first and second tones equals $^{40}/_{39}$ as well. Now, locate the third tone by subtracting 3 parts from 117 parts; this gives 114 parts, or length ratio $^{120}/_{114} = {}^{20}/_{19} = 88.8$ ¢. Therefore, the interval between the second and third tones equals

$$\frac{20}{19} \div \frac{40}{39} = \frac{20}{19} \times \frac{39}{40} = \frac{39}{38} = 45.0\ ¢$$

Finally, locate the fourth tone by subtracting 24 parts from 114 parts; this gives 90 parts, or length ratio $^{120}/_{90} = {}^{4}/_{3} = 498.0$ ¢. Therefore, the interval between the third and fourth tones equals

$$\frac{4}{3} \div \frac{20}{19} = \frac{4}{3} \times \frac{19}{20} = \frac{19}{15} = 409.2\ ¢$$

The illustration below shows these three divisions to scale.

In ascending order, an arithmetic division of Aristoxenus' Enharmonic Tetrachord yields intervals 43.8 ¢, 45.0 ¢, and 409.2 ¢. Table 10.7 shows that the geometric division of this tetrachord yields intervals 49.8 ¢, 49.8 ¢, and 398.4 ¢. Consequently, there exist differences of −6.0 ¢, −4.8 ¢, and +10.8 ¢, respectively, between these two sets of numbers. A further comparison of 15 Parts [249.0 ¢] of the Soft Diatonic Tetrachord in Table 10.7, and Ptolemy's $^{7}/_{6}$ [266.9 ¢] approximation in Section 10.20, Table 10.12, indicates a maximum difference of +17.9 ¢ for all the Aristoxenian tetrachords.

To many scholars, Aristoxenian tetrachords represent abstract divisions of acoustic space. With respect to the flawed proof at the end of Book II, Litchfield states

> Nevertheless, the discrepancy between theory and practice appears not to have bothered Aristoxenus . . . Aristoxenus' concept as he left it neither accommodates nor reflects musical reality. Perhaps he never performed the proof or simply felt the results to be close enough. If either were the case, it would be clear that accuracy in practice was not a major concern to Aristoxenus. Thus, the concept alone must have been Aristoxenus' concern, and he appears not as an empiricist but as a conceptualist or conceptual idealist.[84]

In other words, Aristoxenus' error was at worst a theoretical-conceptual mistake. However, when we compare Ptolemy's maximum error to Aristoxenus' error, the former is smaller than the latter; that is, 17.9 ¢ < 23.5 ¢. Furthermore, due to the proximities of the two different sets of enharmonic cent values, most musicians who listen to tetrachords on low-tension gut strings cannot distinguish errors less than 10–15 ¢. We conclude, therefore, that Ptolemy's *arithmetic approximation*, which he undoubtedly experienced and verified on his canon, constitutes an imperfect yet adequate *geometric representation* of Aristoxenus' tetrachord.

~ 10.17 ~

I believe there is serious doubt that Aristoxenus could have heard in his inner ear, or could have contemplated in his intellect, all that modern scholars have attributed to him. If taken literally, Aristoxenus used irrational numbers in the divisions of his tetrachords. Yet nowhere in his writings are there references to Archytas' or Euclid's monumental solutions. Of the ancient texts that survived, Theon of Smyrna is the only author who cited Euclid's Book VI, Proposition 13, for the computation of geometric means in a musical context.[85] Even so, not a single Greek author ever discussed the geometric divisions of tetrachords, or the computation of irrational ratios.

It seems that Aristoxenus did not reject arithmetic divisions in favor of geometric divisions, but rather, that he disapproved of the quantification and numeration of sound and music. In the following passage, Aristoxenus does not advocate one form of mathematical analysis over another:

> And of our answers we endeavor to supply proofs that will be in agreement with the phenomena — in this unlike our predecessors [i.e., the Pythagoreans]. For some of these introduced extraneous reasoning, and rejecting the senses as inaccurate fabricated rational principles, asserting that height and depth of pitch consist in certain numerical ratios and relative rates of vibration — a theory utterly extraneous to the subject and quite at variance with the phenomena.[86] (Text in brackets mine.)

Instead, his flawed proof, his convenient decision with respect to the smallest diesis, and his insistence that the ear is the final arbiter, all emphasize an individual's perception of sound, not scientific investigation. However, the question still remains, "How did Aristoxenus tune his tetrachords?" Recall the earlier definition, "A tone is the excess of the Fifth over the Fourth." So, with respect to the Enharmonic Tetrachord, Aristoxenus probably tuned two "tones" by ear down from $4/3$, and then divided the remaining "half-tone" by ear into two "quarter-tones." This technique resulted in either two vague arithmetic divisions or, conversely, in two imprecise geometric divisions.

Aristoxenus was probably aware of the arithmetic-geometric asymptote, and used the ear's inherent limitations and inclinations to convince his followers of the supreme importance of acoustic approximations. Furthermore, because Aristoxenus did not discuss the obvious and unavoidable byproducts of prime number division and, thereby, implied that the comma of Pythagoras either was unimportant or did not exist, his music theories represent oversimplifications at best. Perhaps Aristoxenus' private undisclosed knowledge of the comma explains his public refusal to use Pythagorean ratios, and why he chose instead to rely on verbal descriptions and quasi-mathematical definitions. This is ironic, because his ideas depend on mathematics. Even as a "conceptual idealist," Aristoxenus' definition of a "tone" is unintelligible without a foreknowledge of ratios in numeric form. As discussed in Section 10.7, if one performer prefers sharp "fourths" and "fifths," and another prefers flat "fourths" and "fifths," who is to say what a "tone" is?

~ 10.18 ~

It is difficult to imagine the history of music from the Arabian Renaissance and the European Renaissance to modern times without Ptolemy's *Harmonics*. Ptolemy (1) developed scientific methods for the investigation of musical ideas on elaborately constructed canons, (2) defined an enduring theory of relative consonance, and (3) discovered a rich variety of exceptionally beautiful scales. He also recorded an invaluable Catalog of Scales (see Section 10.20), which includes enharmonic, chromatic, and diatonic tetrachords of Archytas, Aristoxenus, Eratosthenes (*c.* 276 B.C. – *c.* 194 B.C.), and Didymus (fl. *c.* A.D. 50). In Section 10.21, we will discuss Gioseffo Zarlino, who recognized the musical importance of Ptolemy's Tense Diatonic, and passionately advocated its implementation. Today we know it as the just-intoned version of the major scale. Furthermore, in Chapter 11, Part IV, we will examine Ptolemy's indelible influence on Arabian music theory and terminology.

Recall that in Section 10.5, we examined Ptolemy's criticism of the Pythagoreans for not recognizing multiple-epimere ratio $8/3$ as a true consonance. In his book, Ptolemy also challenged the Pythagorean legend of weights suspended from strings. In Book I, Chapter 8, he observes

> Let us reject the attempt to base the proof we are seeking . . . on weights suspended from strings, since such demonstrations cannot reach the peak of precision, but serve rather as a source of controversy for those who undertake them.[87]

In other words, in Ptolemy's work one never encounters Nicomachus' "weight ratios" or "vibration ratios." (See Section 3.17.)

Before we discuss Ptolemy's scales in full detail, let us first examine his criticism of Aristoxenian music theory. In Section 10.12, we quoted Aristoxenus as stating that ". . . the Fourth consists of two tones and a half." Ptolemy demonstrated that because ". . . the limma is smaller than a half-tone,"[88] a "fourth" must also be smaller than "two and a half tones." To prove his point, Ptolemy used string length units for his analysis. For example, Ptolemy begins with a string, length ratio $1/1$, which has a length of 1536 units. According to Equation 3.33, a "tone" [$9/8$] below $1/1$ requires $1536 \times 9/8 = 1728$ units; similarly, a "second-tone" [$81/64$] below $1/1$ requires $1536 \times 81/64 = 1944$ units; a "fourth" [$4/3$] below $1/1$ requires $1536 \times 4/3 = 2048$ units; and a "third-tone" [$729/512$] below $1/1$ requires $1536 \times 729/512 = 2187$ units. The illustration to scale below shows how Ptolemy expressed the limma [$256/243$], or the interval between the "second-tone" and the "fourth," as ratio $2048/1944$.

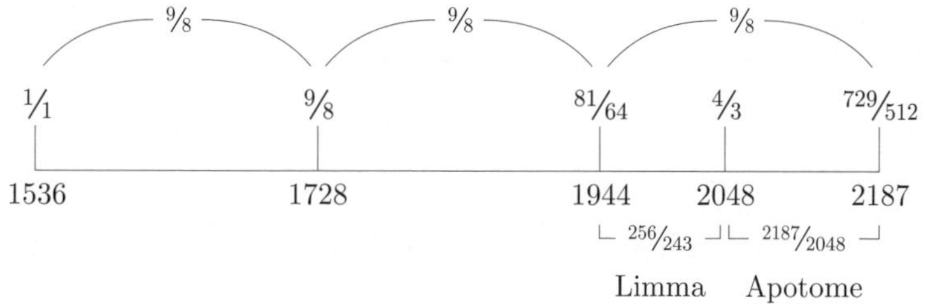

He referred to the limma as the smaller portion of the "third-tone." Now, as discussed in Section 10.15, the larger portion of the "third-tone" — the apotome, ratio $2187/2048$ [113.7 ¢] — exceeds the smaller portion of the "third-tone" — the limma, ratio $256/243$ [90.2 ¢] — by the comma of Pythagoras, ratio $531441/524288$ [23.5 ¢]. Although Ptolemy did not calculate this comma, he was, nevertheless, in a position to correctly argue that because of this discrepancy, ". . . the whole fourth is less than two and a half tones."[89]

To divide the "third-tone" — ratio $9/8$ [203.91 ¢] — into two "Exact semitones," we must first geometrically divide the comma into two exact halves; in other words, we must calculate the square root of the comma. If we then evenly distribute these two halves by "adding" a half-comma to the limma, and by "subtracting" a half-comma from the apotome, both of these intervals will equal an "Exact semitone." Therefore, to calculate this interval, multiply the former ratio by the half-comma, divide the latter ratio by the half-comma, and note that both ratios will then equal $203.91\ ¢ \div 2 = 101.96\ ¢$:

$$\text{“Exact semitone”} = \sqrt{\frac{9}{8}} = \frac{256}{243} \times \sqrt{\frac{531441}{524288}} = \frac{\frac{2187}{2048}}{\sqrt{\frac{531441}{524288}}} = 101.96\ ¢$$

In a startling development, Ptolemy continues this discussion with a simple numerical analysis that enabled him to conclude, ". . . the half-tone [i.e., the "Exact semitone"] is in a ratio very close to that of 258 to 243."[90] That is, Ptolemy proposed ratio

$$\text{“Ptolemy's semitone”} = \frac{258}{243} = 103.70\ ¢$$

as a "very close" rational approximation of the "Exact semitone." The difference between "Ptolemy's semitone" and the "Exact semitone" equals only 103.70 ¢ − 101.96 ¢ = 1.74 ¢, which means that these two ratios are musically indistinguishable and, for all practical purposes, identical. The next illustration to scale shows the proximity of these two intervals.

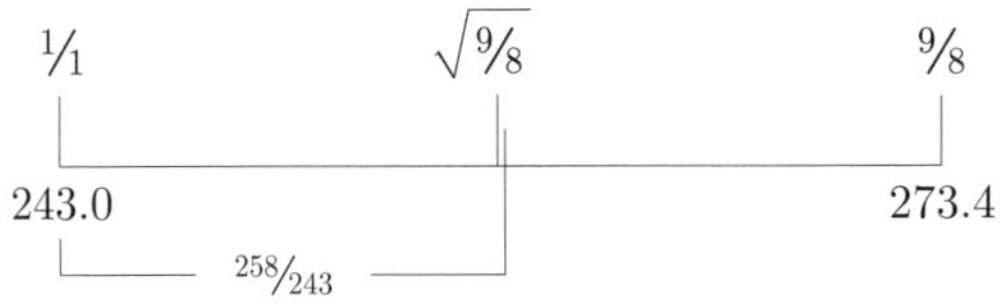

Finally, Ptolemy concludes that the discrepancy between his semitone and the limma is interval ratio $^{129}/_{128}$:

$$\frac{258}{243} \div \frac{256}{243} = \frac{258}{\cancel{243}} \times \frac{\cancel{243}}{256} = \frac{129}{128} = 13.47\ ¢$$

This discovery enabled Ptolemy to challenge the Aristoxenians:

> That so slight a variation [129:128] is capable of being judged by the hearing not even they would say.[91] (Ratio in brackets mine.)

Ptolemy proved that, in the absence of mathematical analysis, even the most careful and well-intentioned listener will produce conceptual mistakes and significant cumulative tuning errors. He argued that since the Aristoxenians did not perceive the interval between the limma and his semitone, they incorrectly defined the "fourth" as consisting of 2½ "tones" exactly. In the illustration to scale below, the ignored or missed interval, $^{129}/_{128}$, appears as the gap between $^{256}/_{243}$ and $^{258}/_{243}$.

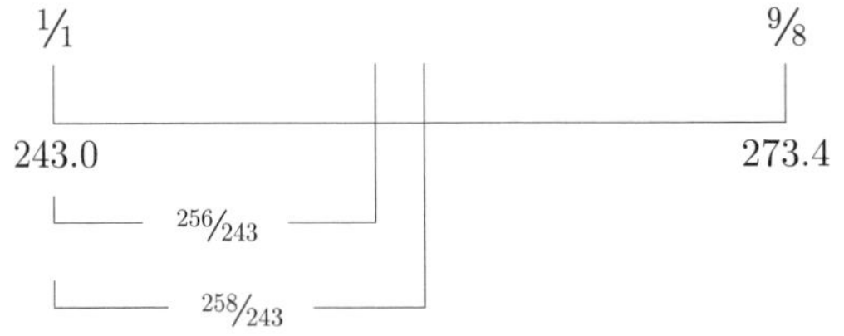

The mathematical beauty of Ptolemy's analysis is that it demonstrates a precise understanding for the distinction between rational numbers and irrational numbers. I have no doubt that Ptolemy could have calculated accurate rational length ratio approximations for all the irrational geometric "parts" of Aristoxenus' tetrachords. A table of rational approximations would have greatly aided the Aristoxenians in dividing canon strings. However, since Ptolemy did not pursue this argument beyond contesting Aristoxenus' "fourth," it seems highly unlikely that the Aristoxenians were interested in numbers, rational or irrational. In other words, if geometric divisions were commonplace in abstract theory or in musical practice, why would Ptolemy go through the trouble of calculating an extremely accurate rational approximation?

His refusal to accept Pythagorean and Aristoxenian orthodox teachings, coupled with a deep scientific and musical interest in carefully tuned canon strings, enabled Ptolemy to discard many ancient misconceptions, and to develop his own original ideas. In Book I, Chapter 8, he described the mathematical principles of canon tuning in full detail. In this context, he also explained an important technique for testing a ". . . [gut] string's evenness of constitution . . ."[92] to ensure that a player obtains consistent and accurate results. Finally, his interdisciplinary approach to sense perception and calculation also enabled Ptolemy to contemplate the physical limits of human hearing. Ptolemy's observation with respect to ratio $^{129}\!/_{128}$ suggests that Greek musicians experienced difficulties perceiving intervals smaller than 10–15 ¢ on low-tension gut canon strings.

10.19

Because many ancient texts were either lost or destroyed, and because many writers did not bother to explain theories of scale construction, we do not know how most Greek music theorists derived their tetrachords. However, in this respect, Ptolemy's work is a notable exception. In his book, Ptolemy carefully described a theory of relative or graduated consonance, which in turn provided him with a mathematical and musical basis for the division of tetrachords.

As discussed below, Ptolemy's theory of consonance consists of two parts: (1) the near-equal division of a given musical interval, and (2) with respect to epimore ratios, expressed by the formula $1 + {}^1\!/_x$, the proximity of the single part $^1\!/_x$ to unity. (See Table 10.2.) Let us begin by examining the latter aspect of the theory in full detail. Consider the following canon tuning description in the *Harmonics I.8:*

III

> . . . we will find that by moving the bridges to each point of division that the differences [in string lengths] of the produced tones will exactly agree with aural perception. If we assume that {EK is four parts of which KG is three}, then the tones of these string sections give the fourth {in *epitritic* ratio}, 4:3. If {EK is three parts of which KG is two}, then the tones of these string sections give the fifth {in *hemiolic* ratio}, 3:2. If again the whole length is divided in such a manner that {EK is two parts of which KG is one}, then the octave emerges {in *diplasios* ratio}, 2:1.[93] (Italics in braces, and text in brackets mine. Text in braces in Ptolemy's original text.)

Quote III describes the same musical intervals as Quote I. (See Section 10.8.) The only technical difference is that Quote I establishes the "octave," "fifth," and "fourth" as intervals between two canon strings, whereas Quote III establishes the "fourth," "fifth," and "octave" as intervals on only one canon string. To illustrate the latter technique, Ptolemy's text includes a line drawing very similar to Figure 10.13. This figure shows that it is possible to adjust a canon bridge so that the string sections on the left and right sides of the bridge produce a desired musical interval. In Quote III, Ptolemy describes the tuning of two epimore ratios, the "fourth" and the "fifth," and a multiple ratio, the "octave." Note that this method emphasizes the distinction between the first component, or 1, and the second component, or $^1\!/_x$, of all epimore ratios. For the "fourth" and "fifth," the first component consists of the right string sections as unity fractions $3/3$ and $2/2$, respectively, relative to the left string sections. Furthermore, for these two intervals, the second component is contained in the right sections as single parts $1/3$ and $1/2$, respectively, relative to the left sections. Hence the "fourth" is expressed as length ratio $3/3 + 1/3 = 4/3$, and the "fifth," as length ratio $2/2 + 1/2 = 3/2$. Consequently, for String I, EK exceeds KG by $1/3$ the length of KG; for String II, EK exceeds KG by $1/2$ the length of KG. In contrast, for String III, EK exceeds KG by the whole length of KG. Hence the duple, or the "octave," is expressed as length ratio $1/1 + 1 = 2/1$. (See Section 3.17.) As discussed below, formal calculations of the former single parts and of the latter whole length — which Ptolemy collectively called *excesses* — require subtraction. In Quote VIII, note that in this context of subtraction, Ptolemy also refers to the excesses as *differences.*

In the *Harmonics I.5*, Ptolemy describes the "octave" by stating

IV

> . . . of the ***consonant*** intervals the octave is most beautiful, and of the ratios the duple [2:1] is best; [1] the octave because it is closest to equal-tension tones [or unisons], and [2] the duple because only with this ratio is the excess equal to the {amount exceeded}. Furthermore, the octave consists of two consecutive symphonic intervals: the fifth and the fourth; and the duple consists of the ***first two consecutive epimores:*** ratios 3:2 and 4:3.[94] (Bold italics, ratio and numbers in brackets mine. Text in braces in Ptolemy's original text.)

Here Ptolemy acknowledges aural and mathematical reasons given by the Pythagoreans for the consonant quality of the "octave," expressed as length ratio $2/1$. Since Ptolemy repeats the latter

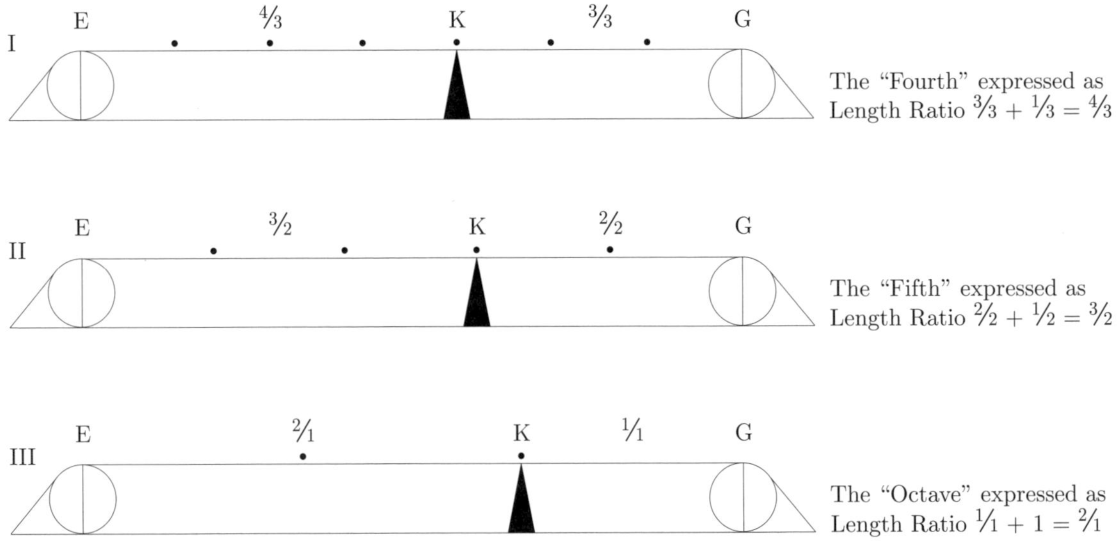

Figure 10.13 An illustration similar to Ptolemy's original line drawing designed to show the tuning of a "fourth," "fifth," and "octave" on one canon string. This technique requires that the string sections on the left and right sides of the bridge produce a desired musical interval. For String I, note that the left section exceeds the right section by a single part, or by $1/3$ the length of the right section; similarly, for String II, the left section exceeds the right section by a single part, or by $1/2$ the length of the right section. Finally, for String III, the left section exceeds the right section by the whole length of the right section.

reason in the *Harmonics I.7* — where he discusses his own theories of consonance — we find that Ptolemy completely agrees with the Pythagoreans on this issue. Condition 1 states that the "octave" is the finest consonance because it sounds most like a unison. Ptolemy refers to unisons as *equal-tension tones*, or to tones that have identical tension. For Ptolemy, tension acts as the most important variable in the tuning of open strings. As such, strings have four variables: density of stringing material, diameter, length, and tension. However, the two most popular stringed instruments of ancient Greece, the *kithara* and *lyre*, were equipped with strings of equal length that were exclusively played as unstopped or open strings. (See Section 11.48.) Consequently, after stringing such instruments, the first three variables become constants, which means that the only remaining variable — tension — accounts for differences in pitch.

Condition 2 states that length ratio 2:1 produces the finest consonance because it is the only ratio whose excess (the difference between numerator and denominator) is equal to the amount exceeded (the denominator). In Figure 10.13, String III shows that the excess of the left section over the right section equals $2 - 1 = 1$; in modern notation, $\frac{2}{1} - \frac{1}{1} = 1$.

Notice, therefore, that in Quote IV, Ptolemy associates proximity to sonorous unity, or the closeness of a given interval to the sound of a unison, with proximity to numeric unity, or the closeness of the excess of a given length ratio to unity. He concludes, therefore, that the "octave" satisfies the first condition based on aural perception, and the second condition based on mathematical calculation.

Before we apply these analytical techniques to other tones and ratios, let us first examine Ptolemy's classification of three basic kinds of intervals: the *homophonic* intervals, the *symphonic* intervals, and the *emmelic* (lit. *melodic*) intervals. In the *Harmonics I.7*, Ptolemy assigns to these intervals a hierarchical order of relative musical quality:

V

> Due to their excellent quality, in first place we put the homophonic intervals, in second place, the symphonic intervals, and in third place, the melodic intervals.
>
> There is a clear distinction between the octave and double-octave and the other symphonic intervals, as there is between the latter and the melodic intervals. For this reason, they are more appropriately called homophonic intervals. We define the homophonic intervals as those, which, when taken together, give the impression of a single tone, like the octave and those intervals composed of octaves. The symphonic [intervals] follow the homophonic [intervals] most closely, like the fifth and fourth, and those composed of these and of the homophonic intervals. The melodic [intervals] follow the symphonic [intervals] most closely, like the whole-tones and other similar intervals. Therefore, the homophonic intervals are somehow composed by combining symphonic intervals, and the symphonic intervals, by combining melodic intervals.[95] (Text in brackets mine.)

Refer back to Section 10.4, Equations 10.2 and 10.3, and note that Ptolemy defines the homophonic intervals as *multiple* ratios, and the symphonic intervals as the first two *epimore* ratios, respectively. Ptolemy's observations regarding these intervals are in basic agreement with the Pythagorean theory of consonance as discussed in Section 10.5. However, in a clear departure from tradition, Ptolemy also considered the musical qualities of epimore ratios smaller than $\frac{4}{3}$. The Pythagoreans classified these epimores *en masse* as dissonant ratios. In contrast, Ptolemy's last sentence emphasizes a parallel relationship between the function of symphonic intervals with respect to homophonic intervals, and the function of melodic intervals with respect to symphonic intervals.

In the next paragraph of the *Harmonics I.7*, Ptolemy synthesizes the definitions and categories described in Quotes IV and V. He restates the Pythagorean concept of consonance as applied to the "octave," but also introduces the idea of relative or graduated consonance as applied to *unequal-tension tones*, or non-unisons.

VI

> We take the same starting point as the Pythagoreans, that is, we assign equal numbers [1:1, 2:2, 3:3, etc.] to equal-tension tones [unisons], and unequal numbers [2:1, 3:2, 4:3, etc.] to unequal-tension tones [non-unisons], which after all is entirely natural. Consequently, from this starting point, we measure the existing differences of the unequal-tension tones according to the degree to which they ***come close to complete equality*** [sonorous and numeric unity]. It is immediately apparent that ratio 2:1 is closest to complete accord [sonorous unity] because the excess is equal to the {amount exceeded}. Of the homophonic intervals, the octave is the most unitary [closest to numeric unity] and the most beautiful interval [closest to sonorous unity] . . .[96] (Bold italics, text and ratios in brackets mine. Text in braces in Ptolemy's original text.)

With regard to the "octave," length ratio ²⁄₁, Ptolemy echoes the musical and mathematical conditions for consonance stated in Quote IV. However, with respect to the concept of relative consonance, he now expands his definition to include unequal-tension tones, or non-unisons. Ptolemy declares that proximity to sonorous unity, and therefore proximity to numeric unity, provide a means by which to evaluate the consonant musical qualities of *all* tones and ratios. As discussed in the next chapter, this ubiquitous approach toward the classification of consonances profoundly influenced the writings of Arabian music theorists who flourished between A.D. 900 and 1300. (See Chapter 11, Part IV.)

Before Ptolemy describes his classification of melodic intervals, he makes a preliminary observation with regard to the symphonic intervals:

VII

> After ratio 2:1, the numbers that are closest to complete accord are those that most nearly divide it into two [equal] parts, i.e. 3:2 and 4:3.[97] (Text in brackets mine.)

Refer to Section 10.8, and note that we must here distinguish between an exactly equal division of a canon string, and a nearly equal division of the corresponding musical interval. For example, in Figure 10.5(b) the C_4 string demonstrates the division of a string that produces the "octave" above the open C_3 string. A vertical arrow at 750.0 mm indicates the exact center of the length whose left and right ends are stopped at 1000.0 mm and 500.0 mm, respectively. Such an arithmetic division of ancient length ratio ²⁄₁ produces two intervals that most nearly divide it into two equal *rational numbers* or rational parts: a lower "fourth," ratio ⁴⁄₃, and an upper "fifth," ratio ³⁄₂. (See the column labeled Arithmetic Mean in Table 10.10.) Now, according to Quote VI, Ptolemy observed a direct relationship between the magnitude of the excess or difference of a given length ratio and the consonant quality of the corresponding musical interval; that is, the larger the size of the excess, the closer it is to unity, and therefore, the more consonant the interval sounds to human ears. The proximity of the excess to unity constitutes the crux of Ptolemy's theory of relative or graduated consonance. With this concept in mind, we may now calculate the proximities of these two intervals to unity, and thereby evaluate their relative consonant qualities. In Figure 10.13, for String I the excess of length ratio $^4/_3$ equals $4 - 3 = 1$; with respect to the denominator 3, a difference of 1 equals $^1/_3$ of 3. (In modern notation, $^4/_3 - ^3/_3 = ^1/_3$.) And for String II the excess of length ratio $^3/_2$ equals $3 - 2 = 1$; with respect to the denominator 2, a difference of 1 equals $^1/_2$ of 2. (In modern notation, $^3/_2 - ^2/_2 = ^1/_2$.) Since $^1/_2$ is closer to unity than $^1/_3$, Ptolemy's theory of graduated consonance states that the "fifth" is more consonant than the "fourth." We conclude, therefore, that the following series of intervals represents a *graduated progression of relative consonance:* $^2/_1$, $^3/_2$, $^4/_3$. This conceptualization marked a clear departure from Pythagorean theory, where all intervals are categorized as either absolute consonances or absolute dissonances.

Ptolemy did not end his analysis here, but extended his theory to include the most important aspect of music making the world over: melody. The dynamic relationship between near-equal division and proximity to unity inspired Ptolemy to divide not only the "octave," but also the "fourth," or the definitive interval of Western scale construction. Furthermore, he also devised a method to compare the relative melodic qualities of intervals that result from such divisions. In the *Harmonics I.7*, Ptolemy simply states

VIII

> After ratio 4:3, the ratios that come closest to complete accord are those that divide it into proportional {excesses}, i.e., ***the smaller epimores.*** With regard to their value, after the symphonic [intervals] come the melodic [intervals], like the whole-tone, and those which make up the smallest symphonic intervals. We identify these as epimore ratios that are smaller than 4:3. Of these, [1] those that divide the latter most nearly into two [equal] parts are — for the same reason — more melodic; [2] also, [the more melodic ratios are] those whose {differences} consist of larger single parts of {the amounts exceeded}. These [small epimores] also come closest to complete accord, just as the half is nearest of all, then the third, ***and so on in sequence.***[98] (Bold italics, and text and numbers in brackets mine. Text in braces in Ptolemy's original text.)

In this passage, Ptolemy gives two conditions for comparing the melodic qualities of two epimore ratios smaller than $^4/_3$. Condition I follows logically from Quote VII, only in this context, the interval meant for division is not the "octave," but the "fourth." An exactly equal division of length ratio $^4/_3$ results in the arithmetic progression 8:7:6, which produces two nearly equal intervals: a lower "large major second," ratio $^8/_7$ [231.2 ¢], and an upper "small minor third," ratio $^7/_6$ [266.9 ¢]. Condition 2 also follows logically from Quote VII. Here, however, Ptolemy does not consider proximity to unity as a standard for evaluation, but rather, differences or excesses that consist of larger single parts of the denominators. For example, the difference of the "small minor third" consists of $^7/_6 - ^6/_6 = ^1/_6$; and the difference of the "large major second" consists of $^8/_7 - ^7/_7 = ^1/_7$. Now, since a single part $^1/_6$ of a unit long is larger than a single part $^1/_7$ of a unit long, Ptolemy's theory of melody states that the "small minor third" is more melodic than the "large major second." So, consistent with this mathematical analysis, the following potentially infinite series of epimores smaller than $^4/_3$ expresses a *graduated progression of relative melodiousness:* $^5/_4$, $^6/_5$, $^7/_6$, $^8/_7$, $^9/_8$, $^{10}/_9$, $^{11}/_{10}$, . . .

Since Greek music theorists based their definitions of three different genera exclusively on divisions of the tetrachord, or the "fourth," Ptolemy did not contemplate the division of the "fifth." An exactly equal division of length ratio $^3/_2$ results in the arithmetic progression 6:5:4, which produces two nearly equal intervals: a lower "minor third," ratio $^6/_5$ [315.6 ¢], and an upper "major third," ratio $^5/_4$ [386.3 ¢]. Because these two consonances are crucially important to the history of Western music theory, I included them in the previous graduated series of epimores. For example, a calculation of the excess of length ratio $^5/_4$ equals $^5/_4 - ^4/_4 = ^1/_4$, and the excess of length ratio $^6/_5$ equals $^6/_5$ –

$\frac{5}{5} = \frac{1}{5}$. Since $\frac{1}{4}$ is closer to unity than $\frac{1}{5}$, Ptolemy's theory of relative consonance states that ratio $\frac{5}{4}$ is more consonant than ratio $\frac{6}{5}$. Or stated differently, since a single part $\frac{1}{4}$ of a unit long is larger than a single part $\frac{1}{5}$ of a unit long, Ptolemy's theory of relative melodiousness states that the "major third" is more melodic than the "minor third." Finally, in the last sentence of Quote VIII, Ptolemy refers to the two symphonic intervals, or to the two large epimores first mentioned in Quote IV. (See also Equation 10.3.) First, he describes the "fifth" with an excess of $\frac{1}{2}$, and then the "fourth" with an excess of $\frac{1}{3}$. Therefore, it is highly likely that the "major third" with an excess of $\frac{1}{4}$, and the "minor third" with an excess of $\frac{1}{5}$, follow next in his sequence of graduated consonances.

With respect to the history of consonance and dissonance, the Arabian theorist Al-Fārābī (d. *c.* 950) incorporated Ptolemy's hierarchical order of homophonic, symphonic, and emmelic intervals into his own writings, and interpreted the concept of graduated consonance to include the 5-limit "major third," and the 5-limit "minor third." (See Section 11.57.) Ibn Sīnā (980–1037) and Ṣafī Al-Dīn (d. 1294) also classified ratios $\frac{5}{4}$ and $\frac{6}{5}$ as bona fide consonances. However, European theorists did not begin to accept the former ratio as a consonance until the 15th century (see Section 10.36), nor the latter ratio until the 16th century (see Section 10.46).

Finally, Table 10.12 compares the intervalic divisions of the diatonic genus to those of the enharmonic and chromatic genera. For the diatonic genus, most intervals between the first and third tones approximate near-equal division because they consist of various kinds of "minor thirds." In contrast, the intervals between the first and third tones of the enharmonic and chromatic genera consist primarily of various kinds of "minor seconds" and "major seconds," respectively. Therefore, Ptolemy's theory also implies that the diatonic genus is more melodic than the enharmonic and chromatic genera. Approximately two thousand years later, we find that Ptolemy was correct. The highly melodic and singable quality of Ptolemy's Tense Diatonic is the principal reason why it will survive into the 21st century as the Western major scale. (See Section 10.21.)

10.20

With these concepts in mind, let us now examine Ptolemy's tetrachords in full detail. Ptolemy begins his discussion by defining two different kinds of intervals contained in a given tetrachord:

IX

> The enharmonic and chromatic [genera] are characterized by the so-called *pyknon*, when the two lower intervals together are smaller than the upper [interval] alone; the diatonic [genus], by the so-called *apyknon*, when none of the three intervals is greater than the two remaining [intervals] together.[99] (Text in brackets mine.)

First, Ptolemy acknowledges an ancient definition of the *pyknon*[100] (lit. *close* or *compressed*). Refer to Figure 10.1 and note that for a typical chromatic and enharmonic tetrachord, the two lower intervals together are *smaller than* the remaining upper interval. In the enharmonic tetrachord example, the *pyknon* consists of a "semitone," or $\frac{32}{31} \times \frac{31}{30} = \frac{16}{15}$, which is smaller than the upper "major third," or $\frac{5}{4}$; and in the chromatic tetrachord example, the *pyknon* consists of a "small whole tone," or $\frac{20}{19} \times \frac{19}{18} = \frac{10}{9}$, which is smaller than the upper "minor third," or $\frac{6}{5}$. Second, Ptolemy also defines a new interval that he calls the *apyknon*. Figure 10.1 shows that a typical diatonic tetrachord does not have a *pyknon*. Consequently, Ptolemy found it necessary to invent the *apyknon*, or the opposite condition when the two lower intervals are *larger than* the upper interval. (Apparently, Ptolemy did not restrict the position of this interval, but defined all two-interval combinations of a diatonic tetrachord as *apyknons.*) In the diatonic tetrachord example, the *apyknon* consists of a "small minor third," or $^{256}/_{243} \times {}^{9}/_{8} = {}^{32}/_{27}$, which is larger than the upper "whole tone," or $^{9}/_{8}$. As discussed below, for Ptolemy the *apyknon* best defines the characteristic feature of his diatonic tetrachords.

If we label the lower, middle, and upper intervals in the following manner:

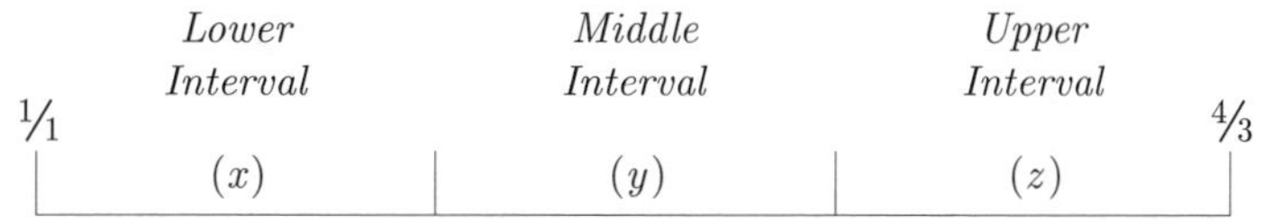

then Figure 10.14 shows a modern interpretation of the generalized size and specific location of the *pyknon* and *apyknon* in Ptolemy's tetrachords.

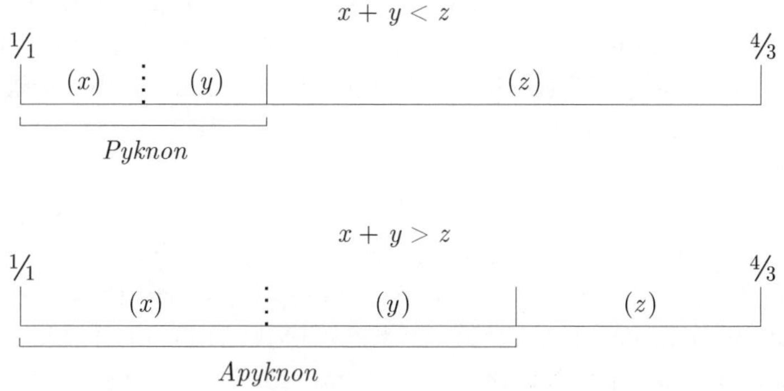

Figure 10.14 Modern interpretation of the generalized size and specific location of the *pyknon* and *apyknon* in Ptolemy's tetrachords. Music theorists associate the traditional *pyknon* with enharmonic and chromatic tetrachords, and Ptolemy's *apyknon*, with diatonic tetrachords.

Finally, Ptolemy cites the following three principles that govern the divisions of all his tetrachords:

X

> In agreement with the verification of the senses, we also assume that for all genera [1] the lower of the intervals are smaller than every one of the remaining [intervals]; [2] especially, however, for those which have a *pyknon*, that the two lower intervals together are smaller than the upper [interval]; [3] for the genera with an *apyknon*, that none of the intervals is larger than the two remaining [intervals] together.[101] (Text and numbers in brackets mine.)

Interval variables x, y, and z enable us to summarize these principles in modern notation.

Principle 1. $x < y;\ x < z$

Principle 2. $x + y < z$

Principle 3. $x + y > z;\ x + z > y;\ y + z > x$

Ptolemy then continues his analysis in the *Harmonics I.15* by stating that we must first divide ratio $4/3$, as many times as possible, into two epimore ratios. He observes that of all possible interval ratio combinations, only three pairs of epimores exist that, when multiplied together, equal ratio $4/3$, namely, $16/15 \times 5/4 = 4/3$; $10/9 \times 6/5 = 4/3$; and $8/7 \times 7/6 = 4/3$. Given these combinations, Ptolemy explains that his tetrachords with *pyknons* have ratios $16/15$, $10/9$, and $8/7$ as lower intervals, and with *apyknons*, ratios $7/6$ and $6/5$ as lower intervals.

Enharmonic Tetrachord: $\mathbf{16/15} \times 5/4 = 4/3$
Soft Chromatic Tetrachord: $\mathbf{10/9} \times 6/5 = 4/3$
Tense Chromatic Tetrachord: $\mathbf{8/7} \times 7/6 = 4/3$

Soft Diatonic Tetrachord: $\mathbf{7/6} \times 8/7 = 4/3$
Tense Diatonic Tetrachord: $\mathbf{6/5} \times 10/9 = 4/3$

To arithmetically divide these *pyknons* and *apyknons* into two smaller intervals, he then employs the mathematical technique shown in Table 10.11. For example, Table 10.11, Row 1, shows how Ptolemy derived his Enharmonic Tetrachord. Begin by arithmetically dividing the $16/15$ *pyknon* into three near-equal intervals. That is, multiply $16/15 \times 3/3 = 48/45$, insert two missing integers, and organize the arithmetic progression 48:47:46:45. Now, because 47 does not make epimore ratios with both outer terms (here $48/47$ is an epimore, but $47/45$ is not an epimore), Ptolemy rejected this number, and chose instead number 46 for the derivation of the lower and middle intervals. This number gives epimores $46/45$, and $48/46 = 24/23$. Since Principle 1 states that $x < y$ and $x < z$, Ptolemy designated $46/45$ as the lower interval, and $24/23$ as the middle interval. Table 10.11, Rows 2–5, summarize similar calculations and distributions of intervals for four other tetrachords. In all rows, the last entries give the three interval ratios of a given tetrachord in ascending order.

Table 10.11

PTOLEMY'S TETRACHORD DERIVATIONS

Ptolemy's Arithmetic Divisions of Three *Pyknons*					Interval Ratios
Enharmonic: $\mathbf{16/15}$	$16 \times 3 = 48$ $15 \times 3 = 45$	48:~~47~~:46:45	$48/46$, $46/45$	$48/46 = 24/23$	$46/45$, $24/23$, $5/4$
Soft Chromatic: $\mathbf{10/9}$	$10 \times 3 = 30$ $9 \times 3 = 27$	30:~~29~~:28:27	$30/28$, $28/27$	$30/28 = 15/14$	$28/27$, $15/14$, $6/5$
Tense Chromatic: $\mathbf{8/7}$	$8 \times 3 = 24$ $7 \times 3 = 21$	24:~~23~~:22:21	$24/22$, $22/21$	$24/22 = 12/11$	$22/21$, $12/11$, $7/6$

Ptolemy's Arithmetic Divisions of Two *Apyknons*					Interval Ratios
Soft Diatonic: $\mathbf{7/6}$	$7 \times 3 = 21$ $6 \times 3 = 18$	21:20:~~19~~:18	$21/20$, $20/18$	$20/18 = 10/9$	$21/20$, $10/9$, $8/7$
Tense Diatonic: $\mathbf{6/5}$	$6 \times 3 = 18$ $5 \times 3 = 15$	18:~~17~~:16:15	$18/16$, $16/15$	$18/16 = 9/8$	$16/15$, $9/8$, $10/9$

Note that Ptolemy did not contemplate a diatonic tetrachord with *apyknon* ratio $\frac{5}{4}$ because such a construction would have resulted in interval ratios $\frac{15}{14}$, $\frac{7}{6}$, $\frac{16}{15}$, or in two "semitones" separated by a "small minor third." Figure 10.1 shows that such a sequence does not produce a diatonic tetrachord.

In Table 10.12, Ptolemy's derivation of the Tonic Diatonic Tetrachord is as follows. Of the two diatonic tetrachords in Table 10.11, ratio $\frac{9}{8}$ is the only "whole tone" that does not appear as the upper interval. Because $\frac{4}{3} \div \frac{9}{8} = \frac{32}{27}$, Ptolemy rejects the latter *apyknon* for further division because it is not an epimore. Furthermore, he observes that in the Tense Diatonic Tetrachord, the "small whole-tone," ratio $\frac{10}{9}$, has already been conjoined with $\frac{9}{8}$. Therefore, he chooses the "large whole-tone," ratio $\frac{8}{7}$, as the middle interval of his tetrachord, because it is the only kind of "whole tone" that has not yet been conjoined with $\frac{9}{8}$. Ptolemy then multiplies these two latter intervals together, $\frac{8}{7} \times \frac{9}{8} = \frac{9}{7}$, and divides $\frac{4}{3}$ by the product: $\frac{4}{3} \div \frac{9}{7} = \frac{28}{27}$, which gives him the lower epimore of the tetrachord. In ascending order, the interval ratios of his Tonic Diatonic Tetrachord are $\frac{28}{27}$, $\frac{8}{7}$, $\frac{9}{8}$.

Ptolemy called his last, and possibly his favorite tetrachord, the Even Diatonic Tetrachord. In the *Harmonics I.16*, he calculates this tetrachord by arithmetically dividing the "fourth" into three near-equal intervals. However, before Ptolemy explains this unique derivation, he contemplates a genus based on the arithmetic division of the "fourth" into two near-equal intervals:

XI

> In addition, the division of the whole tetrachord into two ratios occurs when two consecutive ratios of nearly equal size, namely 7:6 and 8:7, divide the whole distance between the extremes in half. For the indicated reasons [see Quotes VI, VII, and VIII], this genus seems very pleasant to the ears. We find still another such genus when we proceed with [the concept of] equality in the proportions between tones, and examine whether another suitable combination can be made within the fourth that initially divides it into three nearly equal ratios, with [nearly] equally great excesses [i.e., epimore ratios: $1 + \frac{1}{x}$]. Such a genus is expressed by the ratios 10:9, 11:10, 12:11; we obtain it by tripling the . . . {numbers} . . . of ratio 4:3, a calculation that gives us the number sequence 9, 10, 11, 12, together with the consecutive ratios mentioned.[102] (Bold italics, and text and ratios in brackets mine. Text in braces in Ptolemy's original text.)

Ptolemy's Derivation of the Even Diatonic Tetrachord			Interval Ratios
Even Diatonic: $\frac{4}{3}$	$4 \times 3 = 12$ $3 \times 3 = 9$	12:11:10:9	$\frac{12}{11}$, $\frac{11}{10}$, $\frac{10}{9}$

Below, I give three possible derivations of the arithmetic divisions of *pyknons* in tetrachords by Eratosthenes and Didymus. Unlike Ptolemy's six tetrachord derivations that consist of preliminary divisions of *pyknons* and *apyknons* into three near-equal intervals, the latter three derivations consist of *pyknon* divisions into two near-equal intervals.

Possible Derivation of Eratosthenes' Enharmonic Tetrachord				Interval Ratios
Pyknon of Enharmonic: 4/3 ÷ 19/15 = **20/19**	20 × 2 = 40 19 × 2 = 38	40:39:38	40/39, 39/38	40/39, 39/38, 19/15

Possible Derivation of Didymus' Enharmonic Tetrachord				Interval Ratios
Pyknon of Enharmonic: 4/3 ÷ 5/4 = **16/15**	16 × 2 = 32 15 × 2 = 30	32:31:30	32/31, 31/30	32/31, 31/30, 5/4

Possible Derivation of Eratosthenes' Chromatic Tetrachord				Interval Ratios
Pyknon of Chromatic: 4/3 ÷ 6/5 = **10/9**	10 × 2 = 20 9 × 2 = 18	20:19:18	20/19, 19/18	20/19, 19/18, 6/5

Finally, Table 10.12 gives Ptolemy's complete catalog of scales in his *Harmonics II.14*.[103]

Table 10.12

PTOLEMY'S CATALOG OF SCALES

Greek Enharmonic Scales

Archytas Enharmonic

1/1		**28/27**		**16/15**		**4/3**		**3/2**		**14/9**		**8/5**		**2/1**
0 ¢		*63.0 ¢*		*111.7 ¢*		*498.0 ¢*		*702.0 ¢*		*764.9 ¢*		*813.7 ¢*		*1200.0 ¢*
	28/27		36/35		5/4		9/8		28/27		36/35		5/4	
	63.0 ¢		*48.8 ¢*		*386.3 ¢*		*203.9 ¢*		*63.0 ¢*		*48.8 ¢*		*386.3 ¢*	

Aristoxenus and Eratosthenes Enharmonic

1/1		**40/39**		**20/19**		**4/3**		**3/2**		**20/13**		**30/19**		**2/1**
0 ¢		*43.8 ¢*		*88.8 ¢*		*498.0 ¢*		*702.0 ¢*		*745.8 ¢*		*790.8 ¢*		*1200.0 ¢*
	40/39		39/38		19/15		9/8		40/39		39/38		19/15	
	43.8 ¢		*45.0 ¢*		*409.2 ¢*		*203.9 ¢*		*43.8 ¢*		*45.0 ¢*		*409.2 ¢*	

Didymus Enharmonic

1/1		**32/31**		**16/15**		**4/3**		**3/2**		**48/31**		**8/5**		**2/1**
0 ¢		*55.0 ¢*		*111.7 ¢*		*498.0 ¢*		*702.0 ¢*		*756.9 ¢*		*813.7 ¢*		*1200.0 ¢*
	32/31		31/30		5/4		9/8		32/31		31/30		5/4	
	55.0 ¢		*56.8 ¢*		*386.3 ¢*		*203.9 ¢*		*55.0 ¢*		*56.8 ¢*		*386.3 ¢*	

Ptolemy Enharmonic

1/1		**46/45**		**16/15**		**4/3**		**3/2**		**23/15**		**8/5**		**2/1**
0 ¢		*38.1 ¢*		*111.7 ¢*		*498.0 ¢*		*702.0 ¢*		*740.0 ¢*		*813.7 ¢*		*1200.0 ¢*
	46/45		24/23		5/4		9/8		46/45		24/23		5/4	
	38.1 ¢		*73.7 ¢*		*386.3 ¢*		*203.9 ¢*		*38.1 ¢*		*73.7 ¢*		*386.3 ¢*	

Table 10.12
(continued)

Greek Chromatic Scales

Archytas Chromatic

1/1		**28/27**		**9/8**		**4/3**		**3/2**		**14/9**		**27/16**		**2/1**
0 ¢		*63.0 ¢*		*203.9 ¢*		*498.0 ¢*		*702.0 ¢*		*764.9 ¢*		*905.9 ¢*		*1200.0 ¢*
	28/27		243/224		32/27		9/8		28/27		243/224		32/27	
	63.0 ¢		*140.9 ¢*		*294.1 ¢*		*203.9 ¢*		*63.0 ¢*		*140.9 ¢*		*294.1 ¢*	

Aristoxenus Soft Chromatic

1/1		**30/29**		**15/14**		**4/3**		**3/2**		**45/29**		**45/28**		**2/1**
0 ¢		*58.7 ¢*		*119.4 ¢*		*498.0 ¢*		*702.0 ¢*		*760.6 ¢*		*821.4 ¢*		*1200.0 ¢*
	30/29		29/28		56/45		9/8		30/29		29/28		56/45	
	58.7 ¢		*60.8 ¢*		*378.6 ¢*		*203.9 ¢*		*58.7 ¢*		*60.8 ¢*		*378.6 ¢*	

Aristoxenus Hemiolic Chromatic

1/1		**80/77**		**40/37**		**4/3**		**3/2**		**120/77**		**60/37**		**2/1**
0 ¢		*66.2 ¢*		*135.0 ¢*		*498.0 ¢*		*702.0 ¢*		*768.1 ¢*		*836.9 ¢*		*1200.0 ¢*
	80/77		77/74		37/30		9/8		80/77		77/74		37/30	
	66.2 ¢		*68.8 ¢*		*363.1 ¢*		*203.9 ¢*		*66.2 ¢*		*68.8 ¢*		*363.1 ¢*	

Aristoxenus Tonic Chromatic and Eratosthenes Chromatic

1/1		**20/19**		**10/9**		**4/3**		**3/2**		**30/19**		**5/3**		**2/1**
0 ¢		*88.8 ¢*		*182.4 ¢*		*498.0 ¢*		*702.0 ¢*		*790.8 ¢*		*884.4 ¢*		*1200.0 ¢*
	20/19		19/18		6/5		9/8		20/19		19/18		6/5	
	88.8 ¢		*93.6 ¢*		*315.6 ¢*		*203.9 ¢*		*88.8 ¢*		*93.6 ¢*		*315.6 ¢*	

Didymus Chromatic

1/1		**16/15**		**10/9**		**4/3**		**3/2**		**8/5**		**5/3**		**2/1**
0 ¢		*111.7 ¢*		*182.4 ¢*		*498.0 ¢*		*702.0 ¢*		*813.7 ¢*		*884.4 ¢*		*1200.0 ¢*
	16/15		25/24		6/5		9/8		16/15		25/24		6/5	
	111.7 ¢		*70.7 ¢*		*315.6 ¢*		*203.9 ¢*		*111.7 ¢*		*70.7 ¢*		*315.6 ¢*	

Ptolemy Soft Chromatic

1/1		**28/27**		**10/9**		**4/3**		**3/2**		**14/9**		**5/3**		**2/1**
0 ¢		*63.0 ¢*		*182.4 ¢*		*498.0 ¢*		*702.0 ¢*		*764.9 ¢*		*884.4 ¢*		*1200.0 ¢*
	28/27		15/14		6/5		9/8		28/27		15/14		6/5	
	63.0 ¢		*119.4 ¢*		*315.6 ¢*		*203.9 ¢*		*63.0 ¢*		*119.4 ¢*		*315.6 ¢*	

Ptolemy Tense Chromatic

1/1		**22/21**		**8/7**		**4/3**		**3/2**		**11/7**		**12/7**		**2/1**
0 ¢		*80.5 ¢*		*231.2 ¢*		*498.0 ¢*		*702.0 ¢*		*782.5 ¢*		*933.1 ¢*		*1200.0 ¢*
	22/21		12/11		7/6		9/8		22/21		12/11		7/6	
	80.5 ¢		*150.6 ¢*		*266.9 ¢*		*203.9 ¢*		*80.5 ¢*		*150.6 ¢*		*266.9 ¢*	

Table 10.12
(continued)

Greek Diatonic Scales

Archytas Diatonic and Ptolemy Tonic Diatonic

1/1	28/27	32/27	4/3	3/2	14/9	16/9	2/1
0 ¢	63.0 ¢	294.1 ¢	498.0 ¢	702.0 ¢	764.9 ¢	996.1 ¢	1200.0 ¢

28/27	8/7	9/8	9/8	28/27	8/7	9/8
63.0 ¢	231.2 ¢	203.9 ¢	203.9 ¢	63.0 ¢	231.2 ¢	203.9 ¢

Aristoxenus Soft Diatonic

1/1	20/19	8/7	4/3	3/2	30/19	12/7	2/1
0 ¢	88.8 ¢	231.2 ¢	498.0 ¢	702.0 ¢	790.8 ¢	933.1 ¢	1200.0 ¢

20/19	38/35	7/6	9/8	20/19	38/35	7/6
88.8 ¢	142.4 ¢	266.9 ¢	203.9 ¢	88.8 ¢	142.4 ¢	266.9 ¢

Aristoxenus Tense Diatonic

1/1	20/19	20/17	4/3	3/2	30/19	30/17	2/1
0 ¢	88.8 ¢	281.4 ¢	498.0 ¢	702.0 ¢	790.8 ¢	983.3 ¢	1200.0 ¢

20/19	19/17	17/15	9/8	20/19	19/17	17/15
88.8 ¢	192.6 ¢	216.7 ¢	203.9 ¢	88.8 ¢	192.6 ¢	216.7 ¢

Originally Philolaus Diatonic, also Eratosthenes Diatonic, and Ptolemy Ditone Diatonic

1/1	256/243	32/27	4/3	3/2	128/81	16/9	2/1
0 ¢	90.2 ¢	294.1 ¢	498.0 ¢	702.0 ¢	792.2 ¢	996.1 ¢	1200.0 ¢

256/243	9/8	9/8	9/8	256/243	9/8	9/8
90.2 ¢	203.9 ¢	203.9 ¢	203.9 ¢	90.2 ¢	203.9 ¢	203.9 ¢

Didymus Diatonic

1/1	16/15	32/27	4/3	3/2	8/5	16/9	2/1
0 ¢	111.7 ¢	294.1 ¢	498.0 ¢	702.0 ¢	813.7 ¢	996.1 ¢	1200.0 ¢

16/15	10/9	9/8	9/8	16/15	10/9	9/8
111.7 ¢	182.4 ¢	203.9 ¢	203.9 ¢	111.7 ¢	182.4 ¢	203.9 ¢

Ptolemy Soft Diatonic

1/1	21/20	7/6	4/3	3/2	63/40	7/4	2/1
0 ¢	84.5 ¢	266.9 ¢	498.0 ¢	702.0 ¢	786.4 ¢	968.8 ¢	1200.0 ¢

21/20	10/9	8/7	9/8	21/20	10/9	8/7
84.5 ¢	182.4 ¢	231.2 ¢	203.9 ¢	84.5 ¢	182.4 ¢	231.2 ¢

Ptolemy Tense Diatonic

1/1	16/15	6/5	4/3	3/2	8/5	9/5	2/1
0 ¢	111.7 ¢	315.6 ¢	498.0 ¢	702.0 ¢	813.7 ¢	1017.6 ¢	1200.0 ¢

16/15	9/8	10/9	9/8	16/15	9/8	10/9
111.7 ¢	203.9 ¢	182.4 ¢	203.9 ¢	111.7 ¢	203.9 ¢	182.4 ¢

Ptolemy Even Diatonic

1/1	12/11	6/5	4/3	3/2	18/11	9/5	2/1
0 ¢	150.6 ¢	315.6 ¢	498.0 ¢	702.0 ¢	852.6 ¢	1017.6 ¢	1200.0 ¢

12/11	11/10	10/9	9/8	12/11	11/10	10/9
150.6 ¢	165.0 ¢	182.4 ¢	203.9 ¢	150.6 ¢	165.0 ¢	182.4 ¢

10.21

In 1589, Gioseffo Zarlino (1517–1590) published a work entitled *De tutte l'opere del R.M. Gioseffo Zarlino da Chioggia...*, which included, among several previously published books, a newly revised edition of the *Istitutioni harmoniche* (Venice, 1558, reprinted 1562 and 1573). In this *De tutte l'opere...* edition of the *Istitutioni*, Seconda Parte, Cap. 39, Zarlino described Ptolemy's Syntonous (Tense) Diatonic Tetrachord as the most natural of all diatonic scales.[104] Fascinated by the melodic beauty of this scale, Zarlino designed an elaborate engraving to illuminate the scale's intervalic structure.[105] The central portion of this illustration consists of the following note names, string length units, and interval ratios:

C		D		E		F		G		A		H		C
180	$\frac{9}{8}$	160	$\frac{10}{9}$	144	$\frac{16}{15}$	135	$\frac{9}{8}$	120	$\frac{10}{9}$	108	$\frac{9}{8}$	96	$\frac{16}{15}$	90

In this configuration, Ptolemy's scale seems to consist of two different tetrachords: interval ratios $9/8$, $10/9$, $16/15$ before the disjunct, and interval ratios $10/9$, $9/8$, $16/15$ after the disjunct. However, Table 10.12 shows that Ptolemy constructed this scale from a single tetrachord with interval ratios $16/15$, $9/8$, $10/9$ before and after the disjunct:

$16/15$ $9/8$ $10/9$ ($9/8$) $16/15$ $9/8$ $10/9$

To understand the reason for these discrepancies, refer to Figure 10.15, which shows Ptolemy's Tense Diatonic Tetrachord distributed over the Greater Perfect System, and in the context of the Dorian and Lydian Modes. As discussed in Section 10.10, during the Middle Ages, Western musicians preferred to tune Philolaus' so-called Pythagorean scale in the Greek Lydian Mode. This practice continued well into the Renaissance, and explains why Zarlino depicted Ptolemy's scale in the standard C–C′ "octave" range. Although the original order of interval ratios remains undisturbed, the melodic and harmonic character of a given scale changes considerably when one begins the sequence on a different starting note. Zarlino's interpretation is extremely important to the development of Western music because he clearly recognized the scale's musical potential when heard and harmonized in the ancient Lydian Mode. In Part VI, we will discover that Ptolemy's scale is the original just intoned incarnation of the tempered major scale. Also, recall that in Section 8.7, we considered a G-major version of this scale in the construction of a simple flute, and in Section 9.14, a chromatic version in the construction of a musical slide rule.

A		B		C		D		E		F		G		A′		B′		C′		D′		E′		F′		G′		A″
	($9/8$)		$16/15$		$9/8$		$10/9$		$16/15$		$9/8$		$10/9$		($9/8$)		$16/15$		$9/8$		$10/9$		$16/15$		$9/8$		$10/9$	

	E	F	G	A	B	C	D	E′	
Dorian Mode:	$1/1$	$16/15$	$6/5$	$4/3$	$3/2$	$8/5$	$9/5$	$2/1$	(Standard Greek E–E′ Octave)

	C	D	E	F	G	A	B	C′	
Lydian Mode:	$1/1$	$9/8$	$5/4$	$4/3$	$3/2$	$5/3$	$15/8$	$2/1$	(Standard Western C–C′ Octave)

Figure 10.15 Ptolemy's Tense Diatonic in the Dorian and Lydian Modes. Zarlino first advocated the Lydian Mode of this scale in the 16th century. It is now the most sung and played scale in Western music.

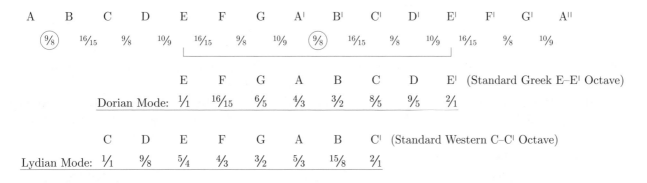

In closing Part IV, I would like to offer a personal observation. After listening to all the ancient Greek scales as they appear in Table 10.12, I was struck by the flowing musical quality of Ptolemy's Soft Diatonic. This is a 7-limit scale, which, in the ancient Dorian Mode, has a strong "minor" sound because it begins with a "flat semitone," ratio 21/20, and progresses to a "flat minor third," ratio 7/6:

1/1		21/20		7/6		4/3		3/2		63/40		7/4		2/1
0 ¢		*84.5 ¢*		*266.9 ¢*		*498.0 ¢*		*702.0 ¢*		*786.4 ¢*		*968.8 ¢*		*1200.0 ¢*
	21/20		10/9		8/7		9/8		21/20		10/9		8/7	
	84.5 ¢		*182.4 ¢*		*231.2 ¢*		*203.9 ¢*		*84.5 ¢*		*182.4 ¢*		*231.2 ¢*	

All major and minor diatonic scales in Western music theory begin with a "whole tone," which means that one cannot identify the musical character of a scale upon hearing the first interval. In contrast, the unique musical quality of this entire scale compelled me to consider its inclusion in the overall tuning of a musical instrument. (Incidentally, note that of the two Ptolemaic diatonic scales in Table 10.11, this tetrachord most nearly divides the "fourth" into two equal parts; that is, the *apyknon* consists of a "small minor third," ratio 7/6 [266.9 ¢], and the upper interval of a "large major second," ratio 8/7 [231.2 ¢].) I decided, therefore, to include three versions of Ptolemy's Soft Diatonic in the tuning of the Glassdance in Plate 9. One may hear this scale starting on 1/1, 4/3, and 3/2 of the instrument's lower "octave." (See Section 12.17.)

Part V

MEANTONE TEMPERAMENTS, WELL-TEMPERAMENTS, AND EQUAL TEMPERAMENTS

10.22

The majority of tempered tunings contain 12 tones. Since the Greeks did not contemplate such a scale, the question naturally arises, "Where did the 12-tone scale originate?" In the East, the oldest extant description of such a scale is in a Chinese work entitled *Shih Chi* by Ssu-ma Ch'ien (*c.* 145 B.C. – *c.* 87 B.C.). (See Chapter 11, Part I.) And in the West, the first account is in an Arabian work entitled *Risāla fī hubr ta'līf al-alḥān*, by Isḥāq Al-Kindī (d. *c.* A.D. 874). (See Chapter 11, Part IV.) The Chinese scale consists of *eleven* ascending just 3/2's. Consequently, Figure 10.16(a) shows that the twelfth interval between E♯ and C′ is a "small fifth":

$$\frac{2}{1} \div \frac{177147}{131072} = \frac{2}{1} \times \frac{131072}{177147} = \frac{262144}{177147} = 678.5\ ¢$$

Since a "pure fifth" equals 702.0 ¢, note that the difference between these two intervals equals 702.0 ¢ − 678.5 ¢ = 23.5 ¢, or the comma of Pythagoras. In contrast, Al-Kindī's 12-tone scale consists of *four* ascending "fifths" and *seven* descending "fifths." (See Figure 11.41 and Table 11.22.) To resolve the comma of Pythagoras, Al-Kindī installed two different "semitone" frets on his *'ūd* (lit. *lute*). The first fret under String I produces the limma, ratio 256/243 [90.2 ¢], between C–D♭; and the second fret produces the apotome, ratio 2187/2048 [113.7 ¢], between C–C♯. As discussed in Section 10.15, the discrepancy between these two intervals equals the comma of Pythagoras. This highly original design enabled Al-Kindī to tune *two identical 12-tone scales,*[106] which means that Al-Kindī is the first theorist in the history of music who tuned a 12-tone "double-octave" scale on a stringed instrument equipped with frets.

In Europe, the first 12-tone scale is in a work entitled *Flores musice omnis cantus Gregoriani*, written in 1332 by Hugo Spechtshart [von Reutlingen] (*c.* 1285 – *c.* 1359), first published in 1488.[107]

Spechtshart's original scale includes two sharps and three flats. Since he tuned the open string of his monochord to F, this scale consists of *eight* ascending "fifths" (F: C, G, D, A, E, B, F♯, C♯) and *three* descending "fifths" (F: B♭, E♭, A♭). However, Spechtshart's scale in C consists of *seven* ascending "fifths" (C: G, D, A, E, B, F♯, C♯) and *four* descending "fifths" (C: F, B♭, E♭, A♭). Figure 10.16(a) identifies the two sharps of the latter mode as ratios $^{729}/_{512}$ and $^{2187}/_{2048}$; and Figure 10.16(b) identifies the three flats as ratios $^{16}/_{9}$, $^{32}/_{27}$, and $^{128}/_{81}$.

Figure 10.16(a) shows in clockwise rotation the note names and frequency ratios of twelve ascending $^{3}/_{2}$'s known as the *spiral of "fifths."* In this figure, all "octave" equivalents have been simplified to ratios larger than $^{1}/_{1}$ and smaller than $^{2}/_{1}$. (See Section 9.4.) On the top of this spiral, notice the overlap at B♯, which indicates that twelve ascending $^{3}/_{2}$'s exceed seven ascending $^{2}/_{1}$'s by the comma of Pythagoras, or by 23.5 ¢. We may calculate this overlap in the following manner:

$$\text{Comma of Pythagoras} = \frac{\left(\frac{3}{2}\right)^{12}}{\left(\frac{2}{1}\right)^{7}} = \frac{\frac{531441}{4096}}{\frac{128}{1}} = \frac{531441}{4096} \times \frac{1}{128} = \frac{531441}{524288} = 23.46\ ¢$$

Conversely, Figure 10.16(b) shows in counterclockwise rotation the note names and frequency ratios of twelve descending $^{3}/_{2}$'s. Similarly, on the top of this spiral observe the gap at D𝄫, which indicates that twelve descending $^{3}/_{2}$'s fall short of seven descending $^{2}/_{1}$'s by the comma of Pythagoras. We may calculate this gap in the following manner:

$$\text{Comma of Pythagoras} = \frac{\frac{2}{1}}{\frac{1048576}{531441}} = \frac{2}{1} \times \frac{531441}{1048576} = \frac{531441}{524288}$$

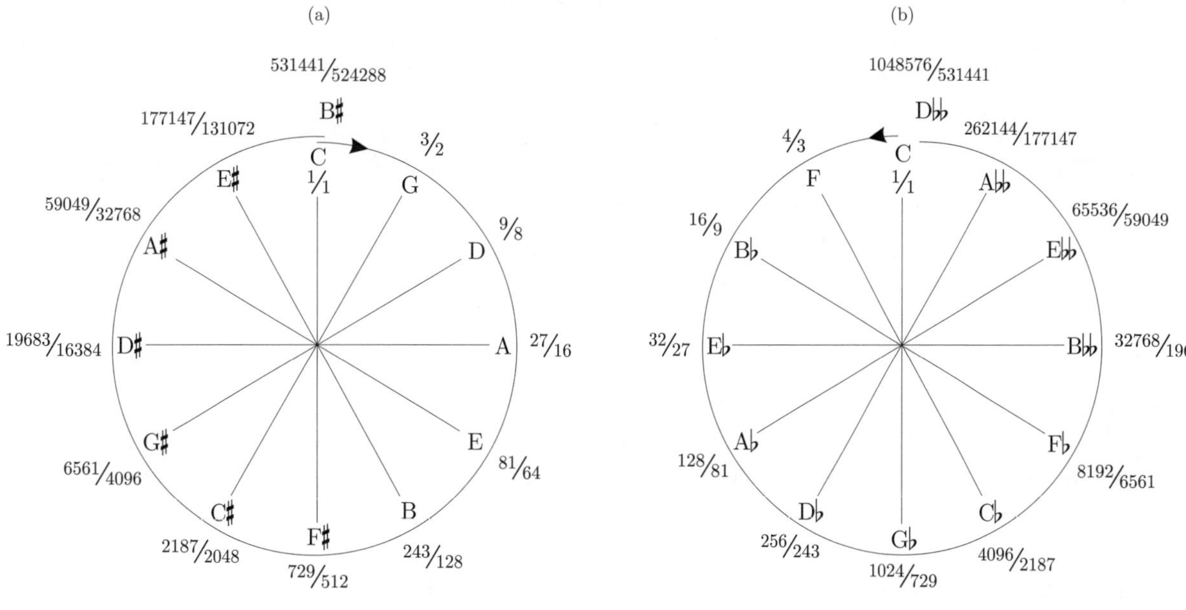

Figure 10.16 Ascending and descending spirals of "fifths." (a) On the top of this spiral an overlap indicates that twelve ascending $^{3}/_{2}$'s exceed seven ascending $^{2}/_{1}$'s by a discrepancy called the comma of Pythagoras, which equals 23.5 ¢. (b) Similarly, on the top of this spiral a gap indicates that twelve descending $^{3}/_{2}$'s fall short of seven descending $^{2}/_{1}$'s by the same discrepancy.

The ratios in Figures 10.16(a) and 10.16(b) are extremely important in the history of Western and Eastern music. In the West, tunings designed with such ratios are collectively called *Pythagorean scales* because both spirals include only 3-limit ratios. (As discussed in Section 10.1, a 3-limit scale consists of ratios whose numerators and denominators contain no prime factors except 2 and 3.) Since the Pythagoreans classified all musical intervals that include prime number 5 as dissonances, they did not construct scales with ratios 5/4, 6/5, 16/15, . . .

Given such a profusion of ratios, Figure 10.17 shows two sample scales that include the most frequently used 3-limit ratios in Western tuning theory. The first example, which I call the *'Apotome Scale'*, consists of *eight* ascending "fifths" that include C♯, F♯, and G♯, and *three* descending "fifths" that include E♭ and B♭. This tuning represents the most common example of a 12-tone Pythagorean scale.[108] However, Marin Mersenne[109] (1588–1648) also proposed a just intoned version of the second example, which I call the *'Limma Scale'*. It consists of *five* ascending "fifths" and *six* descending "fifths," which means that all the altered notes — D♭, E♭, G♭, A♭, and B♭ — are here tuned flat. Finally, Johannes Kepler[110] (1571–1630) proposed a just intoned version of a mixed scale, which consists of *seven* ascending "fifths" that include C♯ and F♯, and *four* descending "fifths" that include E♭, A♭, and B♭. We conclude, therefore, that in analyzing Western 12-tone scales, we must consider all the ratios in Figure 10.17.

The earliest illustration of a European musical instrument tuned to a 12-tone scale appears in *Syntagma musicum II: De organographia* by Michael Praetorius (1571–1621).[111] Here, Praetorius depicts the chromatic keyboard of the Halberstadt organ finished in 1361. Since *tempered* keyboard tunings, including meantone temperaments and well-temperaments, did not take hold in Europe until the early 16th century and the early 18th century, respectively, this instrument was probably tuned to the *'Apotome Scale'* in Figure 10.17.[112]

~ 10.23 ~

During the Renaissance — a period in Europe from the beginning of the 14th century to the end of the 16th century — keyboard musicians gradually replaced various 12-tone Pythagorean scales with meantone temperaments. Later, in the Baroque Era, musicians transformed these tunings into well-temperaments. Although meantone temperaments and well-temperaments are very different, they

'Apotome Scale'

C	C♯	D	E♭	E	F	F♯	G	G♯	A	B♭	B	C'
1/1	2187/2048	9/8	32/27	81/64	4/3	729/512	3/2	6561/4096	27/16	16/9	243/128	2/1
0 ¢	113.7 ¢	203.9 ¢	294.1 ¢	407.8 ¢	498.0 ¢	611.7 ¢	702.0 ¢	815.6 ¢	905.9 ¢	996.1 ¢	1109.8 ¢	1200.0 ¢
	↕					↕		↕				

C	D♭	D	E♭	E	F	G♭	G	A♭	A	B♭	B	C'
1/1	256/243	9/8	32/27	81/64	4/3	1024/729	3/2	128/81	27/16	16/9	243/128	2/1
0 ¢	90.2 ¢	203.9 ¢	294.1 ¢	407.8 ¢	498.0 ¢	588.3 ¢	702.0 ¢	792.2 ¢	905.9 ¢	996.1 ¢	1109.8 ¢	1200.0 ¢

'Limma Scale'

Figure 10.17 The sixteen most important 3-limit ratios in Western tuning theory. The *'Apotome Scale'*, which consists of *eight* ascending "fifths" that include C♯, F♯, and G♯, and *three* descending "fifths" that include E♭ and B♭, represents the most typical 12-tone Pythagorean scale. However, in discussing Western scale theory, we must also consider the ratios of the *'Limma Scale'*, which consist of *five* ascending "fifths" and *six* descending "fifths." Here all the altered notes — D♭, E♭, G♭, A♭, and B♭ — are tuned flat.

have one common feature: irrational length ratios and frequency ratios. Music theorists calculated the string lengths of these tempered tunings through the geometric division of monochords and canon strings. Consequently, many major Renaissance treatises on tuning theory refer to Euclid's *Elements*, Book VI, Proposition 13, for the construction of a mean proportional.[113] (See Section 10.9.)

Before we examine meantone and well-tempered tunings in full detail, refer back to Figure 10.6, which shows the Euclidean construction of a mean proportional between two straight lines AD and BD, whose lengths at 1000.0 mm and 500.0 mm, respectively, represent length ratio $^2\!/_1$. Recall that in this example, we used a ruler to measure the mean proportional, line CD at 707.1 mm, a dimension accurate to within one-tenth of a millimeter (or 0.0039 in.). Such a precise measurement enabled us to avoid a large round-off error in approximating the irrational number 1.4142, or the square root of 2. Before the development of highly accurate measuring instruments, it would have been difficult for music theorists in the Renaissance to achieve similar results for many different kinds of geometric divisions.

As an alternative, Figure 10.18 shows a tuning device for strings that does not require a calibrated ruler. Refer to Figure 10.6 and establish the lengths of AD and BD for length ratio $^2\!/_1$ through the following geometric construction. With an open compass mark the locations of B and D; now turn the compass once on point D, then turn the compass again, and mark point A. (This technique works for all rational lengths.) Open the compass farther, locate the center of AB, draw the semicircle, and construct the mean proportional CD. Finally, to hear the "tritone" $F\sharp_3$ in relation to C_3 and C_4, simply transfer the lengths of AD, CD, and BD, to the top, middle, and

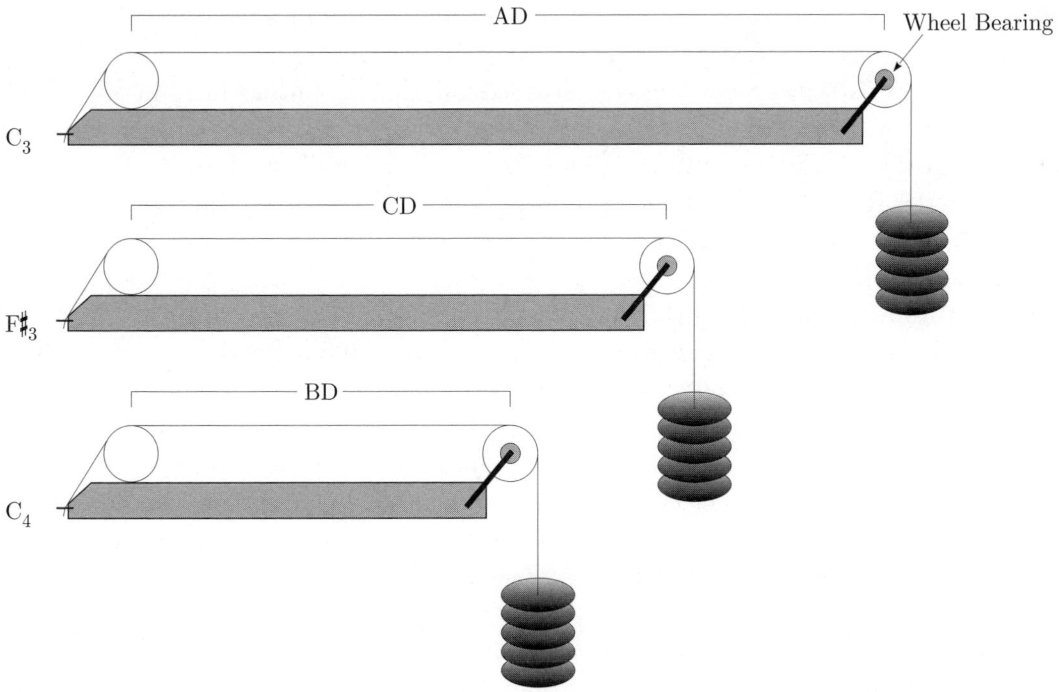

Figure 10.18 A tuning device for the musical evaluation of irrational frequency ratios. If the diameter, density, and tension variables are constant for all three strings, then only changes in length account for the different frequencies of the strings. The lengths of the top, middle, and bottom strings correspond to the lengths of lines AD, CD, and BD in Figure 10.6, respectively. This device makes it possible to hear and evaluate irrational frequency ratios without performing calibrated string length measurements.

bottom strings, respectively, of the tuning device in Figure 10.18. However, to assure accurate tones, the diameter (D), density (ρ), and tension (T) variables must be constant for all three strings. Otherwise, changes in the length (L) variable will not solely determine the different frequencies of the strings. Moreover, my experiments indicate that the accuracy of this apparatus also depends on the quality of the wheel bearing at the location where the string bends through a 90° angle to the floor. A precision needle bearing designed to support a heavy rotating load with a minimum of friction gives the best results. In contrast, a poorly constructed bearing (or worse, no revolving support at all) generates a high level of static friction between the bent string and the rigid frame. Consequently, the string does not experience the full force of the suspended weight, and the device will not produce consistent and predictable results. This is probably why Ptolemy was unable to ". . . reach the peak of precision . . ." with his suspended weight experiments. The relation between frequency and force remained a mystery until approximately 1630, when Galileo and Mersenne independently discovered the laws of vibrating strings. (See Chapter 2, Note 9.) These two scientists undoubtedly used carefully machined parts in the construction of their tuning devices. Furthermore, note that this apparatus also needs strings with consistent diameters and mass densities. By the time Galileo and Mersenne performed their experiments, metal wire drawing technology had advanced to produce high-quality musical instrument strings. In short, although such a device does not depend on intricate length measurements, it too requires advanced technology.

10.24

Zarlino was aware of all these difficulties. As a great innovator, he recognized the inherent inaccuracies of calculating irrational length ratios, and the mechanical problems associated with string tuning devices. In a second treatise entitled *Dimostrationi harmoniche* (Venice, 1571, reprinted in 1578), and in the *Istitutioni harmoniche* (see Section 10.21), Zarlino introduced Euclid's construction in Book VI, Proposition 13 as a method for *direct canon string division.* Except for the dots and the arrowhead, Figure 10.19(a) is an exact copy of the illustration in the *Dimostrationi harmoniche* (1571), Ragionamento Terzo, Proposta X;[114] and except for the English translations, Figure 10.19(b) is an exact copy of the illustration in the *Istitutioni harmoniche* (1573), Seconda Parte, Cap. 24.[115]

In Figure 10.19(a), Zarlino specifically refers to the line *de*, and in Figure 10.19(b), to the line *ab* as a *chorda* (lit. *musical instrument string*). In the former, $de = 9$ units and $eg = 8$ units. Therefore, *he* represents the mean proportional of ancient length ratio $9/8$, or $he = \sqrt{9 \text{ units} \times 8 \text{ units}} \approx 8.485$ units. Note that in Figure 10.19(a), the inner curve indicates that Zarlino adjusted his compass to the length *he* and drew a quarter circle from *h* down to *k*; in other words, a counterclockwise rotation of 90° causes *he* to intersect *de* at *k*, which means that $ke = he$. Suppose we tune the open canon string *de* to C_3. If we place a bridge at *f*, then *fe* produces the "whole tone," ratio $9/8$ [203.9 ¢], or D_3; and if we place a bridge at *k*, then *ke* produces the "exact semitone," ratio $\sqrt{9/8}$ [102.0 ¢], or $C\sharp_3$.

In Figure 10.19(b), $ab = 2$ units and $bd = 1$ unit. Consequently, *eb* represents the mean proportional of ancient length ratio $2/1$, or $eb = \sqrt{2 \text{ units} \times 1 \text{ unit}} \approx 1.4142$ units. A counterclockwise rotation of 90° causes *eb* to intersect *ab* at *f*, which means that $fb = eb$. Now, suppose that we tune the open string *ab* to C_3. If we place a bridge at *c*, then *cb* produces the "octave," ratio $2/1$ [1200.0 ¢], or C_4; and if we place a bridge at *f*, then *fb* produces the "exact tritone," ratio $\sqrt{2/1}$ [600.0 ¢], or $F\sharp_3$.

We conclude, therefore, that Zarlino's method, which geometrically divides a given ratio directly on the string, resolves several mechanical problems associated with irrational length ratios and

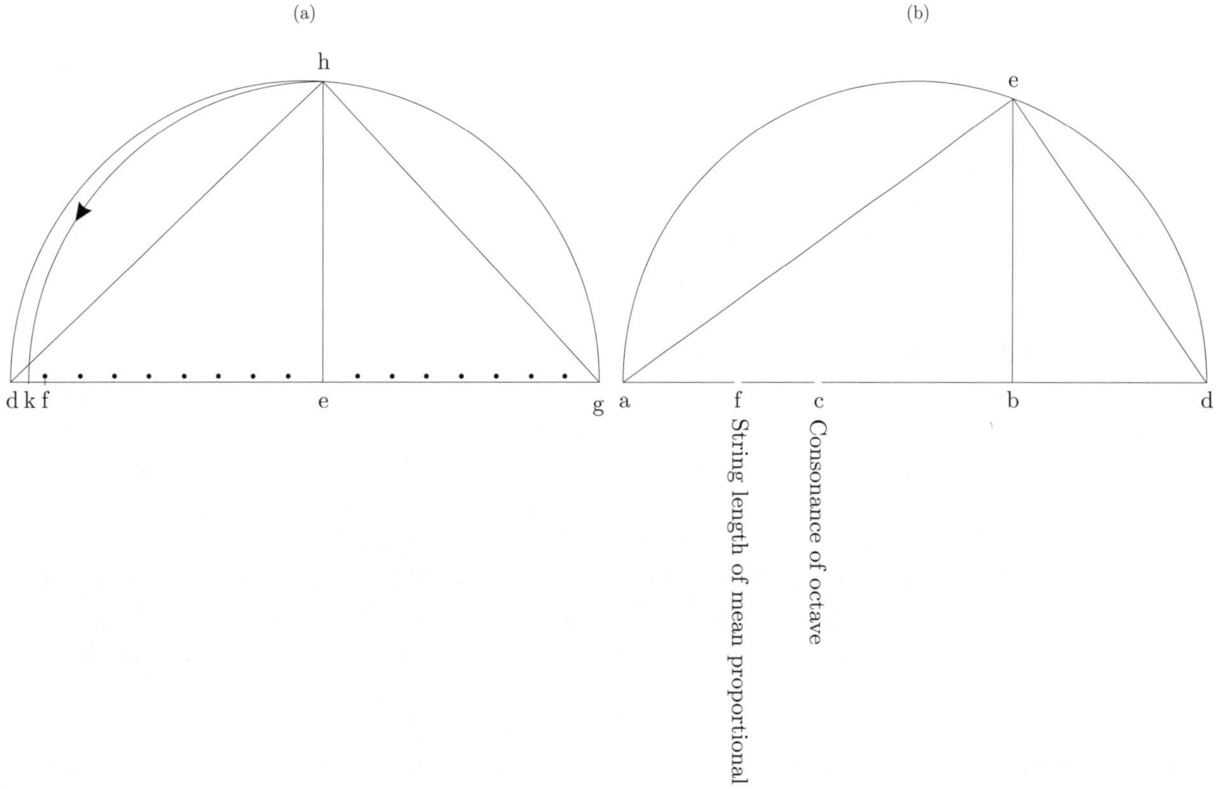

Figure 10.19 Zarlino's interpretation of Euclid's construction of a mean proportional. In his version of these figures, Zarlino specifically refers to line *de* in (a), and line *ab* in (b), as musical instrument strings. These direct canon string divisions enabled Zarlino to avoid difficult line measurements and complicated line transfers associated with the determination of irrational length ratios.

frequency ratios. By simply placing a bridge at the point where the mean proportional intersects the string, a musician can easily determine the location of an irrational length ratio and, thereby, evaluate the musical quality of an irrational frequency ratio. This method avoids all the difficulties of intricate line measurements, and the complications of line transfers to problematic tuning devices.

≈ 10.25 ≈

In 1484, eighty-seven years before the publication of the *Dimostrationi*, the French mathematician Nicolas Chuquet (1445–1488) wrote in a book entitled *The Geometry:*

> By this teaching it is apparent that the square roots of numbers can be given by lines.[116]

Figures 10.20(a), 10.20(b), and 10.20(c) show how Chuquet demonstrated the mean proportionals of 9, 8, and 5, respectively. Chuquet first divides the horizontal and vertical diameters of a circle into six aliquot parts.[117] He then simply states that PD $= \sqrt{9}$, LC $= \sqrt{8}$, HB $= \sqrt{5}$. Although he did not include the lines AP and PG, AL and LG, AH and HG, to indicate the locations of similar triangles (see Note 43), his constructions are identical to Euclid's famous solution as shown in Figures 10.6 and 10.19. However, the inclusion of PG in Figure 10.20(a) suggests that he may have contemplated the geometric progression AG:PG:DG, or the following proportion:

$$\frac{\text{AG}}{\text{PG}} = \frac{\text{PG}}{\text{DG}}$$

Now, suppose AG in (d) represents a musical instrument string. Rotate the hypotenuse PG counterclockwise until P intersects AG at X, which means that XG = PG. This location marks the geometric division of the "octave," expressed as length ratio $^2/_1$. That is, on a string with a length of 6 units, the "octave" is located at 3 units, and the "exact tritone" above the open string at $\sqrt{6 \times 3} = \sqrt{18} \approx 4.2426$ units.

The principal difference between the construction in Figure 10.19(b) and in Figure 10.20(d) is the location and function of the altitude *eb* of $\triangle ade$ in the former figure, and of altitude PD of $\triangle AGP$ in the latter figure. Note carefully that in Figure 10.19(b), the altitude functions as a mean proportional, but in Figure 10.20(d), the altitude does *not* function as a mean proportional. Furthermore, in Figure 10.19(b), *eb* delimits the lengths *ab* and *db*, where *ab represents a string of varying length.* In Zarlino's method, one combines *db* and *ab* to determine the diameter of the semicircle, which means that *db* serves no practical purpose in the actual geometric division of the string *ab*. However, in Figure 10.20(d), the diameter *AG represents a canon string of constant length.* Here the location of D, or the location of the bridge beneath the string, divides AG in half; hence ancient length ratio $^2/_1$. Because $\triangle AGP$ and $\triangle DGP$ are similar triangles, the hypotenuse PG functions as the geometric mean in the progression AG:PG:DG. Therefore, PG represents the geometric mean of length ratio $^2/_1$. Similarly, LG in Figure 10.20(e) and HG in Figure 10.20(f) represent the geometric means of length ratios $^3/_2$ and $^6/_5$, respectively. The mathematical elegance of the latter three constructions is twofold: (1) because AG is constant, determine the bridge locations of all length ratios in the usual manner; (2) because AG is constant, perform all geometric divisions from the same location; i.e., from the right (or left) end of the string.

Although Chuquet did not explicitly perform these latter three constructions, it is extremely likely that he considered them. In any case, Chuquet, Zarlino, or any other Renaissance theorist-musician could have easily understood the practical advantage of this method of geometric string division. Furthermore, in Chuquet's greatest work entitled *The Triparty*, the author gives detailed techniques for the calculation of square roots accurate to four decimal places.[118] Regrettably, Zarlino did not have an opportunity to study either book because *The Triparty* was first published in 1880[119] and *The Geometry* in 1979.[120] Finally, with the imminent publication of Napier's logarithms in 1614,[121] mathematicians no longer faced the problem of calculating irrational numbers in an expeditious manner, and so geometric divisions with ruler and compass fell into disuse.

10.26

The transition from the Pythagorean scale to meantone temperaments ushered in a new musical era. Due to the mechanical requirements of fretted instruments (see Section 10.28), most lute and viol players in the 16th century did not seriously debate the pros and cons of Pythagorean intonation; for these musicians, approximate (inexact) versions of 12-tone equal temperament were the only tunings that worked. (See Section 10.31.) However, keyboard players were often torn between the 3-limit Pythagorean scale that generated pure "fifths" and dissonant "major thirds," and various meantone temperaments that produced impure "fifths," but consonant "major thirds." Bartolomeo Ramis (*c.* 1440 – *c.* 1500), in a treatise entitled *Musica practica*, was the first Renaissance music theorist who advocated replacing the dissonant Pythagorean "major third," ratio $^{81}/_{64}$, with a consonant 5-limit "major third," ratio $^5/_4$. Ramis argued

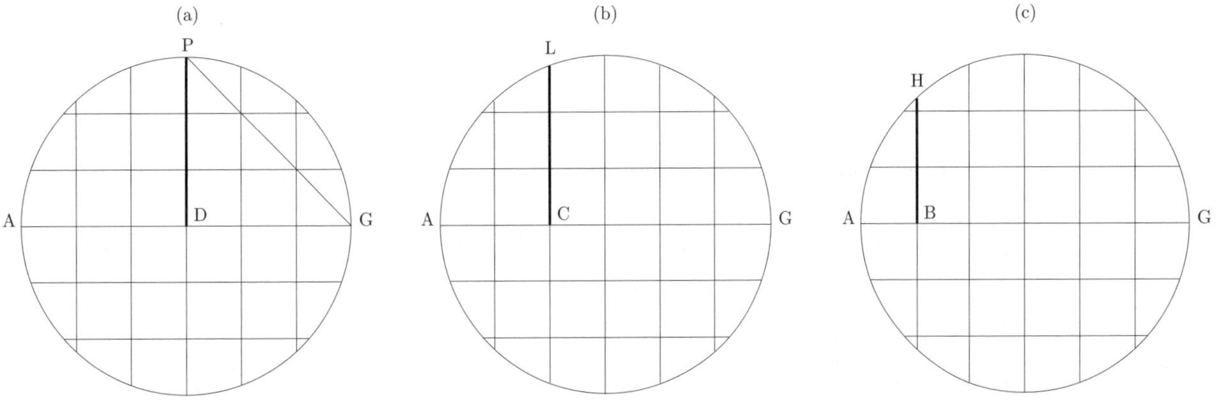

(a)

$$\frac{AD}{PD} = \frac{PD}{GD}$$

$$PD^2 = GD \times AD$$

$$PD = \sqrt{GD \times AD}$$

$$PD = \sqrt{3 \times 3} = \sqrt{9} = 3$$

(b)

$$\frac{AC}{LC} = \frac{LC}{GC}$$

$$LC^2 = GC \times AC$$

$$LC = \sqrt{GC \times AC}$$

$$LC = \sqrt{4 \times 2} = \sqrt{8} \approx 2.8284$$

(c)

$$\frac{AB}{HB} = \frac{HB}{GB}$$

$$HB^2 = GB \times AB$$

$$HB = \sqrt{GB \times AB}$$

$$HB = \sqrt{5 \times 1} = \sqrt{5} \approx 2.2361$$

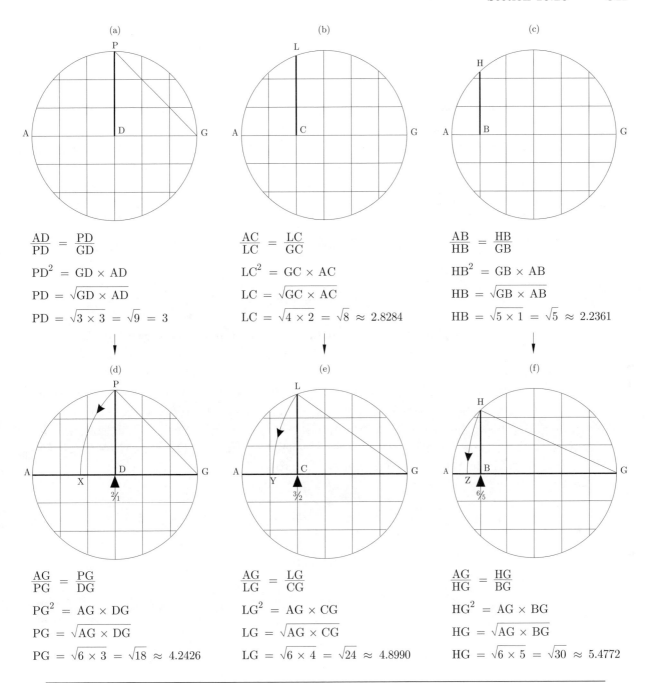

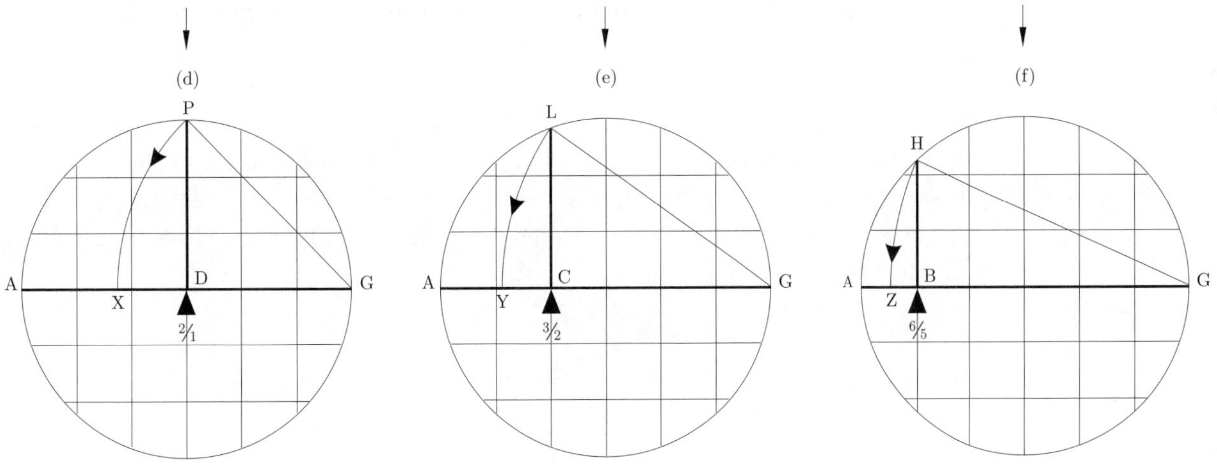

(d)

$$\frac{AG}{PG} = \frac{PG}{DG}$$

$$PG^2 = AG \times DG$$

$$PG = \sqrt{AG \times DG}$$

$$PG = \sqrt{6 \times 3} = \sqrt{18} \approx 4.2426$$

(e)

$$\frac{AG}{LG} = \frac{LG}{CG}$$

$$LG^2 = AG \times CG$$

$$LG = \sqrt{AG \times CG}$$

$$LG = \sqrt{6 \times 4} = \sqrt{24} \approx 4.8990$$

(f)

$$\frac{AG}{HG} = \frac{HG}{BG}$$

$$HG^2 = AG \times BG$$

$$HG = \sqrt{AG \times BG}$$

$$HG = \sqrt{6 \times 5} = \sqrt{30} \approx 5.4772$$

Figure 10.20 Illustrations based on figures in Chuquet's *Geometry*. Chuquet used circular graphs (a), (b), and (c) to demonstrate the construction of three mean proportionals. Although he did not include lines AP and PG, AL and LG, AH and HG, respectively, to indicate the locations of similar triangles, his constructions are identical to Euclid's famous solution as shown in Figures 10.6 and 10.19. However, my inclusion of line PG in (a) suggests that he may have contemplated the geometric progression AG:PG:DG, or the proportion AG:PG = PG:DG. Now, suppose AG in (d) represents a musical instrument string 6 units long. Rotate the hypotenuse PG counterclockwise until P intersects AG at X. This location marks the geometric division of the "octave," expressed as length ratio 2:1. Similarly, Y in (e) marks the geometric division of the "fifth," expressed as length ratio 3:2, and Z in (f), the geometric division of the "minor third," expressed as length ratio 6:5.

> But still, although it [the Pythagorean division] is useful and pleasing to theorists, it is laborious and difficult for singers to understand.[122] (Text in brackets mine.)

Ramis' theory was immediately condemned by his contemporaries. Despite these objections, many theorists, including Zarlino, defended the inclusion of prime number 5, and in the end, Ramis' tuning prevailed. (See Section 10.36.)

In 1523, Pietro Aron (*c.* 1490 – *c.* 1550) published the first general (non-mathematical) description of ¼-comma meantone temperament.[123] This tuning flourished throughout Europe from approximately 1500 to 1700. ¼-comma meantone is distinguished by a characteristic meantone, or a "whole tone," which represents the geometric division of ratio 5⁄4 into two equal interval ratios.

$$\text{Meantone ratio: } \sqrt{\frac{5}{4}} \approx 1.1180$$

$$\text{Meantone cents: } \log_{10}\sqrt{\frac{5}{4}} \times 3986.314 = 193.16\ ¢$$

Before we discuss this temperament in full detail, consider the following geometric division of length ratio 5⁄4. Refer to Figure 10.21, and draw AB to exemplify an open canon string. Next, draw a semicircle with AB as the diameter. Divide AB into five aliquot sections, and place a D at four of these sections. Extend a perpendicular from D to the circumference at C. Now, observe that the hypotenuse CB represents the geometric mean of length ratio 5⁄4. To determine the location of the meantone directly on the canon string, rotate CB counterclockwise until C intersects AB. This point marks the location of the meantone expressed as length ratio $\sqrt{5/4}$. Organize these lengths into the geometric progression AB:CB:DB, and define the proportion

$$\frac{AB}{CB} = \frac{CB}{DB} \tag{10.8}$$

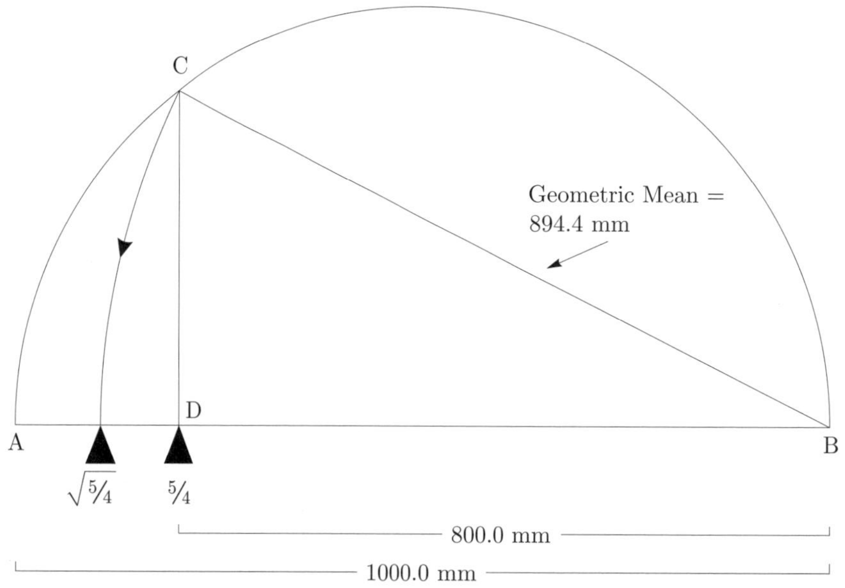

Figure 10.21 The geometric division of length ratio 5⁄4. See Section 10.25 for details on this construction. The geometric progression AB:CB:DB expresses the proportion AB:CB = CB:DB, where CB = $\sqrt{\text{AB} \times \text{DB}}$.

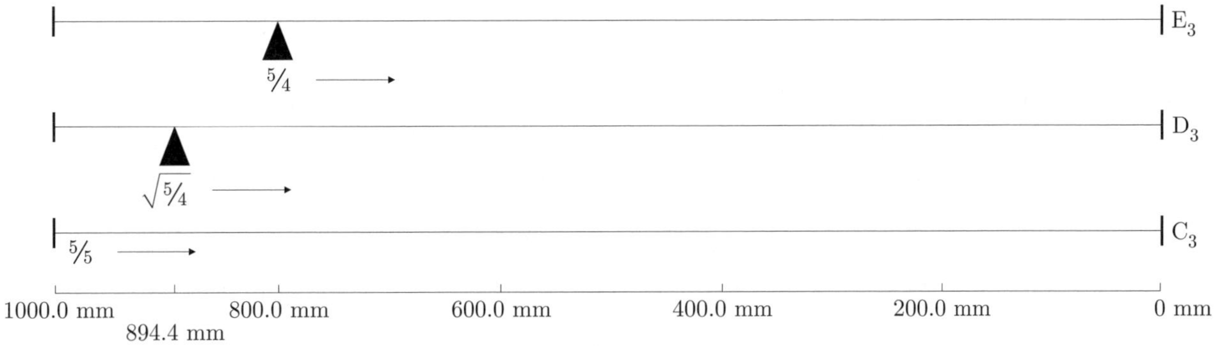

Figure 10.22 The geometric division of the "major third" expressed as ancient length ratio $^5\!/\!_4$. The bridge under the middle string at 894.4 mm represents the geometric mean of the "major third" between C_3–E_3. This meantone is the characteristic interval that gives $^1\!/\!_4$-comma meantone temperament its name.

Suppose AB = 1000.0 mm and DB = 800.0 mm. Place a ruler against the hypotenuse and note that CB = 894.4 mm. We may also calculate the length of CB directly. Substitute the lengths of AB and DB into Equation 10.8, and solve for CB:

$$\frac{1000.0\text{ mm}}{\text{CB}} = \frac{\text{CB}}{800.0\text{ mm}}$$

$$\text{CB}^2 = (1000.0\text{ mm})(800.0\text{ mm})$$

$$\text{CB} = \sqrt{(1000.0\text{ mm})(800.0\text{ mm})}$$

$$\text{CB} \approx 894.4\text{ mm}$$

Now, arrange these three values in a descending geometric progression of string lengths 1000.0 mm : 894.4 mm : 800.0 mm, divide all three lengths by 800.0 mm, and organize the sequence 1.25 : 1.1180 : 1.0. Note that because the middle term represents the common ratio of a geometric progression, this progression expresses an ascending sequence of identical musical intervals; in this case, a low meantone followed by a high meantone.

To verify that the square root of $^5\!/\!_4$ produces two identical meantones, refer to Figure 10.22. Place a bridge at 800.0 mm from the right end of the top string, and at 894.4 mm from the right end of the middle string. The right section of the middle string now sounds D_3, or the geometric division of the "major third" between C_3–E_3. Now, simultaneously play the open string and the right section of the middle string, and listen to the meantone between C_3–D_3; finally, play the right section of the middle string and the top string, and listen to the meantone between D_3–E_3. The meantone ratio $\sqrt{^5\!/\!_4}$ equals 193.16 ¢, which is exactly half the size of the "major third" ratio $^5\!/\!_4$ at 386.31 ¢.

∾ 10.27 ∾

In the *Istitutioni*, Zarlino initially favored a tuning called $^2\!/\!_7$-comma meantone temperament.[124] However, a few years later Zarlino changed his mind and sided with $^1\!/\!_4$-comma meantone temperament. He wrote in the *Dimostrationi:*

> Unlike the first temperament [$^2\!/\!_7$-comma], in which all the ratios (excluding the octaves) are surd and irrational, the second [$^1\!/\!_4$-comma] has true and natural forms in its large thirds . . . This second temperament is very

pleasing to the ear, and not as difficult to make . . .[125] (Text and ratios in brackets mine.)

Before we begin a detailed tuning analysis of $\frac{1}{4}$-comma meantone temperament, let us first calculate the famous "comma" that defines this tuning. At a piano, tune the following sequence of four consecutive just $\frac{3}{2}$'s: C_3–G_3, G_3–D_4, D_4–A_4, and A_4–E_5. Such a sequence produces frequency ratios

$$G_3 = \tfrac{1}{1} \times \tfrac{3}{2} = \tfrac{3}{2}$$
$$D_4 = \tfrac{3}{2} \times \tfrac{3}{2} = \tfrac{9}{4}$$
$$A_4 = \tfrac{9}{4} \times \tfrac{3}{2} = \tfrac{27}{8}$$
$$E_5 = \tfrac{27}{8} \times \tfrac{3}{2} = \tfrac{81}{16}$$

Next, tune C_5 as a $\frac{4}{1}$ up from C_3; then, E_5 as a $\frac{5}{4}$ up from C_5. This results in frequency ratio

$$E_5 = \tfrac{4}{1} \times \tfrac{5}{4} = \tfrac{5}{1}$$

Now, compare the two E_5's, subtract the cent value of the latter from the former, and observe that an $\frac{81}{16}$ exceeds a $\frac{5}{1}$ by 21.51 ¢:

$$\frac{81}{16} = 701.955\ ¢ \times 4 = 2807.820\ ¢$$

$$\frac{5}{1} = 2400.0\ ¢ + 386.314\ ¢ = 2786.314\ ¢$$

$$2807.820\ ¢ - 2786.314\ ¢ = 21.506\ ¢$$

This discrepancy is called the *syntonic comma*, or the comma of Didymus, and it corresponds to interval ratio $\frac{81}{80}$.

$$\text{Syntonic Comma: } \tfrac{81}{16} \div \tfrac{5}{1} = \tfrac{81}{16} \times \tfrac{1}{5} = \tfrac{81}{80}$$

Note that the same discrepancy exists between the "large whole tone," ratio $\frac{9}{8}$, and the "small whole tone," ratio $\frac{10}{9}$.

$$\text{Syntonic Comma: } \tfrac{9}{8} \div \tfrac{10}{9} = \tfrac{9}{8} \times \tfrac{9}{10} = \tfrac{81}{80}$$

To eliminate the syntonic comma and, thereby, reduce an $\frac{81}{16}$ to a $\frac{5}{1}$, geometrically divide this discrepancy into four equal parts, and then distribute these parts by tuning four consecutive flat tempered "fifths." First, calculate the $\frac{1}{4}$ syntonic comma in cents:

$$\tfrac{1}{4}\text{ Syntonic Comma} = \sqrt[4]{\frac{81}{80}} \approx 1.0031105$$

$$\log_{10} 1.0031105 \times 3986.314 = 5.377\ ¢$$

$$\text{Or, } \tfrac{1}{4}\text{ Syntonic Comma} = 21.506\ ¢ \div 4 = 5.377\ ¢$$

Next, refer to Figure 10.23, Step ①, and tune four consecutive "flat fifths"; that is, reduce each "fifth" by 5.38 ¢. The cumulative effect of such tempering is that the first "fifth" G_3, ratio $\frac{3}{2}$, is tuned a $\frac{1}{4}$-comma flat; the second "fifth" D_4, ratio $\frac{9}{4}$, is tuned a $\frac{1}{2}$-comma flat; the third "fifth" A_4, ratio $\frac{27}{8}$, is tuned $\frac{3}{4}$-comma flat; and the fourth "fifth" E_5, ratio $\frac{81}{16}$, is tuned 1-comma flat.

Cent calculations of the frequency ratios in Step ① require three actions. (1) Simplify the previously calculated "octave" equivalents $\frac{9}{4}$, $\frac{27}{8}$, and $\frac{81}{16}$ to standard frequency ratios $\frac{9}{8}$, $\frac{27}{16}$, and

81⁄64, respectively. (2) Calculate the cents of the latter ratios, and (3) subtract the cumulative ¼-comma cent values.[126]

$$\text{G}_3^{-\frac{1}{4}}: \log_{10}\frac{3}{2} \times 3986.314 - (5.377\ ¢ \times 1) = 696.58\ ¢$$

$$\text{D}_4^{-\frac{2}{4}}: \log_{10}\frac{9}{8} \times 3986.314 - (5.377\ ¢ \times 2) = 193.16\ ¢$$

$$\text{A}_4^{-\frac{3}{4}}: \log_{10}\frac{27}{16} \times 3986.314 - (5.377\ ¢ \times 3) = 889.74\ ¢$$

$$\text{E}_5^{-\frac{4}{4}}: \log_{10}\frac{81}{64} \times 3986.314 - (5.377\ ¢ \times 4) = 386.31\ ¢$$

The last step eliminates the syntonic comma from the scale, and produces a just "major third," or E_5 = 81⁄64 ÷ 81⁄80 = 5⁄4 = 386.31 ¢.

Next, proceed to Step ②. First tune a "double-octave" from E_5 down to E_3, and then tune the following four ascending just 5⁄4's: G_3–B_3, D_4–$\text{F}\sharp_4$, A_4–$\text{C}\sharp_5$, and E_5–$\text{G}\sharp_5$. In Figure 10.23, zero cent values between tones indicate just or rational interval ratios, and positive or negative cent values, tempered or irrational interval ratios. Because these "major thirds" are pure and, therefore, do not introduce any new tempered intervals, Step ② extends the *rate of tempering* established in Step ①. Consequently, Step ② produces four consecutive "flat fifths" — E_3–B_3, B_3–$\text{F}\sharp_4$, $\text{F}\sharp_4$–$\text{C}\sharp_5$, $\text{C}\sharp_5$–$\text{G}\sharp_5$ — that are tempered 5⁄4-commas flat, 6⁄4-commas flat, 7⁄4-commas flat, and 2-commas flat, respectively. Since the interval between the first and last tones in Step ①, or between C–E, is a just 5⁄4, the interval between the first and last tones in Step ②, or between E–G♯ is a just 5⁄4 as well. With respect to the tonic, two consecutive just "major thirds" produce a just "minor sixth," or G♯ = 5⁄4 × 5⁄4 = 25⁄16 = 772.6 ¢. Therefore, ¼-comma meantone temperament includes two just intervals: C–E and C–G♯.

	[25⁄16] $\text{G}\sharp_3^{-\frac{8}{4}}$	*+ 35.67*	$\text{E}\flat_4^{+\frac{3}{4}}$	*−5.38*	$\text{B}\flat_4^{+\frac{2}{4}}$	*−5.38*	$\text{F}_5^{+\frac{1}{4}}$	*−5.38*	C_6^{0} [8⁄1]
	0		*+ 41.06*		*+ 41.06*		*+ 41.06*		*+ 41.06*
② ⟶	[5⁄4] $\text{E}_3^{-\frac{4}{4}}$	*−5.38*	$\mathbf{B}_3^{-\frac{5}{4}}$	*−5.38*	$\mathbf{F}\sharp_4^{-\frac{6}{4}}$	*−5.38*	$\mathbf{C}\sharp_5^{-\frac{7}{4}}$	*−5.38*	$\mathbf{G}\sharp_5^{-\frac{8}{4}}$ [25⁄16]
	0		*0*		*0*		*0*		*0*
① ⟶	[1⁄1] $\mathbf{C}_3^{0}$	*−5.38*	$\mathbf{G}_3^{-\frac{1}{4}}$	*−5.38*	$\mathbf{D}_4^{-\frac{2}{4}}$	*−5.38*	$\mathbf{A}_4^{-\frac{3}{4}}$	*−5.38*	$\mathbf{E}_5^{-\frac{4}{4}}$ [5⁄4]
			0		*0*		*0*		*0*
		③ ⟶	$\mathbf{E}\flat_3^{+\frac{3}{4}}$	*−5.38*	$\mathbf{B}\flat_3^{+\frac{2}{4}}$	*−5.38*	$\mathbf{F}_4^{+\frac{1}{4}}$	*−5.38*	C_5^{0} [4⁄1]

Figure 10.23 A tuning lattice of Aron's ¼-Comma Meantone Temperament. In this lattice, all "fifths" appear in the horizontal direction, and all "major thirds," in the vertical direction. The fractional comma notation indicates the amount of tempering each tone receives. Low cent values between tones reveal the strengths, and high cent values, the weaknesses of this temperament.

Next, proceed to Step ③, and tune the following three descending just $5/4$'s: G_3–$E\flat_3$, D_4–$B\flat_3$, and A_4–F_4. Figure 10.23 shows that this tuning produces three descending "flat fifths" below C_5. Note carefully that the principal difference between three *ascending* "flat fifths" in Step ① — G_3–D_4, D_4–A_4, A_4–E_5 — and three *descending* "flat fifths" in Step ③ — C_5–F_4, F_4–$B\flat_3$, $B\flat_3$–$E\flat_3$ — is the sign of the fractional comma notation. This sign indicates whether a given tone is tempered in a negative (flat) direction, or in a positive (sharp) direction. As expected, all "fifths" above C are tempered by negative $1/4$-comma increments, which means that these are all "flat fifths." Now, before we discuss the descending "flat fifths," we must first distinguish between an interval ratio and a frequency ratio or tone in a given scale. Note that the *inversion* of the interval of a "fifth" above the tonic, ratio $1/1$, or above the "octave," ratio $2/1$, sounds the frequency ratio or tone of the "fourth" below the "octave"; here $F_4 = 2/1 \div 3/2 = 4/3 = 498.05$ ¢. Now, examine Figure 10.24, which shows that if one tunes the *interval* of an ascending "fifth" a $1/4$-comma flat, one must subtract 5.377 ¢ (701.955 ¢ – 5.377 ¢ = 696.578 ¢) to define the tone of a "flat fifth" above C. However, if one tunes this *interval* as a descending "flat fifth," one must subtract 696.578 ¢ (1200.0 ¢ – 696.578 ¢ = 503.422 ¢) to define the tone of a "sharp fourth" below C. To calculate the amount by which this "sharp fourth" exceeds a just "fourth," subtract 503.422 ¢ – 498.045 ¢ = 5.377 ¢.

F	$F^{+\frac{1}{4}}$	C	$G^{-\frac{1}{4}}$	G
$4/3$	*1200.00 ¢*	*0.00 ¢* ⟶	*701.96 ¢*	$3/2$
498.05 ¢	*– 696.58 ¢*	⟵ *1200.00 ¢*	*– 5.38 ¢*	*701.96 ¢*
	503.42 ¢		*696.58 ¢*	

Figure 10.24 Since the inversion of the *interval* of the "fifth" above the "octave" produces the tone of the "fourth" below the "octave," the inversion of the *interval* of a "flat fifth" above the "octave" produces the tone of a "sharp fourth" below the octave. Here the "flat fifth" above the "octave" equals 696.58 ¢, and the "sharp fourth" below the "octave" equals 503.42 ¢.

Finally, with respect to the top row in Figure 10.23, tune $G\sharp_3$ as a "double-octave" below $G\sharp_5$ in Step ②, and tune $E\flat_4$, $B\flat_4$, F_5, and C_6 as "octaves" above the respective tones in Step ③. Now observe that the top row reveals a "sharp fifth" that sounds between $G\sharp_3$–$E\flat_4$, and the following four "sharp major thirds" that sound between B_3–$E\flat_4$, $F\sharp_4$–$B\flat_4$, $C\sharp_5$–F_5, and $G\sharp_5$–C_6. We will discuss the musical consequences of these intervals below.

Cent calculations for the tones in Step ② require us to add 386.31 ¢ to the cent values of the tones in Step ①. Conversely, cent calculations for the tones in Step ③ require us to subtract 386.31 ¢ from the cent values of the tones in Step ①. The cent values of the entire $1/4$-comma meantone tempered scale appear in Table 10.13. Note the presence of the characteristic meantone, which represents the geometric division of frequency ratio $5/4$ into two equal interval ratios.

A detailed analysis of the cent values in Figure 10.23 and in Table 10.13 indicates that $1/4$-comma meantone temperament has eleven consonant "flat fifths" that equal 701.96 ¢ – 5.38 ¢ = 696.58 ¢, and eleven consonant "sharp fourths" that equal 498.05 ¢ + 5.38 ¢ = 503.43 ¢. The "fifth" between $G\sharp_3$–$E\flat_4$ is a dissonant *sharp* tempered "wolf fifth" that equals (310.26 ¢ + 1200.0 ¢) – 772.63 ¢ = 737.63 ¢; conversely, the "fourth" between $E\flat_3$–$G\sharp_3$ is a dissonant *flat* tempered "wolf fourth" that equals 772.63 ¢ – 310.26 ¢ = 462.37 ¢. The "wolf fifth" is 737.63 ¢ – 701.96 = 35.67 ¢ larger than a just $3/2$, and the "wolf fourth" is 498.05 ¢ – 462.37 ¢ = 35.68 ¢ smaller than a just $4/3$. In Figure 10.23, the "wolf fifth" appears in the top row between $G\sharp_3$–$E\flat_4$. It occurs in this tuning by default. Renaissance and Baroque musicians avoided the dissonant "wolf fifth" and "wolf fourth"

Table 10.13

Scale		Aron's 1/4-Comma Meantone Temperament	
C	1/1	0	
			76.05
C♯		76.05	
			117.11
D		193.16	
			117.10
E♭		310.26	
			76.05
E	5/4	386.31	
			117.11
F		503.42	
			76.05
F♯		579.47	
			117.11
G		696.58	
			76.05
G♯	25/16	772.63	
			117.11
A		889.74	
			117.10
B♭		1006.84	
			76.05
B		1082.89	
			117.11
C′	2/1	1200.00	

as much as possible. To explain the dissimilarity among "fifths" and "fourths," note that 1/4-comma meantone temperament has *two* different kinds of "semitones." Table 10.13 shows that within an "octave" there are seven "large semitones" that equal 117.11 ¢, and five "small semitones" that equal 76.05 ¢.[127] The "flat fifths" consist of "four large plus three small semitones": (117.11 ¢ × 4) + (76.05 ¢ × 3) = 696.59 ¢. However, the "wolf fifth" consists of "five large plus two small semitones": (117.11 ¢ × 5) + (76.05 ¢ × 2) = 737.65 ¢. Therefore, the difference between these two "fifths" equals 117.11 ¢ − 76.05 ¢ = 41.06 ¢.

A further analysis of Table 10.13 indicates *six* consonant major scales that have just 5/4's, and "small fifths" tempered 5.38 ¢ flat: C-major, G-major, D-major, A-major, F-major, and B♭-major; and *six* consonant minor scales that have "small minor thirds" tempered 5.38 ¢ flat of a just 6/5, and the same "small fifths": A-minor, E-minor, B-minor, F♯-minor, D-minor, G-minor. These account for the best twelve keys in 1/4-comma meantone temperament. Although E-major and E♭-major also have just 5/4's, there is a "wolf fifth" between G♯–D♯ in the former scale, and between A♭–E♭ in the latter scale. Four remaining dissonant major scales — B-major, F♯-major, C♯-major, and A♭-major — have "large major thirds" tempered 41.06 ¢ sharp of a just 5/4. Of the remaining dissonant minor keys, three scales — C♯-minor, G♯-minor, and C-minor — have the previous mentioned "small minor thirds," but also "wolf fourths"; and three final scales — E♭-minor, B♭-minor, and F-minor — have "small minor thirds" tempered 46.43 ¢ flat.

To tune 1/4-comma meantone temperament on a set of canon strings, refer to Equation 9.23 and convert the cent values in Table 10.13 to decimal ratios. For example, the decimal ratio of the "flat fifth" equals

$$10^{\frac{696.58\ ¢}{3986.314}} = 1.4954$$

Therefore, according to Equation 3.32, locate this tone on a 1000.0 mm long canon string by placing a bridge at

$$\Lambda = \frac{1000.0 \text{ mm}}{1.4954} = 668.7 \text{ mm}$$

from either the left or the right end of the string.

~ 10.28 ~

We return now to the topic of lute and viol tunings vs. keyboard tunings. At the beginning of Section 10.26, we observed that during the Renaissance, lutes and viols were tuned to approximate versions of 12-tone equal temperament, while keyboards and organs were tuned to meantone temperaments. To understand the reasons for these two different tunings, consider once more the ¼-comma meantone scale in Table 10.13, and the two different kinds of "semitones" that constitute this tuning. These "large semitones" and "small semitones" are the constituent intervals of the "large major thirds" and the "small major thirds" described in Section 10.27. Note that a just 5⁄4 consists of "two large plus two small semitones": (117.11 ¢ × 2) + (76.05 ¢ × 2) = 386.32 ¢. In contrast, a "large major third" consists of "three large plus one small semitone": (117.11 ¢ × 3) + 76.05 ¢ = 427.38 ¢, which means that a "large major third" exceeds a just 5⁄4 by 427.38 ¢ − 386.31 ¢ = 41.07 ¢. Similarly, a meantone "minor third" consists of "two large plus one small semitone": (117.11 ¢ × 2) + 76.05 ¢ = 310.27 ¢. This meantone "minor third" is a ¼-comma smaller than a just 6⁄5: 315.64 ¢ − 310.27 ¢ = 5.37 ¢. In contrast, a "small minor third" consists of "two small plus one large semitone": (76.05 ¢ × 2) + 117.11 ¢ = 269.21 ¢, which means that a "small minor third" is smaller than a just 6⁄5 by 315.64 ¢ − 269.21 ¢ = 46.43 ¢.

Two different kinds of "semitones" present serious intonational difficulties on fretted stringed instruments. On lutes and viols, a fret serves to stop six or more strings at a fixed location on the fingerboard. However, for a meantone scale that consists of two different "semitones," a fret that accurately stops one string may *not* accurately stop another string. For example, a typical 16th-century lute has six open strings tuned to G_2, C_3, F_3, A_3, D_4, and G_4.[128] The third fret (or the third "semitone") under the G_2 string produces $B\flat_2$, a tone that is 310.26 ¢ higher than the open string. Ideally, the same fret under the F_3 string should also produce $G\sharp_3$, a tone that is only 269.20 ¢ higher than the open string. Unfortunately, this is not possible. The difference in cents between these two stopped tones is 310.26 ¢ − 269.20 ¢ = 41.06 ¢. Therefore, the same fret that produces $B\flat_2$ on the first string would also produce a $G\sharp_3$ on the third string that sounds 41.06 ¢ too sharp.[129] For this mechanical reason, fretted instruments are not suitable for meantone temperaments. Instead, Renaissance musicians tuned lutes and viols to 12-tone equal temperament, a scale that has only one kind of "semitone."[130] However, because this temperament includes a dissonant "large major third" tuned 13.69 ¢ sharp of a just 5⁄4, keyboard instruments were consistently tuned to meantone temperaments. For these reasons, lute and viol players did not perform with clavichord and harpsichord players. Inevitably, during the 17th century unfretted violins and cellos replaced the older fretted viols.[131] Because violin and cello players were able to adjust to meantone temperaments during a performance, the earlier tuning controversies no longer prevented these musicians from playing together.

10.29

From a historical perspective, various meantone temperaments represent the transition from just intoned Pythagorean scales to 12-tone equal temperament. Since ¼-comma meantone constitutes a mixture of just intervals and tempered intervals, we refer to it as an *unequal temperament*. The great reluctance during the 18th and 19th centuries to abandon meantone temperaments was twofold. Many musicians refused to part with (1) consonant just ⁵⁄₄'s and only slightly flat tempered "minor thirds" (see Figure 10.26), and (2) the unique *key color* associated with a given scale. The latter reason is *terra incognita* for musicians who only know 12-tone equal temperament, a tuning in which all scales and all triads sound the same. In an unequal temperament, the presence of two different sizes of "semitones" has a unique effect on the musical quality of a given scale. Consequently, Renaissance and Baroque musicians attributed distinct emotional characteristics to the different keys available in meantone temperaments.

Ultimately, meantone temperament gave way to equal temperament. Modern books on this subject endlessly repeat that the acceptance of equal temperament developed out of the desire to play in all 24 keys. To most music theorists, 12-tone equal temperament is a mathematical prerequisite for unconstrained modulation. Although this argument has some validity, from a musical instrument builder's perspective, modulation is not the only reason that caused the advancement of equal temperament. Equal temperament became a necessity due to the structural limitations of keyboard instruments, and due to the physical limitations of the human hand.[132] Consider, for example, the tuning of an unfretted stringed instrument. On a violin, the performer easily controls the tuning of the instrument. Moreover, only a few strings make it possible to produce a large variety of tones. This principle of sound production also applies to wind instruments and the human voice. However, on keyboard instruments like clavichords and harpsichords the performer cannot adjust the tuning of the strings while playing, which means that any given string produces only one pitch. Similarly, the frets of lutes and viols determine all available tones. On such fixed-pitch instruments, one must add more strings to increase the number of tones. Furthermore, consider a violin player who is able to produce 20 distinct frequencies from a single string. To match such a diversity of sound requires 20 separate strings on a harpsichord, or 20 individual frets under a single lute string.[133]

There are serious mechanical difficulties inherent in building a harpsichord with the intonational flexibility of a violin. If one could build such an instrument, and develop a proficient playing technique, then the need for equal temperament would disappear. Subtle intonational adjustments like those produced on unfretted instruments would be readily available by simply playing the appropriate keys. During the Renaissance, many builders successfully constructed such keyboard instruments. Michael Praetorius (1571–1621) published a detailed tuning chart of an *instrumentum perfectum* with nineteen tones to the "octave."[134] Also, Marin Mersenne published drawings for proposed keyboards with sixteen, eighteen, twenty-six, and thirty-one tones to the "octave";[135] and Zarlino proposed a keyboard with nineteen tones to the "octave."[136] However, the mechanical difficulties to builders, the physical challenges to performers, and monetary costs associated with such complicated instruments proved impractical. So, the success of 12-tone equal temperament became inevitable.

10.30

Before we discuss 12-tone equal temperament in full detail, let us first examine an important paper by John Barnes.[137] During the late 17th century, keyboard players became increasingly dissatisfied with the tuning of their instruments because major keys with more than three sharps, and minor keys with more than two flats, sounded too dissonant in ¼-comma meantone temperament. Twelve dissonant keys (or fifty percent of the available keys) remained unusable on standard keyboards with twelve tones to the "octave." In 1691, Andreas Werckmeister (1645–1706) published a book entitled *Musicalische Temperatur.*[138] Here, Werckmeister proposed several *well-temperaments* for all varieties of keyboard instruments. Barnes argues convincingly that Johann S. Bach (1685–1750) composed the *Well-Tempered Clavier* for a tuning called Werckmeister's No. III Well-Temperament.[139] A careful examination of this tuning shows that (1) musicians during the second half of the 17th century disengaged from hallowed tuning practices; and (2) that this fundamental change culminated in the inevitable adoption of equal temperament.

In summary of Section 10.27, refer back to Figure 10.23 and note that ¼-comma meantone temperament includes eight just 5⁄4's and twelve tempered "fifths." As a result, two dissonant "wolf" intervals, G♯–E♭ and E♭–G♯, significantly limit the musical possibilities of this scale. Werckmeister abandoned this approach to tuning and created a scale that includes the exact opposite distribution of intervals. In his tuning, there are eight just 3⁄2's and twelve tempered "major thirds." Werckmeister achieved this design by reexamining the intonational problem presented by the *open spiral of "fifths"* in Figure 10.16(a). For example, begin on a piano's lowest C_1 note, and play the following sequence of twelve consecutive "fifths":

$$C_1 - G_1 - D_2 - A_2 - E_3 - B_3 - F\sharp_4 - C\sharp_5 - G\sharp_5 - D\sharp_6 - A\sharp_6 - E\sharp_7 - B\sharp_7$$

Observe that the last note in this sequence is enharmonically equivalent to C_8. In other words, in a *closed circle of "fifths"* the last note is an exact number of "octaves" above the first note; here the circle ends seven "octaves" higher than the first note. However, if we measure twelve consecutive 3⁄2's in cents, and seven consecutive 2⁄1's in cents, we find that these two tones are not mathematically equivalent. As discussed in Section 10.22, the discrepancy by which twelve "fifths" exceed seven "octaves" is called the comma of Pythagoras, or the *ditonic comma.* Werckmeister resolved the ditonic comma in his well-temperament in a similar manner used to eliminate the syntonic comma in meantone temperament.

To understand how Werckmeister designed his scale, first calculate the ¼ ditonic comma in cents:

$$\tfrac{1}{4}\text{ Ditonic Comma} = \sqrt[4]{\frac{531441}{524288}} \approx 1.0033935$$

$$\log_{10} 1.0033935 \times 3986.314 = 5.865\ ¢$$

$$\text{Or, } \tfrac{1}{4}\text{ Ditonic Comma} = 23.46\ ¢ \div 4 = 5.865\ ¢$$

Refer to Figure 10.25,[140] and observe that in Werckmeister's scale each of three consecutive "fifths" — C_3–G_3, G_3–D_4, D_4–A_4 — and one separate "fifth" — B_3–$F\sharp_4$ — are tuned 5.87 ¢ flat. Determine the standard frequency ratios of the first three consecutive "fifths," calculate their cents, and subtract the cumulative ¼-comma cent values.[141]

$$G_3^{-\frac{1}{4}}:\ \log_{10}\frac{3}{2} \times 3986.314 - (5.865\ ¢ \times 1) = 696.09\ ¢$$

$$D_3^{-\frac{2}{4}}:\ \log_{10}\frac{9}{8} \times 3986.314 - (5.865\ ¢ \times 2) = 192.18\ ¢$$

$$A_4^{-\frac{3}{4}}:\ \log_{10}\frac{27}{16} \times 3986.314 - (5.865\ ¢ \times 3) = 888.27\ ¢$$

Next, observe that E_5 is a just 3⁄2 above $A_4^{-\frac{3}{4}}$, and B_3 is a just 3⁄2 above E_3, which means that the cumulative effect does not apply to these two tones. Therefore, to indicate that there is no change (no increase or decrease) in the size of these two "fifths," temper these frequency ratios by the same amount as $A_4^{-\frac{3}{4}}$.

$$E_5^{-\frac{3}{4}}\text{: } \log_{10}\frac{81}{64}\times 3986.314 - (5.865\ ¢\times 3) = 390.23\ ¢$$

$$B_3^{-\frac{3}{4}}\text{: } \log_{10}\frac{243}{128}\times 3986.314 - (5.865\ ¢\times 3) = 1092.18\ ¢$$

Finally, $F\sharp_4$ is a flat ¼-comma "fifth" above B_3. First, calculate the just $F\sharp_4$ above just B_3 — $^{243}\!/\!_{128} \times {}^{3}\!/\!_{2} = {}^{729}\!/\!_{512}$ — and then subtract 1 ditonic comma.

$$F\sharp_4^{-\frac{4}{4}}\text{: } \log_{10}\frac{729}{512}\times 3986.314 - (5.865\ ¢\times 4) = 588.27\ ¢$$

This last step eliminates the ditonic comma from the scale, and produces a just "tritone," or $F\sharp_4 = {}^{729}\!/\!_{512} \div {}^{531441}\!/\!_{524288} = {}^{1024}\!/\!_{729} = 588.27\ ¢$. Now, Werckmeister's scale requires that we tune six consecutive just 3⁄2's up from this "tritone": $F\sharp_4$–$C\sharp_5$, $C\sharp_5$–$G\sharp_5$, $G\sharp_5$–$E\flat_6$, $E\flat_6$–$B\flat_6$, $B\flat_6$–F_7, F_7–C'_8, which brings us — after we simplify "octave" equivalents — to 2⁄1. Note, therefore, that within the simplified 1⁄1–2⁄1 range, his scale includes six just ratios: 1024⁄729, 256⁄243, 128⁄81, 32⁄27, 16⁄9, 4⁄3. The result is a well-tempered tuning that forms a closed circle of twelve "fifths" over the span of seven "octaves." However, unlike the piano circle, which consists of twelve *identical* flat tempered "fifths" — (700 ¢ × 12) = (1200 ¢ × 7) — Werckmeister's circle contains a *mixture* of four flat tempered "fifths" and eight just 3⁄2's — (696 ¢ × 4) + (702 ¢ × 8) = (1200 ¢ × 7).

An examination of the cent values in Table 10.14 shows that the former ¼-comma meantone "wolf fifth" G♯–E♭ is now a just 3⁄2, and the "wolf fourth" E♭–G♯ is now a just 4⁄3. Furthermore, four previously dissonant "major thirds" — B–E♭, F♯–B♭, C♯–F, and G♯–C — which sounded 41.06 ¢ sharp, now only sound 15.65 ¢ sharp for the B–E♭ triad, and only 21.51 ¢ sharp for the remaining three triads. However, three consonant just 5⁄4's in meantone temperament — E♭–G, A–C♯, and E–G♯ — now sound 15.65 ¢ sharp, and three more just 5⁄4's — B♭–D, G–B, and D–F♯ — now sound

[128⁄81] $G\sharp_5^{-\frac{4}{4}}$	*0*	$\mathbf{E\flat_6^{0}}$ [32⁄27]	*0*	$\mathbf{B\flat_6^{0}}$ [16⁄9]	*0*	$\mathbf{F_7^{0}}$ [4⁄3]	*0*	C_8^{0} [32⁄1]
+ 15.65		*+ 15.65*		*+ 21.51*		*+ 21.51*		*+ 21.51*
$E_3^{-\frac{3}{4}}$	*0*	$\mathbf{B_3^{-\frac{3}{4}}}$	*−5.87*	$\mathbf{F\sharp_4^{-\frac{4}{4}}}$ [1024⁄729]	*0*	$\mathbf{C\sharp_5^{-\frac{4}{4}}}$ [256⁄243]	*0*	$\mathbf{G\sharp_5^{-\frac{4}{4}}}$ [128⁄81]
+ 3.92		*+ 9.78*		*+ 9.78*		*+ 15.65*		*+ 15.65*
[1⁄1] $\mathbf{C_3^{0}}$	*−5.87*	$\mathbf{G_3^{-\frac{1}{4}}}$	*−5.87*	$\mathbf{D_4^{-\frac{2}{4}}}$	*−5.87*	$\mathbf{A_4^{-\frac{3}{4}}}$	*0*	$\mathbf{E_5^{-\frac{3}{4}}}$
		+ 15.65		*+ 9.78*		*+ 3.92*		*+ 3.92*
		$E\flat_3^{0}$ [32⁄27]	*0*	$B\flat_3^{0}$ [16⁄9]	*0*	F_4^{0} [4⁄3]	*0*	C_5^{0} [4⁄1]

Figure 10.25 A lattice of Werckmeister's No. III Well-Temperament. As in Figure 10.23, all "fifths" appear in the horizontal direction, and all "major thirds," in the vertical direction. Note that within the simplified 1⁄1–2⁄1 range, this masterful tuning includes six just ratios: 1024⁄729, 256⁄243, 128⁄81, 32⁄27, 16⁄9, 4⁄3.

Table 10.14

Scale		Werckmeister's No. III Well-Temperament	
C	1/1	0	
			90.23
C♯	256/243	90.23	
			101.95
D		192.18	
			101.96
E♭	32/27	294.14	
			96.09
E		390.23	
			107.82
F	4/3	498.05	
			90.22
F♯	1024/729	588.27	
			107.82
G		696.09	
			96.09
G♯	128/81	792.18	
			96.09
A		888.27	
			107.82
B♭	16/9	996.09	
			96.09
B		1092.18	
			107.82
C′	2/1	1200.00	

9.78 ¢ sharp. This is probably one of the reasons why Werckmeister wrote almost apologetically, "And our temperaments are not so far removed from the old ones as many people think."[142]

In keeping with the Renaissance tradition of *key color*, note that this scale has *four* different "semitones." However, the largest difference between these "semitones" equals only 107.82 ¢ − 90.22 ¢ = 17.60 ¢, which is less than half the difference between the two "semitones" of 1/4-comma meantone temperament. Finally, refer to Figure 10.26, which compares Aron's and Werckmeister's temperaments. In the former scale, the tuning of eleven moderately flat tempered "fifths" and one dissonant "wolf fifth" produce eight just 5/4's, and four dissonant sharp tempered "major thirds." In the latter scale, the tuning of twelve moderate to strong tempered "major thirds" produce eight just 3/2's, and four moderately flat tempered "fifths." More importantly, observe how this scale distributes the dissonant major and minor triads to the remote keys. As one modulates from the keys without any or only a few sharps and flats, to the keys with many sharps and flats, the dissonance gradually increases. In short, at the beginning of the 18th century, the emphasis in keyboard tuning shifted dramatically from a limited number of consonant keys to a full range of consonant-dissonant keys intentionally designed in a sequence of graduated consonance-dissonance. For this reason alone, Werckmeister's scale is a masterful example of musical mathematics.

10.31

12-tone equal temperament consists of a closed circle of identical "fifths." We may achieve such a tuning in two mathematically equivalent ways. (1) Geometrically divide the comma of Pythagoras

Aron's ¼-Comma Meantone Temperament (*c.* 1500)

	E♭	B♭	F	C	G	D	A	E	B	F♯	C♯	G♯	E♭
"Fifths":	*−5*	*−5*	*−5*	*−5*	*−5*	*−5*	*−5*	*−5*	*−5*	*−5*	*−5*	*+36*	
"Major Thirds":	*0*	*0*	*0*	*0*	*0*	*0*	*0*	*0*	*+41*	*+41*	*+41*	*+41*	
"Minor Thirds":	*−46*	*−46*	*−46*	*−5*	*−5*	*−5*	*−5*	*−5*	*−5*	*−5*	*−5*	*−5*	

Werckmeister's No. III Well-Temperament (*c.* 1700)

	E♭	B♭	F	C	G	D	A	E	B	F♯	C♯	G♯	E♭
"Fifths":	*0*	*0*	*0*	*−6*	*−6*	*−6*	*0*	*0*	*−6*	*0*	*0*	*0*	
"Major Thirds":	*+16*	*+10*	*+4*	*+4*	*+10*	*+10*	*+16*	*+16*	*+16*	*+22*	*+22*	*+22*	
"Minor Thirds":	*−22*	*−22*	*−22*	*−22*	*−16*	*−10*	*−4*	*−10*	*−16*	*−16*	*−16*	*−16*	

Figure 10.26 A comparison of Aron's ¼-Comma Meantone Temperament and Werckmeister's No. III Well-Temperament.

into twelve equal parts, and then distribute these parts by tuning twelve consecutive flat tempered "fifths." (2) Geometrically divide the "octave" into twelve equal parts, and then tune twelve identical flat tempered "semitones."

The first method requires that we calculate a ⅟12 ditonic comma in cents:

$$\tfrac{1}{12}\text{ Ditonic Comma} = \sqrt[12]{\frac{531441}{524288}} \approx 1.00112989$$

$$\log_{10} 1.00112989 \times 3986.314 = 1.955\ ¢$$

$$\text{Or, } \tfrac{1}{12}\text{ Ditonic Comma} = 23.46\ ¢ \div 12 = 1.955\ ¢$$

Now, determine the cent values of twelve consecutive flat tempered "fifths" by subtracting the cumulative ⅟12-comma cent values from the ratios that constitute the spiral of "fifths" in Figure 10.16(a). However, since 12-TET includes only one kind of "semitone," and since this crucial interval first occurs between C_1–$\text{C}\sharp_5$, the sequence below applies the required pattern of calculation to the first three "fifths," and then skips to the defining seventh "fifth."

$$\text{G}_1^{-\frac{1}{12}}:\ \log_{10}\frac{3}{2} \times 3986.314 - (1.955\ ¢ \times 1) = 700.000\ ¢$$

$$\text{D}_2^{-\frac{2}{12}}:\ \log_{10}\frac{9}{8} \times 3986.314 - (1.955\ ¢ \times 2) = 200.000\ ¢$$

$$\text{A}_2^{-\frac{3}{12}}:\ \log_{10}\frac{27}{16} \times 3986.314 - (1.955\ ¢ \times 3) = 900.000\ ¢\ ...$$

$$\text{C}\sharp_5^{-\frac{7}{12}}:\ \log_{10}\frac{2187}{2048} \times 3986.314 - (1.955\ ¢ \times 7) = 100.000\ ¢\ ...$$

The second method establishes the flat tempered "semitone" directly. Simply extract the 12th root of 2 (see Section 9.13), and then calculate this interval in cents.

$$\text{C}\sharp\text{: } \log_{10} \sqrt[12]{2} \times 3986.314 = \log_{10} 1.0594631 \times 3986.314 = 100.000\ ¢$$

Note, therefore, that the latter two methods are mathematically equivalent because

$$\frac{\dfrac{2187}{2048}}{\sqrt[12]{\dfrac{531441}{524288}}^{\,7}} = \sqrt[12]{2} \approx 1.0594631$$

As discussed in Section 10.18, the "Exact semitone" equals

$$\log_{10} \sqrt{\frac{9}{8}} \times 3986.314 = 101.955\ ¢$$

which means that it is a $^1\!/_{12}$-comma too sharp for 12-TET. Because the irrational value of $\sqrt[12]{2}$ remained unknown until Simon Stevin (1548–1620) in the West (see Sections 10.32–10.33), and Chu Tsai-yü (1536–1611) in the East (see Section 11.11), managed to independently calculate this number in 1584, musicians and instrument builders tuned an *approximation of 12-TET* on fretted stringed instruments. In the West, this approximation was based on Ptolemy's arithmetic division of the "whole tone." An exactly equal division of length ratio $^9\!/_8$ results in the arithmetic progression 18:17:16, which produces two nearly equal "semitones": a lower "small semitone," ratio $^{18}\!/_{17}$ [99.0 ¢], and an upper "large semitone," ratio $^{17}\!/_{16}$ [105.0 ¢]. Ptolemy describes this division in the *Harmonics I.10:*

> Since neither 9:8 nor any other epimore ratio can be divided in half, but 17:16 and 18:17, whose values are nearly the same, multiplied together equal 9:8, the value of the semitone may lie approximately between these two [ratios], i.e., [it] is larger than 18:17, [and] smaller than 17:16.[143] (Text in brackets mine.)

Ptolemy used this example to demonstrate that it is impossible to arithmetically divide any given epimore ratio into two equal interval ratios. His analysis is highly accurate because he correctly observed that

$$^{18}\!/_{17} < \sqrt{^9\!/_8} < {}^{17}\!/_{16}$$

Consistent with the technique of string division described in Figure 10.5, Figure 10.27 shows the arithmetic division of length ratio $^{18}\!/_{16}$ [$^9\!/_8$] on the sample string 1000.0 mm long.[144]

The oldest extant description of length ratio $^{18}\!/_{17}$ on a fretted lute exists in a work entitled *Kitāb al-mūsīqī al-kabīr* (Major book on music),[145] by Abū Naṣr Al-Fārābī (d. *c.* 950). Al-Fārābī gives the following description of the arithmetic division of ratio $^4\!/_3$ into two nearly equal intervals 8:7:6, or $^8\!/_7$ and $^7\!/_6$; of ratio $^9\!/_8$ into two nearly equal "semitones" 18:17:16, or $^{18}\!/_{17}$ and $^{17}\!/_{16}$; and finally of ratio $^9\!/_8$ into four nearly equal "quarter-tones" 36:35:34:33:32, or $^{36}\!/_{35}$, $^{35}\!/_{34}$, $^{34}\!/_{33}$, and $^{33}\!/_{32}$:

> We propose, for example, to divide the fourth in half. First of all, we take the numbers representing the notes of this interval, i.e., 4 and 3. We double them, which gives us 8 and 6. We take half of the difference between 8 and 6, i.e., 1, which we add to 6, or which we subtract from 8; either of these two operations gives us the number 7; 7 will be the value of the note that divides the interval of the fourth in half . . .
>
> This rule enables us to divide in half all the intervals that we want. For the interval of the tone divided into two semitones, the ratio of the first

Figure 10.27 The arithmetic division of the "whole tone" expressed as ancient length ratio $^{18}\!/\!_{16}$ [$^{9}\!/\!_{8}$]. Vincenzo Galilei adopted length ratio $^{18}\!/\!_{17}$ as a flat tempered "semitone" on his 12-tone lute.

> note to the second is 18 to 17, and that of the second to the third is 17 to 16. For the quarter-tone, called the *interval of slackness*, the ratio of the first note to the second is that of 36 to 35. The third degree of the tone, thus divided, will be represented by the number 34, the fourth by 33, and the fifth by 32.[146]

In Figure 11.48, length ratio $^{18}\!/\!_{17}$ appears on Al-Fārābī's 10-fret *'ūd*, and in Figure 11.49, on his 22-tone "double-octave" *'ūd*. The "quarter-tone," ratio $^{33}\!/\!_{32}$, also exists in both tunings as the interval between Frets 8 and 9 on the former, and between Frets 9 and 11 on the latter instrument; that is: $^{81}\!/\!_{64} \div {}^{27}\!/\!_{22} = {}^{33}\!/\!_{32}$. Furthermore, because Al-Fārābī knew that the "octave" consists of twelve "semitones,"

> Let us assume that the half step (*faḍlah*) equals half the whole step (*'awdah*). It would follow that if we subtract the half step from the whole step, the remainder would be of the same size. The half step is thus the interval common to all these intervals, an interval which can be measured twice in the whole step. The interval of the fourth, therefore, consists of two whole steps and a half; the interval of a fifth, of three whole steps and a half. If we assume for the half step a measurement of one, ***the octave will measure twelve*** and, accordingly, the fifth will measure seven; the fourth, five; and the whole step, two.[147] (Bold italics mine.)

and because in adjusting the frets on his lute he must have been aware that $^{18}\!/\!_{17} \approx \sqrt{^{9}\!/\!_{8}}$, it is highly probable that Al-Fārābī contemplated the significance of twelve $^{18}\!/\!_{17}$'s six hundred years before music theorists in Europe.

In Europe, the first description of the arithmetic division of ratio $^{9}\!/\!_{8}$ exists in a work entitled *Opera omnia*, written in about 1546 by Jerome Cardan (1501–1576).[148] Cardan gives the following mathematical and musical description of $^{18}\!/\!_{17}$ and $^{17}\!/\!_{16}$:

> And there is another division of the tone into semitones, which is varied by putting the tone between 18 and 16; the middle voice is 17; the major semitone is between 17 and 16, but the minor between 18 and 17, the difference of which is 1/288 [1/272]. It is surprising how the minor semitone should be introduced so pleasingly in concerted music, but the major semitone never.[149] (Ratio in brackets mine.)

Finally, in 1581, Vincenzo Galilei (*c.* 1520 – d. 1591) — the father of Galileo Galilei — proposed in his *Dialogo della musica antica et della moderna* that instrument builders and musicians employ ratio $^{18}\!/\!_{17}$ as a practical solution for tuning an approximation of 12-tone equal temperament on the lute. On pp. 121–122 of Claude V. Palisca's translation of this treatise, Galilei gives the following correct instructions for locating the frets of a complete 12-tone scale on a monochord:

> Therefore, I divide the line AB into eighteen parts, and toward the high end [starting from the low end], where the first segment ends, I place the first fret. Then, I divide the entire remainder of the line again into eighteen parts, and at the end of the first segment I locate the second fret. By this method, I go on to divide the distance that the frets leave empty until I reach the twelfth step.[150]

Unfortunately, on p. 128, Galilei initially gives incorrect instructions for locating the second and third frets on a lute, but then changes ". . . the condition mentioned . . ." and proceeds with correct instructions, which are numerically equivalent to those in the quoted passage above.

Western writers typically cite Vincenzo Galilei as the first theorist to tune ratio $^{18}\!/\!_{17}$ on the lute.

> Vincenzo Galilei must be given the credit for explaining a practical, but highly effective, method of this type. For placing the frets on the lute he used the ratio 18:17 for the semitone, saying that the twelfth fret would be at the mid-point of the string. He went on to say that no other fraction would serve; for 17:16, etc., would give too few frets, and 19:18, etc., too many. Since 18:17 represents 99 cents, 17:16, 105 cents, and 19:18, 94 cents, Galilei was correct in his contention. But he did not give a mathematical demonstration of his method. It remained for him a proof by intuition.[151]

To understand the mathematical technique used to determine the locations of frets on a lute, consider a description from a monumental work entitled *Harmonie universelle: The Books on Instruments*, published in 1636 by Marin Mersenne. The following passage is from the Second Book of String Instruments, Proposition I:

> Many makers of instruments divide the length of the lute or the open string into 18 parts, of which the seventeenth forms the first fret; and then they divide the rest of the string into 18 parts, of which they again take the seventeenth to make the second semitone, and in the same way until they have 8 or 9 semitones.[152]

For example, on a typical lute string with a length of 635.00 mm (25.0 in.), the first three frets are located

$$\text{Fret 1: } \frac{635.00 \text{ mm}}{\frac{18}{17}} = 599.72 \text{ mm}$$

$$\text{Fret 2: } \frac{599.72 \text{ mm}}{\frac{18}{17}} = 566.40 \text{ mm}$$

$$\text{Fret 3: } \frac{566.40 \text{ mm}}{\frac{18}{17}} = 534.93 \text{ mm}$$

from the bridge. Observe that these calculations are equivalent to

$$\text{Fret 1:}\quad \frac{635.00 \text{ mm}}{\left(\frac{18}{17}\right)^1} = 599.72 \text{ mm}$$

$$\text{Fret 2:}\quad \frac{635.00 \text{ mm}}{\left(\frac{18}{17}\right)^2} = 566.40 \text{ mm}$$

$$\text{Fret 3:}\quad \frac{635.00 \text{ mm}}{\left(\frac{18}{17}\right)^3} = 534.94 \text{ mm}$$

Now, the "octave" fret should be located

$$\text{“Octave” Fret:}\quad \frac{635.00 \text{ mm}}{\frac{2}{1}} = 317.50 \text{ mm}$$

from the bridge. However, this approximation places the last fret at

$$\text{Fret 12:}\quad \frac{635.00 \text{ mm}}{\left(\frac{18}{17}\right)^{12}} = 319.81 \text{ mm}$$

or 2.31 mm too low on the neck: that is, too near to the nut, or too far from the bridge. (On lutes, violins, etc. the phrase "low on the neck" describes a location nearer to the nut, and "high on the neck," nearer to the bridge.) Consequently, Fret 12 produces an "octave" that sounds 12.54 ¢ flat:

$$\log_{10}\left(\frac{18}{17}\right)^{12} \times 3986.314 = 1{,}187.46 \text{ ¢}$$

Although the preceding analysis gives a negative impression of this approximation of 12-TET, consider the practical benefits of ratio 18⁄17. Because the last fret sits too low on the neck, we assume that the strings stopped at this location are too long and will sound flat. However, on an actual lute, this is not the case. When a lute player's finger presses down on a string at the location of a fret, such an action slightly stretches the string and therefore increases its tension. Because the frequency (F) of a string is directly proportional to the square root of the tension (T), as the tension increases, the frequency increases as well.[153] For this reason, during the Renaissance many builders preferred using powers of 18⁄17 to calculate the fret locations on their lutes.[154] Even though the strings are slightly too long, such increases in tension compensate for the extra length and raise the strings to the desired frequencies. On modern guitars, the tension problem has a different solution. To correct this difficulty, guitar makers intentionally build instruments with slightly longer strings. The extra string length, which varies between 1–5 mm, is called *string compensation.*[155] This feature also exists on the Harmonic/Melodic Canon in Plate 2, and on the Bass Canon in Plate 3. On these instruments, moveable bridges push against the strings in an upward direction, an action that also stretches and increases the tension of the strings. Consequently, all the strings on both canons are slightly longer than the theoretically correct lengths. (See Sections 12.3 and 12.6.)

Finally, Figure 10.28 shows an edited reproduction of a lute engraving from Mersenne's Second Book of Instruments, Proposition I.[156] This engraving includes lute fret measurements of two critically important scales based on a open string length of 100,000 units. Table 10.15, Column 3, shows that the measurements in the first column in Figure 10.28 represent a 5-limit just intoned version of the Western 12-tone scale. The 5-limit ratios of this chromatic scale were first calculated in a treatise entitled *Musica practica*, published in 1482 by Bartolomeo Ramis. (See Figures 10.32 and 10.33.) Table 10.15, Column 6, shows that the measurements in the second column in Figure 10.28 represent the complete approximation of 12-TET as intended by Galilei's application of interval ratio $^{18}/_{17}$. Observe that in the latter column, the engraver mistranscribed four measurements. Now, refer back to Figure 10.15, and note that we may trace the historic origins of many length ratios in Figure 10.28 to the work of Ptolemy.

Table 10.15

LUTE FRET MEASUREMENTS FROM AN ENGRAVING IN MERSENNE'S *HARMONIE UNIVERSELLE*

Scale		*L*	Scale		*L*
C	$^1/_1$	100,000	C	$^1/_1$	100,000
C♯	$^{16}/_{15}$	93,750	C♯	$(^{18}/_{17})^1$	94,444
D	$^9/_8$	88,889	D	$(^{18}/_{17})^2$	89,198
D♯	$^6/_5$	83,333	D♯	$(^{18}/_{17})^3$	84,242
E	$^5/_4$	80,000	E	$(^{18}/_{17})^4$	79,562
F	$^4/_3$	75,000	F	$(^{18}/_{17})^5$	75,142
F♯	$^{45}/_{32}$	71,111	F♯	$(^{18}/_{17})^6$	70,967
G	$^3/_2$	66,667	G	$(^{18}/_{17})^7$	67,025
G♯	$^8/_5$	62,500	G♯	$(^{18}/_{17})^8$	63,301
A	$^5/_3$	60,000	A	$(^{18}/_{17})^9$	59,784
A♯	$^{16}/_9$	56,250	A♯	$(^{18}/_{17})^{10}$	56,463
B	$^{15}/_8$	53,333	B	$(^{18}/_{17})^{11}$	53,326
C'	$^2/_1$	50,000	C'	$(^{18}/_{17})^{12}$	50,364
(1)	(2)	(3)	(4)	(5)	(6)

10.32

Simon Stevin (1548–1620) was the first known European mathematician to calculate 12-tone equal temperament. Stevin described his findings in a treatise entitled *Vande Spiegeling der Singconst.*[157] Here, Stevin did *not* give the irrational decimal ratios of 12-TET; instead, he listed 12 length ratios for a monochord 10,000 units long. Stevin calculated these length ratios in two distinctly different steps. Table 10.16 shows that in Step 1, he extracted the square, quartic, and cubic roots of 2, which gave him the irrational decimal ratios of the "tritone," the "minor third," and the "major third," respectively.

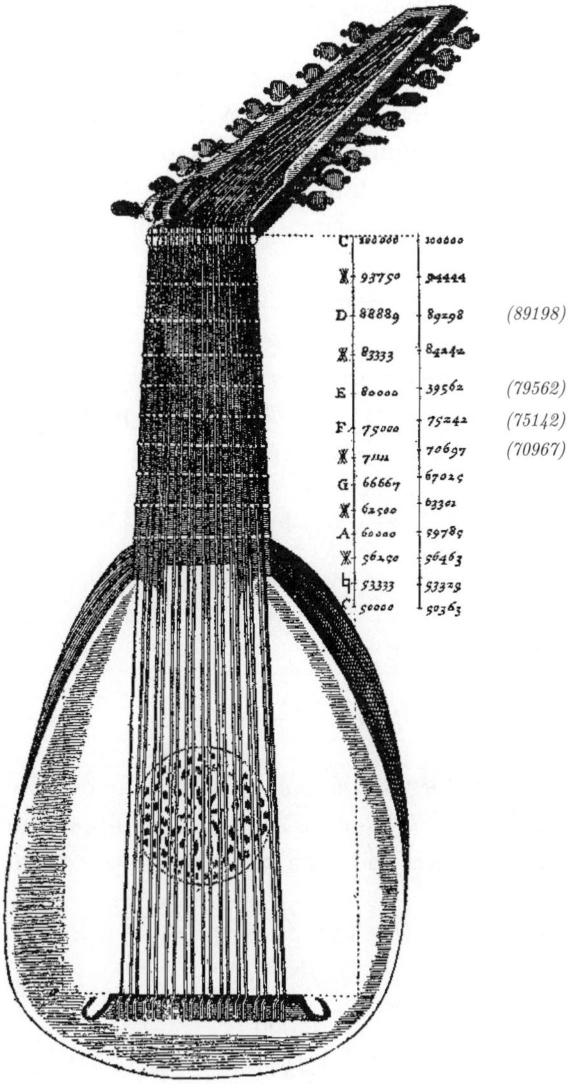

Figure 10.28 An edited reproduction of a lute engraving from Mersenne's *Harmonie universelle: The Books on Instruments.* Refer to Figure 10.15 and Table 10.15, and note that we may trace the origins of the two scales in this engraving to mathematical concepts in Ptolemy's *Harmonics.*

Table 10.16

STEVIN'S CALCULATIONS OF IRRATIONAL DECIMAL RATIOS

Intervals	Notation	Equivalents	Decimal Ratios
"Tritone"	$\frac{2}{\sqrt{2}}$	$\sqrt{2}$	≈ 1.4142
"Minor Third"	$\frac{2}{\sqrt[4]{8}}$	$\sqrt[4]{2}$	≈ 1.1893
"Major Third"	$\frac{2}{\sqrt[3]{4}}$	$\sqrt[3]{2}$	≈ 1.2599

In Step 2, he utilized these three preliminary results to calculate nine additional irrational decimal ratios. Note, therefore, that the precision of the former ratios determines the accuracy of the latter ratios. Because Stevin *miscalculated* the "minor third" in Step 1, he transferred a small error to eight out of nine length ratios in Step 2. However, this inaccuracy produced only a maximum positive error of +0.2 ¢, and a maximum negative error of −0.4 ¢. Stevin's work is a remarkable achievement because he managed to calculate the irrational decimal ratios of 12-TET without the use of logarithms and, therefore, without extracting the twelfth root of 2.[158]

~ 10.33 ~

In Step 1, Stevin calculated the geometric division of length ratio $^{2}/_{1}$ into two, four, and three equal parts.[159] Suppose we choose a C–C′ "octave." Such divisions produce the "tritone" C–F♯, the "minor third" C–E♭, and the "major third" C–E, respectively.

C ———————— F♯ ———————— C′

C ———— E♭ ———— F♯ ———— A ———— C′

C —————— E —————— G♯ —————— C′

For detailed discussions on the extraction of roots, Stevin refers the reader to his French work on arithmetic entitled *L'Arithmetique*.[160] Given the roots as they appear in the fourth column of Table 10.16, Stevin defined three proportions and then calculated these string lengths (Λ).

$$\text{For F}\sharp\text{:}\quad \frac{2}{\sqrt{2}} = 1.4142$$

$$\Lambda = \frac{10{,}000}{1.4142} = 7071$$

$$\text{For E}\flat\text{:}\quad \frac{2}{\sqrt[4]{8}} = 1.1893$$

$$\Lambda = \frac{10{,}000}{1.1893} = 8408$$

$$\text{For E:}\quad \frac{2}{\sqrt[3]{4}} = 1.2599$$

$$\Lambda = \frac{10{,}000}{1.2599} = 7937$$

In the original text, Stevin only gives length ratios $^{10000}/_{7071}$, $^{10000}/_{8408}$, and $^{10000}/_{7937}$. Notice Stevin's miscalculation for the length of the "minor third." The decimal ratio approximation should read 1.1892, which results in a string length E♭ = 8409 units.

Finally, in Step 2, Stevin first derived the decimal ratios of the "semitone" and the "whole tone." Since a "major third" minus a "minor third" equals a "semitone," he calculated the decimal ratio of C♯ by dividing the decimal ratio of E by the decimal ratio of E♭. This exact quotient is equivalent to the twelfth root of 2:

$$\frac{\frac{2}{\sqrt[3]{4}}}{\frac{2}{\sqrt[4]{8}}} = \frac{\sqrt[3]{2}}{\sqrt[4]{2}} = \sqrt[12]{2} \tag{10.9}$$

Similarly, since a "semitone" plus a "semitone" equals a "whole tone," he calculated the decimal ratio of D by squaring the decimal ratio of C♯. Consequently, here are Stevin's string lengths for C♯ and D.

For C♯: "Major Third" (E) – "Minor Third" (E♭) → $\frac{\frac{10{,}000}{7937}}{\frac{10{,}000}{8408}} = 1.0593,\ \Lambda = \frac{10{,}000}{1.0593} = 9440$

For D: "Semitone" (C♯) + "Semitone" (C♯) → $\left(\frac{10{,}000}{9440}\right)^2 = 1.1222,\ \Lambda = \frac{10{,}000}{1.1222} = 8911$

Stevin then derived seven more lengths from various interval combinations.

For F: "Semitone" (C♯) + "Major Third" (E) → $\frac{10{,}000}{9440} \times \frac{10{,}000}{7937} = 1.3347,\ \Lambda = \frac{10{,}000}{1.3347} = 7493$

For G: "Tritone" (F♯) + "Semitone" (C♯) → $\frac{10{,}000}{7071} \times \frac{10{,}000}{9440} = 1.4981,\ \Lambda = \frac{10{,}000}{1.4981} = 6675$

For G♯: "Fifth" (G) + "Semitone" (C♯) → $\frac{10{,}000}{6675} \times \frac{10{,}000}{9440} = 1.5870,\ \Lambda = \frac{10{,}000}{1.5870} = 6301$

For A: "Tritone" (F♯) + "Minor Third" (E♭) → $\frac{10{,}000}{7071} \times \frac{10{,}000}{8408} = 1.6820,\ \Lambda = \frac{10{,}000}{1.6820} = 5945$

For A♯: "Tritone" (F♯) + "Major Third" (E) → $\frac{10{,}000}{7071} \times \frac{10{,}000}{7937} = 1.7818,\ \Lambda = \frac{10{,}000}{1.7818} = 5612$

For B: "Augmented Sixth" (A♯) + "Semitone" (C♯) → $\frac{10{,}000}{5612} \times \frac{10{,}000}{9440} = 1.8876,\ \Lambda = \frac{10{,}000}{1.8876} = 5298$

For C′: "Major Seventh" (B) + "Semitone" (C♯) → $\frac{10{,}000}{5298} \times \frac{10{,}000}{9440} = 1.9995,\ \Lambda = \frac{10{,}000}{1.9995} = 5001$

Note that only the length of the "augmented sixth," A♯ — or the "minor seventh," B♭ — is exact because it is neither directly nor indirectly based on the miscalculated length of E♭.

In Table 10.17, Columns 2 and 3 list Stevin's length ratios and cent values calculated with his decimal ratios accurate to four places. In contrast, Columns 4 and 5 list exact length ratios and cent values calculated with decimal ratios accurate to six places. To compute the decimal ratios of 12-TET, use Equation 9.24,

$$\sqrt[12]{2}^{\,y} = x$$

where y is a given "semitone," any positive integer 1–12. Now, refer to Equation 3.32, and divide 10,000 units by these ratios to obtain the string lengths in Column 4. For cent calculations, substitute the appropriate decimal ratio into Equation 9.21:

$$\log_{10} x \times 3986.314 = ¢$$

Table 10.17

12-TONE EQUAL TEMPERAMENT STRING LENGTH AND CENT VALUES

Scale	Stevin's String Lengths	Stevin's Cent Values	Exact String Lengths	Exact Cent Values
C	10,000	0	10,000	0
C♯	9440	99.7	9439	100.00
D	8911	199.6	8909	200.00
E♭	8408	300.1	8409	300.00
E	7937	400.0	7937	400.00
F	7493	499.8	7492	500.00
F♯	7071	600.0	7071	600.00
G	6675	699.8	6674	700.00
G♯	6301	799.6	6300	800.00
A	5945	900.2	5946	900.00
A♯	5612	1000.0	5612	1000.00
B	5298	1099.9	5297	1100.00
C^I	5001	1199.6	5000	1200.00
(1)	(2)	(3)	(4)	(5)

Because 12-TET has only one kind of "semitone" that equals 100.0 ¢, all musical intervals in this temperament are identical. Consistent with the organizational principles of Figure 10.26, Figure 10.29 shows that all "fifths" of 12-TET are tuned 2 ¢ flat of a just 3/2, all "major thirds," 14 ¢ sharp of a just 5/4, and all "minor thirds," 16 ¢ flat of a just 6/5.

	C	G	D	A	E	B	F♯	C♯	G♯	D♯	A♯	E♯	B♯
"Fifths":	−2	−2	−2	−2	−2	−2	−2	−2	−2	−2	−2	−2	
"Major Thirds":	*+14*	*+14*	*+14*	*+14*	*+14*	*+14*	*+14*	*+14*	*+14*	*+14*	*+14*	*+14*	
"Minor Thirds":	*−16*	*−16*	*−16*	*−16*	*−16*	*−16*	*−16*	*−16*	*−16*	*−16*	*−16*	*−16*	

Figure 10.29 The "fifths," "major thirds," and "minor thirds" of 12-tone equal temperament. When compared to the two examples in Figure 10.26, it is apparent why this scale is called an *equal* temperament.

∾ 10.34 ∾

This last section of Part V on tempered tunings also serves as a transition to Part VI on just intonation. In 1691, Christiaan Huygens (1629–1695) wrote a letter to the editor of *Histoire des Ouvranges des Sçavans* in which he compared 1/4-meantone temperament to 31-tone equal temperament.[161] Huygens was the first music theorist to accurately calculate these two temperaments with logarithms. His analysis is significant because it also sheds new light on the consonant musical qualities of frequency ratios 7/6, 7/5, and 7/4.[162]

The number 12 of the conventional piano scale is not a constant, but a variable. Many different tunings exist in which an open spiral of "fifths" approximates a closed circle of "fifths," or an exact number of "octaves." For example, a spiral of 31 consecutive $^{3}\!/_{2}$'s exceeds 18 consecutive $^{2}\!/_{1}$'s by 160.61 ¢.

$$\frac{\left(\frac{3}{2}\right)^{31}}{\left(\frac{2}{1}\right)^{18}} = 1.09721$$

$$\log_{10} 1.09721 \times 3986.314 = 160.61\ ¢$$

As a result, all "fifths" in 31-TET are tuned 160.61 ¢ ÷ 31 = 5.18 ¢ flat, a quantity that is very close to a ¼ syntonic comma at 5.38 ¢. Table 10.18 lists the cent values of the complete 31-tone equal tempered scale.

Table 10.18

31-TONE EQUAL TEMPERAMENT

Scale	Cents	Scale	Cents
1.	0	17.	619.35
2.	38.71	18.	658.06
3.	77.42	19.	696.77
4.	116.13	20.	735.48
5.	154.84	21.	774.19
6.	193.55	22.	812.90
7.	232.26	23.	851.61
8.	270.97	24.	890.32
9.	309.68	25.	929.03
10.	348.39	26.	967.74
11.	387.10	27.	1006.45
12.	425.81	28.	1045.16
13.	464.52	29.	1083.87
14.	503.23	30.	1122.58
15.	541.94	31.	1161.29
16.	580.65	32.	1200.00

With logarithms, Huygens discovered that 31-TET includes a very close approximation of ¼-comma meantone temperament. This approximation is musically indistinguishable from exact meantone temperament. Refer to Table 10.19, and note that eleven tones of 31-TET are less than 2.0 ¢ removed from the meantone scale. This discovery inspired Huygens to design a transposition mechanism for a harpsichord with 31 strings to the "octave."[163] In place of the upper manual (which sits above the lower manual on a typical French harpsichord),[164] Huygens recommended a moveable keyboard with 12 keys per "octave." In place of the lower manual, Huygens proposed a set of 31 key levers (or *batons*) per "octave" to operate the harpsichord jacks, which in turn pluck the strings. To fit 31 *batons* into the space of 7 standard white keys, each *baton* had a width ⅕ (or more accurately, $^{7}\!/_{31}$) of a conventional key. A set of pins coupled the upper keys to the lower *batons*. The arrangement of these pins activated the following strings: #1, #3, #6, #9, #11, #14, etc. as shown in Table 10.19. By sliding the moveable keyboard to the left or to the right, Huygens' transposition mechanism enabled a performer to play this irregular string pattern on any given starting note.[165] As a result, all the remote keys of ¼-comma meantone temperament sounded as consonant as the near keys. However, although such a transposing harpsichord solved the problem of playing in dissonant keys, it did not resolve the difficulties associated with modulation. Consequently, Huygens' design had only limited appeal.

Table 10.19

CENT COMPARISON OF ¼-COMMA MEANTONE AND 31-TET

Scale	¼-Comma Meantone	Scale	31-TET
C	0	1.	0
C♯	76.05	3.	77.42
D	193.16	6.	193.55
E♭	310.26	9.	309.68
E	386.31	11.	387.10
F	503.42	14.	503.23
F♯	579.47	16.	580.65
G	696.58	19.	696.77
G♯	772.63	21.	774.19
A	889.74	24.	890.32
B♭	1006.84	27.	1006.45
B	1082.89	29.	1083.87
C′	1200.00	32.	1200.00

Finally, Huygens also discovered close approximations of septimal ratios 7/6, 7/5, and 7/4 not only in ¼-comma meantone temperament, but in 31-TET as well. The presence of these intervals in two different scales confirmed for him the *musical* significance of these ratios. In the meantone scale, a septimal "minor third" approximation occurs twice: E♭–G♭ and F–A♭; a septimal "tritone" approximation, six times: C–F♯, D–G♯, E♭–A, F–B, G–C♯, and B♭–E; and a septimal "minor seventh" approximation, also twice: E♭–D♭ and B♭–A♭. Table 10.20 compares the cent values of meantone and 31-TET ratios to the cent values of just intoned ratios. In the first column, sequences of S and L indicate the small and large "semitones" that constitute the ¼-comma meantone intervals in the second column. Observe that the 7/6 meantone approximation is closer to the exact value than the 31-TET approximation, and *vice versa* for 7/5 and 7/4.

Table 10.20

CENT COMPARISON OF THREE SEPTIMAL RATIOS

	¼-Comma Meantone	31-TET	J.I.
SLS	E♭–G♭ = 269.21 ¢	8. = 270.97 ¢	7/6 = 266.87 ¢
SLLSLS	C–F♯ = 579.47 ¢	16. = 580.65 ¢	7/5 = 582.51 ¢
SLSLSLLSLS	E♭–D♭′ = 965.79 ¢	26. = 967.74 ¢	7/4 = 968.83 ¢

As an enlightened scientist, Huygens declared that ratios $7/6$, $7/5$, and $7/4$ are consonant. Huygens arrived at this conclusion because he believed in the validity of experience and reason.

> Now I say that these intervals of 7:5 and 10:7 have something harmonious, when examined attentively (at least I experience it so with my ear), and that one could count them among the consonances, whatever may be said about it by the Messrs composers, who range them among the false relations. [*Marginal Note:*] I won't listen to those who plead authority.[166]

In Section 5.18, we discussed how a *beating phenomenon* between the coincident harmonics of two vibrating strings influences our perceptions of consonance and dissonance. We now find that this phenomenon also occurs in another context and, therefore, offers two different tests for judging the musical quality of a given interval ratio. (1) The first is a direct, aural test; it enables us to evaluate an interval ratio by listening to beats. Huygens applied this test and acknowledged the consonance of ratio $7/4$ because ". . . it emits a sound that is agreeable to the ear, and it does not beat . . ."[167] (2) The second is an indirect, mathematical test; it enables us to evaluate an interval ratio by considering the magnitude of its positive integers. For example, ratio $2/1$ is the most consonant interval because two strings tuned to this ratio move in phase whenever the short string performs two vibrations, and the long string, one vibration. In contrast, ratio $3/2$ is more dissonant because two vibrating strings tuned to this ratio are "in phase" less often. Here the short string performs three vibrations, and the long string, two vibrations, before both strings move in phase again. Note carefully that the first test relies on an audible *production of beats* between two different harmonic frequencies, whereas the second test relies on a mechanical *rate of coincidence* between the vibrations of two different strings. Now, since all music theorists accept the consonance of ratios $6/5$ and $8/5$, it follows logically that ratios $7/6$, $7/5$, and $7/4$ must also be consonant because strings tuned to the latter ratios vibrate in phase about as often as those tuned to the former ratios.[168] To this day, most theorists deny that ratios with prime number 7 are consonant because the conventional piano scale is based on a just intoned scale that excludes all prime numbers except 2, 3, and 5. (See Figure 10.33.) In other words, they do not dismiss prime number 7 for experiential reasons, but for theoretical reasons.

Part VI

JUST INTONATION

~ 10.35 ~

The term *just intonation* has two different definitions. The first is ancient and strictly mathematical. It states that just intonation is a method of tuning intervals and scales based exclusively on rational numbers. The second is modern and strictly acoustic. It states that just intonation is a method of tuning based on the intervals of the harmonic series. In the first context, the term *just* means *exact*, as in *just enough salt*,[169] and in the second context, *just* means *natural*, as in a *just full age*.[170] Recall that flexible strings[171] and columns of air[172] have a natural tendency to subdivide into exact numbers of standing waves and, thereby, produce harmonics that are integer multiples of a fundamental frequency. Since these definitions describe the same physical phenomenon from two different perspectives, we find that a natural event is also an exact occurrence, and *vice versa*.[173]

In Section 10.2, we defined rational numbers as commensurable (measurable) numbers. Before the development of keyboard temperaments in the 16th century,[174] *all* instruments in Europe were tuned in just intonation. During that time, musicians did not think of just intonation as a uniquely defined method for tuning instruments. However, with the implementation of various temperaments, music theorists became conscious of the difference between rational, commensurable, or just intoned intervals on the one hand, and irrational, incommensurable, or tempered intervals on the other. Due to this discrepancy, music theorists in the middle of the 16th century began comparing tempered intervals to just intervals. This practice started approximately one hundred and fifty years *before* the formal scientific discovery of the harmonic series. Once defined, the harmonic series confirmed that integer ratios ${}^{n}/_{1}$ and ${}^{n}/_{x}$ (see Section 3.13), which constitute the core of tuning theory since the time of the ancient Greeks, had a physical reality in nature, and could, therefore, not be dismissed as antiquated entities of long-forgotten civilizations. The convention of comparing intervals continues to this day because for acoustic music the harmonic series is both fundamental and theoretically infinite!

∼ 10.36 ∼

In the West, the modern history of just intonation begins with Bartolomeo Ramis (*c.* 1440 – *c.* 1500), who published a treatise in 1482 entitled *Musica practica.* Ramis proposed a 12-tone chromatic scale, which, for the first time in European music history,[175] included six 5-limit ratios. Although Ramis spent the most productive time of his life in Italy, he was born in a small town called Baéza in southern Spain.[176] After the Moslems invaded Spain in 711, they referred to this region as *al-Andalus,* a word that is etymologically ". . . connected with the name of the Vandals, who had occupied the land before the Arabs."[177] The Moslems controlled various areas of Andalusia until 1492. During this eight hundred year reign, Arabian artists, scientists, and scholars created magnificent cultural centers in the cities of Cordova, Granada, and Seville. Henry George Farmer (1882–1965), an eminent historian of Arabian music, recounts

> Both Adelard of Bath and Roger Bacon had advocated that European students should go to the Arabic fountain head in the schools of Muslim Spain. That some did go is evident from a statement of Ibn al-Ḥijārī (12th century) who said that 'students from all parts of the world flocked to Cordova' to sit at the feet of Arabic scholars.[178]

As discussed in Chapter 11, Part IV, Al-Fārābī, Ibn Sīnā, and Ṣafī Al-Dīn all wrote monumental music treatises in which they classified ratios ${}^{5}/_{4}$ and ${}^{6}/_{5}$ as bona fide consonances. To most music historians the fact that Ramis lived the first thirty-two years of his life in Andalusia before he left for Italy *c.* 1472,[179] and the fact that he was the first European music theorist to advocate the systematic implementation of 5-limit ratios, is a pure coincidence not worthy of investigation. However, the highly likely possibility exists that Ramis not only learned a great deal of musical mathematics from his Arabian counterparts, but that his famous 5-limit chromatic scale has its theoretical origins in Ṣafī Al-Dīn's 17-tone *'ūd* tuning.

Although Ramis' original monochord in A includes a traditional Pythagorean "major third" between A–C♯, ratio ${}^{81}/_{64}$, Ramis broke with European orthodoxy when he specified

${}^{5}/_{4}$'s between B♭–D, C–E, F–A$^{|}$, and G–B$^{|}$,

${}^{6}/_{5}$'s between A–C, D–F, and E–G,

${}^{5}/_{3}$'s between C–A$^{|}$, F–D$^{|}$, and G–E$^{|}$,

${}^{8}/_{5}$'s between D–B♭$^{|}$, E–C$^{|}$, A–F, and B–G.

Recall from the discussion in Section 10.26 that Ramis rejected the 3-limit Pythagorean scale because ". . . although it is useful and pleasing to theorists, it is laborious and difficult for singers . . ."[180] This statement clearly defines Ramis' intent. At the above-mentioned locations, Ramis substituted simple $5/4$'s for complex $81/64$'s, simple $6/5$'s for complex $32/27$'s, simple $5/3$'s for complex $27/16$'s, and simple $8/5$'s for very complex $128/81$'s. (See Figure 10.16.) Ramis included these 5-limit consonances because he observed and experienced the *natural* tendencies of singers, and decided to reject conventional but impractical Pythagorean music theory that excludes all prime numbers except 2 and 3. Again, remember that this breach occurred approximately two hundred years before the discovery of the harmonic series, which means that Ramis did not have the benefit of science to corroborate his theory. Franchino Gaffurio (1451–1522) and other contemporary music theorists cited ancient texts to demonstrate that Ramis' 5-limit chromatic scale subverted venerated Pythagorean traditions.[181] However, these objections soon evaporated, and as a consequence, singing as an art became a more enjoyable experience.

Ramis' monochord consists of two separate parts. He begins by describing the first 16 length ratios of his 12-tone "double-octave" scale:

> Accordingly, let a string of any length be used which may be extended over a somewhat concave piece of wood. Let the end to which the string is tied be shown by point *a;* let the other place, at the opposite end, to which the string is drawn and tightened, be shown by point *q*. Then let the distance *q a*, that is, the length of the entire string, be divided into two equal parts, and let the mid-point be written with the letter *h*. Again we will divide the length of the string *h a* in half and put *d* in the middle of the division. The length *h d* again will be divided and *f* is placed in the middle of the division.
>
> Note that the same is also to be done with the other half of the string, namely, *h q*, for in the first division letter *p* will be written in the middle; in the division of *h p* the letter *l* will be placed equidistantly, and keeping the same intervallic rule let *n* be placed between *l* and *p*. Then when we have divided *f n* in half we will write the letter *i*.
>
> We shall not go further through this median division to the smaller segments until we have made other divisions, but now we will divide the entire string *a q* into three parts, and measuring from *q*, at the [one-] third part *m* is placed and *e* at two-thirds of the string. Then let *e q* again be divided into three parts, and going from *q* to *e* let the sign square ♮ be placed at two-thirds of the distance; where the length of square ♮ and *q* is doubled let *b* be written.
>
> Then we will again divide *m h* in half and at the middle point we will put the letter *k*. Now we duplicate the length of *k q* and place *c* at the end of the duplication; but equidistant between *e* and square ♮ let letter *g* be placed. Then if we divide *g* into two equal parts letter *o* will be put in the middle; thus the entire monochord has been divided in a legitimate partition . . .[182] (Text in brackets mine.)

Figure 10.30 shows these divisions in the order described by Ramis; it also includes the ancient length ratios or modern frequency ratios of this scale, and the modern note names as well. Note carefully that almost all bridge locations depend on previously calculated results. Because of this, a single error near the beginning of Ramis' description will cause many subsequent mistakes. To help simplify the illustration, dots with arrows point to previously calculated divisions; furthermore, brackets that indicate the locations of tones labeled *e*, *b*, and *c* represent a doubling of the string lengths that indicate the locations of tones labeled *m*, ♮, and *k*, respectively.

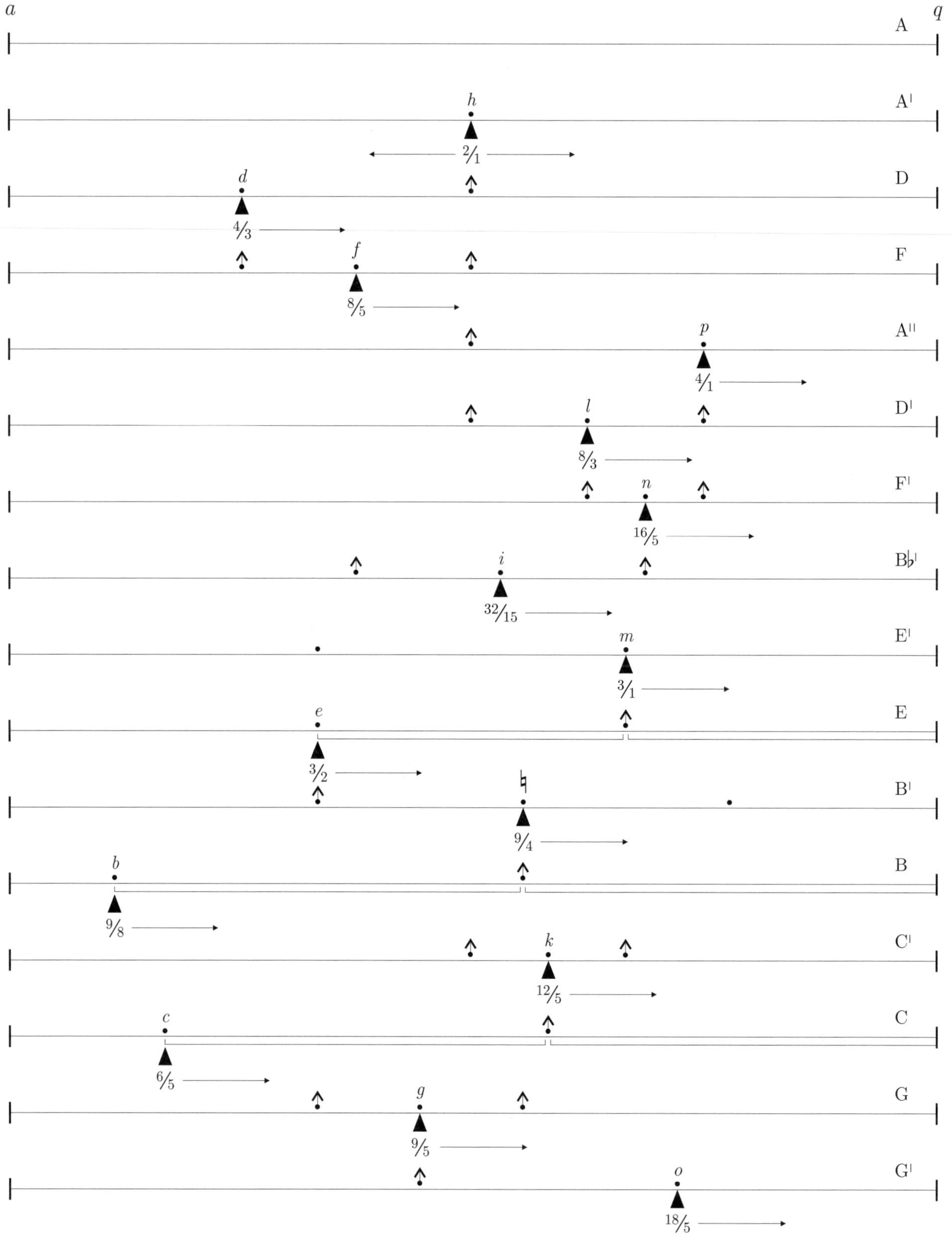

Figure 10.30 The first 16 tones of Ramis' "double-octave" scale. In the West, this is the first 12-tone scale that includes six 5-limit ratios. Figure 10.31 shows the remaining nine tones. (Dots with arrows point to previously calculated divisions.)

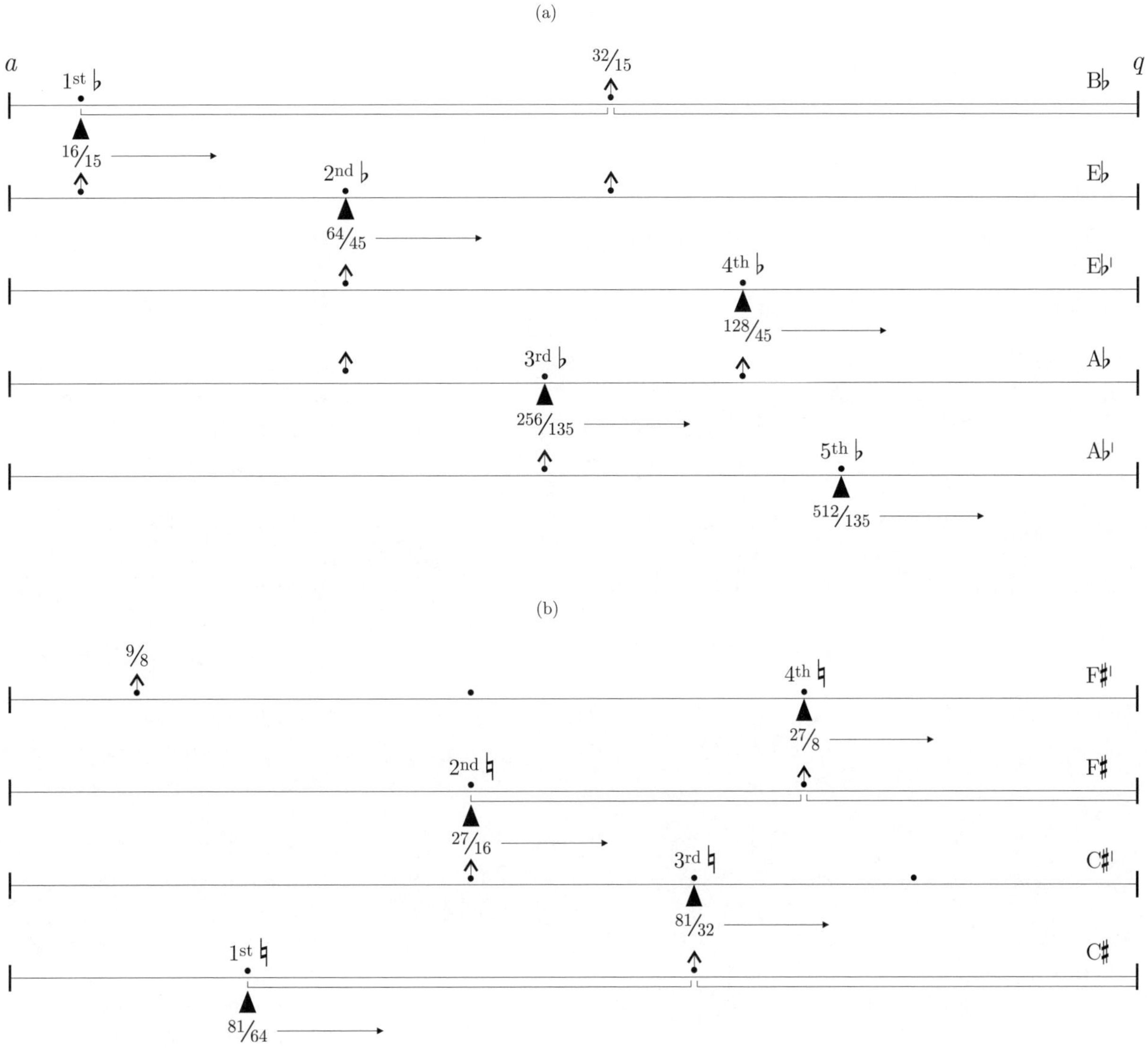

Figure 10.31 The remaining 9 tones of Ramis' "double-octave" monochord. (a) Ramis utilized three flats (B♭ˡ appears in Figure 10.30), and (b) two sharps in his 5-limit chromatic scale. (Dots with arrows point to previously calculated divisions.)

Table 10.21

MODERN LENGTH RATIO TO FREQUENCY RATIO CALCULATIONS OF RAMIS' 5-LIMIT CHROMATIC SCALE

Letters *a–q*, Tone A	$1/1$	Whole string length.
Letter *h*, Tone A^{I}	$1 \times 1/2 = 1/2 \rightarrow 2/1$	Half of string.
Letter *d*, Tone D	$1/2 \times 1/2 = 1/4$ $1/2 + 1/4 = 2/4 + 1/4 = 3/4 \rightarrow 4/3$	Half of $1/2$ section. $1/2$ section plus subsection.
Letter *f*, Tone F	$3/4 - 1/2 = 3/4 - 2/4 = 1/4$ $1/4 \times 1/2 = 1/8$ $3/4 - 1/8 = 6/8 - 1/8 = 5/8 \rightarrow 8/5$	Length of internal section. Half of internal section. $3/4$ section minus subsection.
Letter *p*, Tone A^{II}	$1/2 \times 1/2 = 1/4 \rightarrow 4/1$	Half of $1/2$ section.
Letter *l*, Tone D^{I}	$1/2 - 1/4 = 2/4 - 1/4 = 1/4$ $1/4 \times 1/2 = 1/8$ $1/2 - 1/8 = 4/8 - 1/8 = 3/8 \rightarrow 8/3$	Length of internal section. Half of internal section. $1/2$ section minus subsection.
Letter *n*, Tone F^{I}	$3/8 - 1/4 = 3/8 - 2/8 = 1/8$ $1/8 \times 1/2 = 1/16$ $3/8 - 1/16 = 6/16 - 1/16 = 5/16 \rightarrow 16/5$	Length of internal section. Half of internal section. $3/8$ section minus subsection.
Letter *i*, Tone B♭^{I}	$5/8 - 5/16 = 10/16 - 5/16 = 5/16$ $5/16 \times 1/2 = 5/32$ $5/8 - 5/32 = 20/32 - 5/32 = 15/32 \rightarrow 32/15$	Length of internal section. Half of internal section. $5/8$ section minus subsection.
Letter *m*, Tone E^{I}	$1 \times 1/3 = 1/3 \rightarrow 3/1$	Third of string.
Letter *e*, Tone E	$1/3 \times 2 = 2/3 \rightarrow 3/2$	Double of $1/3$ section.
Square ♮, Tone B^{I}	$2/3 \times 2/3 = 4/9 \rightarrow 9/4$	Two-thirds of $2/3$ section.
Letter *b*, Tone B	$4/9 \times 2 = 8/9 \rightarrow 9/8$	Double of $4/9$ section.
Letter *k*, Tone C^{I}	$1/2 - 1/3 = 3/6 - 2/6 = 1/6$ $1/6 \times 1/2 = 1/12$ $1/2 - 1/12 = 6/12 - 1/12 = 5/12 \rightarrow 12/5$	Length of internal section. Half of internal section. $1/2$ section minus subsection.
Letter *c*, Tone C	$5/12 \times 2 = 10/12 = 5/6 \rightarrow 6/5$	Double of $5/12$ section.
Letter *g*, Tone G	$2/3 - 4/9 = 6/9 - 4/9 = 2/9$ $2/9 \times 1/2 = 2/18$ $2/3 - 2/18 = 12/18 - 2/18 = 10/18 = 5/9 \rightarrow 9/5$	Length of internal section. Half of internal section. $2/3$ section minus subsection.
Letter *o*, Tone G^{I}	$5/9 \times 1/2 = 5/18 \rightarrow 18/5$	Half of $5/9$ section.

Table 10.21
(continued)

1st ♭, Tone B♭	$15/32 \times 2 = 30/32 = 15/16 \rightarrow 16/15$	Double of $15/32$ section.
2nd ♭, Tone E♭	$15/16 - 15/32 = 30/32 - 15/32 = 15/32$ $15/32 \times 1/2 = 15/64$ $15/16 - 15/64 = 60/64 - 15/64 = 45/64 \rightarrow 64/45$	Length of internal section. Half of internal section. $5/16$ section minus subsection.
4th ♭, Tone $E\flat^{\vert}$	$45/64 \times 1/2 = 45/128 \rightarrow 128/45$	Half of $45/64$ section.
3rd ♭, Tone A♭	$45/64 - 45/128 = 90/128 - 45/128 = 45/128$ $45/128 \times 1/2 = 45/256$ $45/64 - 45/256 = 180/256 - 45/256 = 135/256 \rightarrow 256/135$	Length of internal section. Half of internal section. $45/64$ section minus subsection.
5th ♭, Tone $A\flat^{\vert}$	$135/256 \times 1/2 = 135/512 \rightarrow 512/135$	Half of $135/256$ section.
	* * *	
4th ♮, Tone $F\sharp^{\vert}$	$8/9 \times 1/3 = 8/27 \rightarrow 27/8$	Third of $8/9$ section.
2nd ♮, Tone F♯	$8/27 \times 2 = 16/27 \rightarrow 27/16$	Double of $8/27$ section.
3rd ♮, Tone $C\sharp^{\vert}$	$16/27 \times 2/3 = 32/81 \rightarrow 81/32$	Two-thirds of $16/27$ section.
1st ♮, Tone C♯	$32/81 \times 2 = 64/81 \rightarrow 81/64$	Double of $32/81$ section.

In the second part, Ramis describes 9 more length ratios, which are all accidentals. In Ramis' time, the natural sign ♮ represented a tone raised by a "semitone." Therefore, with respect to the "seventh," ♮ signifies B♮, the "major seventh," as opposed to B♭, the "minor seventh." Also, observe that in the following passage, Ramis does not include ratio $32/15$, or $B\flat^{\vert}$ of the upper "octave," because he defined it in the first part:

> And then we will form the conjunctions of soft ♭ in this way: having duplicated the length of *q i* we will mark the first conjunction of soft ♭ [B♭], and so the first will be between *a* and *b*. Then the length of the string *i* and the first ♭ is divided in the middle and is marked as the second ♭ [E♭], which will be between *d e*. But if we have divided the median length of the second ♭ *q* we will mark the fourth ♭ [$E\flat^{\vert}$] between *l m*. By dividing in half the length of the fourth ♭ and the second ♭ we will mark the third ♭ [A♭]. But if the length of the third ♭ *q* is so divided the fifth ♭ [$A\flat^{\vert}$] will be marked. Thus from the division we will have five conjunctions of soft ♭ resulting from a correct division.
>
> But if we wish to obtain square ♮ conjunctions we will divide *b q* into three parts, and coming from letter *q* to *b* we will put forth [the fourth] ♮ [$F\sharp^{\vert}$] at the end of the [one-] third part, namely, between *n o*, and the second square ♮ [F♯] at two-thirds of the length, which will fall between *f g*. If the length of *q* to the second square ♮ is divided into three parts, coming from letter *q* to the second square ♮ we will place the third square ♮ [$C\sharp^{\vert}$] at two-thirds of the length, and it will be between *k l;* if the length of it and of *q* is doubled, accordingly the first ♮ [C♯] between *c d* will result. Thus from

> this division we will have four square ♮ conjunctions arising from a correct division . . .[183] (Text in brackets mine.)

Figure 10.31(a) shows the locations of five flats described in the first paragraph, and Figure 10.31(b), of four sharps described in the second paragraph. Now, refer to Table 10.21, which gives the modern length ratios and inversions that result in the frequency ratios of the complete "double-octave" scale.

Figure 10.32 shows Ramis' original monochord in A, and a modal version in C. Table 10.22 unfolds the inner structures of these two scales. Here Columns 1–3 show that the original scale consists of an ascending spiral of four "fifths" above $1/1$, and a descending spiral of seven "fifths" below $1/1$. The ascending progression represents the ubiquitous pentatonic scale known the world over as ratios: $1/1$, $9/8$, $81/64$, $3/2$, $27/16$, [$2/1$]. In Column 3, note the "flat fifth," interval ratio $40/27$ [680.45 ¢], which indicates the transition from D to G, or from 3-limit ratio $4/3$ to 5-limit ratio $9/5$: $4/3 \div 9/5 = 40/27$. Also, in Column 3, a "schismatic fifth," interval ratio $16384/10935$ [700.00 ¢], indicates the transition from A♭ (i.e., G♯) to C♯, or from 5-limit ratio $256/135$ to 3-limit ratio $81/64$: $256/135 \div 81/64 = 16384/10935$. The latter constitutes an extremely close rational approximation of the irrational "tempered fifth" of 12-TET.

A	B♭	B	C	C♯	D	E♭	E	F	F♯	G	A♭	A′	B♭′	B′	C′
	$16/15$	$135/128$	$16/15$	$135/128$	$256/243$	$16/15$	$135/128$	$16/15$	$135/128$	$16/15$	$256/243$	$135/128$	$16/15$	$135/128$	$16/15$

A	B♭	B	C	C♯	D	E♭	E	F	F♯	G	A♭	A′	
$1/1$	$16/15$	$9/8$	$6/5$	$81/64$	$4/3$	$64/45$	$3/2$	$8/5$	$27/16$	$9/5$	$256/135$	$2/1$	Ramis' Monochord

	C	C♯	D	E♭	E	F	F♯	G	A♭	A	B♭	B	C′
Ramis' Scale in C:	$1/1$	$135/128$	$10/9$	$32/27$	$5/4$	$4/3$	$45/32$	$3/2$	$128/81$	$5/3$	$16/9$	$15/8$	$2/1$

Figure 10.32 Ramis' original 5-limit monochord in A, and a modal version in C. Ramis substituted six 5-limit ratios for traditional Pythagorean 3-limit ratios to make this 12-tone scale more natural for singers.

To understand the origin of the "schismatic fifth," we must first calculate the discrepancy called a *schisma* (lit. *split*), or the imperceptible interval between the ditonic comma and the syntonic comma:

$$\text{Schisma} = \frac{\frac{531441}{524288}}{\frac{81}{80}} = \frac{32805}{32768} = 1.954\ ¢$$

Note that a schisma and a $1/12$ ditonic comma are extremely similar:

$$1/12 \text{ Ditonic Comma} = \sqrt[12]{\frac{531441}{524288}} = 1.955\ ¢$$

Consequently, a "just fifth," ratio $3/2$, reduced by a schisma very closely approximates a "just fifth" reduced by a $1/12$ ditonic comma.

Table 10.22

THE INNER STRUCTURE OF RAMIS' 5-LIMIT 12-TONE SCALE

	Ramis' Ascending Spiral of 4 "Fifths," Descending Spiral of 7 "Fifths"			6 Tones Below A-1/1 Tuned One Syntonic Comma Sharp			6 Tones Above C-1/1 Tuned One Syntonic Comma Flat		
	(1)	(2)	(3)	(4)	(5)	(6)	(7)	(8)	(9)
(4)	C♯	81/64	81/64		C♯^{0}	81/64		C♯$^{-\frac{4}{4}}$	135/128
(3)	F♯	27/16	3/2		F♯^{0}	27/16		F♯$^{-\frac{4}{4}}$	45/32
(2)	B	9/8	3/2		B^{0}	9/8		B$^{-\frac{4}{4}}$	15/8
(1)	E	3/2	3/2		E^{0}	3/2		E$^{-\frac{4}{4}}$	5/4
	A	1/1	3/2		A^{0}	1/1		A$^{-\frac{4}{4}}$	5/3
(1)	D	4/3	3/2; 16384/10935		D^{0}	4/3		D$^{-\frac{4}{4}}$	10/9
(2)	G	9/5	40/27	9/5	G$^{+\frac{4}{4}}$		3/2	G^{0}	
(3)	C	6/5	3/2	6/5	C$^{+\frac{4}{4}}$		1/1	C^{0}	
(4)	F	8/5	3/2	8/5	F$^{+\frac{4}{4}}$		4/3	F^{0}	
(5)	B♭	16/15	3/2	16/15	B♭$^{+\frac{4}{4}}$		16/9	B♭^{0}	
(6)	E♭	64/45	3/2	64/45	E♭$^{+\frac{4}{4}}$		32/27	E♭^{0}	
(7)	A♭	256/135	3/2; 256/135	256/135	A♭$^{+\frac{4}{4}}$		128/81	A♭^{0}	

Ramis' Scale In C, with 6 5-Limit Ratios			Ṣafī Al-Dīn's Scale In C, with 6 *Schisma Variants*		
(10)		(11)	(12)		(13)
C	1/1		C	1/1	
C♯	135/128	92 ¢	D♭	256/243	90 ¢
D	10/9	182 ¢	E♭♭	65536/59049	180 ¢
E♭	32/27		E♭	32/27	
E	5/4	386 ¢	F♭	8192/6561	384 ¢
F	4/3		F	4/3	
F♯	45/32	590 ¢	G♭	1024/729	588 ¢
G	3/2		G	3/2	
A♭	128/81		A♭	128/81	
A	5/3	884 ¢	B♭♭	32768/19683	882 ¢
B♭	16/9		B♭	16/9	
B	15/8	1088 ¢	C♭	4096/2187	1086 ¢
C'	2/1		C'	2/1	

Comma of Pythagoras, or Ditonic Comma = $\frac{531441}{524288}$ = 23.46 ¢

Comma of Didymus, or Syntonic Comma = $\frac{81}{80}$ = 21.51 ¢

Schisma = $\frac{531441}{524288} \div \frac{81}{80} = \frac{32805}{32768}$ = 1.954 ¢

$$\text{Rational "Schismatic Fifth" of Ramis' Scale:}\quad \frac{\frac{3}{2}}{\frac{32805}{32768}} = \frac{16384}{10935} = 700.001\ ¢$$

$$\text{Irrational "Tempered Fifth" of 12-TET:}\quad \frac{\frac{3}{2}}{\sqrt[12]{\frac{531441}{524288}}} = 700.000\ ¢$$

In Table 10.22, Columns 4 and 5, observe that Ramis' scale in A includes a total number of six 3-limit ratios tuned one syntonic comma sharp. Examine the illustration below to see that in a descending spiral of "fifths," which begins on A, the seventh "fifth" is A♭, or 3-limit ratio $4096/2187$.

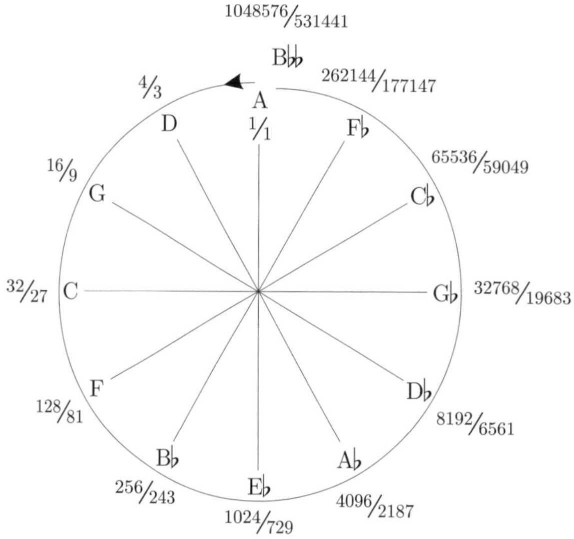

If we increase this ratio by one syntonic comma, the result equals a 5-limit ratio: $A\flat^{+\frac{4}{4}} = 4096/2187 \times 81/80 = 256/135$, the scale's "major seventh." Similarly, $E\flat^{+\frac{4}{4}} = 1024/729 \times 81/80 = 64/45$; $B\flat^{+\frac{4}{4}} = 256/243 \times 81/80 = 16/15$; $F^{+\frac{4}{4}} = 128/81 \times 81/80 = 8/5$; $C^{+\frac{4}{4}} = 32/27 \times 81/80 = 6/5$; $G^{+\frac{4}{4}} = 16/9 \times 81/80 = 9/5$.

Now, turn back to Figure 10.16(a), and to Table 10.22, Columns 7 and 8. A comparison indicates that Ramis' modal version in C includes a total number of six 3-limit ratios tuned one syntonic comma flat. For example, Figure 10.16(a) shows that in an ascending spiral of "fifths" that begins on C, the second "fifth" is D, or 3-limit ratio $9/8$. If we decrease this ratio by one syntonic comma, the result equals a 5-limit ratio: $D^{-\frac{4}{4}} = 9/8 \div 81/80 = 10/9$, the scale's "small whole tone." Similarly, $A^{-\frac{4}{4}} = 27/16 \div 81/80 = 5/3$; $E^{-\frac{4}{4}} = 81/64 \div 81/80 = 5/4$; $B^{-\frac{4}{4}} = 243/128 \div 81/80 = 15/8$; $F\sharp^{-\frac{4}{4}} = 729/512 \div 81/80 = 45/32$; $C\sharp^{-\frac{4}{4}} = 2187/2048 \div 81/80 = 135/128$. Columns 10 and 11 give this 12-tone scale in chromatic order.

Next, refer to Columns 12 and 13, which show 12 selected tones from an *'ūd* tuning described by Ṣafī Al-Dīn (d. 1294) in a treatise entitled *Risālat al-Sharafīya fi'l-nisab al-ta'līfīya* (The Sharafian treatise on musical conformities in composition).[184] Ṣafī Al-Dīn's *First 'Ūd Tuning* is based on an ascending spiral of four "fifths" above $1/1$, and on a descending spiral of fourteen "fifths" below $1/1$. [See Table 11.40(a).] Consequently, his "double-octave" consists of a theoretical 19-tone scale that produces two slightly different 17-tone *'ūd* tunings. [See Table 11.40(b).] However, note carefully that both scales include *all* the ratios in Column 13. If we increase six 3-limit ratios in Column 13 by one schisma, we obtain six 5-limit ratios in Column 11. For example, $C\sharp^{+\frac{4}{4}} = {}^{256}\!/\!_{243} \times {}^{32805}\!/\!_{32768} = {}^{135}\!/\!_{128}$; $D^{+\frac{4}{4}} = {}^{65536}\!/\!_{59049} \times {}^{32805}\!/\!_{32768} = {}^{10}\!/\!_{9}$; . . . Since the finest ear cannot distinguish between two frequencies unless they are at least 2 cents apart, Ramis' scale in Column 11 and Ṣafī Al-Dīn's scale in Column 13 are musically indistinguishable, and for all practical purposes identical. As discussed in Section 11.67, we may interpret the latter six 3-limit ratios as *schisma variants*, because we tend to perceive such *complex* 3-limit ratios as *simple* 5-limit ratios.

Ṣafī Al-Dīn was fully aware of the historic origins and the musical derivations of the schisma variants. As discussed in Sections 11.68–11.69, more than three hundred years before Ṣafī Al-Dīn, Al-Fārābī described how musicians tuned these complex 3-limit ratios on the *ṭunbūr* of Khurāsān by ear. Furthermore, turn to Table 11.38, and notice that one derives the Arabian schisma variants either by extending the ascending spiral to the 7th, 8th, 9th, and 10th "fifth" above ${}^{1}\!/\!_{1}$, or by extending the descending spiral to the 7th, 8th, 9th, and 10th "fifth" below ${}^{1}\!/\!_{1}$. Ṣafī Al-Dīn's uninterrupted spiral of fourteen descending "fifths" below ${}^{1}\!/\!_{1}$ indicates that he was fully aware of the musical and mathematical derivations of the schisma variants. However, since Ramis offered no musical or mathematical explanation for the presence of interval ratio ${}^{16384}\!/\!_{10935}$ — the sole "schismatic fifth" that sounds between C♯–A♭ — it is highly likely that he was unaware of its existence. We conclude, therefore, that Ramis probably modeled his 5-limit scale after Ṣafī Al-Dīn's 3-limit scale; that is, Ramis substituted his six 5-limit ratios for Ṣafī Al-Dīn's six schisma variants. Consequently, the "schismatic fifth" simply occurred by default.

As described by Al-Fārābī and Ṣafī Al-Dīn, the utilization of schisma variants originated in the ancient Persian *ṭunbūr* tuning tradition. Ṣafī Al-Dīn, who was arguably the greatest music theorist of the Arabian Renaissance, was also famous throughout the Arabian empire for his organization and identification of 84 Melodic Modes. (See Sections 11.74–11.75.) In Andalusia, musicians played these melodic modes for two hundred years before Ramis began his formal education. Many modes identified by Ṣafī Al-Dīn are in use to this day. (See Section 11.83.)

Scales that require flat consecutive ${}^{3}\!/\!_{2}$'s are very reminiscent of tempered tunings. So, it would not be entirely incorrect to describe the scales of Ṣafī Al-Dīn and Ramis as "just temperaments." Finally, Ramis' insistence on just ${}^{5}\!/\!_{4}$'s has undoubtedly played a crucial role in later developments of meantone temperament.

∾ 10.37 ∾

Consider now a comparison of the scales by Ramis and Stevin. Select twelve rational frequency ratios from Ramis' scales in Figure 10.32 that most closely represent the irrational frequency ratios of Stevin's tempered scale. Note, however, that tempered intervals emulate just intoned intervals; not the other way around. (Singers are no more capable of singing *a cappella* in 12-tone equal temperament than they are able to sing *a cappella* in pure Pythagorean intonation.) In this case, the choice of just ratios is determined by 12-TET simply because the latter tuning represents the conventional Western scale.

Figure 10.33 shows two scales *effectively* calculated by Ramis and Stevin. Neither scale is an exact replica of original work. Instead, the first scale is a conglomeration of Ramis' frequency ratios, and the second scale accurately reflects Stevin's intent. In other words, if it were possible, Ramis and Stevin would easily recognize their tuning ideas in the first and second scales, respectively.

To measure the differences between these two different sets of ratios, the lowercase of the Greek letter *delta* (δ) represents the departure in cents of a tempered frequency ratio from its just intoned counterpart. Refer to Table 10.23, which lists the departures of the 12-TET ratios from the 5-limit ratios in Figure 10.33.

Frequency Ratios of the Standard 5-Limit Chromatic Scale, Effectively Calculated by Ramis *c.* 1500

C	C♯	D	E♭	E	F	F♯	G	A♭	A	B♭	B	C′
$1/1$	$16/15$	$9/8$	$6/5$	$5/4$	$4/3$	$45/32$	$3/2$	$8/5$	$5/3$	$16/9$	$15/8$	$2/1$
0 ¢	111.7 ¢	203.9 ¢	315.6 ¢	386.3 ¢	498.0 ¢	590.2 ¢	702.0 ¢	813.7 ¢	884.4 ¢	996.1 ¢	1088.3 ¢	1200.0 ¢

Frequency Ratios of the Standard 12-Tone Equal Tempered Scale, Effectively Calculated by Stevin *c.* 1600

C	C♯	D	E♭	E	F	F♯	G	A♭	A	B♭	B	C′
$\sqrt[12]{2}^{0}$	$\sqrt[12]{2}^{1}$	$\sqrt[12]{2}^{2}$	$\sqrt[12]{2}^{3}$	$\sqrt[12]{2}^{4}$	$\sqrt[12]{2}^{5}$	$\sqrt[12]{2}^{6}$	$\sqrt[12]{2}^{7}$	$\sqrt[12]{2}^{8}$	$\sqrt[12]{2}^{9}$	$\sqrt[12]{2}^{10}$	$\sqrt[12]{2}^{11}$	$\sqrt[12]{2}^{12}$
0 ¢	100.0 ¢	200.0 ¢	300.0 ¢	400.0 ¢	500.0 ¢	600.0 ¢	700.0 ¢	800.0 ¢	900.0 ¢	1000.0 ¢	1100.0 ¢	1200.0 ¢

Figure 10.33 Two distinctly different versions of the standard Western 12-tone scale. Neither scale in this figure is an exact replica of original work. Instead, these two scales express the tuning ideas of Ramis and Stevin, respectively. The rational frequency ratios of the just intoned scale were selected from Ramis' monochord in A. (See Section 10.36.) The irrational frequency ratios of the equal tempered scale represent precise values of the numbers first calculated by Stevin without the use of logarithms. (See Section 10.33.)

Table 10.23

DEPARTURES IN CENTS OF 12-TET RATIOS FROM JUST INTONED 5-LIMIT RATIOS

Scale	δ	Scale	δ
		F♯	+9.8 ¢
C	0.0 ¢	G	−2.0 ¢
C♯	−11.7 ¢	A♭	−13.7 ¢
D	−3.9 ¢	A	+15.6 ¢
E♭	−15.6 ¢	B♭	+3.9 ¢
E	+13.7 ¢	B	+11.7 ¢
F	+2.0 ¢	C′	0.0 ¢

Further notable differences between these two scales are as follows: the tempered scale has one "semitone" [100.0 ¢], while the just intoned scale has three "semitones": $16/15$ [111.7 ¢], $135/128$ [92.2 ¢], and $25/24$ [70.7 ¢]; the tempered scale has one "whole tone" [200.0 ¢], while the just intoned scale has three "whole tones": $9/8$ [203.9 ¢], $10/9$ [182.4 ¢], and $256/225$ [223.5 ¢]; and so forth. It is remarkable that many musicians trained on 12-TET instruments have never heard the just intoned intervals on which these tempered intervals are based.

Finally, Table 10.24 compares several different 12-tone scales. Of special interest is a 7-limit just intoned scale in Column 8. I included this scale for two specific reasons. Many modern music historians have attempted to intellectually degrade the importance of just intoned scales by promulgating two serious misconceptions. First, they insist that in a musical context, the ratios of just intoned scales must include only small, positive integers. This bogus rule is based on the premise that the frequency ratios of just intonation are somehow synonymous with consonant tones and intervals like 2/1, 3/2, 4/3, etc. Almost four centuries ago, Marin Mersenne observed, ". . . all the vibrations of air which the consonances and dissonances make are commensurable [i.e., rational] . . ."[185] (Text in brackets mine.) Second, they insist that just intonation is a tuning system, or some specific scale. The 7-limit scale challenges both of these highly opinionated assumptions. First, this scale contradicts the notion that interval ratios with prime numbers larger than 5 are inherently dissonant and musically unacceptable, and therefore serve no purpose in a just intoned scale. Second, it refutes the erroneous conclusion that a specific scale represents just intonation. Just intonation is *not* a tuning system. It is a tuning principle, or a method of tuning. Furthermore, as discussed in Section 10.68, a just intoned scale, like a tempered scale, may have any number of tones. All writers who applaud the "virtues" of tempered tunings while criticizing the "faults" of just intoned tunings argue their case from a very narrow perspective. Ultimately, such criticisms yield irrelevant bits of information, like the kind obtained from comparing apples and oranges.[186]

Table 10.24

COMPARISONS IN CENTS OF FIVE 12-TONE WESTERN SCALES

Scale	A 3-Limit Pythagorean Scale		A 5-Limit Just Intoned Scale		1/4-Comma Meantone Scale	A 7-Limit Just Intoned Scale		12-TET Scale
C		0		0	0		0	0
C♯	2187/2048	113.69	16/15	111.73	76.05	16/15	111.73	100.00
D	9/8	203.91	9/8	203.91	193.16	8/7	231.17	200.00
E♭	32/27	294.14	6/5	315.64	310.26	7/6	266.87	300.00
E	81/64	407.82	5/4	386.31	386.31	5/4	386.31	400.00
F	4/3	498.05	4/3	498.05	503.42	4/3	498.05	500.00
F♯	729/512	611.73	45/32	590.22	579.47	7/5	582.51	600.00
G	3/2	701.96	3/2	701.96	696.58	3/2	701.96	700.00
G♯/A♭	6561/4096	815.64	8/5	813.69	772.63	8/5	813.69	800.00
A	27/16	905.87	5/3	884.36	889.74	12/7	933.13	900.00
B♭	16/9	996.09	16/9	996.09	1006.84	7/4	968.83	1000.00
B	243/128	1109.78	15/8	1088.27	1082.89	15/8	1088.27	1100.00
C′	2/1	1200.00	2/1	1200.00	1200.00	2/1	1200.00	1200.00
(1)	(2)	(3)	(4)	(5)	(6)	(7)	(8)	(9)

~ 10.38 ~

Although Ramis managed to integrate 5-limit ratios into the 12-tone scale, he did not develop a theory of consonance. In 1558, seventy-six years after the publication of Ramis' monochord, Gioseffo Zarlino (1517–1590) published a work entitled *Istitutioni harmoniche* in which he proposed (1) that the *numero Senario* (from the Latin *senarius*, lit. *composed of six in a group;* fig. *the number Series 1–6*) constitutes the source of all possible musical consonances, and (2) that the harmonic division of strings expresses the "nature of Harmony" and produces "the consonances, which the composers call perfect." (See Section 10.44, Quote V.) However, at the end of his life, in the *De tutte l'opere...* edition of the *Istitutioni* (1589),[187] Zarlino argued that the arithmetic division *and* the harmonic division of the "fifth," length ratio 3/2, are equally important to the development of music theory. He thereby became the first European music theorist to mathematically define what we now call the *minor tonality* and the *major tonality*, respectively, of musical composition.

In the *Istitutioni harmoniche* (1573), Zarlino acknowledges a theoretical contribution by the Arabian physician, scientist, and music theorist Avicenna, or Ibn Sīnā (980–1037), and plagiarizes a mathematical contribution by the German mathematician Michael Stifel (1487–1567). Zarlino first quotes a crucial sentence from a Latin translation of a compendium of Ibn Sīnā's writings entitled *Auicene perhypatetici philosophi: ac medicorum facile primi opera in luce redacta...*, published in 1508.[188] Later in the text, Zarlino utilizes a harmonic division of a "double-octave and a fifth," ratio 6/1, into *five interval ratios* as described in Stifel's *Arithmetica integra*, published in 1544.[189] Although in the *Dimostrationi harmoniche* (1571),[190] Zarlino severely criticizes Stifel's geometric division of the "tone," ratio 9/8, two years later he fails to acknowledge Stifel's stunning mathematical solution for the division of musical intervals into two or more harmonic means.

To understand Zarlino's theory of musical consonance, the reader should thoroughly read Sections 3.14–3.19, and carefully study Figures 3.22 and 3.23. These two illustrations show the notation of length ratios and interval ratios in the context of the arithmetic division (Λ_A), and the harmonic division (Λ_H) of the "octave" on canon strings. Throughout Zarlino's treatises, *all* ratios represent either (1) length ratios, or (2) interval ratios between length ratios. This means that frequency ratios, or interval ratios between frequency ratios, do *not* exist in his works.[191] The great Arabian theorist, Al-Fārābī, deliberately set the standard for notating musical ratios as expressions of string length measurements when he stated

> The largest extreme of an interval, that which corresponds to the largest number, is, for certain mathematicians of another time, its lower extreme; for others, it is the upper {extreme}. In our opinion, it matters little, either from the point of view of theory or from the point of view of the ear, whether the large extreme is placed at the lower note or at the upper note. But having regarded up to now the lower note of an interval as being its large extreme, we will abide by this convention; besides, it is suited to the principles we stated, and facilitates our explanation of the rules of music; for it relates the measurement of the notes to the lengths [of strings] from which they come. The longest has the largest measurement and produces the lowest note; the shortest, which has the smallest measurement, gives the highest note.[192] (Text in braces mine. Text in brackets in *La Musique Arabe*.)

Therefore, one finds that in the musical treatises of the Arabian Renaissance,[193] *all* ratios refer exclusively to length ratios, or to interval ratios between length ratios.

During the 16th century, many European artists, scientists, and intellectuals were inspired to observe the physical processes and functions of nature. The Italian term *la scienza naturale* (lit. *the science of natural things;* in other words, *physics*), or the simplified expression *la naturale* (lit. *the natural*), signified this renewed interest in natural phenomena. Consequently, there arose a heated debate between those who based their studies on mathematics, or *abstract* truth, and those who based their studies on physics, or *concrete* truth. The former philosophical approach is known as *rationalism*, and the latter, as *empiricism.*[194] In the *Istitutioni harmoniche*, Prima Parte, Cap. 19, Zarlino maintains that numbers have the capacity to manifest themselves as parts of "sounding bodies," and that only through the quantifications of "sonorous numbers" are human beings able to comprehend the tones and ratios produced by vibrating strings. However, Zarlino resolves the debate between the science of numbers vs. the science of nature in the following chapter heading and passage from Prima Parte, Cap. 20:

The reason why music is the subordinate of arithmetic, and the intermediary between *la Mathematica* [mathematics] and *la Naturale* [physics].

> . . . I am so bold to assert, that music is not only the subordinate of mathematics, but also of physics, not with respect to numbers, but with respect to tone, which is something natural. From it arises every modulation, every consonance, every harmony, and every melodic song. Avicenna [Ibn Sīnā], who also advocates such an interpretation, says: "Music derives its principles from the science of nature [physics] and the science of numbers [mathematics]."[195] (Text in brackets mine. Italics in Zarlino's original text.)

Zarlino here quotes Ibn Sīnā from a chapter (or book) entitled *Sufficientia* (lit. *Physics*, or *Science of Nature*).[196] In short, Ibn Sīnā and Zarlino refused to compromise and, thereby, focused their attention on the best of both worlds. Given the personal nature and emphatic tone of his resolve, it seems to me that Zarlino was greatly influenced not only by Ibn Sīnā, but by other Arabian writers as well.

10.39

To substantiate this assumption, let us prepare an examination of the *Istitutioni harmoniche* by first considering the division of musical intervals on canon strings in Ibn Sīnā's *Kitāb al-shifā'* (Book of the cure) and in Ṣafī Al-Dīn's *Risālat al-Sharafīya fi'l-nisab al-ta'līfīya.* (See Section 10.36.) H.G. Farmer describes the former treatise by stating

> This great work by the famous Avicenna — as he was known to the wide world — contained the entire sum of knowledge in science and philosophy known in Islamic lands, if not western Europe also. It includes a chapter (*fann*) on music which is divided into six discourses (*maqālāt*) dealing respectively with the physics of sound, musical intervals, genres and species of melody, systems, and mutations, as well as rhythm and composition.[197]

Ibn Sīnā describes the arithmetic and harmonic division of the "octave" by noting

> The octave is called the interval of *absolute consonance* [homophonic interval]; the fifth and the fourth are called intervals of *similar notes* [symphonic intervals]; sometimes one attributes to them the ***characteristic of inversion.*** The extreme degrees of the octave are, as we have said, [***equivalent***]; this is a special characteristic of that interval. The property of the two medium intervals is to compose an octave; the latter interval then contains between its two extreme terms an *arithmetic mean* and a *harmonic mean.* The ratio of the octave is, in fact, that of 4 to 2; if we introduce the number 3 between these two terms, we obtain two consecutive ratios [4:3:2] resulting from an ***arithmetic mean term.*** The ratio of the two largest terms is that of the fourth [4:3], and the ratio of the two smallest, that of the fifth [3:2]. Moreover, the ratio of 6 to 3 also constitutes an octave ratio; if between these two terms we introduce a third, i.e., 4, we obtain two consecutive ratios [6:4:3] resulting from a ***harmonic mean term.*** The ratio of the two largest terms is that of the fifth [6:4], and of the two smallest, that of the fourth [4:3]. The two ratios of the fourth and of the fifth form a replica [***or form an "octave" with***] one another, when they have a common degree, and when they are arranged ***in opposite directions.***

> Take, for example, a fourth; it has an upper degree [3] and a lower degree [4]. If its upper degree also belongs to an interval of a fifth [3:2] of which it constitutes the low note [3], that is to say, if it [3] is followed by another higher note whose value is equal to $\frac{2}{3}$ of its own [that is, $3 \times \frac{2}{3} = 2$], by playing the ***common note*** [3] and the uppermost note [2], [or 3:2], followed by the common note [3] and the lowest note [4], [or 4:3], the ear will perceive the ***same*** sensation. It will be the ***same*** if one plays a fourth [4:3] going up and a fifth [3:2] going down. This happens because the ratio of the uppermost degree to the lowest is that of the octave.[198] (Bold italics, and text, ratios, and integers in brackets mine. Bold italics in brackets my correction of the "puissance" translation error in *La Musique Arabe.*)

Figure 10.34 shows that Ibn Sīnā's ratios refer unequivocally to string length measurements. Although so-called Western theorists such as Nicomachus,[199] Theon,[200] and Boethius[201] (see Section 10.4) also described various arithmetic and harmonic divisions of the "octave," Ibn Sīnā was the first music theorist to define both of these divisions in *least terms.* Notice that one cannot reduce Ibn Sīnā's integers of the arithmetic division of the "octave" expressed as interval ratios 4:3:2, or the harmonic division of the "octave" expressed as interval ratios 6:4:3. As discussed in Section 10.43, it is extremely important to notate arithmetic and harmonic divisions in least terms when one attempts to divide a given length ratio into *three or more* interval ratios.

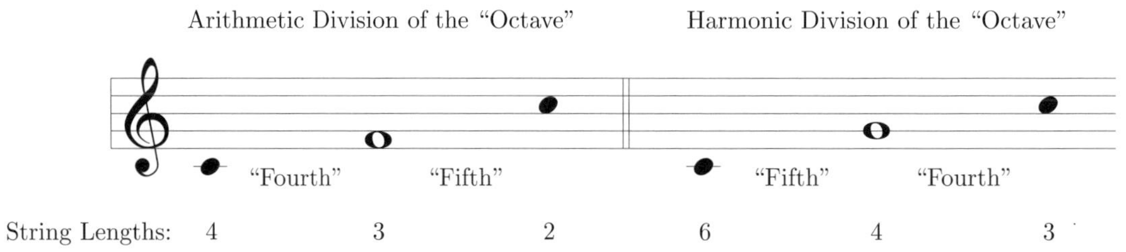

Figure 10.34 The arithmetic and harmonic division of the "octave" according to Ibn Sīnā (980–1037). Ibn Sīnā was the first music theorist to express both of these divisions in least terms. He also observed that although the intervals of these two divisions are identical, "their position has changed." He therefore stated that by simply reversing the order of the intervals of an arithmetic division, one achieves a harmonic division.

Ibn Sīnā also observed that the intervals produced by an arithmetic and a harmonic division of a given interval are identical:

I

> Now, we have already seen that in giving a ratio an arithmetic mean, we obtain two ratios identical to those that result from a harmonic mean; but ***their position has changed.***[202] (Bold italics mine.)

Therefore, since the calculation of a harmonic mean is more difficult than an arithmetic mean, Ibn Sīnā offers the following convenient solution:

II

> When it comes to making this division by way of the harmonic mean, if we do not find any number [integer] that can serve this purpose, it will suffice

> to place in the ***lower [position] the largest of the two ratios obtained by way of the arithmetic mean.***[203] (Bold italics, and text in brackets mine.)

Finally, consider this passage by Ṣafī Al-Dīn, which constitutes the first known description of the arithmetic division of the "fifth":

> If we are then asked which are the two intervals whose ratios are made of consecutive numbers taken in the natural order of numbers, and which together exactly complete the interval of the ratio 1 + ½ [3:2], the fifth, the easiest way to solve the problem will be this: We double the term of this ratio that represents ***the higher note, that is 2***, and we will thereby know that of the two intervals required, the one placed in the upper [position] will be in the ratio 1 + ¼ [5:4], and the one placed in the lower [position] in the ratio 1 + ⅕ [6:5].[204] (Bold italics, and text and ratios in brackets mine.)

Figure 10.35 shows that the arithmetic division of length ratio $3/2$ produces a "minor third," ratio $6/5$, as the lower interval, and a "major third," ratio $5/4$, as the upper interval. In least terms, we may notate this division as interval ratios 6:5:4.

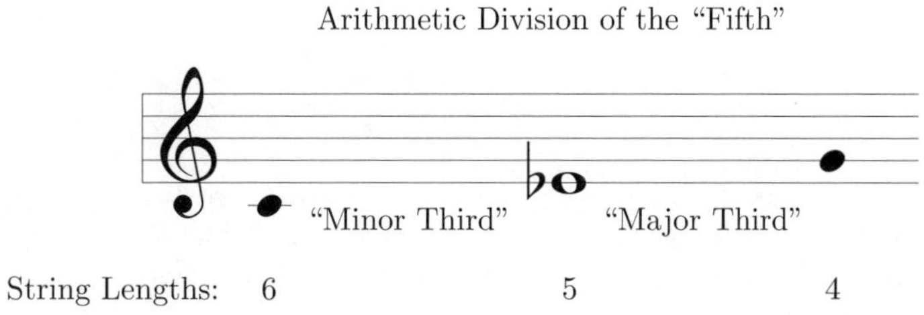

Figure 10.35 The arithmetic division of the "fifth" according to Ṣafī Al-Dīn (d. 1294). Ṣafī Al-Dīn was the first music theorist to describe this division.

10.40

Zarlino introduces the concept of his *Senario* in Prima Parte, Cap. 15:

> I
>
> On the characteristics of the *numero Senario* and its parts, and the relations between them, one finds the form of every musical consonance.
>
> Although the *numero Senario* possesses many special characteristics, I will nevertheless, in order not to deviate, enumerate only those [properties] that are suitable for our purpose. First, it represents the first of the perfect numbers. It contains parts which stand in the following relation to one another: if one picks out two arbitrary parts, they always indicate the relation or the form of a proportion of a musical consonance — whether it concerns a simple or a compound consonance — as one can see in the following figure [see Figure 10.36].[205] (Text in brackets mine. Italics in Zarlino's original text.)

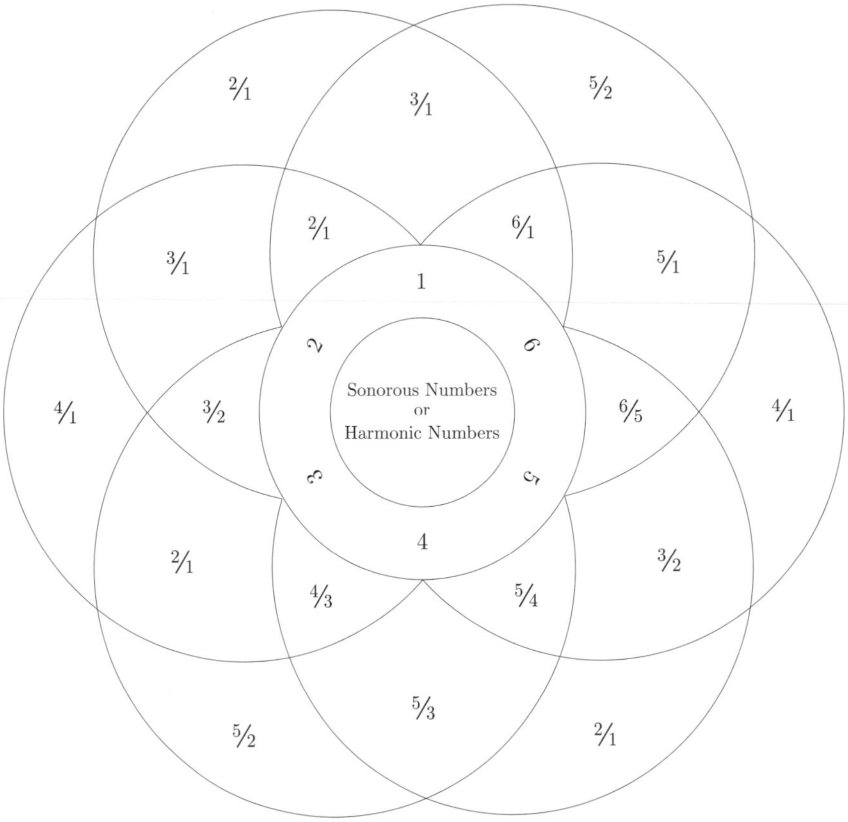

Figure 10.36 An edited copy of an engraving of the *numero Senario* in the *Istitutioni harmoniche, Prima Parte, Cap. 15.* To facilitate a mathematical discussion of Zarlino's illustration, I replaced the original Latin interval names with ratios. For example, in this engraving the *diapente*, or the "fifth," occurs twice; consequently, I substituted ratio $^3\!/_2$ in two locations.

In the original engraving above, Zarlino assigns traditional Latin names to the musical intervals included in the *Senario*. To discuss the mathematical significance of this illustration, Figure 10.36 expresses these interval names as ratios.

When viewed from a historical perspective, Quote I is of paramount importance to the development of European music because it shatters the 3-limit barrier of Pythagorean theory. As described in Section 10.5, the Pythagoreans recognized only five consonances: $^4\!/_1$, $^3\!/_1$, $^2\!/_1$, $^3\!/_2$, $^4\!/_3$. These ratios represent all possible interval combinations in the series 1, 2, 3, 4. Figure 10.37 shows that one obtains these consonances through a division of a canon string into two, three, and four aliquot parts.

Dissatisfied with the limitations of only five consonances, Zarlino proposed the number six, or the first perfect number, as the underlying mathematical principle of all musical consonances. By definition, a perfect number is a positive number that equals the sum of its positive divisors. In this case, $1 + 2 + 3 = 6$. To demonstrate the musical potential of the *Senario*, or of the series 1, 2, 3, 4, 5, 6, Zarlino continues his description with the arithmetic division of the "octave," expressed as interval ratios 4:3:2, and the arithmetic division of the "fifth," expressed as interval ratios 6:5:4. He then states that a "harmonic divisor," or a harmonic division of these two ratios, would have placed the "parts," or these interval ratios, in "reverse order."

II

> Its parts [i.e., the six parts of the *Senario*] are so sequenced and arranged, that the forms of either of the two simplest and largest consonances [i.e.,

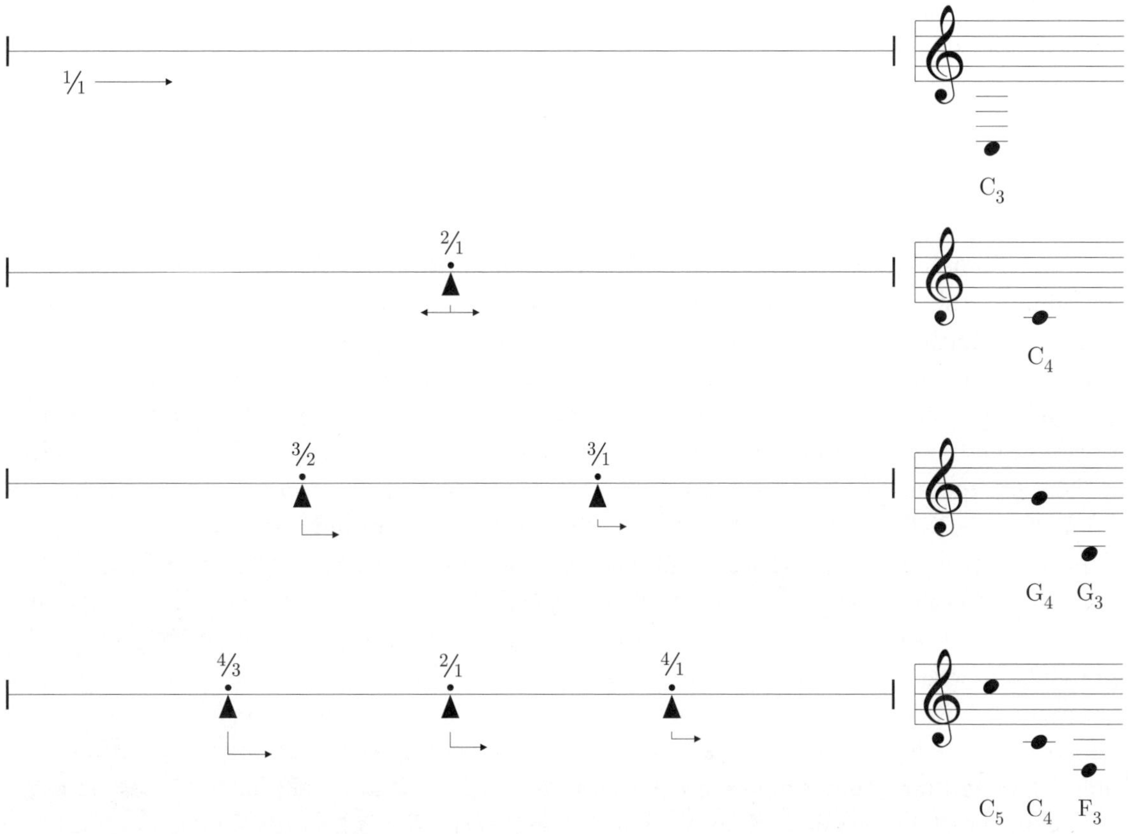

Figure 10.37 The following five Pythagorean consonances — 4/1, 3/1, 2/1, 3/2, 4/3 — result from the division of a canon string into two, three, and four aliquot parts.

2:1 and 3:2] — which the musicians call perfect because they are contained in the parts of the number 3 — may be divided by a middle number into two harmonically proportioned parts. First, one finds the octave, without an inner term, in the form and the relation of 2:1. Then the octave is divided by the number 3, which is situated between 4 and 2, into two consonant parts [4:3:2]; that is, into the fourth, which is between 4 and 3, and into the fifth between 3 and 2. One finds the fifth in turn between the numbers 6 and 4, which is divided by 5 into two consonant parts [6:5:4]; that is, a major third between 5 and 4, and a minor third, which is contained in the numbers 6 and 5.

I wrote that the parts are arranged according to a harmonic proportion. However, this does not concern the order of the proportions (because they are in reality in arithmetic order), [i.e., 4:3:2 or interval ratios 4:3, 3:2; and 6:5:4 or interval ratios 6:5, 5:4], but applies only to the relation of the parts as determined by the middle number. Because these parts exist in such large quantity and in as many relations as there are parts — which are fashioned [into proportions] by a middle number or a ***harmonic divisor*** — although in a ***reverse order***, [i.e., 6:4:3 or interval ratios 3:2, 4:3; and 15:12:10 or interval ratios 5:4, 6:5], as we will see below in the appropriate place.[206] (Bold italics, and text and ratios in brackets mine. Text in parentheses in Fend's German translation.)

In Section 10.42, we will discuss the mathematics of the latter paragraph in full detail. For now, we conclude that while it may be impossible to prove a direct connection between the musical treatises of Ibn Sīnā and Ṣafī Al-Dīn on the one hand, and Quote II from Zarlino's *Istitutioni harmoniche* on the other, we should *not* assume that the latter text states new or original ideas.

~ 10.41 ~

Before we continue this discussion on the arithmetic and harmonic divisions of length ratios, let us first examine Latin expressions for ratios, which appear in countless European treatises on music. Ordinarily, the Latin prefix *sesqui* means *one and a half*, or *one-half more;* consequently, the Latin word *sesquiopus* means the *work of a day and a half*, and *sesquicentennial* literally equals (100 years ÷ 2) + 100 years = 150 years. However, this simple definition of *sesqui* does not apply to mathematical descriptions of epimore or superparticular ratios. (See Section 10.4.) Although medieval and Renaissance theorists retained old Greek names of musical intervals such as *diapente* for "fifth," *diatessaron* for "fourth," *ditonon* for "major third," *tonon* for "whole tone," etc., they substituted new Latin mathematical expressions such as *sesquialtera* for *hemiolios* [3/2], *sesquitertia* for *epitritos* [4/3], *sesquiquarta* for *epitetartos* [5/4], *sesquioctava* for *epogdoos* (*epiogdoos*) [9/8], etc. Except for the first example, note that the Latin prefix *sesqui* replaces the Greek prefix *epi.* To understand the derivations of these new constructions, refer to Table 10.25, which gives the Latin terms for the first ten ordinal numbers. Now, since *sesqui* means *one-half more*, and since *alter* means *second* — as in the *second part* of a whole, or *one-half* — *sesquialtera* literally equals (1/2 ÷ 2) + 1/2 = 3/4. However, turn to Table 10.26 and note that *sesquialtera* actually means 1 + 1/2 = 3/2; similarly, since *tertius* means *third* — as in the *third part* of a whole, or *one-third* — *sesquitertia* literally equals (1/3 ÷ 2) + 1/3 = 1/2; however, *sesquitertia* actually means 1 + 1/3 = 4/3. As a result, we conclude that in the context of *musical ratios*, the Latin prefix *sesqui* simply describes the operation of addition, which means that it has the identical mathematical function as the Greek prefix *epi.* (See Section 3.17.) Consequently, *sesquiquarta* denotes *one-fourth in addition*, and connotes *one and one-fourth:* 1 + 1/4 = 5/4.

Finally, with respect to epimere or superpartient ratios, Table 10.27 lists the Latin terms of seven ratios that appear in Table 10.3. To identify a given ratio, extract the numerator and the denominator contained in the term. First, to determine the denominator, simply identify the last word. Second, to calculate the numerator, identify an inner value — *bi* for 2, *tri* for 3, *quadri* for 4, or *quinque* for 5 — and add this quantity to the denominator. Therefore, *super<u>quadri</u>partiens-<u>quinta</u>* describes a ratio with 5 in the denominator, and 5 + 4 = 9 in the numerator, or ancient length ratio 9/5.

Table 10.25

LATIN TERMS FOR THE FIRST TEN ORDINAL NUMBERS

primus	*first*
alter	*second*
tertius	*third*
quartus	*fourth*
quintus	*fifth*
sextus	*sixth*
septimus	*seventh*
octavus	*eighth*
nonus	*ninth*
decimus	*tenth*

Table 10.26

LATIN TERMS FOR TEN SUPERPARTICULAR RATIOS

sesquialtera	*one and one-half*	$1 + \frac{1}{2}$	Ancient length ratio: $\frac{3}{2}$
sesquitertia	*one and one-third*	$1 + \frac{1}{3}$	Ancient length ratio: $\frac{4}{3}$
sesquiquarta	*one and one-fourth*	$1 + \frac{1}{4}$	Ancient length ratio: $\frac{5}{4}$
sesquiquinta	*one and one-fifth*	$1 + \frac{1}{5}$	Ancient length ratio: $\frac{6}{5}$
sesquisexta	*one and one-sixth*	$1 + \frac{1}{6}$	Ancient length ratio: $\frac{7}{6}$
sesquiseptima	*one and one-seventh*	$1 + \frac{1}{7}$	Ancient length ratio: $\frac{8}{7}$
sesquioctava	*one and one-eighth*	$1 + \frac{1}{8}$	Ancient length ratio: $\frac{9}{8}$
sesquinona	*one and one-ninth*	$1 + \frac{1}{9}$	Ancient length ratio: $\frac{10}{9}$
sesquidecima	*one and one-tenth*	$1 + \frac{1}{10}$	Ancient length ratio: $\frac{11}{10}$
sesquidecimaquinta	*one and one-fifteenth*	$1 + \frac{1}{15}$	Ancient length ratio: $\frac{16}{15}$

Table 10.27

LATIN TERMS FOR SEVEN SUPERPARTIENT RATIOS

superbipartiens-tertia	Ancient length ratio: $\frac{5}{3}$
supertripartiens-quarta	Ancient length ratio: $\frac{7}{4}$
superquadripartiens-quinta	Ancient length ratio: $\frac{9}{5}$
superquinquepartiens-sexta	Ancient length ratio: $\frac{11}{6}$
supertripartiens-quinta	Ancient length ratio: $\frac{8}{5}$
superquadripartiens-septima	Ancient length ratio: $\frac{11}{7}$
superquinquepartiens-nona	Ancient length ratio: $\frac{14}{9}$

~ 10.42 ~

In preparation for a discussion on Zarlino's arithmetic and harmonic division of length ratio $\frac{6}{1}$ on canon strings, we must first review his methods of calculation. With respect to the first kind of division, Zarlino states in Prima Parte, Cap. 36,

> For example, we want to arithmetically divide a sesquialtera, which is formed by the basic numbers 3 and 2. The former includes consecutive prime numbers, which must first be doubled. Then we obtain the numbers 6 and 4. When they are added, the result is 10; when this result is divided into two equal parts, the result is 5. Therefore, I say that 5 is the divisor of our proportion. Because it not only produces the same differences in this proportionality, but also divides the proportion (as is the characteristic of an arithmetic proportionality) into two unequal relations, in such a manner, that one finds between the larger numbers the smaller proportion, and inversely, between the smaller {numbers}, the larger {proportion}. The sesquiquinta {exists} between the 6 and 5, and the sesquiquarta, between the 5 and 4 . . . It is true, that one will refer to this [sequence of numbers] as a progression rather than a proportionality. Because one begins with the smaller number, comes to a middle {number}, and from this, to the larger {number}. One progresses with equal distances. One always finds unity or

> two or three or another number which produces the mentioned distance.[207] (Text in braces mine. Text in parentheses and brackets in Fend's German translation.)

In short, after doubling the outer terms, Zarlino utilizes Equation 3.37A and calculates the *arithmetic division* of length ratio $3/2$ in the following manner:

$$\tfrac{3}{2} \times \tfrac{2}{2} = \tfrac{6}{4}$$

$$(6 + 4) \div 2 = 5$$

$$6{:}5{:}4$$

This arithmetic progression expresses an ascending sequence of musical intervals: a low "minor third," length ratio $6/5$, followed by high "major third," length ratio $5/4$.

With respect to the second kind of division, Zarlino states in Prima Parte, Cap. 39,

> If we want to harmonically divide a sesquialtera, which is formed by the basic numbers 3 and 2, then we will first divide it arithmetically in the manner that I stated above. Then we obtain an arithmetic proportionality in the numbers 6:5:4. Second, to cause it to become a harmonic proportionality, we multiply the 6 and the 4 by the 5, and then [we multiply] the 6 by the 4. From the products we derive the desired [harmonic] division, which is formed by the numbers 30:24:20 . . . Because the relation between the numbers 6 and 4, which indicates the distance between the harmonic numbers, corresponds to that between the numbers 30 and 20. They are the outer terms of the sesquialtera, which are divided into a sesquiquarta between 30:24 [5:4], and into a sesquiquinta with the relation 24:20 [6:5]. Thus, one finds between the larger numbers the larger relation, and between the smaller [numbers], the smaller [relation], and this is the characteristic of this proportionality.[208] (Text and ratios in brackets mine.)

To summarize, Zarlino does not utilize Equation 3.38A, but calculates the *harmonic division* of length ratio $3/2$ based on the three terms of the arithmetic division of $3/2$.

$$\boxed{6{:}5{:}4}$$

$$\tfrac{6}{4} \times \tfrac{5}{5} = \tfrac{30}{20}$$

$$6 \times 4 = 24$$

$$30{:}24{:}20$$

Least Terms, 15:12:10

This harmonic progression expresses the former ascending sequence of musical intervals in "reverse order": a low "major third," length ratio $15/12 = 5/4$, followed by high "minor third," length ratio $12/10 = 6/5$.

10.43

Next, to prepare for Zarlino's arithmetic and harmonic divisions, we must also consider the work of Michael Stifel. In commentaries to his German translation of the Prima Parte and Seconda Parte of the *Istitutioni harmoniche*, Michael Fend gives the following description and translated excerpt from Stifel's *Arithmetica integra* (1544):

> Zarlino owes the realization of the reciprocity of both sequences of ratios indirectly to *Arithmetica integra*, by Michael Stifel who . . . first taught how harmonic sequences can be constructed beyond three terms provided that one derives them from arithmetic sequences. Stifel began with the observation that a cube, which possesses 6 faces, 8 vertices, 12 edges, and 24 face angles, represents a harmonic proportion, and he transferred this sequence of proportions (6:8:12:24) to a ***descending sequence*** of tones: dd, aa, d, D. He compared it to the [descending] sequences cc, gg, c, C; aa, e, a, A; g, d, G, Γut [lit. *Gamma ut*, or *lowest* G], and then unexpectedly advanced the thesis that one
>
> > *"can produce — from any given arithmetic progression — a harmonic [progression], which includes as many terms as the arithmetic [progression]. One proceeds in the following manner: Multiply the terms of your arithmetic proportion in sequence with one another. Then divide the product by the individual terms of your arithmetic progression, beginning with its largest term. From the arithmetic sequence 1, 2, 3, 4, 5, 6 comes the harmonic [sequence] 10, 12, 15, 20, 30, 60. In the same manner, out of a given harmonic sequence comes an arithmetic [sequence]!"*[209]
>
> (Bold italics and text in brackets mine. The harmonic progression in parentheses in Fend's German commentary.)

Regarding Stifel's cube analysis, refer to Equation 3.38A, and for a given string where $a = 6$ units and $c = 12$ units, calculate $\Lambda_H = 8$ units; and where $a = 8$ units and $c = 24$ units, $\Lambda_H = 12$ units. Consequently, Stifel's harmonic progression demonstrates that the "double-octave," ratio $^{24}/_{6} = {}^{4}/_{1}$, has *two harmonic means*, namely, 8 and 12. Now examine Figure 10.38, which shows Stifel's descending tones: dd, aa, d, D, on a canon string with a length of 6 units, 8 units, 12 units, and 24 units, respectively. Because Stifel interprets the harmonic progression 6:8:12:24 as a descending sequence of tones, we must, in turn, interpret his series as a descending sequence of interval ratios: $^{8}/_{6}$, $^{12}/_{8}$, $^{24}/_{12}$, or simply $^{4}/_{3}$, $^{3}/_{2}$, $^{2}/_{1}$, respectively. Now, turn to Figure 3.12, and observe that if we play these three interval ratios in ascending order: $^{2}/_{1}$, $^{3}/_{2}$, $^{4}/_{3}$, Stifel's harmonic division of the "double-octave" produces the first three intervals of the harmonic series, namely, the "octave," "fifth," and "fourth."

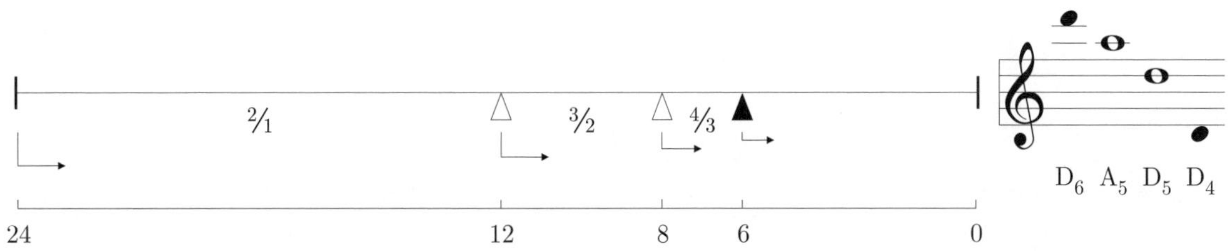

Figure 10.38 The division of the "double-octave" into *two harmonic means* according to Michael Stifel (1487–1567). When Stifel observed that a cube has 6 faces, 8 vertices, 12 edges, and 24 face angles, he interpreted the harmonic progression 6:8:12:24 as a descending sequence of tones: dd, aa, d, D. These tones produce a descending sequence of interval ratios: $^{4}/_{3}$, $^{3}/_{2}$, $^{2}/_{1}$. In this figure, black notes represent the two outer terms of the "double-octave," length ratio $^{24}/_{6} = {}^{4}/_{1}$, and white notes, the two harmonic means.

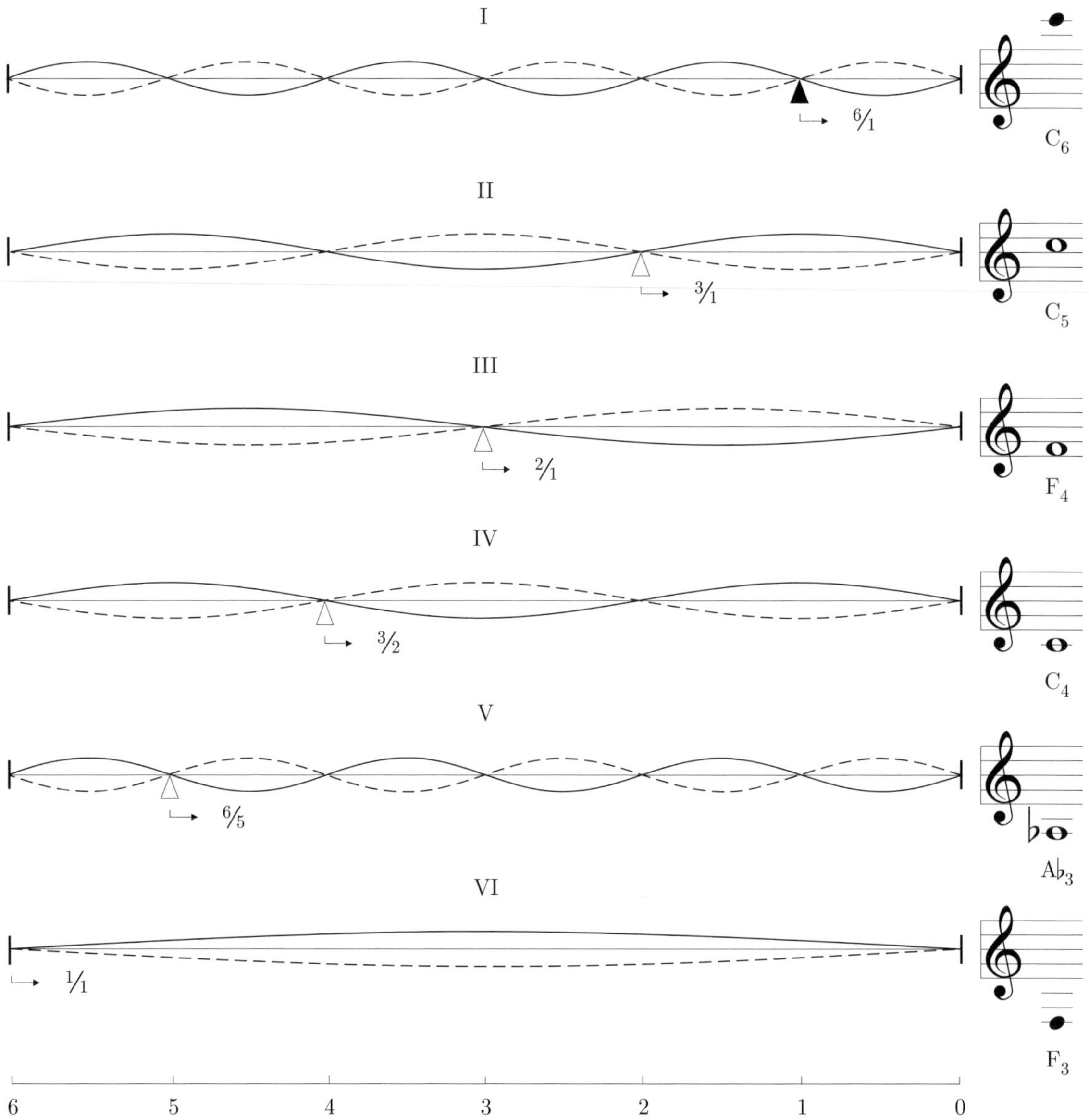

Figure 10.39 The division of the "double-octave and a fifth" into *four arithmetic means* according to Stifel (1544). When we play this arithmetic division of length ratio 6/1 in ascending order, Strings VI–IV sound the F–minor triad: F–A♭–C.

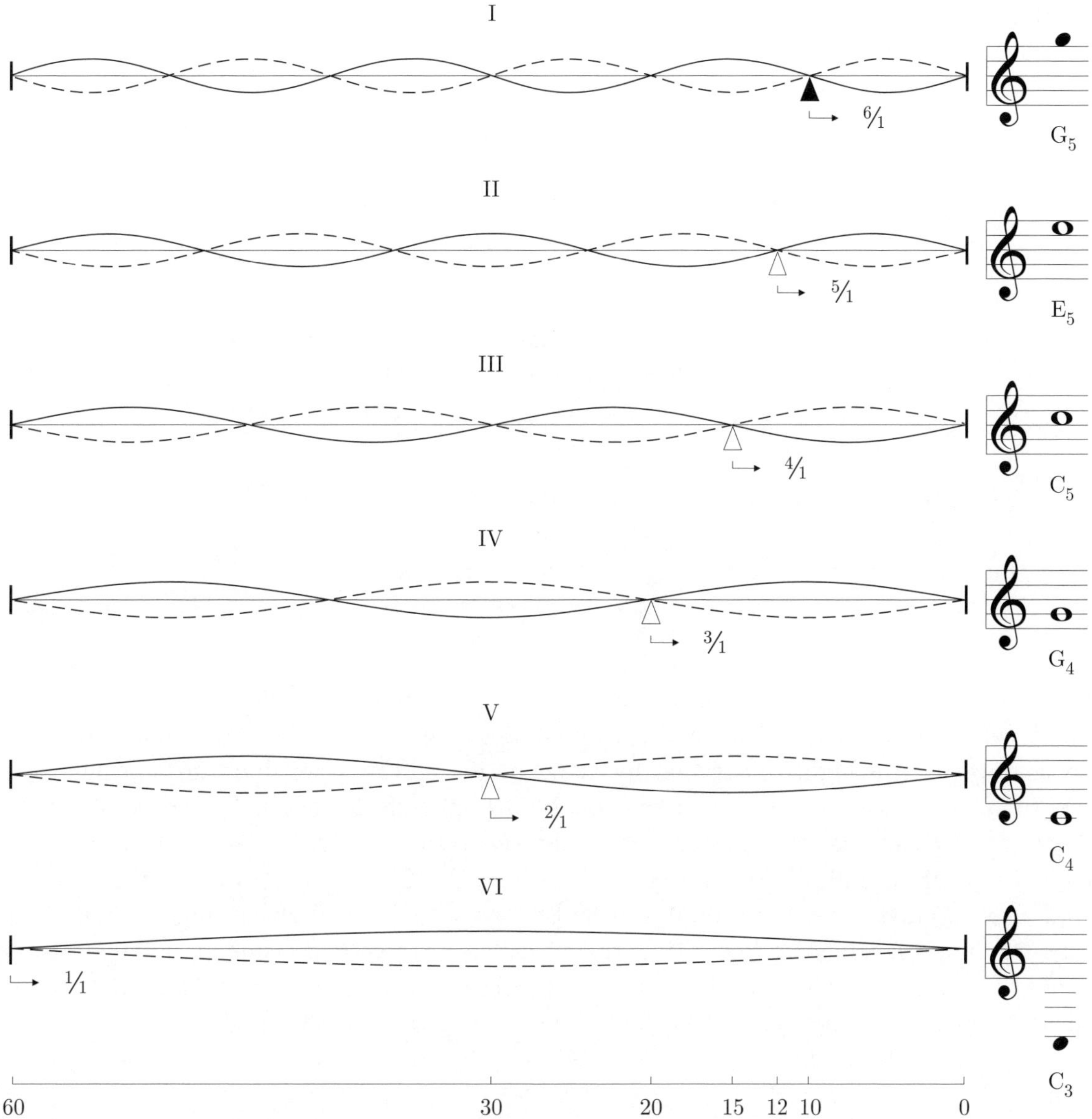

Figure 10.40 The division of the "double-octave and a fifth" into *four harmonic means* according to Stifel (1544). When we play this harmonic division of length ratio $^6\!/\!_1$ in ascending order, Strings III–I sound the C-major triad: C–E–G. In the *Istitutioni harmoniche* (1573), Prima Parte, Cap. 40, Zarlino fails to acknowledge the mathematical and musical significance of Stifel's harmonic division of length ratio $^6\!/\!_1$ in the context of demonstrating the *Senario* on canon strings.

With respect to transforming the arithmetic progression 1, 2, 3, 4, 5, 6 into the harmonic progression 10, 12, 15, 20, 30, 60, Stifel calculated the integers of the latter sequence in three steps.

Step 1. $1 \times 2 \times 3 \times 4 \times 5 \times 6 = 720$

Step 2.
$$720 \div 6 = 120$$
$$720 \div 5 = 144$$
$$720 \div 4 = 180$$
$$720 \div 3 = 240$$
$$720 \div 2 = 360$$
$$720 \div 1 = 720$$

Step 3.
$$120 \div 12 = 10$$
$$144 \div 12 = 12$$
$$180 \div 12 = 15$$
$$240 \div 12 = 20$$
$$360 \div 12 = 30$$
$$720 \div 12 = 60$$

Step 3 reduces the quotients of Step 2 to least terms. Although Stifel did not explicitly interpret the arithmetic and harmonic division of the "double-octave and a fifth," ratio $6/1$, as a descending sequence of tones, it is highly likely that he also experienced these two divisions on canon strings. Figure 10.39 shows the arithmetic progression 1:2:3:4:5:6 as a descending sequence of tones: C_6, C_5, F_4, C_4, $A\flat_3$, F_3, or a descending sequence of interval ratios: $2/1$, $3/2$, $4/3$, $5/4$, $6/5$. If we express each tone as a length ratio, and play them in ascending order: F_3–$1/1$, $A\flat_3$–$6/5$, C_4–$3/2$, F_4–$2/1$, C_5–$3/1$, C_6–$6/1$, we find that the first three tones produced by Strings VI–IV sound the F-minor triad: F–A♭–C. Finally, examine Figure 10.39 to see that this so-called *arithmetic division* actually consists of a sequence of *increasing* string lengths, where each succeeding length is an integer multiple of the first length. That is, String I has a length of 1 unit, String II has a length of 1 unit $\times$ 2 = 2 units, etc. Hence, Stifel's descending division of ancient length ratio $6/1$ into *four arithmetic means:* 1, 2, 3, 4, 5, 6.

In contrast, Figure 10.40 shows Stifel's harmonic progression 10:12:15:20:30:60 as a descending sequence of tones: G_5, E_5, C_5, G_4, C_4, C_3, or a descending sequence of interval ratios: $12/10$, $15/12$, $20/15$, $30/20$, $60/30$, or simply $6/5$, $5/4$, $4/3$, $3/2$, $2/1$, respectively. If we express these tones as length ratios, and play them in ascending order: C_3–$1/1$, C_4–$2/1$, G_4–$3/1$, C_5–$4/1$, E_5–$5/1$, G_5–$6/1$, we find that the last three tones produced by Strings III–I sound the C-major triad: C–E–G. Now, turn back to Figures 3.10, 3.13, and 3.15, and observe that the standing waves in Figure 10.40 represent the first six modes of vibration of a flexible string. The first complete analysis of the mode shapes and mode frequencies of vibrating strings exists in a work entitled *Système général des intervalles des sons...* by Joseph Sauveur (1653–1716), published in 1701. (See Section 10.56.) We conclude, therefore, that Stifel comprehended the mathematical and musical significance of the division of ancient length ratio $6/1$ into *four harmonic means:* 10, 12, 15, 20, 30, 60, approximately 150 years before Sauveur discovered the *harmonic progression* 1, $1/2$, $1/3$, $1/4$, $1/5$, $1/6$, . . . *as a natural phenomenon of subdividing strings.*

10.44

In the *Istitutioni harmoniche*, Prima Parte, Cap. 40, Zarlino begins his formal demonstration of the *Senario* on canon strings by first summarizing the fundamental differences between the "compound unities" of the arithmetic division, and the "sonorous quantities" of the harmonic division.

> The harmonic proportionality possesses the same proportions as the arithmetic [proportionality] because the forms of the consonances are contained (as we saw) in the parts of the *numero Senario;* however, in the case of the arithmetic proportionality, among the smaller numbers exist the larger proportions, and among the larger [numbers], the smaller [proportions]; while one finds the opposite in the case of the harmonic proportionality, that is, we have among the larger numbers the larger proportions, and among the smaller [numbers], the smaller [proportions]. This difference stems from the fact that the one [the former] is associated with pure numbers, and the other [the latter], with sonorous quantities. They progress in opposite directions, that is, one [the former] increases, the other [the latter] decreases in relation to their respective starting point, as I showed. None of them deviates from the natural progression, which one finds in the order of the proportions. This [order] is formed by the numbers in the following manner: in the arithmetic proportionality, the numbers form ***compound unities***, while in the harmonic proportionality, they are parts of ***sonorous quantities***.[210] (Bold italics, and text in brackets mine. Italics in Zarlino's original text. Text in parentheses in Fend's German translation.)

As discussed in Section 10.43, the "compound unities" represent increasing string lengths that are integer multiples of the first string length, and the "sonorous quantities" represent decreasing string lengths of a manually subdivided string. Zarlino then continues with the arithmetic division of an "octave and a fifth," or length ratio $^3\!/_1$.

III

> In order to better understand these things, we will give an example. We draw a line AB, which for an arithmetician represents unity, and for a musician, a sonorous body, hence a string. Its length is one foot. If we want to give it an arithmetic progression, then we must leave it whole and undivided, because one may not divide unity of an arithmetic progression. Thus an [arithmetic] proportion, consisting of three numbers, is given in such a manner, that the proportion of a tripla [3:1] is divided by a mean into two parts.
>
> We must proceed in the following manner: First, the mentioned line (if possible) is to be doubled, so that unity is doubled [to form] a duality, which follows unity directly. After we doubled it, we have the line AC of a two-foot length. If we compare the doubled line AC with the line AB, then we discover between them the proportion of the dupla [2:1], which is first in the natural order of the proportion, as one also finds between the numbers two and one. When we want to find the third term in this kind of progression, we must extend the line AC to a three-foot length, so that it reaches the point D, because three directly follows two. Then we will have the proportion of the tripla between DA and BA, because AD is measured exactly three times by AB, or AD contains AB three times, as in the case of numbers the three contains the one three times. And the proportion from AC can be divided into two parts in the following manner: in a dupla CA and BA, and in a sesquialtera [3:2] DA and CA, indeed an arithmetic proportionality . . .[211] (Ratios in brackets mine.)

At this point in the text, Zarlino includes a simple figure to illustrate his division on a canon string, but he neither describes nor demonstrates the arithmetic division of number six, length ratio $^6\!/\!_1$, in full detail. As an alternative, refer to Figure 10.41, which takes Zarlino's arithmetic method to its logical conclusion. Here Strings I–III illustrate the first three steps described by Zarlino in Quote III, and String III shows the complete arithmetic division of length ratio $^3\!/\!_1$, interval ratios 3:2:1. The column to the left of the string gives Zarlino's method for calculating the arithmetic mean, and the staff to the right of the string shows C_5 as the arithmetic mean between C_6 and F_4. Finally, Strings IV–VI demonstrate three succeeding constructions that result in the arithmetic division of length ratio $^4\!/\!_2$, interval ratios 4:3:2, of ratio $^5\!/\!_3$, interval ratios 5:4:3, and of ratio $^6\!/\!_4$, interval ratios 6:5:4.

Zarlino then continues with the harmonic division of length ratio $^6\!/\!_2$ [$^3\!/\!_1$].

IV

> However, if we want to construct a harmonic progression, we will proceed in the following manner: First, we divide the mentioned line AB at its center, the point C, because the half comes before every other part. I now say that one finds between the given string AB and its half CB . . . the proportion of the dupla [2:1], which is the first in the natural order of the proportions. Then we will decrease the mentioned line AB by $^2\!/\!_3$ at the point D, and we will thus obtain the proportion of the sesquialtera [3:2], which takes the second place in the order of the proportions. I say that the sesquialtera exists between CB and DB, furthermore the tripla [3:1] [exists] between AB and DB, which are [both] divided by CB into two proportions according to the harmonic proportionality . . .[212]

Here again, Zarlino includes a simple figure to illustrate his division on a canon string, but he neither describes nor demonstrates the harmonic division of length ratio $^6\!/\!_1$ in full detail. So, refer to Figure 10.42, which takes Zarlino's harmonic method to its logical conclusion. Strings I–III illustrate the first three steps described by Zarlino in Quote IV, and String III shows the complete harmonic division of length ratio $^6\!/\!_2$ [$^3\!/\!_1$], interval ratios 6:3:2. In conformity with his method of calculating a harmonic division based on the three terms of a corresponding arithmetic division, the column to the left of String III gives the latter three terms in a rectangular frame. Also, the staff to the right of the string shows C_4 as the harmonic mean between C_3 and G_4. Finally, Strings IV–VI demonstrate three succeeding constructions that result in the harmonic division of length ratio $^6\!/\!_3$ [$^2\!/\!_1$], interval ratios 6:4:3, of ratio $^{20}\!/\!_{12}$ [$^5\!/\!_3$], interval ratios 20:15:12, and of ratio $^{30}\!/\!_{20}$ [$^3\!/\!_2$], interval ratios 15:12:10. Note carefully the transition in string length units between Strings IV and V. Although it is possible to extend the fractional string length notation 3.0 : 2.0 : 1.5 of String IV, to 2.0 : 1.5 : 1.2 for String V, and to 1.5 : 1.2 : 1.0 for String VI, in Quote V below Zarlino explicitly gives Stifel's harmonic progression 60:30:20:15:12:10 as the harmonic division of number six. Consequently, the mathematical complication that requires a transition from 6 units for the overall length of Strings I–III, to 60 units for the overall length of Strings IV–VI, probably explains why Zarlino neither described nor illustrated the complete harmonic division of length ratio $^6\!/\!_1$.

Zarlino continues with the following comparison of the arithmetic and the harmonic division of length ratio $^3\!/\!_1$:

> And as the numbers of the arithmetic progression are multiplied unities, so those [numbers] of the harmonic [progression] represent the number of parts that can be determined from a sonorous body, [and] which originate from the subdivision of this body. Therefore, in the former one regards the

multiplication of unity, as in the following sequence: 3:2:1. And in the latter, one regards the multiplication of parts on a divided object, which is formed by the numbers 6:3:2. Because if we regard the whole divided into its parts, then we discover that the line CD is the smallest part of the line AB, and that it measures AB altogether six times, the line CB, three times, and the line DB, two times.[213] (Text in brackets mine.)

With respect to these two different kinds of divisions on canon strings, Zarlino concludes

V

Now it can be seen, that in the harmonic progression [6:3:2], the larger numbers [6:3] contain the larger proportions and the lower sounds [i.e., the "octave"], while the smaller numbers [3:2] correspond to the smaller proportions and the higher sounds [i.e., the "fifth"]. Because they [the higher sounds] are brought forth on strings with smaller dimensions, while in the case of the lower tones, the strings have larger dimensions. Furthermore, we can see: As one progresses in the arithmetic proportionality (provided that one would realize it in the manner shown) from the high to the low sound by multiplying the string length, so one proceeds in the harmonic [proportionality] in reverse from low to high by shortening the string. In the arithmetic progression [3:2:1] the intervals of the smaller proportion [3:2] have their position in the lower [sounds], [i.e., the "fifth"], contrary to the *natura dell'Harmonia* [lit. *nature of Harmony*], whose characteristic it is that the deep sounds possess a larger interval than the high [sounds], and these [the high sounds], in turn, [possess] a smaller [interval].

However, since all the proportions that belong to the arithmetic progression — because they follow the natural order of the proportions — also exist in the same order in the harmonic progression [that is, the "octave," "fifth," "fourth,". . . descend in the arithmetic progression, and the "octave," "fifth," "fourth,". . . ascend in the harmonic progression], we can now understand in which manner one should take the meaning of the words in Chapter 15, which state that in the terms of the *numero Senario* are contained all the forms of the simple musical consonances that can be produced, and that ***the consonances, which the composers call perfect***, are fashioned after the harmonic division of this number. Because when the consonances are transferred to a sounding body with the aid of the consonant ratios 60:30:20:15:12:10, then one recognizes that these consonances are so divided as the parts of the number 6, although they are now arranged in another manner. Likewise, it is comprehensible in which sense the words of the very learned Jacobus Faber Stapulensis in his "Musica" (Prop. III, 34) are to be understood: that the harmonic proportionality is completely indispensable and that, although the magnitudes of its proportions agree with those of the arithmetic proportionality, the sequence and the place [position] of the ratios are different.[214] (Bold italics, and text and ratios in brackets mine. Italics in Zarlino's original text. Text in parentheses in Fend's German translation.)

In the first paragraph of Quote V, Zarlino identifies the "nature of Harmony" — or the very essence of musical harmony — with the harmonic division of strings. His preference for the harmonic division is based on the performance of choral music, where one places large intervals in the bass,

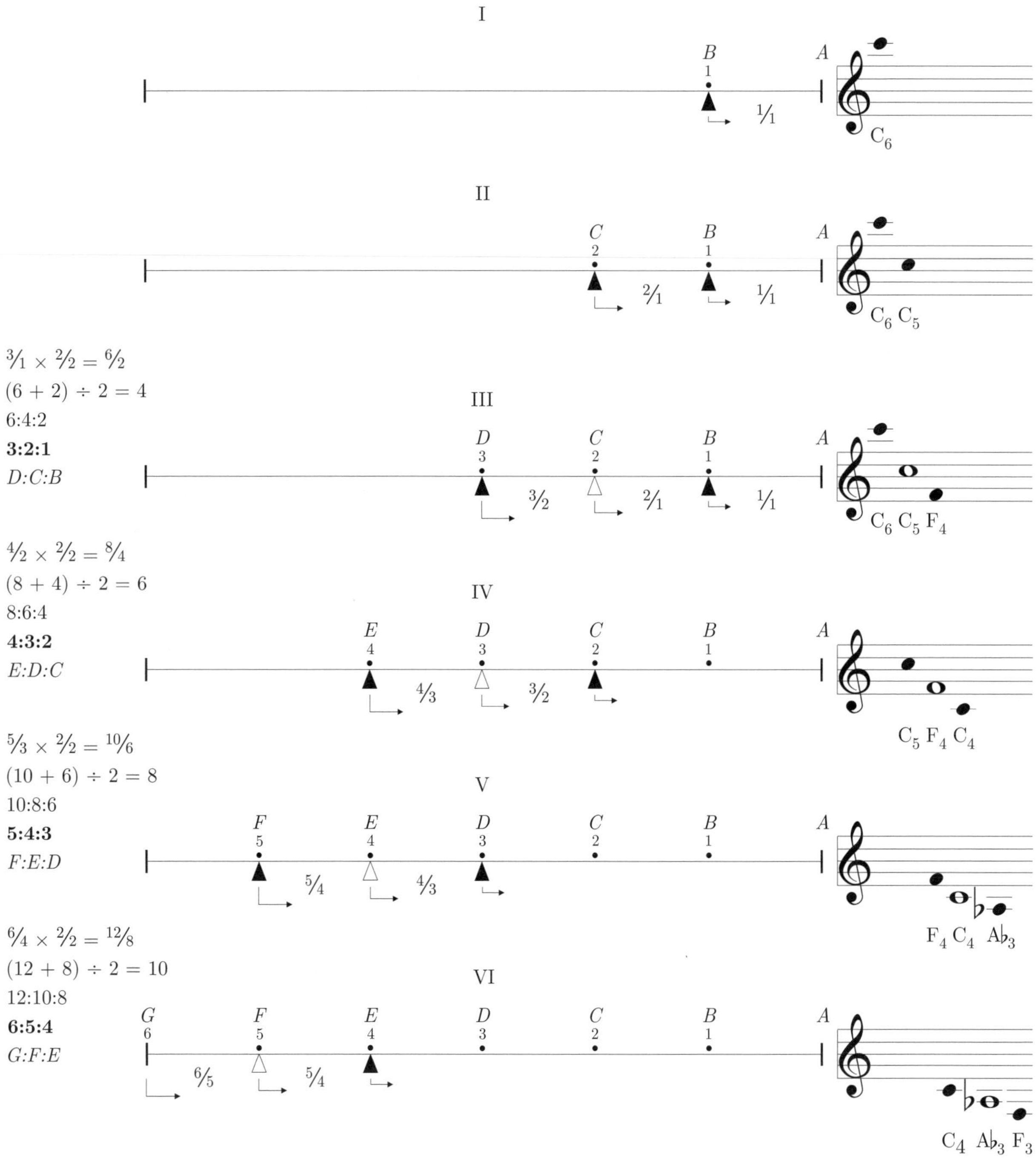

Figure 10.41 The descending arithmetic division of length ratio $6/1$ as described and suggested by Zarlino. According to his text, Strings I–III show the first three steps required for the arithmetic division of length ratio $3/1$. Strings IV–VI take Zarlino's method to its logical conclusion, namely, the arithmetic division of length ratio $6/1$.

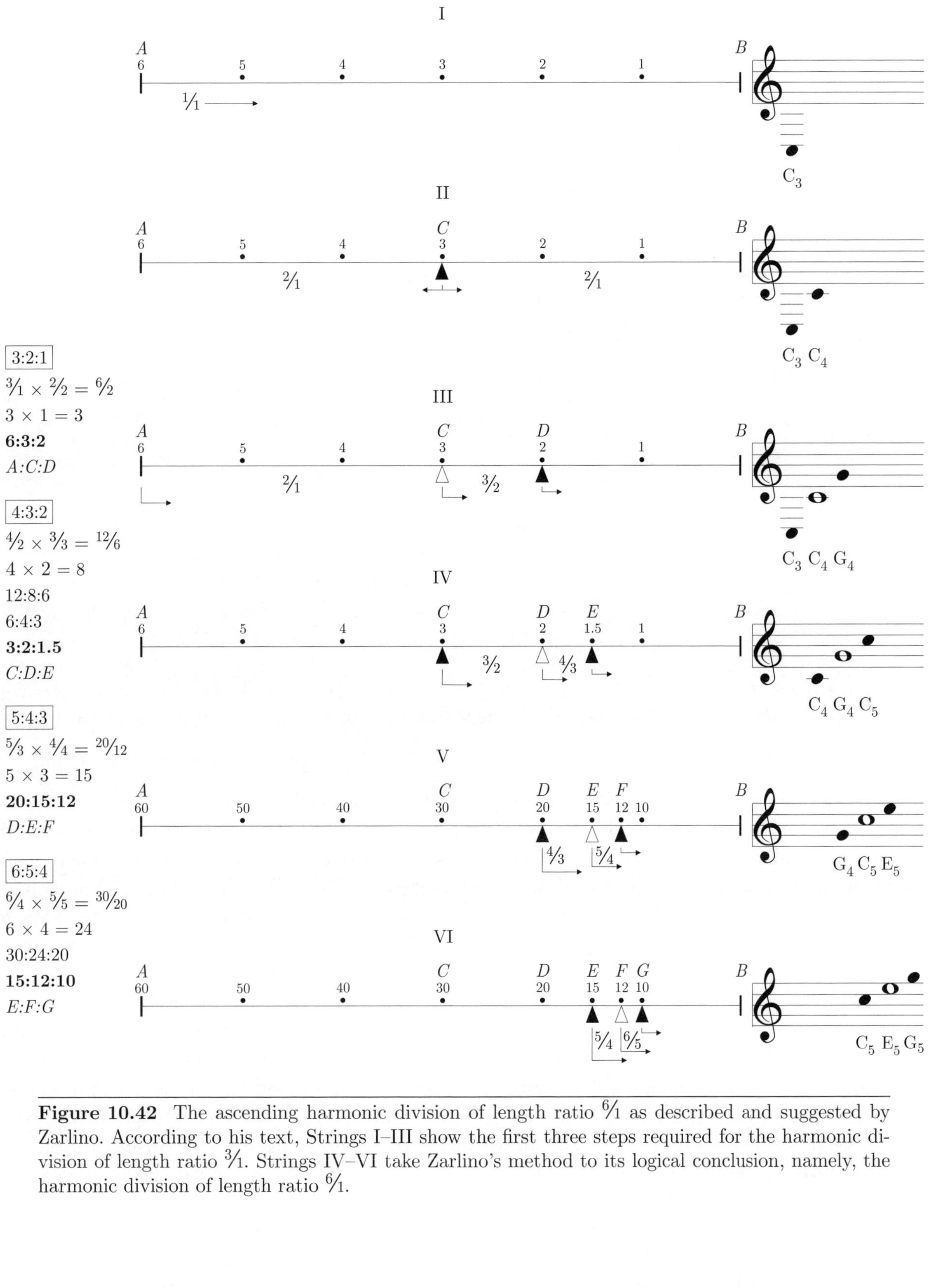

Figure 10.42 The ascending harmonic division of length ratio $6/1$ as described and suggested by Zarlino. According to his text, Strings I–III show the first three steps required for the harmonic division of length ratio $3/1$. Strings IV–VI take Zarlino's method to its logical conclusion, namely, the harmonic division of length ratio $6/1$.

The Arithmetic Division of the "Fifth" Expressed as Ancient Length Ratio $3/2$

Lengths:	$L =$ 30.0 in.	→	$\Lambda_A =$ 25.0 in.	→	$\Lambda =$ 20.0 in.	→	$L =$ 0 in.
Ancient Length Ratios:	$30/30 = 1/1$		$30/25 = 6/5$		$30/20 = 3/2$		
Latter Denominators:	30	:	25	:	20		
Least Terms:	6	:	5	:	4		
Frequencies:	20.0 cps		24.0 cps		30.0 cps		
Frequency Ratios:	$20/20 = 1/1$		$24/20 = 6/5$		$30/20 = 3/2$		
Latter Numerators:	20	:	24	:	30		
Least Terms:	10	:	12	:	15		

Interval Ratio Notation: The longer length for Λ_A, and the higher frequency for F, appear in the numerator.

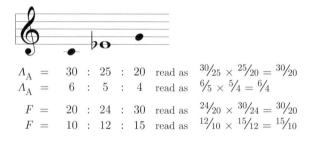

Λ_A	=	30	:	25	:	20	read as	$30/25 \times 25/20 = 30/20$
Λ_A	=	6	:	5	:	4	read as	$6/5 \times 5/4 = 6/4$
F	=	20	:	24	:	30	read as	$24/20 \times 30/24 = 30/20$
F	=	10	:	12	:	15	read as	$12/10 \times 15/12 = 15/10$

Figure 10.43 Arithmetic division of the "fifth" expressed as length ratio $3/2$. On this canon string, the "fifth" is defined by 30.0 in. and 20.0 in. lengths, and the arithmetic mean, by a 25.0 in. length.

or in the lower position of a chord, and small intervals in the treble, or in the upper position of a chord. In the second paragraph, Zarlino establishes an irrefutable nexus between his *numero Senario* and Stifel's harmonic division of length ratio $6/1$, notated here as the harmonic progression 60:30:20:15:12:10, or an ascending sequence of interval ratios: $60/30$, $30/20$, $20/15$, $15/12$, $12/10$, or simply $2/1$, $3/2$, $4/3$, $5/4$, $6/5$. To strengthen his argument, in the next sentence Zarlino paraphrases a passage from a famous mathematical treatise entitled *Musica libris quatuor demonstrata*, by Jacobus Faber Stapulensis (Jacques Le Febvre), (*c.* 1455 – d. 1536), first published in 1496.

Zarlino's unrelenting determination to shift the focus from the arithmetic division to the harmonic division reveals how deeply entrenched the practice of direct canon string division had become. As discussed in Sections 10.4 and 10.8, the latter method always produces an arithmetic division, where the smaller interval appears in the lower position, and the larger interval, in the upper position. With respect to the "octave," it matters little if in playing a chord one utilizes the arithmetic or the harmonic division. The former places the "fourth," ratio $4/3$, in the lower position, and the "fifth," ratio $3/2$, in the upper position; and the latter places the "fifth" in the lower position, and the "fourth" in the upper position. However, with respect to the "fifth," and what would later be called triadic harmony, the difference between the arithmetic division of length ratio $3/2$ and the harmonic division of length ratio $3/2$ literally defines the emotional polarity of Western music. Figure 10.43 shows that the arithmetic division of the "fifth" places the "minor third," ratio $6/5$, in the lower position, and the "major third," ratio $5/4$, in the upper position; we call the chord C–E$\flat$–G a *minor triad*, or *minor tonality*.

The Harmonic Division of the "Fifth" Expressed as Ancient Length Ratio $\frac{3}{2}$

	$L =$		$\Lambda_H =$		$\Lambda =$	$L =$
Lengths:	30.0 in. →		24.0 in. →		20.0 in. →	0 in.
Ancient Length Ratios:	$30/30 = 1/1$		$30/24 = 5/4$		$30/20 = 3/2$	
Latter Denominators:	30	:	24	:	20	
Least Terms:	15	:	12	:	10	
Frequencies:	20.0 cps		25.0 cps		30.0 cps	
Frequency Ratios:	$20/20 = 1/1$		$25/20 = 5/4$		$30/20 = 3/2$	
Latter Numerators:	20	:	25	:	30	
Least Terms:	4	:	5	:	6	

Interval Ratio Notation: The longer length for Λ_H, and the higher frequency for F, appear in the numerator.

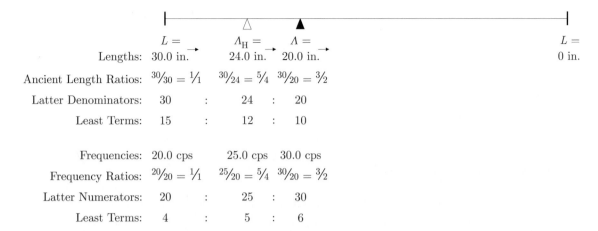

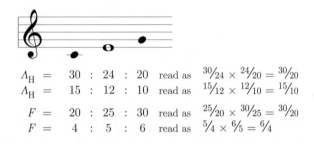

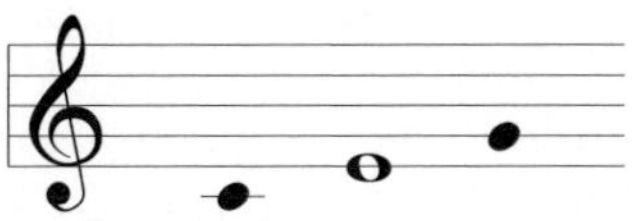

Λ_H = 30 : 24 : 20 read as $30/24 \times 24/20 = 30/20$
Λ_H = 15 : 12 : 10 read as $15/12 \times 12/10 = 15/10$

F = 20 : 25 : 30 read as $25/20 \times 30/25 = 30/20$
F = 4 : 5 : 6 read as $5/4 \times 6/5 = 6/4$

Figure 10.44 Harmonic division of the "fifth" expressed as length ratio $\frac{3}{2}$. On this canon string the "fifth" is defined by 30.0 in. and 20.0 in. lengths, and the harmonic mean, by a 24.0 in. length.

In contrast, Figure 10.44 shows that the harmonic division of the "fifth" places the "major third" in the lower position, and the "minor third" in the upper position; we call the chord C–E–G a *major triad*, or *major tonality.*

Now, turn back to Figure 10.39, and note that the minor triad F–A♭–C occurs in Stifel's arithmetic progression when realized on a string with 6, 5, 4, aliquot parts; and, in Figure 10.40, the major triad C–E–G occurs in Stifel's harmonic progression when realized on a string with 15, 12, 10, aliquot parts.

10.45

Before we examine Zarlino's final analysis of the arithmetic and harmonic division of the "fifth," let us first evaluate two important mathematical aspects of the *Senario.* In his paper, Robert W. Wienpahl states that ". . . the major and minor sixth are not considered by Zarlino to be basic consonances . . ."[215] because they are not superparticular or epimore ratios. In Section 10.4, we noted that a superparticular ratio has a numerator that exceeds the denominator by one. Therefore, since the integers of the "major sixth," ratio $\frac{5}{3}$, and the "minor sixth," ratio $\frac{8}{5}$, do not differ by unity, Zarlino concludes that they are compound or imperfect consonances. Zarlino distinguishes between simple and compound consonances in the *Istitutioni harmoniche*, Prima Parte, Cap. 16. Near the end of this chapter, he concludes

VI

> In the *Senario*, that is, in its parts, one finds every Simple musical consonance *in atto* [lit. *in actuality*], and beyond that, the Compound [musical consonance] *in potenza* [lit. *in potentiality*].[216] (Text in brackets mine. Italics in Zarlino's original text.)

In the middle of this chapter, Zarlino contends

> To the . . . [compound consonances] belongs the mentioned [major] sixth, which consists of the fourth and the major third. It is recognized by the simplest terms of its proportion, 5 and 3, which is divided by 4 into 5:4:3.[217] (Text in brackets mine.)

In other words, because the "major sixth," expressed as interval ratios 5:4:3, consists of two smaller consonances, Zarlino considers it a compound consonance: $5/4 \times 4/3 = 5/3$. He then continues by applying the same argument to the "minor sixth":

VII

> Next to it, I will place the minor sixth, which arises from a union of the fourth and the minor third. Its simplest terms are contained in the genus superpartiens as the ratio supertripartiensquinta, and they can be joined by a middle term. Since one finds this proportion between 8 and 5, a middle harmonic number is included between them, namely, the 6. It divides the proportion 8:5 into two smaller ratios 8:6:5, that is, a sesquitertia and a sesquiquinta. For this reason we can characterize this consonance as a Compound [consonance]. Until now, it has received a friendly reception by musicians, and it is counted among the other consonances. If, under the parts of the *Senario*, one does not come across its form *in atto* [in actuality], one finds it there nevertheless *in potenza* [in potentiality]. Because, it builds its form in truth from the parts that are contained in the number 6, that is, from the fourth and the minor third.[218] (Text in brackets mine. Italics in Zarlino's original text.)

That is, because the "minor sixth," expressed as interval ratios 8:6:5, also consists of two smaller consonances, it too is a compound consonance: $8/6 \times 6/5 = 8/5$. Therefore, both the "major sixth" and "minor sixth" are considered less than perfect consonances.

Although the "major sixth" and the "minor sixth" are both superpartient ratios, note that the *Senario* includes both integers of ratio 5:3, but only one integer of ratio 8:5. Because of this, Zarlino's rationalization with respect to ratio $5/3$ seems unnecessary and contradictory. To resolve this confusion, we may conjecture that if the *Senario* had contained both integers of ratio $8/5$, Zarlino would probably not have given an inconsistent description of ratio $5/3$. In other words, the necessity to rationalize the inclusion of superpartient ratio $8/5$ forced him to rationalize superpartient ratio $5/3$ as well. The inscription in the inner circle of Figure 10.36 is evidence enough that Zarlino primarily regarded ratio $5/3$ as a simple or basic consonance.

As if to acknowledge his inconsistent treatment of ratio $5/3$, Zarlino draws a hard distinction between $5/3$ and $8/5$ by directly stating in Quote VI, and by indirectly stating in Quote VII, that the former is found "in actuality" in the *Senario*, but the latter is only found "in potentiality." When viewed from this perspective, ratio $5/3$ is an *actual* consonance among all the other consonances in Figure 10.36, but ratio $8/5$ is only a *potential* consonance that stands apart from the ratios in this figure. To understand Zarlino's apparent reluctance to classify ratio $8/5$ as a bona fide dissonance, consider this sequence of ratios: $6/5$, $4/3$, $3/2$, $8/5$. Now turn back to Section 10.20, and observe that in the Catalog of Scales, only Ptolemy's Tense Diatonic includes these four ratios. In Section 10.21, Figure 10.15 shows that in the Lydian Mode, the latter sequence transforms to ratios $5/4$, $4/3$, $3/2$, $5/3$. Given Zarlino's fascination with Ptolemy's scale, his artistic predilections led him to regard ratios $5/3$ and $8/5$ as unequal but musically acceptable consonances.

≈ 10.46 ≈

Toward the end of his life, Zarlino abandoned the needlessly conflicted rhetoric of his early writings. In the *De tutte l'opere...* edition of the *Istitutioni harmoniche*, he gives equal consideration to the harmonic and the arithmetic division of the "fifth." With the exception of the modern G-clef, Figure 10.45(a) is an exact copy of Zarlino's illustration as it appears in *De tutte l'opere...*, Terza Parte, Cap. 31, p. 222. Figure 10.45(b) gives a detailed ratio analysis of Figure 10.45(a). For the harmonic division of the "pure fifth," expressed as length ratio $180/120 = 3/2$, Zarlino describes the lower interval, ratio $180/144 = 5/4$ [386.3 ¢], as a *ditono* (lit. *two-tones*) and *sesquiquarta;* and he describes the upper interval, ratio $144/120 = 6/5$ [315.6 ¢], as a *semiditono* (lit. *flat two-tones*) and *sesquiquinta.* To verify his *harmonic mean* calculation, substitute the outer two terms — 180 units and 120 units — into Equation 3.38A to obtain the units:

$$\Lambda_{\mathrm{H}} = \frac{2(180)(120)}{180 + 120} = 144$$

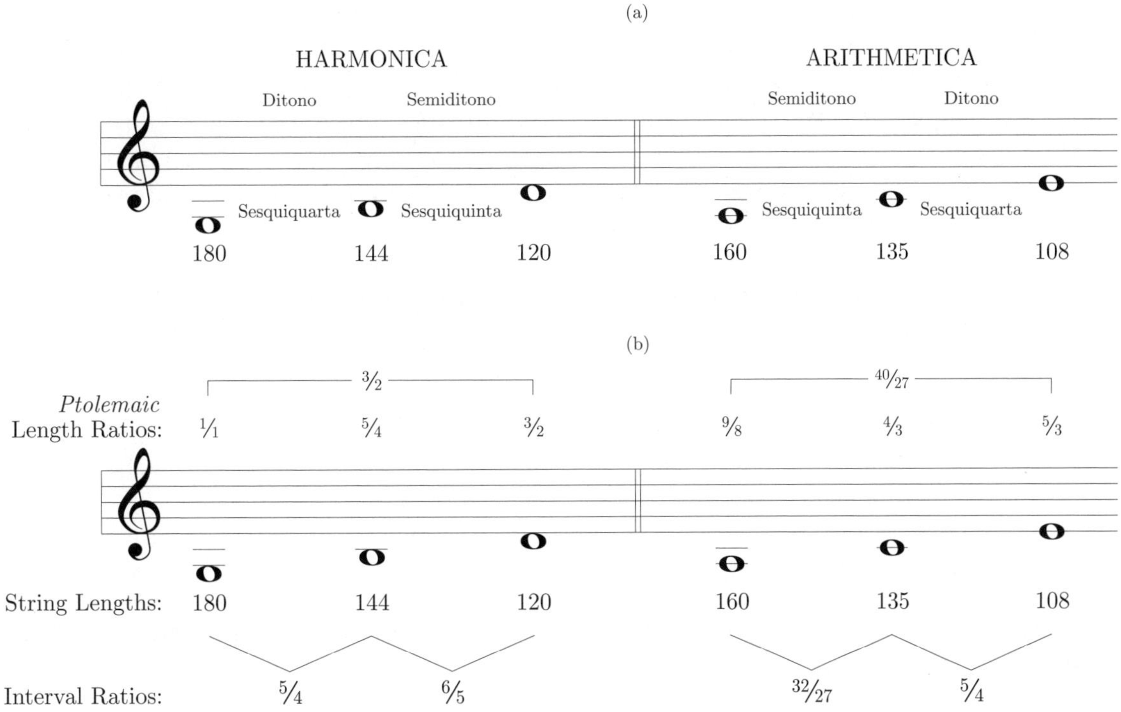

Figure 10.45 Zarlino's harmonic and arithmetic divisions of the "fifth." (a) Except for the modern G-clef, this is an exact copy of Zarlino's illustration as it appears in the *De tutte l'opere...* edition of the *Istitutioni harmoniche.* (b) A ratio analysis shows that Zarlino performed an *exact* harmonic division of the "pure fifth," ratio $3/2$, and an *approximate* arithmetic division of a "flat fifth," ratio $40/27$. The former yields interval ratios $5/4$ and $6/5$, and the latter, interval ratios $32/27$ and $5/4$.

Unfortunately, the arithmetic division of the "fifth" is not so simple. In Figure 10.45(b), observe that the length ratios above the staff represent the first six tones of Ptolemy's Tense Diatonic in the ancient Lydian Mode: $1/1$, $9/8$, $5/4$, $4/3$, $3/2$, $5/3$; hence, string lengths $180 \div 9/8 = 160$, $180 \div 5/4 = 144$, etc. Given this sequence of tones, the interval between the "whole tone," ratio $9/8$, and the "major sixth," ratio $5/3$, is a "flat fifth": $5/3 \div 9/8 = 40/27$ [680.4 ¢], or a "fifth" tuned 1 syntonic comma flat: $3/2 \div 81/80 = 40/27$. A substitution of the outer two terms — 160 units and 108 units — into Equation 3.37A gives the following *arithmetic mean:*

$$\mathit{\Lambda}_{\text{A}} = \frac{160 + 108}{2} = 134$$

Now, if Zarlino had given this exact result in Figure 10.45(a), it would have produced two very complex interval ratios with prime number 67; that is, a lower "flat minor third," ratio $160/134 = 80/67$ [307.0 ¢], and an upper "flat major third," ratio $134/108 = 67/54$ [373.4 ¢]. He avoids this difficulty by increasing 134 units to 135 units, but also incurs a small mathematical error. The lower interval is now a Pythagorean "minor third," ratio $160/135 = 32/27$ [294.1 ¢] — or a 5-limit "minor third" tuned 1 syntonic comma flat: $6/5 \div 81/80 = 32/27$ — and the upper interval, the desired 5-limit "major third," ratio $135/108 = 5/4$, or a true *sesquiquarta.* However, in the final analysis, the "flat fifth" and the Pythagorean "minor third" approximations do not contradict Zarlino's original intent, namely, to demonstrate the major and minor tonalities in the context of a single musical scale.

To clarify the musical distinction between the harmonic division of the "fifth" and major tonality on the one hand, and the arithmetic division of the "fifth" and minor tonality on the other, Zarlino describes Figure 10.45(a) by stating

VIII

> . . . the variety of the harmony . . . consists not only in the variety of the consonances which occur between the parts, but *also* in the variety of the harmonies, which arises from the position of the sound forming the third or tenth above the lowest part of the composition. Either this is minor and the resulting harmony is ordered by or resembles the arithmetical proportion or [arithmetic] mean, or it is major and the harmony is ordered by or resembles the harmonic [proportion].
>
> ***On this variety depend the whole diversity and perfection of the harmonies.*** For . . . in the perfect composition the fifth and third, or their extensions [or "octave" equivalents; i.e., the "twelfth" and "tenth," respectively], must always be actively present, seeing that apart from these two consonances the ear can desire no sound that falls between their extremes or beyond them and yet is wholly distinct and different from those that lie within the extremes of these two consonances combined. For in this combination occur all the different sounds that can form different harmonies.[219] (Italics, bold italics, and text in brackets mine.)

He then continues by attributing a "joyful" sensibility to the major tonality, and a "mournful" sensibility to the minor tonality.

IX

> But since the extremes of the fifth are invariable and always placed subject to the same proportion, apart from certain cases in which the fifth is used imperfectly, the extremes of the thirds are given different positions. I do not say different in proportion; ***I say different in position***, for . . . when

> the major third is placed below, the harmony is made joyful, and when it is placed above, the harmony is made mournful. Thus, from the different positions of the thirds which are placed in counterpoint between the extremes of the fifth or above the octave, the variety of harmony arises.[220] (Bold italics mine.)

We conclude that the *Senario* not only enabled Zarlino to define a theory of consonance, but also provided him with two mathematical means to describe the polar emotions of human existence.

Stifel, who also recognized the musical importance of both means, was not swayed by the rhetorical arguments of his day. He wrote in the *Arithmetica integra*,

> But I do not see what the Harmonic [progression] may explain about musical concords that the Arithmetic [progression] does not explain in equal proportion [i.e., just as well].[221] (Text in brackets mine.)

Zarlino's contributions to Western music are truly monumental. By integrating the mathematical principles of Ptolemy's scale, Ramis' monochord, Stifel's arithmetic and harmonic divisions of length ratio $\frac{6}{1}$, and his theory of consonance as defined by the *Senario*, Zarlino gave Western music its modern roots. Although Zarlino favored $\frac{1}{4}$-comma meantone temperament for the tuning of keyboard instruments,[222] his theory of consonance was exclusively based on rational or just intoned ratios. Irrational or tempered ratios do not play any part in the formulation of his musical ideas. Four hundred years later, Western music theory still agrees with the basic premise of the *Senario*, and teaches that only these ratios constitute desirable consonances.

10.47

Francisco Salinas (1513–1590), a contemporary of Zarlino, agreed with the basic premise of the *Senario*. In 1577, Salinas published a treatise entitled *De musica libri VII*, in which he illustrated the arithmetic and the harmonic divisions of length ratio $\frac{6}{1}$ in full detail.[223] Before we discuss these illustrations, consider the following observations by H.G. Farmer, who, in his introduction to the Arabic-Latin writings of Al-Fārābī, reminds us that Ramis and Salinas were born and educated in Spain:

> His [Al-Fārābī's] treatment of speculative theory was not only an advance on that contributed by the Greeks, but in Western Europe he had no peer as an independent thinker until Ramos de Pareja (*c.* 1440–1521) made his appearance, and he, like another great theorist — Salinas (*c.* 1512–1590), came from Spain, a land that had been greatly influenced by the Arabian sciences.[224] (Text in brackets mine.)

Turn now to Figures 10.46 and 10.47, which show edited copies of two engravings in Salinas' *De musica*, Liber II, Cap. XII. In the original engravings, Salinas assigns traditional Latin names to the musical intervals of the *Senario*. To discuss the mathematical significance of the illustrations, Figures 10.46 and 10.47 express these interval names as ratios. The type of triangular table seen in Figure 10.46 occurs five times in Salinas' book.[225] Although Salinas was the first European music theorist to use this kind of illustration, it originally appears in an Arabian treatise entitled *Sharḥ Maulānā Mubārak Shāh* (The Mubārak Shāh commentary),[226] by Al-Jurjānī (d. 1413). Al-Jurjānī's treatise consists of a lengthy commentary on a work entitled *Kitāb al-adwār* (Book of the modes [of music]), by Ṣafī Al-Dīn (d. 1294). (See Section 11.73.) In Al-Jurjānī's text, the row below the base line of the large triangle gives eighteen note names of Ṣafī Al-Dīn's 17-tone scale (i.e., "octave" included), and the first row of triangular-shaped tiles, the 17 interval ratios of the scale. Al-Jurjānī referred to his figure as the "blessed table." Al-Manūbī al-Sanūsī, the translator and editor of Al-Jurjānī's treatise,[227] describes this figure in the following manner:

> This table was undoubtedly called blessed (*mubārak*) to denote its somewhat miraculous character. In fact, it allows the reader to realize, at a simple glance, the exact ratio between any two degrees of the scale, without having to execute long and tiresome calculations.
>
> Take a large triangle. The base of this triangle is divided into seventeen sections corresponding to the seventeen intervals of the octave scale of Ṣafī Al-Dīn. The seventeen sections are determined by eighteen points, each one given an alphabetical sign corresponding to the eighteen degrees of this scale [i.e., "octave" included]. From each one of these points emanate two lines, each one parallel to one of the two lateral sides of the large triangle. Because of this, [the triangle] amounts to an assembly of spaces, [each] having the form of a diamond, or that of a square resting on one of its angles — except for the spaces of the first row, which are triangular.
>
> The [interval] ratio of any two degrees of the scale is written in the space whose upper angle is determined by the point of intersection of the two lines which emanate from the letters representing the two degrees in question . . .
>
> The [interval] ratio written in a [diamond] space is the sum [product] of the ratios written in [the bottom row of triangular] spaces . . . ; using this blessed table, it becomes easy to find the sum [product] of any series of ratios.
>
> [Although] the copyist of the manuscript of the British Museum (Or. 2361; fol. 78, v.) omitted the inscriptions that were to fill the spaces of the table, it was not difficult for us to reconstruct them using the formula applied by the author [Al-Jurjānī] for the division of his canon string.
>
> Instead of expressing these [length] ratios in the manner of the Arab theorists, i.e., according to the formula $1 + {}^{x}\!/_{n}$, we preferred to express them as ordinary fractions. We gave these ratios their exact expression; but it could be that the author simplified some of them by giving them an approximate value, expressed by numbers whose ratio is easy to comprehend.[228] (Text in brackets mine. Text in parentheses in *La Musique Arabe.*)

Figure 10.46 illustrates the arithmetic division of length ratio $^6\!/_1$. The row of integers — 6, 5, 4, 3, 2, 1 — forms the mathematical substructure of the principal triangle, and above it, the first row of ratios — $^6\!/_5$, $^5\!/_4$, $^4\!/_3$, $^3\!/_2$, $^2\!/_1$ — forms the musical substructure of this triangle. From here, all the upper ratios belong to smaller triangular structures. Notice that each upper ratio sits in a diamond-shaped tile that forms a triangle with at least two triangular-shaped tiles in the base. To compute the value of an upper ratio, multiply the ratios that constitute its base. For example, the diamond-shaped tile of ratio $^5\!/_3$ forms a triangle with $^5\!/_4$ and $^4\!/_3$ in the base; therefore, $^5\!/_4 \times {}^4\!/_3 = {}^5\!/_3$. Similarly, the tile of ratio $^5\!/_2$ forms a triangle with $^5\!/_4$, $^4\!/_3$, and $^3\!/_2$ in the base; therefore, $^5\!/_4 \times {}^4\!/_3 \times {}^3\!/_2 = {}^5\!/_2$. Of course, we may also view this figure from the opposite perspective; namely, the ratios in the base reveal the constituent parts of the upper ratios.

Now, if we increase the base of the principal triangle one increment to the right — or from 1 to 0 — the resulting sequence 6, 5, 4, 3, 2, 1, 0 depicts the division of a canon string into six aliquot parts as shown in Figure 10.39. Under these conditions, the ratios in the diamond-shaped tiles represent the musical intervals produced by canon string sections. Consequently, Figure 10.39 shows that canon strings stopped at 5 parts and 2 parts sound the musical interval of "one octave and a

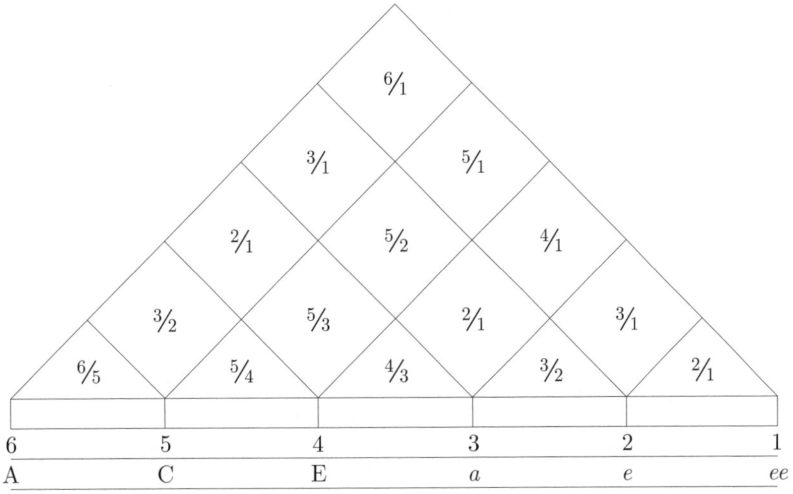
6/1
3/1
5/1
2/1
5/2
4/1
3/2
5/3
2/1
3/1
6/5
5/4
4/3
3/2
2/1
6 5 4 3 2 1
A C E *a* *e* *ee*

Figure 10.46 An edited copy of an engraving in Salinas' *De musica libri VII* (1577). This highly organized table illustrates the arithmetic division of length ratio 6/1 as originally described by Michael Stifel, and later incorporated into the *Senario* by Gioseffo Zarlino. The first appearance of such a triangular musical table occurs in an Arabian treatise on music entitled *Sharḥ Maulānā Mubārak Shāh*, by Al-Jurjānī (d. 1413).

major third," or a "tenth." In Figure 10.39, interval ratio 5/2 occurs between $A\flat_3$–C_5, and in Figure 10.46, between C–*e*.

Figure 10.47 demonstrates the harmonic division of length ratio 6/1. Readers familiar with Figures 10.40 and 10.42 should have no difficulties interpreting the mathematical and musical meaning of this illustration. Finally, Salinas shared Zarlino's enthusiasm for 5-limit ratios, and dismissed all higher prime number ratios, including ratios 7/1 and 7/6, as undesirable dissonances.

> And neither beyond 6:1 in the ratio 7:1 is a consonance to be found, just as not in 7:6 beyond 6:5.[229]

2/1
3/2
4/3
5/4
6/5
60 30 20 15 12 10
A *a* *e* *aa* *cc♯* *ee*

Figure 10.47 An edited copy of an engraving in Salinas' *De musica libri VII*, which shows the harmonic division of length ratio 6/1 on a canon string.

∼ 10.48 ∼

After the publication of Zarlino's works, most musicians and theorists in the 16th and 17th centuries accepted two fundamental ideas: (1) that the *Senario* contains all musical consonances, and (2) that Ptolemy's Tense Diatonic is the definitive example of a diatonic scale. However, clear definitions of what constitutes a major tonality and a minor tonality were not formulated until the 18th century. Meanwhile, during the 17th century, mathematicians and musicians developed a keen interest in the science of sound. Most notable among the writers on musical sound was Marin Mersenne (1588–1648). Before we discuss his observations in full detail, let us first examine what I call Mersenne's harmonic-diatonic system. In 1636, Mersenne published a grand opus entitled *Harmonie universelle.*[230] The largest treatise contained in this work is called *The Books on Instruments.*[231]

Throughout this and many other texts, Mersenne referred to various tones and harmonics by number. To understand Mersenne's numbering system, turn back to Figure 10.15, and recall the length ratios of Ptolemy's Tense Diatonic in the ancient Lydian Mode; and to Figure 10.28 and Table 10.15, which show this diatonic mode in the context of a 12-tone tuning on Mersenne's lute. Now, examine Figure 10.48 to confirm that the length ratios of this diatonic scale define tones 1–8 of Mersenne's first "octave." Finally, observe that the ratios of all upper "octaves" are "octave-multiples" — or "octave" equivalents — of the ratios in the first "octave." The tones of the upper "octaves" are numbered 8–15, 15–22, . . . To calculate an "octave-multiple," divide the denominator of a given ratio by 2; if this is not possible without producing a remainder, multiply the numerator by 2. Repeat either operation for every consecutive "octave-multiple." Note, therefore, that the single, double, and triple "octave-multiples" of 5/4 are 5/2, 5/1, and 10/1, respectively; and that the single, double, and triple "octave-multiples" of 5/3 are 10/3, 20/3, and 40/3, respectively. Of course, throughout his texts, Mersenne also discussed the "minor semitone" 25/24, the "major semitone" 16/15, the "minor tone" 10/9, the "minor third" 6/5, the "minor sixth" 8/5, the "minimum seventh" 16/9, the "minor seventh" 9/5, the "minor tenth" 12/5, etc.[232] Figure 10.48 does not include these tones because they would needlessly clutter the illustration.

In Figure 10.48, Mersenne's harmonic-diatonic system consists of a mixture of round black notes and square white notes. The latter notes represent six correct harmonics discovered by Mersenne. In contrast, one bracketed square white note indicates an incorrect "harmonic." Finally, for comparison, a sequence of round white notes represents the harmonic series as produced by flexible strings and columns of air open at both ends. For more information on these two vibrating systems, see Chapters 3 and 7, respectively.

10.49

Mersenne was the first European to accurately describe and mathematically define the first six harmonics — 1/1, 2/1, 3/1, 4/1, 5/1, 6/1 — of vibrating strings. These discoveries forever changed the sound of Western music theory. Suddenly, scientists and musicians realized that the rational ratios of just intonation not only constitute a convention of man, but also reflect a phenomenon of nature!

In *Harmonie universelle: The Books on Instruments*, Mersenne dedicated Book 4, Prop. IX, to his discoveries of string harmonics. In this text, he used three different terms to describe harmonics. *Petits sons delicats* appears in a general context, and literally means *small, delicate sounds. Sons differens du naturel* appears in a numerical context, and means *sounds different from the natural.* Here *naturel* connotes *son naturel*, or *natural sound*, a term that Mersenne consistently used to describe the lowest and most audible tone of a string, or the fundamental, ratio 1/1. Finally, *sons extraordinaires* also appears in a numerical context, and means *extraordinary sounds.* To simplify the following discussion, I will continue to use the simple word *harmonic* to describe these special sounds discovered by Mersenne. Even though Mersenne accurately identified the first six harmonics of vibrating strings, he had no knowledge of the superposition of traveling waves and the resulting production of standing waves; therefore, he did *not* have an exact mathematical understanding of the harmonic series as a theoretically infinite sequence of integers. Consequently, the following infinite series of ancient length ratios or modern frequency ratios: 1/1, 2/1, 3/1, 4/1, 5/1, 6/1, 7/1, . . . eluded him. Throughout his life, Mersenne agonized in his letters to René Descartes (1596–1650),

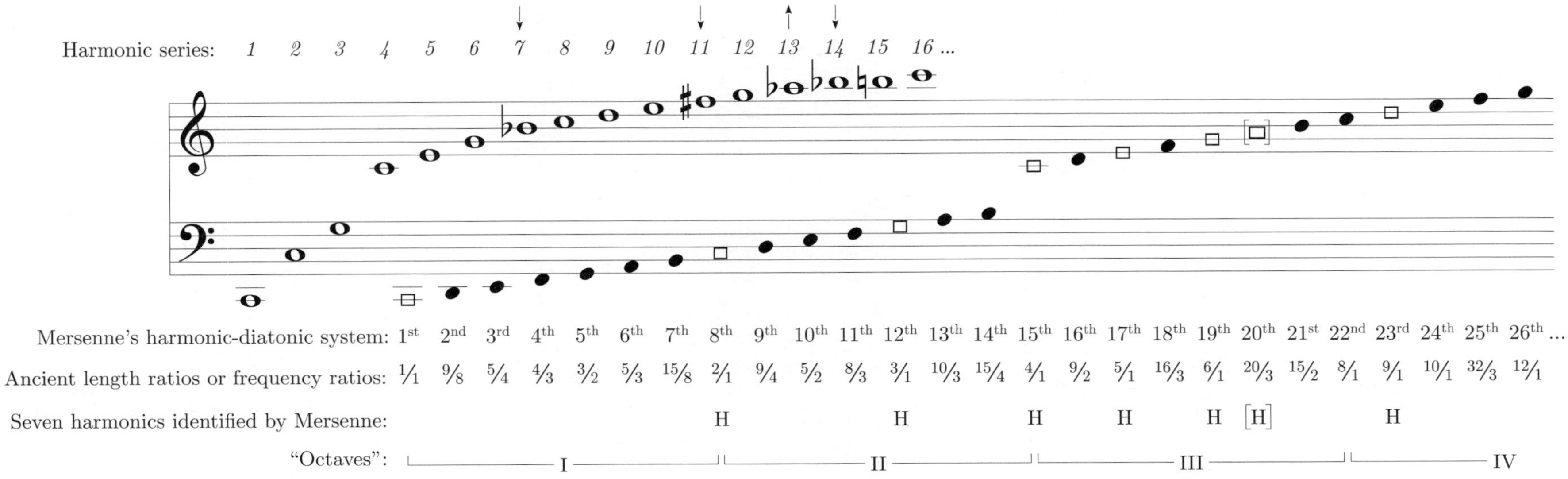

Figure 10.48 A comparison of the harmonic series (round white notes) and Mersenne's harmonic-diatonic system (square white notes and round black notes). Mersenne accurately recorded the first six harmonics of vibrating strings. In his system these are the 1st, 8th, 12th, 15th, 17th, and 19th tones. He also *correctly* identified the 23rd tone as a harmonic, but *incorrectly* identified the 20th tone as a harmonic. Mersenne never acknowledged the presence of the seventh harmonic, ratio $^7/_1$, the eleventh harmonic, ratio $^{11}/_1$, or the thirteenth harmonic, ratio $^{13}/_1$. Throughout his writings, Mersenne suggested improvements in the construction and tuning of musical instruments. For example, he proposed a new design for the trumpet marine that would enhance the resonance and playability of the instrument; and he also proposed a new monochord tuning for this instrument that emphasized the possibility of playing consonant tones *between* harmonics. Trumpet players understood this idea very well since all natural trumpets only produce the tones of the harmonic series. The desire to hear consonances between harmonics inspired later generations of brass instrument builders to make trumpets with valves.

Christophe de Villiers (*c.* 1595 – *c.* 1650), Isaac Beeckman (1588–1637), and other prominent mathematicians and scientists, over a unifying principle that would explain the presence of harmonics in the sounds of strings, organ pipes, and trumpets.[233] Nevertheless, this problem was not solved until one hundred years after Mersenne's death. (See Section 10.56.) Despite these mysteries, difficulties, and frustrations, Mersenne persevered and discovered important truths about the nature of sound because he had phenomenal powers of hearing and observation, and a tenacious curiosity. In his own words, "Some new properties of strings will always be found if one takes the trouble of examining them in all the ways possible."[234]

In the *Harmonie universelle: The Books on Instruments*, Book 4, Prop. IX, Mersenne assures the reader that the harmonics he hears are not due to the sympathetic vibrations of other strings. He then assigns ratios to these harmonics, and ends by comparing four string harmonics — $2/1$, $3/1$, $4/1$, $5/1$ — to the "leaps," that is, to the harmonics of the natural trumpet:[235]

I

> Thus it is very certain that these different tones do not come from other strings which are on the instruments and which tremble without being played . . . since the ***single*** string of the monochords produce the same sounds.
>
> Now these sounds follow the ratio of these numbers, 1, 2, 3, 4, 5, since one hears four *sons differens du naturel*, the first of which is at the upper octave [2:1], the second at the twelfth [3:1], the third at the fifteenth [4:1], and the fourth at the major seventeenth [5:1], as is seen by the said numbers which contain the ratios of these consonances in their lesser terms. At this point, two things must be remarked, that is, [**1**] that no sound is ever heard lower . . . than the *son naturel* of the string [1:1], since they are all higher, and [**2**] these tones follow the same progression as the leaps [i.e., harmonics] of the trumpet . . .[236] (Bold italics, ratios, and numbers in brackets mine. Italics in Mersenne's original text.)

Now, before we continue with Mersenne's description of the "twentieth," we must first look ahead to Book 4, Prop. XIII, and examine his observations of harmonics on a stringed instrument called the *trumpet marine*. (See Sections 10.50–10.51, and Figure 10.50.) Here, Mersenne identifies the 19th tone of his system, ratio $6/1$, as the fifth harmonic, and ends with a comment on the 20th tone:

II

> Nevertheless I add that these leaps and these points [on the string of a trumpet marine], which imitate the sounds of the military trumpet, do nothing else but explain in great volume what the string does being played open, that is, [the string sounds] the octave [2:1], the twelfth [3:1], the fifteenth [4:1], the seventeenth [5:1], the nineteenth [6:1], etc., one after the other . . . which it produces all together at the same time . . .
>
> Now it is a constant fact that they make many different tones, or a single tone composed of many in the same time, and that one hears only those which are in tune together, that is, the repetitions of the octave, the fifths, and the repeated thirds, and sometimes some others, for example the twentieth.[237] (Text and ratios in brackets mine.)

This gives a total number of five harmonics: $2/1$, $3/1$, $4/1$, $5/1$, $6/1$. Now let us return to Book 4, Prop. IX, and read Mersenne's analysis of the "major twentieth." Keep in mind that at the end of Quote I, Mersenne had only identified four harmonics:

> Beyond these four *sons extraordinaires*, I hear still a fifth one higher . . . It produces the major twentieth with the *son naturel*, with which it is ***as three to twenty.***[238] (Bold italics mine. Italics in Mersenne's original text.)

This identification is incorrect. If we assume that he was aware of the sixth harmonic, ratio $6/1$, as described in Quote II, then the next *son extraordinaire* is a prime number harmonic, namely, ratio $7/1$. Although one could argue that Mersenne mistook $7/1$ for $20/3$, this is highly unlikely. Mersenne's hearing was much too accurate to make such an obvious error. Besides, ratio $20/3$ does not have unity in the denominator.

The last harmonic accurately identified by Mersenne is the ninth harmonic. In 1635–36, Mersenne published a work entitled *Harmonicorum libri XII*, in which he makes this assertion:

> Besides the Diapason [2:1] and Disdiapason [4:1], which octave is the one more clearly and distinctly perceived, I always hear the twelfth [3:1] and the major seventeenth [5:1] beyond, and then I easily perceive toward the end of the natural sound the major twenty-third [9:1], which is ***as 1 to 3.***[239] (Bold italics and ratios in brackets mine.)

This last quantification is extremely important because it reveals a tendency in *The Books on Instruments*. Mersenne knew perfectly well that length ratio $3/1$ only produces the 12th tone. So, the question arises, "Why did he assign the latter ratio to the 23rd tone?"

The answer to this question is highly complicated. First, Mersenne accepted the basic premise of Zarlino's *Senario*, which proposed that all musical consonances are contained in the number six. For example, consider the passage in which Mersenne describes his stringing idea for a hurdy-gurdy:

> . . . but if one puts on six bourdons [six drone strings] which make the octave [2:1], the twelfth [3:1], the fifteenth [4:1], the seventeenth [5:1], and the nineteenth [6:1], following the numbers 1, 2, 3, 4, 5, and 6, one will have a perfect harmony . . .[240] (Text and ratios in brackets mine.)

Incidentally, Mersenne also was aware that the *Senario* does not include the "minor sixth," ratio $8/5$, and essentially accepted Zarlino's rationalization. (See Section 10.45.) He wrote

> But 8 makes the minor sixth with 5 [8:5] and the eleventh with 3 [8:3]. Thus the number 8 produces two new consonances which are not met with in the six numbers.[241]

Second, Mersenne realized the significance of Ptolemy's Tense Diatonic, and in *The Books on Instruments* enumerates this scale on three separate occasions. The first two times, he gives the scale in string length units or length ratios,[242] and the third time, as a standard by which to evaluate the frequency ratios of the natural trumpet.[243] Third, as a priest in the Catholic Church, Mersenne harbored deeply felt religious and moral convictions. Throughout his life, Mersenne observed nature as a scientist, and as a priest.

> If the tone of each string is more harmonious and agreeable as it makes a greater number of different tones heard in the same time, and if one may be permitted to compare moral actions to natural, and to translate Physics into human actions, one can say that each action is as much more agreeable and harmonious to God, as it is accompanied by a greater number of motives, provided that they all be good.[244]

In short, Mersenne did not distinguish between observational aspects of science and ethical aspects of religion.

Taken together, these three core issues explain Mersenne's outer and inner focus. Consequently, Mersenne believed and insisted that all harmonics are consonances, or "octave-multiples" of four ratios — $\frac{1}{1}$, $\frac{5}{4}$, $\frac{3}{2}$, $\frac{5}{3}$ — contained in Zarlino's Senario and in Ptolemy's diatonic scale. In his harmonic-diatonic system, ratio $\frac{1}{1}$ generates $\frac{2}{1}$, $\frac{4}{1}$; ratio $\frac{5}{4}$ generates [$\frac{5}{2}$], $\frac{5}{1}$; ratio $\frac{3}{2}$ generates $\frac{3}{1}$, $\frac{6}{1}$; and ratio $\frac{5}{3}$ generates [$\frac{10}{3}$], $\frac{20}{3}$. This conviction compelled him to define the 23rd tone, or the ninth harmonic, as ratio $\frac{3}{1}$; that is, he rationalized the dissonant ninth harmonic as a consonant "twelfth," ratio $\frac{3}{1}$, above the 12th tone, also ratio $\frac{3}{1}$. Although Mersenne accurately perceived the 23rd tone as a harmonic, he avoided describing the ninth harmonic as ratio $\frac{3}{1}$ raised to the second power — $(\frac{3}{1})^2 = \frac{3}{1} \times \frac{3}{1} = \frac{9}{1}$ — because such a definition would have contradicted the notion that all upper harmonics are "octave-multiples" of lower consonances. In contrast, Mersenne incorrectly perceived the 20th tone as a harmonic, but consistent with his convictions, he defined it as ratio $\frac{20}{3}$, or a double "octave-multiple" of the consonant "major sixth," ratio $\frac{5}{3}$. Finally, Mersenne never acknowledged the presence of the seventh harmonic, ratio $\frac{7}{1}$, the eleventh harmonic, ratio $\frac{11}{1}$, and the thirteenth harmonic, ratio $\frac{13}{1}$. Furthermore, since all trumpets produce the frequency ratios of the harmonic series, he was also compelled by a need for consistency to eliminate the latter three ratios and ratio $\frac{14}{1}$ from a table that shows the first 16 harmonics of the natural trumpet.[245]

~ 10.50 ~

These blatant omissions in *The Books on Instruments* do not mean that Mersenne avoided controversies surrounding high prime number ratios. Before we discuss Mersenne's perplexing descriptions of 7-limit ratios, let us first examine the acoustic properties of the trumpet marine, a stringed instrument prominently featured in *The Books on Instruments.* The trumpet marine is a triangular-shaped musical instrument that stands 6–7 ft in height, and is usually equipped with one long string. In playing this instrument, the performer does *not* stop the string by pressing it against a fingerboard. Instead, the performer lightly touches it, and so causes the string to sound *flageolet tones*, also called *natural harmonics.*[246] This playing technique is made possible by the natural occurrence of standing waves in strings. As discussed in Section 3.3, in vibrating strings, the superposition of transverse traveling waves produces transverse standing waves. In a standing wave, we may describe points of minimum and maximum motion as an alternating pattern of nodes and antinodes. By lightly touching a string at the location of a node, a player is able to force the string to vibrate in a standing wave pattern, which in turn produces a frequency associated with that particular mode shape. Since there are many nodes along a vibrating string, the player must know the exact location of a given node to produce a desired tone. The performer sets the string into motion with a short bow *above* where the finger touches the string, or near the upper end of the instrument.[247] Also, the trumpet marine has an asymmetric bridge designed to vibrate against the soundboard. Upon simultaneously touching and bowing the string, Mersenne observed

> Now if there can be found the reason in the trembling bridge, one should be able to say that the points of the string imitate the tone of the trumpet when the number of beatings of the said bridge are in tune with the number of vibrations of the string.[248]

Hence its name trumpet marine, although no one knows why also "marine."

In Mersenne's time, nodes, antinodes, standing waves, and mode shapes were unknown entities. However, because an aliquot division of a string into an integral number of equal parts gives the locations of nodes, 17th-century performers were able to coax flageolet tones from the string of a trumpet marine without having any knowledge of mode shapes. Nevertheless, it is important to realize that an awareness of flageolet tones does *not* lead to an understanding of the harmonic series.

For example, in Figure 10.49 arrows indicate the locations of nodes that, when lightly touched, produce the frequency of a particular harmonic, also called a mode frequency. By lightly touching a string at ½ its length, one forces the string to vibrate in the shape of the second mode, which in turn causes it to sound the second harmonic, or F_2. By touching it at ⅓ its length from either end, a string sounds the third harmonic, or F_3. Similarly, to sound F_4 one must touch a string at ¼ its length from either end, because if one touches it at 2⁄4 its length, F_2 will sound. All this makes perfect sense. Now image you are living in the 17th century, and you notice the following pattern. First, you lightly touch a string at ⅕ its length and hear F_5, or an interval of "two octaves and a major third" above the fundamental, ratio 5⁄1. Next, you lightly touch the same string at ⅖ its length and hear F_5 again. Suddenly the logical relation between shorter string lengths and higher mode frequencies disappears. Why is the pitch not changing? Since you are producing flageolet tones, touching a string at ⅕ and ⅖ its length causes it to assume the standing wave pattern of the fifth mode of vibration. In the context of flageolet tones, a knowledge of string lengths has no bearing on tuning: modern length ratio ⅖ does *not* produce frequency ratio 5⁄2. To explain the acoustic properties of flageolet tones, one must have knowledge of standing wave patterns, or mode shapes. Under these circumstances, the production of mode frequencies depends on the shape of the vibrating string, and not on its stopped — or lightly touched — length. Finally, observe that when one divides a string length into a *prime number* of equal parts, all lightly touched locations produce the *same* harmonic.

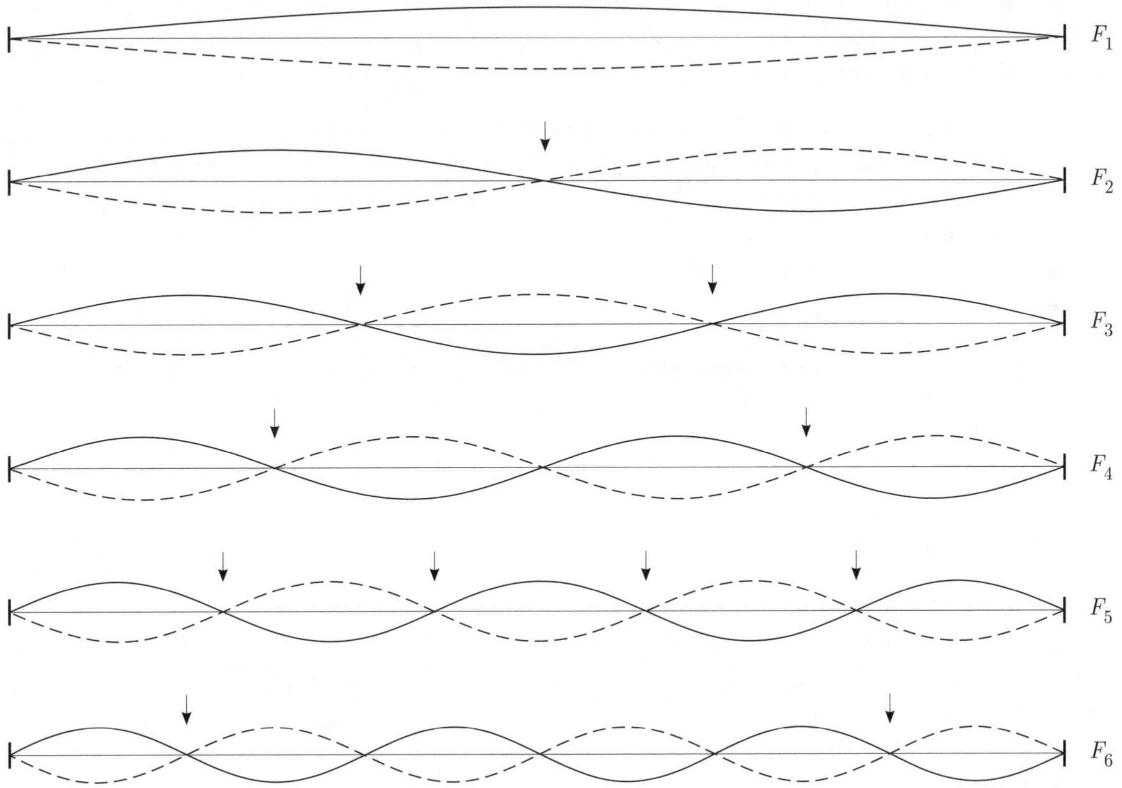

Figure 10.49 Standing wave patterns, or mode shapes, of a vibrating string. By lightly touching a string at the location of a node, the string vibrates in a standing wave pattern, which in turn produces a *flageolet tone* or *natural harmonic* associated with that particular mode shape. Arrows show the locations where one must touch a string to produce the indicated standing wave patterns and mode frequencies.

~ 10.51 ~

In Book 4, Prop. XII, Mersenne included an illustration that shows two trumpet marines. Figure 10.50 is a reproduction of this engraving.

> Now I give here two different figures, of which that on the right hand ACED represents its ***older*** shape, and that on the left [PS] shows the ***new*** form that has been found more comfortable and better for resounding.[249] (Bold italics mine. Letters in brackets in Mersenne's original text.)

In Quote II, Mersenne commented on the similarity between the tones of the trumpet marine and the military trumpet. However, in the engraving, the markings along the strings of these two instruments do not indicate that Mersenne used this instrument to produce flageolet tones. On the contrary, he observed

> And when the string is so pressed with the fingers of the left hand that it touches the table, it sounds equally well in all the places as if it were held on a viol.[250]

The trumpet marine's association with the tones of the natural trumpet undoubtedly attracted Mersenne's attention because he was extremely interested in harmonics, and in promoting his harmonic-diatonic system. Furthermore, the trumpet marine is also a very simple and inexpensive instrument, and so does not present any major barriers to readers who are interested in listening to new tunings. But most important to Mersenne, the trumpet marine has a very long and flexible string that is ideal for exploring and visualizing new tunings. In short, Mersenne converted the trumpet marine into a monochord, and stated in his description of the "new" instrument,

> . . . I have marked all the letters of the gamut, or the harmonic scale . . . on one of the sides of this instrument, so that one can use it as a monochord. For the Γ [lit. *Gamma* or *G*] signifies the lowest tone, which descends a tone lower than the *Proslambanomene* of the Greeks, which corresponds to our A *re*, so that after having played the open string, it rises a tone [9:8] in shortening from Γ to A; and if it is shortened to B, it rises a major third [5:4], which is made of the entire string PΓ against P♮, and the same with the others up to the twentieth row of letters, that is to say to the double *ee*, which make the major twentieth [20:3], or the major hexachord [5:3] on the disdiapason [4:1] against the open string. [That is, $^{20}\!/_3 \div {}^4\!/_1 = {}^5\!/_3$.][251] (Text and ratios in brackets mine.)

Although Mersenne did not offer any information on the "old" trumpet marine tuning, I noticed that eleven marks along the right edge of this instrument indicate very precise monochord divisions. Careful measurements of this figure reveal that the divisions of Mersenne's "old" instrument engraving are more exact than the "new" instrument engraving. Since he offers a verbal description of the "new" instrument tuning, this lack of precision is of little consequence. In the facsimile edition of the *Harmonie universelle* cited in Note 230, the longest string of the "old" trumpet marine engraving measures 144.0 mm, and the sole string of the "new" trumpet marine engraving measures 156.0 mm. Fortunately, the string length of the "old" instrument is long enough and the marks are sufficiently accurate to reveal important tuning information about this instrument.

Turn now to Table 10.28, which consists of two sections. In the left section, Column 1 lists the first 14 harmonics or frequency ratios of the natural trumpet, Column 2, the modern note names of these tones, and Column 3, the corresponding frequencies in cycles per second. In the right section, Column 4 is labeled Mark, and lists the numbers Mersenne used to indicate eleven monochord

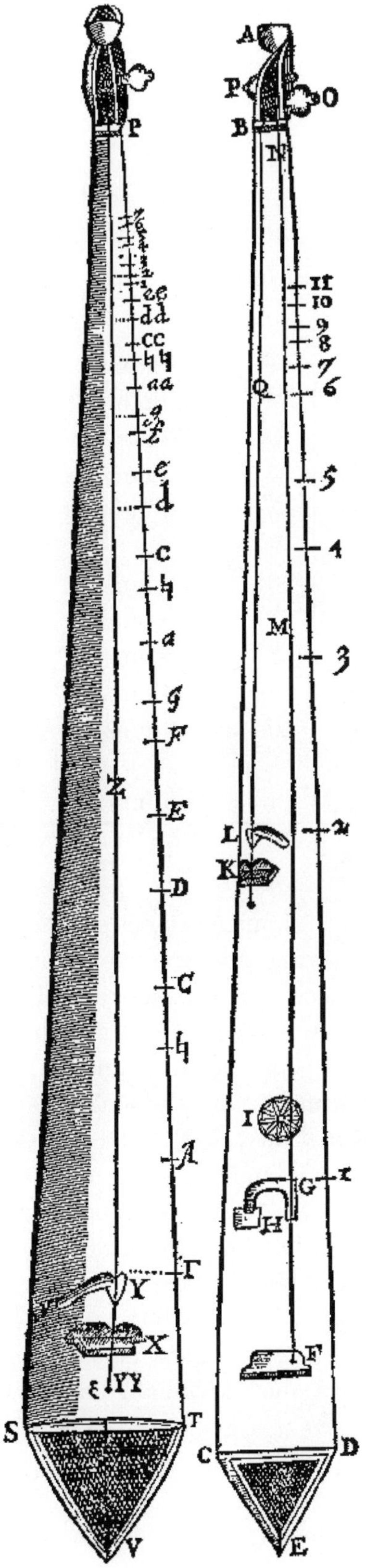

Figure 10.50 A reproduction of two trumpet marine engravings from Mersenne's *Harmonie universelle: The Books on Instruments.* Mersenne refers to ACED on the right as the "older shape," and to PS on the left as the "new form."

Table 10.28

COMPARISON OF THE FREQUENCY RATIOS OF THE NATURAL TRUMPET AND THE LENGTH RATIOS OF MERSENNE'S "OLD" TRUMPET MARINE

First 14 Harmonics of the Natural Trumpet			String Lengths & Length Ratios from an Engraving of Mersenne's "Old" Trumpet Marine				
Harmonics			Mark	*Λ*			
1/1	G_2 ≈	100.0 cps					
2/1	G_3	200.0 cps	1	144.0 mm	1/1	G_3 ≈	200.0 cps
3/1	D_4	300.0 cps	2	96.0 mm	3/2	D_4	300.0 cps
4/1	G_4	400.0 cps	3	72.0 mm	2/1	G_4	400.0 cps
5/1	B_4	500.0 cps	4	57.6 mm	5/2	B_4	500.0 cps
6/1	D_5	600.0 cps	5	48.0 mm	3/1	D_5	600.0 cps
7/1	F_5	700.0 cps			[7/2]		
8/1	G_5	800.0 cps	6	36.0 mm	4/1	G_5	800.0 cps
9/1	A_5	900.0 cps	7	32.0 mm	9/2	A_5	900.0 cps
10/1	B_5	1000.0 cps	8	28.8 mm	5/1	B_5	1000.0 cps
11/1	$C\sharp_6$	1100.0 cps	9	27.0 mm	16/3	C_6	1066.7 cps
12/1	D_6	1200.0 cps	10	24.0 mm	6/1	D_6	1200.0 cps
13/1	$E\flat_6$	1300.0 cps			[13/2]		
14/1	F_6	1400.0 cps	11	21.6 mm	20/3	E_6	1333.3 cps
(1)	(2)	(3)	(4)	(5)	(6)	(7)	(8)

divisions on the "old" trumpet marine. Column 5 is labeled *Λ*, and gives the measurements of the divisions of the longest string in the engraving, from the nut at the top of the instrument to the marks below. My original measurements are accurate to the nearest millimeter. However, Column 5 rounds these lengths to the nearest 1/10 millimeter to equate them with the length ratios in Column 6.

In modern times, the pitch $G_2 = 98.0$ cps. (See Appendix A.) To facilitate a comparison between the frequency ratios of the natural trumpet and the length ratios of the "old" trumpet marine, Column 3 gives the following approximations: $G_2 \approx 100.0$ cps, $G_3 \approx 200.0$ cps, etc. Note, however, that G_2 does not represent the actual fundamental pitch of a natural trumpet: it is much too low. Finally, observe that if the open string at Mark #1 sounds the same frequency as the trumpet's second harmonic, or $G_3 \approx 200.0$ cps, all but four length ratios of the "old" trumpet marine match the frequency ratios of the natural trumpet. On the string, length ratios 7/2 and 13/2 are missing, length ratio 16/3 has replaced frequency ratio 11/2, [200.0 cps × 11/2 = 1100.0 cps], and length ratio 20/3 has replaced frequency ratio 7/1 [200.0 cps × 7/1 = 1400.0 cps]. The omissions of prime numbers 7, 11, and 13 are characteristic of Mersenne's harmonic-diatonic system, and come as no surprise.

10.52

Mersenne describes the tuning of the "new" trumpet marine in full detail:

> Now the side PT is a very exact monochord, which begins with {Γ} *ut* [1:1], A *re* [9:8], and {♮} [B] *mi* [5:4], etc., up to the twentieth diction of the harmonic hand {ee} *la* [20:3]. At this point it must be noted that it contains the first mode, in that after having mounted a fifth from {Γ} *ut* [1:1] to D

> *sol re* [3:2], that is to say that after having formed the first species of the Diapente, it rises from D {*sol re*} [3:2] to G {*sol re ut*} [2:1] by the first species of the fourth, the {major} tone [9:8] is found from {Γ} to A [$9/8 \div 1/1 = 9/8$], and the {minor} tone [10:9] from A to {♮}, [$5/4 \div 9/8 = 10/9$]; the major from C to D, the minor from D to E, and the major from E to F[♯], and so the others in rising. As to the major semitones [16:15], they are from {♮} to C [$4/3 \div 5/4 = 16/15$], and from F[♯] to G, etc., for there is no mean semitone [135:128] in {♮} at all.[252] (Ratios, 'B', and sharp signs in brackets mine. Natural signs in braces my corrections of Chapman's mistranscriptions of Mersenne's original text. 'Γ', 'ee', *'sol re'*, *'sol re ut'*, 'major', and 'minor' in braces my corrections of Mersenne's original text.)

These interval ratios describe Ptolemy's Tense Diatonic in G, which occurs on the "new" trumpet marine between Γ–G, G–g, and g–#2. Hence, Mersenne's explanation that there is no "mean semitone," ratio $135/128$, in this scale.[253] The illustration below shows Ptolemy's scale in the first "octave."

Γ		A		♮		C		D		E		F[♯]		G
$1/1$		$9/8$		$5/4$		$4/3$		$3/2$		$5/3$		$15/8$		$2/1$
	$9/8$		$10/9$		$16/15$		$9/8$		$10/9$		$9/8$		$16/15$	

To verify this tuning, turn to Table 10.29. In the section on the left, Column 1 is labeled Mark, and lists the note names and numbers Mersenne used to indicate 27 monochord divisions on the "new" trumpet marine. Column 2 is labeled Λ, and gives the measurements of the divisions of the sole string in the engraving, from the nut at the top to the marks below; and Column 3, the corresponding length ratios. The section on the right is essentially the same as in Table 10.28.

Mersenne continues his description of the "new" trumpet marine by comparing it to the trumpet:

> The first point where this instrument begins to make the pitch of the trumpet after that of the open string is marked by the first dotted line opposite to *d*, that is to say it makes the twelfth [3:1] with the string played open, inasmuch as P *d* is *sous-triple* {lit. *sub-triple*, or $1/3$} that of PΓ.[254] (Italics in Mersenne's original text. Text in braces my correction of Chapman's mathematical translation error.)

Although Mersenne correctly identifies the inverse proportionality between modern length ratio $1/3$ and frequency ratio $3/1$, Table 10.29 shows that this statement is incorrect. The first point at which the "new" trumpet marine makes the pitch of a trumpet is at Mark G, or l.r. $1/2 \rightarrow$ f.r. $2/1$. Mersenne then describes five additional trumpet tones on the "new" trumpet marine at d, g, ♮♮, dd, and #2, which correspond to ancient length ratios or frequency ratios $3/1$, $4/1$, $5/1$, $6/1$, and $8/1$, respectively. Table 10.29 locates the first four of these divisions on the "old" trumpet marine at Marks #5, #6, #8, and #10. Finally, Mersenne describes the "major twentieth," ratio $20/3$, on the "new" trumpet marine as

> . . . marked by the five numbers following 2, that is, by 3, 4, 5, 6, and 7, which make all the degrees of the major hexachord . . .[255]

On the "new" trumpet marine, this hexachord exists in four different locations, or between Γ–E, G–e, g–ee, and #2–#7. Table 10.29 reveals that on the "old" trumpet marine, only one hexachord exits between Marks #6–#11.

Table 10.29

COMPARISONS OF LENGTH RATIOS FROM MERSENNE'S ENGRAVINGS OF "NEW" AND "OLD" TRUMPET MARINES

"New" Trumpet Marine			"Old" Trumpet Marine			
Mark	Λ		Mark	Λ		
Γ	156.0 mm	1/1	1	144.0 mm	1/1	G_3
A	138.7 mm	9/8				
♮	124.8 mm	5/4				
C	117.0 mm	4/3				
D	104.0 mm	3/2	2	96.0 mm	3/2	D_4
E	93.6 mm	5/3				
F♯	83.2 mm	15/8				
G	78.0 mm	2/1	3	72.0 mm	2/1	G_4
a	69.3 mm	9/4				
♮	62.4 mm	5/2	4	57.6 mm	5/2	B_4
c	58.5 mm	8/3				
d	52.0 mm	3/1	5	48.0 mm	3/1	D_5
e	46.8 mm	10/3				
f♯	41.6 mm	15/4				
g	39.0 mm	4/1	6	36.0 mm	4/1	G_5
aa	34.7 mm	9/2	7	32.0 mm	9/2	A_5
♮♮	31.2 mm	5/1	8	28.8 mm	5/1	B_5
cc	29.3 mm	16/3	9	27.0 mm	16/3	C_6
dd	26.0 mm	6/1	10	24.0 mm	6/1	D_6
ee	23.4 mm	20/3	11	21.6 mm	20/3	E_6
1	20.8 mm	15/2				
2	19.5 mm	8/1				
3	17.3 mm	9/1				
4	15.6 mm	10/1				
5	14.6 mm	32/3				
6	13.0 mm	12/1				
7	11.7 mm	40/3				
(1)	(2)	(3)	(4)	(5)	(6)	(7)

Mersenne undoubtedly tantalized his readers with the possibility of interjecting musical consonances between the tones of the natural trumpet. One encounters his inventiveness with respect to musical instrument designs throughout *The Books on Instruments.* In this case, however, Mersenne did not openly discuss the advantages of his "new" trumpet marine, nor its theoretical application to the natural trumpet. Instead, he simply demonstrated that the "new" tuning encompasses the "old." He thereby challenged the reader to contemplate the possibility of transforming the "old" without detriment into the "new." The idea of mixing tones that exist in nature with tones that exist in man's imagination is both ancient and profound. Every builder, whether violin or marimba maker, knows that the success of a musical instrument depends on how well the properties of nature blend with the intentions of man. No one understood this interweaving of musical sounds better than Mersenne. In the trumpet marine engraving, Mersenne envisioned the future because the desire to hear consonances between harmonics eventually inspired later generations of brass instrument builders to make trumpets with valves.

10.53

Mersenne's omissions of *sons extraordinaires* with prime numbers 7, 11, 13, . . . were intentional. For example, in *The Books on Instruments*, Book 5, Prop. XIII, his contrived heading reads, "To explain why the trumpet does ***not*** produce the sesquisextal [7/6] . . . interval . . ."[256] (Bold italics mine.) Mersenne wrote this proposition for the sole purpose of rationalizing the omissions of interval ratios 7/6 and 8/7 in his description of trumpet tones. These blatantly fallacious statements, which even a novice trumpet player would reject, are not worth repeating. However, Mersenne did examine the musical and mathematical complexities of prime number 7 in a work entitled *Book One on Consonances*. Before we examine his discussion in full detail, let us first review the observations of an important writer on this subject.

In an essay entitled *Scientific Empiricism in Musical Thought*, Claude V. Palisca devoted a large portion to the writings of Giovanni Battista Benedetti (1530–1590).[257] Benedetti was the first scientist to offer a theory of consonance based on the mechanical motions of strings. For Benedetti — as for Ptolemy before him — not all consonances are alike. He noted distinct differences in the musical quality of eight accepted consonances, and decided to classify them in the following order: 1/1, 2/1, 3/2, 4/3, 5/3, 5/4, 6/5, 8/5. The "unison" was the most perfect consonance; next came the "octave," then the "fifth," the "fourth," etc. To explain this sequence of graduated consonances, Benedetti observed that when two strings produce a simple consonance, the "equalization of percussion" (*aephalitione percussionum*), or the "equal concurrence of air waves" (*aequali concursu undarum aeris*) is notably high.[258] In other words, simple consonances occur when there is a high rate of coincidence (or a high rate of synchronicity) between the vibratory motions of two strings of different lengths. Therefore, according to Benedetti, the ". . . order of agreement of the terminations of the percussions of the air waves, by which the sound is generated . . ."[259] has a profound effect on our perceptions of consonance and dissonance. Benedetti came to these conclusions by observing the motions of bridged canon strings.

> But when the bridge so divides the string that a third [l.r. 1/3] of it remains on one side and two thirds [l.r. 2/3] on the other, then the larger part is twice the smaller and the two will sound the consonance of the octave [ratio 2/1, since $2/3 \div 1/3 = 2/1$]. The percussions of the boundary-tones of this octave will have between them such a proportion that in every second percussion of the minor portion of this string, the larger will percuss or concur with the minor at the same instant of time. For everyone knows that the longer the string, the more slowly it is moved. Therefore, since the longer part is twice the shorter, and they are both of the same tension, in the time that the longer completes one period of vibration, the shorter completes two.
>
> Now if the bridge so divides the string that two fifths [l.r. 2/5] remain on one side and three fifths [l.r. 3/5] on the other, the consonance of the fifth [ratio 3/2, since $3/5 \div 2/5 = 3/2$] will be generated . . . Therefore, they will not convene at one instant until three periods of the minor portion and two of the major have been completed.
>
> It follows that the ratio between the number of periods of the minor portion and that of the major will be the same as the ratio between

> the lengths of the two portions. Therefore the product of the number of the minor portion [2 parts] . . . and the number of periods [3 periods] of the same portion [$2 \times 3 = 6$] will be equal to the product of the number of the major portion [3 parts] and the number of periods [2 periods] of the same major portion [$3 \times 2 = 6$].
>
> These products will be therefore: for the diapason 2 [$2 \times 1 = 2$]; for the fifth, 6 [$3 \times 2 = 6$]; for the fourth, 12 [$4 \times 3 = 12$]; for the major sixth, 15 [$5 \times 3 = 15$]; for the ditone, 20 [$5 \times 4 = 20$]; for the semiditone, 30 [$6 \times 5 = 30$]; finally for the minor sixth, 40 [$8 \times 5 = 40$]. These numbers agree among themselves with a certain wonderful logic.[260] (Text, ratios, and numbers in brackets mine.)

We conclude that Benedetti offered two original ideas: (1) Degrees of consonance are determined by how often two strings vibrate in phase.[261] (2) One may evaluate the relative consonance of two given interval ratios by comparing the integer product of one ratio to the integer product of the other ratio: that is, the smaller the product, the greater the consonance, and *vice versa.*

10.54

In *Book One on Consonances*, Mersenne explains his method for evaluating the relative consonance of musical intervals. Early in the discussion, Mersenne reminds us that consonances exist in nature.

III

> Nevertheless, I wish to note all the consonances which are natural, in order to confirm that there are consonances in nature, as the trumpet teaches us.[262]

A few pages later, he points out that changes in pitch are produced by alterations in the magnitude of vibrations in the air.

> Consequently, it would be better to say, properly speaking, that one perceives a certain number of vibrations of air, than to say that one hears a low or a high sound, although one amounts to the other, and one is the cause and the other the effect.
>
> The same thing can be said of the vibrations which form the unison and the other consonances. For example, the octave is nothing other than two vibrations of air compared to one vibration of air. Thus, one can say that two flying birds, one of which strikes the air twice as quickly as the other, form the octave. For although we do not hear these vibrations, they form, nevertheless, sounds which can be heard by ears more acute than ours.[263]

Finally, Mersenne begins his account of relative consonance by describing variations in the *rate of coincidence* between strings of different lengths.

> As for . . . whether the unison is more pleasant and more agreeable than the octave, I say firstly that there is no doubt that it is more pleasant, since it unites its sounds more often and more readily. For since the unison is 1 to 1, all the vibrations of the air are united at each stroke, whereas the vibrations of the octave are united only every two strokes.[264]

Throughout *Book One on Consonances*, the reader encounters many comparisons designed to show why a given ratio is more or less consonant than another ratio. During these discussions, Mersenne consistently uses Benedetti's mechanical model to explain the relative consonance of musical intervals. That is, all consonances are evaluated according to how often two vibrating strings "are united" in their respective motions. For example,

> The minor third [6:5] should, nevertheless, be more pleasant, since its vibrations unite at each sixth stroke of the high sound, and those of the minor sixth [8:5] unite only at each eighth stroke . . .[265] (Ratios in brackets mine.)

And yet, Mersenne the musician quickly adds

> It is difficult to determine which is the better of these two consonances, for each is excellent according to the situations in which it is placed.[266]

Predictably, Mersenne also applies Benedetti's products of multiplication to evaluate the relative consonance of musical intervals. Mersenne observes

> If we wish to determine by how much [one consonance] surpasses [another consonance], the multiplication of their terms by each other will show how much.[267] (Text in brackets mine.)

Toward the end of the book, Mersenne also extends this technique to "replicas" (or "octave-multiples").

IV

> Thus it is evident that the tenth [5:2] is more pleasant than the major third [5:4], and the seventeenth [5:1] more pleasant and more excellent than the tenth, as I have shown in the discourses on the third and on its replicas, inasmuch as its multiple ratio is easier to understand, and its terms are united more often, than those of the superparticular ratios of the [major] third and of the major tenth.[268] (Text and ratios in brackets mine.)

A sequential compilation of the replicas and interval ratios listed in Prop. XXXII, Table 10,[269] yields a graduated sequence of consonances *endorsed* by Mersenne. These consonances appear in the right section of Table 10.30.

Notably absent from the right section of Table 10.30 are 7-limit ratios. However, this does not mean that Mersenne either ignored or was unsympathetic to these omissions. On the contrary, in the first two paragraphs of Prop. XXXIII, Mersenne delineates the mathematical and musical complexities of this subject.

Why there are only seven or eight simple consonances.

> This difficulty is one of the greatest of music, for although we experience that of all the sounds it is only those which are equal [1:1], or which are in double [2:1], sesquialtera [3:2], sesquitertia [4:3], sesquiquarta [5:4], sesquiquinta [6:5], superbipartient three [5:3], and supertripartient five [8:5] ratios, which are agreeable, and which deserve the name of perfect or imperfect consonances, it is, nevertheless, difficult to give the reason for this.
>
> For why are not the two sounds whose ratio is sequisexta, that is, 7 to 6, or sesquiseptima, 8 to 7, agreeable? If we consider the repeated consonances, why do not the sounds whose ratio is 7 to 1 and 9 to 1, that is, septuple and nonuple, please the mind and the ear, since those whose ratio is 8, 10, 12, and 16 to 1 are agreeable? Moreover, those of 7 to 1 or 9 to 1,

> unite more often, and consequently should be more agreeable, according to the reason we have adduced elsewhere on what is more agreeable or less agreeable in music.[270] (Ratios in brackets mine.)

A few pages later, Mersenne restates these difficulties by conceding

> It must be acknowledged that it is quite difficult to know why the sesquiquinta [6:5] is the last superparticular ratio which is pleasing in an interval of sounds . . .[271] (Ratio in brackets mine.)

In Prop. XXXIII, Mersenne carefully describes and discusses these 7-limit ratios: 7/1, 7/2, 7/3, 7/4, 7/5, 7/6.[272] A sequential compilation of the former *endorsed* consonances, and the latter *contemplated* consonances appears in the left section of Table 10.30. Throughout Prop. XXXIII, Mersenne examines both sides of the debate, and lists numerous reasons for and against the inclusion of these intervals. Amazingly, Mersenne also argues against the elimination of these ratios based on ideas advocated by Plato[273] (427–347 B.C.) and Johannes Kepler[274] (1571–1630). In short, Mersenne understood this dilemma in a context more sophisticated than the conventional polemics of his time.

Ultimately, Mersenne rejected 7-limit ratios because the inclusion of such intervals would have introduced an entirely new minor tonality.

V

> If it is said that the sounds do not unite quickly enough to be agreeable in the proportion of 7 to 1 or 7 to 8, the sounds of 5 to 8, of 16 to 1, and of several other consonances unite yet less often, and nevertheless these proportions are agreeable.
>
> Others derive the reason from the fact that the intervals of 7 to 1 . . . cannot be divided into intervals suitable for singing, and that 7 cannot form any harmonic ratio with the numbers which precede it, for it forms the septuple ratio with 1 [7:1] . . . [this also applies to] the sesquisexta [7:6], which does not arise from the difference between consonances . . . Consequently, the sesquisexta, or any other interval of all those which can be found between the minor third and the major tone, cannot be in tune.[275] (Text and ratios is brackets mine.)

The objections raised in the second paragraph of Quote V indirectly identify number 7 as a prime number, a fact acknowledged by Mersenne at the end of Prop. XXXIII.[276] To understand the musical and mathematical challenges associated with the introduction of prime number 7 ratios — *or any new prime number ratio* — consider for a moment Figure 10.51, which illustrates the symmetric substitution of 5-limit ratios into the 3-limit Pythagorean *'Apotome Scale'*. (See Section 10.23.) In the original 3-limit scale, ancient length ratio 81/64 defines the "major third," and length ratio 32/27, the "minor third." All together, this scale includes eight major triads (or major tonalities) with 81/64 as the lower and 32/27 as the upper interval ratio; the first three major tonalities are 1/1–81/64–3/2, 9/8–729/512–27/16, 32/27–3/2–16/9. Furthermore, this scale also includes eight minor triads (or minor tonalities) with 32/27 as the lower and 81/64 as the upper interval ratio; the first three minor tonalities are 1/1–32/27–3/2, 2187/2048–81/64–6561/4096, 9/8–4/3–27/16. Now, if we replace 81/64 with a 5/4 "major third," there will only be one new major tonality: 1/1–5/4–3/2; and if we replace 32/27 with a 6/5 "minor third," there will only be one new minor tonality: 1/1–6/5–3/2. In either case, 5/4 and 6/5 ". . . cannot be in tune . . ." with any of the other 3-limit ratios because, for instance, there is no 15/8 to sound a "fifth" above 5/4, and no 8/5 to sound a "fifth" below 6/5. Consequently, the 5/4 and 6/5 additions are of little practical value unless we maximize the harmonic possibilities of these new consonances by substituting three 5-limit ratio pairs — [16/15, 15/8], [6/5, 5/3], [5/4, 8/5] — into the scale. In this context,

Table 10.30

COMPARISON OF CONSONANCES CONTEMPLATED AND ENDORSED BY MERSENNE

Contemplated Interval Ratio	Contemplated Product	Endorsed Interval Ratio	Endorsed Product
1/1	1	1/1	1
2/1	2	2/1	2
3/1	3	3/1	3
5/1	5	5/1	5
3/2	6	3/2	6
7/1	7		
5/2	10	5/2	10
4/3	12	4/3	12
7/2	14		
5/3	15	5/3	15
5/4	20	5/4	20
7/3	21		
7/4	28		
6/5	30	6/5	30
7/5	35		
8/5	40	8/5	40
7/6	42		

a *pair* refers to a given *ratio and its inversion*, or to two interval ratios that span an "octave." For example, 15/8 is the inversion of 16/15 — and 16/15 is the inversion of 15/8 — because $15/8 \times 16/15 = 2/1$. Therefore, we may also express this "octave" as interval ratios 16:15:8.

Given such requirements, the introduction of prime number 5 into a 3-limit Pythagorean scale seemed feasible to theorists a century before Mersenne, but the prospect of substituting prime number 7 into the same 12-tone scale boggled even the best of minds. It was inconceivable to Mersenne, and most theorists in the 17th century, to sacrifice 5-limit ratios for 7-limit ratios in the same

C	C♯	D	E♭	E	F	F♯	G	G♯	A	B♭	B	C'
1/1	2187/2048	9/8	32/27	81/64	4/3	729/512	3/2	6561/4096	27/16	16/9	243/128	2/1
	↓		↓	↓		↓		↓	↓		↓	
C	C♯	D	E♭	E	F	F♯	G	G♯	A	B♭	B	C'
1/1	16/15	9/8	6/5	5/4	4/3	45/32	3/2	8/5	5/3	16/9	15/8	2/1

Figure 10.51 The substitution of 5-limit ratios into the 3-limit Pythagorean *'Apotome Scale'*. Three 5-limit ratio pairs — [16/15, 15/8], [6/5, 5/3], [5/4, 8/5] — produce a maximum number of harmonic possibilities given the limitations of this 12-tone scale.

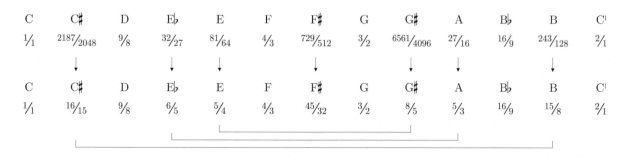

manner that earlier music theorists had replaced 3-limit ratios with 5-limit ratios. However, suppose we leave the 5-limit scale intact, and expand the 12-tone scale to include prime number 7 ratios. A reasonable increase would consist of two new ratio pairs: [8/7, 7/4] and [7/6, 12/7]. These four ratios would produce three new minor tonalities with 7/6 as the lower and 9/7 as the upper interval ratio: 1/1–7/6–3/2, 8/7–4/3–12/7, 3/2–7/4–9/8, and three new major tonalities with 9/7 as the lower and 7/6 as the upper interval ratio: 7/6–3/2–7/4, 4/3–12/7–2/1, 16/9–8/7–4/3. Such a design would require a 16-tone scale and, consequently, new instruments, new systems of notation, and new playing techniques. For centuries, theorists have proposed larger scales to accommodate high prime number ratios, but for practical reasons, most of these ideas perished long ago.[277]

Had Mersenne lived in the 20th or 21st century, he may have joined in the effort to build new instruments with tunings that include 7-limit ratios. (See Chapter 12.) Mersenne confessed his unhappiness over this situation when he noted

> Nevertheless, all these reasons do not satisfy me entirely, inasmuch as if the pleasure of music begins with a consideration of the mind, which is capable of contemplating all kinds of ratios . . .[278]

Finally, and most importantly, Mersenne also understood the dulling effect of cultural conditioning, the force of habit, and the power of musical expression when imbued with an inquisitive spirit.

> Since lengthy usage normally renders pleasant and fluent that which previously seems harsh and tiresome, I do not doubt at all that the dissonant intervals of which I have spoken in this proposition, namely, the ratios of 7 to 6 and of 8 to 7, which divide the fourth [arithmetically, as in 8:7:6], can become agreeable, if we become accustomed to hearing them and enduring them, and if they are used as necessary in solos and in ensemble pieces in order to arouse the passions, and for several effects of which music is ordinarily deprived.[279] (Text and ratios in brackets mine.)

10.55

Mersenne's experiments marked a critical transition in the history of just intonation. Painstaking investigations into the science of sound enabled him to correctly perceive the first six harmonics of a vibrating string, and to accurately identify these harmonics as a progression of five interval ratios: 2/1, 3/2, 4/3, 5/4, 6/5. Under these conditions, a natural string serves a more important function than a natural trumpet because the string produces a sonic spectrum that consists of several harmonics that are simultaneously audible to human ears. However, because Mersenne did not define his *sons extraordinaires* in the context of a potentially infinite series of harmonics, his observations were inconclusive and raised many unanswered questions.

The next step in the discovery of the harmonic series occurred in 1677, when John Wallis (1616–1703) published a short letter ". . . concerning a new musical discovery."[280] In this paper, Wallis described the presence of motionless points (or nodes) along a vibrating string. To prove the *natural* occurrence of these points, Wallis avoided physical contact with his test string, because he knew that the act of plucking a string has a direct effect on the presence of nodes. For example, Wallis observed that if one plucks a string at the location of a node, or at the location that represents an aliquot division of the string, ". . . the sound is incongruous, by reason that the point is disturbed which should be at rest."[281] Consequently, if one plucks a string in the middle, the node at the center of the string will *not* form, and the second harmonic will *not* sound. Because of this, Wallis designed his experiment with two strings, so that by means of sympathetic resonance, the vibrations of the first plucked string would drive the second test string — without human interference — into motion.

> Whereas it hath been long since observed, that, if a Viol string, or Lute string, be touched with the Bow or Hand, another string on the same or another Instrument not far from it, (if an *Unison* to it, or an *Octave*, or the like) will at the same time tremble of its own accord. The cause of it, (having been formerly discussed by divers,) I do not now inquire into. But add this to the former Observation; that, not the whole of that other string doth thus tremble, but the several parts severally, according as they are Unisons to the whole, or the parts of that string which is so struck. For instance, supposing AC to be an upper Octave to $\alpha\gamma$, and therefore an Unison to each half of it, stopped at β:
>
> 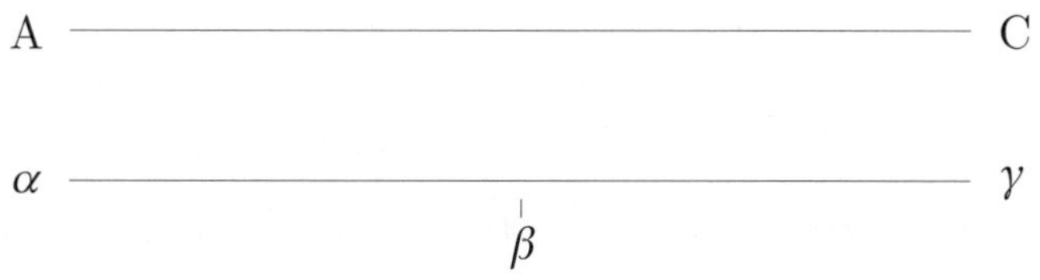
>
>
> Now if, while $\alpha\gamma$ is open, AC be struck; the two halves of this other, that is $\alpha\beta$ and $\beta\gamma$, will both tremble; but not the middle point at β. Which will easily be observed, if a little bit of paper be lightly wrapped about the string $\alpha\gamma$, and removed successively from one end of the string to the other.[282]

Although Wallis correctly observed that strings subdivide into increasingly shorter sections that are separated by nodes, he did not contemplate the possibility of a theoretically infinite number of subdivisions along a string's vibrating length, nor did he discuss the simultaneous presence of many different harmonics.

A few years later, in 1692, Francis Roberts (Robartes), (*c.* 1649 – d. 1718), published an essay that expanded on Wallis' findings.[283] In the previous quotation, note that Wallis referred to ". . . an *Unison* . . . an *Octave*, or the like . . ." because he believed that sympathetic resonance is an exclusive function of consonance. Wallis maintained that as a string subdivides into shorter sections, the node phenomenon occurs only if two strings sound a consonant interval ratio. To challenge this assumption, Roberts used a bowed trumpet marine because the higher modes of vibration of strings have very low amplitudes. Roberts realized that Wallis' motionless points or nodes occurred only at *aliquot* parts of a string, or at locations determined by dividing a string into 2, 3, 4, 5, . . . *equal* parts. By lightly touching a string at aliquot parts corresponding to $\frac{1}{2}$, $\frac{1}{3}$, $\frac{1}{4}$, $\frac{1}{5}$, . . . , $\frac{1}{16}$ of the length of the string (see Figure 10.49), Roberts made audible a progression of discrete flageolet tones — now known as the harmonic series — up to the sixteenth harmonic.[284] Unfortunately, Roberts insisted that the 7th, 11th, 13th, and 14th harmonics produce tones that are defective and ". . . out of Tune . . ." Consequently, he did not comprehend his discovery as a naturally occurring or scientific phenomenon intrinsic to all vibrating strings.

Roberts also applied his principle to the natural trumpet and explained the production of tones based on ". . . breaking the Air within the Tube into the shortest vibrations, but that no Musical sound will arise unless they are suited to some aliquot part . . ." Unlike Wallis, Roberts concluded that for strings and trumpets the ". . . Notes ascending, continually decreased in proportion of $\frac{1}{1}$ $\frac{1}{2}$ $\frac{1}{3}$ $\frac{1}{4}$ $\frac{1}{5}$ in *infinitum*."[285] Nevertheless, Wallis and Roberts did not frame these discoveries in the larger context of a harmonic series. The possibility of a string simultaneously subdividing into many different lengths, and thereby simultaneously sounding many different harmonics, escaped both investigators.

10.56

In 1701, Joseph Sauveur (1653–1716) published a short work entitled *Système général des intervalles des sons, et son application à tous les systèmes et à tous les instrumens de musique,*[286] in which he introduced several new terms used to this day. Sauveur was the first scientist to use *acoustique* to describe the general science of sound:

> I have thus believed that there is a science superior to music, which I have called ***Acoustique***, which has as its object sound in general, whereas music has as its object sound in so far as it is agreeable to the hearing.[287] (Bold italics in Sauveur's original text.)

He invented *son harmonique* and *son fondamental* to distinguish between a string's harmonic sounds or mode frequencies and its fundamental sound or frequency:

> I call ***Son harmonique*** of the ***Son fondamental*** that which makes several vibrations while the fundamental makes only one.[288] (Bold italics in Sauveur's original text.)

Finally, Sauveur introduced *noeuds* (nodes) to define locations of no motion, and *ventres* (antinodes) to define locations of maximum motion along a string's vibrating length. (See Section 10.57, Figures 10.52 and 10.53.)

> I will call the points A, D, E, F, G, and B, the ***Noeuds*** of these undulations and the middles of these undulations, their ***Ventres***.[289] (Bold italics in Sauveur's original text.)

The latter four terms stemmed from a series of experiments conducted by Sauveur.

> While I was meditating on the phenomena of sounds, it came to my attention that, especially at night, you can hear in long strings, in addition to the principal sound, other little sounds at the twelfth and the seventeenth of that sound, and that Trumpets, in addition to these sounds, make others, the number of vibrations of which is a multiple of the number of those of the *Son fondamental.* I found nothing in the explanation of the marine trumpet which satisfied me on this subject. But upon seeking the cause of this phenomenon on my own, I concluded that a string, in addition to the undulations made by its entire length producing the fundamental, divides into two, three, four, ***and so forth***, equal divisions, which produce the octave, twelfth, and fifteenth of that sound; then I inferred the necessity of *noeuds* and *ventres* in these undulations and the manner of perceiving them by touch and sight, as I explain in *Sons harmoniques* [Section IX].[290] (Bold italics, and text in brackets mine.)

In this passage, Sauveur managed to describe for the first time what seemed utterly impossible to Mersenne, namely, that a string simultaneously subdivides into a potentially infinite number of different lengths, and thereby simultaneously produces a potentially infinite number of different mode frequencies. Deeply frustrated by this problem, Mersenne wrote sixty-five years earlier,

> That is why it is necessary to examine how [the movement] can cause the same string to beat the air differently in the same time, for since [the

> string] makes the five or six tones of which I have spoken, it seems that it is entirely necessary that [the string] beat the air 5, 4, 3, and 2 times in the same time that it beats a single time. ***This is difficult to imagine***, unless one say that the half-string beats it twice while the entire string beats it once, and that in the same time the third, fourth and fifth parts beat it 3, 4, and 5 times. ***This is against experience, which shows*** evidently that all the parts of the string make an equal number of vibrations in the same time, for all the string being continuous has a single movement . . .[291] (Bold italics mine.)

Although Mersenne entertained the idea ". . . that [the string] beat the air 5, 4, 3, and 2 times in the same time that it beats a single time," he refused to accept this explanation as the cause for *sons extraordinaires* in vibrating strings. He rejected this possibility because he saw no evidence of it! As an empiricist, he was justified in assuming that such a theory goes "against experience" because no human being can accurately observe the complex motions of a vibrating string. However, as a mathematician, he was unjustified in concluding that because he could not observe such a phenomenon, it did not exist. In time, Sauveur's description turned out to be correct. Nevertheless, note carefully that both men did not contemplate the possibility of traveling waves in strings, and therefore had no knowledge of the *principle of superposition.* (See Sections 3.1 and 3.3.) So, although Sauveur correctly described the process by which a string subdivides into shorter sections, and correctly identified the harmonic frequency ratios associated with such sections, he offered no mechanical or mathematical explanation for this phenomenon.

The solution to this invisible problem came from Jean le Rond D'Alembert (1717–1783), who solved a second order partial differential equation, known as the *wave equation*, which enabled him to formulate an equation for the constant speed of transverse traveling waves in flexible strings.[292] (See Equation 3.11.) D'Alembert also created a purely mathematical model to show that standing waves in strings are caused by the superposition of traveling waves that propagate in opposite directions. (See Figure 3.6.) This principle applies to all acoustic sound-producing systems.

10.57

From a mathematical perspective, Sauveur's most important contribution appears in a table in Section IX of his *Système général des intervalles des sons.* Here, Sauveur lists the frequency ratios of the first 32 harmonics of a vibrating string. Table 10.31 below shows the first two columns of Sauveur's table. Sauveur gives the following description of these columns:

> The first column indicates the number of vibrations which a harmonic makes while the fundamental makes only one. It marks also the order of the harmonics.
>
> The second column supposes that each octave of the fundamental makes 10,000 vibrations and indicates then the number of vibrations made by the harmonic in proportion to the first sound of each octave.[293]

This table includes the first eleven prime numbers — 2, 3, 5, 7, 11, 13, 17, 19, 23, 29, 31 — and accurately gives the frequencies of eleven prime number ratios based on a fundamental frequency of 10,000.0 cps. For example, Sauveur represents the thirteenth harmonic as a "sharp minor sixth," ratio $^{13}/_{8}$ [840.5 ¢], with a frequency of 10,000.0 cps × $^{13}/_{8}$ = 16,250.0 cps; and he represents the seventeenth harmonic as a "sharp minor second," ratio $^{17}/_{16}$ [105.0 ¢], with a frequency of 10,000.0 cps × $^{17}/_{16}$ = 10,625.0 cps. As an objective scientist, Sauveur calculated these frequencies without regard to consonance vs. dissonance polemics of past and present music theorists. In this respect, his table

Table 10.31

FIRST TWO COLUMNS FROM SAUVEUR'S TABLE OF HARMONIC FREQUENCY RATIOS

Ratios of the vibrations to the fundamental.		Ratios of the vibrations to the first sound of the octave.	Ratios of the vibrations to the fundamental.		Ratios of the vibrations to the first sound of the octave.
1	1	10000	1	16	10000
1	2	10000	1	17	10625
1	3	15000	1	18	11250
1	4	10000	1	19	11875
1	5	12500	1	20	12500
1	6	15000	1	21	13125
1	7	17500	1	22	13750
1	8	10000	1	23	14375
1	9	11250	1	24	15000
1	10	12500	1	25	15625
1	11	13750	1	26	16250
1	12	15000	1	27	16875
1	13	16250	1	28	17500
1	14	17500	1	29	18125
1	15	18750	1	30	18750
			1	31	19375
			1	32	10000

is a welcome sight even in the 21st century. At the end of Section X, Sauveur refers to his table one last time. Here, without further elaboration, he simply states that this series of harmonic frequency ratios also occurs when musicians overblow wind instruments:

> This same table also indicates the sounds of the ordinary trumpet, or the hunting horn, and the projections [or tones produced by overblowing] of the wind instruments with holes.[294] (Text in brackets mine.)

From a scientific perspective, Sauveur's most important contribution consists of two line drawings that depict sequential changes in the standing wave pattern of a lightly touched vibrating string. The last two drawings of Figures 10.52 and 10.53 demonstrate — for the first time in the history of acoustics — the standing wave pattern of a mode of vibration other than the obvious fundamental mode. These two figures, which represent exact copies of Sauveur's drawings, illustrate the standing wave pattern of the fifth mode of vibration, or of the fifth harmonic. Knowledge of the distribution of nodes and antinodes along a vibrating string enabled Sauveur to explain why a given string length — when divided into a prime number of aliquot parts — produces the same flageolet tone, or the same harmonic mode frequency. (See Section 10.50.) Sauveur describes his first drawing in this manner:

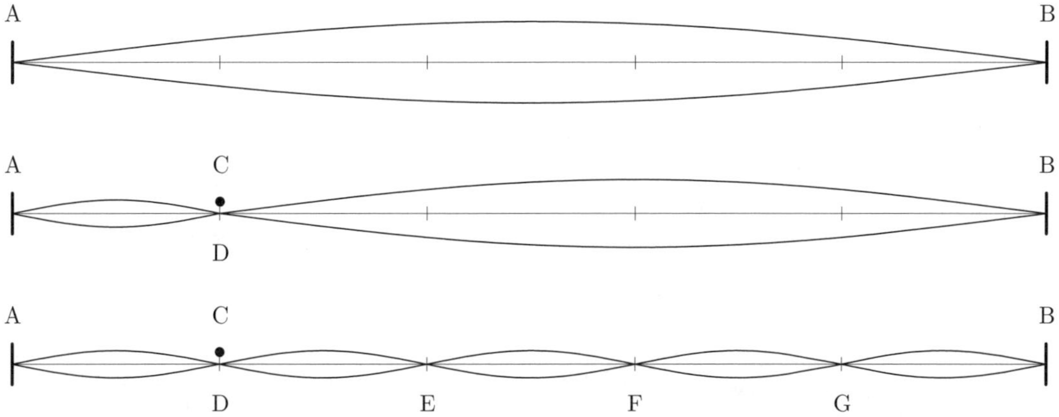

Figure 10.52 An exact copy of Sauveur's first figure that shows the sequential changes in the standing wave pattern of a lightly touched string. In this case, a thin obstacle at ⅕ of the string length produces the fifth harmonic.

> Pluck the open string. It will render a sound that I call the fundamental of that string. Put, immediately, a thin obstacle (like the tip of a pen if the string is thin), C, on one of these divisions, D. The disturbance, then, of the string is communicated to both sides of the obstacle. It will render the 5th harmonic, a XVIIth.
>
> To understand the reason for this effect, note that when the open string, AB, is plucked, it makes its undulations in its whole length. But, when an obstacle, C, is placed on the first division, D, of the string, supposed to be divided into five equal parts, the whole undulation (an undulation of a string is the spindle-like shape made by the vibrations of this string), AB, divides first into two, AD and DB, and, since AD is ⅕ of AB or ¼ of DB, it makes its undulations 5 times more quickly than the total, AB, or 4 times more quickly than the other part, DB. The part, AD, then, involves its neighboring part, DE, and compels it to follow its disturbance. It must, consequently, be equal to it, for a greater part would go more slowly and a smaller one, more quickly. The part, DE, then compels the following one, EF, to follow the same disturbance, one after another, thus, as far as the last. All the parts, then, will make undulations crossing in the divisions D, E, F, and G. Consequently, the string will render the 5th harmonic, or a XVIIth.[295] (Text in parentheses in Maxham's translation.)

He then describes the second figure:

> If the obstacle, C, is at the second division of the string, it will render the ***same*** harmonic. For, (1) the obstacle, C, will first compel the string to make two undulations, AE and EB. (2) The undulation AE, going more quickly than the other, will compel EG, its equal, to follow its disturbance. (3) The remaining part, GB, which is half of it, going twice as quick, will compel its equal, GF, to follow its disturbance and this one will involve the following one, FE, and so forth, one after the other to the last. The whole string, then, will be divided by its undulations into equal parts of the greatest common measure of the parts, AC and CB, divided by the thin obstacle, C.[296] (Bold italics mine.)

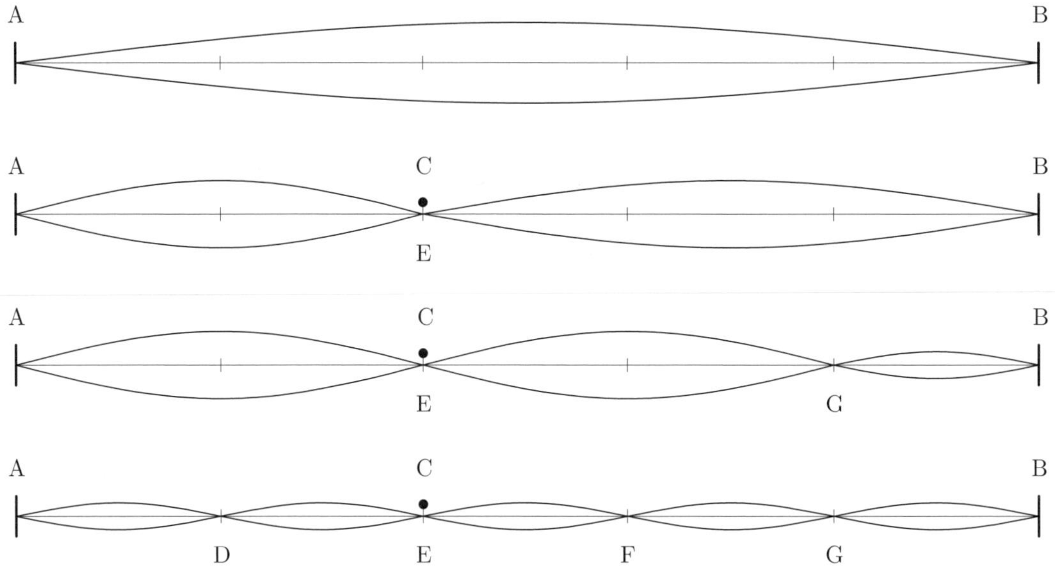

Figure 10.53 An exact copy of Sauveur's second figure that shows the sequential changes in the standing wave pattern of a lightly touched string. In this case, a thin obstacle at $2/5$ of the string length *also* produces the fifth harmonic.

In the next paragraph, Sauveur ends the discussion by acknowledging John Wallis' discovery of nodes.

To some, the study of nodes, antinodes, and mode shapes may seem redundant and inconsequential. Since length and frequency are inversely proportional, musicians have tuned stringed instruments for thousands of years without any knowledge of standing wave patterns. Every location along a vibrating string represents the position of a potential node, so that at any given point, a decrease in length produces an increase in frequency. This general principle also applies to bars. However, recall that in Sections 6.10–6.14, we discussed how decreases in the thickness of a bass marimba bar at the locations of five antinodes decrease the frequency not only of the fundamental, but of the second and third modes as well. Here a knowledge of standing wave patterns is essential because, for example, a removal of material at the locations of nodes does not change these mode frequencies. The first mathematician to calculate the locations of nodes and antinodes in free and clamped bars was Daniel Bernoulli (1700–1782). Bernoulli solved two fourth order partial differential equations, and included with his final solutions accurate line drawings of the mode shapes of free and clamped bars.[297] (See Figures 6.1 and 6.11.) Such discoveries would have been unthinkable without Sauveur's groundbreaking investigations.

10.58

Sauveur's recognition of a potentially infinite harmonic series had an immeasurable effect on the development and conceptualization of Western music. This finding also prompted music theorists to reevaluate the significance of many historical texts. A renewed interest in such works was largely fueled by the realization that rational (1) length ratios, (2) frequency ratios, and (3) interval ratios are inextricably linked to the natural vibrations of flexible strings and columns of air. By the time Sauveur published his treatises, 12-tone equal temperament was rapidly becoming a widely accepted tuning standard throughout Europe. Despite this practice, musicians and theorists continued to use just ratios in their descriptions of scales, and in their attempts to distinguish between major and minor tonalities of Western music. Sauveur's great discovery confirmed that just ratios and just proportions constitute the *only* accurate means by which musicians are able to understand the cultural and physical origins of music. Therefore, before we discuss the influence of the harmonic series on modern musicians and composers, let us first consider Sauveur's term *sons harmoniques.*

Recall that in Section 3.18, we discussed the arithmetic and harmonic division of the "octave" on canon strings. Also, in Section 10.43, we examined Stifel's method for transforming an arithmetic progression of integers — 1, 2, 3, 4, 5, 6 — into a harmonic progression of integers: 10, 12, 15, 20, 30, 60. Now, observe carefully that we may transform an *arithmetic progression of integers* into a *harmonic progression of fractions;* and that we may transform the latter into the former. To achieve the first transformation, simply write the reciprocals of a given arithmetic progression; to achieve the second transformation, simply write the reciprocals of a given harmonic progression. Since 1, 2, 3, 4, 5, 6, constitutes an arithmetic progression of integers, the sequence below constitutes a *harmonic progression of fractions:*

$$\tfrac{1}{1},\ \tfrac{1}{2},\ \tfrac{1}{3},\ \tfrac{1}{4},\ \tfrac{1}{5},\ \tfrac{1}{6}$$

To verify that this is a harmonic progression, substitute the first and third terms into Equation 3.38A, and calculate the second term:

$$\frac{2(\tfrac{1}{1})(\tfrac{1}{3})}{\tfrac{1}{1}+\tfrac{1}{3}} = \tfrac{1}{2}$$

Similarly, substitute the second and fourth terms into this equation, and calculate the third term:

$$\frac{2(\tfrac{1}{2})(\tfrac{1}{4})}{\tfrac{1}{2}+\tfrac{1}{4}} = \tfrac{1}{3}$$

Dimensionless ratios like $\tfrac{1}{2}$, $\tfrac{2}{1}$, $\tfrac{1}{3}$, $\tfrac{3}{1}$ often cause a great deal of confusion because many music theorists do not specify whether such quantities represent length ratios or frequency ratios. For example, we may express the "octave" as an ancient length ratio: 1000.0 mm ÷ 500.0 mm = $\tfrac{2}{1}$, as a modern length ratio: 500.0 mm ÷ 1000.0 mm = $\tfrac{1}{2}$, or as a frequency ratio: 392.0 cps ÷ 196.0 cps = $\tfrac{2}{1}$. Unless a writer specifies what such ratios mean, these and all other dimensionless quantities are completely open to interpretation. In this context, the above-mentioned harmonic progression of fractions has its physical origins *not* in frequency dimensions, but in string length dimensions! In support of this critical distinction, consider the following complete definition from a definitive work entitled *Mathematics Dictionary:*

> **harmonic sequence.** A sequence whose reciprocals form an arithmetic sequence. In *music*, strings of the same material, same diameter, and same torsion, whose lengths are proportional to terms in a harmonic sequence, produce harmonic tones. The sequence $\{1, \tfrac{1}{2}, \tfrac{1}{3}, \ldots, \tfrac{1}{n}\}$ is a harmonic sequence. *Syn.* harmonic progression.[298]

We conclude, therefore, that the sequence 1, $\tfrac{1}{2}$, $\tfrac{1}{3}$, $\tfrac{1}{4}$, $\tfrac{1}{5}$, $\tfrac{1}{6}$, . . . represents a harmonic progression of modern length ratios. (See Figure 3.14.) Flexible strings produce this harmonic progression as they naturally subdivide into shorter loops. In contrast, the reciprocal sequence 1, $\tfrac{2}{1}$, $\tfrac{3}{1}$, $\tfrac{4}{1}$, $\tfrac{5}{1}$, $\tfrac{6}{1}$, . . . represents an arithmetic progression of corresponding mode frequency ratios. Now, in a strict mathematical context, all terms of a harmonic progression — such as $\tfrac{1}{2}$, $\tfrac{1}{3}$, $\tfrac{1}{4}$, $\tfrac{1}{5}$, or 60, 30, 20, 15 — must satisfy Equation 3.38A, and all terms of an arithmetic progression — such as $\tfrac{2}{1}$, $\tfrac{3}{1}$, $\tfrac{4}{1}$, $\tfrac{5}{1}$, or $\tfrac{1}{60}$, $\tfrac{1}{30}$, $\tfrac{1}{20}$, $\tfrac{1}{15}$ — must satisfy Equation 3.37A. However, since in a musical context, the arithmetic sequence of frequency ratios 1, $\tfrac{2}{1}$, $\tfrac{3}{1}$, $\tfrac{4}{1}$, $\tfrac{5}{1}$, $\tfrac{6}{1}$, . . . is called the *harmonic series*, we must carefully distinguish between precise mathematical definitions on the one hand, and conventional figures of speech on the other. (See Section 3.9.)

In conclusion, it is highly likely that Sauveur renamed Mersenne's *sons extraordinaires* and called them *sons harmoniques* to maintain mathematical consistency between the *intervals of the tones* produced by the ancient harmonic divisions of strings and the *intervals of the harmonics* produced by the natural subdivisions of vibrating strings. As depicted in Figure 3.23, only the harmonic division of an "octave" on a string produces a large "fifth," interval ratio $\frac{3}{2}$, in the lower position, and small "fourth," interval ratio $\frac{4}{3}$, in the upper position. This harmonic division of the "octave" is completely consistent with the natural processes of a vibrating string: it sounds a lower "fifth" while subdividing into two $\frac{1}{2}$-sections and three $\frac{1}{3}$-sections, and an upper "fourth" while subdividing into three $\frac{1}{3}$-sections and four $\frac{1}{4}$-sections of its overall vibrating length. (See Figures 3.10, 3.13, and 3.15.)

10.59

During the Enlightenment, an intellectual movement that dominated 18th-century Europe, many mathematicians and philosophers believed that through reason (or rationalism) and scientific observation (or empiricism) all the mysteries of the universe would eventually be revealed. One of the greatest thinkers of this era was Isaac Newton (1642–1727). Many considered his twofold discovery of gravity and mass as a quintessential example of an enlightened mind. The tendency during the Enlightenment to think of Nature as a finely tuned clock, with a mechanism governed solely by mathematical equations, also had a profound effect on the study of music. Jean-Philippe Rameau (1683–1764), prolific composer and author of six major treatises on music, spent his entire intellectual life searching for a universal principle that would explain the origins of all music. In this effort, he was doomed to failure because art, unlike science, depends primarily on the life-experiences of an individual, and on the cultural traditions of a civilization. Rameau's critics were quick to ask, "If a universal principle of music exists, why does music from around the world not sound the same?" Nevertheless, Rameau's relentless pursuit, and above all, his willingness to study new texts and to recant spurious ideas, enabled him to formulate several important concepts of Western music theory. Most books on traditional harmony and musical composition extol Rameau's teachings to this day.

Regarding Rameau's theoretical works, our main objective will be to analyze his derivations of the major and minor tonalities in Western music. However, due to the inherent complexities of this subject, we must examine Rameau's early works. Because Rameau's verbal descriptions of mathematical definitions and procedures are often difficult to understand, we will approach this review from two different perspectives. First, we will examine key passages from Rameau's original texts, and second, consider analytical commentary by Matthew Shirlaw (1873–1961). Large portions of Shirlaw's well-known book entitled *The Theory of Harmony* discuss the music theories of Zarlino and Rameau in exquisite detail. Readers who require more information should consult Rameau's treatises and Shirlaw's text directly.

In 1722, Rameau published his first theoretical work entitled *Traité de l'harmonie*.[299] Although this treatise appeared twenty-one years after Sauveur's *Système général des intervalles des sons*, Rameau does not give any indications that he was aware of the harmonic series as a natural phenomenon of vibrating strings. Instead, he explains his theories in purely mathematical or rational terms. According to Shirlaw,[300] Rameau discusses three principles of music: (1) Harmonic Generation, (2) the Fundamental Bass, and (3) the Inversion of Chords. The first of these is most difficult to comprehend because Rameau was not a mathematician. Turn to Figure 10.54, and observe that

Rameau's first engraving in the *Traité de l'harmonie* shows seven canon strings numbered 1, 2, 3, 4, 5, 6, and 8.[301] Because Rameau included the last string for musical reasons — that is, to produce the "triple-octave," ratio $8/1$, above the first string, and the "minor sixth," ratio $8/5$, above the fifth string — he simply ignored the seventh string and described the sequence 1, 2, 3, 4, 5, 6, 8, as the "first progression," and as an "arithmetic progression." Furthermore, Rameau repeatedly stated that only the arithmetic proportion follows a "natural progression," or a "natural order" of numbers;[302] consequently, it alone satisfies "the rules of arithmetic." Throughout the *Traité*, and in his second work entitled *Nouveau système de musique théorique* (1726), Rameau argues in favor of the arithmetic progression, and repeatedly cites the above-mentioned simple sequence of integers that represents vibration numbers, or frequency ratios. In other words, he avoids the harmonic progression in his mathematical discussions, although he does give an expanded version of Stifel's more complicated sequence of integers that represents string lengths, or length ratios. In the *Traité*, on two occasions in Book One, he refers to the harmonic progression as a "new proportion"; and on two more occasions, he holds Zarlino responsible for the invention of the "harmonic proportion."[303] In the latter passages, Rameau reveals that he is not familiar with the works of the ancient Greeks. (See Section 3.18.) However, in his third and fourth treatises entitled *Génération harmonique* (1737) and *Démonstration du principe de l'harmonie* (1750), Rameau abandons frequency ratios and uses length ratios to describe his observations of vibrating systems.

Rameau describes his sequence of integers in the first engraving by stating that it represents (1) the number of divisions per string, and (2) the number of vibrations per string.

I

> We must remark here that the numbers indicating the ***divisions of the strings or its vibrations*** follow their ***natural progression***, and that everything is thus based on the rules of arithmetic. The numbers measuring the ***lengths of the strings***, however, follow a progression which is the ***inversion of the first progression***, thus destroying some of the rules of arithmetic, or at least obliging us to invert them, as we shall see later.[304] (Bold italics mine.)

Rameau's observation that the "numbers indicating the . . . vibrations follow their natural progression" is central to his theory of harmonic generation because only an arithmetic progression of vibration numbers produces a simple sequence of integers. In contrast, a harmonic progression of string length units does not produce such a "natural order," but a more complicated sequence of integers. To understand the intellectual origins of Rameau's numerical distinctions, consider the following two quotations from Zarlino's *Istitutioni harmoniche*, Prima Parte, Cap. 12:

> Even if *Unità* [lit. *Unity*] itself is not a number, it is nevertheless the origin of numbers. According to Unity, each thing, be it simple or compound, *o corporale o spirituale* [lit. *or corporeal or spiritual*] is characterized by *Una* [lit. *One*, or *Oneness*].[305] (Text in brackets mine. Italics in Zarlino's original text.)

Although Zarlino gives the impression that the number one is not a number, later in the chapter he declares

> Because the natural progression of numbers is the following: 1, 2, 3, 4, 5, 6, 7, 8, 9, 10, one can extend it to infinity by joining Unity to it.[306] (Text in brackets mine.)

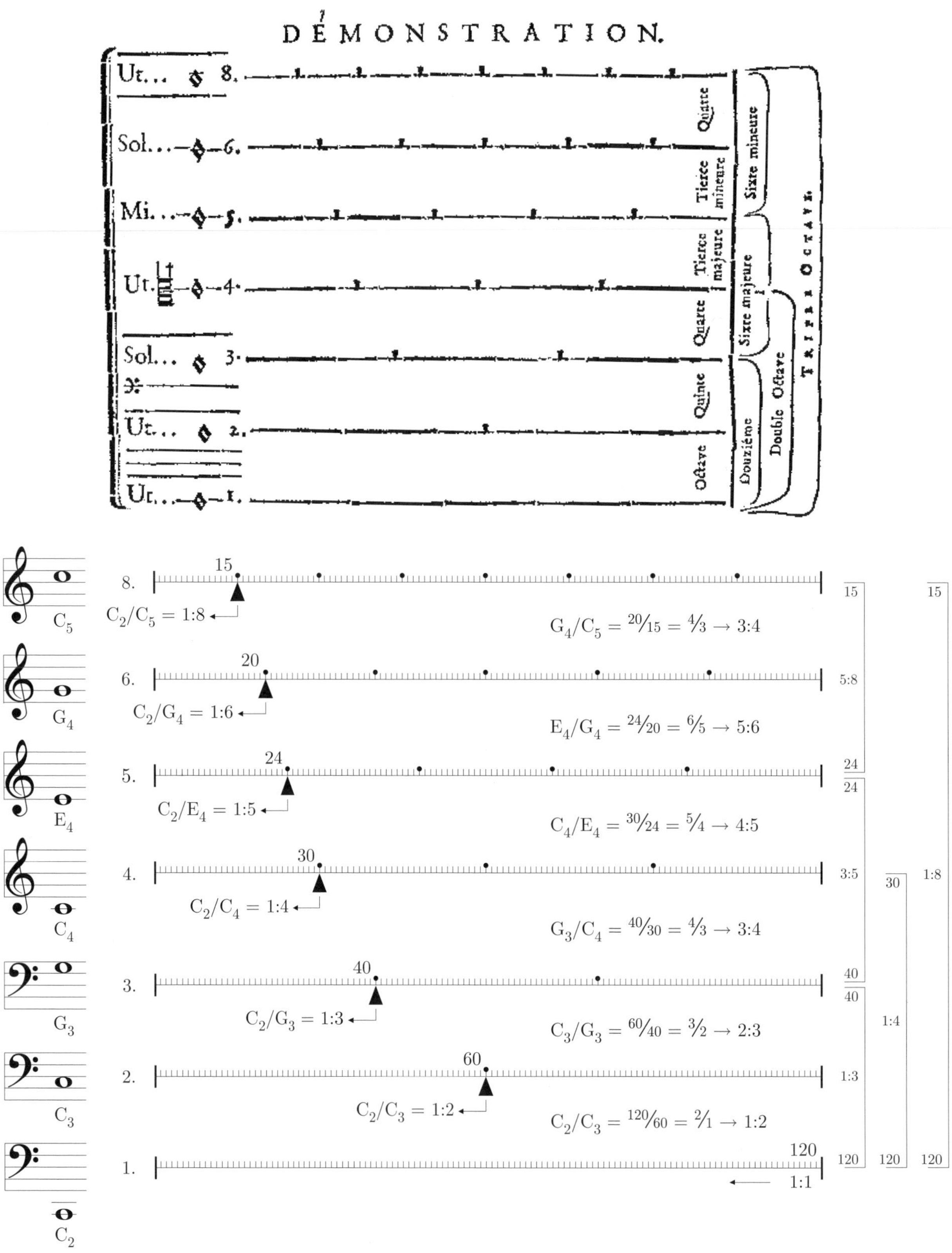

Figure 10.54 A reproduction of Rameau's first engraving in the *Traité de l'harmonie*, followed by my interpretation of this figure. Note that I replaced the original French interval names with vibration ratios used by Rameau in the original text. As discussed in Section 3.7, the l.r. → f.r. notation expresses the *inverse proportionality* between length ratios and frequency ratios of vibrating strings.

For Zarlino, the logical connection between unity and infinity is based on the premise that an entity which only has a beginning, or a beginning and a middle, does not constitute a Unity. Therefore, infinity depends (paradoxically) on the concept of Unity; that is, for an entity to be comprehensible, it must have a beginning, a middle, and an end. In the *Traité*, Chapter One, Article I, *On the source of Harmony or the fundamental Sound*, Rameau accepts Zarlino's definition of *Unità*.

> We should first assume that the undivided string corresponding to 1 produces a given sound; the properties of this sound must be examined by relating them to those of the single string and even to those of the unit [unity], which is the source of all numbers.[307] (Text in brackets mine.)

But in Chapter One, Article III, *On the octave*, Rameau rejects Zarlino's inclusion of the number one in the natural progression of numbers.

> The unit {unity} is the source of numbers, and 2 is the first number; there is a close resemblance between these two epithets, source and first [Fr. *principe* and *premier*], which is quite appropriate.[308] (Text in braces mine. Text in brackets in Gossett's translation.)

Before we continue, let us first reexamine Quote I in the context of Rameau's latter two statements. In the second sentence of Quote I, Rameau observes, "The numbers measuring the lengths of the strings, however, follow a progression which is the inversion of the first progression . . ." Since the first progression is the arithmetic progression of integers: 1, 2, 3, 4, 5, 6, 8, the inversions or reciprocals of these terms produce a harmonic progression. Now, because he claims that unity is not a number, but the source of numbers, we conclude that Rameau did *not* include a sequence of fractional string lengths as the "inversion of the first progression." Had he described such entities, the following harmonic progression of fractional string lengths would have resulted: $\frac{1}{1}$, $\frac{1}{2}$, $\frac{1}{3}$, $\frac{1}{4}$, $\frac{1}{5}$, $\frac{1}{6}$, $\frac{1}{8}$; in this harmonic progression, all terms after unity equal less than one. (Strictly speaking, this is not a harmonic progression because the reciprocal $\frac{1}{7}$ is missing.) Finally, in Rameau's first two treatises, fractional string lengths such as $\frac{1}{2}$, $\frac{1}{3}$, $\frac{1}{4}$, . . . never appear.

In the *Traité*, Book One, Chapter 11, Rameau acknowledges the distinction between ancient length ratios and frequency ratios.

> Thus, we shall not find in [ancient length ratios] 4:3:2 what we find in [frequency ratios] 2:3:4, since the interval generated from the comparison of 2 and 3 [i.e., the "fifth"], which is the first on the one hand [or in the latter sequence], is on the contrary the last on the other [or in the former sequence].[309] (Text in brackets mine.)

Rameau then paraphrases Zarlino's method for converting an arithmetic division of length ratios into a harmonic division of length ratios. As discussed in Section 10.42, this technique consists of two separate steps:

> This obliges us to invert our arithmetic proportion [of ancient length ratios 4:3:2] . . . by multiplying the two extremes by the mean, and then [multiplying] one of the extremes by the other [extreme], thus returning the intervals to their natural order represented by the numbers 12:8:6.[310] (Text and ratios in brackets mine.)

An application of Zarlino's method shows how to "invert" the arithmetic proportion 4:3:2 into the harmonic proportion 12:8:6.

4:3:2

$\frac{4}{2} \times \frac{3}{3} = \frac{12}{6}$

$4 \times 2 = 8$

12:8:6

Least Terms, 6:4:3

Turn to Figure 3.23, which shows that string lengths in harmonic progression 6:4:3 produce string vibrations in arithmetic progression 2:3:4.

In the next sentence, Rameau cites these string length units:

> In short, if the most perfect harmony that the union of the consonances can produce is obtained in the ***divisions [of the strings or its vibrations]*** by the numbers 1:2:3:4:5:6:8, this same harmony can be obtained in the ***multiplication*** of lengths only by the numbers 120:60:[40:]30:24:20:15.[311] (All bold italics and text in brackets mine.)

Table 10.32 shows that Rameau's length numbers are based on Stifel's harmonic progression: 10, 12, 15, 20, 30, 60, which Zarlino used as a harmonic progression of string length units: 60, 30, 20, 15, 12, 10.

Table 10.32

Arithmetic Progression of Vibrations:	1	2	3	4	5	6	8
Stifel's harmonic prog. of lengths as used by Zarlino:	60	30	20	15	12	10	
Stifel's harmonic prog. of lengths as used by Rameau:	120	60	40	30	24	20	15

(Strictly speaking, Rameau's length numbers are not in harmonic progression because, according to Equation 3.38A, the harmonic mean between 24 and 15 approximately equals 18.4615.) Rameau doubled the integers of the harmonic progression he found in Zarlino's *Istitutioni harmoniche* (see Section 10.44, Quote V), and appended a 15-unit length, because he wanted to include the seventh string, frequency ratio $\frac{8}{1}$, without resorting to a fractional string length unit. (Note that on a string 60 units long, a $\frac{1}{8}$ section requires 7.5 units.) To understand the mathematics of Rameau's length numbers, we must compute the least common multiple, or LCM, of his sequence of integers: 1, 2, 3, 4, 5, 6, 8. The LCM — which corresponds to the smallest quantity that is divisible by two or more quantities without producing a remainder — represents an open canon string length divisible by all the terms in Rameau's sequence without requiring fractional units. Calculate an LCM in two separate steps. (1) In this case, determine the prime factors of integers 2, 3, 4, 5, 6, 8; this yields: 2, 3, 2^2, 5, 2×3, 2^3. (2) Now, multiply the ". . . distinct prime factors, each taken the greatest number of times it occurs in any one of the quantities."[312] Therefore,

$$\text{Rameau's LCM} = 3 \times 5 \times 2^3 = 120.$$

Since 120 units $\div$ 8 = 15 units, the "triple-octave," ratio $\frac{8}{1}$, produced by Rameau's seventh string is located 15 units from either the left or the right end of the string.

We are now able to comprehend why, in the context of the arithmetic progression, Rameau refers to "the divisions by the numbers 1:2:3:4:5:6:8," and, in the context of the harmonic progression, he refers to "the multiplication of lengths only by the numbers 120:60:[40:]30:24:20:15." Despite

Rameau's claim in Quote I, that an "inversion" of vibration numbers produces length numbers, it is *impossible* to "invert" an arithmetic progression 1:2:3:4:5:6:8 based on vibration numbers, and thereby generate a harmonic progression 120:60:40:30:24:20:15 based on length numbers. To comprehend the interrelationship between these two inherently different progressions of *dimensionless* ratios in Rameau's *Traité*, turn back to Figure 10.54. Observe that in my interpretation of Rameau's engraving, each string length is divided into 120 units; consequently, one unit represents $1/120$ of a length. In the following passages from Book One of the *Traité*, the "largest number" corresponds to the LCM 120, the "common measure," to the reciprocal $1/120$, and the "smaller numbers," to the doubled integers of Stifel's harmonic progression:

> As for the ***common measure which should be used for each length*** (the length being determined by the quantity of units the numbers contain), we must apply this common measure, and consequently augment the string, as many times as the number contains units. The numbers thus indicate the multiplication of the proposed string, which is the sonorous body representing the unit, and not its division. Since the ***largest number*** marks the undivided string here, the ***smaller numbers*** will thus mark the divisions.[313] (Bold italics mine. Text in parentheses in Gossett's translation.)
>
> To obtain the ratios of the lengths, we need only take two lengths arising from two different divisions, and give each a common measure by means of a compass. We shall find that each length will contain as many times the common measure as the numbers marking the divisions contain units . . .[314]

Now, since $1/120 \times 120 = 1/1$, this multiplication of lengths yields l.r. $1/1 \rightarrow$ f.r. $1/1$, which represents the division of the first string by the number 1, and produces the fundamental frequency tuned to C_2; since $1/120 \times 60 = 1/2$, this multiplication of lengths yields l.r. $1/2 \rightarrow$ f.r. $2/1$, which represents the division of the second string by the number 2, and produces an "octave," or C_3; since $1/120 \times 40 = 1/3$, this multiplication of lengths yields l.r. $1/3 \rightarrow$ f.r. $3/1$, which represents the division of the third string by the number 3, and produces "one octave and a fifth," or G_3; since $1/120 \times 30 = 1/4$, this multiplication of lengths yields l.r. $1/4 \rightarrow$ f.r. $4/1$, which represents the division of the fourth string by the number 4, and produces a "double-octave," or C_4; since $1/120 \times 24 = 1/5$, this multiplication of lengths yields l.r. $1/5 \rightarrow$ f.r. $5/1$, which represents the division of the fifth string by the number 5, and produces a "double-octave and a major third," or E_4; since $1/120 \times 20 = 1/6$, this multiplication of lengths yields l.r. $1/6 \rightarrow$ f.r. $6/1$, which represents the division of the sixth string by the number 6, and produces a "double-octave and a fifth," or G_4; finally, since $1/120 \times 15 = 1/8$, this multiplication of lengths yields l.r. $1/8 \rightarrow$ f.r. $8/1$, which represents the division of the seventh string by the number 8, and produces a "triple-octave," or C_5. These multiplications demonstrate that Rameau had full knowledge of the more complicated harmonic progression of fractional length ratios. However, the aesthetic appeal of a simple sequence or "natural order" of integers caused him to favor the arithmetic progression of frequency ratios.

Consistent with Rameau's numerical notation, my interpretation in Figure 10.54 shows all frequency ratios as $1 : n$, where 1 represents the vibration of the open string, and n represents the number of vibrations of the string sections to the *left* of the bridges; and it shows all sequential interval ratios between successive string sections to the *left* of the bridges as $x : n$, where x represents the small number of vibrations of a long string section, and n represents the large number of vibrations of a short string section. For example, with respect to interval ratios, I expressed the "fourth" between the left sections of Strings 3 and 4, or between G_3–C_4, as $4/3 \rightarrow$ 3:4. As discussed in Section 3.14, this constitutes a non-standard notation, because it places an ancient length ratio greater than one ($4 \div 3 = 1.33$) to the left of the arrow, and a frequency ratio less than one ($3 \div 4 = 0.75$) to the right of the arrow. However, to avoid confusion, in the following discussions I will continue to write all frequency ratios and intervals ratios as $^n/_x$. For instance, although Rameau expresses the "fifth" as frequency ratio 2:3, or as interval ratio 2:3, I will notate this musical tone as frequency ratio $^3/_2$, or as interval ratio $^3/_2$. Review Tables 10.4 and 10.21 to verify that I exclusively refer to ratios $^1/_n$ and $^x/_n$ as modern length ratios. As discussed in Sections 10.62–10.64, in his third and fourth treatises — the *Génération harmonique* and *Démonstration du principe de l'harmonie* — Rameau changed his mind and decided to use ratio $^1/_n$ as a *length ratio.*

~ 10.60 ~

With respect to the theory of harmonic generation, Rameau argued in favor of vibration numbers for two reasons. (1) He found the mathematical simplicity of the arithmetic progression 1, 2, 3, 4, 5, 6, 8, immensely appealing. (2) In dealing exclusively with vibration numbers, he attempted to distance himself from Zarlino. However, in his struggles against the famous master, he was unable to dismiss the musical and intellectual appeal of Zarlino's *numero Senario.* Rameau embraced the *Senario* wholeheartedly, and in doing so, emulated most European music theorists who condemned the number 7 as an intolerable dissonance. Rameau describes his first engraving in this manner:

> . . . we shall take seven strings whose [number of] divisions are indicated by numbers. ... We then put the numbers in their natural order beside each string, as in the following demonstration. Each number indicates the equal parts into which the string corresponding to it is divided. Notice that number 7, which cannot give a pleasant interval (as is evident to connoisseurs), has been replaced by number 8; the latter directly follows 7, is twice one of the numbers contained in ***the senario*** {$4 \times 2 = 8$}, and forms a triple octave {ratio 1:8} with 1. This does not increase the quantity of numbers put forth, since 6 and 8 give the same interval as 3 and 4, every number always representing the number that is its half.[315] (Bold italics mine. Text and numbers in braces mine. Text in brackets and parentheses in Gossett's translation.)

Shirlaw observes

> The question is, does harmony arise arbitrarily, or from a fixed and definite principle? Zarlino, Descartes, Rameau, have all contended that harmony does arise from such a principle, which is certainly sufficiently definite, namely, ***the senario*** or series of numbers 1, 2, 3, 4, 5, 6. This principle of the determination of the consonances which are accepted as such by the ear is constant and invariable. The consonances are judged by the ear to be in perfect tune only when they correspond accurately with the acoustical determinations given by this principle.[316] (Bold italics mine.)

Because Rameau rejected all length numbers and length ratios in favor of vibration numbers and vibration ratios, his mathematical descriptions of the major and the minor tonalities are diametrically opposed to Zarlino's descriptions. Recall that in Figure 10.45, Zarlino identifies the minor tonality as an arithmetic progression of length ratios, and the major tonality as a harmonic progression of length ratios. In Book One, Chapter 3, Article V of the *Traité,* Rameau insists on vibration ratios and, thereby, switches the mathematical identities of Zarlino's time-honored definitions.

II

> The sounds which form the thirds and sixths are all contained in the divisions of the undivided string and are consequently generated by the fundamental sound. With regard to intervals, however, only the octave [$2/1$], the fifth [$3/2$], and the major third [$5/4$] are directly generated by the fundamental sound. The minor third [$6/5$] and the [major and minor] sixths [former: $5/3$; latter: $8/5$] are dependent on the fifth and the octave for they arise from the difference between the major third and the fifth [$3/2 \div 5/4 = 6/5$], and between the . . . [minor and major] thirds and the octave [major sixth: $2/1 \div 6/5 = 5/3$; minor sixth: $2/1 \div 5/4 = 8/5$]. This demands some thought, especially with regard to the minor third.
>
> Since all intervals are generated by the octave and begin and end there, so should the minor third. It should not be found indirectly between the major third and the fifth, but related directly to the fundamental sound or its octave. Otherwise this ***[minor] third*** could no longer change its position; it would have to occupy the middle position in chords [as in, C–E–G–C′] and could never occupy their extremities [as in, C–E♭–G–C′, or F–A♭–C–F′]. This would be entirely contrary to experience and to those properties attributed to the ***arithmetic and harmonic proportions;*** i.e., the former divides the fifth (*according to our system*) by the major third below and the minor above, while the latter divides it on the contrary by the minor third below and the major above. There is a ***new type of inversion*** in the order of these thirds, clearly indicating that all the ***diversity of harmony*** is indeed based on inversion.[317] (Italics, bold italics, and text and ratios in brackets mine. Text in parentheses in Gossett's translation.)

In the following passage from Book One, Chapter 7, Rameau describes the frequency ratios of his "new type of inversion":

III

> 20 and 30 divided at 25 give the perfect chord called major, since the fifth is divided by the major third below [as in the arithmetic progression of frequency ratios 20:25:30]; these same numbers divided at 24 give the perfect chord called minor, since the fifth is divided by the minor third below [as in the harmonic progression of frequency ratios 20:24:30].[318] (Text and ratios in brackets mine.)

In Figure 10.44, the arithmetic progression of interval ratios based on vibration numbers — 20:25:30 — defines the major triad C–E–G; and in Figure 10.43, the harmonic progression of interval ratios based on vibration numbers — 20:24:30 — defines the minor triad C–E♭–G. Now, turn to Section 10.39, Quotes I and II, from Ibn Sīnā's *Kitāb al-shifā'*, and to Section 10.40, Quote II, and Section 10.46, Quote IX, from Zarlino's *Istitutioni harmoniche.* Notice that these two theorists were completely aware of the changed position, reversed order, or "inversion" between arithmetically divided intervals and harmonically divided intervals. Furthermore, provided arithmetic mean calculations and harmonic mean calculations are *dimensionally consistent*, Table 10.33 shows, with respect to the "octave" and the "fifth," that divisions based on lengths produce a diametrically opposed distribution of intervals when compared to divisions based on frequencies. (See Section 3.19. Also, see Section 10.62 and Figure 10.55 for discussions on fractional frequency dimensions as shown in Table 10.33.) Music theorists like Stifel and Zarlino intentionally chose length numbers over vibration numbers to maintain historical continuity with *ancient length ratios* as described in Greek and Arabian sources. Contrary to Rameau's opinion, there is nothing "new" about his "inversion." Finally, compare Rameau's statement on "the diversity of harmony" to Zarlino's observations in Section 10.46, Quote VIII. Again, there is very little originality in Rameau's concluding remark.

~ 10.61 ~

In 1726, Rameau published his second treatise *Nouveau système de musique théorique.* Here, Rameau refers directly to the works of Mersenne and Sauveur, and finds in their discoveries of *harmonics* and the *harmonic series* unequivocal scientific corroboration of his theory of harmonic generation. Rameau's elation over this empirical confirmation is so great that he gives his treatise two subtitles: "In which the Principle of all the Rules Necessary for Practice is Discovered," and "In Order to Serve as an Introduction to the *Traité de l'harmonie.*" The heading of Chapter 1 reads, *Observations On The Experiment Which Serves As The Principle Of This System.* The first two paragraphs state

> A ***single string*** causes all the consonances to sound, among which, principally, is distinguished the twelfth [1:3] and the seventeenth [1:5].* Anyone capable of discerning these consonances may be assured of this by plucking one of the lower strings of the clavecin or by bowing one of the larger strings on a violoncello. Thus, we believe we are able to propose this experiment as a fact which will serve us as the principle in order to establish all our conclusions.
>
> The same consonances may be distinguished on the organ in one of the larger *bourdon* pipes. By just blowing into one of these pipes one will hear at least the twelfth [1:3] almost as distinctly as the dominating sound [1:1].
>
> *Pére Mersenne, [*Harmonie universelle*] Bk. 4, *On instruments*, page 209. M. Sauveur, "Système général des intervalles," *Mémoires de l'Académie Royale des Sciences*, pages 299 and 351.[319] (Bold italics and ratios in brackets mine. Title in brackets in Chandler's translation.)

Note Rameau's asterisk in the first paragraph, which accurately indicates his bibliographical sources. Readers unclear why the "twelfth" tone represents the third harmonic, and the "seventeenth" tone represents the fifth harmonic, should turn to Figure 10.48, which shows Mersenne's harmonic-diatonic system of tones.

A few pages later, Rameau generalizes on the natural production of harmonics in strings and pipes:

> Furthermore, as soon as a similar effect is sensed in a *corps sonore* [lit. *sonorous body*], one cannot be kept from attributing it to all sonorous bodies with this single difference, that the effect can be more perceptible in one body than in another.[320] (Text in brackets mine. Italics in Rameau's original text.)

He then characterizes the third and fifth harmonics as *replicas* (in Rameau's texts: *replica* lit. *octave*, or *octave-multiple;* and *replicas* lit. *octaves*, or *octave-multiples*) of the "fifth" and "major third" in the diatonic scale:

> Since the twelfth [$^3/_1$] and major seventeenth [$^5/_1$] are only ***replicas*** of the fifth [$^3/_2 \times {}^2/_1 = {}^3/_1$] and major third [$^5/_4 \times {}^4/_1 = {}^5/_1$], and since, furthermore,

Table 10.33

DIVISIONS OF AN "OCTAVE"

	Integer Dimensions	Fractional Dimensions
Lengths	Arithmetic: C, F, C′ → 4 : 3 : 2	$\frac{1}{3} : \frac{1}{4} : \frac{1}{6}$, or $\frac{4}{12} : \frac{3}{12} : \frac{2}{12}$, based on a string 12 units long
	Harmonic: C, G, C′ → 6 : 4 : 3	$\frac{1}{2} : \frac{1}{3} : \frac{1}{4}$, or $\frac{6}{12} : \frac{4}{12} : \frac{3}{12}$, based on a string 12 units long
Frequencies	Arithmetic: C, G, C′ → 2 : 3 : 4	$\frac{1}{6} : \frac{1}{4} : \frac{1}{3}$, or C_4-260.0 cps, G_4-390.0 cps, C_5-520.0 cps, based on G_6 at 1560.0 cps
	Harmonic: C, F, C′ → 3 : 4 : 6	$\frac{1}{4} : \frac{1}{3} : \frac{1}{2}$, or C_4-260.0 cps, F_4-346.7 cps, C_5-520.0 cps, based on C_6 at 1040.0 cps

DIVISIONS OF A "FIFTH"

	Integer Dimensions	Fractional Dimensions
Lengths	Arithmetic: C, E♭, G → 6 : 5 : 4	$\frac{1}{10} : \frac{1}{12} : \frac{1}{15}$, or $\frac{6}{60} : \frac{5}{60} : \frac{4}{60}$, based on a string 60 units long
	Harmonic: C, E, G → 15 : 12 : 10	$\frac{1}{4} : \frac{1}{5} : \frac{1}{6}$, or $\frac{15}{60} : \frac{12}{60} : \frac{10}{60}$, based on a string 60 units long
Frequencies	Arithmetic: C, E, G → 4 : 5 : 6	$\frac{1}{15} : \frac{1}{12} : \frac{1}{10}$, or C_3-130.0 cps, E_3-162.5 cps, G_3-195.0 cps, based on B_6 at 1950.0 cps
	Harmonic: C, E♭, G → 10 : 12 : 15	$\frac{1}{6} : \frac{1}{5} : \frac{1}{4}$, or C_3-130.0 cps, $E\flat_3$-156.0 cps, G_3-195.0 cps, based on G_5 at 780.0 cps

> the effect of which we have just spoken is equally proper to all, we will cite them alike in similar cases.[321] (Bold italics, and ratios in brackets mine.)

In Chapter 2 of the *Nouveau système*, Rameau addresses the existence of consonances in a single, naturally vibrating string. Before we discuss this paramount phenomenon, recall that in Section 10.54, Quote III, Mersenne was the first acoustician to observe ". . . that there are consonances in ***nature***, as the trumpet teaches us." (Bold italics mine.) Furthermore, Bernard Le Bovier de Fontanelle (1657–1757), secretary of the prestigious *Académie Royale des Sciences* of Paris, and eloquent exponent of Sauveur's work, also noted the existence of musical consonances in nature. Fontanelle's most concise paper on Sauveur is a 3-page essay entitled *Sur l'application des sons harmoniques aux jeux d'orgues*, written in 1702. Of particular interest to this discussion is one short paragraph from this essay, which Mersenne would have comprehended without further elaboration:

> This new consideration of the relationship of sounds is more natural not only because it is only ***the series of numbers that are all multiples of unity***, but also because it conveys and represents all the music and the only music that ***nature*** gives us by itself without the help of art.[322] (Bold italics mine.)

Rameau completely agrees with the latter interpretation and states

IV

> We shall call the lowest and most predominant sound in the single [***natural***] string the *fundamental sound;* it is designated as unity.
>
> It suffices to hear the twelfth and the major seventeenth in the single [***natural***] string in order to conclude that all the consonances are hidden in that string. Those which are not distinguished come from the octaves, which, as we have just stated in the preceding chapter, are perhaps imperceptible.
>
> The octaves 2, 4 and 8 are products of 1, and the octave 6 is a product of 3, etc., from which we have 1, 2, 3, 4, 5, 6, 8. From these numbers come all the consonances that exist fundamentally in the numbers 1, 3, 5, or, in other words, in the consonances corresponding to these three numbers.[323] (Bold italics in brackets mine.)

He then establishes a general hierarchy of consonances,

V

> It is easy to determine now that the fifth [2:3] and the major third [4:5] recognized in the three numbers 1, 3, 5 are the first of all the consonances. We shall refer to these consonances as being *first* and *direct* in that they are ***directly related to the fundamental sound 1***.[324] (Bold italics mine.)

and gives an exact mathematical description of the most important consonances:

> We cite the fundamental sound at 1, 2, and 4 in order to show that it reposes, so to say, on its octave at each generation. From its first octave, 2, it passes to its fifth, 3, and from there it passes to its second octave, 4, in order to arrive at its third, 5. This operation ought to indicate to us that the fifth 2:3 and the third 4:5 are equal to the twelfth 1:3 and the seventeenth 1:5, ***disregarding the difference in octaves or replicas***.[325] (Bold italics mine.)

This explains Rameau's shorthand notation 1:3:5, which he used throughout his treatises to express the major triad 20:25:30, in least terms, 4:5:6.[326]

During Rameau's time, all musicians agreed that the "minor third," or minor tonality, has the same musical importance as the "major third," or major tonality. However, given Rameau's "new" theories based not only on vibration numbers, but also on the natural phenomenon called a *harmonic series*, Rameau was hard-pressed to find empirical evidence that would prove that the minor perfect chord 20:24:30 — in least terms, 10:12:15 — has the same natural origins as the major perfect chord 4:5:6. Despite all his ideas and observations, Rameau knew that the "minor third" was *not* directly related to the fundamental sound 1, but to the first replica of the fifth harmonic, or to the tenth harmonic, simply because $5 \times 2 = 10$.[327] Nevertheless, this did not prevent him from rationalizing the "minor third" as a naturally occurring consonance.

> Although we will hear only the major third in a single string (not considering the octave and the fifth), the minor third subsists, nevertheless, in a new comparison which must be made between this major third and the fifth. As a result we may still call this [minor] third consonance *first* and *direct*, ***not that it is directly related to the fundamental sound 1***, but because it can relate to a new combination of the chord . . .[328] (Bold italics, and text in brackets mine. Italics and text in parentheses in Chandler's translation.)

> Since the fifth is the most perfect of all consonances, not to mention the octave, and since it may be composed of a major third and a minor third, the order of these thirds must be immaterial. At least it is thus that the ear decides it, and no further proof is necessary.[329]

In other words, since a "fifth" consists of a "major third" and a "minor third," and since one may freely switch the positions of these two "thirds," and, thereby, relate them sequentially to the fundamental, Rameau argued that the minor triad $\frac{1}{1}$–$\frac{6}{5}$–$\frac{3}{2}$ represents the same kind of a "natural" consonance as the major triad $\frac{1}{1}$–$\frac{5}{4}$–$\frac{3}{2}$. Of course, Rameau had no mathematical or empirical proof for this assertion, and so relied on his ear as the final arbiter of this theory. A few pages later in the *Nouveau système*, Rameau reiterates his description in the *Traité* (see Section 10.60, Quotes II and III), which identifies the major perfect chord as an arithmetic progression of frequency ratios:

VI

> . . . the continued arithmetic progression 1:3:5, which we ought at the same time to call harmonic [as in ancient length ratios 15:5:3], gives the most perfect of all chords . . .[330] (Text in brackets mine.)

For a second perspective on the difficulties presented by the minor tonality, consider the following prime number analysis. The "octave," ratio $\frac{2}{1}$, which has prime number 2 in the numerator, is directly related to the fundamental because it is a replica of number 1 in the denominator; in the harmonic series, the former number [2] represents an interval directly above the latter number [1]. Similarly, the "fifth," ratio $\frac{3}{2}$, which has prime number 3 in the numerator, is also directly related to the fundamental because number 2 in the denominator is a replica of the fundamental; in the harmonic series, the former number [3] represents an interval directly above the latter number [2]. Finally, the "major third," ratio $\frac{5}{4}$, which has prime number 5 in the numerator, is also directly related to the fundamental because number 4 in the denominator is a replica of the fundamental; in the harmonic series, the former number [5] represents an interval directly above the latter number [4]. However, the "minor third," ratio $\frac{6}{5}$, which has composite number 6 in the numerator, is *not* directly related to the fundamental because prime number 5 in the denominator is *not* a replica of the fundamental; consequently, in the harmonic series, the former number [6] represents an interval directly above the latter number [5]. Now, with respect to the first three ratios: $^2\!/_1$, $^3\!/_2$, $^5\!/_4$, turn back to Section 9.7, and recall that we may express the latter denominators as a geometric progression where the *common ratio* between terms is prime number 2, as in 2^0, 2^1, 2^2, 2^3, 2^4, . . . or integers 1, 2, 4, 8, 16, . . . Since by definition it is impossible to generate prime number 5 through powers of prime number 2, we conclude that in the harmonic series, the "minor third" will *never* produce a consonant interval directly above the fundamental, or above a replica of the fundamental. In this sense, ratios $^2\!/_1$, $^3\!/_2$, and $^5\!/_4$ are unique because they alone represent such consonances in nature.

10.62

In 1737, Rameau published his third treatise, *Génération harmonique.* Here he reluctantly acknowledges that Zarlino correctly derived the harmonic division of intervals based on *ancient length ratios*,[331] and for the first time uses *modern length ratios* to describe how strings naturally subdivide into shorter loops. In Chapter I, Rameau recounts various experiments designed to demonstrate the inverse proportionality between length ratios and frequency ratios.

> *Experiment 3.* Bow one of the larger strings of a viol or violoncello. You will hear, along with the sound of the whole string, the sounds of its octave [1:2], its double octave [1:4], even perhaps its triple octave [1:8], its twelfth [1:3], and its major seventeenth [1:5], which are in the ratios of 1 : $^1\!/_2$: $^1\!/_3$: $^1\!/_4$: $^1\!/_5$: $^1\!/_8$ . . . You could also hear the sound of $^1\!/_7$ of the string, if not more, but this sound will be so weak that it will doubtless escape you. We have indeed distinguished it, but without being able to perceive its pitch in relation to any other sounds. And, to hear it, we had to take $^1\!/_7$ of the string separately . . . Thus, the sound of this $^1\!/_7$ appears only as a ***lost sound***, so weak that it could not conceivably be heard if it were not pointed out . . .[332] (Bold italics and ratios in brackets mine.)

Rameau's characterization of the seventh harmonic as a "lost sound" is, of course, nothing but an intellectual ploy designed to dismiss all prime numbers not contained in Zarlino's 5-limit *Senario.* Note that in Section 10.61, Quote IV, Rameau also described the near imperceptibility of the "octave," but did not degrade its musical importance simply because as a harmonic it sounds "weak."

Rameau then gives an acoustic explanation of the major tonality based on modern length ratios.

> All these Experiments [on strings and organ pipes] . . . confirm . . . not only that sound needs the resonance of a certain number of its aliquot parts to be appreciable in pitch, but also that this number is fixed in the $^1\!/_3$, $^1\!/_5$, not to mention the octaves giving the $^1\!/_2$, $^1\!/_4$, etc. Our daily experience, in the form of the chord called the ***perfect or natural chord***, which is correctly composed of three different sounds,
>
> | *ut* | *sol* | *mi* |
> |---|---|---|
> | 1 | $^1\!/_3$ | $^1\!/_5$ |
> | [C] | [G] | [E] |
>
> should top everything, since this is the chord which affects us most pleasantly . . .[333] (Bold italics, and text and note names in brackets mine.)

> This proportion, $1 : \frac{1}{3} : \frac{1}{5}$, is just what has been recognized from all times, under the title of *trias harmonica*, or "harmonic proportion."[334]

He then simplifies the harmonic proportion to form the major perfect chord.

VII

> Instead of $1 : \frac{1}{3} : \frac{1}{5}$, we get, by taking 1 and $\frac{1}{3}$ to their octaves, $\frac{1}{4}$ and $\frac{1}{6}$, the proportion $\frac{1}{4} : \frac{1}{5} : \frac{1}{6}$; now everything is reduced to its smallest degrees, and, at the same time, contained within the range of the octave, $\frac{1}{4} : \frac{1}{8}$. See Example I.[335]

I.

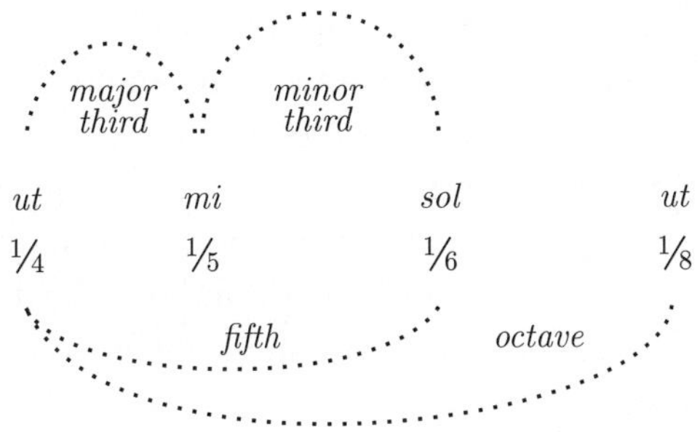

We conclude, therefore, that in Example I of the *Génération harmonique*, Rameau reversed his earlier mathematical definition of the major tonality in music. In the *Traité* (see Section 10.60, Quotes II and III), and in the *Nouveau système* (see Section 10.61, Quote VI), he identified the major tonality as an arithmetic progression of frequency ratios. Now, however, Rameau withdraws his insistence on frequency ratios, and although he uses modern length ratios instead of ancient length ratios, he follows Zarlino's example and identifies the major tonality as a harmonic progression of length ratios. To understand Rameau's description in Quote VII, refer to Figure 10.55(a). The upper portion of this illustration shows the first, third, and fifth modes of vibration of a flexible string. Since the fundamental mode is tuned to C_2 at 65.0 cps, the third mode sounds G_3 at 195.0 cps, and the fifth mode, E_4 at 325.0 cps. We may notate this sequence of tones as a harmonic progression of modern length ratios $\frac{1}{1} : \frac{1}{3} : \frac{1}{5}$. (See Figure 3.14.) Furthermore, notice two horizontal arrows in Figure 10.55(a), which indicate that by substituting the *second replica* of C_2 — namely, C_4 — and the *first replica* of G_3 — namely, G_4 — Rameau simplified $\frac{1}{1} : \frac{1}{3} : \frac{1}{5}$ and expressed the *major tonality as a harmonic progression of modern length ratios* $\frac{1}{4} : \frac{1}{5} : \frac{1}{6}$. Consequently, modern length ratios $\frac{1}{4} : \frac{1}{5} : \frac{1}{6}$ represent the fourth, fifth, and sixth harmonics, or the major triad C_4–E_4–G_4. Finally, observe that an inversion of the latter sequence identifies the *major tonality as an arithmetic progression of frequency ratios* $\frac{4}{1} : \frac{5}{1} : \frac{6}{1}$. Because Rameau heard the "tonic" C_4 as the second replica of the first harmonic C_2, he demonstrated that the major perfect chord is directly related to the fundamental sound 1. Since the fundamental sound provides the tonic of the major perfect chord, Rameau referred to the first harmonic as the *generator*, or the generating tone.[336]

Unfortunately, Rameau's acoustic explanation of the minor tonality based on length ratios is neither simple nor correct.

> *Experiment 2.* Take a viol or violoncello. Tune two of its strings a twelfth apart. Bow the lower [and slower] string. You will see the higher [and faster] string vibrate, and maybe even hear it; you will hear it without fail if you touch it with your fingernail while it is vibrating. Then bow the

> higher [and faster] string. [**1**] You will not only see the lower [and slower] one vibrate ***as a whole***, [**2**] but you will also see it divide itself into three equal parts, forming three loops of vibrations between two nodes or fixed points.[337] (Bold italics, and text and numbers in brackets mine.)

Here Rameau erroneously assumes that a sonorous body — an open string — generates not only higher and faster vibrations *above* its fundamental frequency, but also lower and slower vibrations *below* its fundamental frequency. With respect to Condition 1, refer to Figure 10.55(b). Suppose we have two open strings: the short high string is tuned to C_6 at 1040.0 cps, and the long low string is tuned to "one octave and a fifth" below, or F_4 at 346.7 cps. According to Rameau's text, the C_6 string produces not only a harmonic series that generates an ascending third harmonic, or a tone that sounds "one octave and a fifth" *above* C_6; it also produces a so-called *subharmonic series* that generates a descending third harmonic, or a tone that sounds "one octave and a fifth" *below* C_6. Based on this theory, Rameau claims that if we play the C_6 string, it would cause the F_4 string to vibrate "as a whole." Note carefully: Condition 1 of "Experiment 2" is false. Sympathetic resonance between two different vibrating systems occurs only when both systems have one or more frequencies in common. In this case, the C_6 string cannot induce the F_4 string to vibrate "as a whole" simply because the C_6 does *not* generate a harmonic frequency at 346.7 cps. However, with respect to Condition 2, Rameau is correct: the C_6 does induce the F_4 string to subdivide into three loops, which causes the F_4 to sound its third harmonic, namely, C_6. To experience the latter phenomenon, go to a piano, and gently depress the F_4 key without making a sound; this action lifts the felt damper off the strings. Now, quickly strike the C_6 key. Although the C_6 strings are no longer vibrating, the tone of C_6 at 1040.0 cps continues to sound because the C_6 strings caused the third harmonic of the F_4 strings to vibrate in sympathetic resonance.

Rameau reverted to length ratios and invented the so-called *subharmonic series* for only one reason. He attempted to directly relate the minor tonality to the fundamental sound 1. Had Rameau succeeded in establishing such a direct relation, his demonstration would have established the existence of the minor tonality in *nature*. That is, if it were possible for a short high string with a length of 1 unit to induce a low long string with a length of 3 units, and an even lower and longer string with a length of 5 units, to vibrate as a whole, then the vibrations from these three strings would have produced the tones of a minor triad. Under such bizarre conditions, the question arises, "What is the fundamental frequency of the short high string?" The answer is that the short high string has no fundamental frequency! Figure 10.55(b) shows that in generating a *subharmonic series*, the short high string would have to undergo a theoretically infinite series of elongations to produce the low frequencies. In other words, the C_6 string at 1040.0 cps would have to triple its length to produce F_4 at 346.7 cps, or a tone $1/3$ the frequency of the generating tone $1/1$; and it would have to quintuple its length to produce $A\flat_3$ at 208.0 cps, or a tone $1/5$ the frequency of the generating tone $1/1$. Since length ratio $1/3$ represents a tone "one octave and a fifth" above $1/1$, length ratio $3/1$ represents a tone "one octave and a fifth" below $1/1$; similarly, since length ratio $1/5$ represents a tone "two octaves and a major third" above $1/1$, length ratio $5/1$ represents a tone "two octaves a major third" below $1/1$. In the next passage, Rameau refers to the natural subdivisions of vibrating strings as "sub-multiples," and to his synthetic elongations as "multiples":

> As soon as the octave is known, the octave of this octave can be imagined, as well as the octave of the fifth and of the third. Then, as the [ascending length] ratio of the octave is 1 : $1/2$, or [its descending length ratio is] 1:2, that of the [ascending length ratio of the] fifth [is] 1 : $1/3$, or [its descending length ratio is] 1:3, and that of the [ascending length ratio of the] major third [is] 1 : $1/5$, or [its descending length ratio is] 1:5, the idea immediately

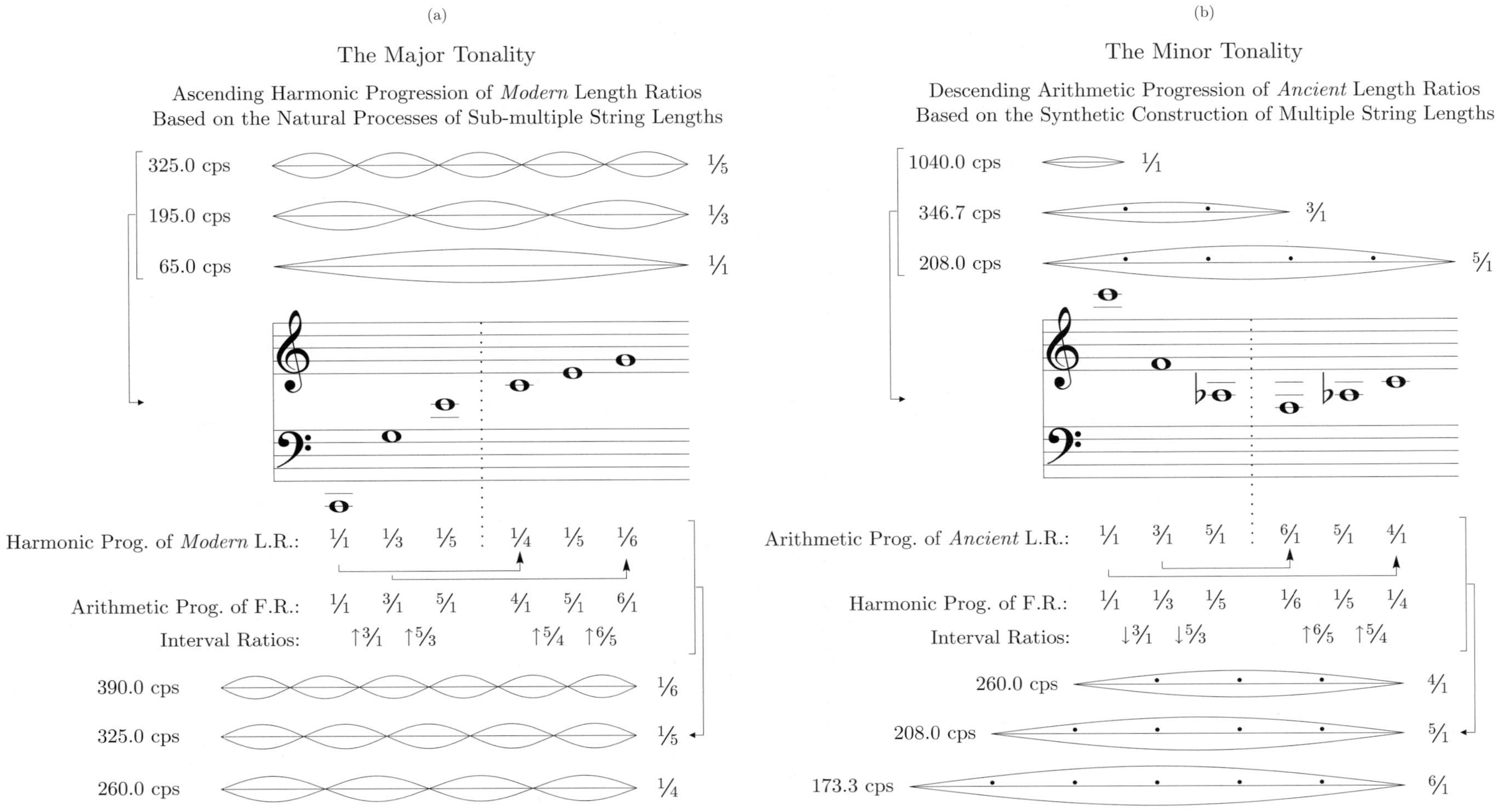

Figure 10.55 The origins of the major and minor tonalities according to Rameau (1737). (a) The major tonality originates in the harmonic progression of *modern* length ratios. Here length ratio $1/3$ represents the harmonic mean between length ratios $1/1$ and $1/5$; and $1/5$, between $1/4$ and $1/6$. Such length ratios produce an ascending sequence of frequency ratios. (b) The minor tonality originates in the arithmetic progression of *ancient* length ratios. Here length ratio $3/1$ represents the arithmetic mean between length ratios $1/1$ and $5/1$; and $5/1$, between $6/1$ and $4/1$. Such length ratios produce a descending sequence of frequency ratios. The major tonality is based on the natural processes of a subdividing string; Rameau referred to these subdivisions as "sub-multiples." In contrast, the minor tonality is based on the synthetic construction of a string with increasing lengths; Rameau referred to these elongations as "multiples."

> springs to mind of numerical progressions that are sub-double [$\frac{1}{2}$ the length] or double [2 times the length], sub-triple [$\frac{1}{3}$ the length] or triple [3 times the length], and sub-quintuple [$\frac{1}{5}$ the length] or quintuple [5 times the length].
>
> We are permitted the relation between the ***multiples*** [length ratios 1:3:5] and ***sub-multiples*** [length ratios $1 : \frac{1}{3} : \frac{1}{5}$] of unity to remain arbitrary for now, for they depend on each other . . . The one comes from the arithmetic proportion [i.e., the minor tonality comes from length ratios 1:3:5], and the other from the harmonic proportion [i.e., the major tonality comes from length ratios $1 : \frac{1}{3} : \frac{1}{5}$].[338] (Bold italics, and text and ratios in brackets mine.)

Rameau illustrated the relation between his string length "multiples" and the minor tonality in Example II.[339]

II.

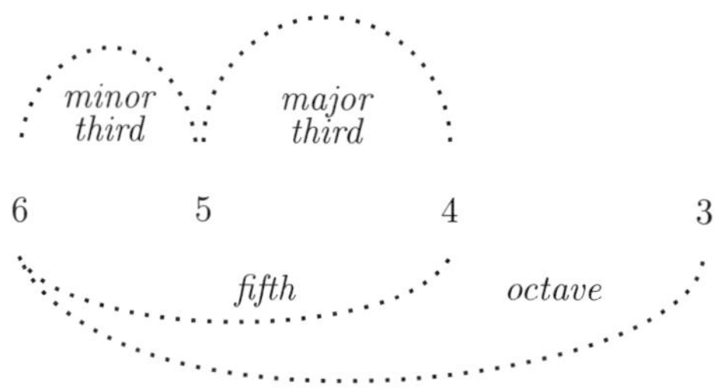

To comprehend this illustration, refer again to Figure 10.55(b). Notice two horizontal arrows, which indicate that by substituting the *second replica below* C_6 — namely, C_4 — and the *first replica below* F_4 — namely, F_3 — Rameau simplified $\frac{1}{1} : \frac{3}{1} : \frac{5}{1}$ and expressed the *minor tonality as an arithmetic progression of ancient length ratios* $\frac{6}{1} : \frac{5}{1} : \frac{4}{1}$. Consequently, ancient length ratios $\frac{6}{1} : \frac{5}{1} : \frac{4}{1}$ represent the minor triad F_3–$A\flat_3$–C_4. Now, observe that an inversion of the latter sequence identifies the *minor tonality as a harmonic progression of frequency ratios* $\frac{1}{6} : \frac{1}{5} : \frac{1}{4}$. Finally, since a *subharmonic series* does not exist, Condition 1 of "Experiment 2" produces *no* audible sympathetic resonances from the long low strings. Rameau conceded this fact when he acknowledged

> And consequently, because the faster vibrations agitate the slower vibrations but weakly, they cannot give the body which is receiving the slower vibrations sufficient agitation for the sound to be transmitted to the ear.[340]

≈ 10.63 ≈

Turn now to Figures 10.56(a) and 10.56(b), which show C_4 as the *dual-generator* of six natural ascending harmonics, and six synthetic descending so-called *subharmonics.* In Figure 10.56(a), the second replica above C_4 — namely, C_6 — represents both the generator and the lowest tone of the ascending major triad C_6–E_6–G_6. In contrast, observe that in Figure 10.56(b), the second replica below C_4 — namely, C_2 — represents the generator but *not* the lowest tone of the descending minor triad C_2–$A\flat_1$–F_1. Therefore, although we hear the generator C_6 as the tonic of the major chord, we do not hear the generator C_2 as the tonic of the minor chord. This dichotomy between the acoustic *generator* (C_2) and the musical *fundamental* (F_1) of the minor chord caused Rameau considerable consternation, and required him to make the following decision:

VIII

> Since the low, predominant sound of a sonorous body is always fundamental for the ear, it must be supposed, first, that this is true in the arithmetic proportion [or in the minor tonality expressed as ancient length ratios $\frac{6}{1}$: $\frac{5}{1}$: $\frac{4}{1}$]. But the fundamental is ***not*** that low sound [or C_2] ***which gives*** the arithmetic proportion, by the reciprocal power of slower and faster vibrations . . . ; rather the fundamental is the lowest sound [or F_1] ***occurring in*** the [arithmetic] proportion.[341] (Bold italics, and text in brackets mine.)

In other words, Rameau admitted that the generator and the fundamental of the minor triad are two different tones.

In the *Génération harmonique*, Rameau attempted to present *ut* (or C) as the dual-generator of an ascending major harmony, and of a descending minor harmony. If we simplify "octave" equivalents

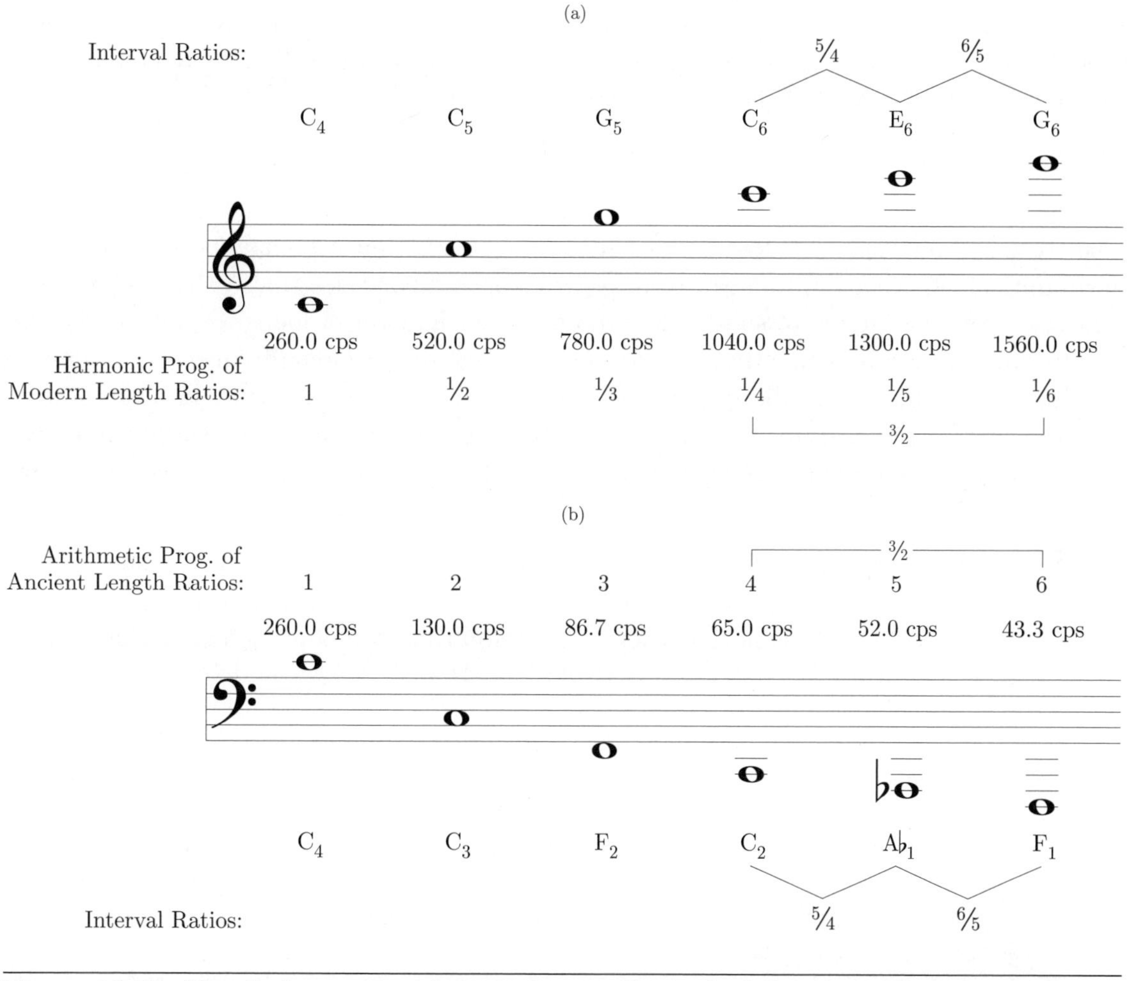

Figure 10.56 The *dual-generator* of the major tonality and of the minor tonality according to Rameau (1737). (a) In the top staff, C_4 acts as the generator of the ascending major triad C_6–E_6–G_6. (b) In the bottom staff, C_4 acts as the generator of the descending minor triad C_2–$A\flat_1$–F_1. In the *Génération harmonique*, Rameau admitted that whereas the replica C_6 functions both as the generator and as the fundamental of the major triad, the replica C_2 functions only as the generator of the minor triad. In the minor chord F_1–$A\flat_1$–C_2, the fundamental (or lowest tone) is not the generator, but F_1. The absence of sound in Condition 1 of "Experiment 2," and this inconsistency with respect to the musical functionality of the generator, caused Rameau insurmountable difficulties in explaining the acoustic origins of the minor tonality in nature.

in Figures 10.55 and 10.56, the illustration below shows C_5 as the generator of the ascending major triad C_5–E_5–G_5, and of the descending minor triad C_5–$A\flat_4$–F_4:

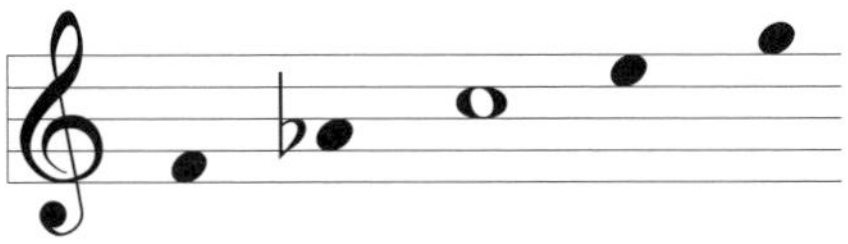

Rameau found the idea of an acoustic dual-generator that produces the major tonality and minor tonality in opposite directions immensely appealing. It represented not only acoustic and musical perfection, but also a clear departure from Zarlino's unidirectional and strictly mathematical approach; as discussed in Section 10.46, Zarlino constructed both the major triad and the minor triad in an ascending direction. Unfortunately, Rameau knew that his theory was flawed. (1) The absence of sound in Condition 1 of "Experiment 2" proves that a string tuned to a relatively high (or fast) frequency cannot "generate" sympathetic vibrations in the fundamental of a string tuned to a relatively low (or slow) frequency. (2) In the previous illustration, C_5 fails to convince the ear that it functions as the tonic of the minor chord.

~ 10.64 ~

In 1750, Rameau published his fourth treatise *Démonstration du principe de l'harmonie.*[342] Near the beginning of this treatise, Rameau recants his error and concedes that a short high string can only induce a long low string to subdivide into an integer number of loops. Consequently, the low string can only vibrate in sympathetic resonance if one of its harmonic frequencies is identical to the fundamental frequency of the high string. Despite this acknowledgment, Rameau states that because the short high generator has the "power" to induce vibrations in strings tuned a 12th and a 17th below the generator, the acoustic explanation of the minor tonality stands as described in the *Génération harmonique.*

> If other sonorous bodies, which are in the same ratio to the source [*principe*] as the [harmonic] sounds that it produces, are tuned with this source [*principe*] — such as not only its ⅓ [i.e., twelfth above] and ⅕ [i.e., major seventeenth above] but also its triple [i.e., twelfth below] and quintuple [i.e., major seventeenth below] — it will make them all vibrate, with the following difference: the former {the ***sub-multiples***, or modern length ratios ⅓ and ⅕} will vibrate in their totality whereas the source [*principe*] will force the latter {the ***multiples***, or ancient length ratios 3⁄1 and 5⁄1} to divide themselves into all the partials {***loops***} which form a unison with the source. Thus, in this case, it has the same power on its multiples as it has on its submultiples. These experiments are equally perceptible to the ear, to the eye, and to the touch.
>
> From this last power of the source [*principe*] on its multiples arise these ratios:

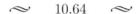

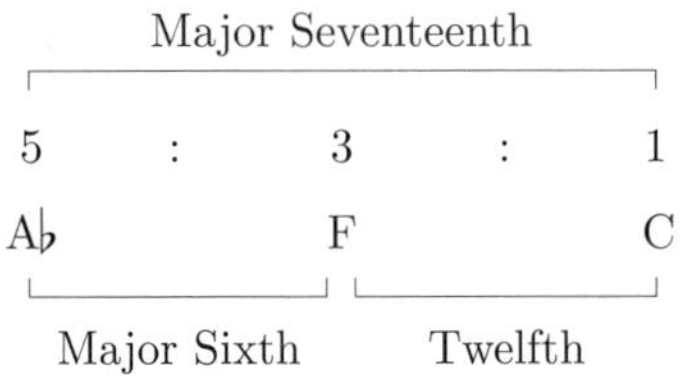

which, reduced to their smallest intervals and applied to [string] lengths give:

Fifth

6 : 5 : 4

F A♭ C

Minor Third Major Third

In 1, $\frac{1}{3}$ and $\frac{1}{5}$, or:

Fifth

$\frac{1}{4}$: $\frac{1}{5}$: $\frac{1}{6}$

Major Third Minor Third

is recognized the *harmonic proportion.* And in 5, 3, 1, or:

Fifth

6 : 5 : 4

Minor Third Major Third

the *arithmetic proportion* is identified.[343] (Text in braces mine. Italics and text in brackets in Briscoe's translation.)

Then, halfway through the *Démonstration*, in a chapter entitled *On the Minor Mode*, Rameau suddenly realizes that he *cannot* rationalize the minor triad, or the arithmetic progression of ancient length ratios 6:5:4, according to natural phenomena.

> The source [principe] C, which directly produces the *major mode* through the pure and simple operation of nature, at the same time ***indicates*** to art the means of forming a *minor mode* from it.
>
> This difference, between nature's own work and that which it is content to ***indicate***, is indeed well delineated, in that there is the resonance of the major genre [inherent] in the sonorous body of C, whereas [for the *minor genre*] there is only ***a simple vibration*** through the effect of [the sonorous body's] power on foreign bodies capable of giving the minor genre, as has been seen in the way that the arithmetic proportion is formed.[344] (Bold italics mine. Italics and text in brackets in Briscoe's translation.)

He assigns nature the passive role of a mere indicator because

> Only the direct major third resounds with the fundamental sound, which is, consequently, the cause of its effect. Consequently still, the fundamental can no longer be the cause of a direct minor third which we suppose it to be. It will, therefore, be necessarily from this same minor third that the difference of the effect between it and the major third will arise.[345]

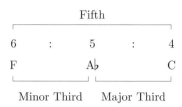

Rameau concludes that because of the latter difference, the *minor third below C* — the tone *A* — is the new fundamental sound of the minor triad. This is an extremely important development in the history of Western music. To this day students of traditional harmony learn that the key of A-minor is the relative minor of C-major. However, we will not pursue Rameau's theories beyond this point.[346] Instead, let us now refocus on the subject of just intonation. In preparation for such a discussion, consider Shirlaw's highly relevant observation:

> But when it is discovered that the same proportions which, applied to a sonorous body, or several sonorous bodies, produce the major harmony, produce also in inverted order the minor harmony, we are presented with a fact which may not only be of service to a maker of musical instruments, but which may and does influence, to a very considerable extent, the whole theory of harmony. In so far as the question is one of proportion, ***the minor harmony must be regarded as an inverted major harmony.***[347] (Bold italics mine.)

∼ 10.65 ∼

In 1929, one hundred and seventy-nine years after the appearance of Rameau's *Démonstration*, Max F. Meyer (1873–1967) published a volume entitled *The Musician's Arithmetic.*[348] Meyer wrote this book as a primer in mathematics for music students.

> The great practical problem for the student of "a musician's arithmetic" consists in *learning to talk of ratios* whose terms contain the prime numbers 1, 3, 5, and 7 . . . as factors, in the numerators and denominators of the fractions expressing the ratios. ("2" is omitted from the list of prime numbers because . . . in "discovering the octave" we have dispossessed ourselves of all even numbers; "11" is omitted because a prime number as large as that is unlikely to be needed, but whoever wants an intellectual chastisement may put it back.)
>
> The student cannot talk intelligently of ratios unless they mean something to his ear. Unfortunately he has never met a teacher (have you met one?) capable of training him to connect melodic phrases with ratios of numbers.[349]

Throughout his text, Meyer is extremely critical of Rameau's theories. He finds Rameau's conclusion ". . . that there are only two modes, the major and the minor . . ."[350] particularly offensive and damaging to the future development of music.

> Rameau's mistake in substituting two modes for the ancient seven modes was an error of over-emphasis . . . His mistake has resulted in denying to the composer the freedom of further inventions, and has thus hampered musical progress.[351]

Despite such criticisms, there are many indications that Rameau had a considerable influence on Meyer's understanding of musical mathematics. For example, Meyer's highly original illustration on p. 22 of his book shows a mathematical and musical structure that would have been unthinkable without knowledge of Rameau's *Génération harmonique.* Figure 10.57(a) is an exact copy of Meyer's illustration. Notice immediately that this figure is remarkably similar to Al-Jurjānī's triangular table in *La Musique Arabe, Volume 3,* p. 230, and to Salinas' triangular table in Figure 10.46. All three figures consist of diamond-shaped tiles organized into a two-dimensional pattern of just intoned ratios. In Meyer's figure, evidence of just ratios is not immediately apparent because with the exception of integers 1, 3, 5, 7, all other numbers represent cent values. However, the ratio

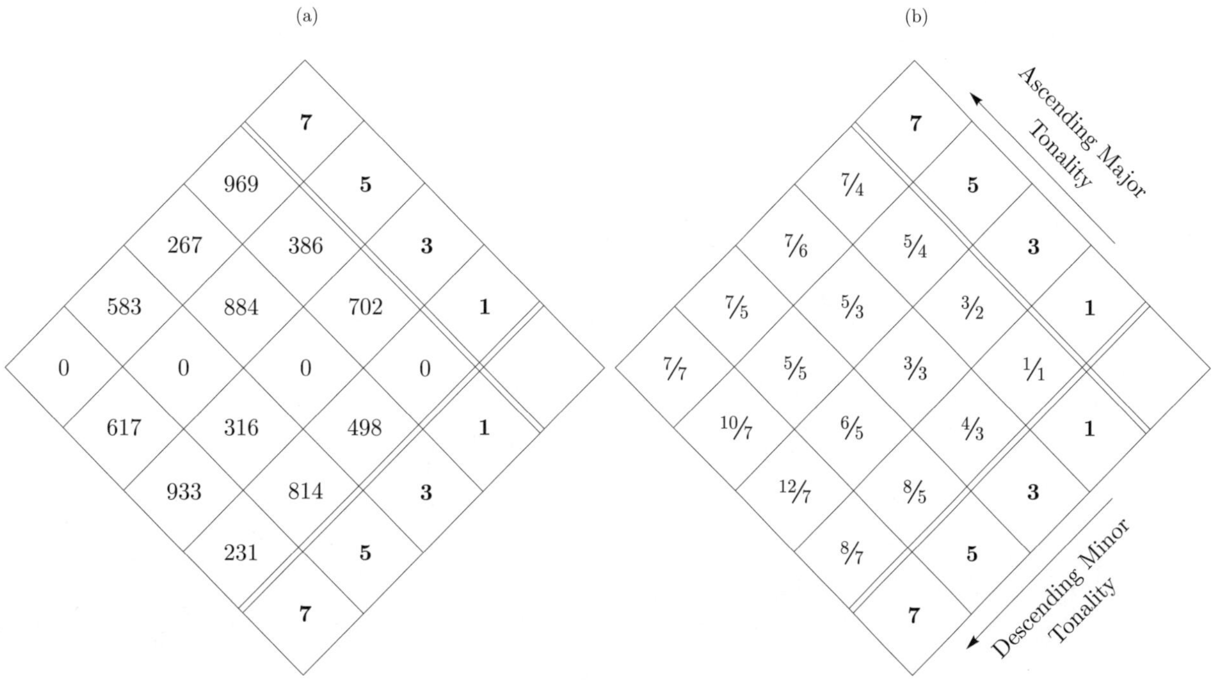

Figure 10.57 Meyer's 7-limit Tonality Diamond. (a) This is an exact copy of Meyer's original diamond-shaped lattice. The numbers enclosed by the double lines represent cent values. (b) A ratio analysis of these cent values reveals four ascending major tonalities, and four descending minor tonalities.

analysis in Figure 10.57(b) reveals that these cent values indicate four ascending major tonalities, and four descending minor tonalities.

As was the custom for Rameau (see Section 10.61, Quotes IV and V), so Meyer also used a shorthand notation that consisted of integers. For example, integers 1–3–5–7 represent frequency ratios 1/1, 3/2, 5/4, 7/4, respectively. Furthermore, Meyer expressly stated that ". . . a *dash* between two numbers will always mean an interval — or 'span,' as we call it, — between the two tones represented by the two numbers."[352] Although such an ordered sequence of integers is numerically appealing, it does not express a graduated progression of intervals: here a large "fifth," ratio 3/2, is followed by a small "major third," ratio 5/4, which in turn is followed by an even larger "minor seventh," ratio 7/4. Therefore, I decided to reverse the order of prime numbers 3 and 5, resulting in the sequence 1–5–3–7. Figure 10.58(a) shows that without changing the contents of the diagonals, every tetrad now expresses the graduated sequence "tonic," "major third," "fifth," "minor seventh." To help clarify these ascending and descending relations, Figure 10.58(b) gives the approximate note names of Meyer's tonality diamond based on a "tonic," ratio 1/1, tuned to middle C, or C_4. We may arrange the thirteen unique frequency ratios of Meyer's 7-limit Tonality Diamond — plus the "octave," ratio 2/1 — into the following scale, which contains three kinds of "thirds," two kinds of "tritones," and three kinds of "sixths":

1/1, 8/7, [7/6][6/5][5/4], 4/3, [7/5][10/7], 3/2, [8/5][5/3][12/7], 7/4, 2/1

The musical organization of Meyer's tonality diamond is based on Rameau's theory of a *dual-generator*. In other words, in Figure 10.58, pitch C_4 generates the first ascending major tonality C_4–E_4–G_4–$B\flat_4$, expressed as ratios 1/1–5/4–3/2–7/4, and pitch C_4 generates the first descending minor tonality ↓C_4–$A\flat_3$–F_3–D_3, expressed as ratios ↓1/1–8/5–4/3–8/7. Turn now to Table 10.34, which lists

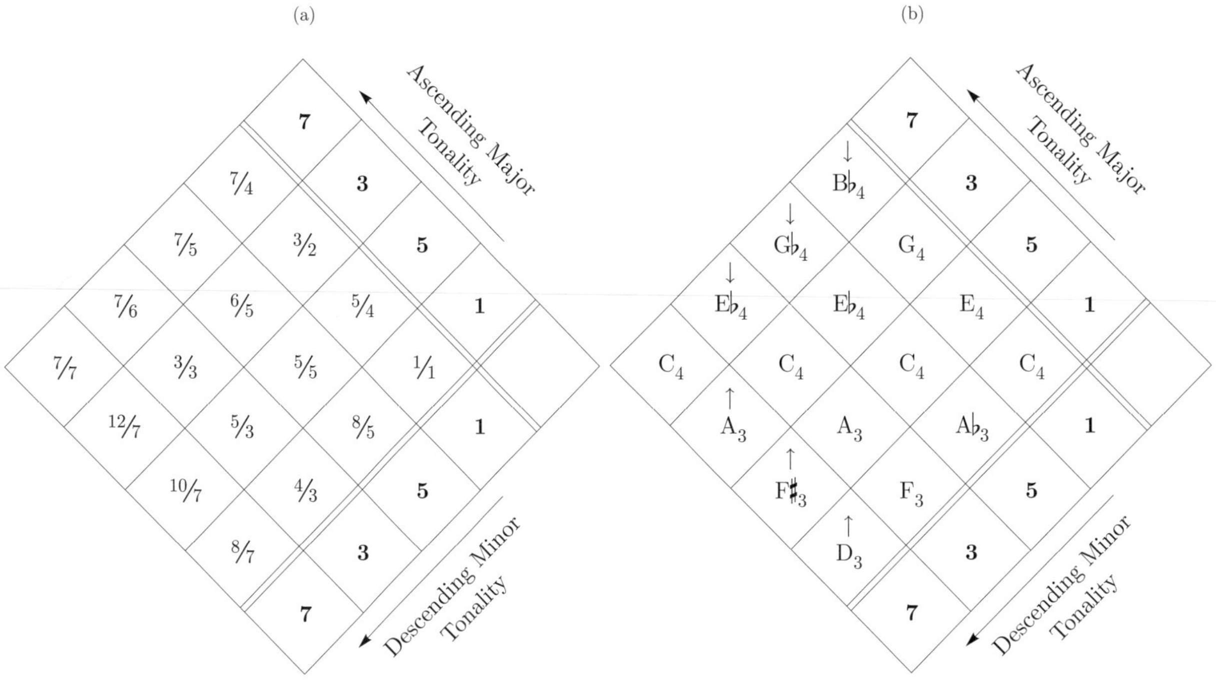

Figure 10.58 Meyer's 7-limit Tonality Diamond revised. (a) Compared to Figure 10.57(b), the locations of bold-faced prime numbers 3 and 5 are here reversed. This change organizes every tetrad into a graduated sequence of tones, as in 1/1–5/4–3/2–7/4 for the first ascending major tonality, and ↓1/1–8/5–4/3–8/7 for the first descending minor tonality. (b) To help clarify the latter organization of ratios, this figure gives the approximate note names of Meyer's tonality diamond based on a "tonic," ratio 1/1 tuned to middle C, or C_4. As in Figure 3.12, arrows pointing upward or downward indicate tones that sound considerably higher or lower than the tones of the conventional piano scale tuned in 12-tone equal temperament.

the exact ratios and approximate note names of Meyer's 7-limit Tonality Diamond. Here the left column lists four ascending diagonals that constitute four ascending major tonalitites, and the right column, four descending diagonals that constitute four descending minor tonalitites. Observe that since the first interval of the first ascending diagonal consists of an ascending "major third," $1/1 \times 5/4 = 5/4$, or interval C_4–E_4, the first interval of the first descending diagonal sounds a descending "major third," $2/1 \div 5/4 = 8/5$, or interval ↓C_4–$A\flat_3$. Consequently, the latter pitch $A\flat_3$, ratio 8/5, acts as the first tone of the second ascending major tonality $A\flat_3$–C_4–$E\flat_4$–$G\flat_4$. Similarly, since the second interval of the first ascending diagonal consists of an ascending "fifth," $1/1 \times 3/2 = 3/2$, or interval C_4–G_4, the second interval of the first descending diagonal sounds a descending "fifth," $2/1 \div 3/2 = 4/3$, or interval ↓C_4–F_3. Consequently, the latter pitch F_3, ratio 4/3, acts as the first tone of the third ascending major tonality F_3–A_3–C_4–$E\flat_4$. Finally, since the third interval of the first ascending diagonal consists of an ascending "minor seventh," $1/1 \times 7/4 = 7/4$, or interval C_4–$B\flat_4$, the third interval of the first descending diagonal sounds a descending "minor seventh," $2/1 \div 7/4 = 8/7$, or interval ↓C_4–D_3. Consequently, the latter pitch D_3, ratio 8/7, acts as the first tone of the fourth ascending major tonality D_3–$F\sharp_3$–A_3–C_4.

With respect to the second column in Table 10.34, observe that E_4, or the "major third" of the first ascending diagonal, acts as the first tone of the second descending minor tonality ↓E_4–C_4–A_3–$F\sharp_3$; similarly, G_4, or the "fifth" of the first ascending diagonal, acts as the first tone of the third descending minor tonality ↓G_4–$E\flat_4$–C_4–A_3; and finally, $B\flat_4$, or the "minor seventh" of the first ascending diagonal, acts as the first tone of the fourth descending minor tonality ↓$B\flat_4$–$G\flat_4$–$E\flat_4$–C_4.

Table 10.34

EIGHT TONALITIES OF MEYER'S 7-LIMIT DIAMOND

Four Ascending Major Tonalities	Four Descending Minor Tonalities
↑ $1/1 - 5/4 - 3/2 - 7/4$ $C_4 - E_4 - G_4 - B\flat_4$	↓ $1/1 - 8/5 - 4/3 - 8/7$ $C_4 - A\flat_3 - F_3 - D_3$
↑ $8/5 - 5/5 - 6/5 - 7/5$ $A\flat_3 - C_4 - E\flat_4 - G\flat_4$	↓ $5/4 - 5/5 - 5/3 - 10/7$ $E_4 - C_4 - A_3 - F\sharp_3$
↑ $4/3 - 5/3 - 3/3 - 7/6$ $F_3 - A_3 - C_4 - E\flat_4$	↓ $3/2 - 6/5 - 1/1 - 12/7$ $G_4 - E\flat_4 - C_4 - A_3$
↑ $8/7 - 10/7 - 12/7 - 7/7$ $D_3 - F\sharp_3 - A_3 - C_4$	↓ $7/4 - 7/5 - 7/6 - 7/7$ $B\flat_4 - G\flat_4 - E\flat_4 - C_4$

Finally, and most importantly to composers and musicians, the tonality diamond furthers the study of just intonation because its unique lattice design of crisscrossed diagonals reveals that every ratio may be taken in two different senses. In this respect, the diamond pattern sheds new light on the Western practice of modulation. Students of traditional harmony learn that modulation from one key to another key — say, from C-major to B♭-major — requires a transitional chord that both keys have in common; in this case, an F-major triad qualifies because it represents the chord of the subdominant in C-major, and the chord of the dominant in B♭-major. Similarly, every just ratio in Meyer's tonality diamond serves a double function. For example, $E\flat_4$, ratio $6/5$, functions as a "major third," ratio $5/4$, in the descending minor tonality that begins on G_4, ratio $3/2$; and $E\flat_4$ also functions as a "fifth," ratio $3/2$, in the ascending major tonality that begins on $A\flat_3$, ratio $8/5$.

On many occasions, Meyer refers to his tonality diamond as a "table of spans." It is his single most important teaching tool. Meyer uses the diamond not only for convenient interval calculations, but also as a musical mandala designed to symbolize myriad mathematical possibilities of just intoned harmonies and scales. Toward the end of his book, Meyer acknowledges Rameau's contributions, and offers his own thoughts on the importance of just ratios in the study of music.

> **Rameau and beyond Rameau.** Rameau brought a certain clearness into the theory of chords by giving each tone *an absolute name* (fundamental, third, fifth, etc.) in the chord without any reference to the actual intervals. This reference to the actual intervals, he discovered, could be avoided by using the concept of the inversion of chords . . .
>
> The limits of this clarifying influence of Rameau we recognized when we studied his "theorem." It is only by substituting *number symbols* for such terms as Rameau's "fundamental, third, fifth, seventh, etc., natural, diminished, augmented" that we can free the theory from artificial fetters . . .
>
> The number symbol has the advantage over all other terms that it is both absolute and relative . . . Only number symbols can simply and directly and without modifying epithets fulfill this double condition. All other names force us to use queer modifiers like "augmented, sharpened," or what not, of little definiteness.

> A number is always absolute, individual, in being distinct from all other numbers. And it is always relative because it permits and invites the formation of a ratio. ***And there is no lower nor upper limit to the quantity of terms which may enter a ratio, — two, three, four, five, any multitude.*** The crazy concept of a "triad" as the only legitimate tone family, outlawing all smaller and larger families as being of illegal size, is safely avoided. For examples compare in the body of our text our numerous "scales" varying in size from two [tones and] up.
>
> Ratios, when *reduced* to their lowest terms or *translated* into "spans" are quickly comparable with other ratios without any possibility of ambiguity. No other terms are safe from ambiguity.[353] (Bold italics, and text in brackets mine. Text in parentheses in Meyer's original text.)

We conclude, therefore, that Meyer considered the four diagonal lines that enclose his tonality diamond as moveable boundaries, and that he did not rigidly limit the musical possibilities of just intoned frequency ratios to prime numbers 2, 3, 5, and 7.

~ 10.66 ~

Before we continue, let us first review three different derivations of the minor tonality. Zarlino calculated the minor triad by constructing an arithmetic division of a "flat fifth," ratio $^{40}\!/_{27}$. In the *De tutte l'opere...* edition of the *Istitutioni*, Zarlino gives the minor triad A_3–C_4–E_4 as ancient length ratios $^{9}\!/_{8}$–$^{4}\!/_{3}$–$^{5}\!/_{3}$ *above* the fundamental G_3, ratio $^{1}\!/_{1}$. On the other hand, in the *Génération harmonique*, Rameau attempted an acoustical explanation of the minor triad as originating in a synthetic *subharmonic series.* In Figure 10.56(b), my interpretation of Rameau's text shows the minor triad $\downarrow C_2$–$A\flat_1$–F_1 as ancient length ratios $\downarrow{}^{4}\!/_{1}$–$^{5}\!/_{1}$–$^{6}\!/_{1}$ *below* the fundamental C_4, ratio $^{1}\!/_{1}$. Finally, Meyer, in agreement with Shirlaw, organized four descending minor triads of his tonality diamond as exact mathematical inversions of four ascending major triads. Here an inversion of the "major third" above $^{1}\!/_{1}$ [$^{2}\!/_{1}$] sounds the "minor sixth" below because $^{2}\!/_{1} \div {}^{5}\!/_{4} = {}^{8}\!/_{5}$; similarly, an inversion of the "fifth" above $^{1}\!/_{1}$ [$^{2}\!/_{1}$] sounds the "fourth" below because $^{2}\!/_{1} \div {}^{3}\!/_{2} = {}^{4}\!/_{3}$. In Figure 10.58(b), I interpret Meyer's descending frequency ratios $\downarrow{}^{1}\!/_{1}$–$^{8}\!/_{5}$–$^{4}\!/_{3}$ as the descending minor triad $\downarrow C_4$–$A\flat_3$–F_3. Note carefully that Rameau's and Meyer's minor triads are for all practical purposes identical. This fact raises the following question: "Could Meyer have conceived of his tonality diamond without Rameau's spurious dual-generator?" The answer is probably no. For example, refer to Figure 10.46, and observe that Salinas did not think of ratios $^{4}\!/_{3}$, $^{8}\!/_{5}$, $^{5}\!/_{3}$, as inversions of $^{3}\!/_{2}$, $^{5}\!/_{4}$, $^{6}\!/_{5}$, respectively. Consequently, Salinas' engraving consists of only an ascending half-diamond.

~ 10.67 ~

Harry Partch (1901–1974), who stated, "I am not an instrument-maker, but a philosophical music-man seduced into carpentry," spent his entire adult life building a unique collection of acoustic musical instruments, composing music for these instruments, and writing about the significance of just intonation. In 1949, Partch published a book entitled *Genesis of a Music*, in which he passionately advocated the musical incorporation of prime numbers 7 and 11.[354] An expanded second edition of this work appeared in 1974.[355] Despite Partch's attempt to recognize Max F. Meyer's ". . . salutary effect . . . [on the] . . . presentation of material . . ."[356] in *Genesis of a Music*, Partch failed to acknowledge Meyer as the creator of the 7-limit Tonality Diamond, and thereby plagiarized his work. In both editions of *Genesis*, Partch included four illustrations based on Meyer's tonality diamond: a 5-limit Incipient Tonality Diamond, an 11-limit Expanded Tonality Diamond, an 11-limit Block

Plan of the Diamond Marimba, and The Tonality Diamond on a 13-Limit.[357] With respect to his Diamond Marimba, Partch states

> This instrument is the theoretical Tonality Diamond brought to practical tonal life . . .[358]

A comparison to Figure 10.57(b) reveals that Partch's marimba pattern introduced three minor changes into Meyer's original design. Refer to Figure 10.59, which shows an exact copy of Partch's block plan, and note that Partch (1) rotated Meyer's tonality diamond 180° on its vertical axis, (2) reversed the locations of prime numbers 3 and 5, and (3) added four new diagonals. The first modification left Meyer's tonality diamond intact and only changed the directions of the major and minor tonalities: they now ascend and descend from *left to right.* The need for the second change has already been discussed in Section 10.65. The third alteration added 20 bars to Meyer's 7-limit nuclear cluster, and enabled Partch to play six major chords with just ninths and just elevenths in an ascending direction and, conversely, six minor chords with just ninths and just elevenths in a descending direction.

We may interpret the frequency ratios of Partch's Diamond Marimba in the following manner. If we think of 1/1 as the fourth harmonic, then the ascending sequence of tones — 1/1, 5/4, 3/2, 7/4, 9/8, 11/16 — represents the 4th, 5th, 6th, 7th, 9th, 11th harmonics of the harmonic series, respectively; and the descending sequence of tones — 1/1, 8/5, 4/3, 8/7, 16/9, 16/11 — represents the exact inversion of the ascending sequence. Partch referred to the former sequence as a 1/1 *Otonality,* which means that the major tonality progresses in an ascending direction "over" 1/1; and he referred to the latter sequence as a 1/1 *Utonality,* which means that the minor tonality progresses in a descending direction "under" 1/1. Similarly, the 11-limit Diamond Marimba also consists of 8/5–, 4/3–, 8/7–, 16/9–, 16/11 Otonalities, and 5/4–, 3/2–, 7/4–, 9/8–, 11/8 Utonalities. However, it is important to point out that for Partch, ". . . neither overtones [harmonics] nor undertones [subharmonics] are predicated as determinants of Monophony's tonalities; these are implicit in small-number ratios."[359] (Text in brackets mine.) In other words, Partch maintained that his musical thinking is not indebted to modern discoveries in acoustics. He thereby renounces all ties to the recent past and claims that his musical theories are solely based on the ancient Greek method of dividing canon strings.

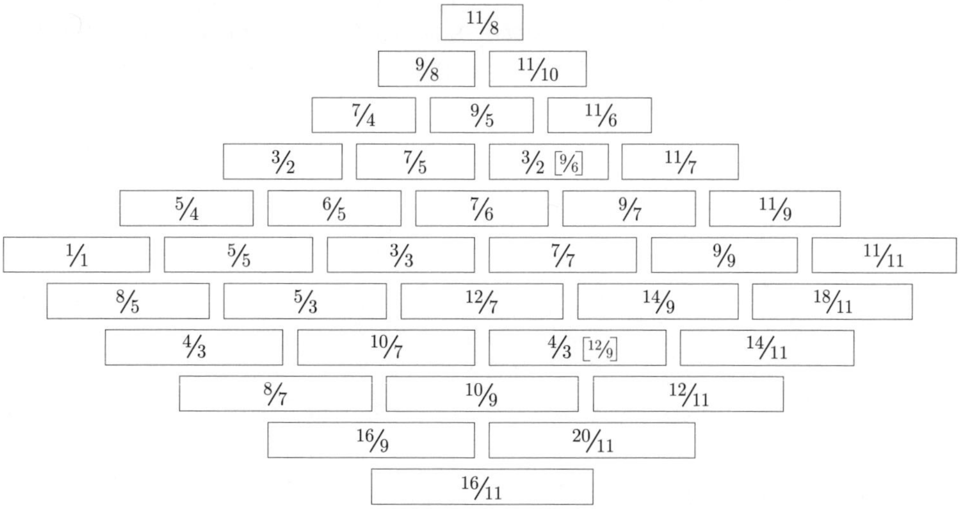

Figure 10.59 Meyer's 7-limit Tonality Diamond as transformed and expanded by Partch into an 11-limit Diamond Marimba. Note Meyer's 16-bar nuclear cluster in the left central portion of Partch's plan. To achieve this pattern, Partch introduced three minor changes into Meyer's original design.

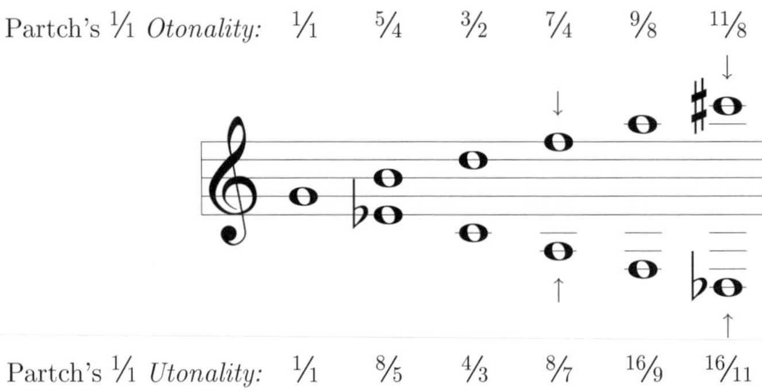

Figure 10.60 Partch's 1/1 Otonality and 1/1 Utonality as realized on his Diamond Marimba tuned one "octave" lower. Partch's marimba is tuned to G_5 at 784.0 cps. To avoid excessive ledger lines, this figure shows the 1/1 Otonality and 1/1 Utonality tuned to G_4 at 392.0 cps.

On Partch's Diamond Marimba, the neutral axis that runs through the center of the diamond — 1/1, 5/5, 3/3, 7/7, 9/9, 11/11 — sounds G_5 at 784.0 cps. If we lower this central pitch by one "octave" to G_4 at 392.0 cps, Figure 10.60 shows the approximate tones of the 1/1 Otonality and the 1/1 Utonality on the conventional treble staff. As in Figure 3.12, arrows pointing downward indicate tones that sound considerably lower than notated, and arrows pointing upward indicate tones that sound considerably higher than notated.

Regarding the debate over generator vs. fundamental, recall Rameau's passage in Section 10.63, Quote VIII, which states that the fundamental of the minor triad is the lowest sounding note. Partch essentially agreed with Rameau's interpretation when he noted

> In Utonality ("minor") the conception is somewhat different, since the series of identities descends in pitch from its unity [that is, descends from the "generator," ratio 1/1, or from the "octave," ratio 2/1], though the practical results are exactly the same; the unity is here the "fifth of the chord" [that is, the "octave" sounds the interval of a "fifth" above 4/3, or 2/1 ÷ 3/2 = 4/3]. The long controversy as to the correct location of the "root" of the "minor" triad is rhetoric, so far as creative music goes, since the composer needs no greater authority than his fancy to put the "root" wherever he wants to put it. In the final chord of a cadence it is quite natural to put the . . . ("root") at the bottom, since the natural position of the unity in the Tonality Diamond is at the top.[360] (Text and ratios in brackets mine. Text in parentheses in Partch's original text.)

10.68

With respect to scales and tunings, Partch is best known for his 43-tone just scale. Refer to Table 10.35, and note that this scale consists of 22 ratio pairs, the first of which is [1/1, 2/1]. Asterisks in Table 10.35 indicate that 29 frequency ratios (or 67% of the total) are contained in the 11-limit Tonality Diamond. However, because these diamond ratios produce eight large gaps between chromatic scale degrees, Partch decided to fill these intervals with the following seven ratio pairs: [81/80, 160/81], [33/32, 64/33], [21/20, 40/21], [16/15, 15/8], [32/27, 27/16], [21/16, 32/21], [27/20, 40/27]. Now, the question naturally arises, "Why did Partch decide to include these particular ratios?" Although he did not

Table 10.35

PARTCH'S 43-TONE SCALE

Scale	Ratios	Scale	Ratios
1.	$1/1$ *	23.	$10/7$ *
2.	$81/80$	24.	$16/11$ *
3.	$33/32$	25.	$40/27$
4.	$21/20$	26.	$3/2$ *
5.	$16/15$	27.	$32/21$
6.	$12/11$ *	28.	$14/9$ *
7.	$11/10$ *	29.	$11/7$ *
8.	$10/9$ *	30.	$8/5$ *
9.	$9/8$ *	31.	$18/11$ *
10.	$8/7$ *	32.	$5/3$ *
11.	$7/6$ *	33.	$27/16$
12.	$32/27$	34.	$12/7$ *
13.	$6/5$ *	35.	$7/4$ *
14.	$11/9$ *	36.	$16/9$ *
15.	$5/4$ *	37.	$9/5$ *
16.	$14/11$ *	38.	$20/11$ *
17.	$9/7$ *	39.	$11/6$ *
18.	$21/16$	40.	$15/8$
19.	$4/3$ *	41.	$40/21$
20.	$27/20$	42.	$64/33$
21.	$11/8$ *	43.	$160/81$
22.	$7/5$ *	44.	$2/1$

answer this question in a musical context, we may, nevertheless, venture several guesses. Because of the highly complex nature of this subject, the following analysis will focus primarily on the dominant-subdominant implications of these inclusions. To begin, the *Pythagorean Pair* [$32/27$, $27/16$] provides a $3/2$ interval ratio below $16/9$, and a $3/2$ interval ratio above $9/8$, respectively; similarly, a *Nexus Pair*[361] [$27/20$, $40/27$] provides a $3/2$ above $9/5$, and a $3/2$ below $10/9$, respectively. Consequently, these two pairs now yield the major triad $32/27 : 40/27 : 16/9$, and the minor triad $9/8 : 27/20 : 27/16$. Furthermore, the *Syntonic Comma Pair* [$81/80$, $160/81$] provides a $3/2$ above $27/20$, and a $3/2$ below $40/27$. This, in turn, yields the major triad $27/20 : 27/16 : 81/80$, and the minor triad $160/81 : 32/27 : 40/27$. Note also that the *Ptolemaic Pair* [$16/15$, $15/8$] provides a $3/2$ below $8/5$, and a $3/2$ above $5/4$; the pair [$21/20$, $40/21$] provides a $3/2$ above $7/5$, and a $3/2$ below $10/7$; and the pair [$21/16$, $32/21$] provides a $3/2$ above $7/4$, and a $3/2$ below $8/7$. These latter three pairs yield three major and three minor triads. Finally, the pair [$33/32$, $64/33$] provides a $3/2$ above $11/8$, and a $3/2$ below $16/11$; this is the only pair that does not serve a major or minor triadic function.

To comprehend and analyze such relations without tedious calculations, Erv Wilson[362] created a unique tuning lattice of Partch's 43-tone scale. Turn to Figure 10.61, and examine the key in the upper right-hand corner of this figure that shows how Wilson organized his lattice. Furthermore, observe that various line combinations in the lattice represent chords and scales. For example, the following six patterns indicate that Partch's scale contains fourteen major and fourteen minor triads,

Major Triad

Minor Triad

nine major triads with just sevenths, and five minor triads with just sevenths,

Major Triad and Just Seventh

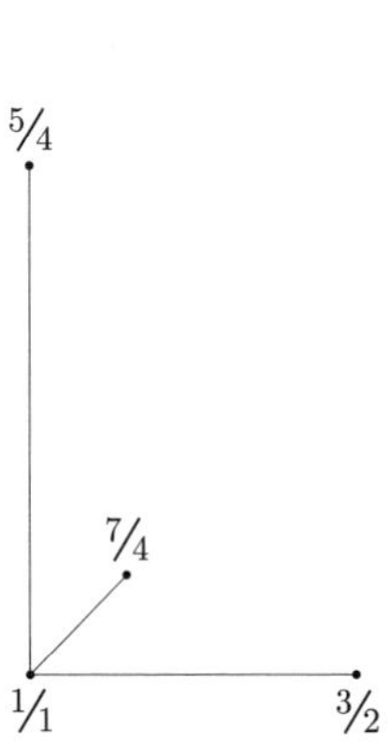

Minor Triad and Just Seventh

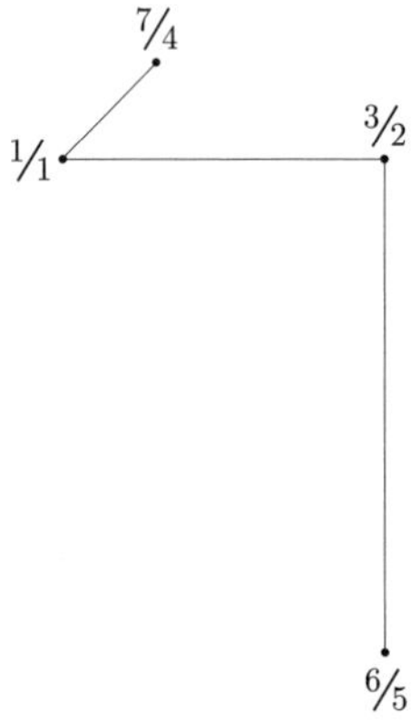

six Ptolemaic major scales, and six natural minor scales:

Ptolemaic Major Scale

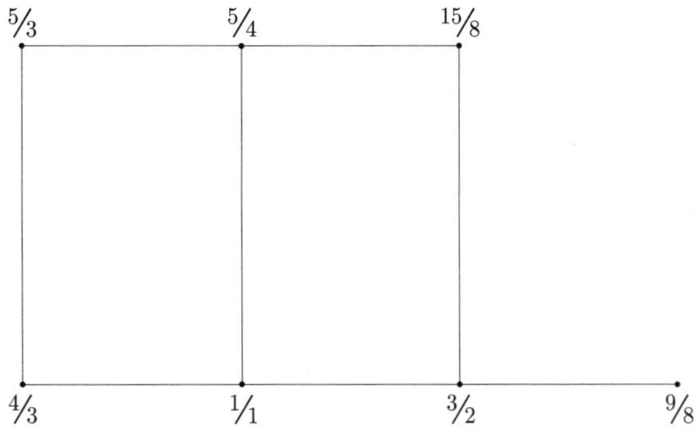

Natural Minor Scale

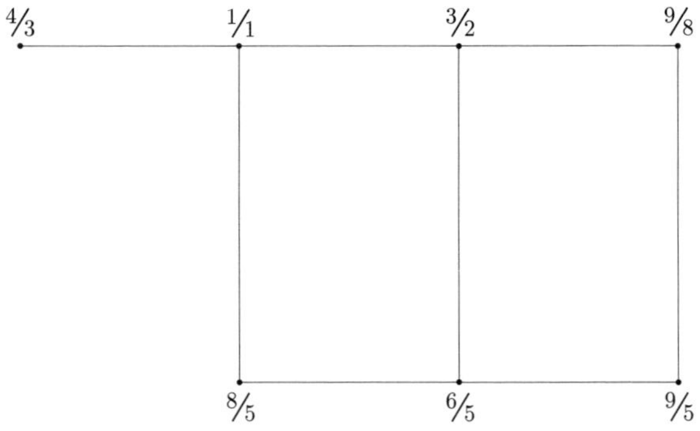

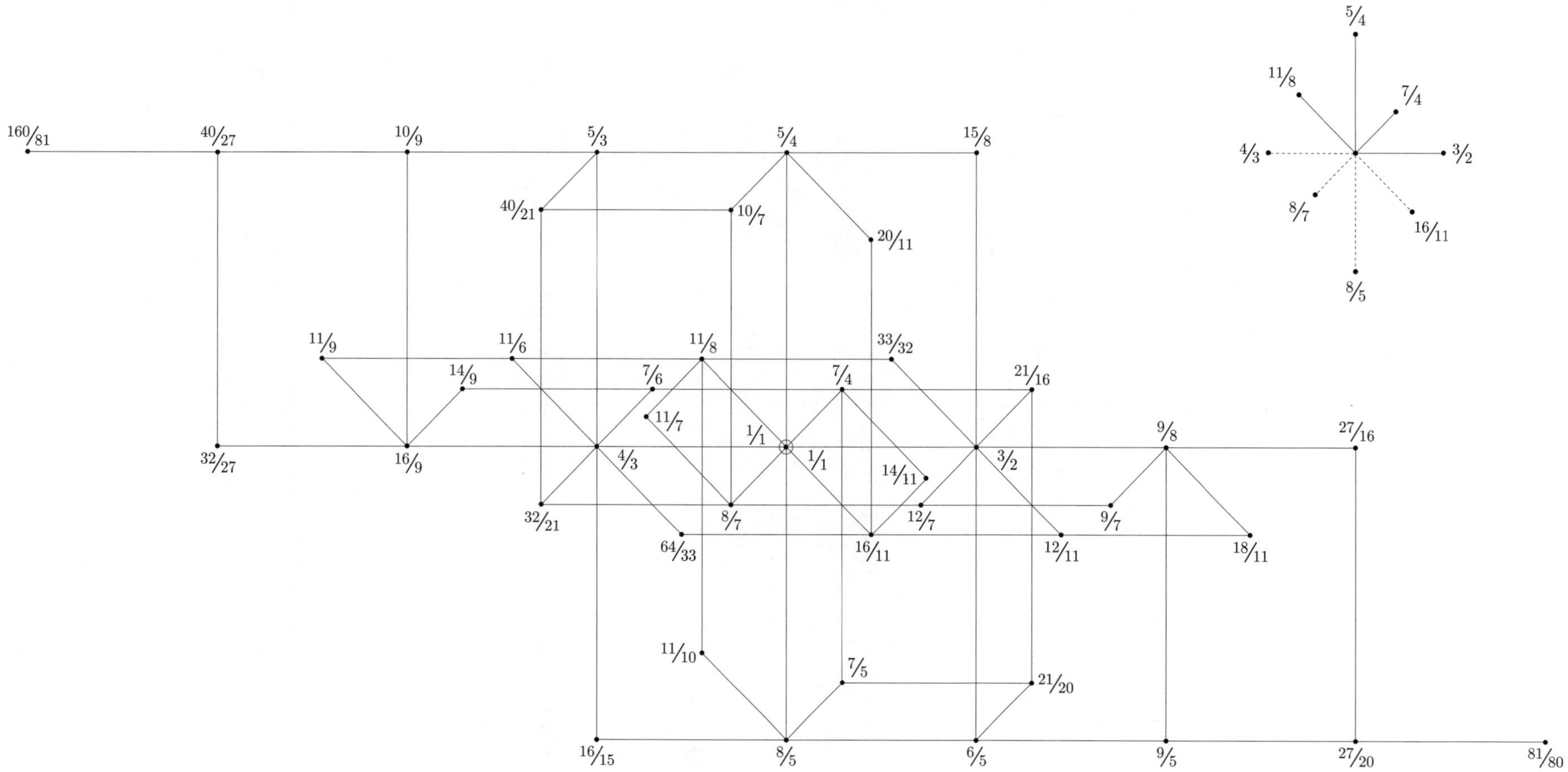

Figure 10.61 Wilson's tuning lattice of Partch's 43-tone scale. The key in the upper right-hand corner of this figure indicates how Wilson organized his lattice. Above the central axis, lines between points going north represent ascending 5/4 interval ratios, and going south represent descending 5/4 interval ratios; similarly, above the central axis, lines between points going northeast represent ascending 7/4 interval ratios, and going southwest represent descending 7/4 interval ratios, etc.

10.69

In closing Part VI, and as a fitting tribute to the subject of just intonation, consider a mathematical technique developed by Viggo Brun[363] to convert a given irrational decimal ratio into a rational integer ratio approximation. In this text, an *integer ratio* consists of a numerator x and a denominator y, where both x and y are positive integers. One encounters a need for such conversions whenever a writer or ethnomusicologist records a scale in cents but fails to include a prime number analysis of the scale. For example, suppose a researcher lists a scale that includes a tone that equals 435 ¢. To identify the prime number composition of such a tone, we must convert 435 ¢ to a rational or just x/y approximation.

Before we calculate this approximation, let us first convert a rational decimal ratio into a rational integer ratio. Brun's method for converting 1.250 into ratio $5/4$ requires six procedures, where each procedure consists of four separate steps.

①	1.250	④	1	0	③
	1.000		0	1	
	0.250	②	1	0	
	1.000		1	1	
	0.750		1	1	
	0.250		2	1	
	0.500		1	1	
	0.250		3	2	
	0.250		1	1	
	0.250		4	3	
	0.000		1	1	
			5	4	

Four Steps Per Procedure:

① Subtract 1.0 from the decimal ratio, or the smaller from the larger amount.
② Bring down the smaller amount.
③ Bring down the row of the array associated with the larger amount.
④ Add the two columns of the array, and bring down the two sums.

The groups of elements on the right-hand side of these procedures constitute arrays. An array is a simple rectangular matrix of numbers. For the initial decimal ratio, the top *horizontal row* of the array always consists of elements 1 and 0; and for the initial value 1.0, the bottom horizontal row of the array always consists of elements 0 and 1. In step ③, bring down the row associated with the larger decimal fraction. Finally, in step ④, think of the array as two *vertical columns;* now add the terms of the first column, then add the terms of the second column, and bring down the two sums. In this example, continuous subtraction of decimal fractions terminates in zero, and continuous addition of array elements yields ratio $5/4$.

Now, to convert 435 ¢ into a just x/y approximation, first refer to Equation 9.23, and calculate a rational decimal ratio approximation accurate to six decimal places:

$$10^{\frac{¢}{1200/\log_{10} 2}} = 10^{\frac{¢}{3986.314}} = x \qquad \text{(Eq. 9.23)}$$

$$10^{\frac{435\ ¢}{3986.314}} = 1.285652$$

Next, apply Brun's method, and note that after seven procedures, subtraction yields 0.000436, and addition yields ratio $^9\!/_7$.

1.285652	1	0
1.000000	0	1
0.285652	1	0
1.000000	1	1
0.714348	1	1
0.285652	2	1
0.428696	1	1
0.285652	3	2
0.143044	1	1
0.285652	4	3
0.142608	4	3
0.143044	5	4
0.000436	5	4
	9	7

Given the initial decimal fraction 1.285652, it is to be expected that seven procedures will not reduce such a complicated number to zero. If we had used a more accurate cent value, $^9\!/_7 = 435.084$ ¢, then the more accurate decimal fraction 1.285714 would have reduced to 0.000002 after seven procedures; the latter number is for all practical purpose equal to zero. In any case, the accuracy of the initial decimal fraction determines the accuracy of the just $^x\!/_y$ approximation. To conclude this discussion, Table 10.36 lists eleven just approximations generated by Brun's method for eleven scale degrees of 12-TET accurate to the nearest cent.[364]

Table 10.36

JUST $^x\!/_y$ APPROXIMATIONS OF 12-TET

Scale	Approx.
100 ¢	$^{71}\!/_{67}$
200 ¢	$^{55}\!/_{49}$
300 ¢	$^{44}\!/_{37}$
400 ¢	$^{63}\!/_{50}$
500 ¢	$^{239}\!/_{179}$
600 ¢	$^{99}\!/_{70}$
700 ¢	$^{355}\!/_{237}$
800 ¢	$^{73}\!/_{46}$
900 ¢	$^{37}\!/_{22}$
1000 ¢	$^{98}\!/_{55}$
1100 ¢	$^{134}\!/_{71}$

Notes

1. Niven, I. (1961). *Numbers: Rational and Irrational*, p. 13. Random House, New York.

   ". . . 1 is not included among the prime numbers. For, if 1 were taken as a prime we then could write, for example,

$$35 = 5 \times 7 = 1 \times 5 \times 7$$

   and so 35 (or any other natural number) could be expressed in more than one way as a product of primes." In other words, the exclusion of 1 ensures that a given composite number can be factored into prime numbers only once.

2. In advanced mathematics, one also encounters imaginary and complex numbers that are not defined as real numbers.

3. A mixed number consists of the sum of an integer and a fraction, such as $3/2 = 1 + 1/2 = 1.50$; or $4/3 = 1 + 1/3 = 1.3333...$; etc. Therefore, a mixed decimal always includes a whole number.

4. Crew, H., and De Salvio, A., Translators (1914). *Dialogues Concerning Two New Sciences*, by Galileo Galilei, p. ix. Dover Publications, Inc., New York.

5. With this pendulum experiment, Galileo intended to explain the difference between consonant (commensurable) and dissonant (incommensurable) ratios. However, he failed to acknowledge that string length ratio 2001:1000 produces an interval that is almost as consonant as length ratio 2:1. So, we will avoid Galileo's acoustic conclusions, and focus instead on the mathematical implications of his experiment.

6. *Dialogues Concerning Two New Sciences*, p. 107.

7. The frequency equation for a pendulum states

$$F = \frac{1}{2\pi}\sqrt{\frac{g}{L}}$$

   where g is the acceleration of gravity; and L is the length of the pendulum. Suppose we consider Galileo's example of a pendulum with a length of 16.0 units, and a frequency of 2.0 cps. If a second pendulum has a frequency of 3.0 cps, what is its length? First, ignore the constants π and g, and construct the following proportion:

$$\frac{\sqrt{\dfrac{1}{16.0 \text{ units}}}}{2.0 \text{ cps}} = \frac{\sqrt{\dfrac{1}{L}}}{3.0 \text{ cps}}$$

   which states that the square root of an inverse length of 16.0 units is to 2.0 cps as the square root of an unknown inverse length L is to 3.0 cps. Solve for L in five steps: (1) cross-multiply the equation; (2) remove the radicals and square the frequencies and the related units; and (3) multiply on both sides of the equation. Next, (4) transform the equation to cancel the frequency units and divide; finally, (5) transform once more and divide again.

$$\sqrt{\frac{1}{L}} \times 2.0 \text{ cps} = \sqrt{\frac{1}{16.0 \text{ units}}} \times 3.0 \text{ cps}$$

$$\frac{1}{L} \times (2.0)^2 \text{ cps}^2 = \frac{1}{16.0 \text{ units}} \times (3.0)^2 \text{ cps}^2$$

$$\frac{4.0 \text{ cps}^2}{L} = \frac{9.0 \text{ cps}^2}{16.0 \text{ units}}$$

$$\frac{16.0 \text{ units}}{L} = \frac{9.0 \cancel{\text{cps}^2}}{4.0 \cancel{\text{cps}^2}} = 2.25$$

$$L = \frac{16.0 \text{ units}}{2.25} = 7.11 \text{ units}$$

In the original text, Galileo mistakenly assigned a length of 9 units to the second pendulum. Nevertheless, Galileo's experiment predicts that after 2 cycles of the long 16.0-unit pendulum, and 3 cycles of the short 7.11-unit pendulum, both pendulums ". . . will reach the same terminus at the same instant, and then begin a repetition of the cycle . . ." because both string lengths represent commensurable or rational numbers.

Now suppose we give the second pendulum an incommensurable string length of $\sqrt{60.0 \text{ units}} \approx$ 7.74597 units. Such a change would mean that the frequency (F) of the second pendulum must result in an incommensurable or irrational rate of vibration with respect to the first pendulum. A solution to the following proportionality:

$$\frac{\sqrt{\dfrac{1}{16.0 \text{ units}}}}{2.0 \text{ cps}} = \frac{\sqrt{\dfrac{1}{7.74597 \text{ units}}}}{F}$$

shows that the second pendulum vibrates at $F \approx 2.87443$ cps. Therefore, these two pendulums will ". . . never complete a definite number of vibrations at the same instant . . . ," or will never vibrate in phase. (See Section 5.18.)

8. (A) Heath, T. (1921). *A History of Greek Mathematics, Volume 1*, pp. 244–249. Dover Publications, Inc., New York, 1981.

   (B) Diels, H. (1903). *Die Fragmente der Vorsokratiker, Griechisch und Deutsch, Volume 1*, pp. 425–427. Weidmannsche Verlagsbuchhandlung, Berlin, Germany, 1951.

   Diels gives Archytas' proof in the original Greek, and a translation in German. The two figures that illustrate the proof are exceptionally clear.

9. Heath, T.L., Translator (1908). *Euclid's Elements, Volume 2*, p. 216. Three Volumes. Dover Publications, Inc., New York, 1956.

   This is a reference to Euclid's Book VI, Proposition 13.

10. D'Ooge, M.L., Translator (1926). *Nicomachus of Gerasa: Introduction to Arithmetic*, pp. 212–229. The Macmillan Company, New York.

11. Lawlor, R. and D., Translators (1978). *Mathematics Useful for Understanding Plato*, by Theon of Smyrna, pp. 48–52. Wizards Bookshelf, San Diego, California, 1979.

12. Bower, C.M., Translator, (1989). *Fundamentals of Music*, by A.M.S. Boethius, pp. 12–13. Yale University Press, New Haven, Connecticut.

13. *A History of Greek Mathematics*, pp. 101–104.

14. For complicated ratios, use the following equation to add two fractions with different denominators:

$$\frac{a}{b} + \frac{c}{d} = \frac{ad + bc}{bd}$$

15. *Nicomachus of Gerasa: Introduction to Arithmetic*, pp. 212–213.

16. *Mathematics Useful for Understanding Plato*, p. 48.

17. (A) *Fundamentals of Music*, p. 96.

In Book 3, Chapter 5, entitled *How Philolaus divided the tone*, Boethius states that Philolaus' division of interval ratio $9/8$ ". . . made two parts, one that is more than half, which he called the 'apotome' [$2187/2048$], and the remainder, which is less than half, which he called the 'diesis' [better known as the *limma*, $256/243$]." (Text and ratios in brackets mine.) In Section 10.18, we will discuss how Ptolemy divided the tone into the *apotome* and *limma* in string length units. Ptolemy's description raises the distinct possibility that Philolaus calculated his interval divisions in the same manner. If this is true, then Philolaus' use of length ratios predates Euclid's method by approximately 120 years.

(B) *Die Fragmente der Vorsokratiker, Griechisch und Deutsch, Volume 1*, p. 405.

Diels identifies Philolaus' description of the division of the tone as authentic fragment A26. This page gives Philolaus' fragment as it appears in Boethius' original Latin text.

(C) Burkert, W. (1962). *Lore and Science in Ancient Pythagoreanism*, p. 380, Footnote 47; pp. 386–400. Translated by E.L. Minar, Jr. Harvard University Press, Cambridge, Massachusetts, 1972.

In Footnote 47, Burkert agrees with Diels that A26 is an authentic fragment.

18. Crocker, R.L. (1963). Pythagorean mathematics and music. *The Journal of Aesthetics and Art Criticism* **XXII**, No. 2, Part I, pp. 189–198, and No. 3, Part II, pp. 325–335.

This article discusses all significant aspects of Pythagorean mathematics and music. Crocker's analysis of Archytas' three tetrachords is especially noteworthy.

19. Guthrie, K.S., Translator (1987). *The Pythagorean Sourcebook and Library*, p. 29. Phanes Press, Grand Rapids, Michigan.

The discovery that the arithmetic progression 1, 2, 3, 4 represents in numeric order the three most important consonances in music — namely, the "octave," the "fifth," and the "fourth" — convinced the early Pythagoreans of the mystical power of integers. The Pythagoreans referred to the following mystic symbol as a Tetraktys. It symbolized consonances $2/1$, $3/2$, and $4/3$ as expressed by the number ten.

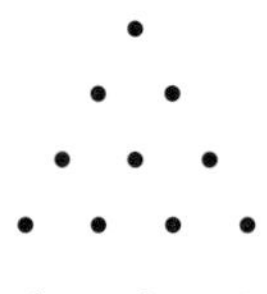

20. (A) Hamilton, E., and Cairns, H., Editors (1966). *The Collected Dialogues of Plato*, p. 763. Quotation from the *Republic* translated by P. Shorey. Random House, Inc., New York.

(B) *Lore and Science in Ancient Pythagoreanism*, p. 372.

Burkert offers a lengthy analysis of the conflict between sound and number as described by Plato in the *Republic*.

21. Barker, A., Translator (1989). *Greek Musical Writings, Volume 2*, pp. 286–287. Cambridge University Press, Cambridge, England.

This volume contains many complete translations of ancient Greek texts on music.

22. Chalmers, J.H., Jr. (1993). *Divisions of the Tetrachord*. Frog Peak Music, Hanover, New Hampshire.

Chalmers cites literally hundreds of tetrachord divisions, mostly by Western theorists.

23. *Greek Musical Writings, Volume 2*, pp. 303–304.

24. Macran, H.S., Translator (1902). *The Harmonics of Aristoxenus*, p. 198. Georg Olms Verlag, Hildesheim, Germany, 1990.

25. See Section 10.7 for a detailed discussion on the early development of the heptachord and octachord.

26. Barbera, A., Translator (1991). *The Euclidean Division of the Canon*, p. 187. University of Nebraska Press, Lincoln, Nebraska.

27. West, M.L. (1992). *Ancient Greek Music*, pp. 219–222. The Clarendon Press, Oxford, England, 1994.

The Greek names for the tones in the GPS describe strings and their position on the lyre. For example, *lichanos* refers to the *forefinger* string.

28. Levin, F.R., Translator (1994). *The Manual of Harmonics, of Nicomachus the Pythagorean*, p. 75. Phanes Press, Grand Rapids, Michigan.

29. Many ancient and contemporary sources give the three intervals, or interval ratios, of a tetrachord in descending order, in this case: Tone, Tone, Semitone.

30. *The Manual of Harmonics*, p. 75.

31. *Ibid.*, p. 77.

32. *Ibid.*, p. 83.

33. *Ibid.*

34. *Ibid.*, pp. 83–84.

Nicomachus' observation with respect to "equal torsion," which I interpret as a reference to stiffness, is very astute. If two strings appear to be identical but the first one is stiffer, it will produce a higher frequency than the second string. See Chapter 4.

35. *Ibid.*, p. 85.

36. *Ibid.*, p. 141.

37. See Sections 3.7 and 3.13.

38. (A) Düring, I., Editor (1930). *Die Harmonielehre des Klaudios Ptolemaios*, p. 33. Original Greek text of Ptolemy's *Harmonics*. Wettergren & Kerbers Förlag, Göteborg, Sweden.

(B) Düring, I., Translator (1934). *Ptolemaios und Porphyrios über die Musik*, p. 49. Georg Olms Verlag, Hildesheim, Germany, 1987.

Düring's German translation of Ptolemy's *Harmonics* is the first modern translation of this great work. Although the Greek text of the quoted passage does not refer directly to canon strings, Düring interprets two occurrences of the word *meros* (lit. *part*) in the context of string length divisions. I completely agree with this interpretation. Furthermore, in Book 1, Chapter 15, entitled *"The division of tetrachords according to rational calculations and sense-perception,"* Ptolemy includes, after his detailed explanations of tetrachord divisions, two tables of length ratios in string length units, and a description of an eight-string canon with moveable bridges. Unfortunately, in *Greek Musical Writings, Volume 2*, pp. 306–307, A. Barker gives a literally and mathematically accurate but musically incomprehensible translation of this crucial passage. For this and similar technical reasons, I translated several important passages from Düring's German translation of Ptolemy's *Harmonics*.

39. See Sections 9.5 and 9.8.

40. Lindley, M. (1984). *Lutes, Viols and Temperaments*, pp. 104–108. Cambridge University Press, Cambridge, England.

41. See Section 3.18.

42. Euclid's famous construction was not applied to the calculation of musical intervals until the Renaissance. See Note 113.

43. Stephan, B. (1991). *Geometry: Plane and Practical*, pp. 6–7, 47–48, 59–60. Harcourt Brace Jovanovich, Publishers, San Diego, California.

The proof of Euclid's Book VI, Proposition 13, is based on the fact that $\triangle CDA$ and $\triangle CDB$ are similar triangles. For further discussions, also consult *Euclid's Elements, Volume 2*, p. 216, and Theon's *Mathematics Useful for Understanding Plato*, p. 78. Euclid's method is limited to the extraction of square roots. It is not possible to extract cube roots with ruler and compass.

44. See Section 9.1.

45. Since the *right* section of the middle string represents an irrational length, $1000.0 \text{ mm} \div \sqrt{2} \approx 707.1$ mm, the *left* section represents an irrational length as well: $1000.0 \text{ mm} - (1000.0 \text{ mm} \div \sqrt{2}) \approx 292.9$ mm. With a Euclidean algorithm (see Section 10.69), we may *approximate* an irrational ratio with a rational ratio. This method shows that $\sqrt{2}$ has the following rational integer ratio approximation:

$$\sqrt{2} \approx \frac{239}{169} = 1.4142$$

Consequently, we may approximate the right section of the middle string with modern length ratio $^{169}/_{239}$, and frequency ratio $^{239}/_{169}$. Calculate $\log_{10} {}^{239}/_{169} \times 3986.314 = 600.0$ ¢ and note that the right section of the middle string sounds a "tritone" above the frequency of the open string. Furthermore, we may approximate the left section of the middle string with *complementary* length ratio $^{70}/_{239}$, and frequency ratio $^{239}/_{70}$. (See Sections 3.13 and 3.15.) Calculate $\log_{10} {}^{239}/_{70} \times 3986.314 = 2125.9$ ¢. Now, subtract 2125.9 ¢ − 1200.0 ¢ = 925.9 ¢ and note that the left section of the middle string sounds one "octave [1200.0 ¢] and a *sharp* major sixth [925.9 ¢]" above the frequency of the open string.

46. (A) *Greek Musical Writings, Volume 2*, pp. 36–38.

Barker identifies this quotation as Fragment 6.

(B) *The Manual of Harmonics*, p. 125.

47. *Lore and Science in Ancient Pythagoreanism*, p. 394.

"These considerations, along with the archaic terminology, allow us to regard Philolaus' Fragment 6 as one of the oldest pieces of evidence for Greek music."

48. Modern theorists refer to the discrepancy between an "octave" and four "minor thirds" as a *large diesis* (lit. *large separation*). Four "minor thirds" $= {}^6/_5 \times {}^6/_5 \times {}^6/_5 \times {}^6/_5 = {}^{1296}/_{625}$. Large Diesis $= {}^{1296}/_{625} \div {}^2/_1 = {}^{648}/_{625} = 62.6$ ¢. And they refer to the discrepancy between an "octave" and three "major thirds" as a *small diesis*. Three "major thirds" $= {}^5/_4 \times {}^5/_4 \times {}^5/_4 = {}^{125}/_{64}$. Small Diesis $= {}^2/_1 \div {}^{125}/_{64} = {}^{128}/_{125} =$ 41.1 ¢. The large diesis is a discrepancy by which four "minor thirds" exceed an "octave," and a small diesis is a discrepancy by which an "octave" exceeds three "major thirds."

49. White, W.B. (1917). *Piano Tuning and Allied Arts*, 5th ed., pp. 86–87. Tuners Supply Company, Boston, Massachusetts, 1972.

50. (A) *Greek Musical Writings, Volume 2*, pp. 205–207.

(B) *The Euclidean Division of the Canon*, pp. 179–185.

51. Barbera, C.A. (1977). Arithmetic and geometric divisions of the tetrachord. *Journal of Music Theory* **21**, No. 2, pp. 294–323.

52. *The Collected Dialogues of Plato*, p. 763. Quotation from the *Republic* translated by P. Shorey.

53. *The Harmonics of Aristoxenus*, p. 204.

54. *Ibid.*, p. 189.

55. (A) Winnington-Ingram, R.P. (1954). "Greek Music (Ancient)." In *Grove's Dictionary of Music and Musicians, Volume 3*, 5th ed., E. Blom, Editor, pp. 770–780. St. Martin's Press, Inc., New York, 1970.

(B) Winnington-Ingram, R.P. (1932). Aristoxenus and the intervals of Greek music. *The Classical Quarterly* **XXVI**, Nos. 3–4, pp. 195–208.

(C) Winnington-Ingram, R.P. (1936). *Mode in Ancient Greek Music.* Cambridge University Press, London, England.

56. Litchfield, M. (1988). Aristoxenus and empiricism: A reevaluation based on his theories. *Journal of Music Theory* **32**, No. 1, pp. 51–73.

57. Crocker, R.L. (1966). "Aristoxenus and Greek Mathematics." In *Aspects of Medieval and Renaissance Music: A Birthday Offering to Gustave Reese*, J. LaRue, Editor. Pendragon Press, New York.

58. *Divisions of the Tetrachord*, pp. 19–20.

59. *Euclid's Elements, Volume 1*, p. 190.

60. *Ibid.*

61. *The Harmonics of Aristoxenus*, pp. 174–176.

62. *Ibid.*, p. 176.

63. *Ibid.*, pp. 183–184.

64. *Journal of Music Theory* **32**, p. 52.

65. *Ibid.*, p. 68.

66. *The Harmonics of Aristoxenus*, p. 182.

67. *Ibid.*, p. 199.

68. *Ibid.*, p. 198.

69. Mackenzie, D.C., Translator (1950). *Harmonic Introduction*, by Cleonides. In *Source Readings in Music History*, O. Strunk, Editor, pp. 34–46. W. W. Norton & Company, Inc., New York.

On p. 39, Cleonides states, "The tone is assumed to be divided into twelve least parts, of which each one is called a twelfth-tone."

70. *Journal of Music Theory* **32**, p. 54.

71. *Ibid.*, p. 58.

72. Archytas' solution for the cube root of 2 cannot be applied to irrational numbers. However, through a process of trial and error it is possible to calculate the cube root of 1.05946:

$$\sqrt[3]{\frac{\sqrt[3]{2}}{\sqrt[4]{2}}} \approx \sqrt[3]{1.05946} = 1.01944$$

73. Although the following solution requires extremely precise length measurements, one can find the fourth root of 1.05946 by performing Euclid's construction twice. With respect to Figure 10.6, the first calculation for the square root when AC = 500.0 mm, and when CB = 500.0 mm × 1.05946 = 529.73 mm, yields CD = 514.65 mm, and common ratio 1.02930. The second calculation for the fourth root when AC = 500.0 mm, and when CB = 500.0 mm × 1.02930 = 514.65 mm, yields CD = 507.27 mm, and common ratio 1.01455.

74. Note that my frequencies compared to Litchfield's frequencies are musically indistinguishable. For example, based on a fundamental frequency of 330.0 cps, Litchfield calculated 4.5 Parts of the Hemiolic Chromatic Tetrachord at 344.55 cps. According to Equation 9.23, I calculated this frequency ratio at 344.61 cps:

$$330.0 \text{ cps} \times \sqrt[30]{\frac{4}{3}}^{\,4.5} = 344.55 \text{ cps}$$

$$330.0 \text{ cps} \times 10^{\frac{75.0\ \text{¢}}{3986.314}} = 344.61 \text{ cps}$$

75. (A) *Greek Musical Writings, Volume 2*, p. 345, Footnote 112.

(B) *Divisions of the Tetrachord*, p. 20.

Barker, Litchfield, and other contemporary critics interpret Aristoxenus' numbers as quarter-, third-, and half-tone divisions of abstract tonal "space." Consequently, they do not consider the question of tuning Aristoxenus' tetrachords as a relevant problem. Furthermore, anyone who proposes to undertake such a task is immediately subject to criticism because no one is able to prove whether arithmetic or geometric divisions of canon strings apply to these tetrachords. The underlying assumption of most modern scholars is that Aristoxenus' work indicates a historic trend among Greek intellectuals who advocated a clear separation between music theory and music practice. In other words, many writers claim that this treatise symbolizes a pure philosophy of music, which has nothing to do with canon strings and moveable bridges.

76. *The Harmonics of Aristoxenus*, p. 175.

77. *Ibid.*, p. 199.

78. *Ibid.*, pp. 207–208.

79. *Greek Musical Writings, Volume 2*, p. 199.

80. *Ibid.*, pp. 298–299.

81. *Ibid.*, p. 299, Footnote 100.

Ptolemy suggests ratio $^{65}/_{64}$ [26.8 ¢] as a close approximation for the comma of Pythagoras [23.5 ¢]. This kind of calculation and frame of mind sets an excellent example. Only by acknowledging the reality of the comma's existence, and by defining its numerical value were mathematicians in the late Renaissance able to calculate the length ratios and frequency ratios of 12-tone equal temperament.

82. See Figures 3.22 and 3.23.

83. (A) *Die Harmonielehre des Klaudios Ptolemaios*, pp. 69–70.

(B) Forster Translation: in *Ptolemaios und Porphyrios über die Musik*, p. 85; also in *Greek Musical Writings, Volume 2*, p. 345.

Düring gives length ratios 3:4, 2:3, and 1:2, which do not appear in Ptolemy's original text.

84. *Journal of Music Theory* **32**, pp. 64–65.

85. *Mathematics Useful for Understanding Plato*, p. 78.

86. *The Harmonics of Aristoxenus*, pp. 188–189.

87. *Greek Musical Writings, Volume 2*, p. 291.

88. *Ibid.*, p. 296.

89. *Ibid.*, p. 297.

90. *Ibid.*, p. 298.

91. *Ibid.*

92. *Ibid.*, p. 292.

93. (A) *Die Harmonielehre des Klaudios Ptolemaios*, p. 19.

(B) Forster Translation: in *Ptolemaios und Porphyrios über die Musik*, p. 36; also in *Greek Musical Writings, Volume 2*, pp. 292–293.

Düring gives "EK is four-thirds of KG," "EK is three-halves of KG," and "EK is twice as long as KG." These modern fractions do not appear in Ptolemy's original text.

94. (A) Forster Translation: in *Ptolemaios und Porphyrios über die Musik*, p. 29; also in *Greek Musical Writings, Volume 2*, p. 285.

Düring gives "original number" for Ptolemy's "amount exceeded."

(B) Solomon, J., Translator (2000). *Ptolemy Harmonics.* Brill, Leiden, Netherlands.

In this new English translation, Solomon includes detailed commentaries on Ptolemy's text. For example, he gives several interpretations of the word *isotonic* (see p. 14, etc.), and on p. 37 translates the term as *equal tension.* In other passages, Solomon simply writes *isotonic*, and gives contextual explanations in his footnotes. However, in Quotes IV and VI, I disagree with Barker and Solomon, and translate Düring's interpretation of *isotonic* as *equal-tension.*

95. Forster Translation: in *Ptolemaios und Porphyrios über die Musik*, pp. 32–33; also in *Greek Musical Writings, Volume 2*, p. 289.

96. Forster Translation: in *Ptolemaios und Porphyrios über die Musik*, p. 33; also in *Greek Musical Writings, Volume 2*, p. 289.

Düring gives "smaller original number" for Ptolemy's "amount exceeded."

97. *Ibid.*

98. Forster Translation: in *Ptolemaios und Porphyrios über die Musik*, p. 34; also in *Greek Musical Writings, Volume 2*, p. 290.

Düring gives "differences" for Ptolemy's "excesses"; he gives "numerators" for Ptolemy's "differences"; and he gives "their denominators" for Ptolemy's "the amounts exceeded."

99. Forster Translation: in *Ptolemaios und Porphyrios über die Musik*, p. 45; also in *Greek Musical Writings, Volume 2*, p. 302.

100. *The Harmonics of Aristoxenus*, p. 182.

Aristoxenus defines the *pyknon* by stating, "Again, we shall apply the term Pycnum to the combination of two intervals, the sum of which is less than the complement that makes up the Fourth."

101. Forster Translation: in *Ptolemaios und Porphyrios über die Musik*, p. 49; also in *Greek Musical Writings, Volume 2*, p. 307.

102. Forster Translation: in *Ptolemaios und Porphyrios über die Musik*, pp. 53–54; also in *Greek Musical Writings, Volume 2*, pp. 311–312.

Düring gives "denominator and numerator" for Ptolemy's "numbers."

103. *Ptolemaios und Porphyrios über die Musik*, pp. 86–88; *Greek Musical Writings, Volume 2*, pp. 347–350.

104. (A) Zarlino, R.M.G. (1573). *Istitutioni harmoniche*, p. 140. Facsimile Edition, The Gregg Press Limited, Farnborough, Hants., England, 1966.

In the *De tutte l'opere...* edition of the *Istitutioni harmoniche* (available in a facsimile edition from Georg Olms Verlag, Hildesheim, Germany), Zarlino improved earlier versions of the *Istitutioni.* Due to these changes, Zarlino's engraving of Ptolemy's scale appears on p. 147 of the 1589 edition of *De tutte l'opere...*, but on p. 140 of this 1573 edition of the *Istitutioni.*

(B) Fend, M., Translator (1989). *Theorie des Tonsystems:* Das erste und zweite Buch der *Istitutioni harmoniche* (1573), von Gioseffo Zarlino, p. 336. Peter Lang, Frankfurt am Main, Germany.

This German translation includes the Prima and Seconda Parte of the *Istitutioni harmoniche.*

105. (A) *Grove's Dictionary of Music and Musicians*, Volume 9, 5th ed., p. 401.

(B) Hawkins, J. (1853). *A General History of the Science and Practice of Music, Volume 1*, p. 399. Dover Publications, Inc., New York, 1963.

These two texts include fairly accurate reproductions of Zarlino's original engraving.

106. As discussed in Section 11.46, the principal purpose of the apotome fret is to produce the same E♭ to E interval on String IV as on String I, and the same A♭ to A on String V as on String II.

107. (A) Beck, C., Translator (1868). *Flores musice omnis cantus Gregoriani*, by Hugo Spechtshart [von Reutlingen], pp. 76–79. Bibliothek des Litterarischen Vereins, Stuttgart, Germany.

This volume contains Spechtshart's original Latin text and a modern German translation.

(B) Adkins, C.D. (1963). *The Theory and Practice of the Monochord*, p. 170, pp. 172–174. Ph.D. dissertation printed and distributed by University Microfilms, Inc., Ann Arbor, Michigan.

On pp. 172–173, Adkins gives a translation of Spechtshart's 12-tone monochord division.

108. Barbour, J.M. (1951). *Tuning and Temperament*, pp. 89–90. Da Capo Press, Inc., New York, 1972.

109. *Tuning and Temperament*, 98.

110. *Ibid.*

111. Crookes, D.Z., Translator (1986). *Syntagma musicum II: De organographia, Parts I and II*, by Michael Praetorius, pp. 66–69. The Clarendon Press, Oxford, England. The first edition of this work was published in 1618.

112. The Halberstadt organ did not have a characteristic split key for playing in a tempered tuning. The absence of an F♯/G♭ key means that this key was probably tuned to $^{729}/_{512}$.

113. Palisca, C.V. (1985). *Humanism in Italian Renaissance Musical Thought*, pp. 241–244. Yale University Press, New Haven, Connecticut.

Palisca gives a brief history of Euclid's construction in several Italian Renaissance treatises.

114. Zarlino, R.M.G. (1571). *Dimostrationi harmoniche*, p. 161. Facsimile Edition, The Gregg Press Incorporated, Ridgewood, New Jersey, 1966.

115. (A) *Istitutioni harmoniche*, p. 110.

(B) *Theorie des Tonsystems:* Das erste und zweite Buch der *Istitutioni harmoniche*, pp. 278–279.

116. Flegg, G., Hay, C., and Moss, B., Translators (1985). *Nicolas Chuquet, Renaissance Mathematician*, p. 261. D. Reidel Publishing Company, Dordrecht, Holland.

This volume contains many translated excerpts from Chuquet's mathematical works.

117. *Ibid.*, p. 260.

118. *Ibid.*, pp. 93–109.

119. *Ibid.*, p. 380.

120. *Ibid.*, p. 379.

121. See Note 158.

122. Miller, C.A., Translator (1993). *Musica practica*, by Bartolomeo Ramis de Pareia, p. 46. Hänssler-Verlag, Neuhausen-Stuttgart, Germany.

This is an English translation.

123. *Tuning and Temperament*, pp. 26–27.

124. (A) Asselin, P. (1985). *Musique et Tempérament*, pp. 195–205. Éditions Costallat, Paris, France.

Appendix 9 contains a catalog of 43 historic temperaments given in cps, decimal ratios, and cents.

(B) *Tuning and Temperament*, pp. 32–33.

125. Kelleher, J.E. (1993). *Zarlino's "Dimostrationi harmoniche" and Demonstrative Methodologies in the Sixteenth Century*, p. 296. Ph.D. dissertation printed and distributed by University Microfilms, Inc., Ann Arbor, Michigan.

This dissertation includes many translated excerpts from Zarlino's *Dimostrationi*. The cited quotation is from the *Dimostrationi*, Ragionamento Quarto, Proposta Prima, p. 221.

126. The fractional comma notation $G^{-\frac{1}{4}}$ was first used by J.M. Barbour and appears in many other texts as well. Here the notes that produce a spiral of "fifths" that ascends from C: G–D–A–E–B–F♯–C♯–G♯, represent Pythagorean ratios 3/2–9/8–27/16–81/64–243/128–729/512–2187/2048–6561/4096, respectively; and the notes that produce a spiral of "fifths" that descends from C: F–B♭–E♭, represent Pythagorean ratios 4/3–16/9–32/27, respectively. Unfortunately, the superscript does *not* indicate whether a given fractional value refers to a syntonic comma or to a ditonic comma.

127. The "large semitone" is also called a "diatonic semitone," and the "small semitone," a "chromatic semitone."

128. Marcuse, S. (1964). *Musical Instruments: A Comprehensive Dictionary*, p. 318. W. W. Norton & Company, Inc., New York, 1975.

129. Refer to Equation 9.22, and calculate the decimal ratio of 310.26 ¢, and of 269.2 ¢.

$$\text{B}\flat_2\text{: } (1.00057779)^{310.26\ \text{¢}} = 1.1963$$

$$\text{G}\sharp_3\text{: } (1.00057779)^{269.20\ \text{¢}} = 1.1682$$

Next, refer to Equation 9.25, and calculate the respective fret location of each tone on a 25.0 in. long lute string.

$$\text{B}\flat_2\text{: } \frac{25.0\ \text{in}}{1.1963} = 20.9\ \text{in}$$

$$\text{G}\sharp_3\text{: } \frac{25.0\ \text{in}}{1.1682} = 21.4\ \text{in}$$

Therefore, $\text{B}\flat_2$ on the G_2 open string requires a fret 20.9 in. from the bridge, but $\text{G}\sharp_3$ on the F_3 open string requires a fret 21.4 in. from the bridge. This example demonstrates that a single fret placed straight across a fingerboard can only produce one of these required frequencies. Consequently, meantone temperaments are impractical on fretted stringed instruments.

130. Because exact 12-tone equal temperament calculations did not occur throughout Europe until the middle of the 17th century, many Renaissance lutes and viols were equipped with moveable gut frets, which musicians tied around the fingerboard and adjusted for proper intonation. With the advent of logarithmic calculations, later instruments were built with permanently seated metal frets.

131. *Tuning and Temperament*, p. 8.

132. From thumb to little finger, the average open human hand spans a distance between 7 in. and 8 in. Any builder of keyboard instruments who attempts to fit a complete scale from "tonic" to "octave" into such a limited space must accept the intonational limitations of relatively small scales.

133. Coelho, V., Editor (1992). *Music and Science in the Age of Galileo*, p. 225. Kluwer Academic Publishers, Dordrecht, Netherlands.

A typical Renaissance lute has only eight frets per string.

134. *Syntagma musicum II: De organographia, Parts I and II*, pp. 66–69.

On p. 68, Praetorius correctly identifies three different sizes of "semitones." (1) The "major semitone" contains 5 commas: 21.51 ¢ × 5 = 107.55 ¢, which is close to 117.11 ¢. (2) The "minor semitone" contains 4 commas: 21.51 ¢ × 4 = 86.04 ¢, which is close to 76.05 ¢. And (3) the "intermediate semitone" on a lute contains 4½ commas: 21.51 ¢ × 4.5 = 96.80 ¢, which is very close to 100.0 ¢, or the modern 12-tone equal tempered "semitone."

135. Chapman, R.E., Translator (1957). *Harmonie universelle: The Books on Instruments*, by Marin Mersenne, pp. 435–441. Martinus Nijhoff, The Hague, Netherlands. The first edition of this work was published in 1636.

136. *Istitutioni harmoniche*, Seconda Parte, Cap. 47, p. 164.

137. Barnes, J. (1979). Bach's keyboard temperament. *Early Music* **7**, No. 2, pp. 236–249.

138. Rasch, R., Editor (1983). *Musicalische Temperatur*, by Andreas Werckmeister. The Diapason Press, Utrecht, Netherlands.

The first part of this book consists of commentary and mathematical analysis in English, and the second part contains a facsimile edition of the original work. For a modern analysis of Werckmeister's No. III, see pp. 26–30, 40–41. On pp. 29–30, Rasch gives historical reasons for the No. III vs. No. 1 confusion mentioned below.

139. *Tuning and Temperament*, p. 162.

Barbour refers to Werckmeister's No. III as "Werckmeister's No. 1."

140. Jorgensen, O. (1977). *Tuning the Historical Temperaments by Ear*, pp. 302–311. The Northern Michigan University Press, Marquette, Michigan.

Unlike Figure 10.23, Figure 10.25 does not give three simple tuning steps because Werckmeister's No. III requires a slightly more complicated approach than ¼-comma meantone temperament. Jorgensen's instructions for tuning this temperament are practical and highly accurate. However, note carefully that Jorgensen also refers to Werckmeister's No. III as "Werckmeister No. 1."

141. See Note 126.

142. *Early Music* **7**, 1979, p. 237.

143. Forster Translation: in *Ptolemaios und Porphyrios über die Musik*, p. 41; also in *Greek Musical Writings, Volume 2*, pp. 297–298.

144. To understand how the division of the left section of the first string into two equal parts is directly related to the arithmetic division of length ratio $\frac{9}{8}$, suppose we divide this string into 18 equal parts. Now, count 16 parts from the right end of the string, and place a bridge at length ratio $\frac{18}{16}$, which reduces to $\frac{9}{8}$, and sounds the "whole tone" D_3. Now, count 17 parts, and place a bridge under the second string at length ratio $\frac{18}{17}$, which sounds the "semitone" $C\sharp_3$. Observe that the bridge at $\frac{18}{17}$ divides the space between $\frac{18}{16}$ and the end of the string at $\frac{18}{18}$ into two equal parts.

145. D'Erlanger, R., Bakkouch, 'A.'A., and Al-Sanūsī, M., Translators (Vol. 1, 1930; Vol. 2, 1935; Vol. 3, 1938; Vol. 4, 1939; Vol. 5, 1949; Vol. 6, 1959). *La Musique Arabe*, Librairie Orientaliste Paul Geuthner, Paris, France.

Volumes 1–4 contain French translations of six Arabian treatises on music. *Volumes 1–2* contain the *Kitāb al-mūsīqī al-kabīr* by Al-Fārābī. See Chapter 11, Part IV.

146. Forster Translation: in *La Musique Arabe, Volume 1*, p. 97.

147. (A) Al-Faruqi, L.I. (1974). *The Nature of the Musical Art of Islamic Culture: A Theoretical and Empirical Study of Arabian Music*, pp. 412–413. Ph.D. dissertation printed and distributed by University Microfilms, Inc., Ann Arbor, Michigan.

Appendix III, pp. 404–455, consists of translated excerpts from Al-Fārābī's *Kitāb al-mūsīqī al-kabīr.*

(B) *La Musique Arabe, Volume 1*, p. 55.

148. Sadie, S., Editor (1980). *The New Grove Dictionary of Music and Musicians, Volume 3*, pp. 772–773. Macmillan Publishers Limited, London, England.

149. *Tuning and Temperament*, p. 57.

150. Palisca, C.V., Translator (2003). *Dialogue on Ancient and Modern Music*, by Vincenzo Galilei, pp. 121–122. Yale University Press, New Haven, Connecticut.

151. (A) *Tuning and Temperament*, pp. 57–58.

(B) *Dialogue on Ancient and Modern Music*, p. 122.

152. *Harmonie universelle: The Books on Instruments*, pp. 76–77.

153. See Section 2.6.

154. *Lutes, Viols and Temperaments*, p. 32.

155. Rossing, T.D. (1990). *The Science of Sound*, p. 212. Addison-Wesley Publishing Co., Inc., Reading, Massachusetts.

156. *Harmonie universelle: The Books on Instruments*, p. 74.

157. De Haan, D.B., Publisher (1884). *Vande Spiegeling der Singconst*, by Simon Stevin, pp. 27–29. Amsterdam.

Stevin's treatise on music was not published during his lifetime. This first edition consists of fragments found in the estate of Constantijn Huygens (1596–1687). The full original text may be found in *The Principal Works of Simon Stevin, Volume 5*, edited by E. Crone, *et al.*, music editor A.D. Fokker, translated by C. Dikshoorn, and published by C.V. Swets & Zeitlinger, Amsterdam, 1966. Unfortunately, this latter edition only gives Stevin's first monochord calculations that are largely inaccurate. Furthermore, it also does not include the method Stevin used to compute nine of the twelve decimal ratios in the second step.

158. *Mirifici logarithmorum canonis descriptio*, by John Napier was first published in 1614. (See Section 9.5.)

159. Crone, E., Editor; Fokker, A.D., Music Editor; Dikshoorn, C., Translator (1966). *The Principal Works of Simon Stevin, Volume 5*, p. 443. C.V. Swets & Zeitlinger, Amsterdam.

160. *Vande Spiegeling der Singconst*, pp. 25–26.

The *L'Arithmetique* was first published in 1585. The year of this publication marks the date for these historically significant calculations.

161. Rasch, R., Editor (1986). *Le cycle harmonique* (1691), *Novus cyclus harmonicus* (1724), by Christiaan Huygens, pp. 155–163. The Diapason Press, Utrecht, Netherlands.

This book contains facsimile editions of Huygens' original letter in French (1691), a Latin translation (1724), plus modern English and Dutch translations.

162. (A) *The Division of the Monochord* (1661), by Christiaan Huygens, pp. 121–127.

The above-mentioned volume also contains this short essay on the monochord. Huygens acknowledged the consonance of ratios $7/5$ and $10/7$ on p. 127.

(B) Cohen, H.F. (1984). *Quantifying Music*, pp. 225–228. D. Reidel Publishing Company, Dordrecht, Netherlands.

163. (A) *Le cycle harmonique*, pp. 69–76.

Here the editor R. Rasch includes descriptions and reproductions of three different keyboards designed by Huygens.

(B) *Quantifying Music*, p. 222.

164. Hubbard, F. (1965). *Three Centuries of Harpsichord Making*, 4th ed., Plate XI. Harvard University Press, Cambridge, Massachusetts, 1972.

165. *Le cycle harmonique*, p. 161.

Although Huygens claimed that he "... had such movable keyboards made ..." it is extremely doubtful that they actually worked. Huygens' plan presents the harpsichord maker with two serious structural problems. (1) The maker must not only fit 31 *batons* in the space of seven standard white keys, but also 31 harpsichord jacks between the closely spaced strings. (2) To accommodate these jacks, the maker must also chisel 31 rectangular mortises (or holes) per "octave" into the box slide that holds the jacks in place. Due to these formidable requirements, it is very unlikely that such an instrument ever existed.

166. *Quantifying Music*, p. 227.

167. *Ibid.*, p. 226.

168. See Sections 10.53–10.54.

169. Soukhanov, A.H., Executive Editor (1992). *The American Heritage Dictionary of the English Language*, 3rd ed., p. 979. Houghton Mifflin Company, Boston, Massachusetts.

170. *The Compact Edition of the Oxford English Dictionary, Volume 1*, p. 638. Oxford University Press, Oxford, England, 1974.

171. See Sections 3.5 and 3.8.

172. See Section 7.10.

173. The harmonic series does *not* apply to other vibrating systems such as stiff strings, bars, and plates. Here the higher modes produce frequencies that are noninteger, or irrational multiples of the fundamental frequency.

174. See Sections 10.26–10.27.

175. (A) Dupont, W. (1935). *Geschichte der musikalischen Temperatur*, pp. 20–21. C.H. Beck'sche Buchdruckerei, Nördlingen, Germany.

In the Erlangen University Library, Dupont discovered an anonymous treatise from the second half of the 15th century entitled *Pro clavichordiis faciendis*, which describes a monochord division intended as a clavichord tuning. Dupont cites the original Old German text and includes a modern synopsis of this passage. To many scholars, the following tuning is the earliest known European 12-tone scale that includes 5-limit ratios:

		↓		5/4					↓		5/4		
C	D♭	D	E♭	E	F	G♭	G	A♭	A	B♭	B	C′	D♭′
$\frac{1}{1}$	$\frac{256}{243}$	$\frac{4096}{3645}$	$\frac{32}{27}$	$\frac{5}{4}$	$\frac{4}{3}$	$\frac{1024}{729}$	$\frac{3}{2}$	$\frac{128}{81}$	$\frac{2048}{1215}$	$\frac{16}{9}$	$\frac{15}{8}$	$\frac{2}{1}$	$\frac{256}{243}$
0 ¢	90 ¢	202 ¢	294 ¢	386 ¢	498 ¢	588 ¢	702 ¢	792 ¢	904 ¢	996 ¢	1088 ¢	1200 ¢	90 ¢

In this scale, D and A are tuned as "major thirds," ratio $\frac{5}{4}$, down from G♭ and D♭, respectively. Consequently, D is a *schisma equivalent* of $\frac{9}{8}$, and A is a *schisma equivalent* of $\frac{27}{16}$. According to Dupont, the anonymous author is unaware of these schisma ". . . comma differences." Finally, B is tuned as a $\frac{5}{4}$ up from G.

(B) *The Theory and Practice of the Monochord*, pp. 238–241.

Adkins includes a detailed diagram of this division.

(C) *Tuning and Temperament*, pp. 92–93.

176. *Musica practica*, p. 15.

Hence, his Spanish name Bartolomé Ramos.

177. Hitti, P.K. (1937). *History of the Arabs*, p. 498. Macmillan and Co. Ltd., London, England, 1956.

178. Farmer, H.G. (1965). *The Sources of Arabian Music*, p. xxi. E.J. Brill, Leiden, Netherlands.

179. *Musica practica*, p. 17.

180. *Ibid.*, p. 46.

181. *Humanism in Italian Renaissance Musical Thought*, pp. 232–234.

On pp. 233–234, Palisca gives excerpts of Gaffurio's attack on Ramis.

182. *Musica practica*, pp. 47–48.

183. *Ibid.*, p. 85.

184. *La Musique Arabe, Volume 3.*

185. Williams, R.F., Translator (1972). *Marin Mersenne: An Edited Translation of the Fourth Treatise of the "Harmonie universelle," Volume 1*, p. 216. Three Volumes. Ph.D. dissertation printed and distributed by University Microfilms, Inc., Ann Arbor, Michigan.

This dissertation contains complete English translations of the following works by Mersenne. *Volume 1: Book One on Consonances*, and *Book Two on Dissonances; Volume 2: Book Three on Genera, Species, Systems, and Modes of Music*, and *Book Four on the Composition of Music; Volume 3: Book Five on the Composition of Music*, and *Book Six on the Art of Singing Well.*

The cited quotation is from Mersenne's *Book One on Consonances*, Prop. XXXIII. All future quotations from Williams' highly accurate translations will be listed in the notes in the following manner: Mersenne's original book title, Mersenne's proposition number, and the pages as numbered in Williams' dissertation.

186. Barbour, J.M. (1933). The persistence of the Pythagorean tuning system. *Scripta Mathematica*, Vol. 1, pp. 286–304.

It is truly ironic that Barbour's arguments against a 12-tone just intoned scale of his own making should appear in a journal dedicated to mathematics.

187. See Section 10.46.

188. Ibn Sīnā (Avicenna): *Auicene perhypatetici philosophi: ac medicorum facile primi opera in luce redacta...* This Latin translation was published in 1508. Facsimile Edition: Minerva, Frankfurt am Main, Germany, 1961.

The second chapter (or book) of this compendium is entitled *Sufficientia.*

189. Facsimile editions or translations of *Arithmetica integra* are not available. See Sections 10.43 and 10.46, and Chapter 9, Note 6, for translated excerpts from this work. Stifel was the first mathematician to use the term *exponent*, and to state the *four laws of exponents.*

190. (A) *Dimostrationi harmoniche*, Ragionamento Terzo, Proposta VIIII, pp. 158–160.

(B) *Zarlino's "Dimostrationi harmoniche" and Demonstrative Methodologies in the Sixteenth Century*, pp. 265–268.

Here Kelleher describes not only Zarlino's criticism, but also quotes several translated passages from Stifel's *Arithmetica integra.*

191. See Section 3.12.

192. Forster Translation: in *La Musique Arabe, Volume 1*, pp. 100–101.

193. See Chapter 11, Part IV.

194. Reichenbach, H. (1951). *The Rise of Scientific Philosophy.* The University of California Press, Berkeley and Los Angeles, California, 1958.

195. Forster Translation: in *Theorie des Tonsystems*, pp. 104–105; in *Istitutioni harmoniche*, pp. 37–38.

196. *Auicene perhypatetici philosophi* . . . I, Cap. 8, p. 18.

197. *The Sources of Arabian Music*, p. 36.

198. Forster Translation: in *La Musique Arabe, Volume 2*, p. 124.

With respect to the "puissance" translation error, see Section 11.55, Note 76.

199. *The Manual of Harmonics*, pp. 107–108.

200. *Mathematics Useful for Understanding Plato*, pp. 76–79.

201. *Fundamentals of Music*, pp. 65–72.

202. Forster Translation: in *La Musique Arabe, Volume 2*, p. 136.

203. *Ibid.*, pp. 136–137.

204. *Ibid.*, *Volume 3*, pp. 36–37.

205. Forster Translation: in *Theorie des Tonsystems*, p. 87; in *Istitutioni harmoniche*, p. 31.

206. Forster Translation: in *Theorie des Tonsystems*, pp. 87–88; in *Istitutioni harmoniche*, pp. 31–32.

207. Forster Translation: in *Theorie des Tonsystems*, pp. 148–149; in *Istitutioni harmoniche*, pp. 54–55.

208. Forster Translation: in *Theorie des Tonsystems*, p. 156; in *Istitutioni harmoniche*, p. 60.

209. Forster Translation: in *Theorie des Tonsystems*, p. 167.

210. Forster Translation: in *Theorie des Tonsystems*, p. 161; in *Istitutioni harmoniche*, p. 61.

211. Forster Translation: in *Theorie des Tonsystems*, pp. 161–162; in *Istitutioni harmoniche*, pp. 61–62.

212. Forster Translation: in *Theorie des Tonsystems*, p. 162; in *Istitutioni harmoniche*, p. 62.

213. Forster Translation: in *Theorie des Tonsystems*, pp. 162–163; in *Istitutioni harmoniche*, p. 62.

214. Forster Translation: in *Theorie des Tonsystems*, pp. 163–164; in *Istitutioni harmoniche*, pp. 62–63.

215. Wienpahl, R.W. (1959). Zarlino, the *Senario*, and tonality, p. 31. *Journal of the American Musicological Society* **XII**, No. 1, pp. 27–41.

 Wienpahl gives a detailed analysis of the "major sixth" and "minor sixth" in Zarlino's *Senario.* This paper also includes many translated excerpts from Zarlino's *Istitutioni harmoniche*, and from Salinas' *De musica libri VII.*

216. Forster Translation: in *Theorie des Tonsystems*, p. 93; in *Istitutioni harmoniche*, p. 34.

217. Forster Translation: in *Theorie des Tonsystems*, p. 91; in *Istitutioni harmoniche*, p. 33.

218. Forster Translation: in *Theorie des Tonsystems*, pp. 91–92; in *Istitutioni harmoniche*, pp. 33–34.

219. (A) *Source Readings in Music History*, p. 242.

 (B) *Journal of the American Musicological Society* **XII**, No. 1, p. 27.

 (C) Shirlaw, M. (1917). *The Theory of Harmony*, p. 50. Da Capo Press Reprint Edition. Da Capo Press, New York, 1969.

220. (A) *Source Readings in Music History*, pp. 242–243.

 (B) *Journal of the American Musicological Society* **XII**, No. 1, p. 28.

221. Forster Translation: in *Theorie des Tonsystems*, p. 168.

 In his commentaries, Fend gives Stifel's original Latin text: "Non enim video quod Harmonica habeat quod ad concentus Musicos pertineat, quod Arithmetica non habeat aequali commoditate."

222. See Section 10.27.

223. Daniels, A.M. (1962). *The De musica libri VII of Francisco de Salinas.* Ph.D. dissertation printed and distributed by University Microfilms, Inc., Ann Arbor, Michigan.

 This dissertation includes many lengthy translated excerpts from Salinas' treatise.

224. Farmer, H.G., Translator (1965). *Al-Fārābī's Arabic-Latin Writings on Music*, p. 4. Hinrichsen Edition Ltd., New York.

225. (A) Kastner, M.S., Editor (1958). *De musica libri VII*, by Francisco Salinas, p. 56, 62, 86, 144, 230. Facsimile Edition. Bärenreiter-Verlag, Kassel, Germany.

(B) Fernandez de la Cuesta, I., Translator (1983). *Siete libros sobre la musica*, by Francisco Salinas, p. 127, 136, 175, 265, 403. Editorial Alpuerto, Madrid, Spain.

This is a modern Spanish translation of Salinas' original Latin text. An English translation of this work does not exist.

226. *La Musique Arabe, Volume 3*, p. 230.

227. *The Sources of Arabian Music*, p. 58.

228. Forster Translation: in *La Musique Arabe, Volume 3*, pp. 576–577.

229. (A) *Journal of the American Musicological Society* **XII**, No. 1, p. 35.

(B) *De musica libri VII*, p. 61.

(C) *Siete libros sobre la musica*, p. 136.

230. Mersenne, M. (1636–37). *Harmonie universelle contenant la théorie et la pratique de la musique.* Three Volumes. Facsimile Edition. Éditions du Centre National de la Recherche Scientifique, Paris, France, 1963.

The works translated by R.F. Williams appear in *Volume 2;* and the work translated by R.E. Chapman appears in *Volume 3.*

231. R.E. Chapman, Translator: *Harmonie universelle: The Books on Instruments.*

232. (A) R.F. Williams, Translator: *Book One on Consonances*, Prop. XL, pp. 263–268.

Here Mersenne lists 100 consonant just ratios, and 50 dissonant just ratios.

(B) R.F. Williams, Translator: *Book Two on Dissonances*, Prop. II, p. 284.

Here Mersenne lists 12 just ratios the size of a "semitone" and smaller.

233. Hyde, F.B. (1954). *The Position of Marin Mersenne in the History of Music*, Part 1, Chapter VII. Two Volumes. Ph.D. dissertation printed and distributed by University Microfilms, Inc., Ann Arbor, Michigan.

This dissertation includes many translated excerpts from Mersenne's works and correspondence.

234. *The Books on Instruments*, Book 4, Prop. XIII, p. 280.

235. As discussed in Chapter 8, Note 38, the act of overblowing a tube open at both ends produces all the tones of the harmonic series. Flutes open at both ends and trumpets are alike in this respect.

236. (A) *The Books on Instruments*, Book 4, Prop. IX, p. 268.

(B) *Harmonie universelle contenant la théorie...*, Volume 3, p. 208.

237. *The Books on Instruments*, Book 4, Prop. XIII, pp. 280–281.

238. (A) *Ibid.*, Book 4, Prop. IX, p. 268.

(B) *Harmonie universelle contenant la théorie...*, Volume 3, p. 209.

239. Green, B.L. (1969). *The Harmonic Series From Mersenne to Rameau: An Historical Study of Circumstances Leading to Its Recognition and Application to Music*, p. 335. Ph.D. dissertation printed and distributed by University Microfilms, Inc., Ann Arbor, Michigan.

This dissertation includes many translated excerpts from Mersenne's works. The cited quotation is from *Harmonicorum libri XII*, Tome II, Book 1, Prop. XXXIII, p. 53.

240. *The Books on Instruments*, Book 4, Prop. X, p. 271.

241. *Ibid.*, Book I, Prop. VI, p. 33.

242. *Ibid.*, Book 2, Prop. I, p. 74; Book 2, Prop. VI, p. 91.

243. *Ibid.*, Book 5, Prop. XI, p. 320.

244. *Ibid.*, Book 4, Prop. IX, p. 270.

245. *Ibid.*, Book 5, Prop. XI, p. 320.

246. Lightly touching a string to sound flageolet tones is analogous to overblowing a trumpet: both techniques produce *only* the tones of the harmonic series.

247. *Musical Instruments: A Comprehensive Dictionary*, p. 542.

248. *The Books on Instruments*, Book 4, Prop. XIII, p. 280.

249. (A) *Ibid.*, Book 4, Prop. XII, p. 277.

On p. 278, Mersenne refers to the second figure on the left as PS.

(B) *Harmonie universelle contenant la théorie...*, Volume 3, p. 218.

250. *The Books on Instruments*, Book 4, Prop. XIII, p. 280.

251. *Ibid.*, Book 4, Prop. XII, p. 278.

252. (A) *Ibid.*

(B) *Harmonie universelle contenant la théorie...*, Volume 3, p. 219.

With respect to the corrections {*sol re*} and {*sol re ut*}, see the article "Solmization" in *The New Groves Dictionary of Music and Musicians, Volume 17*, p. 459, Table 2.

253. We may interpret Mersenne's qualification that "there is no mean semitone [135:128] in {♮} at all" as a reference to Ramis' 5-limit scale, which includes numerous "mean semitones." (See Figure 10.32.) Mersenne defines the "mean semitone" as ratio 135:128 in *Book Two on Dissonances*, Prop. II, p. 284, of the Williams Translation. Ptolemy's Tense Diatonic includes only the "major semitone," ratio $^{16}/_{15}$. (See Figure 10.15.)

254. (A) *The Books on Instruments*, Book 4, Prop. XII, p. 278.

(B) *Harmonie universelle contenant la théorie...*, Volume 3, p. 219.

255. *The Books on Instruments*, Book 4, Prop. XII, p. 279.

256. *Ibid.*, Book 5, Prop. XIII, p. 322.

257. Palisca, C.V. (1961). "Scientific Empiricism in Musical Thought." In *Seventeenth Century Science and the Arts*, H.H. Rhys, Editor, pp. 91–137. Princeton University Press, Princeton, New Jersey.

258. *Scientific Empiricism in Musical Thought*, p. 106.

259. *Ibid.*

260. *Ibid.*, pp. 106–108.

See Sections 3.11 and 3.13, for examples on how to divide strings according to *modern length ratios* $^{1}/_{n}$ and $^{x}/_{n}$, respectively, where the short string length is in the numerator and the long string length is in the denominator; such as $^{1}/_{3}$, $^{2}/_{3}$, $^{2}/_{5}$, $^{3}/_{5}$, etc.

261. See Section 10.34.

262. *Book One on Consonances*, Prop. I, p. 29.

263. *Ibid.*, Prop. II, p. 37.

264. *Ibid.*, Prop. IV, p. 48.

265. *Ibid.*, Prop. XXXII, p. 202.

266. *Ibid.*

267. *Ibid.*, Prop. XXXII, p. 203.

268. *Ibid.*, Prop. XL, p. 273.

269. *Ibid.*, Prop. XXXII, p. 206.

270. *Ibid.*, Prop. XXXIII, pp. 207–208.

271. *Ibid.*, Prop. XXXIII, p. 213.

272. *Ibid.*, Prop. XXXIII, pp. 214–215.

273. *Ibid.*, Prop. XXXIII, p. 217.

274. *Ibid.*, Prop. XXXIII, pp. 215–216.

275. *Ibid.*, Prop. XXXIII, pp. 214–215.

276. *Ibid.*, Prop. XXXIII, p. 223.

277. See Section 10.29.

278. *Book One on Consonances*, Prop. XXXIII, p. 219.

279. *Ibid.*, Prop. XXXIII, p. 222.

280. Wallis, J. (1677). Dr. Wallis' letter to the publisher, concerning a new musical discovery. *Philosophical Transactions of the Royal Society of London* **XII**, pp. 839–842.

281. *Ibid.*, p. 841.

282. *Ibid.*, pp. 839–840.

283. Roberts, F. (1692). A discourse concerning the musical notes of the trumpet, and the trumpet-marine, and of the defects of the same. *Philosophical Transactions of the Royal Society of London* **XVII**, pp. 559–563.

284. *Ibid.*, p. 562.

285. *Ibid.*, p. 563.

286. (A) Maxham, R.E., Translator (1976). *The Contributions of Joseph Sauveur to Acoustics, Volume 2*, pp. 1–97. Two Volumes. Ph.D. dissertation printed and distributed by University Microfilms, Inc., Ann Arbor, Michigan.

Volume 1 of this dissertation discusses the acoustic discoveries of Sauveur in full detail. *Volume 2* contains complete English translations of the following short works by Sauveur: (1) *General System of Intervals, and Its Application to All the Systems and Instruments of Music*, (1701); (2) *Application of Harmonics to the Composition of Organ Stops*, (1702); (3) *General Method for Forming the Tempered Systems of Music, and of the Choice of the One Which Should Be Employed*, (1707); (4) *General Table of the Tempered System of Music*, (1711); (5) *Relationship of the Sounds of Strings of Musical Instruments to the Sags of the Strings; and a New Determination of the Fixed Sounds*, (1713).

All future quotations of Sauveur are from his *General System of Intervals.*

(B) Rasch, R., Editor (1984). *Collected Writings on Musical Acoustics*, by Joseph Sauveur. The Diapason Press, Utrecht, Netherlands.

The first part of this book consists of commentary and mathematical analysis in English. The second part contains facsimile editions of the five papers mentioned above.

287. (A) *General System of Intervals*, p. 1.

(B) *Collected Writings on Musical Acoustics*, p. 99.

288. (A) *General System of Intervals*, p. 70.

(B) *Collected Writings on Musical Acoustics*, p. 149.

289. (A) *General System of Intervals*, p. 75.

(B) *Collected Writings on Musical Acoustics*, p. 152.

290. (A) *General System of Intervals*, pp. 3–4.

(B) *Collected Writings on Musical Acoustics*, p. 101.

291. *The Books on Instruments*, Book 4, Prop. IX, p. 269.

292. Truesdell, C. (1960). *The Rational Mechanics of Flexible or Elastic Bodies: 1638–1788*, pp. 237–244. Orell Füssli, Zürich, Switzerland.

293. (A) *General System of Intervals*, p. 71.

(B) *Collected Writings on Musical Acoustics*, p. 149.

294. (A) *General System of Intervals*, p. 81.

(B) *Collected Writings on Musical Acoustics*, p. 156.

295. (A) *General System of Intervals*, pp. 73–74.

(B) *Collected Writings on Musical Acoustics*, pp. 151–152.

296. (A) *General System of Intervals*, pp. 75–76.

(B) *Collected Writings on Musical Acoustics*, pp. 152–153.

297. *The Rational Mechanics of Flexible or Elastic Bodies*, pp. 192–199.

298. James, G., and James, R.C. (1976). *Mathematics Dictionary*, 4th ed., p. 178. Van Nostrand Reinhold, New York.

299. Gossett, P., Translator (1971). *Traité de l'harmonie* [Treatise on Harmony], by Jean-Philippe Rameau. Dover Publications, Inc., New York.

This is an English translation.

300. *The Theory of Harmony*, p. 68.

301. Rameau, J.P. (1722). *Traité de l'harmonie reduite à ses principes naturels*, p. 4. Facsimile Edition. Biblioteca Nacional de Madrid, Spain, 1984.

302. P. Gossett, Translator: *Traité de l'harmonie*, p. 14, 21, 24, 55.

303. *Ibid.*, p. 14 and 21 describe the "new proportion," and pp. 24–25, Zarlino's "proportion."

304. *Ibid.*, pp. 4–5.

305. Forster Translation: in *Theorie des Tonsystems*, p. 75; in *Istitutioni harmoniche*, p. 27.

306. *Ibid.*

307. *Traité de l'harmonie*, p. 7.

308. *Ibid.*, p. 8.

309. *Ibid.*, p. 55.

310. *Ibid.*

311. *Ibid.*, p. 55.

312. *Mathematics Dictionary*, p. 258.

313. *Traité de l'harmonie*, p. 23.

314. *Ibid.*, p. 54.

315. *Ibid.*, p. 6.

316. *The Theory of Harmony*, p. 69.

317. *Traité de l'harmonie*, p. 15.

318. *Ibid.*, p. 35.

319. Chandler, B.G., Translator (1975). *Rameau's "Nouveau système de musique théorique": An Annotated Translation with Commentary*, p. 213. Ph.D. dissertation printed and distributed by University Microfilms, Inc., Ann Arbor, Michigan.

320. *Ibid.*, p. 216.

321. *Ibid.*, p. 217.

322. *The Harmonic Series from Mersenne to Rameau*, pp. 423–424.

Here Green gives a complete English translation of Fontanelle's important essay.

323. *Nouveau système de musique théorique*, p. 221.

324. *Ibid.*, p. 222.

325. *Ibid.*, p. 227.

326. *Ibid.*, p. 224.

327. *Traité de l'harmonie*, p. 16, pp. 25–26.

328. *Nouveau système de musique théorique*, pp. 223–224.

329. *Ibid.*, p. 225.

330. *Ibid.*, p. 228.

On pp. 208–209, Rameau explains that the arithmetic progression of frequency ratios 1:3:5 is produced by the harmonic progression of length ratios 15:5:3.

331. Hayes, D., Translator (1968). *Rameau's Theory of Harmonic Generation; An Annotated Translation and Commentary of "Génération harmonique" by Jean-Philippe Rameau*, pp. 19–20. Ph.D. dissertation printed and distributed by University Microfilms, Inc., Ann Arbor, Michigan.

Also, see Section 10.46, Figure 10.45.

332. *Ibid.*, pp. 38–39.

333. *Ibid.*, p. 54.

334. *Ibid.*, p. 55.

335. (A) *Ibid.*, p. 62.

As it appears in Section 10.62, Example I is an exact translated version of Rameau's engraving in the following facsimile edition:

(B) Jacobi, E.R., Editor (1968). *Jean-Philippe Rameau (1683–1764): Complete Theoretical Writings, Volume 3*, p. 137. American Institute of Musicology, [Rome, Italy].

In this facsimile edition, the two semicircles are mislabeled and misplaced. The large semicircle should read *"major third"* and appear first; the small semicircle should read *"minor third"* and appear second.

336. *Génération harmonique*, p. 70.

337. *Ibid.*, p. 36.

338. *Ibid.*, p. 69.

339. (A) *Ibid.*, p. 64.

As it appears in Section 10.62, Example II is an exact translated version of Rameau's engraving in the following facsimile edition:

(B) *Jean-Philippe Rameau (1683–1764): Complete Theoretical Writings, Volume 3*, p. 137.

340. *Génération harmonique*, pp. 31–32.

341. *Ibid.*, p. 63.

342. Briscoe, R.L., Translator (1975). *Rameau's "Démonstration du principe de l'harmonie" and "Nouvelles reflections de M. Rameau sur sa démonstration du principe de l'harmonie": An Annotated Translation of Two Treatises by Jean-Philippe Rameau.* Ph.D. dissertation printed and distributed by University Microfilms, Inc., Ann Arbor, Michigan.

343. *Ibid.*, pp. 123–125.

344. *Ibid.*, p. 153.

345. *Ibid.*, p. 157.

346. (A) Jorgenson, D.A. (1957). *A History of Theories of the Minor Triad.* Ph.D. dissertation printed and distributed by University Microfilms, Inc., Ann Arbor, Michigan.

(B) Jorgenson, D.A. (1963). A résumé of harmonic dualism. *Music and Letters* **XLIV**, No. 1, pp. 31–42.

Consult these two works by Dale Jorgenson for a scholarly overview of this discussion.

347. *The Theory of Harmony*, p. 223.

348. Meyer, M.F. (1929). *The Musician's Arithmetic.* Oliver Ditson Company, Boston, Massachusetts.

349. *Ibid.*, p. 20.

350. *Génération harmonique*, pp. 163–164.

351. *The Musician's Arithmetic*, p. 51.

352. *Ibid.*, p. 6.

353. *Ibid.*, pp. 103–105.

354. Partch, H. (1949). *Genesis of a Music.* The University of Wisconsin Press, Madison, Wisconsin.

355. Partch, H. (1949). *Genesis of a Music*, 2nd ed. Da Capo Press, New York, 1974.

356. *Genesis of a Music* (1949), p. 300. *Genesis of a Music* (1974), p. 427.

357. *Genesis of a Music* (1949), p. 110, 158, 213, 327, respectively. *Genesis of a Music* (1974), p. 110, 159, 261, 454, respectively.

358. *Genesis of a Music* (1974), pp. 259–261.

359. *Ibid.*, p. 75.

Partch referred to his general system of tuning as Monophony, and gives the following definition on p. 71: "Monophony: an organization of musical materials based upon the faculty of the human ear to perceive all intervals and to deduce all principles of musical relationships as an expansion from unity, as 1 is to 1, or — as it is expressed in this work — $^1\!/_1$." Compare this statement to Zarlino's definition of *Unità* in Section 10.59: "According to Unity, each thing, be it simple or compound, or corporeal or spiritual, is characterized by oneness."

360. *Ibid.*, p. 112.

361. In Figure 10.61, $^{27}\!/_{20}$ acts as a $^3\!/_2$ nexus between $^9\!/_5$ and the syntonic comma $^{81}\!/_{80}$; and $^{40}\!/_{27}$ acts as a $^3\!/_2$ nexus between $^{10}\!/_9$ and the inversion of the syntonic comma $^{160}\!/_{81}$.

362. Unpublished correspondence, 1976.

363. Brun, V. (1964). Euclidean algorithms and musical theory. *L'Enseignement Mathématique* **X**, pp. 125–137.

364. Williamson, C. (1938). The frequency ratios of the tempered scale. *Journal of the Acoustical Society of America* **10**, pp. 135–136.

Brun's method is based on the famous Euclidean Algorithm for finding the greatest common divisor between any two given integers. This algorithm leads to a technique for representing the quotient of two integers as a continued fraction. Williamson gives an exceptionally lucid explanation for using continued fractions to convert irrational decimal ratios into rational integer ratio approximations.

11 / WORLD TUNINGS

When Westerners speak of music as a universal language, they more than likely think of a symphony orchestra performance in China or Japan, or some other musical product exported from the occident to the orient. Long before I began writing this book, I envisioned discussing Chinese, Indonesian, Indian, and Arabian tuning theory in the same breath as Greek and Renaissance tuning theory. Why not? Music is a universal language not only because human beings have ears and a desire to make music, but also because people all over the world cultivate and investigate the subject of musical mathematics.

Most listeners to whom "foreign" music sounds "funny" never get past a first impression because they lack the artistic and scientific tools to analyze their initial response. If prejudice is the expression of personal opinion without a consideration of facts, then understanding is the expression of personal opinion based on a willingness to consider facts. In this context, a factual examination of another civilization may lead to the following questions: When a Chinese musician tunes the strings of a *ch'in*, and when a European musician tunes the strings of a harpsichord, how are these two tunings alike, and how are they different? However, such comparisons alone do not meet the requirements for true understanding. One must also ask, "Does an examination of facts further the experience of listening to music from distant civilizations?" If your answer is "yes," then read on.

The reading requirements for Chapter 11 are the same as outlined at the beginning of Chapter 10. The reader should also study Sections 10.1–10.2, and know the definitions of prime numbers, composite numbers, rational numbers, and irrational numbers. However, a complete reading of Chapter 10 is not required. Throughout Chapter 11, I have intentionally avoided references to Western tuning and music theory wherever possible. Finally, this chapter consists of four parts. Part I examines Chinese music; Part II, Indonesian music; Part III, Indian music; and Part IV, Arabian, Persian, and Turkish music. Due to the vastness of these subjects, I have selected only a few basic concepts from each civilization. Without these considerations, no fundamental understanding is possible.

Part I

CHINESE MUSIC

11.1

Of the texts that have survived, the earliest detailed description of Chinese tuning practice exists in a book entitled *Lü-shih ch'un-ch'iu* (*The Spring and Autumn of Lü Pu-wei*), written *c.* 240 B.C.[1] According to this narrative, the semi-legendary emperor Huang Ti (fl. *c.* 2700 B.C.) ordered music master Ling Lun to cast a set of sixty bells, and to tune them in twelve sets of five bells each. To accomplish this task, Ling Lun used the original 12-tone scale, where each scale degree provided him with a fundamental tone from which to tune the original pentatonic scale. The oldest extant source that gives detailed calculations for this 12-tone scale is a book by Ssu-ma Ch'ien (*c.* 145 B.C. – *c.* 87 B.C.) entitled *Shih Chi* (*Records of the Historian*), written *c.* 90 B.C.[2] Here, Ssu-ma Ch'ien cites the famous formula

San fen sun i fa: Subtract and add one-third.[3]

for the calculation of 12 pitch pipe lengths. An ancient pitch pipe consists of a tube closed at one end. One plays a pitch pipe like a panpipe by blowing across the open end of the tube. Ssu-ma Ch'ien's formula works equally well for string lengths. Equations 7.18 and 3.10 indicate that these two vibrating systems are very similar. The former equation states that the theoretical wavelength of the fundamental tone of a closed tube equals four times the length of the tube; and the latter equation, that the theoretical wavelength of the fundamental tone of a string equals two times the length of the string. However, because the frequencies of tubes are affected by end corrections,[4] lip coverage at the embouchure hole,[5] and the strength of a player's airstream,[6] the following discussion will focus on strings; the frequencies of the latter are easier to predict and control. Furthermore, since Ssu-ma Ch'ien based his calculations on a closed tube 8.1 units long,[7] and since fractional lengths are inconvenient, we will use an overall string length of 9 units. This length occurs in many historical texts, including a work entitled *Lung-yin-kuan ch'in-p'u* by Wang Pin-lu (1867–1921). Pin-lu's student, Hsü Li-sun, edited and renamed this manuscript *Mei-an ch'in-p'u*, and published it in 1931. Fredric Lieberman translated the latter in his book *A Chinese Zither Tutor.*[8] We will refer to this work throughout Sections 11.5–11.7.

11.2

The ancient formula *subtract and add one-third* consists of two mathematical operations that have opposite effects. Subtraction of a string's ⅓ length yields variable L_{short}, and addition of a string's ⅓ length yields variable L_{long}. However, in the context of scale calculations, one may obtain identical results through the following operations of division and multiplication. (1) The act of subtracting ⅓ from a string's vibrating length (L) is equivalent to dividing L by ancient length ratio $3/2$, or multiplying L by modern length ratio $2/3$:

$$L_{\text{short}} = L - \frac{L}{3} = \frac{L}{\frac{3}{2}} = L \times \frac{2}{3}$$

(2) The act of adding ⅓ to a string's decreased length is equivalent to multiplying L_{short} by ancient length ratio $4/3$:

$$L_{\text{long}} = L_{\text{short}} + \frac{L_{\text{short}}}{3} = L_{\text{short}} \times \frac{4}{3}$$

(3) Similar to the first operation, the act of subtracting ⅓ from a string's increased length is equivalent to dividing L_{long} by ancient length ratio $3/2$, or multiplying L_{long} by modern length ratio $2/3$:

$$L_{\text{short}} = L_{\text{long}} - \frac{L_{\text{long}}}{3} = \frac{L_{\text{long}}}{\frac{3}{2}} = L_{\text{long}} \times \frac{2}{3}$$

For a string 9.0 units long, Table 11.1 shows that the Chinese up-and-down principle of scale generation produces string lengths accurate to five decimal places.

Table 11.1

12 STRING LENGTHS PRODUCED BY THE CHINESE UP-AND-DOWN PRINCIPLE OF SCALE GENERATION

9.00000
$9.00000 \times 2/3 = 6.00000$
$6.00000 \times 4/3 = 8.00000$
$8.00000 \times 2/3 = 5.33333$
$5.33333 \times 4/3 = 7.11111$
$7.11111 \times 2/3 = 4.74074$
$4.74074 \times 4/3 = 6.32099$
$6.32099 \times 4/3 = 8.42799$
$8.42799 \times 2/3 = 5.61866$
$5.61866 \times 4/3 = 7.49155$
$7.49155 \times 2/3 = 4.99437$
$4.99437 \times 4/3 = 6.65916$

To assure that these lengths produce tones within the span of an "octave," or that all lengths are longer than 4.5 units, note two consecutive multiplications of ratio $4/3$ near the center of Table 11.1. Joseph Needham describes this process of scale generation in the same context as discussed in Section 3.18; namely, in ancient musical texts, mathematicians and musicians express scale degrees not as frequency ratios, but as length ratios.

> ***Before the idea of frequency existed***, however, the same relation was expressed simply in terms of length, the length of a resonating agent multiplied by $2/3$ being equivalent to the frequency multiplied by $3/2$. The length of a zither string, then, multiplied by $2/3$ gives a note which when struck is a perfect fifth higher than its fundamental. This is the first step (or *lü*) in a process which evolves an unending spiral of notes. The length of the resonating agent which sounds the perfect fifth is then multiplied by $4/3$, the resulting note being a fourth below the perfect fifth . . .[9] (Bold italics mine.)

Now, starting on C (or F), arrange these ancient length ratios (or frequency ratios) in the same order as shown in Figure 10.16(a). With the exception of B♯, or the *ditonic comma*,[10] ratio $531441/524288$, Table 11.2 shows that the Chinese and Pythagorean progression of ratios are identical, which means that both sequences form an ascending *spiral of "fifths."* (For more accurate results, recalculate the Chinese ratios to a greater number of decimal places.) However, remember that this 12-tone spiral of eleven ascending $3/2$'s represents the basis of Chinese scale theory approximately 1500–2000 years before mathematicians in the West contemplated the musical possibilities of such a scale.[11] Finally, Table 11.3, Column 1, lists the 12 ratios; Column 2, the Chinese names of the scale degrees or *lü;* Column 3, the English translations of these names;[12] Column 4, the Chinese solmization of the *five basic tones* of the original pentatonic scale; Column 5, the note names starting on C; Column 6, the note names starting on F; and Column 7, the cent values of the 12 *lü*. Notice that the ratios of this pentatonic scale originate in the *first five tones* of the up-and-down principle of scale generation; that is, $1/1$ or *do* is *kung*, $3/2$ or *sol* is *chih*, $9/8$ or *re* is *shang*, $27/16$ or *la* is *yü*, and $81/64$ or *mi* is *chiao.* In diatonic order, these ratios are $1/1$ or *Huang-chung* is *kung*, $9/8$ or *T'ai-ts'ou* is *shang*, $81/64$ or *Ku-hsien* is *chiao*, $3/2$ or *Lin-chung* is *chih*, and $27/16$ or *Nan-lü* is *yü*.

Table 11.2

CHINESE 12-TONE SPIRAL OF ELEVEN ASCENDING $\frac{3}{2}$'s

$\frac{9.0}{9.00000} = \frac{1}{1}$	C
$\frac{9.0}{6.00000} = \frac{3}{2}$	G
$\frac{9.0}{8.00000} = \frac{9}{8}$	D
$\frac{9.0}{5.33333} = \frac{27}{16}$	A
$\frac{9.0}{7.11111} = \frac{81}{64}$	E
$\frac{9.0}{4.74074} = \frac{243}{128}$	B
$\frac{9.0}{6.32099} = \frac{729}{512}$	F♯
$\frac{9.0}{8.42799} = \frac{2187}{2048}$	C♯
$\frac{9.0}{5.61866} = \frac{6561}{4096}$	G♯
$\frac{9.0}{7.49155} = \frac{19683}{16384}$	D♯
$\frac{9.0}{4.99437} = \frac{59049}{32768}$	A♯
$\frac{9.0}{6.65916} = \frac{177147}{131072}$	E♯

Table 11.3

RATIOS AND NAMES OF THE ORIGINAL CHINESE 12-TONE SCALE, AND THE SOLMIZATION OF THE ORIGINAL CHINESE PENTATONIC SCALE

$\frac{1}{1}$	*Huang-chung*	Yellow Bell	*KUNG*	C	F	0.0 ¢
$\frac{2187}{2048}$	*Ta-lü*	Greatest Tube		C♯	F♯	113.7 ¢
$\frac{9}{8}$	*T'ai-ts'ou*	Great Frame	*SHANG*	D	G	203.9 ¢
$\frac{19683}{16384}$	*Chia-chung*	Pressed Bell		D♯	G♯	317.6 ¢
$\frac{81}{64}$	*Ku-hsien*	Old, Purified	*CHIAO*	E	A	407.8 ¢
$\frac{177147}{131072}$	*Chung-lü*	Mean Tube		E♯	A♯	521.5 ¢
$\frac{729}{512}$	*Jui-pin*	Luxuriant Vegetation		F♯	B	611.7 ¢
$\frac{3}{2}$	*Lin-chung*	Forest Bell	*CHIH*	G	C	702.0 ¢
$\frac{6561}{4096}$	*I-tse*	Equalizing Rule		G♯	C♯	815.6 ¢
$\frac{27}{16}$	*Nan-lü*	Southern Tube	*YÜ*	A	D	905.9 ¢
$\frac{59049}{32768}$	*Wu-I*	Not Terminated		A♯	D♯	1019.6 ¢
$\frac{243}{128}$	*Ying-chung*	Answering Bell		B	E	1109.8 ¢
(1)	(2)	(3)	(4)	(5)	(6)	(7)

~ 11.3 ~

The Chinese *ch'in* (or *qin*) is one of the most expressive musical instruments created by man. The fact that it has survived without significant modifications for over 3000 years[13] is a testament to its musical beauty and acoustic integrity. Performers on the *ch'in* produce three different kinds of sounds: open string tones, flageolet tones, and stopped tones. Moreover, the underlying mathematical organization of the *ch'in* categorizes these sounds into four distinct yet interdependent tuning systems: (1) the flageolet system, (2) the stopped hui integer system, (3) the open string pentatonic system, and (4) the stopped hui fraction system. Before we discuss these tuning systems in full detail, let us first examine the construction of this instrument.

In a book entitled *The History of Musical Instruments*, Curt Sachs (1881–1959) classifies the *ch'in* as a zither.

> A zither has no neck or yoke; the strings are stretched between the two ends of a body, whether this body is in the usual sense a resonator itself, or whether it requires an attached resonator.[14]

The *ch'in* has a slightly tapered body approximately 4 ft. long, 8 in. wide, and 3 in. thick.[15] It is made from two different kinds of wood.[16] The top piece consists of a relatively soft wood called *t'ung* wood (*Paulownia imperialis*). It has a slightly convex shape and acts as a soundboard against which the performer stops the strings. In contrast, the bottom piece consists of a relatively hard wood called *tzu* wood (*Tecoma radicanus*). It is flat and gives the instrument structural rigidity. These two pieces of wood are jointed together on all four sides of the instrument. Consequently, an air chamber between the convex top and the flat bottom functions as a cavity resonator,[17] and amplifies the sounds of the strings. Two rectangular sound holes in the bottom piece allow the amplified acoustic energy to radiate into the surrounding air.

The *ch'in* has seven identically long strings of varying thickness, but no moveable bridges and no frets for the purposes of tuning. A permanent narrow bridge that spans the instrument's width sits approximately 3 in. from the wide end. Between the bridge and this end, seven holes traverse vertically through the top and bottom pieces. The strings are threaded through the holes and tied to tuning pegs that push up against the bottom of the instrument. Because the pegs reside underneath the instrument, they are not visible to the casual observer. From here, the strings pass over the bridge and around the narrow end of the *ch'in*. This end acts as a nut. The strings are here tied to two large knobs that are fastened to the bottom piece.

Performers place the *ch'in* on a table so that the wide end with the bridge is near the right hand, and the narrow end is near the left hand. Although players use both hands to set the strings into motion, the right hand does most of the plucking, and the left hand, all of the stopping.

~ 11.4 ~

(1) Flageolet System. As discussed in Chapter 10, performers produce flageolet tones by lightly touching a string at the locations of nodes.[18] To find the nodes, *ch'in* players rely on flat circular reference points called *hui*. These markers are inlaid into the soundboard along the outer edge of the lowest string, or String I; this string is farthest from the performer. Turn to Table 11.4 and Figure 11.1, and note that the *hui* are numbered from right to left, or in a direction from bridge to nut. Each *hui* represents the division of a given string into an aliquot number of parts. Furthermore, notice that the arrangement of the *hui* constitutes a symmetric pattern with respect to *hui* 7, which marks the centers of all seven strings. The locations of *hui* 1 and 13 require string divisions into eight equal parts, of *hui* 2 and 12 into six equal parts, of *hui* 3 and 11 into five equal parts, of *hui* 4 and 10 into four equal parts, of *hui* 5 and 9 into three equal parts, and of *hui* 6 and 8 *also* into five equal parts. Table 11.4 gives modern length ratios and frequency ratios of the flageolet tuning system, and it lists the approximate Western tones for String I when tuned to C_2. Finally, Table 11.4 also includes the aliquot parts, and the length and frequency ratios of *theoretical hui* 14; one needs the latter ratios to calculate the closest fraction and the closest ratio of *shang*, ratio $9/8$, in Table 11.5. (See Note 25.)

(2) Stopped Hui Integer System. At the locations of the *hui*, performers also play a series of stopped tones. Again, Table 11.4 gives the modern length ratios, frequency ratios, and approximate Western tones of String I. Observe that the first stopped tone at length ratio $7/8$ sounds a "sharp major second," or frequency ratio $8/7$ [231.2 ¢].

Table 11.4

CH'IN FLAGEOLET AND STOPPED TONES AT THE LOCATIONS OF *HUI* 1–13 AND OF THEORETICAL *HUI* 14 ON STRING I TUNED TO C_2

Hui Integers:	[14]	13	12	11	10	9	8	7	6	5	4	3	2	1
Number of Aliquot Parts:	[10]	8	6	5	4	3	5	2	5	3	4	5	6	8
Flageolet Length Ratios:	[1/10]	1/8	1/6	1/5	1/4	1/3	2/5	1/2	2/5	1/3	1/4	1/5	1/6	1/8
Flageolet Freq. Ratios:	[10/1]	8/1	6/1	5/1	4/1	3/1	5/1	2/1	5/1	3/1	4/1	5/1	6/1	8/1
Approx. Flageolet Tones:	[E_5]	C_5	G_4	E_4	C_4	G_3	E_4	C_3	E_4	G_3	C_4	E_4	G_4	C_5
Stopped Length Ratios:	[9/10]	7/8	5/6	4/5	3/4	2/3	3/5	1/2	2/5	1/3	1/4	1/5	1/6	1/8
Stopped Freq. Ratios:	[10/9]	8/7	6/5	5/4	4/3	3/2	5/3	2/1	5/2	3/1	4/1	5/1	6/1	8/1
Approx. Stopped Tones:	[D_2]	D_2	$E\flat_2$	E_2	F_2	G_2	A_2	C_3	E_3	G_3	C_4	E_4	G_4	C_5

11.5

(3) Open String Pentatonic System. The *ch'in* has both an old and a new open string tuning system. This change in tuning was instigated during the Sung (A.D. 960–1279) and Yüan (A.D. 1279–1368) Dynasties, and codified during the Ming Dynasty (A.D. 1368–1644). For simplicity, Walter Kaufmann[19] describes the old as a pre-Ming *ch'in* tuning, and the new as a post-Ming *ch'in* tuning. Figure 11.2 traces this transformation from the old to new tuning in the context of a parallel change from the original pentatonic scale to a new pentatonic scale.

Figure 11.2(a), Row 1, gives the approximate Western tones of the original pentatonic scale, shown here as a sequence of two identical scales, or a total of ten tones. The numbers above all note names in this figure enumerate the tones in diatonic cipher notation, also known as the Chevé System. (See Figure 11.3.) Row 2 identifies nine exact interval ratios, and Row 3, five exact frequency ratios of the original scale. Row 4 shows that the first five frequency ratios of the old pre-Ming *ch'in* tuning are the same as the original scale. Finally, Row 5 indicates that *ch'in* players tuned this scale on Strings I–V of their instruments (see Figure 11.1), so that *kung* is the first, or lowest string. This means that Strings VI and VII sound one "octave" *above* Strings I and II, respectively.

Figure 11.2(b) suggests that the new pentatonic scale in Figure 11.2(c) has its musical origins in the original pentatonic scale. In Figure 11.2(b), Row 1, observe that the first tone G is vertically aligned with the fourth tone G in Figure 11.2(a), Row 1. Consequently, note that Figure 11.2(b), Row 2, shows the same sequence of interval ratios as between G–G′ in Figure 11.2(a), Row 2. Finally, Figure 11.2(b), Row 3, identifies five exact frequency ratios of the G-mode. Note carefully that the frequency ratios of the original scale and the G-mode are *not* identical. The original pentatonic scale — 1/1–9/8–81/64–3/2–27/16 — sounds a "large major third," ratio 81/64, between the first and third scale degrees, whereas the G-mode — 1/1–9/8–4/3–3/2–27/16 — sounds a "fourth," ratio 4/3, between the first and third degrees.

Figure 11.2(c), Row 1, illustrates the new post-Ming *ch'in* tuning in the context of a new pentatonic scale in C. Figure 11.2(c), Row 2, shows that the derivation of this scale is based on the interval ratios of the G-mode in Figure 11.2(b), Row 2. Consequently, the first six frequency ratios

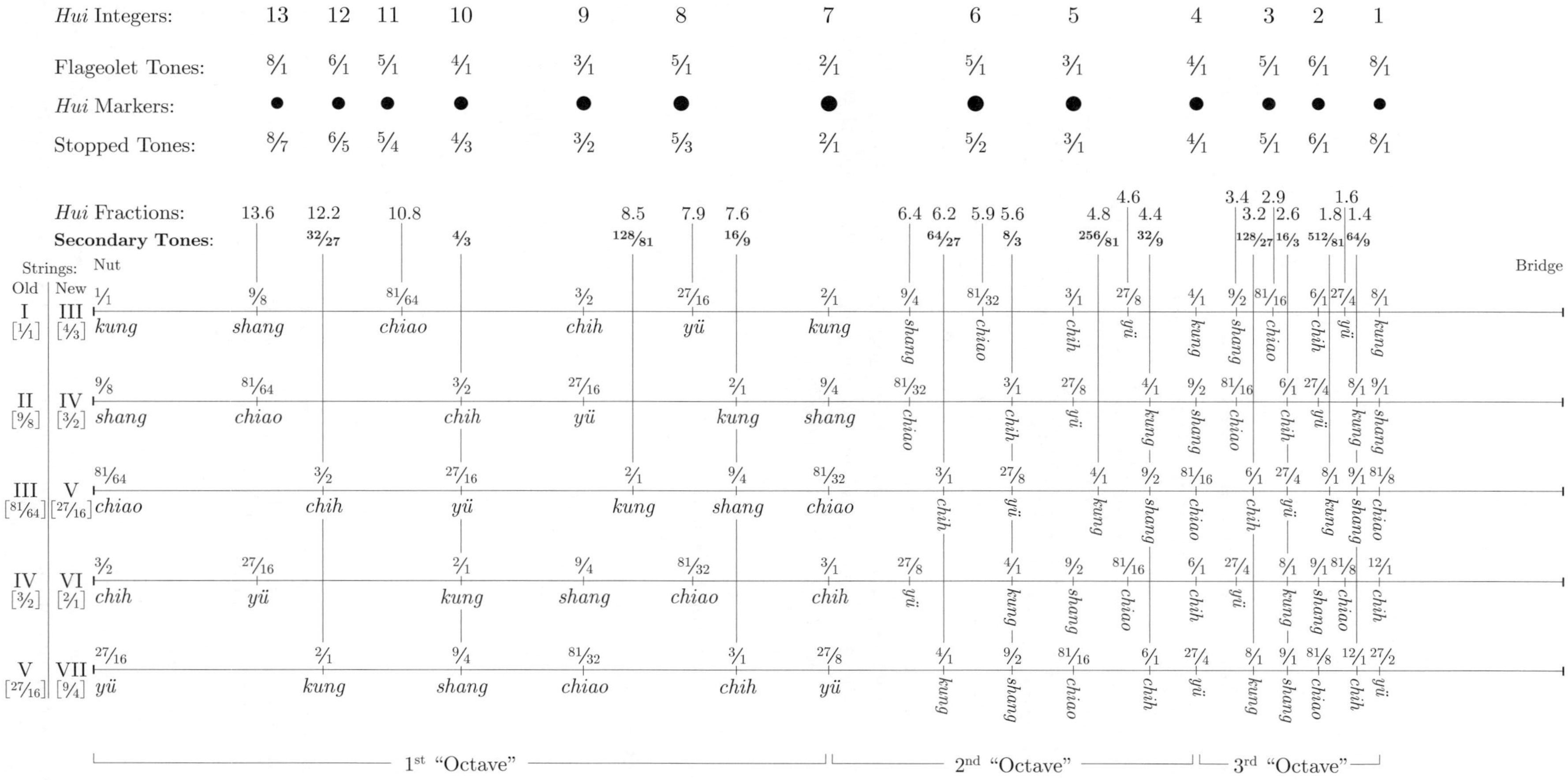

Figure 11.1 Drawing to scale of four different tuning systems on the *ch'in*, a Chinese stringed instrument without bridges and without frets. Circular reference markers called *hui* indicate the exact locations of a unique series of (1) flageolet tones, and (2) stopped tones. Furthermore, in the Old Strings Column, when open Strings VI and VII are tuned an "octave" above Strings I and II, respectively, the *ch'in* sounds (3) the old pre-Ming pentatonic tuning; and in the New Strings Column, when open Strings I and II are tuned an "octave" below Strings VI and VII, respectively, the *ch'in* sounds the new post-Ming pentatonic tuning. Finally, an unmarked sequence of *hui* fractions indicates the stopping locations for playing (4) the original Chinese pentatonic scale on all strings over the span of three "octaves." (Tone locations to scale.)

of the new post-Ming *ch'in* tuning in Figure 11.2(c), Row 3, are identical to the frequency ratios of the G-mode in Figure 11.2(b), Row 3. Finally, Figure 11.2(c), Row 4, shows that musicians shifted the tonic *kung* from C on String I to F on String III. This shift causes Strings I and II to sound one "octave" *below* Strings VI and VII, respectively. As discussed in Sections 11.7–11.8, *kung* on String III establishes the musical and mathematical basis of twelve *mode tunings* called *tiao*.

A comparison between Figure 11.2(a), Row 4, and Figure 11.2(c), Row 3, illustrates the differences between the old and new *ch'in* tunings. String III of the pre-Ming tuning sounds *chiao*, or a "sharp major third," ratio 81/64, above String I. In contrast, String III of the post-Ming tuning also sounds *chiao*, but in this case a "fourth," ratio 4/3, above String I! Chinese musicians have acknowledged the *dual identity of chiao* for almost one thousand years. For example, the scholar Chu Hsi (A.D. 1130–1200) described the difference between the old and new *ch'in* tunings by noting

> If the first string of the *ch'in* is tuned to the pitch *huang-chung* [1/1] and sounds the tone *kung*, the third string should be tuned to the pitch *ku-hsien* [81/64] so it can sound the tone ***chiao***. Now present *ch'in* players all tune the third string not to *ku-hsein* but to *chung-lü* [4/3] using that pitch as ***chiao***. It is done like this, but no one knows why . . .[20] (Bold italics, ratios in brackets mine.)

Recall that Table 11.3 shows *Chung-lü* not as ratio 4/3, but as ratio 177147/131072. To understand the origin of the 4/3-identity, consider how the *ch'in* is tuned. Lieberman states that one tunes String I to C_2,[21] and then gives the following tuning sequence for the open strings of the *ch'in*.[22] In the illustration below, a progression of white notes represents the required scale degrees, and black notes indicate previously tuned degrees in the sequence. In the last step, one tunes String III as a "fifth," or as a 3/2 interval, below String VI. This produces *Chung-lü* as a "fourth," or as frequency ratio 4/3, on the post-Ming *ch'in*.

Tuning the Pentatonic Scale on the New Post-Ming *Ch'in*

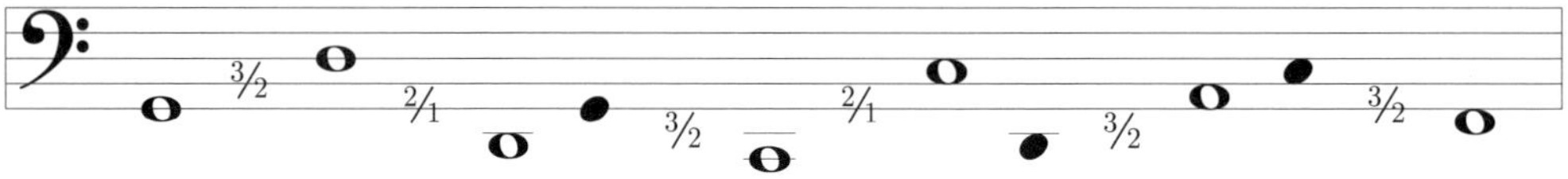

	3/2	9/4	9/8	1/1	2/1	27/16	4/3
Strings:	IV	VII	II	I	VI	V	III
	shang	*yü*	*yü*	*chih*	*chih*	*chiao*	*kung*

∾ 11.6 ∾

(4) Stopped Hui Fraction System. The musical possibilities of the tones designated by the *hui* markers are rather limited. On the C string, the flageolet tones produce 2/1–4/1–8/1 [C], 5/1 [E], and 3/1–6/1 [G]. The stopped tones extend this pattern by contributing two pitches, 5/4–5/2 [E], and 3/2 [G]. However, beyond this accretion, the stopped tones produce only four new pitches: 8/7 [D], 6/5 [E♭], 4/3 [F], and 5/3 [A]. Furthermore, observe that the Stopped Hui Integer System does *not* indicate the location of the original pentatonic scale on the first string because ratios 9/8 [D], 81/64 [E], and 27/16 [A] are missing. To correct this deficiency, Chinese *ch'in* masters developed a unique technique for determining the *approximate* locations of unmarked tones. This technique consists of an invisible system of *hui* fractions. In his translation of the *Mei-an ch'in-p'u*, Lieberman gives the following description of *hui* fractions:

(a)

	1	2	3	5	6	1	2	3	5	6	
Original Chinese Pent. Scale in C:	C	D	E	G	A	C′	D′	E′	G′	A′	(1)
Interval Ratios of Original Scale:		9/8	9/8	32/27	9/8	32/27	9/8	9/8	32/27	9/8	(2)
Frequency Ratios of Original Scale:	1/1	9/8	81/64	3/2	27/16						(3)
Freq. Ratios of Old Pre-Ming *Ch'in:*	1/1	9/8	81/64	3/2	27/16	2/1	9/4				(4)
Pent. note names of Strings I–VII:	I	II	III	IV	V	VI	VII				(5)
	kung	*shang*	*chiao*	*chih*	*yü*	*kung*	*shang*				

(b)

	5	6	1	2	3	5	
Chinese Pentatonic Scale in G:	G	A	C′	D′	E′	G′	(1)
Interval Ratios of G-Mode:		9/8	32/27	9/8	9/8	32/27	(2)
Frequency Ratios of G-Mode:	1/1	9/8	4/3	3/2	27/16	2/1	(3)

(c)

	5	6	1	2	3	5	6	
New Chinese Pentatonic Scale in C:	C	D	F	G	A	C′	D′	(1)
Interval Ratios of G-Mode:		9/8	32/27	9/8	9/8	32/27	9/8	(2)
Freq. Ratios of New Post-Ming *Ch'in:*	1/1	9/8	4/3	3/2	27/16	2/1	9/4	(3)
	kung	*shang*	*chiao*	*chih*	*yü*	*kung*	*shang*	
Kung Shifted to F on String III:	3/2	27/16	1/1	9/8	81/64	3/2	27/16	(4)
Pent. note names of Strings I–VII:	I	II	III	IV	V	VI	VII	(5)
	chih	*yü*	*kung*	*shang*	*chiao*	*chih*	*yü*	

Figure 11.2 Old and new *ch'in* tunings in the context of original and new Chinese pentatonic scales. (a) Strings I–V of the old *ch'in* tuning sound the original pentatonic scale. (b) The G-mode is here depicted in the context of the original scale. (c) In comparison to the old *ch'in* tuning, which sounds interval ratio 81/64 between Strings I and III, the new *ch'in* tuning sounds interval ratio 4/3 between Strings I and III.

> . . . fractions are used to specify points between two *hui.* The convention is to imagine that the distance between each pair of *hui* is divided into ten equal segments, or *fen.* The number y.x then denotes "x *fen* to the left of *hui* y." Since the distance between pairs of *hui* varies, the *fen* do not have a fixed length.[23]

In other words, one counts *fen* segments like *hui* markers from right to left.

Table 11.5 consists of three sections with six rows per section. Since all rows per section show identical categories, the following discussion does not refer to any specific section. In Figure 11.1, and in Table 11.5, Row 1, observe two different kinds of ratios associated with *hui* fractions. Ratios in regular typeface represent "primary tones," or ratios required to play the original pentatonic scale on String I; and ratios in bold typeface represent "secondary tones," or ratios required to play the original pentatonic scale on Strings II–VII. Due to the arbitrary division of the distances between *hui* into ten equal segments, notice that all *hui* fractions represent only approximate locations of the primary and secondary tones. Table 11.5, Rows 2 and 3, list *hui* fractions from two scholarly Chinese sources.[24] Row 4 gives the closest *hui* fractions required by the primary and secondary ratios. Except for two cases, $\frac{9}{8} \leftrightarrow 13.6$, and $\frac{512}{81} \leftrightarrow 1.8$, at least one fraction in Row 2 or Row 3 matches a fraction in Row 4.[25] Row 5 lists the actual ratios of the closest fractions in Row 4. Finally, Row 6 gives the cent differences that result when one subtracts the cent values of the ratios in Row 5 from the cent values of the ratios in Row 1. These differences vary from a minimum of -0.27 ¢ to a maximum of $+21.51$ ¢.

As an example of how to calculate a cent difference in Row 6, consider secondary ratio $\frac{16}{9}$. In Figure 11.1, this ratio sounds *kung* [C_3] on the open $\frac{9}{8}$ string because $\frac{9}{8} \times \frac{16}{9} = \frac{2}{1}$; it sounds *shang* [$D_3$] on the open $\frac{81}{64}$ string because $\frac{81}{64} \times \frac{16}{9} = \frac{9}{4}$; and it sounds *chih* [$G_3$] on the open $\frac{27}{16}$ string because $\frac{27}{16} \times \frac{16}{9} = \frac{3}{1}$. According to Equation 3.32, on a *ch'in* string 1200.0 mm long, ancient length ratio $\frac{16}{9}$ is located

$$\frac{1200.0 \text{ mm}}{\frac{16}{9}} = 675.0 \text{ mm}$$

from the bridge, or from the right end of the string. Now, to establish the location of fraction 7.6, begin by calculating the positions of *hui* 7 and *hui* 8. Observe that these two markers are located 600.0 mm and 720.0 mm, respectively, from the bridge:

$$\textit{Hui } 7 = \frac{1200.0 \text{ mm}}{\frac{2}{1}} = 600.0 \text{ mm}$$

$$\textit{Hui } 8 = \frac{1200.0 \text{ mm}}{\frac{5}{3}} = 720.0 \text{ mm}$$

These two measurements enable us to determine that six *fen* to the left of *hui* 7 equals a distance of 72.0 mm because

$$\text{Distance between } \textit{hui:} \quad 720.0 \text{ mm} - 600.0 \text{ mm} = 120.0 \text{ mm}$$

$$\text{Distance of one } \textit{fen:} \quad \frac{120.0 \text{ mm}}{10} = 12.0 \text{ mm}$$

$$\text{Distance of six } \textit{fen:} \quad 12.0 \text{ mm} \times 6 = 72.0 \text{ mm}$$

Consequently, fraction 7.6 is located 600.0 mm + 72.0 mm = 672.0 mm from the right end of the string. Finally, according to Equation 9.21, length ratio $^{16}/_{9}$ has a cent value of

$$\log_{10} \frac{1200.0 \text{ mm}}{675.0 \text{ mm}} \times 3986.314 = 996.09\ ¢$$

whereas *hui* fraction 7.6 has a cent value of

$$\log_{10} \frac{1200.0 \text{ mm}}{672.0 \text{ mm}} \times 3986.314 = 1003.80\ ¢$$

Table 11.5

HUI FRACTION ANALYSIS OF THE *CH'IN*

	shang		*chiao*		*chih*		*yü*		*kung*	
Required *Ch'in* Ratios:	9/8	**32/27**	81/64	**4/3**	3/2	**128/81**	27/16	**16/9**	2/1	(1)
Hui Fractions in Wang:	13.7	12.2	10.8			8.5	7.9	7.6		(2)
Hui Fractions in Li-sun:	X	X	10.9			8.5	7.9	7.6		(3)
Closest *Hui* Fractions:	13.6	12.2	10.8	[10]	[9]	8.5	7.9	7.6	[7]	(4)
Ratios of Closest Fractions:	100/89	120/101	100/79			30/19	100/59	25/14		(5)
Cent Differences, [Row 1] – [Row 5]:	+2.16	−4.28	−0.27			+1.42	−7.59	−7.71		(6)
Required *Ch'in* Ratios:	9/4	**64/27**	81/32	**8/3**	3/1	**256/81**	27/8	**32/9**	4/1	(1)
Hui Fractions in Wang:	6.4	6.2	5.9	5.6		4.8	4.6	4.3		(2)
Hui Fractions in Li-sun:	6.5	6.2	X	5.6		4.8	4.6	4.4		(3)
Closest *Hui* Fractions:	6.4	6.2	5.9	5.6	[5]	4.8	4.6	4.4	[4]	(4)
Ratios of Closest Fractions:	25/11	50/21	150/59	75/28		60/19	10/3	60/17		(5)
Cent Differences, [Row 1] – [Row 5]:	−17.40	−7.71	−7.59	−7.71		+1.42	+21.51	+12.78		(6)
Required *Ch'in* Ratios:	9/2	**128/27**	81/16	**16/3**	6/1	**512/81**	27/4	**64/9**	8/1	(1)
Hui Fractions in Wang:	3.4	3.2	2.9	2.6		X	X	X		(2)
Hui Fractions in Li-sun:	3.6	3.2	X	2.6		X	1.6	1.4		(3)
Closest *Hui* Fractions:	3.4	3.2	2.9	2.6	[2]	1.8	1.6	1.4	[1]	(4)
Ratios of Closest Fractions:	50/11	100/21	300/59	75/14		120/19	20/3	120/17		(5)
Cent Differences, [Row 1] – [Row 5]:	−17.40	−7.71	−7.59	−7.71		+1.42	+21.51	+12.78		(6)

Note, therefore, a difference of 996.09 ¢ − 1003.80 ¢ = −7.71 ¢, which tells us that ratio $^{16}/_{9}$ is a slightly lower tone than *hui* fraction 7.6.[26] However, since the next smaller fraction 7.5 produces a difference of −38.91 ¢, and since the next larger fraction 7.7 produces a difference of 22.93 ¢, we conclude that 7.6 represents the closest approximation with respect to ratio $^{16}/_{9}$. Finally, verify this analysis in three steps. (1) Reduce the length ratio of *hui* fraction 7.6 to lowest terms; (2) calculate the interval ratio between length ratios $^{25}/_{14}$ and $^{16}/_{9}$; and (3) compute the cent value of interval ratio $^{225}/_{224}$:

$$\frac{1200.0 \text{ mm}}{672.0 \text{ mm}} = \frac{25}{14}$$

$$\frac{25}{14} \div \frac{16}{9} = \frac{25}{14} \times \frac{9}{16} = \frac{225}{224}$$

$$\log_{10} \frac{225}{224} \times 3986.314 = 7.71 ¢$$

At this point in the discussion, it is important to emphasize that the *ch'in* is a microtonal instrument.[27] *Ch'in* masters employ extremely complex playing techniques that include vibratos, sliding through intervals, and bending tones. Consequently, the above *hui* fraction analysis has only minimum musical value. Because the *ch'in* has no moveable bridges and no frets, virtuoso players have no problems adjusting the intonation of their instruments. In this respect, the subtle, intimate, and haunting musical beauty of the Chinese *ch'in* is very reminiscent of the Japanese *shakuhachi*, a large bamboo flute, which, due to its notched embouchure hole, also inspires many intricate microtonal inflections and ornamentations.[28]

11.7

In his text, Lieberman includes two tables to illustrate how *ch'in* players produce mode tunings called *tiao*.[29] Musicians refer to the first set of six *tiao* as the *lowered kung becomes chiao* cycle; and to the second set of six *tiao* as the *raised chiao becomes kung* cycle. Although the first *tiao* in both cycles corresponds to the new post-Ming *ch'in* tuning in Figure 11.2(c), I include the first *tiao* in the overall count and, thereby, arrive at a total number of 12 mode tunings, or 12 *tiao*. Recall the diatonic cipher notation, or Chevé System, discussed in Section 11.5 and used in Figure 11.2. Many musicians and scholars use this system to notate one "octave" of the pentatonic scale as 1–2–3–5–6–1. In the following discussion, I use the notation ①, ②, ③, ⑤, ⑥, ① to represent the tones *kung*, *shang*, *chiao*, *chi*, *yü*, *kung*, respectively.

Turn now to Table 11.6, which shows *lowered kung becomes chiao* as a cycle of six consecutive mode tunings. The first *tiao* — *Huang-chung-tiao* — is identical to the open string tuning depicted in Figure 11.2(c), Rows 4–5; namely, String III sounds *kung* or $^{1}/_{1}$ [F]; String IV sounds *shang* or $^{9}/_{8}$ [G]; String V sounds *chiao* or $^{81}/_{64}$ [A]; etc. The second tuning — *Lin-chung-tiao* — occurs in two steps. (1) Lower *kung*, ratio $^{1}/_{1}$, on String III by one *lü*, or by interval ratio $^{256}/_{243}$, from $^{1}/_{1}$ [F] to $^{243}/_{128}$ [E]; that is, $^{2}/_{1} \div {}^{256}/_{243} = {}^{243}/_{128}$. (2) Rename lowered *kung* and call it *chiao*. In Table 11.6, an arrow that points from Row 1 to Row 2 indicates that lowered *kung*, or ①, in *Huang-chung-tiao* becomes *chiao*, or ③, in *Lin-chung-tiao*. Consequently, *chih*, or ⑤, in *Huang-chung-tiao* now becomes *kung*, or ①, in *Lin-chung-tiao;* etc. The third tuning — *T'ai-ts'ou-tiao* — occurs when one lowers *kung*, or ①, on Strings I and VI by one *lü* from $^{3}/_{2}$ [C] to $^{729}/_{512}$ [B]; that is, $^{3}/_{2} \div {}^{256}/_{243} = {}^{729}/_{512}$. Note that lowered *kung*, or ①, in *Lin-chung-tiao* becomes *chiao*, or ③, in *T'ai-ts'ou-tiao*. Consequently, *chih*, or ⑤, on String IV in *Lin-chung-tiao* now becomes *kung*, or ①, in *T'ai-ts'ou-tiao;* etc.

Table 11.7 shows *raised chiao becomes kung* as a cycle of six consecutive mode tunings. Again, the first *tiao* — *Huang-chung-tiao* — is identical to the open string tuning depicted in Figure 11.2(c), Rows 4–5. The second tuning — *Chung-lü-tiao* — occurs in two steps. (1) Raise *chiao*, ratio $^{81}/_{64}$, on String V by one *lü*, or by interval ratio $^{2187}/_{2048}$, from $^{81}/_{64}$ [A] to $^{177147}/_{131072}$ [A♯]; that is, $^{81}/_{64} \times {}^{2187}/_{2048} = {}^{177147}/_{131072}$. (2) Rename raised *chiao* and call it *kung*. In Table 11.7, an arrow that points from Row 1 to Row 2 indicates that raised *chiao*, or ③, in *Huang-chung-tiao* becomes *kung*, or ①, in *Chung-lü-tiao*. Consequently, *yü*, or ⑥, on Strings II and VII in *Huang-chung-tiao* now becomes *chiao*, or ③, in *Chung-lü-tiao;* etc. The third tuning — *Wu-i-tiao* — occurs when one raises *chiao*, or ③, on Strings II and VII by one *lü* from $^{27}/_{16}$ [D] to $^{59049}/_{32768}$ [D♯]; that is, $^{27}/_{16} \times {}^{2187}/_{2048} = {}^{59049}/_{32768}$. Note that raised *chiao*, or ③, in *Chung-lü-tiao* becomes *kung*, or ①, in *Wu-i-tiao*. Consequently, *yü*, or ⑥, on String IV in *Chung-lü-tiao* now becomes *chiao*, or ③, in *Wu-i-tiao*.

In Table 11.6, an analysis of the first three tiao shows that *Huang-chung-tiao*, *Lin-chung-tiao*, and *T'ai-ts'ou-tiao* are named after the location of their respective *kung* in the 12-tone scale in Table 11.3. For *Huang-chung-tiao*, *kung*, or ①, sounds *Huang-chung* in the scale; etc. Note, however, that the last three tiao, or *Wu-i-tiao*, *Chung-lü-tiao*, and *Huang-chung-tiao*, are *not* named after the location of their respective *kung*. For *Wu-i-tiao*, *kung*, or ①, sounds *Nan-lü* in the scale; etc. Similarly, in Table 11.7, an analysis of the first three tiao shows that *Huang-chung-tiao*, *Chung-lü-tiao*, and *Wu-i-tiao* are named after the location of their respective *kung* in the 12-tone scale. Again, for *Huang-chung-tiao*, *kung*, or ①, sounds *Huang-chung* in the scale; etc. Note, however, that the last three tiao, or *T'ai-ts'ou-tiao*, *Lin-chung-tiao*, and *Huang-chung-tiao*, are *not* named after the location of their respective *kung*. For *T'ai-ts'ou-tiao*, *kung*, or ①, sounds *Chia-chung* in the scale; etc.

To understand the origins of the names of the last three tiao in both cycles, we must examine the pentatonic series of tones. In Table 11.6, the first *tiao* — *Huang-chung-tiao* — consists of the sequence: ⑤, ⑥, ①, ②, ③, ⑤, ⑥. Because the sixth *tiao* — also *Huang-chung-tiao* — has the identical sequence, it also has the identical name. Furthermore, in Table 11.7, because the sixth *tiao* — *Huang-chung-tiao* — has the identical sequence of the first *tiao*, it also has the identical name of the first *tiao*. However, note carefully, that these similarities do not apply to the actual tones of the mode tunings. In Table 11.6, all the tones of the sixth *tiao* sound one *lü* below the first *tiao*. And in Table 11.7, all the tones of the sixth *tiao* sound one *lü* above the first *tiao*.

With respect to the other *tiao*, in Table 11.6, the second *tiao*, *Lin-chung-tiao*, consists of the sequence: ①, ②, ③, ⑤, ⑥, ①, ②. Because the fifth *tiao* in Table 11.7 has the identical sequence, it also has the identical name. Similarly, in Table 11.6, the third *tiao*, *T'ai-ts'ou-tiao*, consists of the sequence: ③, ⑤, ⑥, ①, ②, ③, ⑤. Because the fourth *tiao* in Table 11.7 has the identical sequence, it also has the identical name. Finally, in Table 11.7, the second *tiao*, *Chung-lü-tiao*, and the third *tiao*, *Wu-i-tiao*, determine the names of the fifth and fourth *tiao*, respectively, in Table 11.6. We conclude, therefore, that the pentatonic series of tones of the first three *tiao* of each cycle determine the names of three other *tiao*.

11.8

The 12-tone scale in Table 11.3 has two different kinds of 1-*lü* intervals: a small "semitone," interval ratio $^{256}/_{243}$ [90.2 ¢], and a large "semitone," interval ratio $^{2187}/_{2048}$ [113.7 ¢]. In Table 11.6, musicians always lower *kung* by interval ratio $^{256}/_{243}$; and in Table 11.7, they always raise *chiao* by interval ratio $^{2187}/_{2048}$. However, these patterns do not yield consistent results with respect to the sizes of intervals between tones of the 12 *tiao*. Beginning with *kung*, or ①, the six *tiao* in Table 11.6, and the first and sixth *tiao* in Table 11.7, all produce the following interval sequence:

① $^{9}/_{8}$ [204 ¢] ② $^{9}/_{8}$ [204 ¢] ③ $^{32}/_{27}$ [294 ¢] ⑤ $^{9}/_{8}$ [204 ¢] ⑥ $^{32}/_{27}$ [294 ¢] ①

Table 11.6

LOWERED KUNG BECOMES CHIAO RATIO ANALYSIS:
A CYCLE OF SIX CONSECUTIVE MODE TUNINGS ON THE NEW POST-MING *CH'IN*

Jui-pin	*Lin-chung*	*I-tse*	*Nan-lü*	*Wu-i*	*Ying-chung*	***Huang-chung***	*Ta-lü*	*T'ai-ts'ou*	*Chia-chung*	*Ku-hsien*	*Chung-lü*	*Jui-pin*	*Lin-chung*	*I-tse*	*Nan-lü*	
•	•	•	•	•	•	•	•	•	•	•	•	•	•	•	•	
B	C	C♯	D	D♯	E	F	F♯	G	G♯	A	A♯	B'	C'	C♯'	D'	
729/512	3/2	6561/4096	27/16	59049/32768	243/128	1/1	2187/2048	9/8	19683/16384	81/64	177147/131072	729/512	3/2	6561/4096	27/16	
	chih		*yü*			*kung*		*shang*		*chiao*			*chih*		*yü*	
	⑤		⑥			①		②		③			⑤		⑥	
	3/2		**27/16**			**1/1**		**9/8**		**81/64**			**3/2**		**27/16**	1. *Huang-chung-tiao*
	①		②		③ [256/243] ←			⑤		⑥			①		②	
	3/2		27/16		243/128			9/8		81/64			3/2		27/16	2. *Lin-chung-tiao*
③ ←			⑤		⑥			①		②		③ ←			⑤	
729/512			27/16		243/128			9/8		81/64		729/512			27/16	3. *T'ai-ts'ou-tiao*
⑥			①		②		③ ←			⑤		⑥			①	
729/512			27/16		243/128		2187/2048			81/64		729/512			27/16	4. *Wu-i-tiao*
②		③ ←			⑤		⑥			①		②		③ ←		
729/512		6561/4096			243/128		2187/2048			81/64		729/512		6561/4096		5. *Chung-lü-tiao*
⑤		⑥			①		②		③ ←			⑤		⑥		
729/512		6561/4096			243/128		2187/2048		19683/16384			729/512		6561/4096		6. *Huang-chung-tiao*
←	•	←	•		←	•	←	•	←	•		←	•	←	•	
I		II			III		IV		V			VI		VII		Strings

Table 11.7

RAISED CHIAO BECOMES KUNG RATIO ANALYSIS:
A CYCLE OF SIX CONSECUTIVE MODE TUNINGS ON THE NEW POST-MING *CH'IN*

Lin-chung	*I-tse*	*Nan-lü*	*Wu-i*	*Ying-chung*	***Huang-chung***	*Ta-lü*	*T'ai-ts'ou*	*Chia-chung*	*Ku-hsien*	*Chung-lü*	*Jui-pin*	*Lin-chung*	*I-tse*	*Nan-lü*	*Wu-i*	
•	•	•	•	•	•	•	•	•	•	•	•	•	•	•	•	
C	C♯	D	D♯	E	F	F♯	G	G♯	A	A♯	B	C'	C♯'	D'	D♯'	
3/2	6561/4096	27/16	59049/32768	243/128	1/1	2187/2048	9/8	19683/16384	81/64	177147/131072	729/512	3/2	6561/4096	27/16	59049/32768	
chih		*yü*			*kung*		*shang*		*chiao*			*chih*		*yü*		
⑤ **3/2**		⑥ **27/16**			① **1/1**		② **9/8**		③ **81/64**			⑤ **3/2**		⑥ **27/16**		1. *Huang-chung-tiao*
② 3/2		③ 27/16			⑤ 1/1		⑥ 9/8		↳ [2187/2048]	① 177147/131072		② 3/2		③ 27/16		2. *Chung-lü-tiao*
⑥ 3/2		↳	① 59049/32768		② 1/1		③ 9/8			⑤ 177147/131072		⑥ 3/2		↳	① 59049/32768	3. *Wu-i-tiao*
③ 3/2			⑤ 59049/32768		⑥ 1/1		↳	① 19683/16384		② 177147/131072		③ 3/2			⑤ 59049/32768	4. *T'ai-ts'ou-tiao*
↳	① 6561/4096		② 59049/32768		③ 1/1			⑤ 19683/16384		⑥ 177147/131072		↳	① 6561/4096		② 59049/32768	5. *Lin-chung-tiao*
	⑤ 6561/4096		⑥ 59049/32768		↳	① 2187/2048		② 19683/16384		③ 177147/131072			⑤ 6561/4096		⑥ 59049/32768	6. *Huang-chung-tiao*
•—→ I		•—→ II			•—→ III		•—→ IV		•—→ V			•—→ VI		•—→ VII		Strings

Such a pattern does not apply to four *tiao* in Table 11.7. Table 11.8 shows that in the *raised chiao becomes kung* cycle, *Chung-lü-tiao*, *Wu-i-tiao*, *T'ai-ts'ou-tiao*, and *Lin-chung-tiao* are all different because they contain two unique intervals. The first is a "small whole tone," $\frac{256}{243} \times \frac{256}{243} = \frac{65536}{59049} = 180.5$ ¢, and the second is a "large minor third," $\frac{2187}{2048} \times \frac{2187}{2048} \times \frac{256}{243} = \frac{19683}{16384} = 317.6$ ¢.

Table 11.8

INTERVAL SEQUENCES OF THE *RAISED CHIAO BECOMES KUNG* CYCLE

①		②		③		⑤		⑥		①	
1/1		9/8		81/64		3/2		27/16		1/1	1. *Huang-chung-tiao*
	9/8 204 ¢		9/8 204 ¢		32/27 294 ¢		9/8 204 ¢		32/27 294 ¢		
177147/131072		3/2		27/16		1/1		9/8		177147/131072	2. *Chung-lü-tiao*
	65536/59049 180 ¢		9/8 204 ¢		32/27 294 ¢		9/8 204 ¢		19683/16384 318 ¢		
59049/32768		1/1		9/8		177147/131072		3/2		59049/32768	3. *Wu-i-tiao*
	65536/59049 180 ¢		9/8 204 ¢		19683/16384 318 ¢		65536/59049 180 ¢		19683/16384 318 ¢		
19683/16384		177147/131072		3/2		59049/32768		1/1		19683/16384	4. *T'ai-ts'ou-tiao*
	9/8 204 ¢		65536/59049 180 ¢		19683/16384 318 ¢		65536/59049 180 ¢		19683/16384 318 ¢		
6561/4096		59049/32768		1/1		19683/16384		177147/131072		6561/4096	5. *Lin-chung-tiao*
	9/8 204 ¢		65536/59049 180 ¢		19683/16384 318 ¢		9/8 204 ¢		32/27 294 ¢		
2187/2048		19683/16384		177147/131072		6561/4096		59049/32768		2187/2048	6. *Huang-chung-tiao*
	9/8 204 ¢		9/8 204 ¢		32/27 294 ¢		9/8 204 ¢		32/27 294 ¢		

11.9

Chinese musicians do not employ the 12-tone scale as a single musical entity. Instead, the scale constitutes a theoretical structure. In tuning their instruments, musicians either (1) select patterns of five or seven tones for various pentatonic or heptatonic scales,[30] or (2) use selected scale degrees as fundamental frequency ratios from which to tune smaller scales. Such implementations inspired many generations of Chinese music theorists to contemplate the 12-tone scale as a purely mathematical structure. As a result, they invented many different kinds of tempered scales. However, these temperaments did not influence the tuning of musical instruments. All Chinese instruments are traditionally tuned in just intonation.

The earliest record of a complete 12-tone scale other than the traditional scale exists in a book entitled *Huai-Nan-Tzu*, by Liu An (d. 122 B.C.), the Prince of Huai Nan.[31] Liu An designed his scale on the ancient up-and-down principle of scale generation. However, instead of using ancient length ratios 3/2 [as in 750/500] and 4/3 [as in 1000/750], Liu An employed ratios 749/500 [699.6 ¢] and 1000/749

Table 11.9

THE GENERATION OF A "JUST TEMPERAMENT" BY LIU AN

	81
$81 \times {}^{500}/_{749}$	$= 54$
$54 \times {}^{1000}/_{749}$	$= 72$
$72 \times {}^{500}/_{749}$	$= 48$
$48 \times {}^{1000}/_{749}$	$= 64$
$64 \times {}^{500}/_{749}$	$= 43$
$43 \times {}^{1000}/_{749}$	$= 57$
$57 \times {}^{1000}/_{749}$	$= 76$
$76 \times {}^{500}/_{749}$	$= 51$
$51 \times {}^{1000}/_{749}$	$= 68$
$68 \times {}^{500}/_{749}$	$= 45$
$45 \times {}^{1000}/_{749}$	$= 60$

[500.4 ¢], respectively. Given an overall string length of 81 units, Table 11.9 shows the results of Liu An's calculations, which he rounded to zero decimal places.

Refer to Table 11.10, which gives the length ratios of Liu An's 12-tone scale reduced to lowest terms. Note that his design leaves the original pentatonic scale intact, which means that he changed only seven tones. When compared to the traditional scale in Table 11.3, all *modified* degrees are now closer approximations of 12-tone equal temperament. This technique of changing only a select number of tones by sequentially multiplying and dividing *rational* interval ratios is reminiscent of the method found in a treatise entitled *Musica practica*[32] by Bartolomeo Ramis (*c.* 1440 – *c.* 1500). Six degrees of Ramis' 12-tone scale in A result from multiplying 3-limit ratios by the *syntonic comma*, ratio ${}^{81}/_{80}$, and six degrees of the modal version in C result from dividing 3-limit ratios by the syntonic comma. Consequently, we may refer to all such modified scales as "just temperaments."

Table 11.10

LENGTH RATIOS OF LIU AN'S "JUST TEMPERAMENT"
REDUCED TO LOWEST TERMS

${}^{81}/_{81} = {}^{1}/_{1}$	=	0.0 ¢	C
${}^{81}/_{54} = {}^{3}/_{2}$	=	702.0 ¢	G
${}^{81}/_{72} = {}^{9}/_{8}$	=	203.9 ¢	D
${}^{81}/_{48} = {}^{27}/_{16}$	=	905.9 ¢	A
${}^{81}/_{64} = {}^{81}/_{64}$	=	407.8 ¢	E
${}^{81}/_{43} = {}^{81}/_{43}$	=	1096.3 ¢	B
${}^{81}/_{57} = {}^{27}/_{19}$	=	608.4 ¢	F♯
${}^{81}/_{76} = {}^{81}/_{76}$	=	110.3 ¢	C♯
${}^{81}/_{51} = {}^{27}/_{17}$	=	800.9 ¢	G♯
${}^{81}/_{68} = {}^{81}/_{68}$	=	302.9 ¢	D♯
${}^{81}/_{45} = {}^{9}/_{5}$	=	1017.6 ¢	A♯
${}^{81}/_{60} = {}^{27}/_{20}$	=	519.6 ¢	E♯

11.10

Chinese mathematicians were keenly aware of the existence of *open spirals of "fifths"* that resemble *closed circles of "fifths,"* or an exact number of "octaves."[33] Due to the inherent discrepancies that result from computing with prime numbers 2 and 3, *commas* are by definition inevitable.[34] However, certain open spirals come very close to resembling closed circles. For example, Chiao Yen-shou (fl. *c.* 70 B.C.) discovered that sixty $\frac{3}{2}$'s closely approximate thirty-five $\frac{2}{1}$'s.[35]

$$\frac{\left(\frac{3}{2}\right)^{60}}{\left(\frac{2}{1}\right)^{35}} = 1.07010$$

$$\log_{10} 1.07010 \times 3986.314 = 117.30\ \text{¢}$$

As a result, all "fifths" in this temperament are tuned 117.30 ¢ ÷ 60 = 1.9550 ¢ flat, which is the same amount as 12-tone equal temperament.[36]

There is evidence that Ching Fang (fl. *c.* 45 B.C.), who contemplated the latter spiral, also considered a spiral of fifty-three $\frac{3}{2}$'s.[37]

$$\frac{\left(\frac{3}{2}\right)^{53}}{\left(\frac{2}{1}\right)^{31}} = 1.00209$$

$$\log_{10} 1.00209 \times 3986.314 = 3.6145\ \text{¢}$$

Here all "fifths" are tuned only 3.6145 ¢ ÷ 53 = 0.0682 ¢ flat, an amount that no human ear is capable of detecting. Therefore, we may think of this spiral as a circle.

Finally, in a treatise entitled *Lü-lü sin-p'u*, Ch'ien Lo-chih (425–453) pondered a spiral of 360 "fifths."[38]

$$\frac{\left(\frac{3}{2}\right)^{360}}{\left(\frac{2}{1}\right)^{210}} = 1.50160$$

$$\log_{10} 1.50160 \times 3986.314 = 703.80\ \text{¢}$$

The "fifths" of this temperament are also tuned 703.80 ¢ ÷ 360 = 1.9550 ¢ flat, or by the same amount as 12-tone and 60-tone equal temperament.

11.11

In 1584, one year before the publication of Simon Stevin's *L'Arithmetique*,[39] Prince Chu Tsai-yü (1536–1611) published his monumental work entitled *Lü-hsüeh hsin-shuo*, in which he expounded his theory of 12-tone equal temperament. Before we examine Chu Tsai-yü's approach in full detail, let us first consider a previously mentioned string length equation. Refer to Equation 3.32, and note that this equation has the condition $\Lambda < L$, which states that the calculated or bridged string length (Λ) is smaller than L of the fundamental mode of vibration.

$$\Lambda = \frac{L}{\left(\frac{n}{x}\right)}$$

Use this equation to calculate the string lengths of a given scale in an ascending direction, or from the fundamental to the "octave." On the other hand, in Chu Tsai-yü's work we find the opposite approach, expressed by Equation 3.33:

$$\Lambda = L \times \frac{n}{x}$$

This equation has the condition: $\Lambda > L$, which states that the calculated string length is greater than L. For Chu Tsai-yü, L represents the vibrating string length of the "octave"; consequently, he calculated the string lengths of his 12-tone equal tempered scale in a descending direction, or from the "octave" down to the fundamental.

Because complete translations of Chu Tsai-yü's works into European languages are not available, I am not able to give a thorough account of his process of scale generation. My principal source on this subject consists of translated excerpts by Kenneth Robinson.[40]

The modern algebraic equivalent of Chu Tsai-yü's calculation of the twelfth root of 2 consists of two consecutive square root calculations, followed by a cubic root calculation. In other words, Chu Tsai-yü effectively computed the twelfth root of 2 by extracting the cubic root of the fourth root of 2.[41] We may notate these procedures by writing

$$\sqrt[3]{\sqrt{\sqrt{2}}} = \sqrt[3]{\sqrt[4]{2}} = \sqrt[12]{2}$$

Refer to Equation 10.9, and recall that Simon Stevin discovered a very similar approach. Both men realized that a solution to this problem, although ominous in appearance, requires only square root and cubic root calculations. Before the invention of logarithms, mathematicians could not have extracted the twelfth root of 2 if they had insisted on giving this problem a literal interpretation.

Based on a string length of 10 units for the "octave," or *Huang-chung* [C'], Chu Tsai-yü first calculated the string length of *Jui-pin* [F♯] below C' by computing in effect,[42]

$$\text{For F}\sharp\text{:}\quad \Lambda = 10 \times \sqrt{2} \approx 14.142135623730950488016 89$$

He then calculated the string length of *Nan-lü* [A] below C' by computing in effect,[43]

$$\text{For A:}\quad \Lambda = 10 \times \sqrt{\sqrt{2}} \approx 11.892071150027210667175$$

and finally, the string length of *Ying-chung* [B] below C' by computing in effect,[44]

$$\text{For B:}\quad \Lambda = 10 \times \sqrt[3]{\sqrt{\sqrt{2}}} \approx 10.594630943592952645618 25$$

Divide the latter product by ten and note that the quotient approximates the irrational number $\sqrt[12]{2}$.[45] To finish the scale, Chu Tsai-yü probably performed two more cubic extractions. He most likely calculated the string length of *I-tse* [G♯] by multiplying in effect $10 \times \sqrt[3]{2} \approx 12.59921$, and the length of *Wu-i* [A♯] by multiplying in effect $10 \times \sqrt[3]{\sqrt{2}} \approx 11.22462$. In Table 11.11, these latter five extractions are marked with asterisks. We may calculate the remaining string lengths for 12-tone equal temperament either by raising some of these extractions to the second or third power, or by multiplying various combinations of previously calculated extractions. Table 11.11 also includes six such possible solutions.

Table 11.11

FIVE EFFECTIVE EXTRACTIONS AND SIX POSSIBLE SOLUTIONS FOR STRING LENGTHS OF 12-TONE EQUAL TEMPERAMENT BASED ON CALCULATIONS BY CHU TSAI-YÜ

C′			$= 10.00000$
B*	$10 \times \sqrt[3]{\sqrt{\sqrt{2}}}$	$= 10 \times \sqrt[12]{2}^{1}$	≈ 10.59463
A♯*	$10 \times \sqrt[3]{\sqrt{2}}$	$= 10 \times \sqrt[12]{2}^{2}$	≈ 11.22462
A*	$10 \times \sqrt{\sqrt{2}}$	$= 10 \times \sqrt[12]{2}^{3}$	≈ 11.89207
G♯*	$10 \times \sqrt[3]{2}$	$= 10 \times \sqrt[12]{2}^{4}$	≈ 12.59921
G	$10 \times \sqrt[3]{2} \times \sqrt[3]{\sqrt{\sqrt{2}}}$	$= 10 \times \sqrt[12]{2}^{5}$	≈ 13.34840
F♯*	$10 \times \sqrt{2}$	$= 10 \times \sqrt[12]{2}^{6}$	≈ 14.14214
F	$10 \times \sqrt{2} \times \sqrt[3]{\sqrt{\sqrt{2}}}$	$= 10 \times \sqrt[12]{2}^{7}$	≈ 14.98307
E	$10 \times \sqrt[3]{2}^{2}$	$= 10 \times \sqrt[12]{2}^{8}$	≈ 15.87401
D♯	$10 \times \sqrt{\sqrt{2}}^{3}$	$= 10 \times \sqrt[12]{2}^{9}$	≈ 16.81793
D	$10 \times \sqrt[3]{\sqrt{2}} \times \sqrt[3]{2}^{2}$	$= 10 \times \sqrt[12]{2}^{10}$	≈ 17.81797
C♯	$10 \times \sqrt[3]{\sqrt{2}} \times \sqrt{\sqrt{2}}^{3}$	$= 10 \times \sqrt[12]{2}^{11}$	≈ 18.87749
C	10×2	$= 10 \times \sqrt[12]{2}^{12}$	$= 20.00000$

Notes

1. (A) Kaufmann, W. (1976). *Musical References in the Chinese Classics*, p. 107. Detroit Monographs in Musicology, Detroit, Michigan.

   (B) Needham, J. (1962). *Science and Civilization in China, Volume 4, Part I*, p. 172. Cambridge University Press, Cambridge, England.

2. (A) Kaufmann, W. (1967). *Musical Notations of the Orient*, p. 17. Indiana University Press, Bloomington, Indiana.

   (B) *Science and Civilization in China, Volume 4, Part I*, p. 173.

3. (A) *Musical References in the Chinese Classics*, p. 147.

   (B) *Musical Notations of the Orient*, p. 17.

4. See Sections 7.11 and 8.3.

5. See Section 8.7.

6. *Ibid.*

7. *Science and Civilization in China, Volume 4, Part I*, p. 175.

8. (A) Lieberman, F., Translator (1977). *The Mei-an Ch'in-p'u*, edited by Hsü Li-sun, pp. 186–187. In Lieberman's *The Chinese Long Zither Ch'in: A Study Based on the Mei-an Ch'in-p'u.* Ph.D. dissertation printed and distributed by University Microfilms, Inc., Ann Arbor, Michigan.

   (B) Lieberman, F., Translator (1983). *The Mei-an Ch'in-p'u*, edited by Hsü Li-sun, p. 18. In Lieberman's *A Chinese Zither Tutor.* University of Washington Press, Seattle, Washington.

   The dissertation is 851 pages long and includes everything contained in the tutor, which is only 172 pages long. However, because the illustrations and tables in the tutor are clearer and easier to understand, all Notes (except one) refer to Lieberman's tutor. Readers who need detailed information should consult the dissertation.

9. *Science and Civilization in China, Volume 4, Part I*, pp. 172–173.

10. The ditonic comma, and its geometric division into 12 equal parts, play a crucial role in Western tuning theory and practice because of the mathematical requirements of 12-tone equal temperament. (See Section 10.31.) Since musicians in China tune their instruments in just intonation, the enharmonic distinction between B♯ and the "octave" C$^{\prime}$ is not a determining factor. Consequently, the Chinese *spiral of "fifths"* simply ends on E♯.

11. This time span assumes that Chinese mathematicians defined the spiral of "fifths" in approximately 700–500 B.C., and that Europeans began implementing such a scale in approximately A.D. 1000–1300. Remember, the ancient Greeks did *not* contemplate 12-tone scales. The so-called *comma of Pythagoras* has nothing to do with the original discoveries attributed to Pythagoras. (See Sections 10.15 and 10.22.)

12. Kuttner, F.A. (1965). A musicological interpretation of the twelve lüs in China's traditional tone system. *Journal of the Society for Ethnomusicology* **IX**, No. 1, pp. 22–38.

13. (A) Sachs, C. (1940). *The History of Musical Instruments*, p. 185. W. W. Norton & Company, Inc., New York.

   Sachs cites *ch'in* poetry from about 1100 B.C.

   (B) Gulik, R.H., Translator (1941). *Poetical Essay on the Lute*, by Hsi K'ang (A.D. 223–262), pp. 51–70. In Gulik's *Hsi K'ang and His Poetical Essay on the Lute*, Sophia University, Tokyo, Japan.

   This essay recounts the ancient musical traditions of the *ch'in.*

14. *The History of Musical Instruments*, p. 463.

15. Apel, W., Editor (1944). *Harvard Dictionary of Music*, 2nd ed., pp. 170–171. Harvard University Press, Cambridge, Massachusetts, 1972.

16. *Musical Notations of the Orient*, p. 275.

17. See Section 7.13.

18. For a discussion on the acoustic properties of flageolet tones, and how to calculate the length ratios and frequency ratios of such tones based on standing wave patterns or mode shapes of vibrating strings, see Section 10.50.

19. *Musical Notations of the Orient*, p. 277.

20. Lui, T. (1968). A short guide to *ch'in*, p. 184. *Selected Reports* **I**, No. 2, pp. 180–201. Publication of the Institute of Ethnomusicology of the University of California at Los Angeles.

21. *A Chinese Zither Tutor*, p. 37.

22. *Ibid.*, p. 42.

23. *Ibid.*, p. 25.

24. (A) *Ibid.*, pp. 26–27.

Figures 11 and 12 of Lieberman's book show only *hui* fractions 8.5, 7.9, and 7.6 in Arabic numerals. The remaining *hui* fractions are depicted in Chinese characters.

(B) Wang, K. (1956). *Chung-kuo yin yueh shih*, p. 26. Taipei, Formosa: Chung hua shu chu.

Although Wang's book is in Chinese, the foldout on p. 26 gives *hui* fractions in Arabic numerals. In Table 11.5, I corrected 73.7, 72.2, and 70.8 to read 13.7, 12.2, and 10.8, respectively. Furthermore, I omitted Wang's *hui* fraction 7.5 from Table 11.5, which he defines as the tone "h," or "B natural." This tone does not belong to the pentatonic scale on the *ch'in.*

25. I calculated the relation $9/8 \leftrightarrow 13.6$ based on the logical assumption that theoretical *hui* 14 requires a string division into 10 aliquot parts. Such a division is consistent with the patterns in Table 11.4 because it would produce flageolet length ratio $1/10$, flageolet frequency ratio $10/1$, and the approximate flageolet tone E_5. Furthermore, *hui* 14 also represents stopped length ratio $9/10$, and stopped frequency ratio $10/9$. So, for ratio $9/8$, I used ancient length ratios $10/9$ and $8/7$ to calculate the closest *hui* fraction at 13.6, and the ratio of the closest fraction, $100/89$.

26. Due to complicated round-off errors, I initially calculated all cent values in Table 11.5, Rows 1 and 5, to four decimal places. After subtraction, I then rounded the final cent differences in Row 6 to two decimal places.

27. (A) Sadie, S., Editor (1980). *The New Grove Dictionary of Music and Musicians, Volume 4*, p. 267. Macmillan Publishers Limited, London, England, 1995.

(B) *The Chinese Long Zither Ch'in: A Study Based on the Mei-an Ch'in-p'u*, p. 11.

(C) *Selected Reports* **I**, No. 2, 1968, p. 183.

28. For those readers interested in listening to *ch'in* music, I highly recommend a cassette tape entitled *Music for the Ch'in Performed by Contemporary Masters of the Mei-an Tradition*, compiled and edited by F. Lieberman. For a copy, write to the University of Washington Press, P.O. Box C-50096, Seattle Washington 98105. Throughout the tape, a given composition is performed by two or three *ch'in* masters, so that the listener has a chance to appreciate different interpretations of the same composition. The last two pieces on Side 2 are performed by Hsü Li-sun.

29. *A Chinese Zither Tutor*, pp. 32–33.

30. *Science and Civilization in China, Volume 4, Part I*, pp. 160–165.

Needham traces the historical evolution of pentatonic and heptatonic scales in ancient China.

31. (A) Reinhard, K. (1956). *Chinesische Musik*, 2nd ed., pp. 79–81. Im Erich Röth-Verlag, Kassel, Germany.

(B) Musical Notations of the Orient, pp. 19–21.

32. See Section 10.36.

33. See Section 10.30.

34. See Section 10.15.

35. *Musical Notations of the Orient*, p. 18.

36. See Section 10.31.

37 *Musical Notations of the Orient*, p. 18.

38. *Ibid.*, pp. 18–19.

39. See Chapter 10, Note 160.

40. Robinson, K. (1980). *A Critical Study of Chu Tsai-yü's Contribution to the Theory of Equal Temperament in Chinese Music.* Franz Steiner Verlag GmbH, Wiesbaden, Germany.

41. *Ibid.*, p. 112.

42. *Ibid.*, p. 114.

Through an elaborate geometrical method, Chu Tsai-yü actually calculated the length of *Jui-pin* by extracting the square root of 2 times 10^2, or the square root of 200.

43. *Ibid.*, p. 116.

Chu Tsai-yü actually calculated the length of *Nan-lü* by extracting the square root of the length of *Jui-pin* multiplied times 10, or the square root of 141.42135...

44. *Ibid.*

Chu Tsai-yü actually calculated the length of *Ying-chung* by extracting the cubic root of the length of *Nan-lü* multiplied times 10^2, or the cubic root of 1189.20711...

45. Wang, L., and Needham, J. (1955). Horner's method in Chinese mathematics: Its origins in the root-extraction procedures of the Han Dynasty. *T'oung Pao Archives* **XLIII**, No. 5, pp. 345–401. Leiden, Netherlands.

This paper discusses the spectacular root-extraction procedures developed in ancient China, and thereby suggests how Chu Tsai-yü could have obtained his extraordinarily accurate results.

Part II

INDONESIAN MUSIC

Java

~ 11.12 ~

Indonesia consists of an archipelago of three thousand islands scattered throughout the Indian Ocean in Southeast Asia. It is the birthplace of gamelan music. Gamelan orchestras, composed of many low-lying and stationary musical instruments arranged in rectangular or circular patterns, bring to mind unique islands of sound. Gamelan music defies standard mathematical analysis because among the thousands of orchestras that exist in Indonesia, no two are alike. For unknown reasons, the tradition of monochord division did not flourish in Indonesia, and consequently tuning theory did not evolve as a branch of mathematics. Instead, the subject of musical mathematics developed on a purely *experiential* basis. Each village and town has its own individual sound, and for a given gamelan, professional gamelan makers tune their instruments, without the benefit of acoustic or electronic devices, to within a few cents of a desired scale. Given the inharmonic mode frequencies of vibrating bars[1] and gongs, such precision in the tuning of percussion instruments constitutes a remarkable scientific and musical achievement.

Gamelans on the islands of Java and Bali are tuned to two basic scales, or *laras*, called *sléndro* and *pélog*. Musicians East and West write gamelan music in cipher notation, which consists of a progression of integers that represent the tones of a piece composed in either *sléndro* or *pélog*. Unfortunately, unless one understands the idiosyncrasies of this notation, it is extremely easy to misinterpret the pitches of gamelan tunings. Before we discuss this subject in full detail, let us first review the cipher notation in Section 11.5 and Figure 11.2. Many scholars record the original Chinese pentatonic scale by writing 1–2–3–5–6–1, where the last digit represents a tone an "octave" above the first digit. Figure 11.3 shows that this technique has its origins in the Chevé System,[2] which uses numbers 1 through 7 to identify the sequential tones of the standard Western diatonic scale. For a tone an "octave" above a given pitch, the cipher-dot notation requires a dot above a cipher, and for a tone an "octave" below a given pitch, a dot below a cipher; similarly, it requires two dots above or below a cipher for a tone two "octaves" above or below a given pitch. When one compares the pitches of the original Chinese pentatonic scale to five select pitches of the Western diatonic scale, the sequence 1–2–3–5–6–1 represents the Chinese scale fairly well.

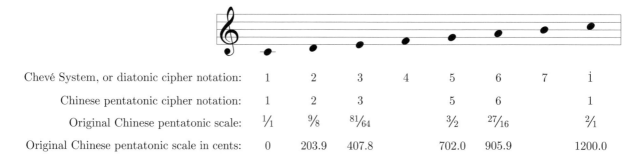

Chevé System, or diatonic cipher notation:	1	2	3	4	5	6	7	$\dot{1}$
Chinese pentatonic cipher notation:	1	2	3		5	6		1
Original Chinese pentatonic scale:	1/1	9/8	81/64		3/2	27/16		2/1
Original Chinese pentatonic scale in cents:	0	203.9	407.8		702.0	905.9		1200.0

Figure 11.3 The Chevé System, or diatonic cipher notation used in many ethnomusicological texts. Here the sequence 1–2–3–4–5–6–7–$\dot{1}$ represents one "octave" of the standard Western diatonic scale. When applied to the original Chinese pentatonic scale in Figure 11.2, the sequence reads 1–2–3–5–6–1, which represents the latter scale fairly well.

Sléndro consists of a 5-tone or pentatonic scale. An application of the latter sequence of ciphers to this scale does not yield favorable results. Regrettably, since most writers do not bother to discuss these inherent difficulties, the transmission of accurate information suffers. Avoidance of such discussions is based on two perplexing facts: (1) No two gamelans have identical tunings, and (2) differences in tuning may vary significantly. This lack of consistency is the hallmark of gamelan tunings and, when viewed from a musical perspective, is the source of endless artistic inspiration. However, given an accurate set of numbers, there is no reason why science should suffer at the expense of art. Reliable tuning data reveal tendencies *not* supported by conventional cipher notation. For example, Figure 11.4, Row 2, indicates that the *sléndro* tuning system is traditionally notated 1–2–3–5–6–$\dot{1}$, which immediately suggests the original Chinese pentatonic scale, or a spiral of "fifths." In contrast, Figure 11.4, Row 3, shows recalculated average cent values of 28 Javanese *sléndro* gamelans analyzed by Wasisto Surjodiningrat, *et al.*[3] Note that in the majority of cases, traditional pitch 3 *tends* to sound like a "flat fourth,"[4] as in frequency ratio $^{21}/_{16}$ [470.8 ¢], and not like a "sharp major third," ratio $^{81}/_{64}$ [407.8 ¢]. Similarly, traditional pitch 6 *tends* to sound like a "flat minor seventh,"[5] as in ratio $^{7}/_{4}$ [968.8 ¢], and not like a "sharp major sixth," ratio $^{27}/_{16}$ [905.9 ¢]. Because traditional pitches 3 and 6 are generally tuned a "semitone" higher than enumerated, we should write *sléndro* as 1–2–4–5–7♭–$\dot{1}$, and if not, we should understand it as such.[6] Furthermore, *sléndro* and *pélog* "octaves" are frequently tuned about a *syntonic comma*, ratio $^{81}/_{80}$ [21.5 ¢], sharp.[7] This technique gives many gamelans a shimmering musical quality because "sharp octaves" cause very noticeable beat rate patterns on powerful percussion instruments made of bronze. So, to acknowledge this unique and vital feature of many Javanese gamelans, it would not be entirely incorrect to notate *sléndro* 1–2–4–5–7♭–$\dot{1}$(♯), as in Figure 11.4, Row 1, to indicate such "sharp octaves."

A complete or double gamelan consists of a set of instruments tuned in *sléndro*, and a set of instruments tuned in *pélog*. Consider now the *sléndro* scale of a *saron demung*, a percussion instrument with seven bronze bars, which belongs to a famous double gamelan called Kyahi Kanjutmesem.[8] (Since Surjodiningrat, *et al.* give all frequencies rounded to zero decimal places, I will do the same with respect to the *related* frequency and cent calculations below. However, wherever warranted, I will also continue to give frequency and cent values carried out to one decimal place.) This instrument is tuned to the following frequencies: 248 cps, 287 cps, 331 cps, 378 cps, 435 cps, 500 cps, and 580 cps. Here *sléndro* begins on the second bar, and the "sharp octave" resides on the seventh bar. Since D_4 of 12-TET vibrates at 293.7 cps, and since the second bar vibrates at 287 cps, or 40.0 ¢ flat of D_4, observe that the first note in Figure 11.4 does *not* reflect this pitch. Instead, the cent values in Figure 11.4, Row 4, were calculated relative to the frequency of the *second* bar, or to the first pitch of the *sléndro* scale. According to Equation 9.21,

$$\text{Pitch 2} = \log_{10}\frac{331 \text{ cps}}{287 \text{ cps}} \times 3986.314 = 247\ ¢$$

$$\text{Pitch 3} = \log_{10}\frac{378 \text{ cps}}{287 \text{ cps}} \times 3986.314 = 477\ ¢\ \ldots$$

The tones in Figures 11.4 and 11.5 only give very rough approximations of the cent averages in Rows 3. Refer to the 5-limit analysis in Figure 11.4, Row 5, and notice that *sléndro* in its simplest form consists of two ascending $^{3}/_{2}$'s, or two ascending "fifths": [Pitch 5 = $^{1}/_{1} \times {}^{3}/_{2} = {}^{3}/_{2}$], [Pitch 2 = $^{3}/_{2} \times {}^{3}/_{2} = {}^{9}/_{4} = {}^{9}/_{8}$], and two descending $^{3}/_{2}$'s, or two descending "fifths": [Pitch 3 = $^{1}/_{1} \div {}^{3}/_{2} = {}^{2}/_{3} = {}^{4}/_{3}$], [Pitch 6 = $^{4}/_{3} \div {}^{3}/_{2} = {}^{8}/_{9} = {}^{16}/_{9}$]. However, because pitch 6 tends to sound like a "flat minor seventh," note carefully that a typical *sléndro* scale does *not* have an interval of a "major third." To help identify extremely sharp or flat sounding pitches, Figures 11.4 and 11.5 show such tones with arrows pointing upward or downward, respectively; these arrows indicate tones that sound

Javanese Sléndro

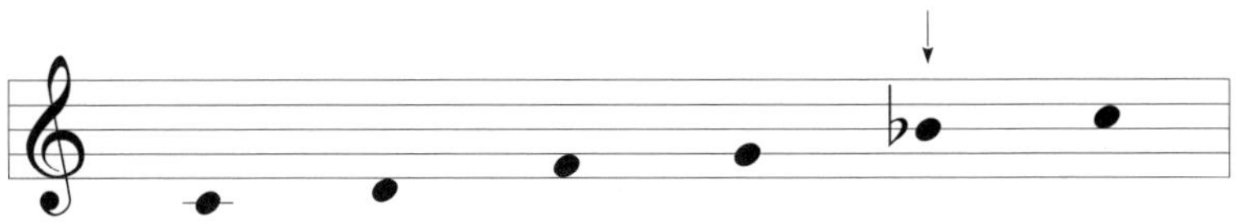

Revised cipher notation:	1		2		4		5		7♭		i̇(♯)	(1)
Traditional cipher notation:	1		2		3		5		6		i̇	(2)
Cent averages in Surjodiningrat:	0		233		472		718		961		1213	(3)
		233		*239*		*246*		*243*		*252*		
Pitches in cents of *Saron demung*, Gamelan Kyahi Kanjutmesem, Java:	0		247		477		720		961		1218	(4)
5-Limit ratio analysis:	1/1		9/8		4/3		3/2		16/9		81/40	(5)
	0		204		498		702		996		1222	(6)
Cent differences, [Row 6] – [Row 3]:			–29		+26		–16		+35		+9	(7)
7-Limit ratio analysis:	1/1		8/7		21/16		32/21		7/4		81/40	(8)
	0		231		471		729		969		1222	(9)
Cent differences, [Row 9] – [Row 3]:			–2		–1		+11		+8		+9	(10)
11-Limit ratio analysis:	1/1		8/7		21/16		50/33		96/55		81/40	(11)
	0		231		471		719		964		1222	(12)
Cent differences, [Row 12] – [Row 3]:			–2		–1		+1		+3		+9	(13)

Figure 11.4 A typical Javanese *sléndro* scale. In Row 3, recalculated cent averages from a study by Surjodiningrat, *et al.* indicate that despite the traditional cipher notation, variations of this gamelan scale have very little in common with the original Chinese pentatonic scale. The revised cipher notation in Row 1 gives a more accurate description of *sléndro* tunings. Furthermore, graduated 5-limit, 7-limit, and 11-limit ratio analyses reveal the intonational complexities of this scale.

approximately 40–50 ¢ higher or lower than the illustrated pitches of 12-tone equal temperament. Now, consider an inclusion of D_5 [233 ¢] above C_5 in Figure 11.4. Such a tone seems to suggest a "major third" between $B\flat_4$ and D_5; but if we give D_5 a stretched "octave" tuning of (1200.0 ¢ + 13.0 ¢) + 233.0 ¢ = 1,446.0 ¢, and then subtract 961.0 ¢, the interval between $B\flat_4$ and D_5 equals 485.0 ¢, which is a "flat fourth."

11.13

Pélog consists of a 7-tone or heptatonic scale. However, as discussed in Section 11.15, musicians utilize *pélog* as a pentatonic scale; that is, for a given composition, performers choose five of seven available tones. The remaining two tones are used as well, but only in the context of embellishments and modulations.

In Figure 11.5, Rows 1 and 2 indicate that with the exception of accidentals, the revised and traditional cipher notations of *pélog* are identical. Of the two, the revised notation of *pélog* as 1–2♭–3♭–4(♯)–5–6♭–7♭–i̇(♯) more accurately conveys the complexity of this tuning system. Figure 11.5, Row 3, shows recalculated average cent values of 30 Javanese *pélog* gamelans analyzed by Surjodiningrat, *et al.*[9] Figure 11.5, Row 4, lists the *pélog* pitches in cents of a *saron demung* and a *saron ritjik* (or *saron barung*) that also belong to gamelan Kyahi Kanjutmesem.[10] The frequencies of these bars are 296 cps, 320 cps, 345 cps, 406 cps, 439 cps, 471 cps, 519 cps, and 598 cps.[11] Here *pélog* begins on the first bar,

Javanese Pélog

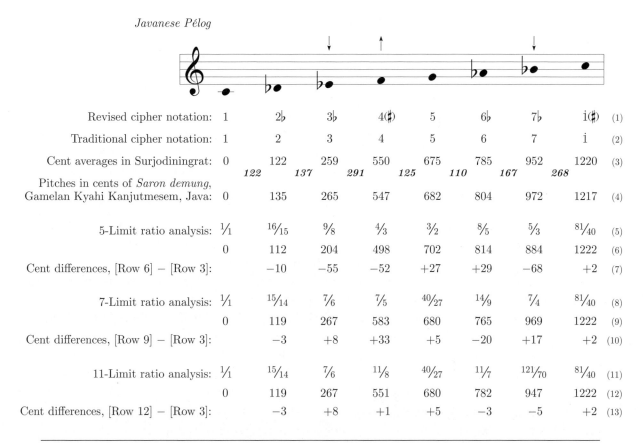

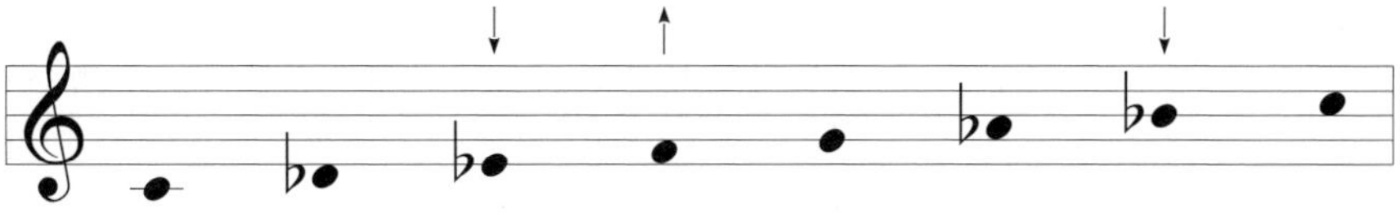

Revised cipher notation:	1	2♭	3♭	4(♯)	5	6♭	7♭	i(♯)	(1)
Traditional cipher notation:	1	2	3	4	5	6	7	i	(2)
Cent averages in Surjodiningrat:	0	122	259	550	675	785	952	1220	(3)
	122	*137*	*291*	*125*	*110*	*167*	*268*		
Pitches in cents of *Saron demung*, Gamelan Kyahi Kanjutmesem, Java:	0	135	265	547	682	804	972	1217	(4)
5-Limit ratio analysis:	1/1	16/15	9/8	4/3	3/2	8/5	5/3	81/40	(5)
	0	112	204	498	702	814	884	1222	(6)
Cent differences, [Row 6] – [Row 3]:		−10	−55	−52	+27	+29	−68	+2	(7)
7-Limit ratio analysis:	1/1	15/14	7/6	7/5	40/27	14/9	7/4	81/40	(8)
	0	119	267	583	680	765	969	1222	(9)
Cent differences, [Row 9] – [Row 3]:		−3	+8	+33	+5	−20	+17	+2	(10)
11-Limit ratio analysis:	1/1	15/14	7/6	11/8	40/27	11/7	121/70	81/40	(11)
	0	119	267	551	680	782	947	1222	(12)
Cent differences, [Row 12] – [Row 3]:		−3	+8	+1	+5	−3	−5	+2	(13)

Figure 11.5 A typical Javanese heptatonic *pélog* scale. In Row 3, recalculated cent averages from a study by Surjodiningrat, *et al.* indicate a very complicated scale that requires an 11-limit ratio analysis to reduce the cent differences to less than ± 10 ¢.

and the "sharp octave" resides on the eighth bar. Again, since D_4 of 12-TET vibrates at 293.7 cps, and since the first bar of the *saron demung* vibrates at 296 cps, or 13.5 ¢ sharp of D_4, observe that the first note in Figure 11.5 does not reflect this pitch. Instead, the cent values in Figure 11.5, Row 4, were calculated relative to the frequency of the *first* bar, or to the first pitch of the *pélog* scale:

$$\text{Pitch 2} = \log_{10} \frac{320 \text{ cps}}{296 \text{ cps}} \times 3986.314 = 135\ ¢$$

$$\text{Pitch 3} = \log_{10} \frac{345 \text{ cps}}{296 \text{ cps}} \times 3986.314 = 265\ ¢\ ...$$

A comparison of the cent differences of the *sléndro* scale in Figure 11.4, Rows 7 and 10, and of the *pélog* scale in Figure 11.5, Rows 7 and 10, reveals that the latter scale is not well served by 5-limit and 7-limit ratios. Consequently, only the 11-limit ratio analysis in Row 11 produces a fairly accurate representation of this scale. Now, unfold the *pélog* scale in Figure 11.5 in the following manner:

D♭		A♭		E♭		B♭		F♯		C		G
	663 ¢		694 ¢		693 ¢		818 ¢		670 ¢		675 ¢	

This configuration reveals three consecutive "flat fifths," a "sharp minor sixth," and two more "flat fifths," respectively. As discussed in Section 11.12, the method of calculating these intervals takes into account the tuning of "sharp octaves" whenever an interval spans cipher $\dot{1}$. For example, consider an inclusion of E♭$_5$ [259 ¢] in Figure 11.5. If we give this tone a stretched "octave" tuning of (1200.0 ¢ + 20.0 ¢) + 259.0 ¢ = 1,479.0 ¢, and then subtract 785.0 ¢, the interval between A♭$_4$ and E♭$_5$ equals 694.0 ¢. In Section 11.14, we will observe that *sléndro* tunings consist mainly of "wide fifths," and in Section 11.15, that *pélog* tunings consist mainly of "narrow fifths."[12]

To further distinguish *pélog* from *sléndro*, and to aid readers interested in listening to gamelan music, observe that the *pélog* scale in Figure 11.5 has four "sharp semitones": [C$_4$–D♭$_4$ = 122 ¢], [D♭$_4$–E♭$_4$ = 137 ¢], [F♯$_4$–G$_4$ = 125 ¢], [G$_4$–A♭$_4$ = 110 ¢], and four "sharp major thirds": [D♭$_4$–F♯$_4$ = 428 ¢], [E♭$_4$–G$_4$ = 416 ¢], [F♯$_4$–B♭$_4$ = 402 ¢], [A♭$_4$–C$_5$ = 435 ¢]. In contrast, *sléndro* has no "semitones," and no "major thirds."

11.14

Gamelan musicians organize their compositions into musical sub-systems called *paṭet*. *Paṭet* consists of hierarchical distributions of tones and cadences in either *sléndro* or *pélog*. There are many factors that influence *paṭet;* these include the tuning of gamelan instruments, the artistic qualities of a composition, and the ceremonial context of a given performance. The subject of *paṭet* is extremely complex and fraught with controversy even among native musicians. Here, as in definitions of *sléndro* and *pélog*, one can only describe tendencies because hundreds of compositions exist in which gamelan musicians establish the resonance and mood of *paṭet* through very unpredictable methods and techniques. In short, since no single abstract theory can explain all manifestations and expressions of *paṭet*, the best way to approach and understand this subject is by listening to gamelan music.

Ki Sindoesawarno gives the following etymological description of the word *paṭet:*

> Pathet is an arrangement, a system, of the roles in melody. In melody there are basic roles, important roles, and completing roles. These roles are invested in tones. Thus the tones in a melody hold the positions of basic tones, important tones, and completing tones. The system which determines the division of roles is called *pathet* ['limited,' 'reined in'] or *pathut* ['proper,' 'fitting,' 'appropriate'], or *surupan* [Sundanese and Indonesian, 'proper']. Changing the distribution of roles as they apply to the tones means changing the system, thus changing the pathet.[13]

Given such a general definition, we may define the practice of *paṭet* as the sounding of musical modes. Mantel Hood, a renowned Western scholar in the field, describes *paṭet* by stating

> Each mode [*paṭet*] is governed by a hierarchy of five pitches; melodic movement is guided by a primary and a secondary interval of the *sléndro* or *pélog* fifth, and melodic resolution is achieved through the use of typical cadential formulas outlining the primary interval of the fifth. The modes are also associated with certain times of the day or night and specific time periods in the presentation of puppet plays and dance dramas . . .[14] (Text in brackets mine.)

And Sumarsam gives the following historical account:

> [Ki Hadjar] Dewantara [1899–1959] felt deeply that Javanese arts and European arts were compatible, so he also discussed gamelan theory in Western musical terms. In his *Sari Swara* [1930] he explained gamelan modal practice (pathet) by using the analogy of the Western concept of the changing of keys (or the concept of movable *do*). He assigns the cipher 1

> as the tonic or *dhasar* of each of the three [*sléndro*] pathet. In *pathet nem*, pitch 2 functions as the dhasar; in *pathet sanga*, 5 functions as dhasar; and in *pathet manyura*, 6 functions as dhasar.[15] (Text in brackets mine.)

All prominent writers on Indonesian music agree on these three basic definitions of *sléndro paṭet*, including Radèn Lurah Martopangrawit,[16] Radèn Mas Kodrat Poerbapangrawit,[17] and Mantle Hood.[18] The latter description also establishes the correct musical order of *sléndro paṭet* with respect to register or range; that is, *sléndro paṭet Nem* is associated with a low register, *sléndro paṭet Sanga* with a middle register, and *sléndro paṭet Manyura* with a high register on various gamelan instruments. Long gamelan performances often modulate slowly through a steady rise in *paṭet* that culminates in the highest mode, *paṭet Manyura* in *sléndro*, and *paṭet Barang* in *pélog*.

Turn now to Figure 11.6, which shows three *sléndro paṭet* based on the theoretical scale in Figure 11.4. Note, however, that these *paṭet* do not appear in correct musical order. Instead, the organizational principle here reveals a staggered progression of "fifths," which suggests that *paṭet Nem* has its musical origin in *paṭet Sanga*, and *paṭet Manyura* has its musical origin in *paṭet Nem.* Observe that the fourth tone of *paṭet Sanga* — or a "fifth" above the tonic — functions as the tonic of *paṭet Nem*, and the fourth tone of *paṭet Nem* — again, a "fifth" above the tonic — functions as the tonic of *paṭet Manyura.* Cent calculations show why these and similar intervals that span any four tones in *sléndro* are called *"wide sléndro fifths."*

The cadential relation between the tonic and the "fifth" above plays a crucial role in determining the musical identity of a particular *paṭet.* Figure 11.7 gives a more detailed and musically meaningful account of these *sléndro paṭet.* Here, as in Figure 11.8, *sléndro paṭet* appear in musical order from low, to middle, to high registers. Also, in Figures 11.7 and 11.8, the traditional cipher notation indicates the distribution of this order on a *gendèr barung*, a gamelan percussion instrument equipped with bronze bars and closed tube resonators.[19] In many gamelan compositions, musicians use the *gendèr* to establish *paṭet.*[20] Figure 11.7 depicts the gong tone of the tonic as G-I, the gong tone a "fifth" above the tonic as G-V, and the gong tone a "fifth" below the tonic as G-IV. These markings are based on Western music theory where musicians identify the "fifth" above the tonic — or the "fourth" below the tonic — with Roman numeral V, and the "fourth" above the tonic — or the "fifth" below the tonic — with Roman numeral IV. Since the interval 2̣–5̣ in *sléndro paṭet Nem*, the interval 5̣–1 in *sléndro paṭet Sanga*, and the interval 6̣–2 in *sléndro paṭet Manyura* all produce various kinds of "fourths" above the tonic, the latter reference to Western music is not too objectionable.

Gamelan musicians assign degrees of importance to these three gong tones. For all *sléndro paṭet*, G-I is the *principal cadential tone.* G-I accentuates the last tone of a final cadence, and is played on one of the largest vertically hanging *gongs* (G). G-V is the second, and G-IV is the third most important cadential tone. Shorter melodic phrases within a large composition usually end on G-V, G-IV, or on the tone immediately above G-I. Musicians stress the last tones of these intermediate cadences on *kempul* (P), which is a small vertically hanging gong, or on *kenong* (N), *kempyang* (p), and *kethuk* (t), which are large, medium, and small horizontally suspended gongs, respectively.[21] The remaining tone (pitch 1 in *paṭet Nem*, pitch 3 in *paṭet Sanga*, and pitch 5 in *paṭet Manyura*) is the weakest and least important cadential tone. Many compositions in *sléndro paṭet Nem* end with cadential sequences that progress from pitch 6 to a very low and powerful *gong* tuned to pitch 2. Figures 11.7(a), 11.7(b), and 11.7(c) indicate *principal descending cadences* from G-V to G-I with a series of arrows between tones. Furthermore, *principal ascending cadences* — as from G-I to G-V — also play a crucial role in establishing *paṭet.* Such cadences, also indicated with arrows between tones, do not exist in traditional Western music. So, the reader should at all times avoid interpreting the cadential possibilities between gong tones from a strictly European perspective. Finally, for all *sléndro paṭet*, musicians perform *secondary ascending and descending cadences* between G-IV and G-I.

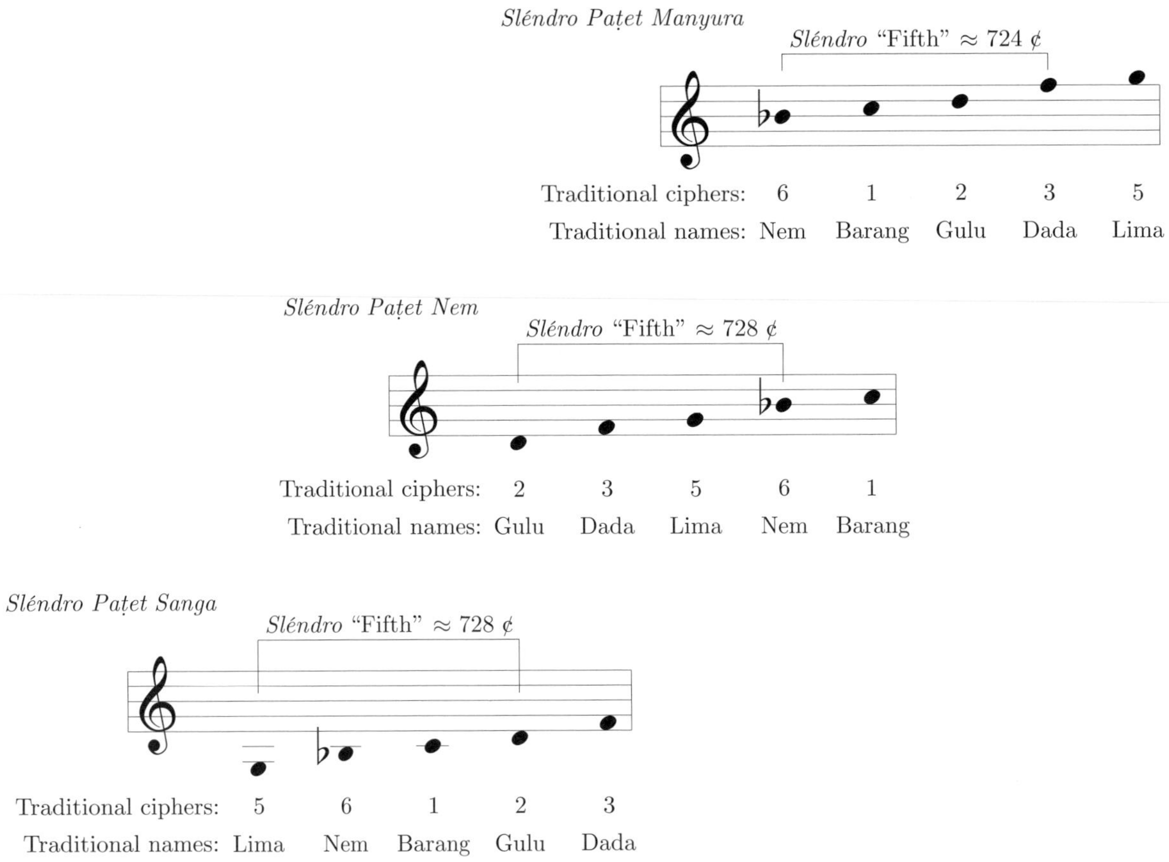

Figure 11.6 Three *sléndro paṭet* based on the theoretical scale in Figure 11.4. These three *paṭet* do not appear in musical order from low, to middle, to high registers (see Figures 11.7 and 11.8). Instead, this figure is designed to reveal a staggered progression of "fifths," which in turn suggests the origins of *paṭet Nem* and *paṭet Manyura*. The cadential relation between the first tone or tonic, and the fourth tone or "fifth" above, plays a crucial role in determining the identity of a particular *paṭet*.

Performances of the latter cadences need special consideration. Refer to Figure 11.8, and observe that a 12-bar *gendèr barung* spans the interval 1̣–2̇, a 13-bar instrument, the interval 1̣–3̇, and a 14-bar instrument, the interval 6̤–3̇. Consequently, one cannot play descending or ascending cadences directly between G-I and G-IV on any of these instruments as indicated in Figure 11.7(a). In *sléndro paṭet Nem*, a so-called *descending cadence* from G-I to G-IV in the lowest range of a 12-bar or 13-bar instrument must be played indirectly as 2̣, 1̣, 6̣, 5̣, and a so-called *ascending cadence*, indirectly as 5̣, 6̣, 1̣, 2̣. On the other hand, on a 14-bar instrument it is possible to descend directly from G-I to G-V below by playing 2̣, 1̣, 6̤. We conclude, therefore, that the direction and location of cadential patterns is often determined by the availability of tones on a given instrument, and by the discretion of the performer. For a given *paṭet*, musicians play variations of these pentatonic patterns in all registers of their instruments. Since the primary function of Figure 11.7 is to distinguish between *sléndro paṭet*, this illustration should *not* be confused with actual performance practice on all gamelan instruments.

Melodic and cadential progressions that terminate on designated tones are crucial in identifying a particular *paṭet*. Even so, observe that *paṭet Nem* is not easily distinguished from the other two modes. In *paṭet Nem*, the cadence 6̣, 5̣, 3̣, 2̣ also appears in *paṭet Manyura* between G-I and G-IV; and in *paṭet Nem*, the cadence 2, 1, 6̣, 5̣ also exists in *paṭet Sanga* between G-V and G-I. Under such

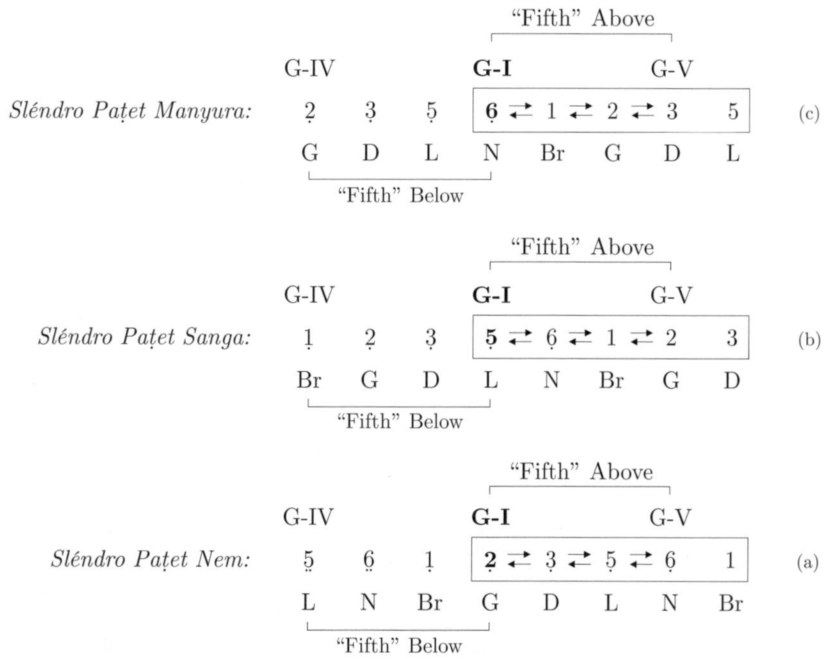

Figure 11.7 Hierarchical distributions of gong tones and cadences that define three *sléndro paṭet*. G-I is the principal, G-V is the second, and G-IV is the third most important gong tone for a given *paṭet*. Arrows between gong tones indicate principal ascending and descending cadences.

circumstances only register (range),[22] orchestration, time of day,[23] or ceremonial context act as vital indicators of a particular *paṭet*.[24] For these *sléndro paṭet*, only two 4-tone cadential sequences — 5̣, 3̣, 2̣, 1̣ and 3, 2, 1, 6̣ — unmistakably identify *paṭet Sanga* and *paṭet Manyura*, respectively. With respect to 3-tone cadential sequences, mode identifications are a bit simpler. For example, in *paṭet Nem*, 2̣, 3̣, 5̣ begins on G-I and ends on G-IV, but the same sequence in *paṭet Manyura* does not end on a gong tone. Similarly, in *paṭet Sanga*, 5̣, 6̣, 1 begins on G-I and ends on G-IV, whereas the same sequence in *paṭet Nem* also does not end on a gong tone. Many other such 3-tone cadences enable composers and musicians to differentiate between very similar sounding *paṭet*.

Finally, Figure 11.8 gives frequencies,[25] cent analyses, and pitch distributions of three *sléndro paṭet* on a 12-bar *gendèr barung* of gamelan Kyahi Kanjutmesem. The cent values in Row 1 were calculated by comparing the actual frequencies in Row 3 to the theoretical frequencies of 12-tone equal temperament in Row 2. For example, since the frequency of bar $\dot{2}$ is 672 cps, and the frequency of E_5 is 659.3 cps, the interval in cents between these two frequencies equals

$$\log_{10} \frac{672 \text{ cps}}{659.3 \text{ cps}} \times 3986.314 = 33 \text{ ¢}$$

Furthermore, in Row 6, a cent analysis of the given frequencies reveals one shimmering "octave" tuned flat, and five shimmering "octaves" tuned sharp. Since the frequency of bar 2 is 333 cps, and of bar $\dot{2}$ is 672 cps, note the following sharp "octave" between these two bars:

$$\log_{10} \frac{672 \text{ cps}}{333 \text{ cps}} \times 3986.314 = 1216 \text{ ¢}$$

A similar analysis also shows a sequence of widening and increasingly more dissonant "fifths" between G-I and G-V as one progresses from the lowest mode in Row 7 to the highest mode in Row 9.

Sléndro Paṭet Manyura (high): G-I 6̣ —— 748 ¢ —— G-V 3; degrees: 6̣ 1 2 3 5; intervals: ***259 ¢*** ***251 ¢*** ***238 ¢*** ***241 ¢*** (9)

Sléndro Paṭet Sanga (middle): G-I 5̣ —— 726 ¢ —— G-V 2; degrees: 5̣ 6̣ 1 2 3; intervals: ***215 ¢*** ***259 ¢*** ***251 ¢*** ***238 ¢*** (8)

Sléndro Paṭet Nem (low): G-I 2̣ —— 685 ¢ —— G-V 6̣; degrees: 2̣ 3̣ 5̣ 6̣ 1; intervals: ***205 ¢*** ***264 ¢*** ***215 ¢*** ***259 ¢*** (7)

"Octaves" in cents:						1200	1195	1227	1204	1224	1218	1216	(6)
Scale degrees in cents:	0	257	462	726	941	0	251	489	730	966	0	249	(5)
Gendèr barung, Gamelan Kyahi Kanjutmesem, Java:	1̣	2̣	3̣	5̣	6̣	1	2	3	5	6	1̇	2̇	(4)
	Barang	Gulu	Dada	Lima	Nem	Barang	Gulu	Dada	Lima	Nem	Barang	Gulu	
Frequencies in Surjodiningrat:	144	167	188	219	248	288	333	382	439	503	582	672	(3)

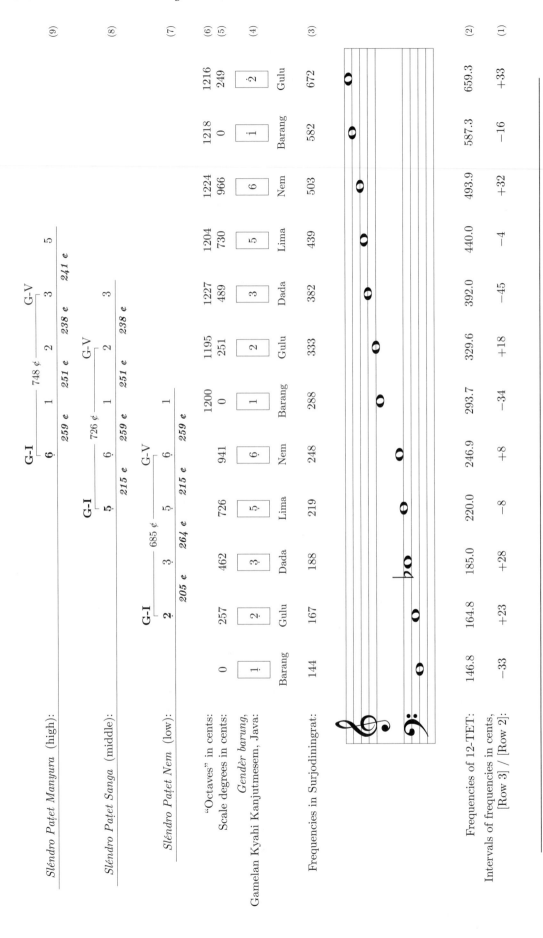

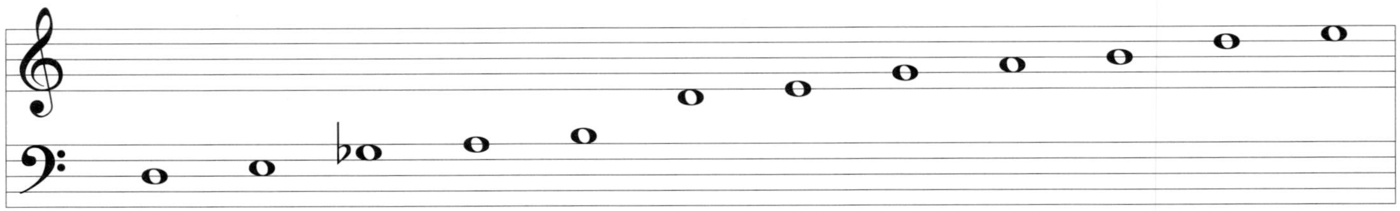

Frequencies of 12-TET:	146.8	164.8	185.0	220.0	246.9	293.7	329.6	392.0	440.0	493.9	587.3	659.3	(2)
Intervals of frequencies in cents, [Row 3] / [Row 2]:	−33	+23	+28	−8	+8	−34	+18	−45	−4	+32	−16	+33	(1)

Figure 11.8 Pitch distributions of three *sléndro paṭet* on a 12-bar *gendèr barung* of gamelan Kyahi Kanjutmesem. G-I signifies the lowest and most important cadential *gong* of a particular *sléndro paṭet*. Frequencies supplied by Surjodiningrat, *et al.* reveal a series of shimmering "octaves" in Row 6, and a sequence of widening "fifths" between G-I and G-V as one progresses from the lowest mode in Row 7 to the highest mode in Row 9.

To avoid cumulative round-off errors, do not calculate large intervals in cents by adding smaller intervals in cents. For example, to compute the cent value of the indicated "fifth" of *sléndro paṭet Nem*, always utilize the original frequency ratio:

$$\log_{10} \frac{248 \text{ cps}}{167 \text{ cps}} \times 3986.314 = 685 ¢$$

∾ 11.15 ∾

As discussed in Section 11.13, *pélog* consists of a theoretical heptatonic scale. From a total number of seven tones, musicians choose five pitches to construct various pentatonic modes called *pélog paṭet*. The dynamics of choice make *pélog paṭet* inherently more complicated than *sléndro paṭet*. To minimize confusion, the following analysis parallels the discussion in Section 11.14. Refer to Figure 11.9, which shows three *pélog paṭet* based on the theoretical scale in Figure 11.5. Observe that the modes appear in correct musical order from low, to middle, to high registers. The organizational principle of Figure 11.9 reveals a staggered progression of "fifths." Here two overlapping patterns suggest that *pélog paṭet Nem* has its musical origin in *pélog paṭet Lima*, and that *pélog paṭet Barang* has its musical origin in *pélog paṭet Nem*. However, not all writers agree on the latter version of *paṭet Barang*. Before we discuss differences of interpretation, note the conspicuous absence of pitch 4 from all modes in Figure 11.9. (The traditional name of pitch 4 is *"pélog"* as well.) The reason for these omissions is due to the evolving nature of gamelan music. In the past, pitch 4 played a prominent role in defining three additional *pélog paṭet*, plus one unusual mode called *pélog paṭet Miring.*[26] Figure 11.10(a) shows that of the three conventional modes that survived, only *pélog paṭet Lima* continues to persist in two different versions between G-I and G-IV. Nevertheless, pitch 4 does serve as an *embellishment tone* and *modulation tone* in all current versions of *pélog paṭet.*[27] Finally, in Figure 11.9, cent calculations show why the indicated "fifths" and similar intervals that span any four tones in *pélog* are called *"narrow pélog fifths."*

Pélog paṭet are also more complex than *sléndro paṭet* because the tonics of *pélog paṭet Lima* and *pélog paṭet Nem* do *not* function as the principal cadential tones. According to Figures 11.10(a) and 11.10(b), Martopangrawit, Poerbapangrawit, and Hood agree that the principal descending cadences for these two modes proceed from G-I to G-IV.[28] Consequently, G-IV is now the principal, G-I is the second, and G-V is the third most important cadential tone. Furthermore, Martopangrawit is the only modern writer who characterizes all three *pélog paṭet* with *two* equally important gong tones, namely, G-IV and G-I. Figure 11.10(c) shows that he extends this interpretation to *pélog paṭet Barang* as well. In contrast, Figure 11.10(d) indicates that Poerbapangrawit and Hood define *paṭet Barang* in a manner consistent with *sléndro paṭet* distributions, which, coincidentally, renders pitch 5 as the least important cadential tone of the mode.[29] Although Martopangrawit acknowledges the theoretical derivation of the latter version of *paṭet Barang,*[30] he rejects it in the context of performance practice.

> According to the theory of gendhing [composition], pathet barang has pitches ***5 and 2*** as dhong tones [tonics], and, indeed, this is borne out in the gendhing left us by our ancestors. A survey of the approximately forty gendhing . . . in pathet barang bequeathed to us by our ancestors indicates that only eight (or 20 percent) have pitch 6 as the gong tone.[31] (Bold italics and text in brackets mine.)

After listening to many *gendhing* in *pélog paṭet Barang*, and examining many gamelan scores,[32] I completely agree with Martopangrawit's interpretation of this mode. For example, Figure 11.11,

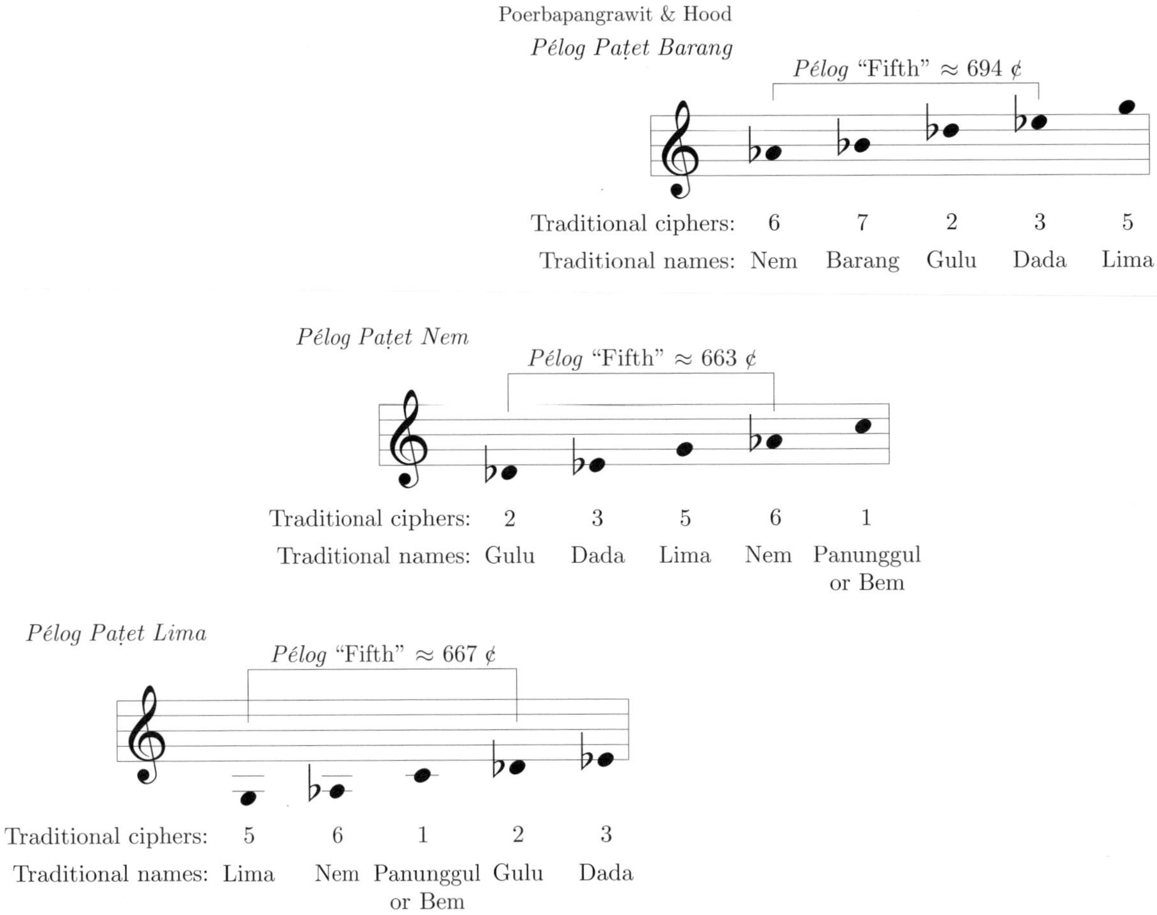

Figure 11.9 Three *pélog paṭet* based on the theoretical scale in Figure 11.5. These three *paṭet* do appear in musical order from low, to middle, to high registers. As in Figure 11.6, note the staggered progression of "fifths," which suggests the origins of *paṭet Nem*, and this particular version of *paṭet Barang*. However, unlike Figure 11.5, observe the conspicuous absence of pitch 4 from all these *paṭet*.

Row 3, gives the tuning of a *saron demung* that belongs to gamelan Kangjéng Kyahi Sirat Madu. I transcribed this scale from a CD recording of a composition entitled *Tunjung Anom*.[33] Since *pélog paṭet Barang* does not include pitch 1, this bar is not heard on the recording. However, in Row 4 note the presence of pitch 4 (*pélog*), which the performers sound several times as an embellishment tone; (the first time occurs exactly 1:13 from the beginning). Throughout this composition and, of course, at the very end, one hears the lowest *gong* as the final tone of the following principal cadence: 7, 6, 7, **5**(G). As discussed in Section 11.14, executions of such cadences are determined by the location and availability of tones on a given instrument.

With respect to mode identification, notice that *paṭet Lima* is not easily distinguished from *paṭet Nem*. In *paṭet Lima* the secondary cadence 5̣, 6̣, 1, 2 also appears in *paṭet Nem* as a primary cadence. Although a similar conflict seems to exist between secondary cadences in Figures 11.10(b) and 11.10(c), *pélog paṭet Barang* is absolutely unique because it alone includes pitch 7, depicted here as G!. In *pélog paṭet Barang*, G! rivals all other pitches because many compositions in this mode end on *gongs* tuned to pitch 7. Since for intermediate cadences, the tone immediately above G-I also continues to serve as an important cadential tone, we see that *all* pitches in *pélog paṭet Barang* constitute important gong tones.

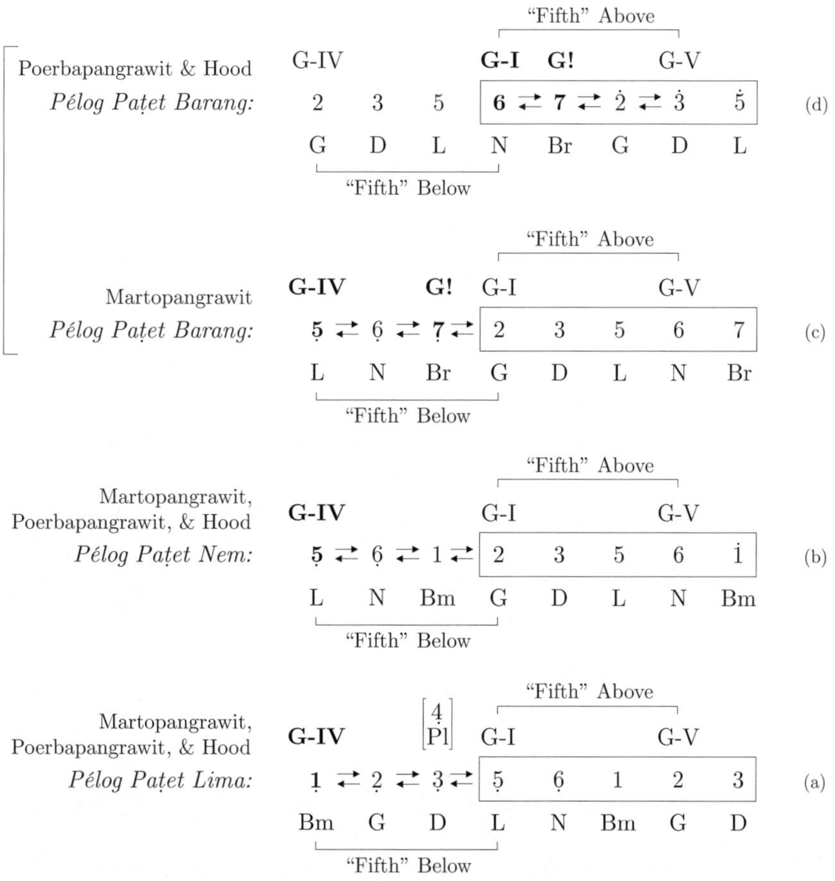

Figure 11.10 Hierarchical distributions of gong tones and cadences that define three *pélog paṭet*. In (a) and (b), three prominent writers give the same interpretations of *pélog paṭet Lima* and *pélog paṭet Nem*, but in (c) and (d) completely disagree with respect to the principal gong tone and principal cadence of *pélog paṭet Barang*.

Finally, refer to Figure 11.12, which gives frequencies,[34] cent analyses, and pitch distributions of three *pélog paṭet* on two 12-bar instruments of gamelan Kyahi Kanjutmesem. As described in the caption, the bars in Row 4 belong to two *gendèr barungs*, with the exception of bar $\dot{3}$, which belongs to a *gendèr panerus*. In Row 6, note that the "octave" between bars 2 and $\dot{2}$ is tuned flat by the same amount as the "octave" between bars $\underset{\cdot}{2}$ and 2 in Figure 11.8, Row 6. Also, observe a sequence of widening "fifths" between G-I and G-V as one progresses from the lowest mode in Row 7 to the highest mode in Row 10. Furthermore, it is significant that the latter tuning pattern extends without interruption into Figure 11.8, Rows 7–9. If we combine the former and latter sequences, the result is the following progression of expanding "fifths": 654 ¢, 664 ¢, 679 ¢, 685 ¢, 726 ¢, 748 ¢.

~ 11.16 ~

Gamelan musicians do not play compositions in *sléndro* and *pélog* simultaneously. To produce smooth transitions between pieces composed in these two different *laras*, performers sound a common tone called *tumbuk*. However, note carefully that in double gamelans, usually two different frequencies qualify as common or interchangeable tones of transition. According to Poerbapangrawit:

Martopangrawit	G-I		679 ¢ (G-I to G-V)	**G-IV**	G-V	**G!**	
Pélog Paṭet Barang:	2	3		**5**	6	7	(6)
Scale degrees in cents:	0	136	429	561	680	851	(5)
		136	***293***	***132***	***119***	***171***	
Six bars of a 7-bar *Saron demung*, Gamelan Kangjéng Kyahi Sirat Madu, Java:	2	3	4	5	6	7	(4)
	Gulu	Dada	Pélog	Lima	Nem	Barang	
Frequencies from CD recording:	306	331	392	423	453	500	(3)

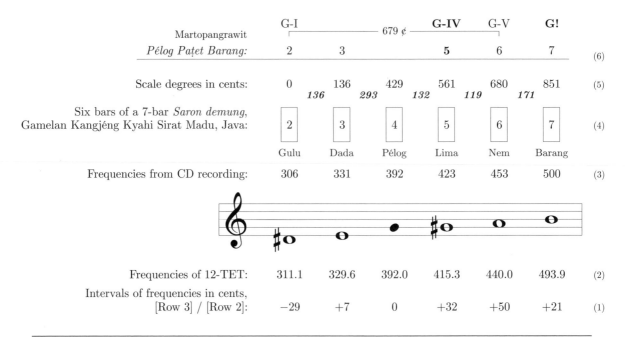

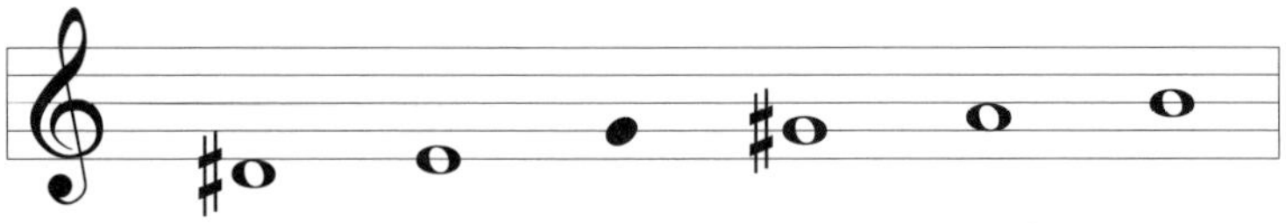

Frequencies of 12-TET:	311.1	329.6	392.0	415.3	440.0	493.9	(2)
Intervals of frequencies in cents, [Row 3] / [Row 2]:	−29	+7	0	+32	+50	+21	(1)

Figure 11.11 The tuning of a *saron demung* that belongs to gamelan Kangjéng Kyahi Sirat Madu, Java. I transcribed this tuning from a CD recording of a composition entitled *Tunjung Anom*. This is a fine example of a composition in *pélog paṭet Barang* that ends on G-IV, or pitch 5.

> In a double set with ***tumbuk on pitch 6***, sléndro pitch 5 is equivalent to pélog pitch 4. In effect, therefore, there are two equivalent tones: sléndro pitch 5 is the same as pélog pitch 4, and sléndro pitch 6 is the same as pélog pitch 6.
>
> In a double set with ***tumbuk on pitch 5***, sléndro pitch 6 will be ***almost*** equivalent to pélog pitch 7 (barang), and sléndro pitch 1 (barang) will be ***almost*** equivalent to pélog pitch 1 (panunggul) [or bem].[35] (Bold italics and text in brackets mine.)

We conclude, therefore, that *tumbuk* 6 demands precision in the tuning of *sléndro-pélog* bars 6-6 and 5-4, respectively, and *tumbuk* 5, precision in the tuning of *sléndro-pélog* bars 5-5, 6-7, and 1-1, respectively. Observe that the latter definition with respect to pitches 1 and 5 describes gamelan Kyahi Kanjutmesem perfectly. Refer to Figure 11.13, which shows the required bars and frequencies previously cited in Figures 11.8 and 11.12. Since these *pélog* bars are consistently tuned sharp of the *sléndro* bars, and since it is mathematically most convenient to organize these pitches into frequency ratios,[36] Figure 11.13 shows the appropriate bars in reverse order, namely, as vertical *pélog-sléndro* ratio pairs. Here the low *pélog-sléndro* pairs 1̣-1̣, 5̣-5̣, and the "octave" pair 5-5 produce near unisons, or slow beat rates of 1 cps. The human ear identifies such a low beat rate as a relatively smooth or consonant interval.[37] In contrast, the pair 7̣-6̣ produces half the beat rate of the "octave" pair 7-6, or very rapid rates of 8 cps and 16 cps, respectively; and the "octave" pair 1-1, nearly half the beat rate of the "double-octave" pair 1̇-1̇, or again very rapid rates of 8 cps and 15 cps, respectively. For the human ear, such high beat rates are associated with rough or dissonant intervals. The following beat rate pattern from pair 1̣-1̣ through pair 1̇-1̇ — 1 cps, 1 cps, 8 cps, 8 cps, 1 cps, 16 cps, 15 cps — leaves no doubt that the sounding of pairs 1̣-1̣, 5̣-5̣, and 5-5 provide the smoothest and most consonant transitions between *laras*, hence the *tumbuk* 5 designation.

Poerbapangrawit & Hood												**G-I**	**G!**	679 ¢		G-V	
Pélog Paṭet Barang (high):												**6**	**7**		2̇	3̇	(10)
												168 ¢		***363 ¢***	***148 ¢***		
Martopangrawit					**G-IV**		**G!**		G-I	664 ¢		G-V					
Pélog Paṭet Barang (high):					**5̣**		**7̣**		2	3	5	6	7				(9)
									125 ¢	***421 ¢***	***118 ¢***	***168 ¢***					
					G-IV				G-I	664 ¢		G-V					
Pélog Paṭet Nem (middle):					**5̣**				2	3	5	6		1̇			(8)
									125 ¢	***421 ¢***	***118 ¢***		***410 ¢***				
		G-IV			G-I		654 ¢		G-V								
Pélog Paṭet Lima (low):		**1̣**			5̣	6̣		1	2	3							(7)
					107 ¢		***407 ¢***	***140 ¢***	***125 ¢***								
"Octaves" in cents:							1214	1235	1227	1215	1200	1211	1224	1215	1195	1217	(6)
Scale degrees in cents:	971	0	149	286	722	829	984	0	140	265	686	804	972	0	120	268	(5)
Two 12-bar *Gendèr barungs*, Gam. Kyahi Kanjutmesem, Java:	7̤	1̣	2̣	3̣	5̣	6̣	7̣	1	2	3	5	6	7	1̇	2̇	3̇	(4)
	Barang	Bem	Gulu	Dada	Lima	Nem	Barang	Bem	Gulu	Dada	Lima	Nem	Barang	Bem	Gulu	Dada	
Frequencies in Surjodiningrat:	127	145	158	171	220	234	256	296	321	345	440	471	519	597	640	697	(3)

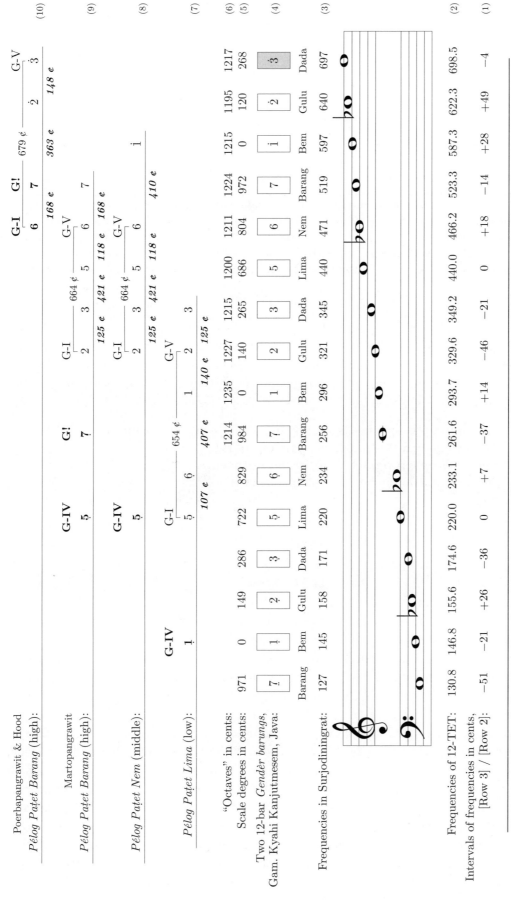

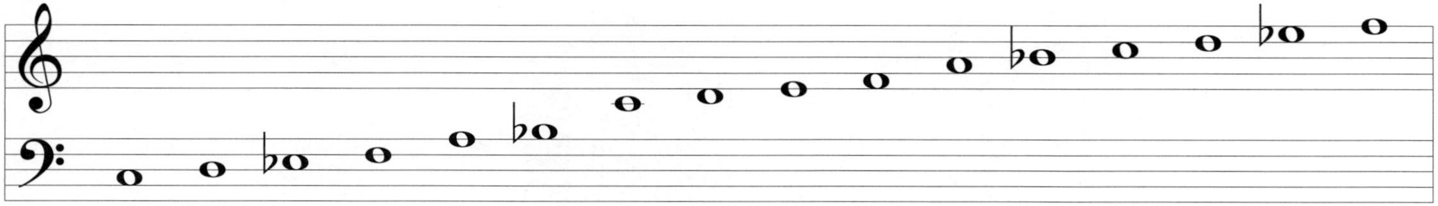

Frequencies of 12-TET:	130.8	146.8	155.6	174.6	220.0	233.1	261.6	293.7	329.6	349.2	440.0	466.2	523.3	587.3	622.3	698.5	(2)
Intervals of frequencies in cents, [Row 3] / [Row 2]:	−51	−21	+26	−36	0	+7	−37	+14	−46	−21	0	+18	−14	+28	+49	−4	(1)

Figure 11.12 Pitch distributions of four *pélog paṭet* on two 12-bar *gendèr barungs* of gamelan Kyahi Kanjutmesem. In Row 4, the low instrument consists of bars 7̤, 2̣, 3̣, 5̣, 6̣, 7̣, 2, etc., and the high instrument, of bars 1̣, 2̣, 3̣, 5̣, 6̣, 1, 2, etc., which means both instruments have bars 2̣, 3̣, 5̣, 6̣, 2, 3, 5, 6, 2̇ in common. According to the data by Surjodiningrat, *et al.*, these latter bars are tuned to perfect unisons. Shaded bar pitch 3̇ belongs to a *gendèr panerus*, tuned one "octave" higher than a *gendèr barung.* This is the highest bar on a 13-bar and 14-bar *gendèr barung;* the lowest bar on a 14-bar instrument is 6̤. In Row 10, pitch 5̇ of *pélog paṭet Barang* does not appear because it is outside the high register of all *gendèr barungs.*

Pélog tuning of *Gendèr barung*, Gamelan Kyahi Kanjutmesem:	1̣	5̣	7̣	1	5	7	1̇
	145	220	256	296	440	519	597
	144	219	248	288	439	503	582
Sléndro tuning of *Gendèr barung*, Gamelan Kyahi Kanjutmesem:	1̣	5̣	6̣	1	5	6	1̇
Frequency differences, or beat rates:	1 cps	1 cps	8 cps	8 cps	1 cps	16 cps	15 cps
Intervals of frequencies in cents:	+12	+8	+55	+47	+4	+54	+44

Figure 11.13 The *tumbuk* 5 tuning of double gamelan Kyahi Kanjutmesem. According to Poerbapangrawit, *tumbuk* 5 requires that *pélog-sléndro* pairs 5-5, 7-6, and 1-1 receive special tuning considerations. Here *pélog-sléndro* pairs 1̣-1̣, 5̣-5̣, 7̣-6̣, 1-1, 5-5, 7-6, 1̇-1̇ produce beat rates of 1 cps, 1 cps, 8 cps, 8 cps, 1 cps, 16 cps, and 15 cps, respectively. Such a pattern indicates a *tumbuk* 5 tuning because pairs 1̣-1̣, 5̣-5̣, and 5-5 produce the most consonant intervals between these two different scales.

In stark contrast, the other pairs — 2̣-2̣, 3̣-3̣, 2-2, 3-3, 2̇-2̇ — produce beat rates of 9 cps, 17 cps, 12 cps, 37 cps, 32 cps, respectively, most of which sound extremely dissonant. These latter pairs are further distinguished from the former pairs in that the *sléndro* bars are consistently tuned sharp of the *pélog* bars. Gamelan builders describe the process of tuning bars to various beat rates in four different ways.

> *Suara pleng:* two pitches, sounding together, perfectly in tune.
> *Suara berombak:* two pitches slightly out of tune.
> *Suara nyliring:* two pitches rather out of tune.
> *Suara bléro:* two pitches very much out of tune.[38]

Bali

11.17

Published posthumously in 1966, the most authoritative study on Balinese gamelan is a work entitled *Music in Bali*[39] by Colin McPhee (1900–1964). Although McPhee studied gamelan tunings and music in the first half of the 20th century, many texts and recordings of the second half of the 20th century confirm the accuracy and relevance of his writings. Unfortunately, an exhaustive tuning analysis like the kind carried out by Surjodiningrat, *et al.* in Java does not exist for gamelan orchestras in Bali.

In Java and Bali, gamelan musicians divide their compositions into two different tuning systems called *sléndro* and *pélog*. However, McPhee reminds us, "These names are not familiar to most Balinese, who have their own terminology."[40] For example, *sléndro* is widely known as *saih gendèr wayang*, because musical performances in this *saih* (scale) occur only on a special *gendèr* quartet used to accompany the *wayang*, or shadow puppet theater. Turn to Figure 11.14, which illustrates various aspects of Balinese *sléndro* scales. In Row 2, notice that traditional Balinese cipher notation is sequential and, therefore, includes number 3. Once again we must take into account that here, as in Javanese cipher notation, pitch 3 does *not* identify a "major third," but a "fourth." In Row 3, cent averages of three *gendèrs* were calculated based on frequencies given by McPhee.[41] For

Balinese Sléndro

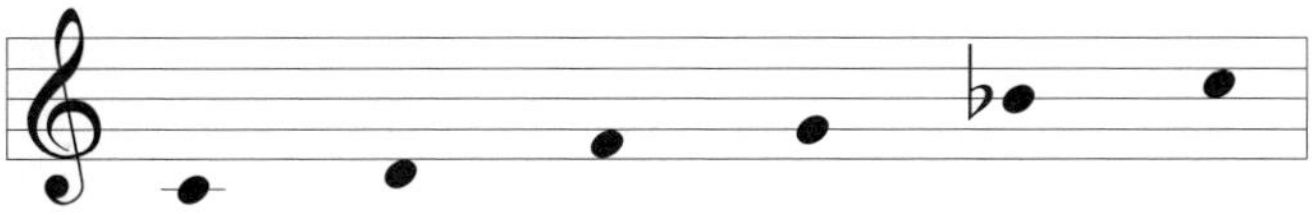

Revised cipher notation:	1		2		4		5		7		i̇	(1)
Traditional cipher notation:	1		2		3		4		5		i̇	(2)
Cent averages of three gamelans in McPhee:	0		241		457		687		958		1200	(3)
		241		***216***		***230***		***271***		***242***		
Pitches in cents of *Gendèr dasa*, Kuta Village, Bali:	0		205		477		737		1006		1200	(4)
		205		***272***		***260***		***269***		***194***		

Figure 11.14 A typical Balinese *sléndro* scale. In Bali, *sléndro* is reserved for the accompaniment of the shadow puppet theater.

comparison, Row 4 gives the tuning of a *gendèr dasa*, an instrument equipped with *dasa* (ten) bars. The first six bars of this instrument were tuned to the following frequencies: 183 cps, 206 cps, 241 cps, 280 cps, 327 cps, and 366 cps.[42] Here *sléndro* begins on the first bar, which means that the cent values in Row 4 were calculated relative to the frequency of the *first* bar. Observe that a typical Balinese *sléndro* scale has the same distinguishing features as its Javanese counterpart: "wide fifths," no "semitones," and no "major thirds." As in Figure 11.4, such characteristics produce a scale with five more-or-less equal intervals; that is, since 1200.0 ¢ ÷ 5 = 240.0 ¢, consecutive intervals in *sléndro* tend to sound like "sharp major seconds." Finally, note that in contrast to Javanese *sléndro paṭet*, in Bali there are no modes or *patutan*[43] associated with *sléndro.* Instead, musicians achieve tonal variety by shifting the tonic to any pitch of the 5-tone scale. With respect to Balinese *pélog*, *patutan* do exist; however, here too, any scale degree may be used to establish the tonal center of a composition. Generally speaking, Balinese musicians do not follow a strict hierarchical distribution of modal tones and, therefore, do not end their compositions on an orthodox set of primary or secondary cadences.

Balinese Pélog

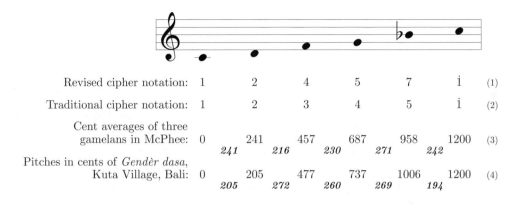

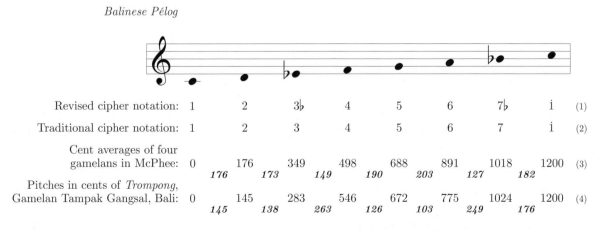

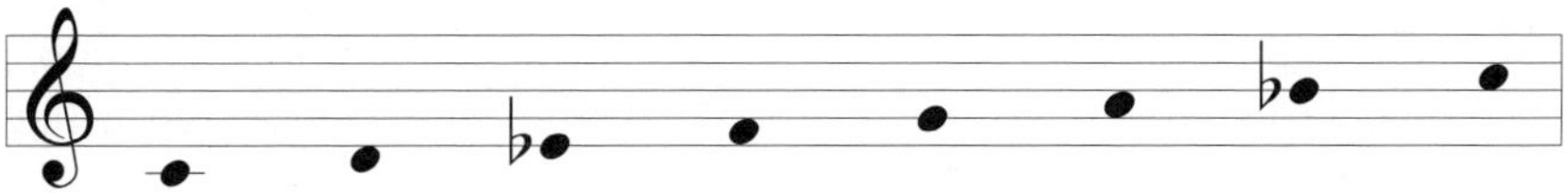

Revised cipher notation:	1		2		3♭		4		5		6		7♭		i̇	(1)
Traditional cipher notation:	1		2		3		4		5		6		7		i̇	(2)
Cent averages of four gamelans in McPhee:	0		176		349		498		688		891		1018		1200	(3)
		176		***173***		***149***		***190***		***203***		***127***		***182***		
Pitches in cents of *Trompong*, Gamelan Tampak Gangsal, Bali:	0		145		283		546		672		775		1024		1200	(4)
		145		***138***		***263***		***126***		***103***		***249***		***176***		

Figure 11.15 A typical Balinese heptatonic *pélog* scale. When compared to the average Javanese *pélog* scale in Figure 11.5, most of the tones of the average Balinese scale sound sharp.

By far the most well known tunings in Bali are pentatonic *pélog* scales derived from large heptatonic *pélog* scales. Throughout Chapter 7, McPhee stresses that these heptatonic scales originate in the tuning of the *suling gambuh.* The *suling* is a long end-blown flute equipped with a duct or windway that directs the airstream against a sharp edge or fipple. European instruments that have whistle-type mouthpieces include the recorder, penny whistle, flageolet, pitch pipe, and organ flue pipe. Unlike transverse and notched flutes, the intonation of fipple flutes is steadier and easier to control because lip coverage at the aperture is *not* a variable.[44] In short, Balinese musicians use the *suling* as a musical instrument, and as a pitch pipe for the tuning of percussion instruments.[45] The word *gambuh* refers to the classical theater of Bali, so that *suling gambuh* means *theater flute.*

Before we discuss a *suling* tuning in full detail, refer to Figure 11.15, Row 2, which shows that the traditional Balinese cipher notation for *pélog* is the same as in Java; notice that this scale also consists of "narrow fifths." In Row 3, cent averages of four percussion gamelans were calculated based on frequencies given by McPhee.[46] For comparison, Row 4 gives the heptatonic *pélog* tuning of a *trompong* that belongs to the Tampak Gangsal gamelan. The *trompong* is a percussion instrument made of ten or more horizontally suspended knobbed kettle-gongs. The first eight kettles were tuned to the following frequencies: 310 cps, 337 cps, 365 cps, 425 cps, 457 cps, 485 cps, 560 cps, and 620 cps.[47] (See also Figure 11.17, Row 3.) Here *pélog* begins on the first kettle, which means that the cent values in Row 4 were calculated relative to the frequency of the *first* kettle.

One crucial aspect not addressed by McPhee is the tuning of "sharp octaves." Consequently, for percussion instruments whose range exceeds one "octave," McPhee does not give the frequencies of the second "octave." Also, McPhee does not give the frequencies of the *penjorog*, or the beat rate between matched sets of instruments. In Bali, bar percussion instruments are built in pairs. The low instrument is called *pengumbang*, and the high instrument, *pengisep.* Gamelan builders establish a beat rate between paired instruments by tuning the *pengisep* slightly higher than the *pengumbang.* Recent studies by Mantle Hood,[48] Ruby Sue Ornstein,[49] Andrew F. Toth,[50] and I Wayan Rai[51] include not only the frequencies of "sharp octaves," but also the frequencies of the *pengumbang* and the *pengisep* instruments. According to Ornstein, in 1964 the average beat rate of the Pliatan gamelan hovered between 7.0 cps and 8.0 cps.[52] For example, a pair of *gendèr jegogans* were tuned to 136.5 cps and 144.0 cps, respectively, which produced a beat rate of 7.5 cps.

11.18

In Bali, the heptatonic *pélog* scale is widely known as *saih pitu* (seven). Regarding the tuning of the *suling gambuh*, McPhee observes

> . . . two examples of the seven-tone scale as found in the *suling gambuh* are included, since the *gambuh* scale system was considered a main source for gamelan tunings in the past.[53]

Turn to Figure 11.16, Row 3, which shows the *suling gambuh* scale McPhee considers most crucial for the study of *saih pitu*,[54] and for the derivations of four *saih lima* (five) or four *patutan* depicted in Rows 6–9.[55] In Row 4, black circles indicate closed tone holes, and white circles, open tone holes on the *suling gambuh.* The fingering of the second "octave" is the same as the first "octave" because flute players achieve the tones of the higher scale by overblowing the *suling;* this basic technique applies to all flutes.[56]

Table 11.12 compares the solmizations of Javanese and Balinese pentatonic scales. In Java and Bali, all *sléndro* scales begin on *dong* and end on *ding.* Although this solmization also applies to Javanese *pélog* scales, Balinese *pélog* scales begin on *ding* and end on *dang.* Consequently, on the

Table 11.12

SOLMIZATIONS OF PENTATONIC SCALES IN JAVA AND BALI

Java: *Sléndro* and *Pélog* Bali: *Sléndro*	Bali: *Pélog*
Dong	*Ding*
Deng	*Dong*
Dung	*Deng*
Dang	*Dung*
Ding	*Dang*

suling gambuh in Figure 11.16, the first tone of *patutan Tembung* is called *ding*, and the fifth tone, *dang;* this also applies to *patutan Selisir*, *patutan Baro*, and *patutan Lebeng*. In Figures 11.16, 11.17, and 11.18, vowels in parentheses express this solmization in symbolic notation.

Before we discuss the four *patutan* in full detail, let us first address a point of confusion. According to McPhee, the *saih lima* ". . . which appears to be known everywhere . . ."[57] is called *patutan Selisir*. On p. 39, McPhee illustrates *Selisir* starting on the fourth tone; however, on p. 133, he states that *Selisir* begins on the fifth degree of the *suling*. The following observation explains the reason for this apparent contradiction:

> In the first octave of the *suling* the lowest tone, produced with all finger-holes closed, ***is never used.***[58] (Bold italics mine.)

So, if we do not include the first unused tone, then *patutan Selisir* starts on pitch 4; but if we do include it, then *patutan Selisir* begins on pitch 5. Therefore, in Figure 11.16, one may interpret $C\sharp_4$ as either the fourth or the fifth tone of the *suling gambuh*.

Figure 11.16, Rows 6–9, show that *patutan Tembung*, *Selisir*, *Baro*, and *Lebeng* begin on the first, fourth, fifth, and sixth tones of the *suling gambuh*, respectively. Observe carefully that each *saih lima* also includes two auxiliary tones called *pemero*. A letter *p* in brackets [*p*] indicates the locations of these tones. In his dissertation, Rai defines *pemero* as follows:

> Pemero: The pitches that are not used as main pitches in a particular patutan.[59]

Now, if in a given *patutan* the *pemero* is pitch 4, then it is called *penyorog;* and if the *pemero* is pitch 7, then it is called *pemanis*. Here are Rai's definitions of these two terms:

> *Penyorog:* For example, Pitch 4 in patutan Selisir. The word "penyorog" derives from the Balinese word "sorog," meaning to push. The prefix "pe" makes it more active. In patutan Selisir, pitch 4 is considered a pitch that gives a "pushing" feeling.
>
> *Pemanis:* For example, Pitch 7 in patutan Selisir. The word "pemanis" derives from word "manis" meaning sweet. To the root word "manis" is added the prefix "pe" (active), becoming pemanis, meaning to sweeten.[60]

Rai clarifies the function of the *penyorog* by stating

> Pitch 4 in gamelan Semar Pagulingan Saih Pitu is considered a pitch that can change subtlely the perceived structure of embat [[the total intervalic

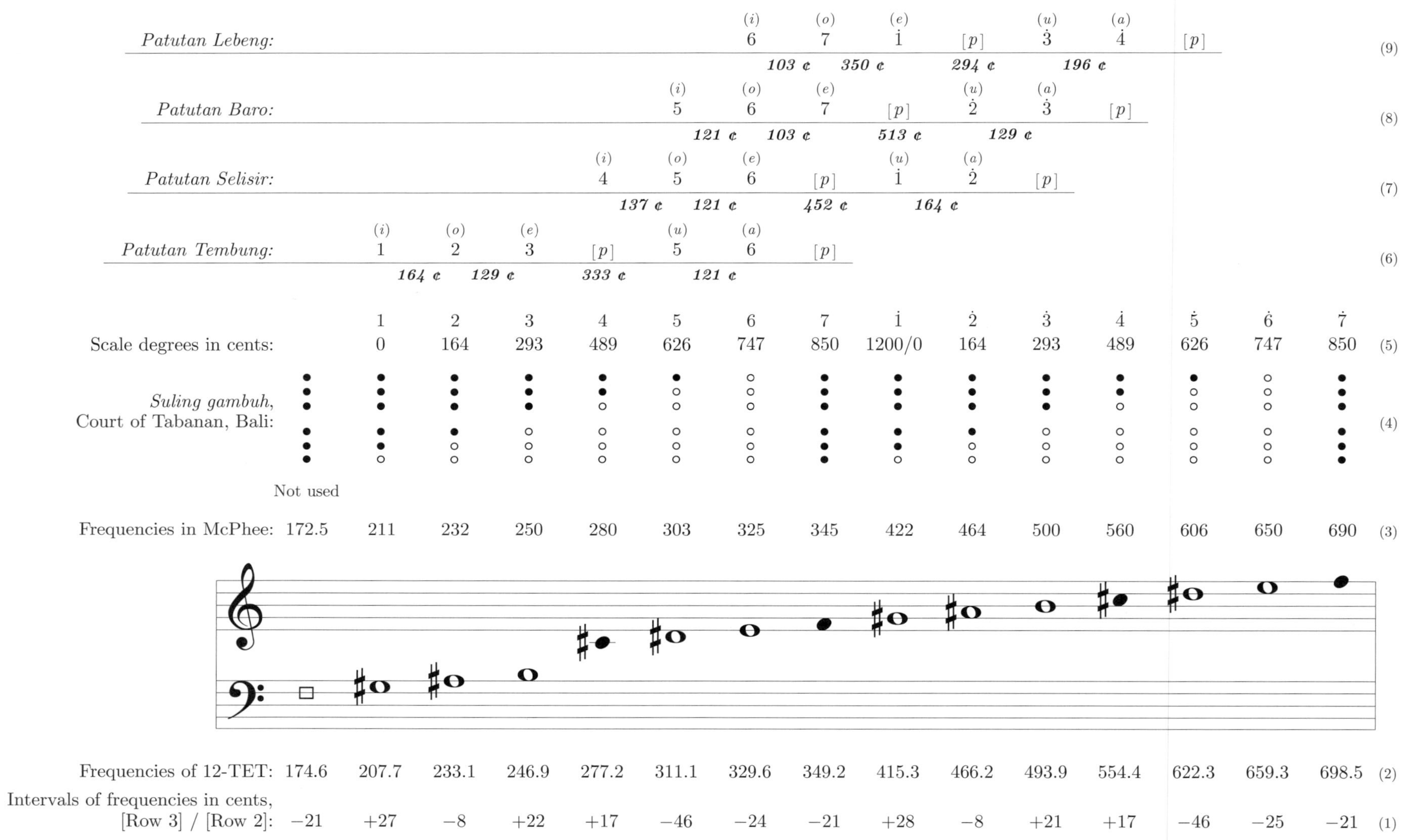

		1	2	3	4	5	6	7	1̇	2̇	3̇	4̇	5̇	6̇	7̇	
Patutan Lebeng:							(*i*) 6	(*o*) 7	(*e*) 1̇	[*p*]	(*u*) 3̇	(*a*) 4̇	[*p*]			(9)
							103 ¢	***350 ¢***		***294 ¢***	***196 ¢***					
Patutan Baro:						(*i*) 5	(*o*) 6	(*e*) 7	[*p*]	(*u*) 2̇	(*a*) 3̇	[*p*]				(8)
						121 ¢	***103 ¢***		***513 ¢***	***129 ¢***						
Patutan Selisir:					(*i*) 4	(*o*) 5	(*e*) 6	[*p*]	(*u*) 1̇	(*a*) 2̇	[*p*]					(7)
					137 ¢	***121 ¢***		***452 ¢***	***164 ¢***							
Patutan Tembung:		(*i*) 1	(*o*) 2	(*e*) 3	[*p*]	(*u*) 5	(*a*) 6	[*p*]								(6)
		164 ¢	***129 ¢***		***333 ¢***	***121 ¢***										
Scale degrees in cents:		0	164	293	489	626	747	850	1200/0	164	293	489	626	747	850	(5)
Suling gambuh, Court of Tabanan, Bali:	●●● ●●● (Not used)	●●● ●●○	●●● ●○○	●●● ○○○	●●○ ○○○	●○○ ○○○	○○○ ○○○	●●● ●●●	●●● ●●○	●●● ●○○	●●● ○○○	●●○ ○○○	●○○ ○○○	○○○ ○○○	●●● ●●●	(4)
Frequencies in McPhee:	172.5	211	232	250	280	303	325	345	422	464	500	560	606	650	690	(3)

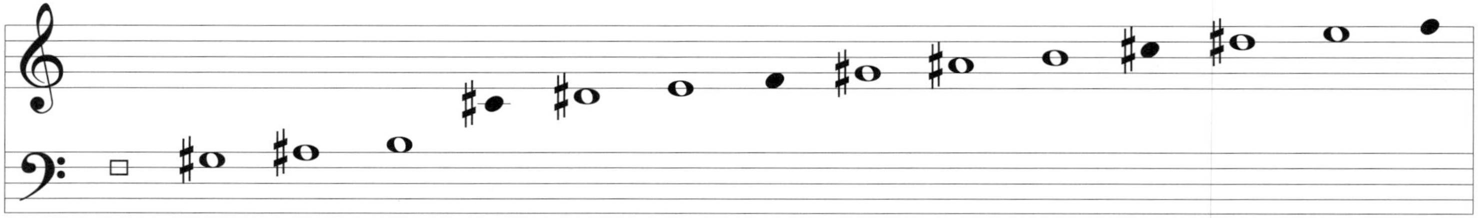

Frequencies of 12-TET:	174.6	207.7	233.1	246.9	277.2	311.1	329.6	349.2	415.3	466.2	493.9	554.4	622.3	659.3	698.5	(2)
Intervals of frequencies in cents, [Row 3] / [Row 2]:	−21	+27	−8	+22	+17	−46	−24	−21	+28	−8	+21	+17	−46	−25	−21	(1)

Figure 11.16 Pitch distributions of four Balinese *patutan* on the *suling gambuh* of the Court of Tabanan. According to McPhee, on the *suling gambuh* the heptatonic *pélog* scale, known as *saih pitu*, acted as a principal source for the pentatonic *pélog* modes, known as *saih lima*. In many texts, *patutan Selisir* is cited as the quintessential Balinese mode.

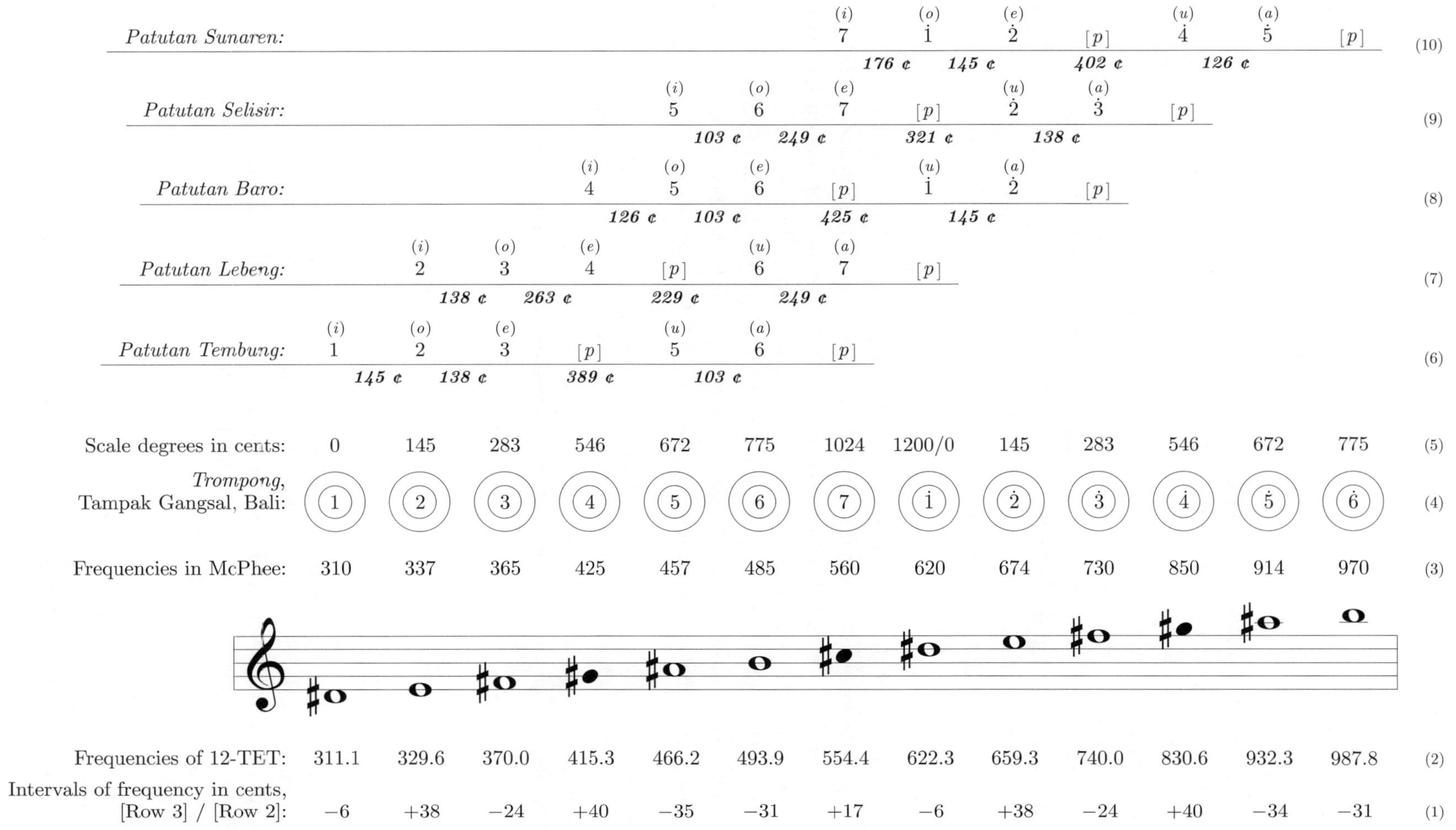

Figure 11.17 Pitch distributions of five Balinese *patutan* on the *trompong* of Tampak Gangsal gamelan. According to McPhee, in gamelan *Semar Pegulingan* the *trompong* replaced the *suling gambuh* as leading melodic instrument. This change caused a completely different and equally important derivation of *patutan*.

> structure of a particular gamelan]]. Said another way, the perception of pitch can be altered by the melodic context in which it appears. In Pak Beratha's word, "Ya lakar ngulehang munyi." (This pitch will make the sound [embat] smooth.)[61] (Text in double brackets in Rai's glossary definition of *embat.* Note differences in spelling; in Rai: *Pagulingan;* in McPhee and Brown: *Pegulingan.*)

In Section 11.15, we discussed a Javanese composition in *pélog paṭet Barang* that uses pitch 4 as an embellishment tone. Similarly, in Section 11.19 we will examine a Balinese composition in *six-tone patutan Selisir* that uses the *penyorog* as a frequently occurring melodic tone.

Musicians used the *suling gambuh* to define four *patutan* for *gamelan gambuh*, the ensemble reserved for performances of *gambuh* theatre, which McPhee described as ". . . the main source for Balinese dances and dance dramas and for the music which accompanies these performances."[62] Figure 11.16, Rows 6 and 7, indicate that on the *suling gambuh, patutan Selisir* begins on the *penyorog* of *patutan Tembung,* or on the fourth tone of the *saih pitu.* Although this relation between *Selisir* and *Tembung* is central in *gamelan gambuh,* other gamelans recognize a completely different and equally important juxtaposition of these two modes. For example, in *gamelan Semar Pegulingan* — originally a palace gamelan that played for Balinese nobility — McPhee states that ". . . the *trompong* . . . replaced the *suling* as leading melodic instrument."[63] Turn to Figure 11.17, Row 3, which shows the *trompong* scale McPhee considered most crucial for the study of *saih pitu,*[64] and for the derivations of five *saih lima* depicted in Rows 6–10.[65] With the exception of *patutan Tembung* in Row 6, the derivations of the other three modes are completely different. Rows 7–9 indicate that *patutan Lebeng, Baro,* and *Selisir* begin on the second, fourth, and fifth tones of the *trompong,* respectively. Furthermore, Rows 6 and 9 indicate that *patutan Selisir* here begins on the *dung* of *patutan Tembung,* or on the fifth tone of the *saih pitu.* Also, Row 10 includes a fifth mode called *patutan Sunaren.* Finally, the reader should consider the derivations of *patutan* in Figures 11.16 and 11.17 equally important and equally representative of the era in which McPhee lived and worked.

With respect to the two previously mentioned gamelans, McPhee observed

> Like the *gambuh* theater, the seven-tone *Semar Pegulingan* had all but vanished by 1931. There were several six-tone orchestras, so formed as to make possible the playing of separate repertories in the two scales, *Tembung* and *Selisir.* But only two seven-tone ensembles could be found in any state of activity.[66]

In 1972, Robert E. Brown recorded an LP entitled *Gamelan Semar Pegulingan: Gamelan of the love god.* The liner notes convey important information about the recording.

> The present recording is the first commercial recording of the *Semar Pegulingan* type of gamelan, except for three 78-rpm discs, now rare collectors' items, issued abroad by Odéon and Beka in 1928. It was the captivating sound of these early recordings, which he encountered by chance, that first drew Colin McPhee to Bali. When he arrived, he found that the *Semar Pegulingan* style had almost vanished. Originally a palace gamelan — played outside the royal sleeping-chambers — and later the standard orchestra for *Lègong* dances, *Semar Pegulingan* had declined in popularity and by the 1930s was preserved in only a few villages. Eager to document the delicate, courtly music, McPhee arranged for the gamelan recorded here to be brought to his village, where he hired a teacher and organized a club of musicians. After McPhee's departure in 1939, the instruments fell into disuse . . .

	(*i*)	(*o*)	(*e*)	(*deung*)	(*u*)	(*a*)	(*daing*)								
Patutan Lebeng:	1	2	3	4	5	6	7								(11)
		143 ¢	***156 ¢***	***286 ¢***	***120 ¢***	***124 ¢***	***177 ¢***								
					(*i*)	(*o*)	(*e*)		(*u*)	(*a*)					
Patutan Sunaren:					5	6	7	[*p*]	$\dot{2}$	$\dot{3}$	[*p*]				(10)
						124 ¢	***177 ¢***	***339 ¢***		***186 ¢***					
				(*i*)	(*o*)	(*e*)		(*u*)	(*a*)						
Patutan Tembung:				4	5	6	[*p*]	$\dot{1}$	$\dot{2}$	[*p*]					(9)
					120 ¢	***124 ¢***	***398 ¢***		***118 ¢***						
		(*u*)	(*a*)	(*i*)		(*o*)	(*e*)								
Patutan Baro:		2	3	4	[*p*]	6	7	[*p*]							(8)
			156 ¢	***286 ¢***	***244 ¢***		***177 ¢***								
	(*i*)	(*o*)	(*e*)		(*u*)	(*a*)									
Patutan Selisir:	1	2	3	[*p*]	5	6	[*p*]								(7)
		143 ¢	***156 ¢***	***406 ¢***		***124 ¢***									
"Octaves" in cents:								1227	1202	1233	1170	1180	1219	1252	(6)
Scale degrees in cents:	0	143	299	585	706	830	1007	0	118	304	528	658	821	1031	(5)
Gendèr rambat (*pengisep*), Puri Agung Gianyar, Bali:	1	2	3	4	5	6	7	$\dot{1}$	$\dot{2}$	$\dot{3}$	$\dot{4}$	$\dot{5}$	$\dot{6}$	$\dot{7}$	(4)
Frequencies in Rai:	287.8	312.6	342.1	403.6	432.6	464.8	514.8	584.8	626.0	697.2	793.3	855.4	939.6	1061.1	(3)

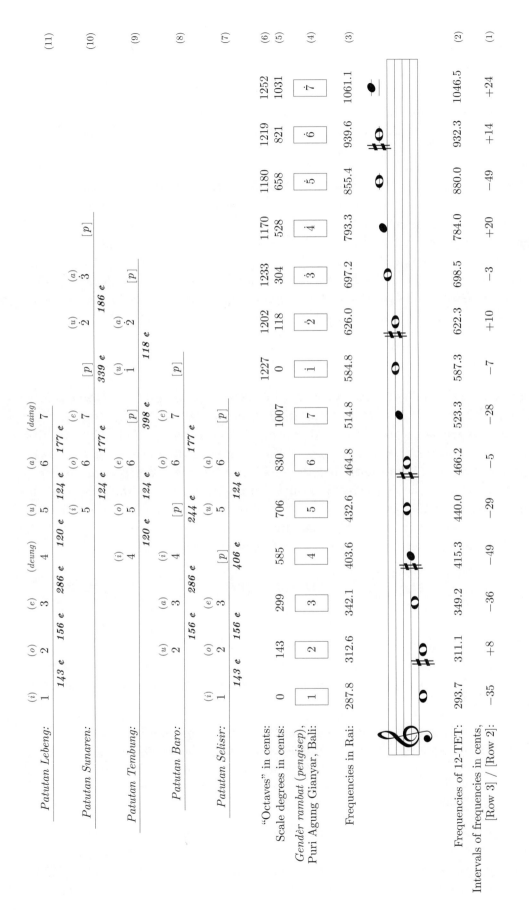

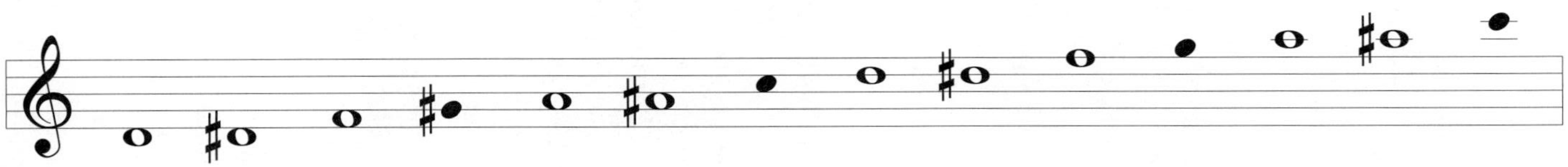

Frequencies of 12-TET:	293.7	311.1	349.2	415.3	440.0	466.2	523.3	587.3	622.3	698.5	784.0	880.0	932.3	1046.5	(2)
Intervals of frequencies in cents, [Row 3] / [Row 2]:	−35	+8	−36	−49	−29	−5	−28	−7	+10	−3	+20	−49	+14	+24	(1)

Figure 11.18 Pitch distributions of five Balinese *patutan* on the *gendèr rambat* of gamelan Puri Agung Gianyar. According to Rai, in the late 20th century the derivation of *patutan* in gamelan *Semar Pegulingan* underwent yet another transformation. Compared to Figure 11.16, the ciphers of "new" *patutan Selisir* are now identical to "old" *patutan Tembung;* and the ciphers of "new" *patutan Tembung* are now identical to "old" *patutan Selisir.* Note Rai's unique solmization of *patutan Baro;* usually, the first pitch of a group of three contiguous pitches is called *ding.*

> Now, however, some thirty-odd years later, the gamelan has been restored to life . . .
>
> . . . A version of *Gambang*, almost identical with the one here recorded, but minus the coda, is transcribed by McPhee on pp. 311–315 of *Music in Bali*.[67]

In the first two chapters of his dissertation, Rai discusses the decline and resurgence of gamelan *Semar Pegulingan;* and in the third chapter, his text informs us that in the late 20th century, the derivations of *patutan* have undergone yet another transformation. Turn to Figure 11.18, Row 3, which gives the frequencies of the *saih pitu* of a *gendèr rambat* (*pengisep*) from gamelan Puri Agung Gianyar,[68] and the derivations of five *saih lima* in Rows 7–11.[69] Rows 7–10 indicate that *patutan Selisir*, *Baro*, *Tembung*, and *Sunaren* now begin on the first, second, fourth, and fifth tones of the *gendèr rambat*, respectively. Compared to Figure 11.16, "new" *patutan Selisir* is the principal mode because its ciphers are now identical to "old" *patutan Tembung;* conversely, the ciphers of "new" *patutan Tembung* are now identical to "old" *patutan Selisir*. Also, in Row 11, note that *patutan Lebeng* includes all seven tones. Rai states that *patutan Lebeng* is based on *patutan Selisir*,[70] which means that if *patutan Selisir* includes pitch 4, or the *penyorog*, and pitch 7, or the *pemanis*, then it is called *patutan Lebeng*.

11.19

Let us now consider a 1952 Columbia LP recording that includes a composition in *six-tone patutan Selisir*. In preparation for an analysis of this composition, refer to Figure 11.19(a), Row 2, which lists cent averages of three gamelans analyzed by McPhee.[71] For comparison, Figure 11.19(b), Row 4, gives exact cent values of *patutan Selisir* from a gamelan analyzed by McPhee in Pliatan, Bali.[72] Turn back to Figure 11.16, Row 3, and note that the first three frequencies of *patutan Selisir* on the *suling gambuh* closely match the first three frequencies in Figure 11.19(b), Row 1. Beyond this point, there are no more similarities between these two versions of the same mode. Figure 11.19(b), Row 4, shows a "sharp tritone" between $C\sharp_4$–$G\sharp_4$ that equals 639 ¢, but in Figure 11.16, Row 3, the complementary interval between pitches 4 and $\dot{1}$ is a "sharp fifth" that equals

$$\log_{10}\frac{422\text{ cps}}{280\text{ cps}} \times 3986.314 = 710\ ¢$$

The difference between these two intervals is 710 ¢ − 639 ¢ = 71 ¢. Also, Figure 11.19(b), Row 4, indicates a "flat minor sixth" between $C\sharp_4$–A_4 that equals 763 ¢, but in Figure 11.16, Row 3, the complementary interval between pitches 4 and $\dot{2}$ is a "flat major sixth" that equals 874 ¢; here the difference is 874 ¢ − 763 ¢ = 111 ¢. With respect to *patutan Selisir*, McPhee describes these apparent inconsistencies by observing

> Yet, as previously stated, the different tunings are no more than variants of a single scale whose norm remains undetermined. In the last analysis, the tones *ding*, *dong*, *dèng*, *dung*, and *dang* are not fixed tones at all, but ***tonal zones*** which allow for endless modification of pitch when it comes to tuning the gamelan.[73] (Bold italics mine.)

Now, before we discuss a third and even greater difference between these two versions of the same mode, refer to Table 11.13, which gives Ornstein's frequencies for *patutan Selisir* on a pair of *gendèr tjalungs* (*jublags*) in Pliatan.[74] These are also the frequencies heard on the recording. When measured against the frequencies in Figure 11.19(b), Row 1, the *pengumbang* frequencies represent

Patutan Selisir:

(a)

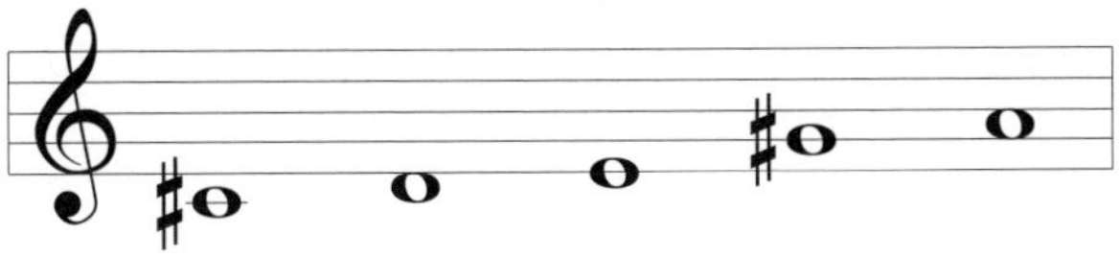

	Ding		*Dong*		*Deng*		*Dung*		*Dang*	
										(1)
Cent averages of three gamelans in McPhee:	0		109		269		670		764	(2)
		109		*160*		*401*		*94*		

(b)

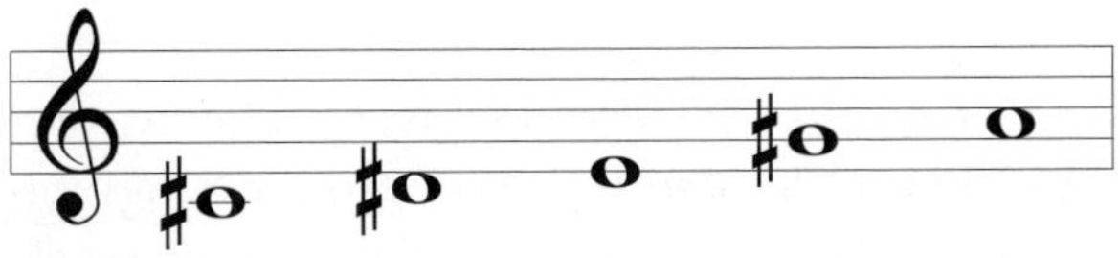

Frequencies in McPhee Pliatan Village, Bali:	280		305		327		405		435	(1)
Frequencies of 12-TET:	277.2		311.1		329.6		415.3		440.0	(2)
Intervals of frequencies in cents:	+17		−34		−14		−43		−20	(3)
Scale degrees in cents:	0		148		269		639		763	(4)
		148		*121*		*370*		*124*		

Six-tone Patutan Selisir:
Pliatan Village, Bali

(c)

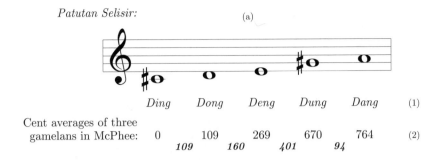

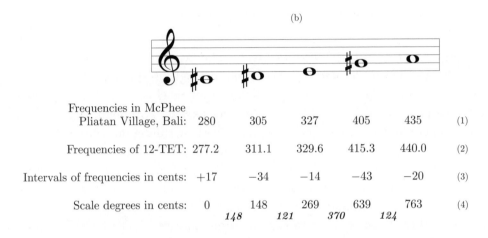

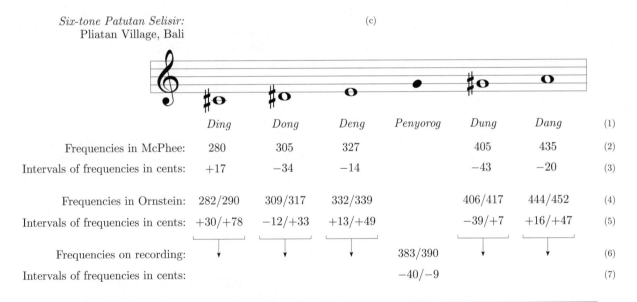

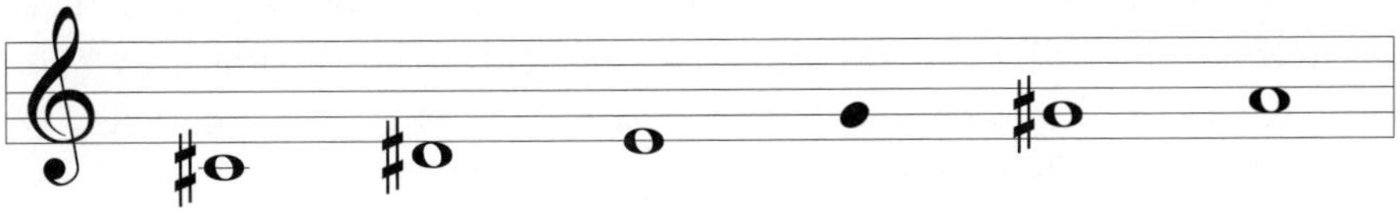

	Ding	*Dong*	*Deng*	*Penyorog*	*Dung*	*Dang*	(1)
Frequencies in McPhee:	280	305	327		405	435	(2)
Intervals of frequencies in cents:	+17	−34	−14		−43	−20	(3)
Frequencies in Ornstein:	282/290	309/317	332/339		406/417	444/452	(4)
Intervals of frequencies in cents:	+30/+78	−12/+33	+13/+49		−39/+7	+16/+47	(5)
Frequencies on recording:	↓	↓	↓	383/390	↓	↓	(6)
Intervals of frequencies in cents:				−40/−9			(7)

Figure 11.19 *Patutan Selisir* as tuned on percussion instruments throughout Bali. (a) Row 2 gives cent averages of three gamelan tunings cited by McPhee. (b) Row 1 gives the exact frequencies as found by McPhee in Pliatan Village in the 1930's. Row 4 shows the scale degrees in cents. (c) Row 2 gives the old frequencies in McPhee's text, and Row 4, the new paired tunings found in Ornstein's dissertation and on a Columbia LP recording. Row 6 includes the low and high frequencies of the *penyorog*, which I obtained from the recording. This additional pitch transforms the original pentatonic mode into a hexatonic mode.

Table 11.13

PATUTAN SELISIR ON A PAIR OF *GENDÈR TJALUNGS*
FROM THE PLIATAN GAMELAN

Pengumbang	*Pengisep*
ding = 282.1 cps	*ding* = 289.5 cps
dong = 309.0 cps	*dong* = 317.3 cps
deng = 331.7 cps	*deng* = 339.3 cps
dung = 406.2 cps	*dung* = 416.7 cps
dang = 443.7 cps	*dang* = 452.0 cps

increases of 12.9 ¢, 22.6 ¢, 24.7 ¢, 5.1 ¢, and 34.3 ¢, respectively. The last and largest difference occurred because gamelan tuners in Pliatan decided to switch from the old international pitch where A_4 = 435.0 cps, to the new international pitch where A_4 = 440.0 cps. This change in standard pitch probably explains the frequency increases of the four other pitches as well. Although McPhee and Ornstein do *not* include frequencies of the *penyorog* and *pemanis* in their tuning data from Pliatan, the recording clearly indicates the presence of the former pitch. Figure 11.19(c), Row 1, shows the *penyorog* as a tone between *deng* and *dung.*[75] Consequently, when Balinese musicians notate a 6-tone composition in cipher notation, they *renumber* the original 5-tone mode by assigning the *penyorog* the number 4, *dung* the number 5, and *dang* the number 6.[76]

For comparison, Figure 11.19(c), Rows 2 and 3 repeat the same data as Figure 11.19(b), Rows 1 and 3, and Figure 11.19(c), Row 4, the same data as in Table 11.13, rounded here to the nearest cent. In Figure 11.19, all intervals in cents are based on A_4 tuned to 440.0 cps. I obtained the low and high frequencies of the *penyorog* in Row 6 from the recording. Figure 11.19(c), Rows 4–7 cite the paired tunings of the *gendèr tjalungs* because on the recording one sometimes hears a prominent melodic note produced by the low *pengumbang*, and at other times, by the high *pengisep*. Finally, in Row 7, calculate the intervals of the *penyorog* based on the frequency of G_4 in 12-TET, which vibrates at 392.0 cps. (See Figure 11.11.)

Table 11.14, Rows 1–4, give exact intervals of *patutan Selisir* produced by instruments described in Figures 11.16, 11.17, 11.18, and 11.19(b), respectively; and Row 5 shows average cent values of these intervals. When compared to frequency ratio $^{16}/_{15}$ [111.7 ¢], the first and fourth intervals tend to sound like "sharp semitones"; when compare to frequency ratio $^{10}/_{9}$ [182.4 ¢], the second interval tends to sound like a "flat small whole tone"; and when compared to frequency ratio $^{5}/_{4}$ [386.3 ¢], the third interval tends to sound like a "major third."

Table 11.14

EXACT AND AVERAGE INTERVALS OF *PATUTAN SELISIR*

	ding		*dong*		*deng*		*dung*		*dang*	
Suling gambuh:		137 ¢		121 ¢		452 ¢		164 ¢		(1)
Trompong:		103 ¢		249 ¢		321 ¢		138 ¢		(2)
Gendèr rambat:		143 ¢		156 ¢		406 ¢		124 ¢		(3)
Gamelan in Pliatan:		148 ¢		121 ¢		370 ¢		124 ¢		(4)
Cent averages:		133 ¢		162 ¢		387 ¢		138 ¢		(5)

In a thorough study entitled *Gamelan Gong Kebyar: The Art of Twentieth-Century Balinese Music*, Michael Tenzer included nearly 100 pages of musical transcriptions designed to illuminate 55 tracks of music on two accompanying CD's. Because most of the musical examples are in *patutan Selisir*, Tenzer utilized a nonlinear key signature where the first accidental is C♯ and the second accidental is G♯. [See Figure 11.19(a).] In the passage below, Tenzer acknowledges the musical pre-eminence of *patutan Selisir*, and the historic significance of *Music in Bali:*

> The staff pitches C♯–D–E–G♯–A represent the *kebyar* scale in Western notation throughout the present study for consistency and for the sake of continuity with McPhee, who mainly used the same system.[77]

We turn now to a performance of *Lagu Chondong*, the first movement of the classic *legong* dance. This is an exceptionally beautiful composition in *six-tone patutan Selisir.* I transcribed the *gendèr tjalung* parts in Figure 11.20 from a 1952 LP recording by the gamelan in Pliatan.[78] After a brief introduction, the performers on the *gendèr tjalungs* play a distinct alto melody heard between deep gongs and low drum rolls in the bass, and rapid interlocking accompaniment on high-pitched *gangsas* (*sarons*) in the treble. In the transcription, the first four measures are repeated three times at the beginning and six times at the end. Throughout the performance, the *penyorog* (G♮) always occurs on the first beat of a measure, which means it is a prominent melodic tone. Also, observe that unlike Javanese music, gong (G) tones in Balinese music occur not only on the last tones of cadences, but also on the first tones of melodic phrases.[79] In this example, all four and eight bar phrases begin on gong tones. This also applies to a very rapid six-measure phrase that begins on the G♯ after the *accelerando.*

Note carefully that the oversimplified Western notation in Figures 11.19(c) and 11.20 does *not* accurately represent the musical intervals of the two *gendèr tjalungs.* For example, observe that on the *pengumbang* and *pengisep* the intervals between $C\sharp_4$–$G\sharp_4$ are *not* "fifths," but "sharp tritones" that equal

$$\textit{Pengumbang:}\ \log_{10}\frac{406\text{ cps}}{282\text{ cps}}\times 3986.314 = 631\ ¢$$

$$\textit{Pengisep:}\ \log_{10}\frac{417\text{ cps}}{290\text{ cps}}\times 3986.314 = 629\ ¢$$

In contrast, notice correctly notated "sharp tritones" between $D\sharp_4$–A_4 that equal

$$\textit{Pengumbang:}\ \log_{10}\frac{444\text{ cps}}{309\text{ cps}}\times 3986.314 = 628\ ¢$$

$$\textit{Pengisep:}\ \log_{10}\frac{452\text{ cps}}{317\text{ cps}}\times 3986.314 = 614\ ¢$$

"Tritones" are seldom heard as melodic intervals in Western music. Here, in the central section of the composition, seven $D\sharp_4$–A_4 intervals conjure a sense of suspended and unresolved tension; that is, each interval occurs at the end of a phrase, or just before a gong tone that marks the beginning of a new phrase. In countless ways, this composition serves as an archetypical example of superb Balinese musicianship. Because of its musical excellence, the Pliatan gamelan has left an indelible impression on musicians throughout the world.

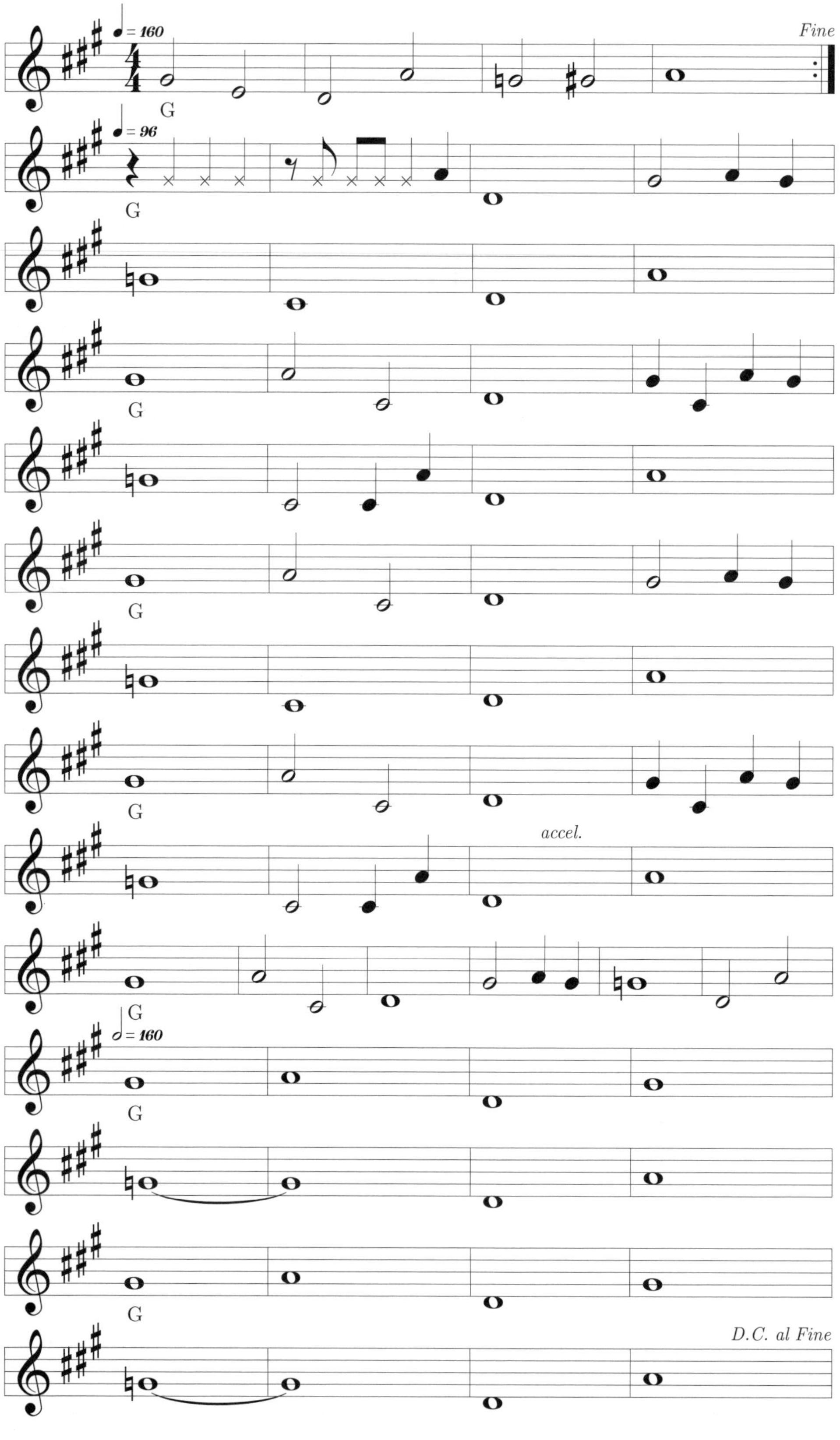

Figure 11.20 The parts of the *gendèr tjalung* in a performance of *Lagu Chondong*, the first movement of the classic *legong* dance. This composition is in *six-tone patutan Selisir*, and was transcribed from a 1952 LP recording by the gamelan in Pliatan, Bali.

Notes

1. See Chapter 6.

2. (A) Blom, E., Editor (1954). *Grove's Dictionary of Music and Musicians, Volume 2*, 5th ed., pp. 204–205. St. Martin's Press, Inc., New York, 1970.

This cipher notation, also called the Galin–Paris–Chevé System, was named after the French mathematician Pierre Galin (1786–1821) and the French physician Émile Chevé (1804–1864).

(B) Randel, D.M., Editor (1986). *The New Harvard Dictionary of Music*, 6th ed., p. 154. The Belknap Press of Harvard University Press, Cambridge, Massachusetts, 1993.

"The notation [Chevé System] was adapted for teaching purposes to Javanese *gamelan* music as the *kepatihan* notation and is still in use in Indonesia."

3. Surjodiningrat, W., Sudarjana, P.J., and Susanto, A. (1972). *Tone Measurements of Outstanding Javanese Gamelans in Jogjakarta and Surakarta*, 2nd ed., p. 51, Table 8. Gadjah Mada University Press, Jogjakarta, Indonesia.

4. (A) Lentz, D.A. (1965). *The Gamelan Music of Java and Bali*, p. 34. University of Nebraska Press, Lincoln, Nebraska.

(B) McDermott, V., and Sumarsam (1975). Central Javanese music: The *paṭet* of laras *sléndro* and the *gendèr barung*, p. 236. *Journal of the Society for Ethnomusicology* **XIX**, No. 2, pp. 233–244.

5. *The Gamelan Music of Java and Bali*, p. 34.

6. (A) Sumarsam (1992). *Gamelan: Cultural Interaction and Musical Development in Central Java*, pp. 111–112, 132–139. The University of Chicago Press, Chicago, Illinois, 1995.

The author discusses the influence of Western musical practice on the notation of gamelan music. During the early part of the twentieth century, Indonesian artists and intellectuals instigated a change from a difficult alphabetic method to a more convenient numeric system of notation by implementing the Chevé System. On p. 112, Sumarsam observes, "For *sléndro*, number 4 was omitted; thus, the [initial] arrangement was 1 2 3 5 6 7, 7 being the upper octave of 1." On pp. 83–89, Sumarsam also lists many non-Indonesian ethnic groups that influenced the art and life of the islands. However, despite prominent patronage of the arts by the Chinese community, Sumarsam offers no explanation why number 4 was omitted. It seems entirely plausible to me that the omission of number 4 was due to the pervasive influence of the Chinese. That is, Indonesian musicians faced for the first time with the daunting task of enumerating their tunings and music, sought to "legitimize" *sléndro* by giving it the same cipher identity as the ancient Chinese pentatonic scale.

(B) Sindoesawarno, K. (1955). *Ilmu Karawitan* [*Knowledge About Gamelan Music*], translated by M.F. Hatch. In *Karawitan, Volume 2*, J. Becker and A.H. Feinstein, Editors, pp. 311–387. Center for South and Southeast Asian Studies, The University of Michigan, 1987.

On p. 338, the author describes how R.M.T. Wreksadiningrat (1848–1913) ". . . compiled a notational system using numbers (*angka*), similar to the Galin–Paris–Chevé system."

7. See Section 10.27.

8. *Tone Measurements of Outstanding Javanese Gamelans*, p. 41, Table 3, Row 7.

9. *Ibid.*, p. 53, Table 9.

10. *Ibid.*, p. 43, Table 4, Rows 10 and 11.

The *saron*, or *gangsa*, is a one-octave percussion instrument equipped with bronze bars. Instead of individually tuned resonators, the bars are mounted over a trough resonator or sound box designed to amplify several different bars simultaneously.

11. The last bar of the *saron demung* is tuned to 519 cps, and sounds the last pitch of the fourth "octave" of the gamelan. The first bar of the *saron ritjik* (or *saron barung*) is tuned to 598 cps; this pitch sounds the first pitch of the fifth "octave" of the gamelan, and the "octave" above the *first* bar of the *saron demung*.

12. Hood, M. (1966). *Sléndro* and *pélog* redefined, pp. 46–47. *Selected Reports* **I**, No. 1, pp. 28–48. Publication of the Institute of Ethnomusicology of the University of California at Los Angeles.

13. Sindoesawarno in *Karawitan, Volume 2*, p. 362.

14. Apel, W., Editor (1944). *Harvard Dictionary of Music*, 2nd ed., p. 436. Harvard University Press, Cambridge, Massachusetts, 1972.

15. *Gamelan: Cultural Interaction...*, pp. 135–136.

16. Martopangrawit, R.L. (1972). *Catatan-Catatan Pengetahuan Karawitan* [*Notes on Knowledge of Gamelan Music*], translated by M.F. Hatch, p. 83. In *Karawitan, Volume 1*, J. Becker and A.H. Feinstein, Editors, pp. 1–244. Center for South and Southeast Asian Studies, The University of Michigan, 1984.

17. Poerbapangrawit, R.M.K. (1955). *Gendhing Jawa* [*Javanese Gamelan Music*], translated by J. Becker, p. 418. In *Karawitan, Volume 1*, J. Becker and A.H. Feinstein, Editors, pp. 409–438. Center for South and Southeast Asian Studies, The University of Michigan, 1984.

18. Hood, M. (1954). *The Nuclear Theme as a Determinant of Paṭet in Javanese Music*, pp. 7–8, p. 123. Da Capo Press, Inc., New York, 1977.

19. See Sections 7.9–7.11.

20. Sumarsam (1975). Gendèr barung, its technique and function in the context of Javanese gamelan. *Indonesia* **20**, pp. 161–172.

21. Sadie, S., Editor (1984). *The New Grove Dictionary of Musical Instruments, Volume 2*, p. 11. Macmillan Press Limited, London, England.

This page gives an excellent ground plan of a typical Javanese gamelan, and silhouette illustrations of the instruments. The abbreviations G, P, N, p, t indicate the required gong tones in gamelan scores. See *Karawitan, Volume 3*.

22. Martopangrawit in *Karawitan, Volume 1*, p. 84.

23. *Karawitan, Volume 1*, p. 355.

24. *Indonesia* **20**, 1975, pp. 167–169.

Sumarsam addresses the difficulties in identifying *sléndro Nem*. Through a series of diagrams, Sumarsam shows how the performance of cadential "fifths" and cadential "octaves" in *sléndro Nem* differ from similar cadential patterns in *sléndro Sanga* and *sléndro Manyura*.

25. *Tone Measurements of Outstanding Javanese Gamelans*, p. 41, Table 3, Row 2.

26. *The Nuclear Theme as a Determinant of Paṭet in Javanese Music*, p. 145.

27. *Ibid.*, p. 223.

28. (A) Martopangrawit in *Karawitan, Volume 1*, pp. 160–161.

(B) Poerbapangrawit in *Karawitan, Volume 1*, pp. 418–419, p. 435.

(C) *The Nuclear Theme as a Determinant of Paṭet in Javanese Music*, p. 145, 224.

29. *Ibid.*, pp. 225–230.

Hood quotes two references from 1934 and 1938 in which J.S. Brandts Buys attempts to explain K.H. Dewantara's interpretations of *pélog paṭet*. Although these accounts are confusing, they do confirm that all *pélog paṭet* are difficult to define because in many compositions principal cadences occur in a descending direction from G-I to G-IV. With respect to *pélog paṭet Barang*, the first reference attributes the principal cadence to pitches 2 and 6 (or the "fifth" above the tonic), and the second reference, to pitches 5 and 2 (or the "fifth" below the tonic). Unfortunately, Hood dispenses with this complexity, and on p. 230 gives all *pélog paṭet* a strictly symmetrical interpretation. His insistence on abstract symmetry effectively eliminates pitch 5 (*lima*) as one of the three most important gong tones in *pélog paṭet Barang*.

30. Martopangrawit in *Karawitan, Volume 1*, p. 168.

31. *Ibid.*, pp. 162–163.

32. See *Karawitan, Volume 3*.

33. This composition is on Track 4 of an Ocora Radio France CD entitled *JAVA: Palais Royal de Yogyakarta, Volume 2, La musique instrumentale*, C-560068.

34. *Tone Measurements of Outstanding Javanese Gamelans*, p. 43, Table 4, Rows 2 and 3.

35. Poerbapangrawit in *Karawitan, Volume 1*, pp. 421–422.

36. See Chapter 3, Parts III–IV.

37. See Section 5.18.

38. *Karawitan, Volume 1*, p. 349.

39. McPhee, C. (1966). *Music in Bali: A Study in Form and Instrumental Organization in Balinese Orchestral Music.* Yale University Press, New Haven, Connecticut.

McPhee was also a renowned American composer. His works for symphony and chamber orchestras, and his transcriptions of Balinese music for piano have recently been reissued on CD.

40. *Ibid.*, p. 37.

41. *Ibid.*, p. 52, Chart 11, Row 1–3.

42. *Ibid.*, p. 51, Chart 10, Row 1.

43. (A) *Ibid.*, p. 374.

McPhee gives this definition: "Patutan: *patut*, right, correct; tuning, the tuning of the gamelan . . . . . . names of different tunings, of which the final standards cannot be determined."

(B) Rai, I, W. (1996). *Balinese Gamelan Semar Pagulingan Saih Pitu: The Modal System*, p. 25. Ph.D. dissertation printed and distributed by University Microfilms, Inc., Ann Arbor, Michigan.

Rai defines *patutan* as follows:

> The term "Patutan" derives from word "patut" plus suffix "an." "Patut" is a Balinese word meaning correct. Patutan, as it is used in gamelan Semar Pagulingan Saih Pitu, is a term used to denote a concept of modality in Balinese music.
>
> I Nyoman Rembang defines patutan as follows: "Patutan is the role or function of pitches within a particular scale in order to create a different feeling in music." According to I Nyoman Rembang, the term "patutan" has a similar meaning with the term "pathet" in Javanese music.

44. See Section 8.7.

45. Schaareman, D., Editor (1992). *Balinese Music in Context: A Sixty-fifth Birthday Tribute to Hans Oesch.* Amadeus Verlag, Winterthur, Switzerland.

This publication contains many articles on current trends in Balinese gamelan music. I highly recommend an article by Karl Richter entitled *Slèndro-Pèlog and the Conceptualization of Balinese Music: Remarks on the Gambuh Tone System*, pp. 195–219, to those readers interested in studying contemporary *suling gambuh* tunings.

46. *Music in Bali*, p. 42, Chart 2, Rows 1–3.

47. *Ibid.*, Chart 2, Row 4.

48. Hood, M. (1966). *Sléndro* and *pélog* redefined, p. 38, pp. 45–48. *Selected Reports* **I**, No. 1, pp. 28–48. Publication of the Institute of Ethnomusicology of the University of California at Los Angeles.

49. Ornstein, R.S. (1971). *Gamelan Gong Kebjar: The Development of a Balinese Musical Tradition*, pp. 94–100. Ph.D. dissertation printed and distributed by University Microfilms, Inc., Ann Arbor, Michigan.

In this study, the measurements of the gamelan in Pliatan were made by Harrison Parker in 1964.

50. (A) Toth, A.F. (1975). The Gamelan Luang of Tangkas, Bali, p. 68. *Selected Reports* **II**, No. 2, pp. 65–79. Publication of the Institute of Ethnomusicology of the University of California at Los Angeles.

(B) Toth, A.F. (1993). "Selera Yang Selaras: Papatutan Gong Ditinjau Dari Segi Akustika dan Estetika," pp. 115–116. *Mudra: Jurnal Seni Budaya*, pp. 92–117. Edisi Khusus.

51. *Balinese Gamelan Semar Pagulingan Saih Pitu: The Modal System*, pp. 44–63.

Rai lists the frequencies for four modern 7-tone gamelans.

52. *Gamelan Gong Kebjar: The Development of a Balinese Musical Tradition*, p. 91.

53. *Music in Bali*, p. 36.

54. *Ibid.*, p. 42, Chart 2, Row 5; and p. 116.

55. *Ibid.*, p. 39.

56. See Section 8.7.

57. *Ibid.*, p. 47.

58. *Ibid.*, p. 117.

59. *Balinese Gamelan Semar Pagulingan Saih Pitu: The Modal System*, p. 276.

60. *Ibid.*, p. 96.

61. *Ibid.*, p. 38.

62. *Music in Bali*, p. 113.

63. *Ibid.*, p. 43.

64. *Ibid.*, p. 42, Chart 2, Row 4; and p. 141.

65. *Ibid.*, p. 39.

66. *Ibid.*, p. 140.

67. Brown, R.E., Recordist (1972). *Gamelan Semar Pegulingan: Gamelan of the love god.* Nonesuch Records, Explorer Series H–72046. Notes by R.E. Brown and P.B. Yampolsky.

68. *Balinese Gamelan Semar Pagulingan Saih Pitu: The Modal System*, p. 46.

69. *Ibid.*, p. 54, 86.

70. *Ibid.*, p. 86.

71. *Music in Bali*, p. 46, Chart 5, Rows 2–4.

72. *Ibid.*, p. 46, Chart 5, Row 1.

73. *Ibid.*, p. 47.

74. *Gamelan Gong Kebjar: The Development of a Balinese Musical Tradition*, p. 95.

75. *Music in Bali*, p. 286.

76. *Ibid.*, p. 291.

77. Tenzer, M. (2000). *Gamelan Gong Kebyar: The Art of Twentieth-Century Balinese Music*, p. 41. The University of Chicago Press, Chicago, Illinois.

78. Mandera, A.A.G., Director (1952). *Dancers of Bali: Gamelan Orchestra From the Village of Pliatan, Bali*, Side 2, Track 4(a). Columbia Masterworks Recording, ML–4618. Notes by C. McPhee.

A different interpretation of this composition entitled *Lègong Kraton* exists on Side 2, Track 2, of Robert E. Brown's recording *Gamelan Semar Pegulingan: Gamelan of the love god.* See Note 67.

79. *Gamelan Gong Kebjar: The Development of a Balinese Musical Tradition*, p. 127.

Part III

INDIAN MUSIC

Ancient Beginnings

∾ 11.20 ∾

One of the oldest and most revered texts on Indian music is a work entitled *Nāṭyaśāstra*, written by Bharata (early centuries A.D.). Although large portions of Bharata's treatise recount performance practices of the theater and dance, Volume 2, Chapters 28–33, deal exclusively with music. In *Nāṭyaśāstra 28.21*, Bharata begins his description of the classical 22-*śruti* scale by giving the names of seven *svaras*, translated below as *notes*, and also interpreted in this discussion as *tones* and *scale degrees*.

> *Nāṭ. 28.21* — The seven notes [*svaras*] are: *Ṣaḍja* [Sa], *Ṛṣabha* [Ri], *Gāndhāra* [Ga], *Madhyama* [Ma], *Pañcama* [Pa], *Dhaivata* [Dha], and *Niṣāda* [Ni].[1] (Text in brackets mine.)

Bharata then defines the musical qualities of four different kinds of sounds, and specifies the consonant and dissonant intervals contained in two different scales called *Ṣaḍjagrāma* (*Sa-grāma*) and *Madhyamagrāma* (*Ma-grāma*).

> *Nāṭ. 28.22* — [According] as they relate to an interval of [more or less] *Śrutis*, they are of four classes, such as Sonant (*vādin*), Consonant (*saṃvādin*), Assonant (*anuvādin*), and Dissonant (*vivādin*).
>
> That which is an *Aṃśa* [note] anywhere, will in this connection, be called there Sonant (*vādin*). Those two notes which are at an interval of nine or thirteen *Śrutis* from each other are mutually Consonant (*saṃvādin*), e.g., *Ṣaḍja* and *Madhyama*, *Ṣaḍja* and *Pañcama*, *Ṛṣabha* and *Dhaivata*, *Gāndhāra* and *Niṣāda* in the *Ṣaḍja Grāma*. Such is the case in the *Madhyama Grāma*, except that *Ṣaḍja* and *Pañcama* ***are not*** Consonant, while *Pañcama* and *Ṛṣabha* ***are so*** . . .
>
> *23* — In the *Madhyama Grāma*, *Pañcama* and *Ṛṣabha* are Consonant while *Ṣaḍja* and *Pañcama* are so in the *Ṣaḍja Grāma* [only].
>
> The notes being at an interval of [two or] twenty *Śrutis* are Dissonant, e.g., *Ṛṣabha* and *Gāndhāra*, *Dhaivata* and *Niṣāda*.
>
> . . . As a note [prominently] sounds it is called Sonant; as it sounds in consonance [with another] it is Consonant; as it sounds discordantly [to another] it is Dissonant, and as it follows [another note] it is called Assonant. These notes become low or high according to the adjustment of the strings . . . of the *Vīṇā* . . .[2] (Bold italics mine.)

With this general background information — which will prove crucial in constructing the scales — Bharata then quantifies these seven scale degrees according to how many *śrutis* (from the Sanskrit *śru*, lit. *to hear; śruti* in music, *an interval*) are contained between each degree.

> *Nāṭ. 28.23* — . . . Now, there are two *Grāmas: Ṣaḍja* and *Madhyama*. Each of these two (lit. there) include twenty-two *Śrutis* in the following manner:

> *24* — *Śrutis* in the *Ṣaḍja Grāma* are shown as follows: ***three*** [in Ri], ***two*** [in Ga], ***four*** [in Ma], ***four*** [in Pa], ***three*** [in Dha], ***two*** [in Ni], and ***four*** [in Sa].
>
> In the *Madhyama Grāma*, *Pañcama* should be made deficient in one *Śruti.* The difference which occurs in *Pañcama* when it is raised or lowered by a *Śruti* and when consequential slackness or tenseness [of strings] occurs, will indicate a ***typical*** (*pramāṇa*) *Śruti.*[3] (Bold italics and text in brackets mine.)

Next, Bharata describes a demonstration on two *vīṇās*, each equipped with seven strings, and tuned exactly alike to the *Sa-grāma.* The tuning of one *vīṇā* remains unchanged. Bharata gives directions for changing the tuning of the other *vīṇā* in four separate steps. Each step requires the lowering of all seven degrees by increments of one *śruti.* Consequently, after the first step, or after lowering all the strings by 1 *śruti*, no two degrees of the two *vīṇās* match because the smallest interval of the *Sa-grāma* consists of 2 *śrutis.* After the second step, or after lowering Ga by 2 *śrutis*, it will sound the same tone as Ri of the *unchanged vīṇā;* and after lowering Ni by 2 *śrutis*, it will sound the same tone as Dha of the unchanged *vīṇā.* Similarly, after the third step, or after lowering Ri by 3 *śrutis*, it will sound the same tone as Sa of the unchanged *vīṇā;* and after lowering Dha by 3 *śrutis*, it will sound the same tone as Pa of the unchanged *vīṇā.* Finally, after the fourth step, or after lowering Ma by 4 *śrutis*, it will sound the same tone as Ga of the unchanged *vīṇā;* after lowering Pa by 4 *śrutis*, it will sound the same tone as Ma of the unchanged *vīṇā;* and after lowering Sa by 4 *śrutis*, it will sound the same tone as Ni of the unchanged *vīṇā.* In a passage translated by N.A. Jairazbhoy,[4] Bharata states, ". . . lower again, in exactly this manner . . ." (*punarapi tadvadevapakarṣāt*),[5] which means that this experiment was intended to prove that all *śruti* intervals are exactly equal in size. Bharata implies that *only* controlled decreases by identical *śrutis* will produce the scale degrees on the changed *vīṇā* that exactly match the degrees of the unchanged *vīṇā.* In this context, the unchanged *vīṇā* represents a scientific control, or an aural reminder of the changed *vīṇā* before it was lowered.

Bharata then summarizes

> *Nāṭ. 28.25–26* — In the *Ṣaḍja Grāma*, *Ṣaḍja* includes four *Śrutis*, *Ṛṣabha* three, *Gāndhāra* two, *Madhyama* four, *Pañcama* four, *Dhaivata* three, and *Niṣāda* two.
>
> *27–28* — [In the *Madhyama Grāma*] *Madhyama* consists of four *Śrutis*, *Pañcama* three, *Dhaivata* four, *Niṣāda* two, *Ṣaḍja* four, *Ṛṣabha* three, and *Gāndhāra* two *Śrutis.* [Thus] the system of [mutual] intervals (*antara*) has been explained.[6]

In the absence of clearly defined length ratios and interval ratios,[7] this mixture of numerical and verbal terms seems completely open to interpretation. However, a historically accurate analysis reveals that the musical possibilities contained in this text are extremely limited and point toward only one plausible explanation. Before we examine this interpretation of Bharata's text, let us first eliminate two possibilities.

In *Nāṭyaśāstra 28.24*, Bharata distinguishes between the *Sa-grāma* and the *Ma-grāma* by stating that in the former scale, Pa contains 4 *śrutis*, and in the latter scale, Pa contains only 3 *śrutis.* He defines this difference based on a *typical śruti*, or a *pramāṇa śruti.* Bharata goes on to describe his experiment with two *vīṇās*, which only works if the *pramāṇa śruti* is a standard interval, or an interval of a constant size. All these formulations lead to one possibility, namely, that Bharata was contemplating *geometric division* of the "octave" into 22 equal parts. To achieve such a "division" requires the calculation of a complicated irrational number called a *common ratio*,[8] which, in this case, leads directly to 22-tone equal temperament. Recall that in 1584 and 1585, Chu Tsai-yü[9] and Simon Stevin,[10] respectively, calculated the "semitone," or the common ratio of 12-tone equal temperament, when they independently discovered simplified solutions for the twelfth root of 2. They were able to calculate this complicated constant without logarithms because composite number 12 is a product of primes $3 \times 2 \times 2$.[11] This factorization enabled Tsai-yü and Stevin to *effectively* extract the required root in two different ways:

$$\text{Logarithmic “Semitone”} = \sqrt[12]{2}$$

$$\text{Tsai-yü's Solution} = \sqrt[3]{\sqrt[4]{2}}$$

$$\text{Stevin's Solution} = \frac{\sqrt[3]{2}}{\sqrt[4]{2}}$$

A similar technique for the *Pramāṇa Śruti* of 22-tone equal temperament does not yield favorable results because a factorization of composite number 22 yields prime numbers 11 and 2. Here a "simplified" solution would require the extraction of the eleventh root of the square root of 2:

$$\text{Logarithmic } \textit{Pramāṇa Śruti} = \sqrt[22]{2}$$

$$\text{“Simplified” Solution} = \sqrt[11]{\sqrt{2}}$$

Because 11 is a relatively large prime number, this equation *cannot* be solved without logarithms. Consequently, even though Bharata was under the impression that the *pramāṇa śruti* represents a constant interval, the fact remains that a scientific or artistic experience of 22-tone equal temperament is impossible without advanced mathematics. No human being is able to accurately and consistently tune such a scale by simply listening and adjusting the tension of the strings on a *vīṇā*.

Although there is no evidence of irrational length ratios in ancient Indian music, the intriguing question remains, "Is there a mathematical theory Indian musicians could have contemplated that explains the origin of 22 divisions per 'octave'?" This question probably has no definitive answer. However, we may attempt an explanation by examining the rational interval ratio $^{32}/_{31}$, which very closely approximates the irrational interval ratio $\sqrt[22]{2}$:

$$\frac{32}{31} = 54.96\ ¢$$

$$\sqrt[22]{2} = 54.55\ ¢$$

Now, raise $^{32}/_{31}$ to the 22nd power, and observe that twenty-two successive rational *pramāṇa śrutis* exceed one "octave" by only 9.2 ¢:

$$\left(\frac{32}{31}\right)^{22} = 1209.2\ ¢$$

This discrepancy is less than half of the spiral of twelve "fifths," which exceeds seven "octaves" by the *ditonic comma*, known as the *comma of Pythagoras*, or by 23.5 ¢.[12]

Unfortunately, to actually tune a scale through 22 powers of $^{32}/_{31}$ is not any easier than through 22 powers of $\sqrt[22]{2}$. Both methods require the precision and control provided by a monochord or canon with moveable bridges. Again, no human being can accurately tune so many successive rational or irrational intervals by ear. Since there is no historical evidence of the construction of monochords in ancient India,[13] these "theories" could *not* have been realized in the tuning of ancient Indian instruments. The only difference is that the rational approximation could have been contemplated in numerical terms, whereas the irrational division could not have been contemplated in numerical terms. We conclude, therefore, that a literal interpretation of Bharata's *pramāṇa śruti* as an irrational interval ratio has no theoretical validity. A "theory" that cannot be realized (under any conditions) at a given moment in time must be distinguished from a theory that can be realized at a given moment in time. Whether ancient or not, Bharata's "theory" of *pramāṇa śruti* was at best an expression of his imagination. Finally, the seductive oversimplification provided by a *pramāṇa śruti* eliminated the development of a rigorous integration of music and mathematics. As long as the *pramāṇa śruti* existed, there was no need to describe subtle differences in intonation with length ratios and interval ratios. The *pramāṇa śruti* prevented ancient Indian writers and musicians from thinking in ratios, and from intentionally tuning to ratios.

~ 11.21 ~

The *vīṇā* in Bharata's text is *not* the stringed instrument that appeared in the second half of the first millennium A.D. This later instrument is called an *ālāpinī vīṇā* and classified as a stick-zither because it has a straight bamboo or wooden tube over which a single string is stretched.[14] The *ālāpinī vīṇā* evolved into the modern stick-zither called *bīṇ* in North India, and into the modern lute also called *vīṇā* in South India. These two instruments now have frets, full gourd resonators, four playing strings, and numerous sympathetic strings. In contrast, Figure 11.21 shows that Bharata's *vīṇā* was an arched bow-harp.[15] The ancient harp-*vīṇā* consisted of a curved arm jointed to a hollow boat-shaped body that acted as a cavity resonator to amplify the strings. This wooden resonator was covered with a soundboard made of leather, through which the strings passed. Most harp-*vīṇās* had seven, nine, ten, or fourteen strings.

Since no specimens survived, two critical aspects about the internal construction of the harp-*vīṇā* remain unknown. (1) We do not know whether the strings were attached to a strip of wood (called a string holder), which in turn was anchored to the inside walls of the resonator, or whether the curved arm extended all the way through the resonator and, thereby, provided a continuous structure that held the strings at both ends. (2) We also do not know by what mechanism the strings were tuned. Ancient sculptures and reliefs show no tuning pegs in the upper part of the arm. Therefore, the strings were probably adjusted with tuning-cords, very much like the modern *saùng-gauk* of Burma, also an arched harp with a boat-shaped resonator.[16] However, if the arm passed through the resonator, then the remote possibility exists that tuning pegs were located in the lower part of the arm. In either case, adjusting the tension of the strings must have been tedious at best because neither design facilitates the demanding process of precision tuning. It is difficult to achieve fine incremental adjustments with tuning-chords because such lashings are subject to creep and slippage; similarly, it is difficult to manipulate tuning pegs inside the resonator because they are situated in a confined and awkward location. Finally, note carefully that the harp-*vīṇā* had *no* post to give it structural rigidity between the lower open end where the resonator terminates in a round corner, and the upper open end where the arm terminates in a scroll. This open semi-circular design severely limited the tuning possibilities of the instrument.

> It is nevertheless very difficult to understand how such harps . . . could be tuned or kept in tune; not so much because no tuning devices are to be seen in the representations, as because it would be impossible to make an instrument with a curved frame and no post, were the frame even of steel, so rigid that a change of tension in one string would not alter that of all the others.[17]

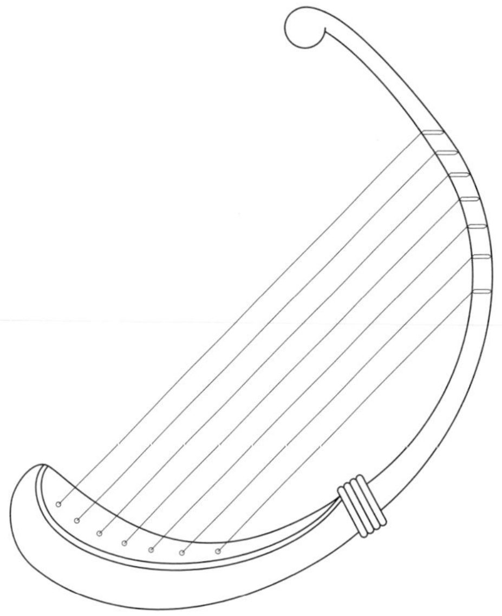

Figure 11.21 Bharata's harp-*vīṇā*. It is extremely unlikely that an arched bow-harp of this design — with no post, and probably no tuning pegs — was used to tune intricate and difficult scales.

We conclude, therefore, that it is extremely unlikely that the ancient harp-*vīṇā* was used to tune technically difficult scales. Bharata's demonstration was at best a "thought experiment" designed to illustrate the distribution of *śruti* intervals. The slightest motion between open ends would have obliterated the subtle intonational differences of scale degrees lowered (or strings loosened) in 1-*śruti* increments.[18] As on most folk harps, the harp-*vīṇā* was probably tuned to "octaves," "fifths," "fourths," and "thirds."

~ 11.22 ~

Among modern Indian and European writers, the greatest controversy surrounding Bharata's text consists of two fundamentally different interpretations regarding the distribution of *śruti* intervals in both the *Sa-grāma* and the *Ma-grāma*. A careful reading of *Nāṭyaśāstra 28.24–28* does not reveal whether these intervals come before (below) or after (above) the indicated tones. However, if we take into consideration Bharata's description of consonant and dissonant intervals, then only one correct interpretation emerges. I can categorically say that all the writers who advocate the incorrect interpretation never take Bharata's interval descriptions in *Nāṭyaśāstra 28.22–23* into consideration; it is as if the original text does not exist. Table 11.15 gives the correct and incorrect interpretations of the *Sa-grāma* and *Ma-grāma.*[19] In the correct version of the *Sa-grāma*, the *śruti* intervals — 4, 3, 2, 4, 4, 3, 2 — come before the indicated tones, and in the incorrect version, after the indicated tones. Only the correct version complies with Bharata's demonstration on the two *vīṇās*. For example, recall that in the fourth step, Bharata requires that after *lowering* Sa by 4 *śrutis*, it will have the same tone as Ni of the unchanged *vīṇā*. In the *Sa-grāma*, such a retuning would be impossible if a 4-*śruti* interval did not *precede* Sa.

In *Nāṭyaśāstra 28.22*, Bharata specifically defines consonant intervals as containing either nine or thirteen *śrutis*. Since 9 *śrutis* + 13 *śrutis* = 22 *śrutis*, let us express 9 *śrutis* as ratio $4/3$, 13 *śrutis* as ratio $3/2$, and 22 *śrutis* as ratio $2/1$, because $4/3 \times 3/2 = 2/1$. Therefore, if Ma is a "fourth," and if Pa is a "fifth," then the interval between Ma and Pa is $3/2 \div 4/3 = 9/8$. Now, since in the *Sa-grāma* the interval between Ma and Pa contains 4 *śrutis*, we conclude that all such intervals in the scale

Table 11.15

CORRECT AND INCORRECT INTERPRETATIONS OF THE *SA-GRĀMA* AND *MA-GRĀMA* IN INDIAN AND EUROPEAN TEXTS

Correct *Sa-grāma:*	Sa	3	Ri	2	Ga	4	Ma	4	Pa	3	Dha	2	Ni	4	Sa^{l}
Correct *Ma-grāma:*	Ma	3	Pa	4	Dha	2	Ni	4	Sa	3	Ri	2	Ga	4	Ma^{l}
Incorrect *Sa-grāma:*	Sa	4	Ri	3	Ga	2	Ma	4	Pa	4	Dha	3	Ni	2	Sa^{l}
Incorrect *Ma-grāma:*	Ma	4	Pa	3	Dha	4	Ni	2	Sa	4	Ri	3	Ga	2	Ma^{l}

represent a "tone," ratio $9/8$. Refer to Figure 11.22(a), Row 1, and notice that Sa, Ma, Pa, and Sa^{l} are vertically aligned with ratios $1/1$, $4/3$, $3/2$, and $2/1$, respectively, in Row 4; and that all 4-*śruti* intervals in Row 2 are vertically aligned with interval ratios $9/8$ in Row 3. With these values, compute two *svara* ratios in Row 4: Ni = $2/1 \div 9/8 = 16/9$, and Ga = $4/3 \div 9/8 = 32/27$. Next, suppose that a 3-*śruti* interval represents a "small whole tone," ratio $10/9$, and that a 2-*śruti* interval represents a "semitone," ratio $16/15$. With the latter ratio, calculate one more *svara* ratio in Row 4: Dha = $16/9 \div 16/15 = 5/3$. Finally, according to this interpretation, interval ratio $10/9$ occurs between Sa–Ri and Pa–Dha by default; and interval ratio $16/15$ occurs between Ri–Ga by default.

To confirm these assumptions, return to *Nāṭyaśāstra 28.22* and observe that Bharata insists that in the *Sa-grāma*, intervals Sa–Ma, Sa–Pa, Ri–Dha, and Ga–Ni are consonant. A sequence of solid brackets in Figure 11.22(a) confirms that these tones span interval ratios $4/3$, $3/2$, $3/2$, and $3/2$, respectively. In the last sentence of *Nāṭyaśāstra 28.22*, and in the first sentence of *Nāṭyaśāstra 28.23*, Bharata juxtaposes the *Ma-grāma* and *Sa-grāma* and observes the following opposite conditions: in the *Ma-grāma*, Sa–Pa [or C–G^{l}] is not consonant while Pa–Ri [or G–D] is consonant, and in the *Sa-grāma*, Sa–Pa [or C–G] is consonant while Pa–Ri [or G–D^{l}] is not consonant. (With respect to the *Ma-grāma*, in Figure 11.22(b) the tone G^{l} is immediately above F^{l}, and with respect to the *Sa-grāma*, in Figure 11.22(a) the tone D^{l} is immediately above C^{l}.) Although Bharata does not explicitly define Pa–Ri as a dissonant interval in the *Sa-grāma*, we may deduce this description based on a logical analysis of his juxtaposition. In Figure 11.22(a) the dashed bracket shows that the inversion of Pa–Ri — interval Ri–Pa — is a dissonant "sharp fourth," as in $3/2 \div 10/9 = 27/20 = 519.6$ ¢, which means that Pa–Ri is a dissonant "flat fifth," as in $20/9 \div 3/2 = 40/27 = 680.4$ ¢.

Further evidence that these distributions of *śrutis* in the *Sa-grāma* and *Ma-grāma* are authentic may be found in a text entitled *Dattilam*, written by Dattila (early centuries A.D.). Bharata refers to Dattila as an authority on music (*Nāṭyaśāstra 1.26*), but Dattila does not mention Bharata. Two English translations of the *Dattilam* exist, one by E. Wiersma-Te Nijenhuis,[20] and the other by Mukund Lath.[21] The latter states, "The whole testimony shows that Dattila was at least as ancient as Bharata and that the *Dattilam* is almost certainly his authentic creation."[22] In *Dattilam 12–14*, the author explicitly states that in the *Sa-grāma*, *Ṣadja* is the first degree, and that three *śrutis* higher, *Ṛṣabha* is the second degree, etc. Similarly, in the *Ma-grāma*, *Madhyama* is the first degree, and three *śrutis* higher, *Pañcama* is the second degree, etc. The Nijenhuis translation reads

> *Dat. 12* — The sound (*dhvani*), which is indicated by the term *Ṣadja* is [the starting point] in the *Ṣadjagrāma*. From this one the third [*śruti*] upwards is, no doubt, *Ṛṣabha*.
>
> *13* — From this one the second [*śruti*] is *Gāndhāra*, from this one the fourth [*śruti*] is *Madhyama*. From *Madhyama* in the same way *Pañcama;* from this one the third [*śruti*] is *Dhaivata*.

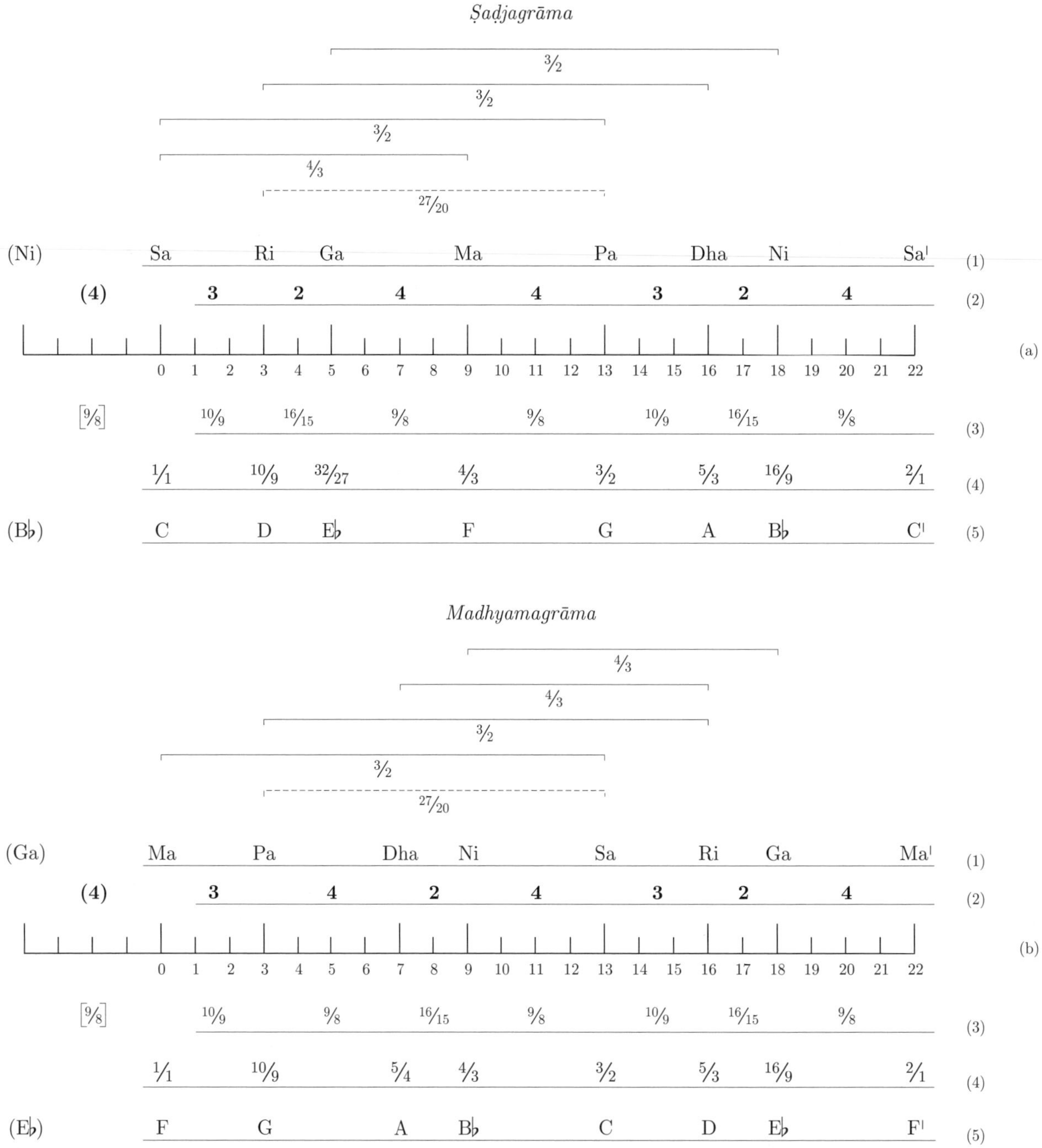

Figure 11.22 The two parent scales of ancient India projected over the 22-*śruti* scale. (a) For the *Sa-grāma*, Bharata specifies the four consonant intervals indicated by solid brackets, and one dissonant Pa–Ri — or Ri–Pa — interval indicated by a dashed bracket. (b) Similarly, for the *Ma-grāma*, he specifies four consonant intervals and one dissonant Pa–Sa interval. Although Bharata's text does not utilize ratios of any kind, the analyses depicted here are perfectly consistent with his numerical and verbal descriptions.

> *14* — From this one the second [*śruti*] is *Niṣāda;* from this one the fourth [*śruti*] is *Ṣaḍja.* In the *Madhyamagrāma*, *Pañcama* is the third [*śruti*] from *Madhyama.*[23]

With respect to the *Madhyamagrāma*, the Lath translation reads

> *Dat. 14* — In the *Madhyama-grāma*, *Pañcama* is the third higher [*śruti*] commencing with *Madhyama.*[24]

We turn now to the *Ma-grāma*, which Bharata describes in *Nāṭyaśāstra 28.24* as having a Ma–Pa interval reduced by one *pramāṇa śruti.* Given that in the *Sa-grāma*, the interval between Ma–Pa contains 4 *śrutis*, in the *Ma-grāma* it therefore contains 3 *śrutis.* Since 4 *śrutis* represents ratio $9/8$, and 3 *śrutis*, ratio $10/9$, calculate the difference between these two intervals by dividing the larger ratio by the smaller ratio: $9/8 \div 10/9 = 81/80 = 21.5$ ¢. In Western tuning theory, this discrepancy is called the *syntonic comma*, or the *comma of Didymus.*[25] Unfortunately, $81/80$ is less than half the size of $32/31$ [55.0 ¢], the closest rational approximation of the common ratio of 22-TET. If Bharata either heard or thought of $81/80$ (or some similar microtonal interval) as a *pramāṇa śruti*, then it is understandable given the structural imperfections and mathematical limitations of the ancient harp-*vīṇā.* In any case, the same shift that decreases the Ma–Pa interval by one *śruti*, increases the Pa–Dha interval by one *śruti;* therefore, in the *Ma-grāma*, the interval Pa–Dha contains 4 *śrutis.*

Refer to Figure 11.22(b), and note that it shows the *Ma-grāma* based on the same organizational principles as the *Sa-grāma* in Figure 11.22(a). Again, to verify the authenticity of these ratios, return to the second paragraph of *Nāṭyaśāstra 28.22.* Here, Bharata clearly indicates that in the *Ma-grāma*, intervals Sa–Ma or inversion Ma–Sa, Ri–Dha or inversion Dha–Ri, Ga–Ni or inversion Ni–Ga, and Pa–Ri are consonant. The solid brackets in Figure 11.22(b) confirm that these tones span interval ratios $3/2$, $4/3$, $4/3$, and $3/2$, respectively. And in the same sentence, Bharata observes that the interval Sa–Pa is *not* consonant. In Figure 11.22(b), the dashed bracket shows that this interval is a dissonant "sharp fourth," ratio $27/20$.

If we now assign Sa, ratio $1/1$, to C, then Figure 11.22(a), Row 5, shows that in Western music theory, the *Ṣaḍjagrāma* is a kind of minor scale, which includes a Pythagorean "minor seventh" [996.1 ¢], ratio $16/9$ [B♭], that sounds a "fifth" below Ma$^{\prime}$ [$8/3 \div 3/2 = 16/9$], and a Pythagorean "minor third" [294.1 ¢], ratio $32/27$ [E♭], that sounds a "fifth" below Ni [$16/9 \div 3/2 = 32/27$].[26] In contrast, if we assign Ma, ratio $1/1$, to F, then Figure 11.22(b), Row 5, shows that the *Madhyamagrāma* is a kind of major scale, which includes a 5-limit "major third" [386.3 ¢], ratio $5/4$ [A], and the "minor seventh," ratio $16/9$ [E♭] as before.

Finally, let us reflect on the meaning of some ancient terms. Although Western musicians may think of the *Sa-grāma* and *Ma-grāma* as scales, *grāma* in the purest sense of the word does *not* mean scale. The abstract concept of "scale" remained unknown in India until the 19th century. (See Section 11.32.) We should understand the word *grāma* to mean tone-system, or tuning. As such, these two tone-systems serve no musical purpose. A *grāma* refers to the tuning of a musical instrument, or to the quantification and distribution of *svaras* and *śrutis.* However, many texts do refer to the two *grāmas* as the parent scales of ancient Indian music. In the final analysis, musicians recognized organizations of *svaras* and *śrutis* as *musical entities* only when they are endowed with *technical properties* called *lakṣaṇa*, and *expressive qualities* called *rasa.* We will consider these two terms in Sections 11.23 and 11.27, respectively.

∾ 11.23 ∾

One of the most important discussions in Bharata's book occurs in *Nāṭyaśāstra 28.38–149.* Here Bharata describes a highly organized system of melodic modes called *jātis.* At the end Chapter 28, and almost as an aside, Bharata explains the functions of the *jātis:*

> *Nāṭ. 28.150–151* — These are the *Jātis* with their ten characteristics [*lakṣaṇa*]. These should be applied in the song (*pada*) with dance movements (*Karaṇas*) and gestures suitable to them (lit. their own). I shall now speak of their distinction in relation to the Sentiments (*rasa*) . . .[27] (Text in brackets mine.)

Dattila confirms the monumental significance of the *jātis* in a single unequivocal statement:

> *Dat. 97* — . . . anything which is sung is based on the *jātis.*[28]

Bharata divides his *jātis* into two different technical categories: *śuddha* (pure) and *vikṛta* (modified). The description below of the *śuddha jātis* is from a major treatise entitled *Saṅgītaratnākara* by Śārṅgadeva (1210–1247). (See Sections 11.30–11.31.)

> *Saṅ. Ch. I, Sec. 7, A. (i) (b)* — The definition of *śuddhatā:* To define *śuddhatā*, it is stated that the *jātis*, which have their ***denominative*** note [descriptive note] as the [1] final note (*nyāsa*), [2] the semi-final note (*apanyāsa*), [3] the fundamental note (*aṃśa*) [prominent note], and [4] the initial note (*graha*), which do not have the final note in the high register and which are complete [i.e., heptatonic] are known as *śuddhā jātis.*[29] (Bold italics and text in brackets mine.)

Dattilam 62 gives a similar description. The text (translation?) of Bharata is less precise because it excludes the Semi-final note. Therefore, in the next passage we will assume that a single tone — which acts as Initial, Prominent, Semi-final, and Final note — is the denominative note of a given *śuddha jāti.*[30] (See Figure 11.24.)

I

> *Nāṭ. 28.44* — . . . In the *Ṣaḍja Grāma* the pure (*Jātis*) are *Ṣāḍjī* [after *Ṣaḍja*], *Ārṣabhī* [after *Ṛṣabha*], *Dhaivatī* [after *Dhaivata*] and *Naiṣādī* [after *Niṣāda*] and in the *Madhyama Grāma* they are *Gāndhārī* [after *Gāndhāra*], *Madhyamā* [after *Madhyama*] and *Pañcamī* [after *Pañcama*]. 'Pure' (*śuddha*) in this connection means having *Svarāṃśa* (= *Aṃśa*), *Graha*, and *Nyāsa* consisting of all the seven notes (lit. not deficient in notes). When some of these *Jātis* lack two or more of the prescribed characteristics except the *Nyāsa*, they are called 'modified' (*vikṛta*) . . .[31] (Text in brackets mine.)

Here, as in Dattila's and Śārṅgadeva's texts, the terms *aṃśa*, *graha*, *nyāsa*, and *apanyāsa* belong to the *lakṣaṇa*, or to ten technical properties, which, when uniquely applied to the *jātis*, give each mode its distinctive musical identity. Bharata describes the *lakṣaṇa* thus:

> *Nāṭ. 28.74* — Ten characteristics [*lakṣaṇa*] of the *Jātis* are: *Graha* [Initial note], *Aṃśa* [Prominent note], *Tāra* [High register], *Mandra* [Low register], *Nyāsa* [Final note], *Apanyāsa* [Semi-final note] . . . *Alpatva* [Rare note] . . . *Bahutva* [Copious note] . . . *Ṣāḍava* [Hexatonic mode], and . . . *Auḍava* [Pentatonic mode].[32] (Text in brackets mine.)

The seven *śuddha jātis* are by definition heptatonic modes. However, in *Nāṭyaśāstra 28.103–149*, Bharata describes eighteen more *jātis*. Seven of these have the *same* names as the *śuddha jātis* but, due to their modified nature, are here classified as *vikṛta jātis;* the remaining eleven have *unique* names and are classified as *saṃsarga jātis*, or *jātis* comprised from a combination of *śuddha jātis.*[33] Therefore, it is best to think of Bharata's *jātis* in three separate categories: *śuddha*, *vikṛta*, and *saṃsarga*. Bharata divides these eighteen *jātis* into the following mode-types:

> *Nāṭ. 28.56* — Of these, four [are] heptatonic (*saptasvarā*) . . . ten [are] pentatonic (*pañcasvarā*) . . . and . . . four [are] hexatonic (*ṣaṭsvarā*).[34] (Text in brackets mine.)

An analysis of the text shows that all four heptatonic modes belong to the *saṃsarga jātis*, six of the ten pentatonic modes belong to the *vikṛta jātis*, and therefore only one of the four hextonic modes belongs to the *vikṛta jātis*.

We will not discuss the eleven *saṃsarga jātis* in full detail,[35] but we will analyze Bharata's seven *śuddha jātis* and seven *vikṛta jātis*. To do this, we must first familiarize ourselves with an extremely important development in ancient Indian music: the utilization of auxiliary notes called *svarasādhāraṇa*, translated into English as Overlapping notes. Bharata defines *sādhāraṇa* and *svarasādhāraṇa* thus:

II

> *Nāṭ. 28.34* — . . . The Overlapping (*sādhāraṇa*) means the quality of a note rising between two [consecutive] notes [in a *Grāma*].
>
> *35* — . . . [1] The *Kākalī* and [2] the transitional note (*antarasvara*) are the Overlapping notes (*svarasādhāraṇa*). Now if ***two*** *Śrutis* are added to *Niṣāda*, it is called *Kākalī Niṣāda* and not *Ṣaḍja;* as it is a note rising between the two (pure *Niṣāda* and *Ṣaḍja*), it becomes Overlapping. Similarly, [the ***two*** *Śrutis* being added to it] *Gāndhāra* becomes transitional *Gāndhāra* {*Antara Gāndhāra*} and not *Madhyama*, because it is a transitional note (*antarasvara*) between the two (*Madhyama* and *Gāndhāra*). Thus the Overlapping notes [occur].[36] (Numbers in brackets, bold italics, and text in braces mine.)

And again, Dattila gives a terse description:

> *Dat. 16* — *Niṣāda* is called *Kākalī*, when [the note] is raised by two *śrutis*. Similarly, *Gāndhāra* is called *Antarasvara*.[37]

For convenience, we will simply refer to *Antara Gāndhāra* as "An," and to *Kākalī Niṣāda* as "Ka." With respect to the *Sa-grāma*, calculate the *svara* ratio of An by first increasing the interval between Ri and Ga from 2 *śrutis* to 4 *śrutis*, and then multiplying the *svara* ratio of Ri by a 4-*śruti* interval: An $= \frac{10}{9} \times \frac{9}{8} = \frac{5}{4}$. Similarly, calculate the *svara* ratio of Ka by first increasing the interval between Dha and Ni from 2 *śrutis* to 4 *śrutis*, and then multiplying the *svara* ratio of Dha by a 4-*śruti* interval: Ka $= \frac{5}{3} \times \frac{9}{8} = \frac{15}{8}$. With respect to the *Ma-grāma*, calculate the *svara* ratio of Ka by first increasing the interval between Dha and Ni from 2 *śrutis* to 4 *śrutis*, and then multiplying the *svara* ratio of Dha by a 4-*śruti* interval: Ka $= \frac{5}{4} \times \frac{9}{8} = \frac{45}{32}$. Similarly, calculate the *svara* ratio of An by first increasing the interval between Ri and Ga from 2 *śrutis* to 4 *śrutis*, and then multiplying the *svara* ratio of Ri by a 4-*śruti* interval: An $= \frac{5}{3} \times \frac{9}{8} = \frac{15}{8}$. (See Figure 11.23.)

Bharata describes the general implementation of the *svarasādhāraṇa* in *Nāṭyaśāstra 28.36–37*. Because in the previously quoted M. Ghosh translation the meaning of this passage is not clear, consider now an alternate translation found in the commentary of Mukund Lath's *A Study of Dattilam.* (See Section 11.22.) Lath translated this passage from a different source and identifies it as *Nāṭyaśāstra 28.35–36:*

> *Nāṭ. 28.35–36* — The *antara-svara* [An] should always be associated (with the *jāti*) when making an ascending movement; its use should be exceedingly spare and never in making descending movements. If the *antara-svara* be used in descending movements, whether sparingly or with profusion, it destroys the *śruti* and the *jati-rāga.*[38] (Text in brackets mine.)

Lath then adds the following interpretation of this passage based on a famous commentary of the *Nāṭyaśāstra* by Abhinava Gupta (fl. *c.* A.D. 1000):

> Abhinava points out that the word *antara-svara* in these verses denoted not only the *auxiliary ga* [An] but also the *kākalī ni* [Ka] and the maxim applies equally to both the auxiliary notes: *"antarasvaraśabdena cātra kākalyapi saṃgṛhīta iti kṛtopyayameva kramaḥ"* (A.B. on N.S. 28, 36).[39] (Text in brackets mine.)

Bharata describes the specific implementation of the *svarasādhāraṇa* with respect to the *jātis* in *Nāṭyaśāstra 28.38.* Again, consider this translation by Lath, which he cites as *Nāṭyaśāstra 28.37:*

III

> *Nāṭ. 28.37* — There are three *jātis* which are connected with the use of the *sādharāṇa svaras* (i.e., *antara ga* and *kākalī ni*), namely, *Madhyamā*, *Pañcamī*, and *Ṣaḍjamadhyā.*[40]

Madhyamā and *Pañcamī* are classified as both *śuddha* and *vikṛta jātis*, and *Ṣaḍjamadhyā*, as a *saṃsarga jāti.*

11.24

Before we begin a ratio analysis of the *śuddha jātis* and the *vikṛta jātis*, consider first a tuning sequence designed to produce the *Sa-grāma* on an ancient harp-*vīṇā* with nine open strings. In the illustration below, a progression of white notes represents the required scale degrees, and black notes indicate previously tuned degrees in the sequence. Notice that this procedure only requires tuning "octaves," "fifths," "fourths," and one "major third."

Tuning the *Sa-grāma* on the Ancient *Vīṇā*

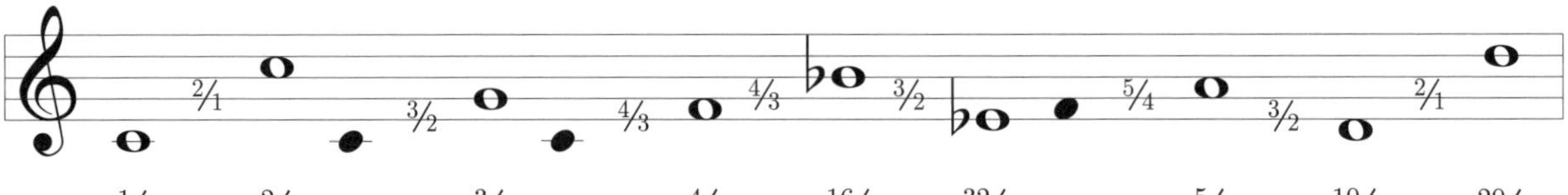

	1/1	2/1	3/2	4/3	16/9	32/27	5/3	10/9	20/9
Strings:	1	8	5	4	7	3	6	2	9
	Sa	Sa'	Pa	Ma	Ni	Ga	Dha	Ri	Ri'

Refer to Figure 11.23(a), Rows 1 and 2, which give the ratios and note names, respectively, of the *Sa-grāma* from the lowest tone Sa, ratio 1/1, on String 1 to the highest tone Ri', ratio 20/9, on String 9. Now, if we were to tune this *vīṇā* to the *Ma-grāma* as illustrated in Figure 11.22(b), Row 5,

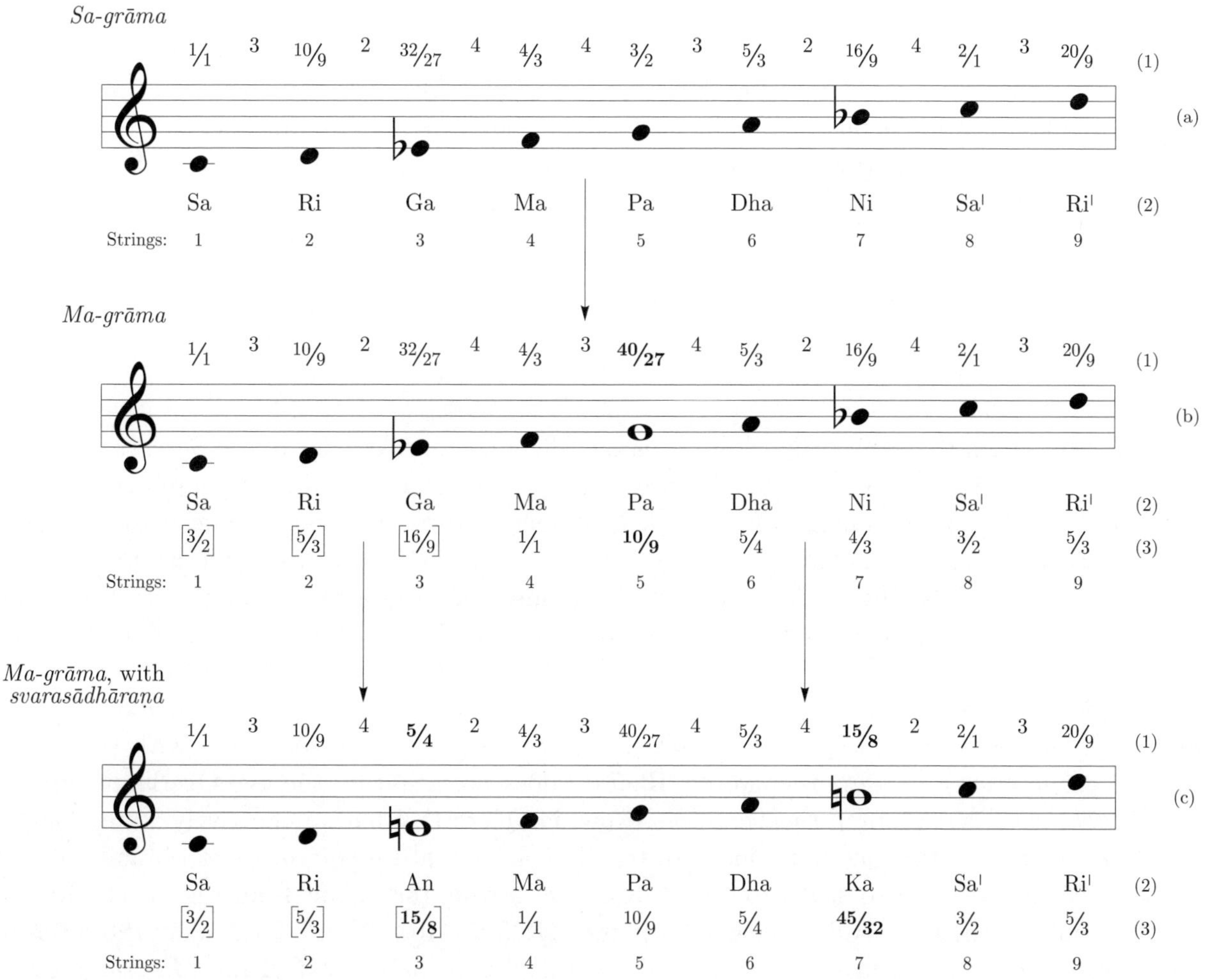

Figure 11.23 Retuning the ancient *vīṇā.* (a) Rows 1 and 2 give the ratios and note names of the *Sa-grāma.* (b) Upon retuning String 5 to ratio 40/27, Row 3 gives the ratios of the *modulated Ma-grāma* tuning; observe that such a change modulates the *old* tonic Sa, ratio 1/1, on String 1 to a *new* tonic Ma, ratio 1/1, on String 4. A modal version of the *Ma-grāma* tuning now appears in Row 1. (c) Upon retuning String 3 to ratio 5/4, and String 7 to ratio 15/8, Row 3 gives the ratios of the modulated *Ma-grāma* with *svarasādhāraṇa.*

then we would (1) change the frequency of the lowest tone from C_4 to F_4, and (2) retune all the remaining strings. However, given the structural instability of the *vīṇā*, such an increase in tension would pose significant mechanical difficulties. It is far more likely that musicians in ancient India rendered the *Ma-grāma* as a *modulated* scale on the *vīṇā*. One may produce a *modulated Ma-grāma* by retuning only a single string of the original *Sa-grāma* tuning. As explained below, such a modulation shifts ratio 1/1 from Sa on String 1 to Ma on String 4.

Recall from the discussion in Section 11.22 that the principal difference between the *Sa-grāma* and the *Ma-grāma* is that the Ma–Pa interval contains 4 *śrutis* in the former tuning, and 3 *śrutis* in the latter tuning. An arrow that points from Figure 11.23(a) to 11.23(b) indicates this difference. To reduce this interval, and thereby produce a modulated *Ma-grāma* tuning based on the original *Sa-grāma* tuning, requires two simple steps. (1) In Figure 11.23(b), Row 1, identify the tone of String 5 of the *Ma-grāma* tuning by multiplying the tone of String 4 of the *Sa-grāma* tuning by a 3-*śruti* interval: String 5 of *Ma-grāma* $= \frac{4}{3} \times \frac{10}{9} = \frac{40}{27}$. (2) Tune the *new* Pa, ratio 40/27 on String 5 as a "fourth," ratio 4/3, above String 2: that is $\frac{10}{9} \times \frac{4}{3} = \frac{40}{27} = 680.4$ ¢. Figure 11.23(b), Row

3, shows that such a simple retuning modulates the *old* tonic Sa, ratio $\frac{1}{1}$, on String 1 to the *new* tonic Ma, ratio $\frac{1}{1}$, on String 4. However, this shift does *not* render the modulated *Ma-grāma* as a continuous heptatonic scale from the tonic, ratio $\frac{1}{1}$ [F_4], to the "minor seventh," ratio $\frac{16}{9}$ [$E\flat_5$], because the latter string is missing; but since String 3 sounds a $\frac{16}{9}$ [$E\flat_4$] one "octave" below, note that the entire scale does exist on the *vīṇā*. To confirm that $\frac{32}{27}$ in Figure 11.23(b), Row 1, is mathematically equivalent to $\frac{16}{9}$ in Row 3, verify the proportion[41]

$$\frac{\frac{32}{27}}{\frac{1}{1}} = \frac{\frac{16}{9}}{\frac{3}{2}}$$

In Figure 11.23(a), I arbitrarily chose C_4 as the fundamental frequency of the *Sa-grāma* tuning. Furthermore, observe that the tones in Figures 11.23(b) and 11.23(c), Rows 1, represent *modes* of the modulated *Ma-grāma* tuning in Rows 3. Do not confuse these *Ma-grāma* modes with the original *Sa-grāma* tuning. For example, in Figures 11.23(b) and 11.23(c), Rows 1, the Sa–Pa intervals are not $\frac{3}{2}$'s, but $\frac{40}{27}$'s. Since a mode may begin on any degree of a given tuning, one could also construct various *Ma-grāma* modes in Figures 11.23(b) and 11.23(c) by assigning ratio $\frac{1}{1}$ to Ri, Ga, Pa, etc.

In Quote I, Bharata explains that the *śuddha jātis* called *Madhyamā* and *Pañcamī* are derived from the *Ma-grāma*, and in Quote III, that these two *jātis* ". . . are connected with the use of the *sādharāṇa svaras* . . ." In other words, Bharata does *not* associate the two Overlapping notes with *śuddha jātis* derived from the *Sa-grāma*. Now, in Quote II, Bharata effectively states that to tune the *svarasādhāraṇa*, one must increase the Ri–Ga interval by two *śrutis* to obtain An, and the Dha–Ni interval by two *śrutis* to obtain Ka. Two arrows that point from Figure 11.23(b) to 11.23(c) indicate these intervalic changes. In Figure 11.23(c), Rows 1 and 3, calculate the ratios of the *svarasādhāraṇa* as discussed in Section 11.23. Finally, in the context of the *Ma-grāma* mode in Row 1, tune the new *sādharāṇa* An, ratio $\frac{5}{4}$, on String 3 as a $\frac{5}{4}$ interval above String 1, and the new *sādharāṇa* Ka, ratio $\frac{15}{8}$, on String 7 as a $\frac{3}{2}$ interval above String 3. With respect to the modulated *Ma-grāma* in Row 3, the latter two ratios are mathematically equivalent to ratios $\frac{15}{8}$ [An] and $\frac{45}{32}$ [Ka], respectively.

11.25

Turn now to Figures 11.24 and 11.25, which give the *svara* ratios, *śruti* intervals, approximate Western tones, and *lakṣaṇa* of Bharata's seven *śuddha jātis* and seven *vikṛta jātis*, respectively. Notes marked with letters I, P, S, O, and F signify Initial, Prominent, Semi-final, Omitted (O_H for Hexatonic modes, and O_P for Pentatonic modes), and Final notes. Figure 11.24 illustrates the *śuddha jātis* as defined in Quote I, and Figure 11.25, the *vikṛta jātis* as defined in *Nāṭyaśāstra 28.103–112, 121–123, 128–130*, and *132–134*. Although in the latter passages, Bharata does not specify the I notes, he defines the following relation between Prominent (*aṃśa*) notes and Initial (*graha*) notes:

> *Nāṭ. 28.91* — . . . *Aṃśas* are always *Grahas* in all these *Jātis*.[42]

In Figure 11.25, therefore, all P notes appear as I notes as well. The *vikṛta jātis* definitions also include references to "Rare" (or "Reduced") and "Amplified" notes, and to the melodic "movement" of notes. Because some of these descriptions are not clear and are open to interpretation, and because these additional *lakṣaṇa* would hopelessly clutter the illustration, I decided not to include them in Figure 11.25.

Figure 11.24 shows seven *śuddha jātis* arranged in ascending order. Such a pattern requires organizing the *jātis* into three sections. As specified in Quote I, a column marked Origins indicates that the first two *śuddha jātis* are derived from the *Ṣaḍjagrāma*, the next three *śuddha jātis*, from the *Madhyamagrāma*, and the last two *śuddha jātis*, from the *Ṣaḍjagrāma* as well. As discussed in Section 11.24 and illustrated in Figure 11.23, modes derived from the *Ṣaḍjagrāma*, the *Madhyamagrāma*, and the *Madhyamagrāma* with *svarasādhāraṇa* require three fundamentally different tunings. Notice, however, that in Figure 11.24, *all śuddha jātis* are shown as beginning on Sa, ratio 1/1, or C_4, and ending on Sa$^{|}$, ratio 2/1, or C_5. To understand the reason for representing all modes with common tonic and "octave" frequencies, consider the following three *śuddha jātis: Ārṣabhī, Gāndhārī*, and *Madhyamā*. Starting on D_4, $E\flat_4$, and F_4, the *śruti* intervals and translated *svara* ratios of these *jātis* are

Ārṣabhī starting on D_4:	1/1	2	16/15	4	6/5	4	27/20	3	3/2	2	8/5	4	9/5	3	2/1
Gāndhārī starting on $E\flat_4$:	1/1	4	9/8	3	5/4	4	45/32	2	3/2	4	27/16	3	15/8	2	2/1
Madhyamā starting on F_4:	1/1	3	10/9	4	5/4	4	45/32	2	3/2	3	5/3	4	15/8	2	2/1

Given these tones, it is not at all obvious that *Ārṣabhī* and *Gāndhārī* have all but one ratio (3/2 vs. 40/27) in common, and *Gāndhārī* and *Madhyamā* have all but two ratios (32/27 vs. 5/4, and 16/9 vs. 15/8) in common. By interpreting these *śuddha jātis* according to the *Sa-grāma* or *Ma-grāma* (*Sa-tuning* or *Ma-tuning*) from which they are derived, we avoid the possibility of mistakenly assigning differences where there are none. In Figures 11.24 and 11.25, intonational discrepancies between the *jātis* — *which require crucial changes in tuning* — emerge as actual differences in the translated *svara* ratios of the two *grāmas*, not as seeming differences in the *śruti* intervals of the *jātis*. In short, common tonic and "octave" frequencies provide two mathematical constants to evaluate the tuning adjustments required by the *jātis* on a *vīṇā*. These adjustments, in turn, indicate genuine performance practices. Given the intonational limitations of the *vīṇā*, Figure 11.24 shows that musicians achieved musical variety (1) by retuning the fifth string, and combinations of the third and seventh strings, and (2) by systematically rotating the I, P, S, and F notes from the first through the seventh tones of the seven *jātis*.

With regard to Western tuning theory and practice, the most remarkable *śuddha jātis* are *Ārṣabhī* and *Naiṣādī*. All but one of the translated *svara* ratios of the *Ārṣabhī* match a scale conceived by Ptolemy (*c.* A.D. 100 – *c.* 165) called the Tense Diatonic in the ancient Dorian Mode; similarly, all but one of the translated *svara* ratios of the *Naiṣādī* match the Tense Diatonic in the ancient Lydian Mode. This latter scale was proclaimed by Gioseffo Zarlino (1517–1590) as the most "natural" of all diatonic scales. (See Section 10.21.) These four scales constitute a remarkable coincidence in the history of music when one considers the possibility that Ptolemy and Bharata were contemporaries. Bharata's *Ārṣabhī* has a "sharp fourth," ratio 27/20, whereas Ptolemy's Dorian Mode has a "just fourth," ratio 4/3; and Bharata's *Naiṣādī* has a Pythagorean "major sixth," ratio 27/16, whereas Ptolemy's Lydian Mode has a 5-limit "major sixth," ratio 5/3.

Bharata's *śuddha jāti*, the *Ārṣabhī:* 1/1, 16/15, 6/5, 27/20, 3/2, 8/5, 9/5, 2/1
Ptolemy's Tense Diatonic, Dorian Mode: 1/1, 16/15, 6/5, 4/3, 3/2, 8/5, 9/5, 2/1

Bharata's *śuddha jāti*, the *Naiṣādī:* 1/1, 9/8, 5/4, 4/3, 3/2, 27/16, 15/8, 2/1
Ptolemy's Tense Diatonic, Lydian Mode: 1/1, 9/8, 5/4, 4/3, 3/2, 5/3, 15/8, 2/1

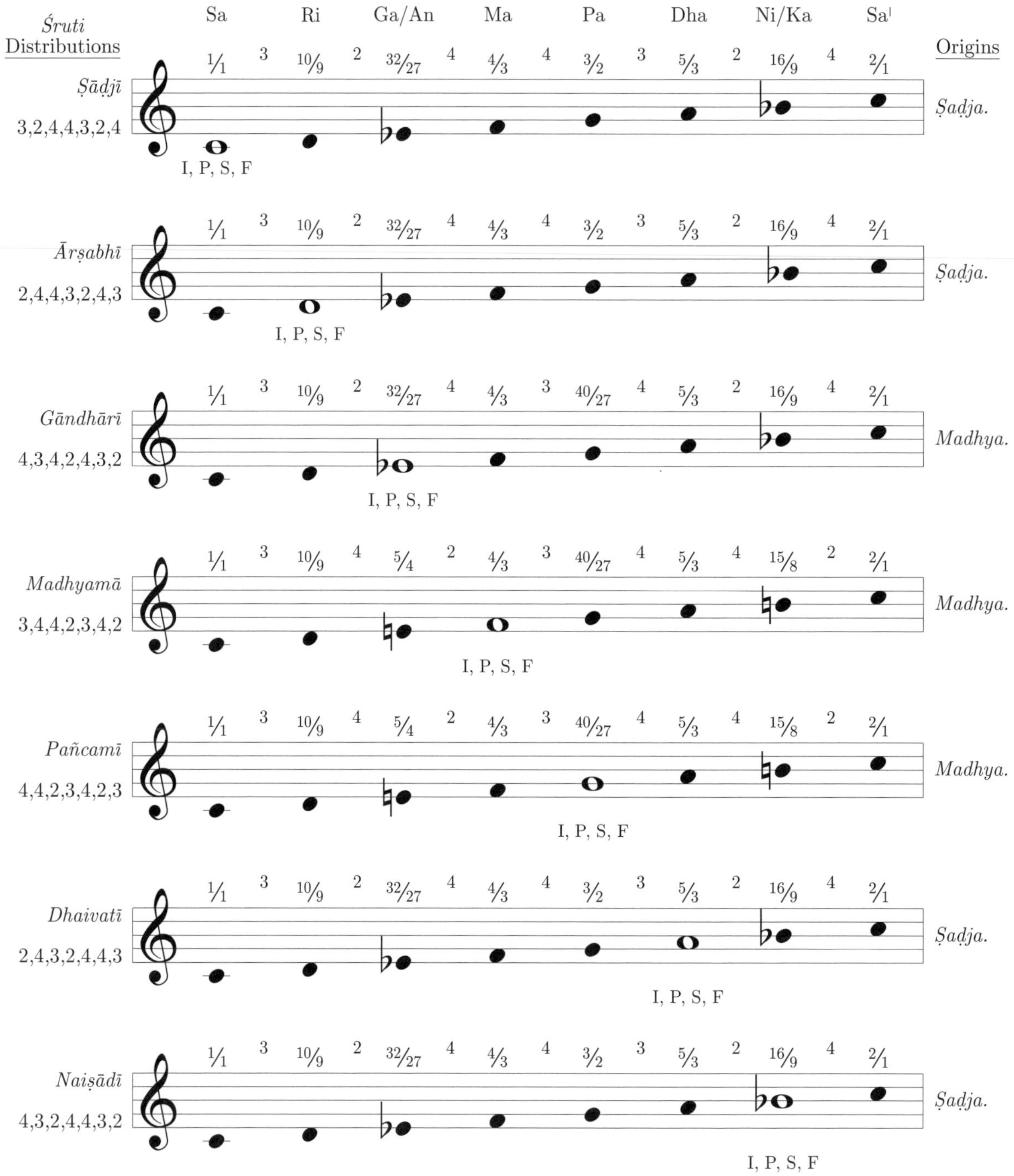

Figure 11.24 Bharata's seven *śuddha jātis*. Notice the systematic rotation of the I, P, S, and F notes from the first through the seventh tones of the seven *jātis*. As depicted in Figure 11.23, tone Ga = $^{32}/_{27}$, An = $^{5}/_{4}$, Ni = $^{16}/_{9}$, Ka = $^{15}/_{8}$, and Pa = $^{3}/_{2}$ or $^{40}/_{27}$.

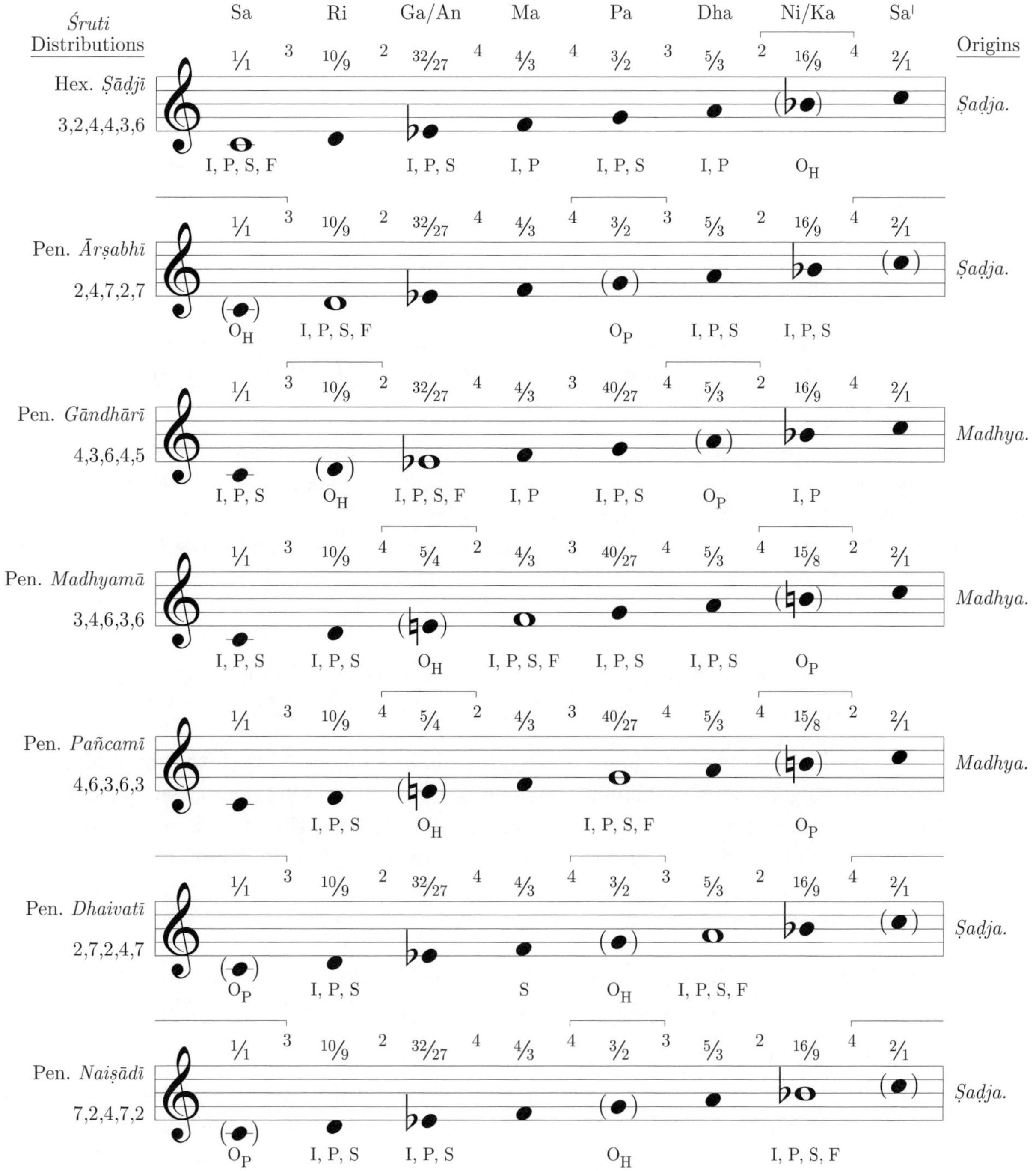

Figure 11.25 Bharata's seven *vikṛta jātis*. Notice the systematic rotation of the I, P, S, and F notes from the first through the seventh degrees of seven modes. For hexatonic modes, Bharata specifies the omission of notes marked O_H, and for pentatonic modes, the omission of notes marked O_H and O_P.

~ 11.26 ~

Figure 11.25 lists Bharata's seven *vikṛta jātis*. Of these, *Ṣāḍjī* is the only one defined as a pure hexatonic *jāti;* the remaining six *jātis* are described as both hexatonic and pentatonic modes. With respect to hexatonic and pentatonic *Ārṣabhī*, in *Nāṭyaśāstra 28.105–107* the Ghosh translation specifies the elimination of Ni and Pa, respectively. However, E. Wiersma-Te Nijenhuis mentions in the commentary of her translation of *Dattilam* (see Section 11.22) that the Sanskrit text of the Baroda edition of the *Nāṭyaśāstra* calls for the omission of Sa and Pa.[43] This construction also appears in *Dattilam 65*, and in a historically significant treatise entitled *Bṛhaddeśi* by Mataṅga (late first millennium A.D.). (See Section 11.30.)

> *Bṛh. [Anu. 148]* — In *Ārṣabhī . . . Ṣāḍava* [Hexatonic mode] is devoid of *Ṣaḍja* and *Auḍuvita* [Pentatonic mode] is devoid of *Ṣaḍja-Pañcama.*[44] (Text in brackets mine.)

I agree with the latter three descriptions because all three pentatonic *vikṛta jātis* with *Ṣaḍjagrāma* origins follow the clearly defined pattern of 1 omitted tone [C], 3 modal tones [D–E♭–F], 1 omitted tone [G], 2 modal tones [A–B♭], 1 omitted tone [C′].

In Figure 11.25, the column marked *Śruti* Distributions indicates that for the pentatonic *jātis*, the elimination of O_H and O_P results in three new *śruti* intervals:

$$5\ \textit{śrutis} = 3\ \textit{śrutis} + 2\ \textit{śrutis} = {}^{10}\!/_{9} \times {}^{16}\!/_{15} = {}^{32}\!/_{27} = 294.1\ ¢$$
$$6\ \textit{śrutis} = 4\ \textit{śrutis} + 2\ \textit{śrutis} = {}^{9}\!/_{8} \times {}^{16}\!/_{15} = {}^{6}\!/_{5} = 315.6\ ¢$$
$$7\ \textit{śrutis} = 4\ \textit{śrutis} + 3\ \textit{śrutis} = {}^{9}\!/_{8} \times {}^{10}\!/_{9} = {}^{5}\!/_{4} = 386.3\ ¢$$

The introduction of two different "minor third" intervals and one "major third" interval, respectively, immediately suggests the possibility that one of these *vikṛta jātis* may closely resemble the original Chinese pentatonic scale. (See Sections 11.2 and 11.5.) A ratio analysis of the pentatonic *Gāndhārī* shows that all but one of the translated *svara* ratios match the Chinese pentatonic; the pentatonic *Gāndhārī* has a 5-limit "major third," ratio 5/4, whereas the Chinese scale has a Pythagorean "major third," ratio 81/64.

Bharata's *vikṛta jāti*, the pentatonic *Gāndhārī:*	1/1, 9/8, 5/4, 3/2, 27/16, 2/1
Original Chinese pentatonic scale:	1/1, 9/8, 81/64, 3/2, 27/16, 2/1

Finally, notice that the method of extracting pentatonic modes from heptatonic modes is very reminiscent of the process by which Indonesian musicians define three different modes in *pélog paṭet.* (See Section 11.15.) Furthermore, the various *lakṣaṇa* properties — particularly the emphasis on the Final notes of the *śuddha* and *vikṛta jātis* — are also very similar to the hierarchical distributions of tones and cadences in *sléndro paṭet* and *pélog paṭet.* Although it is impossible to prove that the Indonesian civilization inherited these musical practices from India, consider a brief account by Curt Sachs, who traces the history and influence of the Indian civilization in Southeast Asia.

> History in the southeast began in the first centuries A.D. when it became an immense, though loosely knit, Indian colony. Nearly the entire coast from Burma to the boundaries of China . . . and the large Malayan islands, Sumatra and Java, formed numerous states under the predominance of Indian civilization.
>
> One state, the Sumatran empire of the Salendra dynasty, became particularly important, in the eighth century, extending its hegemony as far as western and Central Java. The outstanding monument that is left in

Central Java, the gigantic stupa at Borobudur, is a fertile source of information not only about Indian religion, architecture and sculpture in the Archipelago, but also about Hindu-Malayan music. Many musical scenes are depicted on the two thousand reliefs which adorn its walls.

There we find several kind of bells and cymbals; conical, cylindrical, hourglass and pot drums; cross flutes, single and double trumpets and shell trumpets; arched harps, stick-zithers and lutes. All instruments of ancient India are represented . . .

. . . [The post-Indian period] begins with the end of Sumatran supremacy in Java in the ninth century. A short time afterwards, about 920, Central Java was deserted, we do not know why, and East Java became the political and cultural center.[45] (Text in brackets mine.)

11.27

From an artistic perspective, the most remarkable aspects of Bharata's musical discussions are the *rasa*, or *expressive qualities* attributed to the *jātis*. The quaint English translation of *rasa* as "Sentiments" belies the powerful human emotions portrayed by the characters of ancient Indian plays:

> *Nāṭ. 6.15* — The eight Sentiments (*rasa*) recognized in drama are as follows: Erotic, Comic, Pathetic, Furious, Heroic, Terrible, Odious, and Marvelous.[46]

To emphasize the religious source of the *rasa*, Bharata associates each emotion with a principal deity in Hindu mythology:

> *Nāṭ. 6.44–45* — *Viṣṇu* is the god of the Erotic, *Pramathas* of the Comic, *Rudra* of the Furious, *Yama* of the Pathetic, *Śiva* (*Mahākāla*) of the Odious, *Yama* (*Kāla*) of the Terrible, *Indra* of the Heroic, and *Brahman* of the Marvelous Sentiments.[47]

In *Nāṭyaśāstra 6.45–83*, Bharata continues the discussion with a detailed description of the psychological complexities of every *rasa*. For example, in an amazingly insightful comment on human nature — rediscovered by Sigmund Freud (1856–1939) seventeen hundred years later — Bharata shrewdly observes, ". . . the Erotic Sentiment includes conditions available in all other Sentiments."[48]

In *Nāṭyaśāstra 29.1–16*, Bharata discusses the musical settings appropriate for every *rasa:*

> *Nāṭ. 29.13–14* — [For example,] a song in the Erotic and the Comic Sentiments should abound in many *Madhyamas* and *Pañcamas* (i.e., should be *Jātis* containing these notes in profusion), and in the Heroic, the Furious and the Marvelous Sentiments, songs should be made with many *Ṣaḍjas* and *Ṛṣabhas.* And the song in the Pathetic Sentiment should be full of many *Gāndhāras* and *Niṣādas* (lit. the seventh). Similarly a song in the Odious and the Terrible Sentiments should have many *Dhaivatas.*[49]

Ghosh explains the historical significance of these descriptions by observing

> As songs included in the performance of a play were to serve its principal purpose, which was the evocation of Sentiments, the author discusses here how *jātis* can be applied for this purpose. The seven notes which have

> already been assigned to different Sentiments (XXIX. 13–14), played an important part in this connection. All these ultimately led to the formation of the *Rāgas* in the later Indian Music, in which the particular melody-types were meant not only to create a Sentiment appropriate to a situation in a play, [i.e., appropriate to the stylized and predetermined situations of theatrical productions] but also to act on the hearers' emotion in such a way that they might experience in imagination the particular situations described in isolated songs as well.[50] (Text in brackets mine.)

In other words, this early synthesis of *lakṣaṇa properties* and *rasa qualities* provided the intellectual and emotional basis for the development of *rāga*. The principal distinction between *jāti* and *rāga* is that whereas the former exists in public or religious/theatrical environments, the latter thrives in private or meditative surroundings. All religious and theatrical productions have one element in common: ritual. Large events require the full cooperation of priests-performers and congregations-audiences. In a ritualistic setting, all participants come together with a common understanding over what is about to happen. An individual's artistic creation, and its effect on the hearer's imagination, stands in stark contrast to such communal experiences. Under these circumstances, the artist abandons public spectacles in favor of intimate performances. To voice the discoveries of inner explorations, the artist develops a technique largely absent from ritual: improvisation. In this context, the evolution of Indian music serves as a shining example of how an ancient civilization transformed public art to private art. To fully understand the transition from *jāti* to *rāga*, let us begin by focusing on an art form common to both musical expressions: the song.

~ 11.28 ~

Richard Widdess, a renowned scholar in the field, carefully distinguishes between two different songs — the *gītaka* and the *dhruvā* — of early Indian dramatic music.

> In considering the functions of the *jātis* in dramatic music, however, a distinction must be drawn between the mainly ritual role of music in the *pūrvaraṅga*, and its dramatic function during the play proper. [That is, starting in the *mukha* and afterwards. See Quote V.] [1] The purpose of the *pūrvaraṅga* was to propitiate the gods, especially *Śiva*, on whose blessing the success of the whole performance depended; it comprised a sequence of songs (*gītaka*) and dances of mainly ritual character. [2] During the play proper, which could be based on religious or secular subjects, music served as an occasional accompaniment or interlude: songs (*dhruvā*) were sung by the stage musicians at specific junctures to heighten the emotional force of the situation depicted by the actors. Some scenes evidently lent themselves to a high degree of musical elaboration . . . [and were] intended to be sung by the actors and musicians.[51] (Numbers and text in brackets mine.)

Recall the following quote in Section 11.23:

> *Dat. 97* — . . . anything which is sung is based on the *jātis*.

which establishes an unequivocal relation between the religious *and* secular music of the theater and the *jātis*. Since Dattila and Bharata only give detailed descriptions of the *jātis*, we may safely assume that these modes provided the musical structure of the *gītaka and dhruvā* repertory. Bharata clearly specifies the latter association:

IV

Nāṭ. 29.5 — The *Jātis* should be made in the application of *Dhruvās* by the producers, after [very carefully] considering the Sentiments, the action and the States [in a play].[52]

However, in *Nāṭyaśāstra 32.484*, Bharata suddenly contradicts himself and defines the two original parent scales, the *Madhyamagrāma* and *Ṣaḍjagrāma*, as bona fide musical modes. And in *Nāṭyaśāstra 32.485–486* he interjects three completely new modes without giving the *śruti* intervals of these modes. Furthermore, he does not indicate the *lakṣaṇa* properties of any of these five modes.

V

Nāṭ. 32.484 — Hence [i.e., after the *pūrvaraṅga*] [the] notes in the two *Grāmas* as well as the Overlapping note[s] [*sādhāraṇas*] should be applied to plays which express the various States.

32.485–486 — In the Opening of the drama there should be the songs {*gāna*[*ṃ*]} of the *Madhyama Grāma*, *Ṣaḍja* in the Progression, the Overlapping [*Sādhārita*] in the Development, *Pañcama*(*mī*) in the Pause, and *Kaiśika*(*kī*) in the conclusion.[53] (Text in brackets mine. Text in braces in Bharata's original text.)

With respect to the previously mentioned contradiction, Widdess observes

> Although the term *rāga* as such does not occur in it, this passage is regarded as important evidence for the early history of *rāga* . . . Verse [*32.484* of the Ghosh translation] tells us that we are referring not to the *pūrvaraṅga* . . . but to the play proper. The verse states that the modes appropriate to the play proper are the two *grāmas* [*Madhyamagrāma* and *Ṣaḍjagrāma*] — which elsewhere in [the *Nāṭyaśāstra*] are treated exclusively as scales, not modes — together with various *sādhāraṇas*, which might be interpreted as mixed modes, or modes into which the two secondary (*sādhāraṇa*) [overlapping] pitches are introduced. The two *grāmas* are furthermore connected with 'various emotions', showing that they are here regarded as more than simply tunings or interval-sets.[54] (Text in brackets mine.)

In other words, nowhere in the *Nāṭyaśāstra* does Bharata describe the *lakṣaṇa* properties nor the *rasa* qualities of the *Ma-grāma* and *Sa-grāma*. So, it is extremely doubtful that these two *grāmas* were endowed with technical and performance attributes during Bharata's time.

Approximately five centuries after Bharata, in a work entitled *Nāradīyā Śikṣā* by Nārada (mid-first millennium A.D.), we find the following seven carefully defined *grāmarāgas: Madhyamagrāma, Ṣaḍjagrāma, Ṣāḍava, Sādhārita, Pañcama, Kaiśika-madhyama*, and *Kaiśika*. Only five of these modes appear in *Nāṭyaśāstra 32.485–486*. This collection of seven *grāmarāgas* is of paramount importance to the history of Indian music because it represents the earliest origins of the modern *rāgas*. (See Section 11.31.) Due to the *incomplete and undefined* inclusion of these modes very near the end of the *Nāṭyaśāstra*, Chapter 32, Widdess suspects that this text ". . . probably constitutes a late accretion."[55] Although historically informative and relevant, we may also regard such "late" additions as spurious and anachronistic texts designed to bestow on Bharata unimaginable powers of prediction.

~ 11.29 ~

In Quote V, the five modes are *not* called *dhruvās* or *grāmarāgas*, but *gānas*, or songs. Since Bharata does not make a distinction between the musical function of the *dhruvās* and the *gānas*, consider Nijenhuis' possible explanation of the latter:

> The term *gāna* occurring in the older texts, including the *Nāradīyā Śikṣā*, may refer to the melodies to which the hymns (*sāman*) of the *Sāmaveda* were sung, and which are contained in the four manuals for chanting . . .[56]

Bharata's spurious text bestows on the five *gānas* ten expressive characteristics:

> *Nāṭ. 32.492* — That which [1] includes full notes, *Varṇas*, [2] is embellished by instruments, [3] relates to the three voice-registers, [4] has three *Yatis* and three *Mātrās*, [5] gives joy, [6] is harmonious (*sama*) [7] and delicate, [8] contains *Alaṃkāras*, [9] is performed with ease, and [10] has sweetness, is called a song {*gānam*}.[57] (Numbers in brackets mine. Text in braces in Bharata's original text.)

Nārada first describes the characteristics of his *grāmarāgas* as ". . . qualities of singing . . ."[58] and then offers detailed explanations of six of these characteristics plus four more, for a grand total of ten *guṇa* qualities. To match the order in *Nāṭyaśāstra 32.492*, Nijenhuis gives the following translation of Nārada's text, which begins with the phrase, "The qualities (*guṇa*) are: *pūrṇa* . . ."

> *Nār. 1.3.1* — [1] This is called *pūrṇa* (complete) . . . [2] This is called *rakta* (lovely) . . . [6] This is called *sama* (equal) . . . [7] This is called *ślakṣṇa* (soft) . . . [8] This is called *alaṅkṛta* (decorated) . . . [10] This is called *madhura* (sweet).[59] (Six sequentially matching numbers in brackets mine.)

These expressive characteristics of Bharata's *gānas* and Nārada's *grāmarāgas* are significant because they indicate a transitional period in the history of Indian music where song emerges as a flexible art form. That is, none of the ritualistically expressive *rasa* qualities of the ancient theater resemble the poetically expressive *guṇa* qualities of the Sāmavedic chants. An intimation that Bharata may have been aware of such a development occurs in *Nāṭyaśāstra 28.76*, where he uses the word *rāga* to describe the critical function of *aṃśa*, the Prominent note:

VI

> *Nāṭ. 28.76* — The *Aṃśa* [is that note in the song] on which its charm (*rāga*) depends, and from which the charm proceeds . . .[60]

Here *rāga* epitomizes an intrinsic quality, applicable not only to the *jātis* of dramatic music, but to all musical forms of expression.

The oldest extant reference to the word *grāmarāga* as an independently derived musical concept occurs in Nārada's *Nāradīyā Śikṣā*. Widdess translated this important passage as follows:

VII

> *Nār. 1.2.7* — They are called *grāmarāgas* on account of a particularity of musical pitch and aesthetic ethos (*svararāgaviśeṣeṇa grāmarāga iti smṛtāḥ*).[61]

Widdess then distinguishes between the old and new conceptualizations of music by noting

> But there is an important difference between *rāga* and *rasa*, one that is closely paralleled by the difference between *rāga* and *jāti*. In the aesthetic

> sense, the *rāga* of each song or mode is unique, whereas the *rasas* are very broad categories of feeling. Similarly, each musical *rāga*, in the technical sense, is unique, and precisely defined, whereas the *jātis* are comparatively broad modal categories.[62]

Quotes VI and VII express a common theme. Bharata and Nārada are aware that inspired musical performances require exceptional comprehension and understanding, without which music as an art does not exist. The former passage stresses the significance of a particular note, and the latter, of an entire mode.

11.30

Approximately one hundred years after Nārada's *Nāradīyā Śikṣā*, the same *grāmarāgas* appear in an extraordinary 7th or 8th century A.D. inscription at Kuḍimiyāmalai in the state of Madras.[63] This remarkable epigraph was engraved on a rock wall behind the Śikhānāthasvāmi temple. Although much of the text is obscure and insufficiently consistent, the basic seven *svara* — Sa, Ri, Ga, Ma, Pa, Dha, Ni — are precisely defined, as well as the two *svarasādhāraṇa: Kākalī Niṣāda* (abbreviated "Ka") and *Antara Gāndhāra* (abbreviated "A"). From this source, one is also able to determine the Initial, Prominent, and Final notes of each *grāmarāga*. It is highly significant that neither the *Nāradīyā Śikṣā* nor the Kuḍimiyāmalai Inscription mention *jātis*. Instead, both sources focus exclusively on *grāmarāgas*. We conclude, therefore, that in the second half of the first millennium A.D., Indian theorists made a concerted attempt to liberate music from the confines of ritualistic environments.

The first theorist to precisely define *rāga* was Mataṅga. In a translation by P.L. Sharma, this historically significant definition appears in *Bṛhaddeśi 261–266.*[64] Widdess translated this passage from a different source and identifies it as *Bṛhaddeśi 279–283:*

> *Bṛh. 279* — The form (*rūpa*) of the classic method (*mārga*) of *rāga*, which has ***not*** been stated by Bharata and others, is outlined by me in connection with practice (*lakṣya*) and theory (*lakṣaṇa*).
>
> In this connection, [there are two definitions of *rāga*,] first:
>
> *280* — In the opinion of the wise, that particularity of notes ***and*** melodic movements (*svaravarṇaviśeṣeṇa*), or that distinction of melodic sound (*dhvanibhedena*), by which one is delighted (*rajyate*), is *rāga*.
>
> Alternatively:
>
> *281* — That particularity of melodic sound (*dhvaniviśeṣa*), adorned with notes ***and*** melodic movements (*svaravarṇavibhūṣita*), which is pleasing (*rañjaka*) to the minds of men, is declared to be *rāga*.
>
> *282* — The definition [of *rāga*] is considered to comprise ***two*** elements: 'generality' (*sāmānya;* i.e. those features common to all *rāgas*) ***and*** 'particularity' (*viśeṣa;* i.e. those features peculiar to individual *rāgas*). 'Generality' is of four parts; 'particularity' [means] Predominant {Prominent note} and other [features].*
>
> *283* — Thus the etymology of the word *rāga* is explained. *Rāga* derives from *rañjana* (colouring): the etymology is stated.
>
> *This sentence seems to refer, first, to the four terms *vādī* 'Sonant', *saṃvādī* Consonant', *anuvādī* 'Assonant' and *vivādī* 'Dissonant'—fundamental

> intervallic relationships inherent in the musical system and hence common to all *rāgas* . . .; and secondly to the combination of melodic features (the position of the Predominant, etc.) that is unique to a particular *rāga* and by which it is distinguished.[65] (Bold italics and text in braces mine.)

Mataṅga's synthesis of "generality" and "particularity" is a familiar theme in Bharata's work. He too emphasizes in *Nāṭyaśāstra 28.23* (see Section 11.20) the general acoustic aspects of music, and in *Nāṭyaśāstra 28.74* (see Section 11.23), the particular technical properties of modes. The outstanding idea asserted by Mataṅga is that because pure *melodic sound* has the power to delight and please the listener, the concept of *rāga* alone justifies the development of a new theory of music.

Of the seven original *grāmarāgas*, Mataṅga describes only four in full detail. However, he also briefly mentions the origin of *Pañcama*. Here Mataṅga quotes Kaśyapa (mid-first millennium A.D.), an authority on music:

> *Bṛh. [Anu. 170] — Ṣāḍava, Pañcama, and Kaiśika obtain in Madhyamagrāma. Sādhārita and Kaiśika-madhyama, similarly, obtain in Ṣaḍjagrāma.*[66]

Mataṅga describes the four *grāmarāgas* in Chapter 3 of the *Bṛhaddeśi*,[67] and refers to them as *Śuddharāgas*, or pure *rāgas*. Furthermore, *Ṣāḍava* is called *Śuddhaṣāḍava*, *Sādhārita* is called *Śuddhasādhārita*, etc. This practice also occurs in Śārṅgadeva's *Saṅgītaratnākara*. As in the *Nāradīyā Śikṣā* and Kuḍimiyāmalai Inscription, the *Saṅgītaratnākara* mentions all seven original *grāmarāgas*.[68]

11.31

Refer to Figure 11.26, which documents the *grāmarāgas* as described in the latter four sources. In this figure, the texts are listed in chronological order: for each mode the oldest text appears first, followed by the second oldest, etc. Most importantly, Figure 11.26 presents us with two noteworthy considerations. (1) Observe that *Ṣaḍjagrāma* and *Madhyamagrāma* are here endowed with *lakṣaṇa*, which means that starting in approximately A.D. 500, musicians began considering these tunings as musical modes. This probably explains the term *grāmarāga: rāgas* derived from two musically defined *grāmas*. (2) Notice that contrary to first impression, Mataṅga and Śārṅgadeva derive the *Kaiśika-madhyama* not from *Madhyamagrāma*, but from *Ṣaḍjagrāma*.

Also, consider the following six common features:

(1) Where indicated, all sources agree on the origins of the *grāmarāgas*. In Figure 11.26, the order of the modes is the same as in the Kuḍimiyāmalai Inscription. In this arrangement, notice the alternating pattern of origins (*Madhyamagrāma*, *Ṣaḍjagrāma*, *Madhyamagrāma*, etc.).

(2) Where indicated, all sources agree that the systematic rotation of the I, P, and F notes is no longer relevant.

(3) Where indicated, all sources agree on the placement of F notes, which means (1) all F notes are restricted to either Ma or Pa, and (2) for all *grāmarāgas* attributed to *Ṣaḍjagrāma*, the F note is Ma.

(4) Where indicated, all sources agree with the *Nāṭyaśāstra* that P notes also represent I notes.

(5) Where indicated, the only disagreement with respect to the I–P combination is *Ṣāḍava:* Kuḍimiyāmalai Inscription identifies Sa as I and P notes, whereas *Bṛhaddeśi* and *Saṅgītaratnākara* identify Ma as I and P notes.

(6) Where indicated, *Ṣāḍava* and *Pañcama* are the only two modes that retain the ancient I–P–F combination.

Madhyamagrāma

	Origins	Sa	Ri		Ma	Pa	Dha		Sa$'$	*Śruti intervals starting on Sa*
Nāradīyā Śikṣā:				Ga			R	Ni		3,2,4,3,4,2,4
Kuḍimiyāmalai Inscription:		I, P		Ga	F			Ni		3,2,4,3,4,2,4
Saṅgītaratnākara:	*Madhya.*	I, P		Ga	F			Ka		3,2,4,3,4,4,2

Ṣaḍjagrāma

	Origins	Sa	Ri		Ma	Pa	Dha		Sa$'$	
Nāradīyā Śikṣā:				Ga				Ni		3,2,4,4,3,2,4
Kuḍimiyāmalai Inscription:		I, P		Ga	F			Ni		3,2,4,4,3,2,4
Saṅgītaratnākara:	*Ṣaḍja.*	I, P		An	F			Ka		3,4,2,4,3,4,2

Ṣāḍava

	Origins	Sa	Ri		Ma	Pa	Dha		Sa$'$	
Nāradīyā Śikṣā:	*Madhya.*			'Ga'				Ni		3,2,4,3,4,2,4
Kuḍimiyāmalai Inscription:		I, P		An	F			Ni		3,4,2,3,4,2,4
Bṛhaddeśī:	*Madhya.*			An	I, P, F			Ka		3,4,2,3,4,4,2
Saṅgītaratnākara:	*Madhya.*			An	I, P, F			Ka		3,4,2,3,4,4,2

Sādhārita

	Origins	Sa	Ri		Ma	Pa	Dha		Sa$'$	
Nāradīyā Śikṣā:				An				Ka		3,4,2,4,3,4,2
Kuḍimiyāmalai Inscription:		I, P		An	F			Ka		3,4,2,4,3,4,2
Bṛhaddeśī:	*Ṣaḍja.*	I, P		Ga	F			Ni		3,2,4,4,3,2,4
Saṅgītaratnākara:	*Ṣaḍja.*	I, P		Ga	F			Ni		3,2,4,4,3,2,4

Pañcama

	Origins	Sa	Ri		Ma	Pa	Dha		Sa$'$	
Nāradīyā Śikṣā:				An		F		Ni		3,4,2,3,4,2,4
Kuḍimiyāmalai Inscription:				An		I, P, F		Ni		3,4,2,3,4,2,4
[*Bṛhaddeśī:*	*Madhya.*]									
Saṅgītaratnākara:	*Madhya.*			An		I, P, F		Ka		3,4,2,3,4,4,2

Kaiśika-madhyama

	Origins	Sa	Ri		Ma	Pa	Dha		Sa$'$	
Nāradīyā Śikṣā:				'Ga'	F			Ka		3,2,4,4,3,4,2
Kuḍimiyāmalai Inscription:		I, P		An	F	O		Ka		3,4,2,7,4,2
Bṛhaddeśī:	*Ṣaḍja.*	I, P	O	Ga	F	O		Ka		5,4,7,4,2
Saṅgītaratnākara:	*Ṣaḍja.*	I, P	O	Ga	F	O		Ka		5,4,7,4,2

Kaiśika

	Origins	Sa	Ri		Ma	Pa	Dha		Sa$'$	
Nāradīyā Śikṣā:	*Madhya.*			'Ga'		F		Ka		3,2,4,3,4,4,2
Kuḍimiyāmalai Inscription:		I, P		An		F		Ka		3,4,2,3,4,4,2
Bṛhaddeśī:	*Madhya.*	I, P		Ga		F		Ka		3,2,4,3,4,4,2
Saṅgītaratnākara:	*Madhya.*	I, P		Ga		F		Ka		3,2,4,3,4,4,2

Figure 11.26 Seven *grāmarāgas* as described in four different sources ranging from *c.* A.D. 500 to *c.* 1200. These modes represent the earliest known *rāgas*.

For three modes, the *Nāradīyā Śikṣā* does not mention the identity of the third scale degree, hence the 'Ga' notation in Figure 11.26, which represents the default note. However, the *Nāradīyā Śikṣā* and the Kuḍimiyāmalai Inscription explicitly describe two *svarasādhāraṇa* of the *Sādhārita*, a mode attributed to *Ṣaḍjagrāma*. (Recall that in Bharata's time, musicians associated the two Overlapping notes only with *jātis* derived from *Madhyamagrāma;* Figure 11.24 shows that on a *vīṇā* tuned to modulated *Ma-grāma* scales, Pa = $^{40}/_{27}$.)[69] Since all modes attributed to *Ṣaḍjagrāma* sound a "just fifth," and since the *Sādhārita* contains two *svarasādhāraṇa*, this *grāmarāga* specifies An = $^{5}/_{4}$, Pa = $^{3}/_{2}$, and Ka = $^{15}/_{8}$.[70] Consequently, on a tuned *vīṇā*, the following *śruti* intervals of the *Sādhārita* — 3, 4, 2, 4, 3, 4, 2 — result in *svara* ratios where all but the second degree match Ptolemy's Tense Diatonic in the ancient Lydian Mode:[71]

$$^{1}/_{1},\ ^{10}/_{9},\ ^{5}/_{4},\ ^{4}/_{3},\ ^{3}/_{2},\ ^{5}/_{3},\ ^{15}/_{8},\ ^{2}/_{1}$$

Unlike the *Naiṣādī*,[72] a comparable *śuddha jāti* that has *svara* ratios $^{5}/_{4}$, $^{3}/_{2}$, and $^{15}/_{8}$ starting on Ni or B♭, the *Sādhārita* may be played on a *vīṇā* starting on Sa or C. We conclude, therefore, that an increased interest in *melodic sound* and *melodic features* may have inspired musicians to tune *svarasādhāraṇa* in *grāmarāgas* derived from *Ṣaḍjagrāma*. The profound melodic simplicity and beauty of *Sādhārita*-like modes has enamored musicians for hundreds of years the world over.

Finally, notice that the double-headed arrows in Figure 11.26 point to identical modes. With respect to Ga and Ni, the *Nāradīyā Śikṣā* gives the same description to *Madhyamagrāma* and *Ṣāḍava;* however, Nārada defines Dha in the former mode as a Rare note. Similarly, with respect to An and Ni, the Kuḍimiyāmalai Inscription assigns the same identity to *Ṣāḍava* and *Pañcama;* however, note the differences in the placements of the I and P notes, and the F notes. Also, with respect to An and Ka, the *Saṅgītaratnākara* gives the same description to *Ṣāḍava* and *Pañcama*, and with respect to Ga and Ka, it gives the same description to *Madhyamagrāma* and *Kaiśika;* however, note the difference in the placement of the I, P, and F notes in the former, and the F note in the latter. Lastly, with respect to An and Ka, the Kuḍimiyāmalai Inscription assigns the same description to *Sādhārita* and *Kaiśika-madhyama;* however, observe the omission of Pa in the latter mode. This latter difference seems obvious on paper, but is less noticeable during musical performances. In modern times, many *rāgas* have five, six, or all seven tones in common. The tradition of distinguishing between such *rāgas* according to varying technical properties continues to this day. (See Section 11.35.)

South India

11.32

An imaginary east-to-west diagonal from Calcutta, near the Bay of Bengal, to Mumbai (Bombay), on the coast of the Arabian Sea, roughly divides the subcontinent of India into two geographical and cultural areas called North India and South India. The former region is known for Hindustani music, and the latter, for Carnatic music. Although both cultures evolved from the same ancient tradition, by the 17th century each had developed a separate musical vocabulary and unique styles in the performance of *rāgas*.

Before we discuss these two traditions, let us first address the question, "What is a *rāga*?" The answer is extremely complex because *rāgas* are musical expressions that continuously change in time. Most *rāgas* consist of two basic elements: (1) a set of technical definitions and instructions, transformed into music through (2) spontaneously improvised performances.[73] Because Indian music is inherently melodic in nature, musicians have created literally thousands of different *rāgas*. In the 16th and 17th centuries, theorists attempted to organize this incomprehensible plethora of *rāgas* by creating organizational systems based on mathematically defined tunings and combinatorics. However, because such efforts compelled theorists and musicians to closely examine the quintessential relation between the technical and musical aspects of *rāgas*, these systems profoundly influenced not only intellectual definitions of *rāgas*, but artistic interpretations as well.

In the next five sections, we will examine the evolution of South Indian *rāgas* in the writings of Rāmāmātya (fl. *c.* 1550), Venkaṭamakhi (fl. *c.* 1620), and Govinda (*c.* 1800). These three writers focused on a theme common to all organizational systems, namely, the principle of abstraction. Rāmāmātya was the first Indian theorist to formulate a system based on a mathematically determined tuning. He defined (1) a theoretical 14-tone scale, (2) a practical 12-tone tuning, and (3) a distinction between abstract *mēḷa rāgas* and musical *janya rāgas*. He then combined these three concepts to identify 20 *mēḷa rāgas*, under which he classified more than 60 *janya rāgas*. Venkaṭamakhi extended Rāmāmātya's approach, and proposed a system that consists of 72 heptatonic permutations called *mēḷakartas*. He then identified 19 *mēḷakartas*, which he used to classify dozens of *janya rāgas*. Finally, Govinda extended Venkaṭamakhi's basic concept, and defined the present-day system, which consists of 72 modern *mēḷa rāgas*, or 72 theoretically constructed heptatonic scales.

We may think of these developments as representing three *interrelated* stages in the history of South Indian music. Rāmāmātya, Venkaṭamakhi, and Govinda created organizational systems based on the principle of *musical abstraction*, *combinatorial abstraction*, and *theoretical abstraction*, respectively. As such, these underlying principles do not tell us how to understand the resulting systems. Therefore, consider the following three interpretations. In the writings of Rāmāmātya and Venkaṭamakhi, the terms *mēḷa rāgas* and *mēḷakartas*, respectively, refer to prototypes — or collections of seven tones — that function as *abstract rāga*-categories. In the 16th, 17th, and 18th centuries, theorists and musicians used *mēḷas* for only *one* purpose: to organize and classify musical *rāgas*. Consequently, in the original sense, *mēḷas* never represented regular scales, or musical *rāgas*. Figure 11.30 shows two *mēḷas* identified by Rāmāmātya enclosed in separate circles to convey the impression of pools of seven tones that similar musical *janya rāgas* have in common. In most texts, *mēḷas* are represented as linear sequences of notes on a treble staff. Westerners, when presented with progressions of notes in regular ascending and/or descending order, unwittingly interpret such sequences as scales. Because this tendency seriously interferes with a historical understanding of South Indian music, I have chosen to equate the *original mēḷas* with the terms *rāga*-categories, prototypes, and *tone pools*.

This definition of *mēḷa* also applies to Venkaṭamakhi's 72 *mēḷakartas* in Figure 11.32. Here too, the reader should not confuse sequential progressions of tones in the lower and upper tetrachords with scales or *rāgas*. If I had chosen to ignore the logical and mathematical sequences of tones required to generate this twelve-by-six array, then Venkaṭamakhi's combinatorics would be completely incomprehensible. In the final analysis, Venkaṭamakhi's *mēḷakartas* also function as abstract *rāga*-categories, prototypes, or tone pools.

Finally, in Govinda's text, the term *mēḷa rāgas* does mean scales — or heptatonic sequences of tones in regular order — which he used to identify (1) 72 *abstract rāga*-categories or prototypes, and (2) a new class of 72 *musical mēḷa rāgas*. Here, for the first time in the history of Indian music, the theoretical concept of a symmetric scale has a musical function. (Therefore, while we may consider Govinda's *mēḷa rāgas* as prototypes, we should *not* think of them as tone pools.) By definition, all *mēḷa rāgas* must consist of seven straight ascending and seven straight descending tones, and a given *mēḷa rāga* as *musical rāga* must include *all* seven tones in at least one *krama* (lit. *straight*) or *vakra* (lit. *crooked*, or *zigzag*) ascending and descending sequence. As discussed in Section 11.38, modern writers have deplored the latter development because theoretically constructed scales tend to obliterate unique technical and musical characteristics for which musical *rāgas* are known. Such oversimplifications, they argue, lead to mechanized and homogenized musical performances.

11.33

Approximately three hundred years after Śārṅgadeva's *Saṅgītaratnākara* — an encyclopedic work used by musicians to this day — Rāmāmātya wrote a short work in 1550 entitled *Svaramēlakalānidhi*. In this 25-page treatise, Rāmāmātya revolutionized the theory and practice of music not only in South India, but in North India as well. Near the beginning of the treatise, Rāmāmātya explains his motivations for writing the *Svaramēlakalānidhi*, and thereby demonstrates that he was fully aware of the intellectual and musical challenges of his time.

> *Sva. 1.24* — The Science of Music has, both ***in theory and practice***, degenerated into conflicting views. Let [me] reconcile . . . all (the conflicting views) and write a (new) science.[74] (Bold italics and text in brackets mine.)

Later writers and theorists followed Rāmāmātya's lead regarding these three incipient contributions:

(1) Rāmāmātya defined a theoretical 14-tone scale, which he realized as a 12-tone tuning.

(2) He specified this tuning by describing the locations of six frets on his *vīṇā*.

(3) Based on this 12-tone scale and tuning, Rāmāmātya defined 20 *mēḷa rāgas* and used them to classify over 60 *janya rāgas*.

In South India, Venkaṭamakhi theoretically resolved the *mēḷa* issue seventy years after the publication of the *Svaramēlakalānidhi*, but in North India, the classification of *rāgas* according to *ṭhāṭs* remains steeped in controversy to this day. The first theorist who attempted to expand the traditional 7-tone scale was Śārṅgadeva. In a well-known passage,[75] Śārṅgadeva defined twelve *vikṛta svaras* (modified notes), which he assigned to locations on or between the positions held by the *śuddha svaras* (pure notes) in the traditional Sa–Ri–Ga–Ma–Pa–Dha–Ni–Sa' sequence. Unfortunately, Śārṅgadeva's idea remained obscure because he did not address two key difficulties. (1) He neglected to observe that five of these twelve *vikṛta svaras* are enharmonically equivalent and, therefore, musically identical; this lack of precision probably confused later generations of readers. (2) He did not offer a tuning example by which musicians could test his theory. In contrast, Rāmāmātya not only fully comprehended the first problem, but also dispelled the second by giving a verifiable demonstration on his fretted *vīṇā*.

Due to the historical significance of the *Svaramēlakalānidhi*, let us first review Rāmāmātya's description of the *Ṣaḍjagrāma:*

> *Sva. 2.27–30* — The *Svaras* arise from the *Śrutis* in such a manner that *Ṣaḍja* takes the fourth *Śruti* of the *Vīṇā; Ṛṣabha*, the seventh; *Gāndhāra*, the ninth; *Madhyama*, the thirteenth; *Pañcama*, the seventeenth; *Dhaivata*, the twentieth; and *Niṣāda*, the twenty-second.[76]

Refer to Figure 11.27(a), Rows 1 and 2, which show the familiar seven ancient *śuddha svaras* and their modern counterparts, respectively. In *Svaramēlakalānidhi 5.17*, Rāmāmātya states, "All . . . *Rāgas* are those of the *Ṣaḍjagrāma*,"[77] which tells us that by the 16th century, the *Madhyamagrāma*, and with it, the concept of *grāma* origins were considered obsolete relics of the past. (See Section 11.35.) Now, Figure 11.27(a), Row 3, illustrates the *śruti* distributions of the *śuddha svaras* as described by Rāmāmātya. Many Indian theorists prefer to number the *Sa-grāma* by starting on Ni, or four *śrutis* before (below) Sa. However, because Ni *never* functions as a first degree or tonic of the *Sa-grāma*, this distribution has no effect on the traditional locations of the ancient *śuddha svaras* as enumerated in Figure 11.27(a), Row 4. In the following passage, Rāmāmātya confirms this point beyond doubt, establishes the existence of seven *śuddha svaras* and seven *symmetric vikṛta svaras*, and concludes with his critique of Śārṅgadeva's twelve *vikṛta svaras:*

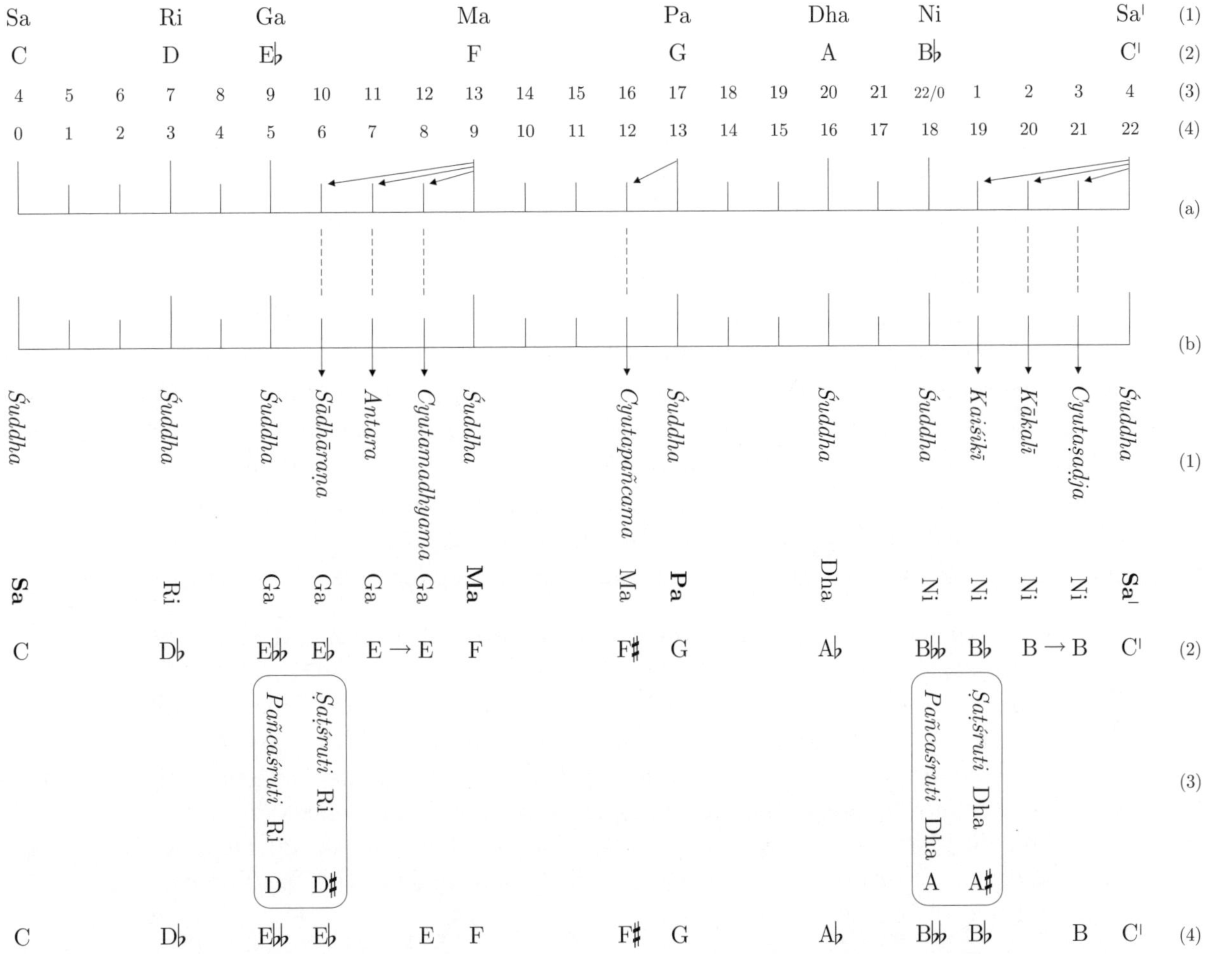

Figure 11.27 Rāmāmātya's original 14-tone scale, simplified on his *śuddha mēḷa vīṇā* as a 12-tone tuning. (a) Arrows pointing in a downward direction toward Sa show that Rāmāmātya conceived of his seven *vikṛta svaras* as reduced or flattened tones. (b) Rāmāmātya's distribution of *vikṛta svaras* in 1-*śruti* intervals indicates that the ratio analyses depicted in Figures 11.22–11.25 no longer apply. Furthermore, all *śuddha svaras* — except Sa, Ma, Pa, and Sa' — now sound one "semitone" lower.

> *Sva. 2.32–33* — These seven *Svaras*, beginning with *Ṣaḍja*, are called *Śuddha Svaras.* While, the *Vikṛta Svaras* are also seven. In all, there are fourteen *Svaras* — *Śuddha* and *Vikṛta.*
>
> *33–34* — How is it that . . . only *seven Vikṛta Svaras* [are given here], while Śārṅgadeva mentioned, in his *Saṅgītaratnākara*, so many as *twelve*?
>
> *34–38* — It is true that, from the theoretical point of view, the number *twelve* may be desirable. But, ***in actual practice***, there are only seven *Vikṛta Svaras*, as being different from the seven *Śuddha Svaras.*[78] (Bold italics mine.)

Rāmāmātya then accounts for the five enharmonic equivalents in Śārṅgadeva's text, and continues by giving the definitions of his own seven *vikṛta svaras:*

> *Sva. 2.44–49* — *'Cyutaṣaḍja'* is the name given to that *Ṣaḍja* which gives up its own fourth *Śruti* and takes the third one. The same rule equally

> applies to *'Cyutamadhyama'* and *'Cyutapañcama'.* When *Śuddha Madhyama* takes the first *Gāndhāra Śruti*, it is called *'Sādhāraṇa Gāndhāra';* but when the same *Śuddha Madhyama* takes the second *Gāndhāra Śruti*, it goes by the name of *'Antara Gāndhāra'.* When, again, *Śuddha Ṣaḍja* takes the first *Niṣāda Śruti*, it is called by expert musicians *'Kaiśikī Niṣāda';* but when it takes the second *Niṣāda Śruti*, it goes by the name of *'Kākalī Niṣāda'.* Thus, the seven (*Vikṛta Svaras*) have been described.[79]

(The prefix *cyuta* means *lowered*, and the modern term *sādhāraṇa* means *common*, or *ordinary.*) According to this text, all seven *vikṛta svaras* are defined by three different *śruti* reductions of Sa and Ma, and a 1-*śruti* reduction of Pa. Arrows in Figure 11.27(a) illustrate Rāmāmātya's tendency to define the *vikṛta svaras* as lowered tones, and the vertical dashed lines that lead to Figure 11.27(b) indicate the locations of the *vikṛta svaras* on his 22-*śruti* scale. However, because in North and South Indian music the Sa–Pa interval represents ratio $3/2$ — or an immutable consonance — Rāmāmātya associates *Cyutaṣaḍja* with Ni and calls it '*Cyutaṣaḍja* Ni', and associates *Cyutapañcama* with Ma and calls it '*Cyutapañcama* Ma'. As indicated in Figure 11.27(b), Rows 1 and 2, Rāmāmātya assigns seven alternate names to the following *śuddha* and *vikṛta svaras:*

> *Sva. 2.49–57* — . . . [1] On account of its identity with *Niṣāda*, *Cyutaṣaḍja* is also called *Cyutaṣaḍja* Ni. [2] On account of its identity with *Gāndhāra*, *Cyutamadhyama* is also called by me *Cyutamadhyama* Ga. [3] On account of its identity with *Madhyama*, *Cyutapañcama* is also called by me *Cyutapañcama* Ma . . . [4] *Śuddha Gāndhāra* [E𝄫] is called by me *Pañcaśruti* Ri [D] . . . [5] *Sādhāraṇa Gāndhāra* [E♭] is, in practice, also called *Ṣaṭśruti* Ri [D♯]. [6] Likewise . . . *Śuddha Niṣāda* [B𝄫] is called *Pañcaśruti* Dha [A]; [and] . . . [7] *Kaiśikī Niṣāda* [B♭] is called *Ṣaṭśruti* Dha [A♯].[80] (Numbers and text in brackets mine.)

(*Pañcaśruti* defines a 5-*śruti* interval above Sa or Pa, and *ṣaṭśruti*, a 6-*śruti* interval above Sa or Pa.) As indicated in Figure 11.27(b), Row 3, the latter four enharmonic equivalents — D, D♯, A, A♯ — are absolutely vital to South Indian music because they enable theorists and musicians to describe chromatic intervals without notating two consecutive *svaras* of the same name. For example, in his definition of *Śrī-rāga* (see Section 11.35), Rāmāmātya correctly describes the first chromatic step as a *Pañcaśruti* Ri [D]–*Sādhāraṇa* Ga [E♭] interval; although he could have described it as a *Śuddha* Ga [E𝄫]–*Sādhāraṇa* Ga [E♭] interval, this notation is incorrect because it utilizes two consecutive Ga's.

In Section 11.34, we will examine the tuning of Rāmāmātya's *vīṇā*. This discussion will show that the ratio analyses depicted in Figures 11.22–11.25 no longer apply to Figure 11.27. Note that Rāmāmātya distributed his *vikṛta svaras* in 1-*śruti* intervals, a division strictly avoided in all ancient texts. Furthermore, a comparison between Figure 11.27(a), Row 2, and Figure 11.27(b), Row 2, reveals that all *śuddha svaras* — except Sa, Ma, Pa, and Sa$^{\prime}$ — now sound one "semitone" lower. Consequently, former *Śuddha* Ri [D] sounds D♭, former *Śuddha* Ga [E♭] sounds E𝄫, former *Śuddha* Dha [A] sounds A♭, and former *Śuddha* Ni [B♭] sounds B𝄫. Finally, with respect to Figure 11.27(b), Row 4, Rāmāmātya made a deliberate decision *not* to include frets for *Antara* Ga [E] and *Kākalī* Ni [B], and thereby tuned a 12-tone scale on his *vīṇā*.

∼ 11.34 ∼

During the second half of the first millennium A.D., ancient harp-*vīṇās* were gradually replaced by stick-zithers, initially called *ālāpinī vīṇās*. The latter instruments had only one string. However, in later centuries they were built with two and three strings. When compared to harp-*vīṇās*, zither-*vīṇās* have two distinguishing features. (1) All playing strings are identical in length. (2) Although the *ālāpinī vīṇā* from the 7th century A.D. did not have frets, by the 13th century, the *kinnarī vīṇā* had 12 to 14 frets.[81] Rāmāmātya's *śuddha mēḷa vīṇā*, presumably built to demonstrate the feasibility of his 12-tone scale, had four open stings tuned to *anumandra* (very low) Sa, ratio 1/1 [C], *anumandra* Pa, ratio 3/2 [G], *mandra* (low) Sa, ratio 2/1 [C′], and *mandra* Ma, ratio 8/3 [F′]. Because Rāmāmātya's tuning description does not refer to "octave" equivalents, the following text includes bracketed notes with primes [′] to indicate pitches that sound one "octave" higher. We will go on to discuss the enharmonic conflict between C♯/D♭ and F♯/G♭ found below.

> *Sva. 3.26–31* — . . . On the ***first*** *Anumandra Sa*-wire [C], should be placed frets Nos. 1, 2, 3, 4, 5, 6, so that they may produce respectively the following *Svaras: Śuddha* Ri [D♭], *Śuddha* Ga [E𝄫], *Sādhārana* Ga [E♭], *Cyutamadhyama* Ga [E], *Śuddha* Ma [F], and *Cyutapañcama* Ma [F♯].
>
> *31–34* — We shall consider what *Svaras* these six frets produce on the other three (upper) wires. On the ***second*** wire, called *Anumandra Pañcama* [G], the same six frets produce respectively the following *Svaras: Śuddha* Dha [A♭], *Śuddha* Ni [B𝄫], *Kaiśikī* Ni [B♭], *Cyutaṣaḍja* Ni [B], *Śuddha* Sa [C′], and *Śuddha* Ri [not D♭′, **but** C♯′].
>
> *35–36* — The two *Svaras*, namely, *Śuddha* Sa [C′] and *Śuddha* Ri [C♯′] produced on the second wire, ***occur again*** on the third wire . . . and are therefore of ***no use on the second wire***.
>
> *37–39* — The *Svaras*, which the same six frets produce on the ***third*** *Mandra Sa*-wire [C′], are, as in the case of the *Anumandra Sa*-wire, as follows: *Śuddha* Ri [D♭′], *Śuddha* Ga [E𝄫′], *Sādhārana* Ga [E♭′], *Cyutamadhyama* Ga [E′], *Śuddha* Ma [F′], and *Cyutapañcama* Ma [F♯′].
>
> *39–40* — Since *Śuddha* Ma [F′] and *Cyutapañcama* Ma [F♯′], ***occur again*** on the fourth wire, they are of ***no use on the third wire***.
>
> *41–43* — The *Svaras*, which the same six frets produce on the ***fourth*** *Mandra Ma*-wire [F′], are: *Cyutapañcama* Ma [not F♯′, **but** G♭′], *Śuddha* Pa [G′], *Śuddha* Dha [A♭′], *Śuddha* Ni [B𝄫′], *Kaiśikī* Ni [B♭′], and *Cyutaṣaḍja* Ni [B′].[82] (Bold italics and text in brackets mine.)

Since there is no historical evidence that an Indian mathematician in *c.* A.D. 1550 calculated the 12th root of 2 (i.e., before Chu Tsai-yü in 1584, and before Simon Stevin in 1585; see Section 11.20), we will assume that Rāmāmātya described a just intoned tuning. This conclusion is also supported in *Svaramēlakalānidhi 3.35–36* and *3.39–40*. Before we discuss these two passages, let us first examine Rāmāmātya's description in full detail. Refer to Figure 11.28, which shows his fret design and gives a ratio analysis of the text. The six steps below describe how Rāmāmātya may have determined the locations of his six frets.

(1) Locate String IV, Fret 2 [G′] to sound an "octave" above *Open String* II [G].
(2) Locate String IV, Fret 4 [B𝄫′] to sound an "octave" above String II, Fret 2 [B𝄫].
(3) Locate String IV, Fret 6 [B′] to sound an "octave" above String II, Fret 4 [B].
(4) Locate String II, Fret 5 [C′] to sound an "octave" above *Open String* I [C].
(5) Locate String II, Fret 3 [B♭] to sound an "octave" below String IV, Fret 5 [B♭′].
(6) Locate String II, Fret 1 [A♭] to sound an "octave" below String IV, Fret 3 [A♭′].

In the following passage, Rāmāmātya confirms this basic approach to fretting his *vīṇā:*

> *Sva. 3.44–62* — . . . Inasmuch as the . . . *Śuddha* Ni [B𝄫], produced on the second wire by the second fret, is of the same value as the *Śuddha* Ni

> [B♭♭′], produced on the fourth wire by the fourth fret . . . Inasmuch, again as the . . . *Cyutaṣaḍja* Ni [B], produced on the second wire by the fourth fret, is of the same value as the . . . *Cyutaṣaḍja* Ni [B′], produced on the fourth wire by the sixth fret . . . Inasmuch, again, as the . . . *Kaiśikī* Ni [B♭′], produced on the fourth wire by the fifth fret, is of the same value as the . . . *Kaiśikī* Ni [B♭], produced on the second wire by the third fret . . . Inasmuch, further again, as the . . . *Śuddha* Dha [A♭′], produced on the fourth wire by the third fret, is of the same value as the . . . *Śuddha* Dha [A♭], produced on the second wire by the first fret; all the *Svaras* have been shown to be of definitely determined values. In this manner Rāmāmātya determined the values of all the *Svaras* produced on all the four wires by all the six frets.[83]

Consider now the two passages in question. In *Svaramēlakalānidhi 3.35–36*, Rāmāmātya's first observation that C′ on String II, Fret 5 sounds the same tone as Open String III is true, but his second observation that C♯′ on String II (Fret 6) sounds the same tone as D♭′ on String III (Fret 1)

	I	II	III	IV
	Anumandra Sa [C] 1/1	*Anumandra* Pa [G] 3/2	*Mandra* Sa [C′] 2/1 [1/1]	*Mandra* Ma [F′] 8/3 [4/3]
Nut				
1	*Śuddha* Ri [D♭] 256/243	*Śuddha* Dha [A♭] 128/81	*Śuddha* Ri [D♭′]* 256/243	*Cyutapañcama* Ma [G♭′]† 1024/729
2	*Pañcaśruti* Ri [D] *Śuddha* Ga [E♭♭] 9/8	*Pañcaśruti* Dha [A] *Śuddha* Ni [B♭♭] 27/16	*Pañcaśruti* Ri [D′] *Śuddha* Ga [E♭♭′] 9/8	*Śuddha* Pa [G′] 3/2
3	*Ṣaṭśruti* Ri [D♯] *Sādhāraṇa* Ga [E♭] 32/27	*Ṣaṭśruti* Dha [A♯] *Kaiśikī* Ni [B♭] 16/9	*Ṣaṭśruti* Ri [D♯′] *Sādhāraṇa* Ga [E♭′] 32/27	*Śuddha* Dha [A♭′] 128/81
4	*Cyutamadhyama* Ga [E] 81/64	*Cyutaṣaḍja* Ni [B] 243/128	*Cyutamadhyama* Ga [E′] 81/64	*Pañcaśruti* Dha [A′] *Śuddha* Ni [B♭♭′] 27/16
5	*Śuddha* Ma [F] 4/3	*Śuddha* Sa′ [C′] 2/1	*Śuddha* Ma [F′] 4/3	*Ṣaṭśruti* Dha [A♯′] *Kaiśikī* Ni [B♭′] 16/9
6	*Cyutapañcama* Ma [F♯] 729/512	*Śuddha* Ri [C♯′]* 2187/2048	*Cyutapañcama* Ma [F♯′]† 729/512	*Cyutaṣaḍja* Ni [B′] 243/128

Figure 11.28 Rāmāmātya's fretting and tuning of his *śuddha mēḷa vīṇā*. This 12-tone scale marked a radical departure from traditional tunings in both North and South India. Soon after the publication of the *Svaramēlakalānidhi*, many Indian musicians and theorists began exploring the musical possibilities of 12-tone scales. Contrary to Rāmāmātya's text, the two pairs of pitches marked * and † are not identical. (Fret locations to scale.)

is not true. Similarly, in *Svaramēlakalānidhi 3.39–40*, Rāmāmātya's first observation that F$^{|}$ on String III, Fret 5 sounds the same tone as Open String IV is true, but his second observation that F♯$^{|}$ on String III (Fret 6) sounds the same tone as G♭$^{|}$ on String IV (Fret 1) is also not true. In both cases, Rāmāmātya insists that because the first observations are true, the second observations are by association also true. Indeed, if this were a 12-tone equal tempered tuning, then the second observations would be true, but would not require comment. In other words, Rāmāmātya is forcing the issue and avoiding an inevitable encounter with the comma of Pythagoras.[84] To understand why the second observation in *Svaramēlakalānidhi 3.35–36* is untrue, refer to Figure 11.29(a). Here a pattern of horizontal arrows that begins on String IV, Fret 2 indicates a *descending* sequence of "fourths," ratio $4/3$. Now, if we simplify "octave" equivalents,[85] or if we ignore changes in register indicated by the diagonal arrows, then this sequence of descending $4/3$'s emerges:

$$\downarrow 3/2\ [\text{G}],\ 9/8\ [\text{D}],\ 27/16\ [\text{A}],\ 81/64\ [\text{E}],\ 243/128\ [\text{B}],\ 729/512\ [\text{F}\sharp],\ 2187/2048\ [\text{C}\sharp] \qquad \text{(A)}$$

Similarly, in Figure 11.29(b) a pattern of horizontal arrows that begins on String II, Fret 5 indicates an *ascending* sequence of "fourths." Again, if we simplify "octave" equivalents, then this sequence of ascending $4/3$'s emerges:

$$\uparrow 2/1\ [\text{C}],\ 4/3\ [\text{F}],\ 16/9\ [\text{B}\flat],\ 32/27\ [\text{E}\flat],\ 128/81\ [\text{A}\flat],\ 256/243\ [\text{D}\flat],\ 1024/729\ [\text{G}\flat] \qquad \text{(B)}$$

Observe carefully that if we begin on $3/2$ [G], then after six descending $4/3$'s, Sequence A generates $2187/2048$ [C♯], or the *apotome* [see Sections 10.15 and 10.18, and Figure 10.16(a)]; and if we begin on $2/1$ [C], then after five ascending $4/3$'s, Sequence B generates $256/243$ [D♭], or the *limma* [see Sections 10.10, 10.15, 10.18, and Figure 10.16(b)]. These two tones are not identical; the former is a comma of Pythagoras *sharper* than the latter: $2187/2048 \div 256/243 = 2187/2048 \times 243/256 = 531441/524288$. We also encounter the same discrepancy in the second observation of *Svaramēlakalānidhi 3.39–40.* After five descending $4/3$'s, Sequence A produces $729/512$ [F♯], whereas after six ascending $4/3$'s, Sequence B produces $1024/729$ [G♭]. Divide the former by the latter, and find once again the comma of Pythagoras: $729/512 \div 1024/729 = 729/512 \times 729/1024 = 531441/524288$.

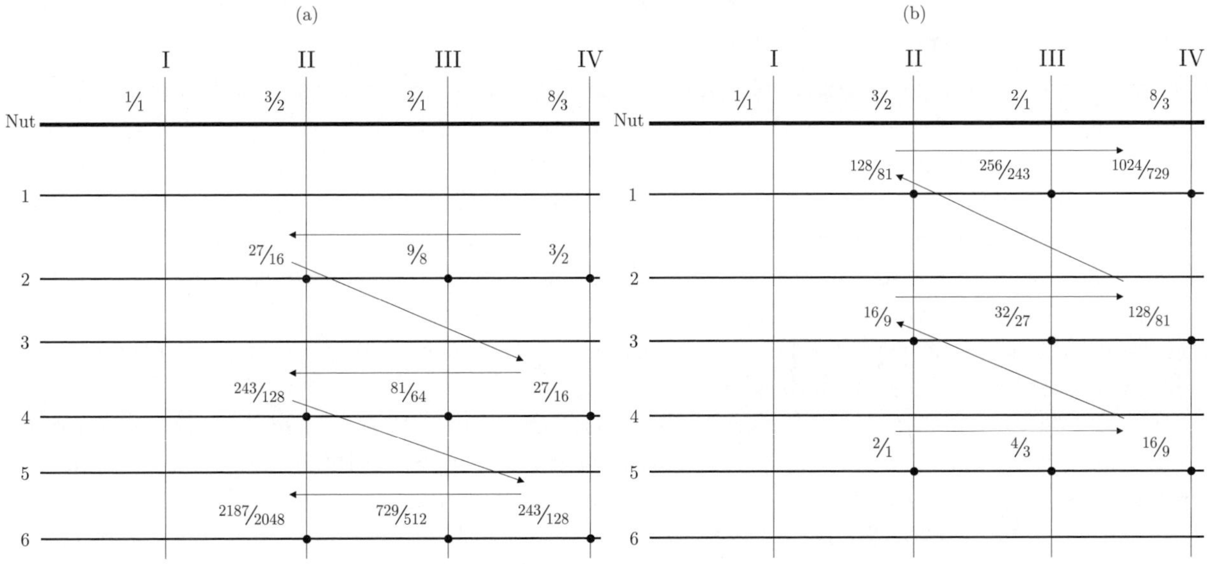

Figure 11.29 Patterns of "descending" and "ascending" $4/3$'s on Rāmāmātya's *vīṇā*. Contrary to his text, in (a) the tone at String II, Fret 6, is not identical to the tone at String III, Fret 1, in (b); similarly, in (a) the tone at String III, Fret 6, is not identical to the tone at String IV, Fret 1, in (b).

Note that there are two D♭'s and one C♯ on the *vīṇā*. In *Svaramēlakalānidhi 3.35–36*, Rāmāmātya eliminates C♯ˡ, ratio $^{2187}/_{2048}$, on String II, Fret 6. This is a *consistent* choice because the two remaining D♭'s — ratio $^{256}/_{243}$ on String I, Fret 1 and String III, Fret 1 — represent *two identical* "semitones." However, observe there are also two F♯'s and one G♭. In *Svaramēlakalānidhi 3.39–40*, Rāmāmātya eliminates F♯ˡ, ratio $^{729}/_{512}$, on String III, Fret 6. This is an *inconsistent* choice because F♯, ratio $^{729}/_{512}$ on String I, Fret 6, and G♭ˡ, ratio $^{1024}/_{729}$ on String IV, Fret 1, represent *two different* "tritones." Two different "tritones" means two different "octaves," "fifths," "fourths," etc., exist in the scale. For example, the interval between G♭ˡ on String IV, Fret 1, and D♭ˡ on String III, Fret 1, is a "just fourth": $^{1024}/_{729} \div {}^{256}/_{243} = {}^{4}/_{3} = 498.0$ ¢, but the interval between F♯ on String I, Fret 6, and D♭ on String I, Fret 1, is a "sharp fourth" that is a comma of Pythagoras [23.5 ¢] higher: $^{729}/_{512} \div {}^{256}/_{243} = {}^{144209}/_{106701} = 521.5$ ¢.

The latter choice indicates that Rāmāmātya did not mathematically define the *svara* ratios of his *vīṇā*, which means that he did not base his scale and tuning theory on formal length ratio calculations. Nevertheless, because Rāmāmātya's description of fret locations admits only one possible realization, we may consider his work a significant expression of musical mathematics.

With respect to the disparities between the theoretical 14-tone scale in Figure 11.27 and the practical 12-tone tuning in Figure 11.28, Rāmāmātya explains the elimination of *Antara* Ga and *Kākalī* Ni as follows:

> *Sva. 3.64–72* — While all the hitherto-discussed *Svaras* have been fourteen in number, the theory of twelve *Svaras* will now be explained, without any confusion. First, the question as to why a couple of frets was not fixed to produce *Kākalī* Ni and *Antara* Ga may be taken up. If two frets were fixed to produce *Kākalī* Ni and *Antara* Ga, the resulting sound is a ***disagreeable beat;*** and hence the absence of the two frets to produce those two *Svaras*. How then can they be otherwise produced? The learned musicians are of opinion that *Kākalī* Ni can be produced, in a way, even by the *Cyutamadhyama Ga*-fret. In fact, all the *Rāgas*, in which *Kākalī* Ni and *Antara* Ga play any part, may likewise be sung. Some practical musicians consider *Cyutamadhyama* Ga and *Cyutaṣaḍja* Ni as the representatives respectively of *Antara* Ga and *Kākalī* Ni, on account of the ***very small difference*** in sound between them.[86] (Bold italics mine.)

Let us assume that the "disagreeable beat" occurred when Rāmāmātya tuned *Antara* Ga to a 5-limit "major third," ratio $^{5}/_{4}$, and *Kākalī* Ni to a 5-limit "major seventh," ratio $^{15}/_{8}$. This would produce the following interval between *Cyutamadhyama* Ga and *Antara* Ga: $^{81}/_{64} \div {}^{5}/_{4} = {}^{81}/_{80} =$ 21.5 ¢, and between *Cyutaṣaḍja* Ni and *Kākalī* Ni: $^{243}/_{128} \div {}^{15}/_{8} = {}^{81}/_{80} = 21.5$ ¢. In both cases, the discrepancy is called the comma of Didymus, which is 2.0 ¢ less than the comma of Pythagoras. Since most musicians are unable to musically distinguish between these two extremely similar commas, we find Rāmāmātya's interpretations perfectly consistent. On the one hand, he dismisses the Pythagorean comma between C♯/D♭ and F♯/G♭, and on the other hand, he eliminates the Didymic comma between two different kinds of E's and B's.[87]

Table 11.16 gives the ancient length ratios of Rāmāmātya's 12-tone *śuddha mēḷa vīṇā* tuning, their cent values, plus four alternate note names. Turn to Figure 10.16(a) and 10.16(b), and note that his scale consists of *six ascending* $^{3}/_{2}$'s, *five descending* $^{3}/_{2}$'s, and an "octave." Consequently, Table 11.16 gives the "tritone" as F♯, ratio $^{729}/_{512}$, not only because this tone represents a consistent choice, but also because the note name *Cyutapañcama* Ma clearly refers to a variant of F. If we were to interpret the "tritone" as G♭, ratio $^{1024}/_{729}$, then its note name would have to refer to a variant of Pa.

Finally, unless Rāmāmātya knew less than Bharata, Nārada, Mataṅga, and Śārṅgadeva about the art of tuning musical instruments — a highly unlikely possibility — all these difficulties

Table 11.16

THE 12-TONE *ŚUDDHA MĒḶA VĪṆĀ* TUNING
AS DEFINED BY RĀMĀMĀTYA

1. Sa	C	$1/1$	0.0 ¢
2. *Śuddha* Ri	D♭	$256/243$	90.2 ¢
3. *Śuddha* Ga (or) *Pañcaśruti* Ri	E♭♭ (or) D	$9/8$	203.9 ¢
4. *Sādhāraṇa* Ga (or) *Ṣaṭśruti* Ri	E♭ (or) D♯	$32/27$	294.1 ¢
5. *Cyutamadhyama* Ga	E	$81/64$	407.8 ¢
6. *Śuddha* Ma	F	$4/3$	498.0 ¢
7. *Cyutapañcama* Ma	F♯	$729/512$	611.7 ¢
8. Pa	G	$3/2$	702.0 ¢
9. *Śuddha* Dha	A♭	$128/81$	792.2 ¢
10. *Śuddha* Ni (or) *Pañcaśruti* Dha	B♭♭ (or) A	$27/16$	905.9 ¢
11. *Kaiśikī* Ni (or) *Ṣaṭśruti* Dha	B♭ (or) A♯	$16/9$	996.1 ¢
12. *Cyutaṣaḍja* Ni	B	$243/128$	1109.8 ¢
13. Sa	C'	$2/1$	1200.0 ¢

associated with commas prove two points. (1) The notion that musicians in ancient India tuned a 22-tone equal tempered scale has no basis in fact. Mathematicians and theorists design equal tempered tunings for only one reason: to disperse various kinds of commas.[88] (2) The 22-*śruti* scale provided an intellectual framework for the conceptualization and actualization of 5-tone, 6-tone, 7-tone, and 12-tone scales, but never 22-tone scales. Theorists who have the mathematical knowledge needed to construct sophisticated tempered or just 22-tone scales also demonstrate awareness and mastery over the intonational difficulties presented by commas. Rāmāmātya's treatise constitutes a critical step in the evolution of Indian music because he was the first writer to wrestle with these complex problems, not as a mathematician, but as an inventive and visionary musician.

~ 11.35 ~

The theoretical 14-tone scale and the practical 12-tone tuning provided Rāmāmātya with two prerequisite tools to realize his final goal: an objective system for the classification of hundreds of *rāgas*. To accomplish this task, Rāmāmātya defined a highly effective distinction. He divided all *rāgas* into two categories: a primary set called *janaka rāgas* or *mēḷa rāgas*, and a secondary set, called *janya rāgas*. Rāmāmātya describes the fundamental difference between these two classes of *rāgas* in the following manner:

> *Sva. 4.1–2* — . . . I shall duly proceed to speak about the *Mēḷas*, which ***cause*** their respective *Rāgas* to be formed and which are distinguished by *Rāga*-names, coined after the fashion of the languages prevailing in various provinces.[89] (Bold italics mine.)

This terse definition is significant for what it states, and for what it omits. (1) The key word here is *cause.* Rāmāmātya's concept of cause and effect revolutionized Indian music because it permanently eliminated the earlier concept of *origin.* Rāmāmātya realized that no theorist could derive a plethora of *rāgas* from only two *grāmas.* (2) Conspicuously absent from his definition is the *lakṣaṇa-rasa* or *lakṣaṇa-guṇa* principle of his predecessors. Rāmāmātya probably decided against hierarchical classifications based on traditional technical properties and performance qualities because he knew that such considerations would complicate his system beyond comprehension. For an organizational arrangement to be effective, it must be simple, which in turn makes it memorable.

From his 12-tone tuning, Rāmāmātya selected various 7-tone scales. Since Sa and Pa are not subject to change, Rāmāmātya achieved diversity by selecting different combinations of five tones from the remaining ten tones. His objective was to identify, among the musical *rāgas* of his time, one *janaka* (lit. *parent*) *rāga*, or *mēḷa* (lit. *unifier*) *rāga*,[90] with seven tones that represents the largest number of *janya* (lit. *born*, or *derived*) *rāgas.* The *janya rāgas* have five, six, or seven tones in common with the *mēḷa rāgas.* When, in the latter case, two *rāgas* consist of seven identical tones, Rāmāmātya named the *mēḷa rāga* after the best-known or exemplary *rāga.* In this capacity, I refer to all such 7-tone *rāgas* as *denominative rāgas.* By definition, a denominative *rāga* serves a double function: (1) it assumes a new technical identity as an abstract *mēḷa rāga*, and (2) it retains its original identity as a musical *janya rāga.* Consequently, denominative *rāgas* always occur twice in Rāmāmātya's catalogs: the first time as *mēḷa rāgas*, and the second time as *janya rāgas.* Furthermore, because Rāmāmātya considered all *janya rāgas* equally important, the denominative *rāgas* did *not* represent outstanding technical or musical characteristics. We conclude, therefore, that Rāmāmātya was the first theorist in the history of Indian music who used a mathematically determined tuning to define a system of *rāga* classification based on the principle of musical abstraction. We may think of his *mēḷa rāgas* as tone pools that reflect the living musical *rāga* traditions of his time!

Rāmāmātya's *mēḷa rāgas* are now exclusively known as *janya rāgas.* Some of these have vanished, others are known by different names, and a few have survived intact. For example, Figure 11.30(a) shows Rāmāmātya's *Mēḷa Māḷavagauḷa*, which has the same tones as Govinda's modern *Mēḷa Māyāmāḷavagauḷa.* However, in Rāmāmātya's treatise, *Rāga Māḷavagauḷa* is described as a *pentatonic rāga*;[91] this *rāga* is now extinct. On the other hand, Venkaṭamakhi identifies the latter prototype as *Mēḷa Gauḷa* and describes *Rāga Gauḷa* as a *hexatonic rāga* shown in Figure 11.30(a).[92] Rāmāmātya also lists a *janya rāga* of *Mēḷa Māḷavagauḷa* called *Rāga Mēchabauḷi*,[93] which, like *Rāga Gauḷa*, has survived into modern times as a *janya rāga* of *Mēḷa Māyāmāḷavagauḷa.* In contrast, Figure 11.30(b) shows Rāmāmātya's *Mēḷa Śrī-rāga* and *Rāga Śuddhabairavī*,[94] both of which exist today as *janya rāgas* of Govinda's modern *Mēḷa Kharaharapriyā.* Rāmāmātya describes his two *mēḷas* thus:

> *Sva. 4.11–12* — Rāmāmātya characterizes, with the approval of those that are well-versed in *Rāga* (*-Lakṣaṇa*), the *Mēḷa* of *'Māḷavagauḷa'* as consisting of these seven *svaras*, namely, *Śuddha* Sa [C], *Śuddha* Ri [D♭], *Śuddha* Ma [F], *Śuddha* Pa [G], *Śuddha* Dha [A♭], *Cyutamadhyama* Ga [E], and *Cyutaṣaḍja* Ni [B].
>
> *13–15* — Then do I enumerate some of the *Rāgas* derived from this *Mēḷa* (of *Māḷavagauḷa*); and they are: *Māḷavagauḷa*, . . . , *Mēchabauḷi*, [etc.] . . .
>
> *16–17* — The *Mēḷa* of *'Śrī-rāga'* consists of these seven *svaras*, namely, *Śuddha* Sa [C], *Pañcaśruti* Ri [D], *Sādhāraṇa* Ga [E♭], *Śuddha* Ma [F], *Śuddha* Pa [G], *Pañcaśruti* Dha [A], and *Kaiśikī* Ni [B♭].
>
> *18–19* — Then do I enumerate some of the *Rāgas* derived from this *Mēḷa* (of *Śrī-rāga*); and they are: *Śrī-rāga*, . . . , *Śuddhabairavī*, [etc.] . . . These and a few others also are derived from this *Mēḷa*.[95] (Text in brackets mine.)

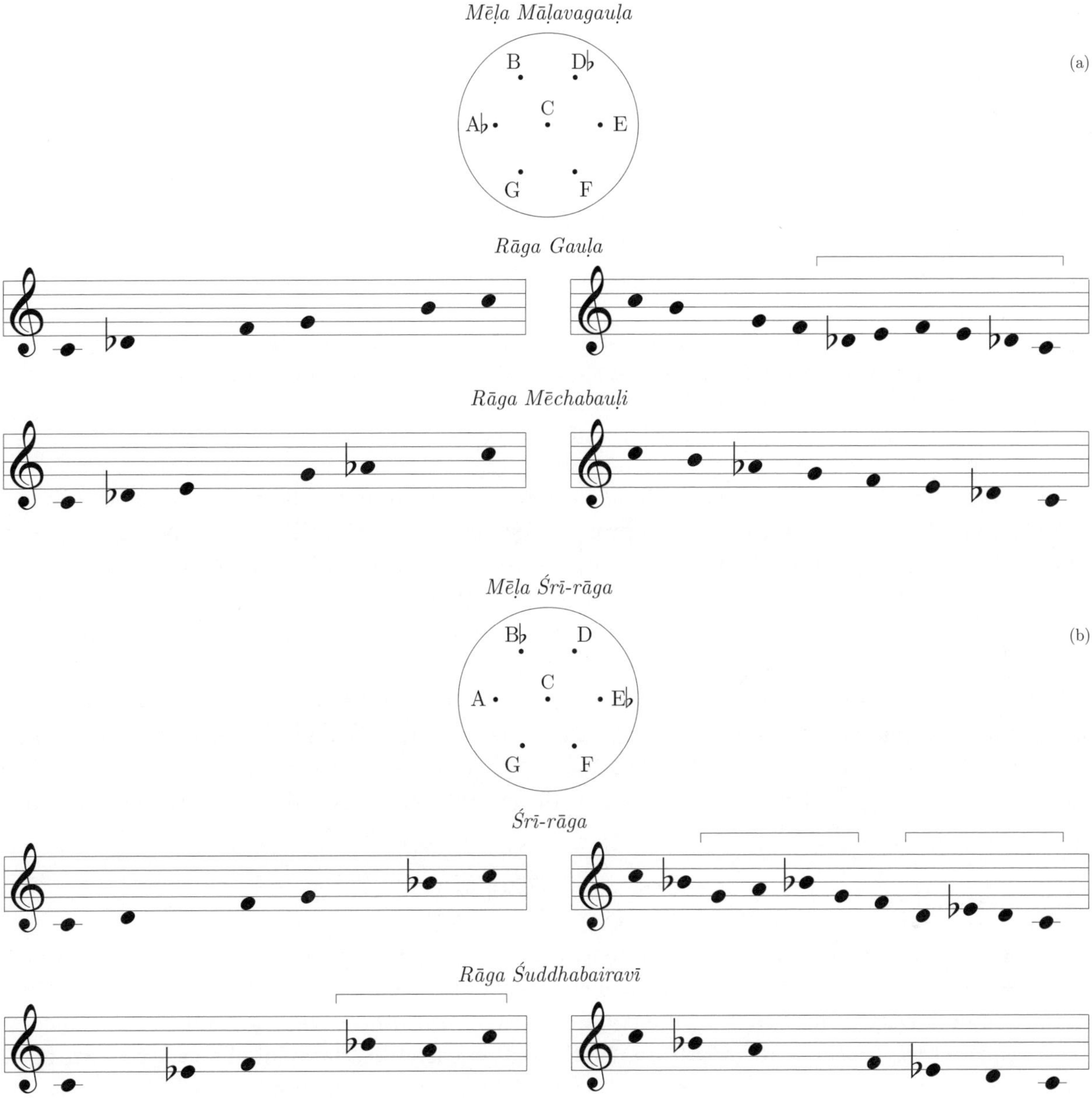

Figure 11.30 Two *mela ragas* identified by Rāmāmātya. Both examples show that *mēḷa rāgas* represent abstract *rāga*-categories, or pools of seven tones that similar musical *janya rāgas* have in common.

Figure 11.33 shows that *Mēḷa Māḷavagauḷa* and *Mēḷa Śrī-rāga* are identified in Venkaṭamakhi's system as No. 15 and No. 22, respectively. In the previous quotation, note that the *mēḷa rāgas* always appear *first* in their respective list of *janya rāgas*. Rāmāmātya applied this organizational principle throughout his catalogs of more than 60 *janya rāgas*. Finally, as discussed in Section 11.32, do not confuse the *mēḷa rāgas* in Figure 11.30 with scales or musical *rāgas*. Before Govinda's time, most *rāgas* did *not* consist of seven straight ascending tones and seven straight descending tones. Refer to Figure 11.30, which illustrates how Rāmāmātya would have intentionally performed a given *janya rāga* on his *vīṇā* by observing (1) *varjya svara(s)*: omitting one or two notes in the ascent or descent, (2) *vakra svaras:* playing notes out of order in the ascent or descent, and/or (3) *anya svara:* using a foreign note not specified by the *mēḷa*.[96] For example, with respect to the first two characteristics, Figure 11.30(b) shows that musicians play *Śrī-rāga* by omitting Ga and Dha in the ascent, and by playing two *vakra* passages — C', B♭, G–A–B♭–G, F, D–E♭–D–C — in the descent. With regard to the third characteristic, Rāmāmātya's *Mēḷa Hindōḷa* — called *Mēḷa Bhairavī* by Venkaṭamakhi, and *Mēḷa Naṭabhairavī* by Govinda (see Figure 11.33) — is now played as *Rāga Bhairavī* with a foreign A♮ in the ascent, and A♭ in the descent.[97] In Rāmāmātya's *Svaramēlakalānidhi*, therefore, each *mēḷa rāga* functions as a tone pool from which musicians derive vast musical possibilities.

Śrī-rāga is the modern equivalent of the ancient *Ṣaḍjagrāma*. In a highly insightful article, T.V. Subba Rao characterizes this *rāga* by observing

> . . . *Śrī-rāga* is the foremost and most auspicious . . . There is no doubt that the glory and sanctity attaching to this *rāga* is to be attributed, apart from mythology, to its being the oldest of all scales, derived as it was as the first offspring of *Ṣaḍjagrāma* . . .[98]

Although Rāmāmātya mentions the *graha*, *aṃśa*, and *nyāsa* notes, he does not use traditional *lakṣaṇa* properties to distinguish between groups of similar *janya rāgas* that have five, six, or seven tones in common. Instead, he differentiates between such *rāgas* according to pentatonic, hexatonic, or heptatonic forms. For example, Rāmāmātya classifies *Rāga Bhairavī* and *Rāga Dhanyāsi* as *janya rāgas* of *Mēḷa Śrī-rāga*, but describes the former as a heptatonic *rāga*, and the latter as a pentatonic *rāga* because it ". . . leaves [out] Ri and Dha."[99] Later, in Venkaṭamakhi's work, we encounter distinctions based on various *varjya*, *vakra*, and *anya svara* features. We conclude, therefore, that theorists gradually replaced the old *lakṣaṇa* properties — i.e., the I, P, S, and F notes — with these new *lakṣaṇa* properties. However, the Indian tradition of creating large groups of very similar sounding *rāgas*, distinguished primarily by exquisite melodic subtleties, exists today as in the ancient past.

~ 11.36 ~

In 1620, Venkaṭamakhi wrote a treatise entitled *Caturdaṇḍiprakāśika*,[100] in which he brought Rāmāmātya's *mēḷa rāga* concept to its logical conclusion. Before we analyze this organizational system in full detail, let us first consider Venkaṭamakhi's 12-tone scale, and the names he assigned to the *śuddha* and *vikṛta svaras*. Refer to Table 11.17, and note that Venkaṭamakhi's scale consists of *six ascending* $3/2$'s, *five descending* $3/2$'s, and an "octave." Consequently, he used exactly the same *svara* ratios as originally defined by Rāmāmātya.[101] Observe, however, that Venkaṭamakhi substituted the terms *Catuśśruti* Ri for *Pañcaśruti* Ri, and *Catuśśruti* Dha for *Pañcaśruti* Dha.[102] (*Catuśśruti* defines a 4-*śruti* interval above Sa or Pa.) Śārṅgadeva was the first theorist who used *catuśśruti* to define a *modified* 4-*śruti* interval between Sa and Ri.[103] We initially encountered this interval as the difference between Pa and Ma: 13 *śrutis* − 9 *śrutis* = 4 *śrutis*, which yields interval ratio $3/2 \div 4/3 = 9/8$.[104] Venkaṭamakhi substituted this *catuśśruti* definition because it is mathematically more accurate than Rāmāmātya's *pañcaśruti* description. In Section 11.34, we interpreted Rāmāmātya's scale as consisting of six ascending $3/2$'s, and five descending $3/2$'s. The former sequence generates a "major second" expressed by the product of two ascending consecutive "fifths": $3/2 \times 3/2 = 9/4 = 9/8$. Venkaṭamakhi observed that when applied to ratios above Sa and Pa, this 4-*śruti* interval produces *Catuśśruti* Ri, ratio $9/8$, and *Catuśśruti* Dha, ratio $27/16$, respectively. Rāmāmātya incorrectly described ratio $9/8$ as *Pañcaśruti* Ri, or as a 5-*śruti* interval above Sa, because his primary focus was not on ratio definitions, but on general *śruti* descriptions of the *śuddha* and *vikṛta svaras* of his new scale. This conflict between *ratio definitions* and *śruti descriptions* teaches a crucial lesson about all forms of Indian music: unless a theorist or musician specifically identifies *svaras* in

Table 11.17

THE *SVARAS* OF THE MODERN SOUTH INDIAN 12-TONE SCALE
AS DESCRIBED BY VENKAṬAMAKHI

1.	Sa	C	$1/1$	0.0 ¢
2.	*Śuddha* Ri	D♭	$256/243$	90.2 ¢
3.	*Śuddha* Ga (or) *Catuśśruti* Ri	E𝄫 (or) D	$9/8$	203.9 ¢
4.	*Sādhāraṇa* Ga (or) *Ṣaṭśruti* Ri	E♭ (or) D♯	$32/27$	294.1 ¢
5.	*Antara* Ga	E	$81/64$	407.8 ¢
6.	*Śuddha* Ma	F	$4/3$	498.0 ¢
7.	*Prati* Ma	F♯	$729/512$	611.7 ¢
8.	Pa	G	$3/2$	702.0 ¢
9.	*Śuddha* Dha	A♭	$128/81$	792.2 ¢
10.	*Śuddha* Ni (or) *Catuśśruti* Dha	B𝄫 (or) A	$27/16$	905.9 ¢
11.	*Kaiśikī* Ni (or) *Ṣaṭśruti* Dha	B♭ (or) A♯	$16/9$	996.1 ¢
12.	*Kākalī* Ni	B	$243/128$	1109.8 ¢
13.	Sa	C′	$2/1$	1200.0 ¢

terms of ancient length ratios or modern frequency ratios, and *śrutis* in terms of interval ratios, *the identity of a scale or tuning may be completely open to interpretation.* Therefore, correctly stated, Rāmāmātya's introduction of the "major second," ratio $9/8$ — i.e., *Catuśśruti* Ri — rendered the "flat major second," ratio $10/9$, of the ancient *Ṣaḍjagrāma* obsolete. Venkaṭamakhi also substituted *Antara* Ga for *Cyutamadhyama* Ga, and *Kākalī* Ni for *Cyutaṣaḍja* Ni; he probably considered these two *svara* names more prestigious because they first appeared in Bharata's venerated *Nāṭyaśāstra.* In addition, Venkaṭamakhi introduced the term *prati*, which means *substitute*, and changed *Cyutapañcama* Ma to *Prati* Ma. These latter three changes eliminated Rāmāmātya's *cyuta* prefixes from the 12-tone scale. Table 11.17 shows the *svara* ratios and note names as they are known in South India to this day.

Venkaṭamakhi's organizational system consists of 72 mathematically determined *mēḷa rāgas*, which he called *mēḷakartas.*[105] In the *Caturdaṇḍiprakāśika*, Venkaṭamakhi simply proposes this system without actually listing all 72 heptatonic permutations.[106] He does, however, give detailed descriptions of 19 *mēḷakartas*, and includes their numeric identities as specified by the system.[107] The naming of all 72 *mēḷakartas* was undertaken by Muddu Venkaṭamakhi, the grandson of the theorist.[108]

To understand how Venkaṭamakhi used combinatorics to generate his system, recall that in South Indian music theory one may *not* write a chromatic interval by notating two consecutive *svaras* of the same name.[109] Given this limitation, the 72 *mēḷakartas* represent all possible heptatonic permutations of the 12-tone scale. A convenient demonstration of this fact takes several steps. First, refer back to Table 11.17, and observe that the 12-tone South Indian scale includes sixteen different *svara* names, because four of these represent enharmonic equivalents. Now, turn to the schematic in Figure 11.31, and note that variants of Ri, Ga, Ma, Dha, and Ni account for fourteen of these names. For example, the schematic shows Ri with three *svara* name subscripts,

D♭	D	D♯	E♭♭	E♭	E	F	F♯	A♭	A	A♯	B♭♭	B♭	B
	Ri			Ga		Ma			Dha			Ni	
Śud.	*Cat.*	*Ṣaṭ.*	*Śud.*	*Sād.*	*Ant.*	*Śud.*	*Pra.*	*Śud.*	*Cat.*	*Ṣaṭ.*	*Śud.*	*Kai.*	*Kāk.*
1	2	3	1	2	3	1	2	1	2	3	1	2	3

Figure 11.31 A schematic that depicts the scale degrees associated with *svaras* Ri, Ga, Ma, Dha, and Ni. In Figure 11.32, the numeric subscripts of these *svaras* conveniently demonstrate how Venkaṭamakhi used combinatorics to generate his system of 72 *mēḷakartas*.

three numeric subscripts, and three musical note superscripts. These indices appear aligned in three separate columns to indicate three scale degrees associated with Ri. Here $\text{Ri}_{\text{Śud. 1}}$ depicts *Śuddha* Ri, the first (lowest) degree of Ri, or the musical note D♭; $\text{Ri}_{\text{Cat. 2}}$ depicts *Catuśśruti* Ri, the second (middle) degree of Ri, or the musical note D♮; and $\text{Ri}_{\text{Ṣaṭ. 3}}$ depicts *Ṣaṭśruti* Ri, the third (highest) degree of Ri, or the musical note D♯. Similarly, variants of Ga, Dha, and Ni also depict three degrees each in the scale.[110] Now, since Ma represents two scale degrees, F and F♯, Venkaṭamakhi divided his 72 permutations into two distinct sets: *Mēḷakartas* 1–36 consist of tetrachords C–F and G–C′, and *Mēḷakartas* 37–72 consist of tetrachords C–F♯ and G–C′.

Venkaṭamakhi realized his 72 *mēḷakartas* by defining six *upward* progressions from Ri to Ga in the lower tetrachords, and six *upward* progressions from Dha to Ni in the upper tetrachords. His system requires that degrees of Ri always represent notes lower than degrees of Ga, and degrees of Dha always represent notes lower than degrees of Ni. (Consequently, he did not include combinations such as Ri_3–Ga_1 because the latter represents a *downward* progression from D♯ to E♭♭.) Finally, Figure 11.32 shows at a glance that we may represent all possible upward progressions by assigning the following six combinations of subscripts — 1-1, 1-2, 1-3, 2-2, 2-3, 3-3 — to six Ri–Ga pairs, and to six Dha–Ni pairs. *Mēḷakartas* 1–36 express these pairs with Ma_1, or F, and *Mēḷakartas* 37–72, with Ma_2, or F♯. The result is a twelve-by-six matrix that generates Venkaṭamakhi's 72 *mēḷakartas*, or 72 heptatonic permutations.

By Venkaṭamakhi's admission, only 19 *mēḷakartas* — Nos. 1, 3, 8, 13, 14, 15, 20, 21, 22, 28, 29, 30, 35, 36, 39, 45, 51, 58, 65 — served as relevant *rāga*-categories of his time.[111] The vast majority, or 53 *mēḷakartas*, had little or no musical value in the early 17th century. For this reason, when compared to Rāmāmātya's *mēḷa rāgas*, Venkaṭamakhi's system seemed at first to be needlessly abstract. Whereas Rāmāmātya relied on the principle of musical abstraction, which originated from a contemplation of living *rāgas*, Venkaṭamakhi relied instead on the principle of combinatorial abstraction, which originated from a contemplation of inanimate permutations. However, Venkaṭamakhi's system proved irresistible for two reasons. (1) Since the 72 *mēḷakartas* represent all possible permutations, Venkaṭamakhi's twelve-by-six array is foolproof: the most popular and the most obscure *rāgas* are by default included in the system. (2) Since the system is all-inclusive, it has the power to predict future developments: inquisitive and innovative musicians found in this vast repository myriad unexplored possibilities. Walter Kaufmann traces this history of slow acceptance by noting

> This system [i.e., Venkaṭamakhi's *mēḷakartas*] and a second one [i.e., Govinda's *mēḷa rāgas*] . . . did not become popular immediately. There were numerous musicians and writers who opposed this "dehumanized" manner of artificially creating scales and ignoring the many subtleties, the real refinement of the *rāgas*. The storm of objections abated to some degree when it became known that the great Tyāgarāja (1767–1847) used some of the new scales in his (approximately) two-thousand *kīrtaṇas* and *kṛtis* [*rāga* songs].[112] (Text in brackets mine.)

	$P\ D_1\ N_1\ S'$ **G A♭ B♭♭ C'**	$P\ D_1\ N_2\ S'$ **G A♭ B♭ C'**	$P\ D_1\ N_3\ S'$ **G A♭ B C'**	$P\ D_2\ N_2\ S'$ **G A B♭ C'**	$P\ D_2\ N_3\ S'$ **G A B C'**	$P\ D_3\ N_3\ S'$ **G A♯ B C'**
$S\ R_1\ G_1\ M_1$ **C D♭ E♭♭ F**	1	2	3	4	5	6
$S\ R_1\ G_2\ M_1$ **C D♭ E♭ F**	7	8	9	10	11	12
$S\ R_1\ G_3\ M_1$ **C D♭ E F**	13	14	15	16	17	18
$S\ R_2\ G_2\ M_1$ **C D E♭ F**	19	20	21	22	23	24
$S\ R_2\ G_3\ M_1$ **C D E F**	25	26	27	28	29	30
$S\ R_3\ G_3\ M_1$ **C D♯ E F**	31	32	33	34	35	36
$S\ R_1\ G_1\ M_2$ **C D♭ E♭♭ F♯**	37	38	39	40	41	42
$S\ R_1\ G_2\ M_2$ **C D♭ E♭ F♯**	43	44	45	46	47	48
$S\ R_1\ G_3\ M_2$ **C D♭ E F♯**	49	50	51	52	53	54
$S\ R_2\ G_2\ M_2$ **C D E♭ F♯**	55	56	57	58	59	60
$S\ R_2\ G_3\ M_2$ **C D E F♯**	61	62	63	64	65	66
$S\ R_3\ G_3\ M_2$ **C D♯ E F♯**	67	68	69	70	71	72

Figure 11.32 A twelve-by-six matrix that generates Venkaṭamakhi's 72 *mēḷakartas.* The numeric subscripts of Ri, Ga, Ma, Dha, and Ni demonstrate at a glance that this organizational system produces all possible heptatonic permutations of the 12-tone scale as specified by South Indian music theory. The underlined numbers indicate 36 *vivādi mēḷas*, or *dissonant mēḷas*, because they contain two consecutive half-steps, or two consecutive "semitones" within one or both tetrachords. (See Section 11.38.)

~ 11.37 ~

Rāmāmātya's and Venkaṭamakhi's works are alike because in both systems the abstract *rāga*-categories called *mēḷa rāgas* and *mēḷakartas*, respectively, are neither (1) technical scales, nor (2) musical *rāgas*. This basic approach to *rāga* classification came to a gradual end sometime in the late 18th or early 19th century when Govinda wrote a book entitled *Saṃgraha Cūḍa Maṇi.*[113] In this work, Govinda proposed that all modern *mēḷa rāgas* must be two-directional *krama* (lit. *straight*) *sampūrṇa* (lit. *complete;* i.e., heptatonic): that is, must consist of seven straight ascending and seven straight descending tones. Furthermore, he decided to model the scales of his *mēḷa rāgas* on the progressions of tones generated by Venkaṭamakhi's 72 heptatonic permutations. Govinda then renamed the resulting *mēḷa rāgas* by appending alphanumeric prefixes to their names. Finally, he insisted that these theoretically constructed and theoretically named *mēḷa rāgas* represent traditional abstract *rāga*-categories, and a newly created class of musical *mēḷa rāgas.* Eventually his notion gained acceptance by those who believed in 7-tone uniformity. These followers became convinced that the new *mēḷa rāgas* exemplify ideal or musically superior *rāgas.* The latter assertion has caused a great deal of controversy and dissension among many modern writers, theorists, and musicians.

Govinda's 72 scales are collectively known as the *Kanakāṅgī-Ratnāṅgī* system, a title derived from the names of his first two *mēḷa rāgas.* With respect to the history of *rāga* classification, Govinda's system demoted Rāmāmātya's and Venkaṭamakhi's *mēḷas* to the status of *janya rāgas* because most musical *rāgas* do not conform to the two-directional *krama sampūrṇa* requirement. Strict adherence to this condition meant that Govinda's uniform scales replaced the tone pools of his predecessors. N.S. Ramachandran, a renowned scholar of South Indian music, observes

> . . . Govinda restricts the term *'pūrṇa'* to apply to *rāgas* or scales with 7 notes in consecutive or regular succession in both *āroha* [ascent] and *avaroha* [descent] . . .
>
> Venkaṭamakhi and Govinda differ fundamentally in their treatment of the *mēḷakarta rāgas.* Govinda defines everyone of the 72 scales as *sampūrṇa* in *ārohaṇa* and *avarohaṇa.* Consequently he classifies Venkaṭamakhi's scales as *janyas* wherever they are not *sampūrṇa* in ascent and descent. He seems to be guided by the rule that ***a scale should be*** *pūrṇa* in *āroha* and *avaroha.*[114] (Bold italics and text in brackets mine.)

Despite all these new restrictions and definitions, Govinda was unable to improve on Venkaṭamakhi's system. However, since he needed to distinguish his 72 *mēḷa rāgas* from the original 72 *mēḷakartas,* he decided to append alphanumeric prefixes to all his *mēḷa rāga* names. Note carefully that Govinda's prefixes conform exactly to Venkaṭamakhi's *mēḷakarta* numbers. This strategy guaranteed success because theorists and musicians are able to identify Govinda's *mēḷa rāgas* by simply referring to the original twelve-by-six matrix. We conclude, therefore, that Govinda's theoretical considerations are the only differences that exist between the old *mēḷakartas* and the modern *mēḷa rāgas.*

To create his alphanumeric system, Govinda numbered the consonants of the Sanskrit alphabet.[115] He then simultaneously named and numbered a given *mēḷa rāga* by appending a prefix, which consists of two consonances in reverse order, to the *mēḷa rāga* name. For example, in his system, M is 5, and Y is 1. Therefore, to determine the numeric identity of *Mēḷa Māyāmālavagauḷa,* *reverse* the order of the consonants in the prefix, which yields 15. Similarly, since Ch is 6, and K is also 1, *Mēḷa Chakravākam* is number 16. Refer to Figure 11.33, and note that in the column labeled South Indian *Mēḷas,* the first are the modern *mēḷa rāga* names given by Govinda to his scales and musical *mēḷa rāgas,* and the second are the old *mēḷakarta* names given by Venkaṭamakhi to his tone pools. Numbers in parentheses indicate the matrix identities of the fourteen most popular *mēḷa rāgas* of modern South Indian music.[116] Many writers do not acknowledge Govinda's system, and instead continue to use Venkaṭamakhi's names.

~ 11.38 ~

Before the 19th century, not many *janya rāgas* were *krama sampūrṇa* in *āroha* or *avaroha,* and even fewer were *krama sampūrṇa* in *āroha and avaroha.* In Figure 11.30(a), *Rāga Mēchabauḷi* is, therefore, a somewhat rare occurrence of the former kind of *rāga.* Harold S. Powers, a noted writer on South Indian music, observes

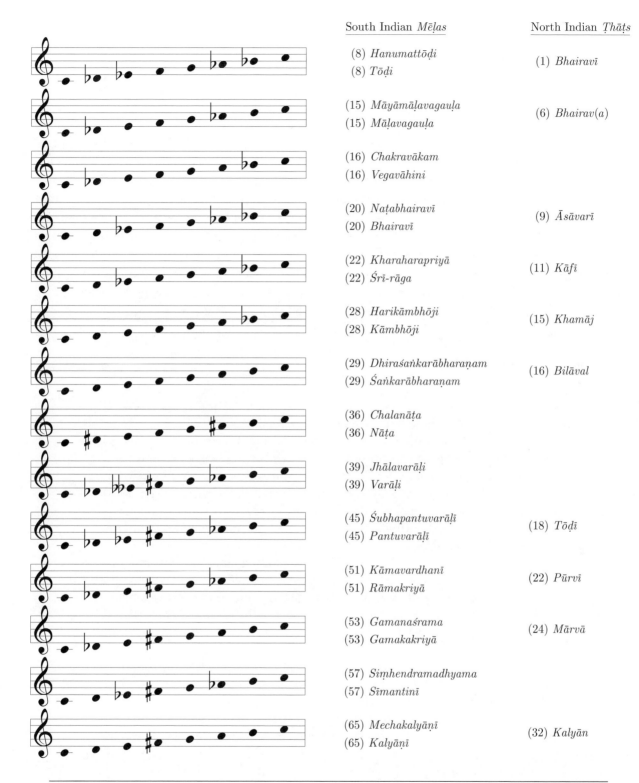

South Indian *Mēḷas*	North Indian *Ṭhāṭs*
(8) *Hanumattōḍi* (8) *Tōḍi*	(1) *Bhairavī*
(15) *Māyāmāḷavagauḷa* (15) *Māḷavagauḷa*	(6) *Bhairav(a)*
(16) *Chakravākam* (16) *Vegavāhini*	
(20) *Naṭabhairavī* (20) *Bhairavī*	(9) *Āsāvarī*
(22) *Kharaharapriyā* (22) *Śrī-rāga*	(11) *Kāfī*
(28) *Harikāmbhōji* (28) *Kāmbhōji*	(15) *Khamāj*
(29) *Dhiraśaṅkarābharaṇam* (29) *Śaṅkarābharaṇam*	(16) *Bilāval*
(36) *Chalanāṭa* (36) *Nāṭa*	
(39) *Jhālavarāḷi* (39) *Varāḷi*	
(45) *Śubhapantuvarāḷī* (45) *Pantuvarāḷī*	(18) *Tōḍī*
(51) *Kāmavardhanī* (51) *Rāmakriyā*	(22) *Pūrvī*
(53) *Gamanaśrama* (53) *Gamakakriyā*	(24) *Mārvā*
(57) *Siṃhendramadhyama* (57) *Sīmantinī*	
(65) *Mechakalyāṇī* (65) *Kalyāṇī*	(32) *Kalyān*

Figure 11.33 The most popular fourteen from a total of seventy-two modern South Indian *mēḷa rāgas*, and the most popular ten from a total of thirty-two modern North Indian *ṭhāṭs*. In the South Indian column, the first are new names given by Govinda in the 19th century, and the second are old names given by Venkaṭamakhi in the 17th century; the latter names still appear in many modern texts. In the North Indian column, the list was defined and named by Bhatkhande in the early 20th century. However, because he recognized only ten *ṭhāṭs*, some modern theorists and musicians advocated a more comprehensive system of thirty-two *ṭhāṭs*.

> . . . By ca. 1800 . . . the general principle of regular ascending-descending order [i.e., two-directional *krama sampūrṇa*] had been accepted. Though actual compositions in *mēḷa rāgas* [i.e., as *janya rāgas*] at first by no means adhered to the principle of regular ordering, it has by now become a requirement that *mēḷas* and hence compositions in *mēḷas*, must fulfill this condition.[117] (Text in brackets mine.)

This reluctance toward the musical implementation of two-directional *krama sampūrṇa* is rooted in the melodic traditions of Carnatic Music. Refer back to Figure 11.32, and note that 36 *mēḷakartas* are *vivādi* (lit. *dissonant*) *mēḷas*. Powers defines *vivādi mēḷas* as having ". . . two consecutive half-steps within one or both tetrachords";[118] hence, the concept of *chromatic mēḷas*. According to T.L. Venkatarama Iyer, Venkaṭamakhi was fully aware of the so-called *vivādi doṣas* (lit. *dissonant defects*) generated by his system, and in the *Caturdaṇḍiprakāśika*, addressed this problem by including many musical examples designed to reflect authentic South Indian melodic practice. In the following discussion, Iyer explains that Venkaṭamakhi intentionally avoided all *vivādi mēḷa* combinations, and unequivocally discouraged the implementation of two consecutive half-steps in *janya rāgas:*

> Now I must explain what the notion of *mēḷa* according to Venkaṭamakhi is. From the earliest days of Carnatic Music down to recent times a *mēḷa* was understood to be a *rāga* wherein the 7 notes occurred whether in the ascent or in the descent. It was then called *Sampūrṇa* and was then taken as a *Mēḷa Rāga*. It was not necessary that a *Mēḷa Rāga* should be a *sampūrṇa* both in ascent and in descent. Thus *Śrī-rāga* is a *Mēḷa* according to all the writers and that is the 22nd *mēḷa* of Venkaṭamakhi . . .
>
> Now when Venkaṭamakhi propounded the possibility of 72 *mēḷas* according to the value of the *svara*, he found that while some of them were represented by *rāgas* actually in existence others were not. Now 40 [in my opinion, ***only 36***] of these *mēḷas* represented what is known as *vivādi svara* combinations. Venkaṭamakhi adopted with reference to them the conception that a *mēḷa* need not be *sampūrṇa* in *ārohaṇa* and *avarohaṇa* ***but that it should be melodious*** . . .
>
> Thus in his scheme of 72 *mēḷas*, Venkaṭamakhi avoided *vivādi* combinations such as do not conduce to melody, and evolved the *mēḷas*, avoiding the *sampūrṇa* scale if it was a mere scale, and did not possess melodic properties such as would be necessary if it was to be a [*janya*] *rāga*. Therefore his system represents an evolution on lines which are in consonance with the genius of Carnatic Music. In his system there are no scales miscalled *"Rāgas,"* while his scientific classification provided a background for all Carnatic *rāgas*, those which were then in existence and those which might come into existence thereafter.
>
> Lovers of Carnatic Music must regret that this scheme which combined both melody and science should have been departed from. A change has, in recent years, come over the system. A new idea of *mēḷa* [Govinda's *Kanakāṅgī-Ratnāṅgī* system] has sprung up. It is stated that a *mēḷa* must be *sampūrṇa* both in ascent and descent . . . This classification is again recent; and unknown to writers of recognized authority — such as Rāmāmātya, Govinda Dīkṣita [the author of *Saṅgīta Sudhā*, and father of Venkaṭamakhi], and Venkaṭamakhi. This innovation cannot be earlier than the end of the 18th century . . .
>
> Under this system, even in *vivādi mēḷas*, the *ārohaṇam* and *avarohaṇam* must be *sampūrṇa*. That this conception stresses the *Svaras* and ignores

the requirements of melody must be conceded. For example take the very first *mēḷa* [#**1**] under the new dispensation; the *ārohaṇa* is Sa [C], [*Śuddha*] Ri [D♭], [*Śuddha*] Ga [E𝄫], [*Śuddha*] Ma [F], Pa [G], [*Śuddha*] Dha [A♭], [*Śuddha*] Ni [B𝄫], Sa [C']; that is to satisfy the new concept of *mēḷa;* and it is called *Kanakāṇgī* [#**1**, so named by Govinda]. Now Venkaṭamakhi, acting under the old conception of *mēḷa* and emphasizing melody adopted only Sa Ri Ma Pa Dha Sa as the *ārohaṇa;* and under the revised scheme it ceased to be a *mēḷa* and became a *janya.* But *Kanakāṇgī* is a scale and *Kanakāmbarī* [#**1**, so named by Venkaṭamakhi] is a *Rāga.* In the same manner we find that under the new scheme many of the *mēḷas* of Venkaṭamakhi are classed as *janyas*, and new *mēḷas* which are merely scales take their place. Thus the criticism that the scheme of 72 *mēḷas* is destructive of *rāga-bhāva* [lit., *rāga-emotion*] and tends to mechanize music is true to a large extent of the modified system which is now in vogue but is not true of the system as originally featured by Venkaṭamakhi.

From this it should follow that the revised scheme of 72 *mēḷas* which has latterly come to be adopted should be condemned as an innovation for the worse, as tending to destroy the best elements in the Carnatic Music. It is therefore surprising to find that the new scheme should find support from not a few of the present day theorists. One reason for this is that Śri Tyāgarāja is supposed to have lent his support to it. It would be strange indeed if the great Tyāgarāja set his approval on the theory of scales in *Kanakāṇgī* and the like *mēḷas* . . . In the *vivādi mēḷas* the authentic *kīrtaṇas* of Tyāgarāja show that he adopted the system of Venkaṭamakhi. For example, *Manōrañjanī* [#**5**], *Chhāyānāṭa* [#**34**], and *Nabhomani* [#**40**] and the like, are all *mēḷas* of Venkaṭamakhi and in them we have great pieces of Tyāgarāja. And there are no authentic compositions in which Tyāgarāja adopts *vivādi* combinations such as Sa [C'], [*Kākalī*] Ni [B], Dha [A♯], Pa [G], with *Ṣaṭśruti Dhaivata* [A♯]; [*Śuddha*] Ma [F], [*Antara*] Ga [E], Ri [D♯], Sa [C], with *Ṣaṭśruti Ṛṣabha* [D♯]; Sa [C], [*Śuddha*] Ri [D♭], Ga [E𝄫], [*Śuddha*] Ma [F], with *Śuddha Gāndhāra* [E𝄫]; and Pa [G], [*Śuddha*] Dha [A♭], Ni [B𝄫], Sa [C'], with *Śuddha Niṣāda* [B𝄫]. The only exception is in the case of *rāgas* like *Varāḷi* [#**39**] where according to tradition *Śuddha Gāndhāra* [E𝄫] is [tuned] slightly higher than the *Catuśśruti Ṛṣabha* [D] and thus the *vivādi doṣa* is ***avoided.*** This is in accordance with the practice of Venkaṭamakhi.

. . . For example take the piece *"Evvare Rāmayya"* [by Tyāgarāja]. It is said to be in *Gāṅgeyabhuṣanī* [#**33**, so named by Govinda]. But there is no [*Śuddha*] Ma [F], [*Antara*] Ga [E], [*Ṣaṭśruti*] Ri [D♯], Sa [C] in it, and without Ma Ga Ri Sa it loses its character as a scale under the new scheme. It has only Ma Ri Sa and it is therefore clearly a piece in *Gāṅgātaraṅgiṇī* [#**33**, so named by Venkaṭamakhi] . . . A critical analysis of the pieces of Tyāgarāja in these *mēḷas* will reveal that he was quite against the scale invention of *Kanakāṇgī* and its sister-*mēḷas;* and that he . . . followed only . . . [Venkaṭamakhi's] system of melody; and that he does not lend any countenance to scales theory. There is no authentic composition of his in *Kanakāṇgī* and similar *mēḷas* . . .

And finally there are those who prefer . . . [Govinda's] system because of its simplicity and perfection on paper. But art does not thrive on mere arithmetical formulae or mechanized rules. And however satisfactory the *"Kanakāṅgī"* system may be for purpose of mass teaching in schools and

> institutions, it has no place where there is an artistic ideal to be put forward and sustained.
>
> . . . It requires imagination to develop *rāgas;* it requires only practice to manipulate *svaras.* The former is a gift; the latter is an acquisition. The system of *svaras* and scale is a gift to plodding men without imagination; and thus its adoption has tended to destroy the *Rāga-chāyā* [*Rāga-resemblance*], and discount imagination.
>
> . . . I think, lovers of music should take a serious view of the situation, and rescue Carnatic Music and Śri Tyāgarāja from the baneful effects of the scales-theory embodied in the *Kanakāṅgī* system; and restore the concept of *rāga* for which Carnatic Music has always stood and restore in full the system of Venkaṭamakhi which is based upon it.[119] (Bold italics and text in brackets mine.)

This dichotomy between abstract *mēḷa rāgas* and musical *janya rāgas* was also addressed in a series of three lectures given by K.V. Ramachandran at the Madras Music Academy in South India. Ramachandran's aesthetic considerations center on the unique musical images of *rāgas* versus the predictable mechanical constructions of *mēḷa rāgas.* However, in this context, he does *not* distinguish between Rāmāmātya's and Venkaṭamakhi's *mēḷa rāgas*, which serve only an organizational function, and Govinda's *mēḷa rāgas*, which as scales, serve both organizational and musical functions. Instead, Ramachandran deplores the concept and presence of *mēḷa rāgas*, and urges his audience to consider all *rāgas* as incomparable expressions of human music making. For example, with respect to *Rāga Śaṅkarābharaṇam*, #29 in Figures 11.32 and 11.33, he warns his listeners not to be influenced by Western music theory.

> I would just stress this point here, that there is little straight movement and that the *Rāga* is all twists and bends and gaps and full of stylized decorations; and to call this the diatonic major scale, is to miss its rich epic content . . .[120]

More importantly, K.V. Ramachandran is most concerned with *apurva* (lit. *uncommon*) *rāgas*, or *rāgas* that defy all attempts at categorization.

> I had referred to the vocabulary and idiom of which each *Rāga* had and which could ***not*** be defined by the mere *āroha* and *avaroha.* That was why Vidvan Rajamanickam Pillai [a famous contemporary violinist] said that such a definition was as absurd as defining a man by his height and girth. The *Rāgas* constituted the substance of our music; and the theorists who during the past five centuries have written about them have attempted to classify them under hypothetical labels called *Mēḷas*, because there was a need at the time to stress the *Svaras* more than the character of the melody as previously. The *mēḷa* was just a label and at no time did it have anything other than a classifying sense, like the terms vowel and consonant. All that it did indicate was the more prominent notes employed by the *Rāgas* grouped under it. Thus the *Mēḷa Māḷavagauḷa* [**#15**] was called variously as *Sāvēri*, *Bauḷi*, *Gurjari*, *Nādanāmakriyā* etc. by various writers and they knew quite well what they meant. It did not imply any taboo that *Svaras* not comprehended under the *Mēḷa* should not be employed. When the theorists generalized from a dozen *Rāgas* that employed *Śuddha* Ri [D♭], [*Śuddha*] Ma [F], and [*Śuddha*] Dha [A♭], *Antara* Ga [E], and *Kākalī* Ni [B], and called the *mēḷa Māḷavagauḷa*, it was this *mēḷa* which was derived from the *Rāgas* which it sought to group. But how could *Rāgas* in existence

long before the need for *Mēḷas* arose be said to be born from them? — a late label that came in the succession of labels beginning with the *Grāmas*. The very idea of *Janya* and *Janaka* is basically wrong.

Then the taboos of untouchability that the so-called *Janyas* born long before the so-called parents, should not touch any *svara* not found in the parent; that the *Sampūrṇa Rāgas* should pass through all the seven notes of the gamut up and down regularly as though it was a ladder or staircase! As I showed you in *Śaṅkarābharaṇa* [#**29**], irregularity is the very essence of the *Rāga;* the *Rāga* could flex itself according to its own genius, omit what notes it chose, make what combination it pleased. After the advent of the new idea of the *mēḷa*, all such irregularities had to be drastically ironed out and the *Rāgas* made straight. That is why in *Śaṅkarābharaṇa* people argue, Sa [C$^{\prime}$], [*Kākalī*] Ni [B], [*Catuśśruti*] Dha [A], Pa [G] is proper and not Sa Dha Pa. Then there were *Rāgas* like *Bhairavī* [#**20**], . . . , that found use for a variety of notes not found in the supposed parent *mēḷa* [see Section 11.35] . . . Thus the most beautiful *Rāgas* like *Bhairavī* were thought of as mixed, impure, hybrid and not pure like the *Mēḷa* . . . Why should something external to the *Rāga* be set up as its standard? If we would understand *Rāgas* at all, we should give up all such assumptions for which I have searched in vain for a basis.[121] (Bold italics and text in brackets mine.)

. . . I said that the *Svara* was one of the materials out of which the *Rāgas* were fashioned, even as out of bricks, the architect makes the dome. The end product dome is entirely different from the bricks of which it is made. And each *Rāga* has its own vocabulary and idiom; b[e]nds and twists and omissions are the rule and very rarely do *Rāgas* progress regularly . . . So in comparing *Rāgas* you will not be able to see the dome if you look only at the bricks. You should therefore listen to the *Rāga* and compare resemblances. So the term *Chaya* with reference to the melodic contours of the *Rāgas* are far more important than the omission or addition of a *svara*. The tone poem should be seen whole and not alone the members of which it is made.[122] (Correction in brackets mine.)

11.39

North Indian music and South Indian music are alike in two technical respects: (1) Musicians in both cultures do not tune their instruments to a given concert pitch or "absolute" pitch like A_4-440.0 cps. Instead, instruments are tuned to accommodate the natural range of an individual singer, or to accommodate the range of instruments in a particular ensemble. (2) Because musical ensembles in both cultures are small, the tuning of fixed-pitch instruments is not standardized. Consequently, one may hear a wide variety of "major thirds," "minor thirds," etc. throughout both regions. Musical groups typically vary between three and six players: (i) a lead singer, a lead stringed instrument, or a flute, (ii) a drone, called the *tamburā*, and (iii) various kinds of drums. When present, the fourth, fifth, or sixth instruments usually consist of additional stringed instruments. As long as musical groups are small, standardized tunings are not a crucial factor. Furthermore, the improvisational character of Indian music requires musical flexibility not just during performances of *rāgas*, but with respect to intonation as well. For example, in South Indian music there exists no significant fretless instruments, so the latter requirement is a little less demanding than in North Indian music, where the *sarod*, *sāraṅgī*, and *vicitra vīṇā* are all fretless instruments.

The seminal instrument of South Indian music is the modern *vīṇā*, classified as a lute. Its predecessor, the *kinnarī vīṇā*, is a stick-zither. However, when the lower gourd of the latter instrument was replaced with a round wooden body equipped with soundboard and bridge, it transformed the stick into a neck: hence the lute classification.[123] The *vīṇā* has seven strings and twenty-four fixed frets that span two "octaves." Four open playing strings pass over the frets, and are usually tuned to G_2, C_3, G_3 and C_4; the last string — which is nearest the player — is the most important melodic string. Three more fretless strings, stretched along the side of the neck, are commonly tuned to C_4, G_4, and C_5; the highest string is again nearest the player. These latter three strings are played by the little finger of the right hand in time with the rhythm, or *tāla* of the *rāga*.

C. Subrahmanya Ayyar, in his book entitled *The Grammar of South Indian (Karnatic) Music*, gives the following just scale for the Sa-string tuned to C_4: $^{16}/_{15}$ [$D\flat_4$], $^{10}/_{9}$ [D_4], $^{32}/_{27}$ [$E\flat_4$], $^{5}/_{4}$ [E_4], $^{4}/_{3}$ [F_4], $^{45}/_{32}$ [$F\sharp_4$], $^{3}/_{2}$ [G_4], $^{8}/_{5}$ [$A\flat_4$], $^{5}/_{3}$ [A_4], $^{16}/_{9}$ [$B\flat_4$], $^{15}/_{8}$ [B_4], $^{2}/_{1}$ [C_5].[124] After simplifying "octave" equivalents, the locations of these frets produce — relative to the latter string — the following scale on the Pa-string tuned to G_3: $^{8}/_{5}$ [$A\flat_3$], $^{5}/_{3}$ [A_3], $^{16}/_{9}$ [$B\flat_3$], $^{15}/_{8}$ [B_3], $^{1}/_{1}$ [C_4], $^{135}/_{128}$ [$D\flat_4$], $^{9}/_{8}$ [D_4], $^{6}/_{5}$ [$E\flat_4$], $^{5}/_{4}$ [E_4], $^{4}/_{3}$ [F_4], $^{45}/_{32}$ [$F\sharp_4$], $^{3}/_{2}$ [G_4]. Ayyar observes that this just tuning generates two different D♭'s, D's, and E♭'s on the *vīṇā*.[125] According to Powers, the second fret under the Sa-string of his *vīṇā* produces ratio $^{9}/_{8}$.[126] This is very plausible because all the frets of the *vīṇā* are not permanently attached to the instrument like the frets of a guitar, but are held in place with a removable mixture of hardened wax. Performers may, thereby, change the tuning of the *vīṇā* to suit their individual needs and circumstances.

In closing this discussion on South Indian music, consider the following analysis by Powers, which synthesizes Rāmāmātya's great tuning achievement and Venkaṭamakhi's great combinatorial achievement in the context of South Indian performance practice on the *vīṇā*:[127]

> The importance of the definitive fixing, through immobile frets, of twelve *svarasthānas* [tone-locations, equivalent to fret locations] to the octave cannot be overestimated in its importance for South Indian theory, and, in my opinion, in its importance for the peculiar tremulous style as well. The effect of reducing the number of theoretically available pitches to twelve must have been two-fold. First and foremost, it paved the way for the construction of a self-contained system of theoretical scales [modern *mēḷa rāgas*], based ***not*** on pitches derived from sung music but on twelve *svarasthānas* arrived at on an instrument, systematically permuted, as we have seen. Second, it meant that other notes produced by the voice, such as those alternative varieties of E and B [see Section 11.34], would have to be produced on the instrument by deflecting [bending] the playing string across the frets and thus increasing the tension. It is my belief that this is one of the principal causative factors underlying the undulating style so characteristic of the Southern music. In the North to this day the principal stringed instrument, the *sitar*, has seven movable frets to the octave, frets which can be adjusted to produce minute harmonic differences of pitch from *rāga* to *rāga;* such fine distinctions of pitch the South Indian *vainika* [*vīṇā* player] can only approximate by pulling the playing string slightly out of line across the fret.[128] (Bold italics and text in brackets mine.)

North India

11.40

Approximately one hundred and twenty years after the appearance of Rāmāmātya's *Svaramēlakalānidhi*, two theorists in North India wrote treatises that included mathematically defined tunings based on string length divisions. According to V.N. Bhatkhande (1860–1936), a great scholar of North Indian music, the descriptions of *vīṇā* tunings in Hṛdaya Nārāyaṇa's *Hṛdayaprakāśa* (*c.* 1660), and in Ahobala's *Saṅgītapārijāta* (*c.* 1680), are so similar that

> . . . we are not sure whether he [Ahobala] copied from Hṛdaya's book or *vice versa.*[129] (Text in brackets mine.)

Since no complete English translation of either work exists, we turn now to Bhatkhande's partial translation of the *Hṛdayaprakāśa.* Nārāyaṇa begins his description of the *vīṇā* tuning by giving the string divisions of the *śuddha svaras:*

Śuddha Svaras

> Exactly in the center of the wire (that portion of the wire which is capable of producing sound) will stand the *Tāra Ṣaḍja* [C']. If the whole wire is divided into three equal parts, the *Pañcama* [G] of the middle octave will stand at the end of the first part.
>
> The *Madhyama* [F] of the middle octave will be exactly between the two *Ṣaḍjas.* The *Śuddha Gāndhāra* [E♭] will stand exactly between Sa and Pa. If the distance between Sa and Pa be divided into three equal parts, then the *Śuddha Ṛṣabha* [D] will stand at the end of the first part.
>
> The *Śuddha Dhaivata* [A] ought to be placed in the interval between Pa and *Tāra* Sa. If the distance between the Pa and *Tāra* Sa be divided into three parts, the *Śuddha Niṣāda* [B♭] will come at the end of the second part.[130] (Text in brackets mine.)

(The prefix *tāra* means *high.*) Figure 11.34 shows these seven divisions in the order described by Nārāyaṇa;[131] note carefully that many bridge locations depend on previously calculated results. Consequently, a single error near the beginning of Nārāyaṇa's description will cause many subsequent mistakes. To help simplify the illustration, dots with arrows point to previously calculated divisions.

Table 11.18 gives a detailed analysis of the calculations of the ratios below the bridges in Figure 11.34. As described in Section 3.7, I use arrows in this table to indicate the inverse proportionality between modern length ratio x/n and frequency ratio n/x, or l.r. $x/n \rightarrow$ f.r. n/x. Therefore, to identify a given ratio in Nārāyaṇa's text, calculate a sequence of modern length ratios, and then invert the result to identify the frequency ratio.[132] This technique provides a method of analysis that is universally applicable to all tuning descriptions based on string length divisions. Finally, as described in Section 3.20, ancient length ratio n/x is indistinguishable from frequency ratio n/x. For this reason, the frequency ratios in Figure 11.34 define ancient length ratios as well.

Nārāyaṇa concludes his description of the *vīṇā* tuning by giving the string divisions of the *vikṛta svaras:*

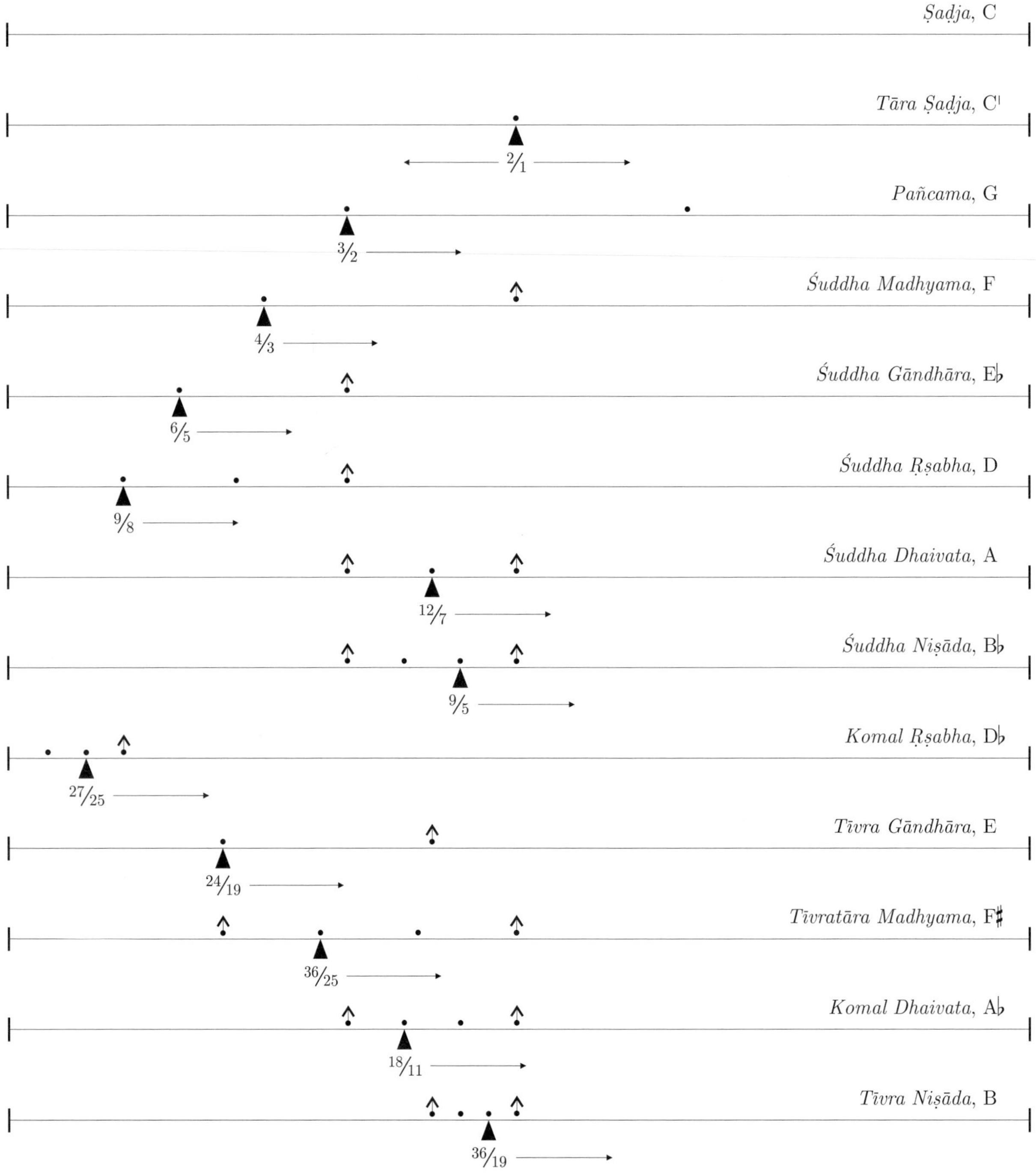

Figure 11.34 Nārāyaṇa's and Ahobala's string length divisions. Both theorists defined identical tunings by dividing a *vīṇā* string, or a section of the string, into two or three equal parts. Note that such simple divisions rapidly generate large prime numbers. (In Figures 11.34 and 11.35, dots with arrows point to previously calculated divisions.)

Table 11.18

MODERN LENGTH RATIO TO FREQUENCY RATIO CALCULATIONS OF NĀRĀYAṆA'S AND AHOBALA'S 12-TONE *VĪṆĀ* TUNING

Ṣaḍja, Tone C	$1/1$	Whole string length.
Tāra Ṣaḍja, Tone C'	$1 \times 1/2 = 1/2 \rightarrow 2/1$	Half of string.
Pañcama, Tone G	$1 \times 1/3 = 1/3$ $1 - 1/3 = 3/3 - 1/3 = 2/3 \rightarrow 3/2$	Third of string. Whole minus subsection.
Śuddha Madh., Tone F	$1/2 \times 1/2 = 1/4$ $1 - 1/4 = 4/4 - 1/4 = 3/4 \rightarrow 4/3$	Half of $1/2$ section. Whole minus subsection.
Śuddha Gāndhāra, Tone E♭	$1/3 \times 1/2 = 1/6$ $1 - 1/6 = 6/6 - 1/6 = 5/6 \rightarrow 6/5$	Half of $1/3$ section. Whole minus subsection.
Śuddha Ṛṣabha, Tone D	$1/3 \times 1/3 = 1/9$ $1 - 1/9 = 9/9 - 1/9 = 8/9 \rightarrow 9/8$	Third of $1/3$ section. Whole minus subsection.
Śuddha Dhaivata, Tone A	$2/3 - 1/2 = 4/6 - 3/6 = 1/6$ $1/6 \times 1/2 = 1/12$ $2/3 - 1/12 = 8/12 - 1/12 = 7/12 \rightarrow 12/7$	Length of internal section. Half of internal section. $2/3$ section minus subsection.
Śuddha Niṣāda, Tone B♭	$2/3 - 1/2 = 4/6 - 3/6 = 1/6$ $1/6 \times 2/3 = 2/18 = 1/9$ $2/3 - 1/9 = 6/9 - 1/9 = 5/9 \rightarrow 9/5$	Length of internal section. Two-thirds of internal section. $2/3$ section minus subsection.
Komal Ṛṣabha, Tone D♭	$1/9 \times 2/3 = 2/27$ $1 - 2/27 = 27/27 - 2/27 =$ $25/27 \rightarrow 27/25$	Two-thirds of $1/9$ section. Whole minus subsection.
Tīvra Gāndhāra, Tone E	$12/12 - 7/12 = 5/12$ $5/12 \times 1/2 = 5/24$ $1 - 5/24 = 24/24 - 5/24 =$ $19/24 \rightarrow 24/19$	Complement of $7/12$ section. Half of complement. Whole minus subsection.
Tīvratāra Madh., Tone F♯	$19/24 - 1/2 = 19/24 - 12/24 = 7/24$ $7/24 \times 1/3 = 7/72$ $19/24 - 7/72 = 57/72 - 7/72 = 50/72 =$ $25/36 \rightarrow 36/25$	Length of internal section. Third of internal section. $19/24$ section minus subsection.
Komal Dhaivata, Tone A♭	$2/3 - 1/2 = 4/6 - 3/6 = 1/6$ $1/6 \times 1/3 = 1/18$ $2/3 - 1/18 = 12/18 - 1/18 =$ $11/18 \rightarrow 18/11$	Length of internal section. Third of internal section. $2/3$ section minus subsection.
Tīvra Niṣāda, Tone B	$7/12 - 1/2 = 7/12 - 6/12 = 1/12$ $1/12 \times 2/3 = 2/36 = 1/18$ $7/12 - 2/36 = 21/36 - 2/36 =$ $19/36 \rightarrow 36/19$	Length of internal section. Two-thirds of internal section. $7/12$ section minus subsection.

Vikṛta Svaras

> If the distance between the *meru* [nut] and the *Śuddha Ṛṣabha* be divided into three parts the *Komal* Ri [D♭] will fall at the end of the second part. The *Tīvra Gāndhāra* [E] will come exactly between the *meru* and the *Śuddha Dhaivata*. If the distance between the *Tīvra* Ga and *Tāra* Sa be divided into three equal parts, the *Tīvratāra* Ma [F♯] will appear at the end of the first part. If the distance between Pa and *Tāra* Sa be divided into three parts, the *Komal Dhaivata* [A♭] will stand at the end of the first part. If the distance between the *Dhaivata* and the *Tāra* Sa is divided into three parts, the *Tīvra Niṣāda* [B] will come at the end of the second part.[133] (Text in brackets mine.)

(The prefix *komal* means *soft*, *tīvra* means *sharp*, and *tīvratāra* means *sharper*.) Figure 11.34 also shows these five divisions in the same order, and Table 11.18, the required calculations.

A great controversy exists with respect to the string division and subsequent identity of *Śuddha Dhaivata* [A].[134] In the following passage, Nārāyaṇa suggests that in actual practice, *Śuddha Dhaivata* was not tuned as ratio $^{12}/_{7}$, but as ratio $^{27}/_{16}$. First, consider what I call Nārāyaṇa's qualifying statement:

Qualifying Statement

> I have adopted this simple method of locating the *svaras* in the interests of those who have not a good *svaradhyāna* [sense of pitch]. The exact places of the *svaras* have to be fixed with the help of *saṃvāditva* [consonant intervals of the "fourth" and "fifth"]. It must always be remembered that the *svaras* in my *Ṣaḍjagrāma* [*suddha* scale] ***must*** stand in *saṃvādi* relationship.[135] (Bold italics and text in brackets mine.)

Given the concept of *saṃvāditva*, we conclude that Nārāyaṇa's scale consists of two tetrachords, tuned a "fifth" apart. However, since *Śuddha Ṛṣabha* [D] is ratio $^{9}/_{8}$, *Śuddha Dhaivata* [A], or a pure

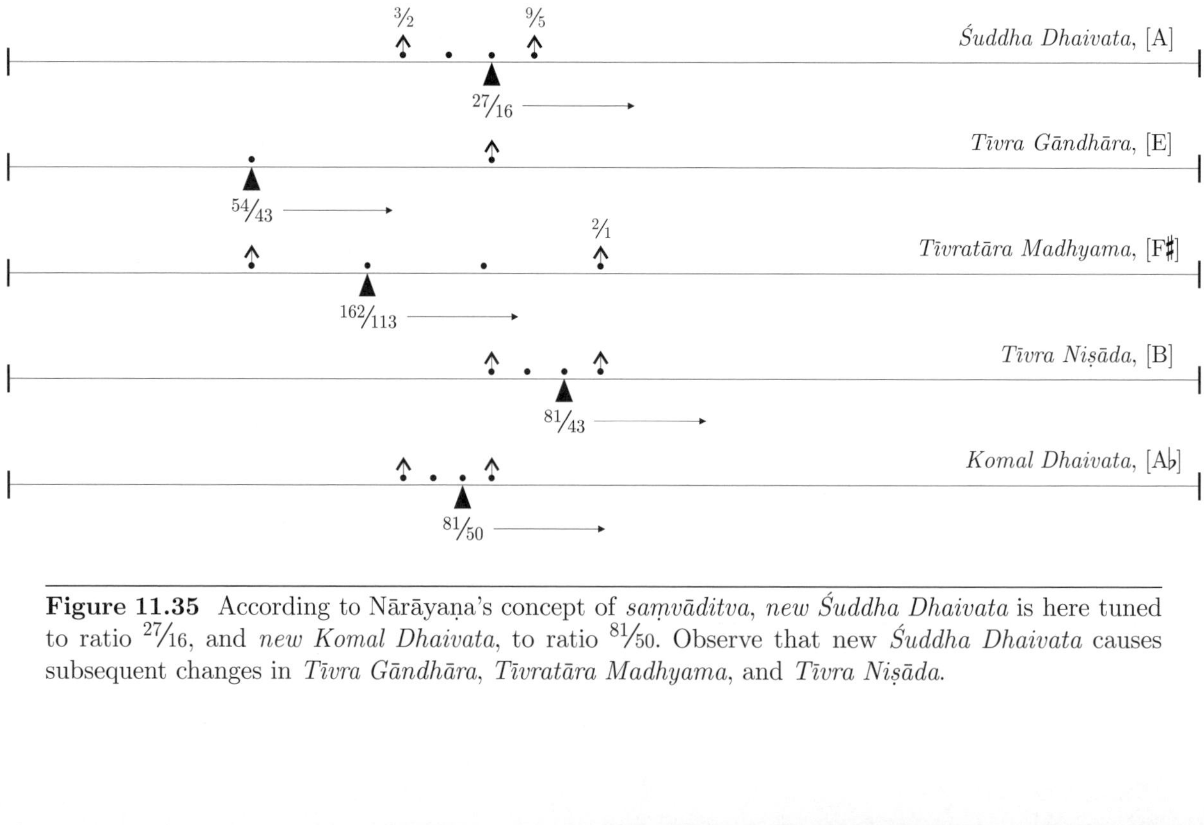

Figure 11.35 According to Nārāyaṇa's concept of *saṃvāditva*, *new Śuddha Dhaivata* is here tuned to ratio $^{27}/_{16}$, and *new Komal Dhaivata*, to ratio $^{81}/_{50}$. Observe that new *Śuddha Dhaivata* causes subsequent changes in *Tīvra Gāndhāra*, *Tīvratāra Madhyama*, and *Tīvra Niṣāda*.

Table 11.19

MODERN LENGTH RATIO TO FREQUENCY RATIO CALCULATIONS FOR NEW *ŚUDDHA DHAIVATA* AS RATIO $27/16$, FOR THREE SUBSEQUENT *SVARAS*, AND FOR *NEW KOMAL DHAIVATA* AS RATIO $81/50$

Śuddha Dhaivata, Tone A	$2/3 - 5/9 = 6/9 - 5/9 = 1/9$	Length of internal section.
	$1/9 \times 2/3 = 2/27$	Two-thirds of internal section.
	$2/3 - 2/27 = 18/27 - 2/27 =$	
	$16/27 \rightarrow 27/16$	$2/3$ section minus subsection.
Tīvra Gāndhāra, Tone E	$27/27 - 16/27 = 11/27$	Complement of $16/27$ section.
	$11/27 \times 1/2 = 11/54$	Half of complement.
	$1 - 11/54 = 54/54 - 11/54 =$	
	$43/54 \rightarrow 54/43$	Whole minus subsection.
Tīvratāra Madh., Tone F♯	$43/54 - 1/2 = 43/54 - 27/54 = 16/54 = 8/27$	Length of internal section.
	$8/27 \times 1/3 = 8/81$	Third of internal section.
	$43/54 - 8/81 = 129/162 - 16/162 =$	
	$113/162 \rightarrow 162/113$	$43/54$ section minus subsection.
Tīvra Niṣāda, Tone B	$16/27 - 1/2 = 32/54 - 27/54 = 5/54$	Length of internal section.
	$5/54 \times 2/3 = 10/162 = 5/81$	Two-thirds of internal section.
	$16/27 - 5/81 = 48/81 - 5/81 =$	
	$43/81 \rightarrow 81/43$	$16/27$ section minus subsection.
Komal Dhaivata, Tone A♭	$2/3 - 16/27 = 18/27 - 16/27 = 2/27$	Length of internal section.
	$2/27 \times 2/3 = 4/81$	Two-thirds of internal section.
	$2/3 - 4/81 = 54/81 - 4/81 = 50/81 \rightarrow 81/50$	$2/3$ section minus subsection.

Table 11.20

TWO VERSIONS OF NĀRĀYAṆA'S AND AHOBALA'S 12-TONE *VĪṆĀ* TUNING

Svara Ratios as Described by Nārāyaṇa and Ahobala				*Svara* Ratios as Intended by Nārāyaṇa and Ahobala			
1. Sa	C	$1/1$	0.0 ¢	Sa	C	$1/1$	0.0 ¢
2. *Komal* Ri	D♭	$27/25$	133.2 ¢	*Komal* Ri	D♭	$27/25$	133.2 ¢
3. *Śuddha* Ri	D	$9/8$	203.9 ¢	*Śuddha* Ri	D	$9/8$	203.9 ¢
4. *Śuddha* Ga	E♭	$6/5$	315.6 ¢	*Śuddha* Ga	E♭	$6/5$	315.6 ¢
5. *Tīvra* Ga	E	$24/19$	404.4 ¢	*Tīvra* Ga	E	$54/43$	394.4 ¢
6. *Śuddha* Ma	F	$4/3$	498.0 ¢	*Śuddha* Ma	F	$4/3$	498.0 ¢
7. *Tīvratāra* Ma	F♯	$36/25$	631.3 ¢	*Tīvratāra* Ma	F♯	$162/113$	623.6 ¢
8. Pa	G	$3/2$	702.0 ¢	Pa	G	$3/2$	702.0 ¢
9. *Komal* Dha	A♭	$18/11$	852.6 ¢	*Komal* Dha	A♭	$81/50$	835.2 ¢
10. *Śuddha* Dha	A	$12/7$	933.1 ¢	*Śuddha* Dha	A	$27/16$	905.9 ¢
11. *Śuddha* Ni	B♭	$9/5$	1017.6 ¢	*Śuddha* Ni	B♭	$9/5$	1017.6 ¢
12. *Tīvra* Ni	B	$36/19$	1106.4 ¢	*Tīvra* Ni	B	$81/43$	1096.3 ¢
13. *Tāra* Sa	C′	$2/1$	1200.0 ¢	*Tāra* Sa	C′	$2/1$	1200.0 ¢

"fifth" above, should be ratio $\frac{9}{8} \times \frac{3}{2} = \frac{27}{16}$. So, the question arises, "Why did Nārāyaṇa neglect to tune this *Śuddha* Dha?" In his qualifying statement, Nārāyaṇa makes two observations: (1) he states that his "simple method" is for those who do not have a good sense of pitch; (2) more to the point, he concedes that the *"svaras* have to be fixed with the help of *saṃvāditva."* Nārāyaṇa requires the *saṃvāditva* because he does not think the required consonances can be tuned by simply dividing his string subsections into two or three equal parts. Unfortunately, in the case of *Śuddha Dhaivata*, Nārāyaṇa is not aware of this fact: If the distance between *Pañcama*, ratio $\frac{3}{2}$ [G], and *Śuddha Niṣāda*, ratio $\frac{9}{5}$ [B♭], is divided into three equal parts, then *new Śuddha Dhaivata*, as ratio $\frac{27}{16}$, comes at the end of the second part. Because most *svara* computations depend on previously calculated results, Figure 11.35 and Table 11.19 show that new *Śuddha Dhaivata* causes subsequent changes in *Tīvra Gāndhāra* [E], *Tīvratāra Madhyama* [F♯], and *Tīvra Niṣāda* [B].

We may also apply the same reasoning to the interval between the "minor second" and the "minor sixth." Since *Komal Ṛṣabha* [D♭] is ratio $\frac{27}{25}$, *Komal Dhaivata* [A♭], or a pure "fifth" above, should be ratio $\frac{27}{25} \times \frac{3}{2} = \frac{81}{50}$. Now, if the distance between *Pañcama*, ratio $\frac{3}{2}$ [G], and new *Śuddha Dhaivata*, ratio $\frac{27}{16}$ [A], is divided into three equal parts, then *new Komal Dhaivata*, as ratio $\frac{81}{50}$, comes at the end of the second part. Figure 11.35 and Table 11.19 also account for this adjustment, which is completely consistent with Nārāyaṇa's "simple method" of string division.

Table 11.20 is a summary of the data discussed so far. The left section gives the *svara* ratios of Nārāyaṇa's description; here brackets indicate four *saṃvādi* "fifths" between the tones of the lower and upper tetrachords. The right section of Table 11.20 gives the *svara* ratios as intended by Nārāyaṇa's qualifying statement; here there are six *saṃvādi* "fifths" between tetrachords. Finally, notice that in the left section, a *saṃvādi* "fourth" also exists between D♭ [$\frac{27}{25}$] and F♯ [$\frac{36}{25}$].

~ 11.41 ~

The formal names of the North Indian *svaras* are as follows: *Khaḍaj* [Sa], *Rikhabh* [Re], *Gāndhāra* [Ga], *Madhyama* [Ma], *Pañcama* [Pa], *Dhaivata* [Dha], and *Nikhād* [Ni].[136] Consider now a comparison of the old and modern versions of the North Indian *śuddha* scales. Table 11.20 shows that the

Table 11.21

THE *SVARAS* OF THE MODERN NORTH INDIAN 12-TONE SCALE

1.	Sa	C
2.	*Komal* Re	D♭
3.	*Śuddha* Re	D
4.	*Komal* Ga	E♭
5.	*Śuddha* Ga	E
6.	*Śuddha* Ma	F
7.	*Tīvra* Ma	F♯
8.	Pa	G
9.	*Komal* Dha	A♭
10.	*Śuddha* Dha	A
11.	*Komal* Ni	B♭
12.	*Śuddha* Ni	B
13.	Sa	C$^{\prime}$

old śuddha scale includes two *komal* tones (two *flat* notes): *Śuddha* Ga [E♭], and *Śuddha* Ni [B♭]. In Figure 11.33, this scale is called *Kāfī Ṭhāṭ*. In contrast, Table 11.21 shows that the *modern śuddha scale*[137] has no *komal* tones. In Figure 11.33, this scale is called *Bilāval Ṭhāṭ*.

A further comparison of modern theory and practice reveals that musicians in South and North India (1) utilize virtually identical 12-tone scales, and (2) observe the melodic principle that prohibits the performance of *two consecutive svaras of the same name.* However, because South Indian theory recognizes three variants of Ri, Ga, Dha, and Ni, and North Indian theory, only two variants of Re, Ga, Dha, and Ni, these seemingly negligible enharmonic differences cause notable musical dissimilarities. For example, the left column in Figure 11.36 shows five South Indian *vivādi* tetrachords, or tetrachords that include two consecutive "semitones," and the right column, five North Indian chromatic tetrachord equivalents. Musicians in the North do *not* perform these chromatic

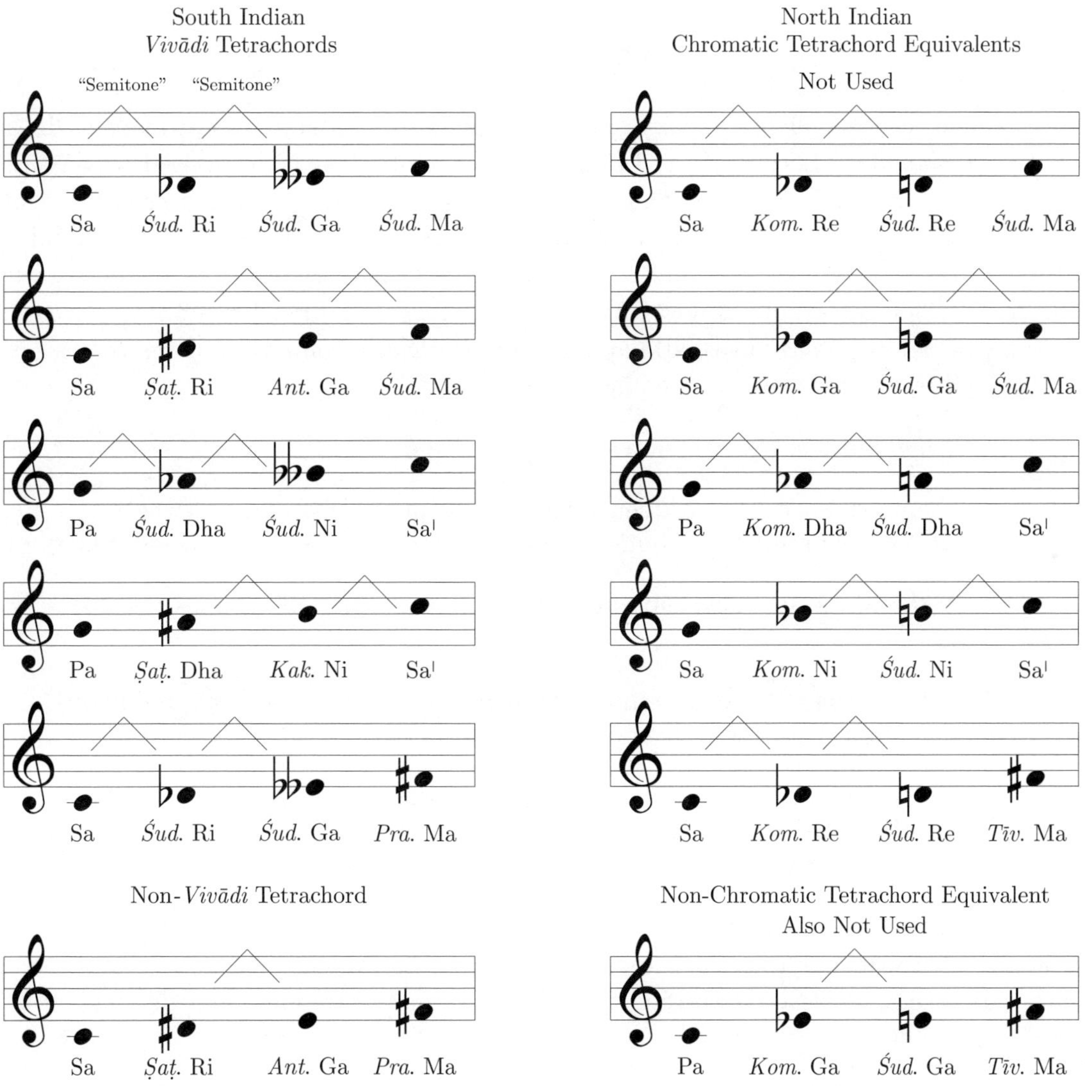

Figure 11.36 A comparison of South Indian *vivādi* tetrachords and North Indian chromatic tetrachord equivalents. The left column shows that musicians in the South perform *vivādi* tetrachords that include two "semitones" without violating the melodic principle that prohibits the use of two consecutive *svaras* of the same name. In contrast, musicians in the North do not perform the chromatic tetrachord equivalents, as well as the last tetrachord in the right column, since all these examples violate the above-mentioned melodic principle.

tetrachords because of the above-mentioned melodic principle. Now, refer back to Figure 11.32, and recall that we first encountered the five South Indian *vivādi* tetrachords in the context of Venkaṭamakhi's twelve-by-six matrix. As discussed in Note 118, tetrachord C–D♯–E–F♯ in Row 12 is a non-*vivādi* tetrachord, which means that it does not have two consecutive "semitones." Notice that this South Indian non-*vivādi* tetrachord appears as the sixth or last example in the left column of Figure 11.36. Now, observe that the North Indian non-chromatic tetrachord equivalent appears as the sixth or last example in the right column of Figure 11.36. Musicians in the North do *not* perform this tetrachord for the *same* reason as the other five tetrachords: namely, it contains two consecutive *svaras* of the same name. Therefore, in Figure 11.32, they exclude all the tetrachords in Rows 1, 6, 7, and 12, and in Columns 1 and 6, or a grand total of 40 *mēḷas* in Venkaṭamakhi's twelve-by-six matrix. The remaining prototypes, 72 *mēḷas* − 40 *mēḷas* = 32 *mēḷas*, constitute the maximum number of theoretically available *rāga*-categories in the music of North India.

∼ 11.42 ∼

The North Indian concept of *ṭhāṭ* is very similar to the South Indian concept of *mēḷa*. In a work entitled *Rāgataraṅgiṇī*,[138] Locana (fl. *c.* 1400) identified 12 *ṭhāṭs*, which he used to classify more than seventy *janya rāgas*.[139] In recent times, the writings of Bhatkhande are frequently mentioned in conjunction with 10 *ṭhāṭs*, which he utilized to organize more than one hundred and twenty North Indian *janya rāgas*.[140] Unfortunately, because none of his large works have been translated into European languages, we must now turn to secondary accounts of his writings. According to N.A. Jairazbhoy, a key passage in Bhatkhande's *Kramik Pustak Mālikā* stipulates that all modern *ṭhāṭs* are defined by the following five requirements:

> 1. A *ṭhāṭ* must have seven notes.
>
> 2. The notes must be in sequence Sa Re Ga Ma Pa Dha and Ni (whether *śuddh* or *vikrit* position — both versions of a single note being forbidden).
>
> 3. A *ṭhāṭ* does not have separate ascending and descending lines (as do *rāgs*).
>
> 4. A *ṭhāṭ* does not have any emotional quality (in contrast with *rāgs* which, by definition, have the power to convey emotions).
>
> 5. *Ṭhāṭs* are named after prominent *rāgs* in order to make them ***easy to remember and recognize***, whether or not these *rāgs* are heptatonic.[141] (Bold italics mine.)

In other words, modern North Indian *ṭhāṭs* are very similar to modern South Indian *mēḷas* (or *mēḷa-kartas*) because theorists define both *rāga*-categories as mechanical scales that are *krama sampūrṇa* in ascent and descent. However, according to Walter Kaufmann, we must also distinguish between *ṭhāṭs* and *mēḷas* in one critical respect:

> *Ṭhāṭa* (or *ṭhāṭ*) is a Prakrit word which means "model," "prototype," "array," or "mold." North Indian Sanskrit theorists use the word for "head-scale," the material of which dominates to a greater or lesser degree a whole group of *rāgas*. The *ṭhāṭa* itself is ***no*** *rāga*, but only a scale, an "array" of notes.[142] (Bold italics mine.)

We conclude, therefore, that *ṭhāṭs* serve no musical function in North Indian music.

D♭	D	E♭	E	F	F♯	A♭	A	B♭	B
Re		Ga		Ma		Dha		Ni	
Kom.	*Śud.*	*Kom.*	*Śud.*	*Śud.*	*Tīv.*	*Kom.*	*Śud.*	*Kom.*	*Śud.*
1	2	1	2	1	2	1	2	1	2

Figure 11.37 A schematic that depicts the scale degrees associated with *svaras* Re, Ga, Ma, Dha, and Ni. In Figure 11.38, these numeric subscripts conveniently demonstrate how one may use combinatorics to generate Roy's 32 *ṭhāṭs*.

Hemendra Lal Roy echoes these basic requirements in his highly analytic and critical work entitled *Problems of Hindustani Music.*

> Bhatkhande finds he can accommodate all the *rāgas* within ten scales and thinks that modern Hindustani music uses only ten scales out of a possible seventy-two found out mathematically by Venkaṭamakhi (See App. III). He says that a scale or *ṭhāṭa* should be a series of seven notes using all the notes Sa, Re, Ga, Ma, Pa, Dha and Ni (*śuddha* or *vikṛta*). It is not necessary, he remarks, for a *ṭhāṭa* should sound sweet, for the *ṭhāṭa* is ***not*** a *rāga*. He uses ten *ṭhāṭas* and names them after the most characteristic *rāgas* called *āśraya-rāgas* . . .[143] (Bold italics mine.)

	P D_1 N_1 S' **G A♭ B♭ C'**	P D_1 N_2 S' **G A♭ B C'**	P D_2 N_1 S' **G A B♭ C'**	P D_2 N_2 S' **G A B C'**
S R_1 G_1 M_1 **C D♭ E♭ F**	1	2	3	4
S R_1 G_2 M_1 **C D♭ E F**	5	6	7	8
S R_2 G_1 M_1 **C D E♭ F**	9	10	11	12
S R_2 G_2 M_1 **C D E F**	13	14	15	16
S R_1 G_1 M_2 **C D♭ E♭ F♯**	17	18	19	20
S R_1 G_2 M_2 **C D♭ E F♯**	21	22	23	24
S R_2 G_1 M_2 **C D E♭ F♯**	25	26	27	28
S R_2 G_2 M_2 **C D E F♯**	29	30	31	32

Figure 11.38 An eight-by-four matrix that generates Roy's 32 *ṭhāṭs*. The numeric subscripts indicate that this organizational system produces all possible heptatonic permutations of the 12-tone scale as specified by North Indian music theory.

In Appendix III, Roy reviews several problems associated with the classification of Hindustani music, and then makes this recommendation:

> If mathematical counting of possible seven-note scales is at all necessary, in the Hindustani system thirty-two scales will suffice with the help of simple arithmetic.*
>
> *I wrote this to Panditji [Bhatkhande] in 1932 and he replied, ". . . I quite agree that the 32 scales you point out would be quite enough for modern music."[144] (Text in brackets mine.)

Although Roy does not give the exact results of his "simple arithmetic," he is the first known writer to propose a system of 32 *ṭhāṭs*. Similar to Venkaṭamakhi's 72 *mēḷakartas* (see Section 11.36), we may conveniently demonstrate that 32 *ṭhāṭs* represent all possible heptatonic permutations of the North Indian 12-tone scale. Refer to the schematic in Figure 11.37, which shows that two variants of Re, Ga, Ma, Dha, and Ni account for ten of a total number of twelve *svara* names in Table 11.21.

Figure 11.38 shows that we may represent all possible upward progressions from Re to Ga, and from Dha to Ni, by applying the following four combinations of subscripts — 1-1, 1-2, 2-1, 2-2 — to four Re–Ga pairs in the lower tetrachords, and to four Dha–Ni pairs in the upper tetrachords. *Ṭhāṭs* 1–16 express these pairs with Ma_1, or F, and *Ṭhāṭs* 17–32, with Ma_2, or F♯. The result is an eight-by-four matrix that generates Roy's 32 *ṭhāṭs*, or 32 heptatonic permutations.

Jairazbhoy also advocates the implementation of Roy's system.[145] Unfortunately, because he decided to map the 32 *ṭhāṭs* over the extremely complicated three-dimensional surface of an icosahedron,[146] musicians and readers of Jairazbhoy's book are unaware that the simple yet highly effective two-dimensional eight-by-four matrix yields *exactly* the same results.

Now, turn back to Figure 11.33, and note that the second column of numbers in parentheses indicates the identities of Bhatkhande's ten scales as they appear in the eight-by-four matrix. However, in the *Hindustānī Saṅgīta Paddhati*, Bhatkhande organized his *ṭhāṭs* in the numerical order shown below:[147]

1. *Kalyān*
2. *Bilāval*
3. *Khamāj*
4. *Bhairav(a)*
5. *Pūrvī*
6. *Mārvā*
7. *Kāfī*
8. *Āsāvarī*
9. *Bhairavī*
10. *Tōḍi*

Although Bhatkhande agreed in theory that Roy's 32 *ṭhāṭs* account for all possible *rāga*-prototypes in North Indian music, he never officially endorsed the idea.

I agree with Roy that his simple arithmetic approach best describes all possible *ṭhāṭ* permutations. While Bhatkhande may have rendered a valuable service in cataloging a large body of North Indian *rāgas* under only ten *ṭhāṭs*, his contribution is essentially academic. Bhatkhande focused primarily on the known. Unlike Venkaṭamakhi and Roy, he did not attempt to address the unknown; apparently, the future development of music did not concern him. I often wonder how many musicians advocate the false premise that North Indian music offers only 10 *ṭhāṭs*. According to Figure 11.38, Bhatkhande's *ṭhāṭs* include less than a third of the total number of available scales.

I would like to end this theoretical discussion by offering the following observation. At times, the subject of Indian music seems hopelessly complex and fragmented. The South Indian matrix and the North Indian matrix serve as a unifying principle that provides a basic conceptual framework for a fundamental understanding of *all* Indian music.

~ 11.43 ~

In the West, the best-known and musically most influential instrument of India is the *sitar*. The name *sitar* originates from the Persian *setār* (lit. *three strings*). Curt Sachs classifies the *sitar* as a lute.

> A lute is composed of a body, and of a neck which serves both as a handle and as a means of stretching the strings beyond the body. In most cases the strings are stopped . . .
>
> Most primitive and oriental lutes are *long lutes*, in which the neck or stick is longer than the body. We distinguish an older *pierced lute*, with a stick penetrating, or at least entering, the body and a less primitive *long neck lute*, with an attached neck instead of the piercing stick, for instance the Persian *sitar-tanbur*.[148]

The modern concert *sitar*, called *tarafdār sitar* — *sitar with sympathetic strings* — has a standard length of approximately 4 feet. The body or shell, made of a gourd cut in half and covered with a wood soundboard, is about 1 foot long; the neck, therefore, is about 3 feet long. From the tuning pegs at the top of the neck, the playing strings pass over the frets to a uniquely shaped parabolic bridge;[149] from here, they pass to the string holder, which is attached to the far end of the shell. A concert *sitar* has between eighteen and twenty frets. In his book entitled *My Music, My Life*, Ravi Shankar includes two line drawings of a *sitar* with twenty frets.[150] The frets are made of brass or silver, and have a convex oval shape that enables the player to easily bend the string in the production of ornaments, as well as macrotonal and microtonal inflections. The frets are held against the neck with silk bindings, which enable the player to move the frets and, thereby, change the tuning. As discussed below, because *sitars* are very rarely equipped with 24 frets, players regularly adjust the locations of four frets to perform *rāgas* in ten different *ṭhāṭs*.

Sitars have either six or seven playing strings, and between eleven and thirteen sympathetic strings. Refer to Figure 11.39, which illustrates the fretting and tuning of five playing strings. This figure does not show two additional strings called *cikārī* strings that are located to the left of String V and numbered Strings VI and VII. For a *sitar* tuned in C, the latter strings sound C_4 and C_5, respectively. The *cikārī* strings are stretched along the side of the neck nearest the player, and ". . . are never stopped, but plucked in the gaps between the melody notes in order to maintain a pervasive (if not constant) drone."[151] This playing technique produces not a passive background drone, but a rhythmic drone pulse.

Figure 11.39 shows that String I is the primary melodic string. Although sitarists also use String II for melodic purposes, its chief function in the music of Ravi Shankar is as a drone. Manfred M. Junius describes the function of String II by noting

> The second string is touched lightly, it provides the sound of the drone, which is heard most of the time. The prominence with which players sound the drone strings varies from one Sitarist to another. With some it is never silent, while others use it very discreetly and increase or decrease its volume at will. The transparent lucidity of *Pandit* Ravi Shankar's style is rather largely based on the perfect control of the second string.[152]

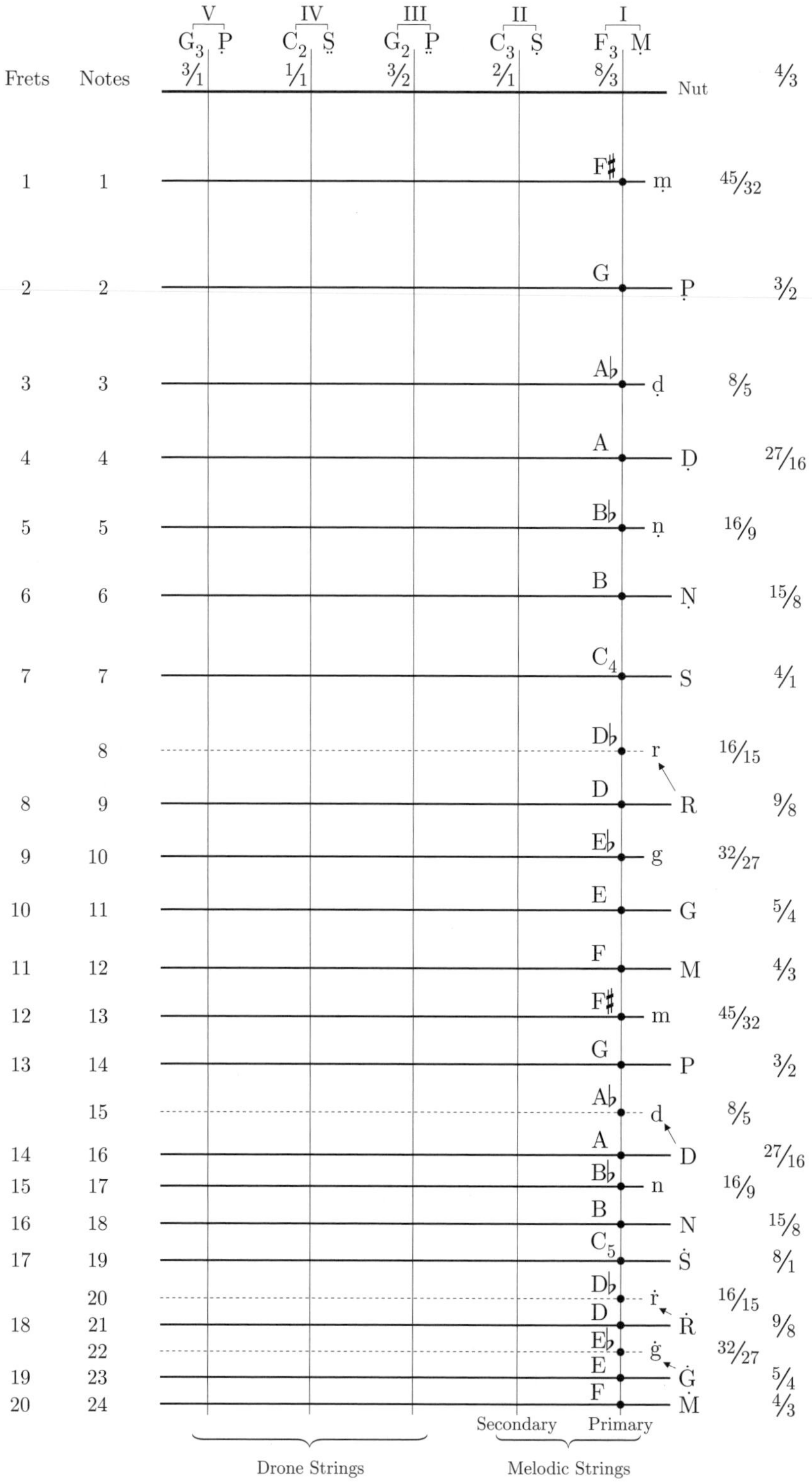

Figure 11.39 A possible tuning of the North Indian *sitar*. Musicians in India do not tune fixed-pitch instruments to a standard scale. In agreement with the general requirements of North Indian scale theory in Table 11.21, I chose Bharata's *Naiṣādī śuddha jāti* as the *śuddha* scale on String I between C_4 and C_5. (See Section 11.25.) Solid horizontal lines indicate frets on String I between C_4 and C_5 that are suitable for *rāgas* in these *ṭhāṭs: Bilāval, Kalyān, Khamāj, Kāfī.* Within this "octave," two arrows that point to dashed lines indicate fret adjustments required by *rāgas* in the remaining six *ṭhāṭs.*

In contrast, Vilayat Khan, who has pioneered a unique adjustable 6-string *sitar* tuning,[153] uses Strings I and II for playing *rāga* melodies.[154] Finally, Strings III, IV, and V are mainly used as drones.

Musicians in North India have adapted the Chevé System (see Section 11.12) for notating music. In many *sitar* primers, the original cipher-dot notation has been replaced with a letter-dot notation. As indicated in the illustration below, uppercase letters without dots represent *śuddha svaras* in the central heptatonic span, which includes tones C_4 through B_4. Uppercase letters with one or two dots below represent *śuddha svaras* one "octave" or two "octaves" below the central span, respectively, and uppercase letters with one dot above represent *śuddha svaras* one "octave" above the central span.

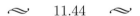

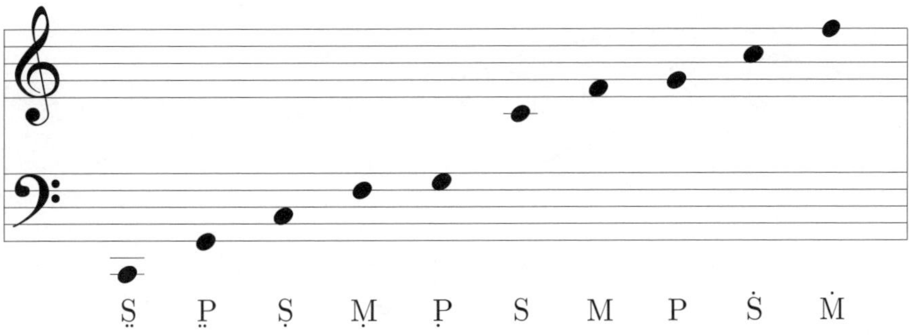

Furthermore, Figure 11.39 shows that lowercase letters without dots represent *vikṛta svaras* in the central heptatonic span, etc. Whereas r, g, d, and n are *komal* (flat) variants of Re, Ga, Dha, and Ni, m is the *tīvra* (sharp) variant of Ma.

On the modern *sitar*, Open Strings IV–I are tuned to the same frequency ratios as Open Strings I–IV of Rāmāmātya's *śuddha mēḷa vīṇā*. (See Section 11.34.) As discussed in Section 11.39, musicians in India do not tune their instruments to a given concert pitch; consequently, the tuning of Strings II and IV typically vary between B and D. Furthermore, because Indian musicians also do not tune fixed-pitch instruments to a standard scale, the tuning in Figure 11.39 represents only one of many possibilities. In conformity with the general requirements of North Indian scale theory as depicted in Table 11.21, I chose Bharata's *Naiṣādī śuddha jāti* as the *śuddha* scale on String I between C_4 and C_5.[155] (See Section 11.25.)

Now, given a tuning in C, Figure 11.39 shows that Strings I and II are tuned to F_3 and C_3, respectively. When compared to the scales in Figure 11.33, we see that the fret locations on String I between C_4 and C_5 are suitable for *rāgas* in the following *ṭhāṭs: Bilāval, Kalyān, Khamāj*, and *Kāfī*. To play *rāgas* in *Mārvā*, move only the R-fret to the r-fret location; similarly, to play *rāgas* in *Āsāvarī*, move only the D-fret to the d-fret location. To play *rāgas* in the four remaining *ṭhāṭs: Bhairavī, Bhairav, Tōdī*, and *Pūrvī*, move both the R-fret and the D-fret to their respective *komal* positions. Finally, Figure 11.39 also shows two similar adjustments for frets Ṙ and Ġ above C_5.

~ 11.44 ~

Since recordings of North Indian music are easily obtained, I would like to end this discussion by recommending two rather unusual musical sources. First, consider listening to the music of Gopal Krishan, who is a great innovator and virtuoso of the Hindustani *vicitra vīṇā*.[156] On this *fretless vīṇā*, classified as a zither, performers stop the melodic strings with a glass ball held in the left hand.[157] Due to the unlimited intonational possibilities of this instrument, it is very reminiscent of the Chinese *ch'in.* (See Sections 11.3–11.8.) Second, for those who may be overwhelmed by the profound complexity and general unfamiliarity of Indian music, consider watching a film entitled *Pather Panchali — Song of the Little Road* — directed by Satyajit Ray, with music by Ravi Shankar.[158] This film chronicles the life and struggles of a poor rural family in the northern state of Bengal. Figure 11.40 shows that the film's music is based on a theme appropriately composed in *Bilāval Ṭhāṭ.* One hears this melody performed on a transverse flute, *sitar*, and *sāraṅgī;* the latter is a highly developed short-necked bowed lute with three playing strings. Ravi Shankar's improvisations are especially noteworthy. Western listeners, who are accustomed to clearly discernible melodies, will find it easy not only to follow these instruments, but also to enjoy a style of improvisation that is uniquely Indian in character.

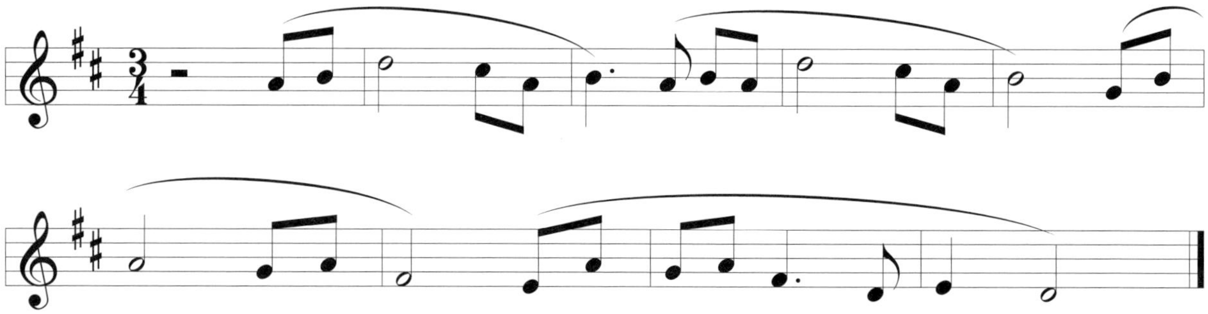

Figure 11.40 The musical theme of Satyajit Ray's *Pather Panchali*, music by Ravi Shankar. The simple penetrating beauty of this melody may be heard throughout the film, which is a moving testament to the sorrows and passions of life and love.

Notes

1. Ghosh, M., Translator (Vol. 1, Ch. 1–27, 1950; Vol. 2, Ch. 28–36, 1961). *The Nāṭyaśāstra*, by Bharata, *Volume 2*, p. 5. Bibliotheca Indica, The Asiatic Society, Calcutta, India.

2. *Ibid.*, pp. 5–7.

3. *Ibid.*, p. 7.

4. Jairazbhoy, N.A. (1975). An interpretation of the 22 *śrutis. Asian Music* **VI**, Nos. 1–2, pp. 38–59.

5. *Ibid.*, p. 41.

6. *The Nāṭyaśāstra, Volume 2*, pp. 8–9.

7. See Chapter 3, Parts III–IV.

8. See Sections 9.1 and 9.8.

9. See Section 11.11.

10. See Sections 10.32–10.33.

11. See Section 10.1.

12. See Sections 10.15 and 10.22.

13. *Asian Music* **VI**, 1975, p. 41.

14. Sadie, S., Editor (1984). *The New Grove Dictionary of Musical Instruments, Volume 3*, pp. 729–730. Macmillan Press Limited, London, England.

15. Coomaraswamy, A.K. (1930). The parts of a *vīṇā*. *Journal of the American Oriental Society* **50**, No. 3, pp. 244–253.

16. *The New Grove Dictionary of Musical Instruments, Volume 3*, pp. 304–305.

17. *Journal of the American Oriental Society* **50**, No. 3, p. 250.

18. To avoid significant cumulative errors in tuning scales with many small intervals requires sophisticated instruments that are physically stable and acoustically accurate. In contrast, tuning scales with only a few large intervals on simple instruments may produce errors that are less objectionable.

19. Bhandarkar, R.S.P.R. (1912). Contribution to the study of ancient Hindu music. *The Indian Antiquary* **XLI**, pp. 157–164, 185–195, 254–265.

    In this remarkably thorough study, Bhandarkar traces the inaccuracies found in works on ancient Indian music by both Asian and European writers. He also stresses correct interpretations of *śruti* distributions and *grāma* constructions.

20. Nijenhuis, E.W., Translator (1970). *Dattilam: A Compendium of Ancient Indian Music.* E. J. Brill, Leiden, Netherlands.

    This translation of the *Dattilam* spans pp. 17–61, whereas Nijenhuis' commentary spans pp. 62–425. Throughout the commentary, Nijenhuis includes many translated excerpts from the works of Bharata, Nārada, Mataṅga, and Sārṅgadeva. On several occasions, Notes below refer the reader to these translations in Nijenhuis' *Dattilam.*

21. Lath, M., Translator (1978). *A Study of Dattilam: A Treatise on the Sacred Music of Ancient India.* Impex India, New Delhi, India.

22. *Ibid.*, p. x.

23. *Dattilam*, p. 19.

24. *A Study of Dattilam*, p. 218.

25. See Section 10.27.

26. See Section 10.22.

27. *The Nāṭyaśāstra, Volume 2*, p. 28.

28. *Dattilam*, p. 33.

29. Shringy, R.K., and Sharma, P.L., Translators (Vol. 1, Ch. 1, 1978; Vol. 2, Ch. 2–4, 1989). *Saṅgītaratnākara*, by Sārṅgadeva, *Volume 1*, p. 267. *Volume 1*, Motilal Banarsidass, Delhi, India; *Volume 2*, Munshiram Manoharlal, New Delhi, India.

30. Rowell, L. (1981). Early Indian musical speculation and the theory of melody. *Journal of Music Theory* **25.2**, pp. 217–244.

The following quotations appear on pp. 232–235 in Rowell's excellent article:

> The most vital choices are those which direct the course of a melody into one of the prescribed *jātis*, the ancestors of the modern concept of *rāga*. The word *jāti* is one of those bland words so useful in musical terminology; it is a past passive participle of the verbal root *jan* [cognate with the Greek word *genesis*] meaning "to be born, arise," and thus its developed meaning: "kind, type, species." A glance at the standard ten characteristics of *jāti* discloses most of the familiar standards by which a mode is recognized in Medieval Western theory — incipit, final, confinal, and ambitus (high and low): 1. *graha*, initial; 2. *aṃśa*, prominent, usually called "sonant" by Indian authors; 3. *tāra*, high; 4. *mandra*, low; 5. *ṣāḍava*, hexatonic; 6. *auḍuvita*, pentatonic; 7. *alpatva*, scarce, weak; 8. *bahutva*, copious; 9. *nyāsa*, final; 10. *apanyāsa*, confinal, an internal cadence tone.
>
> . . . *Aṃśa*, according to the *Nāṭyaśāstra*, had its own list of ten *lakṣaṇas:* it is the generating tone, it determines not only the low tone but the interval between low and high tones, it is the tone most frequently heard, it determines the initial, the final, the three types of confinals, and is the tone which all the others follow. *Aṃśa*, one gathers, is no trivial concept.
>
> . . . *Vādi* or "sonance" is treated formally as a subtonic of *grāma* (scale), but the concept first becomes operational when applied to the structure of an individual *jāti*. Here are four possibilities: 1. *vādi*, sonant, "ruling note" (*aṃśa*); 2. *saṃvādi*, consonant, harmonic affinity; 3. *vivādi*, dissonant, distorted; 4. *anuvādi*, neutral. The commentator Abhinava quotes an old analogy: "*Vādi* is the king, *saṃvādi* is the minister who follows him, *vivādi* is like the enemy and should be sparingly employed, and *anuvādi* denotes the retinue of the followers."

31. *The Nāṭyaśāstra, Volume 2*, pp. 15–16.

32. (A) *The Nāṭyaśāstra, Volume 2*, pp. 18–19.

(B) *Dattilam*, p. 177.

33. (A) *The Nāṭyaśāstra, Volume 2*, pp. 16–17.

(B) *Dattilam*, p. 168.

(C) Widdess, R. (1995). *The Rāgas of Early Indian Music*, pp. 54–56. The Clarendon Press, Oxford, England.

34. *The Nāṭyaśāstra, Volume 2*, p. 17.

35. Because the *saṃsarga jātis* have no recognizable symmetries and no internal patterns, they have little theoretical or practical value for tracing the evolution of Indian music.

36. *The Nāṭyaśāstra, Volume 2*, p. 13.

37. *Dattilam*, p. 19.

38. *A Study of Dattilam*, p. 227.

39. *Ibid.*

40. *Ibid.*, p. 228.

41. See Section 3.6.

42. *The Nāṭyaśāstra, Volume 2*, p. 21.

43. *Dattilam*, p. 229.

44. Sharma, P.L., Editor and Translator (Vol. 1, Ch. 1, 1992; Vol. 2, Ch. 2–6, 1994). *Bṛhaddeśī* of Śrī Mataṅga Muni, *Volume 2*, p. 47. Indira Gandhi National Centre for the Arts in association with Motilal Banarsidass Publishers, Delhi, India.

45. Sachs, C. (1940). *The History of Musical Instruments*, pp. 235–236. W. W. Norton & Company, Inc., New York.

46. *The Nāṭyaśāstra, Volume 1*, p. 102.

47. *Ibid.*, p. 108.

48. *Ibid.*, p. 109.

49. *The Nāṭyaśāstra, Volume 2*, p. 31.

50. *Ibid.*, p. 29, Footnote (1), 2. In this footnote, the reference (XIX. 31–40) should read (XXIX. 13–14).

51. *The Rāgas of Early Indian Music*, pp. 36–37.

52. *The Nāṭyaśāstra, Volume 2*, p. 30.

53. (A) *Ibid.*, pp. 155–156.

    (B) *Dattilam*, p. 173.

    Nijenhuis gives Bharata's original text, which includes the term *gāna[ṃ]*.

54. *The Rāgas of Early Indian Music*, p. 43.

55. *Ibid.*, p. 9, and also p. 37.

56. *Dattilam*, p. 175.

57. (A) *The Nāṭyaśāstra, Volume 2*, p. 156.

    See *Nāṭyaśāstra*, Chapter 29, for numerous descriptions of the *Alaṃkāras* (or *alaṅkāras*), the ornaments (embellishments or decorations) of music.

    (B) *Dattilam*, p. 174.

    Nijenhuis gives Bharata's original text, which ends on the term *gānam.*

58. Bhise, U.R., Translator (1986). *Nāradīyā Śikṣā*, by Nārada, p. 84. Bhandarkar Institute Press, Poona, India.

59. (A) *Dattilam*, pp. 174–175.

    (B) *Nāradīyā Śikṣā*, pp. 84–86.

60. *The Nāṭyaśāstra, Volume 2*, p. 19.

61. (A) *The Rāgas of Early Indian Music*, p. 41.

 (B) *Nāradīyā Śikṣā*, p. 82.

62. *The Rāgas of Early Indian Music*, p. 40.

63. (A) Sathyanarayana, R., Editor (1957). *Kuḍimiyāmalai Inscription on Music.* Śri Varalakshmi Academies of Fine Arts, Parimala Press, Mysore, India.

 (B) Bhandarkar, R.S.P.R. (1913–1914). Kuḍimiyāmalai inscription on music. *Epigraphia Indica* **XII**, No. 28, pp. 226–237.

 This article contains detailed photographs of the inscriptions, and compares this ancient text to Nārada's *Nāradīyā Śikṣā* and Sārṅgadeva's *Saṅgītaratnākara.*

 (C) *The Rāgas of Early Indian Music*, Chapter 4 and Appendix 2.

 Chapter 4 deals exclusively with the Kuḍimiyāmalai Inscription, and Appendix 2 gives a detailed musical analysis of the inscription according to Widdess' interpretation of the text.

64. *Bṛhaddeśi, Volume 2*, pp. 78–79.

65. *The Rāgas of Early Indian Music*, p. 41.

66. *Bṛhaddeśi, Volume 2*, p. 93.

67. *Ibid.*, pp. 87–93.

68. *Saṅgītaratnākara, Volume 2. Śuddhasādhārita*, *Ṣaḍjagrāma*, and *Śuddhakaiśika*, pp. 20–26; *Madhyamagrāma*, pp. 61–62; *Ṣāḍava*, pp. 67–68; *Śuddhakaiśikamadhyama*, pp. 85–86; and *Śuddhapañcama*, pp. 118–119.

69. See Section 11.24.

70. *Epigraphia Indica* **XII**, 1913–1914, p. 228.

71. See Section 11.25.

72. Discussed in this context at the end of Section 11.25.

73. Notable exceptions to the second generality are thousands of *rāga* songs written by master composers Tyāgarāja (1767–1847), Śyāma Śāstri (1763–1827), Muthuswami Dīkṣitar (1775–1835), and others.

74. Aiyar, M.S.R., Translator (1932). *Svaramēlakalānidhi*, by Rāmāmātya, p. 43. The Annamalai University, India.

75. *Saṅgītaratnākara, Volume 1*, pp. 141–146.

76. *Svaramēlakalānidhi*, p. 48.

77. *Ibid.*, p. 61.

78. *Ibid.*, pp. 48–49. Text in brackets from a slightly different translation on p. xxiii.

79. *Ibid.*, pp. 49–50.

80. *Ibid.*, p. 50.

81. *The New Grove Dictionary of Musical Instruments, Volume 3*, p. 730.

82. *Svaramēlakalānidhi*, pp. 52–53.

83. *Ibid.*, pp. 53–54.

84. See Section 10.15.

85. See Section 9.4.

86. *Svaramēlakalānidhi*, pp. 54–55.

87. Since Rāmāmātya did not calculate the length ratios of his *vīṇā* tuning, the possibility exists that even though he experienced the comma of Didymus, he was *not* aware of the comma of Pythagoras. A "disagreeable beat" between near-unisons or two tones that are close (as between two different E's or two different B's) is much easier to hear than between near-"octaves" or two tones that are distant (as between D♭–C♯ꞌ or F♯–G♭ꞌ). (For a description of the beat phenomenon, see Section 5.18.) This predicament illustrates a valuable lesson: sometimes the mind teaches the body to recognize distinctions not easily experienced through the senses. See Section 10.56 for a discussion of a similar problem encountered by Mersenne.

88. See Section 10.15.

89. *Svaramēlakalānidhi*, p. 55.

90. Kaufmann, W. (1976). *The Rāgas of South India*, pp. xvi–xviii. Indiana University Press, Bloomington, Indiana.

Rāga names and technical terms differ significantly among various Indian texts. In most cases, I have chosen to use Kaufmann's spellings throughout the sections on South Indian and North Indian music.

91. On p. 63 of the *Svaramēlakalānidhi*, Rāmāmātya states,

"*Sva. 5.40* — That [*Janya*] *Rāga* is called *Māḷavagauḷa*, which is *Auḍava* [Pentatonic], for it leaves Ri and Pa, though, at times they are retained." (Text in brackets mine.)

In pentatonic or hexatonic forms, *Rāga Māḷavagauḷa* or *Rāga Gauḷa*, respectively, do *not* include all seven tones of the *mēḷa*. With respect to *Mēḷa Māḷavagauḷa*, T.V. Subba Rao observes in his essay "The *rāgas* of the Sangita Saramrita," p. 127, that theorists have questioned ". . . the wisdom of calling a *mēḷa* by the name of a *rāga* which is not *sampūrṇa* [lit. *complete;* i.e., heptatonic]." See Note 98.

92. *The Rāgas of South India: Mēḷa Gauḷa*, pp. xx–xxi, is the same as *Māḷavagauḷa* in Figure 11.33; *Rāga Gauḷa*, p. 123.

93. *Ibid.*, p. 143.

94. *Ibid.*, p. 263, 311.

95. *Svaramēlakalānidhi*, p. 56.

96. Sambamoorthy, P. (Vol. 1, A–F, 1952; Vol. 2, G–K, 1959; Vol. 3, L–N, 1971). *A Dictionary of South Indian Music and Musicians.* The Indian Music Publishing House, Madras, India.

I have used this useful but unfortunately incomplete dictionary throughout the chapter on Indian music. Definitions for *varjya rāgas*, *vakra rāgas*, and *anya rāgas* (*bhāṣāṅga rāgas*) occur in Volume 2, p. 253.

97. (A) Powers, H.S. (1958). *The Background of the South Indian Rāga-System*, pp. 20–21. Ph.D. dissertation printed and distributed by University Microfilms, Inc., Ann Arbor, Michigan.

This dissertation is a valuable source for the study of South Indian music and terminology. The last part includes transcriptions of LP recordings of compositions by Tyāgarāja, Śāstri, Dīkṣitar, and others.

(B) *The Rāgas of South India*, pp. 206–207.

98. Rao, T.V.S. (1945 and 1946). The *rāgas* of the Sangita Saramrita, pp. 63–64. *The Journal of the Music Academy* **XVI**, Parts I–IV, pp. 45–64, and **XVII**, Parts I–IV, pp. 104–134, Madras, India.

99. *Svaramēlakalānidhi*, pp. 62–63.

100. No translations in European languages available.

101. Sastri, S.S. (1931). Venkaṭamakhi and his twelve notes. *The Journal of the Music Academy* **II**, No. 1, pp. 22–23, Madras, India.

Here, Sastri makes a serious attempt to codify the *svara* ratios of Venkaṭamakhi's 12-tone scale. Since Venkaṭamakhi referred to the "tritone" as *Prati* **Ma**, or a variant of F, we must identify his "tritone" as F♯, ratio $^{729}/_{512}$. Unfortunately, Sastri gives the "tritone" as G♭, ratio $^{1024}/_{729}$. (See Section 11.34.)

102. *The Rāgas of South India*, p. xix.

103. (A) *Saṅgītaratnākara*, Vol. 1, p. 143, Footnote 6.

(B) Sadie, S., Editor (1980). *The New Grove Dictionary of Music and Musicians, Volume 9*, p. 93. Macmillan Publishers Limited, London, England, 1995.

104. See Section 11.22.

105. *The New Grove Dictionary of Music and Musicians, Volume 9*, p. 97.

106. *The Rāgas of South India*, p. xix.

107. *Ibid.*, pp. xx–xxi.

Here, Kaufmann gives a detailed description of Venkaṭamakhi's nineteen *mēḷakartas* and their respective numeric identities.

108. Ramachandran, K.V. (1938). The *mēḷakarta* — a critique, p. 31. *The Journal of the Music Academy* **IX**, Parts I–IV, pp. 31–33, Madras, India.

109. See Section 11.33.

110. On first impression, it may seem that because four of these variants are enharmonically equivalent, Venkaṭamakhi's system is flawed and will produce redundant, or duplicate heptatonic permutations. This is decidedly not the case. Three scale degrees per Ri, Ga, Dha, and Ni generate a maximum of 72 heptatonic permutations. As discussed in Section 11.42, because the North Indian system recognizes only two variants per Re, Ga, Dha, and Ni, it generates a maximum of 32 heptatonic permutations.

111. (A) Gangoly, O.C. (1935). *Rāgas and Rāginīs*, p. 209. Nalanda Publications, Bombay, India, 1948.

(B) *The Rāgas of South India*, pp. xx–xxi.

112. *Ibid.*, p. xxi.

113. No English translation available.

114. Ramachandran, N.S. (1938). *The Rāgas of Karnatic Music*, p. 208. University of Madras, Madras, India.

115. (A) Krishnaswamy, A. (1981). *Mēḷakarta and Janya Rāga Chart.* Sakthi Priya Publication, Madras, India.

(B) *The Rāgas of South India*, pp. xxiii–xxiv.

116. *The New Grove Dictionary of Music and Musicians, Volume 9*, pp. 97–98.

117. *The Background of the South Indian Rāga-System*, p. 18.

118. *Ibid.*, p. 98.

119. Iyer, T.L.V. (1940). The scheme of 72 *mēḷas* in Carnatic Music. *The Journal of the Music Academy* **XI**, Parts I–IV, pp. 80–86, Madras, India.

On pp. 81–82 and p. 84 of this article (and in the second paragraph of the quotation), in N.S. Ramachandran's *The Rāgas of Karnatic Music*, p. 44, and in H.S. Powers' *The Background of the South Indian Rāga-System*, p. 54 and 98, we find references to 40 *vivādi mēḷas.* Refer to Figure 11.32, and note that in my opinion there are only 36 *vivādi mēḷas.* If pressed to explain why these writers identify 40 *vivādi mēḷas*, it is probably because 20 *vivādi mēḷas* exist in the first set of *Mēḷakartas* 1–36, which includes *Śuddha* Ma, or F. This fact leads most writers to erroneously assume that 20 *vivādi mēḷas* also exist in the second set of *Mēḷakartas* 37–72, which includes *Prati* Ma, or F♯. However, a careful examination of the underlined numbers in Figure 11.32 shows that Rows 1 and 6, which belong to the first set, consist exclusively of 12 *vivādi mēḷas*, but Rows 7 and 12, which belong to the second set, contain only 8 *vivādi mēḷas.* In Row 7, all 6 *mēḷakartas* are *vivādi mēḷas*, but in Row 12 only two *mēḷakartas* — #67 and #72 — are *vivādi mēḷas*, which means that *Mēḷakartas* 68, 69, 70, and 71 are *not vivādi mēḷas.* There are two reasons that explain this discontinuity in Row 12. (1) In Figure 11.32, only Columns 1 and 6 contain *vivādi* tetrachords: G–A♭–B𝄫–C' and G–A♯–B–C', respectively. (2) In Row 12, tetrachord C–D♯–E–F♯ is a non-*vivādi* tetrachord. By definition, a *vivādi* tetrachord has two consecutive "semitones," which means that a non-*vivādi* tetrachord does *not* have two consecutive "semitones." See Section 11.41, Figure 11.36. We conclude, therefore, that Venkaṭamakhi's 72 *mēḷakartas* contain 36 *vivādi mēḷas*, and 36 non-*vivādi mēḷas.*

With respect to Iyer's identification of the "very first *mēḷa*" — identified by Venkaṭamakhi as *Mēḷa Kanakāmbarī*, and by Govinda as *Mēḷa Kanakāṅgī* — Rāmāmātya calls it *Mēḷa Mukhāri*, and states on p. 56 of the *Svaramēlakalānidhi:*

"Sva. 4.10 — The *Mēḷa* of *Mukhāri* consists of seven *Śuddha svaras."*

This is the simplest description of *Mēḷakarta* #1, which is also the first *vivādi rāga.*

120. Ramachandran, K.V. (1950). Carnatic *rāgas* from a new angle — *Śaṅkarābharaṇa*, p. 97. *The Journal of the Music Academy* **XXI**, Parts I–IV, pp. 88–99, Madras, India.

121. Ramachandran, K.V. (1950). Carnatic *rāgas* and the textual tradition, pp. 104–106. *The Journal of the Music Academy* **XXI**, Parts I–IV, pp. 99–106, Madras, India.

122. Ramachandran, K.V. (1950). *Apurva rāgas* of Tyāgarāja songs, pp. 107–108. *The Journal of the Music Academy* **XXI**, Parts I–IV, pp. 107–109, Madras, India.

123. *The History of Musical Instruments*, pp. 224–226.

124. Ayyar, C.S., (1939). *The Grammar of South Indian (Karnatic) Music*, p. 28. Smt. Vidya Shankar, Madras, India, 1976.

125. *Ibid.*

126. *The Background of the South Indian Rāga-System*, p. 37, pp. 118–119.

127. As an introduction to South Indian music, I would like to recommend two CD's by The Master Recording Company entitled *Raga Sudha Rasa, Volume 1*, KDV 049, and *Volume 2*, KDV 055. These CD's include authentic performances of Carnatic music from composers who lived between the 16th and 19th centuries. Also of great value is a three-disk CD set produced under the patronage of UNESCO and the International Music Council by Auvidis Distribution entitled *Anthology of Indian Classical Music: A Tribute to Alain Daniélou*, D 8270. These CD's include compositions and performances of both North and South Indian vocal music and instrumental music. All major Indian musical instruments are represented.

128. (A) *The Background of the South Indian Rāga-System*, p. 38.

(B) *The New Grove Dictionary of Music and Musicians, Volume 9*, p. 91.

In his dissertation, Powers writes *svarastanas*, and in the latter article, *svarasthānas*.

129. Bhatkhande, V.N. (1930). *A Comparative Study of Some of the Leading Music Systems of the 15th, 16th, 17th, and 18th Centuries*, p. 23. Indian Musicological Society, Baroda, India, 1972.

130. *Ibid.*, pp. 27–28.

131. For several *svaras*, Nārāyaṇa and Ahobala use similar string length divisions as described by Bartolomeo Ramis (*c.* 1440 – *c.* 1500) in his *Musica practica.* (See Section 10.36.)

132. See Section 3.13.

133. *A Comparative Study*, p. 30.

134. *Ibid.*, p. 28.

135. *Ibid.*

136. *The New Grove Dictionary of Music and Musicians, Volume 9*, p. 91.

137. *Ibid.*, p. 96.

138. No English translation available.

139. (A) *Rāgas and Rāginīs*, pp. 196–197.

(B) *A Comparative Study*, pp. 13–23.

140. *Rāgas and Rāginīs*, pp. 223–224.

141. Jairazbhoy, N.A. (1971). *The Rāgs of North Indian Music*, p. 46. Wesleyan University Press, Middletown, Connecticut.

142. Kaufmann, W. (1968). *The Rāgas of North India*, p. 608. Indiana University Press, Bloomington, Indiana.

143. Roy, H.L. (1937). *Problems of Hindustani Music*, pp. 68–69. Bharati Bhavan, Calcutta, India.

On p. 29, Roy includes a short translation of Ahobala's text that describes how to locate the seven *śuddha svaras* on a *vīṇā* string. This account is almost identical to Nārāyaṇa's description. See Note 129.

144. *Ibid.*, p. 118.

145. *The Rāgs of North Indian Music*, pp. 48–49.

146. *Ibid.*, pp. 181–185.

147. (A) *The Rāgas of North India*, p. 14.

(B) *The New Grove Dictionary of Music and Musicians, Volume 9*, p. 98.

148. *The History of Musical Instruments*, p. 464.

149. Marcotty, T. (1974). *Djovari: Giving Life to the Sitar.* This essay on how to make a parabolic *sitar* bridge is in *The Sitar*, by Manfred M. Junius. Heinrichshofen's Verlag, Wilhelmshaven, Germany.

150. Shankar, R. (1968). *My Music, My Life*, p. 99, 102. Simon and Schuster, New York, New York.

151. Sorrell, N., and Narayan, R. (1980). *Indian Music in Performance*, p. 45. New York University Press, New York, New York. This book comes boxed with an excellent cassette tape recording.

152. Junius, M.M. (1974). *The Sitar*, p. 23. Heinrichshofen's Verlag, Wilhelmshaven, Germany.

153. *The Rāgs of North Indian Music*, pp. 186–189.

154. *Indian Music in Performance*, p. 46.

155. Rough measurements from photographs and line drawings indicate that the *śuddha* scale in Figure 11.39 is a reasonable example of a modern *sitar* tuning. In this figure, the entire 12-tone scale consists of two *saṃvādi* tetrachords tuned a "fifth" apart and separated by a $^{45}/_{32}$ "tritone."

156. Gopal Krishan's music may be heard on two CD's by Ocora Radio France, C 560048–49 and C 560078. The latter recording is most impressive.

157. *The New Grove Dictionary of Music and Musicians, Volume 9*, p. 131.

158. *Pather Panchali* is available on Columbia Tristar Home Video.

Part IV

ARABIAN, PERSIAN, AND TURKISH MUSIC

~ 11.45 ~

North American musicians who do not read Arabic, French, or German have very limited opportunities to study ancient Arabian music and tuning theory from original sources. Of the treatises on music written by Al-Fārābī (d. *c.* 950), Ibn Sīnā (980–1037), Ṣafī Al-Dīn (d. 1294), Al-Jurjānī (d. 1413), Al-Lādhiqī (d. 1494), and Al-Shirwānī (d. 1626), not a single work has ever been translated into English. Furthermore, due to intractable religious, linguistic, and intellectual prejudices against Islam, Christian-dominated institutions throughout Europe — such as Catholic and Protestant churches, schools and universities, and the craft guilds — managed by 1600 to completely eradicate the Arabian influence from the written history of European music. For example, the works of Michael Praetorius (1571–1621) and Marin Mersenne (1588–1648) offer no information on the origins of one of the most important instruments of their time: the lute. First in Arabian history (from approximately 700) and later in European history (to approximately 1700), the fretted lute served for a thousand years as an instrument of scientific exploration and musical expression. Henry George Farmer (1882–1965), an eminent historian of Arabian music, gives this etymology of lute (from the Arabic *al-'ūd*, *the lute;* lit. *flexible stick* or *branch*):

> Western Europe owes both the instrument and its name to the Arabic *al-'ūd*, as we see in the Portuguese *alaud*, the Spanish *laud*, the German *Laute*, the Dutch *Luit*, the Danish *Lut*, the Italian *liuto*, the English *lute*, and the French *luth.*[1]

Are we to naïvely accept the highly improbable possibility that while Europeans inherited the lute from the Arabs, European musicians learned absolutely nothing about tuning from Arabian musicians? Consider the following fact: by the end of the 13th century, Arabian literature included not only a voluminous and highly sophisticated collection of works on the art and science of music, but on the precise mathematics of lute tunings as well.

Between approximately A.D. 750 and 1250, many nations in the West experienced the religious, scientific, and artistic influences of what I call the Arabian Renaissance. After the life and death of the prophet Mohammed (*c.* 570 – d. 632), a stunning series of military campaigns brought Spain, Sicily, North Africa, Egypt, Syria, al-'Iraq, Persia (modern Iran), Farghānah (Central Asia), Ṭukhāristān (modern Afghanistan), and Western India (modern Pakistan) under Moslem control. Coincidentally, most of these territories were conquered by Alexander the Great (356–323 B.C.) a thousand years earlier. To administer their newly conquered empire, Moslem rulers created two great cultural centers. In 762 Baghdād became the capital of the empire in the east, and subsequent to the invasion of 711 into Spain, in 756 Cordova became the capital of the empire in the west. The former was destroyed by Mongols in 1258, and the latter, reconquered by Christians in 1236. The *Reconquista* (Reconquest) of Spain continued until the final defeat of the Moslems at Granada in 1492.[2]

Reminiscent of the building of Alexandria by Alexander the Great, Baghdād and Cordova boasted running water, paved and lighted streets, world-renowned architectural monuments, international markets, universities, hospitals, and above all, libraries that contained hundreds of thousands of volumes. If it were not for these libraries, and the care Arabian translators and scholars bestowed on ancient texts, the works of Homer, Hippocrates, Plato, Aristotle, Euclid, Archimedes, Nicomachus, and Ptolemy, to name only a few, would probably not have survived. The task of translating these volumes began in Baghdād in approximately 750, and later became centralized at the famous Bayt al-Ḥikmah (House of Wisdom) in 830. By the end of the 10th century, most of the translations were completed. This phenomenal achievement raises the inevitable question, "Is the Italian Renaissance indebted to the Arabian Renaissance?" To contemplate the profound interdependence of these two civilizations, consider this biographical account from Philip K. Hitti's exhaustive work entitled *History of the Arabs:*

> Al-Kindi . . . flourished in Baghdād. His pure Arabian descent earned him the title "the philosopher of the Arabs," and indeed he was the first and last example of an Aristotelian student in the Eastern caliphate who sprang from Arabian stock. Eclectic in his system, Al-Kindi endeavored in Neo-Platonic fashion to combine the views of Plato and Aristotle and regarded the Neo-Pythagorean mathematics as the basis of all science. Al-Kindi was more than a philosopher. He was astrologer, alchemist, optician and music theorist. No less than two hundred and sixty-five works are ascribed to him, but most of them unhappily have been lost. His principal work on geometrical and physiological optics, based on the *Optics* of Euclid in Theon's recension, was widely used in both East and West until superseded by the greater work of ibn-al-Haytham [d. *c.* 1039]. In its Latin translation, *De aspectibus*, it influenced Roger Bacon [*c.* 1214 – d. 1292]. Al-Kindi's three or four treatises on the theory of music are the earliest extant works in Arabic showing the influence of Greek writers on that subject. In one of these treatises Al-Kindi describes rhythm (*īqā'*) as a constituent part of Arabic music. Measured song, or mensural music, must therefore have been known to the Moslems centuries before it was introduced into Christian Europe. Of Al-Kindi's writings more have survived in Latin translations, including those of Gerard of Cremona [d. 1187], than in the Arabic original.[3] (Dates in brackets mine.)

11.46

The oldest extant source on Arabian music is a work entitled *Risāla fī hubr tā'līf al-alḥān* (On the composition of melodies), by Isḥāq Al-Kindī (d. *c.* 874). Because this text only survived as a fragmented 17th-century transcription of a 13th-century copy, many pages are missing; this explains why the text begins in mid-sentence. Fortunately, the fragments provide enough information to impart Al-Kindī's *'ūd* tuning, which bestows the following six incipient contributions on the history of music:

(1) Outside China, this is the first mathematical description of a 12-tone chromatic scale. Although Al-Kindī's scale also consists of a spiral of "fifths," it differs from the Chinese model in that the tonic, ratio $1/1$, simultaneously functions as the origin of two different spirals: one ascends four "fifths," or four $3/2$'s, and the other descends seven "fifths," or seven $3/2$'s. (See Section 11.47, Table 11.22.)

(2) Al-Kindī's 12-tone scale is the first tuning that uses identical note names to identify the tones of the lower and upper "octave." In his text, Al-Kindī specifically states that the musical *qualities* of tones separated by an "octave" are identical.

(3) This is the first mathematically verifiable scale that accounts for the comma of Pythagoras. In his *'ūd* tuning, Al-Kindī distinguishes between the *apotome* [C♯], ratio $2187/2048$, and the *limma* [D♭], ratio $256/243$.

(4) This is the first mathematically verifiable example of a Greek tetrachord on an actual musical instrument.

(5) On the *Bamm*, or the lowest sounding string, Al-Kindī defines four ancient length ratios — $9/8$, $32/27$, $81/64$, $4/3$ — which appear in all subsequent *'ūd* tunings through the 17th century.

(6) Al-Kindī gives the first mathematical description of a fifth string, which I call *'Zīr 2'*, for the purpose of taking his 12-tone scale to its logical conclusion, namely, to sound the "double-octave," ratio $4/1$, above the open *Bamm*.

Although an English translation of this work exists,[4] for technical reasons I translated excerpts — from two out of a total of six chapters — from a German translation by Robert Lachmann and Mahmud el-Hefni.[5] Note carefully that these selections deal primarily with discussions on tuning, and that I excluded several sentences that include missing text, that make no sense, or that violate mathematical logic.[6] Even though the copyist complains, "The model copied was written at the end of Sawwal in 621 [A.D. 1224] in Damascus from a defective, unreliable copy,"[7] I seriously doubt that he fully comprehended, and was therefore unable to correctly interpret, muddled or spurious passages of the 13th-century copy.

[Chapter 1.]

[1.] . . . and K to A is a whole plus an eighth of a whole (1 + $1/8$, or 9:8) of it, and we have already explained, that the difference between a fifth (3:2) and a fourth (4:3) is a whole plus an eighth of a whole. From this, the distance of the W, which is the of the *Mathlath*, from the A, which is the first fret of the *Mathnā*, is the interval of a fifth. And the octave is composed of a fifth and a fourth. From this, the distance of the A of the *Bamm* from the A of the *Mathnā* is the octave. From this, the relationship of the A of the *Bamm* to the A of the *Mathnā* is the relationship of the doubling 2:1. Consequently, according to the previous statement, the A of the *Mathnā* is of the quality as the A of the *Bamm*.

[2.] From this example, the tones that succeed one another on the basis of similarity, succeed one another on the basis of quality. Therefore, the B of the *Mathnā* is of the same quality as the B of the *Bamm;* the ***utilization*** of the B of the *Bamm* with respect to the frets is already clarified. Likewise, the G of the *Mathnā* is equal to the G of the *Bamm*, and the D of the *Mathnā* is equal to the D of the *Bamm* and the D of the *Zīr* (*Zīr 1*). Likewise the W of the *Zīr* is equal to the W of the *Mathlath*, and the Z of the *Zīr* is equal to the Z of the *Mathlath*, which is ***not used;*** and the Ḥ of the *Zīr* is equal to the Ḥ of the *Mathlath*, and the Ṭ of the *Zīr* is equal to the Ṭ of the *Mathlath* and to the Ṭ of the lower *Zīr* (*'Zīr 2'*), and the I of the lower *Zīr* is equal to I of the *Mathlath*, and the K of the lower *Zīr* is equal to the K of the *Mathlath* and to the K of the *Mathnā*, and the L of the lower *Zīr* is equal to the ***unused*** L of the *Mathnā;* and the A of the lower *Zīr* is equal to the A of the *Mathnā*, and the B of the lower *Zīr* is equal to the B of the *Mathnā*, and the G of the lower *Zīr* is equal to the G of the *Mathnā*, for compelling reasons which we indicated before. ...

[4.] In order now to give an example in numbers, we assign the number 16 to the A of the *Bamm*. Then the W of the *Bamm* equals 12; because A is a whole plus a third of a whole (1 + $1/3$, or 4:3) from W. And the W of the *Bamm* equals the W of the *Mathlath*. Then the K of the *Mathlath* equals 9; because the W of the *Mathlath* is a whole plus a third of a whole from the K of the *Mathlath*. ...

[Chapter 2.]

[2.] Of the double octave, there are two kinds. One is called the conjunct (system); it is the one in which the A of the *Mathnā* participates at the end of the first and in the beginning of the second octave. In the disjunct system, the beginning of the first octave is the A of the *Bamm*, and its end the A of the *Mathnā*, and the beginning of the second, the G of the *Mathnā*, and its end, the G of the second *Zīr* (*'Zīr 2'*); these two systems are disjointed by the distance from A up to G of the *Mathnā*, which forms the interval of the whole tone, i.e., the relationship of a whole plus an eighth of a whole. These indicated tones limit the disjunct system, and that which is below it.

[3.] After the locations of the tones and the used tones, we must discuss the tones in the system of the double octave. We account for the number of their locations. They amount to 20; because on each string there are 4 (stopped) tones in the range of the fourth (tetrachord), and there are 5 strings; in addition to this, comes the tone G of the second *Zīr*, so that through it, the whole range of the octave completes itself, if it is used instead of the A of the second *Zīr*. And with respect to the number of used tone-locations, so W of the *Bamm* and of the *Mathlath* are identical, and K of the *Mathlath* and of the *Mathnā* are identical, and D (of the *Mathnā* and) of the first *Zīr* (*Zīr 1*) are identical, and Ṭ of the first and of the second *Zīr* are identical . . .

[4.] . . . Of the total number of tones used in the genera, 10 are firm and do not change their locations . . . The unchangeable (tones) lie at the two ends of the frets (that is, at the two ends of the vertical fret pattern, which includes 5 tones of Fret 1: *G*, *Ḥ*, *A*, *W*, *K* at the top end, and 5 tones of Fret 4: *W*, *K*, *D*, *Ṭ*, *B* at the bottom end); the changeable (tones) lie in between. The utilization of the modes change the ones lying between the ends (of the fret pattern); because the first mode of the diatonic genus is used differently than the second and third . . .

[5.] . . . Since in the diatonic genus the first and second mode is used most often, its beginning is at the first fret; in contrast, the beginning of the third mode is at the open string . . . of the *Bamm*. ...

[9.] Regarding the number of tones, and their quality in the system of the double octave, there are 7 tones from which all the melodies arise. Since the A of the *Mathnā* has the same quality as the A of the *Bamm*, the octave consists of 7 tones, because its two ends, with respect to quality, are one and the same tone.[8] (Bold italics, and text and ratios in parentheses mine. Text in brackets in Lachmann's and El-Hefni's translation.)

Figure 11.41 is a fret diagram of Al-Kindī's *'ūd* tuning. The only note not mentioned in the fragment is *H*, ratio $^{81}/_{64}$ [E], of the *Bamm*, and *H*, ratio $^{81}/_{32} = {}^{81}/_{64}$ [E^{I}], of the *Zīr 1*. However, since the text explains that Al-Kindī named the twelve notes of the lower and upper "octaves" after the first twelve letters of the old Arabic alphabet: *A*, *B*, *G*, *D*, *H*, *W*, *Z*, *Ḥ*, *Ṭ*, *I*, *K*, *L*, the presence of *H* is self-evident. A close examination of the treatise reveals the following tuning. Chapter 1, Paragraph 4 assigns 16 units to *A* [C], ratio $^{1}/_{1}$, of the open *Bamm*, and defines *W* [F] — Fret 4 — of the *Bamm* as *ancient length ratio* 16:12, or $^{4}/_{3}$. Al-Kindī then tunes *W* [F] — open *Mathlath* — in unison to the latter fret; therefore, *K* [B♭] — Fret 4 — of the *Mathlath* must be ratio $^{4}/_{3} \times {}^{4}/_{3} = {}^{16}/_{9}$. Chapter 2, Paragraph 3 defines *K* [B♭] — open *Mathnā* — tuned in unison to the latter fret, which means *D* [E♭^{I}] — Fret 4 — of the *Mathnā* must be ratio $^{16}/_{9} \times {}^{4}/_{3} = {}^{64}/_{27} = {}^{32}/_{27}$. He then defines *D*

[E♭′] — open *Zīr 1* — tuned in unison to the latter fret, which means *Ṭ* [A♭′] — Fret 4 — of the *Zīr 1* must be ratio $32/27 \times 4/3 = 128/81$. At the end of the paragraph, he defines *Ṭ* [A♭′] — open *ʿZīr 2ʾ* — tuned in unison to the latter fret, which means *B* [D♭″] — Fret 4 — of the *ʿZīr 2ʾ* must be ratio $128/81 \times 4/3 = 512/243 = 256/243$. Although the *ʿūd* (pl. *ʿīdān, aʿwād*) is not specifically mentioned in the fragment, the open strings of short-necked lutes were traditionally tuned in ascending "fourths."

Chapter 1, Paragraph 2 states that *D* [E♭′] of the *Mathnā* is equal to *D* [E♭] — Fret 2 — of the *Bamm*, which means that the latter sounds an "octave" below the former. Since we know that all open strings are tuned in "fourths," the Fret 2 location determines the ratios of *Ṭ* [A♭], *B* [D♭′], *Z* [G♭′], and *L* [C♭′] above *D* [E♭]. Al-Kindī also states that *B* [D♭′] of the *Mathnā* has the same quality as *B* [D♭] — Anterior Fret 1 — of the *Bamm*, which means that the latter sounds an "octave" below the former fret. (The special function of Anterior Frets 1 and 2 is discussed below.) The Anterior Fret 1 location determines the ratios of *Z* [G♭] and *L* [C♭] above *B* [D♭].

Chapter 1, Paragraph 1 states that *A* [C] of the *Bamm* and *A* [C′] — Fret 1 — of the *Mathnā* constitute an "octave," which means that the latter sounds a $2/1$ above the former; the Fret 1 location determines the ratios of *G* [D] and *Ḥ* [G] below *A* [C′], and of *W* [F′] and *K* [B♭′] above *A* [C′].

Chapter 2, Paragraph 2 states that the span from *A* [C′] — Fret 1 — of the *Mathnā* to *G* [D′] — Fret 3 — of the *Mathnā* is interval ratio $9/8$. Therefore, the Fret 3 location determines the ratios of *H* [E] and *I* [A] below *G* [D′], and of *Ḥ* [G′] and *A* [C″] above *G* [D′].

Chapter 1, Paragraph 2 states that *I* [A′] — Anterior Fret 2 — of the *ʿZīr 2ʾ* is equal to *I* [A] of the *Mathlath*, which means that the former sounds an "octave" above the latter; the Anterior Fret 2 location determines the ratio of *H* [E′] below *I* [A′].

Finally, Chapter 2, Paragraph 2 states that *G* [D′] of the *Mathnā* and *G* [D″] of the *ʿZīr 2ʾ* constitute an "octave," which means that the latter sounds an "octave" above the former, and a "double-octave" above *G* [D] of the *Bamm*. The *G* [D″] of the *ʿZīr 2ʾ* does not indicate the location of a fret. Musicians played this tone through a "shift" of the hand, which places the index finger at the location of *L* [C♭′], and the ring finger at the location of *G* [D″]. (See Ibn Sīnā's explanation in Section 11.59.) Many modern scholars insist that the fifth string constitutes a theoretical addition, included solely to complete the "double-octave" between the open *Bamm* and Fret 3 of the *ʿZīr 2ʾ*. However, the renowned poet and musician Ziryāb (*c.* 789 – d. 857), who lived in the southern region of Spain called Andalusia, already added a fifth string to his *ʿūd* sometime between 822 and 852.[9] So, while Ziryāb is credited with this invention in the West, Al-Kindī was first to implement it in the East.

The greatest difficulty with respect to fret locations occurs in Chapter 1, Paragraph 2. Here Al-Kindī states that *Z* [G♭] of the *Mathlath* and *L* [C♭] of the *Mathnā* are *not* used. However, he also reminds the reader that ". . . the utilization of the *B* [D♭] of the *Bamm* with respect to the frets is already clarified." This statement refers to a discussion that did not survive in the fragment. Since a careful analysis of the treatise reveals that tones *B* [D♭], *Z* [G♭], and *L* [C♭] reside on the same fret, the extant text does not give a consistent description of the function of this fret. To resolve this apparent contradiction, first consider Sequence A, which gives the ratios of an ascending sequence of seven $3/2$'s, and then Sequence B, which gives the ratios of a descending sequence of seven $3/2$'s. (See Figure 10.16.)

$$\uparrow 1/1\ [C],\ 3/2\ [G],\ 9/8\ [D],\ 27/16\ [A],\ 81/64\ [E],\ 243/128\ [B],\ 729/512\ [F\sharp],\ 2187/2048\ [C\sharp] \qquad (A)$$

$$\downarrow 1/1\ [C],\ 4/3\ [F],\ 16/9\ [B\flat],\ 32/27\ [E\flat],\ 128/81\ [A\flat],\ 256/243\ [D\flat],\ 1024/729\ [G\flat],\ 4096/2187\ [C\flat] \qquad (B)$$

Now, imagine *L* and *Z* occur on Anterior Fret 2, which determines the *H* [E′] of the *Zīr 1* and the *I* [A′] of the *ʿZīr 2ʾ*. Under such circumstances, *L* would sound a "fourth" below *H* [E′ $= 81/64$],

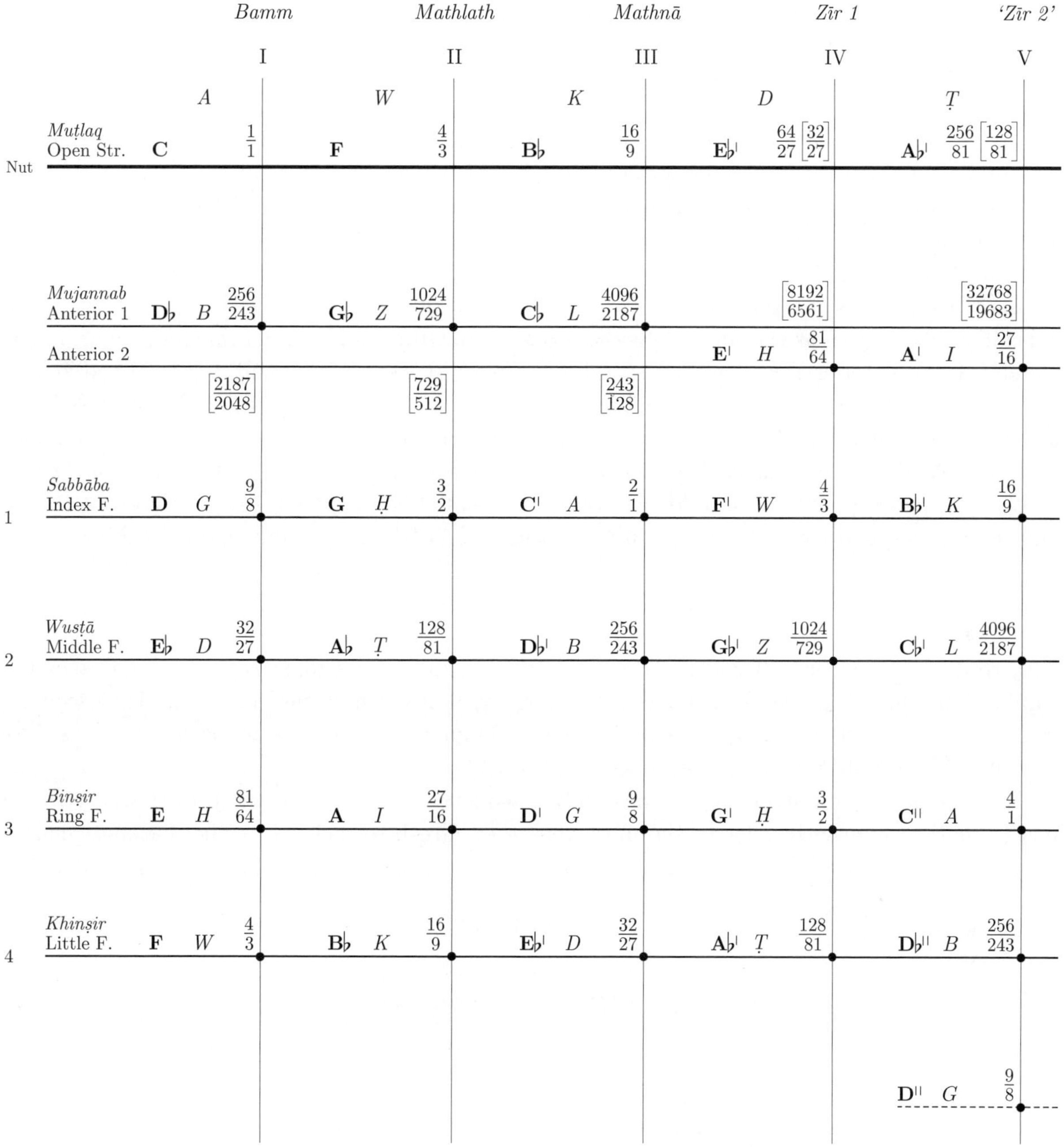

Figure 11.41 Fret locations on the short-necked *'ūd* as described by Al-Kindī (d. *c.* 874). Of the works that have survived in the West, Al-Kindī's treatise is the first to define a 12-tone chromatic scale. Note that the ratios and names of the tones in the lower and upper "octaves" are identical. To achieve this tuning — or, to resolve the comma of Pythagoras — Al-Kindī installed two anterior frets. On these frets, Al-Kindī did not assign letters from the Arabian alphabet to the five ratios shown in brackets. Consequently, he intentionally excluded these tones from his scale. (Fret locations to scale.)

which yields ratio $^{81}\!/_{64} \div {}^{4}\!/_{3} = {}^{243}\!/_{128}$ [B]; and *Z* would sound a "fourth" below *L*, which yields ratio $^{243}\!/_{128} \div {}^{4}\!/_{3} = {}^{729}\!/_{512}$ [F♯]. Since Sequences A and B indicate that the interval between the former *L* [B] and the *L* of the *'Zīr 2'* [C♭] is not an "octave," and since the interval between the latter *Z* [F♯] and the *Z* of the *Zīr 1* [G♭] is also not an "octave," Al-Kindī's earlier statement with respect to *L* and *Z* makes perfect sense. He advises against these two tones because they produce "octaves" that are a comma of Pythagoras flat, or “octaves” that are a comma of Pythagoras too narrow. The interval between B and C♭′ is $243/128 \div 4096/2187 = 531441/524288$, and the interval between F♯ and G♭′ is $729/512 \div 1024/729 = 531441/524288$. Next, suppose *B* of the *Bamm* sounds a “fourth” below *Z* [F♯]; such an interval yields ratio $729/512 \div 4/3 = 2187/2048$ [C♯], also known as the *apotome.* (See Sections 10.15 and 10.18.) With respect to the *B* [D♭′] of the *Mathnā*, this tone also produces an “octave” that is a comma of Pythagoras flat, which means the interval between C♯ and D♭′ is $2187/2048 \div 256/243 = 531441/524288$. However, remember that Al-Kindī explicitly states, “. . . the *B* [D♭′] of the *Mathnā* is of the same quality as the *B* [D♭] of the *Bamm* . . .” Therefore, to sound an exact “octave,” we must move the *B* [C♯] of the *Bamm* from Anterior Fret 2 to Anterior Fret 1. If we position the latter fret a comma of Pythagoras above the former fret,[10] such a location produces ratio $2187/2048 \div 531441/524288 = 256/243$ [D♭], also known as the *limma.* (See Sections 10.10, 10.15, and 10.18.) Suppose we also move *Z* and *L* from Anterior Fret 2 to Anterior Fret 1. Now *B* [D♭], *Z* [G♭], and *L* [C♭] of the *Bamm*, *Mathlath*, and *Mathnā*, respectively, produce three exact “octaves” with *B* [D♭′], *Z* [G♭′], and *L* [C♭′] of the *Mathnā*, *Zīr 1*, and *‘Zīr 2’*, respectively. This construction resolves the apparent contradiction and leaves Al-Kindī’s original scale intact; that is, the frets of the *‘ūd* produce two identical 12-tone scales that span the interval of a “double-octave.” Finally, observe that Anterior Fret 1 provides only three tones, and Anterior Fret 2, only two tones of Al-Kindī’s “double-octave” tuning.

11.47

With respect to the tonic, Table 11.22 shows that Al-Kindī’s *‘ūd* tuning consists of an ascending spiral of four “fifths” above $1/1$, and of a descending spiral of seven “fifths” below $1/1$. The ascending progression represents the ubiquitous pentatonic scale known the world over as ratios $1/1$, $9/8$, $81/64$, $3/2$, $27/16$, [$2/1$]; in Al-Kindī’s notation, *A*, *G*, *H*, *Ḥ*, *I*, [*A*′].

We may attribute portions of the descending sequence to Greek tetrachordal theory. Arabian music theorists frequently refer to the most venerated Greek tetrachord — the diatonic genus of

Table 11.22

THE INNER STRUCTURE OF
AL-KINDĪ’S *‘ŪD* TUNING

	Standard Western Notation	Ratios	Cents	Al-Kindī’s Notation
(4)	E	$81/64$	408 ¢	*H*
(3)	A	$27/16$	906 ¢	*I*
(2)	D	$9/8$	204 ¢	*G*
(1)	G	$3/2$	702 ¢	*Ḥ*
	C	$1/1$	0 ¢	*A*
(1)	F	$4/3$	498 ¢	*W*
(2)	B♭	$16/9$	996 ¢	*K*
(3)	E♭	$32/27$	294 ¢	*D*
(4)	A♭	$128/81$	792 ¢	*Ṭ*
(5)	D♭	$256/243$	90 ¢	*B*
(6)	G♭	$1024/729$	588 ¢	*Z*
(7)	C♭	$4096/2187$	1086 ¢	*L*

Philolaus[11] (fl. *c.* 420 B.C.) — in their descriptions of four cardinal frets on the *'ūd*. These frets represent ratios 9/8, 32/27, 81/64, 4/3. In Chapter 2, Paragraphs 4 and 5, Al-Kindī describes three different modes of the diatonic genus. Because the extant text does not specify an exact order of intervals, let us assume Al-Kindī's first mode constitutes Philolaus' original tetrachord. If we now systematically rotate the limma from its initial position as first interval ratio, to the next position as second interval ratio, and to the final position as third interval ratio, the pattern below emerges.

Mode 1 (Dorian)	D: 9/8	**256/243**	E♭: 32/27	9/8	F: 4/3	9/8	G: 3/2
Mode 2 (Phrygian)	D: 9/8	9/8	E: 81/64	**256/243**	F: 4/3	9/8	G: 3/2
Mode 3 (Lydian)	C: 1/1	9/8	D: 9/8	9/8	E: 81/64	**256/243**	F: 4/3

The Greeks called these the Dorian, Phrygian, and Lydian *harmoniai.*[12] Al-Kindī states in Chapter 2, Paragraph 5, that the first two modes begin on the first fret, and the third mode, on the *muṭlaq* (lit. *free;* hence, fig. *open string*). His descriptions refer to the ancient Arabic *majrā* (lit. *course* or *path;* hence, fig. *mode*) of the *wusṭā* (lit. *middle finger*), and the *majrā* of the *binṣir* (lit. *ring finger*). One distinguished these two *majārī* by a "semitone" interval between the *sabbāba* (lit. *index finger*) and middle finger, and by a "whole tone" interval between the index finger and ring finger. Figure 11.41 confirms Mode 1 in *sabbāba fī majrā al-wusṭā* because this sequence begins with the index finger and proceeds to the middle finger; Mode 2, in *sabbāba fī majrā al-binṣir* because it begins with the index finger and proceeds to the ring finger; and, Mode 3, in *muṭlaq fī majrā al-binṣir* because it begins with the open string, followed by the index finger and ring finger. In Western terms, *sabbāba fī majrā al-binṣir* sounds a tetrachord with a "minor third": 1/1, 9/8, 32/27, 4/3, and *muṭlaq fī majrā al-binṣir*, a tetrachord with a "major third": 1/1, 9/8, 81/64, 4/3. Because ancient Arabian music theory decreed that 32/27 [E♭] and 81/64 [E] are 'incompatible' (see Section 11.50), musicians abstained from playing these two tones in the same mode. This simple rule foreshadowed what would eventually become the distinction between the minor and major tonalities of Western music.

~ 11.48 ~

Before we continue this discussion on Arabian scales and modes, let us first consider the historic and scientific significance of the invention of the *'ūd* by examining the two most popular stringed instruments of ancient Greece: the *kithara* and *lyre.* Curt Sachs gives the following description of these two instruments:

> In the following centuries [after Homer], the names *phorminx and kítharis* were replaced by new terms, *kithara* and *lyra*, which corresponded to new types of lyres.
>
> *The kithara* had a heavy, solidly joined body, a wooden soundboard and strong arms. In most cases the strings were wound around the crossbar and held fast by greasy rolls of oxskin. By turning or shifting the sticky rolls on the crossbar, the player was able to tune his instrument . . .
>
> *The lyra* belonged to beginners and amateurs. It was more primitive than the kithara, although more recent. It was doubtless a retrogressive

> form of the rounded Syrian lyre, though the Greeks attributed it to the Thracians.
>
> Lyras were loosely constructed. The body was either a tortoise shell or a shallow wooden bowl placed on edge and covered by a piece of skin as a soundboard. Two horns of an animal, or wooden arms, projected from the bowl and supported the horizontal crossbar. The strings, fastened on the underside of the bowl and held away from the soundboard by a bridge, were attached in the same way as those of the kithara . . .
>
> There seems to have been no difference in the strings of the lyra and the kithara. The earliest strings were probably made of hemp . . . [which were later] replaced . . . by gut strings.[13] (Text in brackets mine.)

Like the harp-*vīṇā* of ancient India, neither the *kithara* nor the *lyre* was equipped with tuning pegs. Instead, the friction of greasy oxskin lashings provided the only mechanical means for tensioning the strings. As discussed in Section 11.21, it is difficult to achieve fine incremental adjustments with lashing that are continuously subject to slippage and creep.

Sachs neglected to mention that all *kitharas* and *lyres* had strings of equal length, which were *only* played as open strings. Therefore, musicians could only achieve varieties of pitch by changing either string diameters or tension. In this respect, triangular-shaped harps with posts, which were known to the Greeks, provide far greater stability because for a given tuning, strings that gradually decrease in length require less tension than strings of equal length. Furthermore, for a string, frequency is inversely proportional to diameter and length.[14] On *kitharas* and *lyres*, gut string diameters probably varied at most by an $1/8$ in., whereas on small harps, string lengths typically vary by more than a foot. Given the severe tension requirements and tuning limitations caused by strings of equal length, most of these instruments had only seven or fewer strings. My own calculations show that it is very nearly impossible to tune an "octave" on a *kithara* or *lyre* with gut strings; as one approaches the "octave," long and thin gut strings begin to break. No one knows why the Greeks — with their sophisticated mathematical calculations of scales and modes — did not fully develop the intonational possibilities of harps.

Also, the Greeks did not build their *kitharas* and *lyres* with mechanical components that would have provided maximum tuning stability. Although beautiful and graceful in appearance, these instruments were built with only two arms to support the crossbar and lashings. A third arm that would have eliminated bending in the center of the bar was never included. Consequently, the crossbar acted like a spring that bent and unbent with increases and decreases in string tension.

Such changes in tension occurred on a regular basis because neither instrument was equipped with frets. Only by retuning the open strings were musicians able to play in different modes. Moreover, the lack of frets required that all musicians tune these modes by ear. Given that *kitharas* and *lyres* had (1) no tuning pegs, (2) no graduated string lengths, (3) no central crossbar support, and (4) no frets, I cannot image how practicing musicians managed to quickly and accurately retune their instruments to interval ratios such as $32/31$, $28/27$, and $22/21$.[15] Even with the aural assistance of a monochord or canon standing close by, the tuning of enharmonic and chromatic tetrachords must have been a tough assignment at best. This probably explains why after the decline of the Greek and Roman empires, *kitharas* and *lyres* rapidly became extinct. No advancing civilization continued to build these types of instruments simply because they did not work very well. In a noteworthy work entitled *Stringed Instruments of Ancient Greece*, Martha Maas and Jane McIntosh Snyder conclude

> The instruments of least importance in Greek culture, harps and lutes, have become the more important instruments in the West. Although the

> kithara has left its name in words like *gittern*, *guitar*, and *zither*, all of these are in fact instruments of the lute [or] psaltery types. Indeed, instruments of the lyre type survived, as plucked instruments, only in certain areas of Asia and East Africa.[16] (Text in brackets mine.)

For the remaining discussion on Arabian music, I urge the reader to consider not so much the physical and acoustical perfection of the *'ūd* — equipped with tuning pegs, a solid unyielding neck, and a large soundboard, bridge, and resonator designed to optimally amplify the strings — but to ponder the mathematical and musical significance of its frets. Historians and archeologists will probably never prove who invented the fret, but there is no doubt that the Arabs were first to mathematically describe the scales and modes that naturally fall under the human hand on a fretted fingerboard. Figure 11.41 shows that Al-Kindī realized his 25-tone "double-octave" scale with only five strings and six frets, whereas a Greek version of the 15-tone "double-octave" scale would have required fifteen separate strings. Ironically, the Greeks who invented the "double-octave" as a conceptual entity and called it the Greater Perfect System[17] were unable to tune it on a *kithara* or *lyre*. The structural design and mechanical components of these instruments fell short of the demanding physical requirements of this scale.

11.49

In the first half of the 9th century, the most famous teacher and exponent of traditional Arabian music was Isḥāq Al-Mauṣilī (d. 850). Unfortunately, all of his books, including the *Kitāb al-aghānī al-kabīr* (Grand book of songs)[18] and *Kitāb al-naghm wa'l-īqā'* (Book of melody and rhythm)[19] are lost. However, two important related works by different authors have survived. The first, written by Ibn Al-Munajjim (d. 912),[20] is called *Risāla fi'l-mūsīqī* (Treatise on music);[21] in two critical passages cited below, Al-Munajjim refers to Al-Mauṣilī as an authority on the subject of Arabian modes. The second, written by Abu'l-Faraj Al-Iṣfahānī (d. 976), is also called *Kitāb al-aghānī al-kabīr*, after Al-Mauṣilī's work. According to the historian Ibn Khallikān (d. 1282), Al-Iṣfahānī took fifty years to complete this book, which consists of twenty-one volumes and contains nearly 2,000,000 words. Al-Iṣfahānī characterizes Al-Mauṣilī's accomplishments by noting

> [Isḥāq] re-established the genres (*ajnās*) of music (*ghinā*), its [melodic and rhythmic] modes (*ṭarā'iq*) and their classification in a way unknown before him . . . He had, by his own genius, accomplished the labors of Euclid and other (Greek) savants in the theory of music without having known any of their books.[22]

Al-Mauṣilī was primarily concerned with the preservation of Arabian music before his time. Consequently, modern scholars interpret these later works by Al-Munajjim and Al-Iṣfahānī as expressions of the Old Arabian School, a musical tradition that began with Ibn Misjaḥ (d. *c.* 715).[23] Therefore, most if not all the ancient Arabian modes discussed below originated in the 7th century. Farmer gives a brief description and translation of a typical song caption from Al-Iṣfahānī's book. The translation describes a composition by Ibn Suraij (d. *c.* 726), who is credited with the introduction of the Persian lute *'ūd al-fārisī;*[24] this instrument later developed into the classic Arabian *al-'ūd*.

> What we generally find in Al-Iṣfahānī is a song caption which gives the names of the singer, author, and composer, followed by an indication of the rhythmic mode and the melodic mode, together with the occasional mention of the metre of the verse, and perhaps the particular verses which were sung to one mode and what verses were sung to another mode. A fairly common example of that would be as follows:

> "The verse is by 'Umar ibn Abī Rabī'a : the music by Ibn Suraij : with the *ramal* [rhythmic mode] in the *sabbāba fī majrā al-binṣir* [melodic mode], according to [the authority of] Iṣḥāq [al-Mauṣilī], but with the *khafīf thaqīl* [rhythmic mode] in the *binṣir* [melodic mode] according to 'Amr [ibn Bāna]."[25]

Because Al-Iṣfahānī did not discuss scales, we turn now to Al-Munajjim's text. Farmer gives a brief description of the *Risāla fi'l-mūsīqī.*

> This is the only complete textbook on the theory and practice of music in the Old Arabian School. In it the author states that what he has written was based on the teaching of Isḥāq Al-Mauṣilī . . . The writer deals specially with the differences between the theories in the Old Arabian School and those of the Greek scholiasts, or — in his own words — between
>
> 'the masters of Arabian music (*aṣḥāb al-ghinā' al-'arabī*) and the masters of [Greek] music (*aṣḥāb al-mūsīqī*).'
>
> He demonstrates the precise position of every note of the Arabian system by reference to the fingerboard of the lute (*al-'ūd*), and uses an alphabetic notation or tablature (*ḥurūf al-jumal*) for that purpose. He then explains that the Old Arabian System was based on what was termed 'courses' (*majārī*), there being two of these — the course of the third finger (*majrā al-binsir*) and the course of the second finger (*majrā al-wusṭā*). In each of these courses there were four finger scales or modes (*aṣābi'*) which the author describes.[26]

Farmer also informs us that Al-Munajjim tuned his *'ūd* as shown in Figure 11.42(a).[27] With respect to Strings I–IV, this is exactly the same tuning described by Al-Kindī with one notable exception: there is no fret between the nut and the index finger fret. In other words, the *mujannab* (lit. *neighbor;* also translated as *anterior* or *assistant*)[28] fret is missing. This omission is understandable given the difficulties presented by the comma of Pythagoras. (See Section 11.46.) We are here again reminded of Al-Kindī's genius in solving this difficult problem. Given the absence of the *mujannab* fret — and the overall simplicity of this fingerboard when compared to the scales of later theorists discussed below — there is little doubt that this is a very early example of an *'ūd* tuning.

Because a European translation of Al-Munajjim's treatise does not exist, consider a description of the tuning in Figure 11.42(a), which is contained in a work entitled *Rasā'il Ikhwān al-Ṣafā* (*Treatises of the Brothers of Sincerity*),[29] written by a highly educated group of scholars that published many original works in the 10th century. Again, although an English translation of the chapter on music exists,[30] for technical reasons I translated the following passages from a German translation by Friedrich Dieterici:[31]

> The most perfect instrument [which produces] the most beautiful effect is the instrument [called] "Lute." It has a body in which length, width, and depth stand in noble proportions. Length to width = 1 : ½. Width to depth = 1 : ½. Length to depth = 1 : ¼.
>
> The top plate [soundboard] is thin, derived from hard light wood, which resounds when one strikes it. ...
>
> The length of the string is divided into four equal parts and the fret of the little finger {*khinṣir*} is placed at three-quarters of the neck of the lute. Then the string from the upper end is divided into nine equal parts, and the fret of the index finger {*sabbāba*} is placed on the first ninth part of the same neck.

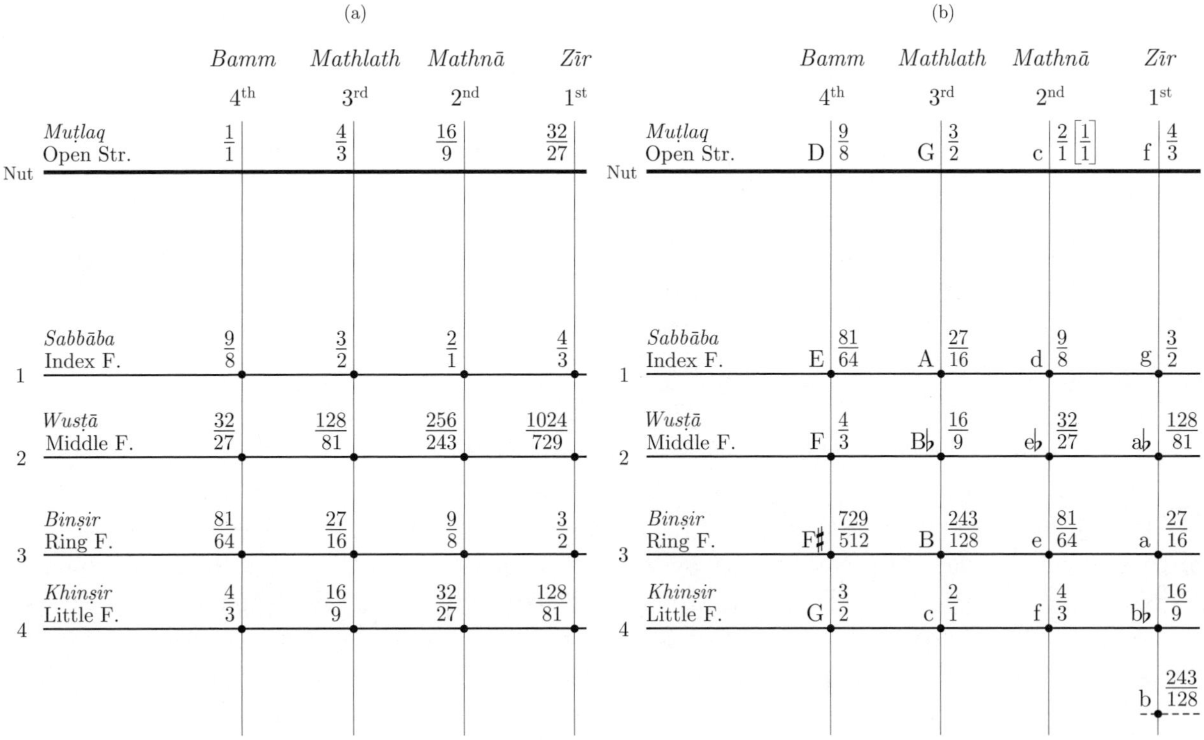

Figure 11.42 One of the oldest and simplest *'ūd* tunings in the history of Arabian music. (a) The fret locations and open string tuning as described by the Ikhwān al-Ṣafā, or the Brothers of Sincerity. (b) According to Farmer and Wright, Al-Munajjim (d. 912) used this tuning to describe eight ancient Arabian modes, which originated in the 7th century. In Al-Munajjim's text, the *Mathnā* string serves as tonic, or provides the lowest tone of all the modes. To maintain consistency with other *'ūd* tunings discussed throughout these sections on Arabian music, the *Mathnā* is here tuned to *'c'*. (Fret locations to scale.)

Then one again divides [the string] from the fret of the index finger to the bridge [*musht*, lit. *comb*] into nine equal parts and places the fret of the ring finger {*binṣir*} on the next [or first] ninth part, since [this fret] lies above the little finger in the direction of the index finger.

Then one divides the length of the string from the fret of the little finger toward the bridge into eight parts, [and] — on the string section above [the latter fret] and at the distance of such [a ⅛ part] — one places here the fret of the middle finger {*wusṭā*}. This fret lies therefore between the fret of the index finger and that of the ring finger. ...

One stretches the treble string [*Zīr*], and tensions it so tightly as it can bear without breaking; then one stretches the next string [*Mathnā*] above the treble and tensions it considerably; one stops the latter with the little finger and strikes it while releasing the treble string. If one hears that their tones sound the same, they are good; if not, one tensions the second tighter or loosens it, until both are equal to each other and their tones ring out as one tone. Next, one stretches the third string [*Mathlath*], one stops it with the small finger and strikes it — while one releases the second [string] — until one hears that the tones of both are equal [and ring out] as if one tone.

> Then one stretches the bass string [*Bamm*], stops it, and strikes it while releasing the third string. If one hears the tones of both [strings] as one tone, they are of equal measure, and likewise all strings in the same manner. ...
> The tone of every string stopped with the little finger is directly equal to the tone of the open string {*muṭlaq*} beneath it.[32] (Text in brackets mine. Text in braces in the original text.)

For a ratio analysis of these fret locations see Sections 11.53 and 11.70, which discuss the *'ūd* tunings of Al-Fārābī and Ṣafī Al-Dīn, respectively. Both theorists give exactly the same mathematical methods (string divisions) for determining the locations of the index, middle, and ring finger frets, as well as the *khinṣir* (lit. *little finger*) fret.

11.50

In a thoughtful paper entitled *Ibn al-Munajjim and the early Arabian modes*,[33] Owen Wright chronicles three different versions of the early modes by Western scholars, and at the end of the discussion offers his own interpretation. Even though Al-Munajjim makes eight descriptive statements with respect to the tones and tone combinations that constitute these melodic modes, his text does not eliminate the possibility of multiple interpretations. Consequently, out of a total number of eight modes, Figure 11.43 shows that Wright proposes two different interpretations of Modes 1, 4, 7, and 8.

Before we consider these eight statements in full detail, I must alert the reader to several problems with respect to notation. (1) Al-Munajjim uses the open *Mathnā* string as tonic; therefore, in his system the *Mathnā* provides the lowest tone for all eight modes. Unfortunately, Western scholars have not always agreed on the letter identity of this pitch. Since I will analyze several different *'ūd* tunings in this discussion on Arabian music, and since I would like to maintain continuity with respect to Western notation, I have consistently assigned the tone C to the open *Bamm* string, or to the lowest tone on the *'ūd*. In the context of this discussion and for reasons described below, Figure 11.42(b) illustrates the open *Mathnā* tuned to *'c'*, which means that the open *Mathlath* sounds G below, and the open *Bamm*, D below. (2) In his paper, Wright does not give a translation of Al-Munajjim's eight statements, but rather offers carefully worded synopses that include Western note names. In Wright's system, the open *Mathnā* sounds *'f'*, but in the following quotation I transposed all tones for an open *Mathnā* tuned to *'c'*:

> 1. According to Isḥāq [Al-Mauṣilī] there are only ten notes, viz.: *c*, *d*, *e*♭, *e*, *f*, *g*, *a*♭, *a*, *b*♭, *b* (B♭ and *B* are used as well as *b*♭ and b).
>
> 2. According to Isḥāq there are nine notes, the tenth note being the octave of the first. (These two contradictory statements are not juxtaposed in the text.)
>
> 3. The modes are divided into two sets (*majrā*), one containing *e*♭ and the other *e*. These two notes are mutually exclusive, i.e. cannot both occur in any one mode.
>
> 4. The notes *c*, *d*, *f*, *g*, *a*, *b*♭ are 'compatible', i.e. may all occur in a single mode. In conjunction with *e* they form the '*e* set' (*majrā al-binṣir*).
>
> 5. The notes *e*♭, *e*, *a*♭, *B* are 'incompatible'. The rule of mutual exclusion applicable to *e*♭ and *e* (cf. statement 3) is also valid for the other pair, *a*♭ and *B*.

1. *Muṭlaq fī majrā al-wusṭā*

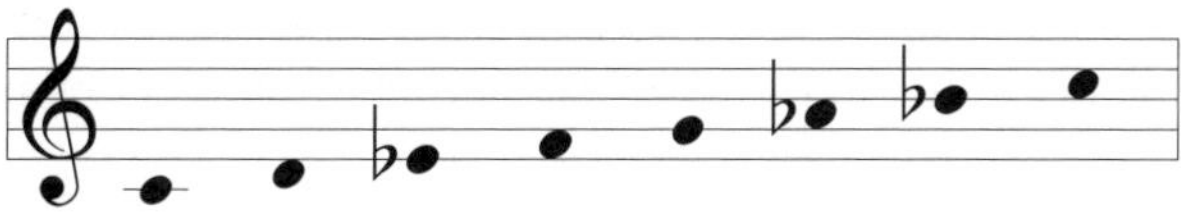

Wright #1:	1	2	3♭	4	5	6♭	7♭	$\dot{1}$
Wright #2:	1	2	3♭	4	5	[6]	7♭	$\dot{1}$
Farmer:	1	2	3♭	4	5	[6]	7♭	$\dot{1}$

2. *Muṭlaq fī majrā al-binṣir*

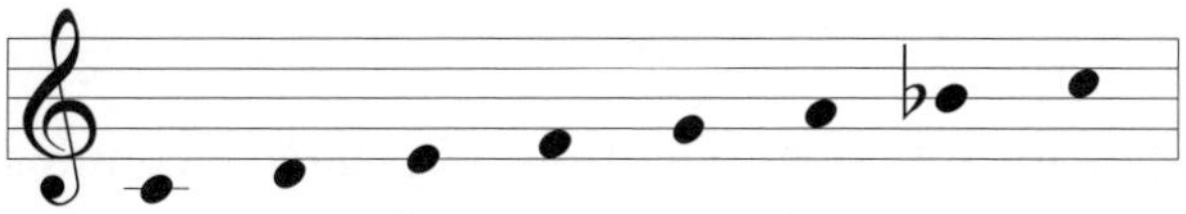

Wright and Framer:	1	2	3	4	5	6	7♭	$\dot{1}$

3. *Sabbāba fī majrā al-wusṭā*

Wright:	1	2♭	3♭	4	5♭	6♭	7♭	$\dot{1}$
Farmer:	1	2♭	3♭	4	[5]	6♭	7♭	$\dot{1}$

4. *Sabbāba fī majrā al-binṣir*

Wright #1:	1	2	3♭	4	5	6♭	7♭	$\dot{1}$
Wright #2:	1	2	3♭	4	5	[6]	7♭	$\dot{1}$
Farmer:	1	2	3♭	4	5	6♭	7♭	$\dot{1}$

5. *Wusṭā fī majrāhā*

Wright:	1	2	3	4	5	6	7	$\dot{1}$
Farmer:	1	2	3	[4♯]	5	6	7	$\dot{1}$

6. *Binṣir fī majrāhā*

Wright:	1	2♭	3♭	4	5	6♭	7♭	$\dot{1}$
Farmer:	1	2♭	3♭	4	[5♭]	6♭	7♭	$\dot{1}$

7. *Khinṣir fī majrā al-wusṭā*

Wright #1:	1	2	3♭	4	5	6	7♭	$\dot{1}$
Wright #2:	1	2	[3]	4	5	6	7♭	$\dot{1}$
Farmer:	1	2	3♭	4	5	6	[7]	$\dot{1}$

8. *Khinṣir fī majrā al-binṣir*

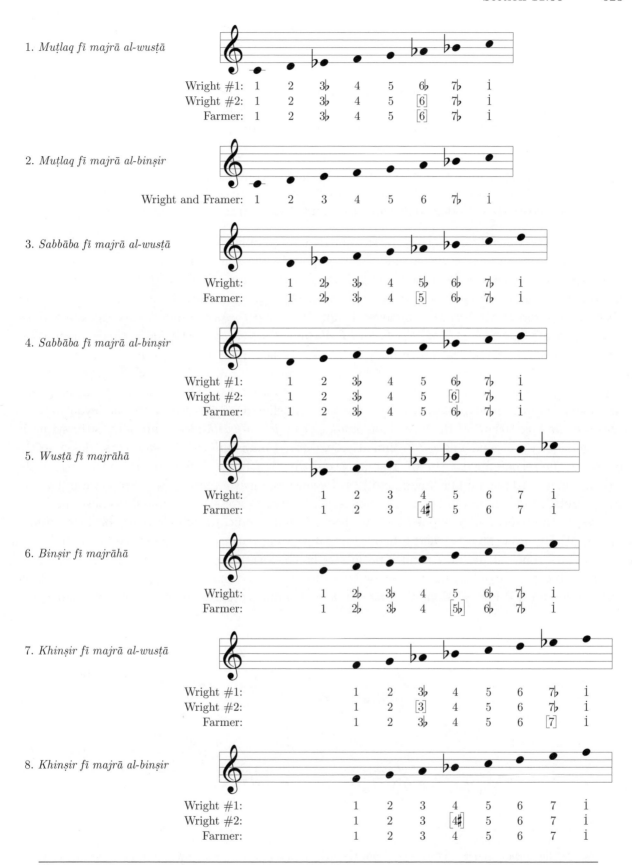

Wright #1:	1	2	3	4	5	6	7	$\dot{1}$
Wright #2:	1	2	3	[4♯]	5	6	7	$\dot{1}$
Farmer:	1	2	3	4	5	6	7	$\dot{1}$

Figure 11.43 Two similar interpretations of the ancient Arabian modes by Wright and Farmer based on very general descriptions by Al-Munajjim.

6. *a*♭ is 'compatible' with *e*♭ in its course, except for one particular place where it does not agree with it: one cannot pass from *a*♭ to *a*, nor from *a* to *a*♭.

7. *B* is 'compatible' with *e* in its course, except for one particular place where it does not agree with it: one cannot pass from *B* to B♭, nor from B♭ to *B;* equally impossible are the movements *B* to *b*♭, *b*♭ to *B*, *b*♭ to *b*, and *b* to *b*♭.

8. The greatest number of notes upon which a composition may be based is eight out of the ten. This is a characteristic feature of Arabian music, and most types of song conform to this standard.[34] (Text in brackets mine.)

These very general descriptive statements require complicated processes of deduction, association, and elimination in the arrangement of permissible tone combinations. Because Wright discusses his reasoning in full detail, we will not repeat these methods here. Instead, let us focus on four intrinsic features of these modes. (1) Since Al-Munajjim uses the open *Mathnā* as tonic, there are no frets to produce the "octaves" *c*ˡ, *d*ˡ, *e*♭ˡ, *e*ˡ, and *f*ˡ. As a result, it was necessary to use lower "octave" equivalents *C, D, E*♭, *E,* and *F.* Farmer observes, "To the Arabs there was nothing irregular or unmusical in that proceeding, since they looked upon a note and its octave as one and the same *musically.*"[35] For ease of comprehension, all modes in Figure 11.43 include upper "octave" tones. (2) With respect to Al-Iṣfahānī's work, Wright informs us, "The names of the eight modes are taken from the *Kitāb al-aghānī.* They are a sort of shorthand description of the layout of each scale on the fingerboard of the lute. Thus *muṭlaq fī majrā al-wusṭā* means literally 'open string in the course of the second finger'."[36] Similarly, *sabbāba fī majrā al-wusṭā* means 'first finger in the course of the second finger'. (In all Arabian texts, the 'first finger' refers to the 'index finger', the 'second finger', to the 'middle finger', etc.) (3) Because the *wusṭā* represents the interval of two adjacent frets, Modes 1, 3, and 7 indicate "semitones" between Frets 1 and 2; and because the *binṣir* represents the interval of a skipped fret, Modes 2, 4, and 8 indicate "whole tones" between Frets 1 and 3. (4) However, Modes 5 and 6 break this alternating pattern of a "semitone" mode followed by a "whole tone" mode. Statement 3 prohibits the co-existence of *e*♭ and *e* in the same mode, so Mode 5, *Wusṭā fī majrāhā*, must progress by a "whole tone" from *e*♭ to *f;* since the only available fret above Fret 3 is Fret 4, Mode 6, *Binṣir fī majrāhā*, must progress by a "semitone" from *e* to *f.*

5. *Wusṭā fī majrāhā*

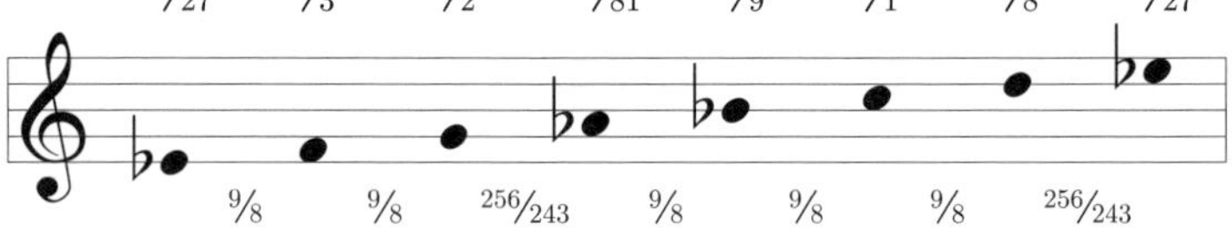

8. *Khinṣir fī majrā al-binṣir*

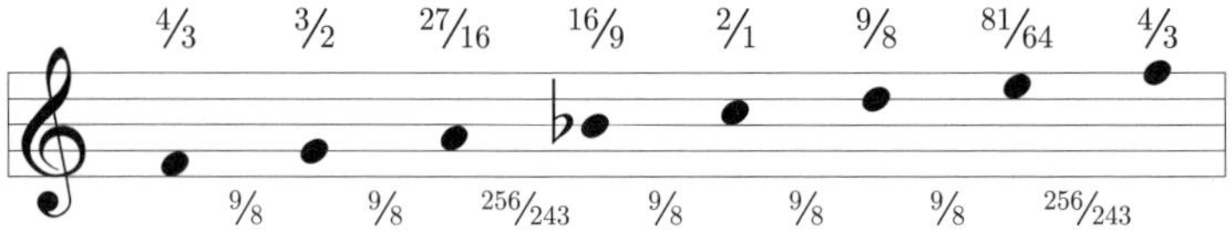

Figure 11.44 Philolaus' diatonic scale in the context of ancient Arabian modes. Although the tunings of the earliest short-necked lutes from the 6th, 7th, and 8th centuries remain unknown, there is no doubt that in the 9th century Arabian musicians played these modes on the classic *al-'ūd.* This cross-cultural achievement comes as no surprise because the Arabs possessed complete translations of Plato, Aristoxenus, Euclid, Nicomachus, and Ptolemy.

As previously mentioned, Figure 11.43 shows that Wright admits two possible interpretations of Modes 1, 4, 7, and 8. In contrast, Farmer gives only one possible version for each mode.[37] Both Wright and Farmer agree on Mode 2. Furthermore, in my opinion, Wright convincingly argues in favor of changing Farmer's versions of Modes 3, 5, and 6.

Finally, note that Wright's version of Mode 5, his first interpretation of Mode 8, and Farmer's version of Mode 8 all express Philolaus' diatonic scale. Figure 10.9 shows Philolaus' scale in the standard Greek Dorian Mode between E and E', and in the standard Western Lydian Mode between C and C'. This latter mode consists of the following sequence of interval ratios: $^9/_8$, $^9/_8$, $^{256}/_{243}$, $^9/_8$, $^9/_8$, $^9/_8$, $^{256}/_{243}$. In Figure 11.44, this sequence appears in the context of Modes 5 and 8. It is, therefore, highly probable that this Pythagorean version of the diatonic scale — based on prime numbers 2 and 3 — was imported into Europe as part and parcel of the fretting and tuning of the *'ūd.*

The manifestation of Greek music theory on Arabian musical instruments comes as no surprise because the Arabs possessed complete translations of Plato, Aristoxenus, Euclid, Nicomachus, and Ptolemy.[38] Farmer reminds us that the infusion of Arabian and Greek scientific knowledge into southern Spain had far-reaching consequences throughout central Europe.

> The music school at the University of Cordova, one of the most famous in the world in its day, was the *Alma Mater* of many of the rising musicians of Europe . . . Students flocked to the Andalusian universities, where they studied and translated the Arabian arithmetician, Al-Khwārizmī, the geometrician, Ibn al-Haitham, the astronomer, Al-Battānī, and the music theorists, Al-Fārābī and Ibn Sīnā, all of whom came to be known in Western Europe under the Latinized names of Algaurizim, Alhazen, Albategnius, Alpharabius, and Avicenna.[39]
>
> It is perfectly true that most of the Arabic treatises on the theory of music remained untranslated, or at least such translations have not been preserved, although we possess Averroës' 'Commentary on *De Anima*' in both Latin and Hebrew. Two Arabic compends on the sciences — including that on music — were translated into Latin, and both became textbooks in European centers of culture, being quoted by Gundisalvus, Magister Lambert, Vincent of Beauvais, Roger Bacon, Jerome of Moravia, Walter Oddington, and other theorists of European music. Even if we suppose that the more important of the Arabic works on music remained untranslated, it is not without reasonable supposition that their contents could have been passed on orally. Both Adelard of Bath and Roger Bacon had advocated that European students should go to the Arabic fountain head in the schools of Muslim Spain. That some did go is evident from a statement of Ibn al-Ḥijārī (12th century) who said that 'students from all parts of the world flocked to Cordova' to sit at the feet of Arabic scholars.[40]

~ 11.51 ~

Before we continue with this discussion on scales and modes, we must first address several problems with respect to modern French and English translations of ancient Arabic texts. The treatises of the six theorists mentioned at the beginning of Section 11.45 appear in the first four volumes of a six-volume work entitled *La Musique Arabe*,[41] published posthumously by Baron Rodolphe D'Erlanger (1872–1932). Regrettably, with regard to mechanical instrument components, the translations of critical words in these volumes are often incorrect. For example, the translators consistently translate the Arabic word *musht* with the French word "cordier." The modern term "cordier" refers to the "tailpiece" found on all instruments of the violin family. On a violin, a cordier consists of a tapered piece of curved wood to which one fastens the strings at the ends opposite to the tuning pegs. The cordier is situated between the bridge and the lower end of the violin, and the tension of the strings suspends the cordier above the violin's top plate, or soundboard. Consequently, the cordier does not contact the top plate, which means that it does not transmit mechanical energy from the vibrating strings to the soundboard. Furthermore, with the exception of a few plucked instruments like mandolins and banjos, the vast majority of instruments that have Western-style tailpieces are bowed instruments. Finally, note that on an instrument equipped with a cordier, all strings have two different lengths: a measured length between nut and bridge, which defines the critical vibrating length of the open strings, and an extended length between nut and tailpiece, which is completely irrelevant to the tuning and playing of the instrument.

In contrast, Figure 11.45(a) shows that the Arabian *'ūd* is not equipped with a suspended tailpiece, but with a mechanical component that functions as a bridge *and* as a string holder. The Arabic term for a *bridge-string holder* is *mushṭ*. This simple part consists of a long, narrow, and flat piece of wood that has numerous notches and holes through which one threads and fastens the strings. As such, a *mushṭ* functions exactly like the bridge-string holder of a modern acoustic guitar. It is glued directly to the top plate near the round end of the *'ūd*, and therefore transmits mechanical energy from the vibrating strings to the soundboard. On an *'ūd*, the measured length of an open string is defined by the distance between the nut — or *'anf* (lit. *nose*) — and the bridge — or *mushṭ* (lit. *comb*).

Because this basic principle applies to *all* stringed instruments equipped with a nut and a bridge, the renowned music theorist Ṣafī Al-Dīn labeled the ends of his *theoretical strings* with letters A for *'anf* and M for *mushṭ*. (See Section 11.70.) In the passage below, Al-Jurjānī quotes Ṣafī Al-Dīn, and then follows the quotation with his own description:

> ". . . The end of the string that corresponds to the *Mushṭ* will be *M;* that which corresponds to the *'Anf* will be *A* . . ."
>
> The *'Anf* is the end of the tapered part of the instrument, or neck, behind which the strings are attached. Leaving the tuning pegs, these strings pass over this end, which is elevated by means of a piece of wood . . . that has as many notches as there are strings. As for the *Mushṭ*, it is a piece of wood that one attaches at the end on the round side [the top plate or soundboard] of the instrument, and that is used to attach the strings.[42] (Text in brackets mine.)

Farmer's overly fussy translation of *mushṭ* as "bridge-tail-piece" does little to obviate this error. In 1928, Farmer wrote, "The *mushṭ* on the lute served the double purpose of bridge and tail-piece."[43] Apparently, Farmer felt compelled to emphasize that a *mushṭ* serves two mechanical functions because on other Arabian stringed instruments — including the famous long-necked lute called *ṭunbūr* — the bridge and tailpiece consist of two separate components. In 1929, Farmer gave this description of a Meccan lute called *qabūs:*

> Unlike the classical lute (*'ūd*), the *qabūs* has no *mushṭ* or bridge-tail-piece. It is mounted with a separate bridge (*ḥāmila*, *faras*), as well as a separate tail-pin (*zubaiba*) to which the strings (*awtār*) are fastened.[44]

Western instrument builders refer to this so-called tail-pin as a hitch pin because musicians use it to fasten the ends of strings directly to an instrument. However, be aware that many ancient and modern instruments are also equipped with separate string holders. Some string holders consist of a piece of wood with holes for threading and fastening strings, while others consist of metal plates with pins for looping and fastening strings. In either case, the Persian *'ūd* in Figure 11.45(b) demonstrates that a string holder — unlike a tailpiece — is directly attached to the lower end of an instrument with glue or screws. On all instruments equipped with a nut, bridge, and string holder or hitch pins, the measured length of an open string is defined by the distance between nut and bridge. Again, the extended length of a string between nut and string holder, or between nut and hitch pin, is mathematically and musically irrelevant.

Numerous problems also exist in the French translation of Al-Jurjānī's canon description. (See Section 11.52.) A canon or polychord is like a monochord in that both instruments are used to experience the mathematical principles of musical ratios.[45] On a canon, all open strings are tuned to the same frequency. To facilitate this requirement, canon strings are made from the same material(s), and have identical lengths, diameters, and tensions. Strings of equal length require that a canon must be built with two nuts, or two downbearing surfaces for the strings, that are parallel, or equally spaced apart. (See Plates 2 and 3.) According to Al-Jurjānī's description, one nut near the tuning pegs consists of a semi-cylindrical rod, while the other nut at the opposite ends of the strings consists of a string holder, or alternatively, of a set of individual hitch pins. Note, therefore, that in Figure 11.46(a) the latter mechanical component functions as a *nut-string holder*. The translation in *La Musique Arabe* refers to the string holder as a "cordier," and to the hitch pins as *boutons* (lit. *buttons*). Here the incorrectness of "cordier" comes full circle and thoroughly distorts Al-Jurjānī's description. Unlike the *musht* of an *'ūd*, the "cordier" of a canon does not function as a bridge, and because the string holder is directly attached to the canon, it does not function as a suspended "tailpiece."

(a) (b)

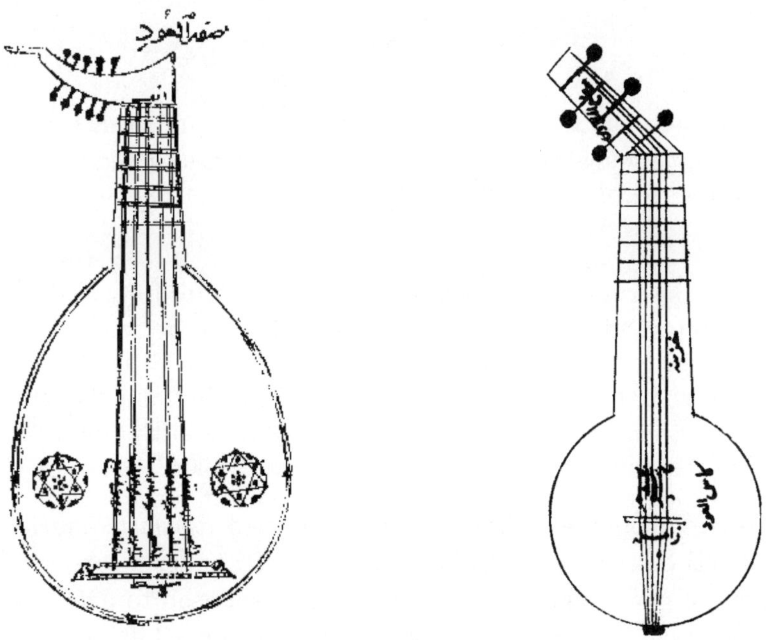

Figure 11.45 Two different lute constructions. (a) This Arabian *'ūd* equipped with five double strings, seven frets, and a *musht* is from a treatise entitled *Kitāb al-adwār*, by Ṣafī Al-Dīn (d. 1294). (b) This Persian *'ūd* equipped with five single strings, seven frets, a *ḥāmila*, and a separate string holder is from a treatise entitled *Kanz al-tuḥaf*, written in 1345 by an unknown author. Farmer states that the former manuscript was copied in the years 1333–1334,[46] and the latter, in the years 1661–1668.[47]

In the above-mentioned quotation, Farmer suggests that Arabian writers use the word *musht* exclusively to describe the bridge of an *'ūd*, and employ terms like *ḥāmila* and *faras* to describe bridges on stringed instruments that have separate string holders, or alternatively, separate hitch pins. The translations in *La Musique Arabe* support this observation. The generic French word "chevalet" for "bridge" appears consistently in the context of stringed instruments other than the *'ūd*. Since in many Arabian treatises the primary purpose of musical instrument descriptions is to explain the underlying mathematical principles of music, I simply translate "chevalet" *and* "cordier" as "bridge." In the original texts, Arabian writers use different terms like *ḥāmila*, *faras*, and *dāmā* to distinguish between various *stand-alone bridges*, like the kind shown in Figure 11.45(b). However, in the final analysis, on all hand-held plucked and bowed instruments the clearly delineated span between nut and bridge is the only distance that accurately describes the vibrating lengths of open strings. Similarly, with respect to Al-Jurjānī's canon description, I simply translate "cordier" as "string holder," because in this case the clearly delineated span between the left nut (semi-cylindrical rod) and the right nut (string holder) is the only distance that accurately describes the vibrating lengths of open strings.

Consistent with this analysis, in the English translations of passages from *La Musique Arabe*, I bracketed "string holder" for "cordier" the first time it appears in a quotation from Al-Jurjānī's text, and "bridge" for "cordier" the first time it appears in a quotation from Al-Fārābī's text. From these points onward, "string holder" and "bridge" appear without brackets to emphasize their correct usage. Finally, in this context, I categorically reject the French term "cordier" and the English term "tail-piece." I know of no Arabian instrument that uses a suspended piece of wood with holes for fastening strings. A tailpiece serves a highly specialized function in the construction of Western instruments and, as such, should not be confused with fastening devices of plucked and bowed stringed instruments found in other parts of the world.

11.52

With respect to fretted lutes, the term *ḥāmila* signifies a stationary bridge. However, on stringed instruments without frets, *ḥāmila* also refers to a moveable bridge situated between two immovable nuts. In his treatise entitled *Kitāb al-kāfī fi'l-mūsīqī* (Book of sufficiency on music),[48] Al-Ḥusain ibn Zaila (d. 1048) observes

> And of those (instruments) possessed of strings ***without*** frets to determine the places (pitch) of the notes, but whose difference between the places (pitch) is in the length or shortness of the string itself, as in the *ṣanj* and the *shahrūd*, or in the length or shortness of the string and the similarity of the bridges (*ḥāmilāt*) and the supports (*ā'mida*) as in the *'anqā'*.[49] (Bold italics mine. Text in parentheses in Farmer's translation.)

Furthermore, in a passage quoted later from a treatise entitled *Risāla fi'l-mūsīqī* (Treatise on music),[50] Abu'l-Ṣalt (d. 1134) describes the placement of a *ḥāmila* under a canon string. These definitions and references are of paramount importance because they lead to irrefutable theoretical and musical connections between the Arabian canon and the Arabian lute. For example, significant passages in the treatises of Al-Fārābī (d. *c.* 950), Ibn Sīnā (980–1037), and Abu'l-Ṣalt indicate that Arabian music theorists and musicians considered a *dastān* (Persian, lit. *fret*) on the fingerboard of an *'ūd* as having the same mathematical and musical function as a *ḥāmila* (Arabic, lit. *carrier*) on the soundboard of a *qānūn*. Here the Arabicized word *qānūn* does not refer to the modern zither, built in the form of a trapezoid and equipped with strings of different lengths, but rather to the ancient Greek *kanon*, described at length in Ptolemy's *Harmonics*.[51] Before we discuss these passages in full detail, let us first acquaint ourselves with an Arabian version of this instrument as described by Al-Jurjānī (d. 1413).

On the construction of an instrument to test the rules of music.

Having shown everything that relates to the elements of melody: the notes, the small intervals, the genera . . . all that remains is for us to explain *the large elements*, those whose role, in a melody, is comparable to that of verses in a poem. ...

You know now, in theory, everything that relates to the ratios of notes. If you want to realize [the theory] through experience and sensation, you need only to play an instrument; I am going to tell you how to build it. It will allow you to easily distinguish consonance from dissonance, whether it concerns notes, intervals, genera, or systems.

Here are the requirements for building the instrument.

Take a wood frame with four sides . . . at right angles, in the shape of a parallelepiped. It may be either rectangular or square. Choose one of the sides of this frame for the base [right side] of the instrument, and the one that is opposite it, for the top [left side]; if it is a rectangle, these will be the two short sides. These two sides must, however, be long enough to accommodate a line of fifteen tuning pegs. Cover the face [soundboard] of the instrument with a flat surface made of thin wood, and its back [bottom], with a surface of curved wood.

Fasten a semi-cylindrical rod, made of ivory or hardwood, and of the thickness of at least one finger, along the edge of the face, on the [left side]. On the other edge of the face, on the [right side], attach a type of [***string holder***], similar to that of the lute; or else place fifteen hitch pins at the [right side] of the instrument, [along] the side of the face, in the same way that one attaches the hitch pin[s] of the *ṭunbūr*. Place each one of these hitch pins opposite one of the fifteen tuning pegs that are aligned [along] the [left side].

Next, equip the instrument with strings. Coming from the hitch pins, or the holes made in the string holder, these strings go towards the tuning pegs, after passing over the semi-cylindrical rod through notches cut opposite the tuning pegs on one side, and opposite the string holder holes or hitch pins on the other.

Tension the strings equally so that they all produce identical notes.

Then make a ruler having the length of the distance from the [left side] to the [right side], or a little more; and determine on it a distance equal to the vibrating section of the [open] strings. Divide the edge of this ruler according to the various divisions . . . of a particular genus . . . ; and inscribe on each division the sign of the note to which it corresponds.

Next, make fourteen bridges of ivory or of hardwood. The base of these bridges must be flat so that they can be positioned at a right angle to the face of the instrument and stay perfectly fixed there. The top of each of these bridges, i.e., their surface over which the string passes, must be rounded and must include one notch, so that its contact with the string approaches the ideal contact of a point with a straight line. The top of the bridges must be slightly higher than the semi-cylindrical [rod].

Then determine on the strings the points that correspond to each of the divisions on the ruler. Move the bridges to place them in line with each of these points, so as to make each of the strings produce one of the notes of

> the desired system. Once this is done, when the strings are set in motion, they will make audible the system that we have organized . . . ; all that we know in theory will then be made perceptible to the ear, and we will thus be able to realize, through sensation, the consonance of intervals, and their dissonance . . .
>
> We can, without difficulty, call this a perfect instrument; in fact, it serves the theory as completely as the practice of the Art of Music.[52] (Text in brackets mine. Bold italics in brackets my correction of the "cordier" translation error in *La Musique Arabe*.)

Since no illustrations of ancient Arabian canons have survived, Figures 11.46(a) and 11.46(b) depict my interpretations of these two different canon descriptions. Many years of canon building and playing have sensitized me to recognize key passages in Al-Jurjānī's text. In my opinion, the following quotations attest to Al-Jurjānī's direct experiences with such instruments. I find his observations (1) that the contact of a bridge ". . . with the string approaches the ideal contact of a point with a straight line . . .", and (2) that ". . . the top of the bridges must be slightly higher than the semi-cylindrical [rod] . . ." especially noteworthy. Observation 1 has two consequences: a triangular-shaped bridge with a sharp point (i) gives an accurate pitch at the exact measured location along a string's length; in contrast, a wide or blunt point has the effect of shortening the string, which in turn causes an inadvertent increase in the string's frequency. (ii) A sharp point also produces accurate length ratios on *both* sides of the bridge. (See Figures 3.15 and 3.17, and Section 12.3.) Observation 2 is a caveat against using a bridge that is too high; such a bridge stretches a string in an upward direction, which effectively increases the string's tension, and thereby causes an unintentional increase in frequency.

Now, let us consider a less detailed but equally significant description of a canon by Abu'l-Ṣalt, who lived approximately 300 years before Al-Jurjānī. Abu'l-Ṣalt was born in Andalusia in 1067, and spent most of his life in Egypt and Tunis. His treatise on music has survived in a Hebrew translation; the Arabic original is lost. Hanoch Avenary, who translated this treatise into English,[53] states that it was a part of a much larger opus entitled *Sefer ba-Haspaqah* (Book of Sufficiency), a work of encyclopedic proportions. In any event, the Hebrew text gives the following title on the first page: "Fourth Discipline of the Second Section: The Science of Music." Apparently, the "fourth discipline" refers to the *quadrivium*, or to the four branches of mathematics: arithmetic, geometry, astronomy, and music. As such, the *quadrivium* was taught in all leading Medieval and Renaissance universities throughout Europe. In Chapter 4, Paragraph 1, Abu'l-Ṣalt states

Al-Qānūn

> When you want to determine the above-mentioned intervals by means of the [measuring-] cord, take for that purpose two strings of the same substance, equal with regard to all the qualities of length, thickness and smoothness, and assemble them on any instrument. Divide the surface of the instrument in parallel to one of them according to the ratio of any System and Genus you wish, and inscribe marks at the single dividing points; these will be on the straight line parallel to the string, and will determine the place of the ***frets**** when they are touched. Next put your finger on the place of any note, and touch the other [string] by putting your finger wherever you wish: thus you will hear the notes of the intervals accurately . . . You can hear them [the notes of an interval] also from one string alone which is divided lengthwise according to the demanded ratios. Touch it as an open string, then put the finger on the place of the required note, and touch a second time. However, this transition of the hand formerly mentioned is difficult

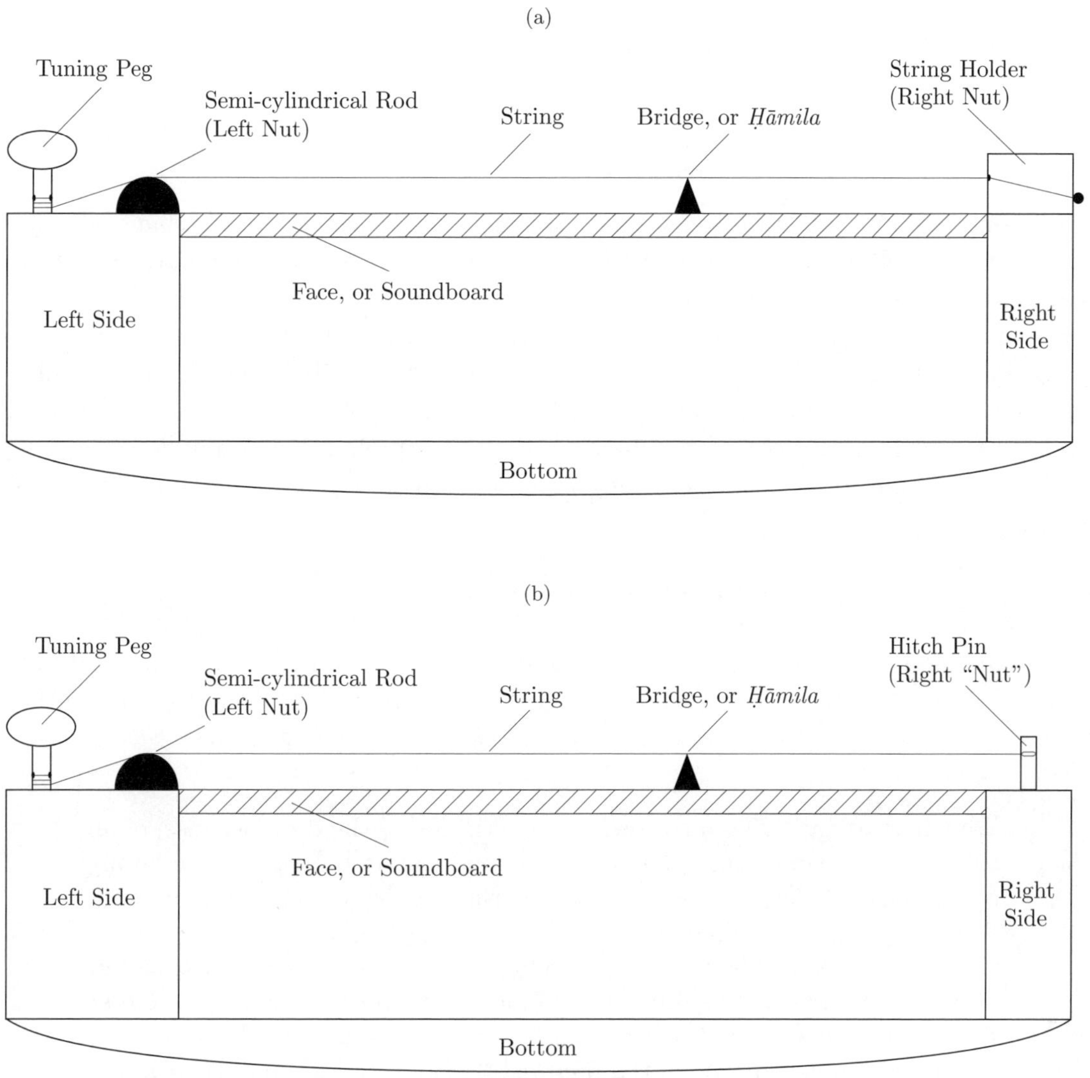

Figure 11.46 Longitudinal cross-sections of two different canon designs described by Al-Jurjānī (d. 1413). (a) On the right side, this canon is equipped with a string holder, which provides a clearly delineated edge to ensure that all strings are equal in length between the semi-cylindrical rod (left nut) and the string holder (right nut). (b) On the right side, this canon is equipped with a set of individual hitch pins. Because the hitch pin holes must all be drilled in a perfectly straight line, the equal string length requirement on this canon is more difficult to achieve.

and troublesome on this instrument. The most advantageous and perfect [method] is to take 15 strings, equal in every respect, and to stretch them on a rectangular instrument. Then take a measuring stick [*al-miṣṭara*] as long as one of them, and divide it according to the intervals of that System which you want to investigate by means of the [measuring-] cord. Then fix it alongside the string next to the first string from which the first note shall be sounded. At the place of the second of the fifteen notes put a ***bridge*** [*ḥāmila*] made of a body with a broad seat and a sharp edge, and let the second string ride on it in a notch [*fī taḥzīz*] at the upper end. Fix the measuring stick near the third string as well. Let the third note be above it, and in this manner go on till the last string. This is the instrument on which

> all the mentioned notes can be heard, and it is the most perfect of all the given instruments and contains their entire compass.
>
> *On p. 53 the translators note, "In the original text, the term fret or stopping place is always rendered by the Persian-Arabic designation *al-dastān*."[54] (Bold italics mine.)

In this quote, Abu'l-Ṣalt establishes the mechanical and conceptual interchangeability of the *dastān* and the *ḥāmila*. Both components serve exactly the same function, namely, to provide a mechanical means for stopping a string at a theoretically infinite number of measured locations along its vibrating length. Since the *ḥāmila* of the *qānūn* is much older than the *dastān* of the *'ūd*, the intriguing possibility exists that the inventors-developers of the fretted *'ūd* consciously conceived of this instrument as a highly practical and portable *qānūn*. In any event, when viewed from this perspective, the evolutionary process from *qānūn* to *'ūd* is both profound and unique because it stems from a desire to bestow on the *'ūd* the tuning accuracy and tuning flexibility for which all *kanons* are known.

11.53

The most famous and complex Arabian treatise on music is a work entitled *Kitāb al-mūsīqī al-kabīr* (Major Book on Music),[55] by Abū Naṣr Al-Fārābī (d. *c.* 950). Although the author does not describe the construction of a canon in his *Instrumentarium*,[56] he makes this pivotal observation:

> We will start by giving a concise . . . description of the lute, because, of all the stringed instruments, it is the most popular. It belongs to the family of instruments that are equipped with strings on which one plays different sections to produce different notes.
>
> On the neck of this instrument, frets pass under the strings and delimit on each one of them the different sections that produce the notes. ***These frets play the role of bridges;*** one places them parallel to the lower part of the instrument known as the [***bridge***].[57] (Bold italics mine. Bold italics in brackets my correction of the "cordier" translation error in *La Musique Arabe*.)

I interpret the statement, "These frets play the role of bridges," as a reference to canon bridges. As discussed above, canon bridges may be moved and repositioned anywhere along a string's length. By now, this observation seems redundant, but a careful reading of the *Kitāb al-mūsīqī al-kabīr* reveals that Al-Fārābī defined many scales and modes that are not playable given the notes of his 10-fret and 12-fret *'ūd* tunings. For example, a tetrachord discussed in Section 11.56 requires ancient length ratio $^{81}\!/_{70}$. Because this ratio does not exist on the latter *'ūd*, Al-Fārābī accurately describes the exact location that, when provided with a moveable fret, produces the desired tone. So, we must be extremely cautious *not* to begin this discussion on Al-Fārābī by assuming that his fret descriptions represent inflexible tuning systems. Unlike a modern guitar that has rigid metal frets embedded in the fingerboard, an authentic lute built in either the Middle East[58] or in Europe[59] has moveable frets that consist of gut strings tied around the instrument's neck. Consequently, a lute player tunes and retunes a lute by moving its frets in the same manner as a canon player tunes and retunes a canon by moving its bridges.

Al-Fārābī describes the 10-fret *'ūd* tuning in the following manner:

> The most commonly used frets are four in number; they are placed on the neck [of the lute] so that the fingers may reach them as easily as possible . . .

The first [fret] is that of the *index finger*, the second, of the *middle finger*, the third, of the *ring finger*, and the fourth, of the *little finger*. The sections we generally use on each string of the lute are, of course, equal in number to the commonly used frets. The first note generated by each string is rendered by the whole string; it is known as the *open string*. The second [note] is called that of the *index finger;* the fret that delimits the string section which generates it is placed at $\frac{1}{9}$ of the distance between the meeting point of the strings [the nut] and the bridge.

$$[\text{Fret } 5 \rightarrow \tfrac{9}{8} = 203.9\ ¢]$$

The third note is that of the *middle finger;* we will not discuss here the fret that delimits the string section which produces it. We will return to it when we deal with that note. The fourth is that of the *ring finger;* the fret that delimits the section which produces it is placed at $\frac{1}{9}$ of the distance between the index finger fret and the bridge.

$$[\text{Fret } 9 \rightarrow \tfrac{81}{64} = 407.8\ ¢]$$

The fifth note is that of the *little finger;* its fret is placed at $\frac{1}{4}$ of the distance between the meeting point of the strings and their other ends attached to the bridge.

$$[\text{Fret } 10 \rightarrow \tfrac{4}{3} = 498.0\ ¢]$$

We see that the notes produced by one of the strings of the lute played open, then with the little finger fret, are at an interval of a fourth; those generated by the open string and the index finger fret are at an interval of a tone; and those rendered by the open string and the ring finger fret, at a ditone. The notes produced by a string stopped at the ring finger fret, then at the little finger [fret], are thus separated by the interval called a *remainder* [limma].

$$[\text{Interval ratio: } \tfrac{4}{3} \div \tfrac{81}{64} = \tfrac{256}{243} = 90.2\ ¢]$$

The most commonly used frets of the lute therefore delimit the intervals of the strong diatonic genus.

The strings of the lute are stretched, according to common practice, so that the second [*Mathlath*] produces, when it is played open, a note identical to that given by the first [*Bamm*] stopped at the little finger fret; the third open string [*Mathnā*] must produce a note identical to that of the little finger fret of the second [*Mathlath*]; and the open fourth [*Zīr*] gives a note like that of the little finger fret of the third [*Mathnā*].

Each open string therefore produces a note that is at an interval of a fourth from . . . the string placed below it. ...

Let us call the meeting point of the strings A. ...

Let us also label the points of contact of the strings with the frets: the points of contact of the index finger fret will be respectively Z, Ḥ, Ṭ, Y; those of the ring finger fret: K, L, M, N; and those of the little finger fret: S, ʿA, F, Ḍ. ...

We sometimes place the middle finger fret above that of the little finger, towards the nut, at a distance corresponding to $\frac{1}{8}$ of that which separates the latter fret [the little finger] from the bridge.

$$[\text{Fret } 6 \rightarrow \tfrac{32}{27} = 294.1\ ¢]$$

The note of the middle finger fret and that of the little finger fret are then in the ratio of $1 + \frac{1}{8}$ [9:8].

$$[\text{Interval ratio: } \tfrac{4}{3} \div \tfrac{32}{27} = \tfrac{9}{8} = 203.9\ ¢]$$

We use this middle finger when the intervals of the strong diatonic genus are arranged [descending] from the upper [note] . . . [as in descending from $\frac{4}{3}$, or $\frac{4}{3} \div \frac{9}{8} = \frac{32}{27}$]; in that case, the note delimiting the second interval of the diatonic genus inverted [as in descending from $\frac{32}{27}$, or $\frac{32}{27} \div \frac{9}{8} = \frac{256}{243}$] falls between the open string [$\frac{1}{1}$] and that of the index finger fret [$\frac{9}{8}$]; we sometimes use this note [$\frac{256}{243}$], but more often it is omitted.

Other musicians place the middle finger fret halfway between that of the index finger and that of the [***ring finger***]; it is then called the *Persian middle finger.*

$$[\text{Fret 7} \rightarrow \tfrac{81}{68} = 302.9\ ¢]$$

Finally, others place it halfway between the Persian middle finger we have just discussed and the ring finger fret; it is then the fret of the *middle finger of Zalzal.*

$$[\text{Fret 8} \rightarrow \tfrac{27}{22} = 354.5\ ¢]$$

The middle finger fret that results from the inversion of the intervals of the strong diatonic genus is not considered by musicians to be a middle finger fret; when they use it, they call it the *neighbor of the middle finger*, but they recognize as a true middle finger only the fret of the *Persian middle finger*, or that of the *middle finger of Zalzal.*

We again represent the four strings of the lute, but this time we show the fret of the [Persian] middle finger; the points of contact of this fret with the strings will be respectively: Q, R, Š, T.

In the playing of the lute, we also use frets placed between that of the index finger and the nut; they are called the *neighbors* {sing. *mujannab*, pl. *mujannabāt*} [or, anterior frets] *of the index finger.* [Al-Fārābi does not give instructions for calculating the location of the first anterior, which I call Fret 1, and which is the first fret in Al-Fārābī's table below; in the context of ratios, he only mentions the following interval ratio between Fret 1 and Fret 10.] One of these is at an interval of a ditone [or, $\frac{9}{8} \times \frac{9}{8} = \frac{81}{64}$] from the little finger;

$$[\text{Fret 1: } \tfrac{4}{3} \div \tfrac{81}{64} = \tfrac{256}{243} = 90.2\ ¢]$$

another is placed halfway between the nut and the index finger fret;

$$[\text{Fret 2} \rightarrow \tfrac{18}{17} = 99.0\ ¢]$$

another [is] halfway between the nut and the fret of the *Persian middle finger,*

$$[\text{Fret 3} \rightarrow \tfrac{162}{149} = 144.8\ ¢]$$

or [halfway between the nut and the fret] of the *middle finger of Zalzal.*

$$[\text{Fret 4} \rightarrow \tfrac{54}{49} = 168.2\ ¢]$$

If we count the notes provided by all the frets we have just discussed, plus those given by the strings in their open length, we find that each string produces [***eleven***] notes. In the table below, we give the numeric value of each of these notes, using the smallest integers that allow us to express their ratios exactly.

NAMES OF THE FRETS	LENGTH[S] of string sections that [the frets] delimit
Open string	20.736
[1] *Neighbor of the index finger*, that results from the inversion of the diatonic genus [256/243]	19.683
[2] *Neighbor of the index finger*, that results from dividing the first interval of a tone in half [18/17]	19.584
[3] *Neighbor of the index finger*, placed halfway between the nut and the Persian middle finger [162/149]	19.072
[4] *Neighbor of the index finger*, placed halfway between the nut and the middle finger of Zalzal [54/49]	18.816
[5] *Index finger* [9/8]	18.432
[6] *Neighbor of the middle finger* [32/27]	17.496
[7] *Persian middle finger* [81/68]	17.408
[8] *Middle finger of Zalzal* [27/22]	16.896
[9] *Ring finger* [81/64]	16.384
[10] *Little finger* [4/3]	15.552

We will again represent the four strings of the lute, and mark on them the two frets of the *middle finger*, the *neighbor of the middle finger*, and the *neighbor of the index finger* resulting from the inversion of the diatonic genus. The points of contact of the fret of the *middle finger of Zalzal* with the four strings are labeled: Th, Ḫ, Dh, Ṣ; those of the *neighbor of the index finger:* B, J, D, H; and those of the *neighbor of the middle finger:* Ḍh, Ġ, W, LA.[60] (Text, numbers, and ratios in brackets mine. Bold italics in brackets my corrections of unedited errors in *La Musique Arabe*. *Mujannab* in braces in Farmer's *The Music of Islam.*)

Figure 11.47 illustrates these ten divisions in the order described by Al-Fārābī, Table 11.23 gives detailed ratio calculations, and Figure 11.48 is a fret diagram of the tuning. In the quote below, Al-Fārābī explains that these frets do not belong to an actual instrument, but rather, that they represent the maximum number of tones utilized by practicing musicians. Furthermore, Al-Fārābī probably neglected to include the note names of Frets 2, 3, and 4 because "certain musicians" did not use them.

The frets we have enumerated are nearly all those that one ordinarily uses on the lute. However, one does not find them all together on the same instrument. There are some that are essential to the playing of the lute and used by all musicians. These are the index finger fret [9/8], that of the

> ring finger [$^{81}/_{64}$], that of the little finger [$^{4}/_{3}$], and one among those that are placed between the index finger and the ring finger frets and which everyone calls *middle finger frets;* for some this will be the *middle finger of Zalzal* [$^{27}/_{22}$], for others the *Persian middle finger* [$^{81}/_{68}$], for still others the fret that we have called the *neighbor of the middle finger* [$^{32}/_{27}$].
>
> As for the frets called the *neighbors of the index finger*, certain musicians reject them and do not use any of them. Others use one of the middle finger frets and employ with it the neighbor of the middle finger, which they consider to be a unique entity and not as a middle finger fret, but they don't use any of those called *neighbors of the index finger;* still others use all together one of the two middle finger frets, the neighbor of the middle finger, and one of the frets known as *neighbors of the index finger*, namely, the one that is separated by an interval of a limma from the index finger fret.[61] (Ratios in brackets mine.)

Al-Fārābī does not include the last fret — $^{9}/_{8} \div {}^{256}/_{243} = {}^{2187}/_{2048} = 113.7$ ¢ — which produces the Greek apotome. However, it does appear in Al-Fārābī's 12-fret tuning. (See Section 11.54.) In his commentary on the 10-fret tuning, Al-Fārābī also describes a second extra fret that functions as an *alternate middle finger of Zalzal.*

> The fret of the middle finger of Zalzal is sometimes placed above that of the ring finger, towards the index finger, at a distance corresponding to an interval of a limma.[62]

This unusual fret — $^{81}/_{64} \div {}^{256}/_{243} = {}^{19683}/_{16384} = 317.6$ ¢ — represents D♯, or the ninth "fifth" in the ascending *spiral of "fifths"* in Figure 10.16(a). Although this tone may be found on the traditional *ṭunbūr* of Khurāsān (see Figure 11.70), it does not appear in any other *'ūd* tuning.

Figures 11.47 and 11.48 include several historically significant ratios. As discussed in Section 10.31, length ratio $^{18}/_{17}$, which results from an arithmetic division of length ratio $^{9}/_{8}$, was first defined by Claudius Ptolemy (*c.* A.D. 100 – *c.* 165) in his great work *Harmonics.* Al-Fārābī's descriptions of "semitone" $^{18}/_{17}$, and of just "quarter-tones" $^{36}/_{35}$, $^{35}/_{34}$, $^{34}/_{33}$, and $^{33}/_{32}$ appear in Section 10.31 as well.

Al-Fārābī is the first theorist to record two second finger frets called the *Persian middle finger* and the *middle finger of Zalzal.* The former, ratio $^{81}/_{68}$ [302.9 ¢] is slightly higher than the Pythagorean "minor third," ratio $^{32}/_{27}$ [294.1 ¢], of the Old Arabian School. A factorization shows that composite number 68 is a product of primes $2 \times 2 \times 17$, which means this is a 17-limit scale.[63] As a result, the denominators of the Persian middle finger fret, ratio $^{81}/_{68}$, and of the Ptolemaic index finger fret, ratio $^{18}/_{17}$, have prime number 17 in common. Consequently, the interval of a "whole tone" exists between these two frets: $^{81}/_{68} \div {}^{18}/_{17} = {}^{9}/_{8}$.

The *middle finger of Zalzal* was named after the famous lutenist Manṣūr Zalzal (d. 791).[64] He is credited with the implementation of length ratio $^{27}/_{22}$ [354.5 ¢], known in the West as the "neutral third" because it approximates the average between the Pythagorean "major third," ratio $^{81}/_{64}$ [407.8 ¢], and the Pythagorean "minor third"; or (407.8 ¢ + 294.1 ¢) ÷ 2 = 351.0 ¢. Throughout the following discussions on Al-Fārābī and Ibn Sīnā, we will use the modern Persian *koron* sign: ᑭ, which indicates a tone that is approximately 30–70 ¢ flat of a given standard Pythagorean pitch, and the modern Persian *sori* sign: ⧺, which indicates a tone that is approximately 30–70 ¢ sharp of given standard Pythagorean pitch. In his book and dissertation entitled *The Dastgāh Concept in Persian Music*, Hormoz Farhat[65] distinguishes between such tones and the notorious tempered "quarter-tone" — 50.0 ¢ exactly — of Western music.

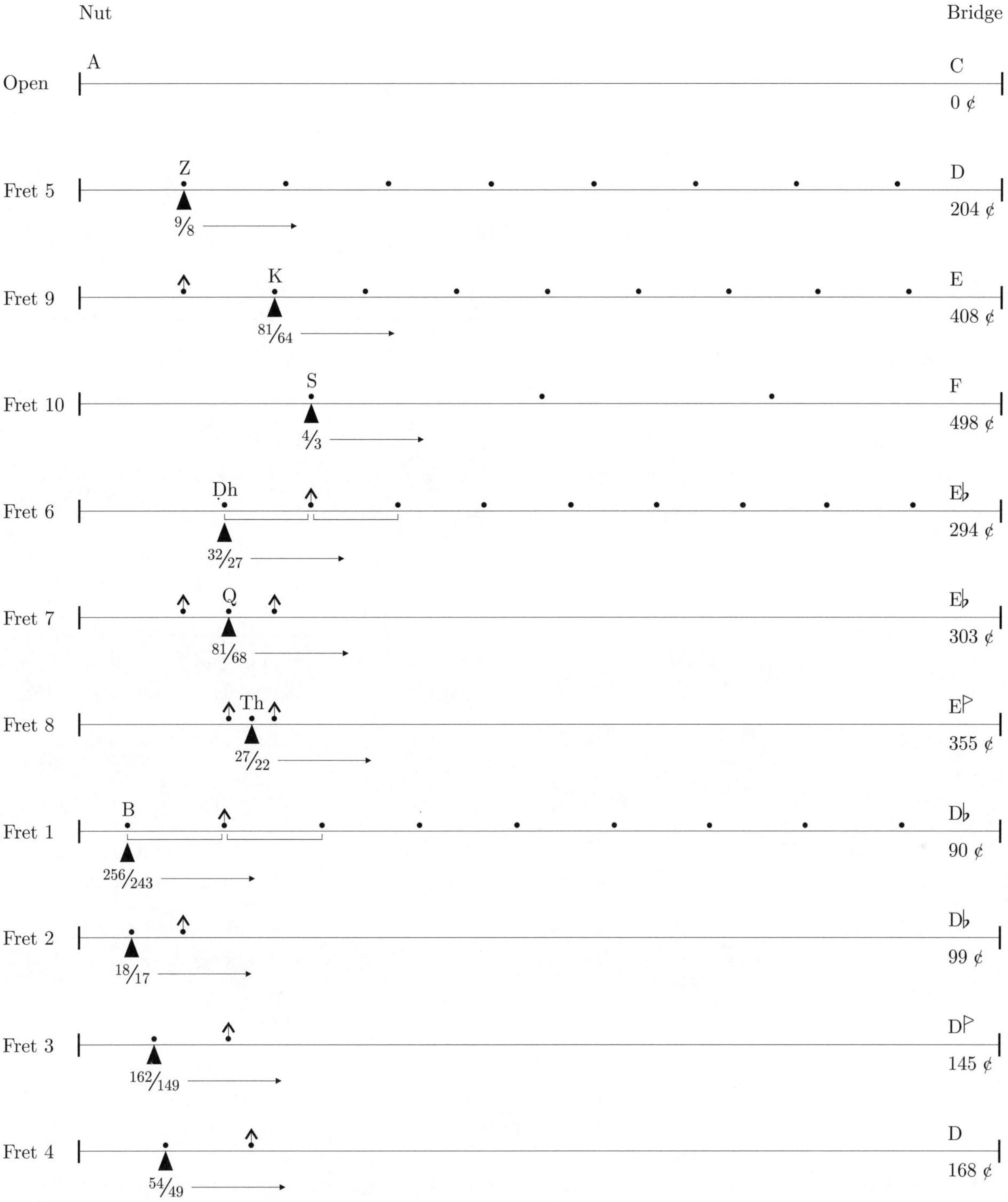

Figure 11.47 Al-Fārābī's string length divisions used to determine the locations of ten frets on the *'ūd*. Ptolemy's $^{18}/_{17}$, Zalzal's $^{27}/_{22}$, and the Persian $^{81}/_{68}$ constitute historically significant inclusions. (Dots with arrows point to previously calculated divisions.)

Table 11.23

MODERN LENGTH RATIO TO FREQUENCY RATIO CALCULATIONS
OF Al-FĀRĀBĪ'S 10-FRET *'ŪD* TUNING

Open String, Tone C	$1/1$	Whole string length.
Fret 5, Tone D	$1 \times 1/9 = 1/9$ $1 - 1/9 = 9/9 - 1/9 = 8/9 \rightarrow 9/8$	Ninth of string. Whole minus subsection.
Fret 9, Tone E	$8/9 \times 1/9 = 8/81$ $8/9 - 8/81 = 72/81 - 8/81 = 64/81 \rightarrow 81/64$	Ninth of $8/9$ section. $8/9$ section minus subsection.
Fret 10, Tone F	$1 \times 1/4 = 1/4$ $1 - 1/4 = 4/4 - 1/4 = 3/4 \rightarrow 4/3$	Quarter of string. Whole minus subsection.
Fret 6, Tone E♭	$3/4 \times 1/8 = 3/32$ $3/4 + 3/32 = 24/32 + 3/32 = 27/32 \rightarrow 32/27$	Eighth of $3/4$ section. $3/4$ section plus subsection.
Fret 7, Tone E♭	$8/9 - 64/81 = 72/81 - 64/81 = 8/81$ $8/81 \times 1/2 = 4/81$ $8/9 - 4/81 = 72/81 - 4/81 = 68/81 \rightarrow 81/68$	Length of internal section. Half of internal section. $8/9$ section minus subsection.
Fret 8, Tone E𝄳	$68/81 - 64/81 = 4/81$ $4/81 \times 1/2 = 2/81$ $68/81 - 2/81 = 66/81 = 22/27 \rightarrow 27/22$	Length of internal section. Half of internal section. $68/81$ section minus subsection.
Fret 1, Tone D♭*	$27/32 \times 1/8 = 27/256$ $27/32 + 27/256 =$ $216/256 + 27/256 = 243/256 \rightarrow 256/243$	Eighth of $27/32$ section. $27/32$ section plus subsection.
Fret 2, Tone D♭	$1/9 \times 1/2 = 1/18$ $1 - 1/18 = 18/18 - 1/18 = 17/18 \rightarrow 18/17$	Half of $1/9$ section. Whole minus subsection.
Fret 3, Tone D𝄳†	$1 - 68/81 = 81/81 - 68/81 = 13/81$ $13/81 \times 1/2 = 13/162$ $1 - 13/162 = 162/162 - 13/162 =$ $149/162 \rightarrow 162/149$	Complement of $68/81$ section. Half of complement. Whole minus subsection.
Fret 4, Tone D	$1 - 22/27 = 27/27 - 22/27 = 5/27$ $5/27 \times 1/2 = 5/54$ $1 - 5/54 = 54/54 - 5/54 = 49/54 \rightarrow 54/49$	Complement of $22/27$ section. Half of complement. Whole minus subsection.

*Although Al-Fārābī gives a verbal description of Fret 1, and includes an exact string length for this fret in his table, he does not offer a mathematical method for determining its location on the string. The method shown here is described by Ṣafī Al-Dīn. (See Section 11.70.)

†In Figure 11.48, two tones on Fret 8: D𝄳ˈ, $12/11$, and G𝄳ˈ, $16/11$, do not produce exact "octaves" with two tones on Fret 3: D𝄳, $162/149$, and G𝄳, $216/149$, respectively. Cent calculations show that the former tones sound 5.8 ¢ sharp of the latter tones.

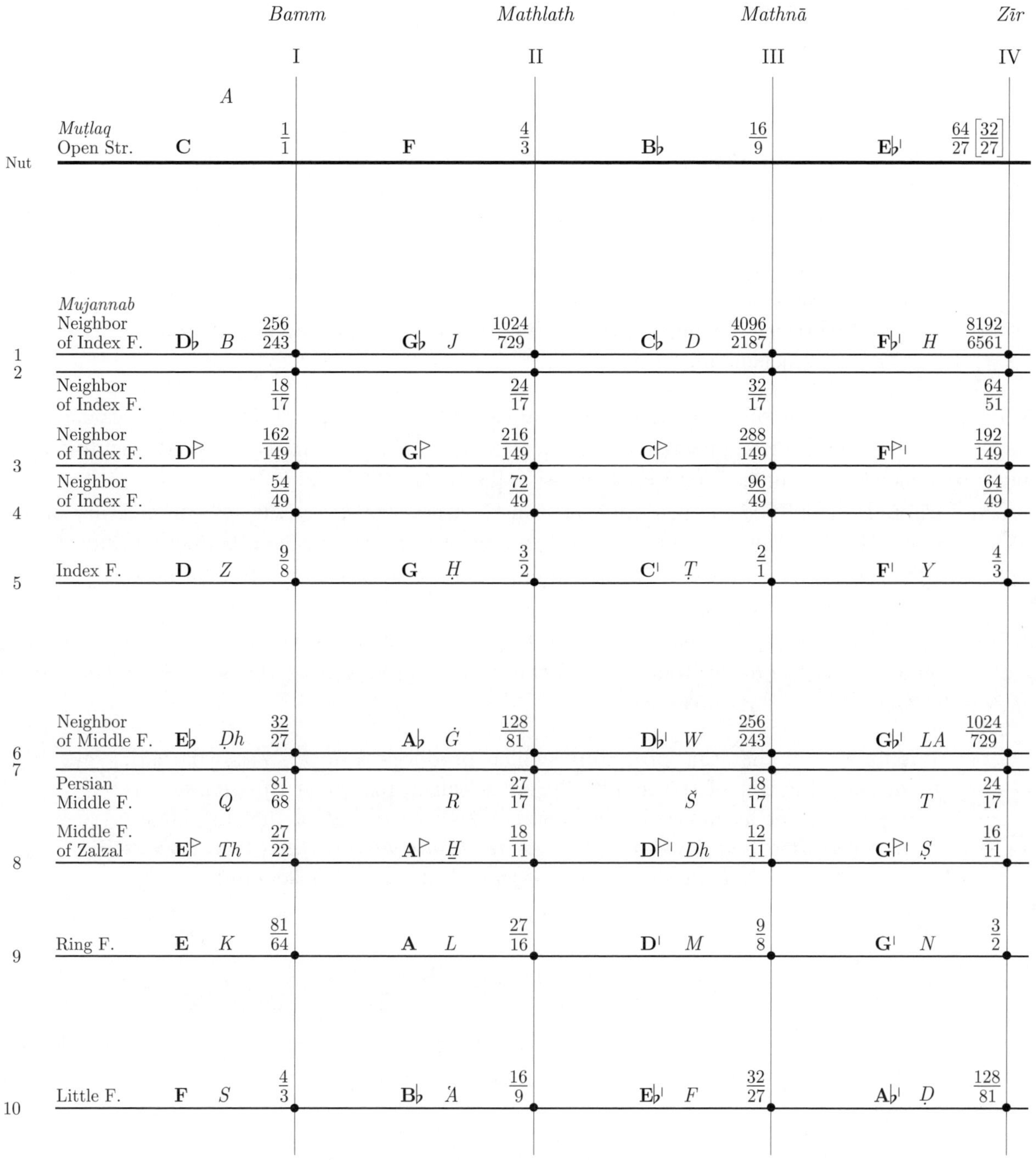

Figure 11.48 Ten theoretical fret locations on the *'ūd* as defined by Al-Fārābī (d. *c.* 950). In his treatise, Al-Fārābī expressly states that one does not encounter all these frets on a given *'ūd*. Instead, practicing musicians choose various kinds of fret combinations for their instruments. Most Arabian lutes were equipped with 4, 5, 6, or 7 frets. (Fret locations to scale.)

> In our notation, the neutral step above *c* is shown as *d*𝄳, and the neutral step above *d* is shown as *e*𝄳, after the accepted system of notation in Persia today. Even though the signs 𝄳 and 𝄲 were invented by A.N. Vaziri [1886–1981], and were to suggest a quarter-tone flat, and a quarter-tone sharp, respectively, and although we have discussed and rejected the quarter-tone system, we see no reason why these signs which are now part of the Persian alphabet of notation, cannot be used to good advantage.[66] (Dates in brackets mine.)

> *Koron* stands for the half flattening of a pitch, or, shall we say, for the lowering of a pitch by a microtone. ...
>
> [*Sori*] stands for half sharp, or [the] raising of a pitch by a microtone.[67] (Text in brackets mine.)

Note, therefore, that in the context of Al-Fārābī's 10-fret tuning, the descending chromatic sequence that includes Fret 8 appears as 81/64 [E], 27/22 [E𝄳], 32/27 [E♭]; similarly, the descending chromatic sequence that includes Fret 3 appears as 9/8 [D], 162/149 [D𝄳], 18/17 [D♭].

Al-Fārābī also identified the just "quarter-tone," interval ratio 33/32, in his commentary on the 10-fret tuning. He gives this description in the context of the *alternate middle finger of Zalzal*, ratio 19683/16384 [D♯], discussed above. Al-Fārābī criticizes the use of the latter fret because the interval between the *ring finger*, ratio 81/64, and the *middle finger of Zalzal* should *not* be a limma: 81/64 ÷ 19683/16384 = 256/243 = 90.2 ¢. Instead, the interval between the *ring finger* and the *middle finger of Zalzal* should be a just "quarter-tone," which can only be produced by the *standard middle finger of Zalzal:* 81/64 ÷ 27/22 = 33/32 = 53.3 ¢.

> But we say that this procedure [which produces ratio 19683/16384] is bad, because the fret of the middle finger of Zalzal, placed in this manner, is necessarily at an interval of a limma [256/243] with that of the ring finger, and ***not at a quarter-tone*** [33/32] ***as it should be*** according to what was said above . . .[68] (Bold italics, and text and ratios in brackets mine.)

~ 11.54 ~

Before we continue with Al-Fārābī's 12-fret *'ūd* tuning — which results in a 22-tone "double-octave" scale — let us first consider his intellectual reasons and musical motivations for creating this scale.

> Let us now proceed to the instruments which give us the natural notes, and to the one of them which gives us the greatest quantity and the most perfect of notes — namely, the *'ūd.*
>
> Evidently, if we assume pitches separated by definite intervals, we may equally assume within those intervals, ***other pitches***. However, since our purpose is to select therefrom the pitches of a single *jins* {Arabicized from the Greek "genus"; Arabic pl. *ajnās*} (from which alone natural tunes are composed) we would not need to consider those, {or} all the pitches which can emerge ***between*** these intervals. The first intervals are natural; the [other] intervals in ***between*** them which might be used are considered unnatural, even though they are similar.
>
> It may happen that some of the intervals ***between*** the notes of a *jamā'ah* ["collection" or scale] are natural while others are unnatural. For

> the most part, the well known intervals used on the instruments are those which should be regarded as essentially natural. On the other hand, it is also necessary to count as somewhat natural those intervals which are sometimes or rarely regarded as natural. ***This results from the fact that much of that which is unnatural in itself would become natural if it were combined with something else.*** Let us then consider all [the intervals] that are used in the tunes reproducible by the *ʿūd*, even if they are only used rarely.[69] (Bold italics, and text in braces mine. Text in parentheses and brackets in Al-Faruqi's dissertation.)

Al-Fārābī's perspective on the presence of "other pitches," on the possibility of "intervals between notes," and on the process by which the "unnatural becomes natural" expresses the conviction of a powerful intellect and the expanse of a limitless imagination. He then continues with this *ʿūd* tuning description:

> Let us tune the lute in the usual manner, and assign the lowest tone to the open string *Bamm*. Its octave equivalent is the note produced by the index finger on the *Mathnā* string. Evidently, this instrument is not meant for a single octave, but also [includes] those notes which are beyond the limits of the first octave collection.
>
> If, thereafter, we seek the upper octave equivalent of the index finger on the *Mathnā* string, we would not find it in the finger positions of the *ʿūd*. In order to complete the second of the octaves of pitches, let us stretch a fifth string. We would then find completion of the second octave in the ring finger tone of the *Ḥādd* or fifth string.
>
> It is evident that the notes in the second octave ought to be notes [equivalent to] the first octave and *vice versa*. Whenever the notes of a melody are found in one of the octaves produced by certain instruments, and not in the other octave, we would conclude that the latter octave has some notes missing and that one octave had been made shorter than the other. The two octaves should be made equal in the number of notes [they contain] so that every note from one octave matches one from the other octave . . .
>
> If we compare the notes of the first octave and those of the second, we find that the tone produced by the index finger on the *Mathnā* {$^2/_1$} has the same pitch as that of the open string *Bamm* {$^1/_1$}. And if we move from the open string *Bamm* to its index finger position {$^9/_8$}, we find an equivalent [for the latter] produced in the second octave by the ring finger on the *Mathnā*. We may then conclude that the interval between the tones produced by the open string *Bamm* and its index finger fret is equal to that between the index finger fret on the *Mathnā* and its ring finger fret.
>
> Of the three middle finger positions used, let it suffice for us to consider one of them, the *wusṭā al Zalzal*. If we descend to the *Zalzal* middle finger position on the *Bamm* {$^{27}/_{22}$}, we would find no note equivalent to it in the second octave. The same is true of the ring finger position on the *Bamm* {$^{81}/_{64}$}. If we were to establish equivalencies for them in the second octave, the pitch of the ring finger on the *Bamm* would be found above the index finger position, close to the *ʿanf* on the *Zīr* string. The note equivalent to that produced by the middle finger on the *Bamm* is above that found near the *ʿanf* of the *ʿūd* on the *Zīr* string.
>
> The note equivalent to that of the little finger on the *Bamm* {$^4/_3$} and the open string *Mathlath* {$^4/_3$} is the index finger note on the *Zīr*. That

> comparable to the index finger note on the *Mathlath* {3/2} is found by the ring finger on the *Zīr*. Finally, for the middle and ring finger notes on the *Mathlath* {18/11 and 27/16}, we do not find any positions in the second octave. If we sought to reproduce them, we would find an equivalent to the note produced by the ring finger on the *Mathlath* {27/16} above the index finger on the fifth string. The {equivalent of the note} of the . . . middle finger {position} on the *Mathlath* {18/11} {is} still farther up on the fifth string. The note of the open string *Mathnā* {16/9} is equivalent to the index finger note on the fifth string. The note produced by the index finger on the *Mathnā* {2/1} is equivalent to that produced by the ring finger on the fifth {4/1}. ***The second octave therefore includes all the notes of the first octave.***[70] (Bold italics, and text and ratios in braces mine. Text in parentheses and brackets in Al-Faruqi's dissertation.)

Although Al-Fārābī begins by stating, "Let us tune the lute in the usual manner . . ." not until this last sentence are we able to deduce his original set of frets that produce the lower "octave." In Figure 11.49, circles indicate that his original tuning consists of a 9-tone scale: 1/1 [C], 9/8 [D], 27/22 [E𝄳], 81/64 [E], 4/3 [F], 3/2 [G], 18/11 [A𝄳], 27/16 [A], 16/9 [B♭], 2/1 [C′].[71] The latter nine tones are located on the following four frets: 9/8, 3/2, and 2/1 on Fret 6; 27/22 and 18/11 on Fret 9; 81/64 and 27/16 on Fret 11; and 4/3 and 16/9 on Fret 12. Consequently, to realize upper "octave" equivalents for 27/22 and 81/64 on the *Bamm*, and for 18/11 and 27/16 on the *Mathlath*, Al-Fārābī installs Frets 1 and 4 across the *Zīr* and *Ḥādd*. All the tones marked with circles in the lower "octave" now have equivalents marked with circles in the upper "octave."

With respect to the tones contained in the upper "octave" but missing in the lower "octave," in Figure 11.49 diamonds indicate five such scale degrees. Al-Fārābī continues his description by observing that ratios 12/11, 16/11, and 64/33 on Fret 9 have no equivalents, and ratios 32/27 and 128/81 on Fret 12 also have no equivalents. To remedy these deficiencies he installs Fret 5 to match the three former tones of Fret 9, and Fret 7 to match the two latter tones of Fret 12. He then decides that ratios 256/243, 1024/729, and 4096/2187 on Fret 7 should also have equivalents, and therefore installs Fret 2. Next, he decides that ratios 8192/6561 and 32768/19683 on Fret 2 of the *Zīr* and *Ḥādd*, respectively, should have equivalents, and so he installs Fret 10. Then, Al-Fārābī states that if one includes the *Persian middle finger* fret, which produces ratios 18/17, 24/17, and 32/17 on the *Mathnā*, *Zīr*, and *Ḥādd*, respectively, one must also install Fret 3 to realize equivalents for these three degrees in the lower "octave."[72] Al-Fārābī concludes

> After these, no note of the *'ūd* remains which needs to be reproduced. In each octave, there are twenty-two notes; and these are all the notes used by the *'ūd*. Some of them are more frequently used than others.[73]

An examination of Al-Fārābī's 22-tone "double-octave" scale reveals that it contains all the degrees of Al-Kindī's 12-tone "double-octave" scale. Al-Fārābī's comments regarding the tuning of two identical "octaves" is a lesson he undoubtedly learned from Al-Kindī. Throughout his writing, Al-Fārābī demonstrates a capacity to assimilate the knowledge of masters who lived before him. As discussed below, he fully incorporated the works of Aristoxenus and Ptolemy into his theory of tetrachords. Moreover, he always interlaced such discussions with his own ideas and interpretations. Like Marin Mersenne in the West, Al-Fārābī consistently contemplated the possibility of expanding his experiences through instruments and tunings designed to transcend ordinary musical standards.[74] This explains why we will encounter minor contradictions in his description of customary practices. (See Section 11.55 and Figure 11.53.)

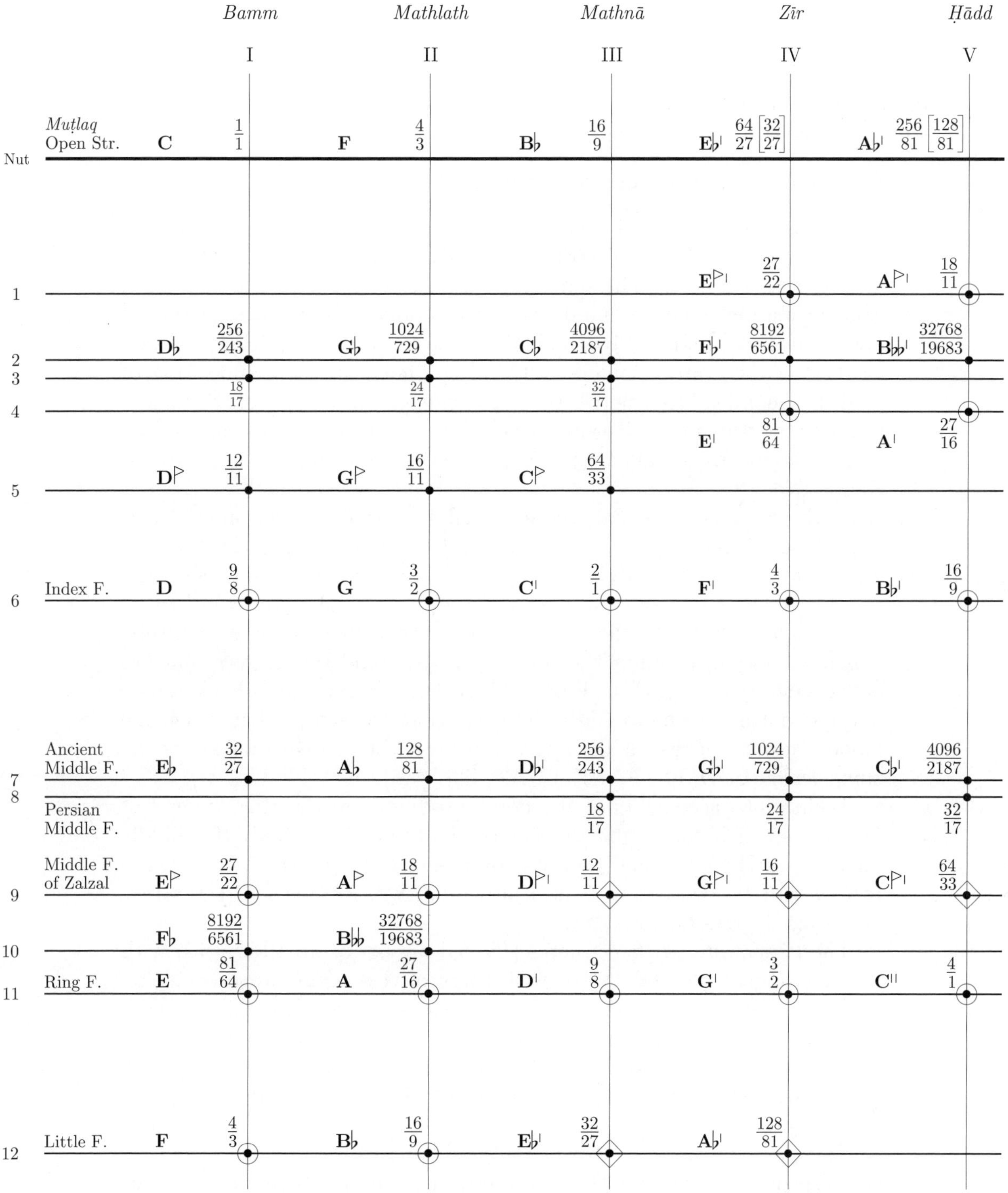

Figure 11.49 Al-Fārābī's 22-tone "double-octave" *'ūd* tuning. This remarkable scale contains all the tones of Al-Kindī's 12-tone "double-octave" *'ūd* tuning shown in Figure 11.41. Al-Fārābī explains that he was motivated to create this scale because "it is also necessary to count as somewhat natural those intervals which are sometimes or rarely regarded as natural." In other words, the 22-tone scale expresses Al-Fārābī's desire to expand his musical experiences beyond conventional norms. (Fret locations to scale.)

~ 11.55 ~

Reminiscent of Al-Munajjim's statements that describe permissible tone combinations of eight ancient modes, Al-Fārābī continues the discussion by defining compatible and incompatible notes, and ends his analysis with three standard modes.

Groupings of compatible notes and scales

Among these frequently used notes, those of the ring finger and the middle finger on the same string ***cannot*** be used together in the same melody as basic notes. The same applies to their upper and lower octave equivalents. On the other hand, the notes produced by the strings played open and those produced by the little finger fret on each {string}, as well as their octaves, are combined with all the notes in the composition of modes. The index finger note on a string will agree with that of the middle finger or the ring finger; likewise, the octave equivalents of these notes. The ring finger and the middle finger notes of the same string are therefore not compatible.

In the same cycle (scale), the notes of the strings played open {C, F, B♭}, those of the little finger {F, B♭} and the index finger {D, G}, will agree ***either*** with those of the middle finger {E$^{\triangleright}$, A$^{\triangleright}$} ***or*** with those of the ring finger {E, A}; they {the notes C, D, F or F, G, B♭} are (compatible) in the *same genus* with the notes of one or the other of those two frets. When one (scale) contains the ring finger notes and the degrees that are of the *same genus* {C, D, E, F or F, G, A, B♭}, to associate other notes to it would not always be to add to its perfection; the same is true when the mode is formed of the middle finger notes and the degrees that are of the *same genus* {C, D, E$^{\triangleright}$, F or F, G, A$^{\triangleright}$, B♭}.

Taking into account only the notes produced by the ring finger fret {E, A} and their compatible degrees {C, D, F, G, B♭}, or only the middle finger notes {E$^{\triangleright}$, A$^{\triangleright}$} and their compatible degrees {C, D, F, G, B♭}, the two cycles (the two octave scales) altogether will include fourteen notes, i.e., seven degrees for each {scale}.

The *Persian middle finger* notes {E♭, A♭} are not compatible either with the ring finger notes {E, A} or with those of the *middle finger of Zalzal* {E$^{\triangleright}$, A$^{\triangleright}$}, but they are of the *same genus* as those of the index finger, the little finger, and the strings played open. Taking into account only the *Persian middle finger* notes {E♭, A♭} and their compatible degrees {C, D, F, G, B♭}, each cycle (each octave scale) will include seven degrees of the *same genus*.

These are the various kinds of compatible notes used by the aforementioned peoples to compose their melodies. As a result, there are three categories of compatible notes that we can organize in each of the two cycles of the scale [of the double octave].

The first kind of notes of the same genus will include the following notes: that which is produced by the first open string of the lute, the index finger note of this same string, that of its ring finger, and that of its little finger, which is identical to that of the second open string; then the index finger of the second string, its ring finger and its little finger {C, D, E, F, G, A, B♭}.

The second will include the following degrees: the note of the first open string, that of its index finger, its middle finger of Zalzal, and its little finger; then the index finger of the second string, its middle finger of Zalzal, and its little finger {C, D, E𝄳, F, G, A𝄳, B♭}.

Finally, the third kind of compatible notes will include: the note of the first string played open, that of the index finger of this same string, that of its Persian middle finger, that of its little finger; then those of the index finger of the second string, its Persian middle finger, and its little finger {C, D, E♭, F, G, A♭, B♭}.

These are the three categories of natural and compatible notes used in the composition of melodies. We could admit others, but they would give birth to a weakly consonant and non-harmonious music.[75] (Bold italics, and text in braces mine. Text in parentheses and brackets in *La Musique Arabe.*)

Figure 11.50 shows that all three modes consist of seven tones, or two *identical conjunct tetrachords* that span the intervals from 1/1 to 4/3, and from 4/3 to 16/9. In response to Al-Fārābī's repeated use of "equivalents," this figure also includes the "octave" of each mode. Finally, I named these genera the *'Diatonic Mode'*, the *'Mode of Zalzal'*, and the *'Persian Mode'* to emphasize the musical quality that gives each mode a unique identity. In the context of scales, the *'Diatonic Mode'* is distinguished by a "major third" and "major sixth," the *'Mode of Zalzal'*, by a "neutral third" and "neutral sixth," and the *'Persian Mode'*, by a "minor third" and "minor sixth." The latter two tones, 81/68 [302.9 ¢] and 27/17 [800.9 ¢], are musically indistinguishable from the "minor third" [300.0 ¢] and the "minor sixth" [800.0 ¢] of 12-tone equal temperament.

Given a tuning where the tonic sounds C, Al-Munajjim and Al-Fārābī both agree that the note of the ring finger — 81/64 [E] — and the notes of the middle finger — either 27/22 [E𝄳] or 81/68 [E♭] — are incompatible in the same melody. We are here again reminded of the profound consequences of these ". . . three categories of compatible notes . . ." The *'Diatonic Mode'* and the *'Persian Mode'* are essentially identical with the major tonality and the minor tonality, respectively, of Western music. In contrast, for most occidental musicians the *'Mode of Zalzal'* remains unknown.

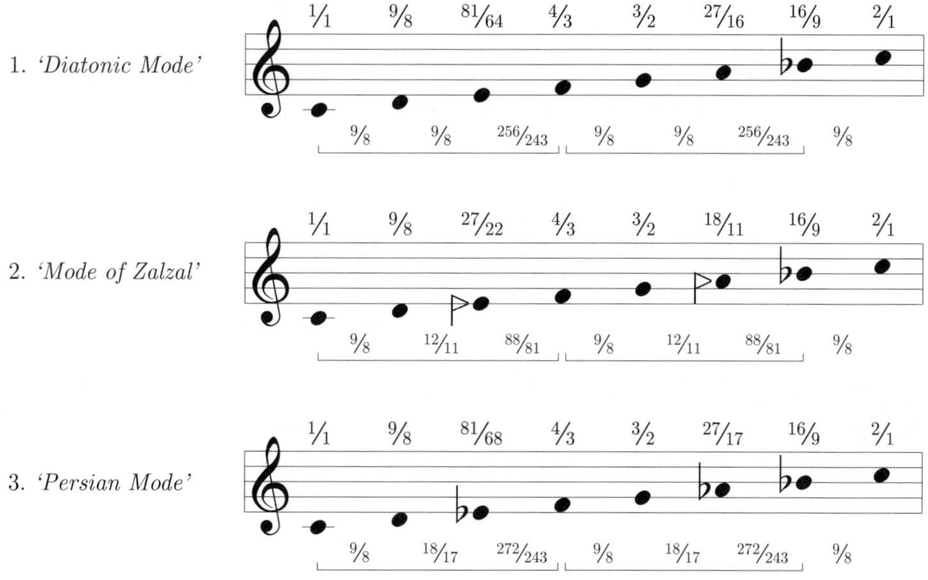

Figure 11.50 Al-Fārābī's three standard modes. Each mode consists of two *identical conjunct tetrachords*, followed by the "octave," C'. I named these genera the *'Diatonic Mode'*, the *'Mode of Zalzal'*, and the *'Persian Mode'* to emphasize the musical quality that gives each mode its unique identity.

Al-Fārābī concludes this discussion on the three standard modes with the following observations:

> We therefore say that a cycle will always include seven degrees of the same genus. This is derived from the statements of certain skillful musicians {like Al-Kindī}, who have long practiced this art and who have investigated the natural notes, contrary to what may be taught by certain masters incapable of furnishing tangible evidence for what they assert in their books, not having educated their ear by listening to music. What the latter say may be partly true; but the notes they include between the two ends of the scale are not all compatible. Their statements enable us, however, to prove that these degrees can be but seven in number, neither more nor less, {although the number of degrees} of the {***octave***} in general is infinite.
>
> The majority of theorists known to us do not seek to establish the compatible notes *within octaves.* Some are solely concerned with the notes capable of having an octave equivalent; others want to establish the number of all the musical notes, whether or not they have an octave equivalent. These theorists therefore cannot agree upon the number of musical degrees. Among those who wanted to establish in books the number of all the notes *reproducible at the octave*, we have to count the Greek mathematicians of antiquity and the Arab empire theorists of our time. Among the latter, some followed the way of the Greek mathematicians, others disregarded it; as skillful practitioners, trained in music, they trusted only their ears. Their vast experience dictated to them what to assert in their writings. Their musical instinct, driving them to the realization of the aforementioned three musical forms, led them to assign a number to the degrees of the scale. They are thus closer to the truth than those theorists of our time who wanted to follow the way of the ancient Greek mathematicians. They followed them, but they did not possess their knowledge or the experience and esthetic sense of more recent practitioners. Confident in the science of the ancients, they merely repeated their words; but one sees that they are incapable of explaining or proving what they assert. In a work where we report the opinions of all authors who have dealt with music, we mention those writers of whom we have just spoken, by pointing out the questions they could solve and those they were unable to solve.
>
> It is evident that, for instruments with open strings, the number of notes in octaves will still be that which we have established. If a string of one of these instruments is tuned to the ring finger [of one of the strings] of the lute, one cannot tune another to the middle finger [of this same string], and if one tunes to the middle fingers, one cannot tune at the same time to the ring fingers. The scale of sounds produced by instruments with open strings will thus contain no more than seven degrees.[76] (Text in braces mine. Bold italics in braces my correction of the "dynamis" translation error in *La Musique Arabe.* Text in brackets in *La Musique Arabe.*)

11.56

In the three remaining sections devoted to Al-Fārābī, we will analyze his writings in the context of two Greek music theorists: Aristoxenus (fl. *c.* 300 B.C.) and Ptolemy (*c.* A.D. 100 – *c.* 165). In preparation for this discussion, I urge the reader to read, study, and absorb Sections 10.12–10.13

and 10.19–10.20, which cover Aristoxenus' tetrachords and Ptolemy's tetrachords, respectively. Without a background in Greek tetrachordal theory, the next sections will be incomprehensible. Because Al-Fārābī's discussion on Aristoxenus' tetrachords is highly condensed, I divided the following continuous passage into five separate quotes to assist in the identification of specific issues under consideration.

I

Let us assume that the half step (*faḍlah*) equals half the whole step (*'awdah*). It would follow that if we subtract the half step from the whole step, the remainder would be of the same size. The half step is thus the interval common to all these intervals, an interval which can be measured twice in the whole step. The interval of the fourth, therefore, consists of two whole steps and a half; the interval of a fifth, of three whole steps and a half. If we assume for the half step a measurement of one, the octave will measure twelve, and, accordingly, the fifth will measure seven; the fourth, five; and the whole step, two.

II

Since the open string *Bamm* $\{1/1\}$ and the index finger position on the *Mathlath* produce the fifth interval $\{3/2\}$, and since the open string *Bamm* $\{1/1\}$ and the open string *Mathlath* produce the fourth $\{4/3\}$, the interval between the open string *Mathlath* and its index finger position is equal to a ***whole step*** $\{3/2 \div 4/3 = 9/8\}$. The same is true of the interval between the open string *Mathnā* $\{16/9\}$ and its index finger position $\{2/1\}$, since it is the difference between the octave and the combination of two fourths $\{2/1 \div (4/3)^2 = 2/1 \div 16/9 = 9/8\}$. The same is true of the interval between the index finger $\{9/8\}$ and ring finger $\{81/64\}$, $\{81/64 \div 9/8 = 9/8\}$. The remaining interval between the ring finger $\{81/64\}$ and little finger $\{4/3\}$ is equal to ***half a step*** $\{4/3 \div 81/64 = 256/243\}$.

III

{**1**} The first *jins* consists therefore of 1 step–1 step–½ step. {**2**} Since the *wusṭā* ("middle finger") *al Zalzal* position is nearer by a quarter of a step to the ring finger position [than the ancient *wusṭā* position], the second *jins* using [the former] becomes 1 step–¾ step–¾ step. {**3**} When the *mujannab al wusṭā*, i.e., the ancient *wusṭā*, is positioned at a point ***three-quarters of the way between the index and ring finger***, a third *tajnīs* or *jins* becomes possible, namely: 1¼ steps–¾ step–½ step. {**4**} When {or since} the Persian *wusṭā* position is halfway between the index and the ring finger stops, a fourth *jins* is derived: 1½ steps–½ step–½ step.

All these *ajnās* derivable from this instrument are popularly used . . .

IV

It is equally possible to derive other *ajnās* than the above-mentioned. This is done ***by dividing the interval of a whole step*** in fourths, eighths, thirds, half-thirds {or sixths: $1/3 \times 1/2 = 1/6$}, and quarter-thirds {or twelfths: $1/3 \times 1/4 = 1/12$}, and then combining them. Other *ajnās* result from these combinations. Examples of such combinations are the following: {**5**} 2 steps–¼ step–¼ step; {**6**} 1⅚ steps–⅓ step–⅓ step; {**7**} 1¾ steps–⅜ step–⅜ step; {**8**} ¾ plus ¼ of ⅓ step–¾ plus ¼ of ⅓ step–¾ plus ¼ of ⅓ step {or ⅚ step–⅚ step–⅚ step}. Thus far, we have eight *ajnās*.

V

> Assuming the measurement of . . . the interval of a fourth would equal 60 {parts} . . . the first *jins* of the first four [*ajnās*] would equal {**1**} 24-24-12. The second *jins* of the first four [*ajnās*] would equal {**2**} 24-18-18; the third *jins:* {**3**} 30-18-12; the fourth *jins:* {**4**} 36-12-12. The first of the second four . . . would equal {**5**} 48-6-6; the second: {**6**} 44-8-8; the third: {**7**} 42-9-9; and the fourth: {**8**} 20-20-20.[77] (Roman numerals, bold italics, and text, numbers, and ratios in braces mine. Text in parentheses and brackets in Al-Faruqi's dissertation.)

In Quote II, Al-Fārābī equates a "whole step," or a "whole tone," with interval ratio $9/8$, and "half a step," or a "semitone," with interval ratio $256/243$; in Quotes III and IV, he then proceeds to define *Ajnās* 1–8 based on various *fractional parts* of a "whole step." Table 11.24 lists these *ajnās* and their fractional parts in the order given by Al-Fārābī.

Table 11.24

AL-FĀRĀBĪ'S EIGHT *AJNĀS* IN ARABIAN ASCENDING ORDER

Jins 1	1	+	1	+	½
Jins 2	1	+	¾	+	¾
Jins 3	1¼	+	¾	+	½
Jins 4	1½	+	½	+	½
Jins 5	2	+	¼	+	¼
Jins 6	1⅚	+	⅓	+	⅓
Jins 7	1¾	+	⅜	+	⅜
Jins 8	⅚	+	⅚	+	⅚

If we invert the intervalic order of *Ajnās* 5, 6, 7, 4, 3, and 1, a comparison to Table 10.5 reveals that these *ajnās* are identical to Aristoxenus' tetrachords.

With respect to *Jins* 1, note that a more accurate interpretation of Al-Fārābī's tetrachord indicates an intervalic inversion of Philolaus' diatonic tetrachord. Here, Al-Fārābī specifies the sequence "tone," "tone," "semitone" in *ascending* order. Figure 11.51(a) shows that ascending interval ratios

(Table 10.5)

ARISTOXENUS' TETRACHORDS IN GREEK ASCENDING ORDER

Enharmonic					
	¼	+	¼	+	2
Chromatic					
Soft	⅓	+	⅓	+	1⅚
Hemiolic	⅜	+	⅜	+	1¾
Tonic	½	+	½	+	1½
Diatonic					
Soft	½	+	¾	+	1¼
Tense	½	+	1	+	1

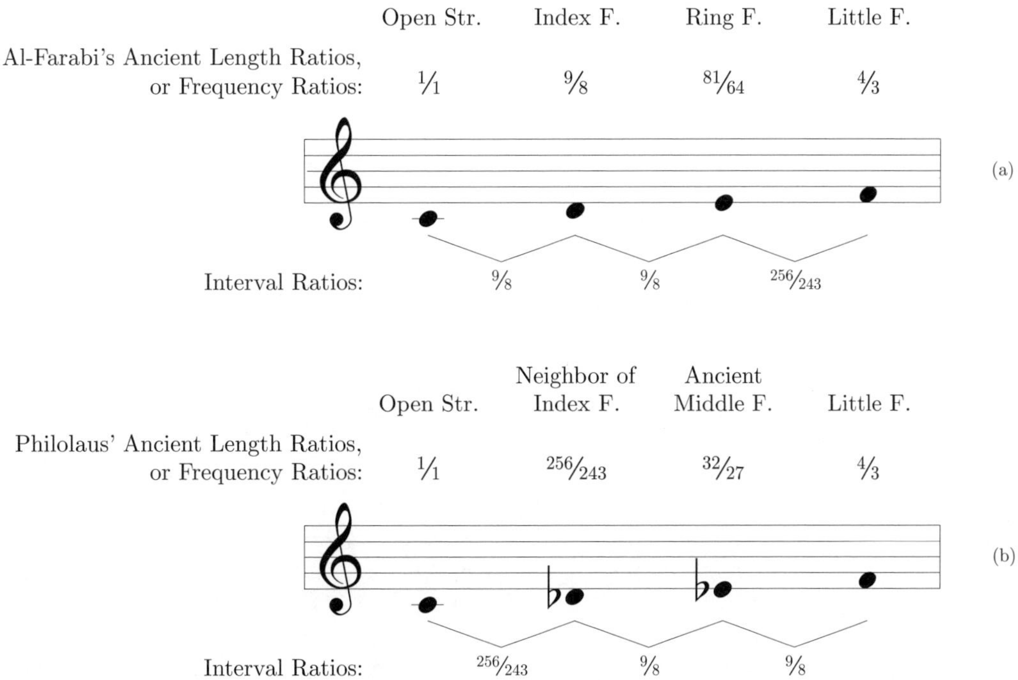

Figure 11.51 Arabian and Greek diatonic tetrachords on the *'ūd*. (a) According to Al-Fārābī (d. *c.* A.D. 950), this tetrachord consists of intervals "tone," "tone," "semitone" in *ascending* order. (b) According to Philolaus (fl. *c.* 420 B.C.), it consists of intervals "tone," "tone," "semitone" in *descending* order.

$9/8$, $9/8$, $256/243$ require ancient length ratios or frequency ratios $1/1$, $9/8$, $81/64$, $4/3$ in ascending order. However, according to Greek music theory, Figure 11.51(b) illustrates the sequence "tone," "tone," "semitone" in *descending* order, which means that descending interval ratios $9/8$, $9/8$, $256/243$ require ancient length ratios or frequency ratios $1/1$, $256/243$, $32/27$, $4/3$ in ascending order. Because Al-Fārābī systematically inverted the intervalic order of *all* Greek tetrachords, his interpretations on the fretted *'ūd* profoundly influenced countless musicians in future generations. Indeed, the tendency to place the largest intervals first, and the smallest intervals last, is very familiar to Western musicians.

Now, unlike Cleonides (fl. *c.* A.D. 50) who assigned Aristoxenus' "fourth" 30 *integer parts*,[78] in Quote V, Al-Fārābī assigns the "fourth" 60 *integer parts*, which means that 1 Step = 24 parts, $1/2$ Step = 12 parts, $1/3$ Step = 8 parts, $1/4$ Step = 6 parts, $1/6$ Step = 4 parts, and $1/8$ Step = 3 parts. Table 11.25 shows *Ajnās* 1–8 given this particular distribution of parts.

Table 11.25

AL-FĀRĀBĪ'S INTEGER PARTS OF HIS EIGHT *AJNĀS*

Jins 1	24	+	24	+	12
Jins 2	24	+	18	+	18
Jins 3	30	+	18	+	12
Jins 4	36	+	12	+	12
Jins 5	48	+	6	+	6
Jins 6	44	+	8	+	8
Jins 7	42	+	9	+	9
Jins 8	20	+	20	+	20

Table 11.26 gives the cent values of Al-Fārābī's integer parts in Table 11.25. Since ratio $^4/_3 = 498.0$ ¢, calculate the cent values of these x-number of parts by solving the following proportion for ¢:

$$\frac{x}{60} = \frac{¢}{498.0\ ¢}$$

$$\frac{x \times 498.0\ ¢}{60} = ¢$$

For example, when $x = 24$ parts, ¢ $= 199.2$ ¢:

$$\frac{24 \times 498.0\ ¢}{60} = 199.2\ ¢$$

Table 11.26

Jins 1	199.2 ¢	+	199.2 ¢	+	99.6 ¢
Jins 2	199.2 ¢	+	149.4 ¢	+	149.4 ¢
Jins 3	249.0 ¢	+	149.4 ¢	+	99.6 ¢
Jins 4	298.8 ¢	+	99.6 ¢	+	99.6 ¢
Jins 5	398.4 ¢	+	49.8 ¢	+	49.8 ¢
Jins 6	365.2 ¢	+	66.4 ¢	+	66.4 ¢
Jins 7	348.6 ¢	+	74.7 ¢	+	74.7 ¢
Jins 8	166.0 ¢	+	166.0 ¢	+	166.0 ¢

Finally, Table 11.27 provides a detailed mathematical analysis and description of Al-Fārābī's *ajnās*, and Figure 11.52 shows the fret locations, and the point locations between frets to scale. According to Al-Fārābī's description in Quote III, *Ajnās* 1, 2, and 4 may be played on the *Bamm* as depicted in Figures 11.48 and 11.49; that is, *Ajnās* 1 and 4 require only the *standard locations* of the index finger [$^9/_8$], Persian middle finger [$^{81}/_{68}$], ring finger [$^{81}/_{64}$], and little finger [$^4/_3$] frets. However, Al-Fārābī's description of *Jins* 2 is slightly more complex. If we disregard his reference to the *ancient wusṭā*, he states in essence that the *wusṭā al Zalzal* is a $^1/_4$ Step from the ring finger: $^{81}/_{64} \div {}^{27}/_{22} = {}^{33}/_{32} = 53.3$ ¢. Therefore, since the interval from the ring finger to the little finger is a $^1/_2$ Step: $^4/_3 \div {}^{81}/_{64} = {}^{256}/_{243} = 90.2$ ¢, the interval from the middle finger of Zalzal to the little finger equals $^1/_4$ Step + $^1/_2$ Step = $^3/_4$ Step, or $^4/_3 \div {}^{27}/_{22} = {}^{88}/_{81} = 143.5$ ¢.

With respect to *Jins* 3, Al-Fārābī gives specific instructions for moving the *ancient wusṭā* fret, ratio $^{32}/_{27}$, to a new location ". . . three-quarters of the way between the index and the ring finger." Table 11.27 indicates that the "new" *ancient wusṭā* fret now represents ancient length ratio or frequency ratio $^{81}/_{70}$.

In Quote IV, the calculations of *Ajnās* 5, 6, 7, and 8 are *not* straightforward. Nevertheless, Al-Fārābī explicitly stated that we must calculate all fret locations ". . . by dividing the interval of the whole step . . ." into various fractional steps. For *Jins* 3, recall that Al-Fārābī required a fractional location, or a $^3/_4$ Step in the *upper whole step interval* between the *index finger fret* [$^9/_8$] and the *ring finger fret* [$^{81}/_{64}$]: $^{81}/_{64} \div {}^9/_8 = {}^9/_8$. For this reason, Table 11.27 gives the length of the $^8/_9$ section of the *upper whole step:* $^8/_9 - {}^{64}/_{81} = {}^{72}/_{81} - {}^{64}/_{81} = {}^8/_{81}$, as the internal section meant for subdivision. In contrast, I interpret the text in Quote IV as requiring fractional steps in the *lower whole step interval* between the *ancient wusṭā* [$^{32}/_{27}$] and the *little finger* [$^4/_3$]: $^4/_3 \div {}^{32}/_{27} = {}^9/_8$. Therefore, with respect to *Ajnās* 5–8, Table 11.27 gives the length of the $^8/_9$ section of the *lower whole step:* $^{27}/_{32} - {}^{3}/_{4} = {}^{27}/_{32} - {}^{24}/_{32} = {}^{3}/_{32}$, as the internal section meant for further subdivisions. Given this requirement, Table 11.27 presents in full detail the calculations of *Ajnās* 5, 6, and 7. In Quote IV, Al-Fārābī states that for *Jins* 8, all three intervals consist of $^{3}/_{4}$ plus $^{1}/_{4}$ of $^{1}/_{3}$ Step. Since $^{1}/_{4}$ of $^{1}/_{3}$ Step equals [$^{1}/_{3}$ Step $\times$ $^{1}/_{4}$] $=$ $^{1}/_{12}$ Step, the required fractional part equals [$^{3}/_{4}$ Step $+$ $^{1}/_{12}$ Step] $=$ [$^{9}/_{12}$ Step $+$ $^{1}/_{12}$ Step] $=$ $^{10}/_{12}$ Step $=$ $^{5}/_{6}$ Step. In the history of Western tuning theory, *Jins* 8 is significant because it represents a very close rational approximation of the geometric division of the "fourth" into three equal intervals. For *Jins* 8, a comparison of the cent values in Tables 11.26 and 11.27 reveals a maximum difference of only 9.9 ¢.

Further comparisons of Al-Fārābī's cent values in Table 11.27, and Ptolemy's cent values in Table 10.12 reveal that *all* of Al-Fārābī's approximations on the *'ūd* are more accurate than Ptolemy's approximations on the canon. For example, in Greek ascending order, Table 10.7 demonstrates that a modern geometric division of Aristoxenus' Enharmonic Tetrachord requires intervals 49.8 ¢, 49.8 ¢, and 398.4 ¢. Ptolemy's arithmetic approximation yields 43.8 ¢, 45.0 ¢, and 409.2 ¢; and Al-Fārābī's arithmetic approximation in *Jins* 5 yields 53.3 ¢, 51.7 ¢, and 393.1 ¢. Furthermore, recall that in Section 10.16, a comparison of 15 Parts [249.0 ¢] in Aristoxenus' Soft Diatonic Tetrachord, and Ptolemy's approximation $^{7}/_{6}$ [266.9 ¢], indicates a maximum difference of +17.9 ¢ for all the Aristoxenian tetrachords. Now, a comparison of 6 Parts [99.6 ¢] in Aristoxenus' Tense Diatonic,

Table 11.27

INTERVAL RATIOS AND MODERN LENGTH RATIO TO FREQUENCY RATIO CALCULATIONS OF AL-FĀRĀBĪ'S EIGHT *AJNĀS* ON THE FRETTED *'ŪD*

Jins 1: Interval Ratios	
$^{9}/_{8} = 203.9$ ¢	1 Step from Nut down to Index F.
$^{81}/_{64} \div {}^{9}/_{8} = {}^{9}/_{8} = 203.9$ ¢	1 Step from Index F. down to Ring F.
$^{4}/_{3} \div {}^{81}/_{64} = {}^{256}/_{243} = 90.2$ ¢	$^{1}/_{2}$ Step from Ring F. down to Little F.
Jins 2: Interval Ratios	
$^{9}/_{8} = 203.9$ ¢	1 Step from Nut down to Index F.
$^{27}/_{22} \div {}^{9}/_{8} = {}^{12}/_{11} = 150.6$ ¢	$^{3}/_{4}$ Step from Index F. down to Middle F.
$^{4}/_{3} \div {}^{27}/_{22} = {}^{88}/_{81} = 143.5$ ¢	$^{3}/_{4}$ Step from Middle F. down to Little F.
Jins 3: Modern Length Ratios → Frequency Ratios	
$^{8}/_{9} - {}^{64}/_{81} = {}^{72}/_{81} - {}^{64}/_{81} = {}^{8}/_{81}$	Length of *upper* $^{8}/_{9}$ section.
$^{8}/_{81} \times {}^{3}/_{4} = {}^{2}/_{27}$	Three-quarters of internal section.
$^{64}/_{81} + {}^{2}/_{27} = {}^{64}/_{81} + {}^{6}/_{81} = {}^{70}/_{81} \rightarrow {}^{81}/_{70} = 252.7$ ¢	Middle F. Fret up from Ring F. Fret.
Interval Ratios	
$^{81}/_{70} = 252.7$ ¢	$1^{1}/_{4}$ Steps from Nut down to Middle F.
$^{81}/_{64} \div {}^{81}/_{70} = {}^{35}/_{32} = 155.1$ ¢	$^{3}/_{4}$ Step from Middle F. down to Ring F.
$^{4}/_{3} \div {}^{81}/_{64} = {}^{256}/_{243} = 90.2$ ¢	$^{1}/_{2}$ Step from Ring F. down to Little F.
Jins 4: Interval Ratios	
$^{81}/_{68} = 302.9$ ¢	$1^{1}/_{2}$ Steps from Nut down to Middle F.
$^{81}/_{64} \div {}^{81}/_{68} = {}^{17}/_{16} = 105.0$ ¢	$^{1}/_{2}$ Step from Middle F. down to Ring F.
$^{4}/_{3} \div {}^{81}/_{64} = {}^{256}/_{243} = 90.2$ ¢	$^{1}/_{2}$ Step from Ring F. down to Little F.

Table 11.27
(continued)

Jins 5: Modern Length Ratios → Frequency Ratios	
$27/32 - 3/4 = 27/32 - 24/32 = 3/32$	Length of *lower* $8/9$ section.
$3/32 \times 1/4 = 3/128$	Quarter of internal section.
$3/4 + 3/128 = 96/128 + 3/128 = 99/128 \rightarrow 128/99 = 444.8$ ¢	Ring F. Fret up from Little F. Fret.
$99/128 + 3/128 = 102/128 = 51/64 \rightarrow 64/51 = 393.1$ ¢	Middle F. Fret up from Ring F. Fret.
Interval Ratios	
$64/51 = 393.1$ ¢	2 Steps from Nut down to Middle F.
$128/99 \div 64/51 = 34/33 = 51.7$ ¢	$1/4$ Step from Middle F. down to Ring F.
$4/3 \div 128/99 = 33/32 = 53.3$ ¢	$1/4$ Step from Ring F. down to Little F.
Jins 6: Modern Length Ratios → Frequency Ratios	
$27/32 - 3/4 = 27/32 - 24/32 = 3/32$	Length of *lower* $8/9$ section.
$3/32 \times 1/3 = 1/32$	Third of internal section.
$3/4 + 1/32 = 24/32 + 1/32 = 25/32 \rightarrow 32/25 = 427.4$ ¢	Ring F. Fret up from Little F. Fret.
$25/32 + 1/32 = 26/32 = 13/16 \rightarrow 16/13 = 359.5$ ¢	Middle F. Fret up from Ring F. Fret.
Interval Ratios	
$16/13 = 359.5$ ¢	$1\,5/6$ Steps from Nut down to Middle F.
$32/25 \div 16/13 = 26/25 = 67.9$ ¢	$1/3$ Step from Middle F. down to Ring F.
$4/3 \div 32/25 = 25/24 = 70.7$ ¢	$1/3$ Step from Ring F. down to Little F.
Jins 7: Modern Length Ratios → Frequency Ratios	
$27/32 - 3/4 = 27/32 - 24/32 = 3/32$	Length of *lower* $8/9$ section.
$3/32 \times 3/8 = 9/256$	Three-eighth of internal section.
$3/4 + 9/256 = 192/256 + 9/256 = 201/256 \rightarrow 256/201 = 418.7$ ¢	Ring F. Fret up from Little F. Fret.
$201/256 + 9/256 = 210/256 = 105/128 \rightarrow 128/105 = 342.9$ ¢	Middle F. Fret up from Ring F. Fret.
Interval Ratios	
$128/105 = 342.9$ ¢	$1\,3/4$ Steps from Nut down to Middle F.
$256/201 \div 128/105 = 70/67 = 75.8$ ¢	$3/8$ Step from Middle F. down to Ring F.
$4/3 \div 256/201 = 67/64 = 79.3$ ¢	$3/8$ Step from Ring F. down to Little F.
Jins 8: Modern Length Ratios → Frequency Ratios	
$27/32 - 3/4 = 27/32 - 24/32 = 3/32$	Length of *lower* $8/9$ section.
$3/32 \times 5/6 = 5/64$	Five-sixth of internal section.
$3/4 + 5/64 = 48/64 + 5/64 = 53/64 \rightarrow 64/53 = 326.5$ ¢	Middle F. Fret up from Little F. Fret.
$53/64 + 5/64 = 58/64 = 29/32 \rightarrow 32/29 = 170.4$ ¢	Index F. Fret up from Middle F. Fret.
Interval Ratios	
$32/29 = 170.4$ ¢	$5/6$ Step from Nut down to Index F.
$64/53 \div 32/29 = 58/53 = 156.1$ ¢	$5/6$ Step from Index F. down to Middle F.
$4/3 \div 64/53 = 53/48 = 171.5$ ¢	$5/6$ Step from Middle F. down to Little F.

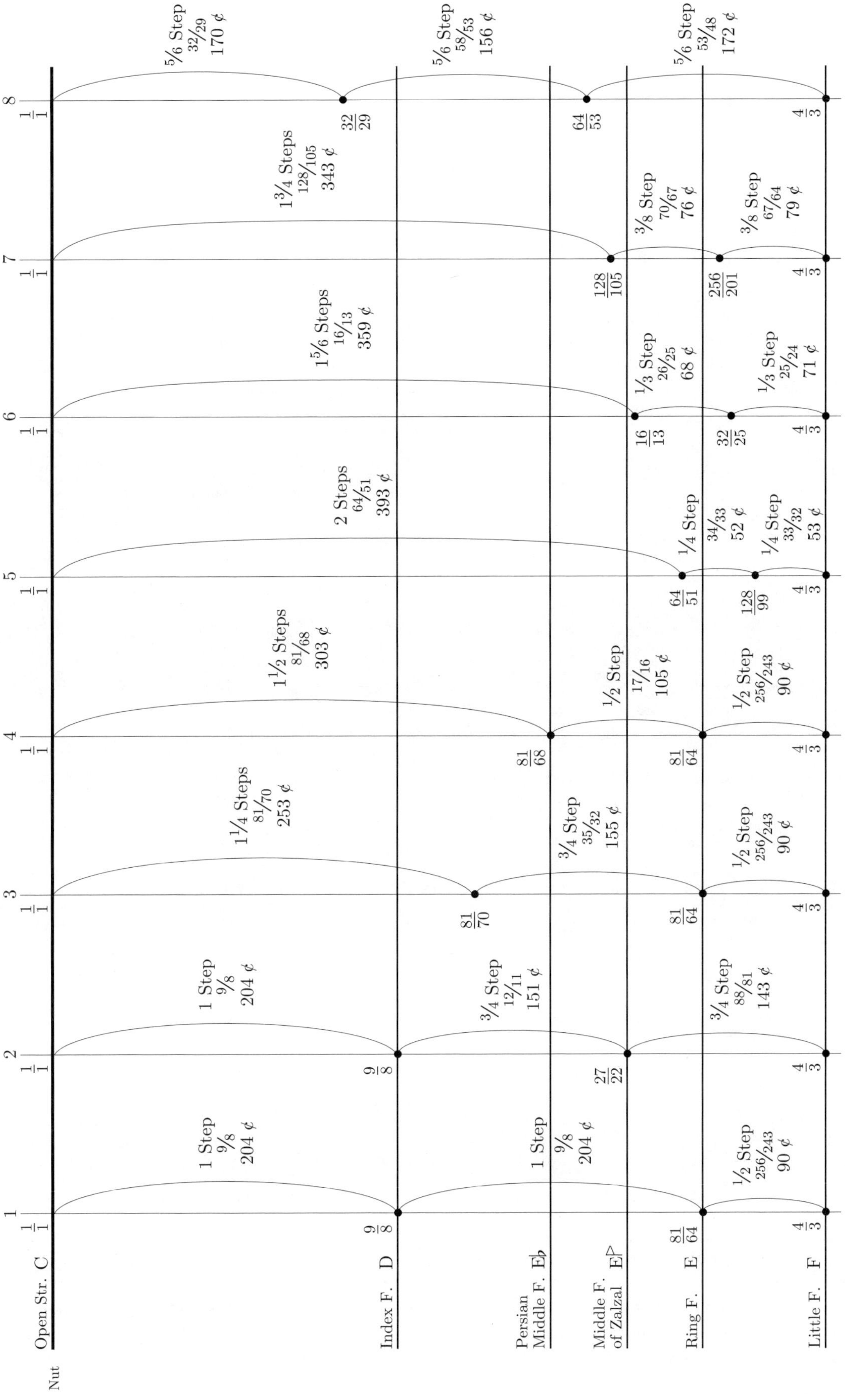

Figure 11.52 Al-Fārābī's Eight *Ajnās.* The *steps* of *Ajnās* 1, 3, 4, 5, 6, and 7 represent the *parts* of six tetrachords by Aristoxenus. For all these genera, Al-Fārābī's calculations on the *'ūd* yield more accurate approximations than those calculated by Ptolemy on the canon. (Fret locations and point locations between frets to scale.)

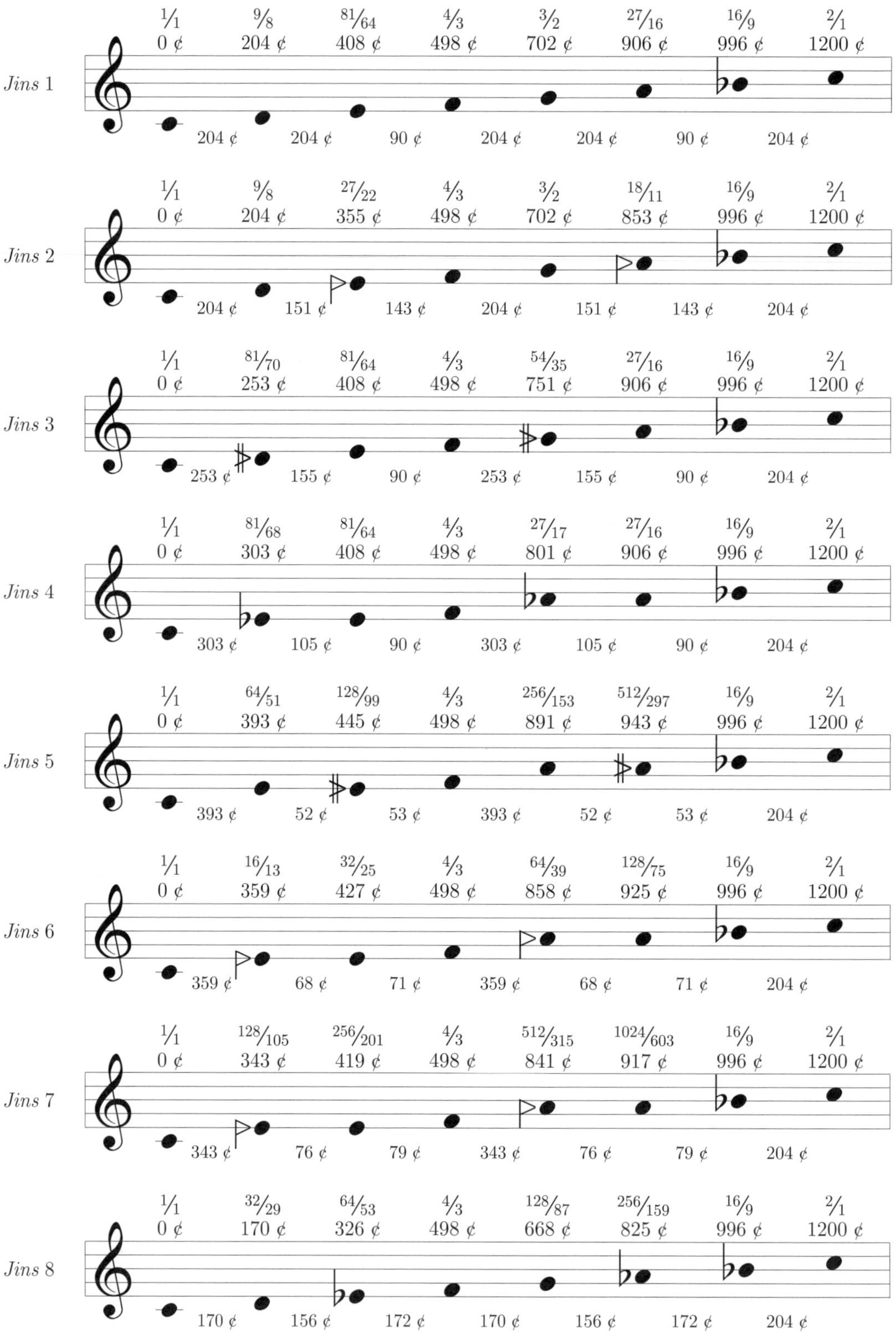

Figure 11.53 An attempt to represent Al-Fārābī's Eight *Ajnās* in Western musical notation. The notes of *Ajnās* 6 and 7 do not indicate any differences between these two modes. The second and fifth degrees of *Jins* 8 sound much flatter than shown. Also, despite Al-Fārābī's statement in Section 11.55 regarding notes that are not compatible, *Jins* 4 shows a progression from E♭ to E, or from the middle finger to the ring finger.

Soft Diatonic, and Tonic Chromatic Tetrachords, and Al-Fārābī's approximation $^{256}/_{243}$ [90.2 ¢] in *Ajnās* 1, 3, and 4, respectively, indicates a maximum difference of −9.4 ¢ for all the Aristoxenian tetrachords. Admittedly, these are not monumental differences. However, these figures suggest that developments in the construction of musical instruments advanced not only the art of music, but the science of mathematics as well. Figure 11.53 illustrates Al-Fārābī's Eight *Ajnās* in Western musical notation. Remember, according to Al-Fārābī, musicians played these *ajnās* on the *'ūd* as *conjunct tetrachords.*

In closing this section, recall that in Sections 10.14–10.17, I argued against geometric interpretations of "fractional parts" and "integer parts." In my opinion, Al-Fārābī's text confirms these objections. Although equal parts such as **4**-**4**-22 and **6**-**6**-18 have convinced many European and American writers that Aristoxenus and Cleonides advocated equal tempered scales, Al-Fārābī gives no indications that equal parts such as 44-**8**-**8** and 36-**12**-**12** must represent mathematically identical intervals on a musical instrument. On the contrary, Al-Fārābī's divisions on the fretted *'ūd* demonstrate that when musical intervals are musically indistinguishable they are for all practical purposes identical. For us, equipped with logarithms, it is easy to prove that ratio $^{34}/_{33}$ [51.7 ¢] more closely approximates Al-Fārābī's 6 Parts [49.8 ¢] than ratio $^{33}/_{32}$ [53.3 ¢]. But in the context of Al-Fārābī's treatise, such a mathematical distinction merely expresses a musical anachronism. Moreover, had Al-Fārābī felt compelled to define two identical "semitones," he could have resolved the comma of Pythagoras in Figure 11.49 by replacing the limma $^{256}/_{243}$ [90.2 ¢] on Fret 2, and the apotome $^{2187}/_{2048}$ [113.7 ¢] on Fret 4, with a single fret. He could have moved this fret to a compromised location just below ancient length ratio $^{18}/_{17}$ [99.0 ¢], and thereby intoned a tempered "semitone," frequency ratio $\sqrt{^9/_8}$ [102.0 ¢]. However, such a possibility never occurred to him simply because the need to resolve the comma did not exist.

~ 11.57 ~

When one considers the overall complexities of Al-Fārābī's 10-fret and 12-fret *'ūd* tunings, it seems that he was unaware of 5-limit ratios. As we will see, this is not the case. Al-Fārābī neither ignored nor dismissed such consonances. Before we examine Al-Fārābī's organization of tetrachords — where small prime number ratios play a crucial role in defining two basic types of Arabian genera — let us first consider his instructions for finding the "major third," ancient length ratio $^5/_4$, on the fingerboard of the *'ūd.*

> When a person has assimilated all that we have explained concerning the tuning of the lute, he will be able to tune not only one lute, but several, and each of them in a different way, thus causing them to produce scales of various tonalities . . . We can, for example, tune a lute so that its scale is at the octave, at the fifth, or at an interval of an entirely different ratio, relative to that of another lute. Moreover, we will be able to do this not only for several lutes, but for a lute and another kind of instrument.
>
> These same rules allow us to tune a lute mounted with five strings or equipped with frets in addition to those that are generally used. We can apply them to whatever arrangement we want. We must also determine the number of intervals and [the number] of consonant degrees by comparing each note of the scale obtained in each kind of tuning. We will not make this list; the reader may supply that himself, and thereby practice applying the rules we have explained.
>
> Note that it is often necessary in lute playing to superimpose the *strong conjunct moderate* genus [$^9/_8$, $^{10}/_9$, $^{16}/_{15}$] over the *diatonic genus* [$^9/_8$, $^9/_8$,

> $^{256}/_{243}$], while organizing their intervals in the same [ascending] direction. For that, above the ring finger fret [$^{81}/_{64}$], another [fret] must be placed at a distance corresponding to ***one-tenth*** of that which separates the index finger fret from the bridge, and a fifth string must be added to the instrument. By equipping the lute with this fret [$^{5}/_{4}$], we obtain many very beautiful and useful consonances.
>
> When it is a matter of passing from the ring finger fret [$^{81}/_{64}$] to the little finger fret [$^{4}/_{3}$], separated by a limma [$^{256}/_{243}$], we replace the ring finger fret with this new fret [$^{5}/_{4}$]; the consonance [$^{16}/_{15}$] of the two notes thus obtained [as in passing from $^{5}/_{4}$ to $^{4}/_{3}$, or $^{4}/_{3} \div {}^{5}/_{4} = {}^{16}/_{15}$] will be more beautiful. This fret, however, cannot replace the ring finger fret when it is a matter of passing from the ring finger note to another having a given special consonance. With these conditions, the lute will be complete, and the notes that it will produce will be perfectly consonant.[79] (Italics, bold italics, and text and ratios in brackets mine.)

Figure 11.54 shows that Al-Fārābī's mathematical method is highly accurate: if we divide the string section between the $^{9}/_{8}$ Fret and the bridge into ten equal parts, the first $^{1}/_{10}$ subsection marks the location of the $^{5}/_{4}$ Fret; this position is located just *above* the $^{81}/_{64}$ Fret in the direction of the nut. Here are the formal calculations.

Location of the $^{5}/_{4}$ Fret on Al-Fārābī's *ʿŪd*

Tone E	$^{8}/_{9} \times {}^{1}/_{10} = {}^{8}/_{90} = {}^{4}/_{45}$	Tenth of $^{8}/_{9}$ section.
	$^{8}/_{9} - {}^{4}/_{45} = {}^{40}/_{45} - {}^{4}/_{45} = {}^{36}/_{45} = {}^{4}/_{5} \rightarrow {}^{5}/_{4} = 386.3$ ¢	$^{8}/_{9}$ section minus subsection.

If we follow Al-Fārābī's advice and equip an *ʿūd* with five strings, this new fret produces ratios $^{5}/_{4}$, $^{5}/_{3}$, $^{10}/_{9}$, $^{40}/_{27}$, and $^{160}/_{81}$ on the *Bamm*, *Mathlath*, *Mathnā*, *Zīr*, and *Ḥādd*, respectively.

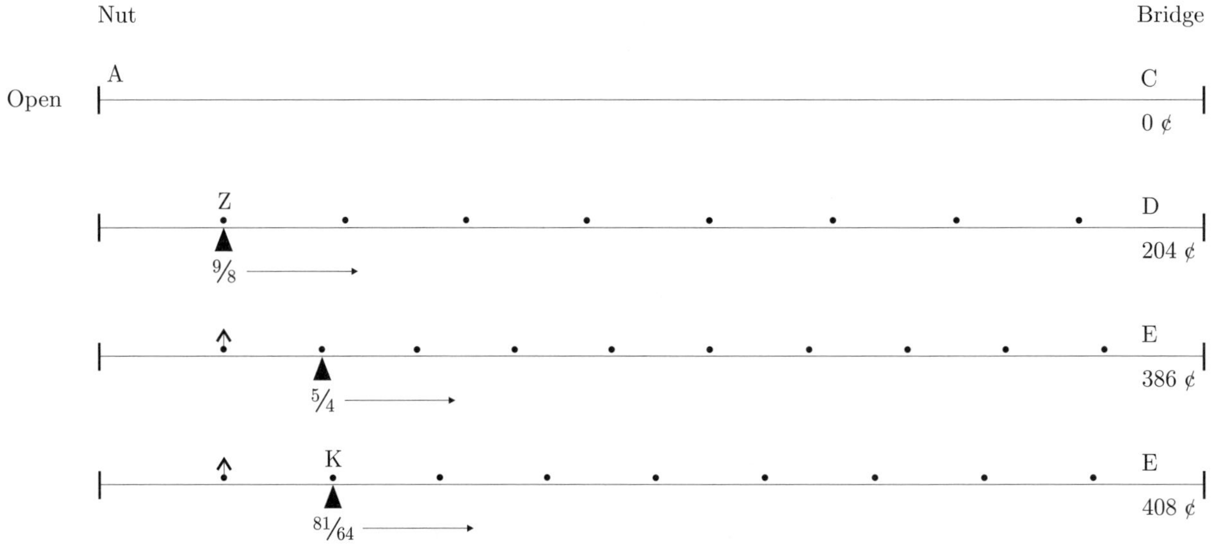

Figure 11.54 Al-Fārābī's technique for locating the $^{5}/_{4}$ Fret on the *ʿūd*. Al-Fārābī states that he needs this new fret to play the *strong conjunct moderate genus*. Table 11.28 shows that this tetrachord consists of ascending interval ratios $^{9}/_{8}$, $^{10}/_{9}$, $^{16}/_{15}$.

With regard to the "minor third," ratio $6/5$, Al-Fārābī's description is unique. He defines this tone not as a string length ratio on the fingerboard of the *'ūd*, but as a clearly perceived consonance while tuning two open harp strings by ear.

> In summary, to pass from a given medium interval to another larger [interval], it is necessary to loosen the lower string of the first interval or to tighten its upper string . . . ; [conversely] to pass from a given interval to another smaller [interval], it is necessary to loosen the upper string of the first interval, or tighten its lower string . . .
>
> For example, let us reduce a ratio of the fourth [$4/3$] to the ratio 1 + $1/5$ [6:5]. The pitches of the fourth will be given by the strings H and Z, H giving the lower note and Z the upper note. We then lower the tension of the Z string just until the consonance of the fourth disappears; Z will then produce a dissonant note in relation to H. Next, we continue to progressively lower the tension of the Z string, just until it produces another note ***consonant*** with H; the ratio of these two notes will be 1 + $1/4$ [5:4]. We again lower the tension of the Z string; the consonance will then disappear, and the note heard from Z will again become dissonant in relation to H. By continuing in this manner, the note heard from Z will be found ***consonant*** a second time relative to H, and the interval obtained will be at that moment in the ratio 1 + $1/5$ [6:5]. By continuing the procedure, one would obtain an interval whose ratio would be less than 1 + $1/5$.[80] (Bold italics, and text and ratios in brackets mine.)

If asked to give a modern description of interval ratios $5/4$ and $6/5$, it would be difficult to imagine a better explanation than the one given here. Al-Fārābī knew that without the aid of mathematics, human ears naturally tend to identify interval ratios $5/4$ and $6/5$ — the Western "major third" and "minor third" — as unequivocal consonances. Furthermore, as a scholar of Greek music theory, he was perfectly aware of Ptolemy's criticism of the Pythagoreans for not including the epitetartic [5:4] as a consonance. (See Section 10.5.) Hence, on a fretless harp equipped only with open strings, Al-Fārābī demonstrates that musicians instinctively gravitate toward these two simple consonances without the need or influence of mathematics. To confirm his findings, Al-Fārābī undoubtedly stopped his tuning procedure at interval ratio $5/4$ and verified the identify of this consonance on a mathematically controlled instrument like the *qānūn* or *'ūd*. Similarly, upon reaching interval ratio

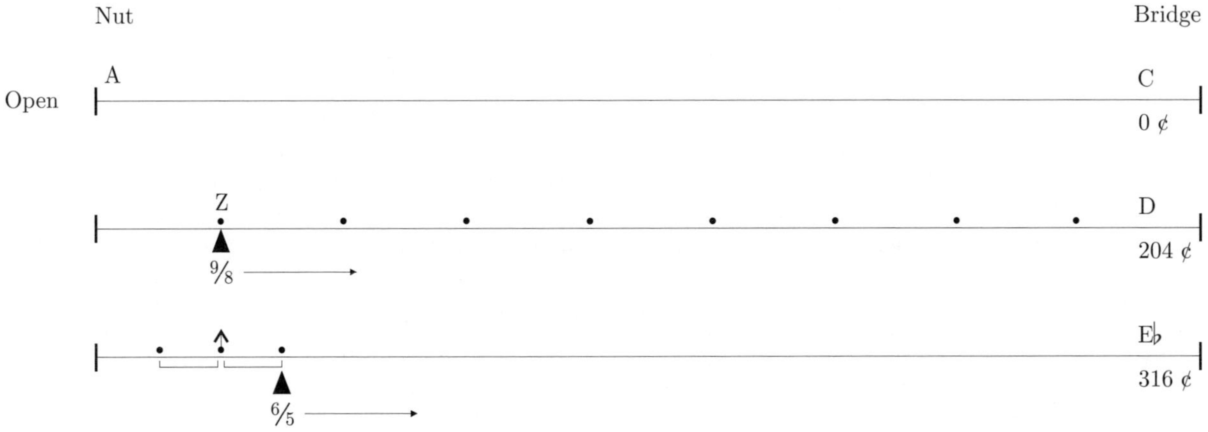

Figure 11.55 A solution for locating the $6/5$ Fret on Al-Fārābī's *'ūd*. Al-Fārābī describes this consonance in the context of tuning two open harp strings by ear.

$^6\!/\!_5$, he stopped and verified again. In a manner consistent with Al-Fārābī's *'ūd* tunings, Figure 11.55 demonstrates that the location of the $^6\!/\!_5$ Fret is extremely easy to find. First, divide the section above the $^9\!/\!_8$ Fret in the direction of the nut in half. Figure 11.47 indicates that this point marks the location of the $^{18}\!/\!_{17}$ Fret. Next, measure the distance of this subsection *below* the $^9\!/\!_8$ Fret in the direction of the bridge, and place the $^6\!/\!_5$ Fret at this location. Here are the formal calculations.

Location of the $^6\!/\!_5$ Fret on Al-Fārābī's *'Ūd*

Tone E♭	$^1\!/\!_9 \times {}^1\!/\!_2 = {}^1\!/\!_{18}$	Half of $^1\!/\!_9$ section.
	$^8\!/\!_9 - {}^1\!/\!_{18} = {}^{16}\!/\!_{18} - {}^1\!/\!_{18} = {}^{15}\!/\!_{18} = {}^5\!/\!_6 \rightarrow {}^6\!/\!_5 = 315.6$ ¢	$^8\!/\!_9$ section minus subsection.

On a 5-string *'ūd*, this fret produces ratios $^6\!/\!_5$, $^8\!/\!_5$, $^{16}\!/\!_{15}$, $^{64}\!/\!_{45}$, and $^{256}\!/\!_{135}$ on the *Bamm*, *Mathlath*, *Mathnā*, *Zīr*, and *Ḥādd*, respectively.

~ 11.58 ~

We turn our attention now to Al-Fārābī's organization of tetrachords. Although significant portions of the French translation in *La Musique Arabe, Volume 1*, are inconsistent with respect to Greek musical terms, we will assume that Ptolemy's terminology inspired the following passage in Al-Fārābī's text:

> Among these intervals we just discussed, the octave, the double octave and, in general, multiples of the octave are called *large consonant intervals.* The fifth, the fourth, the octave plus the fifth, and the octave plus the fourth are known as *medium consonant intervals.* The tone and in general all intervals whose notes comprise a ratio smaller than the fourth, are known as *small consonant intervals.* For certain ancient mathematicians [Ptolemy], the large consonant intervals are called (homophonic) intervals . . . , the medium consonant intervals, (symphonic) intervals . . . , and the small consonant intervals, (emmelic) [Greek, lit. *melodic*] intervals . . .[81] (Text in brackets mine. Text in parentheses in *La Musique Arabe.*)

Al-Fārābī then describes the origins of the *emmelic* intervals.

> Continuing the subject studied above, we will examine how the small consonant intervals known as . . . (melodic intervals) are obtained and combined. They result from the division of large and medium intervals, but more often from the division of small intervals. We can create the {melodic} intervals by {mathematically} dividing all the {intervals} discussed above, or by {aurally} subtracting them from one another. However, when the tone or the intervals of the same kind, in other words the small [melodic] intervals, are divided, the intervals thus obtained are frequently too small, and our ear generally cannot perceive their consonance. To produce the melodic intervals, it is therefore preferable to divide the medium and the large consonant intervals.
>
> The ratios of the melodic intervals are all smaller than the fourth.[82] (Text in braces mine. Text in parentheses and brackets in *La Musique Arabe.*)

Al-Fārābī continues by admitting that although it is theoretically possible to divide the "fourth" into any number of intervals, he prefers the Greek model and will, thereby, divide the "fourth" into only three intervals.

> There are several ways of dividing the fourth. One can divide it into a large number of intervals; but these would become so small that even a musician endowed with vast experience would be unable to determine their number or to perceive their consonance. In this division, the intervals should not become so numerous that the ear of a layman, or that of a professional musician, or a moderately trained ear is unable to recognize their consonance. The number of *melodic* intervals combined inside the fourth must therefore be limited. There can be two, three, or more of them; but if there are more than three, it will be excessive; . . . Some are mistaken, however, when they believe that it is by its very nature or by the nature of intervals, that the fourth can be divided into only three intervals. In fact, we can indeed divide the fourth into more than three intervals or into less, but we prefer to adhere to three, because this division is simpler, gives numbers easier to find and to retain, and is enough, as we will demonstrate, to give us all the small consonant intervals.[83]

Finally, Al-Fārābī describes two basic types of genera — the *strong genus* and the *soft genus* — which he uses to organize all the tetrachords.

> The mathematicians of antiquity called the fourth divided into three intervals a *genus*. In a genus, the ratio of one of the three intervals can be larger or smaller than the sum of the other two. [1] A genus that does ***not*** include an interval whose ratio is larger than the sum of the other two is known as a *strong genus;* [2] when it ***does*** include [such an interval], the genus is known as *soft.*[84] (Bold italics, and text and numbers in brackets mine.)

In these two definitions, Al-Fārābī refers indirectly to Ptolemy's descriptions of the *pyknon* and *apyknon.*[85] Definition 1 describes the *apyknon*, which belongs to the *strong genus*, and Definition 2, the *pyknon*, which belongs to the *soft genus.* Because Al-Fārābī states Definition 1 in negative terms, it is convoluted and not easily grasped. Consider instead a description of the *strong genus* in positive terms:

> Definition 1. A genus that includes an interval whose ratio is smaller than the sum of the other two is known as a *strong genus.*

Similarly, consider a positive description of the *soft genus:*

> Definition 2. A genus that includes an interval whose ratio is larger than the sum of the other two is known as a *soft genus.*

Figure 11.56 illustrates modern interpretations of the generalized size and specific location of the *pyknon* and *apyknon* in Al-Fārābī's tetrachords.

Al-Fārābī's text continues with two tetrachord classifications:

> The largest of the intervals of a soft genus can be found inserted between the other two, or placed at either the lower or upper end; in the first case, we will call the genus *soft non-ordered* and in the second, *soft ordered.* The latter [genus] is subdivided according to whether the larger of the other

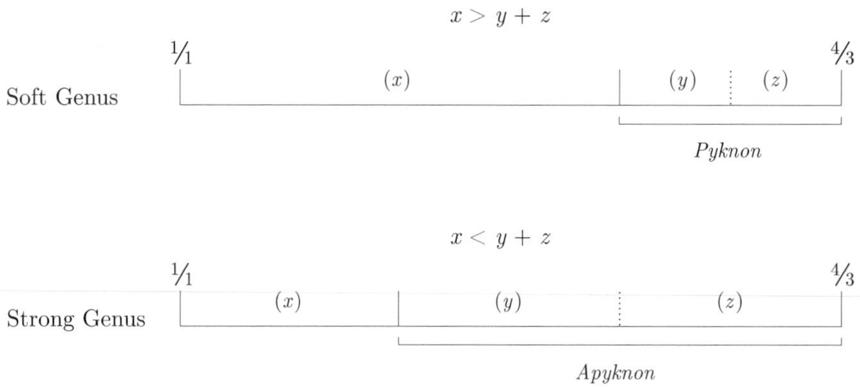

Figure 11.56 Modern interpretations of the generalized size and specific location of the *pyknon* and *apyknon* in Al-Fārābī's tetrachords. In the West, music theorists associate the *pyknon* with enharmonic and chromatic tetrachords, and the *apyknon*, with diatonic tetrachords.

> two intervals [i.e., the medium interval] occupies the center or one of the ends of the fourth; in the first case, the genus will be known as *soft ordered consecutive*, and in the second, *soft ordered non-consecutive*.[86] (Text in brackets mine.)

Figure 11.57 shows at a glance the intervallic structures of Al-Fārābī's *soft ordered consecutive genus* and *soft ordered non-consecutive genus.* Here the regular progression of large, medium, and small intervals applies to the former genus, and the irregular progression of large, small, and medium intervals applies to the latter genus.

Al-Fārābī then imposes certain restrictions to ensure that only consonant tetrachords result:

> We will not consider the *soft non-ordered* genera, because their types are not at all consonant to the ear. We will examine only the *strong* genera and the *soft ordered* genera. We will explain the ratios of their intervals and how to obtain them, while limiting ourselves to those whose consonance is clearly perceptible to the ear.
>
> The previously stated rules, regarding the division of intervals and their subtraction from one another, allow us to find the ratios of the intervals of all the kinds of *strong* and *soft ordered* genera. The division of intervals can be done in several ways, but we will adopt only one of them. This consists of removing . . . an interval from the fourth so that this subtraction leaves

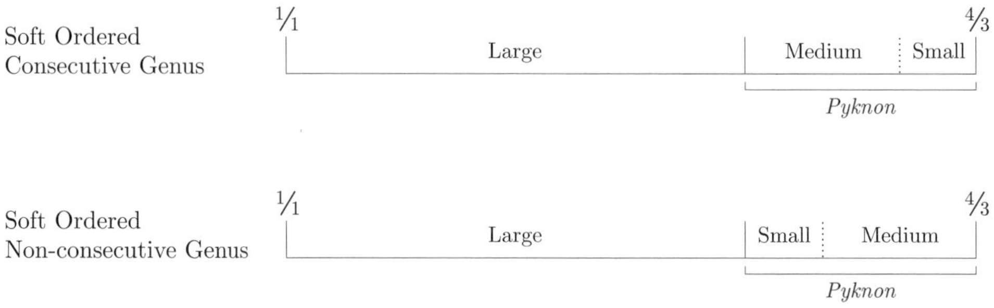

Figure 11.57 The intervalic progressions of Al-Fārābī's *soft ordered consecutive genus* and *soft ordered non-consecutive genus.* Both of these genera contain a *pyknon.*

> a ***remainder*** whose ratio is smaller than the ***subtracted interval***, and then dividing this remainder in two; we thereby obtain all of the kinds of *soft ordered non-consecutive* genera.[87] (Bold italics mine.)

Note that Al-Fārābī does *not* explicitly state that the "subtracted interval" and the subsequent *pyknon* or "remainder" must be an epimore or superparticular ratio. Even so, in his subsequent discussions, Al-Fārābī demonstrates that the *pyknons* of three genera of the Soft Ordered Non-consecutive Tetrachords, and the *pyknons* of three genera of the Soft Ordered Consecutive Tetrachords, consist exclusively of epimore ratios. Turn to Section 10.20, and observe that Ptolemy's and Al-Fārābī's derivations of these *pyknons* are identical.

Al-Fārābī's Tetrachords With *Pyknons*

1. Soft Ordered Non-consecutive, and Soft Ordered Consecutive, Slack: $4/3 \div 5/4 = \mathbf{16/15}$
2. Soft Ordered Non-consecutive, and Soft Ordered Consecutive, Moderate: $4/3 \div 6/5 = \mathbf{10/9}$
3. Soft Ordered Non-consecutive, and Soft Ordered Consecutive, Firm: $4/3 \div 7/6 = \mathbf{8/7}$

With respect to tetrachords that have *apyknons*, Al-Fārābī does not follow Ptolemy's example. Turn to Table 10.11 to see that Ptolemy only used epimore ratios in the derivations of his tetrachords; this generality also applies to his Even Diatonic: $12/11$, $11/10$, $10/9$. However, in Al-Fārābī's derivations of three additional strong genera, two *apyknons* — $32/27$ and $40/33$ — are epimere or superpartient ratios. His tetrachord divisions are therefore not strictly formulaic. Al-Fārābī's consistent inclusion of the Pythagorean "minor third," ratio $32/27$, is especially noteworthy.

Al-Fārābī's Tetrachords With *Apyknons*

1. Strong Doubling, and Strong Conjunct, Slack: $4/3 \div 8/7 = \mathbf{7/6}$
2. Strong Doubling, and Strong Conjunct, Moderate: $4/3 \div 9/8 = \mathbf{32/27}$
3. Strong Doubling, and Strong Conjunct, Firm: $4/3 \div 10/9 = \mathbf{6/5}$

1. Strong Disjunct, Slack: $4/3 \div 8/7 = \mathbf{7/6}$
2. Strong Disjunct, Moderate: $4/3 \div 9/8 = \mathbf{32/27}$
3. Strong Disjunct, Firm: $4/3 \div 11/10 = \mathbf{40/33}$

He then employs various mathematical techniques to divide these *pyknons* and *apyknons* into two smaller interval ratios.[88]

An examination of Table 11.28, Rows 1–3 shows that Al-Fārābī derived his Soft Ordered Non-consecutive Tetrachords by arithmetically dividing the *pyknons* $16/15$, $10/9$, and $8/7$ of the Slack, Moderate, and Firm Genera, respectively, into *two* near-equal intervals. (See Section 10.8.) Next, he arithmetically divided the same *pyknons* of the Soft Ordered Consecutive Tetrachords in Rows 4–6 into *three* near-equal intervals. A comparison to Ptolemy's divisions of the same *pyknons* in Table 10.11 reveals that Al-Fārābī used exactly the same technique as Ptolemy. However, subsequent to these divisions, Al-Fārābī then calculated the medium intervals $24/23$, $15/14$, and $12/11$ of the Slack, Moderate, and Firm Genera, respectively, by multiplying together the first two interval ratios of the latter divisions. For example, he computed the medium interval of the Soft Ordered Consecutive Slack Genus in this way: $48/47 \times 47/46 = 48/46 = 24/23$. The small and final intervals $46/45$, $28/27$, and $22/21$ of these three genera, respectively, he left unchanged from the initial arithmetic divisions into three near-equal intervals.

Now, in Table 11.28, Rows 7–9, Al-Fārābī divided the "fourth" by two identical interval ratios; hence the term "doubling." It is interesting to note that in Ptolemy's Catalog of Scales in Table

10.12, only one tetrachord contains two identical interval ratios, namely, Philolaus' original Diatonic Tetrachord. In Greek ascending order, this tetrachord consists of interval ratios $^{256}/_{243}$, $^{9}/_{8}$, $^{9}/_{8}$. Al-Fārābī called this tetrachord the Strong Doubling Moderate Genus. However, he and all other Arabian music theorists also referred to it as the *diatonic tetrachord.*

Finally, in Table 11.28, Rows 10–12 and Rows 13–15 show Al-Fārābī's conjunct and disjunct tetrachords. In this context, Al-Fārābī did *not* use the terms *conjunct* and *disjunct* in the manner of the ancient Greeks. Here conjunct refers to numerically ordered sequences of *consecutive epimore ratios* from large to small, as in $^{8}/_{7}$, $^{9}/_{8}$; or $^{9}/_{8}$, $^{10}/_{9}$; or $^{10}/_{9}$, $^{11}/_{10}$. In contrast, disjunct refers to numerically ordered sequences of *non-consecutive epimore ratios* from large to small; in these sequences he *skips over* one ratio, as in $^{8}/_{7}$, [not $^{9}/_{8}$], $^{10}/_{9}$; or $^{9}/_{8}$, [not $^{10}/_{9}$], $^{11}/_{10}$; or $^{11}/_{10}$, [not $^{12}/_{11}$], $^{13}/_{12}$.

Al-Fārābī envisioned all these tetrachords in the context of the Greater Perfect System of the ancient Greeks;[89] this system consists of a 15-tone "double-octave" scale. However, because Al-Fārābī played the *'ūd*, he expanded this system to include three different scale types. He explains the three systems in the following manner:

> We are given various ways to combine the intervals that can comprise the perfect system: we may begin, for example, with the interval of a tone {$^{9}/_{8}$}, then place after that the intervals of any genus {i.e., two tetrachords: $^{4}/_{3} \times {}^{4}/_{3} = {}^{16}/_{9}$} until the first octave is reached {$^{9}/_{8} \times {}^{16}/_{9} = {}^{2}/_{1}$}, then follow again with a tone, then the intervals of the chosen genus, until the second octave is completed {$^{2}/_{1} \times {}^{2}/_{1} = {}^{4}/_{1}$}. We may also begin with the intervals of a chosen genus and compose a double fourth {$^{16}/_{9}$}, then complete the octave by means of a tone {$^{16}/_{9} \times {}^{9}/_{8} = {}^{2}/_{1}$}, which we again follow with a double fourth and with a tone to reach the double octave. Finally, we can begin with the three intervals of a genus {i.e., a tetrachord: $^{4}/_{3}$}, follow these with an interval of a tone {$^{4}/_{3} \times {}^{9}/_{8} = {}^{3}/_{2}$}, then the three intervals of the chosen genus to compose the first octave {$^{3}/_{2} \times {}^{4}/_{3} = {}^{2}/_{1}$}, which will be followed by another, constructed in the same manner, to reach the double octave.
>
> The tone placed inside the systems that we have just constructed is called the interval of *disjunction,* because it is used as a separation between genera that are repeated. When the interval of disjunction is placed first in {the [lower or upper] position of} each of the two octaves, the lower double fourth and the upper double fourth are separated by one of the intervals of disjunction, and the system is called the *perfect disjunct.* When, on the contrary, the interval of disjunction is not inserted between the first octave and intervals of the genus that follow it, the system is known as *conjunct;* one also calls it *compact.*
>
> In each of the three systems that we have just constructed, the intervals combined inside the two octaves, lower and upper, are arranged in the same manner, so that one is at ease going from one octave to another, from one combination to another similar one, where the second gives the impression of the first; it is for this reason that one calls them *invariable.* If the system is disjunct, it is called ***perfect invariable disjunct***, and ***perfect invariable conjunct*** if it is conjunct. The intervals of the upper octave and those of the lower octave may still be arranged similarly between themselves in combinations other than the three that we have explained; but these are the best. It sometimes happens that in playing instruments one uses others; the reader will know, with a little attention, how to determine them himself; we will not discuss it here.[90] (Bold italics, and text and ratios in braces mine. Text in brackets in *La Musique Arabe.*)

Table 11.28

AL-FĀRĀBĪ'S TETRACHORD DERIVATIONS

Al-Fārābī's Arithmetic Divisions of Three *Pyknons*					Interval Ratios
1. Soft Ordered Non-consecutive, Slack:	**16/15**	16 × 2 = 32 15 × 2 = 30	32:31:30	32/31, 31/30	5/4, 32/31, 31/30
2. Soft Ordered Non-consecutive, Moderate:	**10/9**	10 × 2 = 20 9 × 2 = 18	20:19:18	20/19, 19/18	6/5, 20/19, 19/18
3. Soft Ordered Non-consecutive, Firm:	**8/7**	8 × 2 = 16 7 × 2 = 14	16:15:14	16/15, 15/14	7/6, 16/15, 15/14

Al-Fārābī's Arithmetic Divisions of Three *Pyknons*					Interval Ratios
4. Soft Ordered Consecutive, Slack:	**16/15**	16 × 3 = 48 15 × 3 = 45	48:47:46:45 48/47 × 47/46 = 24/23	24/23, 46/45	5/4, 24/23, 46/45
5. Soft Ordered Consecutive, Moderate:	**10/9**	10 × 3 = 30 9 × 3 = 27	30:29:28:27 30/29 × 29/28 = 15/14	15/14, 28/27	6/5, 15/14, 28/27
6. Soft Ordered Consecutive, Firm:	**8/7**	8 × 3 = 24 7 × 3 = 21	24:23:22:21 24/23 × 23/22 = 12/11	12/11, 22/21	7/6, 12/11, 22/21

Al-Fārābī's Divisions of Three *Apyknons*				Interval Ratios
7. Strong Doubling, Slack:	**7/6**	4/3 ÷ **8/7** = 7/6	7/6 ÷ **8/7** = 49/48	8/7, 8/7, 49/48
8. Strong Doubling, Moderate or *Diatonic:*	**32/27**	4/3 ÷ **9/8** = 32/27	32/27 ÷ **9/8** = 256/243	9/8, 9/8, 256/243
9. Strong Doubling, Firm:	**6/5**	4/3 ÷ **10/9** = 6/5	6/5 ÷ **10/9** = 27/25	10/9, 10/9, 27/25

Al-Fārābī's Divisions of Three *Apyknons*				Interval Ratios
10. Strong Conjunct, Slack:	**7/6**	4/3 ÷ **8/7** = 7/6	7/6 ÷ **9/8** = 28/27	8/7, 9/8, 28/27
11. Strong Conjunct, Moderate:	**32/27**	4/3 ÷ **9/8** = 32/27	32/27 ÷ **10/9** = 16/15	9/8, 10/9, 16/15
12. Strong Conjunct, Firm:	**6/5**	4/3 ÷ **10/9** = 6/5	6/5 ÷ **11/10** = 12/11	10/9, 11/10, 12/11

Al-Fārābī's Divisions of Three *Apyknons*				Interval Ratios
13. Strong Disjunct, Slack:	**7/6**	4/3 ÷ **8/7** = 7/6	7/6 ÷ **10/9** = 21/20	8/7, 10/9, 21/20
14. Strong Disjunct, Moderate:	**32/27**	4/3 ÷ **9/8** = 32/27	32/27 ÷ **11/10** = 320/297	9/8, 11/10, 320/297
15. Strong Disjunct, Firm:	**40/33**	4/3 ÷ **11/10** = 40/33	40/33 ÷ **13/12** = 160/143	11/10, 13/12, 160/143

Figure 11.58 gives an overview of Al-Fārābī's three systems. (a) In the *perfect invariable disjunct system* the interval of disjunction precedes the "double-fourth" of the lower and upper "octaves"; (b) in the *perfect invariable conjunct system* the interval of disjunction follows the "double-fourth" of the lower and upper "octaves"; (c) and in what remained an *unnamed system* — which I call the *'second disjunct system'* — the interval of disjunction occurs between the two "fourths" of the lower and upper "octaves."

Because these three systems require too much space to compile a complete catalog of scales, I have chosen only one tetrachord for further discussion, namely, Al-Fārābī's *strong conjunct moderate genus*, interval ratios $9/8$, $10/9$, $16/15$. As discussed in Section 11.56, Al-Fārābī systematically inverted the intervalic order of *all* the Greek tetrachords. So, if we invert the latter progression to form the sequence $16/15$, $10/9$, $9/8$, observe that in Table 10.12, Ptolemy gives this progression as Didymus' Diatonic Tetrachord. Furthermore, if we distribute Al-Fārābī's interval ratios as specified by his three systems, Figure 11.59 depicts three different manifestations of the *strong conjunct moderate genus* in the lower "octave" starting on C_4.

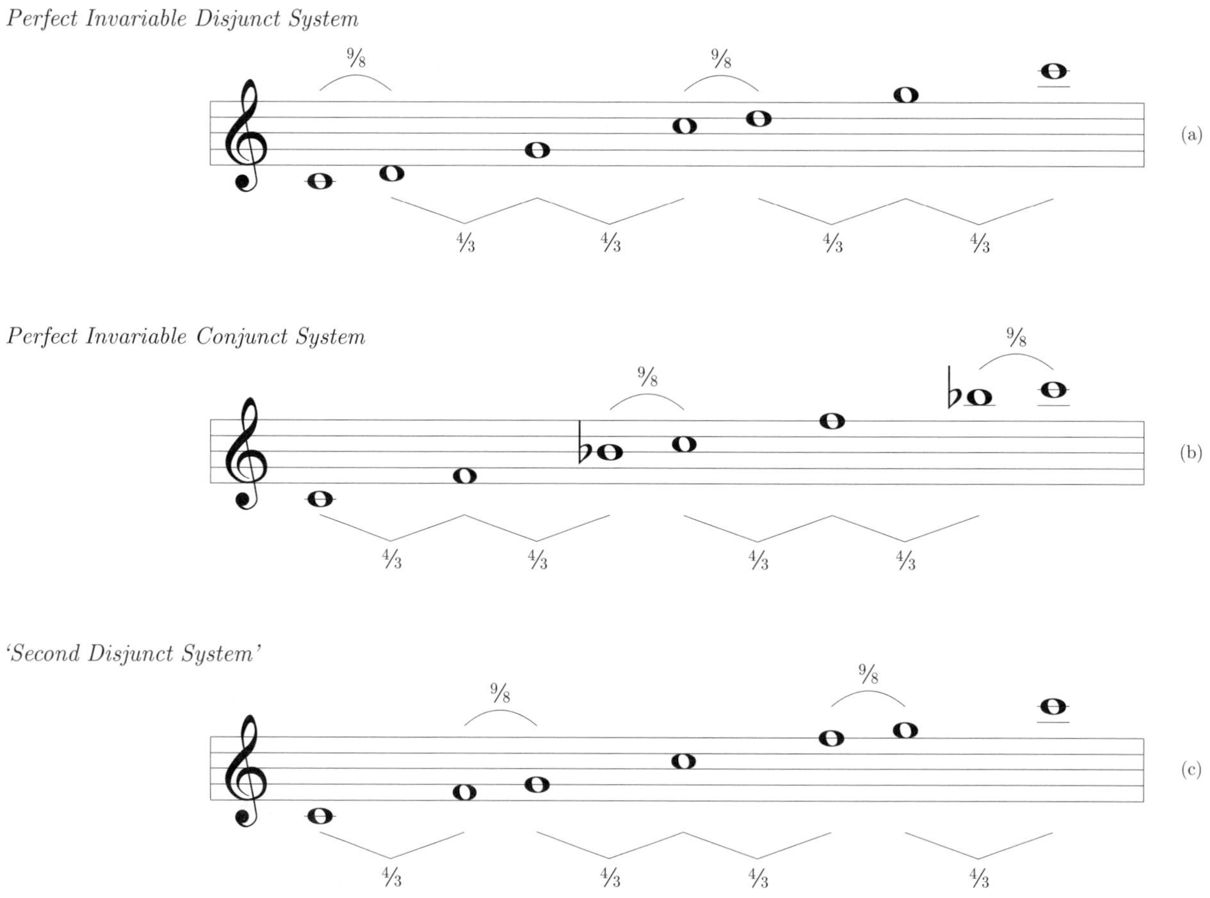

Figure 11.58 Three different distributions of tetrachords and tones within the Greater Perfect System of Greek music theory according to Al-Fārābī. (a) The interval of disjunction precedes the "double-fourth"; (b) the interval of disjunction follows the "double-fourth"; (c) the interval of disjunction occurs between the two "fourths" of the lower and upper "octaves." When the same tetrachord is used to form both the lower and upper "octaves," Al-Fārābī referred to the first group as the *perfect invariable disjunct system*, and to the second group as the *perfect invariable conjunct system*; the third group remained an *unnamed system*, which I call the *'second disjunct system'*.

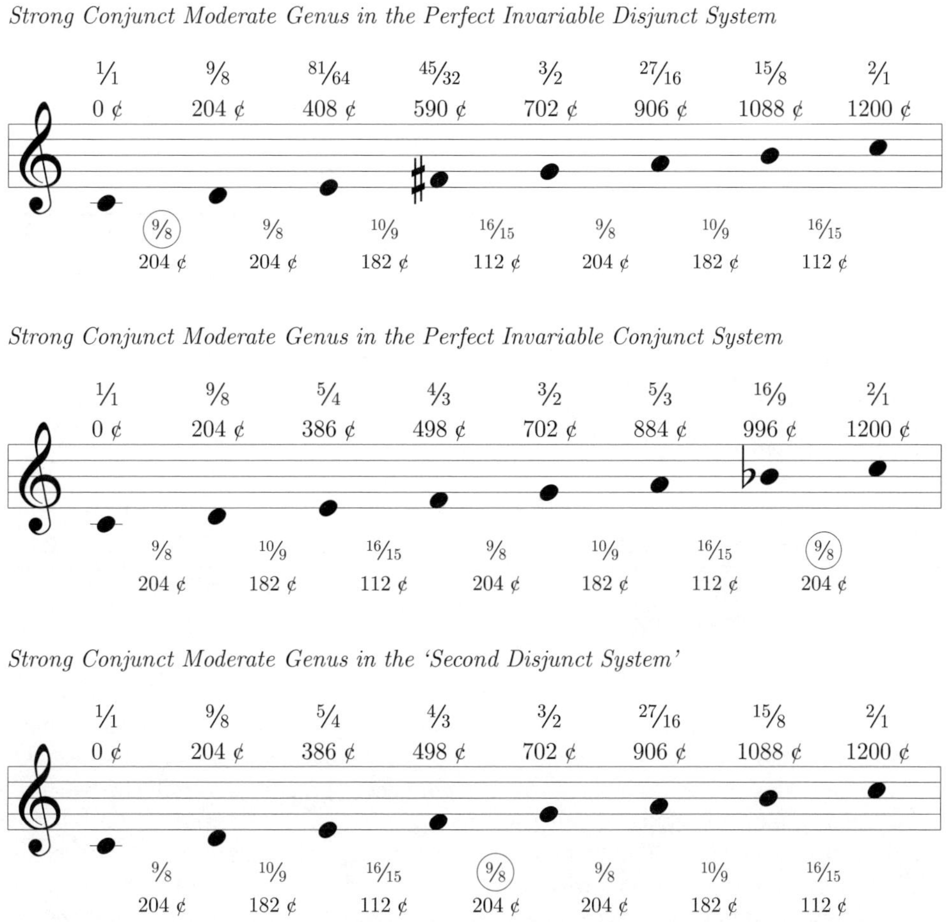

Figure 11.59 Three manifestations of Al-Fārābī's *strong conjunct moderate genus*, a tetrachord that consists of ascending interval ratios 9/8, 10/9, 16/15. Figure 11.58 shows the distributions of tetrachords and tones that govern these three systems.

Let us now compare the fret requirements of these three systems in the lower "octave" of the *'ūd*. Begin by noting that the *disjunct system* includes four consecutive "fourths" within the "double-fourth" D_4–C_5: 9/8–3/2, 81/64–27/16, 45/32–15/8, 3/2–2/1; the *conjunct system* includes four consecutive "fourths" within the "double-fourth" C_4–$B\flat_4$: 1/1–4/3, 9/8–3/2, 5/4–5/3, 4/3–16/9; and the *second disjunct system* includes four consecutive "fifths" within the "octave" C_4–C_5: 1/1–3/2, 9/8–27/16, 5/4–15/8, 4/3–2/1. Consequently, Figure 11.60 illustrates that the *disjunct system* needs three frets, the *conjunct system*, only two frets, and the *second disjunct system*, four frets. These differences occur because the open strings of the *'ūd* are tuned in "fourths." Since the *conjunct system* includes two "fourths" — 1/1–4/3 and 4/3–16/9 — which are playable on open strings, this system requires one less fret than the *disjunct system*. Finally, as discussed in the caption of Figure 11.60, since the *second disjunct system* consists of four consecutive "fifths," it requires a total number of four frets. This added complication probably explains why the latter system remained an *unnamed system*, or why Al-Fārābī included it only for theoretical reasons.[91] However, turn back to Section 11.25, and observe that the *strong conjunct moderate genus* in the *second disjunct system* is identical to Bharata's *śuddha jāti*, the *Naiṣadī*, and almost identical to Ptolemy's Tense Diatonic in the Lydian Mode. The *second disjunct system* is also extremely important in modern Turkish music (see Section 11.77), and in modern Arabian music (see Sections 11.78–11.83).

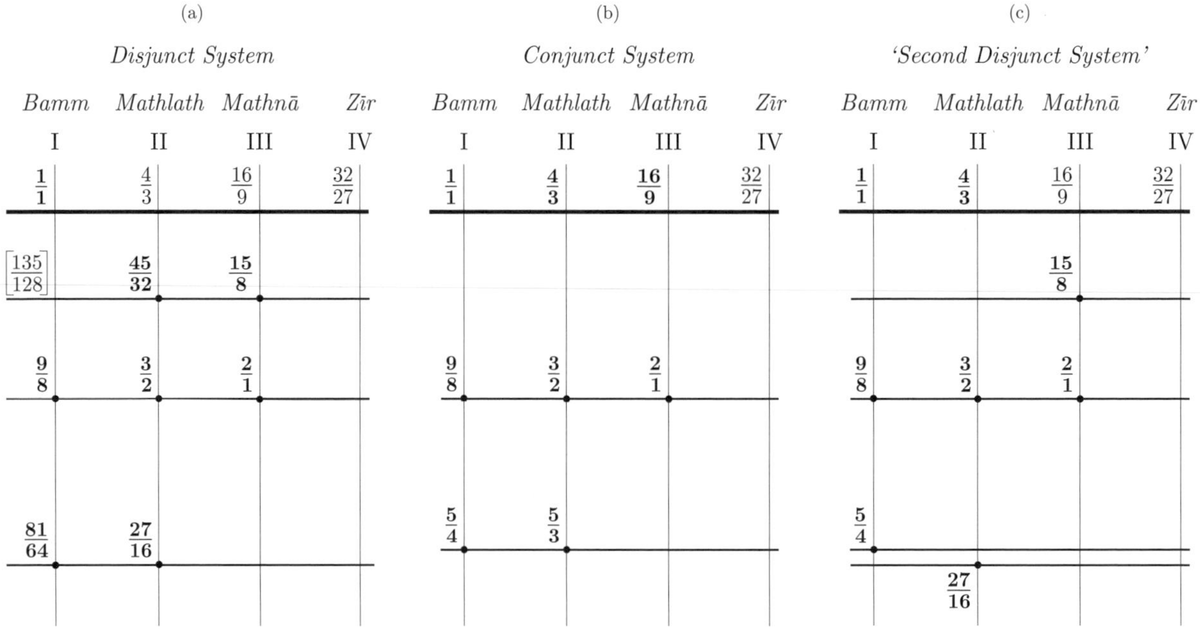

Figure 11.60 Three versions of the *strong conjunct moderate genus* in the lower "octave" of Al-Fārābī's *'ūd*. Refer to Figure 11.59, and note that (a) produces the *perfect invariable disjunct system*, (b) the *perfect invariable conjunct system*, and (c) the *'second disjunct system'*. Because the *disjunct system* includes four consecutive "fourths," this system needs three frets. Similarly, because the *conjunct system* includes four consecutive "fourths," two of which — $1/1$–$4/3$ and $4/3$–$16/9$ — are playable on open strings, this system needs only two frets. In contrast, the *second disjunct system* includes four consecutive "fifths," which means that this system needs four frets. Since the required $5/4$ fret on the *Bamm* does not sound the required $27/16$ on the *Mathlath*, we must install an $81/64$ fret on the *Bamm;* this fret also produces the $27/16$ on the *Mathlath*. And since a $4/3$ fret on the *Bamm* would not sound the required $15/8$ on the *Mathlath*, we must install a $45/32$ fret on the *Mathlath;* this fret also produces the $15/8$ on the *Mathnā*. This added complication probably explains why the latter system remained an *unnamed system*.

~ 11.59 ~

The illustrious successor to Al-Fārābī was Ibn Sīnā (980–1037). The next discussion will focus on Ibn Sīnā's musical treatises in the *Kitāb al-shifā'* (Book of the cure) and in the *Kitāb al-najāt* (Book of the delivery). A French translation of the former exists in D'Erlanger's *La Musique Arabe, Volume 2*, and a German translation of the latter is contained in Mahmoud el-Hefny's dissertation *Ibn Sīnā's Musiklehre* (Ibn Sīnā's teaching on music).[92] Although these two texts give slightly different procedures for the division of lute strings, in the final analysis both tunings are identical. Here is Ibn Sīnā's description of the 7-fret *'ūd* tuning in the *Kitāb al-shifā':*

I

> The best known, most widely used, most popular instrument is the lute. If there exists an instrument more noble than this, it is not in general use among practitioners. It is therefore necessary for us to discuss the lute and the ratio[s] of its frets. We leave to others the task of applying this theory to other instruments, when they have accepted the principles that we are going to explain.

Let us state, therefore, that one has considered on the lute the distance between the bridge and the anterior part which holds the tuning pegs; and at $\frac{1}{4}$ of this distance, on the side of the tuning pegs, one has placed the last fret, which is assigned to the *little finger.*

$$[\text{Fret } 7 \rightarrow \tfrac{4}{3} = 498.0 \text{ ¢}]$$

Between the open string and the little finger, there is thus an interval of a fourth. One has then taken $\frac{1}{9}$ of the length of the instrument [the string], on the side of the anterior part [the nut], and one has placed the *index finger* fret there.

$$[\text{Fret } 3 \rightarrow \tfrac{9}{8} = 203.9 \text{ ¢}]$$

Between the open string and the index finger, there is thus an interval of a tone [9:8]. Next, one has divided the distance between the index finger and the bridge so as to establish another interval of a tone; at the limit of that interval, one has placed the *ring finger* fret.

$$[\text{Fret } 6\text{: } \tfrac{9}{8} \times \tfrac{9}{8} = \tfrac{81}{64} = 407.8 \text{ ¢}]$$

As a result, between the open string and the index finger, one has established an interval of a tone, and another between the index finger and the ring finger. The interval that separates the ring finger and the little finger is therefore a limma.

$$[\text{Interval ratio: } \tfrac{4}{3} \div \tfrac{81}{64} = \tfrac{256}{243} = 90.2 \text{ ¢}]$$

Thus, we have a diatonic genus.

Furthermore, the distance between the little finger and the bridge has been divided in eight [parts]; a length equal to one of these eighths has been taken back above the little finger to place a fret called the *ancient* or *Persian middle finger.*

$$[\text{Fret } 4 \rightarrow \tfrac{32}{27} = 294.1 \text{ ¢}]$$

Between this fret and that of the little finger, there is an interval of a tone;

$$[\text{Interval ratio: } \tfrac{4}{3} \div \tfrac{32}{27} = \tfrac{9}{8} = 203.9 \text{ ¢}]$$

it is separated from the index finger by a limma.

$$[\text{Interval ratio: } \tfrac{32}{27} \div \tfrac{9}{8} = \tfrac{256}{243} = 90.2 \text{ ¢}]$$

Modern [musicians] have placed another fret for the middle finger [i.e., the middle finger of Zalzal], approximately halfway between the index finger and the little finger. Some place it lower, others higher, thereby obtaining various kinds of fourths [tetrachords]. But nowadays one no longer distinguishes between these differences. It would be best, however, to establish from the index finger to the middle finger [of Zalzal] the ratio $1 + \frac{1}{12}$ [13:12].

$$[\text{Fret } 5\text{: } \tfrac{9}{8} \times \tfrac{13}{12} = \tfrac{39}{32} = 342.5 \text{ ¢}]$$

The approximate ratio of [this] middle finger and the little finger will then be $1 + \frac{1}{11}$ [12:11], **the real ratio being $\frac{128}{117}$,**

$$[\text{Interval ratio: } \tfrac{4}{3} \div \tfrac{39}{32} = \tfrac{128}{117} = 155.6\ ¢]$$

which allows the composition of some of the genera we have cited.

Above the index finger fret, one has then placed another at a tone from the latter middle finger indicated above. This fret is a kind of *assistant* {*mujannab*} [or, anterior] to the middle finger [of Zalzal];

$$[\text{Fret 2: } \tfrac{39}{32} \div \tfrac{9}{8} = \tfrac{13}{12} = 138.6\ ¢]$$

it provides thc low octave of [the middle finger of Zalzal] on the third string.

$$[\text{Interval ratio: } \tfrac{13}{6} \div \tfrac{2}{1} = \tfrac{13}{12} = 138.6\ ¢]$$

Above this last fret, one has placed yet another that many consider to be an *assistant* {*mujannab*} [or, anterior] *to the ancient middle finger* [on the third string];

[Anterior to the Ancient- or Persian Middle Finger Fret, *not* used:

$$\tfrac{512}{243} \div \tfrac{2}{1} = \tfrac{256}{243} = 90.2\ ¢]$$

but this is false, because this [anterior] fret is in the ratio of $1 + \frac{1}{7}$ [8:7] with the more recent of the two middle finger frets, known by the name of the *middle finger of Zalzal.*

$$[\text{Fret 1: } \tfrac{39}{32} \div \tfrac{8}{7} = \tfrac{273}{256} = 111.3\ ¢]$$

These are the frets of the lute.

This is how one usually tunes the lute: one makes each open string produce the same pitch as that of the little finger [fret] of the string placed above it, in such a way that one of these [open] strings plays the same role as three-quarters of the other [or stopped string]. Because of that, the notes of the lute will be contained within four fourths.[93] (Bold text, and text and ratios in brackets mine. *Mujannab* in braces in Farmer's translation.)

Figure 11.61 illustrates these seven divisions in the order described by Ibn Sīnā, Table 11.29 gives detailed ratio calculations, and Figure 11.62 is a fret diagram of the tuning.

Ibn Sīnā explains the two extra locations on the *Zīr* in the following manner:

The lute was sometimes given a fifth string, on which the index finger and the ring finger provided the two intervals of a tone necessary to complete the double octave. The fifth string provided an extra limma {$\frac{256}{243}$ above $\frac{4}{1}$} that was not needed; this string has therefore been disregarded . . . {Instead,} to complete the double octave {$\frac{4}{1}$} one uses two fingers and descends below the little finger [of the fourth string] at a distance of two intervals of a tone {$\frac{256}{81} \times \frac{9}{8} = \frac{32}{9}$ [$\frac{16}{9}$], and $\frac{32}{9} \times \frac{9}{8} = \frac{4}{1}$}. Therefore, there exists below the little finger of the [fourth] string, {as ***octave equivalents***}, a note higher than that of the little finger {$\frac{32}{9}$} and another even higher {$\frac{4}{1}$}.

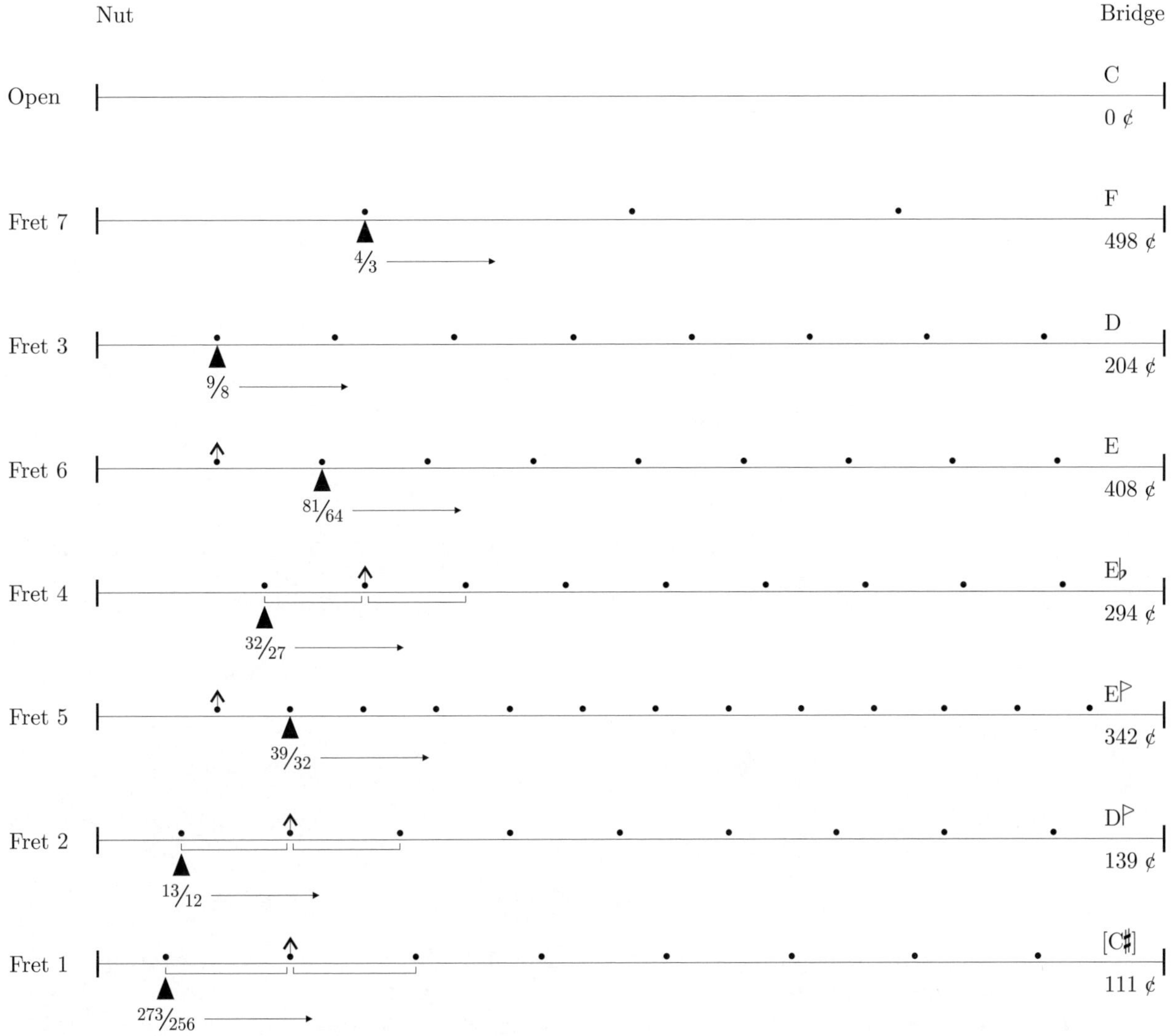

Figure 11.61 Ibn Sīnā's string length divisions used to determine the locations of seven frets on the *'ūd*. The numerators of the last three divisions include prime factor 13. As discussed in Section 11.60, Ibn Sīnā substituted three ratios: $^{273}\!/_{256}$, $^{13}\!/_{12}$, and $^{39}\!/_{32}$, for six similar ratios in Al-Fārābī's 10-fret tuning. These substitutions greatly simplified the mathematical complexity of the *'ūd* without sacrificing two essential intervals required by Arabian music, namely, the "neutral second," which approximately equals 150.0 ¢, and the "neutral third," which approximately equals 350.0 ¢. (Dots with arrows point to previously calculated divisions.)

> One tunes the lute in several other ways; the majority of those differ from what we have just explained only by the tuning of one single string {*Ḥādd*}.[94] (Text and ratios in braces mine. Bold italics in braces my correction of the "puissance" translation error in *La Musique Arabe.* Text in brackets in *La Musique Arabe.*)

Like the *kanon* of ancient Greece, the *'ūd* of ancient Arabia was regarded as a supremely flexible musical instrument, which by its very nature inspired scientific and artistic development.[95] We must, therefore, always consider two essential features in the playing and tuning of the *'ūd.* (1) As discussed in Section 11.53, an authentic lute has moveable frets; consequently, musicians did not

Table 11.29

MODERN LENGTH RATIO TO FREQUENCY RATIO CALCULATIONS
OF IBN-SĪNĀ'S 7-FRET *'ŪD* TUNING

Open String, Tone C	$1/1$	Whole string length.
Fret 7, Tone F	$1 \times 1/4 = 1/4$ $1 - 1/4 = 4/4 - 1/4 = 3/4 \rightarrow 4/3$	Quarter of string. Whole minus subsection.
Fret 3, Tone D	$1 \times 1/9 = 1/9$ $1 - 1/9 = 9/9 - 1/9 = 8/9 \rightarrow 9/8$	Ninth of string. Whole minus subsection.
Fret 6, Tone E	$8/9 \times 1/9 = 8/81$ $8/9 - 8/81 = 72/81 - 8/81 = 64/81 \rightarrow 81/64$	Ninth of $8/9$ section. $8/9$ section minus subsection.
Fret 4, Tone E♭	$3/4 \times 1/8 = 3/32$ $3/4 + 3/32 = 24/32 + 3/32 = 27/32 \rightarrow 32/27$	Eighth of $3/4$ section. $3/4$ section plus subsection.
Fret 5, Tone E𝄳	$8/9 \times 1/13 = 8/117$ $8/9 - 8/117 =$ $104/117 - 8/117 = 96/117 = 32/39 \rightarrow 39/32$	Thirteenth of $8/9$ section. $8/9$ section minus subsection.
Fret 2, Tone D𝄳	$32/39 \times 1/8 = 32/312 = 4/39$ $32/39 + 4/39 = 36/39 = 12/13 \rightarrow 13/12$	Eighth of $32/39$ section. $32/39$ section plus subsection.
Fret 1, Tone [C♯]*	$32/39 \times 1/7 = 32/273$ $32/39 + 32/273 =$ $224/273 + 32/273 = 256/273 \rightarrow 273/256$	Seventh of $32/39$ section. $32/39$ section plus subsection.

*In Figure 11.62, the tones on the anterior fret, C♯: $273/256$, F♯: $91/64$, B: $91/48$, E: $91/72$, A: $91/54$, appear in brackets because they very closely approximate, but do not exactly represent, a Pythagorean spiral of ascending "fourths." One could construct such a spiral by taking five consecutive ratios from Figure 10.16(a), and arranging them in the ascending order, C♯: $2187/2048$, F♯: $729/512$, B: $243/128$, E: $81/64$, A: $27/16$. Cent calculations show that the tones on the anterior fret are only 2.4 ¢ flat of the Pythagorean tones in the spiral, which means that the former ratios are musically indistinguishable from the latter ratios.

experience great difficulties in actualizing "unofficial" tunings. (2) By shifting the hand to locations beyond the last fret, musicians easily accessed notes not included in "official" tunings. Observe that in the description below, Ibn Sīnā fuses the concept of *qānūn* and *'ūd* as he instructs his reader to use small moveable bridges to determine (1) four exact locations of frets by ear, and (2) three approximate locations of frets by measurement.

> To lay out the frets in order to reconcile theory with practice, one needs a trained ear to guide oneself; otherwise, it is advisable to rely upon a procedure. This procedure consists of mounting on the lute three strings {from the player's perspective, the strings are arranged in the following order: Upper String = *Bamm*, Middle String = *Mathlath*, Lower String = *Mathnā*} of the same kind and the same thickness. Lightly tension one of these strings {*Bamm* = $1/1$}, enough to produce a sound when the string is struck. Loosen it as much as possible to make it produce the lowest sound

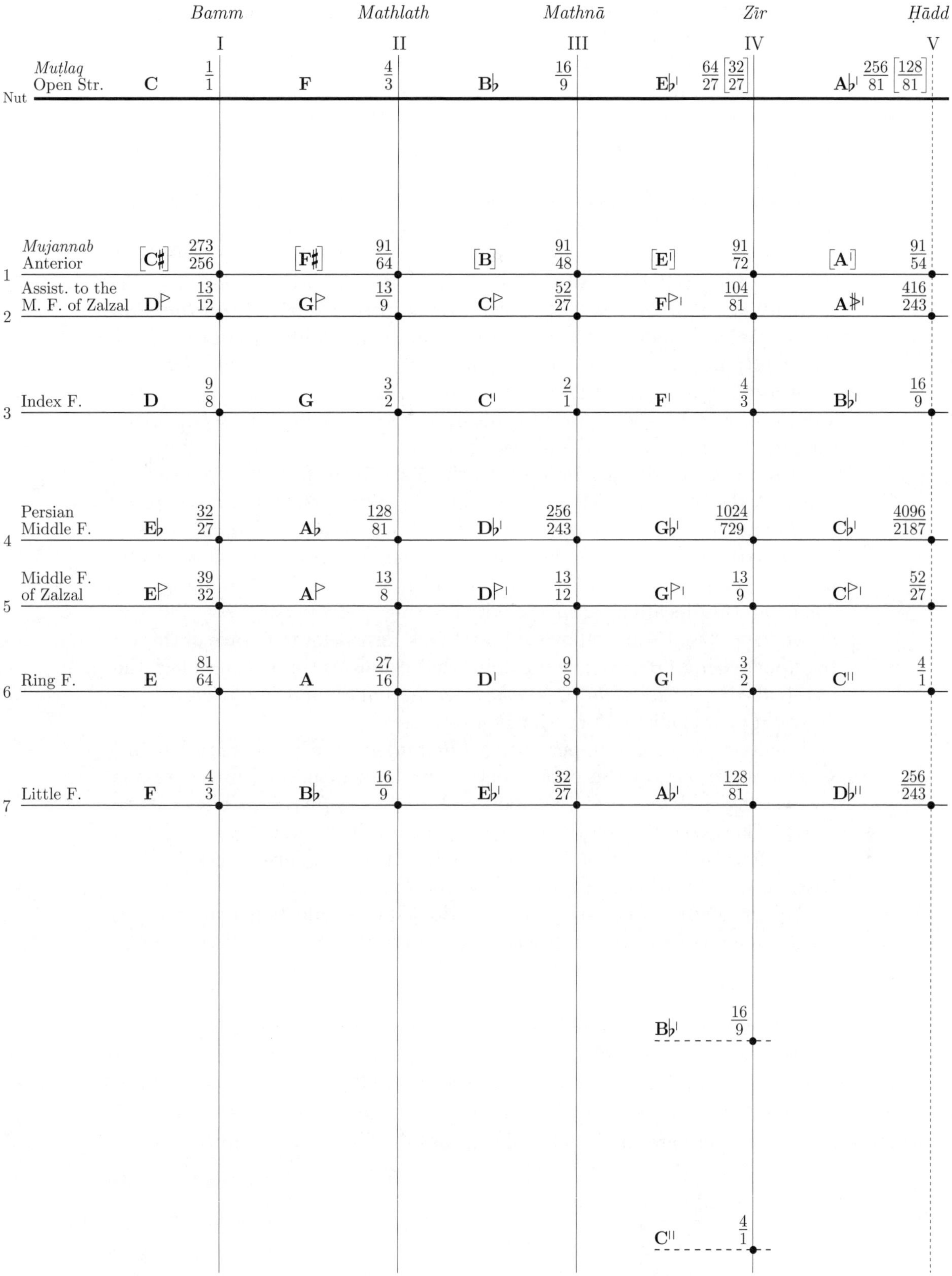

Figure 11.62 Seven fret locations on the *'ūd* as defined by Ibn Sīnā (980–1037). Two extra locations on the *Zīr* string produce the "minor seventh," ratio $^{32}/_{9}$ [$^{16}/_{9}$], and the "double-octave," ratio $^{4}/_{1}$, without the need for a *Ḥādd* string. (Fret locations to scale.)

that is clearly perceptible. Next, moderately tension the third string, so that the sound produced is an octave higher {*Mathnā* = $^2\!/_1$} than the first. Then take a small, thin, properly sized bridge whose height, in raising the string, will not increase the tension {of the string}. Then slide the bridge under . . . the first string {*Bamm*} in the direction of the tuning pegs, just until this string produces, ***on the side of the tuning pegs***, an octave higher than the third {*Mathnā*}, {i.e., on the *Bamm* on the side of the tuning pegs: l.r. $^1\!/_4 \rightarrow$ f.r. $^4\!/_1$}. At this location place the *little finger* fret {i.e., on the *Bamm* on the side of the bridge: l.r. $^3\!/_4 \rightarrow$ f.r. $^4\!/_3$}.

Next, tune the three strings according to the usual tuning: tune each string to the little finger of the one immediately above it {*Bamm* = $^1\!/_1$, *Mathlath* = $^4\!/_3$, *Mathnā* = $^{16}\!/_9$}. On the lower string {*Mathnā*}, ***on the side of the [bridge]***, look for the point that is an octave higher than the upper string {*Bamm*}, and place the *index finger* fret there {$^2\!/_1$ on the *Mathnā*}.

Stop the upper string {*Bamm*} at the index finger fret {$^9\!/_8$ above $^1\!/_1$}, and look for the higher octave of this on the lower string {*Mathnā*}; place the *ring finger* fret there {$^9\!/_8$ above $^2\!/_1$}.

Stop the lower string {*Mathnā*} at the little finger fret {$^{32}\!/_{27}$ above $^2\!/_1$}, and look for the lower octave of this on the upper string {*Bamm*}; place the *Persian middle finger* fret there {$^{32}\!/_{27}$ above $^1\!/_1$ on the *Bamm*}.

Approximately halfway between the index finger and the little finger, place the *middle finger of Zalzal* {$^{72}\!/_{59}$ [344.7 ¢] $\approx$ $^{39}\!/_{32}$ [342.5 ¢] above $^1\!/_1$}. Then, at this location, stop the lower string {*Mathnā*}, {$^{64}\!/_{59}$ [140.8 ¢] above $^2\!/_1 \approx$ $^{13}\!/_{12}$ [138.6 ¢] above $^2\!/_1$}, and look for the lower octave of this on the upper string {*Bamm*}; at the point that produces this octave, place the fret {called} the *assistant* or *neighbor to the middle finger of Zalzal* {$^{64}\!/_{59}$ above $^1\!/_1 \approx$ $^{13}\!/_{12}$ above $^1\!/_1$ on the *Bamm*}.

Finally, look [on the upper string] {*Bamm*} for the {theoretical} point, {$^{256}\!/_{243}$ above $^1\!/_1$}, of the octave below the Persian middle finger [of the lower string] {*Mathnā*}, {$^{256}\!/_{243}$ above $^2\!/_1$}, and at ***approximately*** $^1\!/_4$ of the distance between this point and the assistant to the middle finger of Zalzal, place a fret; this one will be *in front of* all the others {*anterior fret*}, {$^{1024}\!/_{965}$ [102.7 ¢] $\approx$ $^{273}\!/_{256}$ [111.3 ¢] above $^1\!/_1$ on the *Bamm*}.

This is how the frets are placed.[96] (Bold italics, and text and ratios in braces mine. Bold italics in brackets my correction of an unedited error in *La Musique Arabe.* Text in brackets in *La Musique Arabe.*)

In the last two paragraphs, Ibn Sīnā gives approximate locations of the middle finger of Zalzal fret, of the assistant to the middle finger of Zalzal fret, and of the anterior fret because the ratios of these three frets include prime factor 13. (See Section 11.60.) For some, such approximations are necessary and convenient because it is difficult to determine intervals with relatively large prime numbers solely by ear. Here are the formal calculations of the first two approximations.

Zalzal on *Bamm:*	$^8\!/_9 - {^3\!/_4} = {^5\!/_{36}}$	Length of internal section.
	$^5\!/_{36} \times {^1\!/_2} = {^5\!/_{72}}$	Half of internal section.
	$^8\!/_9 - {^5\!/_{72}} =$	
	$^{64}\!/_{72} - {^5\!/_{72}} = {^{59}\!/_{72}} \rightarrow {^{72}\!/_{59}} = 344.7$¢	$^8\!/_9$ section minus subsection.
Zalzal on *Mathnā:*	$^{72}\!/_{59} \times {^4\!/_3} \times {^4\!/_3} = {^{128}\!/_{59}}$	
Assistant on *Bamm:*	$^{128}\!/_{59} \div {^2\!/_1} = {^{64}\!/_{59}} = 140.8$ ¢	Simplified "octave" equivalent.

With respect to the last approximation, notice that the Persian middle finger on the *Mathnā* produces $^{256}\!/_{243}$ above $^{2}\!/_{1}$. Therefore, if we locate a *theoretical point* one "octave" below this fret on the *Bamm*, ratio $^{256}\!/_{243}$ above $^{1}\!/_{1}$, and then measure one quarter of the distance between this point and the approximation of the assistant to the middle finger of Zalzal, ratio $^{64}\!/_{59}$, we find that Ibn Sīnā's approximation of the anterior fret is ratio $^{1024}\!/_{965}$, or 102.7 ¢. Since the exact location of the anterior fret is $^{273}\!/_{256}$, or 111.3 ¢, Ibn Sīnā's approximate location is only 8.6 ¢ flat. Here are the formal calculations of the third approximation.

Anterior on *Bamm:*	$^{243}\!/_{256} - {}^{59}\!/_{64} = {}^{243}\!/_{256} - {}^{236}\!/_{256} = {}^{7}\!/_{256}$	Length of internal section.
	$^{7}\!/_{256} \times {}^{1}\!/_{4} = {}^{7}\!/_{1024}$	Quarter of internal section.
	$^{243}\!/_{256} - {}^{7}\!/_{1024} =$	
	$^{972}\!/_{1024} - {}^{7}\!/_{1024} =$	
	$^{965}\!/_{1024} \rightarrow {}^{1024}\!/_{965} = 102.7$ ¢	$^{243}\!/_{256}$ section minus subsection.

Figure 11.62 shows that Ibn Sīnā's lower "octave" between $^{1}\!/_{1}$–$^{2}\!/_{1}$ consists of a 17-tone scale. In Section 11.70, we will discuss the work of Ṣafī Al-Dīn, who emulated Ibn Sīnā's basic fret design and transformed it into one of the most spectacular musical scales known to mankind.

11.60

To understand why Ibn Sīnā created a 7-fret tuning, turn to Figure 11.63. A comparison between Al-Fārābī's 10-fret tuning and Ibn Sīnā's 7-fret tuning reveals an intentional process of elimination. Ibn Sīnā reduced Al-Fārābī's Frets 1–4 to only two frets, and Al-Fārābī's Frets 7 and 8 to only one fret. In all other respects, the two tunings are identical. A numerical analysis reveals that Al-Fārābī's length ratios include six prime factors: 2, 3, 7, 11, 17, 149, and Ibn Sīnā's, only four prime factors: 2, 3, 7, 13. So, we see that Ibn Sīnā's simplified design (1) eliminated Al-Fārābī's two largest prime factors: 17 and 149, and (2) replaced prime factor 11 with prime factor 13. Furthermore, consistent with Greek music theory, Ibn Sīnā's implementation of prime factor 13 produces two characteristic intervals of the diatonic genus:[97] a "large whole tone," ratio $^{8}\!/_{7}$, between Frets 1 and 5: $^{39}\!/_{32} \div {}^{273}\!/_{256} = {}^{8}\!/_{7}$, and the Pythagorean "whole tone," ratio $^{9}\!/_{8}$, between Frets 2 and 5: $^{39}\!/_{32} \div {}^{13}\!/_{12} = {}^{9}\!/_{8}$.

Predictably, Ibn Sīnā introduces his discussion of tetrachord divisions by stating a clear preference for the diatonic genus over the chromatic and enharmonic genera:

> . . . however . . . ***neither*** the *genus rāsim* [or the *chromatic genus* which includes a "minor third," and is called the *soft genus* because it contains a *pyknon*], ***nor*** the *genus mulawwan* [or the *enharmonic genus* which includes a "major third," and is also called the *soft genus* because it too contains a *pyknon*], is used in our country. Being accustomed to the *strong genera* [or the *diatonic genus* which includes at least one "whole tone," and is called the *strong genus* because it contains an *apyknon*], we quite naturally dislike the others each time one tries to use them.[98] (Italics, bold italics, and text in brackets mine.)

Ibn Sīnā then describes his first method of diatonic tetrachord construction, in which he systematically combines the "large whole tone," ratio $^{8}\!/_{7}$, with the interval ratios of this decreasing sequence of epimore ratios: $^{8}\!/_{7}$, $^{9}\!/_{8}$, $^{10}\!/_{9}$, $^{11}\!/_{10}$, $^{12}\!/_{11}$, $^{13}\!/_{12}$, $^{14}\!/_{13}$. Consequently, his first three tetrachords include the pairs [$^{8}\!/_{7}$, $^{8}\!/_{7}$], [$^{8}\!/_{7}$, $^{9}\!/_{8}$], and [$^{8}\!/_{7}$, $^{10}\!/_{9}$], respectively. Next, he rejects the pairs [$^{8}\!/_{7}$, $^{11}\!/_{10}$] and

Frets 1–4 on Al-Fārābī's *'Ūd*	Ibn Sīnā's Simplifications
1. $\frac{2^8}{3^5} = \frac{256}{243} = 90\ ¢$	
2. $\frac{2 \times 3^2}{17} = \frac{18}{17} = 99\ ¢$	1. $\frac{3 \times 7 \times 13}{2^8} = \frac{273}{256} = 111\ ¢$
3. $\frac{2 \times 3^4}{149} = \frac{162}{149} = 145\ ¢$	2. $\frac{13}{2^2 \times 3} = \frac{13}{12} = 139\ ¢$
4. $\frac{2 \times 3^3}{7^2} = \frac{54}{49} = 168\ ¢$	
Frets 7 and 8 on Al-Fārābī's *'Ūd*	**Ibn Sīnā's Simplification**
7. $\frac{3^4}{2^2 \times 17} = \frac{81}{68} = 303\ ¢$	
	5. $\frac{3 \times 13}{2^5} = \frac{39}{32} = 342\ ¢$
8. $\frac{3^3}{2 \times 11} = \frac{27}{22} = 355\ ¢$	

(Brackets: Fret 1 to Fret 5 = 8⁄7; Fret 2 to Fret 5 = 9⁄8)

Figure 11.63 A comparison of Al-Fārābī's and Ibn Sīnā's *'ūd* tunings. Ibn Sīnā replaced Al-Fārābī's Frets 1–4 with Frets 1 and 2, and Al-Fārābī's Frets 7 and 8 with Fret 5. Since Al-Fārābī's length ratios include six prime factors: 2, 3, 7, 11, 17, 149, and Ibn Sīnā's, only four prime factors: 2, 3, 7, 13, this reduction (1) eliminated the two largest primes — 17 and 149 — from the tuning, and (2) replaced prime factor 11 with prime factor 13. Ibn Sīnā's consistent utilization of prime factor 13 shows that his scale includes two diatonic intervals: a "large whole tone," ratio 8⁄7, between Frets 1 and 5, and the Pythagorean "whole tone," ratio 9⁄8, between Frets 2 and 5.

[8⁄7, 12⁄11] because they sound too dissonant.[99] Finally, in his fourth tetrachord, he combines interval ratio 8⁄7 with the last two epimores, 13⁄12 and 14⁄13; that is, 8⁄7 × 13⁄12 × 14⁄13 = 4⁄3. In the following passage, Ibn Sīnā describes the derivation of this 13-limit tetrachord:

II

IV. — When, to the interval 1 + 1⁄7 [8:7], one joins 1 + 1⁄12 [13:12], the complementary interval [the upper interval] will be 1 + 1⁄13 [14:13]. By establishing this ***very noble genus***, one has realized the last division of the intervals in half. The interval of the double octave [4⁄1] divided in half has provided the octave [2⁄1]. This last interval divided by a mean has given the fifth [3⁄2] and the fourth [4⁄3], [multiply: 2⁄1 × 2⁄2 = 4⁄2; insert the arithmetic mean 4:3:2]. Dividing the interval of the fourth in the same manner has produced the intervals 1 + 1⁄7 [8:7] and 1 + 1⁄6 [7:6], [multiply: 4⁄3 × 2⁄2 = 8⁄6; insert the arithmetic mean 8:7:6]; this last in turn has given 1 + 1⁄12 [13:12] and 1 + 1⁄13 [14:13], [multiply: 7⁄6 × 2⁄2 = 14⁄12; insert the arithmetic mean 14:13:12]. Above all others, Ptolemy prefers the genus that we have just completed. The numeric expression of it is as follows:

$$\begin{bmatrix} & \frac{8}{7} & & \frac{13}{12} & & \frac{14}{13} & \\ 104 & & 91 & & 84 & & 78 \end{bmatrix}$$

> Furthermore, when one joins to the interval $1 + \frac{1}{7}$ [8:7] the interval $1 + \frac{1}{13}$ [14:13], the complement [the upper interval] will be $1 + \frac{1}{12}$ [13:12], and the genus obtained will be ***identical*** to the one preceding.
>
> $$16 \quad \tfrac{8}{7} \quad 14 \quad \tfrac{14}{13} \quad 13 \quad \tfrac{13}{12} \quad 12$$
>
> The truly consonant genera that are based upon the interval $1 + \frac{1}{7}$ [8:7] are the four that we have just cited. Each of these genera should be given a name that the reader chooses as he pleases.[100] (Bold italics, and text, ratios, and string lengths in brackets mine.)

In Quote II, the first ratio analysis of *Diatonic Genus* 4: $\frac{8}{7}$, $\frac{13}{12}$, $\frac{14}{13}$, and the respective string lengths in least terms: 104, 91, 84, 78, appear in brackets because *La Musique Arabe, Volume 2,* does *not* give this tetrachord. Instead, D'Erlanger incorrectly cites the second ratio analysis: $\frac{8}{7}$, $\frac{14}{13}$, $\frac{13}{12}$, and the respective string length in least terms: 16, 14, 13, 12, where the first ratio analysis should appear.

Ibn Sīnā then proceeds with his second method of diatonic tetrachord construction, in which he systematically combines the "whole tone," ratio $\frac{9}{8}$, with the interval ratios of the same decreasing sequence of epimores. As a result, the fifth and sixth diatonic tetrachords include the pairs [$\frac{9}{8}$, $\frac{9}{8}$] and [$\frac{9}{8}$, $\frac{10}{9}$], respectively. Next, he rejects the pairs [$\frac{9}{8}$, $\frac{11}{10}$] and [$\frac{9}{8}$, $\frac{12}{11}$] because they sound too dissonant.[101] He then constructs the seventh tetrachord by combining interval ratios $\frac{9}{8}$ and $\frac{13}{12}$. The passage below describes this 13-limit tetrachord:

III

> VII. — When the interval adjacent to the tone [$\frac{9}{8}$] has the ratio $1 + \frac{1}{12}$ [13:12], the interval [$\frac{128}{117}$] that completes the fourth [$\frac{4}{3}$] will not be consonant, but its ratio will be very close to $1 + \frac{1}{11}$ [12:11]. ***Because this genus is in favor***, we give its numeric expression:[102]
>
> $$468 \quad \tfrac{13}{12} \quad 432 \quad \tfrac{9}{8} \quad 384 \quad \left[\tfrac{128}{117}\right] \quad 351$$
>
> (Bold italics, and ratios in brackets mine.)

In Quote III, ". . . the interval that completes the fourth . . ." of *Diatonic Genus* 7 appears in brackets because *La Musique Arabe, Volume 2,* does *not* include this ratio. Instead, D'Erlanger only shows a blank space between string lengths 384 and 351. Turn back to Section 11.59, Quote I, and recall that in his 7-fret *'ūd* tuning, Ibn Sīnā specifically mentions this crucial interval between the middle finger fret, ratio $\frac{39}{32}$, and the little finger fret, ratio $\frac{4}{3}$; that is, $\frac{4}{3} \div \frac{39}{32} = \frac{128}{117}$; he then stresses the musical importance of interval ratio $\frac{128}{117}$ because it ". . . allows the composition of some of the genera we have cited." Ibn Sīnā then gives the last diatonic pair [$\frac{9}{8}$, $\frac{14}{13}$], and finishes with non-systematic derivations of six chromatic and three enharmonic tetrachords. Table 11.30 lists Ibn Sīnā's catalog of tetrachords, where the interval ratios of each tetrachord appear in the same order as in the original text.

Table 11.30

IBN SĪNĀ'S 16 TETRACHORDS IN THE *KITĀB AL-SHIFĀ*

		Interval Ratios in Arabian Ascending Order		
Strong Genus Diatonic	1.	$8/7$,	$8/7$,	$49/48$
	2.	$9/8$,	$8/7$,	$28/27$
	3.	$8/7$,	$10/9$,	$21/20$
	4.	$8/7$,	$13/12$,	$14/13$
	5.	$9/8$,	$9/8$,	$256/243$
	6.	$10/9$,	$9/8$,	$16/15$
	7.	$13/12$,	$9/8$,	$128/117$
	8.	$9/8$,	$14/13$,	$208/189$
Soft Genus Chromatic	9(a).	$16/15$,	$15/14$,	$7/6$
	9(b).	$7/6$,	$12/11$,	$22/21$
	10.	$10/9$,	$36/35$,	$7/6$
	11.	$20/19$,	$19/18$,	$6/5$
	12.	$6/5$,	$15/14$,	$28/27$
	13.	$6/5$,	$25/24$,	$16/15$
Soft Genus Enharmonic	14.	$5/4$,	$32/31$,	$31/30$
	15.	$40/39$,	$26/25$,	$5/4$
	16.	$36/35$,	$5/4$,	$28/27$

~ 11.61 ~

Throughout his discussions on the divisions of tetrachords, Ibn Sīnā selected only two tetrachords for special consideration: *Diatonic Genus* 4: $8/7$, $13/12$, $14/13$, and *Diatonic Genus* 7: $13/12$, $9/8$, $128/117$. In Quote II, he describes the former as a ". . . very noble genus . . .", and in Quote III, he states that the latter ". . . genus is in favor . . ." As previously mentioned, in Quote I he stresses the indispensability of interval ratio $128/117$ in the tuning of the *'ūd*. We conclude that in Quotes I, II, and III, Ibn Sīnā draws our attention to the musical importance of 13-limit interval ratios.

In Quote II, Ibn Sīnā also observes that a change in the order of interval ratios of a given tetrachord does *not* change the musical identity of the genus; he explicitly states that the second genus ". . . obtained will be identical to the one preceding." Suppose we change the order of the first two interval ratios of *Diatonic Genus* 7. This results in interval ratios $9/8$, $13/12$, $128/117$, which in turn produce ancient length ratios or frequency ratios $1/1$, $9/8$, $39/32$, $4/3$. Now, turn to Figure 11.64, which presents a comparison between Al-Fārābī's *Jins* 2 and Ibn Sīnā's *Diatonic Genus* 7. This former tetrachord contains one "neutral third," ratio $27/22$, and two "neutral seconds," ratios $12/11$ and $88/81$, while the latter tetrachord also contains one "neutral third," ratio $39/32$, and two "neutral seconds," ratios $13/12$ and $128/117$. In summary, observe that on a *Bamm* string tuned to C (or on any other *'ūd* string tuned to any frequency), one plays Al-Fārābī's tetrachord and Ibn Sīnā's tetrachord in the following manner: *Open String, Index Finger, Middle Finger of Zalzal, Little Finger*. Ibn Sīnā's

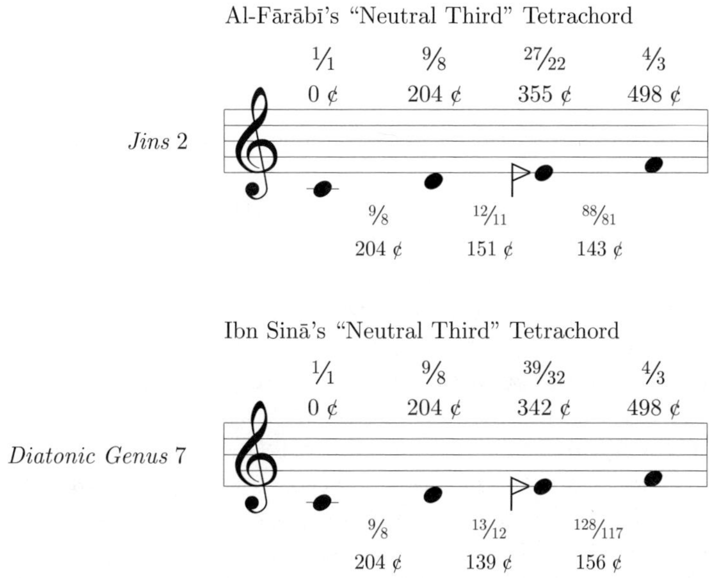

Figure 11.64 A comparison of Al-Fārābī's and Ibn Sīnā's "neutral third" tetrachords. On the *Bamm* (or any other *'ūd* string), one plays Al-Fārābī's and Ibn Sīnā's tetrachords in the following manner: *Open String, Index Finger, Middle Finger of Zalzal, Little Finger.*

process of elimination is, therefore, complete because it simplifies the mathematical complexity of the *'ūd* without sacrificing the playability of this quintessential Arabian tetrachord.

~ 11.62 ~

In preparation for a discussion on Ibn Sīnā's 11 Melodic Modes, let us first reexamine the theory and practice of *near-equal divisions of intervals* in the tetrachords of Ptolemy, Al-Fārābī, and Ibn Sīnā. As discussed in Sections 10.15–10.16 and 11.56, music theorists of antiquity preferred near-equal arithmetic divisions over exactly-equal geometric divisions for two reasons. (1) The musical necessity to resolve various kinds of commas by means of exact geometric divisions did *not* exist. (2) During a musical performance, it is extremely difficult to perceive tuning discrepancies less than 10–15 ¢ on low-tension gut strings. In short, for Ptolemy, Al-Fārābī, and Ibn Sīnā, two intervals that are mathematically different, but that sound nearly the same are for all practical purposes interchangeable. In his dissertation, Farhat observes

> The difference between the two [neutral seconds], however, in a practical sense is too small and too much subject to fluctuation to warrant separate recognition of each one. [We] will therefore refer to all sizes of this interval as neutral 2nd.[103] (Text in brackets mine.)

Obviously, music theorists of antiquity were perfectly capable of perceiving and calculating very small discrepancies between intervals. Even so, had they dwelled on such purely acoustical and mathematical minutiae, the musical art of tetrachord classification would not have developed.

In support of this interpretation of near-equal divisions, consider the next passage from the *Kitāb al-shifā'*, where Ibn Sīnā classifies the most important consonant intervals, and defines the limits of human aural perception and musical instrument construction with respect to very small and very large intervals:

Consonant intervals of the first class.
Homophonic, symphonic, and emmelic intervals.

We will first discuss intervals whose consonance is fundamental; we will call them consonants of the first class. There are three kinds: large, medium, and small.

The ***large*** are those whose ratio is that of the double. When one of the two notes is relative to the other in the double ratio, the interval is described as *complete;* we will later explain what gave it this name.

The ***medium*** intervals are those where the excess of one . . . note {the longer length} over the other {the shorter length} represents a *large portion* of the latter note {the shorter length}. A large portion of a thing is that which is not greater than its half and not less than its third; this will be its half or its third, but not its fourth or its sixth, its fifth or its seventh . . . First, . . . {when} one of the notes exceeds the other by its half, i.e., . . . {when} one of the degrees is represented by 2 and the other by 3, that interval is called the *fifth.* Second, . . . {when} one of the notes exceeds the other by its third, i.e., . . . {when} one of the degrees has the value of 3 and the other of 4, that interval is called the *fourth.* We will later show why they were so named. The series of medium consonant intervals of the first class includes only these two intervals.

All the intervals other than the fourth are known as ***small.*** The first among these has a ratio of $1 + \frac{1}{4}$ {5:4} and the last {is} the last of the series of superparticular {epimore} ratios {or $\frac{36}{35}$, as discussed below}. The small consonant intervals of the first class are also called *emmelic.* It is, indeed, their arrangement that ***gives birth to melody***, as we will later demonstrate.

Music is made to be performed; therefore the number of musical intervals does not extend to all those that nature provides; they will be limited to those that man can produce, and moreover in the noblest and most perfect way. They will lack nobility and perfection when the difference between one of their degrees and the other ***is so small that it can no longer be perceived***, or, again, when it is very small, though still perceptible, or, finally, when it is so large that the voice or instruments cannot reproduce them. If, for example, the excess of a degree over another is equivalent to the 200th part of the latter {$1 + \frac{1}{200} = \frac{201}{200} = 8.6$ ¢}, ***it will escape the ear;*** if it is the 60th {$1 + \frac{1}{60} = \frac{61}{60} = 28.6$ ¢}, or the 70th {$1 + \frac{1}{70} = \frac{71}{70} = 24.6$ ¢}, it will be perceptible, but barely so; the degrees of the interval will be so close that their consonance will be negligible.

If, on the contrary, the excess of one degree over the other equals several times the latter — one of them is, for example, represented by 6 or 7, and the other by 1 {as in $\frac{6}{1}$ or $\frac{7}{1}$} — musical instruments will not lend themselves to such a division [of a string]; or, supposing that this difficulty is overcome, the upper degree of the interval will be far from musical; it will not be appreciated, and will be considered bad. As for the lower note, it will not be perceptible. Our voice, on the other hand, cannot produce such notes, and should it have the capability to do so, it would succeed only with difficulty . . .

. . . This is why a large or small interval, even though consonant, is not always used in practice. With respect to the large intervals, one limits oneself . . . to the interval whose ratio is the double of the double, i.e., that of 4 to 1. With respect to the small intervals, one ends the series of

> superparticular {epimore} ratios with half of the half {$\frac{1}{2} \times \frac{1}{2} = \frac{1}{4}$; $1 + \frac{1}{4} = \frac{5}{4}$}, of the half {$\frac{1}{4} \times \frac{1}{2} = \frac{1}{8}$; $1 + \frac{1}{8} = \frac{9}{8}$}, of the half {$\frac{1}{8} \times \frac{1}{2} = \frac{1}{16}$; $1 + \frac{1}{16} = \frac{17}{16}$}, of the half {$\frac{1}{16} \times \frac{1}{2} = \frac{1}{32}$; $1 + \frac{1}{32} = \frac{33}{32} = 53.3$ ¢}. This ratio ***approaches*** the one wherein one of {its} two numbers exceeds the other by its [***35th***], {$1 + \frac{1}{35} = \frac{36}{35} = 48.8$ ¢}; this last ratio is ***one-fourth*** of one of the small intervals so important in music called the tone {multiply: $\frac{9}{8} \times \frac{1}{4} = \frac{36}{32}$; insert three arithmetic means 36:35:34:33:32}.[104] (Bold italics, and text and ratios in braces mine. Bold italics in brackets my correction of an unedited error in *La Musique Arabe*. Text in brackets in *La Musique Arabe*.)

In the following passage from the *Kitāb al-najāt*, Ibn Sīnā also defines the smallest musical epimore as interval ratio $\frac{36}{35}$; he then states that smaller epimores from $\frac{46}{45}$ [38.1 ¢] to $\frac{49}{48}$ [35.7 ¢] also serve a useful function:

> It is appropriate that the smallest intervals are limited by the relation where one [length] exceeds the other by approximately $\frac{1}{35}$. A smaller [interval] can also be used, which approaches [the relation] where one [length] exceeds the other by approximately a $\frac{1}{45}$ to a $\frac{1}{48}$ part.[105] (Text in brackets mine.)

Note, therefore, that in both of these texts, Ibn Sīnā sets a minimum intervalic limit of about 25–35 ¢. On an *'ūd* equipped with low-tension gut strings, musical intervals become increasingly difficult to distinguish when their differences are less than 25 ¢. With respect to the former passage from the *Kitāb al-shifā'*, we conclude that the two "neutral seconds" in Ibn Sīnā's *Diatonic Genus* 7 — interval ratios $\frac{13}{12}$ [138.6 ¢], and $\frac{128}{117}$ [155.6 ¢] — sound nearly the same because the difference between them equals only 17.0 ¢.

For a historical overview of near-equal divisions by Ptolemy, Al-Fārābī, and Ibn Sīnā, turn to Table 11.31. Row 1(a) demonstrates the derivation of Ptolemy's *Even Diatonic*,[106] and Row 1(b), the same tetrachord with the largest interval, ratio $\frac{10}{9}$, rotated to the first position. As discussed in Section 11.56, Al-Fārābī initiated the Arabian tradition of organizing the interval ratios of a given tetrachord in ascending order, where the largest interval appears first. If we now compare Ptolemy's tetrachord to Al-Fārābī's tetrachords, notice that the *Even Diatonic* more closely approximates *Jins* 2, rather than *Jins* 8. The largest difference between intervals in Row 1(b) equals 31 ¢, in Row 2, it equals 53 ¢, but in Row 3, it equals only 14 ¢. Consequently, Ptolemy's so-called *Even Diatonic* is actually quite uneven when compared to *Jins* 8.

Consider a comparison between Ibn Sīnā's *Diatonic Genus* 4 in Row 4 and Al-Fārābī's *Jins* 8 in Row 3. Observe that Ibn Sīnā did not emulate Al-Fārābī's division of a tetrachord into *three* equal steps: $\frac{5}{6} + \frac{5}{6} + \frac{5}{6}$, but contemplated Ptolemy's *Even Diatonic* and Al-Fārābī's *Jins* 2, both of which consist of a "whole step," or a "whole tone," plus *two* $\frac{3}{4}$-steps, or *two* near-equal "neutral seconds": $1 + \frac{3}{4} + \frac{3}{4}$. This explains Ibn Sīnā's reference to Ptolemy in Quote II. However, be aware that the *Even Diatonic:* $\frac{10}{9}$, $\frac{12}{11}$, $\frac{11}{10}$, only appears in Ptolemy's *Harmonics* and, as such, is not considered an integral part of ancient Greek music theory. In contrast, Al-Fārābī's and Ibn Sīnā's comparable divisions retain distinct Perso-Arabian identities to this day. (See Section 11.66.)

In *Diatonic Genus* 4, rotate interval ratio $\frac{13}{12}$ and place it in the first position; then substitute interval ratio $\frac{9}{8}$ for $\frac{8}{7}$, and place ratio $\frac{9}{8}$ in the second position; the result is Ibn Sīnā's *Diatonic Genus* 7 in Row 5. Turn back to Figure 11.62, and observe that we may play this tetrachord on Ibn Sīnā's *'ūd* in the following manner: *Open String, Assistant to the Middle Finger of Zalzal, Middle Finger of Zalzal, Little Finger.*

In *Diatonic Genus* 7, switch the positions of interval ratios $\frac{13}{12}$ and $\frac{9}{8}$. Two crisscrossed arrows show that such a change results in interval ratios $\frac{9}{8}$, $\frac{13}{12}$, $\frac{128}{117}$. A long vertical arrow that

Table 11.31

NEAR-EQUAL DIVISIONS OF INTERVALS IN THE TETRACHORDS OF PTOLEMY, AL-FĀRĀBĪ, AND IBN SĪNĀ

	Origins	Interval Ratios	Ancient Length Ratios or Frequency Ratios
1(a). Ptolemy, *Even Diatonic*	4/3 × 3/3 = 12/9; 12:11:10:9	12/11, 11/10, 10/9 151 ¢, 165 ¢, 182 ¢	1/1, 12/11, 6/5, 4/3 0 ¢, 151 ¢, 316 ¢, 498 ¢
1(b). Arabian Order, *Even Diatonic*	10/9, 12/11, 11/10	10/9, 12/11, 11/10 182 ¢, 151 ¢, 165 ¢	1/1, 10/9, 40/33, 4/3 0 ¢, 182 ¢, 333 ¢, 498 ¢
2. Al-Fārābī, *Jins* 2	1 + 3/4 + 3/4	9/8, 12/11, 88/81 204 ¢, 151 ¢, 143 ¢	1/1, 9/8, 27/22, 4/3 0 ¢, 204 ¢, 355 ¢, 498 ¢
3. Al-Fārābī, *Jins* 8	5/6 + 5/6 + 5/6	32/29, 58/53, 53/48 170 ¢, 156 ¢, 172 ¢	1/1, 32/29, 64/53, 4/3 0 ¢, 170 ¢, 326 ¢, 498 ¢
4. Ibn Sīnā, *Diatonic Genus* 4	8/7 × 7/6 = 4/3; 7/6 × 2/2 = 14/12; 14:13:12	8/7, 14/13, 13/12 231 ¢, 128 ¢, 139 ¢	1/1, 8/7, 16/13, 4/3 0 ¢, 231 ¢, 359 ¢, 498 ¢
5. Ibn Sīnā, *Diatonic Genus* 7	9/8, [*not* 9/8, 10/9, 11/10, 12/11], 13/12, 128/117	13/12, 9/8, 128/117 139 ¢, 204 ¢, 156 ¢	1/1, 13/12, 39/32, 4/3 0 ¢, 139 ¢, 342 ¢, 498 ¢
6. Ibn Sīnā, *Diatonic Genus* 7 in Melodic Modes 1, 3(b), and 8 or *Mustaqīm*		9/8, 13/12, 128/117 204 ¢, 139 ¢, 156 ¢	1/1, 9/8, 39/32, 4/3 0 ¢, 204 ¢, 342 ¢, 498 ¢
7. Ibn Sīnā, *Diatonic Genus* 7 in Melodic Mode 2		9/8, 13/12, 128/117 204 ¢, 139 ¢, 156 ¢	4/3, 3/2, 13/8, 16/9 498 ¢, 702 ¢, 841 ¢, 996 ¢
8. Ibn Sīnā, Descending *Diatonic Genus* 7 in Melodic Mode 7(c) or *Nawā*		↓ 9/8, 128/117, 13/12 204 ¢, 156 ¢, 139 ¢	2/1, 16/9, 13/8, 3/2 1200 ¢, 996 ¢, 841 ¢, 702 ¢

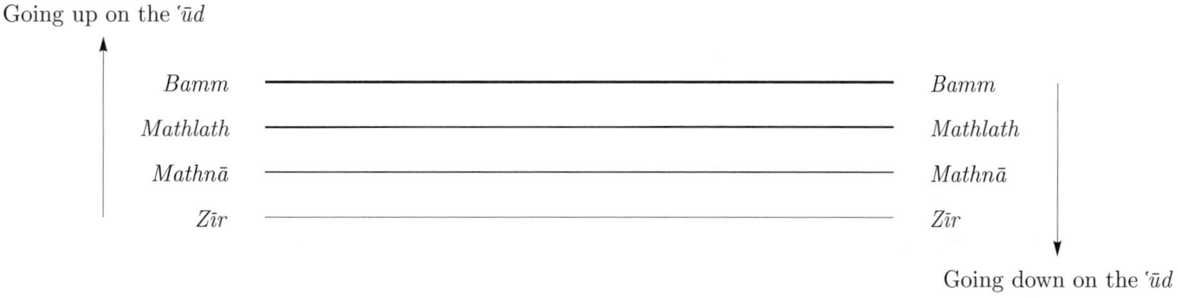

Figure 11.65 Going up and down on the lute. When one holds the *'ūd* in the normal playing position, observe that the *Bamm* is the upper string, and the *Zīr* is the lower string. Therefore, when one goes up, or ascends on the lute, the tones of a given mode descend in frequency; conversely, when one goes down, or descends on the lute, the tones of a given mode ascend in frequency.

points from Rows 1(b) and 2 to Row 6 indicates the intervalic similarities between Ptolemy's *Even Diatonic*, Al-Fārābī's *Jins* 2, and Ibn Sīnā's *Diatonic Genus* 7.

In Section 11.63, we will discuss Ibn Sīnā's 11 Melodic Modes. Turn to Table 11.32, and observe that in Modes 1, 3(b), and 8, *Diatonic Genus* 7 ascends from the tonic, ratio 1/1. Ibn Sīnā refers to Mode 8 as *Mustaqīm*, an Arabic word that literally means *direct*, or *straight*.[107] Now, turn back to Table 11.31, Row 7, which shows that in Mode 2, the *Mustaqīm* tetrachord ascends from the "fourth," ratio 4/3, to the "minor seventh," ratio 16/9. Finally, switch the positions of interval ratios 13/12 and 128/117. Two crisscrossed arrows indicate that such a change results in interval ratios 9/8, 128/117, 13/12. Row 8 verifies that in Mode 7(c), also called *Nawā*, the latter tetrachord descends from the "octave," ratio 2/1.

11.63

Before we examine these modes, let us first address two difficulties. The first problem is strictly technical. Ibn Sīnā states that in playing the modes one ". . . goes up . . ." on the lute, and ". . . descends . . ." on the lute. To dispel the possibility of confusion, Figure 11.65 indicates the locations of the *Bamm*, *Mathlath*, *Mathnā*, and *Zīr* when one holds the *'ūd* in the normal playing position, like a guitar. Contemplate that the upper string, or the string tuned to the lowest frequency, is the *Bamm* and, conversely, the lower string, or the string tuned to the highest frequency, is the *Zīr*.

The second problem is strictly interpretive. In *La Musique Arabe, Volume 2*, pp. 239–243, I do not agree with the musical interpretations of Modes 1, 4 and 11. Immediately below the following English translation, I give brief explanations for these objections. Readers who need to examine these differences of opinion in full detail should consult *La Musique Arabe* directly.

{Mode 1}

> As for the modes that one usually plays on the lute, first are all those built with the help of the *diatonic* genus; then all those built with the help of a genus made of the intervals . . . {1 + 1/8 = 9/8}, 1 + 1/12 {13:12}, and a *complement* . . . {1 + 11/117 = 128/117} which can be produced by an open string, its *index finger*, its *middle finger of Zalzal*, and its *little finger*.

{Mode 2}

> One also plays a mode on the lute composed of the two previously mentioned genera {Philolaus' Greek diatonic tetrachord, and Ibn Sīnā's

Arabian diatonic tetrachord}; the mode is organized over two strings and includes the intervals (. . . that begin on the upper) {string, or *Bamm*}.

{Modes 3(a), 3(b)}

One also could have added a tone {$9/8$} to one of the two genera, and the whole (a fifth) would have been contained between the index finger of one string {*Mathlath*} and the string placed above . . . played open {*Bamm*}.

{Mode 4, or *Unspecified Mode*}

One also uses a mode that begins with the little finger [of the fourth string] {*Zīr*} and ends with the note of the open second {*Mathlath*}, and whose notes follow each other thus, tan, tan, tan, etc.

{Modes 5(a), 5(b)}

One also plays a mode that proceeds not like the previous ones, but as follows:

Second String {*Mathlath*} { little finger
Persian middle finger
index finger
open string

One sometimes goes until reaching the middle finger of Zalzal on the first string {*Bamm*} . . .

{Modes 6(a), 6(b), 6(c)}

One also plays a mode that begins with the index finger of the fourth string {*Zīr*} and continues as follows: tone, tone, limma, tone, tone, note of the middle finger of Zalzal; sometimes, one goes up {on the lute} just to the index finger [of the second string] {*Mathlath*} and to the open string . . . Other times, one descends {on the lute} a tone beyond the index finger of the fourth string.

{Modes 7(a), 7(b), 7(c), or *Nawā*}

As for the mode assigned the name *Nawā*, it proceeds by descending . . . {in frequency} over two strings (4th and 3rd) {*Zīr* and *Mathnā*} and playing on them the intervals: limma, tone, tone, limma, tone, tone; then, advancing from the third string (to the 2nd from the lowest) {*Mathlath*} to the note of the middle finger of Zalzal.

One sometimes descends {on the lute} . . . one tone, thus going beyond the little finger of the fourth string. {On the *Zīr*, this position is not a fret, but the location of ratio $32/9$ [$16/9$ above $2/1$]. See Figure 11.62.} And one sometimes ascends {on the lute} above the middle finger of Zalzal (of the 2nd string) {*Mathlath*} just to the index finger, or even higher still . . .

{Mode 8, or *Mustaqīm*}

One also plays on the lute a mode called "regular" (*Mustaqīm*), using for this purpose all the open strings, their index fingers, and their middle fingers of Zalzal.

{Mode 9}

One plays yet another mode containing a genus based on the interval $1 + \frac{1}{7}$ {8:7}. One begins on the middle finger of Zalzal [of the 4th string] {*Zīr*}; one then plays the *anterior fret* {the first fret}, (i.e., the one at $1 + \frac{1}{7}$ of the middle finger of Zalzal) {$\frac{13}{9} \div \frac{91}{72} = \frac{8}{7}$} and the open string; then the middle finger of Zalzal of the next string up {*Mathnā*} . . . and the index finger. It is customary to then play, giving it emphasis . . . , the *anterior fret* of this last string {$\frac{91}{48}$}, and to return to the index finger.

{Mode 10, or *Iṣfahān*}

One also plays another mode similar to the previous one yet distinct. One uses, for example, the middle finger of Zalzal of the fourth string {*Zīr*}, then the anterior fret; then the open fourth string, the middle finger of Zalzal of the third string {*Mathnā*}, its anterior fret, and the open string, then the ring finger of the second string {*Mathlath*} and its anterior fret. This mode is named *Iṣfahān.*

{Mode 11, or *Salmakī*}

Furthermore, one plays a mode known by the name of *Salmakī*, composed of the intervals: tone, tone, limma, tone, limma, ***approximately*** $1 + \frac{1}{5}$ {6:5}.

One achieves it by starting from the ring finger of the fourth string {*Zīr*}, and by playing its index finger, then the open string, the ring finger of the third string {*Mathnā*}, its index finger, its anterior fret and the anterior fret of the second string {*Mathlath*}.[108] (Bold italics, and text and ratios in braces mine. Text in parentheses and brackets in *La Musique Arabe.*)

Mode 1. I disagree with the musical interpretation of this mode in *La Musique Arabe, Volume 2*, p. 239, Figure 2. In the French translation, serious inconsistencies exist between numeric descriptions of interval ratios and verbal descriptions of frets. Since numeric errors are commonplace, I give this mode a strictly verbal interpretation. In the English translation, interval ratios in braces are consistent with Ibn Sīnā's *implicit* description of intervals between frets.

Mode 4. This is an *Unspecified Mode.* I disagree with the musical interpretation of this mode in *La Musique Arabe, Volume 2*, p. 240, Figure 5. Based on Ibn Sīnā's numeric and verbal descriptions, Table 11.32, Mode 4, gives my interpretation of the *Unspecified Mode*, which, *like all other modes*, upholds the following two principles of scale construction: (1) The first four tones must span a tetrachord, ratio $\frac{4}{3}$. (2) Throughout the 11 Melodic Modes, Ibn Sīnā does not use the second fret called the "assistant to the middle finger of Zalzal."

Mode 11, or *Salmakī.* In *La Musique Arabe, Volume 2*, p. 243, the subsequent commentary in brackets correctly observes that the last two notes do not produce the interval of a "minor third," ratio $\frac{6}{5}$, but the interval of a "fourth," ratio $\frac{4}{3}$. The commentary then gives the middle finger of Zalzal of the second string as the final tone. The interval thus created is ratio $\frac{7}{6}$: $\frac{91}{48} \div \frac{13}{8} = \frac{7}{6}$, and is, therefore, incorrect. To achieve Ibn Sīnā's $\frac{6}{5}$ approximation, the final tone must be the Persian middle finger of the second string: $\frac{91}{48} \div \frac{128}{81} = \frac{2457}{2048} \approx \frac{6}{5}$.

Turn now to Table 11.32, which illustrates my musical interpretations of Ibn Sīnā's 11 Melodic Modes. Square brackets below each staff indicate that every mode begins with either an ascending or a descending tetrachord. Furthermore, combinations of square brackets and curly brackets indicate ascending or descending modal versions of Ibn Sīnā's *Diatonic Genus* 7. Finally, a sole

Table 11.32

IBN SĪNĀ'S 11 MELODIC MODES

Table 11.32
(continued)
IBN SĪNĀ'S 11 MELODIC MODES

Nawā

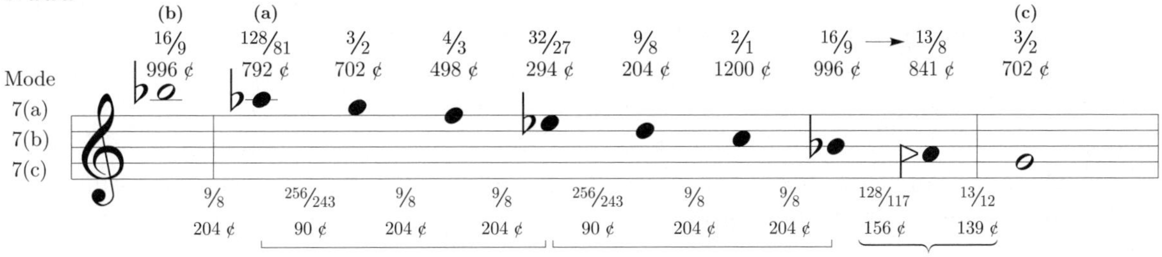

Mustaqīm

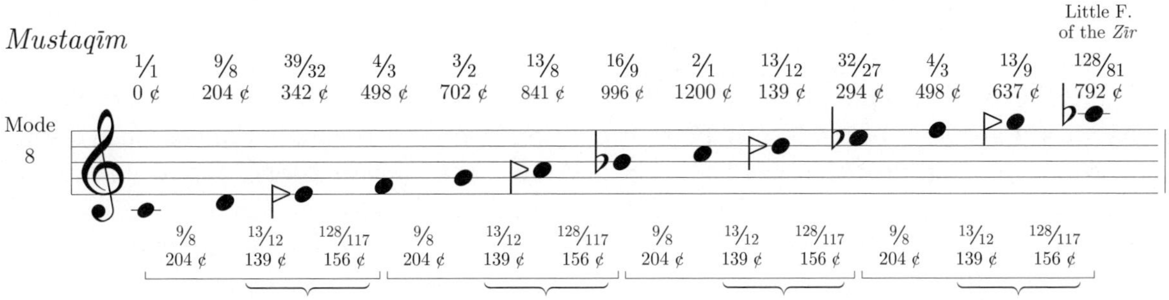

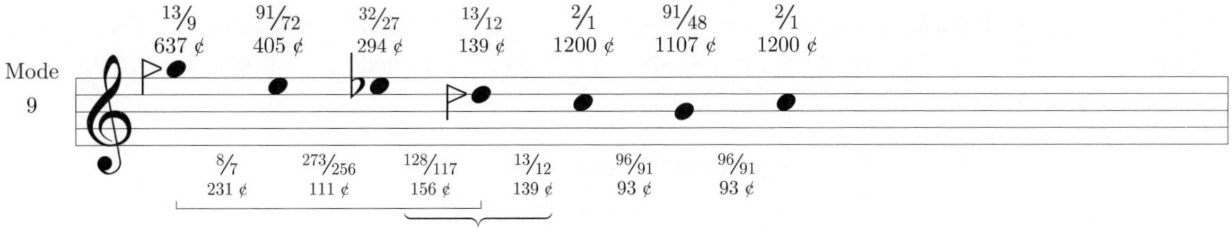

Iṣfahān

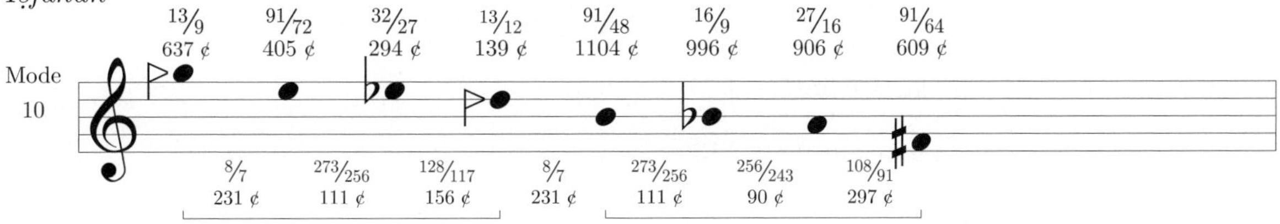

Salmakī

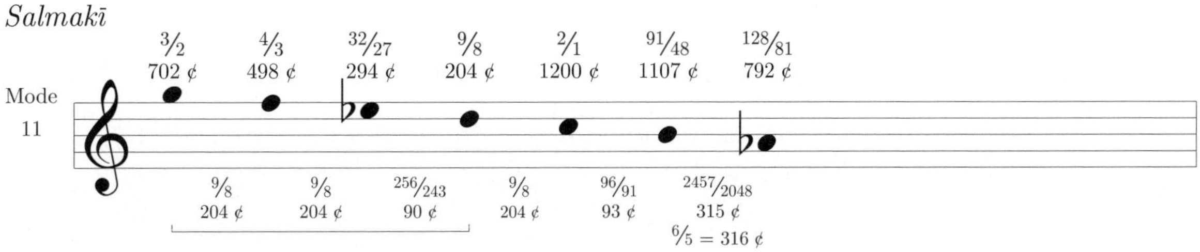

curly bracket in Mode 7(b) identifies descending interval ratios: $^{128}/_{117}$, $^{13}/_{12}$, which first appear in Mode 3(a); similarly, an overlapping square bracket and curly bracket in Mode 9 identifies the same descending sequence: $^{128}/_{117}$, $^{13}/_{12}$.

Although some modern writers have criticized these modes because they lack consistency with regard to the idealized structures of Greek music theory, I do not share these concerns. On the contrary, Ibn Sīnā's mastery of musical mathematics leaves no doubt that his melodic modes are exuberant expressions of an enlightened mind. He is not in the least intimidated to compare, combine, and juxtapose Philolaus' Diatonic Tetrachord with his own *Diatonic Genus* 7. Moreover, arrows that point from $^{4}/_{3}$ to $^{39}/_{32}$ in Modes 5(a) and 5(b), from $^{128}/_{81}$ to $^{13}/_{8}$ in Mode 6(a), and from $^{16}/_{9}$ to $^{13}/_{8}$ in Mode 7(a) indicate that he intentionally disrupted the flow of conventional 3-limit ratios through the interjection of 13-limit ratios.

11.64

Born in 980 at Afshana, near Bukhārā, and buried in Hamadān in 1037, Ibn Sīnā spent his entire life within the territory of the former Persian Empire. The most celebrated philosopher of the Islamic world, Ibn Sīnā wrote most of his works in Arabic, the *lingua franca* of the Arabian Empire. However, because Ibn Sīnā was a theorist of Persian descent, we must now examine modern Persian music to determine the historical significance of his 17-tone scale and his 13-limit ratios.

In 1959 and 1964, Hormoz Farhat measured the intervals of three *setārs* and two *tārs*, all fretted and played by professional musicians.[109] He conducted his research with the aid of a stroboconn, an electronic instrument that converts frequencies into cents. With this data, Farhat concluded that Persian music primarily consists of *nine melodic intervals*.[110] Of these, the most important are the five smallest intervals.

A "minor second": $(m) \approx 90$ ¢.
A "major second": $(M) \approx 204$ ¢.
A "small neutral second": $(n) \approx 135$ ¢.
A "large neutral second": $(N) \approx 160$ ¢.
A "plus second": $(P) \approx 270$ ¢.

The remaining four are the largest intervals.

A "minor third": *c.* 135 ¢ + *c.* 160 ¢ ≈ 295 ¢.
A "major third": *c.* 135 ¢ + *c.* 270 ¢ ≈ 405 ¢.
A "small neutral third": *c.* 204 ¢ + *c.* 135 ¢ ≈ 339 ¢.
A "large neutral third": *c.* 270 ¢ + *c.* 90 ¢ ≈ 360 ¢.

In his dissertation (1965) and book (1990), Farhat states that the "small neutral third" ≈ 335 ¢.

> . . . as a result of the combination of a ***major 2nd and a neutral 2nd*** . . . a smaller neutral 3rd of about 335 cents will result.[111] (Bold italics mine.)

Actually, this is not quite accurate because his derivation ". . . a major 2nd and a neutral 2nd . . ." yields *c.* 204 ¢ + *c.* 135 ¢ ≈ 339 ¢, or a "small neutral third," which is closer to 340 ¢. Also, a comparison between these two texts reveals that Farhat decreased the average cent value of the "large neutral third" from *c.* 365 ¢ to *c.* 360 ¢.[112] He describes this interval in the following manner:

> . . . a result of the combination of a . . . ***plus 2nd and a minor 2nd*** . . . will always be of the larger type [of neutral 3rd] close to 360 cents.[113] (Bold italics, and text in brackets mine.)

Finally, with respect to the "minor third" and the "major third," Farhat specifies the order of the constituent intervals.

> Often two neutral 2nds occur in succession to complete the range of a minor 3rd (295 cents). In such situations, ***the lower of the two tends to be the smaller*** (e.g. 135 + 160 = 295).[114] (Bold italics mine.)
>
> In Persian modal structures, [the "plus second"] ***is always preceded by a small neutral 2nd***, thus the succession of the two completes the range of a major 3rd (135 + 270 = 405).[115] (Bold italics, and text in brackets mine.)

Turn now to Figure 11.66, which shows Farhat's nine melodic intervals in the left sections of Rows 1–9, and the closest intervals on Ibn Sīnā's *'ūd* in the right sections of Rows 1–9. Note carefully that the largest discrepancy between these two sets of intervals equals only 4 ¢. Such a high rate of coincidence is truly mind boggling given a span of about 950 years between Ibn Sīnā's *'ūd* tuning description and Farhat's cent analysis.

Farhat's analysis consists of average cent values taken from two *tārs* and three *setārs*.[116] These fretted Persian instruments have identical ranges of approximately "two octaves and a fifth," or from C_3 (one "octave" below middle C_4), to G_6 (one "fifth" above high C_5). Since every string on a *tār* or *setār* has between twenty to twenty-seven frets, each string produces at least one 17-tone "octave."

Figure 11.67, Column 1, gives the average cent values of the intervals between frets, Column 2, the cumulative cent values of the scale degrees as one ascends from C_4 to C_5, Column 3, Farhat's note names, and Column 4, Ibn Sīnā's 17-tone scale in cents. In the last column, underlined cent values indicate the four largest discrepancies between these two scales: Ibn Sīnā's [C♯], ratio 273/256, is 21 ¢ sharp of D♭; [F♯], ratio 91/64, is 44 ¢ sharp of F𝄲; [B], ratio 91/48, is 67 ¢ sharp of B𝄳; and C𝄳, ratio 52/27, is 25 ¢ sharp of B. For the remaining 13 intervals, the greatest difference is Ibn Sīnā's G𝄳, ratio 13/9, which is only 7 ¢ sharp of the *tār's* G𝄳.

These former four discrepancies are not as severe as they appear. Farhat explains that in Persian music there is no chromaticism, which means that musicians do not play intervals between successive frets.

> It must also be understood that the fretting system shown here has been provided to accommodate all the Persian modes within the given range. Any one mode does not require more than seven or eight pitches. Indeed, some modes may be adequately expressed within the range of a tetrachord or a pentachord. No chromaticism is used, e.g., *e*♭ and *e*♮, or *f*𝄲 and *g*𝄳 are not used in succession. Accordingly a 45-cents or a 70-cents interval, as shown in the above fretting, have no consecutive application in any one of the modes. ***No interval smaller than a semi-tone (ca. ninety cents) is ever used.*** The only exception is an ornamental trill from, for example, *e*♭ to *e*𝄳 which is used in certain modes but is not essential to the structure of those modes.[117] (Bold italics mine.)

Furthermore, the previously mentioned scale degrees: D♭, F𝄲, B𝄳, and B occur only rarely; one encounters them in the context of secondary melodic modes, which are based on twelve primary melodic modes. As discussed and demonstrated in Section 11.66, one may play all twelve primary melodic modes of modern Persian music on Ibn Sīnā's *'ūd* without incurring any significant intonational distortions.

(1) Farhat: "minor second" $(m) \approx 90$ ¢ — Ibn Sīnā: $^{32}/_{27} \div {}^{9}/_{8} = {}^{256}/_{243} = 90$ ¢; $^{4}/_{3} \div {}^{91}/_{72} = {}^{96}/_{91} = 93$ ¢

---

(2) Farhat: "major second" $(M) \approx 204$ ¢ — Ibn Sīnā: $^{9}/_{8} = 204$ ¢; $^{91}/_{48} \div {}^{27}/_{16} = {}^{91}/_{81} = 202$ ¢

---

(3) Farhat: "small neutral second" $(n) \approx 135$ ¢ — Ibn Sīnā: $^{13}/_{12} = 139$ ¢

---

(4) Farhat: "large neutral second" $(N) \approx 160$ ¢ — Ibn Sīnā: $^{32}/_{27} \div {}^{13}/_{12} = {}^{128}/_{117} = 156$ ¢

---

(5) Farhat: "plus second" $(P) \approx 270$ ¢ — Ibn Sīnā: $^{81}/_{64} \div {}^{13}/_{12} = {}^{243}/_{208} = 269$ ¢; $^{91}/_{48} \div {}^{13}/_{8} = {}^{7}/_{6} = 267$ ¢

---

(6) Farhat: "minor third" ≈ 295 ¢ — Ibn Sīnā: "minor third" $= {}^{32}/_{27} = 294$ ¢

Farhat: C —n, 135 ¢— D$^{\triangleright}$ —N, 160 ¢— E♭; 135 ¢ + 160 ¢ = 295 ¢

Ibn Sīnā: C —$^{13}/_{12}$, 139 ¢— D$^{\triangleright}$ —$^{128}/_{117}$, 156 ¢— E♭; $^{13}/_{12} \times {}^{128}/_{117} = {}^{32}/_{27} = 294$ ¢

---

(7) Farhat: "major third" ≈ 405 ¢ — Ibn Sīnā: "major third" $= {}^{81}/_{64} = 408$ ¢

Farhat: C —n, 135 ¢— D$^{\triangleright}$ —P, 270 ¢— E; 135 ¢ + 270 ¢ = 405 ¢

Ibn Sīnā: C —$^{13}/_{12}$, 139 ¢— D$^{\triangleright}$ —$^{243}/_{208}$, 269 ¢— E; $^{13}/_{12} \times {}^{243}/_{208} = {}^{81}/_{64} = 408$ ¢

---

(8) Farhat: "small neutral third" ≈ 340 ¢ — Ibn Sīnā: "small neutral third" $= {}^{39}/_{32} = 342$ ¢

Farhat: C —M, 204 ¢— D —n, 135 ¢— E$^{\triangleright}$; 204 ¢ + 135 ¢ = 339 ¢

Ibn Sīnā: C —$^{9}/_{8}$, 204 ¢— D —$^{13}/_{12}$, 139 ¢— E$^{\triangleright}$; $^{9}/_{8} \times {}^{13}/_{12} = {}^{39}/_{32} = 342$ ¢

---

(9) Farhat: "large neutral third" ≈ 360 ¢ — Ibn Sīnā: "large neutral third" $= {}^{16}/_{13} = 359$ ¢

Farhat: D$^{\triangleright}$ —P, 270 ¢— E —m, 90 ¢— F; 270 ¢ + 90 ¢ = 360 ¢

Ibn Sīnā: D$^{\triangleright}$ —$^{243}/_{208}$, 269 ¢— E —$^{256}/_{243}$, 90 ¢— F; $^{243}/_{208} \times {}^{256}/_{243} = {}^{16}/_{13} = 359$ ¢

Figure 11.66 A comparison between the nine melodic intervals of modern Persian music as described in Farhat's texts, and the closest intervals on Ibn Sīnā's *'ūd*. The greatest discrepancy between these two sets of intervals equals only 4 ¢.

Average Cents of Modern *Tārs* and *Setārs*	(1)	Cumulative Cents (2)	(3)	Ibn Sīnā's 17-Tone *'Ūd* Scale in Cents (4)
Open String			C_4	1/1 = 0 ¢
c. 205 ¢	*c.* 90 ¢	90 ¢	D♭	273/256 = 111 ¢
	c. 45 ¢	135 ¢	D𝄳	13/12 = 139 ¢
	c. 70 ¢	205 ¢	D	9/8 = 204 ¢
c. 205 ¢	*c.* 90 ¢	295 ¢	E♭	32/27 = 294 ¢
	c. 45 ¢	340 ¢	E𝄳	39/32 = 342 ¢
	c. 70 ¢	410 ¢	E	81/64 = 408 ¢
c. 90 ¢	*c.* 90 ¢	500 ¢	F	4/3 = 498 ¢
c. 200 ¢	*c.* 65 ¢	565 ¢	F𝄲	91/64 = 609 ¢
	c. 65 ¢	630 ¢	G𝄳	13/9 = 637 ¢
	c. 70 ¢	700 ¢	G	3/2 = 702 ¢
c. 205 ¢	*c.* 90 ¢	790 ¢	A♭	128/81 = 792 ¢
	c. 45 ¢	835 ¢	A𝄳	13/8 = 841 ¢
	c. 70 ¢	905 ¢	A	27/16 = 906 ¢
c. 205 ¢	*c.* 90 ¢	995 ¢	B♭	16/9 = 996 ¢
	c. 45 ¢	1040 ¢	B𝄳	91/48 = 1107 ¢
	c. 70 ¢	1110 ¢	B	52/27 = 1135 ¢
c. 90 ¢	*c.* 90 ¢	1200 ¢	C_5	2/1 = 1200 ¢

Figure 11.67 A comparison between Farhat's average intervals of modern Persian 17-tone *tār* and *setār* scales (*c.* 1965), and Ibn Sīnā's 17-tone *'ūd* scale (*c.* 1015). Column 1 gives Farhat's average cent values, Column 2, the cumulative cents, Column 3, Farhat's note names, and Column 4, Ibn Sīnā's scale in cents. In Column 4, underlined values indicate the four largest discrepancies between these two scales. For the remaining 13 intervals, the greatest difference is Ibn Sīnā's 13/9, which is only 7 ¢ sharp of G𝄳. (Fret locations to scale.)

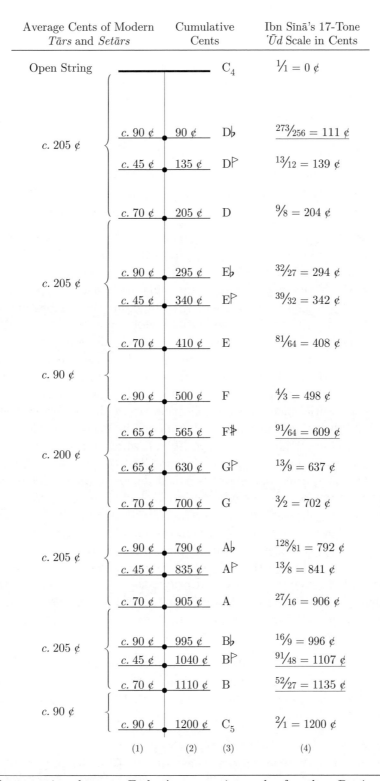

∼ 11.65 ∼

The concept of primary and secondary modes is reminiscent of *janaka* and *janya rāgas* described in Section 11.35. Before we discuss similarities between Indian music and Persian music, let us first draw two critical distinctions. In Indian music, musicians improvise on a given *rāga*, and never modulate to a different *rāga*. In Persian music, however, (1) musicians improvise on a collection of modes, (2) which requires them to modulate to different modes. Such a group of three to fifteen individual modes is called a *dastgāh* (pl. *dastgāha;* lit. *organization*, or *system*). The name of a *dastgāh* also refers to a specific mode heard at the beginning, during cadential patterns in the middle, and often at the end of a performance. One of several individual modes of a *dastgāh* is called a *gushe* (pl. *gushehā;* lit. *corner*, *section*, or *piece*). Farhat describes the relation between *dastgāh* and *gushe* in this way:

> Two separate ideas are, in fact, addressed by the *dastgāh* concept. [1] It identifies a set of pieces, traditionally grouped together, most of which have their own individual modes [or *gushehā*]. [2] It also stands for the modal identity of the initial piece in the group. This mode has a position of dominance as it is brought back frequently, throughout the performance of the group of pieces, in the guise of cadential melodic patterns.
>
> Accordingly, a *dastgāh* signifies both the title of a grouping of modes, of which there are twelve, and the initial mode presented in each group. When we say, for example, *dastgāh-e Homāyun*, we mean a group of pieces under the collective name *Homāyun;* as a mode, however, *Homāyun* only identifies the initial piece of that collection. It would be wrong, therefore, to conclude that there are only twelve modes in Persian music; there are twelve groupings of modes, the totality of which represents some sixty modes. Each mode has its own proper name, but the opening section of the *dastgāh* has no specific name and is called *darāmad* (entry, introduction). The proper name of this opening section is that of the *dastgāh* itself.
>
> The practice of grouping pieces into collections and the application of the term *dastgāh* is of a relatively recent origin. There is no evidence for the practice having existed prior to the Qājār period [or dynasty], (1787–1925). For all we know, before the nineteenth century, modes or *maqāms* were performed individually, as they still are in the Turko-Arabian traditions. Presumably a series of improvisations and compositions were performed in the same mode to cover the desired length of time.[118] (Text and numbers in brackets mine.)

Modern Persian theorists disagree over the classification of *dastgāhā*. Some recognize seven original or primary modes, and five derived or secondary modes. Others maintain that all twelve are original and equally independent modes. In the text below, Farhat explains various aspects of this controversy, and gives his reasons for classifying all twelve *dastgāhā* as primary modes:

> A further clarification of the *dastgāh* concept is required here. The prevailing notion among Persian musicians assigns the title *dastgāh* to only seven of the modal systems: *Shur*, *Segāh*, *Chahārgāh*, [*Māhur*], *Homāyun*, *Navā*, and *Rāst-Panjgāh.* Four of the remaining five, *Abuatā*, *Bayāt-e Tork* (or *Bayāt-e Zand*), *Dashti*, and *Afshāri* are classified as derivatives of *Shur;* the remaining, *Bayāt-e Esfahān* is considered to be a derivative of *Homāyun.* These five are not called *dastgāh*, but the word *āvāz* (song) is used as their generic title.
>
> I have preferred to classify all twelve as *dastgāhs.* In so doing I am not defying a weighty or a long-standing tradition. It must be borne in mind

> that the whole system of the twelve groupings is not very old, and the classifications are fairly arbitrary and without strong reasoning . . .
>
> The reason for recognizing five, or seven, of the twelve as being derivative is that tradition, or [A.N.] Vaziri [1886–1981] as the case may be, has viewed the five, or the seven, as less distinct in their initial modes than the others. The view has been that the dominant mode of a *dastgāh* must have very striking characteristics, including a very distinct structure of intervals. If the initial modes in two *dastgāhs* make use of the same pitch material, even when their functions and melodic dictates are different, then one of the modes is considered a dependent of the other. For example, it is said that if we begin and build from the fourth degree of the mode of *Homāyun*, we shall obtain *Bayāt-e Esfahān*. For that reason *Bayāt-e Esfahān* is known as a derivative of *Homāyun*. This is clearly a fallacious argument. If this were a valid basis for classification then western music would have but one mode; Phrygian [white piano keys between E–E′] could be regarded as a derivative of Dorian [white keys between D–D′], as it begins on the second degree of that mode . . .
>
> The prevailing opinions, as well as those of Vaziri and others, have misunderstood what a mode is. A mode is not a mere assortment of pitches and the resultant intervals. ***Far more important is the function of the tones in the creation of music.*** Notes by themselves do not constitute music; it is in how they are put together that music is made.
>
> In all modal concepts, and certainly in a musical tradition such as the Persian, where improvisation on the basis of certain melodic patterns is fundamental to musical creativity, ***functions of tones are of paramount importance.*** Any similarity in the pitch material of the modes of, say, *Homāyun* and *Bayāt-e Esfahān* is of little significance. What is important is whether or not the melodic patterns that form the frame of reference in both modes are the same. They certainly are not; had they been the same they would not have been identified with two different titles. I have therefore applied the term *dastgāh* equally to all the twelve groupings, some of which are more extensive than others in the number of pieces (*gushes*) which they include.[119] (Bold italics, and text in brackets mine.)

In his musical examples, Farhat marks specific tones of the *dastgāhā* and *gushehā* with letters Ā, S, Ī, F, and M, to define the initial, prominent, semi-final, final, and fluctuating tones, respectively, of a given mode. Table 11.33 gives English translations of the Indian and Persian terms for such tones; the former represent the *lakṣaṇa* properties of early Indian music. (See Section 11.23.) We conclude, therefore, that in both Indian and Persian music, musicians assign different musical functions to the tones of similar sounding modes. This practice enables them to distinguish between such modes.

Table 11.33

English Translations	Indian Terms	Persian Terms
I, *initial*	*graha*	Ā, *āqāz*
P, *prominent*	*aṃśa*	S, *shāhed*
S, *semi-final*	*apanyāsa*	Ī, *īst*
F, *final*	*nyāsa*	F, [*finalis*]*
fluctuating tone		M, *moteqayyer*

*Farhat does not give the Persian term for *finalis*.

Table 11.34

FARHAT'S 12 MODERN PERSIAN *DASTGĀHĀ* AS REALIZED ON IBN SĪNĀ'S *'ŪD*

Dastgāh-e Shur

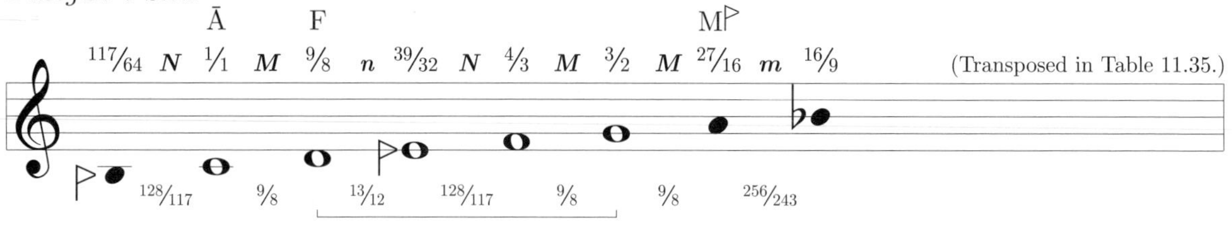

Dastgāh-e Abutā

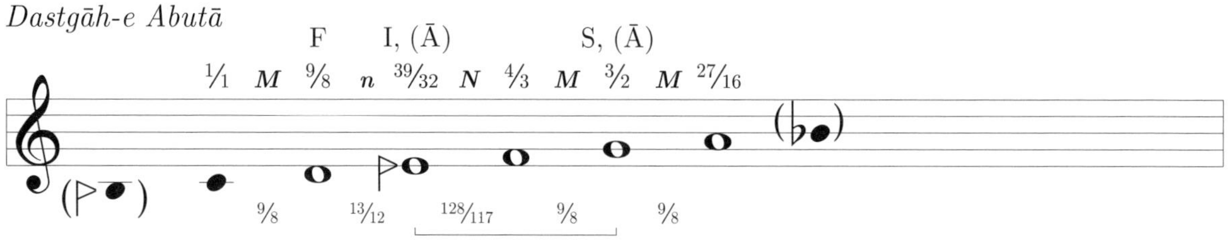

Dastgāh-e Dashti

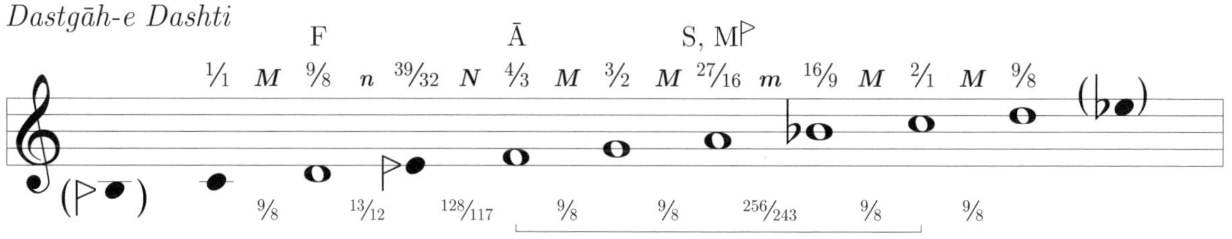

Dastgāh-e Bayāt-e Tork

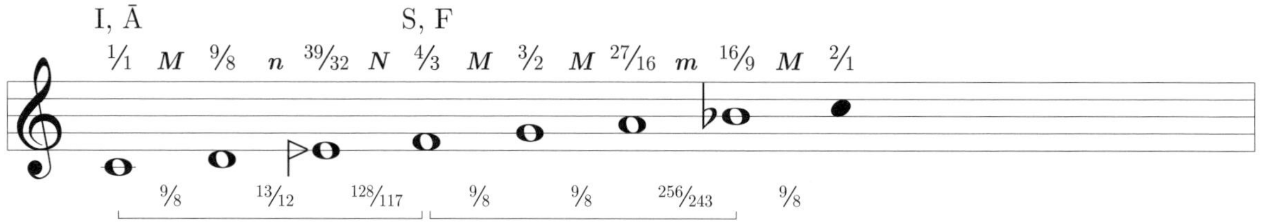

Dastgāh-e Afshari

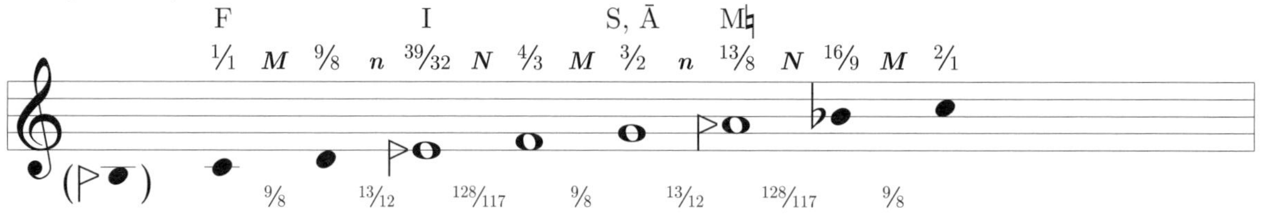

Dastgāh-e Segāh

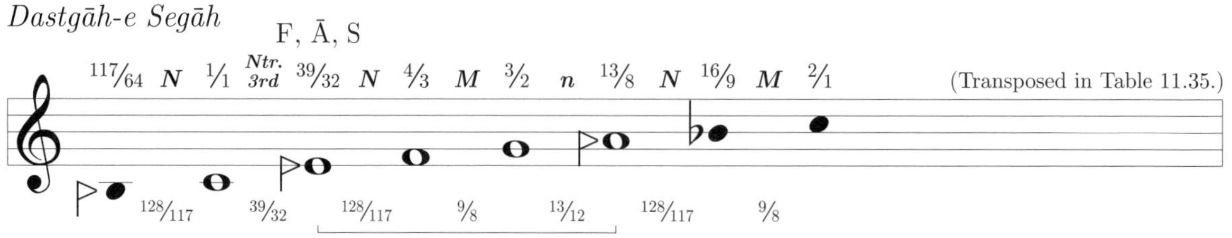

Table 11.34
(continued)

FARHAT'S 12 MODERN PERSIAN *DASTGĀHĀ* AS REALIZED ON IBN SĪNĀ'S *'ŪD*

Dastgāh-e Chahārgāh

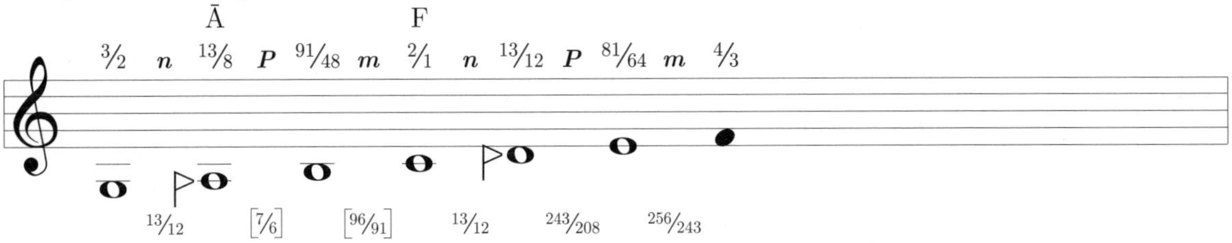

Dastgāh-e Homāyun

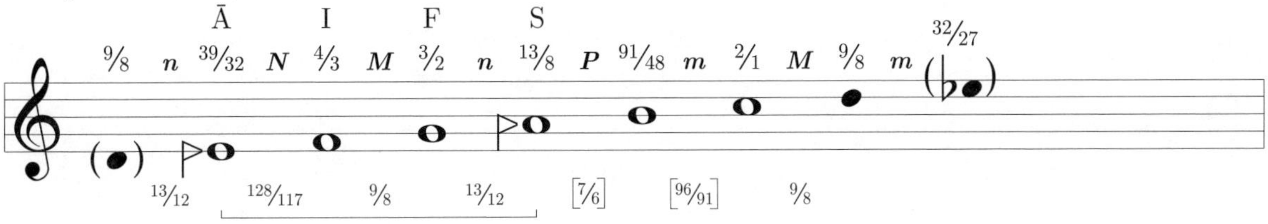

Dastgāh-e Esfahān

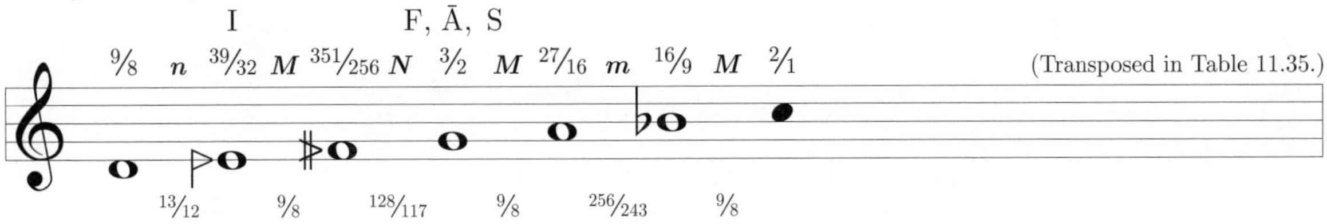

Dastgāh-e Navā

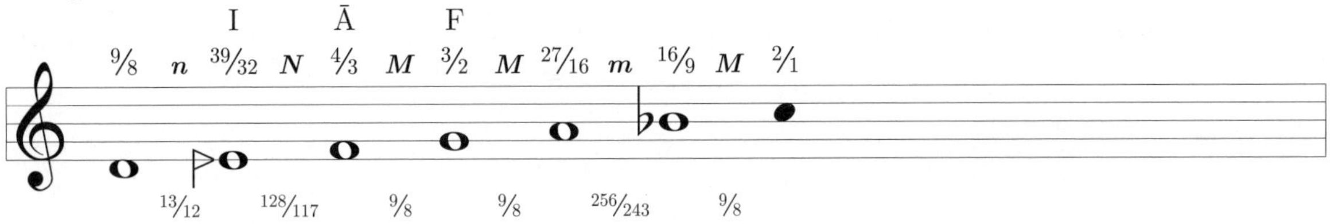

Dastgāh-e Māhur

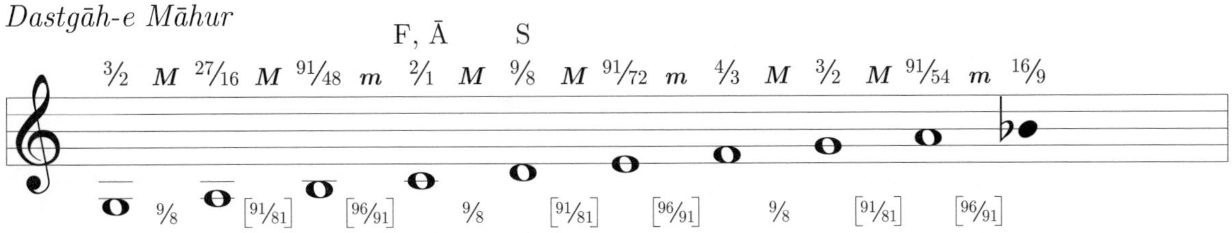

Dastgāh-e Rāst

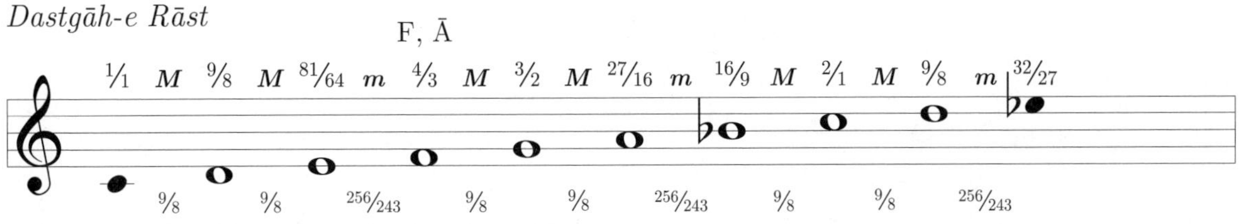

Table 11.35

THREE MODERN PERSIAN MODES TRANSPOSED ON IBN SĪNĀ'S *'ŪD*

Dastgāh-e Shur

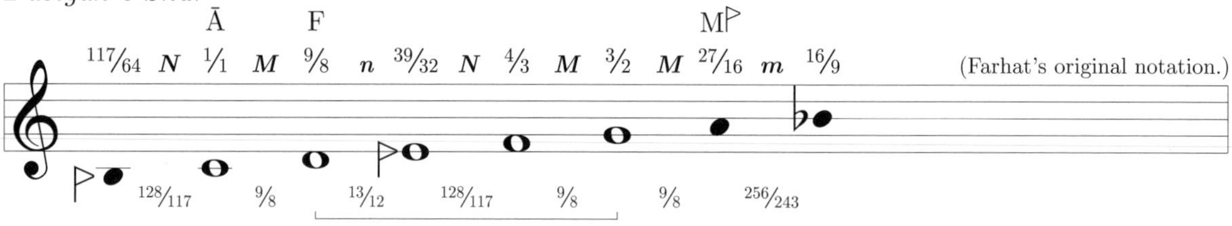

Dastgāh-e Shur

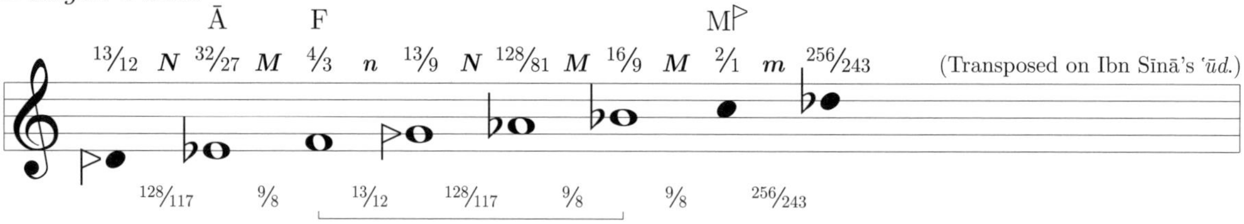

Dastgāh-e Segāh

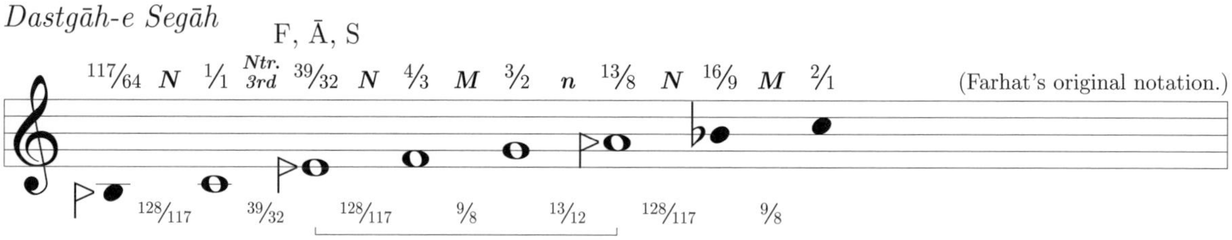

Dastgāh-e Segāh

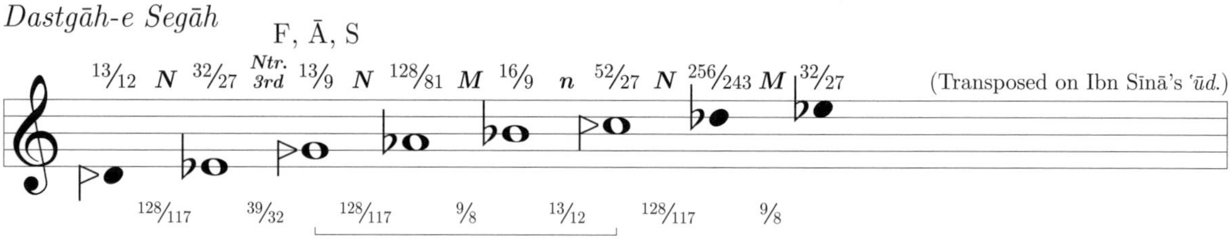

Dastgāh-e Esfahān

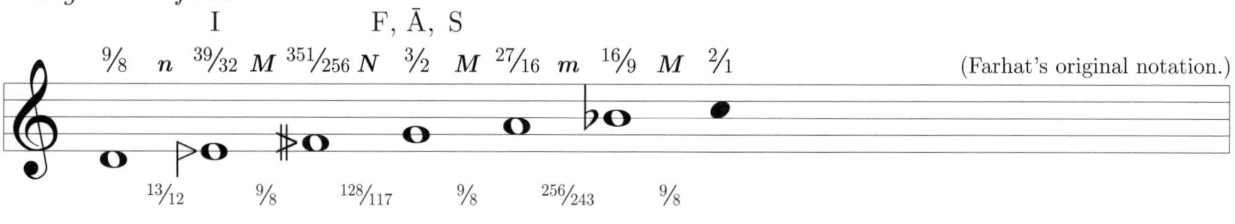

Dastgāh-e Esfahān

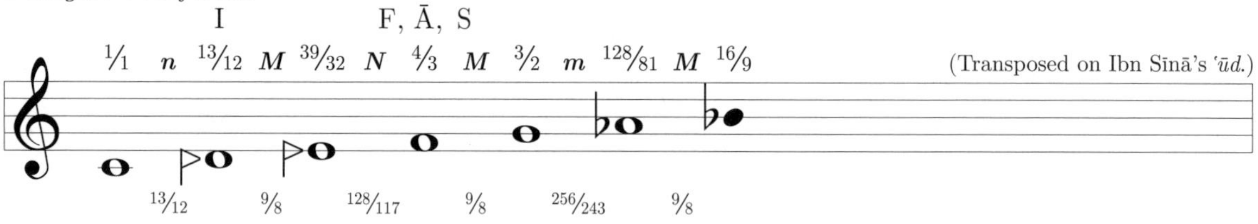

∼ 11.66 ∼

With this background information, we are now prepared to investigate the historical relevance of Ibn Sīnā's 17-tone *'ūd* tuning. Table 11.34 illustrates (1) the tones, (2) the intervals: *m*, *M*, *n*, *N*, *P*, and *Neutral Third*, (3) the musical functions of tones, and (4) the square brackets of twelve modern Persian *dastgāhā* as recorded in Farhat's book and dissertation.[120] For a given *dastgāh*, white notes signify the most important tones, black notes, less important tones, and parenthetical notes, least important tones. For some *dastgāhā*, a square bracket indicates a musical interval in which most of the melodic activity takes place.

Let us now resolve several technical difficulties regarding these musical examples. Turn back to Figure 11.66. The right sections of Rows 1, 2 and 5 confirm that Ibn Sīnā's 17-tone scale includes two "minor seconds" [256/243, 96/91], two "major seconds" [9/8, 91/81], and two "plus seconds" [243/208, 7/6]. For the first pair, the difference between interval ratios equals only 3 ¢, and for the second and third pairs, only 2 ¢. Consequently, the two interval ratios that constitute a given pair are musically indistinguishable and for all practical purposes identical. Farhat defines the first ratios of these pairs as $m \approx$ 256/243, $M \approx$ 9/8, and $P \approx$ 243/208. In Table 11.34, we must also define the second ratios of these pairs as $m \approx$ [96/91], $M \approx$ [91/81], and $P \approx$ [7/6], because on Ibn Sīnā's fretted *'ūd*, three *dastgāhā* — *Chahārgāh*, *Homāyun*, and *Māhur* — would otherwise not be playable.

Also, in Table 11.34, we cannot perform three *dastgāhā* on Ibn Sīnā's *'ūd* as notated in Farhat's texts. Since the *'ūd* does not include B𝄳$_3$ [117/64], or interval ratio 128/117 *below* C$_4$, we must transpose *Shur* and *Segāh*. Similarly, since the *'ūd* does not produce F𝄲$_4$ [351/256], or interval ratio 9/8 *above* E𝄳$_4$, we must also transpose *Esfahān*. Table 11.35 shows that if we transpose the lowest tones of *Shur* and *Segāh* from B𝄳$_3$ to D𝄳$_4$, and the lowest tone of *Esfahān* from D$_4$ to C$_4$, we may play these three *dastgāhā* on Ibn Sīnā's *'ūd* without producing any intervalic modifications.

With respect to *Chahārgāh* and *Māhur*, the ancient length ratios or modern frequency ratios above the tones in Table 11.34 indicate that I transposed these two modes one "octave" higher than

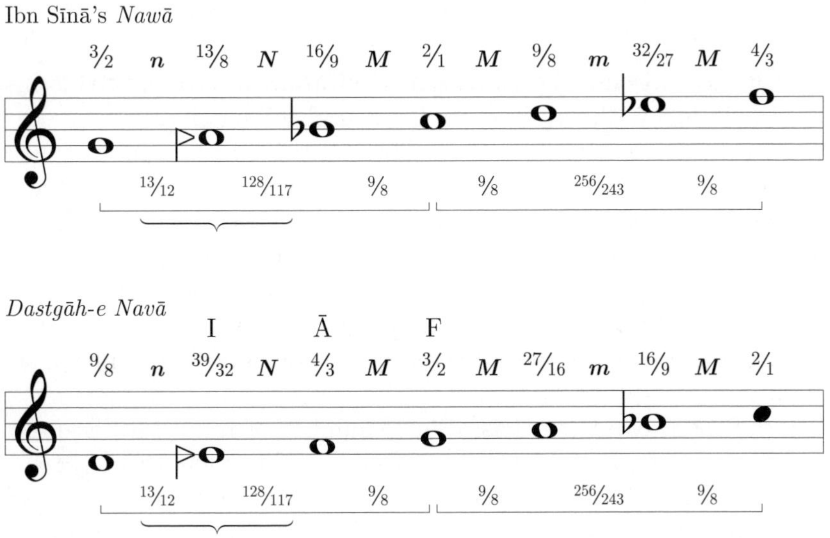

Figure 11.68 A comparison between Ibn Sīnā's description of the ancient melodic mode called *Nawā*, and Farhat's musical notation of the modern mode call *Dastgāh-e Navā*. The conjunct tetrachords of these two modes are identical. Based on Ibn Sīnā's record, we conclude that this mode has not changed for more than 1000 years.

notated. Turn back to Figure 11.62, and observe that if the open *Bamm* on Ibn Sīnā's *'ūd* sounds middle C_4, ratio $^1\!/\!_1$, then the index finger fret of the *Mathnā* sounds high C_5, ratio $^2\!/\!_1$. Furthermore, to play the last two tones of *Māhur*, ratios $^{91}\!/\!_{54}$ and $^{16}\!/\!_9$, it may be desirable to equip the *'ūd* with a fifth string called *Ḥādd.*

Finally, and most importantly, Figure 11.68 verifies that the first six ascending interval ratios of Ibn Sīnā's *Nawā* in Table 11.32 are *identical* to the six ascending interval ratios of the modern Persian mode called *Dastgāh-e Navā* in Table 11.34. Examine the intervals encompassed by the curly brackets in Table 11.32, and notice that these markers indicate the division of the Pythagorean "minor third," interval ratio $^{32}\!/\!_{27}$, into two near-equal "neutral seconds," ratios $^{13}\!/\!_{12}$ and $^{128}\!/\!_{117}$. (See Figure 11.64.) Table 11.32 shows that Ibn Sīnā divided this "minor third" into two "neutral seconds" in four different locations on the *'ūd:* between D–F, or $^4\!/\!_3 \div {}^9\!/\!_8 = {}^{32}\!/\!_{27}$; between F–A♭, or $^{128}\!/\!_{81} \div {}^4\!/\!_3 = {}^{32}\!/\!_{27}$; between G–B♭, or $^{16}\!/\!_9 \div {}^3\!/\!_2 = {}^{32}\!/\!_{27}$, and between C^{I}–E♭^{I}, or $^{64}\!/\!_{27} \div {}^2\!/\!_1 = {}^{32}\!/\!_{27}$. Now, recall Farhat's observation that one divides this "minor third" so that ". . . the lower of the two ["neutral seconds"] tends to be the smaller . . ." In seven of Ibn Sīnā's 11 Melodic Modes, and in eight of the twelve modern *dastgāhā: Shur*, *Abutā*, *Dashti*, *Bayāt-e Tork*, *Afshari*, *Segāh*, *Homāyun*, and *Navā*, this division of the "minor third," and the hierarchical order of the "neutral seconds," defines one of the most essential melodic features of Persian music.

There is no doubt that Ibn Sīnā accurately comprehended and recorded the distinctive intonational characteristics of Persian music. His entire work is a living testament to the enduring significance of the 17-tone scale and 13-limit ratios.

~ 11.67 ~

Ibn Sīnā was succeeded by the renowned Ṣafī Al-Dīn (d. 1294). Before we discuss Ṣafī Al-Dīn's 17-tone *'ūd* tuning, and his array of 84 Melodic Modes, let us first return to Al-Fārābī's *Kitāb al-mūsīqī al-kabīr.* Among the many instruments and tunings described by Al-Fārābī, none is more important than the *ṭunbūr* of Khurāsān. Because the territory of Khurāsān belonged to the former Persian Empire, we again acknowledge the profound influence of Persian musicians on the development of Arabian music. Al-Fārābī begins his description in the following manner:

> The *Ṭunbūr* of Khurāsān.
>
> We will now discuss the *ṭunbūr* of Khurāsān; in studying this instrument, we will follow the method we have applied thus far.
>
> The form, the length, [and] the volume of this instrument vary according to different regions. It is always equipped with two strings of the same thickness. Attached to the same hitch pin, they pass over a bridge, each one in a notch, which prevents their contact. They then extend in parallel along the face of the instrument to reach the nut. There, they pass into two grooves placed at the same distance from one another; they are then wound around two tuning pegs fixed opposite one another, on each side of the neck.
>
> The *ṭunbūr* of Khurāsān has a large number of frets; they are distributed over the neck, from the nut to about half the length of the instrument. Some of them [i.e., the ***fixed frets***] always occupy the same position, regardless of the musician or the region where the instrument is played. In contrast, the others [i.e., the ***moveable frets***] vary and change position in the different regions . . .[121] (Text in brackets mine.)

In preparation for discussions on the tuning of the ancient *ṭunbūr* of Khurāsān and Ṣafī Al-Dīn's *'ūd*, refer to Figure 11.69(a), which subdivides the "fourth" into two "whole tones" (T) and

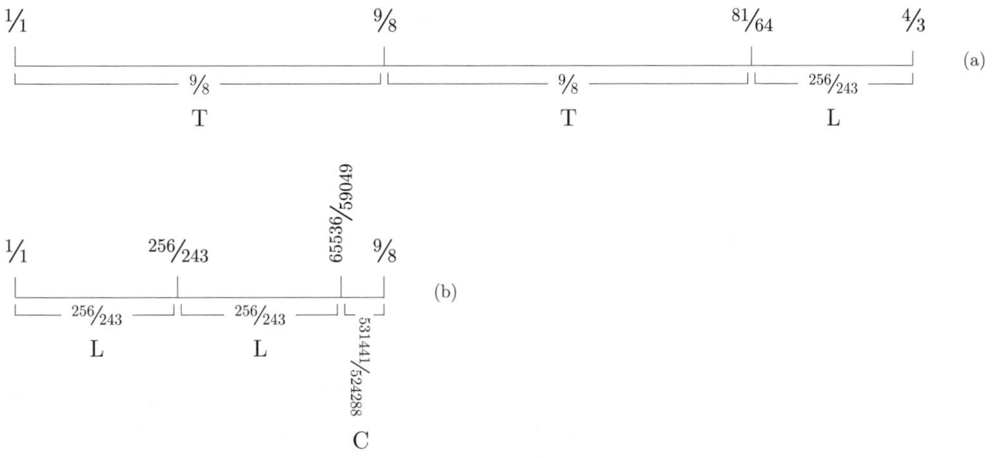

Figure 11.69 Two basic subdivisions on the Perso-Arabian *ṭunbūr* and *'ūd.* (a) The "fourth" is divided into two "whole tones" and one limma. (b) The "whole tone" is divided into two limmas and one comma of Pythagoras. The double-limma yields 3-limit ratio $^{65536}/_{59049}$ [180.5 ¢], or a *schisma variant* that is musically indistinguishable from 5-limit ratio $^{10}/_{9}$ [182.4 ¢]. In this text, we notate the schisma variant as D$\overset{\S}{\downarrow}$ $\sim^{10}/_{9}$. (Interval divisions to scale.)

one limma (L); and to Figure 11.69(b), which subdivides the "whole tone" into two limmas and one comma of Pythagoras (C). The latter subdivision is unique in the history of world tunings. The systematic utilization of the double-limma [L×L], and the double-limma times one comma [L×L×C], produces eight scale degrees in the traditional tuning of the *ṭunbūr* of Khurāsān, which have dual identities as 3-limit and 5-limit ratios. (See Figure 11.70.) Such tones require special consideration. If we fail to understand the function of these scale degrees, all meaning will be lost, and the result will be a mathematically accurate but musically incomprehensible sequence of ratios.

To begin, we must calculate the discrepancy called a *schisma*, or the interval between the *ditonic comma*, known as the *comma of Pythagoras:* $^{531441}/_{524288}$ = 23.5 ¢, and the *syntonic comma*, known as the *comma of Didymus:* $^{81}/_{80}$ = 21.5 ¢.[122]

$$\textit{Schisma} = \frac{\;\frac{531441}{524288}\;}{\;\frac{81}{80}\;} = \frac{32805}{32768} = 1.954\ \text{¢}$$

Since the finest ear cannot distinguish between two frequencies unless they are at least 2 cents apart, an increase or decrease of a given interval by one schisma does *not* affect our aural perception of such an interval.

Turn to Table 11.36(a), Columns 1 and 2, which give the last seven note names and complex frequency ratios of the spiral of twelve ascending "fifths" from Figure 10.16(a). When we divide the 3-limit ratios in Column 2 by a schisma in Column 3, we obtain the 5-limit ratios in Column 5. Conversely, when we multiply the 5-limit ratios by a schisma, we obtain the 3-limit ratios. Schisma divisions decrease the ratios in Column 2 by 1.954 ¢, and schisma multiplications increase the ratios in Column 5 by 1.954 ¢. Nevertheless, as stated above, all such changes are musically imperceptible.

Now, if we divide F♯, ratio $^{729}/_{512}$, by a schisma the result is G♭, ratio $^{64}/_{45}$: $^{729}/_{512} \div {}^{32805}/_{32768} = {}^{64}/_{45}$. In contrast, observe that in Columns 6 and 7, the equality F♯ = G$\overset{\S}{\flat}$ states the inverse operation in schisma notation; namely, if we multiply G♭, ratio $^{64}/_{45}$, by a schisma, the result is G$\overset{\S}{\flat}$, which equals F♯, ratio $^{729}/_{512}$. Although we may musically interpret ratio $^{729}/_{512}$ as a *schisma variant* (*s.v.*)

Table 11.36

ARABIAN SCHISMA AND COMMA VARIANTS
OF THE ASCENDING SPIRAL OF "FIFTHS"

(a)

Ascending Spiral of "Fifths" 3-Limit *Schisma Variants*		*Schisma* $32805/32768$	Ascending Spiral of "Fifths" 5-Limit Ratios		*Schisma Variants* in Schisma Notation		Arabian *Schisma Variants* Perceived As Chromatic 5-Limit Ratios
F♯:	$729/512 = 611.7$ ¢		G♭:	$64/45 = 609.8$ ¢	F♯ =	[G$\overset{\S}{\flat}$]	
C♯:	$2187/2048 = 113.7$ ¢		D♭:	$16/15 = 111.7$ ¢	C♯ =	D$\overset{\S}{\flat}$	D$\overset{\S}{\flat}$ $\sim 16/15$
G♯:	$6561/4096 = 815.6$ ¢		A♭:	$8/5 = 813.7$ ¢	G♯ =	A$\overset{\S}{\flat}$	A$\overset{\S}{\flat}$ $\sim 8/5$
D♯:	$19683/16384 = 317.6$ ¢	÷	E♭:	$6/5 = 315.6$ ¢	D♯ =	E$\overset{\S}{\flat}$	E$\overset{\S}{\flat}$ $\sim 6/5$
A♯:	$59049/32768 = 1019.6$ ¢		B♭:	$9/5 = 1017.6$ ¢	A♯ =	B$\overset{\S}{\flat}$	B$\overset{\S}{\flat}$ $\sim 9/5$
E♯:	$177147/131072 = 521.5$ ¢		"F":	$27/20 = 519.6$ ¢	E♯ =	["F$\overset{\S}{\uparrow}$"]	
B♯:	$531441/524288 = 23.5$ ¢		"C":	$81/80 = 21.5$ ¢	B♯ =	["C$\overset{\S}{\uparrow}$"]	
(1)	(2)	(3)	(4)	(5)	(6)	(7)	(8)

(b)

Ascending Spiral of "Fifths" 3-Limit *Comma Variants*		Comma of Pythagoras $531441/524288$	Ascending Spiral of "Fifths" 3-Limit Ratios		*Comma Variants* in Comma Notation		Arabian *Comma Variants* Perceived As Sharp Consonances
F♯:	$729/512 = 611.7$ ¢		G♭:	$1024/729 = 588.3$ ¢	F♯ =	[G$\overset{\text{ç}}{\flat}$]	
C♯:	$2187/2048 = 113.7$ ¢		D♭:	$256/243 = 90.2$ ¢	C♯ =	[D$\overset{\text{ç}}{\flat}$]	
G♯:	$6561/4096 = 815.6$ ¢		A♭:	$128/81 = 729.2$ ¢	G♯ =	[A$\overset{\text{ç}}{\flat}$]	
D♯:	$19683/16384 = 317.6$ ¢	÷	E♭:	$32/27 = 294.1$ ¢	D♯ =	[E$\overset{\text{ç}}{\flat}$]	
A♯:	$59049/32768 = 1019.6$ ¢		B♭:	$16/9 = 996.1$ ¢	A♯ =	[B$\overset{\text{ç}}{\flat}$]	
E♯:	$177147/131072 = 521.5$ ¢		F:	$4/3 = 498.0$ ¢	E♯ =	F$\overset{\text{ç}}{\uparrow}$	F$\overset{\text{ç}}{\uparrow}$
B♯:	$531441/524288 = 23.5$ ¢		C:	$1/1 = 0.0$ ¢	B♯ =	C$\overset{\text{ç}}{\uparrow}$	C$\overset{\text{ç}}{\uparrow}$
(1)	(2)	(3)	(4)	(5)	(6)	(7)	(8)

of ratio $64/45$ — that is, although we may interpret G$\overset{\S}{\flat}$ as G♭ — we will not do so. [G$\overset{\S}{\flat}$] appears in brackets because it is difficult to musically perceive 3-limit ratio $729/512$ as 5-limit ratio $64/45$. For this reason, we will continue to notate ratio $729/512$ as F♯.

However, when we divide ratio $2187/2048$ in Column 2 by a schisma, the result is ratio $16/15$ in Column 5: $2187/2048 \div 32805/32768 = 16/15$. In this case, we will interpret ratio $2187/2048$ as a schisma variant of ratio $16/15$ — that is, we will interpret D$\overset{\S}{\flat}$ as D♭ — because we tend to perceive *complex* 3-limit ratio $2187/2048$ as *simple* 5-limit ratio $16/15$. Consequently, in Column 8, D$\overset{\S}{\flat}$ identifies $2187/2048$ as a *s.v.* of $16/15$; A$\overset{\S}{\flat}$ identifies $6561/4096$ as a *s.v.* of $8/5$; E$\overset{\S}{\flat}$ identifies $19683/16384$ as a *s.v.* of $6/5$; and B$\overset{\S}{\flat}$ identifies $59049/32768$ as a *s.v.* of $9/5$. To notate the musical interchangeability of such tones, I have adapted the similarity sign ($\sim$) from geometry, which states that two geometric objects have exactly the same

Table 11.37

ARABIAN SCHISMA AND COMMA VARIANTS
OF THE DESCENDING SPIRAL OF "FIFTHS"

(a)

Descending Spiral of "Fifths" 3-Limit *Schisma Variants*		*Schisma* $^{32805}/_{32768}$	Descending Spiral of "Fifths" 5-Limit Ratios		*Schisma Variants* in Schisma Notation		Arabian *Schisma Variants* Perceived As Diatonic 5-Limit Ratios
G♭:	$^{1024}/_{729}$ = 588.3 ¢		F♯:	$^{45}/_{32}$ = 590.2 ¢	G♭ =	[F♯$\overset{s}{\downarrow}$]	
C♭:	$^{4096}/_{2187}$ = 1086.3 ¢		B:	$^{15}/_{8}$ = 1088.3 ¢	C♭ =	B$\overset{s}{\downarrow}$	B$\overset{s}{\downarrow}$ ~$^{15}/_{8}$
F♭:	$^{8192}/_{6561}$ = 384.4 ¢		E:	$^{5}/_{4}$ = 386.3 ¢	F♭ =	E$\overset{s}{\downarrow}$	E$\overset{s}{\downarrow}$ ~$^{5}/_{4}$
B♭♭:	$^{32768}/_{19683}$ = 882.4 ¢	×	A:	$^{5}/_{3}$ = 884.4 ¢	B♭♭ =	A$\overset{s}{\downarrow}$	A$\overset{s}{\downarrow}$ ~$^{5}/_{3}$
E♭♭:	$^{65536}/_{59049}$ = 180.5 ¢		D:	$^{10}/_{9}$ = 182.4 ¢	E♭♭ =	D$\overset{s}{\downarrow}$	D$\overset{s}{\downarrow}$ ~$^{10}/_{9}$
A♭♭:	$^{262144}/_{177147}$ = 678.5 ¢		"G":	$^{40}/_{27}$ = 680.4 ¢	A♭♭ =	["G$\overset{s}{\downarrow}$"]	
D♭♭:	$^{1048576}/_{531441}$ = 1176.5 ¢		"C¹":	$^{160}/_{81}$ = 1178.5 ¢	D♭♭ =	["C$\overset{s}{\downarrow}$"]	
(1)	(2)	(3)	(4)	(5)	(6)	(7)	(8)

(b)

Descending Spiral of "Fifths" 3-Limit *Comma Variants*		Comma of Pythagoras $^{531441}/_{524288}$	Descending Spiral of "Fifths" 3-Limit Ratios		*Comma Variants* in Comma Notation		Arabian *Comma Variants* Perceived As Flat Consonances
G♭:	$^{1024}/_{729}$ = 588.3 ¢		F♯:	$^{729}/_{512}$ = 611.7 ¢	G♭ =	[F♯$\overset{c}{\downarrow}$]	
C♭:	$^{4096}/_{2187}$ = 1086.3 ¢		B:	$^{243}/_{128}$ = 1109.8 ¢	C♭ =	[B$\overset{c}{\downarrow}$]	
F♭:	$^{8192}/_{6561}$ = 384.4 ¢		E:	$^{81}/_{64}$ = 407.8 ¢	F♭ =	[E$\overset{c}{\downarrow}$]	
B♭♭:	$^{32768}/_{19683}$ = 882.4 ¢	×	A:	$^{27}/_{16}$ = 905.9 ¢	B♭♭ =	[A$\overset{c}{\downarrow}$]	
E♭♭:	$^{65536}/_{59049}$ = 180.5 ¢		D:	$^{9}/_{8}$ = 203.9 ¢	E♭♭ =	[D$\overset{c}{\downarrow}$]	
A♭♭:	$^{262144}/_{177147}$ = 678.5 ¢		G:	$^{3}/_{2}$ = 702.0 ¢	A♭♭ =	G$\overset{c}{\downarrow}$	G$\overset{c}{\downarrow}$
D♭♭:	$^{1048576}/_{531441}$ = 1176.5 ¢		C¹:	$^{2}/_{1}$ = 1200.0 ¢	D♭♭ =	C$\overset{c}{\downarrow}$	C$\overset{c}{\downarrow}$
(1)	(2)	(3)	(4)	(5)	(6)	(7)	(8)

shape, but not the same size. Here the similarity sign indicates that two tones produce the same *musically perceived* interval, but do not have the same mathematical size. For example, D$\overset{s}{\flat\uparrow}$ ~$^{16}/_{15}$ states, "D$\overset{s}{\flat\uparrow}$, or the schisma variant $^{2187}/_{2048}$, is musically equivalent to D♭, ratio $^{16}/_{15}$." If in reading such a statement, the identity of a schisma variant is not immediately apparent, use the following procedure. Observe the direction of the arrow; multiply the appropriate 5-limit ratio by a schisma if the arrow points up, or divide the appropriate 5-limit ratio by a schisma if the arrow points down: D$\overset{s}{\flat\uparrow}$ = $^{16}/_{15}$ × $^{32805}/_{32768}$ = $^{2187}/_{2048}$.

Now, if we divide E♯, ratio $^{177147}/_{131072}$, by a schisma the result is "F," ratio $^{27}/_{20}$, or a "sharp fourth." Although we may interpret $^{177147}/_{131072}$ as a schisma variant of ratio $^{27}/_{20}$ — that is, although we may interpret "F$\overset{s}{\uparrow}$" as "F" — we will not do so. ["F$\overset{s}{\uparrow}$"] appears in brackets because it is difficult to musically perceive 3-limit ratio $^{177147}\!/_{131072}$ as 5-limit ratio $^{27}\!/_{20}$. Due to the proximity of the strong consonance of the "fourth," Table 11.36(b), Column 8, shows that we will interpret ratio $^{177147}\!/_{131072}$ as a *comma variant* (*c.v.*) of ratio $^{4}\!/_{3}$ because we tend to perceive ratio $^{177147}\!/_{131072}$ as ratio $^{4}\!/_{3}$ raised by a comma of Pythagoras: $\text{F}\overset{¢}{\uparrow} = {}^{4}\!/_{3} \times {}^{531441}\!/_{524288} = {}^{177147}\!/_{131072}$. Finally, ["$\text{C}\overset{\S}{\uparrow}$"] also appears in brackets because it is difficult to perceive 3-limit ratio $^{531441}\!/_{524288}$ as 5-limit ratio $^{81}\!/_{80}$. Due to the proximity of the strong consonance of the tonic, Table 11.36(b), Column 8, shows that we will interpret ratio $^{531441}\!/_{524288}$ as a *c.v.* of $^{1}\!/_{1}$ because we tend to perceive ratio $^{531441}\!/_{524288}$ as ratio $^{1}\!/_{1}$ raised by a comma of Pythagoras: $\text{C}\overset{¢}{\uparrow} = {}^{1}\!/_{1} \times {}^{531441}\!/_{524288} = {}^{531441}\!/_{524288}$.

Refer now to Table 11.37(a), Columns 1 and 2, which give the last seven note names and complex frequency ratios of the spiral of twelve descending "fifths" from Figure 10.16(b). When we multiply the 3-limit ratios in Column 2 by a schisma in Column 3, we obtain the 5-limit ratios in Column 5. Conversely, when we divide the 5-limit ratios by a schisma, we obtain the 3-limit ratios.

For reasons discussed above, we will continue to notate ratio $^{1024}\!/_{729}$ as G♭. Then, in Column 8, $\text{B}\overset{\S}{\downarrow}$ identifies $^{4096}\!/_{2187}$ as a *s.v.* of $^{15}\!/_{8}$; $\text{E}\overset{\S}{\downarrow}$ identifies $^{8192}\!/_{6561}$ as a *s.v.* of $^{5}\!/_{4}$; $\text{A}\overset{\S}{\downarrow}$ identifies $^{32768}\!/_{19683}$ as a *s.v.* of $^{5}\!/_{3}$; and $\text{D}\overset{\S}{\downarrow}$ identifies $^{65536}\!/_{59049}$ as a *s.v.* of $^{10}\!/_{9}$. Also, for reasons already explained, Table 11.37(b), Column 8, shows that we will interpret ratio $^{262144}\!/_{177147}$ as a *c.v.* of $^{3}\!/_{2}$; here $\text{G}\overset{¢}{\downarrow} = {}^{3}\!/_{2} \div {}^{531441}\!/_{524288} = {}^{262144}\!/_{177147}$. And we will interpret ratio $^{1048576}\!/_{531441}$ as a *c.v.* of $^{2}\!/_{1}$; here $\text{C}\overset{¢}{\downarrow} = {}^{2}\!/_{1} \div {}^{531441}\!/_{524288} = {}^{1048576}\!/_{531441}$.

When viewed from a strictly mathematical perspective, all schisma variants in Table 11.36(a) have dual identities as comma variants in Table 11.36(b), and all schisma variants in Table 11.37(a) have dual identities as comma variants in Table 11.37(b). For example, observe that in Figures 11.70 and 11.71, the interval of a double-limma [L×L]

$$\text{Double Limma} = \left(\frac{256}{243}\right)^2 = \frac{65536}{59049}$$

has 3-limit and 5-limit derivations:

$$\text{D}\overset{¢}{\downarrow} = \frac{9}{8} \div \frac{531441}{524288} = \frac{65536}{59049}$$

$$\text{D}\overset{\S}{\downarrow} = \frac{10}{9} \div \frac{32805}{32768} = \frac{65536}{59049}$$

$\text{D}\overset{¢}{\downarrow}$ identifies the double-limma as a comma variant of 3-limit ratio $^{9}\!/_{8}$; and $\text{D}\overset{\S}{\downarrow}$ identifies the double-limma as a schisma variant of 5-limit ratio $^{10}\!/_{9}$. Similarly, the interval of a quadruple-limma times a double-comma [L×L×L×L×C×C] also has 3-limit and 5-limit derivations:

$$\text{E}\overset{¢}{\downarrow} = \frac{81}{64} \div \frac{531441}{524288} = \frac{8192}{6561}$$

$$\text{E}\overset{\S}{\downarrow} = \frac{5}{4} \div \frac{32805}{32768} = \frac{8192}{6561}$$

Because it is musically meaningless to give two derivations for all such tones, Figures 11.70 and 11.71 identify the schisma variants and comma variants as discussed above. However, because these scale degrees are subject to interpretation, some readers may prefer different notations. For instance, in Figure 11.71, one could state that $\text{G}\overset{\S}{\downarrow}$ identifies $^{262144}\!/_{177147}$ as a *s.v.* of $^{40}\!/_{27}$ because this tone has two mathematical derivations:

$$G\overset{c}{\downarrow} = \frac{3}{2} \div \frac{531441}{524288} = \frac{262144}{177147}$$

$$G\overset{s}{\downarrow} = \frac{40}{27} \div \frac{32805}{32768} = \frac{262144}{177147}$$

In summary, the symbol $\overset{c}{\uparrow}$ or $\overset{c}{\downarrow}$ indicates a 3-limit *diatonic* scale degree increased or decreased by a comma of Pythagoras; and the symbol $\overset{c}{\flat}$ signifies a 3-limit *chromatic* scale degree increased by a comma of Pythagoras. In contrast, the symbol $\overset{s}{\uparrow}$ or $\overset{s}{\downarrow}$ indicates a 5-limit *diatonic* scale degree increased or decreased by a schisma; and the symbol $\overset{s}{\flat}$ signifies a 5-limit *chromatic* scale degree increased by a schisma.

~ 11.68 ~

Al-Fārābī continues his account of the *ṭunbūr* of Khurāsān by describing the locations and letter names of the fixed frets.

> There are usually five standard fixed frets, but there can be more. The first is placed at 1/9 of the distance between the nut and the bridge; the second at 1/4 of this distance; the third at its 1/3; the fourth at its 1/2; the fifth at 1/9 of the distance between the bridge and half of the string.
>
> Take the two strings A–B and J–D. The points of contact of these two strings with the fret at 1/9 will be represented by the letters H and Z; with that at 1/4 , by Ḥ and Ṭ; with that at 1/3, by Y and K; with that at 1/2, by L and M. The points of contact of the two strings with the fret placed beyond this last one, at 1/9 of half the strings, will be represented by the letters N and S.[123]

Given a short length of 1/9 the string between nut and fret, the long playing length is the complementary length, or 8/9 of the string;[124] therefore, since l.r. 8/9 → f.r. 9/8, the first fixed fret produces a "whole tone," ratio 9/8 = 203.9 ¢. Similarly, the second fixed fret produces the "fourth," ratio 4/3 = 498.0 ¢; the third fixed fret produces the "fifth," ratio 3/2 = 702.0 ¢; the fourth fixed fret produces the "octave," ratio 2/1 = 1200.0 ¢; and the fifth fixed fret produces "one octave and a whole tone," or the "ninth," ratio 9/4 = 1403.9 ¢.

Al-Fārābī then describes the distribution of the moveable frets.

> Let us begin then with the most common of the moveable frets that are thirteen in number. There are two of them between A and H; three between H and Ḥ; two between Ḥ and Y; four between Y and L; two between L and N; therefore, the *ṭunbūr* of Khurāsān usually contains eighteen frets. Let us label all of them on the two strings of the instrument. We will give the fixed frets two letters, one on each of the strings, while the moveable frets will have only one [letter]. The first of the moveable frets will be given the letter 'A and so forth, following the Arabic alphabetical order called *jummal*, up to the last moveable fret which will be given the letter Ġ.[125] (Text in brackets mine.)

Next, Al-Fārābī gives instructions for finding the locations of the fixed frets by ear. Since it is easy to determine these positions by simply dividing the string into the required aliquot number of parts, we proceed with Al-Fārābī's instructions for finding the locations of the moveable frets by ear.

We will now show how to position the moveable frets, choosing those that are frequently used.

We make [open] string J–D produce a note identical to the note H. [That is, open string J-D is tuned to the "whole tone," ratio $9/8$.] Next, we search on string A–B for the location of note Z; at this point we place fret R. R and Ḥ–Ṭ will be in the interval of a limma.

We then seek the point on string J–D where it must be stopped to produce note Ḥ, and at this point, we place fret Ḍ. The frets Ḍ and H–Z will be in the interval of a limma.

We search for the location on string J–D [where it must be stopped to produce] note Ḍ [of string] A–B, and we place at this point fret ʿA. Between the notes produced by the open strings and those of fret ʿA, there will be an interval of a limma.

[From] the point where string J–D produces a note identical to that of fret R, we establish fret T on string A–B; it will be separated from Y–K by an interval of a limma.

At the point where string A–B generates a note identical to K, we place fret H̱.

Where this same string [A–B] produces a note identical to that of fret T on string J–D, we position fret Th; and, at the point where [string A–B] produces the same note as fret H̱ on string J–D, we place fret Ṣ. [The latter] is separated from fret L–M by the interval of a limma.

We search on string A–B for the location of a note identical to that of fret Ṣ on string J–D, and at that point we establish fret Ġ, which will be separated from fret N–S by an interval of a limma.

At the point where string J–D gives a note identical to L, we place fret Dh.

We position a supplementary fret at the point where string J–D produces a note identical to that of fret Dh on string A–B. This supplementary fret, extraneous to the thirteen moveable frets previously mentioned, will be given the letter W, and will be at an interval of a limma from fret Y–K.

We establish fret Š at the point where string J–D produces the note given by fret W on string A–B.

We place fret Q where string J–D gives the same note as fret Š on string A–B. Frets Q and Ḍ will have the interval of a limma between them. An interval equal to the excess of a tone over a double limma [i.e., the comma of Pythagoras: $9/8 \div (256/243)^2 = 531441/524288$] will separate fret Q from fret R, and it will be the same with frets Š and T, [and] W and Th.

Fret F will be positioned at the point where string J–D gives a note identical to that of fret Q on string A–B. F and ʿA will be at an interval of a limma, and F and H–Z, at a distance corresponding to the excess of a tone over a double limma.

We place another supplementary fret at the point where string A–B gives the same note as fret Th on string J–D. This fret, extraneous to the thirteen previously mentioned frets, will be labeled 0 [Zero in Figures 11.70 and 11.71].

Where string A–B gives a note identical to that of string J–D at the location of fret 0, we place fret Ḏh; this last fret will be separated from L–M by an interval equal to the excess of a tone over a double limma, whereas an interval of a limma will separate it from Ġ.

> The fret 0 will be separated from [***Dh***] by an interval of a comma [of Pythagoras], and from Ṣ by an interval of a limma. ...
>
> Frets W and 0 are not used in playing this instrument. We have positioned them because they allow us to establish the other frets. One can remove them or keep them, although they remain unused. It is best to leave them; the notes they would produce would correspond to those given by frets called *neighbors* in lute playing.[126] (Text in brackets mine. Bold italics in brackets my correction of an unedited error in *La Musique Arabe.* Text in parentheses in *La Musique Arabe.*)

Turn now to Figure 11.70, which illustrates the fret locations, the ancient length ratios or modern frequency ratios, and the schisma variants of the traditional *ṭunbūr* of Khurāsān as described by Al-Fārābī. Also, notice a vertical sequence of braces that shows the distribution of limmas and commas throughout the tuning. The first six braces indicate that the "octave" between C–C′ on String A–B contains five "whole tones" and one double-limma:

$$\left(\frac{9}{8}\right)^5 \times \left(\frac{256}{243}\right)^2 = \frac{2}{1}$$

Because each "whole tone" consists of three separate tones (or, 5 × 3 tones = 15 tones), and the double-limma consists of two separate tones, the "octave" contains a total number of 15 tones + 2 tones = 17 tones. We conclude that this division of the "octave" explains the origin of the 17-tone scale in the Perso-Arabian musical traditions.

Analogous to Ibn Sīnā's claim that in Persian lands people are ". . . accustomed to the *strong genera* . . ."[127] Al-Fārābī gives a musical explanation for this tuning:

> We have already indicated that the genus usually used on the *ṭunbūr* of Khurāsān is the strong diatonic genus [see Figures 11.50 and 11.51, which show Al-Fārābī's strong diatonic genus: 9⁄8, 9⁄8, 256⁄243]. Indeed, one plays a large number of diatonic combinations on this instrument, and that is why its frets are numerous. Because the strong diatonic genus also constitutes the basis for the lute scale, it is possible for us to reproduce on . . . [the *'ūd*] practically all that one plays on the *ṭunbūr* of Khurāsān.[128] (Text in brackets mine.)

∼ 11.69 ∼

In a subsequent section entitled

> Correspondence between the notes of the *ṭunbūr* of Khurāsān and those of the scale of the lute.[129]

Al-Fārābī proposes tuning open String J–D a "fourth" above open String A–B:

> If we tension string J–D so that it produces, when open, the note Ḥ [4⁄3], the tuning will be at the fourth, and is called the *tuning of the lute*. The [seven] notes heard on string A–B from [***A to R***] will be encountered only once in this tuning; string J–D will not produce any of them. The same applies to [seven] notes heard on string J–D between [***Dh and S***]; string A–B will not produce any of them. Furthermore, four notes of string J–D [G$\overset{c}{\downarrow}$, A$\overset{s}{\downarrow}$, B$\overset{s}{\downarrow}$, and D♭′] will not find their equals among those generated by string

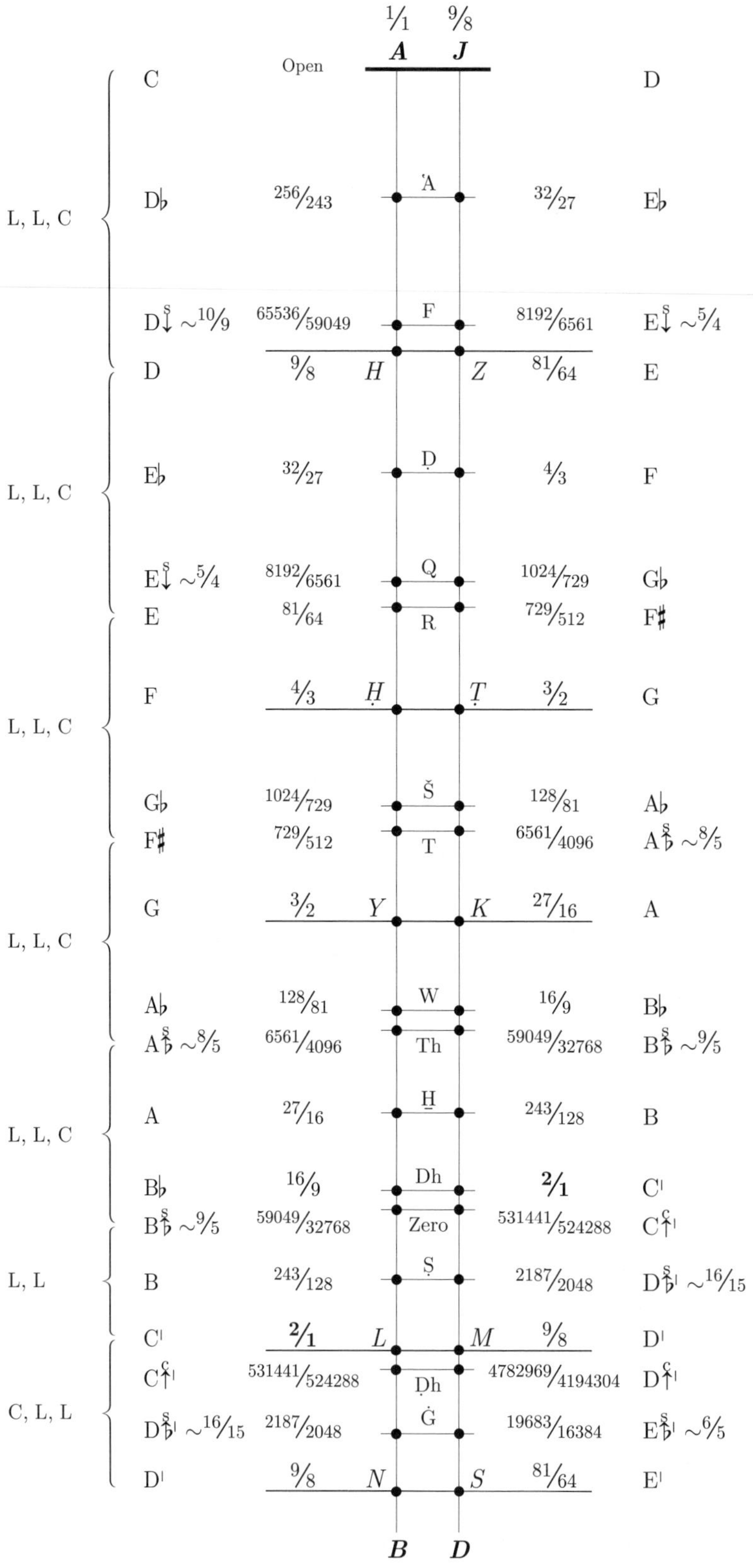

Figure 11.70 According to Al-Fārābī, the traditional *ṭunbūr* of Khurāsān consists of two identical 17-tone scales, each comprising 5 "whole tones" [L×L×C], and 2 limmas [L×L]. This 3-limit tuning includes 6 schisma variants: D ~10/9, E ~5/4, A ~8/5, B ~9/5, D ~16/15, and E ~6/5. (Fret locations to scale.)

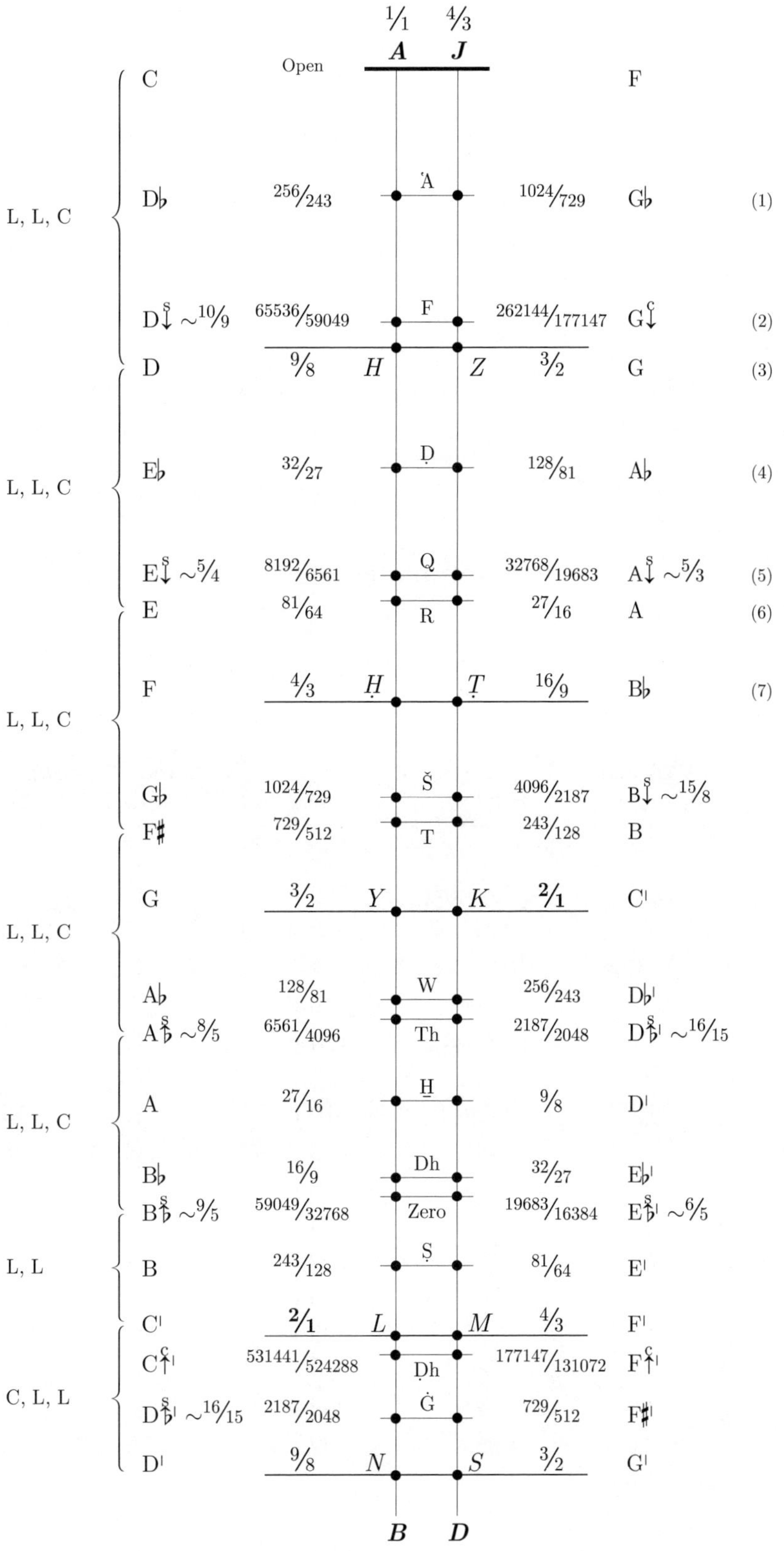

Figure 11.71 Al-Fārābī contemplated a tuning for the *ṭunbūr* where string J–D sounds a "fourth" above string A–B. This tuning includes 2 additional schisma variants: A$\updownarrow$ ~5/3, and B$\updownarrow$ ~15/8. Note carefully, Frets 1–7 now produce the *same* tones as the *Bamm* and *Mathlath* strings of Ṣafī Al-Dīn's *First ʿŪd Tuning* in Figure 11.74. (Fret locations to scale.)

> A–B; and four [notes] of string A–B [F♯, A$\overset{s}{\flat}$, B$\overset{s}{\flat}$, and C$\overset{\varsigma}{\uparrow}$'] will not have identical ones on J–D.[130] (Text in brackets mine. Bold italics in brackets my corrections of unedited errors in *La Musique Arabe.*)

Figure 11.71 presents this tuning in full detail, and Table 11.38 demonstrates that Al-Fārābī's *ṭunbūr* tuning consists of an ascending spiral of twelve "fifths" above 1/1, and of a descending spiral of eleven "fifths" below 1/1. Although we do not know whether Arabian music theorists intentionally patterned their scales after these kinds of ascending and descending spirals, the *ṭunbūr* of Khurāsān proves that such systems do exist in the music of people who tune their instruments by ear! Furthermore, this instrument also establishes that in Persian and Arabian lands, two completely different tuning traditions existed during the same period of time. On the *ṭunbūr*, musicians tuned a "schisma second," D$\overset{s}{\downarrow}$ [180.5 ¢], and a "schisma third," E$\overset{s}{\downarrow}$ [384.4 ¢], while on the *'ūd*, they tuned various "neutral seconds," D$^{\triangleright}$ [$\approx$ 150 ¢], and "neutral thirds," E$^{\triangleright}$ [$\approx$ 350 ¢]. In two elaborate tables,[131] Al-Fārābī compared his *ṭunbūr* tuning in Figure 11.71 to his *'ūd* tuning in Figure 11.48.

Table 11.38

THE INNER STRUCTURE OF
AL-FĀRĀBĪ'S *ṬUNBŪR* TUNING

	Standard Western Notation	Ratios	Cents	*Schisma/Comma* Notation
(12)	B♯	531441/524288	23 ¢	C$\overset{\varsigma}{\uparrow}$
(11)	E♯	177147/131072	522 ¢	F$\overset{\varsigma}{\uparrow}$
(10)	A♯	59049/32768	1020 ¢	B$\overset{s}{\flat}$
(9)	D♯	19683/16384	318 ¢	E$\overset{s}{\flat}$
(8)	G♯	6561/4096	816 ¢	A$\overset{s}{\flat}$
(7)	C♯	2187/2048	114 ¢	D$\overset{s}{\flat}$
(6)	F♯	729/512	612 ¢	F♯
(5)	B	243/128	1110 ¢	B
(4)	E	81/64	408 ¢	E
(3)	A	27/16	906 ¢	A
(2)	D	9/8	204 ¢	D
(1)	G	3/2	702 ¢	G
	C	1/1	0 ¢	C
(1)	F	4/3	498 ¢	F
(2)	B♭	16/9	996 ¢	B♭
(3)	E♭	32/27	294 ¢	E♭
(4)	A♭	128/81	792 ¢	A♭
(5)	D♭	256/243	90 ¢	D♭
(6)	G♭	1024/729	588 ¢	G♭
(7)	C♭	4096/2187	1086 ¢	B$\overset{s}{\downarrow}$
(8)	F♭	8192/6561	384 ¢	E$\overset{s}{\downarrow}$
(9)	B♭♭	32768/19683	882 ¢	A$\overset{s}{\downarrow}$
(10)	E♭♭	65536/59049	180 ¢	D$\overset{s}{\downarrow}$
(11)	A♭♭	262144/177147	678 ¢	G$\overset{\varsigma}{\downarrow}$

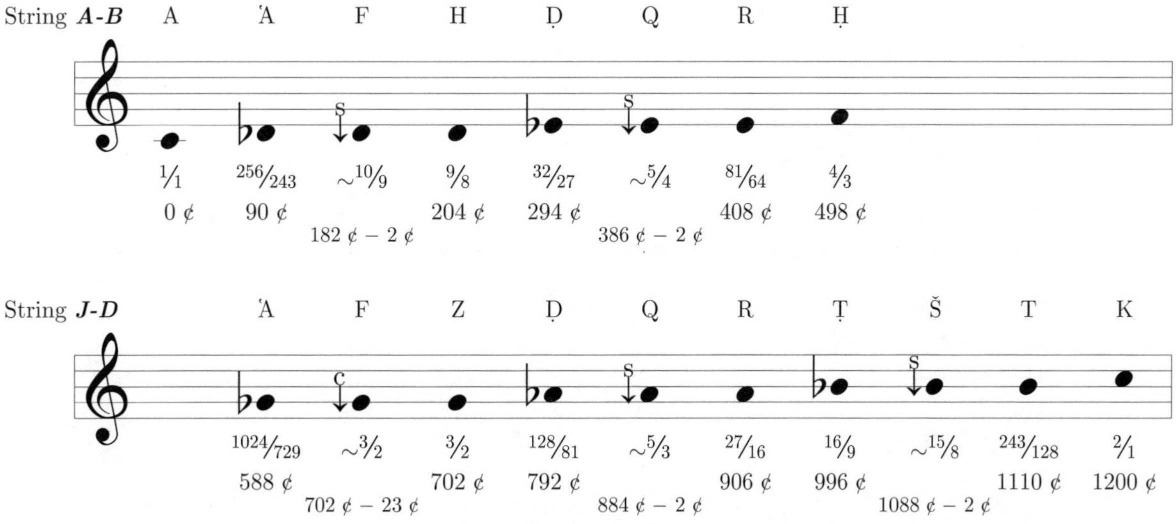

Figure 11.72 An interpretation of Al-Fārābī's 17-tone scale as played on the *ṭunbūr* in Figure 11.71. This scale includes four schisma variants: D$\overset{S}{\downarrow}$ ~10/9, E$\overset{S}{\downarrow}$ ~5/4, A$\overset{S}{\downarrow}$ ~5/3, and B$\overset{S}{\downarrow}$ ~15/8, and one comma variant: G$\overset{c}{\downarrow}$.

He identified the tones that these two instruments have in common, and the tones on the *ṭunbūr* that closely approximate those on the *'ūd*. Al-Fārābī did not dwell on pedantic distinctions, but contemplated a fluid exchange of possibilities in the tunings of both instruments.

Figure 11.72 is my interpretation of Al-Fārābī's 17-tone *ṭunbūr* scale in Western musical notation. When we lower four 5-limit ratios: 10/9 [182 ¢], 5/4 [386 ¢], 5/3 [884 ¢], and 15/8 [1088 ¢] by 2.0 ¢, we obtain four schisma variants: 65536/59049 [180 ¢], 8192/6561 [384 ¢], 32768/19683 [882 ¢], and 4096/2187 [1086 ¢], respectively. Since such decreases are musically imperceptible, the former simple 5-limit ratios indicate how we hear the latter complex 3-limit ratios in the context of a musical scale. Below, notice that Al-Fārābī's scale includes the unique rendition of Ptolemy's Tense Diatonic in the Lydian Mode. (See Section 11.25.)

Ptolemy's Tense Diatonic, Lydian Mode:	1/1,	9/8,	5/4,	4/3,	3/2,	5/3,	15/8,	2/1
On Al-Fārābī's *ṭunbūr* of Khurāsān:	C,	D,	E$\overset{S}{\downarrow}$,	F,	G,	A$\overset{S}{\downarrow}$,	B$\overset{S}{\downarrow}$,	C′
	1/1,	9/8,	~5/4,	4/3,	3/2,	~5/3,	~15/8,	2/1

~ 11.70 ~

Given the traditions of the *ṭunbūr* and *'ūd*, and the interdisciplinary approach to tuning analysis exemplified by Al-Fārābī, we are now prepared to examine two treatises by Ṣafī Al-Dīn: *Risālat al-Sharafīya fi'l-nisab al-ta'līfīya* (The Sharafian treatise on musical conformities in composition), and *Kitāb al-adwār* (Book of the modes [of music]). The latter treatise is contained in a work entitled *Sharḥ Maulānā Mubārak Shāh* (The Mubārak Shāh commentary), by Al-Jurjānī (d. 1413). Al-Jurjānī's treatise consists of a lengthy and highly sophisticated commentary on the *Kitāb al-adwār*. All three works appear in *La Musique Arabe, Volume 3.*

In the *Risālat al-Sharafīya*, Ṣafī Al-Dīn describes his principal tuning, which I call his *First 'Ūd Tuning.* He then discusses several other locations for Frets 2 and 5. In Section 11.72, we will consider one of these alternate tunings, which I call his *Second 'Ūd Tuning.* As discussed in Section

11.77, when we examine the *First ʿŪd Tuning* in the context of Ṣafī Al-Dīn's 84 Melodic Modes in Figure 11.78, the origins of modern Turkish music come to light. And as discussed in Section 11.83, when we examine the *Second ʿŪd Tuning* in the context of Ṣafī Al-Dīn's 84 Melodic Modes in Figure 11.79, the origins of modern Arabian music come to light.

Consider his description of the *First ʿŪd Tuning* in the *Risālat al-Sharafīya:*

> X. — Know that the most renowned and perfect of the instruments is the one that carries the name *ʿūd*, or lute. It is strung with five strings;
>
> the uppermost is called *Bamm;* coming after it:
> the *Mathlath,*
> the *Mathnā,*
> the *Zīr,*
> and the *Ḥadd.*
>
> To tune the strings one makes each open string produce the same note as three-quarters of the [stopped string] above it. ...
>
> Take a string, A–M; divide it into nine equal parts, and at the end of the first of these divisions mark D.
>
> $$[\text{Fret } 3 \rightarrow 9/8 = 203.9\ ¢]$$
>
> The note A [open string] will then be with D in the ratio 1 + ⅛ [9:8].
>
> We then divide the portion of the string extending from D to M into nine parts, and at the end of the first of these divisions, we mark Z;
>
> $$[\text{Fret } 6 \rightarrow 81/64 = 407.8\ ¢]$$
>
> this gives us the ratio 1 + ⅛ between the notes D and Z.
>
> It is evident that the meeting of the note Z with that of three-quarters of the string, which we mark Ḥ,
>
> $$[\text{Fret } 7 \rightarrow 4/3 = 498.0\ ¢]$$
>
> corresponds to the interval of the *remainder* [limma], of the diatonic genus;
>
> $$[\text{Interval ratio: } 4/3 \div 81/64 = 256/243 = 90.2\ ¢]$$
>
> and it clearly appears that these frets delimit the intervals of the diatonic genus, arranged in a direct order [as in ascending interval ratios 9/8, 9/8, 256/243].
>
> The first of these three frets, D, is called the *index finger;* the second, which is Z, is called the *ring finger;* and the third, Ḥ, the *little finger.*
>
> To place the frets that correspond to the inverse combination . . . [as in descending interval ratios 256/243, 9/8, 9/8], we divide Ḥ–M into eight equal parts, to which we add another of the same length, taken in [the direction of] A–Ḥ, and whose end will be marked H;
>
> $$[\text{Fret } 4 \rightarrow 32/27 = 294.1\ ¢]$$
>
> the notes H and Ḥ will be in the ratio 1 + ⅛.
>
> We then divide H–M into eight equal parts and we add to them another of the same length, taken in [the direction of] section A–H; at the end of this last part, we mark B.
>
> $$[\text{Fret } 1 \rightarrow 256/243 = 90.2\ ¢]$$
>
> The note B will be with H in the ratio 1 + ⅛.

The fret marked H is called the *ancient middle finger;* the one marked B is known as the *surplus* {*zā'id*}. ...

We then divide B–M into four parts, and at the end of the first, we mark Ṭ;

[Theoretical Reference Point $\rightarrow$ $^{1024}\!/_{729} = 588.3$ ¢]

then, dividing Ṭ–M into eight parts, we add to it [in the direction of A–Ṭ] a length equal to one of these parts; its end will be marked W,

[Fret 5 $\rightarrow$ $^{8192}\!/_{6561} = 384.4$ ¢]

and the fret that it determines will be called the *middle finger of Zalzal.* The note W will be with Ṭ in the ratio $1 + {}^{1}\!/_{8}$.

Finally, we divide W–M into eight parts, to which we add [in the direction of A–W] another section of the same length, at the end of which we mark J;

[Fret 2 $\rightarrow$ $^{65536}\!/_{59049} = 180.5$ ¢]

the fret determined by J is called the *neighbor* or the *assistant* {*mujannab*} [or anterior].

These are the seven well-known frets placed on the neck of the lute, and contained within the [first] quarter of the strings [near the nut]. Now here is the nomenclature for the signs that will mark the point[s] of contact of the strings and the frets:

The first string [*Bamm*] will be given the letters we have already indicated.

The second open string [*Mathlath*] will be Ḥ; its *surplus* will be Ṭ, its [*anterior*] Y, its *index finger* YA, its *ancient middle finger* YB, its *middle finger of Zalzal* YJ, its *ring finger* YD, its *little finger* YH.

The note of the third open string [*Mathnā*] is identical to YH; its *surplus* will be YW, its [*anterior*] YZ, and its *index finger* YḤ.

The note YḤ completes the lower octave [$^{2}\!/_{1}$ on the *Mathnā*]; it is, in fact, the higher octave of the note A [$^{1}\!/_{1}$ on the *Bamm*]; and it constitutes at the same time the high end of the low octave, and the low end of the high octave [$^{4}\!/_{1}$ on the *Ḥadd*].

The notes of the high octave will be marked respectively: YṬ, K, KA, KB, KJ, KD, KH, KW, KZ, KḤ, KṬ, L, LA, LB, LJ, LD, LH. The note marked LH completes the high octave . . .[132] (Text and ratios in brackets mine. *Zā'id* and *mujannab* in braces in Farmer's *The Music of Islam.*)

Figure 11.73 illustrates these seven divisions in the order described by Ṣafī Al-Dīn, Table 11.39 gives detailed ratio calculations, and Figure 11.74 is a fret diagram of Ṣafī Al-Dīn's *First ʿŪd Tuning.*

To understand the historic origins of the string divisions in Figure 11.73, observe that the tones of Frets 1, 3, 4, 6, and 7 also exist on Al-Kindī's *ʿūd* (see Figure 11.41), and on Al-Fārābī's *ʿūd* (see Figure 11.48). However, Ṣafī Al-Dīn then describes the position of a Theoretical Reference Point that does *not* function as a fret. Instead, Ṣafī Al-Dīn uses this Point to determine the locations of Frets 2 and 5. The former fret sounds D$\overset{\mathrm{s}}{\downarrow}$, ratio $^{65536}\!/_{59049}$, and the latter fret, E$\overset{\mathrm{s}}{\downarrow}$, ratio $^{8192}\!/_{6561}$. Consequently, notice that *all* the tones of Frets 1–7 in Figure 11.73 also occur on Frets 1–7 of String A–B on the *ṭunbūr* in Figure 11.70. We conclude, therefore, that Ṣafī Al-Dīn based his *First ʿŪd Tuning* on the tradition of the *ṭunbūr* of Khurāsān. (Incidentally, recall that in the *ṭunbūr* description in Section 11.68, Al-Fārābī states that two theoretical points — W and Zero — do not function

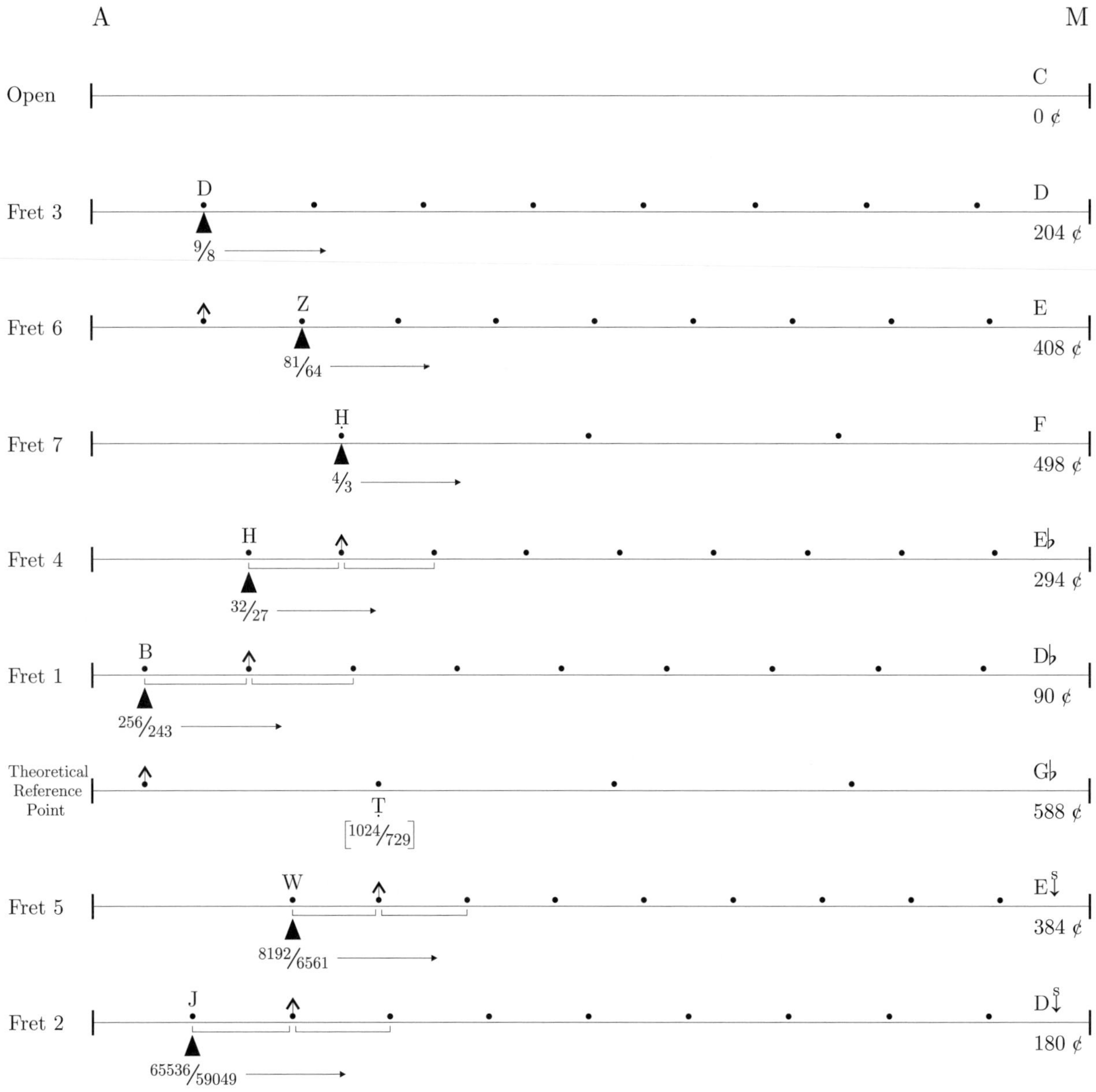

Figure 11.73 Ṣafī Al-Dīn's string length divisions used to determine the locations of seven frets of his *First ʿŪd Tuning*. The tones produced by Frets 3, 6, 7, 4, and 1 also exist on Al-Kindī's *ʿūd* (see Figure 11.41), and on Al-Fārābī's *ʿūd* (see Figure 11.48). Furthermore, *all* the tones of Frets 1–7 also occur on Frets 1–7 of String A–B on the *ṭunbūr* of Khurāsān in Figure 11.70. (Dots with arrows point to previously calculated divisions.)

as frets, but are only used to determine the locations of other frets.) Finally, since Ṣafī Al-Dīn tuned his five open strings in the tradition of the *ʿūd* — that is, in "fourth's," or 4/3's — Frets 1–7 of the *Bamm* and *Mathlath* in Figure 11.74 produce the *same* tones as Frets 1–7 of Strings A–B and J–D on Al-Fārābī's *ṭunbūr* in Figure 11.71.

An analysis of Ṣafī Al-Dīn's *First ʿŪd Tuning* reveals that it consists of an ascending spiral of four "fifths" above 1/1, and of a descending spiral of fourteen "fifths" below 1/1. Table 11.40(a) shows that the ascending spiral represents the ubiquitous pentatonic scale known the world over as ratios 1/1, 9/8, 81/64, 3/2, 27/16, [2/1]. When we combine the first twelve "fifths" of the descending spiral with

Table 11.39

MODERN LENGTH RATIO TO FREQUENCY RATIO CALCULATIONS
OF ṢAFĪ AL-DĪN'S *FIRST ʿŪD TUNING*

Open String, Tone C	$1/1$	Whole string length.
Fret 3, Tone D	$1 \times 1/9 = 1/9$ $1 - 1/9 = 9/9 - 1/9 = 8/9 \rightarrow 9/8$	Ninth of string. Whole minus subsection.
Fret 6, Tone E	$8/9 \times 1/9 = 8/81$ $8/9 - 8/81 = 72/81 - 8/81 = 64/81 \rightarrow 81/64$	Ninth of $8/9$ section. $8/9$ section minus subsection.
Fret 7, Tone F	$1 \times 1/4 = 1/4$ $1 - 1/4 = 4/4 - 1/4 = 3/4 \rightarrow 4/3$	Quarter of string. Whole minus subsection.
Fret 4, Tone E$\flat$	$3/4 \times 1/8 = 3/32$ $3/4 + 3/32 = 24/32 + 3/32 = 27/32 \rightarrow 32/27$	Eighth of $3/4$ section. $3/4$ section plus subsection.
Fret 1, Tone D$\flat$	$27/32 \times 1/8 = 27/256$ $27/32 + 27/256 =$ $216/256 + 27/256 = 243/256 \rightarrow 256/243$	Eighth of $27/32$ section. $27/32$ section plus subsection.
Point, Tone G$\flat$	$243/256 \times 1/4 = 243/1024$ $243/256 - 243/1024 =$ $972/1024 - 243/1024 = 729/1024 \rightarrow 1024/729$	Quarter of $243/256$ section. $243/256$ section minus subsection.
Fret 5, Tone E$\downarrow$	$729/1024 \times 1/8 = 729/8192$ $729/1024 + 729/8192 =$ $5832/8192 + 729/8192 = 6561/8192 \rightarrow 8192/6561$	Eighth of $729/1024$ section. $729/1024$ section plus subsection.
Fret 2, Tone D$\downarrow$	$6561/8192 \times 1/8 = 6561/65536$ $6561/8192 + 6561/65536 =$ $52488/65536 + 6561/65536 =$ $59049/65536 \rightarrow 65536/59049$	Eighth of $6561/8192$ section. $6561/8192$ section plus subsection.

the pentatonic scale of the ascending spiral, the total number equals 12 tones + 5 tones = 17 tones, or the 17-tone scale of the *lower* "octave" of Ṣafī Al-Dīn's *First ʿŪd Tuning.* Now, when we combine the following tones: the first ten "fifths," the thirteenth "fifth," and the fourteenth "fifth" of the descending spiral with the pentatonic scale of the ascending spiral, the total number equals 10 tones + 2 tones + 5 tones = 17 tones, or the 17-tone scale of the *upper* "octave" of Ṣafī Al-Dīn's *First ʿŪd Tuning.* Figure 11.74 indicates that in the second "octave," Fret 2 of the *Zīr* and *Ḥadd* does *not* sound E, ratio $81/64$, and A, ratio $27/16$; instead, it produces F$\downarrow$ and B$\flat\downarrow$, respectively. In Table 11.40(b), two arrows indicate these substitutions in the context of Ṣafī Al-Dīn's theoretical 19-tone scale.

The question naturally arises, "Why did Ṣafī Al-Dīn base his *First ʿŪd Tuning* on the *ṭunbūr* of Khurāsān?" Although no one has answered this question satisfactorily, I would like to offer these observations. Given my explanations of the schisma and comma variants in Tables 11.36 and 11.37, and my subsequent interpretation of Ṣafī Al-Dīn's *First ʿŪd Tuning* in Figure 11.74, a pattern emerges. With the exception of B$\flat\downarrow$, Ṣafī Al-Dīn may have associated the comma variants

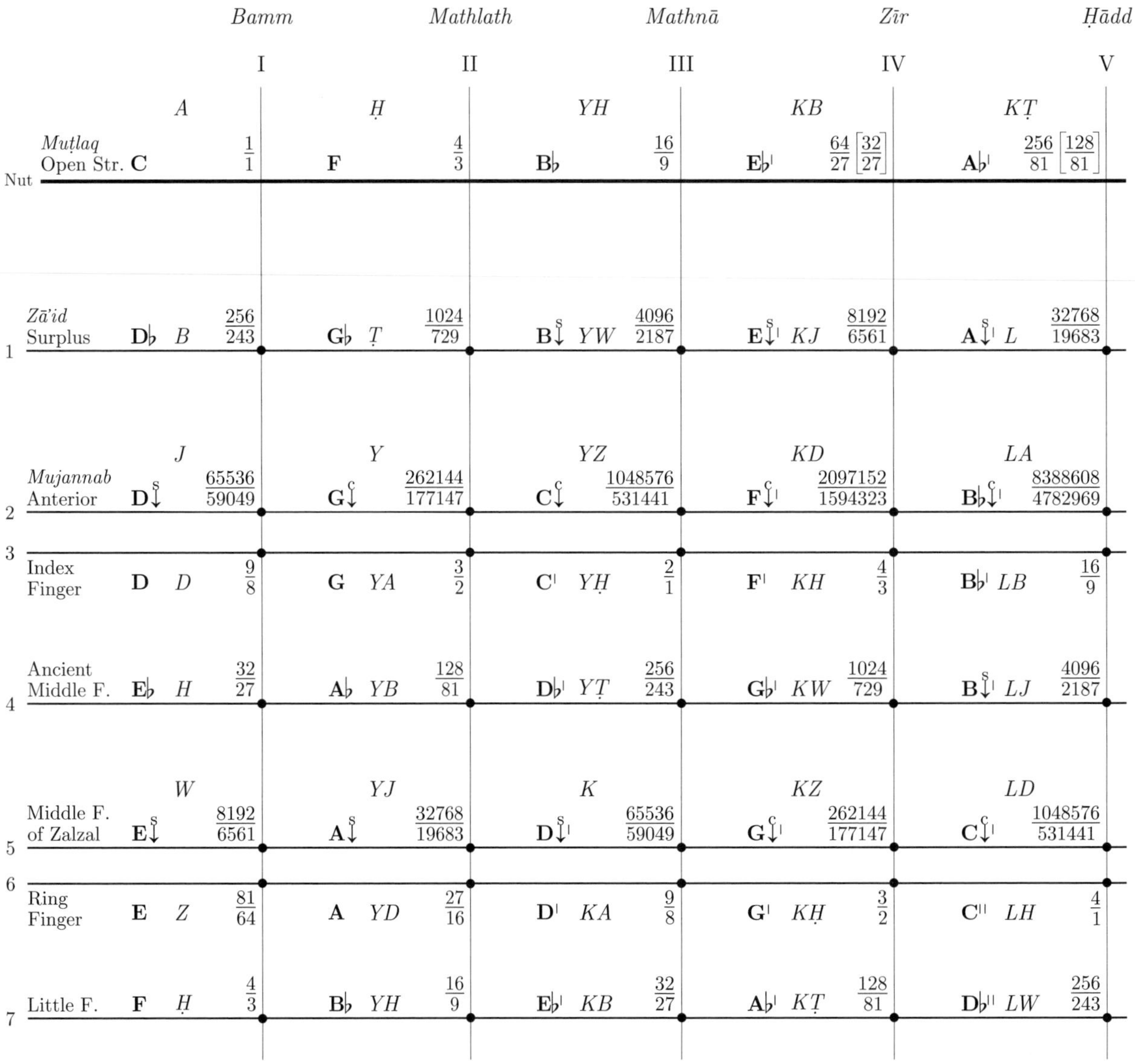

Figure 11.74 Seven fret locations of the *First 'Ūd Tuning* as defined by Ṣafī Al-Dīn (d. 1294). Frets 1–7 of the *Bamm* and *Mathlath* produce the same tones as Strings A–B and J–D of Al-Fārābī's *ṭunbūr* in Figure 11.71. (Fret locations to scale.)

with Ptolemy's *homophonic* interval C–C$^{|}$ [$1/1$–$2/1$], and with the *symphonic* intervals C–G [$1/1$–$3/2$], and C–F [$1/1$–$4/3$]; and he may have associated the schisma variants with Ptolemy's *emmelic* intervals C–D$\overset{s}{\downarrow}$ [$1/1$– $\sim 10/9$] and C–E$\overset{s}{\downarrow}$ [$1/1$– $\sim 5/4$] in the lower tetrachord C–F; the *emmelic* interval F–A$\overset{s}{\downarrow}$ [$4/3$– $\sim 5/3$] in the upper tetrachord F–B♭; and the *emmelic* interval G–B$\overset{s}{\downarrow}$ [$3/2$– $\sim 15/8$] in the upper tetrachord G–C$^{|}$.[133] The intonational variability of these and many other *emmelic* intervals may explain why the *ṭunbūr* of Khurāsān in Figure 11.70 offers choices between [D$\overset{s}{\downarrow}$, D], [E$\overset{s}{\downarrow}$, E], [A♭, A$\overset{s}{\flat}$], and [B♭, B$\overset{s}{\flat}$]; and why Ṣafī Al-Dīn's *First 'Ūd Tuning* in Figure 11.74 offers choices between [D$\overset{s}{\downarrow}$, D], [E$\overset{s}{\downarrow}$, E], [A$\overset{s}{\downarrow}$, A], and also [B♭, B$\overset{s}{\downarrow}$]. For example, in Table 11.43, which lists Ṣafī Al-Dīn's 84 Melodic Modes, the two tones that constitute the three *schisma pairs* — [D$\overset{s}{\downarrow}$, D], [E$\overset{s}{\downarrow}$, E], [A$\overset{s}{\downarrow}$, A], and also the pair [B♭, B$\overset{s}{\downarrow}$] — do *not* co-exist in any modes. In contrast, the two tones that constitute the two *comma pairs* — [G$\overset{c}{\downarrow}$, G], and [C$\overset{c}{\downarrow}$, C$^{|}$] — *do* co-exist in 21 modes, such as Modes 8–10, 20–22, etc. As a result, we conclude that some schisma variants tend to function as *emmelic* intervals that

Table 11.40

THE INNER STRUCTURE OF THE 19 TONES OF ṢAFĪ AL-DĪN'S *FIRST ʿŪD TUNING*

(a)

(4)	E	81/64	408 ¢
(3)	A	27/16	906 ¢
(2)	D	9/8	204 ¢
(1)	G	3/2	702 ¢
	C	1/1	0 ¢
(1)	F	4/3	498 ¢
(2)	B♭	16/9	996 ¢
(3)	E♭	32/27	294 ¢
(4)	A♭	128/81	792 ¢
(5)	D♭	256/243	90 ¢
(6)	G♭	1024/729	588 ¢
(7)	B$\overset{S}{\downarrow}$	4096/2187	1086 ¢
(8)	E$\overset{S}{\downarrow}$	8192/6561	384 ¢
(9)	A$\overset{S}{\downarrow}$	32768/19683	882 ¢
(10)	D$\overset{S}{\downarrow}$	65536/59049	180 ¢
(11)	G$\overset{C}{\downarrow}$	262144/177147	678 ¢
(12)	C$\overset{C}{\downarrow}$	1048576/531441	1177 ¢
(13)	[F$\overset{C}{\downarrow}$]	2097152/1594323	475 ¢
(14)	[B♭$\overset{C}{\downarrow}$]	8388608/4782969	973 ¢

(b)

1/1			**9/8**			**81/64**					**3/2**			**27/16**					**2/1**
C	D♭	D$\overset{S}{\downarrow}$	**D**	E♭	E$\overset{S}{\downarrow}$	**E**	[F$\overset{C}{\downarrow}$]	F	G♭	G$\overset{C}{\downarrow}$	**G**	A♭	A$\overset{S}{\downarrow}$	**A**	[B♭$\overset{C}{\downarrow}$]	B♭	B$\overset{S}{\downarrow}$	C$\overset{C}{\downarrow}$	**C'**
0 ¢	90 ¢	180 ¢	204 ¢	294 ¢	384 ¢	408 ¢	475 ¢	498 ¢	588 ¢	678 ¢	702 ¢	792 ¢	882 ¢	906 ¢	973 ¢	996 ¢	1086 ¢	1177 ¢	1200 ¢

accentuate the subtle melodic differences between modes; whereas some comma variants tend to function as leading tones that accentuate the basic consonances, that is, the *homophonic* and *symphonic* intervals of a given mode.

∾ 11.71 ∾

Before we continue with Ṣafī Al-Dīn's *Second ʿŪd Tuning*, let us first discuss two new musical symbols. Recall that in Section 11.53, I introduced the modern Persian *koron* sign: ⊳, and the modern Persian *sori* sign: ⊳. I used these signs for two reasons: (1) they remind us of the historic precedence of Persian music; (2) they are essential to the notation of the Persian *dastgāha*. However, now that we are preparing for a discussion on modern Arabian music, I would like to substitute the Western *half flat sign:* 𝄳, which indicates a tone that is approximately 30–70 ¢ flat of a given standard

Pythagorean pitch; and the Western *half sharp sign:* 𝄲, which indicates a tone that is approximately 30–70 ¢ sharp of a given standard Pythagorean pitch. These two signs have the same musical function as the *koron* and *sori* signs, and frequently appear in discussions and transcriptions of Arabian music.

~ 11.72 ~

In the *Risālat al-Sharafīya*, Ṣafī Al-Dīn continues his *'ūd* tuning description by giving three alternate locations for Fret 2, and one alternate location for Fret 5.

> XI. — ***We most frequently find the fret J*** halfway between B [256/243] and D [9/8]. Yet sometimes it is placed at an equal distance from the *ancient middle finger* [32/27] and the nut [1/1], or again, halfway between the nut [1/1] and the *middle finger of Zalzal* [8192/6561]. It is still called [anterior] when it occupies any of these three positions.
>
> Also, sometimes the fret W is placed halfway between the index finger [9/8] and the little finger [4/3]; it is then called the *Persian middle finger* [72/59]. ***This fret is often used in our time*** whereas one rarely uses the *middle finger of Zalzal* [8192/6561] or the surplus fret [256/243].[134] (Bold italics, and text and ratios in brackets mine.)

Figure 11.75 illustrates the four divisions in the order described by Ṣafī Al-Dīn, Table 11.41 gives detailed ratio calculations, and Figure 11.76 is a fret diagram of Ṣafī Al-Dīn's *Second 'Ūd Tuning.*

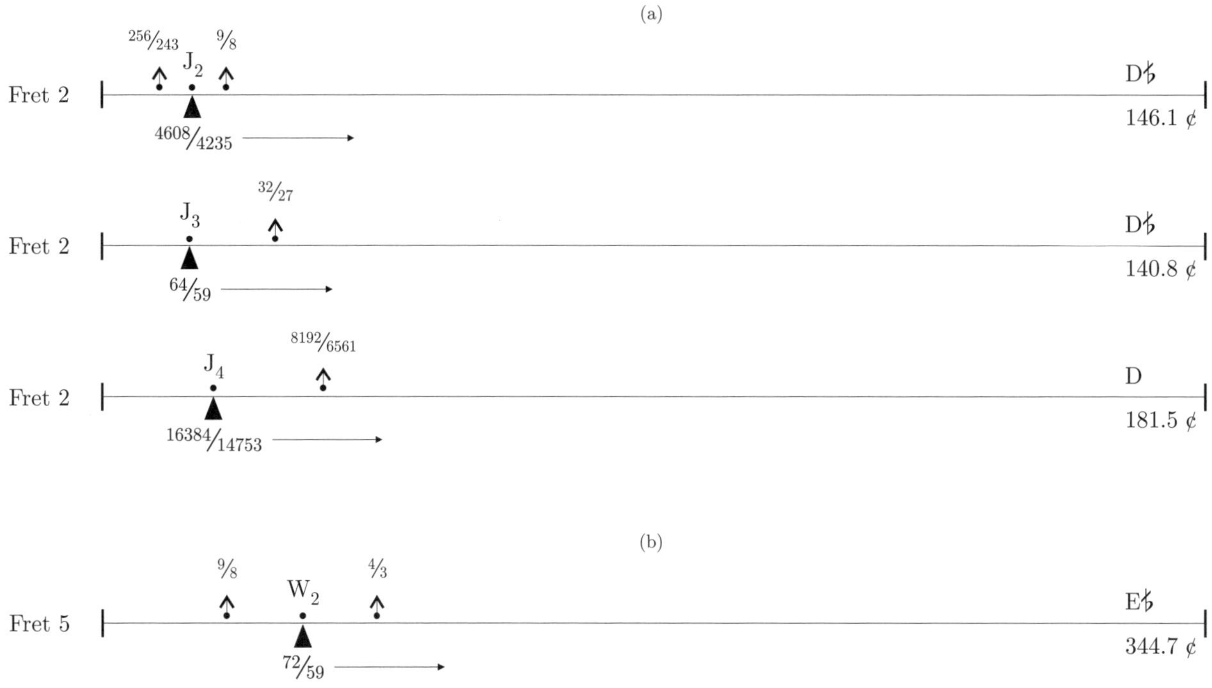

Figure 11.75 In his second *'ūd* tuning description in the *Risālat al-Sharafīya*, Ṣafī Al-Dīn also specified (a) three alternate locations for Fret 2, and (b) one alternate location for Fret 5. Suppose we tune Fret 2 to D𝄳, or the "neutral second," ratio 4608/4235 [146 ¢], and Fret 5 to E𝄳, or the "neutral third," ratio 72/59 [345 ¢]. Figure 11.76 shows that in the lower "octave," Fret 2 produces G𝄳 [644 ¢] on the *Mathlath*, and C𝄳 [1142 ¢] on the *Mathnā;* and Fret 5 produces A𝄳 [843 ¢] on the *Mathlath.* (Dots with arrows point to previously calculated divisions.)

Table 11.41

MODERN LENGTH RATIO TO FREQUENCY RATIO CALCULATIONS OF THREE ALTERNATE LOCATIONS FOR FRET 2, AND ONE ALTERNATE LOCATION FOR FRET 5, OF ṢAFĪ AL-DĪN'S *SECOND ʿŪD TUNING*

	J_2	
Fret 2, Tone D$\not\flat$	$^{243}/_{256} - {}^{8}/_{9} =$	
	$^{2187}/_{2304} - {}^{2048}/_{2304} = {}^{139}/_{2304}$	Length of internal section.
	$^{139}/_{2304} \times {}^{1}/_{2} = {}^{139}/_{4608}$	Half of internal section.
	$^{243}/_{256} - {}^{139}/_{4608} =$	
	$^{4374}/_{4608} - {}^{139}/_{4608} =$	
	$^{4235}/_{4608} \rightarrow {}^{4608}/_{4235} = 146.1$ ¢	$^{243}/_{256}$ section minus subsection.
	J_3	
Fret 2, Tone D$\not\flat$	$^{32}/_{32} - {}^{27}/_{32} = {}^{5}/_{32}$	Complement of $^{27}/_{32}$ section.
	$^{5}/_{32} \times {}^{1}/_{2} = {}^{5}/_{64}$	Half of complement.
	$^{64}/_{64} - {}^{5}/_{64} = {}^{59}/_{64} \rightarrow {}^{64}/_{59} = 140.8$ ¢	Whole minus subsection.
	J_4	
Fret 2, Tone D	$^{8192}/_{8192} - {}^{6561}/_{8192} = {}^{1631}/_{8192}$	Complement of $^{6561}/_{8192}$ section.
	$^{1631}/_{8192} \times {}^{1}/_{2} = {}^{1631}/_{16384}$	Half of complement.
	$^{16384}/_{16384} - {}^{1631}/_{16384} =$	
	$^{14753}/_{16384} \rightarrow {}^{16384}/_{14753} = 181.5$ ¢	Whole minus subsection.
	* * *	
	W_2	
Fret 5, Tone E$\not\flat$	$^{8}/_{9} - {}^{3}/_{4} = {}^{32}/_{36} - {}^{27}/_{36} = {}^{5}/_{36}$	Length of internal section.
	$^{5}/_{36} \times {}^{1}/_{2} = {}^{5}/_{72}$	Half of internal section.
	$^{8}/_{9} - {}^{5}/_{72} = {}^{64}/_{72} - {}^{5}/_{72} =$	
	$^{59}/_{72} \rightarrow {}^{72}/_{59} = 344.7$ ¢	$^{8}/_{9}$ section minus subsection.

Of the three possibilities discussed for Fret 2, Ṣafī Al-Dīn acknowledges that the first alternate location, ratio $^{4608}/_{4235}$ [146.1 ¢], occurs most frequently in the *ʿūd* tuning tradition. This fret is musically indistinguishable from Al-Fārābī's "neutral second," ratio $^{162}/_{149}$ [144.8 ¢], in Figure 11.48; and it closely approximates Ibn Sīnā's "neutral second," ratio $^{13}/_{12}$ [138.6 ¢], in Figure 11.62.

With respect to the second possibility for Fret 5, Ṣafī Al-Dīn also acknowledges that the alternate location, ratio $^{72}/_{59}$ [344.7 ¢], most frequently occurs on the *ʿūd.* This fret closely approximates Al-Fārābī's "neutral third," ratio $^{27}/_{22}$ [354.5 ¢], in the former figure; and it is musically indistinguishable from Ibn Sīnā's "neutral third," ratio $^{39}/_{32}$ [342.5 ¢], in the latter figure. Turn back to Section 11.59, Quote I, and note that Ṣafī Al-Dīn followed Ibn Sīnā's instruction for placing this fret ". . . halfway between the index finger and the little finger." Therefore, the only significant difference between the texts of these three theorists is that Al-Fārābī and Ibn Sīnā referred to Fret 5 as the *middle finger of Zalzal,* whereas Ṣafī Al-Dīn referred to this alternative as the *Persian middle*

Fret		*Bamm* I (*A*)	*Mathlath* II (*Ḥ*)	*Mathnā* III (*YH*)	*Zīr* IV (*KB*)	*Ḥādd* V (*KṬ*)
Nut	*Muṭlaq* Open Str.	**C** 1/1	**F** 4/3	**B♭** 16/9	**E♭ˡ** 64/27 [32/27]	**A♭ˡ** 256/81 [128/81]
1	*Zā'id* Surplus	**D♭** *B* 256/243	**G♭** *Ṭ* 1024/729	**B↓** *YW* 4096/2187	**E↓ˡ** *KJ* 8192/6561	**A↓ˡ** *L* 32768/19683
2	***Mujannab* Anterior**	**D𝄳** *J* 4608/4235	**G𝄳** *Y* 6144/4235	**C𝄳** *YZ* 8192/4235	**F𝄳ˡ** *KD* 16384/12705	**A‡ˡ** *LA* 65536/38115
3	Index F.	**D** *D* 9/8	**G** *YA* 3/2	**Cˡ** *YḤ* 2/1	**Fˡ** *KH* 4/3	**B♭ˡ** *LB* 16/9
4	Ancient Middle F.	**E♭** *H* 32/27	**A♭** *YB* 128/81	**D♭ˡ** *YṬ* 256/243	**G♭ˡ** *KW* 1024/729	**B↓ˡ** *LJ* 4096/2187
5	**Persian Middle F.**	**E𝄳** *W* 72/59	**A𝄳** *YJ* 96/59	**D𝄳ˡ** *K* 64/59	**G𝄳ˡ** *KZ* 256/177	**C𝄳ˡ** *LD* 1024/531
6	Ring F.	**E** *Z* 81/64	**A** *YD* 27/16	**Dˡ** *KA* 9/8	**Gˡ** *KḤ* 3/2	**Cˡˡ** *LH* 4/1
7	Little F.	**F** *Ḥ* 4/3	**B♭** *YH* 16/9	**E♭ˡ** *KB* 32/27	**A♭ˡ** *KṬ* 128/81	**D♭ˡˡ** *LW* 256/243

Figure 11.76 I derived this 17-tone *'ūd* tuning from Ṣafī Al-Dīn's description of alternate locations for Frets 2 and 5. Throughout this text, I refer to this scale as Ṣafī Al-Dīn's *Second 'Ūd Tuning.* (Fret locations to scale.)

finger. Since Ibn Sīnā was a Persian, and since he accurately described the older Persian musical tradition, Ṣafī Al-Dīn did not name this fret incorrectly. Furthermore, Farmer reminds us, "[Fret 5] was a neutral third, an interval which appears to have been used much earlier than [Manṣūr] Zalzal [d. 791], and still persists in Arabic-speaking lands."[135] (Text in brackets mine.)

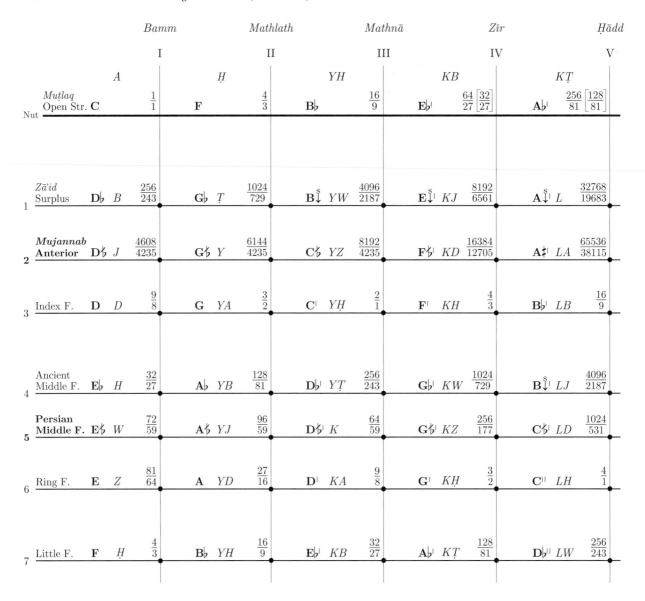

In the last sentence, Ṣafī Al-Dīn concedes that ". . . one rarely uses the *middle finger of Zalzal* [8192/6561] or the surplus fret [256/243]." Because he acknowledged the possibility of tuning a "neutral third," Ṣafī Al-Dīn knew that the surplus fret, or the "semitone," ratio 256/243, is of little use. Consequently, to produce a "whole tone" below the Persian middle finger, ratio 72/59, he provided a new *mujannab* fret between the *zā'id* fret and the index finger fret. So, in Figure 11.76, the "whole tone" between D𝄳–E𝄳 now sounds interval ratio $72/59 \div 4608/4235 = 4235/3776$ [198.6 ¢], which closely approximates interval ratio 9/8 [203.9 ¢]. Also, notice that the "octaves" between Fret 2 and Fret 5 — or between D𝄳–D𝄳ˡ, G𝄳–G𝄳ˡ, C𝄳–C𝄳ˡ — sound interval ratio 4235/2124 [1194.7 ¢], which closely approximates interval ratio $2/1$ [1200.0 ¢]. On this *'ūd*, the former "whole tone" and the latter "octaves" are only 5.3 ¢ flat of their respective Pythagorean counterparts.

Finally, if we once more ask why Ṣafī Al-Dīn preferred his *First 'Ūd Tuning* in Figure 11.74 over his *Second 'Ūd Tuning* in Figure 11.76, the answer may again reside in the schisma variants. Apparently, Ṣafī Al-Dīn had a greater musical affinity for the subtle melodic differences of the *schisma intervals*, which originated in the older Persian *ṭunbūr* tradition, than for the obvious melodic differences of the *neutral intervals*, which originated in the newer Arabian *'ūd* tradition. However, in the final analysis, his record is complete. Like Al-Fārābī before him, Ṣafī Al-Dīn was fully aware that two completely different tuning traditions existed during the same period of time.

11.73

Before we continue with Ṣafī Al-Dīn's 84 Melodic Modes, let us first examine a second description of the *First 'Ūd Tuning*, which appears in Al-Jurjānī's *Sharḥ Maulānā Mubārak Shāh* (The Mubārak Shāh commentary). Throughout this work, Al-Jurjānī cites quotations from Ṣafī Al-Dīn's second treatise entitled *Kitāb al-adwār* (Book of the modes [of music]), and gives commentaries on such excerpted passages. Therefore, in the following description of a 17-tone monochord tuning, all text that appears in quotation marks belongs to the *Kitāb al-adwār.*

> ". . . The notes upon which all melodies move are seventeen in number, all capable of being drawn from the monochord . . ."
>
> We have already said that the author [Ṣafī Al-Dīn] set the number of notes at seventeen and, in our days, this is the number of [***contact points between strings and frets***] placed in the lower octave on the neck of the *'ūd.* All melodies known among us can be drawn from these points; this is why the author said that all melodies move on these notes. Although all these notes are within the range of the monochord, it is difficult to use this instrument in actual practice [because] performances [on it] would lack brilliance and beauty. We were able, however, to see a man draw most of these melodies from a single-stringed instrument called a *KANKARAH;* he was able to do this thanks to his mastery and skill in the practice of the art, and to a certain knowledge of musical theory.
>
> The author divides the string and determines on it the seventeen sections [[which correspond to notes]] of which he speaks.
>
> [1] ". . . Take string A–M. Divide it into two equal parts and mark the point which results from the division *YḤ* . . ."
>
> [*YḤ* → $2/1$ = 1200.0 ¢]
>
> [2] ". . . Next, we divide the string into three parts and we mark *YA* at the end of the first, counting from below [or, counting from the left end of the string marked A] . . ."
>
> [*YA* → $3/2$ = 702.0 ¢]
>
> [3] ". . . Then divide the string into fourths, and mark the end of the first of these fourths *Ḥ* . . ."
>
> [*Ḥ* → $4/3$ = 498.0 ¢]

[4] ". . . Divide the section Ḥ–M into fourths, and mark the end of the first of these fourths YH . . ."

$$[YH \rightarrow {}^{16}\!/_{9} = 996.1\ ¢]$$

[5] ". . . Then divide the whole string into nine [parts], and mark the end of the first ninth D . . ."

$$[D \rightarrow {}^{9}\!/_{8} = 203.9\ ¢]$$

[6] ". . . Next, divide section D–M into nine parts, and at the end of the first of these ninths, mark Z . . ."

$$[Z \rightarrow {}^{81}\!/_{64} = 407.8\ ¢]$$

[7] ". . . We divide section Ḥ–M into eighths; then to these eighths we ***add*** another, on the lower side [or, in the direction of the left end marked A], at the end of which we mark H . . ."

$$[H \rightarrow {}^{32}\!/_{27} = 294.1\ ¢]$$

[8] ". . . We next divide section H–M into eighths; then to these eighths we ***add*** another lower [or, in the direction of A], at the end of which we mark B . . ."

$$[B \rightarrow {}^{256}\!/_{243} = 90.2\ ¢]$$

[9] ". . . We divide section B–M first of all into thirds and we mark YB at the end of the first third;

$$[YB \rightarrow {}^{128}\!/_{81} = 792.2\ ¢]$$

[10] then into fourths and we mark Ṭ at the end of the first fourth . . ."

$$[Ṭ \rightarrow {}^{1024}\!/_{729} = 588.3\ ¢]$$

[11] ". . . We then divide section Ṭ–M into fourths, and we mark YW at the end of the first fourth . . ."

$$[YW \rightarrow {}^{4096}\!/_{2187} = 1086.3\ ¢]$$

[12] ". . . We divide section YW–M into two equal parts, then we ***add*** to the lower part of this section [or, in the direction of A] a portion equal to one of these halves, and at the end of this portion we mark W . . ."

$$[W \rightarrow {}^{8192}\!/_{6561} = 384.4\ ¢]$$

[13] ". . . We divide section W–M into eighths; then to these eighths, we ***add*** another lower [or, in the direction of A], at the end of which we mark J . . ."

$$[J \rightarrow {}^{65536}\!/_{59049} = 180.5\ ¢]$$

[14] ". . . Divide the section J–M into fourths, and mark the end of the first fourth Y . . ."

$$[Y \rightarrow {}^{262144}\!/_{177147} = 678.5\ ¢]$$

[15] ". . . Divide the section W–M into fourths, and mark the end of the first of these fourths YJ . . ."

$$[YJ \rightarrow {}^{32768}\!/_{19683} = 882.4\ ¢]$$

[16(a)] ". . . We divide section Z–M into thirds, and at the end of the first third we mark YZ . . ."

$$[YZ \rightarrow {}^{243}\!/_{128} = 1109.8\ ¢]$$

[16(b)] *According to other copies of the book* [Ṣafī Al-Dīn's *Kitāb al-adwār*] *that we are commenting on, section Y–M is divided into fourths, and the end of the first fourth is marked YZ.*

$$[YZ \rightarrow {}^{1048576}\!/_{531441} = 1176.5\ ¢]$$

The first method is better for whoever gives more importance to ratios of the fifth, which is preferable. But the second division agrees more with the fretting system of the lute, as will be seen further on.

[17] ". . . Finally, we divide section Z–M into fourths, and at the end of the first fourth we mark YD . . ."

$$[YD \rightarrow {}^{27}\!/_{16} = 905.9\ ¢]$$

These are the locations of all the frets . . .[136] (Italics, bold italics, and text, numbers, and ratios in brackets mine. Bold italics in brackets my correction of an unedited error in *La Musique Arabe.* Text in double brackets in *La Musique Arabe.*)

The most difficult aspect of this description is that it vacillates between a tuning intended for a monochord, and a tuning intended for an *'ūd.* Al-Jurjānī begins with Ṣafī Al-Dīn's comments on a monochord, and ends with his own reference to the frets on an *'ūd.* This confusion between a monochord tuning and an *'ūd* tuning has negative repercussions throughout the French translation of Al-Jurjānī's treatise in *La Musique Arabe, Volume 3.*

Observe that in this tuning description, the sixteenth division consists of two completely different possibilities. Division 16(a) produces $YZ = {}^{243}\!/_{128}$; but Division 16(b) produces $YZ = {}^{1048576}\!/_{531441}$. To calculate the former division, note that in Division 6, we may interpret Section Z–M as modern length ratio ${}^{64}\!/_{81}$.[137] With this ratio, the calculations below demonstrate that Division 16(a) yields

Tone YZ	${}^{64}\!/_{81} \times {}^{1}\!/_{3} = {}^{64}\!/_{243}$	Third of ${}^{64}\!/_{81}$ section.
	${}^{64}\!/_{81} - {}^{64}\!/_{243} = {}^{192}\!/_{243} - {}^{64}\!/_{243} = {}^{128}\!/_{243} \rightarrow {}^{243}\!/_{128}$	${}^{64}\!/_{81}$ section minus subsection.

In contrast, to calculate the latter division, note that in Division 14, we may interpret Section Y–M as modern length ratio ${}^{177147}\!/_{262144}$. With this ratio, the calculations below demonstrate that Division 16(b) yields

Tone YZ	${}^{177147}\!/_{262144} \times {}^{1}\!/_{4} = {}^{177147}\!/_{1048576}$	Quarter of ${}^{177147}\!/_{262144}$ section.
	${}^{177147}\!/_{262144} - {}^{177147}\!/_{1048576} =$	
	${}^{708588}\!/_{1048576} - {}^{177147}\!/_{1048576} =$	
	${}^{531441}\!/_{1048576} \rightarrow {}^{1048576}\!/_{531441}$	${}^{177147}\!/_{262144}$ minus subsection.

In his commentary, Al-Jurjānī states that Division 16(a) ". . . gives more importance to ratios of the fifth." For example, to play the interval of a "fifth," ratio ${}^{3}\!/_{2}$, above the Pythagorean "major third," ratio ${}^{81}\!/_{64}$, requires Pythagorean ratio ${}^{81}\!/_{64} \times {}^{3}\!/_{2} = {}^{243}\!/_{128}$. On the other hand, he then acknowledges that Division 16(b) ". . . agrees more with the fretting system of the lute . . ." Why? Because the open strings of the traditional *'ūd* are tuned in "fourth's," or ${}^{4}\!/_{3}$'s. Figure 11.74 shows that if Ṣafī Al-Dīn tunes $\mathrm{D}\overset{\mathrm{s}}{\downarrow}$, or the "schisma second" on the *Bamm*, then Fret 2 must produce $\mathrm{C}\overset{\mathrm{c}}{\downarrow}$, or the "comma octave," on the *Mathnā*. Consequently, Al-Jurjānī's qualifying statement is potentially confusing because Division 16(b) does not in some arbitrary or mysterious manner ". . . agree more . . ." with the fretting of an *'ūd*. The fact is, Division 16(b) is the only tuning that works on a traditional *'ūd*.

Unfortunately, in *La Musique Arabe, Volume 3*, p. 230, the *Blessed Table* — discussed at length in Section 10.47 — was filled out by Al-Manūbī al-Sanūsī (the translator and editor of Al-Jurjānī's treatise), not according to Division 16(b) for the *'ūd*, but according to Division 16(a) for the monochord. As a result, directly below ratio $2/1$ at the top of the triangular-shaped table, two diamond-shaped spaces do not indicate the *'ūd* ratio $1048576/531441$, but the monochord ratio $243/128$. Since Ṣafī Al-Dīn primarily based his 84 Melodic Modes on the *First 'Ūd Tuning*, al-Sanūsī's interpretation of

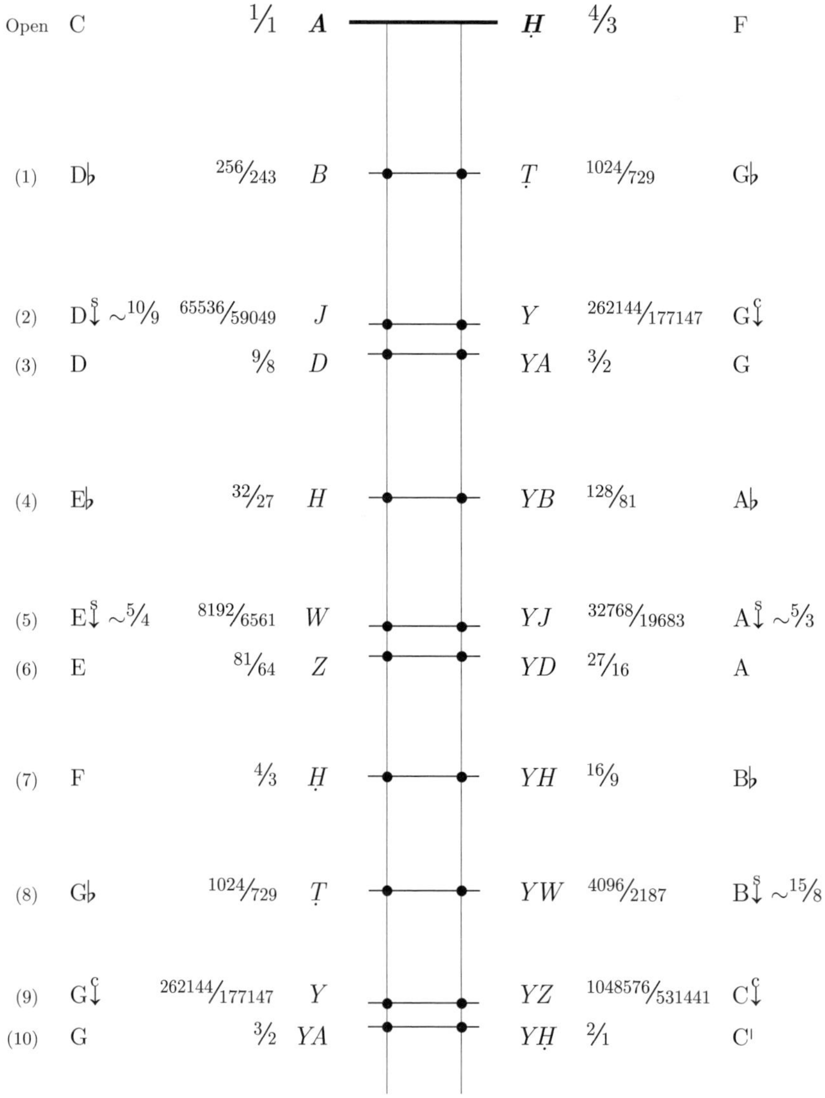

Figure 11.77 Ṣafī Al-Dīn and Al-Jurjānī discuss and demonstrate that the lower 17-tone "octave" of the *First 'Ūd Tuning* may be played on a *ṭunbūr* with only two strings and ten frets. When compared to Al-Fārābī's *ṭunbūr* in Figure 11.71, all but one of the first ten frets match the ten frets of Ṣafī Al-Dīn's *ṭunbūr*. Fret 9 on Al-Fārābī's instrument sounds F♯, ratio $729/512$, on the first string, and B, ratio $243/128$, on the second string. (Fret locations to scale.)

the magnificent *Blessed Table* introduces an element of doubt and confusion that is completely unnecessary. Indeed, had Al-Jurjānī failed to include Division 16(b), his entire work would be subject to question. However, such is not the case.

Another serious error occurs in *La Musique Arabe, Volume 3*, p. 370. This page includes a fret diagram of a *ṭunbūr* of Khurāsān equipped with two strings and ten frets. According to Ṣafī Al-Dīn and Al-Jurjānī, the second open string is tuned a "fourth," ratio $\frac{4}{3}$, above the first open string, ratio $\frac{1}{1}$. Turn to Figure 11.77, which illustrates an edited version of this diagram. In *L.M.A.*, the figure shows the strings and frets, the Arabic note names, and a solfège notation that is incorrect.

To understand this error, we must first analyze the solfège notation. In the key of G (or sol_1), *La Musique Arabe* illustrates Division 16(a) by notating the "major third," ratio $\frac{81}{64}$, as B (or *si*), and the "fifth" above, ratio $\frac{243}{128}$, as F♯ (or *fa*♯). (See the monochord diagram in *L.M.A., Vol. 3*, p. 224.) In contrast, *La Musique Arabe* illustrates Division 16(b) by notating the "comma fifth," ratio $\frac{262144}{177147}$, as D^{-c} (or *rè*$^{-c}$), and the "fourth" above, ratio $\frac{1048576}{531441}$, as G_2^{-c} (or sol_2^{-c}). (See the *'ūd* diagram in *L.M.A., Vol. 3*, p. 372.) Observe the difference between the former F♯ and the latter G_2^{-c}, expressed in *La Musique Arabe* as the difference between *fa*♯ and sol_2^{-c}.

On Ṣafī Al-Dīn's *ṭunbūr*, Fret 9 of the first string sounds Tone *Y*, ratio $\frac{262144}{177147}$. In the key of C, Figure 11.77 correctly identifies this tone on Fret 9 of the first string as G$\overset{c}{\downarrow}$. *La Musique Arabe* shows this tone as D^{-c} (or *rè*$^{-c}$). Since the second string is tuned a "fourth" above the first string, Fret 9 of the second string sounds Tone *YZ*, ratio $\frac{1048576}{531441}$. Figure 11.77 correctly identifies this tone on Fret 9 of the second string as C$\overset{c}{\downarrow}$. In contrast, *La Musique Arabe* shows this tone as F♯ (or *fa*♯). This is incorrect because F♯ (or *fa*♯) results from Division 16(a) for the monochord. *La Musique Arabe* should have shown Tone *YZ* as G_2^{-c} (or sol_2^{-c}), which results from Division 16(b) for the *'ūd*. In short, on Ṣafī Al-Dīn's *ṭunbūr* and *'ūd* — equipped with open strings tuned in "fourth's" — ratio $\frac{243}{128}$ simply does *not* exist.

Some readers may consider such an error a simple oversight. However, throughout Al-Jurjānī's text on Ṣafī Al-Dīn's 84 Melodic Modes, *La Musique Arabe, Volume 3*, identifies Tone *YZ* as (*fa*♯). In the context of Ṣafī Al-Dīn's *First 'Ūd Tuning*, all such parenthetical interpretations are incorrect. Also, in Al-Jurjānī's treatise, the fret diagram of the *ṭunbūr* of Khurāsān occurs immediately before Article Eight. This chapter discusses the fingering chart of Ṣafī Al-Dīn's *First 'Ūd Tuning* in full detail. Therefore, the critical distinction between the tuning for a monochord, and the tuning for a *ṭunbūr* or an *'ūd*, is essential for an accurate understanding of the figure. Furthermore, Ṣafī Al-Dīn's and Al-Jurjānī's transition from *ṭunbūr* tuning to *'ūd* tuning has historic precedence. More than three hundred years before Ṣafī Al-Dīn, Al-Fārābī described a similar musical transition in his *Kitāb al-mūsīqī al-kabīr*.[138]

11.74

In the *Risālat al-Sharafīya* and *Kitāb al-adwār*, Ṣafī Al-Dīn described three *emmelic* intervals called Ṭ, J, and B, which he used to construct his melodic modes.[139] The large interval Ṭ (for *ṭanīnī;* lit. *resonant;* traditionally, the name for the "whole tone," ratio $\frac{9}{8}$) spans four consecutive tones; the medium interval J (as in interval *A–J*) spans three consecutive tones; and the small interval B (for *baqiyyah;* lit. *remainder*, or *remnant*) spans two consecutive tones. Unfortunately, these three definitions are ambiguous because every such interval has two completely different interpretations in the context of Ṣafī Al-Dīn's *First 'Ūd Tuning.* The first music theorist to address this problem was Al-Jurjānī. In the *Sharḥ Maulānā Mubārak Shāh*, Al-Jurjānī accurately observed that there are two different 4-tone intervals, two different 3-tone intervals, and two different 2-tone intervals on Ṣafī Al-Dīn's *First 'Ūd.*[140]

For a ratio analysis of Ṭ, J, and B, turn to Table 11.42. Here Rows 1 and 3 give the Arabian and Western note names of the lower "octave" of Ṣafī Al-Dīn's *First ʿŪd Tuning* as depicted in Figure 11.74; and Row 2 shows the distribution of limmas and commas throughout the scale. Now, two *large* brackets above Row 1 indicate two different 4-tone intervals in the scale. (1) In Row 4, interval *A–D*, or $Ṭ_1$, represents interval ratio (i.r.) 9⁄8, which consists of a double-limma times a comma [L×L×C]. (2) In contrast, in Row 5, interval *Z–Y*, or $Ṭ_2$, represents i.r. 16777216⁄14348907, which consists of a triple-limma [L×L×L]. Ṣafī Al-Dīn considered the latter interval a dissonance.[141] Consequently, the triple-limma does not appear in his melodic modes.

Two *medium* brackets above Row 1 indicate two different 3-tone intervals in the scale. (1) In Row 6, interval *A–J*, or J_1, represents i.r. 65536⁄59049, which consists of a double-limma [L×L]. Al-Jurjānī refers to this interval as a *tatimmah* (lit. *complement*, or *conclusion*), and states that when one increases it by a comma, one obtains the *ṭanīnī* [L×L×C]. (2) In contrast, in Row 7, interval *B–D*, or J_2, represents the Greek *apotome*, or i.r. 2187⁄2048, which consists of a limma times a comma [L×C]. Al-Jurjānī refers to this interval as a *mutammam* (lit. *that which is complete*), and states that when one increases it by a limma, one obtains the *ṭanīnī* [L×L×C]. In short, the term *tatimmah* refers to the large interval called J, and *mutammam*, to the small interval called J.

The two *small* brackets below Row 2 indicate two different 2-tone intervals in the scale. (1) In Row 8, interval *A–B*, or B_1, represents the Greek *limma* [L], or i.r. 256⁄243. Al-Jurjānī refers to this interval as a *baqiyyah*. (2) In contrast, in Row 9, interval *J–D*, or B_2, represents i.r. 531441⁄524288, which is the comma of Pythagoras [C]. Al-Jurjānī refers to this interval as a *faḍlah* (lit. *surplus*, or *remainder*) and, thereby, intentionally distinguishes it from the *baqiyyah*. (In the earlier writings of Al-Fārābī and Ibn Sīnā, *faḍlah* referred to the limma. This caused a great deal of confusion. Al-Jurjānī's terminology alleviated the problem because he exclusively used the term *baqiyyah* to describe the limma, and *faḍlah* to describe the comma.)[142] In short, the term *baqiyyah* refers to the large interval called B, and *faḍlah*, to the small interval called B.

A further examination of Rows 4–9 reveals that we may identify T_1 by a 2-tone gap, or [2]; J_1 and J_2 by a 1-tone gap, or [1]; and B_1 and B_2 by a 0-tone gap, or [0]. Although such a system of notation is not perfect, it makes the task of identifying interval patterns of tetrachords and pentachords a little easier. For example, in the *Risālat al-Sharafīya*, Ṣafī Al-Dīn defines two different kinds of tetrachords.[143] The first kind includes three permutations of two Ṭ's and one B — Ṭ, Ṭ, B; Ṭ, B, Ṭ; and B, Ṭ, Ṭ. We may notate this type as: 2, 2, 0; 2, 0, 2; 0, 2, 2. The second kind includes three permutations of one Ṭ and two J's — Ṭ, J, J; J, J, Ṭ; J, Ṭ, J. We may notate this type as: 2, 1, 1; 1, 1, 2; 1, 2, 1. Ṣafī Al-Dīn then defines a unique 5-tone tetrachord. (In this context, we do not give the word *tetrachord* a literal interpretation, "four strings," but a theoretical interpretation, interval ratio 4⁄3.) This type of tetrachord includes three J's and one B — J, J, J, B; or 1, 1, 1, 0.

Turn to Table 11.43, which shows Ṣafī Al-Dīn's 84 Melodic Modes according to his *First ʿŪd Tuning* and *Second ʿŪd Tuning*. I transcribed these modes from a table in Al-Jurjānī's commentary on Ṣafī Al-Dīn's *Kitāb al-adwār*.[144] However, Al-Jurjānī gives the 84 Melodic Modes only in the context of the *First ʿŪd Tuning*. Observe that the modes are organized in seven groups of twelve modes each; that is, $7 \times 12 = 84$. Each of the seven groups (1) includes a lower tetrachord *A–Ḥ*, or C–F, and (2) begins with a tetrachord in the same order discussed above. Therefore, Modes 1–12 begin with tetrachord 2, 2, 0; Modes 13–24, with tetrachord 2, 0, 2; Modes 25–36, with tetrachord 0, 2, 2; Modes 37–48, with tetrachord 2, 1, 1; Modes 49–60, with tetrachord 1, 1, 2; Modes 61–72, with tetrachord 1, 2, 1; and Modes 73–84, with tetrachord 1, 1, 1, 0. In Table 11.43, one may recognize these patterns by simply comparing the sizes of the 2-tone, 1-tone, and 0-tone gaps between tones.

Now, notice that all the tones of interval *Ḥ–YḤ*, or F–C′, of the first group — or of Modes 1–12 — also constitute all the tones of interval *Ḥ–YḤ*, or F–C′, of the six other groups. Furthermore,

Table 11.42

THREE TYPES OF EMMELIC INTERVALS — Ṭ, J, AND B — USED BY ṢAFĪ AL-DĪN TO DEFINE 84 MELODIC MODES

Not Used (Z–Y)

A	*B*	*J*	*D*	*H*	*W*	*Z*	*Ḥ*	*Ṭ*	*Y*	*YA*	*YB*	*YJ*	*YD*	*YH*	*YW*	*YZ*	*YḤ*	(1)
L	L	C	L	L	C	L	L	L	C	L	L	C	L	L	L	C		(2)
C	D♭	$D\overset{s}{\downarrow}$	D	E♭	$E\overset{s}{\downarrow}$	E	F	G♭	$G\overset{c}{\downarrow}$	G	A♭	$A\overset{s}{\downarrow}$	A	B♭	$B\overset{s}{\downarrow}$	$C\overset{c}{\downarrow}$	C′	(3)

Two 4-Tone Intervals

Ṭ$_1$ (*Ṭanīnī*)

A [*B*, *J*] *D*

C [D♭, $D\overset{s}{\downarrow}$] D

$1/1$ [**2**] $9/8$

i.r. = $9/8$ = [L×L×C] = 204 ¢ (4)

Not Used

Ṭ$_2$

Z [*Ḥ*, *Ṭ*] *Y*

E [F, G♭] $G\overset{c}{\downarrow}$

$81/64$ [**2**] $262144/177147$

i.r. = $262144/177147 \div 81/64 = 16777216/14348907$ = [L×L×L] = 271 ¢ (5)

Two 3-Tone Intervals

J$_1$ (*Tatimmah*)

A [*B*] *J*

C [D♭] $D\overset{s}{\downarrow}$

$1/1$ [**1**] $65536/59049$

i.r. = $65536/59049$ = [L×L] = 180 ¢ (6)

J$_2$ (*Mutammam*)

B [*J*] *D*

D♭ [$D\overset{s}{\downarrow}$] D

$256/243$ [**1**] $9/8$

i.r. = $9/8 \div 256/243 = 2187/2048$ = [L×C] = 114 ¢ (7)

Two 2-Tone Intervals

B$_1$ (*Baqiyyah*)

A, *B*

C, D♭

$1/1$ [**0**] $256/243$

i.r. = $256/243$ = [L] = 90 ¢ (8)

B$_2$ (*Faḍlah*)

J, *D*

$D\overset{s}{\downarrow}$, D

$65536/59049$ [**0**] $9/8$

i.r. = $9/8 \div 65536/5904 = 531441/524288$ = [C] = 23 ¢ (9)

Table 11.43

ṢAFĪ AL-DĪN'S 84 MELODIC MODES IN THE *KITĀB AL-ADWĀR*

	A	*B*	*J*	*D*	*H*	*W*	*Z*	*Ḥ*	*Ṭ*	*Y*	*YA*	*YB*	*YJ*	*YD*	*YH*	*YW*	*YZ*	*YḤ*	
Second ʿŪd Tuning:			**D𝄳**			**E𝄳**				**G𝄳**			**A𝄳**				**C𝄳**		
	C	D♭	D$\overset{s}{\downarrow}$	D	E♭	E$\overset{s}{\downarrow}$	E	F	G♭	G$\overset{c}{\downarrow}$	G	A♭	A$\overset{s}{\downarrow}$	A	B♭	B$\overset{s}{\downarrow}$	C$\overset{c}{\downarrow}$	C$^{\prime}$	
I: 2 2 0																			
(1)	C			D			E	F			G			A	B♭			C$^{\prime}$	I
(2)	C			D			E	F			G	A♭			B♭			C$^{\prime}$	II
(3)	C			D			E	F	G♭			A♭			B♭			C$^{\prime}$	III
(4)	C			D			E	F			G		**A𝄳**/A$\overset{s}{\downarrow}$		B♭			C$^{\prime}$	IV
(5)	C			D			E	F		**G𝄳**/G$\overset{c}{\downarrow}$		A♭			B♭			C$^{\prime}$	V
(6)	C			D			E	F		**G𝄳**/G$\overset{c}{\downarrow}$			**A𝄳**/A$\overset{s}{\downarrow}$		B♭			C$^{\prime}$	VI
(7)	C			D			E	F		**G𝄳**/G$\overset{c}{\downarrow}$		A♭		A	B♭			C$^{\prime}$	VII
(8)	C			D			E	F			G		**A𝄳**/A$\overset{s}{\downarrow}$		B♭		**C𝄳**/C$\overset{c}{\downarrow}$	C$^{\prime}$	VIII
(9)	C			D			E	F		**G𝄳**/G$\overset{c}{\downarrow}$			**A𝄳**/A$\overset{s}{\downarrow}$		B♭		**C𝄳**/C$\overset{c}{\downarrow}$	C$^{\prime}$	IX
(10)	C			D			E	F		**G𝄳**/G$\overset{c}{\downarrow}$	G			A		B$\overset{s}{\downarrow}$		C$^{\prime}$	X
(11)	C			D			E	F		**G𝄳**/G$\overset{c}{\downarrow}$		A♭	**A𝄳**/A$\overset{s}{\downarrow}$			B$\overset{s}{\downarrow}$		C$^{\prime}$	XI
(12)	C			D			E	F			G		**A𝄳**/A$\overset{s}{\downarrow}$			B$\overset{s}{\downarrow}$		C$^{\prime}$	XII
II: 2 0 2																			
(13)	C			D	E♭			F			G			A	B♭			C$^{\prime}$	I
(14)	C			D	E♭			F			G	A♭			B♭			C$^{\prime}$	II
(15)	C			D	E♭			F	G♭			A♭			B♭			C$^{\prime}$	III
(16)	C			D	E♭			F			G		**A𝄳**/A$\overset{s}{\downarrow}$		B♭			C$^{\prime}$	IV
(17)	C			D	E♭			F		**G𝄳**/G$\overset{c}{\downarrow}$		A♭			B♭			C$^{\prime}$	V
(18)	C			D	E♭			F		**G𝄳**/G$\overset{c}{\downarrow}$			**A𝄳**/A$\overset{s}{\downarrow}$		B♭			C$^{\prime}$	VI
(19)	C			D	E♭			F		**G𝄳**/G$\overset{c}{\downarrow}$		A♭		A	B♭			C$^{\prime}$	VII
(20)	C			D	E♭			F			G		**A𝄳**/A$\overset{s}{\downarrow}$		B♭		**C𝄳**/C$\overset{c}{\downarrow}$	C$^{\prime}$	VIII
(21)	C			D	E♭			F		**G𝄳**/G$\overset{c}{\downarrow}$			**A𝄳**/A$\overset{s}{\downarrow}$		B♭		**C𝄳**/C$\overset{c}{\downarrow}$	C$^{\prime}$	IX
(22)	C			D	E♭			F		**G𝄳**/G$\overset{c}{\downarrow}$	G			A		B$\overset{s}{\downarrow}$		C$^{\prime}$	X
(23)	C			D	E♭			F		**G𝄳**/G$\overset{c}{\downarrow}$		A♭	**A𝄳**/A$\overset{s}{\downarrow}$			B$\overset{s}{\downarrow}$		C$^{\prime}$	XI
(24)	C			D	E♭			F			G		**A𝄳**/A$\overset{s}{\downarrow}$			B$\overset{s}{\downarrow}$		C$^{\prime}$	XII
III: 0 2 2																			
(25)	C	D♭			E♭			F			G			A	B♭			C$^{\prime}$	I
(26)	C	D♭			E♭			F			G	A♭			B♭			C$^{\prime}$	II
(27)	C	D♭			E♭			F	G♭			A♭			B♭			C$^{\prime}$	III
(28)	C	D♭			E♭			F			G		**A𝄳**/A$\overset{s}{\downarrow}$		B♭			C$^{\prime}$	IV
(29)	C	D♭			E♭			F		**G𝄳**/G$\overset{c}{\downarrow}$		A♭			B♭			C$^{\prime}$	V
(30)	C	D♭			E♭			F		**G𝄳**/G$\overset{c}{\downarrow}$			**A𝄳**/A$\overset{s}{\downarrow}$		B♭			C$^{\prime}$	VI
(31)	C	D♭			E♭			F		**G𝄳**/G$\overset{c}{\downarrow}$		A♭		A	B♭			C$^{\prime}$	VII
(32)	C	D♭			E♭			F			G		**A𝄳**/A$\overset{s}{\downarrow}$		B♭		**C𝄳**/C$\overset{c}{\downarrow}$	C$^{\prime}$	VIII
(33)	C	D♭			E♭			F		**G𝄳**/G$\overset{c}{\downarrow}$			**A𝄳**/A$\overset{s}{\downarrow}$		B♭		**C𝄳**/C$\overset{c}{\downarrow}$	C$^{\prime}$	IX
(34)	C	D♭			E♭			F		**G𝄳**/G$\overset{c}{\downarrow}$	G			A		B$\overset{s}{\downarrow}$		C$^{\prime}$	X
(35)	C	D♭			E♭			F		**G𝄳**/G$\overset{c}{\downarrow}$		A♭	**A𝄳**/A$\overset{s}{\downarrow}$			B$\overset{s}{\downarrow}$		C$^{\prime}$	XI
(36)	C	D♭			E♭			F			G		**A𝄳**/A$\overset{s}{\downarrow}$			B$\overset{s}{\downarrow}$		C$^{\prime}$	XII
IV: 2 1 1																			
(37)	C			D		**E𝄳**/E$\overset{s}{\downarrow}$		F			G			A	B♭			C$^{\prime}$	I
(38)	C			D		**E𝄳**/E$\overset{s}{\downarrow}$		F			G	A♭			B♭			C$^{\prime}$	II
(39)	C			D		**E𝄳**/E$\overset{s}{\downarrow}$		F	G♭			A♭			B♭			C$^{\prime}$	III
(40)	C			D		**E𝄳**/E$\overset{s}{\downarrow}$		F			G		**A𝄳**/A$\overset{s}{\downarrow}$		B♭			C$^{\prime}$	IV
(41)	C			D		**E𝄳**/E$\overset{s}{\downarrow}$		F		**G𝄳**/G$\overset{c}{\downarrow}$		A♭			B♭			C$^{\prime}$	V
(42)	C			D		**E𝄳**/E$\overset{s}{\downarrow}$		F		**G𝄳**/G$\overset{c}{\downarrow}$			**A𝄳**/A$\overset{s}{\downarrow}$		B♭			C$^{\prime}$	VI

Table 11.43
(continued)

ṢAFĪ AL-DĪN'S 84 MELODIC MODES IN THE *KITĀB AL-ADWĀR*

Second ʿŪd Tuning: **D𝄳** **E𝄳** **G𝄳** **A𝄳** **C𝄳**

	A	*B*	*J*	*D*	*H*	*W*	*Z*	*Ḥ*	*Ṭ*	*Y*	*YA*	*YB*	*YJ*	*YD*	*YH*	*YW*	*YZ*	*YḤ*	
	C	D♭	D$\downarrow^{s}$	D	E♭	E$\downarrow^{s}$	E	F	G♭	G$\downarrow^{c}$	G	A♭	A$\downarrow^{s}$	A	B♭	B$\downarrow^{s}$	C$\downarrow^{c}$	C′	
IV: **2** **1** **1**																			
(43)	C			D		**E𝄳**/E$\downarrow^{s}$		F		**G𝄳**/G$\downarrow^{c}$		A♭		A	B♭			C′	VII
(44)	C			D		**E𝄳**/E$\downarrow^{s}$		F			G		**A𝄳**/A$\downarrow^{s}$		B♭		**C𝄳**/C$\downarrow^{c}$	C′	VIII
(45)	C			D		**E𝄳**/E$\downarrow^{s}$		F		**G𝄳**/G$\downarrow^{c}$			**A𝄳**/A$\downarrow^{s}$		B♭		**C𝄳**/C$\downarrow^{c}$	C′	IX
(46)	C			D		**E𝄳**/E$\downarrow^{s}$		F		**G𝄳**/G$\downarrow^{c}$	G			A		B$\downarrow^{s}$		C′	X
(47)	C			D		**E𝄳**/E$\downarrow^{s}$		F		**G𝄳**/G$\downarrow^{c}$		A♭	**A𝄳**/A$\downarrow^{s}$			B$\downarrow^{s}$		C′	XI
(48)	C			D		**E𝄳**/E$\downarrow^{s}$		F			G		**A𝄳**/A$\downarrow^{s}$			B$\downarrow^{s}$		C′	XII
V: **1** **1** **2**																			
(49)	C		**D𝄳**/D$\downarrow^{s}$		E♭			F			G			A	B♭			C′	I
(50)	C		**D𝄳**/D$\downarrow^{s}$		E♭			F			G	A♭			B♭			C′	II
(51)	C		**D𝄳**/D$\downarrow^{s}$		E♭			F	G♭			A♭			B♭			C′	III
(52)	C		**D𝄳**/D$\downarrow^{s}$		E♭			F			G		**A𝄳**/A$\downarrow^{s}$		B♭			C′	IV
(53)	C		**D𝄳**/D$\downarrow^{s}$		E♭			F		**G𝄳**/G$\downarrow^{c}$		A♭			B♭			C′	V
(54)	C		**D𝄳**/D$\downarrow^{s}$		E♭			F		**G𝄳**/G$\downarrow^{c}$			**A𝄳**/A$\downarrow^{s}$		B♭			C′	VI
(55)	C		**D𝄳**/D$\downarrow^{s}$		E♭			F		**G𝄳**/G$\downarrow^{c}$		A♭		A	B♭			C′	VII
(56)	C		**D𝄳**/D$\downarrow^{s}$		E♭			F			G		**A𝄳**/A$\downarrow^{s}$		B♭		**C𝄳**/C$\downarrow^{c}$	C′	VIII
(57)	C		**D𝄳**/D$\downarrow^{s}$		E♭			F		**G𝄳**/G$\downarrow^{c}$			**A𝄳**/A$\downarrow^{s}$		B♭		**C𝄳**/C$\downarrow^{c}$	C′	IX
(58)	C		**D𝄳**/D$\downarrow^{s}$		E♭			F		**G𝄳**/G$\downarrow^{c}$	G			A		B$\downarrow^{s}$		C′	X
(59)	C		**D𝄳**/D$\downarrow^{s}$		E♭			F		**G𝄳**/G$\downarrow^{c}$		A♭	**A𝄳**/A$\downarrow^{s}$			B$\downarrow^{s}$		C′	XI
(60)	C		**D𝄳**/D$\downarrow^{s}$		E♭			F			G		**A𝄳**/A$\downarrow^{s}$			B$\downarrow^{s}$		C′	XII
VI: **1** **2** **1**																			
(61)	C		**D𝄳**/D$\downarrow^{s}$			**E𝄳**/E$\downarrow^{s}$		F			G			A	B♭			C′	I
(62)	C		**D𝄳**/D$\downarrow^{s}$			**E𝄳**/E$\downarrow^{s}$		F			G	A♭			B♭			C′	II
(63)	C		**D𝄳**/D$\downarrow^{s}$			**E𝄳**/E$\downarrow^{s}$		F	G♭			A♭			B♭			C′	III
(64)	C		**D𝄳**/D$\downarrow^{s}$			**E𝄳**/E$\downarrow^{s}$		F			G		**A𝄳**/A$\downarrow^{s}$		B♭			C′	IV
(65)	C		**D𝄳**/D$\downarrow^{s}$			**E𝄳**/E$\downarrow^{s}$		F		**G𝄳**/G$\downarrow^{c}$		A♭			B♭			C′	V
(66)	C		**D𝄳**/D$\downarrow^{s}$			**E𝄳**/E$\downarrow^{s}$		F		**G𝄳**/G$\downarrow^{c}$			**A𝄳**/A$\downarrow^{s}$		B♭			C′	VI
(67)	C		**D𝄳**/D$\downarrow^{s}$			**E𝄳**/E$\downarrow^{s}$		F		**G𝄳**/G$\downarrow^{c}$		A♭		A	B♭			C′	VII
(68)	C		**D𝄳**/D$\downarrow^{s}$			**E𝄳**/E$\downarrow^{s}$		F			G		**A𝄳**/A$\downarrow^{s}$		B♭		**C𝄳**/C$\downarrow^{c}$	C′	VIII
(69)	C		**D𝄳**/D$\downarrow^{s}$			**E𝄳**/E$\downarrow^{s}$		F		**G𝄳**/G$\downarrow^{c}$			**A𝄳**/A$\downarrow^{s}$		B♭		**C𝄳**/C$\downarrow^{c}$	C′	IX
(70)	C		**D𝄳**/D$\downarrow^{s}$			**E𝄳**/E$\downarrow^{s}$		F		**G𝄳**/G$\downarrow^{c}$	G			A		B$\downarrow^{s}$		C′	X
(71)	C		**D𝄳**/D$\downarrow^{s}$			**E𝄳**/E$\downarrow^{s}$		F		**G𝄳**/G$\downarrow^{c}$		A♭	**A𝄳**/A$\downarrow^{s}$			B$\downarrow^{s}$		C′	XI
(72)	C		**D𝄳**/D$\downarrow^{s}$			**E𝄳**/E$\downarrow^{s}$		F			G		**A𝄳**/A$\downarrow^{s}$			B$\downarrow^{s}$		C′	XII
VII: **1** **1** **1** **0**																			
(73)	C		**D𝄳**/D$\downarrow^{s}$		E♭		E	F			G			A	B♭			C′	I
(74)	C		**D𝄳**/D$\downarrow^{s}$		E♭		E	F			G	A♭			B♭			C′	II
(75)	C		**D𝄳**/D$\downarrow^{s}$		E♭		E	F	G♭			A♭			B♭			C′	III
(76)	C		**D𝄳**/D$\downarrow^{s}$		E♭		E	F			G		**A𝄳**/A$\downarrow^{s}$		B♭			C′	IV
(77)	C		**D𝄳**/D$\downarrow^{s}$		E♭		E	F		**G𝄳**/G$\downarrow^{c}$		A♭			B♭			C′	V
(78)	C		**D𝄳**/D$\downarrow^{s}$		E♭		E	F		**G𝄳**/G$\downarrow^{c}$			**A𝄳**/A$\downarrow^{s}$		B♭			C′	VI
(79)	C		**D𝄳**/D$\downarrow^{s}$		E♭		E	F		**G𝄳**/G$\downarrow^{c}$		A♭		A	B♭			C′	VII
(80)	C		**D𝄳**/D$\downarrow^{s}$		E♭		E	F			G		**A𝄳**/A$\downarrow^{s}$		B♭		**C𝄳**/C$\downarrow^{c}$	C′	VIII
(81)	C		**D𝄳**/D$\downarrow^{s}$		E♭		E	F		**G𝄳**/G$\downarrow^{c}$			**A𝄳**/A$\downarrow^{s}$		B♭		**C𝄳**/C$\downarrow^{c}$	C′	IX
(82)	C		**D𝄳**/D$\downarrow^{s}$		E♭		E	F		**G𝄳**/G$\downarrow^{c}$	G			A		B$\downarrow^{s}$		C′	X
(83)	C		**D𝄳**/D$\downarrow^{s}$		E♭		E	F		**G𝄳**/G$\downarrow^{c}$		A♭	**A𝄳**/A$\downarrow^{s}$			B$\downarrow^{s}$		C′	XI
(84)	C		**D𝄳**/D$\downarrow^{s}$		E♭		E	F			G		**A𝄳**/A$\downarrow^{s}$			B$\downarrow^{s}$		C′	XII

in the first seven modes of each group, Ṣafī Al-Dīn sequentially repeated the lower tetrachords as conjunct upper tetrachords, followed by the "octave," C'. Consequently, Modes 1–7 include the following intervals between *Ḥ–YH*, or F–B♭: 2, 2, 0; 2, 0, 2; 0, 2, 2; 2, 1, 1; 1, 1, 2; 1, 2, 1; and 1, 1, 1, 0, respectively. Note that the latter seven tetrachords constitute the interval F–B♭ of Modes 13–19, Modes 25–31, Modes 37–43, etc. as well.

Finally, consider these derivations of the intervals between *Ḥ–YḤ*, or F–C', of Modes 8–12. Suppose we regard F–C' of Mode 7 as a 6-tone pentachord that consists of intervals 1, 1, 1, 0, 2. (In this context, we do not give the word *pentachord* a literal interpretation, 'five strings', but a theoretical interpretation, interval ratio $\frac{3}{2}$.) If we rotate the last interval into first position, we obtain the pentachord F–C' of Mode 8: 2, 1, 1, 1, 0. If we then switch the positions of the first two intervals of Mode 8, we obtain the pentachord F–C' of Mode 9: 1, 2, 1, 1, 0. If we then rotate the last interval of Mode 9 into second position, we obtain the pentachord F–C' of Mode 10: 1, 0, 2, 1, 1. If we then rotate the last interval of Mode 10 into second position, we obtain the pentachord F–C' of Mode 11: 1, 1, 0, 2, 1. The interval F–C' of the last mode is unique because it is an actual 5-tone pentachord. Ṣafī Al-Dīn gives the intervals of Mode 12 as 2, 1, 2, 1. The latter five pentachords constitute the interval F–C' of Modes 20–24, Modes 32–36, Modes 44–48, etc. as well.

In summary, Table 11.44 lists the 12 genera used by Ṣafī Al-Dīn in the construction of his 84 Melodic Modes. Although he did not notate the seven tetrachords and five pentachords in the manner shown here, I hope this table will be of some assistance to the reader.

~ 11.75 ~

Turn to Figure 11.78, which is a seven-by-twelve matrix that generates Ṣafī Al-Dīn's 84 Melodic Modes according to his *First 'Ūd Tuning*, and to Figure 11.79, which is a seven-by-twelve matrix that generates the 84 Melodic Modes according to his *Second 'Ūd Tuning*. Both figures give the names of twelve modes that Ṣafī Al-Dīn and Al-Jurjānī called *shudūd*[145] (sing. *shadd;* Persian, to

Table 11.44

12 GENERA USED IN THE CONSTRUCTION OF
ṢAFĪ AL-DĪN'S 84 MELODIC MODES

Tetrachords: C–F and F–B♭	
Genus I:	2, 2, 0
Genus II:	2, 0, 2
Genus III:	0, 2, 2
Genus IV:	2, 1, 1
Genus V:	1, 1, 2
Genus VI:	1, 2, 1
Genus VII:	1, 1, 1, 0
Pentachords: F–C'	
Genus VIII:	2, 1, 1, 1, 0
Genus IX:	1, 2, 1, 1, 0
Genus X:	1, 0, 2, 1, 1
Genus XI:	1, 1, 0, 2, 1
Genus XII:	2, 1, 2, 1

sing according to rules).[146] This term referred to twelve primary or principal modes. The first music theorist to give a general description of these twelve *shudūd* was Ibn Sīnā.

> Ibn Sīnā . . . says, — "It behooves that the musician should tune the time of the false dawn (*ṣubḥ al-kādhib*) with the [mode] *Rāhawī*, and the time of the true dawn (*ṣubḥ al-ṣādiq*) with the *Ḥusain*, and the rising of the sun with the *Rāst*, and the time of the forenoon (*ḍuḥā*) with the *Būsalīk* {= *Abū Salīk*}; and the time of midday (*niṣf al-nahār*) with the *Zankūlā*, and the time of noon (*ẓuhr*) with the *'Ushshāq*, and between the prayers with the *Ḥijāz*, and the time of the afternoon (*'aṣr*) with the *'Irāq*, and the time of sunset (*ghurūb*) with the *Iṣfahān*, and the time of nightfall (*maghrib*) with the *Nawā*, and after the evening prayer (*'ashā'*) with the *Buzurk*, and the time of sleep with the *Mukhālif* (= *Zīrāfkand*)."[147] (Text in brackets and parentheses in Farmer's translation; text in braces in Farmer's footnote.)

In addition, Ṣafī Al-Dīn and Al-Jurjānī defined six modes called *āwāzāt*,[148] (sing. *āwāz;* Persian, lit. *voice*, or *sound*).[149] This term referred to six secondary or derived modes, also known as *shu'ab*,[150] (sing. *shu'bah;* lit. *branch*, or *division*).[151] *La Musique Arabe, Volume 3*, p. 388 translates *shu'bah* as "modal combination." We will discuss these modes at the end of this section.

In Figures 11.78 and 11.79, five *shudūd* — *'Ushshaq, Nawā, Abū Salīk, Rāst, and Ḥusainī* — consist of identical conjunct tetrachords followed by the "octave," C$^{|}$. Of these, *Rāst* is the quintessential melodic mode of Arabian music. Now, the Arabic word *mustaqīm* is equivalent to the Persian word *rāst*, (lit. *straight*, *direct*, or *regular*).[152] So, although Ṣafī Al-Dīn was the first theorist to define a *shadd* called *Rāst*, we may trace the historic origins of this mode to Al-Fārābī's *Jins* 2, and to Ibn Sīnā's *Diatonic Genus* 7 and Melodic Mode 8, which he called *Mustaqīm.* (See Sections 11.61–11.63, and Tables 11.31–11.32.)

Ṣafī Al-Dīn used Al-Fārābī's *perfect invariable conjunct system* to organize the tetrachords of *Rāst.* Turn back to Figure 11.58, which shows that in this system the interval of disjunction, interval ratio $\frac{9}{8}$, follows two conjunct tetrachords, or the "double-fourth," ratio $\frac{16}{9}$. According to my numerical interpretation of Ṣafī Al-Dīn's interval Ṭ in Table 11.42, I will notate the Arabian interval of disjunction as ②. In the context of Ancient Arabian *Rāst*, the interval of disjunction exists between B♭–C$^{|}$; that is, $\frac{2}{1} \div \frac{16}{9} = \frac{9}{8}$. Consequently, Ṣafī Al-Dīn's *Rāst* consists of the interval pattern 2, 1, 1, 2, 1, 1, ②. In Figure 11.78 we see that the *First 'Ūd Tuning* generates *Rāst* with a "schisma third" and a "schisma sixth,"

C, D, E$\overset{\S}{\downarrow}$, F, G, A$\overset{\S}{\downarrow}$, B♭, C$^{|}$

and in Figure 11.79, the *Second 'Ūd Tuning* generates *Rāst* with a "neutral third" and a "neutral sixth." This *shadd* is a very close approximation of the lower "octave" of Ibn Sīnā's *Mustaqīm:*

C, D, E$\not\flat$, F, G, A$\not\flat$, B♭, C

Suppose we use Al-Fārābī's *second disjunct system* to reorganize the tetrachords of *Rāst.* The interval of disjunction now occurs between two tetrachords, which means Ṣafī Al-Dīn's *Rāst* consists of the interval pattern 2, 1, 1, ②, 2, 1, 1. Therefore, the *First 'Ūd Tuning* generates *Rāst* with a "schisma third" and "schisma seventh." This *shadd* is *identical* to a modern Turkish *maqām* called *Rast:*

C, D, E$\overset{\S}{\downarrow}$, F, G, A, B$\overset{\S}{\downarrow}$, C$^{|}$

The *Second 'Ūd Tuning* generates *Rāst* with a "neutral third" and a "schisma seventh." This *shadd* closely approximates a modern Arabian *maqām* called *Mahur:*

C, D, E$\not\flat$, F, G, A, B$\overset{\S}{\downarrow}$, C$^{|}$

	I	II	III	IV	V	VI	VII	VIII	IX	X	XI	XII
	F,G,A,B♭,C′ 2 2 0 ②	F,G,A♭,B♭,C′ 2 0 2 ②	F,G♭,A♭,B♭,C′ 0 2 2 ②	F,G,A↓,B♭,C′ 2 1 1 ②	F,G↓,A♭,B♭,C′ 1 1 2 ②	F,G↓,A↓,B♭,C′ 1 2 1 ②	F,G↓,A♭,A,B♭,C′ 1 1 1 0 ②	F,G,A↓,B♭,C↓,C′ 2 1 1 1 0 ②	F,G↓,A↓,B♭,C↓,C′ 1 2 1 1 0 ②	F,G↓,G,A,B↓,C′ 1 0 2 1 1 ②	F,G↓,A♭,A↓,B↓,C′ 1 1 0 2 1	F,G,A↓,B↓,C′ 2 1 2 1
I C,D,E,F 2 2 0	*ʿUshshāq* 1	2	3	4	5	6	7	8	9	10	11	12
II C,D,E♭,F 2 0 2	13	*Nawā* 14	15	16	17	18	19	20	21	22	23	24
III C,D♭,E♭,F 0 2 2	25	26	*Abū Salīk* 27	28	29	30	31	32	33	34	35	36
IV C,D,E↓,F 2 1 1	37	38	39	*Rāst* 40	41	*Zankūlah* 42	43	*Iṣfahān* 44	45	46	47	48
V C,D↓,E♭,F 1 1 2	49	50	51	52	*Ḥusainī* 53	*Ḥijāzī* 54	55	56	57	58	*Zīrāfkand* 59	60
VI C,D↓,E↓,F 1 2 1	61	62	63	64	*Rāhawī* 65	66	67	68	*ʿIrāq* 69	*Buzurg* 70	71	72
VII C,D↓,E♭,E,F 1 1 1 0	73	74	75	76	77	78	79	80	81	82	83	84

Figure 11.78 A seven-by-twelve matrix that generates Ṣafī Al-Dīn's 84 Melodic Modes. This matrix shows the modes in the context of his *First ʿŪd Tuning.* The inclusion of F's in the top row indicates that these modes consist of either conjunct tetrachords (followed by the "octave," C′) or conjunct tetrachord-pentachord combinations. The named and underlined modes represent Ṣafī Al-Dīn's 12 *shudūd*, or principal modes. In Section 11.77, we will trace the historic significance of these modes in modern Turkish music.

	I F,G,A,B♭,C' 2 2 0 ②	II F,G,A♭,B♭,C' 2 0 2 ②	III F,G♭,A♭,B♭,C' 0 2 2 ②	IV F,G,A𝄳,B♭,C' 2 1 1 ②	V F,G𝄳,A♭,B♭,C' 1 1 2 ②	VI F,G𝄳,A𝄳,B♭,C' 1 2 1 ②	VII F,G𝄳,A♭,A,B♭,C' 1 1 1 0 ②	VIII F,G,A𝄳,B♭,C𝄳,C' 2 1 1 1 0 ②	IX F,G𝄳,A𝄳,B♭,C𝄳,C' 1 2 1 1 0 ②	X F,G𝄳,G,A,B↓§,C' 1 0 2 1 1 ②	XI F,G𝄳,A♭,A𝄳,B↓§,C' 1 1 0 2 1	XII F,G,A𝄳,B↓§,C' 2 1 2 1
I C,D,E,F 2 2 0	*'Ushshāq* <u>1</u>	2	3	4	5	6	7	8	9	10	11	12
II C,D,E♭,F 2 0 2	13	*Nawā* <u>14</u>	15	16	17	18	19	20	21	22	23	24
III C,D♭,E♭,F 0 2 2	25	26	*Abū Salīk* <u>27</u>	28	29	30	31	32	33	34	35	36
IV C,D,E𝄳,F 2 1 1	37	38	39	*Rāst* <u>40</u>	41	*Zankūlah* <u>42</u>	43	*Iṣfahān* <u>44</u>	45	46	47	48
V C,D𝄳,E♭,F 1 1 2	49	50	51	52	*Ḥusainī* <u>53</u>	*Ḥijāzī* <u>54</u>	55	56	57	58	*Zīrāfkand* <u>59</u>	60
VI C,D𝄳,E𝄳,F 1 2 1	61	62	63	64	*Rāhawī* <u>65</u>	66	67	68	*'Irāq* <u>69</u>	*Buzurg* <u>70</u>	71	72
VII C,D𝄳,E♭,E,F 1 1 1 0	73	74	75	76	77	78	79	80	81	82	83	84

Figure 11.79 A seven-by-twelve matrix that generates Ṣafī Al-Dīn's 84 Melodic Modes. This matrix shows the modes in the context of his *Second 'Ūd Tuning*. Similar to Figure 11.78, the inclusion of F's in the top row indicates that these modes consist of either conjunct tetrachords (followed by the "octave," C') or conjunct tetrachord-pentachord combinations. Again, the named and underlined modes represent Ṣafī Al-Dīn's 12 *shudūd*, or principal modes. In Section 11.83, we will examine the historic significance of these modes in modern Arabian music. With the exception of B↓§ (see Figure 11.76, Fret 1), all *schisma and comma variants* in the lower "octave" of Ṣafī Al-Dīn's *First 'Ūd Tuning* have been replaced with the *neutral tones* of his *Second 'Ūd Tuning.*

Table 11.45

Ṣafī Al-Dīn's 12 *Shudūd*	Ṣafī Al-Dīn's 6 *Āwāzāt*
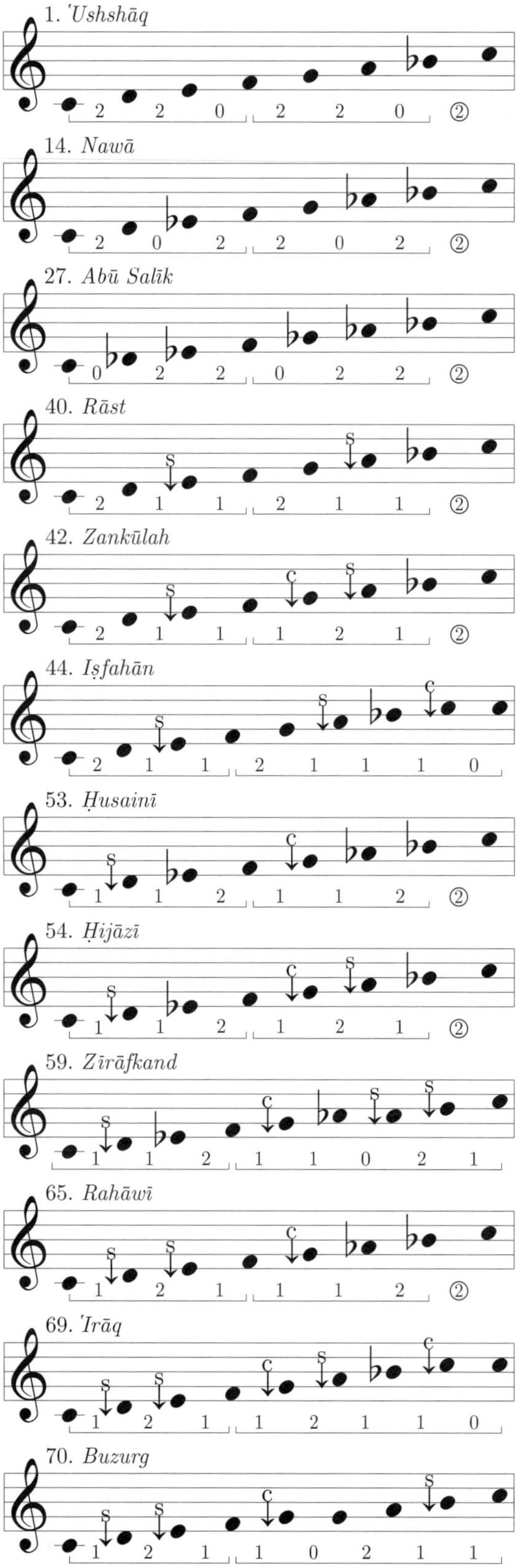	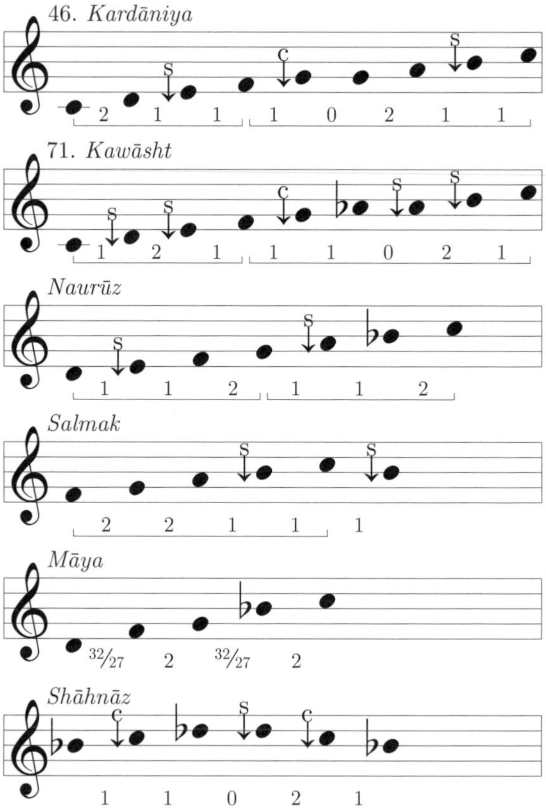

In Sections 11.78–11.80, we will discuss how Ancient Arabian *Rāst* evolved into Modern Turkish *Rast* and Modern Arabian *Rāst.*

Table 11.45 shows twelve *shudūd* and six *āwāzāt* described by Ṣafī Al-Dīn in the context of his *First ʿŪd Tuning.* In his commentary, Al-Jurjānī cites two derivations of the first *āwāz* called *Kardāniya.* In preparation for the first derivation, refer once again to Figures 11.78 and 11.79. Observe that I marked the last two intervals of the upper pentachord of *Iṣfahān* with a tie: 2, 1, 1, 1‿0. These two intervals define the last three tones of *Iṣfahān:* B♭–C$\overset{c}{\downarrow}$–C′. Now, if we remove C$\overset{c}{\downarrow}$, we obtain interval ratio $^{2}/_{1} \div {}^{16}/_{9} = {}^{9}/_{8}$, or an upper interval of disjunction — ② — between B♭–C′. Consequently, *Iṣfahān* now has the simpler interval pattern of a true pentachord: 2, 1, 1, ②.

Al-Jurjānī gives these two descriptions of *Kardāniya:*

I

> Cycle No. 46 is a *"shuʿbah"* derived from *Iṣfahān.* In Persian, this modal combination is called: *Kardāniya,* i.e., "turned over." [1] In fact, it is merely the *Iṣfahān* mode with the interval of disjunction shifted from the upper [position] to the lower [position]. [2] It is thus *Iṣfahān* on the 17th tone . . .[153] (Text and numbers in brackets mine.)

Regarding the first derivation, note that *Iṣfahān* consists of the interval pattern 2, 1, 1, 2, 1, 1, 1‿0; or simply 2, 1, 1, 2, 1, 1, ②. Therefore, if we shift the interval of disjunction from the upper to the lower position, the interval pattern of *Kardāniya,* or of Mode 46, results: 2, 1, 1, 1‿0, 2, 1, 1; or simply 2, 1, 1, ②, 2, 1, 1.

The second derivation is not so simple because Ṣafī Al-Dīn devised a unique system to number the 34 tones of the two "octaves" of his *First ʿŪd Tuning.* He used this system to explain the

Table 11.46

ṢAFĪ AL-DĪN'S ASCENDING SPIRAL OF "FOURTHS" AND THE NUMBERING OF 17 TONES IN THE LOWER AND UPPER "OCTAVES"

(17)	*YA, KḤ*	G	$^{3}/_{2}$	$^{4}/_{3}$
(16)	*D, KA*	D	$^{9}/_{8}$	$^{4}/_{3}$
(15)	*YD, LA*	A	$^{27}/_{16}$	$^{4}/_{3}$
(14)	*Z, KD*	E	$^{81}/_{64}$	$^{43046721}/_{33554432}$
(13)	*YZ, LD*	C$\overset{c}{\downarrow}$	$^{1048576}/_{531441}$	$^{4}/_{3}$
(12)	*Y, KZ*	G$\overset{c}{\downarrow}$	$^{262144}/_{177147}$	$^{4}/_{3}$
(11)	*J, K*	D$\overset{s}{\downarrow}$	$^{65536}/_{59049}$	$^{4}/_{3}$
(10)	*YJ, L*	A$\overset{s}{\downarrow}$	$^{32768}/_{19683}$	$^{4}/_{3}$
(9)	*W, KJ*	E$\overset{s}{\downarrow}$	$^{8192}/_{6561}$	$^{4}/_{3}$
(8)	*YW, LJ*	B$\overset{s}{\downarrow}$	$^{4096}/_{2187}$	$^{4}/_{3}$
(7)	*Ṭ, KW*	G♭	$^{1024}/_{729}$	$^{4}/_{3}$
(6)	*B, YṬ*	D♭	$^{256}/_{243}$	$^{4}/_{3}$
(5)	*YB, KṬ*	A♭	$^{128}/_{81}$	$^{4}/_{3}$
(4)	*H, KB*	E♭	$^{32}/_{27}$	$^{4}/_{3}$
(3)	*YH, LB*	B♭	$^{16}/_{9}$	$^{4}/_{3}$
(2)	*Ḥ, KH*	F	$^{4}/_{3}$	$^{4}/_{3}$
(1)	*A, YḤ*	C	$^{1}/_{1}$	

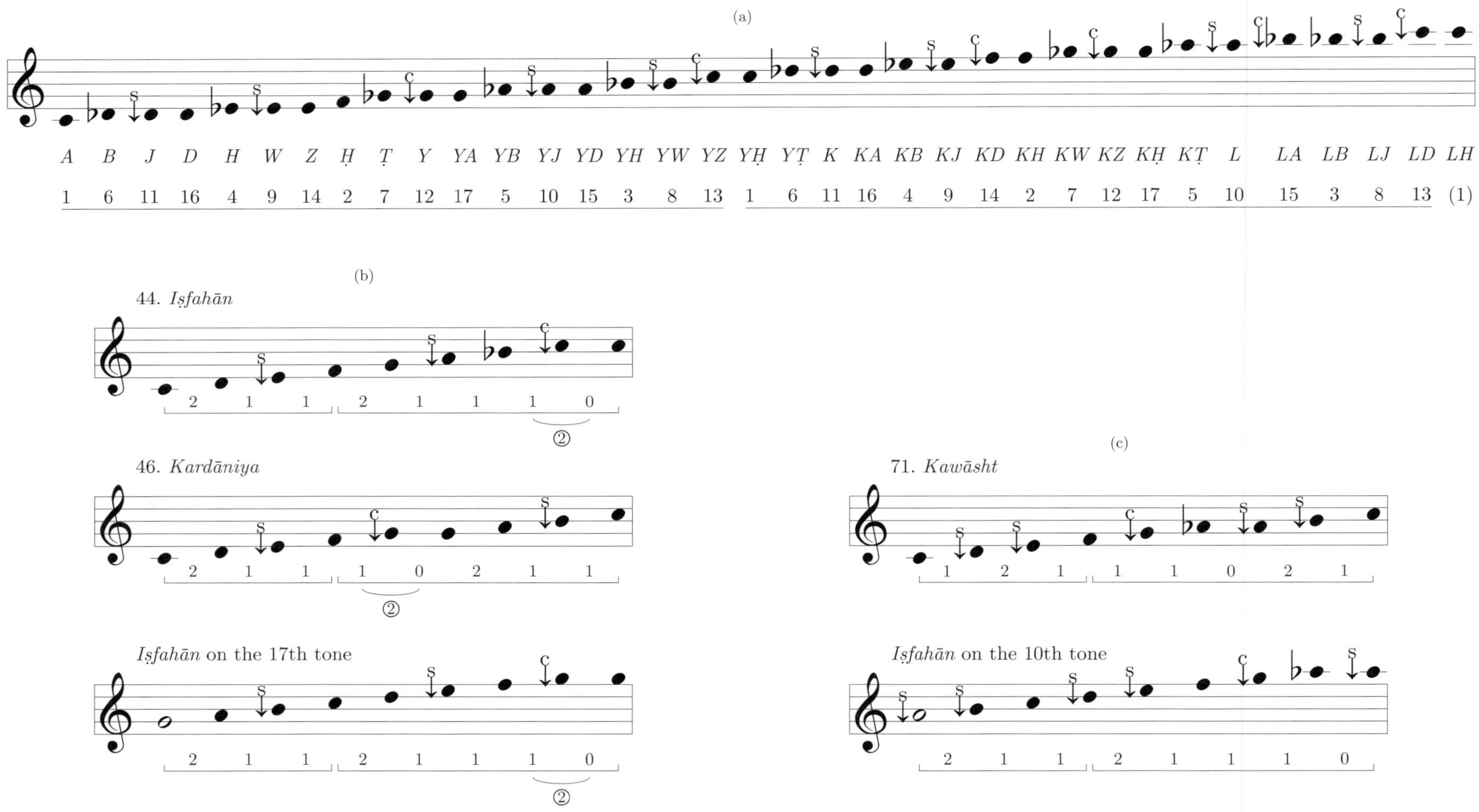

Figure 11.80 Two consecutive "octaves" of Ṣafī Al-Dīn's *First ʿŪd Tuning*, and the derivations of two complete *āwāzāt.* (a) The note names appear as shown in Figure 11.74, and the tone numbers, as determined by Ṣafī Al-Dīn's ascending spiral of "fourths" in Table 11.46. (b) Ṣafī Al-Dīn and Al-Jurjānī give two derivations of No. 46 *Kardāniya:* (1) either move the interval of disjunction of No. 44 *Iṣfahān* from the upper position to the lower position; (2) or identify the tones of *Kardāniya* by constructing *Iṣfahān* on the 17th tone of the spiral. (c) Similarly, identify the tones of No. 71 *Kawāsht* by constructing *Iṣfahān* on the 10th tone of the spiral.

derivations of many modes in Figure 11.78 that have obscure names, or no names at all; and he employed this system to derive two complete *āwāzāt: Kardāniya* and *Kawāsht.* The four remaining *āwāzāt* contain fewer than eight tones, and therefore have origins in musical traditions rather than in systematic derivations.

Ṣafī Al-Dīn numbered the tones of his *First ʿŪd Tuning* according to an ascending spiral of "fourths." To my knowledge, the table in *La Musique Arabe, Volume 3,* p. 410, is the first occurrence of such a spiral in the history of music theory. Table 11.46 gives the note names and tone numbers as depicted in Ṣafī Al-Dīn's table, with the exception that it shows the spiral ascending from the bottom to the top of the page. Observe that the numbers of the seventeen tones of the lower "octave" apply to the seventeen tones of the upper "octave" as well. This causes a minor discrepancy because on Ṣafī Al-Dīn's fretted *ʿūd*, the tonal pairs (*Z*, *KD*) and (*YD*, *LA*) do not produce perfect "octaves." (See Figure 11.74.) Also, in the lower "octave," note a second discrepancy in the spiral as it ascends from the thirteenth tone C$\overset{c}{\downarrow}$, ratio $^{1048576}/_{531441}$, to the fourteenth tone E, ratio $^{81}/_{64}$. Interval ratio $^{43046721}/_{33554432}$ is a "neutral fourth" that equals only 431.3 ¢.

We are now prepared to understand why *Kardāniya* is ". . . *Iṣfahān* on the 17th tone." Turn to Figure 11.80(a), which gives the note names and tone numbers of two consecutive "octaves" of Ṣafī Al-Dīn's *First ʿŪd Tuning.* The first staff of Figure 11.80(b) illustrates *Iṣfahān*, and the second staff, the first derivation of *Kardāniya*, which shifts the interval of disjunction from the upper position to the lower position. The third staff demonstrates the interval pattern of *Iṣfahān:* 2, 1, 1, 2, 1, 1, 1, 0 — on the 17th tone of the spiral, which results in this mode: G, A, B$\overset{s}{\downarrow}$, C$^{|}$, D, E$\overset{s}{\downarrow}$, F, G$\overset{c}{\downarrow}$, G. When we compare the tones of this mode to the tones of Mode 46, we find that they are the same, although the order has changed. Consequently, Ṣafī Al-Dīn and Al-Jurjānī considered *āwāz Kardāniya* as a derivative of *shadd Iṣfahān.*

Similarly, Ṣafī Al-Dīn stated

> . . . As for *Kawāsht*, it is *Iṣfahān* transposed on the 10th tone . . .[154]

Figure 11.80(c) demonstrates that when we begin *Iṣfahān* on the 10th tone of the spiral, the following mode results: A$\overset{s}{\downarrow}$, B$\overset{s}{\downarrow}$, C$^{|}$, D$\overset{s}{\downarrow}$, E$\overset{s}{\downarrow}$, F, G$\overset{c}{\downarrow}$, A♭, A$\overset{s}{\downarrow}$. Even though the order is different, the tones of this mode are the same as Mode 71. For this reason, Ṣafī Al-Dīn and Al-Jurjānī considered *āwāz Kawāsht* as a derivative of *shadd Iṣfahān.*

The remarkable works of Ṣafī Al-Dīn and Al-Jurjānī do not represent relics of the past. In Section 11.77, we will see that when played in the *second disjunct system, shudūd ʿUshshāq, Abū Salīk, Rāst,* and *Ḥusainī* continue to flourish in the music of the modern Turkish fretted *ṭunbūr.* Similarly, in Section 11.83 we will see that when played in the *Second ʿŪd Tuning,* close approximations of *shudūd Nawā, Abū Salīk, Rāst,* and *Ḥusainī* exist in the music of the modern Arabian fretless *ʿūd.*

∼ 11.76 ∼

Born *c.* 870 in the town of Wāsīj, in the district of the city of Fārāb, Turkestan, and died *c.* 950 in Damascus, Syria, Abū Naṣr Al-Fārābī was a renowned philosopher and teacher of Turkish descent. Although music historians will probably never establish a direct connection between Al-Fārābī's *ṭunbūr* tuning in Figure 11.71 and the tuning of the modern Turkish *ṭunbūr* in Figure 11.81, the possibility that such a nexus exists is truly amazing. As discussed in Section 11.69, Al-Fārābī's *ṭunbūr* tuning consists of an ascending spiral of *twelve* "fifths," and a descending spiral of *eleven* "fifths." Remarkably, the Turkish *ṭunbūr* consists of an ascending spiral of *eleven* "fifths," and a descending spiral of *twelve* "fifths." The principal difference between these tunings is that Al-Fārābī's

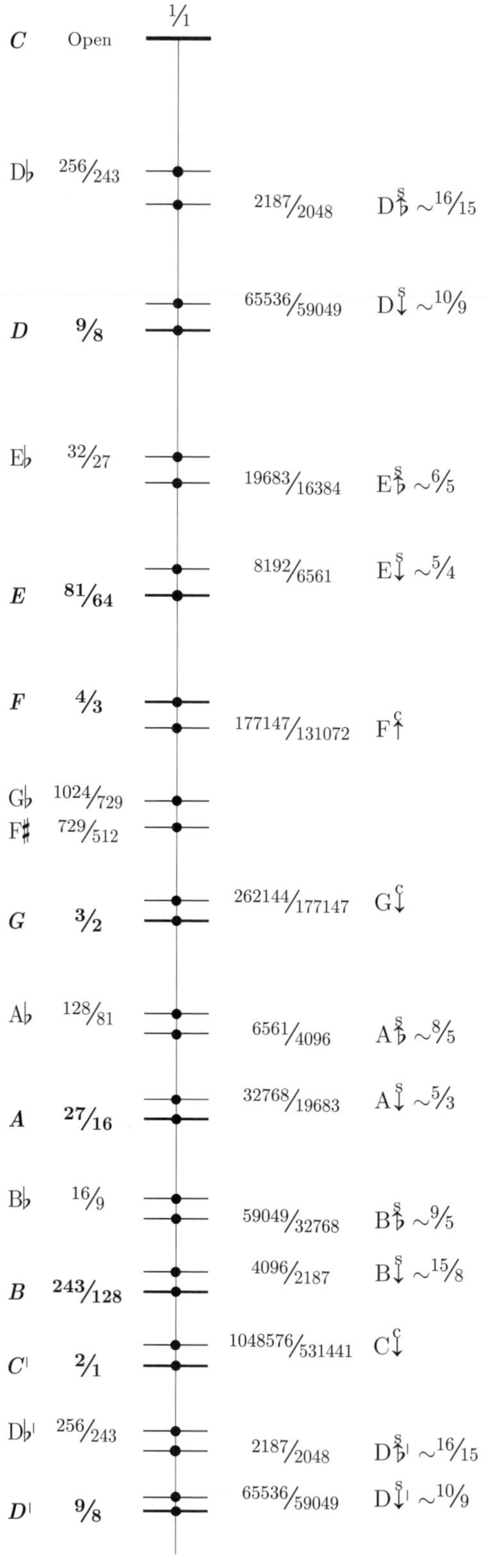

Figure 11.81 The 24 frets of the lower 24-tone "octave," and the first 4 frets of the upper 24-tone "octave" of the modern Turkish *ṭunbūr*. Turn to Figure 11.71, and note that a comparison of the tones between C and G' on Al-Fārābī's *ṭunbūr*, and between C and C' on the Turkish *ṭunbūr* reveals only two discrepancies. Due to many different arrangements and tunings of other open strings, Figure 11.81 shows the first 29 tones of only one string. (Fret locations to scale.)

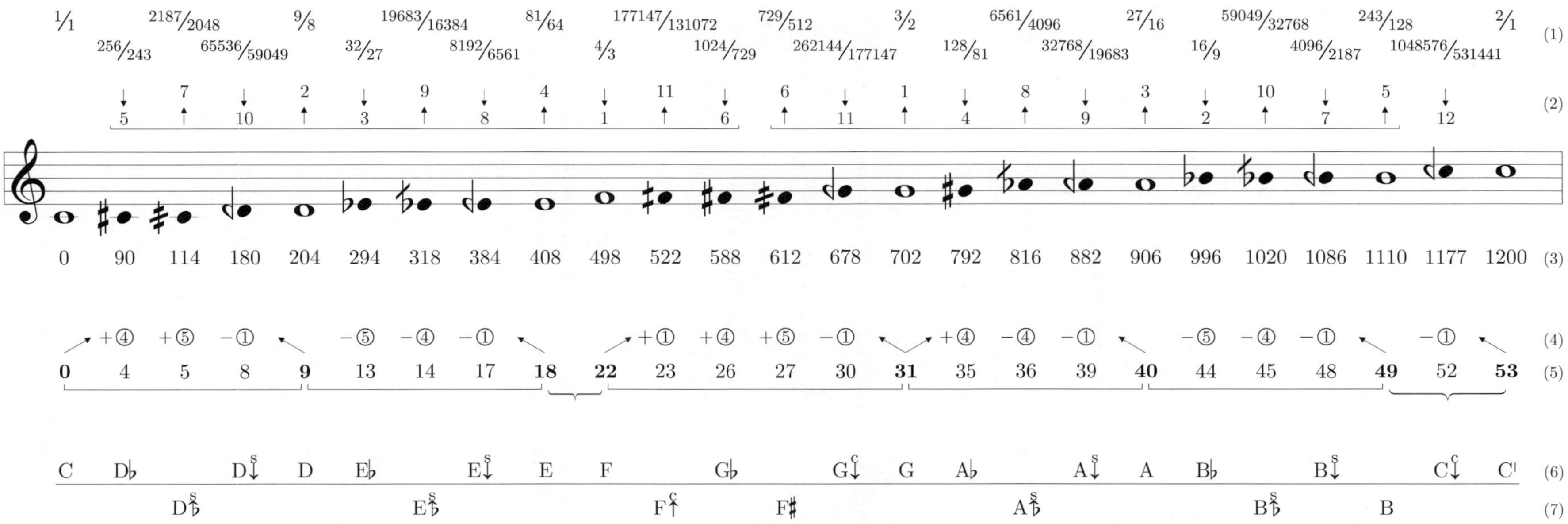

Figure 11.82 The 24-tone just intoned scale of the modern Turkish *ṭunbūr*. Row 1 shows the frequency ratios of the scale, and arrows in Row 2, whether a given ratio belongs to an ascending or descending spiral of "fifths." A corresponding place number identifies the location of a given ratio in its spiral. Row 3 gives the frequency ratios in cents. Row 4 shows the comma intervals of the chromatic tones in relation to the diatonic tones, and Row 5, the cumulative comma values of the scale degrees. Row 6 indicates a 17-tone scale that is identical to Ṣafī Al-Dīn's *First ʿŪd Tuning* in Figure 11.74. With the exception of C↓, Rows 6 and 7 show 23 tones found on Al-Fārābī's *ṭunbūr* in Figure 11.71.

ṭunbūr contains two nonidentical 17-tone "octaves" between C–C^{I}, whereas the Turkish *ṭunbūr* has two identical 24-tone "octaves" between C–C^{II}. However, when we compare the tones of the interval C–G^{I} on Al-Fārābī's *ṭunbūr* to the tones of the interval C–C^{I} on the Turkish *ṭunbūr*, we find only two discrepancies: C↑^{I}, ratio $^{531441}/_{524288}$, exists in the former tuning, but is absent from the latter; and C↓, ratio $^{1048576}/_{531441}$, exists in the latter tuning, but is absent from the former.

In his published dissertation entitled *Makam: Modal Practice in Turkish Art Music*, Karl L. Signell discusses the tuning and musical notation of the modern Turkish *ṭunbūr*.[155] Refer to Figure 11.82, Row 1, which gives the frequency ratios of the 24-tone just intoned scale.[156] In Row 2, vertical arrows indicate whether a given ratio belongs to an ascending or descending spiral of "fifths," and a corresponding place number identifies the location of a given ratio in its spiral. Row 3 gives the frequency ratios in cents.

Eight white notes, which constitute the tones of the diatonic scale — $^{1}/_{1}$ [C], $^{9}/_{8}$ [D], $^{81}/_{64}$ [E], $^{4}/_{3}$ [F], $^{3}/_{2}$ [G], $^{27}/_{16}$ [A], $^{243}/_{128}$ [B], $^{2}/_{1}$ [C^{I}] — play a crucial role in determining the intonation of the black notes, which constitute the chromatic tones of the scale. To understand the function of six different accidentals in Turkish music, consider these definitions:[157]

‡ – a chromatic tone raised by 1 comma
♯ – a chromatic tone raised by ≈ 4 commas
⧣ – a chromatic tone raised by ≈ 5 commas
𝄳 – a chromatic tone lowered by 1 comma
♭̸ – a chromatic tone lowered by ≈ 4 commas
♭ – a chromatic tone lowered by ≈ 5 commas

The common unit of measure is the comma of Pythagoras, ratio $^{531441}/_{524288}$ [23.46 ¢]. Even though 1-comma intervals do *not* occur in Turkish music, musicians use the comma to gauge the relative sizes of intervals in the scale. In Turkish music, the smallest interval is the limma, ratio $^{256}/_{243}$ [90 ¢]. Furthermore, although ‡ and 𝄳 represent the raising and lowering of a given tone by *exactly* 1 comma, the other accidentals represent the raising or lowering of a given tone by *approximately* 4 or 5 commas. We will examine the reason for this difference below.

Return to Figure 11.82, Row 4, which places the chromatic tones in relation to the diatonic tones. Observe that I indicated the former tones with slanted arrows that point in an ascending or descending direction from the latter tones. For example, one tunes F‡ one comma above F; F♯ ≈ 4 commas above F; and F⧣ ≈ 5 commas above F. In contrast, one tunes E𝄳 one comma below E; E♭̸ ≈ 4 commas below E; and E♭ ≈ 5 commas below E. Given this distribution of exact and approximate comma intervals,[158] Row 5 compiles the cumulative comma values of the scale degrees as one ascends from C_4 to C_5. Altogether, there are approximately 53 commas in the scale.

Consider the distinction between approximate and exact comma intervals. Table 11.47, Column 1, shows five approximate comma intervals, and Column 2, the corresponding exact interval ratios. We observed earlier that one tunes E♭̸ ≈ 4 commas below E, but it is more accurate to state that one tunes E♭̸ exactly 1 limma below E, because $^{81}/_{64} \div {}^{19683}/_{16384} = {}^{256}/_{243} = 1$ limma. Hence, Column 3 indicates the exact interval ratios as comma-limma equivalents, and Column 4, the exact cent values of the intervals in Columns 2 and 3. Now, if in Column 1, we interpret the *approximate* multiple comma intervals as *exact* multiple comma intervals, then Column 5 shows the cent values of the latter. For instance, to calculate an exact 4-comma interval, raise ratio $^{531441}/_{524288}$ to the fourth power, and then convert the result, which equals 94 ¢. Cent values in Columns 4 and 5 indicate that 1 limma is 4 ¢ less than 4 commas.

Since interval ratio $^{531441}/_{524288}$ raised to the 53rd power equals 1243.38 ¢, or since 23.46 ¢ × 53 = 1243.38 ¢, note immediately that the total and exact comma cent value of the scale exceeds the

Table 11.47

VARIOUS INTERPRETATIONS OF THE BASIC INTERVALS OF THE TURKISH 24-TONE JUST INTONED SCALE, AND OF THE MELODIC INTERVALS OF TURKISH *MAQĀMĀT*

Approximate Comma Intervals	Exact Interval Ratios	Comma-Limma Equivalents	Exact Cents	Powers of Exact Commas in Cents	Powers of 53-TET in Cents
1 comma	$^{531441}/_{524288}$	C	23 ¢	$\frac{531441}{524228} = 23.46$ ¢	$\sqrt[53]{2} = 22.64$ ¢
≈ 4 commas	$^{256}/_{243}$	L	90 ¢	$\left(\frac{531441}{524228}\right)^4 = 94$ ¢	$\sqrt[53]{2}^4 = 91$ ¢
≈ 5 commas	$^{2187}/_{2048}$	L×C	114 ¢	$\left(\frac{531441}{524228}\right)^5 = 117$ ¢	$\sqrt[53]{2}^5 = 113$ ¢
≈ 8 commas	$^{65536}/_{59049}$	L×L	180 ¢	$\left(\frac{531441}{524228}\right)^8 = 188$ ¢	$\sqrt[53]{2}^8 = 181$ ¢
≈ 9 commas	$^{9}/_{8}$	L×L×C	204 ¢	$\left(\frac{531441}{524228}\right)^9 = 211$ ¢	$\sqrt[53]{2}^9 = 204$ ¢
≈ 12 commas	$^{16777216}/_{14348907}$	L×L×L	271 ¢	$\left(\frac{531441}{524228}\right)^{12} = 282$ ¢	$\sqrt[53]{2}^{12} = 272$ ¢
(1)	(2)	(3)	(4)	(5)	(6)

"octave" by 1243.38 ¢ − 1200.00 ¢ = 43.38 ¢. In other words, by definition no powers of a rational number can produce a prime number, in this case ratio $^2/_1$. So, although *exact* 1-comma intervals do exist within the span of the "octave," all others must be *approximate* multiple comma intervals. However, it is possible to resolve the former discrepancy by means of a geometric division (see Chapter 9, Part III). Such a procedure requires the extraction of the 53rd root of 2, which equals

$$\sqrt[53]{2} = 22.641511 \text{ ¢}$$

when rounded to six decimal places. This is the smallest interval of 53-tone equal temperament; consequently, 22.641511 ¢ × 53 = 1200.000 ¢. In contrast, if we divide the former discrepancy by 53, or 43.38 ¢ ÷ 53 = 0.82 ¢, and then subtract the quotient from the comma of Pythagoras, or 23.46 ¢ − 0.82 ¢ = 22.64 ¢, we obtain an *average* comma cent value for the smallest interval in the 24-tone just scale. When rounded to six decimal places, this value equals 22.641509 ¢, which is practically identical to 53-TET.

Finally, in Table 11.47, compare the values in Columns 6 and 4, and those in Columns 5 and 4. Observe that the cent values of 53-TET more closely approximate the intervals of the 24-tone just scale than the cent values of the exact multiple comma intervals. This is truly ironic. We conclude, therefore, that Turkish musicians use the approximate comma notation to describe the intervals of the 24-tone scale in practical, yet very accurate terms. However, to understand a second historic connection between the 12 *shudūd* of Ṣafī Al-Dīn and the 13 *maqāmāt* of modern Turkish music, we must continue to focus on the exact interval ratios in Column 2, and on the comma-limma equivalents in Column 3.

~ 11.77 ~

Modern Persian *dastgāha* and modern Turkish and Arabian *maqāmāt* (sing. *maqām;* lit. *position* or *place*)[159] are similar in three respects: authentic musical performances require (1) hierarchical distributions of tones, (2) identifiable melodic and cadential patterns, and (3) modulations to intermediary melodic modes. Table 11.48 gives English translations of Turkish[160] and Arabic[161] terms used to describe the hierarchical functions of tones.

Table 11.48

English Translations	Turkish Terms	Arabic Terms
tonic, or *finalis*	*karar*	*qarār*
upper tonic (*octave*)	*tiz durak*	*quwwah*
leading tone	*yeden*	*ẓahīr*
prominent	*güçlü*	*ghammāz*
semi-final	*asma karar*	*markaz*
initial	*giriṣ*	*mabdaʼ*

According to Signell, H. Sadettin Arel (1880–1955), the most influential 20th-century Turkish music theorist

> . . . determined that there were six ***basic*** tetrachords: *Çargâh*, *Puselik*, *Kürdi*, *Rast*, *Uṣṣak*, and *Hicaz*. Each is named for a known makam and the tetrachord delineates the most characteristic part of that makam scale (with the exception of *Çargâh*, a makam not in use today). Extending each tetrachord upwards by a large whole tone, as indicated by parentheses . . . [see Table 11.49(a)], produces the pentachord of the same name. ...
>
> Some other, non-"basic" tetrachords in common use are mentioned by Arel. Though very familiar, they were excluded from the "basic" category because either: (1) the fourth degree did not form a perfect fourth with the base note, or (2) the dominant [or the *prominent tone*] was neither on the fourth nor the fifth degree. Six of these ***"other"*** tetrachords and pentachords are given . . . [see Table 11.49(b)]: *Sabâ*, *Segâh*, *Hüzzam*, *Nikriz*, *Pençgâh*, and *Ferahnâk*.[162] (Bold italics, and text in brackets mine. Text in parentheses in Signell's dissertation.)

Except for the addition of two square brackets and two bracketed notes, Tables 11.49(a) and 11.49(b) illustrate the Turkish tetrachords and pentachords exactly as shown in Signell's Examples 7 and 8.[163] Here whole notes represent tonics, and half notes, dominants.[164] To avoid confusion with the so-called dominant, or "fifth," of Western music theory, I have consistently avoided this term throughout Chapter 11. Signell describes what I call the *prominent tone* in this manner:

> The dominant is the main tonal center midway between the entry tone [or *initial tone*] and the finalis. At the beginning of an improvisation, a secondary drone is sometimes held on the dominant. The dominant is most often located a fifth (in *Rast*, *Hüseyni*, etc.) or a fourth (in *Uṣṣak*, *Nevâ*, etc.) above the tonic. Occasionally, the dominant is a third (in *Segâh*, *Sabâ*, etc.) above the tonic.[165] (Text in brackets mine. Text in parentheses in Signell's dissertation.)

So, in Table 11.49(a), if we interpret the first four tones as a tetrachord, then the fourth tone functions as the *prominent tone* in a given *maqām;* and if we interpret the first five tones as a pentachord, then the fifth tone functions as the *prominent tone* in a given *maqām.*

In Table 11.49(b), note that *Sabâ* has a *prominent tone* 13 commas above the tonic, and *Segâh* has a *prominent tone* 14 commas above the tonic. According to Figure 11.82, 13 commas represent interval ratio $^{32}/_{27}$ [294.1 ¢], and 14 commas, interval ratio $^{19683}/_{16384}$ [317.6 ¢]. Furthermore, in *Segâh*, I included a square bracket to indicate that one primarily identifies this tetrachord by the first four tones, or first three intervals.[166] However, because *Segâh* often extends a "fourth" above the *prominent tone*, I also added G_5 in brackets.[167]

Table 11.49

(a) Signell's 6 Modern Turkish Basic Tetrachords and Pentachords	(b) Signell's 6 Modern Turkish 'Variant' Tetrachords and Pentachords
1. *Çargâh* 9 9 4 9 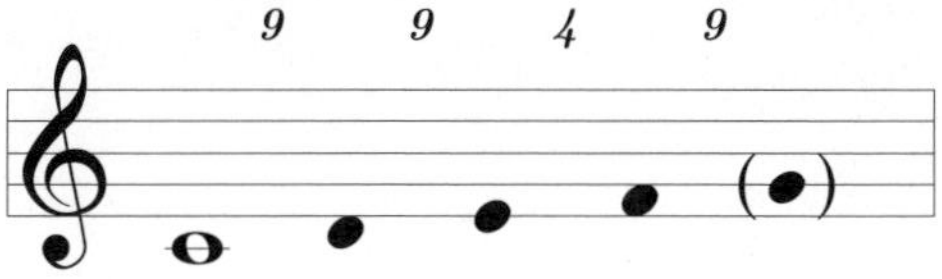	1. *Sabâ* 8 5 5 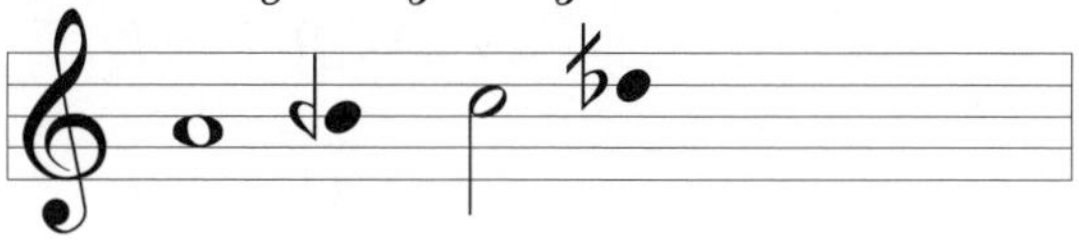
2. *Puselik* 9 4 9 9 	2. *Segâh* 5 9 8 9 5 
3. *Kürdi* 4 9 9 9 	3. *Hüzzam* 5 9 5 12 5 
4. *Rast* 9 8 5 9 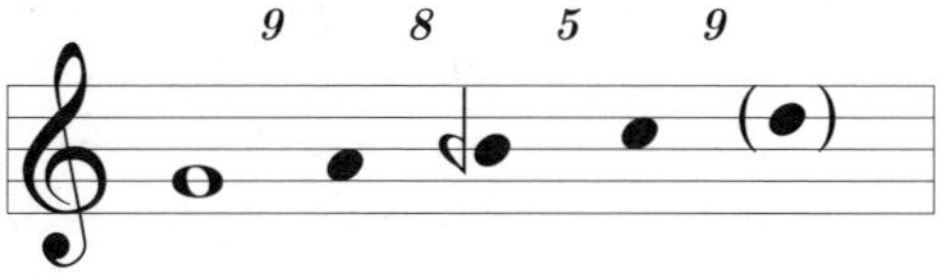	4. *Nikriz* 9 5 12 5 
5. *Uşşak* 8 5 9 9 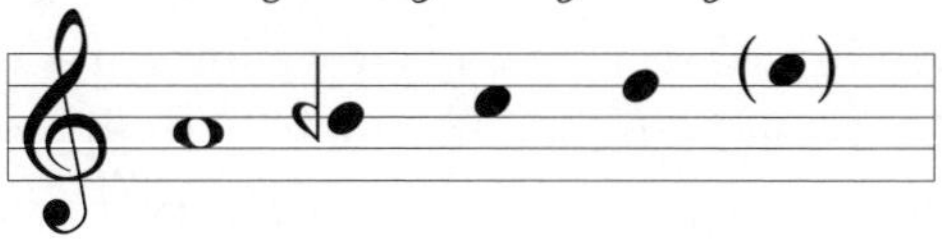	5. *Pençgâh* 9 9 8 5 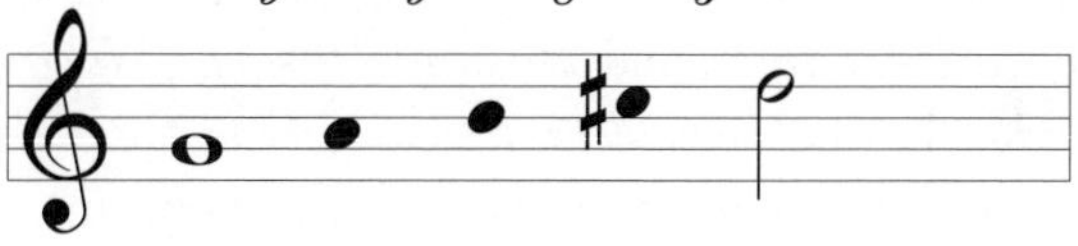
6. *Hicaz* 5 12 5 9 	6. *Ferahnâk* 5 9 9 8 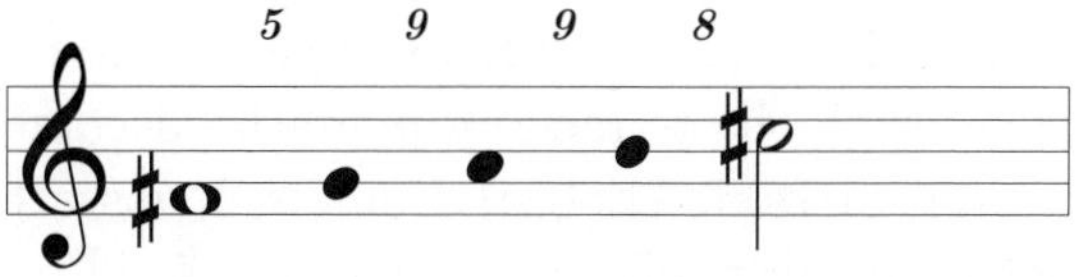

Next, compare *Segâh* to *Hüzzam*. Observe that all tones but one are identical. The “fourth” of *Segâh*, B𝄳$_4$–E𝄳$_5$, interval ratio $^4\!/_3$ [498.0 ¢], equals 22 commas, whereas the “fourth” of *Hüzzam*, B𝄳$_4$–E♭̸$_5$, interval ratio $^{43046721}\!/_{33554432}$ [431.3 ¢], equals 19 commas. (See Table 11.46.) Due to these similarities, one primarily identifies *Hüzzam* by the tetrachord above the *prominent tone*.[168] Consequently, I added G_5 in brackets, and a square bracket to indicate the location of this important upper tetrachord.

Given the tetrachords and pentachords in Table 11.49(a), consider the constructions below of 13 modern Turkish *maqāmāt*.[169]

1. *Çargâh:* *Çargâh* plus *Çargâh*
2. *Puselik:* *Puselik* plus *Hicaz*
3. *Kürdi:* *Kürdi* plus *Puselik*
4. *Rast:* *Rast* plus *Rast*
5. *Suzinâk:* *Rast* plus *Hicaz*
6. *Hüseyni:* *Uşşak* plus *Uşşak*
7. *Nevâ:* *Uşşak* plus *Rast*
8. *Karciğar:* *Uşşak* plus *Hicaz*
9. *Uşşak:* *Uşşak* plus *Puselik*
10. *Hicaz:* *Hicaz* plus *Rast*
11. *Uzzal:* *Hicaz* plus *Uşşak*
12. *Zengüle:* *Hicaz* plus *Hicaz*
13. *Hümayun:* *Hicaz* plus *Puselik*

Turn now to Tables 11.50(a), 11.50(b), and 11.50(c). Column 1 gives Ṣafī Al-Dīn’s 12 *shudūd* in numerical order; Column 2, the basic *maqāmāt* in the above-mentioned order;[170] and Column 3, the *maqāmāt* transposed on Ṣafī Al-Dīn’s *First ʿŪd.* First and foremost, note that of the thirteen *maqāmāt*, the following ten are playable on his *ʿūd: Çargâh, Puselik, Kürdi, Rast, Hüseyni, Nevā, Uşşak, Hicaz, Uzzal,* and *Hümayun.*

To understand this analysis, return to Figure 11.82, Row 6, which shows Ṣafī Al-Dīn’s *First ʿŪd Tuning* from Figure 11.74. Since the modern Turkish *ṭunbūr* includes this 17-tone scale, we may utilize the cumulative comma values in Row 5 to verify the playability of the modern *maqāmāt* on this *ʿūd.* For example, in Table 11.50(a), Column 2, *maqām Çargâh* consists of the following comma intervals: 9, 9, 4, 9, 9, 9, 4; and the corresponding cumulative comma values: 9, 18, 22, 31, 40, 49, 53. Column 3 confirms that if we transpose the lowest tone of *Çargâh* from C_4 to D♭$_4$, we may play this *maqām* on Ṣafī Al-Dīn’s *First ʿŪd.* (For *Çargâh, Puselik, Hicaz,* and *Uzzal,* only one transposition is possible, but for the remaining six playable *maqāmāt*, numerous transpositions are possible.) Also, Column 3 indicates that *Çargâh* consists of two identical disjunct tetrachords: 2, 2, 0, ②, 2, 2, 0. Hence, Column 1 demonstrates that we may attribute the origins of *Çargâh* to Ṣafī Al-Dīn’s *ʿUshshāq* when played in the *second disjunct system.* In Tables 11.50(a) and 11.50(b), four *shudūd* appear with asterisks [*] to signify that four *shadd-maqām* pairs — *ʿUshshāq-Çargâh, Abū Salīk-Kürdi, Rāst-Rast,* and *Ḥusainī-Hüseyni/Nevā* — are identical in two respects: (1) if we interpret the *shudūd* in the *second disjunct system,* then the tetrachord-pentachord combinations of the paired melodic modes are the same; (2) the comma intervals of the *maqāmāt*, or the *exact interval ratios* of the *maqāmāt*, correspond to Ṣafī Al-Dīn’s definitions of intervals Ṭ, J, and B in Table 11.42.

One *shadd* appears with a dagger [†] to indicate that the two modes in the *shadd-maqām* pair — *Rahāwī-Hicaz/Uzzal* — are identical in one respect: if we interpret the *shadd* in the *second disjunct system,* then the tetrachord-pentachord combinations of the paired melodic modes are the same. However, in Table 11.50(c), Column 2, observe that *Hicaz/Uzzal* include a 12-comma interval, or an exact triple-limma [L×L×L = L^3 = 271 ¢], in the lower tetrachord. As discussed in Section 11.74,

Table 11.50(a)

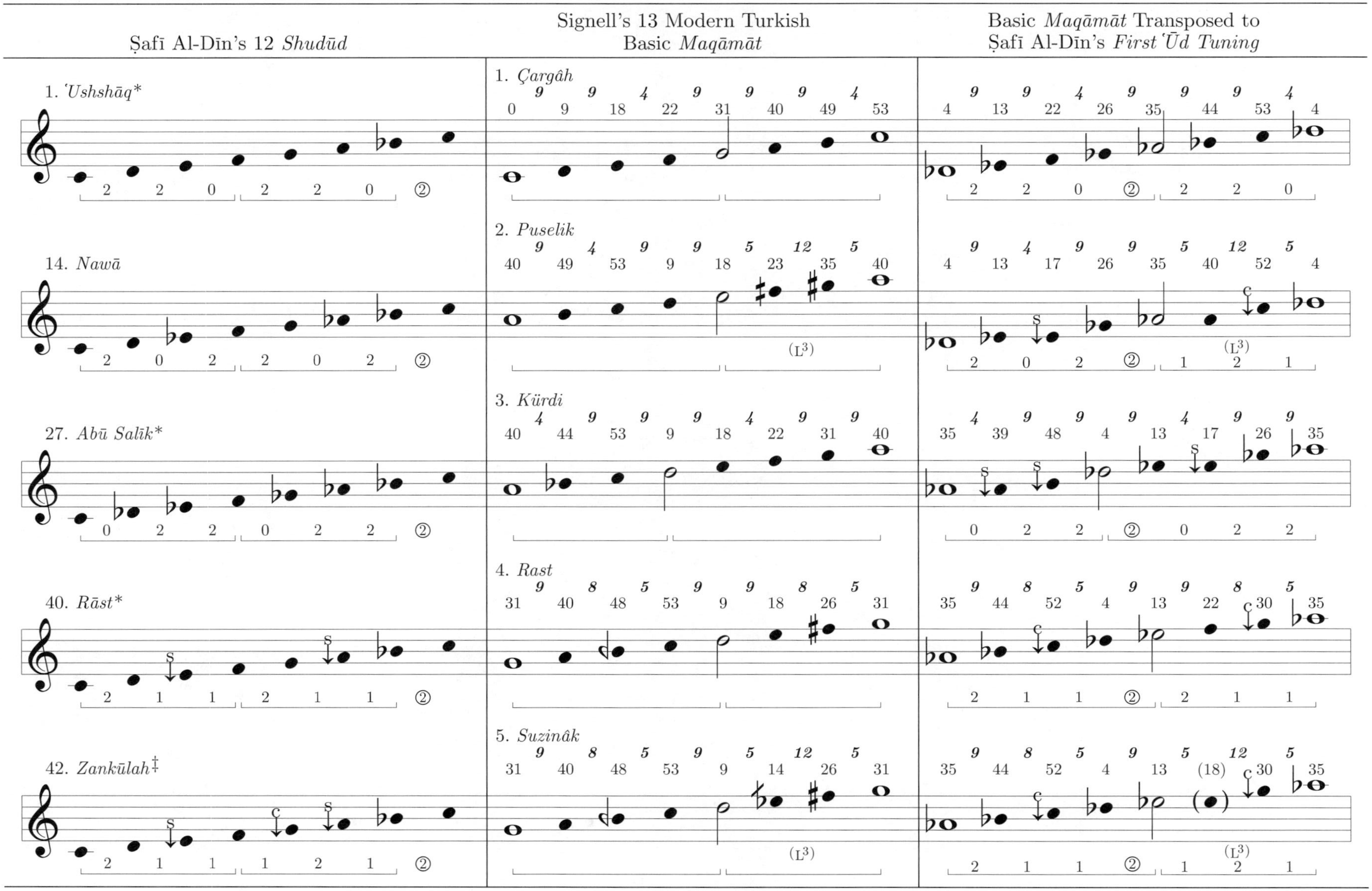
Ṣafī Al-Dīn's 12 *Shudūd*
Signell's 13 Modern Turkish Basic *Maqāmāt*
Basic *Maqāmāt* Transposed to Ṣafī Al-Dīn's *First ʿŪd Tuning*
1. *ʿUshshāq**
2 2 0 2 2 0 ②
1. *Çargâh*
9 9 4 9 9 9 4
0 9 18 22 31 40 49 53
9 9 4 9 9 9 4
4 13 22 26 35 44 53 4
2 2 0 ② 2 2 0
14. *Nawā*
2 0 2 2 0 2 ②
2. *Puselik*
9 4 9 9 5 12 5
40 49 53 9 18 23 35 40
(L3)
9 4 9 9 5 12 5
4 13 17 26 35 40 52 4
2 0 2 ② 1 2 1
(L3)
27. *Abū Salīk**
0 2 2 0 2 2 ②
3. *Kürdi*
4 9 9 9 4 9 9
40 44 53 9 18 22 31 40
4 9 9 9 4 9 9
35 39 48 4 13 17 26 35
0 2 2 ② 0 2 2
40. *Rāst**
2 1 1 2 1 1 ②
4. *Rast*
9 8 5 9 9 8 5
31 40 48 53 9 18 26 31
9 8 5 9 9 8 5
35 44 52 4 13 22 30 35
2 1 1 ② 2 1 1
42. *Zankūlah*‡
2 1 1 1 2 1 ②
5. *Suzinâk*
9 8 5 9 5 12 5
31 40 48 53 9 14 26 31
(L3)
9 8 5 9 5 12 5
35 44 52 4 13 (18) 30 35
2 1 1 ② 1 2 1
(L3)

Table 11.50(b)

Ṣafī Al-Dīn's 12 *Shudūd*	Signell's 13 Modern Turkish Basic *Maqāmāt*	Basic *Maqāmāt* Transposed to Ṣafī Al-Dīn's *First 'Ūd Tuning*

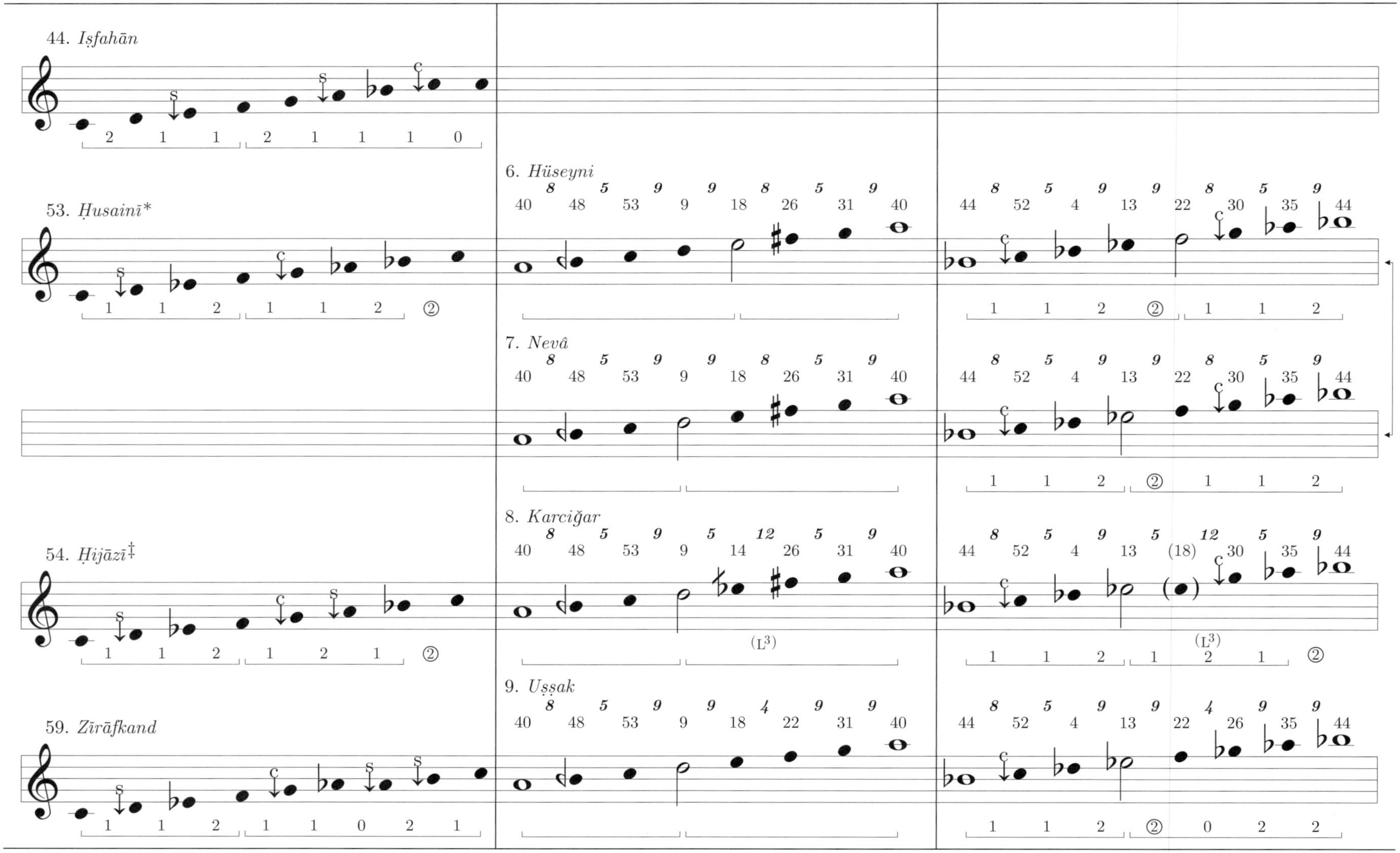

Table 11.50(c)

Ṣafī Al-Dīn's 12 *Shudūd*	Signell's 13 Modern Turkish Basic *Maqāmāt*	Basic *Maqāmāt* Transposed to Ṣafī Al-Dīn's *First ʿŪd Tuning*

Ṣafī Al-Dīn did not use this interval. As a result, the interval ratios of these paired modes are not consistent.

Before we proceed, turn back to the modern Persian *dastgāhā* in Table 11.34. Notice that an interval that is musically indistinguishable from the triple-limma occurs twice in *Dastgāh-e Chahārgāh*, and once in *Dastgāh-e Homāyun.* Farhat calls this interval a "plus second" [$P \approx 270$ ¢]. (See Section 11.64.) In Figure 11.66, Row 5, I interpret it as ratio $^{243}/_{208}$ [269 ¢], and as ratio $^{7}/_{6}$ [267 ¢], on Ibn Sīnā's *'ūd.* So, despite Ṣafī Al-Dīn's exclusion, it is highly likely that the triple-limma occurred frequently in the ancient musical traditions of the *ṭunbūr* and *'ūd.* For evidence of interval ratios larger than $^{9}/_{8}$ [203.9 ¢], turn back to Ibn Sīnā's 11 Melodic Modes in Table 11.32, and to Ṣafī Al-Dīn's 6 *Āwāzāt* in Table 11.45. In the former table, Mode 9 includes $^{8}/_{7}$ [231.2 ¢]; Mode 10, or *Iṣfahān* includes $^{8}/_{7}$ and $^{108}/_{91}$ [296.5 ¢]; and Mode 11, or *Salmakī* includes $^{2457}/_{2048}$ [315.2 ¢]. In the latter table, *Māya* includes two Pythagorean "minor thirds," ratio $^{32}/_{27}$ [294.1 ¢].

Three more *shudūd* — *Zankūlah, Ḥijāzī,* and *'Irāq* — appear with double daggers [‡] to signify that three *maqāmāt* — *Suzinâk, Karciğar,* and *Zengüle,* respectively — are not playable because the upper "octave" of Ṣafī Al-Dīn's *First 'Ūd* does *not* include the tone E_5, or the Pythagorean "major third," ratio $^{81}/_{64}$. Consequently, one cannot play the triple-limma E_5–$G\overset{c}{\downarrow}_5$. Although these three *maqāmāt* suggest that this instrument does not provide such an interval in a given upper tetrachord, observe that the transposition of *Puselik* in Table 11.50(a), Column 3, contradicts this assumption. Here the triple-limma A_4–$C\overset{c}{\downarrow}_4$ is playable. Finally, all other unmarked *shudūd* are considerably different from the closest corresponding *maqāmāt.*

In Tables 11.50(b) and 11.50(c), Column 3, double-headed arrows in the right margins indicate that *maqāmāt Hüseyni* and *Nevâ,* and *maqāmāt Hicaz* and *Uzzal* differ only in the identity of the *prominent tone.*

In conclusion, consider the playability of Signell's "other" tetrachords and pentachords. When viewed from a musical perspective, I refer to these as the 'variant' *maqāmāt.* Table 11.51 confirms that we may transpose five of the six 'variant' *maqāmāt* on Ṣafī Al-Dīn's *First 'Ūd. Hüzzam* appears with an asterisk because a transposition of the entire mode requires the missing tone E_5.

~ 11.78 ~

The Turkish notation is extremely useful because it distinguishes between 9 comma intervals, exact interval ratio $^{9}/_{8}$ [203.9 ¢], and 12 comma intervals, exact interval ratio $^{16777216}/_{14348907}$ [270.7 ¢]; and it distinguishes between 5 comma intervals, exact interval ratio $^{2187}/_{2048}$ [113.7 ¢], and 8 comma intervals, exact interval ratio $^{65536}/_{59049}$ [180.5 ¢]. In this system of notation, it is easy to determine whether or not a given mode contains two identical tetrachords.

Recall that Ṣafī Al-Dīn and Al-Jurjānī failed to differentiate between these two groups of intervals. Turn back to Table 11.42, and notice that interval Ṭ — or interval 2 in this text — represents either a "large whole tone," ratio $^{9}/_{8}$, or a triple-limma, ratio $^{16777216}/_{14348907}$; similarly, interval J — or interval 1 in this text — represents either a "semitone," ratio $^{2187}/_{2048}$, or a "small whole tone," ratio $^{65536}/_{59049}$. Consequently, when one writes a mode as 2, 1, 1, 2, 1, 1, ②, the notation does not immediately indicate whether or not this mode contains two identical conjunct tetrachords; similarly, when one writes a mode as 2, 1, 1, ②, 2, 1, 1, the notation also does not immediately indicate whether or not this mode contains two identical disjunct tetrachords. To resolve this difficulty, I will use a double underline notation. Modes that consist of two identical conjunct tetrachords followed by the interval of disjunction appear as $\underline{\underline{2\text{–}1\text{–}1}}\text{–}\underline{\underline{2\text{–}1\text{–}1}}$–②; and modes that consist of two identical disjunct tetrachords, where the interval of disjunction occurs between the tetrachords, appear as $\underline{\underline{2\text{–}1\text{–}1}}$–②–$\underline{\underline{2\text{–}1\text{–}1}}$.

Table 11.51

Signell's 6 Modern Turkish 'Variant' *Maqāmāt*	6 'Variant' *Maqāmāt* Transposed to Ṣafī Al-Dīn's *First ʿŪd Tuning*

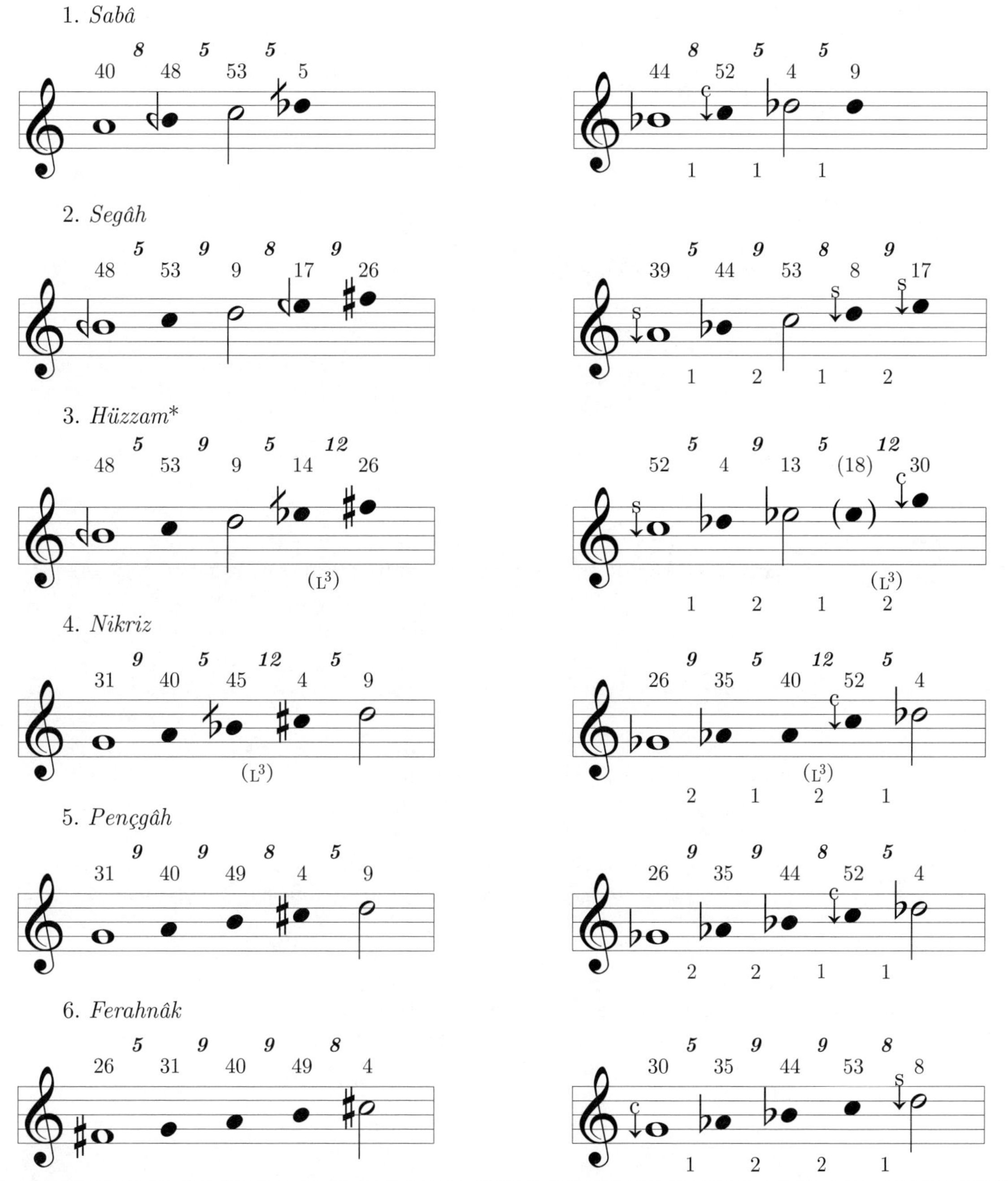

By definition, two *identical conjunct tetrachords* produce a maximum number of *four consecutive "fourths"* within the "double-fourth," or a "minor seventh," ratio $^{16}\!/\!_{9}$. (See Section 11.58.) Therefore, in all such modes, a "fourth" occurs between these scale degrees: 1–4, 2–5, 3–6, 4–7. By definition, two *identical disjunct tetrachords* produce a maximum number of *four consecutive "fifths"* within the "octave," ratio $^{2}\!/\!_{1}$. Therefore, in all such modes, a "fifth" occurs between these scale degrees: 1–5, 2–6, 3–7, and 4–8.

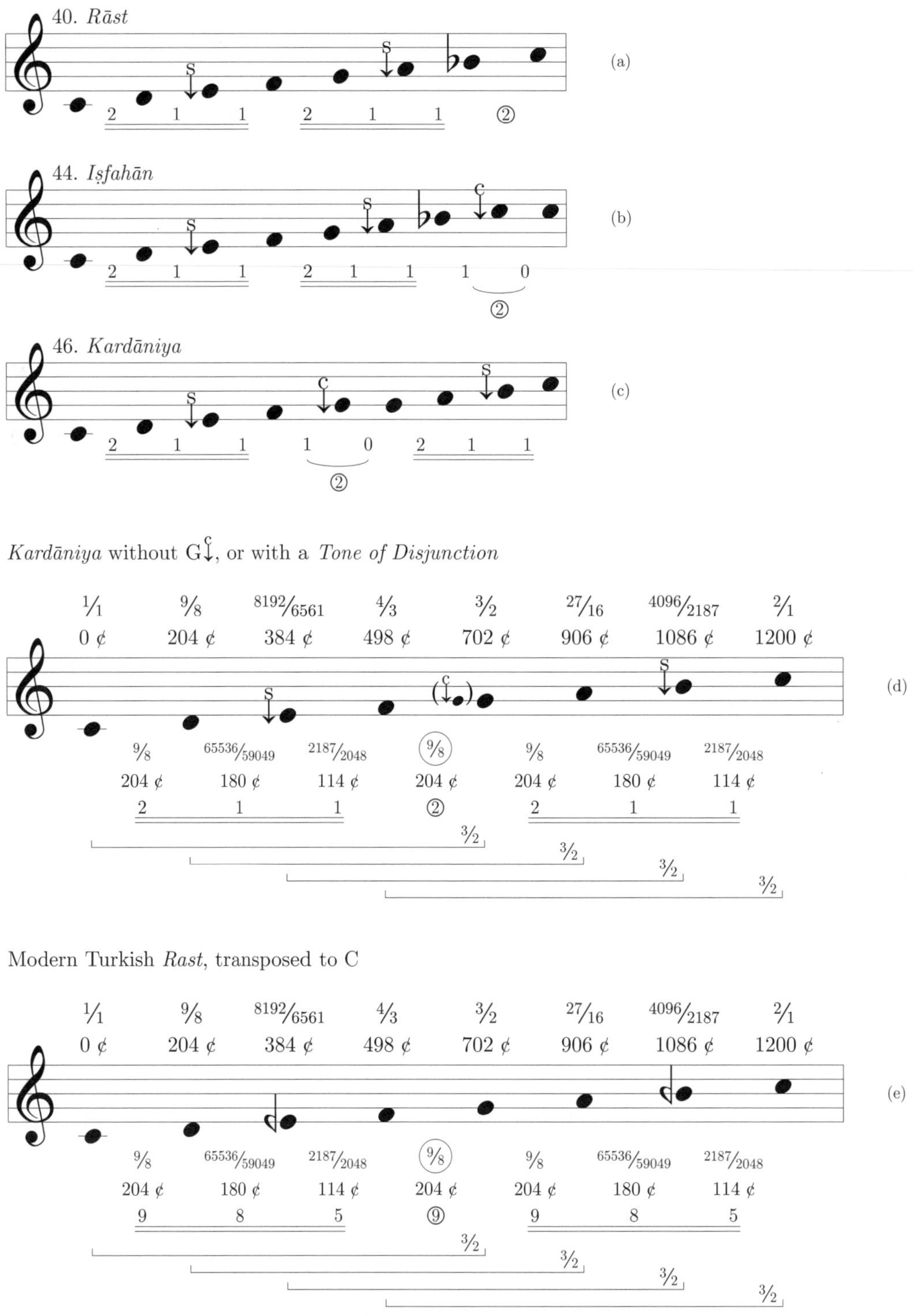

Figure 11.83 The evolution of Modern Turkish *Rast.* (a) *Rāst*, (b) *Iṣfahān*, and (c) *Kardāniya* appear as shown in Table 11.45. Al-Jurjānī derives *Kardāniya* by shifting the tone of disjunction of *Iṣfahān* from the upper to the lower position. In *Iṣfahān* without C↓, the interval of disjunction occurs between B♭–C′; so, in *Kardāniya* without G↓, the interval of disjunction occurs between F–G. (d) This is a detailed analysis of *Kardāniya* and (e), of Modern Turkish *Rast.* Note that both modes have identical interval ratios and frequency ratios, and consist of two identical disjunct tetrachords.

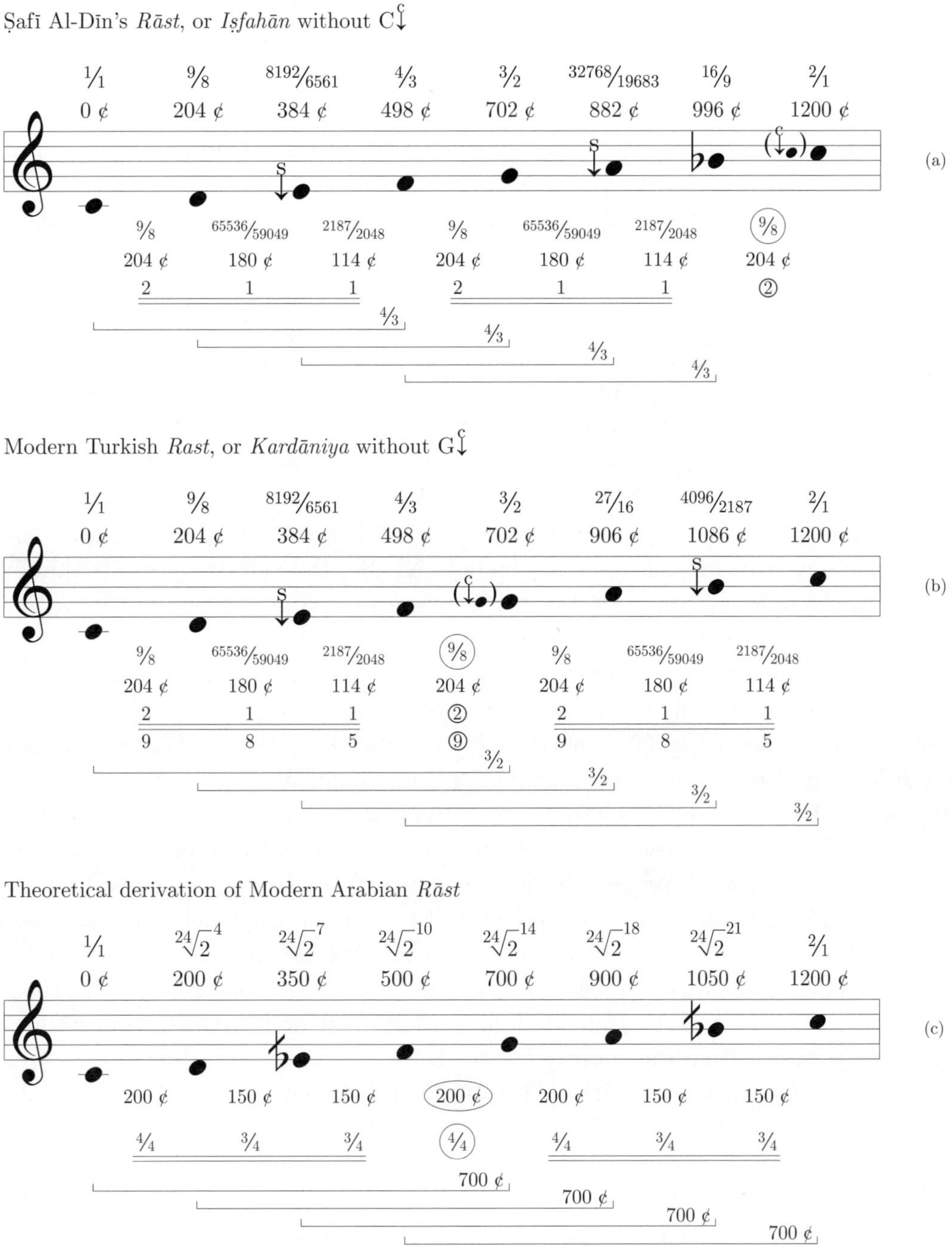

Figure 11.84 The evolution of Modern Arabian *Rāst*. (a) Ṣafī Al-Dīn's *Rāst*, or *Iṣfahān* without C↓, contains two identical conjunct tetrachords. (b) Modern Turkish *Rast*, or *Kardāniya* without G↓, consists of two identical disjunct tetrachords. (c) Based on 24-tone equal temperament, Modern Arabian *Rāst* also consists of two identical disjunct tetrachords. Therefore, with respect to the distribution of tetrachords, Modern Turkish *Rast* and Modern Arabian *Rāst* are identical.

Turn back to Tables 11.50(a), 11.50(b), and 11.50(c), Column 3, and observe that with the exception of *Karciğar*, twelve *maqāmāt* contain two disjunct tetrachords. Of these, six *maqāmāt: Çargâh, Kürdi, Rast, Hüseyni, Nevâ,* and *Zengüle* contain two identical disjunct tetrachords. Now, with respect to *Rast*, the question naturally arises, "Did Ṣafī Al-Dīn's *Rāst*, which consists of two identical conjunct tetrachords: 2–1–1–2–1–1–②, evolve into Modern Turkish *Rast*, which consists of two identical disjunct tetrachords: 9–8–5–⑨–9–8–5?" Although this question may be impossible to answer, I would like to offer the following analysis as a plausible explanation for the origins of Modern Turkish *Rast*, and for the origins of Modern Arabian *Rāst* as well.

Figures 11.83(a), 11.83(b), and 11.83(c) bring back *Rāst*, *Iṣfahān*, and *Kardāniya* as depicted in Table 11.45. *Rāst* consists of two identical conjunct tetrachords, followed by the interval of disjunction: 2–1–1–2–1–1–②. Although *Iṣfahān* consists of the same conjunct tetrachords: 2–1–1–2–1–1, it does *not* end with an interval of disjunction, B♭–C′, but with the intervals B♭–C↓–C′.

Now, according to Section 11.75, Quote I, Al-Jurjānī derived *Kardāniya* from *Iṣfahān*. He extracted *Kardāniya* by shifting the interval of disjunction of *Iṣfahān* ". . . from the upper [position] to the lower [position] . . ." However, since *Iṣfahān* does *not* have an interval of disjunction, this passage probably means that — *in the context of the derivation of Kardāniya* — Al-Jurjānī interpreted *Iṣfahān* as a mode that does *not* include C↓. So, the possibility exists that Al-Jurjānī assigned *Iṣfahān* two different interpretations. For this reason, Figure 11.83(b) shows *Iṣfahān* with a tie, which indicates an interval of disjunction — ② — between B♭–C′. Notice that without C↓, *Iṣfahān* and *Rāst* are identical. The possibility also exists that Al-Jurjānī assigned *Kardāniya* two different interpretations. For this reason, Figure 11.83(c) shows *Kardāniya* with a tie, which indicates an interval of disjunction — ② — between F–G. Notice that without G↓, *Kardāniya* in Figure 11.83(d) and Modern Turkish *Rast* in Figure 11.83(e) are identical.

Al-Jurjānī's derivation signifies an important moment in the history of Arabian music. By shifting the interval of disjunction from the upper to the lower position, musicians changed *Iṣfahān*, which consists of two *identical conjunct tetrachords*, into *Kardāniya*, which consists of two *identical disjunct tetrachords*. Figures 11.84(a) and 11.84(b) illustrate the musical consequences of this transformation. Four brackets in Figure 11.84(a) indicate that Ṣafī Al-Dīn's *Rāst*, or *Iṣfahān* without C↓, includes four consecutive "fourths" within the "double-fourth," ratio 16⁄9. In contrast, four brackets in Figure 11.84(b) indicate that Modern Turkish *Rast*, or *Kardāniya* without G↓, includes four consecutive "fifths" within the "octave," ratio 2⁄1.

Since *Rāst* and *Iṣfahān* (without C↓) are identical, the question arises, "Why did Al-Jurjānī not simply derive *Kardāniya* (without G↓) from *Rāst*?" In reply to this question, notice that on a 17-tone *'ūd* equipped with a fret for a "neutral third" — E𝄳 or E𝄭 — it *is* possible to play the interval pattern of *Rāst:* 2–1–1–2–1–1–②, but it is *not* possible to play the interval pattern of *Kardāniya:* 2–1–1–②–2–1–1, if one starts from the open *Bamm;* this generality also applies to Ṣafī Al-Dīn's *Second 'Ūd.* (See Figure 11.76.) If one begins on C, one can play two identical conjunct tetrachords, or four consecutive "fourths" — C, D, E↓, F, G, A↓, B♭, C′ — and two identical disjunct tetrachords, or four consecutive "fifths" — C, D, E↓, F, G, A, B↓, C′ — *only* on Ṣafī Al-Dīn's *First 'Ūd.* (See Figure 11.74.) Above Fret 5, or above E↓, this is the only *'ūd* that provides both a "fourth," interval E↓–A↓, and a "fifth," interval E↓–B↓. Because musicians regarded *Rāst* as a *regular* or *standard* mode, they probably did not want to associate it with another mode that (1) does not include four consecutive "fourths," and (2) is not playable from the open *Bamm.* This may explain why *Kardāniya* (1) was *not* derived from *Rāst*, but from *Iṣfahān*, and (2) was *not* considered a *shadd*, but an *āwāz.* Apparently, musicians in Ṣafī Al-Dīn's time did not fully accept melodic modes that consisted of two identical disjunct tetrachords. However, the fact that such modes were popular and given names is beyond doubt. Therefore, in response to the first question at the beginning of this section, I would answer, "Modern Turkish *Rast* did not evolve from *Rāst*, but from *Kardāniya.*"

~ 11.79 ~

Figure 11.84(c) depicts Modern Arabian *Rāst.* To my knowledge, the first time this mode appears as a complete 8-tone entity is in a work entitled *Kitāb al-Mūsīqá al-Sharqī* [*The Book of Oriental Music*], by M. Kāmil Al-Khulaʿī (*c.* 1879 – d. 1938), published in 1904. In the excerpt below, translated by Scott Lloyd Marcus in his exhaustive dissertation *Arab Music Theory in the Modern Period*, Al-Khulaʿī gives the note names[171] of Modern Arabian *Rāst:*

> *Rāst* – *Dūkāh* – *Sīkāh* – *Jahārkāh* – *Nawā* – *Ḥusaynī* – *Awj* – *Kirdān* [i.e., C D E𝄳 F G A B𝄳 c]. When it is necessary to ascend beyond or descend below these notes, [this] modal complex [*ṭarīqah*] uses the higher and lower octaves of these same notes. The settling at the end is on the note *Rāst* [C]. In terms of Turkish practice, [this] modal complex starts from *Rāst* [C].[172] (All text in brackets in Marcus' dissertation.)

All the authors I have read on modern Arabian music agree on the tones of Modern Arabian *Rāst.* Despite this fact, none of them explain the historic or mathematical origins of this scale. For this reason, the possibility exists that Modern Arabian *Rāst* merely typifies an academic artifice. The *regular* or *standard* mode — if there is such a mode — of the indigenous people of Arabic-speaking lands remains a mystery.

Figure 11.84(c) indicates that Modern Arabian *Rāst* is theoretically based on 24-tone equal temperament. Recall that in 1584, Prince Chu Tsai-yü (1536–1611) in China,[173] and Simon Stevin (1548–1620) in Holland,[174] managed to extract the 12th root of 2 without the benefit of logarithms. The works of these two music theorists provided the mathematical foundations of 12-tone equal temperament in the Far East and in Europe. Because no evidence exists that such a musically minded Arabian mathematician lived during the last three or four centuries, I am of the opinion that 24-tone equal temperament constitutes little more than a formulaic imposition to inappropriately simplify the profound complexities of Arabian music.

Despite this attempt at numeric reduction, Figure 11.84(c) shows that Modern Arabian *Rāst* consists of two identical disjunct tetrachords. With respect to the distribution of tetrachords, we conclude, therefore, that Modern Turkish *Rast* and Modern Arabian *Rāst* are identical. Before we discuss the tuning theories and melodic modes of the modern era, let us reexamine the *ʿūd* tunings of Al-Fārābī and Ibn Sīnā one last time. Hopefully, this analysis will enable us to avoid anachronisms and half-truths in our attempt to understand a few principles of modern Arabian music.

~ 11.80 ~

Modern Turkish *Rast* on the *ṭunbūr*,

C, D, E𝄬, F, G, A, B𝄬, C′

and Modern Arabian *Rāst* on the *ʿūd*,

C, D, E𝄳, F, G, A, B𝄳, C′

consist of two identical disjunct tetrachords. The only differences between these two modes are the identities of the "third," and of the "seventh," of each mode. Modern Turkish *Rast* has a 17 comma "major third," which is equivalent to Ṣafī Al-Dīn's "schisma third," ratio $^{8192}/_{6561}$ [384.4 ¢]; and it has a 48 comma "minor seventh," which is equivalent to Ṣafī Al-Dīn's "schisma seventh," ratio $^{4096}/_{2187}$ [1086.3 ¢]. Because the *ṭunbūr* provides these two tones above the lowest open string (see Figure 11.81), one may play this mode by starting on C. In contrast, Modern Arabian *Rāst* has a

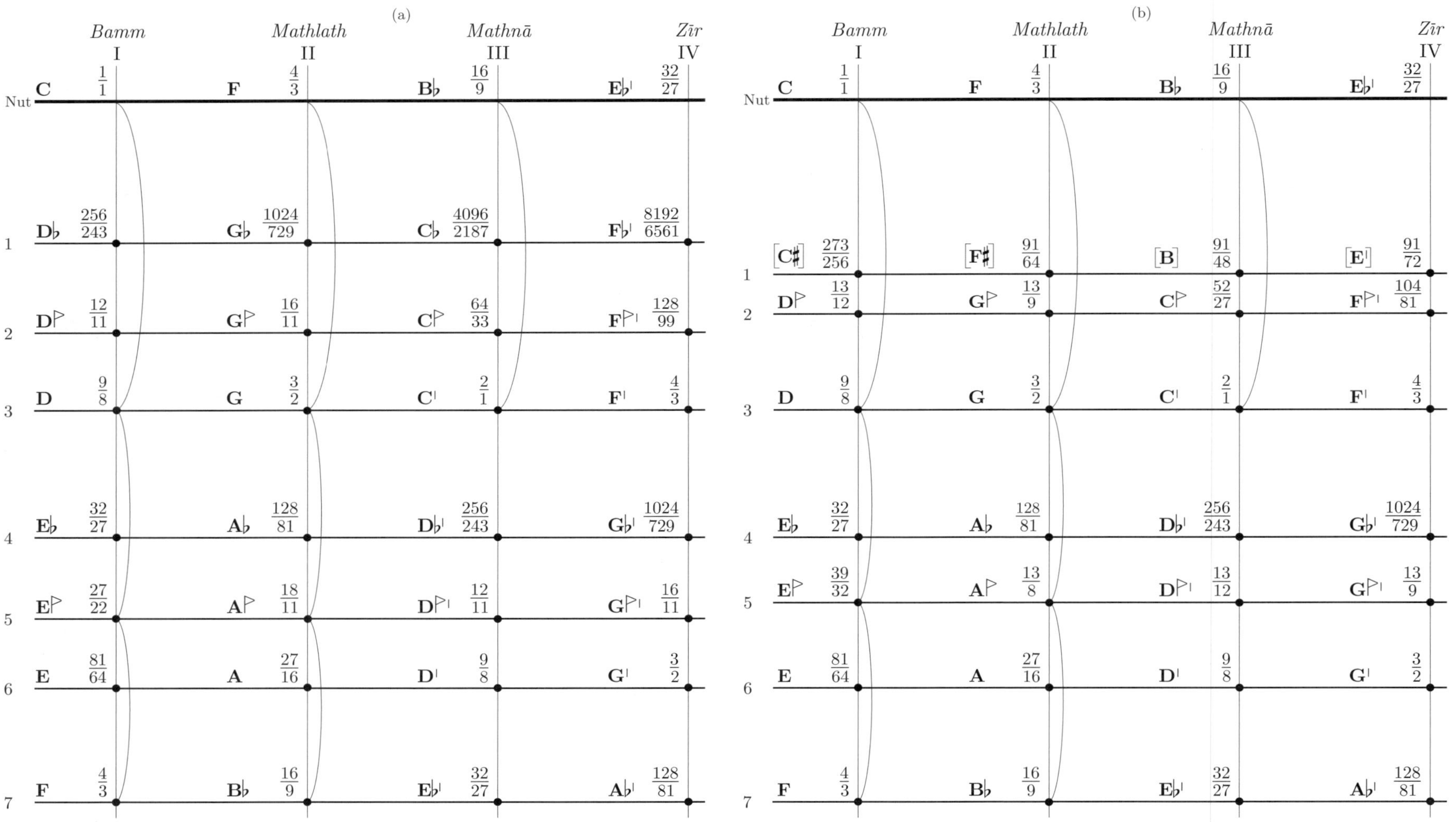

Figure 11.85 Ancient Arabian *Rāst* on Al-Fārābī's *'ūd* and Ibn Sīnā's *'ūd.* (a) I derived this 17-tone tuning from Al-Fārābī's 22-tone scale, which is based on his *Jins* 2 tetrachord: $^1\!/_1$, $^9\!/_8$, $^{27}\!/_{22}$, $^4\!/_3$. (See Figure 11.49.) Ties indicate the interval pattern of Ancient *Rāst:* 2–1–1–2–1–1–②, which consists of two *identical conjunct tetrachords* within the C–C' "octave." (b) Ibn Sīnā's 17-tone *'ūd* tuning is based on his *Diatonic Genus* 7 tetrachord: $^1\!/_1$, $^9\!/_8$, $^{39}\!/_{32}$, $^4\!/_3$. (See Figure 11.62.) Ties between frets indicate the same interval pattern. Ancient *Rāst* is identical to the lower "octave" of Ibn Sīnā's Mode 8, which he called *Mustaqīm.* (See Table 11.32.)

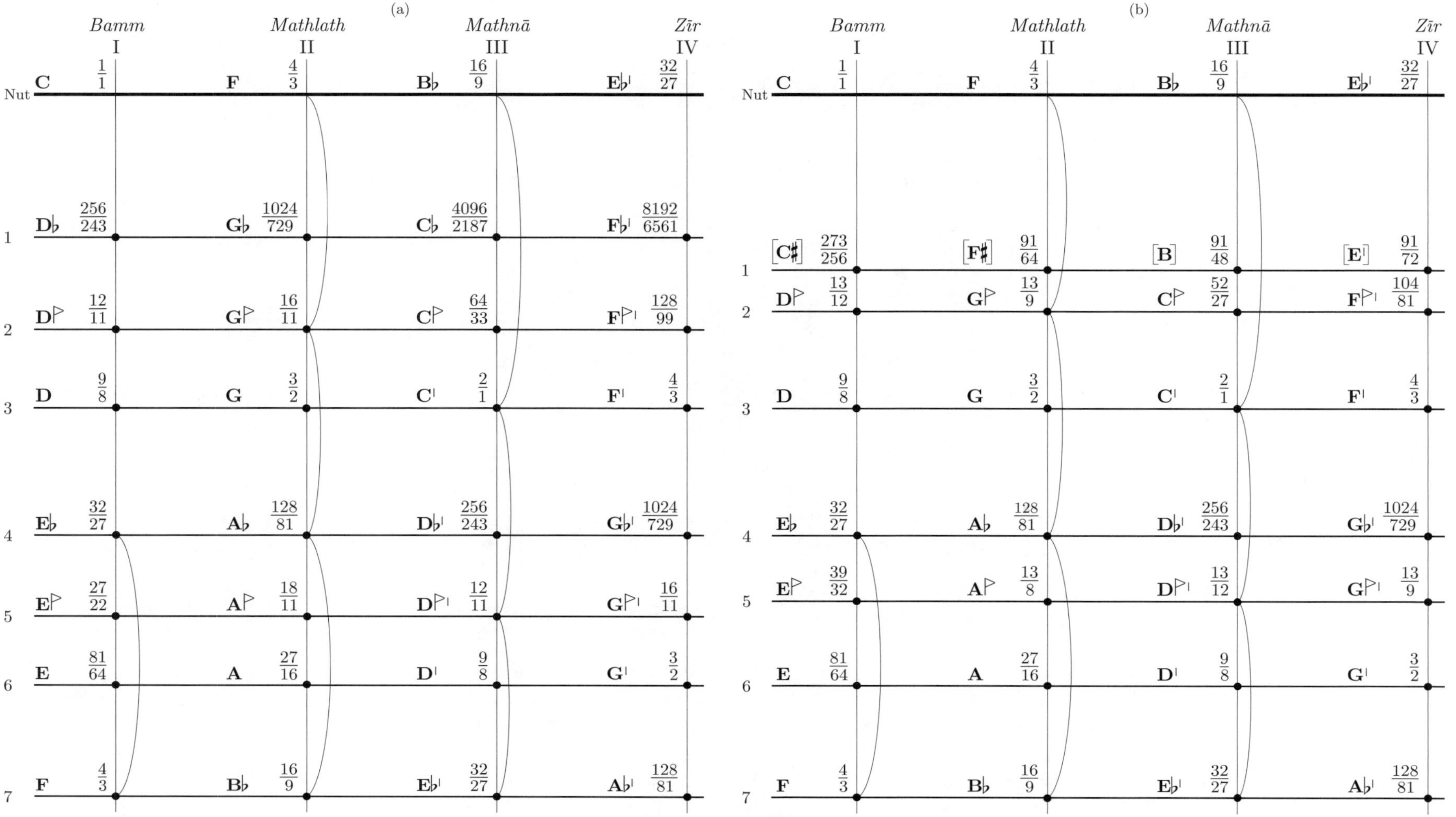

Figure 11.86 Modern Arabian *Rāst* on Al-Fārābī's *'ūd* and Ibn Sīnā's *'ūd*. (a) As discussed in Figure 11.85, I derived this 17-tone *ūd* tuning from Al-Fārābī's 22-tone scale. Ties indicate the interval pattern of Modern *Rāst:* 2–1–1–②–2–1–1, which consists of two *identical disjunct tetrachords* shown here within the E♭–E♭ "octave." (b) Ibn Sīnā's 17-tone *'ūd* tuning. Ties between frets indicate the same interval pattern. On both instruments, Modern *Rāst* also occurs within the A♭–A♭ "octave."

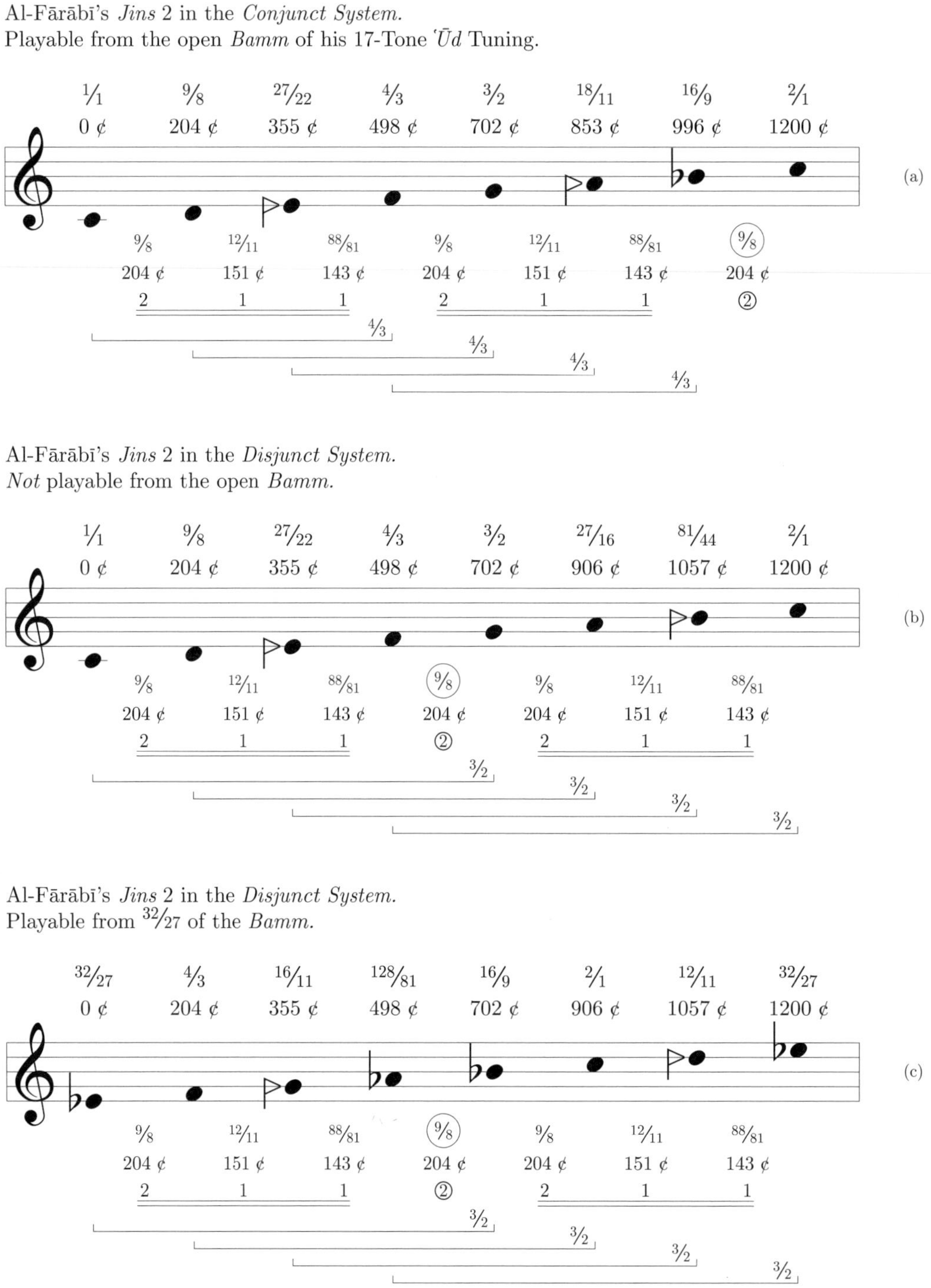

Figure 11.87 Exact interval ratios and frequency ratios to verify the playability of Al-Fārābī's *Jins* 2 tetrachord on his 17-tone *ʿūd.* (a) In the conjunct system, it is possible to play *Jins* 2 as two identical tetrachords from the open *Bamm.* (b) However, in the disjunct system, it is not possible to play *Jins* 2 as two identical tetrachords from the open *Bamm* because the "neutral seventh," ratio 81/44, does not exist on Al-Fārābī's *ʿūd.* (c) Finally, in the disjunct system, it is possible to play *Jins* 2 as two identical tetrachords by starting on the "minor third," ratio 32/27, of the *Bamm* because the required "neutral seventh," ratio 24/11 [12/11], exists on the *Mathnā.* [See Figure 11.86(a).]

Ibn Sīnā's *Diatonic Genus* 7 in the *Conjunct System.*
Playable from the open *Bamm* of his 17-Tone *'Ūd* Tuning.

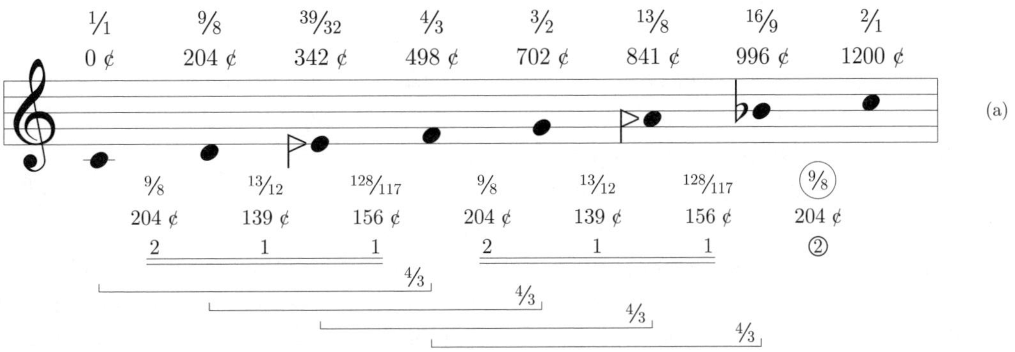

Ibn Sīnā's *Diatonic Genus* 7 in the *Disjunct System.*
Not playable from the open *Bamm.*

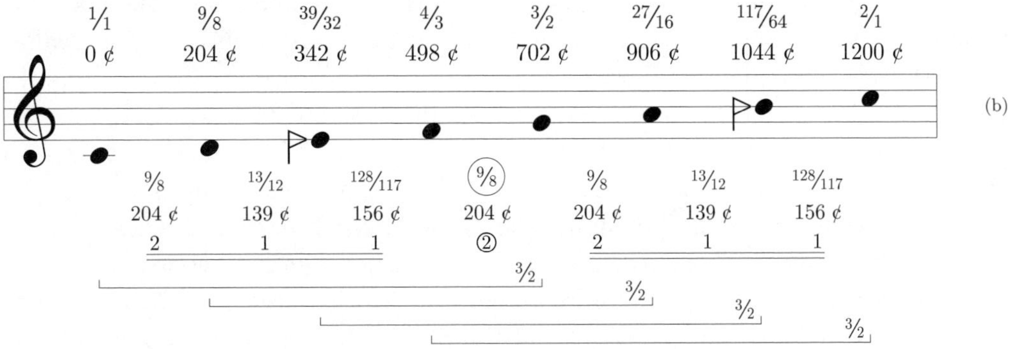

Ibn Sīnā's *Diatonic Genus* 7 in the *Disjunct System.*
Playable from 32/27 of the *Bamm.*

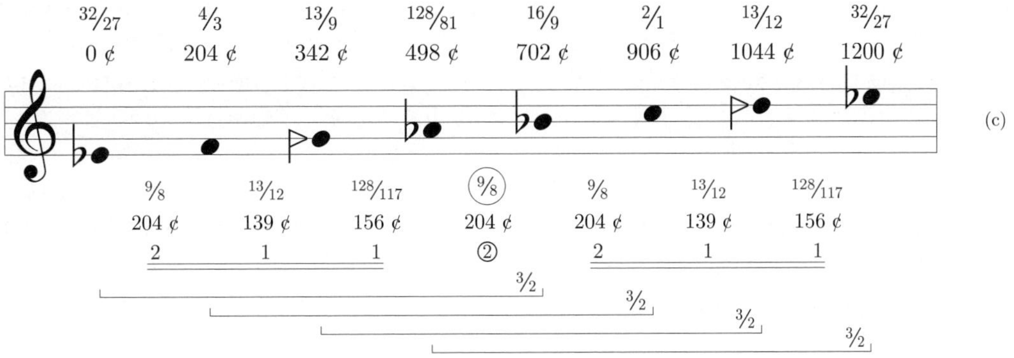

Figure 11.88 Exact interval ratios and frequency ratios to verify the playability of Ibn Sīnā's *Diatonic Genus* 7 on his 17-tone *'ūd.* (a) In the conjunct system, it is possible to play *Diatonic Genus* 7 as two identical tetrachords from the open *Bamm.* (b) However, in the disjunct system, it is not possible to play *Diatonic Genus* 7 as two identical tetrachords from the open *Bamm* because the "neutral seventh," ratio 117/64, does not exist on Ibn Sīnā's *'ūd.* (c) Finally, in the disjunct system, it is possible to play *Diatonic Genus* 7 as two identical tetrachords by starting on the "minor third," ratio 32/27, of the *Bamm* because the required "neutral seventh," ratio 13/6 [13/12], exists on the *Mathnā.* [See Figure 11.86(b).]

"neutral third," which contemporary theorists evaluate at approximately 350 ¢; and it has a "neutral seventh," at approximately 1050 ¢. On Al-Fārābī's *ʿūd* (see Figure 11.48), on Ibn Sīnā's *ʿūd* (see Figure 11.62), and on Ṣafī Al-Dīn's *Second ʿŪd* (see Figure 11.76), a fret for a "neutral third" — E𝄳 or E♭̸ — above the open *Bamm* has *always* existed on the *Bamm;* however, a fret for a "neutral seventh" — B𝄳 or B♭̸ — *never* existed above the open *Bamm;* that is, such a fret never existed on the *Mathnā*. So, two questions naturally arise: (1) Why was a "neutral seventh" fret not included? (2) Does a "neutral seventh" interval occur anywhere else on these ancient *ʿūds*?

(1) In response to the first question, turn back to Section 11.58. Because the open strings of the *ʿūd* are tuned in "fourths," most ancient melodic modes contain two conjunct tetrachords that span the interval of a "double-fourth," or a "minor seventh," ratio $16/9$ [996.1 ¢]. Figure 11.60 illustrates that all such modes require the least number of frets. Furthermore, recall that Fret 1, which produces a "semitone" on the *Bamm*, typically ratio $256/243$ [90.2 ¢], also produces a "major seventh" on the *Mathnā*, typically ratio $4096/2187$ [1086.3 ¢]. So, we see that the *ʿūd* provides the required "minor seventh" between the open *Bamm* and the open *Mathnā*, and it provides a "major seventh" on Fret 1 of the *Mathnā*. For these reasons, Al-Fārābī, Ibn Sīnā, and Ṣafī Al-Dīn never considered the need for another fret to produce an additional "neutral seventh" [≈ 1050 ¢] above the open *Bamm*.

Figure 11.85(a) is a 17-tone *ʿūd* tuning that I derived from Al-Fārābī's 22-tone scale in Figure 11.49. The latter scale is based on Al-Fārābī's *Jins* 2 tetrachord: 1-step, $3/4$-step, $3/4$-step. (See Figure 11.52.) As discussed in Section 11.56, we may express *Jins* 2 as interval ratios $9/8$, $12/11$, $88/81$, or frequency ratios $1/1$, $9/8$ $27/22$, $4/3$. Similarly, Figure 11.85(b) is Ibn Sīnā's 17-tone *ʿūd* tuning, based on his *Diatonic Genus* 7 tetrachord: interval ratios $9/8$, $13/12$, $128/117$, or frequency ratios $1/1$, $9/8$, $39/32$, $4/3$. (See Figure 11.62.) A sequence of ties in each figure shows the interval pattern of Ancient Arabian *Rāst:* 2–1–1–2–1–1–② within the C–C′ "octave." Since this *regular* or *standard* mode consists of two identical conjunct tetrachords, it does not require a "neutral seventh" fret. Finally, recall that Ancient Arabian *Rāst* is identical to the lower "octave" of Ibn Sīnā's Mode 8, which he called *Mustaqīm*. As discussed in Section 11.75, the Arabic term *mustaqīm* is equivalent to the Persian term *rāst*.

(2) My answer to the second question is, "Yes. The interval of a 'neutral seventh' exists on the ancient *ʿūds*." Because most ancient modes were based on conjunct tetrachords, Modern Arabian *Rāst*, which consists of two identical disjunct tetrachords, was probably unknown to Al-Fārābī and Ibn Sīnā as a musical mode. Nevertheless, it is possible to play this modern mode on these ancient instruments. In Figures 11.86(a) and 11.86(b), a sequence of ties shows the interval pattern of Modern Arabian *Rāst:* 2–1–1–②–2–1–1 within the E♭–E♭′ "octave." On Al-Fārābī's *ʿūd*, a "neutral seventh" occurs between E♭–D𝄳′, interval ratio $24/11 \div 32/27 = 81/44 = 1056.5$ ¢; and on Ibn Sīnā's *ʿūd* a "neutral seventh" occurs between E♭–D𝄳′, interval ratio $13/6 \div 32/27 = 117/64 = 1044.4$ ¢. [Astonishingly, the average cent value of these two "neutral sevenths" equals (1056.6 ¢ + 1044.4 ¢) ÷ 2 = 1050.5 ¢.] On both instruments, one may also play Modern Arabian *Rāst* within the A♭–A♭′ "octave." When transposed to A♭, a "neutral seventh" occurs between A♭–G𝄳′. These observations apply to Ṣafī Al-Dīn's *Second ʿŪd* as well.

In summary, Figures 11.87 and 11.88 give exact interval ratios and frequency ratios of Al-Fārābī's *Jins* 2, and of Ibn Sīnā's *Diatonic Genus* 7, in both the conjunct and disjunct systems. The ratios in Figure 11.87(a) indicate that when realized in the conjunct system, it is possible to play Ancient Arabian *Rāst* from the open *Bamm* of Al-Fārābī's *ʿūd*. However, the ratios in Figure 11.87(b) indicate that when realized in the disjunct system, it is not possible to play Modern Arabian *Rāst* from the open *Bamm*. Nevertheless, the ratios in Figure 11.87(c) indicate that it is possible to play Modern Arabian *Rāst* from E♭, ratio $32/27$, of the *Bamm*. Figures 11.88(a), 11.88(b), and 11.88(c) illustrate corresponding patterns of possible and impossible systems on Ibn Sīnā's *ʿūd*. One may use similar ratio calculations to demonstrate the playability of Modern Arabian *Rāst* from A♭ of the *Mathlath*. Again, these observations also apply to Ṣafī Al-Dīn's *Second ʿŪd*.

11.81

The transformation of ancient Rast in the conjunct system — via Kardaniya — to modern Rast in the disjunct system introduced two appealing musical modifications: (1) the prominent consonance throughout the mode changed from four consecutive "fourths" to four consecutive "fifths," and (2) the *leading tone* of the "octave" ascended from B♭ [996.1 ¢] to B𝄳 [1050.0 ¢]. However, to achieve this transformation, music theorists like Al-Khulaʿī encountered two significant problems. (1) Because all ancient 17-tone *ʿūds* equipped with five strings do not include these three intervals (in half-flat notation): C–B𝄳, F–E𝄳ˡ, B♭–A𝄳ˡ, one cannot play a "neutral seventh" *above* an open string on these instruments. The reason why the last two intervals are missing is that the lower "octave" C–Cˡ, and the upper "octave" Cˡ–Cˡˡ, are *not* identical. Although all such instruments produce E𝄬 or E𝄳, and A𝄬 or A𝄳, in the lower "octave," they do not provide "octave" equivalents E𝄬ˡ or E𝄳ˡ, and A𝄬ˡ or A𝄳ˡ, in the upper "octave." Since one cannot play Modern Arabian *Rāst* without a "neutral seventh," modern theorists faced a dilemma. Either leave the ancient instruments as they are, which renders Modern Arabian *Rāst* unplayable from an open string, or interject the "neutral seventh," which permanently changes the musical traditions. (2) The decision to take the latter course led to the problem of "incorporation." The theorists did not consider the possibility of simply adding one new fret directly below the nut to produce the missing tones: B𝄬, E𝄬ˡ, A𝄬ˡ, or B𝄳, E𝄳ˡ, A𝄳ˡ. Instead, they insisted on a mathematical formula to justify these inclusions. In my opinion, the desire to "incorporate" the "neutral seventh" into a historically unprecedented 24-tone scale constitutes the primary reason for the imposition of 24-tone equal temperament on Arabian music.

A second reason for 24-TET stemmed from the need to "explain" the existence of seven *neutral tones* — D𝄳, E𝄳, G𝄳, A𝄳, C𝄳, F𝄳ˡ, A𝄲ˡ — found on Al-Fārābī's 22-tone *ʿūd*,[175] Ibn Sīnā's 17-tone *ʿūd*,[176] and Ṣafī Al-Dīn's *Second ʿŪd*.[177] In *La Musique Arabe, Volume 5*, D'Erlanger describes his rationalization of 24-TET in the following manner. He begins by stating that "The diatonic, Pythagorean scale . . .", which consists exclusively of 3-limit ratios, is ". . . the only natural scale, the only one . . . given by Nature."[178] Based on this premise, he then describes the neutral tones as ". . . irrational intervals . . ."[179] and ". . . artificial sounds . . ."[180] because he is unable to derive them from Pythagorean 3-limit ratios, or from the "octave," ratio 2/1, the "fifth, ratio 3/2, and the fourth, ratio 4/3.[181] D'Erlanger resorts to calling the neutral tones ". . . empirical degrees . . ."[182] because, according to him, musicians determined them by ". . . traditional processes of empirical lute string division[s] . . ."[183] Here he gives the impression that since the time of the famous lutenist Manṣūr Zalzal (d. 791), Persian and Arabian musicians relegated the tuning of the neutral tones to arbitrary experience. His term "empirical degrees" connotes that musicians did not intentionally tune the neutral tones to exact string length ratios. Furthermore, in his text he omits the fact that during the Arabian Renaissance, artists and scientists had full knowledge of Greek music theory. As discussed in numerous previous sections, since the time of Al-Kindī (d. *c.* 874), the frets of *all* ancient *ʿūds* enabled musicians to play the Pythagorean diatonic scale: 1/1, 9/8, 81/64, 4/3, 3/2, 27/16, 16/9, 2/1.[184] (See Figure 11.50.) We conclude, therefore, that Persian and Arabian musicians tuned the neutral tones not because they were ignorant of Greek scale theory, but because they experienced these tones as vital musical expressions of their respective civilizations.

D'Erlanger ends his discussion by asking the rhetorical question

> What formula of division is needed to include these empirical intervals in a regular structure?[185]

Predictably, he and other like-minded intellectuals resolved the problematic "incorporation" of the so-called *empirical intervals* by advocating 24-tone equal temperament. In *La Musique Arabe, Volume 5*, p. 20, D'Erlanger shows a 24-tone equal tempered scale in Western musical notation,

Table 11.52

TWO "OCTAVES" OF THE MODERN ARABIAN 24-TONE EQUAL TEMPERED SCALE

1.	**GG**-3	0 ¢			*YAKĀH*	
2.	GG𝄲	50 ¢				*qarār nīm Ḥiṣār*
3.	**AA♭/GG♯**	100 ¢			*qarār Ḥiṣār*	
4.	AA𝄳	150 ¢				*qarār tīk Ḥiṣār*
5.	**AA**	200 ¢			*ʿUSHAYRĀN*	
6.	AA𝄲	250 ¢				*nīm ʿAjam ʿUshayrān*
7.	**BB♭/AA♯**	300 ¢			*ʿAjam ʿUshayrān*	
8.	**BB𝄳**	350 ¢			*ʿIRĀQ*	
9.	**BB**	400 ¢			*Kawasht*	
10.	BB𝄲/CC𝄳	450 ¢				*tīk Kawasht*
11.	**C**-4	500 ¢	**C**	0 ¢	*RĀST*	
12.	C𝄲	550 ¢				*nīm Zirkūlāh*
13.	**C♯/D♭**	600 ¢	**D♭**	100 ¢	*Zirkūlāh*	
14.	D𝄳	650 ¢				*tīk Zirkūlāh*
15.	**D**	700 ¢	**D**	200 ¢	*DŪKĀH*	
16.	D𝄲	750 ¢				*nīm Kurd*
17.	**E♭/D♯**	800 ¢	**E♭**	300 ¢	*Kurd*	
18.	**E𝄳**	850 ¢	**E𝄳**	350 ¢	*SĪKĀH*	
19.	**E**	900 ¢	**E**	400 ¢	*Būsalik*	
20.	E𝄲/F𝄳	950 ¢				*tīk Būsalik*
21.	**F**	1000 ¢	**F**	500 ¢	*JAHĀRKĀH*	
22.	**F𝄲**	1050 ¢	**F𝄲**	550 ¢		*nīm Ḥijāz*
23.	**F♯/G♭**	1100 ¢	**F♯**	600 ¢	*Ḥijāz*	
24.	G𝄳	1150 ¢				*tīk Ḥijāz*
25.	**G**-4	1200 ¢	**G**	700 ¢	*NAWĀ*	
26.	G𝄲	50 ¢				*nīm Ḥiṣār*
27.	**A♭/G♯**	100 ¢	**A♭**	800 ¢	*Ḥiṣār*	
28.	**A𝄳**	150 ¢	**A𝄳**	850 ¢		*tīk Ḥiṣār*
29.	**A**	200 ¢	**A**	900 ¢	*ḤUSAYNĪ*	
30.	A𝄲	250 ¢				*nīm ʿAjam*
31.	**B♭/A♯**	300 ¢	**B♭**	1000 ¢	*ʿAjam*	
32.	**B𝄳**	350 ¢	**B𝄳**	1050 ¢	*AWJ*	
33.	**B**	400 ¢	**B**	1100 ¢	*Māhūr (or Nihuft)*	
34.	B𝄲/C𝄳	450 ¢				*tīk Māhūr*
35.	**c**-5	500 ¢	**C**ᴵ	1200 ¢	*KIRDĀN*	
36.	c𝄲	550 ¢				*nīm Shahnāz*
37.	**c♯/d♭**	600 ¢			*Shahnāz*	
38.	d𝄳	650 ¢				*tīk Shahnāz*
39.	**d**	700 ¢			*MUḤAYYAR*	
40.	d𝄲	750 ¢				*nīm Sinbulah*
41.	**e♭/d♯**	800 ¢			*Sinbulah*	
42.	**e𝄳**	850 ¢			*BUZRAK (or BUZURK)*	
43.	**e**	900 ¢			*jawāb Būsalik (or Ḥusaynī Shadd)*	
44.	e𝄲/f𝄳	950 ¢				*jawāb tīk Būsalik*
45.	**f**	1000 ¢			*MĀHŪRĀN*	
46.	f𝄲	1050 ¢				*jawāb nīm Ḥijāz*
47.	**f♯/g♭**	1100 ¢			*jawāb Ḥijāz*	
48.	g𝄳	1150 ¢				*jawāb tīk Ḥijāz*
49.	**g**-5	1200 ¢			*JAWĀB NAWĀ* *(or RAMAL TŪTĪ)*	
	(1)	(2)	(3)	(4)	(5)	(6)

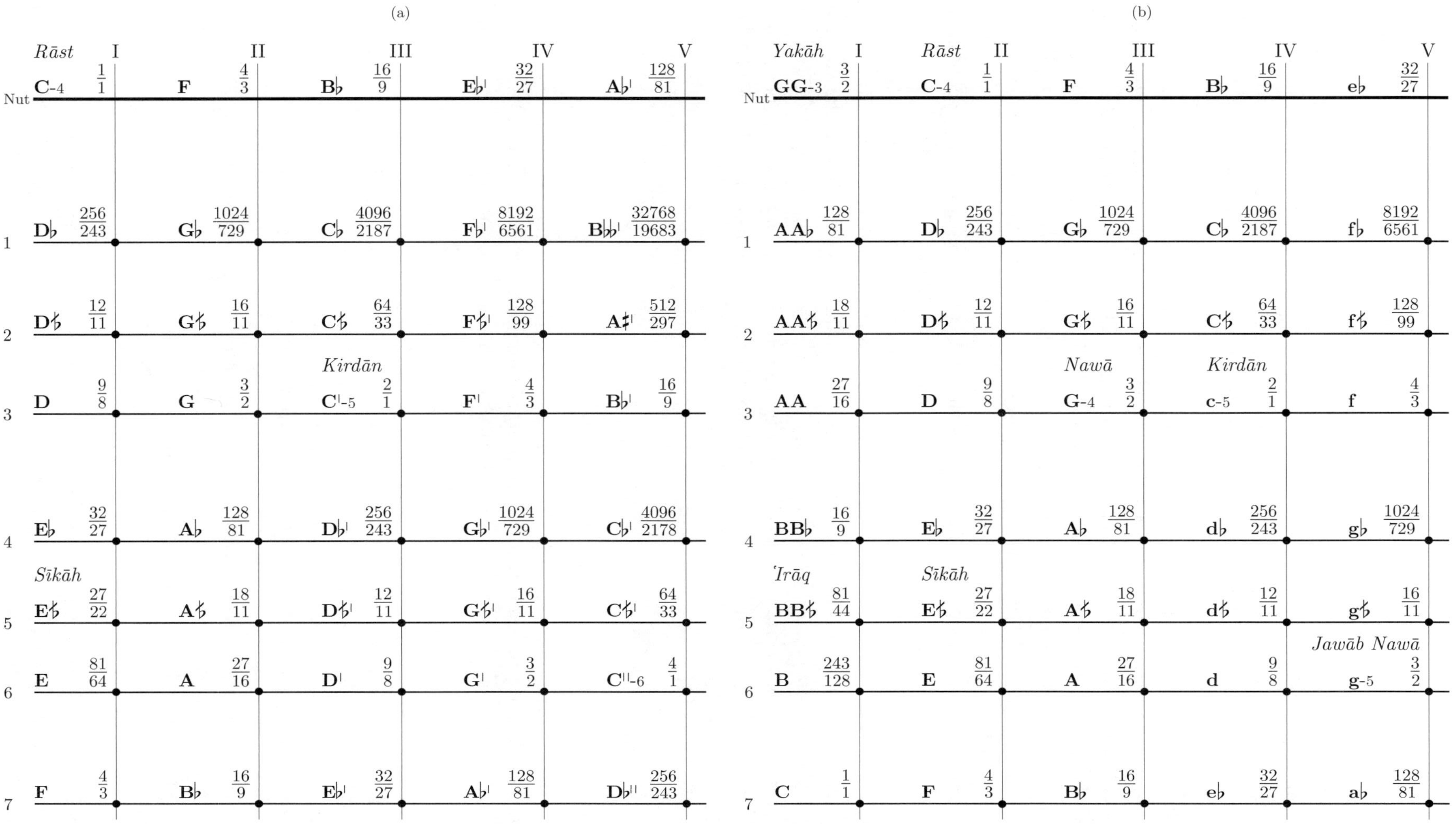

Figure 11.89 Al-Fārābī's 17-tone ʿūd tuning as shown in Figures 11.85(a) and 11.86(a), and an interpretation of the modern Arabian "double-octave" scale as shown in Table 11.52. (a) Open String I of the standard tuning sounds C_4 (modern *Rāst*), and Fret 5, E𝄳$_4$ (modern *Sīkāh*). (b) In this transposed tuning, open String II sounds the tonic *Rāst*, and String I, the "fifth" below *Rāst*, or GG_3 (modern *Yakāh*). Consequently, Fret 5 produces BB𝄳$_3$ (modern *ʿIrāq*). However, because the "octave," or B𝄳$_4$ (modern *Awj*), does not occur above *Rāst*, it is not possible to play the modern Arabian mode called *Rāst* from the tonic, C_4, on this ancient instrument.

complete with half-sharp signs [‡], and half-flat signs [♭̸]. Patterned after the Greater Perfect System of the Greeks, this "double-octave" scale spans the interval between G_3 (196.0 cps) and G_5 (784.0 cps), which means that it includes a total number of 49 tones. Table 11.52, Column 1, gives the Western note names, Columns 5 and 6, the Arabic note names, and Column 2, the cent values of this scale. Finally, Columns 3 and 4 indicate that for contemporary musicians, the central "octave" between *Rāst* [C_4] and *Kirdān* [C_5] constitutes the regular or standard scale of modern Arabian music.

In his characterization of the *empirical intervals*, D'Erlanger fails to distinguish between the *presence* of E♭̸ in the lower "octave" between C–C^{I}, and the *absence* of B♭̸ in the upper "octave" between C^{I}–C^{II} of the ancient *'ūds*. He confounds this critical distinction by discussing the "neutral third" — *Sīkāh* [E♭̸] — and the "neutral seventh" — *Awj* [B♭̸] — in the same sentence, thereby giving the impression that both tones belong to the ancient Perso-Arabian musical traditions.[186] To understand this obfuscation in greater detail, turn to Figure 11.89. In Figure 11.89(a), Strings I–IV are tuned to the same scale as in Figures 11.85(a) and 11.86(a). I derived this tuning from Al-Fārābī's 22-tone scale, which is based on his *Jins* 2 tetrachord. (See Section 11.80.) In Figure 11.89(a), I also included String V to demonstrate beyond any doubt that *Awj* [B♭̸] does not occur in the upper "octave" of this instrument.

Figure 11.89(b) shows my interpretation of the modern "double-octave" scale in the context of this ancient instrument. Note carefully that the tunings in Figures 11.89(a) and 11.89(b) are identical. The only difference is that I transposed *Rāst*, or C_4, from *String I* in Figure 11.89(a) to *String II* in Figure 11.89(b). Consequently, I do not hear String I in Figure 11.89(b) as the tonic *Rāst* [C_4] of the scale, but as the "fifth" of the scale below *Rāst*, or *Yakāh* [GG_3]. Although the "neutral seventh" — *'Irāq* [BB♭̸] — now occurs *below Rāst*, the "octave" of the "neutral seventh" — *Awj* [B♭̸] — does not occur *above Rāst*. In other words, on this ancient 17-tone *'ūd*, it is not possible to play the modern Arabian mode called *Rāst* from the tonic, C_4. This also applies to Ibn Sīnā's *'ūd*, and to Ṣafī Al-Dīn's *Second 'Ūd*.

In summary, consider D'Erlanger's description of Modern Arabian *Rāst:*

RĀST

$\frac{4}{4}, \frac{3}{4}, \frac{3}{4} + (\frac{4}{4})$

> [1] ***This genus plays a role in Arabian music identical to that of the Pythagorean diatonic in ancient Greek music.*** Indeed, the standard octave of the Greek theorists, that of the Dorian harmony, is composed of two diatonic tetrachords separated by the disjunctive tone, whereas Arabian musicians currently attribute an equally important role to the octave comprised of two disjunct fourths [500 ¢ each] divided according to the *Rāst* genus: i.e., one whole tone [200 ¢], and two intervals of a $\frac{3}{4}$ tone [150 ¢] each; [that is, 200 ¢ + (150 ¢ × 2) = 500 ¢].
>
> The name *Rāst* attributed to this genus, both currently and in the time of Ṣafī Al-Dīn, [2] ***was applied to the disjunct octave which results from it,*** as well as to the degree of the general scale on which this standard octave usually begins. The constant usage of this term (which means regular in Persian) by several generations of musicians . . . proves that [3] ***this scale has always been considered by the Arabs and the Persians to be the most regular, the most natural, melodic progression.***[187] (Bold italics, and numbers and text in brackets mine.)

This statement contains three misleading opinions. In Opinion 1, D'Erlanger compares Modern Arabian *Rāst* to an ancient Greek "Pythagorean diatonic"; presumably the latter is the diatonic scale in the Dorian Mode by Philolaus (fl. *c.* 420 B.C.). (See Section 10.10 and Figure 10.9.) As discussed in Sections 3.19, 10.11, and 10.20, we may trace the illustrious history of this scale in the *Timaeus* by Plato (427–347 B.C.), the *Division of the Canon* by Euclid (fl. *c.* 300 B.C.), and the *Harmonics* by Ptolemy (*c.* A.D. 100 – *c.* 165). In Europe, variations of this scale lasted well into the 15th century. Whether or not Modern Arabian *Rāst* will play a role identical to Philolaus' Diatonic Scale is not subject to anyone's whim. Only time will tell. In Opinion 2, D'Erlanger attributes Modern Arabian *Rāst* to Ṣafī Al-Dīn. As discussed in Section 11.78, in the works of Ṣafī Al-Dīn, the closest musical mode to Modern Arabian *Rāst* is *Kardāniya.* Finally, in Opinion 3, D'Erlanger attributes Modern Arabian *Rāst* to the Persians. The works of Ibn Sīnā and the research of H. Farhat do not support this claim. (See Section 11.66.)

11.82

In a work entitled *A Treatise on Arab Music*, Mīkhā'īl Mashāqah (1800–1888) was the first proponent of 24-tone equal temperament.[188] Mashāqah, who wrote his treatise *c.* 1840, did not formally extract the 24th root of 2, and thus did not base his string length calculations on the *common ratio*[189] of 24-TET:

$$\sqrt[24]{2} \approx 1.02930$$

However, his verbal descriptions of the 24-tone scale, and his instructions for dividing the strings of a *ṭunbūr*, indicate that he intended an equal tempered scale. According to Marcus:

> Significantly, Mashāqah is perhaps the first of the Arabic writers to discuss the scale using the term "quarter" tone (*rub'*, literally, "quarter"; pl. *arbā'*).[190]

Mashāqah gives the following description of the two characteristic intervals of 24-TET:

> . . . sound is divided from its tonic to its octave into twenty-four quarters and . . . these quarters are located within seven main notes, and . . . some of these, within them, have four quarters (*arbā'*) and some three quarters, as has been mentioned at the beginning of this treatise.[191] (Text in parentheses in Marcus' dissertation.)

Now, since a ¼-tone has the value of

$$\log_{10} 1.02930 \times 3986.314 = 50.00 \text{ ¢}$$

the interval of a "whole tone," or of a 4⁄4-tone, equals 4 × 50.00 ¢ = 200.00 ¢, and a ¾-tone equals 3 × 50.00 ¢ = 150.00 ¢. This explains the fractional interval notation in Figure 11.84(c).

Modern theorists classify the notes of the 24-tone equal tempered scale in Table 11.52 into three hierarchical categories. (1) With respect to the standard "octave" between *Rāst* and *Kirdān*, Column 5 lists seven fundamental notes [*naghamāt* (notes), *asāsiyyah* (fundamental)]:[192] *Rāst, Dūkāh, Sīkāh, Jahārkāh, Nawā, Ḥusaynī*, and *Awj;* (2) and seven *'arabāt* (sing. *'arabah;* lit. *half note*):[193] *Zirkūlāh, Kurd, Būsalik, Ḥijāz, Ḥiṣār, 'Ajam*, and *Māhūr.* Observe carefully, only *Zirkūlāh, Ḥijāz*, and *Ḥiṣār* function as true half notes, or "semitones." *Zirkūlāh* is located exactly halfway between *Rāst* and *Dūkāh; Ḥijāz* between *Jahārkāh* and *Nawā;* and *Ḥiṣār* between *Nawā* and *Ḥusaynī.* Column 5 also gives four alternate note names in parentheses: *Nihuft, Buzurk, Ḥusaynī Shadd*, and *Ramal Tūtī* that frequently appear in other texts. (3) Finally, within the standard "octave," Column 6 lists five *tīk* (Persian, lit. *raised*) and five *nīm* (Persian, lit. *lowered*) notes. Throughout this column, the term *qarār* (lit. *resting place*) refers to the lower "octave" of *Ḥiṣār*, and the *jawāb* (lit. *answer*) to the upper "octaves" of *Būsalik* and *Ḥijāz.*[194]

Before we continue, let us first discuss two practical aspects of this scale. (1) Most modern writers and theorists agree that Arabian musicians do *not* use all 24 tones.[195] For example, Lois I. Al-Faruqi states, ". . . only fourteen of the twenty-four tones are included in the important *maqāmāt*."[196] She dispenses with five *nīm* and five *tīk* notes in the "octave" between GG_3 and G_4. Similarly, Habib H. Touma acknowledges, ". . . [20] pitches . . . are differentiated as . . . less important (seldom occurring)."[197] (Number in brackets mine.) He dispenses with ten *nīm* and ten *tīk* notes in the "double-octave" between GG_3 and G_5. And Marcus declares, ". . . four notes . . . can be said to be used rarely or not at all in the present day."[198] He dispenses with D𝄳, G𝄳, G𝄲, and B𝄲. However, in his list of 64 *basic maqāmāt*, which does not include ornamental tones and tones of modulation, Marcus only cites the sixteen notes listed in Table 11.52, Column 3. Within the central "octave" between C_4 and C_5, he utilizes the standard fourteen notes in Column 5, plus *nīm Ḥijāz* [F𝄲] and *tīk Ḥiṣār* [A𝄳] in Column 6. (See Section 11.84, Figure 11.91.)

(2) Although the upper four strings of the five-course *'ūd* are still tuned in "fourths"[199] — G_2, A_2, D_3, G_3, C_4 — the modern *'ūd* is a fretless instrument. As such, 24-tone equal temperament is a moot issue; in a musical context, no one is able to accurately play such a scale without frets. Furthermore, contemporary Arabian theorists and musicians do not think in equal tempered steps. In the passage below, Marcus gives his analysis of the situation, and ends with a quotation from an article by the contemporary scholar, composer, and musician Ali Jihad Racy.

> Although a number of theorists have sought to prove that the quarter-tone scale is an equal-tempered system or a modified Pythagorean system, the nature of Arab musical instruments has imbued the new scale with an aspect of ambiguity in this regard. Arab theory books stress that Arab and Western instruments differ because the latter confine the musician to a specific tuning system. (These Western instruments are called *alāt thābitah*, literally "bound" or "tied instruments.") Arab instruments, on the other hand, such as the fretless *'ūd*, leave the musician free to play the Western scale of half-steps or the Arab scale of quarter-steps. They also allow the musician to tune his notes as he wishes. This has allowed the focus of the new scale to be, not on cycles per second or frequency ratios or cents (all ways of specifying exact intonation), but rather on the approximate placement of the notes within the octave. Thus we find that most modern theorists introduce the quarter-tone system in their works but ***do not mention the concept of equal temperament.*** When presenting the quarter-tone scale, most theorists are not refuting the existence of the Pythagorean third of $^{81}/_{64}$ or the just third of $^{5}/_{4}$ in Arab music, in part, because most Arab instruments do not confine performers to any one tuning system. Musicians are free to respond to a variety of acoustical issues and artistic urges . . . Racy expresses this perception of the quarter-tone scale when he comments that the symbol for half-flat (𝄳) "lowers a note by *approximately* a quarter-tone while the symbol 𝄲 [for half-sharp] raises a note by *roughly* a quarter-tone."[200] (Bold italics mine. Italics, text in parentheses, and text in brackets in Marcus' dissertation.)

Unfortunately, Marcus justifies the theoretical admissibility of 24-tone equal temperament on the same grounds as D'Erlanger. Both writers confound the origins of half-flats *Sīkāh* [E𝄳] and *Awj* [B𝄳]. Like D'Erlanger before him, Marcus gives the impression that *Sīkāh* needs "incorporation."

> There is significant evidence that Pythagorean intonation plays an important role in Arab music performance. However, this system is not able to account for half-flats and half-sharps (especially the notes *'Irāq* [BB𝄳],

> *Sīkāh* [E$\flat$], and *Awj* [B$\flat$]). The new quarter-tone scale, thus, fulfills a need in that it fully incorporates these notes into a single coherent theoretical system.[201] (Note names in brackets mine.)

We conclude, therefore, that similar to Persian and Turkish music, Arabian music has successfully resisted Western attempts at logarithmic codification. In the Perso-Arabian context, *Sīkāh* predates the quantification of ≈ 350.0 ¢ by more than a thousand years. It remains a mystery why some writers prefer a faceless numeric derivation over testimonies in works of genius.

Finally, contrary to the impression given by most modern writers and theorists, Modern Arabian *Rāst* is not the *regular* or *standard* mode in all Arabic-speaking lands. In his dissertation, Racy reports

> Also according to A.Z. Idelsohn, in the early twentieth century *Bayyāti* was "the most popular Arabic mode." In Egypt today *Bayyāti* and *Ṣabā* are undoubtedly among the most frequently used *maqāmāt*.[202]

See Section 11.83, Tables 11.54(a)–11.54(d), for a list of 45 modern Arabian *maqāmāt*.

11.83

An exact number of modern Arabian *maqāmāt* does not exist. Descriptions typically vary from 119 *maqāmāt* in *La Musique Arabe, Volume 5*, to 12 *maqāmāt* in introductory texts. Most *maqāmāt* are given as "octave" scales that consist of a primary lower tetrachord called *jins al-jidhʿ* (*jidhʿ*, lit. *stem* or *trunk*), or *jins al-aṣl* (*aṣl*, lit. *principle*), and a secondary upper tetrachord called *jins al-farʿ* (*farʿ*, lit. *branch*).[203] Contemporary theorists classify *maqāmāt* that have identical or very similar lower tetrachords into groups called *faṣāʾil* (sing. *faṣīlah;* lit. *family*, or *genus*).[204] For example, the *jins al-aṣl* of *maqām Shawq Afzā* identifies this mode as a member of the *ʿAjam faṣīlah.* [See Table 11.54(a).] In the next two excerpts, Ṣalāh al-Dīn describes this process of classification in his work entitled *Miftāh al-Alḥān al-ʿArabiyyah*, first published in 1946.

> *Maqāmāt* are from one and the same *faṣīlah* if they are identical in the root or trunk tetrachord [*jins al-rukūz* (*al-jidhʿ*)] even if [they differ in their] branch tetrachord [*jins al-farʿ*].[205] (All text in brackets in Marcus' dissertation.)

> In order to know the *faṣīlah* of a *maqām* which one is asked to analyze, one needs to know the name of its trunk [lower] tetrachord [*jins al-jidhʿ*]. [This knowledge is obtained] by examining this tetrachord (which begins from its first degree until its fourth) and if its intervals correspond to the intervals of one of the principal tetrachords . . . then you know the name of the trunk tetrachord and you know its *faṣīlah* — if the intervals of the trunk tetrachord correspond to the intervals of the *Huzām* tetrachord, for example, then the *maqām* is from the *Huzām faṣīlah* and if they correspond to the *Bayyāti* tetrachord then the *maqām* is from the *Bayyāti faṣīlah* and so on.[206] (Ellipses, and all text in brackets and parentheses in Marcus' dissertation.)

Marcus observes

> In the modern-day theory, modes which share a common lower tetrachord, but differ in the makeup of their upper tetrachord, are said to be from the same *faṣīlah* . . .[207]

To classify the *maqāmāt*, modern theorists usually employ either nine or eleven *faṣā'il*. Table 11.53 lists nine *faṣā'il* used throughout this text. Marcus uses these nine *faṣā'il* to classify 64 *maqāmāt*.[208]

Table 11.53

QUARTER-TONE INTERVAL PATTERNS OF NINE *FAṢĀ'IL* IN MODERN ARABIAN MUSIC THEORY

1. *'Ajam*	4, 4, 2	= 500 ¢	Tetrachord: "Fourth"
2. *Nahāwand*	4, 2, 4	= 500 ¢	Tetrachord: "Fourth"
3. *Kurd*	2, 4, 4	= 500 ¢	Tetrachord: "Fourth"
4. *Rāst*	4, 3, 3	= 500 ¢	Tetrachord: "Fourth"
5. *Bayyāti*	3, 3, 4	= 500 ¢	Tetrachord: "Fourth"
6. *Sīkāh*	3, 4	= 350 ¢	Trichord: "Neutral Third"
7. *Ṣabā*	3, 3, 2	= 400 ¢	Tetrachord: "Major Third"
8. *Nawā Athar*	4, 2, 6, 2	= 700 ¢	Pentachord: "Fifth"
9. *Ḥijāz*	2, 6, 2	= 500 ¢	Tetrachord: "Fourth"

In Table 11.53, we see that *Faṣā'il* 1–3 consist of 4/4-tone [200 ¢] and 2/4-tone [100 ¢] intervals; *Faṣā'il* 4–6, of 4/4-tone and 3/4-tone [150 ¢] intervals; *Faṣīlah* 7, of 3/4-tone and 2/4-tone intervals; and *Faṣā'il* 8–9, of 4/4-tone, 2/4-tone, and 6/4-tone [300 ¢] intervals. Also, we see that *Faṣīlah* 6 is a trichord that spans the interval of a "neutral third"; *Faṣīlah* 7 is a *tetrachord* that only spans a "major third"; and *Faṣīlah* 8 is a pentachord that spans a "fifth."

Tables 11.54(a)–11.54(d) classify 45 *maqāmāt*, most of which appear in contemporary sources,[209] according to these nine *faṣā'il*. In Table 11.54(c), notice that contrary to Ṣalāh al-Dīn's description, *jins Huzām* is not a tetrachord, but a trichord. Marcus explains the reason for this discrepancy in the following manner:

> When *Sīkāh* is conceived as a trichord [3 4], then the "standard" number of tetrachords [*faṣā'il*] is given as ***nine***. When *Sīkāh* is presented as a tetrachord (3 4 4), then *Huzām* (3 4 2) and *'Irāq* (3 4 3) emerge as ***separate entities***, resulting in the "standard" number of tetrachords increasing to ***eleven***.[210] (Bold italics, and quarter-tones and text in brackets mine. Quarter-tones in parentheses in Marcus' dissertation.)

The left columns of these four tables organize 45 *maqāmāt* into 9 *faṣā'il*. In these tables, seven double-headed arrows connect seven pairs of *maqāmāt* that differ only in the identity of the tonic, and one quadruple-headed arrow in Table 11.54(d) connects four *maqāmāt* that differ only in the identity of the tonic. So, of the 45 *maqāmāt* listed in these tables, only 45 − 7 − 3 = 35 *maqāmāt* have uniquely different interval patterns. The principal reason for including the ten extra modes is tradition. When Arabian musicians and theorists distinguish between modes, they consider not only interval patterns, but register as well. For example, Table 11.54(a) shows that when *Nahāwand* begins on G_3 instead of C_4 it is called *Sulṭanī Yakāh*. The difficulty of classifying *maqāmāt* is further complicated by the fact that many modern modes are not given distinctly different names when they are transposed to new tonic pitches. For instance, *maqām Rāst*, based on C, is simply called *Rāst Nawā* when transposed to G.[211] (See Table 11.52.) Marcus describes this situation by noting

Table 11.54(a)

45 Modern Arabian *Maqāmāt*		Ṣafī Al-Dīn's *Second ʿŪd Tuning*
ʿAjam Faṣīlah		
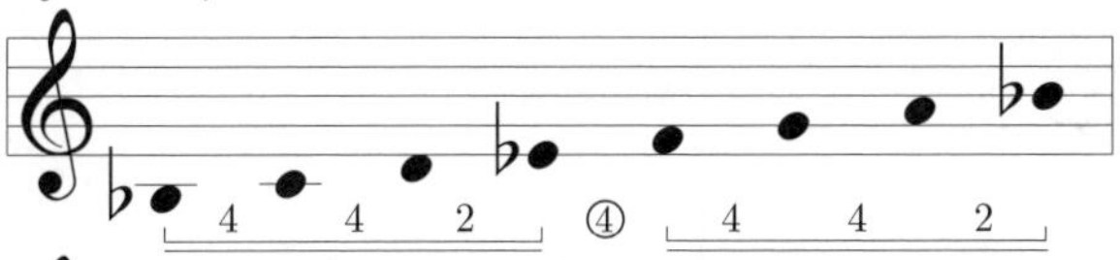	*ʿAjam ʿUshayrān*	Tetrachord I
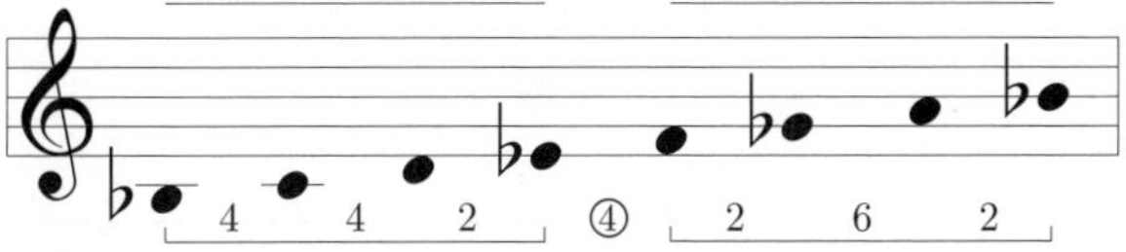	*Shawq Afzā*	Tetrachord I
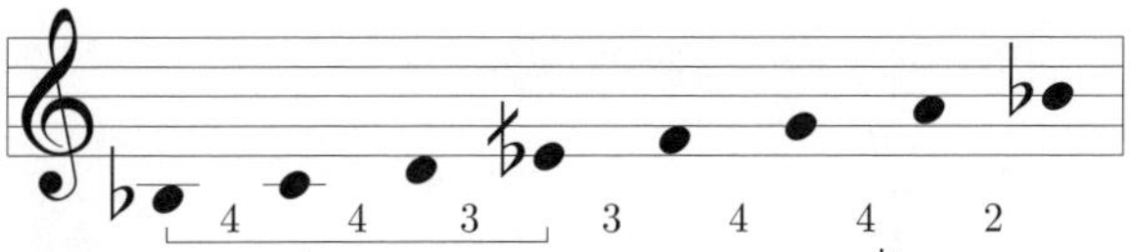	*ʿAjam Murassa*	
	*Jahārkāh*	Tetrachord I
Nahāwand Faṣīlah		
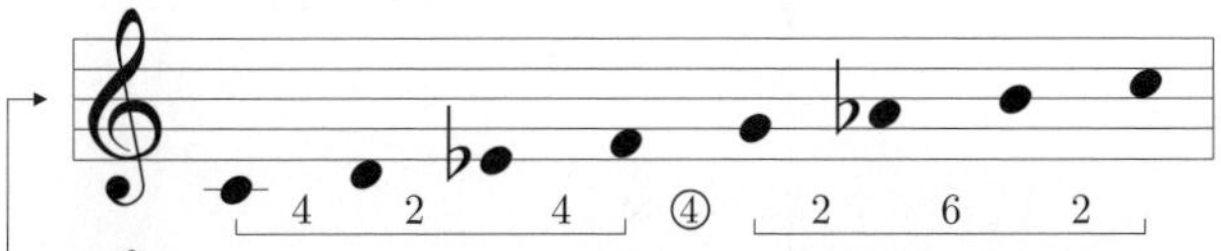	*Nahāwand*	Tetrachord II
	*Nahāwand Muraṣṣa*	Tetrachord II
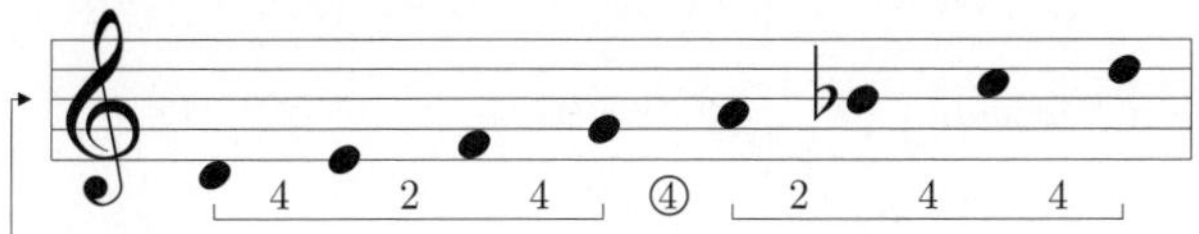	*Būsalik*	Mode #14 (*Nawā*)
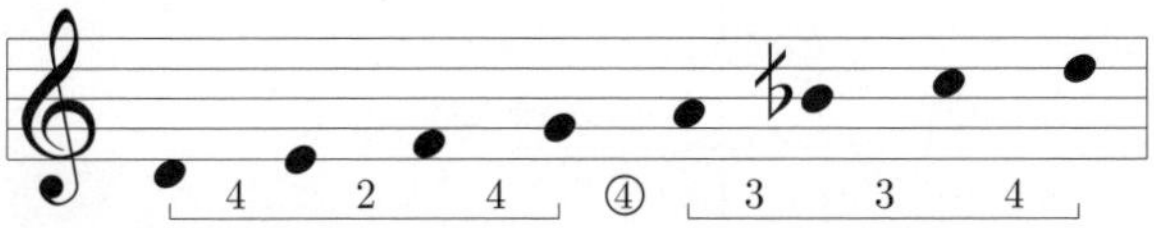	*ʿUshāq Masrī*	Mode #16
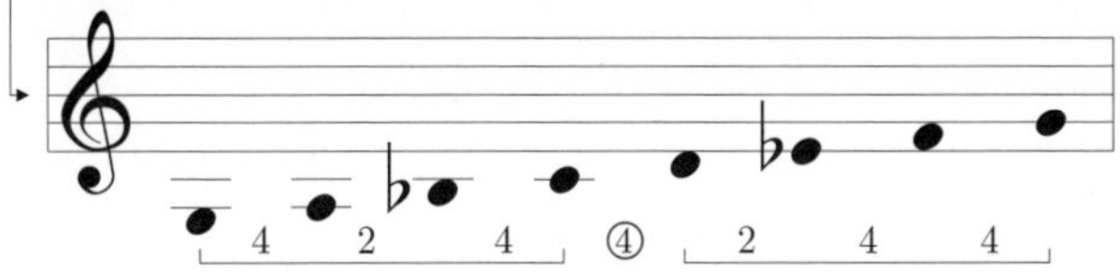	*Faraḥfazā*	Mode #14 (*Nawā*)
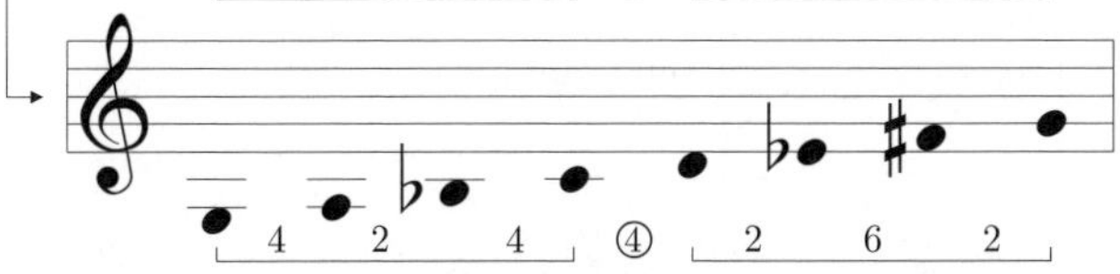	*Sulṭānī Yakāh*	Tetrachord II

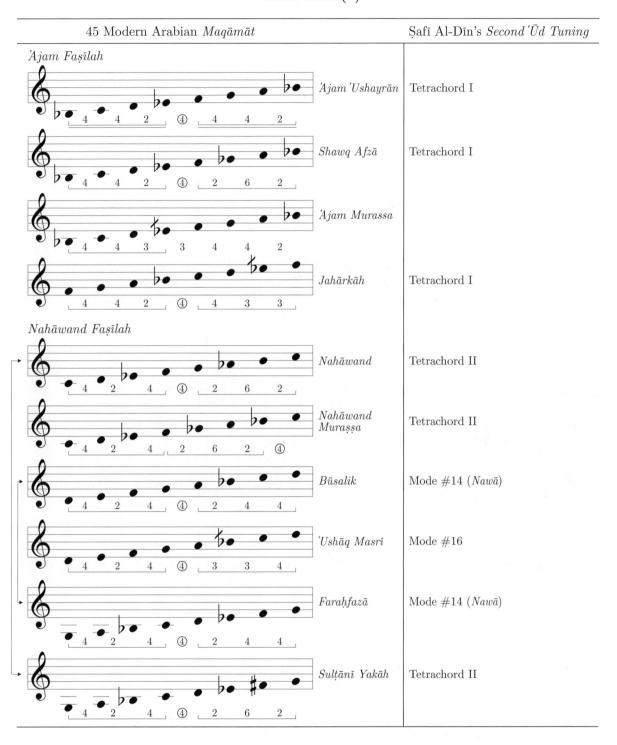

Table 11.54(b)

45 Modern Arabian *Maqāmāt*		Ṣafī Al-Dīn's *Second ʿŪd Tuning*
Kurd Faṣīlah		
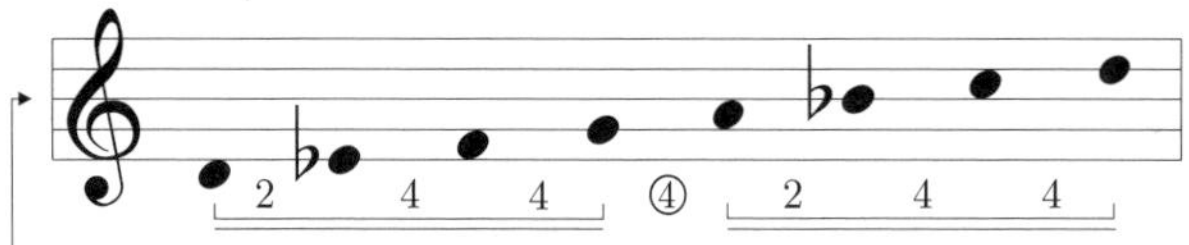	*Kurd*	Mode #26
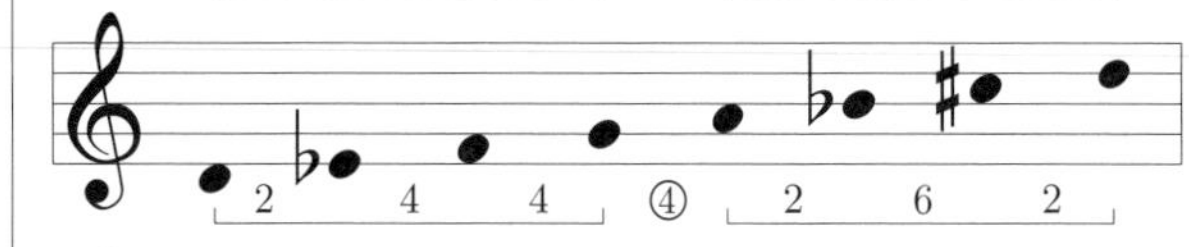	*Shahnāz Kurdī*	Tetrachord III
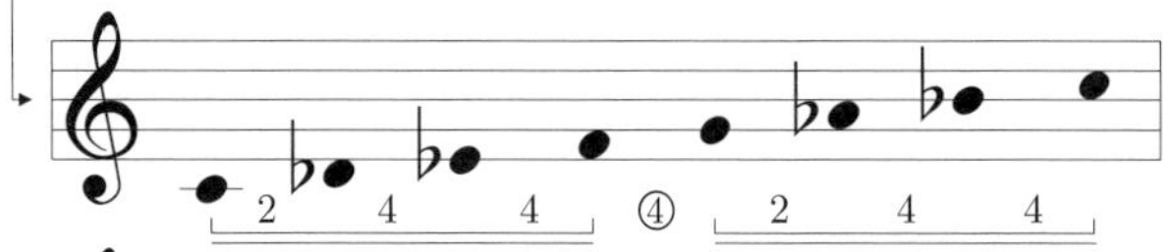	*Ḥijāz Kār Kurd*	Mode #26
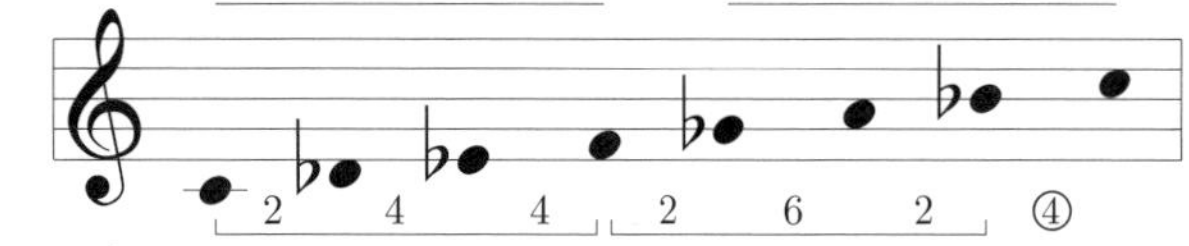	*Ṭarz Nuwīn*	Tetrachord III
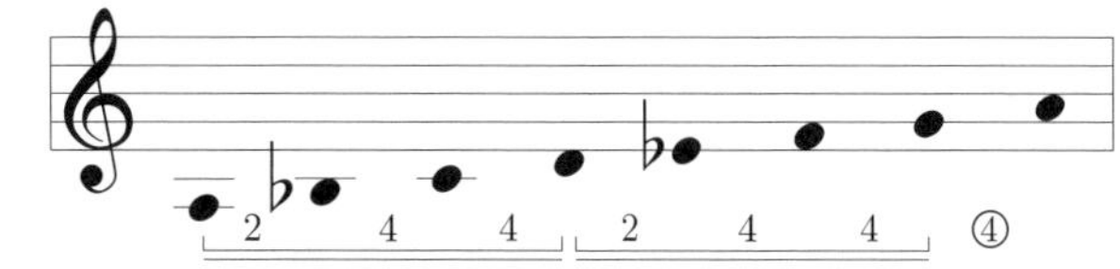	*Shawq Ṭarab*	Mode #27 (*Abū Salīk*)
Rāst Faṣīlah		
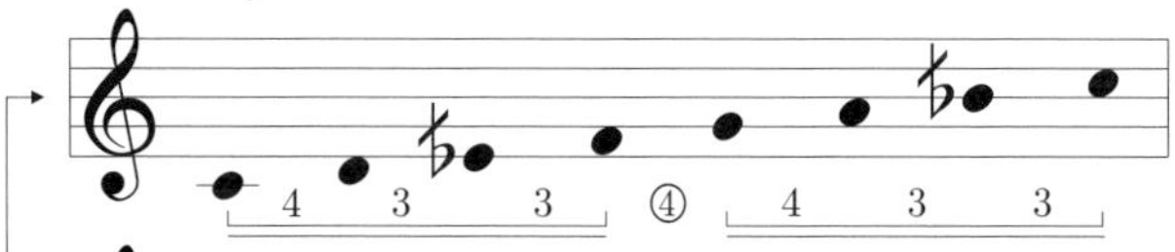	*Rāst*	Tetrachord IV
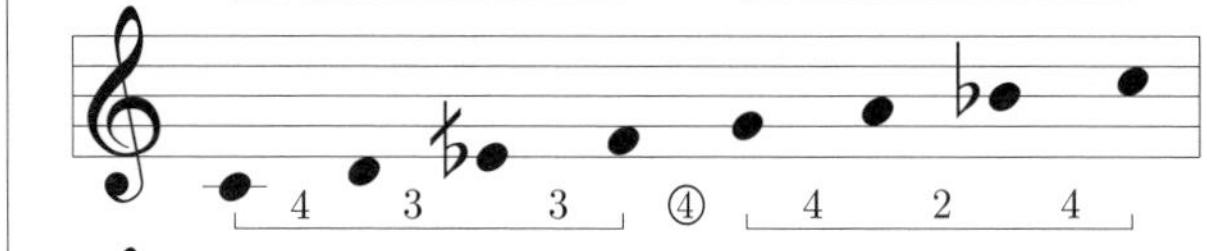	*Sūzdulār*	Mode #37
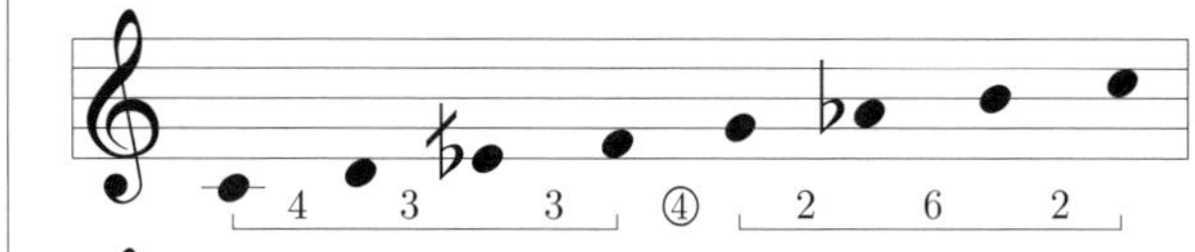	*Sūznāk*	Tetrachord IV
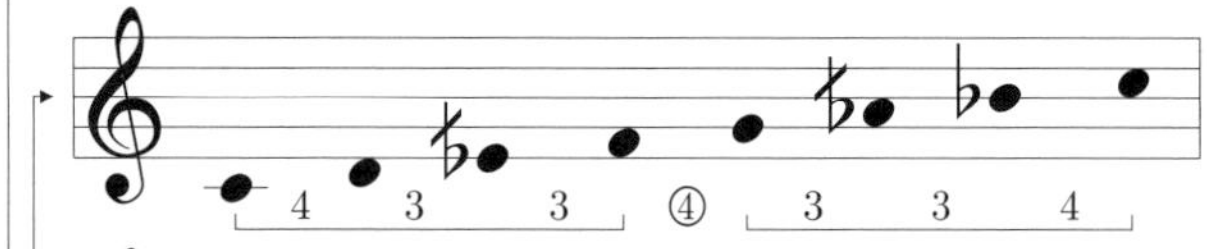	*Nīrz*	Mode #40 (*Rāst*)
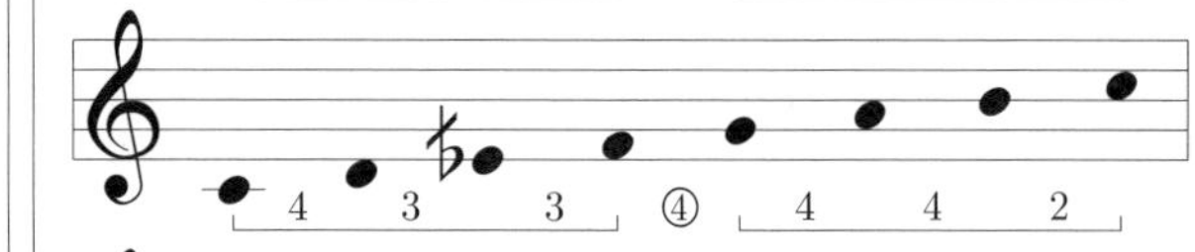	*Māhūr*	Tetrachord IV
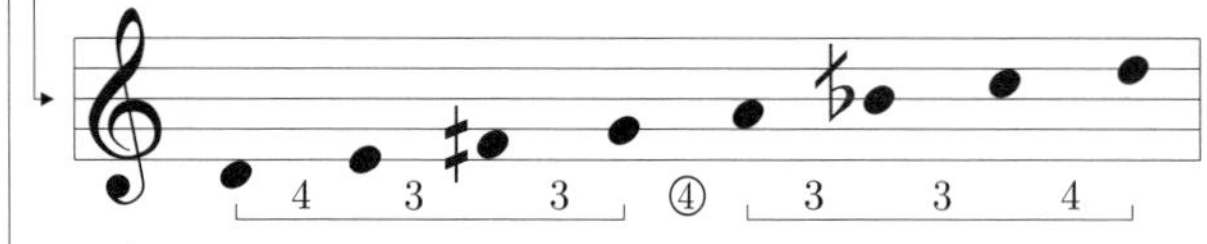	*Nishābūrk*	Mode #40 (*Rāst*)
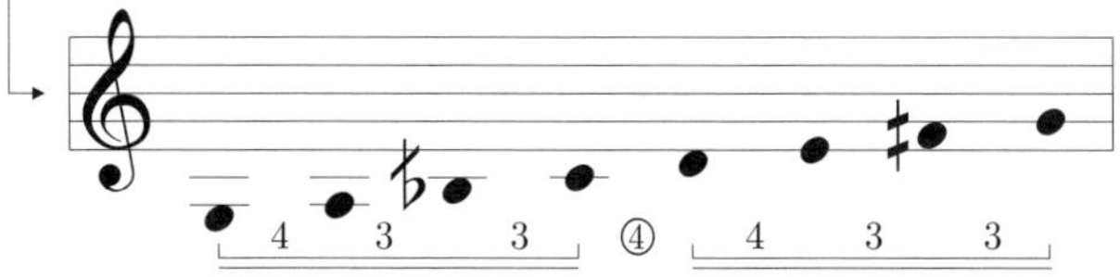	*Yakāh*	Tetrachord IV

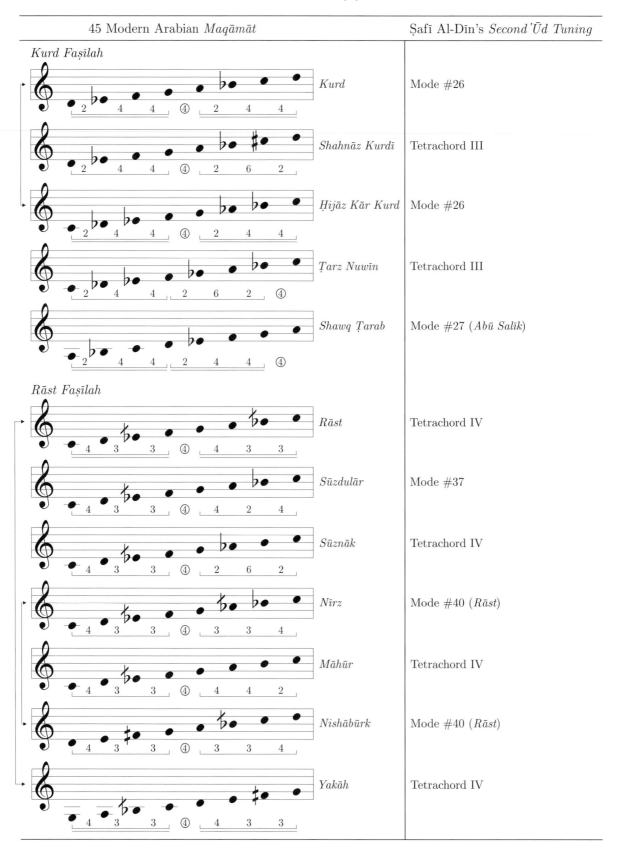

Table 11.54(c)

45 Modern Arabian *Maqāmāt*		Ṣafī Al-Dīn's *Second ʿŪd Tuning*
Bayyāti Faṣīlah		
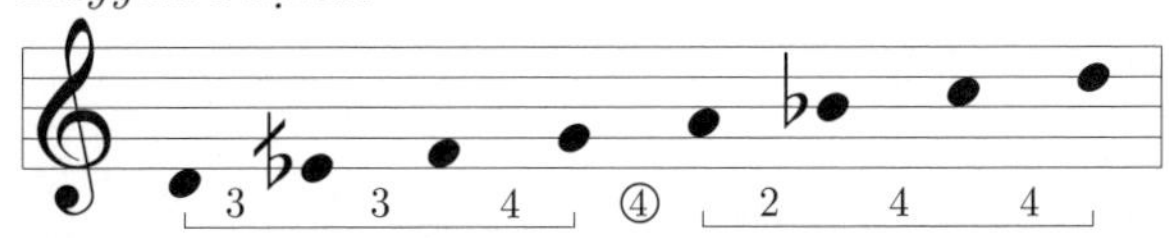	*Bayyāti*	Mode #50
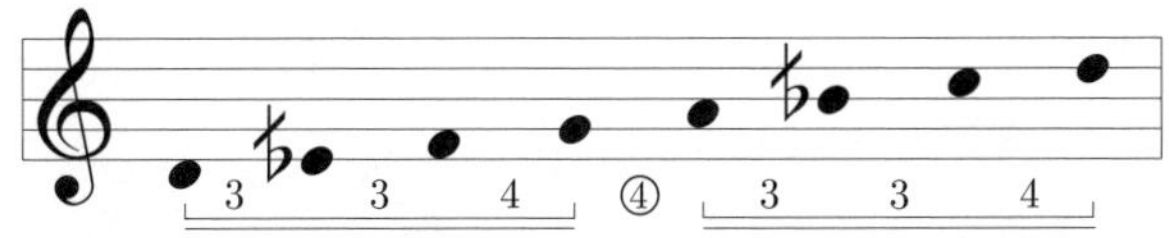	*Ḥusaynī*	Mode #52
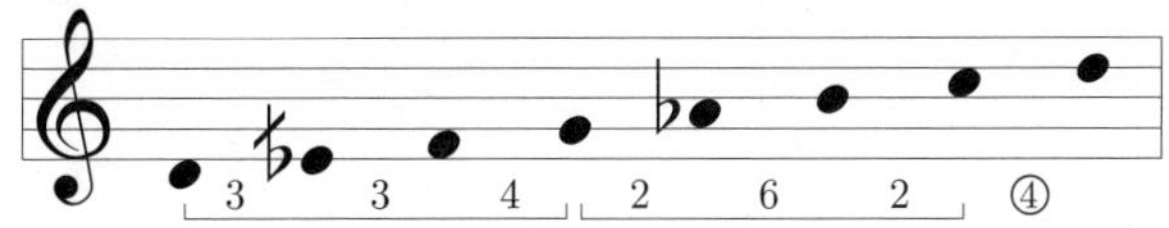	*Shūrī*	Tetrachord V
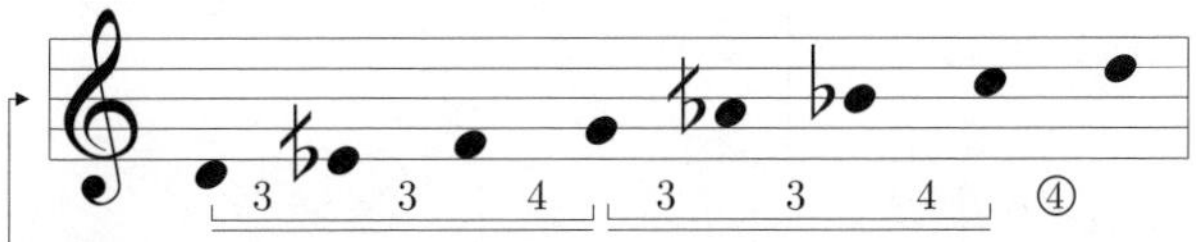	*Bayyātayn*	Mode #53 (*Ḥusainī*)
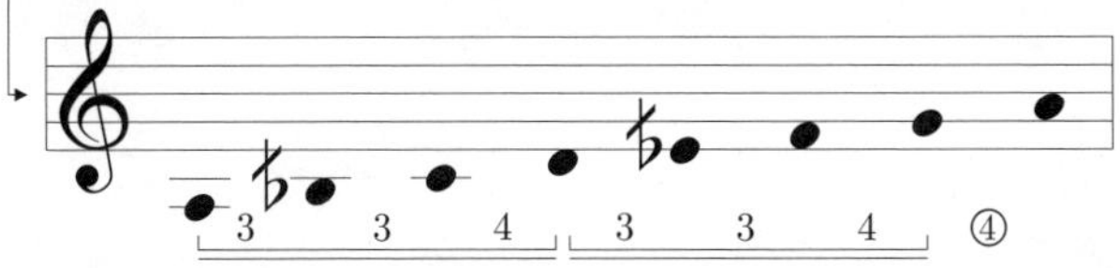	*Ḥusaynī ʿUshayrān*	Mode #53 (*Ḥusainī*)
Sīkāh Faṣīlah		
	*Sīkāh*	Tetrachord VI (3, 4)
	*Huzām*	Tetrachord VI (3, 4)
	*Sīkāh Māyah*	Tetrachord VI (3, 4)
	*Mustaʿār*	
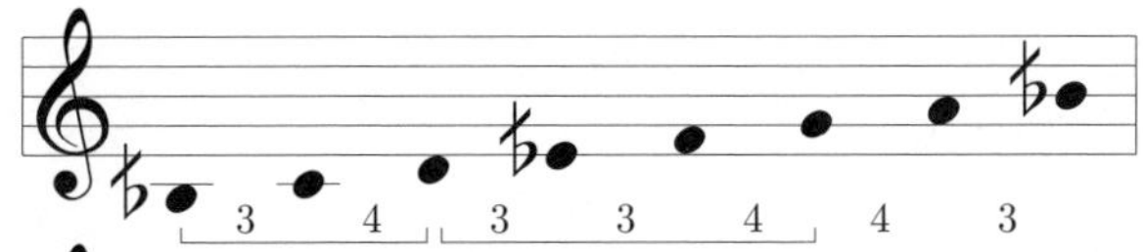	*ʿIrāq*	Tetrachord VI (3, 4, 3)
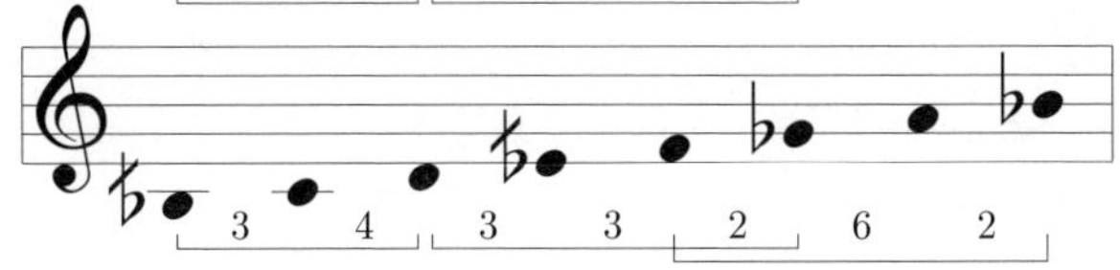	*Bastanikār*	Tetrachord VI (3, 4, 3)

Table 11.54(d)

45 Modern Arabian *Maqāmāt*	Ṣafī Al-Dīn's *Second 'Ūd Tuning*
	(none)

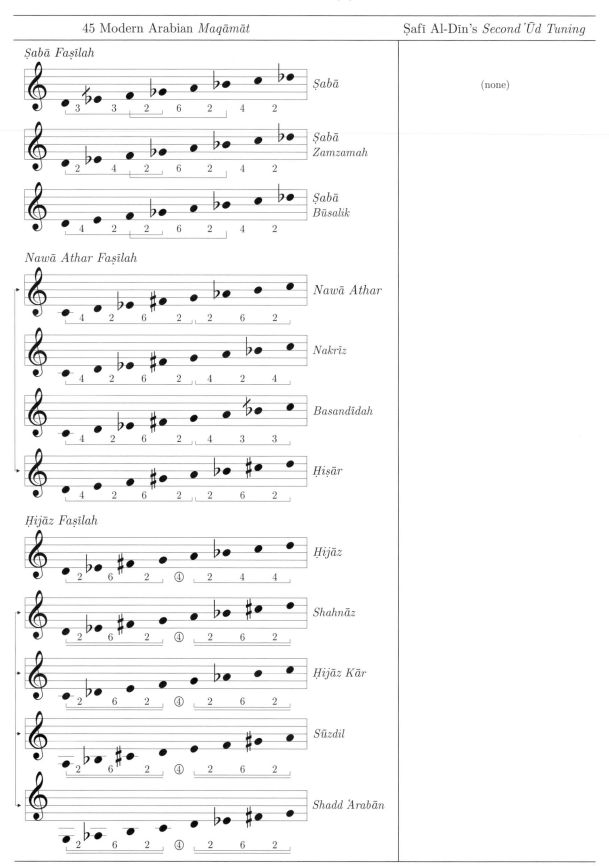

Ṣabā Faṣīlah

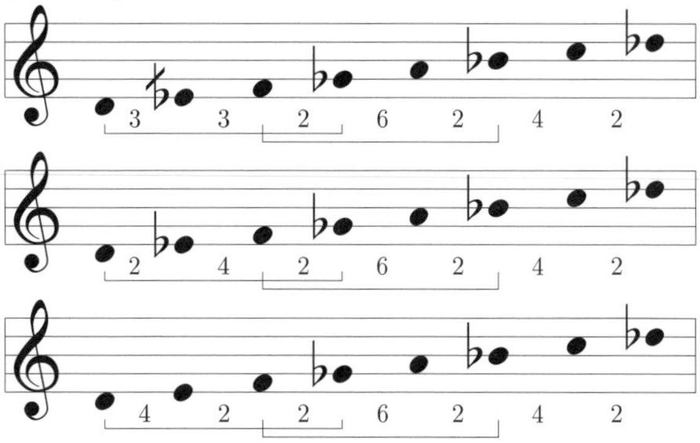

Ṣabā

Ṣabā Zamzamah

Ṣabā Būsalik

Nawā Athar Faṣīlah

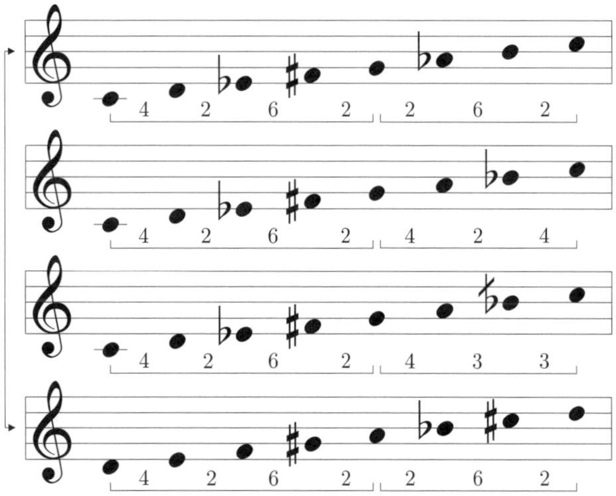

Nawā Athar

Nakrīz

Basandīdah

Ḥiṣār

Ḥijāz Faṣīlah

Ḥijāz

Shahnāz

Ḥijāz Kār

Sūzdil

Shadd 'Arabān

> Most writers choose to list transposed modes which have distinct names but ignore those modes which are not given independent names. While this approach accurately records the existing independently-named modes, it is highly unsatisfactory from the point of view of documenting performance practice for many of the independently-named transpositions are exceedingly rare while many of the transpositions which lack independent names are among the most frequently played modes (*Sūzdil*, i.e., *Ḥijāz* on AA, is an example of the former while *Rāst* and *Bayyāti* transposed to G are examples of the latter)."[212]

The right columns of these tables list the corresponding interval patterns in the tetrachords and modes of Ṣafī Al-Dīn's *Second ʿŪd Tuning.* To verify the historic origins of the modern modes, turn to Figure 11.90, which shows the same tetrachords and pentachords as the seven-by-twelve matrix in Figure 11.79. Observe that Figure 11.90 gives the intervals between notes in quarter-tones. (1) First and foremost, Tetrachords I–V are for all practical purposes identical to the tetrachords that define *ʿAjam faṣīlah, Nahāwand faṣīlah, Kurd faṣīlah, Rāst faṣīlah,* and *Bayyāti faṣīlah,* respectively; also, the first two intervals of Tetrachord VI are identical to the first two intervals that define the trichord of *Sīkāh faṣīlah.* (2) Ṣafī Al-Dīn's *shudūd* #14 (*Nawā*), #27 (*Abū Salīk*), #40 (*Rāst*), and #53 (*Ḥusainī*) are identical to *maqāmāt Būsalik, Shawq Ṭarab, Nīrz,* and *Bayyātayn,* respectively. (3) Modes #16, #26, #37, #50, #52 are identical to *maqāmāt ʿUshāq Masrī, Kurd, Sūzdulār, Bayyāti,* and *Ḥusaynī,* respectively. Asterisks specify that four of the latter nine *maqāmāt* have different names when played on lower tonics. (4) In the right columns of Tables 11.54(a)–11.54(c), eighteen additional references to Tetrachords I–VI indicate that the lower tetrachord or trichord of a modern *maqām* matches an interval pattern in Figure 11.90. (5) The right column of Table 11.54(d) is empty because the lower tetrachords of *Ṣabā faṣīlah* and *Ḥijāz faṣīlah,* and the lower pentachords of *Nawā Athar faṣīlah,* do not match any interval patterns in Figure 11.90. A principal reason for the differences between ancient and contemporary modes is the 6/4-tone [300 ¢] interval of modern Arabian music, which is analogous to the triple-limma [271 ¢] interval of modern Turkish music. In Section 11.74, we discussed that Ṣafī Al-Dīn considered the latter interval a dissonance. (6) Finally, given 45 modern Arabian *maqāmāt,* and 31 references in the right columns of these tables, it is significant that we may trace 69% of the Arabian modes to Ṣafī Al-Dīn's *Second ʿŪd Tuning.*

Modern theorists use three terms to define trichord, tetrachord, and pentachord patterns of the *maqāmāt:* (1) *muttaṣil* means *conjunct,* (2) *munfaṣil* means *disjunct,* and (3) *mutadākhil* means *overlapping.*[213] However, not all theorists agree on the arrangements of these patterns. Consequently, the subdivisions of the modes in Tables 11.54(a)–11.54(d) are subject to interpretation.

> The discussion of present-day tetrachordal theory . . . should not give the impression that there is complete agreement when it comes to the tetrachordal analysis of a given mode. In fact, disagreements arise concerning even the primary tetrachordal structures of some of the more common modes. *Maqām Bayyāti,* for example, is commonly described today as having a *Nahāwand* tetrachord [4, 2, 4] . . . on **G** as its *jins al-farʿ.* [ʿAbdullah] al-Kurdī . . . however, analyzes the *maqām* as having *Kurd* [2, 4, 4] on **A** as its . . . [primary] *jins al-farʿ,* and *Nahāwand* on **G** as a secondary *jins al-farʿ.*[214] (Bold note names, and text and numbers in brackets mine.)

Marcus interprets *maqām Bayyāti* as two (nonidentical) conjunct tetrachords: 3–3–4–4–2–4–④, where the second tetrachord begins on G. In contrast, Al-Kurdī recognizes two different versions of this mode. He first interprets *maqām Bayyāti* as two disjunct tetrachords: 3–3–4–④–2–4–4, where the second tetrachord begins on A; he then acknowledges that the second tetrachord may also begin

	I	II	III	IV	V	VI	VII	VIII	IX	X	XI	XII
	F,G,A,B♭,C' 4 4 2 ④	F,G,A♭,B♭,C' 4 2 4 ④	F,G♭,A♭,B♭,C' 2 4 4 ④	F,G,A𝄳,B♭,C' 4 3 3 ④	F,G𝄳,A♭,B♭,C' 3 3 4 ④	F,G𝄳,A𝄳,B♭,C' 3 4 3 ④	F,G𝄳,A♭,A,B♭,C' 3 3 2 2 ④	F,G,A𝄳,B♭,C𝄳,C' 4 3 3 3 1	F,G𝄳,A𝄳,B♭,C𝄳,C' 3 4 3 3 1	F,G𝄳,G,A,B§↓,C' 3 1 4 ≈4 ≈2	F,G𝄳,A♭,A𝄳,B§↓,C' 3 3 1 ≈5 ≈2	F,G,A𝄳,B§↓,C' 4 3 ≈5 ≈2
I: *'Ajam* C,D,E,F 4 4 2	1	2	3	4	5	6	7	8	9	10	11	12
II: *Nahāwand* C,D,E♭,F 4 2 4	13	*Būsalik** 14	15	*'Ushāq Masrī* 16	17	18	19	20	21	22	23	24
III: *Kurd* C,D♭,E♭,F 2 4 4	25	*Kurd** 26	*Shawq Ṭarab* 27	28	29	30	31	32	33	34	35	36
IV: *Rāst* C,D,E𝄳,F 4 3 3	*Sūzdulār* 37	38	39	*Nīrz** 40	41	42	43	44	45	46	47	48
V: *Bayyāti* C,D𝄳,E♭,F 3 3 4	49	*Bayyāti* 50	51	*Ḥusaynī* 52	*Bayyātayn** 53	54	55	56	57	58	59	60
VI: *Sīkāh* (3,4) C,D𝄳,E𝄳,F 3 4 3	61	62	63	64	65	66	67	68	69	70	71	72
VII C,D𝄳,E♭,E,F 3 3 2 2	73	74	75	76	77	78	79	80	81	82	83	84

Figure 11.90 A modern interpretation of Ṣafī Al-Dīn's 84 Melodic Modes according to his *Second 'Ūd Tuning.* (See Figure 11.79.) Here all intervals between notes are given in quarter-tones. Observe that of the 45 modern Arabian *maqāmāt* listed in Tables 11.54(a)–11.54(d), nine modes have identical interval patterns. Furthermore, asterisks indicate that four of these modes have other names when transposed to a different tonic. Finally, four underlined modern Arabian *maqāmāt: Būsalik, Shawq Ṭarab, Nīrz,* and *Bayyātayn*, are identical to four of Ṣafī Al-Dīn's 12 *shudūd*, or principal modes.

on G. The first illustration below shows *Bayyāti* with a *Nahāwand* tetrachord on G_4 as its *jins al-farʿ*, and the second illustration shows *Bayyāti* with a *Kurd* tetrachord on A_4 as its *jins al-farʿ*.

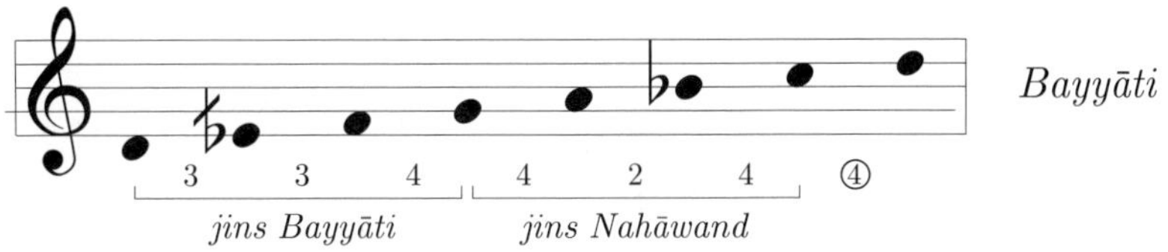

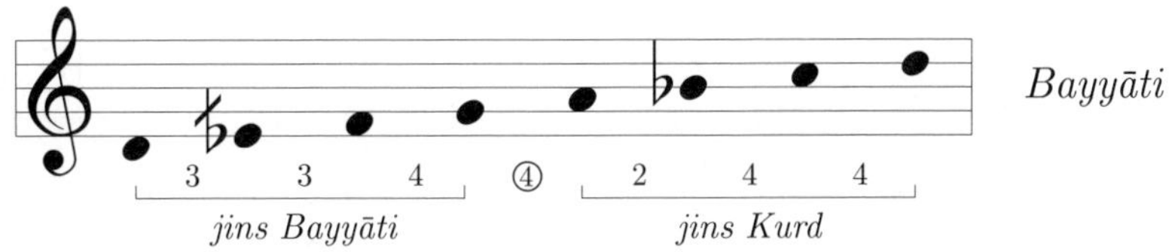

These two interpretations not only express theoretical differences, but have significant musical implications because musicians often consider the first tone of a *jins al-farʿ* as the prominent tone, or the *ghammāz*,[215] of a given mode. In practice, the *ghammāz* functions as a pivot tone for modulation.

> Modulations to a degree other than the tonic are most commonly to the note that starts the upper tetrachord (the *jins al-farʿ*). This note, called the *ghammāz* in present-day Arab music theory, is G for most modes [1] (for example, for *Rāst*, *Nahāwand*, *Nawā Athar*, *Nakrīz*, *Bayyāti*, *Ḥijāz*, *Kurd*, *Sīkāh*, and *Huzām*). [2] For *maqām ʿAjam* (or *ʿAjam ʿUshayrān*) and *Ṣabā* this note is F, while [3] for a few C-based modes this note is either F or G (for example, for *Ḥijāz Kār* and *Ḥijāz Kār Kurd*).[216] (Group numbers in brackets mine. All text in parentheses in Marcus' dissertation.)

Although many theorists concur with these observations, Marcus also includes numerous examples in agreement with the subdivisions of *maqāmāt* as illustrated in Tables 11.54(a)–11.54(d). In all *maqāmāt* where a $\frac{4}{4}$-tone appears as the fourth interval and as the seventh interval (for example, in *Būsalik*, *ʿUshāq Masrī*, *Kurd*, *Sūzdulār*, etc.), I interpreted the $\frac{4}{4}$-tone as a lower interval of disjunction; that is, I interpreted all such modes as consisting of two disjunct tetrachords. Now, in Group 1 of Marcus' description, there are no differences with respect to *Rāst*, *Nahāwand*, *Nawā Athar*, *Nakrīz*, *Sīkāh*, and *Huzām*. However, Marcus also organizes *Bayyāti* with an upper tetrachord on A,[217] and he cites Al-Kurdī's *Ḥijāz* with an upper tetrachord on A.[218] In Group 2, there are no differences with respect to *ʿAjam ʿUshayrān* and *Ṣabā*. Observe carefully, Table 11.54(d) shows *Ṣabā* with a lower tetrachord that spans a narrow $\frac{8}{4}$-tone [400 ¢] interval, or a "major "third," and with an overlapping upper tetrachord that spans a standard $\frac{10}{4}$-tone [500 ¢] interval, or a "fourth." Finally, in Group 3, there is agreement with respect to *Ḥijāz Kār* in Table 11.54(d), and *Ḥijāz Kār Kurd* in Table 11.54(b): both modes have upper tetrachords on G. Space does not permit a detailed discussion on modulation in Arabian music, but Marcus' experiences and observations are worth noting.

> From these lessons [on the *ʿūd* and *nāy*], I learned that each *maqām* is part of a fabric that includes all the *maqāmāt* (or at least a large number of neighboring *maqāmāt*). To know any one *maqām* fully, a student must know all the places to which one can modulate. This stands in marked contrast to Indian music, where the *rāgas* are understood to exist independently. In North Indian music, it is commonly felt that a student can spend three to five years learning a given *rāga* and, in a sense, master it without having studied a second *rāga*. This is not the case in Arab music, where

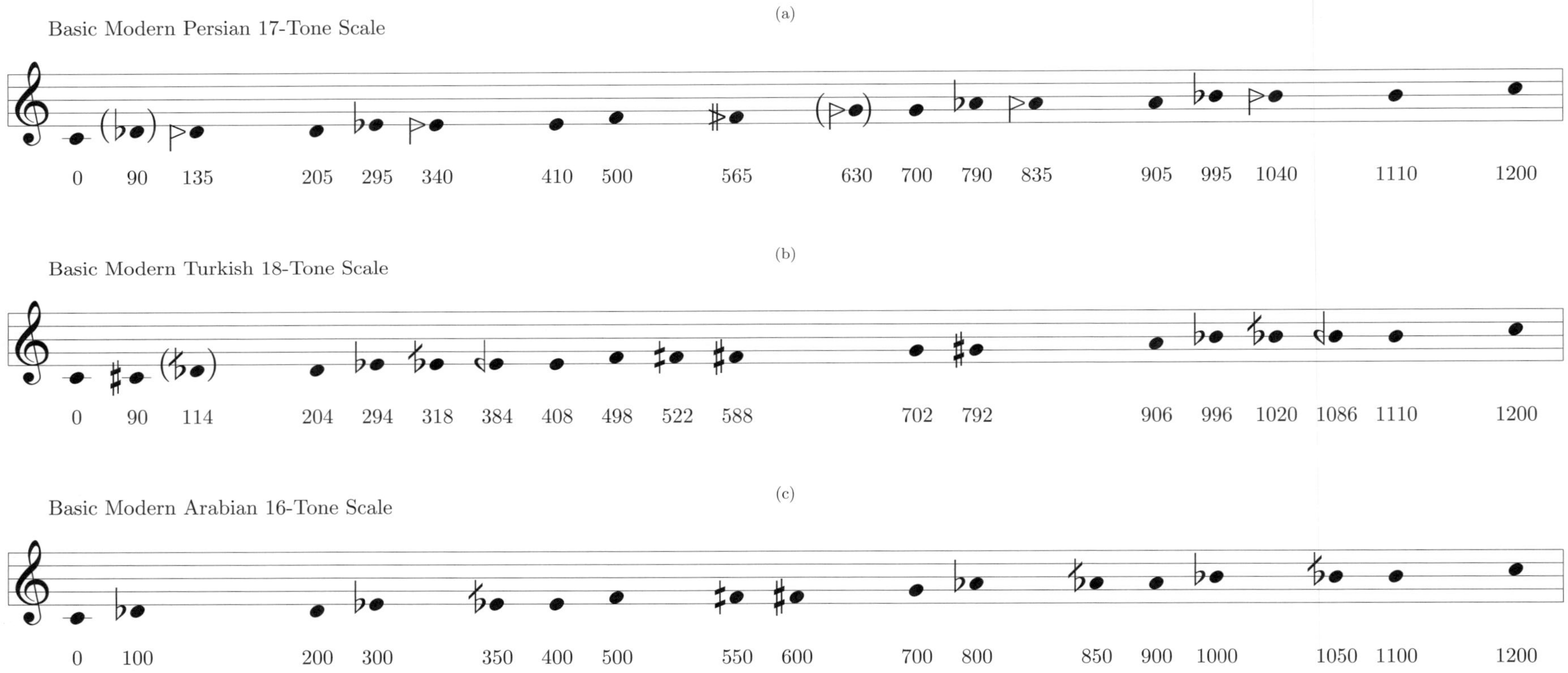

Figure 11.91 Three modern scales that originated in the ancient Perso-Arabian musical traditions. (a) This Persian 17-tone scale appears in Figure 11.67. All but two tones of this scale are used to play 12 *dastgāhā* in Table 11.34; D♭ and G𝄲 occur only in the derived modes called *gushehā*. (b) This Turkish 18-tone scale is used to play 19 *maqāmāt* in Tables 11.50(a)–11.50(c) and Table 11.51; D𝄳 occurs only in *Sabâ*. (c) This Arabian 16-tone scale is used to play 45 *maqāmāt* in Tables 11.54(a)–11.54(d); here F𝄲 does not appear without B𝄳, and A𝄳 does not appear without E𝄳. The above-mentioned tables only give *basic or primary* tones; ornamental tones and tones of modulation are not included.

> to master one *maqām* is to master virtually all the *maqāmāt*.[219] (Text in brackets mine. Text in parentheses in Marcus' article.)

∾ 11.84 ∾

In summary of these discussions on modern Persian, Turkish, and Arabian music, turn to Figure 11.91, which compares the principal scales of these three civilizations. Figure 11.91(a) illustrates the Persian 17-tone scale from Figure 11.67. Musicians utilize all but two tones of this scale to play 12 *dastgāhā* in Table 11.34; that is, D♭ and G𝄬 occur only in the derived modes called *gushehā*. In Figures 11.91(b) and 11.91(c), I transcribed the tones used throughout the modern Turkish and Arabian modes within the span of the C_4–C_5 "octave." Therefore, Figure 11.91(b) illustrates a Turkish 18-tone scale used to play 19 *maqāmāt* in Tables 11.50(a)–11.50(c) and Table 11.51; here D𝄳 occurs only in *Sabâ*. And Figure 11.91(c) shows an Arabian 16-tone scale used to play 45 *maqāmāt* in Tables 11.54(a)–11.54(d). Be aware that in *maqāmāt Nishābūrk* and *Yakāh*, F𝄲 does not appear without B𝄳, and in *maqāmāt Nīrz* and *Bayyātayn*, A𝄳 does not appear without E𝄳. We conclude, therefore, that F𝄲 (*nīm Ḥijāz*) and A𝄳 (*tīk Ḥiṣar*) are both rare and dependent tones.

In Figures 11.91(a)–11.91(c), I attempted to organize tones with similar musical functions into vertical columns. Even so, the reader should be cautious not to confuse the intonational characteristics of some tones in these columns. For example, in Figure 11.91(b), the Turkish "major third," E𝄭 [384 ¢], is equivalent to Al-Fārābī's and Ṣafī Al-Dīn's "schisma third," E↓, which is only 2 ¢ flat of the just "major third," ratio 5⁄4 [386 ¢]. However, directly beneath E𝄭, in Figure 11.91(c), the Arabian "neutral third," E𝄳 [350 ¢], has a completely different mathematical derivation and musical identity.

∾ 11.85 ∾

Regarding CD's, I would like to begin by recommending an Ocora Radio France recording entitled *Iran: Musique Persane*,[220] with liner notes by Hormoz Farhat. This recording presents two *dastgāhā*, *Māhur* and *Segāh*, performed on the following instruments: *tār*, *'ūd*, *kamānche*, *santūr*, *nāy*, *tombak*, and voice. The performance of *Māhur* begins with a *pishdarāmad*. Farhat states

> A *pishdarāmad* is intended as an overture to precede the *darāmad* section of the *dastgāh*, and the name simply means pre-*darāmad*, or pre-opening. It is a composed piece in a set meter, with its melodic ideas drawn from the *darāmads* and some of the *gushes* of the *dastgāh* for which it is composed. A *pishdarāmad*, therefore, uses not only the basic mode of the *dastgāh*, but also the modes and the melodic ideas of some of the main *gushes* in that *dastgāh*. Accordingly, as the *dastgāh* includes modulations to other modes, the *pishdarāmad* for the *dastgāh* also contains those modulations.[221]

Figure 11.92 gives the score of the *pishdarāmad*. Notice that both the initial and the final note is F. Furthermore, with the exception of two A♭'s in the second bar, the entire mode appears to be in the Western key of F-major. Farhat defines *Māhur* in this manner:

> The intervalic structure of the mode of *Māhur* parallels that of the major mode in western music. Yet, because of the other elements which go into the making of Persian modes, probably ***no*** melody in the major mode can be said to be in the mode of *Māhur*. Persian musicians fail to appreciate this fact and are very eager to point out that the major mode is the same as the mode of *Māhur*.* ...

> . . . The *finalis* has a central position; it is the linking tone of two conjunct major tetrachords. It is also the usual *āqāz*. ... Leaps of thirds, both ascending and descending are common.
>
> *A.N. Vaziri, *Musiqi-ye Nazari*, p. 68, states that "The scale of *Māhur* is, without any difference, that of the major scale."[222] (Bold italics mine. Quotation from Vaziri's work in Farhat's notes.)

Table 11.34 shows Farhat's interpretation of *Māhur*, a mode that spans the interval between G_3–$B\flat_4$, with an *āqāz* and a *finalis* on C_4. Although Farhat's book and dissertation give many examples to support this rendition of *Māhur*, and although his CD liner notes give exactly the same scale as in Table 11.34, the score in Figure 11.92 clearly indicates that this *pishdarāmad* begins and ends on F. The next six musical sections of the recording, called *cahārezrāb*, *dād*, *shekaste*, *delkash*, *tasnif*, *and reng* all end on F as well.

I chose this recording of *dastgāh Māhur* for several reasons. (1) The musical performances are authentic and virtuosic. (2) Throughout the compositions and improvisations, Westerners will not easily recognize the key of F-major. (3) In the *pishdarāmad*, the ascending melodic patterns, and the descending cadential patterns that end on half notes, are very popular in contemporary Arabian art music. For example, in a Cinq Planètes recording entitled *Oud: Saïd Chraïbi*,[223] the Moroccan *'ūd* player Saïd Chraïbi plays his interpretation of the above-mentioned *pishdarāmad* on Track 7. The liner notes refer to this *maqām* as *Raast Danjikah*, "Improvisation in an ancient Arabo-Persian mode." Furthermore, in an Ocora Radio France recording entitled *Iraq: L'art du 'ūd*,[224] Munir Bashir plays similar descending cadential patterns throughout his improvisations.

Also noteworthy is an Ocora Radio France collection entitled *Turquie: Archives de la musique turque* (1) and (2).[225] These two CD's contain 41 recordings of Turkish music from 1904–1935, and constitute a treasure-trove of authentic musical performances. The liner notes are very informative.

My favorite performances of Arabian art music are on a CD produced by ETHNIC recordings entitled *AL KINDI: Musique Classique Arabe.*[226] On p. 14, the liner notes give the following description of *AL KINDI:*

> *AL KINDI* group has drawn its repertoire from the so-called Arab-Andalusian tradition of North Africa, the heir of the magnificent Islamic civilization of Spain; it delved into the Syro-Egyptian tradition which flourished during the artistic renaissance (*AL NAHDA*) of the 19th century, and found inspiration in the Iraqi tradition in the footsteps of the Abbassid dynasty, and as well in the Turkish instrumental music of the Ottoman Empire.

This recording features masterful performances by a musical trio that includes the *nāy*, *qānūn*, and *riqq*. An interpretation of the *pishdarāmad* in Figure 11.92 may be heard on Track 4. Finally, my favorite performances of Arabian folk music are on a CD produced by Celestial Harmonies entitled *The Music of Islam, Volume Two: Music of the South Sinai Bedouins.*[227] Tracks #1, #6, #9, and #15 feature the seldom-heard *simsimīyya*,[228] a shimmering 5-sting lyre. A 50-page liner booklet to these exuberant performances informs us

> This recording presents the traditional folk music of the legendary desert nomads, specifically the South Sinai Bedouins. It was recorded in a single night under a full moon in a dry riverbed in the South Sinai desert. Although there were no available recording facilities this setting was much more conductive, acting as a doorway into this ancient culture, people, and music, capturing their very essence.

Figure 11.92 The *pishdarāmad* of *dastgāh Māhur* from a 1987 CD recording by an ensemble from Iran. Musicians frequently perform variations on this composition throughout Farsi- and Arabic-speaking lands.

Notes

1. Farmer, H.G. (1954). "'Ūd." In *Grove's Dictionary of Music and Musicians, Volume 8*, 5th ed., E. Blom, Editor, p. 631. St. Martin's Press, Inc., New York, 1970.

2. Lewis, B., Editor (1976). *Islam and the Arab World*, p. 225. This volume consists of an anthology of many excellent articles. For a history of the Arabian influence in Andalusia, consult "Moorish Spain," by Emilio García Gómez, and for a survey of Arabian music, "The Dimension of Sound," by A. Shiloah. Alfred A. Knopf, New York.

   On p. 225, Gómez quotes the famous Spanish philosopher José Ortega y Gasset (1883–1955), "I do not understand how something which lasted eight centuries can be called a reconquest."

3. Hitti, P.K. (1937). *History of the Arabs*, pp. 370–371. Macmillan and Co. Ltd., London, England, 1956.

4. Cowl, C., Translator (1966). Al-Kindī's essay on the composition of melodies. *The Consort*, No. 23, pp. 129–159.

5. Lachmann, R. and El-Hefni, M., Translators (1931). *Risāla fī hubr tā'līf al-alḥān* [Über die Komposition der Melodien], by Al-Kindī. Fr. Kistner & C.F.W. Siegel, Leipzig, Germany.

6. For example, in the Lachmann/El-Hefni and Cowl translations, Chapter 2, Paragraph 5, Sentences 8 and 9 contradict the first four and a half lines of Chapter 2, Paragraph 7. Since the former passage makes perfect sense, and the latter passage is confused and has missing text, I excluded the latter from the discussion.

7. *The Consort*, 1966, p. 149.

8. Forster Translation: in *Risāla fī hubr tā'līf al-alḥān* [Über die Komposition der Melodien], pp. 21–25.

9. (A) Farmer, H.G. (1978). *Studies in Oriental Musical Instruments, First and Second Series.* Second Series, p. 47, 90. Longwood Press Ltd., Tortola, British Virgin Islands.

   This volume consists primarily of articles by Henry George Farmer first published in *The Journal of the Royal Asiatic Society of Great Britain and Ireland.* In this book, the division into *First and Second Series* means that the first set of articles is numbered pp. 3–107, and the second set is numbered pp. 3–98.

   (B) Ribera, J. (1929). *Music in Ancient Arabia and Spain*, pp. 100–107. This work was translated and abridged from the Spanish by Eleanor Hague and Marion Leffingwell. Stanford University Press, Stanford University, California.

10. In Figure 11.41, the physical distance between Anterior Frets 1 and 2 indicates the aural interval of the comma of Pythagoras, which equals 23.5 ¢.

11. See Section 10.10.

12. See Section 10.6.

13. Sachs, C. (1940). *The History of Musical Instruments*, pp. 130–131. W. W. Norton & Company, Inc., New York.

14. See Section 2.6.

15. See Table 10.12.

16. Maas, M. and Snyder, J.M. (1989). *Stringed Instruments of Ancient Greece*, p. 203. Yale University Press, New Haven, Connecticut.

17. Section 10.6.

18. (A) Farmer, H.G. (1965). *The Sources of Arabian Music*, p. 3. E.J. Brill, Leiden, Netherlands.

This work consists of an annotated bibliography of 353 Arabian texts on music from the eighth through the 16th century. Throughout my text, book titles in parentheses refer to Farmer's English translations of Arabian titles.

(B) Shiloah, A. (1979). *The Theory of Music in Arabic Writings (c. 900–1900).* G. Henle Verlag, München, Germany.

This work also consists of an annotated bibliography of Arabian texts, although much more elaborate than Farmer's book. Shiloah gives the following subtitle: Descriptive Catalogue of Manuscripts in Libraries of Europe and the U.S.A.

19. *The Sources of Arabian Music*, p. 3.

20. *Studies in Oriental Musical Instruments, Second Series*, p. 47.

Here Farmer refers to Al-Munajjim as Yaḥyā b. 'Alī b. Yaḥyā b. Abī Manṣur.

21. *The Sources of Arabian Music*, p. 24.

22. Farmer, H.G. (1953–1954). The song captions in the *Kitāb al-aghānī al-kabīr*, p. 5. *Transactions of the Glasgow University Oriental Society* **XV**, pp. 1–10.

23. Farmer, H.G. (1929). *A History of Arabian Music*, pp. 69–70, 77–78. Luzac Oriental, London, England, 1994.

24. *Ibid.*, p. 73, pp. 79–80.

25. *Transactions of the Glasgow University Oriental Society*, 1953–1954, p. 3.

26. *The Sources of Arabian Music*, p. 24.

27. (A) Farmer, H.G. (1957). "The Music of Islam." In *New Oxford History of Music, Volume 1: Ancient and Oriental Music*, E. Wellesz, Editor, p. 457. Oxford University Press, London, England, 1960.

(B) *Studies in Oriental Musical Instruments, Second Series*, p. 47.

(C) *Transactions of the Glasgow University Oriental Society*, 1953–1954, p. 6.

(D) *A History of Arabian Music*, p. 69.

With respect to the history of the earliest *'ūd* tunings, Farmer states, "When Al-Naḍr ibn al Ḥārith [d. 624] introduced the *'ūd* from Al-Ḥīra about the close of the 6th century, some foretaste of the Pythagorean scale may have been introduced at the same time. Yet there is no certainty on this question." The same uncertainty also applies to the tuning used by Ibn Suraij (d. *c.* 726) on his Persian lute *'ūd al-fārisī*. So, although it is possible to fairly accurately reconstruct the ancient Arabian modes from Al-Munajjim's descriptions, the actual tones of the modes of the 6th, 7th, and 8th centuries remain in doubt simply because the tunings of the earliest short-necked lutes are not known. However, there is no doubt concerning the tuning of the classic Arabian *'ūd* in the 9th century. Al-Kindī's *'ūd* is perfectly suited for the performance of Al-Munajjim's and Al-Iṣfahānī's ancient modes as depicted in Figure 11.43.

28. Al-Faruqi, L.I. (1981). *An Annotated Glossary of Arabic Musical Terms*, p. 197. Greenwood Press, Westport, Connecticut.

This is an invaluable reference work. Al-Faruqi gives literal translations of *mujannab* as *adjoining* and *neighbor* intervals. However, in the context of frets, Al-Faruqi gives Farmer's translation of *mujannab* as *anterior* fret. (See Farmer's *Studies in Oriental Musical Instruments, First and Second Series.* Second Series, p. 55.) Finally, D'Erlanger translates *mujannab* as *neighbor* or *assistant* fret. (See *La Musique Arabe, Volume 2*, p. 238.)

29. *The Sources of Arabian Music*, pp. 33–34.

30. Shiloah, A., Translator (1978). *The Epistle on Music of the Ikhwān Al-Ṣafā*. Tel-Aviv University, Tel-Aviv, Israel.

31. Dieterici, F., Translator (1858–1890; 16 Volumes). *Die Philosophie der Araber im IX. und X. Jahrhundert n. Chr. aus der Theologie des Aristoteles, den Abhandlungen Alfarabis und den Schriften der Lautern Brüder.* The quoted passage on music is in *Volume 6*, entitled: *Die Propaedeutik der Araber im zehnten Jahrhundert.* E.S. Mittler und Sohn, Berlin, Germany, 1865.

32. (A) Forster Translation: in *Die Propaedeutik der Araber im zehnten Jahrhundert*, pp. 117–119.

(B) *The Epistle on Music of the Ikhwān Al-Ṣafā*, pp. 33–34.

In his translation, Shiloah includes some original text in parentheses. However, note carefully, not all the text in parentheses constitutes original text.

33. Wright, O. (1966). Ibn al-Munajjim and the early Arabian modes. *The Galpin Society Journal* **XIX**, pp. 27–48.

34. *Ibid.*, pp. 28–29.

35. *Transactions of the Glasgow University Oriental Society*, 1953–1954, p. 9.

36. *The Galpin Society Journal*, 1966, p. 46.

37. (A) *Transactions of the Glasgow University Oriental Society*, 1953–1954, p. 8.

(B) *New Oxford History of Music, Volume 1: The Music of Islam*, p. 448.

38. (A) *The Sources of Arabian Music*, p. xx.

(B) See Section 3.19 for a discussion of Plato's plagiarism of Philolaus' tetrachord.

39. Farmer, H.G. (1925). Clues for the Arabian influence on European musical theory, pp. 72–73. *The Journal of the Royal Asiatic Society*, First Quarter, pp. 61–80.

40. (A) *The Sources of Arabian Music*, pp. xx–xxi.

(B) Farmer, H.G., Translator (1965). *Al-Fārābī's Arabic-Latin Writings on Music.* Hinrichsen Edition Ltd., New York.

In the above-mentioned quote, Farmer refers to "two Arabic compends." This volume contains translations and commentary on these short compendiums on music by Al-Fārābī. The first is entitled

Iḥṣā' al-'ulūm (Book of the register of the sciences), which was translated in the 12th century into Latin by both John of Seville and Gerard of Cremona under the title *De scientiis.* The second did not survive in the Arabic original, and is therefore only known under the Latin title *De ortu scientiarum* (Concerning the Rise of the Sciences).

41. (A) D'Erlanger, R., Bakkouch, 'A.'A., and Al-Sanūsī, M., Translators (Vol. 1, 1930; Vol. 2, 1935; Vol. 3, 1938; Vol. 4, 1939; Vol. 5, 1949; Vol. 6, 1959). *La Musique Arabe,* Librairie Orientaliste Paul Geuthner, Paris, France.

Volume 1: Kitāb al-mūsīqī al-kabīr, Books 1 and 2, by Al-Fārābī.

Volume 2: Kitāb al-mūsīqī al-kabīr, Book 3, by Al-Fārābī.
Kitāb al-shifā', by Ibn Sīnā.

Volume 3: Risālat al-Sharafīya fi'l-nisab al-ta'līfīya, by Ṣafī Al-Dīn.
Sharḥ Maulānā Mubārak Shāh [on the *Kitāb al-adwār*], by Al-Jurjānī.

Volume 4: Risāla fī 'ilm al-mūsīqī, by Al-Shirwānī.
Risālat al-fatḥīya fi'l-mūsīqī, by Al-Lādhiqī.

Volume 5: Attempt at codification of the customary rules of modern Arabic music:
General scale[s] of sounds.
Modal system.

Volume 6: Attempt at codification of the customary rules of modern Arabic music:
The rhythmic system.
Various forms of artistic composition.

In *The Sources of Arabian Music,* Farmer credits Al-Sanūsī as translator of all six treatises contained in Volumes 1–4.

(B) Shiloah, A. (1981). The Arabic concept of mode, pp. 23–24. *Journal of the American Musicological Society* **XXXIV**, No. 1, pp. 19–42.

The first treatise in *La Musique Arabe, Volume 4,* is attributed to an anonymous author. However, Amnon Shiloah made the following discovery:

"The work . . . was published by Rodolphe d'Erlanger in 1939, in French translation, under the title *Traité anonyme dédié au Sultan Osmanli.* This work of course is listed in its own right in Farmer's *Sources* as Number 320, followed by the statement: 'This treatise has neither a title nor the author's name.' Our discovery of a second manuscript of the same work in the library of the Topkapi Saray has now made it possible to identify both the author and the work and to fill in a long lacuna in the British Museum version. The author's name is al-Mu'min Al-Shirwānī and his work is entitled *Risāla fī 'ilm al-mūsīqī (Tract on the Science of Music).*"

42. *La Musique Arabe, Volume 3,* p. 223.

43. Farmer, H.G. (1928). Ibn Khurdādhbih on musical instruments, p. 517. *The Journal of the Royal Asiatic Society,* Third Quarter, pp. 509–518.

44. *Studies in Oriental Musical Instruments, First Series,* p. 74.

45. See Sections 3.10–3.15.

46. *New Oxford History of Music, Volume 1,* p. xvi.

47. *Studies in Oriental Musical Instruments, First Series, Frontispiece.*

48. *The Sources of Arabian Music*, p. 38.

49. *Studies in Oriental Musical Instruments, First Series*, p. 8.

50. *The Sources of Arabian Music*, p. 41.

51. Barker, A., Translator (1989). *Greek Musical Writings, Volume 2.* Cambridge University Press, Cambridge, England.

52. Forster Translation: in *La Musique Arabe, Volume 3*, pp. 360–362.

53. Avenary, H., Translator (1974). The Hebrew version of Abū l-Ṣalt's treatise on music. *Yuval* **III**, pp. 7–82.

54. *Ibid.*, p. 52.

55. *The Sources of Arabian Music*, p. 28.

56. *Ibid.*, p. xx.

    Farmer observes, "The first description of instruments of music in any language was contributed by Al-Fārābī, and that was six hundred years before any other land had considered the subject sufficiently interesting for serious study."

57. (A) *La Musique Arabe, Volume 1*, p. 166.

    (B) *Studies in Oriental Musical Instruments, Second Series*, p. 65.

58. *Studies in Oriental Musical Instruments, Second Series*, pp. 64–65.

59. Crookes, D.Z., Translator (1986). *Syntagma musicum II: De organographia, Parts I and II*, by Michael Praetorius, p. 69. The Clarendon Press, Oxford, England. The first edition of this work was published in 1618.

60. (A) Forster Translation: in *La Musique Arabe, Volume 1*, pp. 166–174.

    (B) *New Oxford History of Music, Volume 1: The Music of Islam*, p. 460.

61. Forster Translation: in *La Musique Arabe, Volume 1*, p. 179.

62. *Ibid.*, p. 174.

63. See Section 10.1.

64. *Studies in Oriental Musical Instruments, Second Series*, p. 49.

65. (A) Farhat, H. (1965). *The Dastgāh Concept in Persian Music.* Ph.D. dissertation printed and distributed by University Microfilms, Inc., Ann Arbor, Michigan.

    (B) Farhat, H. (1990). *The Dastgāh Concept in Persian Music.* Cambridge University Press, Cambridge, England.

66. *The Dastgāh Concept in Persian Music* (1965), p. 26.

67. *Ibid.*, p. 44.

68. Forster Translation: in *La Musique Arabe, Volume 1*, p. 174.

69. (A) Al-Faruqi, L.I. (1974). *The Nature of the Musical Art of Islamic Culture: A Theoretical and Empirical Study of Arabian Music*, pp. 406–407. Ph.D. dissertation printed and distributed by University Microfilms, Inc., Ann Arbor, Michigan.

In Appendix III, pp. 404–455 consist of translated excerpts from Al-Fārābī's *Kitāb al-mūsīqī al-kabīr.*

(B) *La Musique Arabe, Volume 1*, pp. 44–45.

70. (A) *The Nature of the Musical Art of Islamic Culture*, pp. 407–411.

(B) *La Musique Arabe, Volume 1*, pp. 45–48.

71. Note that Al-Fārābī's original 9-tone scale is similar to the 10-tone scale of the Old Arabian School in Figure 11.42(b).

72. (A) *The Nature of the Musical Art of Islamic Culture*, pp. 411–412.

(B) *La Musique Arabe, Volume 1*, pp. 48–49.

73. (A) *The Nature of the Musical Art of Islamic Culture*, p. 412.

(B) *La Musique Arabe, Volume 1*, p. 49.

74. Comparisons to Marin Mersenne (1588–1648) are truly striking. For example, Table 10.29 shows Mersenne's expansion of the trumpet marine tuning, which in principle resembles Al-Fārābī's expansion of the *'ūd* tuning. Also, in the last quotation of Section 10.54, Mersenne acknowledges the importance of embracing new musical intervals, which resembles Al-Fārābī's desire, ". . . to count as somewhat natural those intervals which are sometimes or rarely regarded as natural."

More than thirty years ago, I coined the term *ambisonance.* From the Greek *amphi* as in amphibian, and the Latin *ambi* as in ambidextrous, these two prefixes literally mean *on both sides.* For me, figuratively, they mean *partaking of two worlds.* Ambisonance describes hearing a musical interval for the first time with the sudden realization that such an interval produces neither a consonance nor a dissonance. Experiences of ambisonance inspire new ways to hear, and then new ways to tune and to compose.

75. Forster Translation: in *La Musique Arabe, Volume 1*, pp. 49–51.

76. *Ibid.*, pp. 51–52.

In *La Musique Arabe, Volume 1*, p. 313, D'Erlanger explains why he translated the Arabic word *quwwah,* — literally "power," "force," or "strength," — with the Greek word *dynamis,* also "power," "force," or "strength." Furthermore, D'Erlanger arbitrarily interjects the French word *puissance* — also "power" or "force" — in places where the original Arabic is not given.

In *An Annotated Glossary of Arabic Music Terms*, p. 269, Al-Faruqi gives the following three definitions for *quwwah:* "1. The relationship or identity that occurs between two tones one octave apart, i.e., either the upper octave equivalent or the lower octave equivalent of a tone. 2. The term also referred to any tone produced on the *'ūd* which had one or more octave equivalent tones within the range of that instrument. Other tones, which had no octave equivalents within the range of the *'ūd* were termed *mufradah.* 3. Tension of a string, therefore pitch."

Note, therefore, that in a musical context, the hierarchical meaning of the word *quwwah* is *octave*, then *octave equivalent*, and finally *pitch.* Although *quwwah* may connote the "power," "force," or "strength" of an octave, of an octave equivalent, or of a pitch, in the context of tuning descriptions, *quwwah* specifically refers to ancient length ratio or frequency ratio $^2\!/_1$, which is the octave of $^1\!/_1$; similarly, it may refer to ancient length ratio or frequency ratio $^9\!/_4$, which is the octave equivalent of $^9\!/_8$; etc. (See Section 9.4.)

D'Erlanger gives the following three reasons for using the Greek word *dynamis:* (1) *Dynamis* means *quwwah* because an octave or an octave equivalent acts to give "power," "force," or "strength," to a given lower tone. (2) D'Erlanger states that since the Greeks used *dynamis* to describe the *function* of a tone, *dynamis* also means the "place" or "position" that a given tone occupies in a tetrachord or scale. (3) D'Erlanger claims that because one may express a progression of octaves and octave equivalents through a so-called *power* series of ratios, as in

$$\text{modern length ratio } \frac{1}{2^1} \text{ produces frequency ratio } \frac{2^1}{1}, \text{ or the "octave" } \frac{2}{1};$$

$$\text{modern length ratio } \frac{1}{2^2} \text{ produces frequency ratio } \frac{2^2}{1}, \text{ or the "double-octave" } \frac{4}{1};$$

$$\text{modern length ratio } \frac{1}{2^3} \text{ produces frequency ratio } \frac{2^3}{1}, \text{ or the "triple-octave" } \frac{8}{1},$$

there exists a mathematical justification to translate *quwwah* as *dynamis*. Finally, consistent with the first and third reasons, D'Erlanger also interjects the French word *puissance* where the topic under consideration centers on such a "power" series.

I categorically reject D'Erlanger's use of *dynamis* and *puissance* as explained by the first and third reasons. In a musical context, and in the context of tuning descriptions, the Greek word *dynamis* and the French word *puissance* do *not* mean octave or octave equivalent. Since the Arabic word *quwwah does* mean octave or octave equivalent, I have consistently translated *dynamis* and *puissance* as either octave or octave equivalent. For example, in Section 11.59, Ibn Sīnā's highly accurate tuning description of two extra tones on the fourth string of the *'ūd* does *not* refer to *puissance*, but to two *octave equivalents*, namely, ancient length ratios or frequency ratios $^{32}\!/_{9}$ and $^{4}\!/_{1}$. Readers who, through no fault of their own, fail to understand this sentence as a reference to two highly specific scale degrees will also fail to comprehend the meaning of Ibn Sīnā's description. Finally, D'Erlanger's utilization of *dynamis* to mean the *function* or position of a given tone in a tetrachord or scale is correct. However, to minimize confusion and to avoid costly mistakes, a translator should never translate a given foreign language (Arabic) into another foreign language (Greek) that the reader of the translation (French) may not understand.

77. (A) *The Nature of the Musical Art of Islamic Culture*, pp. 412–416.

(B) *La Musique Arabe, Volume 1*, pp. 55–59.

78. See Section 10.13.

79. Forster Translation: in *La Musique Arabe, Volume 1*, pp. 214–215.

80. *Ibid.*, p. 303.

81. *Ibid.*, pp. 100–101.

On p. 101 of this French translation, Ptolemy's terms *homophonic*, *symphonic*, and *emmelic* appear only in parentheses. However, in the following two quotations from *La Musique Arabe, Volume 1*, p. 102, the term *emmelic* appears three times without parentheses or brackets. We conclude, therefore, that in these passages, Al-Fārābī refers directly to Ptolemy's classification of intervals, and indirectly to Ptolemy's theory of graduated consonance as discussed in Section 10.19.

82. *Ibid.*, pp. 101–102.

83. *Ibid.*, pp. 102–103.

84. *Ibid.*, p. 103.

85. See Section 10.20, Quotes IX and X.

86. Forster Translation: in *La Musique Arabe, Volume 1*, p. 103.

87. *Ibid.*, p. 103.

88. *La Musique Arabe, Volume 1*, pp. 103–114.

89. *Ibid.*, p. 120, 122.

90. Forster Translation: in *La Musique Arabe, Volume 1*, pp. 118–119.

91. Note carefully that the fret requirements of the *strong conjunct moderate genus* do *not* apply to all other genera in the lower "octave" of the *'ūd*. For example, the *strong conjunct firm genus* — $^{10}/_{9}$, $^{11}/_{10}$, $^{12}/_{11}$ — requires three frets in the *disjunct system*, three frets in the *conjunct system*, and five frets in the *'second disjunct system'*.

92. El-Hefny, M., Translator (1931). *Ibn Sīnā's Musiklehre* [Ibn Sīnā's teaching on music]. Ph.D. dissertation printed by Otto Hellwig, Berlin, Germany.

93. (A) Forster Translation: in *La Musique Arabe, Volume 2*, pp. 234–235.

(B) *Studies in Oriental Musical Instruments, Second Series*, pp. 54–55.

Here Farmer gives an English translation of Ibn Sīnā's *'ūd* tuning in the *Kitāb al-shifā'*.

94. Forster Translation: in *La Musique Arabe, Volume 2*, pp. 235–237.

95. See Section 11.52.

96. Forster Translation: in *La Musique Arabe, Volume 2*, pp. 238–239.

See Sections 3.7 and 3.11 for discussions on the l.r. → f.r. notation.

97. See Section 10.6.

98. Forster Translation: in *La Musique Arabe, Volume 2*, p. 145.

99. *La Musique Arabe, Volume 2*, p. 147.

100. Forster Translation: in *La Musique Arabe, Volume 2*, p. 148.

101. *La Musique Arabe, Volume 2*, pp. 149–150.

102. Forster Translation: in *La Musique Arabe, Volume 2*, p. 150.

103. *The Dastgāh Concept in Persian Music* (1965), p. 43.

104. Forster Translation: in *La Musique Arabe, Volume 2*, pp. 119–121.

In Section 10.31, I cite a passage in which Al-Fārābī describes the arithmetic division of a "tone" into four "quarter-tones."

105. Forster Translation: in *Ibn Sīnā's Musiklehre* [Ibn Sīnā's teaching on music], p. 62.

106. See Section 10.20, Quote XI.

107. *An Annotated Glossary of Arabic Musical Terms*, p. 213.

108. Forster Translation: in *La Musique Arabe, Volume 2*, pp. 239–243.

109. (A) *The Dastgāh Concept in Persian Music* (1965), p. 25.

(B) *The Dastgāh Concept in Persian Music* (1990), p. 15.

110. (A) *The Dastgāh Concept in Persian Music* (1965), pp. 25–27, 42–44.

(B) *The Dastgāh Concept in Persian Music* (1990), pp. 15–16, 25–26.

111. (A) *The Dastgāh Concept in Persian Music* (1965), p. 44.

(B) *The Dastgāh Concept in Persian Music* (1990), p. 26.

112. (A) *The Dastgāh Concept in Persian Music* (1965), p. 44.

(B) *The Dastgāh Concept in Persian Music* (1990), p. 26.

113. *The Dastgāh Concept in Persian Music* (1990), p. 26.

114. *Ibid.*

115. *Ibid.*

116. (A) *The Dastgāh Concept in Persian Music* (1990), p. 17.

(B) *The Dastgāh Concept in Persian Music* (1965), p. 29.

117. (A) *The Dastgāh Concept in Persian Music* (1990), p. 18.

(B) *The Dastgāh Concept in Persian Music* (1965), p. 28.

118. *The Dastgāh Concept in Persian Music* (1990), p. 19.

119. *Ibid.*, pp. 20–21.

120. The musical examples in these two texts are not completely consistent. Where there are minor differences, I utilized Farhat's dissertation.

121. Forster Translation: in *La Musique Arabe, Volume 1*, p. 242.

122. See Section 10.36.

123. Forster Translation: in *La Musique Arabe, Volume 1*, pp. 242–243.

124. See Sections 3.13 and 3.15.

125. Forster Translation: in *La Musique Arabe, Volume 1*, p. 245.

126. *Ibid.*, pp. 246–249.

127. See Section 11.60.

128. Forster Translation: in *La Musique Arabe, Volume 1*, pp. 250–251.

129. *Ibid.*, p. 249.

130. *Ibid.*, p. 253.

131. *La Musique Arabe, Volume 1*, p. 251, 254.

132. (A) Forster Translation: in *La Musique Arabe, Volume 3*, pp. 110–113.

(B) *New Oxford History of Music, Volume 1: The Music of Islam*, p. 463.

133. See Section 10.19, for detailed discussions on Ptolemy's classifications of intervals.

134. Forster Translation: in *La Musique Arabe, Volume 3*, p. 115.

135. *Studies in Oriental Musical Instruments, Second Series*, p. 49.

136. Forster Translation: in *La Musique Arabe, Volume 3*, p. 221, pp. 224–229.

137. See also Figure 11.73, and Table 11.39.

138. See Section 11.69.

139. (A) *La Musique Arabe, Volume 3*, pp. 116–117.

(B) *Ibid.*, p. 238.

140. *Ibid.*, p. 238.

141. *Ibid.*, p. 288.

142. *An Annotated Glossary of Arabic Musical Terms*, p. 72.

143. *La Musique Arabe, Volume 3*, p. 119.

144. *Ibid.*, pp. 337–343.

145. *La Musique Arabe, Volume 3*, pp. 376–379.

146. Farmer, H.G. (1965). The old Arabian melodic modes, p. 101. *Journal of the Royal Asiatic Society*, Parts 3 & 4, pp. 99–102.

147. *A History of Arabian Music*, p. 197.

148. *La Musique Arabe, Volume 3*, pp. 388–392.

149. *An Annotated Glossary of Arabic Musical Terms*, p. 23.

150. *La Musique Arabe, Volume 3*, p. 388.

151. *An Annotated Glossary of Arabic Musical Terms*, p. 310.

152. *Ibid.*, p. 213, 278.

153. Forster Translation: in *La Musique Arabe, Volume 3*, p. 377.

154. *Ibid.*, p. 389.

155. (A) Signell, K.L. (1973). *The Turkish 'Makam' System in Contemporary Theory and Practice.* Ph.D. dissertation printed and distributed by University Microfilms, Inc., Ann Arbor, Michigan.

(B) Signell, K.L. (1977). *Makam: Modal Practice in Turkish Art Music.* Da Capo Press, New York, New York, 1986.

These two texts are almost identical in content. However, because the latter is a little more complete, I refer to it exclusively.

156. *Makam: Modal Practice in Turkish Art Music*, p. 27.

157. *Ibid.*, p. 24.

158. *Ibid.*, p. 27.

Notice that many other enharmonic versions of the 24-tone scale are possible. For example, one could notate $C\sharp_4$ as $D\flat_4 \approx 5$ commas below D; that is, since 9 commas − 5 commas = 4 commas, $C\sharp_4 = D\flat_4$.

159. *An Annotated Glossary of Arabic Musical Terms*, p. 169.

160. *Makam: Modal Practice in Turkish Art Music*, pp. 48–49.

161. *An Annotated Glossary of Arabic Musical Terms.* Each Arabic word is defined on the appropriate page.

162. *Makam: Modal Practice in Turkish Art Music*, p. 31.

163. *Ibid.*, pp. 32–33.

164. *Ibid.*, p. 24.

165. *Ibid.*, p. 49.

166. *Ibid.*, p. 87.

167. *Ibid.*, p. 74(a).

168. *Ibid.*, pp. 74–76.

169. *Ibid.*, p. 36.

170. *Ibid.*, pp. 34–35.

The order of the *maqāmāt* shown in my text is not the same as in Signell's book and dissertation. Refer to Table 11.50, and note that I changed the sequence according to Ṣafī Al-Dīn's *shudūd.* In other words, given the numerical order of Ṣafī Al-Dīn's *shudūd* in Column 1, the *maqāmāt* in Column 2 are closest in musical content. To construct Signell's order of *maqāmāt*, rearrange my numbers in the following sequence: 1, 2, 3, 4, 9, 6, 7, 10, 13, 11, 12, 8, 5.

171. See Section 11.81.

172. Marcus, S.L. (1989). *Arab Music Theory in the Modern Period*, p. 681, 455. Ph.D. dissertation printed and distributed by University Microfilms, Inc., Ann Arbor, Michigan.

173. See Section 11.11.

174. See Sections 10.32–10.33.

175. In Figure 11.49, the seven neutral tones are D𝄳, E𝄳, G𝄳, A𝄳, C𝄳, F𝄳|, A𝄲|. The latter two tones occur on Fret 5 of the *Zīr* and *Ḥādd*, respectively. Observe that unlike traditional 17-tone *ʿūd*s, Al-Fārābī's 22-tone *ʿūd* includes two "neutral sevenths": F–E𝄳| and B♭–A𝄳|. Consequently, we also find the "neutral seventh" C–B𝄳 between the open *Bamm* and Fret 1 of the *Mathnā*. The reason why his *ʿūd* includes B𝄳, E𝄳|, and A𝄳| is that the lower and upper "octaves" of this instrument are identical.

176. In Figure 11.62, the seven neutral tones are D𝄳, E𝄳, G𝄳, A𝄳, C𝄳, F𝄳|, A𝄲|.

177. See Figure 11.76.

178. *La Musique Arabe, Volume 5*, p. 3.

179. *Ibid.*, p. 3.

180. *Ibid.*, p. 3, 45.

181. See Section 10.5.

182. *La Musique Arabe, Volume 5*, p. 7.

183. *Ibid.*

184. This scale consists of two identical conjunct tetrachords, followed by an interval of disjunction, or interval ratios $9/8$, $9/8$, $256/243$, $9/8$, $9/8$, $256/243$, $9/8$. We may interpret this scale as Philolaus' original tetrachord: $256/243$, $9/8$, $9/8$ (see Figure 10.9) as it occurs between G–G$^{\prime}$ of the Greater Perfect System. The Greeks referred to this scale as the Hypophrygian Mode (see Figure 10.4).

185. Forster Translation: in *La Musique Arabe, Volume 5*, p. 45.

186. *La Musique Arabe, Volume 5*, p. 7.

187. Forster Translation: in *La Musique Arabe, Volume 5*, p. 82.

188. (A) Smith, E., Translator (1847). *A Treatise on Arab Music*, by Mīkhā'īl Mashāqah. *Journal of the American Oriental Society* **I**, No. 3, pp. 173–217. Boston, Massachusetts.

(B) Ronzevalle, P.L., Translator (1913). *Un Traité de Musique Arabe Moderne*, by Mīkhā'īl Mashāqah. *Mélanges de la Faculté Orientale* **VI**, pp. 1–120. Université Saint-Joseph, Beirut, Lebanon.

The latter translation contains Mashāqah's Arabic text with commentary by Ronzevalle.

189. See Sections 9.1–9.2 and 9.8.

190. *Arab Music Theory in the Modern Period*, p. 70.

191. (A) *Ibid.*

(B) *A Treatise on Arab Music*, p. 211.

192. *Arab Music Theory in the Modern Period*, p. 73, pp. 324–325.

193. *Ibid.*, p. 88.

194. *Arab Music Theory in the Modern Period*, Chapter II.

In this chapter, Marcus describes the modern derivation of this scale.

195. *Ibid.*, p. 105.

Marcus states that Mashāqah did not include two tones — B𝄲/C𝄳, and G𝄳 — in his description of 95 modes.

196. *The Nature of the Musical Art of Islamic Culture*, p. 67.

197. Touma, H.H. (1996). *The Music of the Arabs*, pp. 25–27. Amadeus Press, Portland, Oregon.

198. *Arab Music Theory in the Modern Period*, p. 106.

199. Sadie, S., Editor (1984). *The New Grove Dictionary of Musical Instruments, Volume 3*, p. 690. Macmillan Press Limited, London, England.

200. (A) *Arab Music Theory in the Modern Period*, pp. 198–199.

(B) Racy, A.J. (1978). "Music." In *The Genius of Arab Civilization*, 2nd ed., J.R. Hayes, Editor, p. 131. MIT Press, Cambridge, Massachusetts, 1983.

201. *Arab Music Theory in the Modern Period*, p. 200.

202. Racy, A.J. (1977). *Musical Change and Commercial Recording in Egypt, 1904–1932*, p. 75. Ph.D. dissertation printed and distributed by University Microfilms, Inc., Ann Arbor, Michigan.

On pp. 220–320, Racy includes detailed discussions and transcriptions of commercial recordings. In particular, pp. 319–320 give examples of modulations in ten of these recordings.

203. (A) *Arab Music Theory in the Modern Period*, p. 476, 497.

(B) *An Annotated Glossary of Arabic Musical Terms*, p. 21, 125.

204. *Arab Music Theory in the Modern Period*, p. 377.

205. *Ibid.*, p. 378.

206. *Ibid.*

207. (A) Marcus, S.L. (1992). Modulation in Arab music: Documenting oral concepts, performance rules and strategies, p. 176. *Ethnomusicology* **36**, No. 2, pp. 171–195.

(B) *Arab Music Theory in the Modern Period*, pp. 377–396.

208. *Ibid.*, pp. 842–844.

209. (A) *Ibid.*

(B) *La Musique Arabe, Volume 5*, pp. 117–333.

(C) *The Nature of the Musical Art of Islamic Culture*, pp. 95–96.

(D) *Musical Change and Commercial Recording in Egypt, 1904–1932*, pp. 319–320.

(E) *The Music of the Arabs*, pp. 29–36.

210. *Arab Music Theory in the Modern Period*, p. 301.

211. (A) *Ibid.*, p. 349.

(B) *Ethnomusicology* **36**, No. 2, p. 173.

212. *Arab Music Theory in the Modern Period*, p. 350.

213. (A) *The Nature of the Musical Art of Islamic Culture*, pp. 91–92.

(B) *Arab Music Theory in the Modern Period*, pp. 310–311, p. 470.

214. *Arab Music Theory in the Modern Period*, pp. 504–505.

On p. 561, Marcus states that ʿAbdullah Al-Kurdī is a teacher of music theory, and a player and teacher of the modern *qānūn*.

215. See Section 11.77, Table 11.48.

216. *Arab Music Theory in the Modern Period*, p. 762.

217. *Ibid.*, p. 505.

218. *Ibid.*, p. 561.

219. *Ethnomusicology* **36**, No. 2, p. 175.

The *nāy* is a vertical flute made of cane or wood, with an open blowhole at the upper end. Similar to the notched embouchure hole of the Japanese *shakuhachi*, a player covers most of the opening with the lips, and blows an air stream against a beveled rim.

220. *Iran: Musique Persane*, Ocora Radio France recording, C-559008.

221. *The Dastgāh Concept in Persian Music* (1990), p. 113.

The Dastgāh Concept in Persian Music (1965), p. 254.

222. *The Dastgāh Concept in Persian Music* (1990), p. 89, 194.

The Dastgāh Concept in Persian Music (1965), pp. 195–196.

223. *Oud: Saïd Chraïbi*, Cinq Planètes recording, CP-10196.

224. *Iraq: L'art du ʿūd*, Ocora Radio France recording, C-580068.

225. *Turquie: Archives de la musique turque* (1) and (2), Ocora Radio France recordings, C-560081 and C-560082, respectively.

226. *AL KINDI: Musique Classique Arabe*, ETHNIC recording, B-6735.

227. *The Music of Islam, Volume Two: Music of the South Sinai Bedouins*, Celestial Harmonies, #13141-2.

228. Shiloah, A. (1972). The *simsimīyya:* A stringed instrument of the Red Sea area. *Asian Music* **IV**, No. 1, pp. 15–26.

On p. 19, Shiloah gives the following four *simsimīyya* tunings for five open strings:

1. c d e f g
2. c d e♭ f g
3. c d e𝄳 f g
4. a b c𝄲 d e

12 / ORIGINAL INSTRUMENTS

Acoustic music is the most difficult music. Building musical instruments from the ground up is an expression of freedom and, therefore, an expression of imagination. Nothing about this art is hewn in stone. The creative builder examines all aspects of musical instrument construction, and on a case-by-case basis decides which traditions to keep, and which to throw out.

I build because the tunings and timbres I want to hear do not exist on store shelves. Robinson Crusoe built because he had no choice. And yet, his creations also had no critics, and so his imagination became his life. Often when I hike through forests or climb mountains, I am reminded that only man knows what time it is. When I enter Crusoe's world, or when in building an instrument time ceases to exist, I live with the knowledge that success is only a function of thought, work, and patience.

The desire for perfection is the juggernaut of creativity. All my instruments are flawed. A bar may not ring as long as another bar; a canon bridge may be too high or too low; or a tone hole may be too wide or too narrow. I know where all the flaws are, and could find many more. But what is the point? The only thing that matters is to build and to make a music that is sustainable in time. I was born a musician, and have built musical instruments since 1975. In the words of Walt Whitman (1819–1892), "I . . . begin, hoping to cease not till death."

I also hope that this book and Chapters 12–13 will inspire others to think critically about acoustic music, and perhaps to build an original instrument or two. One of the happiest moments of my life is to finish a project, step back, and declare in a state of complete surprise, "I'd like to meet the person who built this instrument."

Stringed Instruments

CHRYSALIS

12.1

The Chrysalis in Plate 1, my first concert-size instrument, was inspired by a large, round, stone-hewn Aztec calendar. I asked myself, "What if there was a musical instrument in the shape of a wheel? And what if this wheel had strings for spokes, could spin, and when played, would sound like the wind?" As described below, the Chrysalis wheel has two sides, or two circular soundboards, covered by eighty-two strings on each side.

Figure 12.1(A) shows that a steel axle (a) passes through the center of an octagonal oak hub (b). This hub acts as the central structural component of the wheel. Eight birch spokes (c) radiate from the hub to the centers of eight maple dowel spacers (d), which in turn hold two birch plywood rings (e). Figure 12.1(B) illustrates two Sitka spruce soundboards (f) glued to the rings. The rings

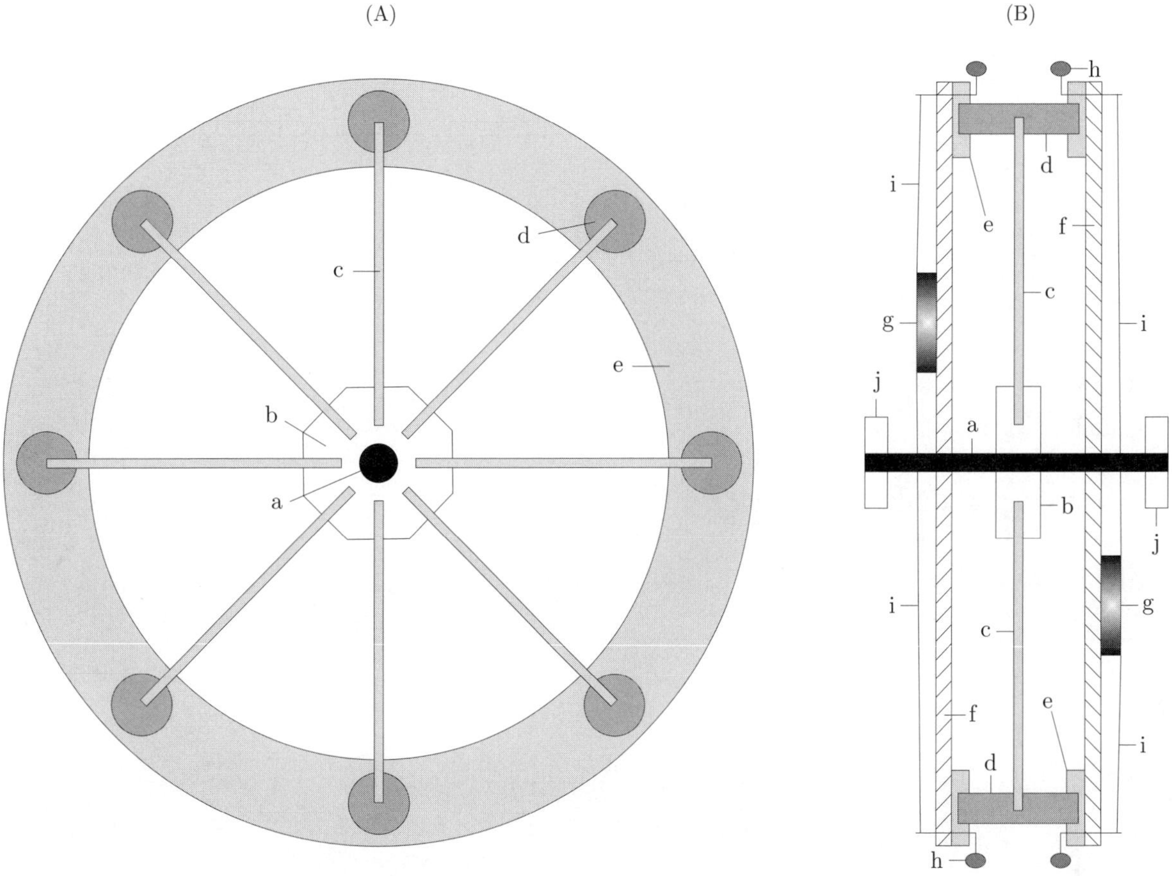

Figure 12.1 Parts and construction of the Chrysalis wheel. (A) This longitudinal cross-section shows a steel axle (a) that passes through the center of an octagonal hub (b). This hub acts as the central structural component of the wheel. Eight spokes (c) radiate from the hub to the centers of eight dowel spacers (d), which in turn hold two plywood rings (e). (B) This transverse cross-section illustrates two soundboards (f) glued to the rings, and two aluminum bridges (g) fastened to the soundboards. Tuning gears (h) encircle both soundboards. From here, long and short steel strings (i) pass to the bridges. Two sealed ball bearings (j) support the wheel at the ends of the steel axle. These bearings enable the performer to turn the wheel in either direction. (Not to scale.)

reinforce the edges of the soundboards while leaving the inner soundboard surface areas unobstructed for maximum resonance. The soundboards consist of several jointed strips of spruce 6.0 in. wide by $\frac{1}{4}$ in. thick. On the back sides, spruce ribs glued against the grain give the soundboards structural support. Furthermore, two bridges (g) fastened at off-center locations on the soundboards provide the instrument with varying string lengths. The original rosewood bridges exploded from the force of the strings; so, I replaced them with aluminum bridges. I located the bridges directly opposite each other, which enables the performer to reach both long and short strings from the playing position to the left of the wheel; this configuration of the bridges also balances the motion of the wheel. Eighty-two tuning gears (h) encircle each soundboard. From here, steel strings (i) pass to the bridges. Note that the two longest strings go through holes in the axle. Two sealed ball bearings (j) support the wheel at the ends of the axle. These bearings enable the performer to turn the wheel in either direction. Finally, the wave-like stand — inspired by my love of the ocean and many years of surfing along the coasts of California and Mexico — affords maximum access to the strings; at any given position of the wheel, all but a few strings are within reach of the performer.

CHRYSALIS

Built: 1975–1976

Dimensions		
Total number of strings		164
Longest string		20.0 in.
Shortest string		8.0 in.
Wheel diameter		36¾ in.
Wheel width		5.0 in.
Length of stand		61.0 in.
Height of stand		41¾ in.
Width of stand		10½ in.
Height from floor to top of wheel		57½ in.
Extension of wheel beyond stand:	At top	16½ in.
	At bottom	9.0 in.
Aluminum bridges		7.0 in. × ⅝ in.
Steel axle		1.0 in. × 8⅜ in.

HARMONIC/MELODIC CANON

12.2

The Harmonic/Melodic Canon in Plate 2 essentially consists of a 6-sided box. Figure 12.2 shows a Sitka spruce soundboard (a) with ten spruce ribs (b). Channels cut into end pieces (c) secure the soundboard without adhesives. Consequently, one can easily remove the soundboard for repairs or replacement. I made the end pieces from a very dense black plastic called acetal, also known as Delrin. This material is extremely stable. Because it does not expand or contract very much due to climatic changes, the H/M Canon stays in tune for a very long time. The end pieces are fastened to a ¾ in. solid birch plywood base (d), which, like the Delrin, is a very dense and stable material. Two teak sides (e) enclose the canon's resonating chamber. However, they do not contribute to the structural stability of the instrument. If one removes the sides to gain access to the space between the soundboard and base, the instrument does not go out of tune.

I made the V-shaped tuning gear brackets (f) from cold rolled steel. After heating a length of bar stock with a welding torch, I bent it around a steel form to give it the triangular shape. I then drilled the mounting holes, and the holes for the tuning gears (g). The posts of the tuning gears fit through holes in black anodized strips of aluminum fastened to the inside surfaces of the brackets. These strips minimize unwanted motion of the posts caused by the tension of the strings.

At the apex of each bracket, I attached a stainless steel turnbuckle (h), like the kind found on sailboats; I secured the other end of the buckle to the base of the canon. When one turns and tensions the buckle, it pulls the bracket in a downward direction toward the base. Once locked in place, the buckle prevents the bracket from bending in an upward direction when the strings are tensioned. This device also greatly contributes to the tuning stability of the instrument.

A Delrin strip (i) protects the teak veneer that covers the exterior surface of the left end piece. Finally, I drove hitch pins (j) into the right end piece, and stretched strings (k) from here to the tuning gears.

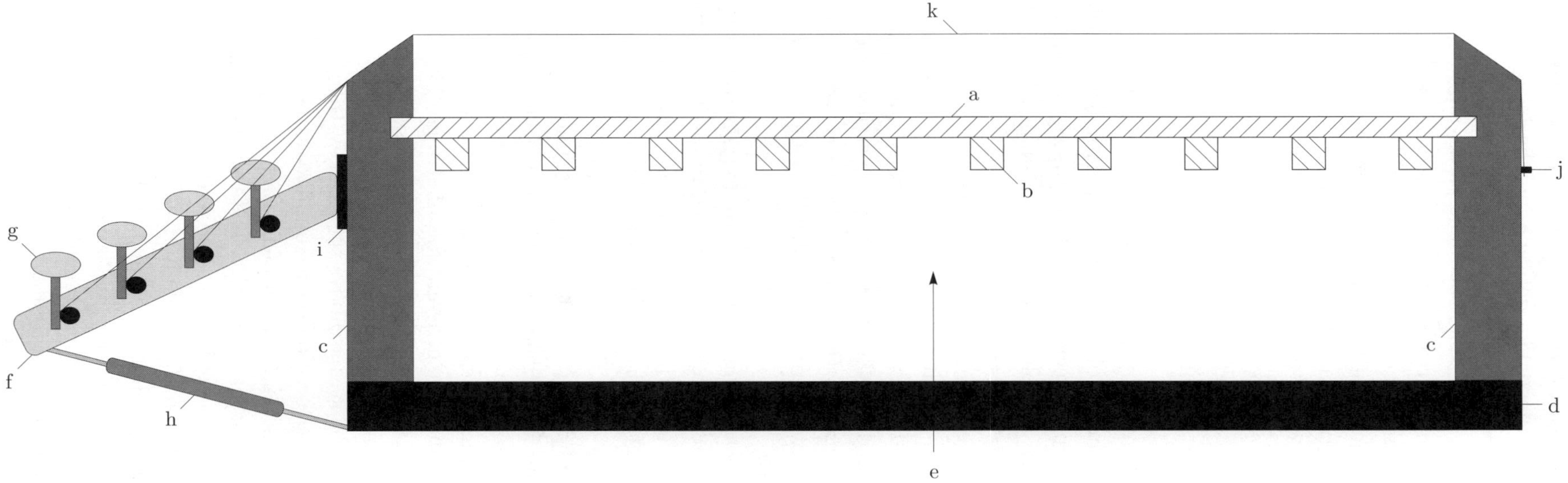

Figure 12.2 Parts and construction of the Harmonic/Melodic Canon. This longitudinal cross-section shows a Sitka spruce soundboard (a) with ten ribs (b). Channels cut into two Delrin end pieces (c) secure the soundboard without adhesives. The end pieces are fastened to a solid birch plywood base (d). Two teak sides (e) enclose the canon's resonating chamber. Six V-shaped steel brackets (f) hold the tuning gears (g). At the apex of each bracket, I attached a stainless steel turnbuckle (h), and secured the other end of the buckle to the base of the canon; the buckle prevents the bracket from bending in an upward direction when the strings are tensioned. A Delrin strip (i) protects the teak veneer that covers the exterior surface of the left end piece. Finally, I drove hitch pins (j) into the right end piece, and stretched strings (k) from here to the tuning gears. (Not to scale.)

Plate 2 shows that I engraved the soundboard with one hundred lines, or one line every 10.0 mm. These lines eliminate the need to juggle a ruler while determining the locations of bridges. Ten columns of holes on the soundboard indicate the locations of ten ribs beneath the soundboard. As explained in Section 12.3 and illustrated in Figure 12.3, each hole passes through the soundboard, the upper portion of a rib, and terminates in a threaded insert located in the lower portion of the rib. One uses these inserts to secure the infinitely adjustable canon bridge assemblies to the soundboard. Since there are forty-eight strings, the soundboard has four hundred and eighty holes.

All open strings of the H/M Canon are tuned to G_3 at 196.0 cps. As calculated in Section 2.8, each string exerts 78.98 pounds-force (lbf), which means that the H/M Canon withstands a total of 3,791.01 lbf, or a little less than 2 tons of force.

12.3

The canon as described in the works of Ptolemy (see Section 10.19) and Al-Jurjānī (see Section 11.52) represents the mathematical embodiment of tuning theory. Although this instrument has a noteworthy history, it did not develop into a precise musical instrument because of a persistent mechanical problem: rattling bridges! When one places a triangular-shaped bridge under a string, and then plucks the string, the applied force causes the bridge to rattle against the soundboard. To avoid this difficulty, it is possible to make a long bridge, so when one plucks a given string the other strings hold the bridge in place. Even so, after much playing such a bridge begins to creep due to the vibratory motion of the strings. To prevent the bridge from moving, it becomes necessary to increase the downbearing force (or downward force) that the strings exert on the bridge. An increase in the height of the bridge increases the strings' deflection, which in turn increases this vertical force. However, because the downbearing force effectively increases the tension of the strings, all the stopped strings sound sharp.

To qualify as a precision instrument, a canon must satisfy two mathematical requirements. For example, if a canon bridge stops the right side of a string at length ratio ⅔, then the right section *must* sound a "fifth" above the open string, or frequency ratio 3⁄2. Also, since this bridge stops the left side of the string at complementary length ratio ⅓, the left section *must* sound an "octave and a fifth" above the open string, or frequency ratio 3⁄1. (See Sections 3.11 and 3.13.) Now, suppose that a canon bridge is too high, so that the "fifth" on the right side sounds 30.0 ¢ sharp, and the "octave and a fifth" on the left side sounds 50.0 ¢ sharp. Under such circumstances, we would be correct to call this instrument a kind of *zither* (see Section 11.3), but incorrect to call it a canon.

A fundamental principle of canon tuning states that the mass density of the string material, the string diameter, and the string tension must be constant for all strings. Therefore, the only acceptable variable is string length. To achieve this requirement, an accurately built canon must have bridges that are only slightly higher than the strings above the soundboard.

If we rule out the downbearing force of the strings above the bridges, then the only alternative is to design a mechanical device that exerts a force onto the soundboard below the bridges. Since a canon should have moveable bridges for the exploration of myriad tuning systems, simply gluing bridges to the soundboard is not a meaningful alternative. Instead, the force below the bridges should act over a relatively wide surface area to facilitate the unrestricted placement of bridges.

Figure 12.3 shows a longitudinal cross-section of the infinitely adjustable canon bridge assembly. Ribs (a) provide structural support for the soundboard (b), and anchorage for threaded inserts (c). The latter are called knife thread inserts because on the outside they have sharp threads designed for turning into wood, and on the inside, standard machine screw threads. Above the soundboard, the bridge carriage (d) consists of ½ in. square aluminum tubing with rounded edges. In Plate 2, notice a long slot milled into the top side of each carriage. Two socket head cap screws (e) pass all the way

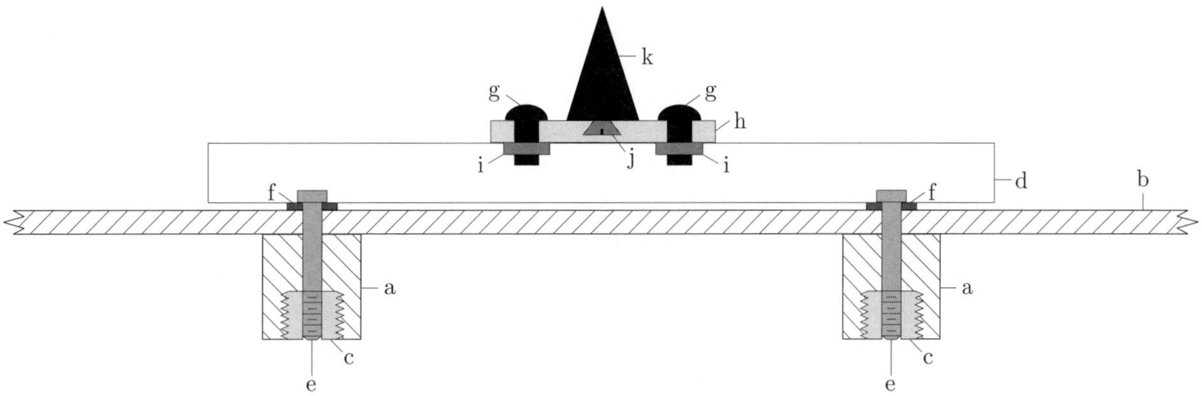

Figure 12.3 Parts and construction of the infinitely adjustable canon bridge assembly. This longitudinal cross-section shows that ribs (a) provide structural support for the soundboard (b), and anchorage for threaded inserts (c). In Plate 2, notice a long slot milled into the top side of the bridge carriage (d). Two socket head cap screws (e) pass all the way through this slot and into two holes in the bottom of the carriage; from here, they go through synthetic washers (f), the soundboard, the ribs, and finally screw into the inserts. Two round head cap screws (g), designed to hold the brass plate (h) against the carriage, slide back and forth in the long slot. Two nuts (i), which have a close fit inside the carriage, will not turn when one tightens or loosens the cap screws. Finally, a flat head countersunk tapping screw (j) fastens the Delrin bridge (k) to the brass plate. (Not to scale.)

through this slot and into two holes in the bottom of the carriage; from here, they go through the synthetic washers (f), the soundboard, the upper portion of a rib, and finally screw into the inserts in the lower portion of the rib. This secures the carriage to the soundboard. The washers consist of a material called E.A.R., which is an acronym for *energy absorbing resin.* I used this material to dampen the high mode frequencies produced by the metal parts of the assembly, and to prevent the carriage from marring the finish of the soundboard. Two round head cap screws (g), designed to hold the brass plate (h) against the carriage, slide back and forth in the long slot. Two nuts (i), which have a close fit inside the carriage, will not turn when one tightens or loosens the cap screws. Finally, a flat head countersunk tapping screw (j) fastens the Delrin bridge (k) to the brass plate. By simply securing the bridge assembly anywhere on the soundboard, sliding the bridge to a desired location along the carriage, and tightening the cap screws, a musician may achieve any tuning imaginable. For this reason, I like to refer to the Harmonic/Melodic Canon as a “limited form of infinity.”

On the H/M Canon, the adjustable bridge assembly works for all strings except the first string. For String 1, the bottom of the bridge slides in an aluminum slot in the shape of a dovetail track. A vertical slit divides the lower portion of the bridge into two symmetrical halves. When one turns the knob, a machine screw widens this slit and, thereby, pushes the bottom sides of the bridge against the angled edges of the dovetail track. This enables one to lock the bridge anywhere under String 1. After tuning String 1, a musician slides its bridge to a location in line with another bridge on the canon soundboard, locks it in place, and then tunes the other string in unison to String 1.

The H/M Canon is as much a musical instrument as a scientific instrument. Since the bridge assemblies fasten directly to the soundboard, (1) rattling bridges do not exist, (2) every string has its own bridge, and (3) the tuning is accurate on both sides of the bridges. However, a tuning accuracy limit does exist. As strings become shorter than 200.0 mm ($\approx$ 8 in.), they sound progressively sharp. The cause for this imperfection is string deflection. Every bridge must deflect its string to some extent; otherwise, the string does not make full contact with the bridge, which results in a weak tone because the transfer of mechanical energy from the vibrating string to the bridge is inefficient.

Now, when one moves a bridge closer to either end of the string, the angle of deflection of the string between the end piece and bridge increases. As the angle of deflection increases, the downbearing force that the string exerts on the bridge increases as well. Consequently, the vertical force has a greater sharpening effect on short strings than on long strings. To minimize this tendency, I intentionally gave the soundboard of the H/M Canon a length of 1000.0 mm plus 4.0 mm; that is, both the left and right sides of the soundboard are 502.0 mm long. For all bridged strings, and especially for short strings with lengths from 250.0 mm to 200.0 mm, this added length — called *string compensation* — counteracts the sharpening effect of string deflection. (See Section 10.31.) But for strings shorter than 200.0 mm, string compensation no longer produces favorable results.

HARMONIC/MELODIC CANON

Built: 1976
Rebuilt: 1981, 1987

Dimensions	
Total number of strings	48
String length	1000.0 mm
String compensation on each side of the soundboard	2.0 mm
Length of canon	41 9/16 in.
Height of canon	5 1/2 in.
Width of canon	40 5/8 in.
Height of left and right end pieces	6 3/4 in.
Thickness of left and right end pieces	1.0 in.
Thickness of soundboard	3/8 in.
Thickness of plywood base	3/4 in.
Length of stand	44.0 in.
Upper height of stand	47.0 in.
Lower height of stand	25.0 in.
Upper width of stand	43 5/8 in.
Lower width of stand	36 7/8 in.
Height from floor to string on upper side of canon	51 1/2 in.
Height from floor to string on lower side of canon	31 3/4 in.
Length of triangular tuning gear bracket	7.0 in.
Height of triangular tuning gear bracket	3/4 in.
Width at base of triangular tuning gear bracket	6 1/4 in.
Height of strings above soundboard	1 5/8 in.
Height of bridges above soundboard	1 7/8 in.

~ 12.4 ~

In 1976, I wrote a composition entitled *Song of Myself: Intoned Poems of Walt Whitman.* "Song of Myself" is the title given by Walt Whitman to the third book of his *Leaves of Grass*, which contains fifty-two poems. I chose eleven poems for this composition.

I scored *Song of Myself* for voice, Chrysalis, and Harmonic/Melodic Canon. This composition represents a departure from the usual practice of combining instrumental music with the language of poetry. At the heart of this composition and its performance is the oral tradition of the storyteller who, since the beginning of poetry and music, has relied on a limited stage set in the fulfillment of his art. He lives today as then to inspire and ignite the imagination of his audience. He rejoices in the conviction of his performance because it is founded on clarity of speech, so that anyone may understand and sense the meaning of the poet's few precious words as they combine with the sounds of the instruments.

Standard musical terms (plainsong, chant, inflected speech, etc.) left me discontent in describing or directing the motivating forces of this musical setting of Whitman's poems. I finally chose the verb to *intone* because I sense within it a quality of restraint. Musicians approaching a set of great poems should always exercise restraint; the poetry will not get any better with the music. Intoning means having and developing a sensitivity for pitch. The inflections of the human voice indicate emotions, reflections, and ideas, not only on stage but everywhere. Intimately connected to and inseparable from pitch is the rhythm, the speed, timing, and accentuation of the poetic line. Only after many months of reflection, and after having thoroughly memorized all the poems, did I approach the question of sound and music because I wanted to preserve as best I could Whitman's internal voice. In this context, the two musical instruments and their mathematical tunings are of secondary importance. I built them to explore in a scientific and aesthetic manner new musical resources. The poems come first: words, thoughts, ideas, and emotions intact.

The tuning of *Song of Myself* is in just intonation. Table 12.1 gives the tuning chart for the left and right sides of the Chrysalis, and Table 12.2, the tuning chart for the H/M Canon distributed over two facing pages. Prime factorization of the integers of the frequency ratios reveals utilization of all prime numbers from 2 through 13. Four additional ratios go beyond 13: $^{28}/_{17}$, $^{32}/_{17}$, and $^{20}/_{19}$ on the H/M Canon, and $^{19}/_{13}$ on the Chrysalis. Furthermore, I organized the charts to demonstrate the concept of *melodic modulation* by showing multiple interpretations of a given ratio when heard or calculated from two or more different tonal centers ($^{1}/_{1}$'s). A definition of what constitutes a "tonality" or "key" is here intentionally avoided. Within a given musical context, three sequential tones are enough to define a tonal center.

Open Strings 1 and 34 on the H/M Canon are tuned to C_3 at 130.0 cps, or to an "octave" below middle C_4 at 260.0 cps. "Double-octaves" at 520.0 cps may be found on the Chrysalis, Strings 18–21 left side, and Strings 29–31 right side. With the exception of "octaves," ratio $^{2}/_{1}$, "double-octaves," ratio $^{4}/_{1}$, . . . , above C_3, I simplified all other "octave" equivalents to ratios larger than $^{1}/_{1}$ and smaller than $^{2}/_{1}$. (See Section 9.4.) For example, in Table 12.2, Strings 15–16 on the left side are 200.0 mm long. Consequently, they produce modern length ratio $^{200.0\text{ mm}}/_{1000.0\text{ mm}} = {}^{1}/_{5}$, or frequency ratio $^{5}/_{1}$, which sounds the interval of "two octaves and a major third" above the fundamental, ratio $^{1}/_{1}$. This simplifies to frequency ratio $^{5}/_{4}$, or the interval of a "major third." (See Section 9.4.)

For the H/M Canon, I used steel music wire gage #10, 0.024 in., for all strings except String 34 (gage #14, 0.033 in.) and String 48 (gage #17, 0.039 in.). For the Chrysalis, I used gage #9, 0.022 in., right side, and gage #6, 0.016 in., left side.

I printed a First Edition of the score of *Song of Myself* in 1980, and an edited and corrected Second Edition in 2000. Tables 12.1 and 12.2 give the tuning charts as they appear in the Second Edition. The tables also show poetic lines in the composition that have distinct tonal centers. Table 12.1 indicates four different poems for voice and Chrysalis, and Table 12.2, five different poems for voice and H/M Canon, or a total number of nine poems. Two remaining poems — Whitman's Poem 1: "I celebrate myself..." and Poem 34: "Now I tell what I knew..." — are for voice only.

Table 12.1

CHRYSALIS

Left Side Tuning

Strings:	Ratios				
1-3:	1/1	(13/9)	375.6 cps	← "There is that in me....."	Poem 50
4-6:	9/8				
7-9:	6/5				
10-13:	16/13.............16/9				
14-17:	20/11				
18-21:	4/1	(4/1)	C_5 at 520.0 cps	← "I wish I could translate....."	Poem 6
22-25:	10/9				
26-29:	14/11.............56/33				
30-33:	3/2 ... 1/1	(3/2)	780.0 cps	← "I also say....."	Poem 18
34-36:	28/27				
37-39:	6/5..............54/35				
40-43:	5/4 ... 45/28				
44-48:	6/5 ... 54/35				
49-51:	7/5				
52-54:	13/11				
55-58:	35/33				
59-61:	1/1	(7/6)	606.7 cps	Poem 38 "I troop forth....." →	
62-64:	20/13				
65-67:	32/21				
68-70:	11/9				
71-74:	7/6				
75-78:	12/11				
79-82:	21/20				
1-3:	1/1	(13/9)	375.6 cps	Poem 6 "It may be you transpire....." →	

Table 12.1
(continued)

CHRYSALIS

Right Side Tuning

Strings: Ratios

1-3: 1/1 (15/8) 243.8 cps ←——— "Something it swings on....." Poem 50

4-6: 7/5

7-8: 10/7

9-10: 19/13

11-13: 3/2

14-16: 20/13

17-18: 11/7

19-20: 5/3

21-22: 26/15

23-24: 16/9

25-26: 25/13

27-28: 2/1 (15/8) 487.6 cps

29-31: 16/15............1/1 (4/1) C_5 at 520.0 cps ←——— "I beat and pound....." Poem 18

32-36: 8/5 3/2

37-41: 5/3 25/16

42-45: 10/7...............3/2 ←——— "A child said....." Poem 6

46-49: 260/189 13/9

50-53: 320/273 16/13

54-57: 7/6

58-62: 1/1 (40/21) 495.2 cps

63-65: 32/21

66-68: 3/2

69-71: 27/20

72-73: 7/5

74-76: 40/27

77-79: 5/4

80-82: 6/5

Poem 38 "Enough....." ———→ 1-3: 1/1 (15/8) 243.8 cps

Table 12.2

	1	2-6	7	8	9-10	11-2	13-4	15-6	17	18	19	20	21	22	23	
													HARMONIC/MELODIC			
Strings:	1	2-6	7	8	9-10	11-2	13-4	15-6	17	18	19	20	21	22	23	
Right Side* m.m.	open	open	500	250	333.3	475	600	800	333.3	437.5	392.9	468.7	500	62.5	625	
	1/1	9/8	2/1	4/1	3/2	20/19	5/3	5/4	3/2	8/7	14/11	16/15	2/1	16/1	8/5	
	C_3	D_3	C_4	C_5									C_4	C_7		
Left Side m.m.			500	750	666.7	525	400	200**	666.7	562.5	607.1	531.3	500	937.5	375	
			2/1	4/3	3/2	40/21	5/4	5/4	3/2	16/9	28/17	32/17	2/1	16/15	4/3	
			C_4										C_4			
Poem 7:																
				3/2					9/8		21/11	8/5	3/2			
Poem 19:			2/1 C_4	4/3		20/19 40/21	5/3		3/2							← "This is the meal....."
							5/3	5/4	3/2				2/1 C_4			
		9/8		4/1 C_5	3/2	20/19										← "Do you guess....."
Poem 21:												24/17			6/5	"I am the poet....." →
									9/8		21/11	8/5 24/17	3/2			
Poem 51:						320/171	40/27		4/3		112/99		16/9		64/45	
									3/2				2/1 C_4			
		1/1 D_3	16/9	16/9	4/3	320/171	40/27	10/9								← "Will you speak....."
		1/1 D_3	16/9	32/27	4/3	320/189	10/9	10/9								
Poem 52:															8/5	
										15/14	105/88	2/1 $C\#_4$	15/8	1/1 $C\#_3$	3/2	

*Underlined frequency ratios occur on the right sides of the bridges.

**Strings shorter than 200 mm sound sharp of the indicated frequency ratios.

Table 12.2

(continued)

CANON I TUNING

24-5	26-8	29	30	31	32	33	34	35	36	37-9	40-2	43-5	46	47	48	
500 2/1 C_4	750 4/3	937.5 16/15	888.9 9/8	833.3 6/5	777.8 9/7	750 4/3	open 1/1 C_3	475 20/19	500 2/1 C_4	641 3/2 unison to 666.7	600 5/3	500 2/1 C_4	259.3 27/14	111.1 9/8	open 3/2 octave below 666.7	
500 2/1 C_4	250 4/1 C_5	62.5 16/1 C_7	111.1 9/8	166.7 3/2	222.2 9/8	250 4/1 C_5		525 40/21	500 2/1 C_4	359 27/20 octave above 740.7	400 5/4	500 2/1 C_4	740.7 27/20	888.9 9/8		
		8/5	27/16	9/5	27/14	2/1 F_3	3/2									← "Has any one supposed....."
	(2/1) F_3															← "Every kind for itself....."
	4/3		9/8				1/1 C_3	40/21								← "The kept-woman, sponger....."
3/2	(2/1) F_3										15/8					
3/2	2/1 F_3															← "Smile, O voluptuous....."
	32/27		1/1 D_3	16/15												← "The past and present wilt....."
	4/3		9/8				1/1 C_3	40/21								← "Do I contradict myself....."
2/1 C_4	4/1 C_5	16/1 C_7	9/8	3/2	9/8	4/1 C_5	1/1 C_3	40/21	2/1 C_4							← "The spotted hawk....."
15/8	5/4															← "I bequeath myself....."
										9/5	5/3	4/3	9/5	3/2	(1/1) G_2	"You will hardly know.....", "But I shall be....." →
										2/1 G_3	10/9	4/3			1/1 G_2	"And filter and fiber your blood....." →

12.5

Musical Examples 12.1 and 12.2 give the first two pages of poems for voice and Chrysalis, and voice and Harmonic/Melodic Canon, respectively. Because the tuning of the instruments and the intonation of the voice are more complex than 12-tone equal temperament, I wrote the entire score in tablature notation. The numbers in the score identify string numbers as shown in Tables 12.1 and 12.2. For all poems, the top staff of the score always indicates the voice part.

In Example 12.1, the middle staff represents the left-hand side, and the bottom staff, the right-hand side of the Chrysalis. A single number means play all the strings of a given group in glissando fashion. So, number 42 for the right hand means play Strings 42–45 in the time of one eighth note. The notation of the voice part follows the numbering and, therefore, the intonation of the strings. However, I decided not to specify "octave" ranges for the voice. A male voice would probably be most comfortable intoning these poems an "octave" below the strings. Throughout the score, I used three different verbs to describe the vocal part. *Intone* means enunciate the poetic line in the rhythm and on the pitch of the score. *Recite* means enunciate in the indicated rhythm, but on any pitch natural to the speaking voice. And *speak* means enunciate on the indicated pitch, but in any rhythm natural to the speaking voice. Furthermore, a dot to the left of a number in the top staff means intone the pitch of the string on the left side of the Chrysalis; no dot means intone the pitch of the string on the right side of the Chrysalis.

In Example 12.2, the organization of the lower two staffs is more complicated. On the H/M Canon, the middle staff carries the melodies and chords that predominate the musical material in the bottom staff. For this reason, the right and left hands play on both staffs. Both hands also play on both sides of the bridges. I avoided awkward hand crossings whenever possible; where some ambiguity arises, L for left hand and R for right hand appear in the score. On the H/M Canon, a dot to the left of a string number means play the indicated string on the left side of the bridge; no dot means play the string on the right side of the bridge.

BASS CANON

12.6

The parts and materials of the Bass Canon in Plate 3, including the infinitely adjustable canon bridge assemblies, are identical to those of the Harmonic/Melodic Canon. Since the open strings of the Bass Canon are tuned to G_2 at 98.0 cps, or an "octave" below the H/M Canon, I increased the lengths of these strings to 1200.0 mm (47.24 in.). To achieve this low frequency without resorting to thick and stiff plain steel strings, the Bass Canon requires thin and flexible wound strings. Because such strings are not available from commercial manufacturers, I built a string winding machine to make custom wound strings. See Section 12.7 for a detailed description of the String Winder.

When compared to the H/M Canon, the Bass Canon is different in three key respects. First, the twelve tuning gear brackets were made by a professional machinist on a computerized milling machine. Each bracket was milled from a rectangular plate of cold rolled steel. Second, to simplify length calculations, I engraved the soundboard of the Bass Canon with lines every 12.0 mm. Consequently, with respect to counting lines, the bridge locations of ratios on *both* the H/M Canon and the Bass Canon are the same. For example, on the H/M Canon ratio $\frac{3}{2}$ requires a bridge at

$$\frac{100.0 \text{ cm}}{\frac{3}{2}} = 66.7 \text{ cm}$$

Example 12.1

6

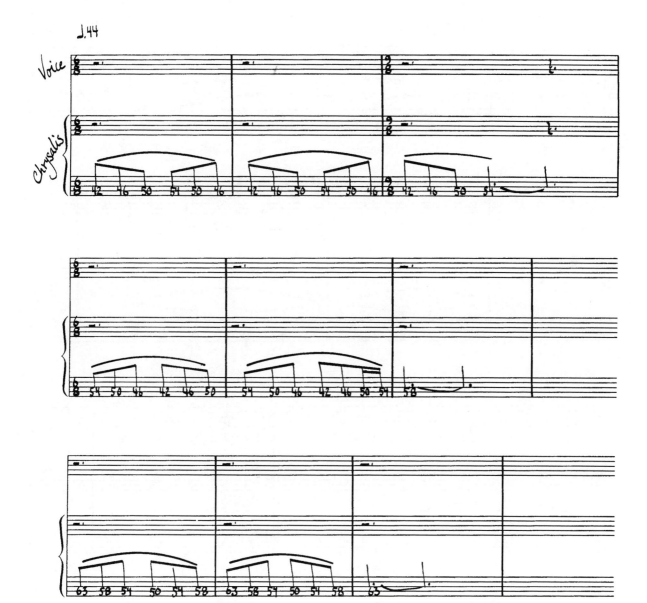

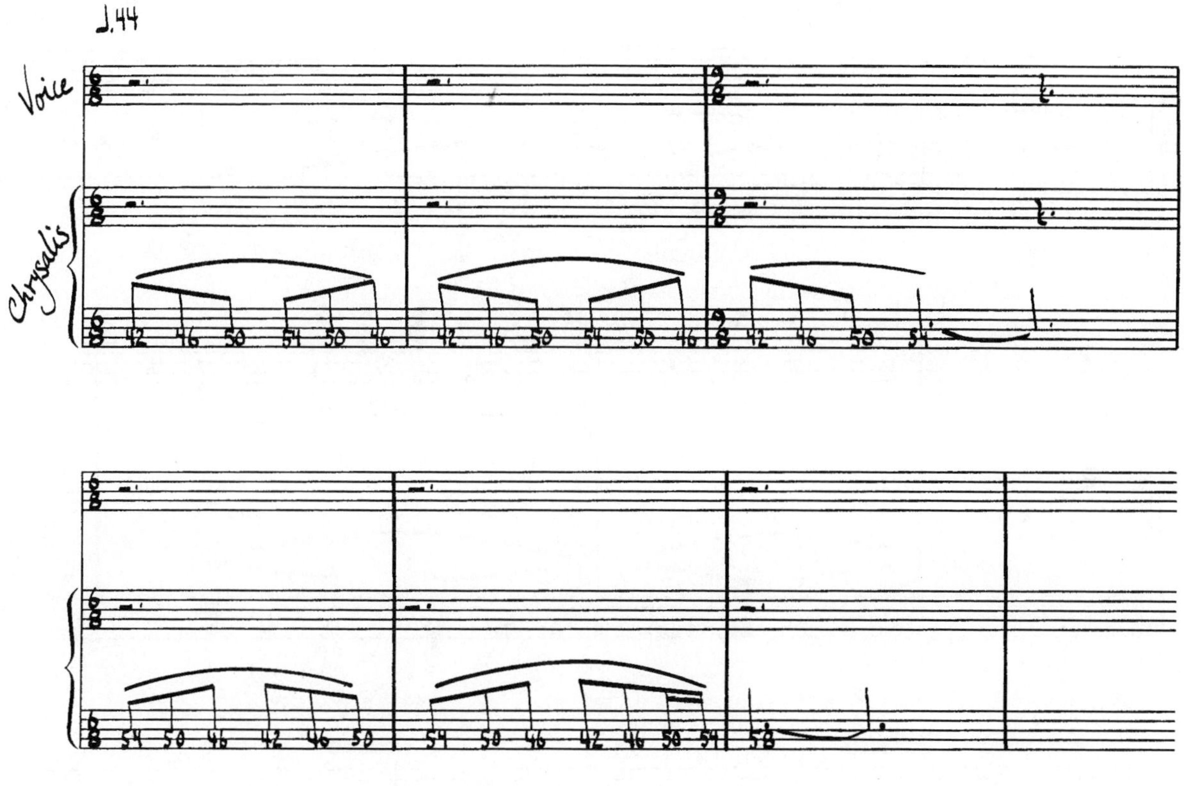

Example 12.1
(continued)

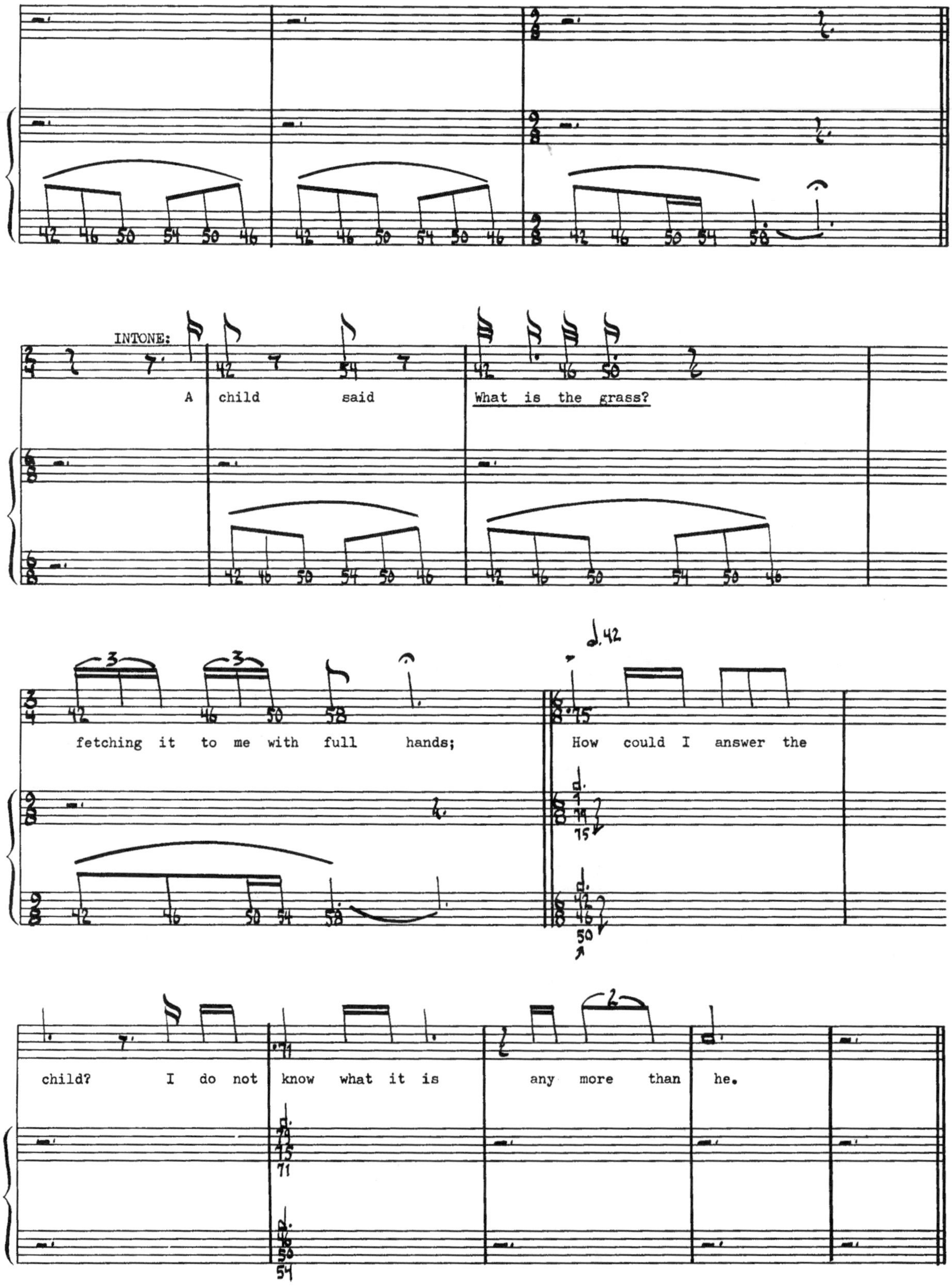

Example 12.2

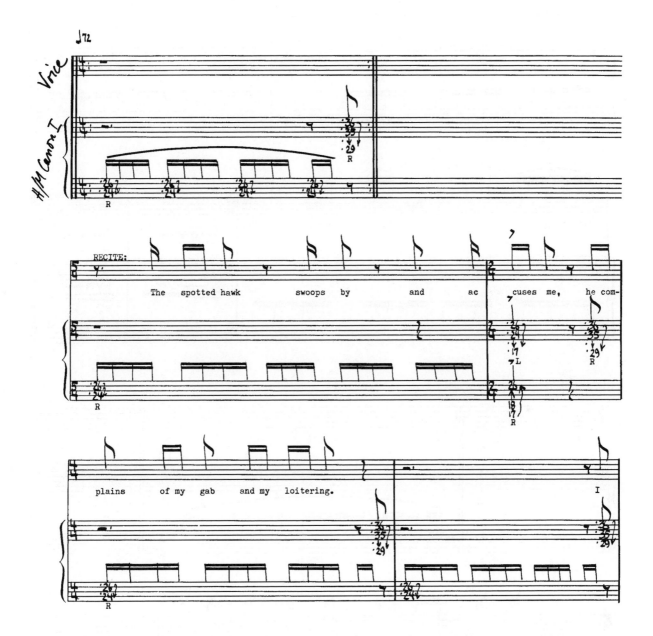

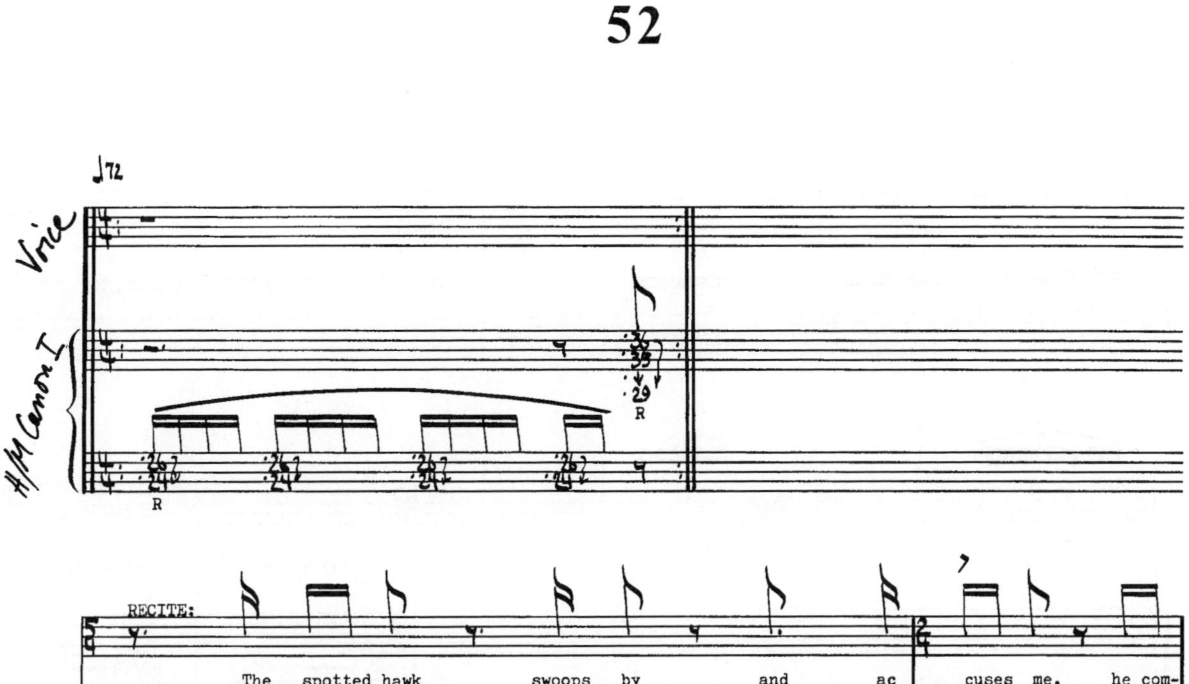
52
♩72
Voice
H/M Canon I
RECITE:
The spotted hawk swoops by and ac cuses me, he com-
plains of my gab and my loitering.
I
R
L

Example 12.2
(continued)

BASS CANON

Built: 1989

Dimensions	
Total number of strings	72
String length	1200.0 mm
String compensation on each side of the soundboard	4.0 mm
Length of canon	50½ in.
Height of canon	5½ in.
Width of canon	42.0 in.
Height of left and right end pieces	6¾ in.
Thickness of left and right end pieces	1$\frac{7}{16}$ in.
Thickness of soundboard	⅜ in.
Thickness of plywood base	¾ in.
Length of stand	53.0 in.
Upper height of stand	47⅝ in.
Lower height of stand	25.0 in.
Upper width of stand	45.0 in.
Lower width of stand	38$\frac{3}{16}$ in.
Height from floor to string on upper side of canon	52.0 in.
Height from floor to string on lower side of canon	31¾ in.
Length of triangular tuning gear bracket	6¾ in.
Height of triangular tuning gear bracket	¾ in.
Width at base of triangular tuning gear bracket	2$\frac{7}{16}$ in.
Height of strings above soundboard	1⅝ in.
Height of bridges above soundboard	1$\frac{29}{32}$ in.

To find this location, first count 66 lines, or 66.0 cm, from either the left or the right end piece; then determine the position of 0.7 cm by judging a point approximately ¾ of the distance between lines 66 and 67, or between 66.0 cm and 67.0 cm. Now, since the open strings of the Bass Canon have a length of 120.0 cm, or 1200.0 mm, ratio 3/2 requires a bridge at

$$\frac{120.0 \text{ cm}}{\frac{3}{2}} = 80.0 \text{ cm}$$

or at 800.0 mm. However, because I spaced the lines 12.0 cm apart, proceed as before. First count 66 lines from either the left or the right end piece; then determine a point approximately ¾ of the distance between lines 66 and 67. This point is located 800.0 mm from the end piece because $66.7 \times 12 = 800$. Third, the Bass Canon has 72 strings, or 24 more strings than the H/M Canon. As calculated in Section 2.12, each wound string exerts 72.0 lbf, which means that the Bass Canon withstands a total of 5,184.0 lbf, or more than 2½ tons of force.

12.7

I designed and built the String Winder in Plate 4 to make wound strings for the Bass Canon. However, the versatility and accuracy of this machine also enable me to produce wound strings for other musical instruments such as harps, guitars, and pianos. With the String Winder, tolerances of wound string diameters typically vary in the vicinity of ± 0.0005 in.

Because several important parts are not visible in Plate 4, turn to Figure 12.4, which illustrates the basic drive components of the String Winder. Motor (a) turns pulley (b) and V-belt (c), which turns pulley (d) and drive shaft (e), which turns timing pulleys (f) and timing belts (g), which turns timing pulleys (h) and chucks (i), which turns a steel string (j). The timing pulleys and timing belts have equally spaced notches to prevent slippage. The two timing belts and four timing pulleys ensure that the two chucks and the string revolve in perfect synchronicity. Therefore, while the steel string above revolves with the same speed as the drive shaft below, the string does *not* twist (torque) and break. Before making a string, a bronze wrap wire from a spool is attached to the steel string. When the machine is turned on, the steel string spins and pulls the bronze wrap wire from the spool. This action transforms the plain steel string into a wound string.

Plate 5 is a detail shot of the spool carriage. Near the right border of this photograph, note a chain that loops around at the far left end of the machine. This chain attaches via an aluminum coupling to the bottom of the carriage. A variable speed DC motor that drives the chain is not visible. It is located at the far right end of the machine. The motor and chain drive the spool carriage from right to left along the entire length of the steel string during the winding operation. Immediately below the carriage, Plate 5 shows two of four precision linear bearings that support the carriage on two long steel shafts; these shafts function as tracks for the carriage. Furthermore, observe that the two carriages, which support the green timing pulleys and chucks, are also mounted on linear bearings and short steel shafts. However, these two chuck carriages do not move during the winding operation. Instead, they are locked into place at varying distances from each other. The distance between the chuck carriages depends on whether one is making long or short wound strings.

Plate 5 also reveals two small wheels mounted between the bronze spool and the steel string. The wheel closest to the spool moves back and forth on a steel shaft mounted parallel to the spool. This motion guides the bronze wire as it unwinds from the spool. An aluminum tracking device, operated by two black knobs, supports the other wheel closest to the string. When one turns the knobs, the location of the wheel shifts sideways and parallel to the steel string. The position of this wheel determines the angle of the bronze wire as it winds over the steel string. I prefer that the wheel maintains a position about ¼ inch to the right of where the winding occurs. Such a location provides a moderate back angle for the bronze wire. This angle ensures that the individual coils of the winding are tightly pressed against each other. The result is a uniform winding — or an evenly distributed mass — that covers the entire length of the steel string.

The steel string in Plates 4 and 5 appears white instead of silver because I placed a nylon fiber bedding over the string. As discussed in Section 2.10, this bedding prevents the bronze wrap wire from buzzing against the steel core wire when the string vibrates on a musical instrument.

Finally, Plate 4 shows two large hand wheels. One is located below and the other above the worktable; the latter is also partially visible in Plate 5. The hand wheel below turns a threaded rod, which moves a platform that supports the motor. This motion shifts the location of the motor and, therefore, the position of motor pulley (b) in relation to drive shaft pulley (d) in Figure 12.4. When V-belt (c) engages different pulley groove diameters, the speed of drive shaft (e) and, therefore, of steel string (j) changes. Since the two pulleys are identical, but have four different groove diameters, the String Winder has 13 speeds between 793–3860 revolutions per minute.

The hand wheel above drives a chain that moves the right chuck carriage on the bearing shafts. After mounting a steel string on hooks between the two chucks, one turns this hand wheel in a clockwise direction, which moves the right chuck to the *right*. This motion increases the distance between the two chucks and places the steel string under tension. A ratchet wheel and pawl, visible behind

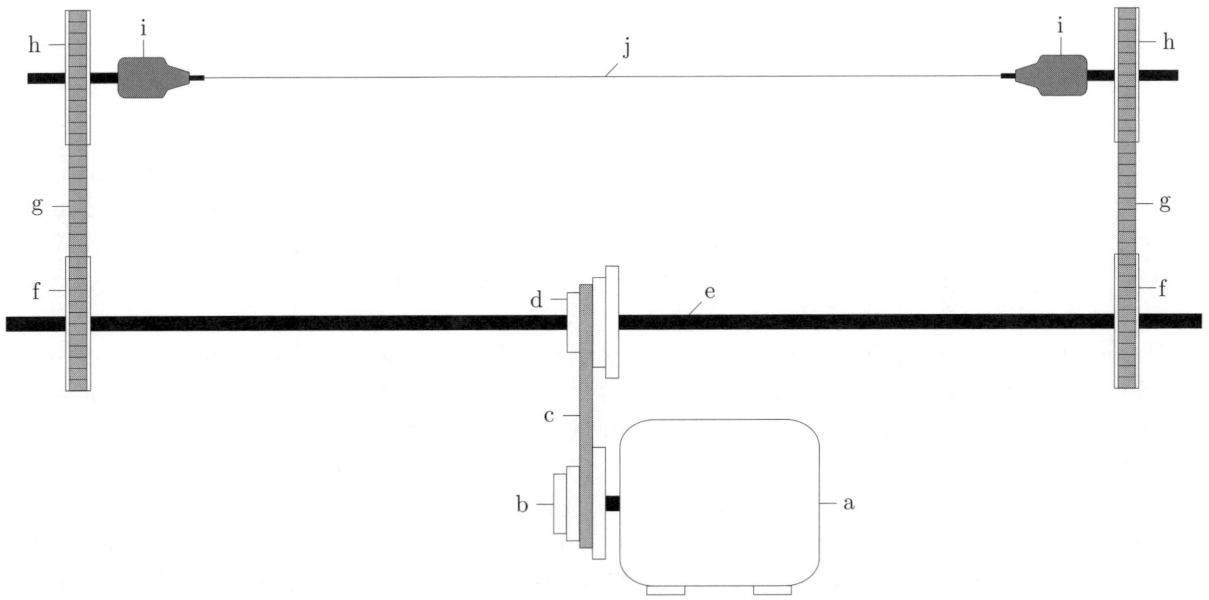

Figure 12.4 The basic drive components of the String Winder. The string (j) revolves with the same speed as the drive shaft (e) below. (Not to scale.)

the hand wheel in Plate 4, prevents the chuck carriage from moving back to the left. The steel string must be under tension during the winding operation for three reasons. (1) A tensioned core wire provides a linear surface for the wrap wire. (2) A wire under tension also produces resistance to deflection from the downward pull of the wrap wire as it unwinds from the spool. (3) Tension causes the steel string to stretch. By winding the wrap wire over a tensioned core wire, the individual coils of the winding wrap as closely as possible around the stretched diameter of the steel string. Because this condition simulates the state of the wound string on a musical instrument, the wrap wire will remain tightly wound around the core wire once the string is mounted on an instrument.

STRING WINDER

Built: 1988

Dimensions	
Length of string winder	114¼ in.
Height of string winder to the top of the timing gear	49⅛ in.
Height of string winder to the top of the work table	33.0 in.
Width of string winder	36 3/16 in.
Length of spool carriage	11.0 in.
Height of spool carriage	½ in.
Width of spool carriage	24½ in.
Lengths of chuck carriages	7.0 in.
Heights of chuck carriages	⅝ in.
Widths of chuck carriages	10½ in.
Diameter of drive shaft	¾ in.
Diameter of bearing shafts	¾ in.

JUST KEYS

12.8

Just Keys is a medium upright or console piano that I restrung three times and retuned four times in 1990. Plate 6 shows the complete keyboard from the first key in the bass to the last key in the treble. Note that the B-3 key identifies ratio $1/1$, which is the fundamental frequency of the tuning. This key sounds G_1 at 49.0 cps. Since the G-11 key normally produces this frequency, observe that I eliminated most of the tones that constitute the first "octave" of the standard piano. Consequently, the A-1 key now sounds frequency ratio $8/5$, or a just "major third," interval ratio $5/4$ below $1/1$, which is $E\flat_1$ at 39.2 cps; and the A♯-2 key now sounds frequency ratio $16/9$, or a just "major second," interval ratio $9/8$ below $1/1$, which is F_1 at 43.6 cps.

Turn to Table 12.3, which is a detailed tuning chart of the Just Keys keyboard. Note a 10-tone "octave," ratios $1/1$–$2/1$, from the B-3 key to the A-13 key, a 17-tone "octave," ratios $2/1$–$4/1$, from the A-13 key to the D-30 key, and another 17-tone "octave," ratios $4/1$–$8/1$, from the D-30 key to the G-47 key. From here, three consecutive 12-tone "octaves," ratios $8/1$–$16/1$, ratios $16/1$–$32/1$, and ratios $32/1$–$64/1$ span the distance from the G-47 key to the G-83 key. These 12-tone scales resemble the tuning of a conventional piano. Prime factorization of the integers of the frequency ratios reveals that the Just Keys has a 7-limit tuning. (See Sections 10.1 and 10.5.) In Plate 6, the Lexan-covered colored labels on the keys identify three different tuning patterns.

Pattern I utilizes dark blue, yellow, red, and large green labels to represent prime numbers 2, 3, 5, and 7, respectively. *Dark Blue Labels* indicate ratio $1/1$, prime number 2, as in ratio $2/1$, and "octave-multiples" $2^2 = 4/1$, $2^3 = 8/1$, $2^4 = 16/1$, $2^5 = 32/1$, and $2^6 = 64/1$. *Yellow Labels* indicate prime number 3, and "octave-multiple" $3 \times 2 = 6$. *Red Labels* indicate prime number 5, and "octave-multiples" $5 \times 2 = 10$, $5 \times 4 = 20$, and $5 \times 8 = 40$. *Large Green Labels* indicate prime number 7.

Pattern II uses light blue and brown labels to specify composite numbers. *Light Blue Labels* indicate composite $3 \times 3 = 9$, and *Brown Labels*, composites $3 \times 5 = 15$, $3 \times 7 = 21$, and $7 \times 9 = 63$.

Pattern III utilizes small green labels to indicate five tempered tones. With respect to G, the $1/1$-tonality is the most consonant tonality, and with respect to C♯, the $7/5$-tonality is the most dissonant tonality on the Just Keys. For reasons discussed in Section 12.10, I slightly tempered five tones within each "octave" to increase the consonance of the $7/5$-tonality. (1) On all $9/8$-keys, a small green label identifies ratio $8/5$, or a tempered "minor sixth" between C♯–A. (2) On all $5/4$-keys, a small green label identifies ratio $16/9$, or a tempered "minor seventh" between C♯–B. (3) On all $3/2$-keys, a small green label identifies ratio $16/15$, or a tempered "minor second" between C♯–D. (4) On all $5/3$-keys, a small green label identifies ratio $6/5$, or a tempered "minor third" between C♯–E. (5) And on all $15/8$-keys, a small green label identifies ratio $4/3$, or a tempered "fourth" between C♯–F♯. Section 12.10 describes the mathematics of these tempered tones in full detail.

12.9

Several factors influenced the development of these tuning patterns. (1) As discussed in Section 2.6, recall that a string made from a given material has four variables: length (L), diameter (D), frequency (F), and tension (T). However, since all pianos have fixed bridges glued directly to the soundboard, L is not a variable, but a predetermined constant. This structural limitation severely restricts the tuning possibilities of the Just Keys.

(2) Components such as large soundboards, heavy cast-iron plates, and thick steel strings cause all pianos to sound loud. (See Chapter 5.) Consequently, great amplitude also means that the dissonant frequencies of the inharmonic modes of vibration become exceedingly noticeable. As every

piano builder knows, inharmonicity affects the tunability and, therefore, the overall musical quality of all pianos. Now, Equation 4.20 states that the coefficient of inharmonicity ($\bar{\cancel{c}}$) is directly proportional to the diameter squared (D^2); therefore, as D decreases, $\bar{\cancel{c}}$ decreases as well. Although I restrung the entire instrument with thin strings, just intoned frequency ratios with prime numbers greater than 7, such as 11 and 13, sounded extremely dissonant due to the great amplitude of the inharmonic modes. In this respect, Just Keys represents an unfinished experiment. I can easily imagine restringing the entire instrument with even thinner strings to further reduce the devastating effects of inharmonicity.

(3) Equation 4.20 also states that the coefficient of inharmonicity is inversely proportional to the frequency squared (F^2), and inversely proportional to the length raised to the fourth power (L^4); therefore, as F increases, and L increases, $\bar{\cancel{c}}$ decreases. Because I intentionally increased all the frequencies between the A-1 key and the D♯-43 key, these changes also decreased the dissonance of the inharmonic modes. Furthermore, since the strings in this location of the instrument are consistently long by design, the tuning in the lower half of Just Keys is more diverse than in the upper half. The fortuitous combination of long, thin, and higher frequency strings enabled me to tune two consecutive 17-tone "octaves" from the A-13 key to the G-47 key. However, because the strings in the upper half of the instrument become rapidly short by design, "octaves" that exceed 12-tones are more difficult to achieve in this location.

12.10

For all practical purposes, Just Keys is a piano tuned in just intonation. Although Section 12.8, Pattern III, describes five tempered tones contained in all G–G "octaves," these slightly altered pitches do not interfere with the overall impression of a musical instrument tuned in just intonation. I challenge anyone to identify the altered tones by name during a musical performance.

I chose to temper these five tones because I wanted to increase the consonance of the 7/5-tonality, which is the most dissonant tonality of the tuning. As described in Section 12.9, inharmonic dissonance — caused by thick strings, thick soundboards, and massive cast-iron plates — severely restricts the tuning possibilities of all pianos. By slightly modifying a few pitches that the 1/1-tonality (the G-tonality) and the 7/5-tonality (the C♯-tonality) have in common, I was able to further counteract the dissonant tendencies of the instrument.

In Table 12.3, the letter *T* identifies the tempered tones of the Just Keys tuning. For example, let us begin with the C♯-17 key, which sounds the tempered combination 9/8–8/5. In relation to the 1/1-tonality, a "major second," ratio 9/8, above 1/1 is ratio 1/1 × 9/8 = 9/8, which according to Equation 9.21 equals

$$\log_{10} \frac{9}{8} \times 3986.314 = 203.91\ \cancel{c}$$

And in relation to the 7/5-tonality, a "minor sixth," ratio 8/5, above 7/5 is ratio 7/5 × 8/5 = 56/25. This "octave" equivalent simplifies to ratio 28/25, which equals

$$\log_{10} \frac{28}{25} \times 3986.314 = 196.20\ \cancel{c}$$

The difference between these two ratios equals 203.91 ¢ − 196.20 ¢ = 7.71 ¢. Divide the difference in half: 7.71 ¢ ÷ 2 = 3.86 ¢. Finally, subtract one-half from ratio 9/8: 203.91 ¢ − 3.86 ¢ = 200.1 ¢, and add the other half to ratio 28/25: 196.20 ¢ + 3.86 ¢ = 200.1 ¢. Observe that the former and the latter cent values are now identical. Since I lowered ratio 9/8 by approximately 4 ¢, or conversely, since I raised 28/25 by approximately 4 ¢, this pitch constitutes a tempered tone in the tuning. A

Table 12.3

JUST KEYS TUNING CHART

A 1	A♯ 2	**B** 3	C 4	C♯ 5	D 6	D♯ 7	E 8	F 9	F♯ 10	G 11	G♯ 12	**A** 13	A♯ 14	B 15	C 16	C♯ 17	D 18	D♯ 19	E 20	F 21	F♯ 22
8/5	16/9	**1/1**	9/8	5/4	4/3	7/5	3/2	8/5	5/3	16/9	15/8	**2/1**	21/20	16/15	10/9	9/8	7/6	6/5	5/4	21/16	4/3
			T	*T*			*T*		*T*		*T*					*T*			*T*		
814	996	G_1	200	383	C_2	583	698	814	891	996	1085	G_2	84	112	182	200	267	316	383	471	C_3
		49.0 cps										98.0 cps									
G 23	G♯ 24	A 25	A♯ 26	B 27	C 28	C♯ 29	**D** 30	D♯ 31	E 32	F 33	F♯ 34	G 35	G♯ 36	A 37	A♯ 38	B 39	C 40	C♯ 41	D 42	D♯ 43	E 44
7/5	3/2	63/40	8/5	5/3	16/9	15/8	**4/1**	21/20	16/15	9/8	7/6	6/5	5/4	4/3	7/5	3/2	63/40	8/5	5/3	7/4	16/9
	T			*T*		*T*				*T*			*T*			*T*			*T*		
583	698	786	814	891	996	1085	G_3	84	112	200	267	316	383	C_4	583	698	786	814	891	969	996
							196.0 cps														
F 45	F♯ 46	**G** 47	G♯ 48	A 49	A♯ 50	B 51	C 52	C♯ 53	D 54	D♯ 55	E 56	F 57	F♯ 58	**G** 59	G♯ 60	A 61	A♯ 62	B 63	C 64	C♯ 65	D 66
9/5	15/8	**8/1**	21/20	9/8	6/5	5/4	4/3	7/5	3/2	8/5	5/3	16/9	15/8	**16/1**	21/20	9/8	6/5	5/4	4/3	7/5	3/2
	T			*T*		*T*			*T*		*T*		*T*			*T*		*T*			*T*
1018	1085	G_4	84	200	316	383	C_5	583	698	814	891	996	1085	G_5	84	200	316	383	C_6	583	698
		392.0 cps												784.0 cps							
D♯ 67	E 68	F 69	F♯ 70	**G** 71	G♯ 72	A 73	A♯ 74	B 75	C 76	C♯ 77	D 78	D♯ 79	E 80	F 81	F♯ 82	**G** 83	G♯ 84	A 85	A♯ 86	B 87	C 88
63/40	5/3	16/9	15/8	**32/1**	21/20	9/8	6/5	5/4	4/3	7/5	3/2	8/5	5/3	16/9	15/8	**64/1**	16/15	9/8	6/5	5/4	4/3
	T		*T*			*T*		*T*			*T*		*T*		*T*			*T*		*T*	
786	891	996	1085	G_6	84	200	316	383	C_7	583	698	814	891	996	1085	G_7	112	200	316	383	C_8
				1568 cps												3136 cps					

mathematical analysis shows that I tempered combinations $^5\!/\!_4$–$^{16}\!/\!_9$, $^3\!/\!_2$–$^{16}\!/\!_{15}$, and $^{15}\!/\!_8$–$^4\!/\!_3$ by precisely the same amount.

With respect to combination $^5\!/\!_3$–$^6\!/\!_5$, the tempered amount is a bit larger. In relation to the $^1\!/\!_1$-tonality, a "major sixth," ratio $^5\!/\!_3$, above $^1\!/\!_1$ is ratio $^1\!/\!_1 \times {^5\!/\!_3} = {^5\!/\!_3}$, which equals

$$\log_{10} \frac{5}{3} \times 3986.314 = 884.36\ ¢$$

And in relation to the $^7\!/\!_5$-tonality, a "minor third," ratio $^6\!/\!_5$, above $^7\!/\!_5$ is ratio $^7\!/\!_5 \times {^6\!/\!_5} = {^{42}\!/\!_{25}}$, which equals

$$\log_{10} \frac{42}{25} \times 3986.314 = 898.15\ ¢$$

The difference between these two ratios equals 898.15 ¢ − 884.36 ¢ = 13.79 ¢. Again, divide the difference in half: 13.79 ¢ ÷ 2 = 6.90 ¢. Finally, add one-half to ratio $^5\!/\!_3$: 884.36 ¢ + 6.90 ¢ = 891.3 ¢, and subtract the other half from ratio $^{42}\!/\!_{25}$: 898.15 ¢ − 6.90 ¢ = 891.3 ¢. Notice that the former and the latter cent values are now identical. Since I raised ratio $^5\!/\!_3$ by approximately 7 ¢, or conversely, since I lowered ratio $^{42}\!/\!_{25}$ by approximately 7 ¢, this pitch also constitutes a tempered tone in the tuning. For all five combinations, a small amount of tempering enhanced the musical versatility of the instrument. I very much doubt that a highly skilled violin or flute player would be able to play a just 12-tone, or a just 17-tone scale without incurring similar negligible imperfections in intonation.

12.11

Musical Example 12.3 is a composition for Just Keys called "The Letter." This score belongs to a larger work entitled *Ellis Island/Angel Island: A Vision of the American Immigrants. Ellis Island/Angel Island* is a composition for musicians and dancers that recounts the experiences of immigrants who confront the arduous task of assimilation. "The Letter" tells the story of immigration from the perspective of wives and children left behind. During the 19th century, hundreds of thousands of men came from Europe and Asia with the intent to earn enough money to bring their families to America. However, despite such hopeful dreams, many families were never reunited.

"The Letter" takes place in a simple courtyard where a mother is tending a small garden. From Measures 1–24, three children enter the scene; they are running and laughing because one of them is waving a letter in the air. The mother joins the happy chase and finally succeeds in grabbing the letter. Measures 25–46, she reads the first page to her children, who are delighted to hear from their father; the kids then continue playing and leave the scene. Measures 47–71, the mother turns the letter over and reads her husband's expressions of love and loneliness. Measures 72–89, the news turns bad and prospects for reunification begin to fade. Measures 90–98, the mother turns inward with the thought that she and the children must survive alone.

Example 12.3 is a tablature score of "The Letter" for Just Keys, and Example 12.4 is a traditional score of the same piece for conventional piano. The latter score includes five linear key signatures. Measure 1 shows F♯-minor; Measure 25, E-minor; Measure 47, C♯-minor; Measure 72, F♯-minor; and Measure 90, D-major. Traditional piano scores serve two requirements: (1) each note represents a key, and (2) each note represents a pitch of the standard 12-tone equal tempered scale. Now, since one "octave" of Just Keys consists of a 10-tone scale, and since two more "octaves" consist of 17-tone scales, the tablature score in Example 12.3 only fulfills the first requirement. That is, even though the notes in the tablature score represent the keys of Just Keys, they do not simultaneously represent the pitches of the standard 12-tone scale. Consequently, in Example 12.3,

Example 12.3

The Letter

For Just Keys

Tablature Score

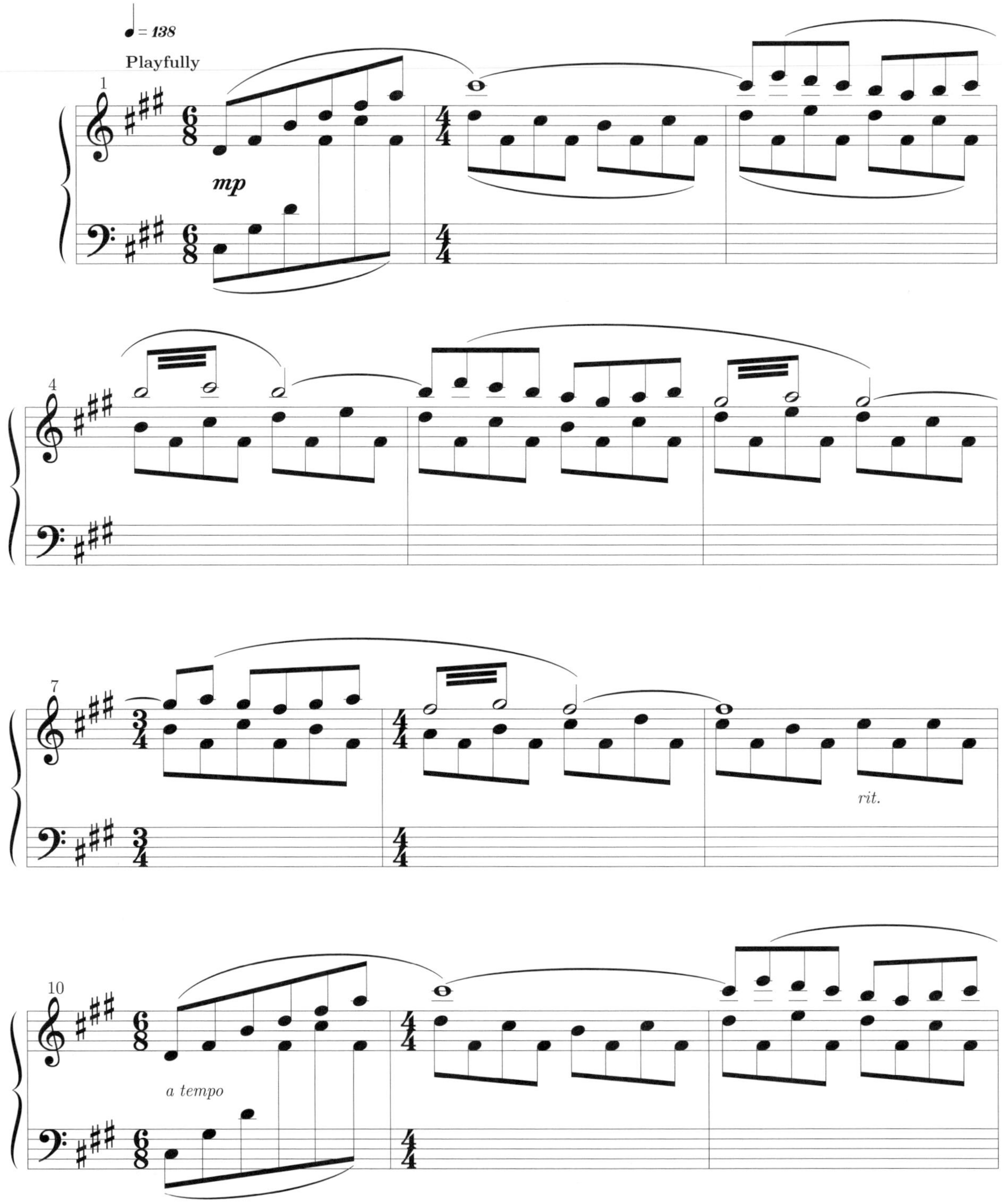

© 1990 Cristiano Forster

All Rights Reserved

Tablature Score

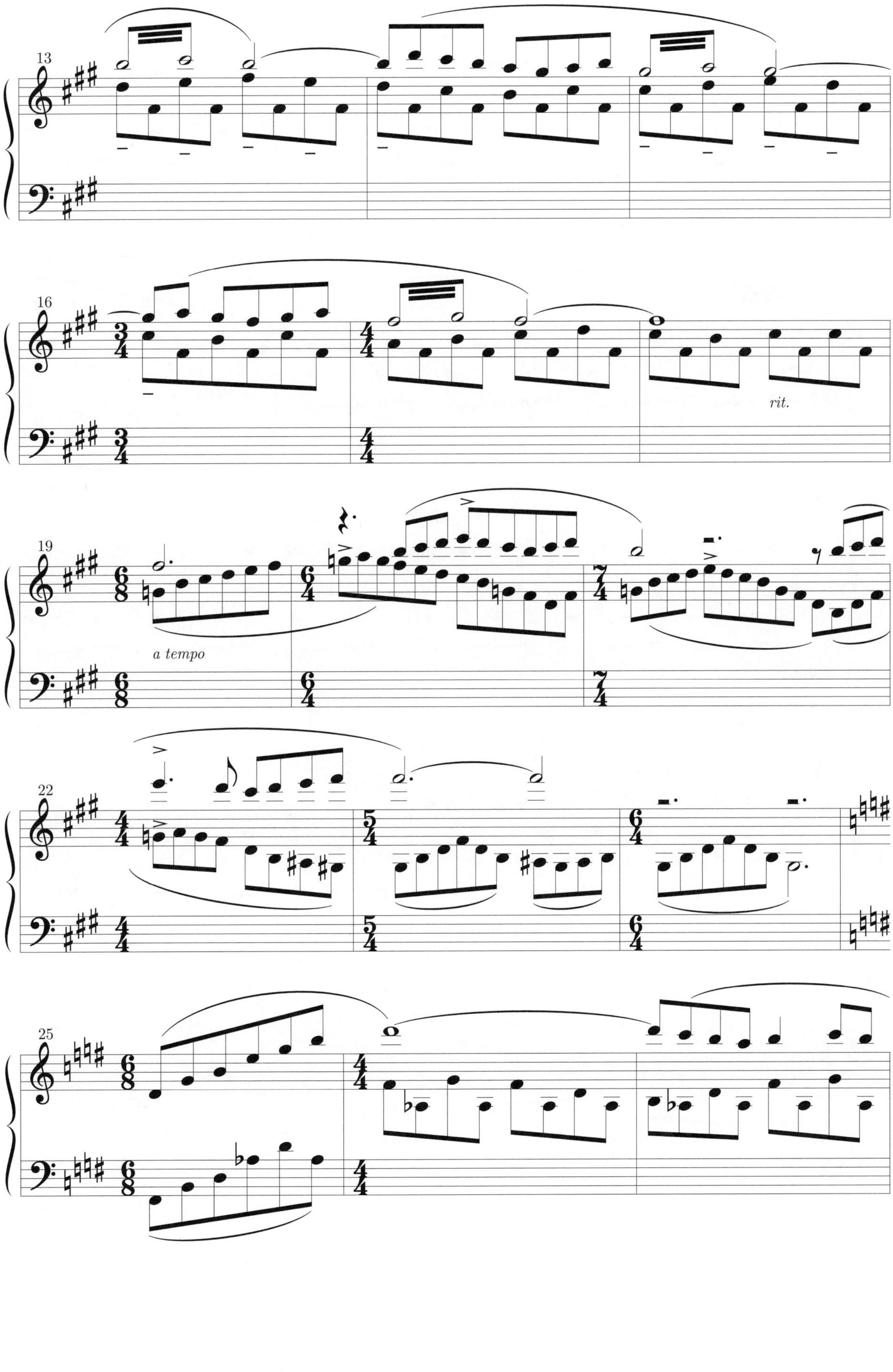

Tablature Score

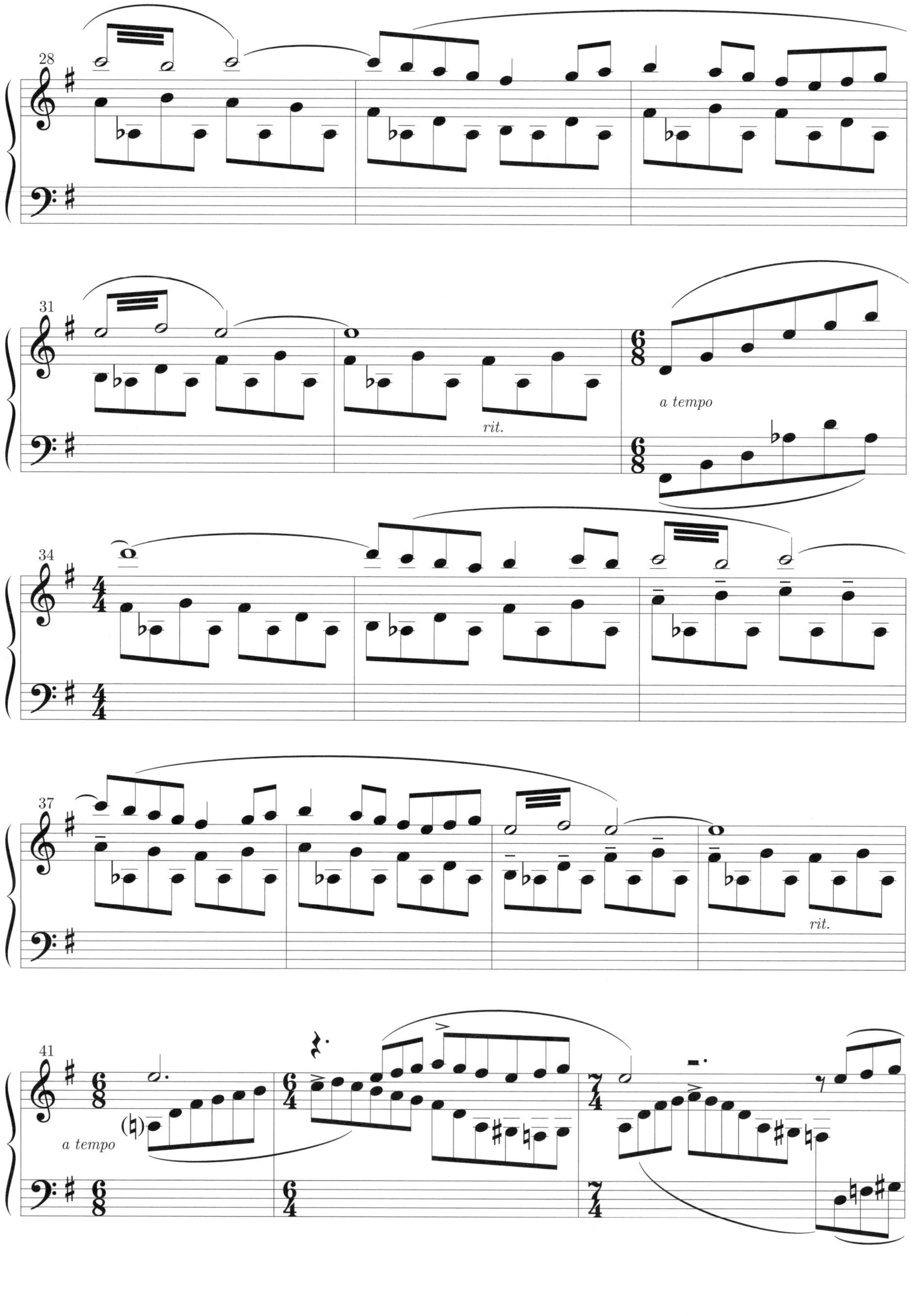

Tablature Score

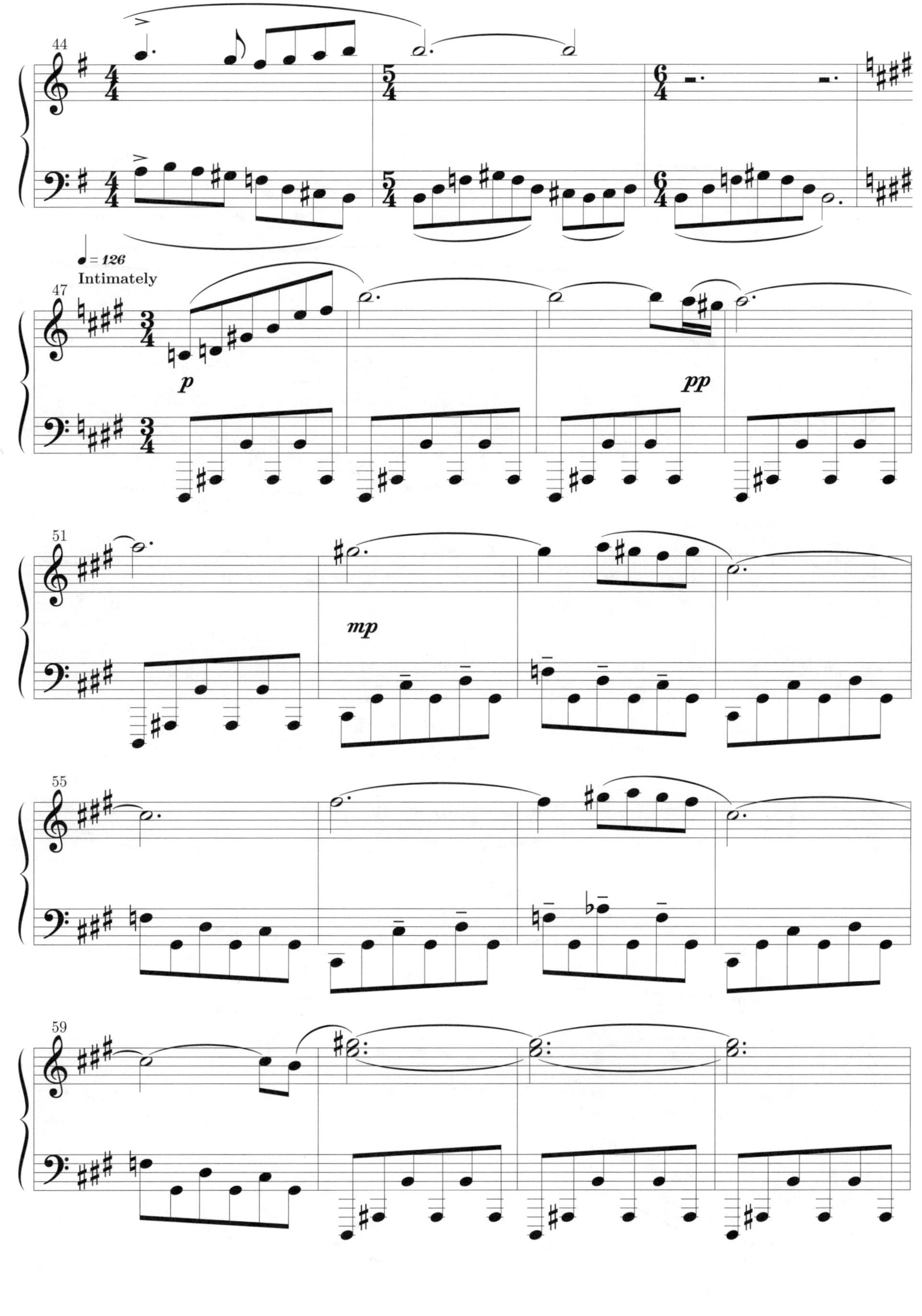

Tablature Score

Tablature Score

Example 12.4

The Letter

For 12-TET Piano

Traditional Score

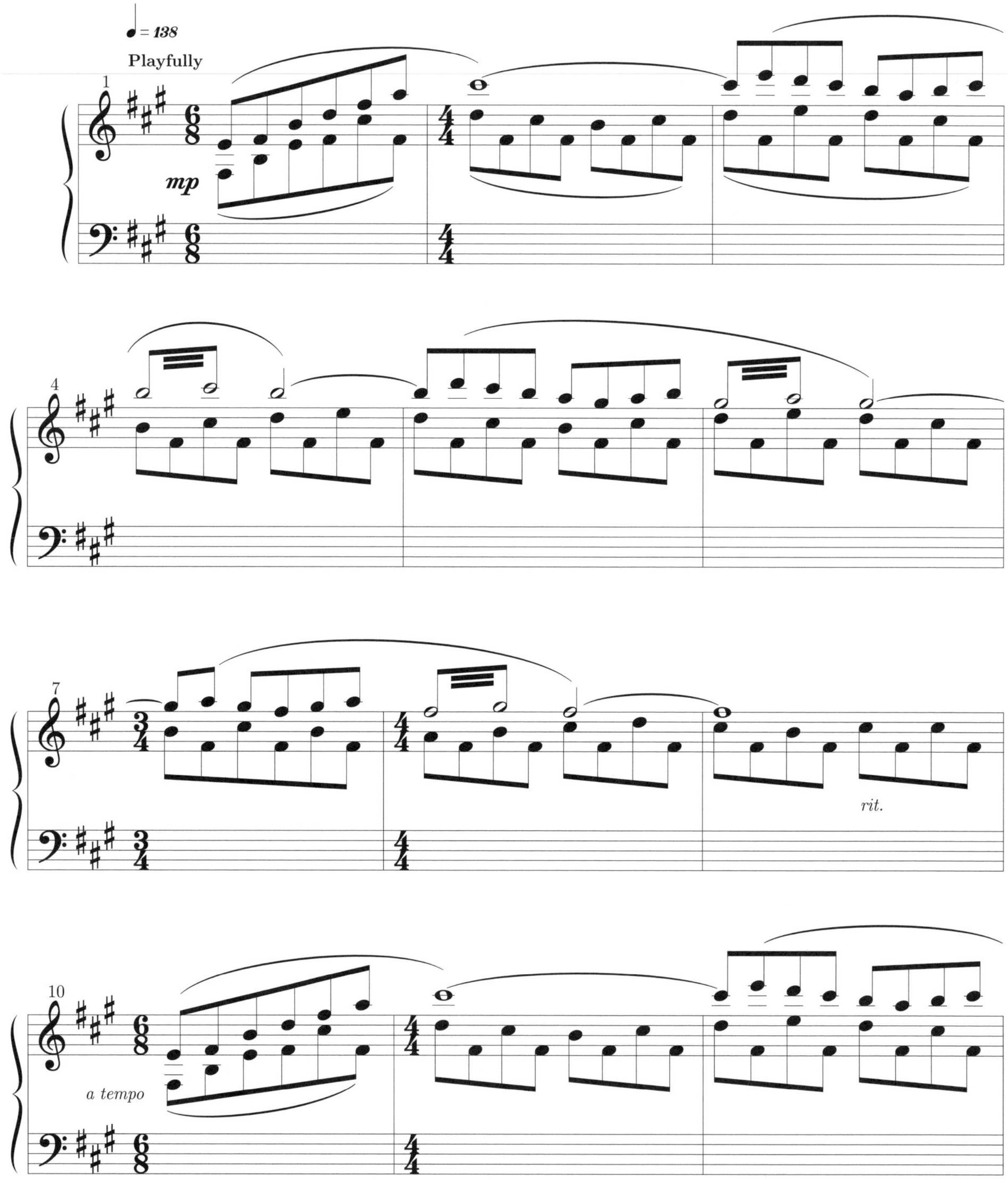

© 1990 Cristiano Forster

All Rights Reserved

Traditional Score

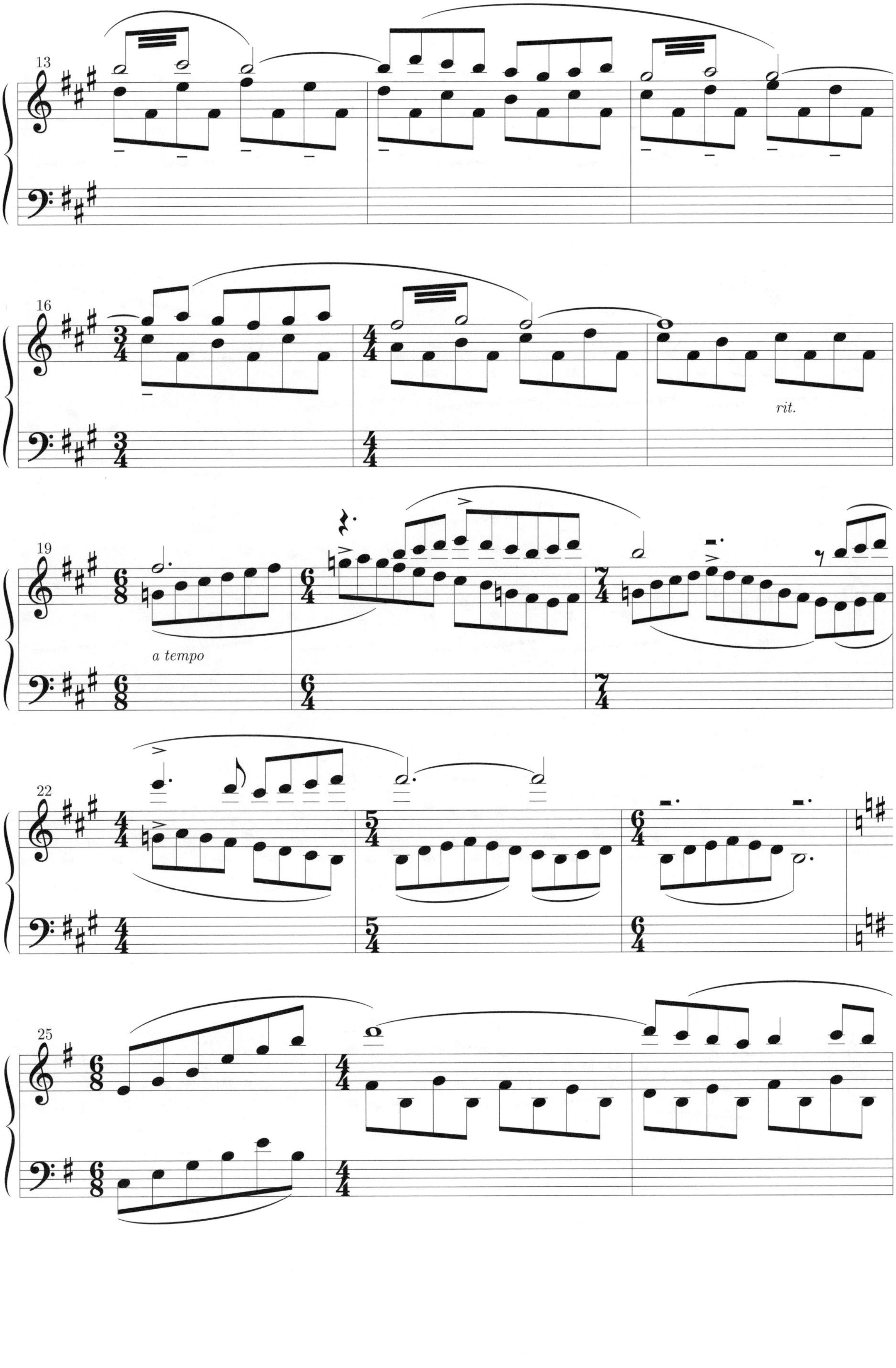

Traditional Score

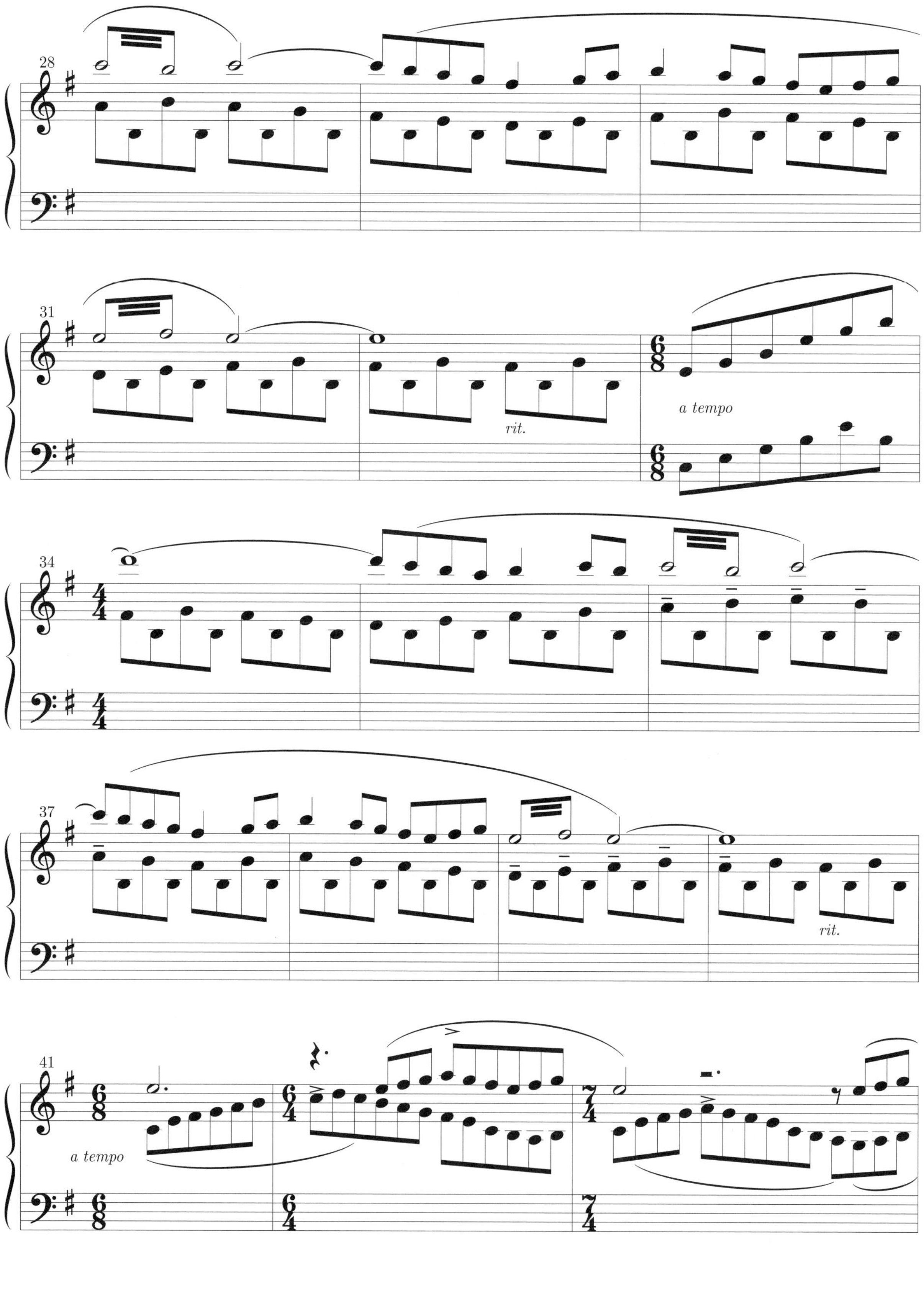

Traditional Score

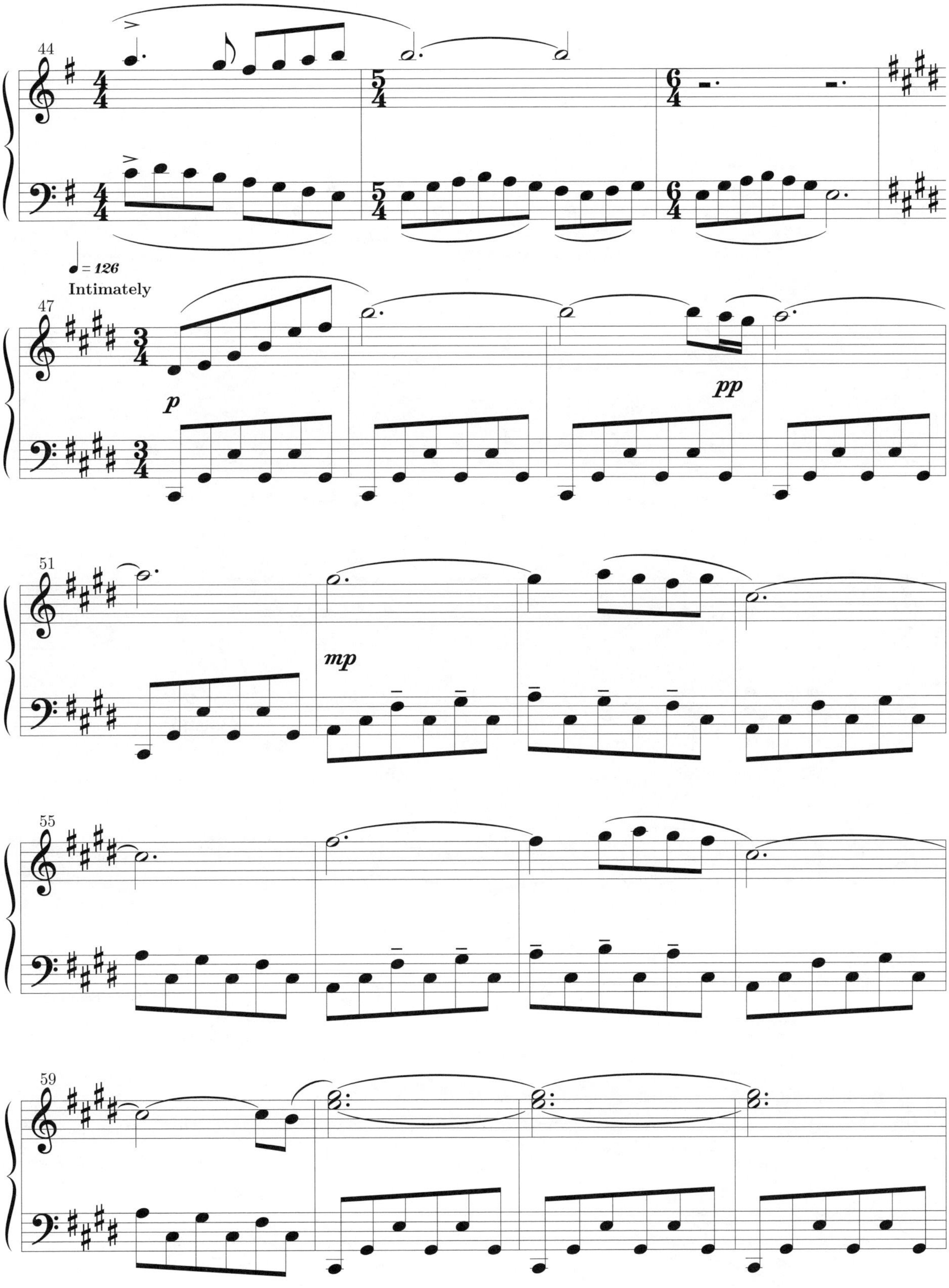

Traditional Score

Traditional Score

I used nonlinear key signatures at Measures 1, 25, 47, 72, and 90. The accidentals of these key signatures are deliberately out of order to alert the musician that the notes in the tablature score do not represent the pitches of the 12-tone scale. The sole purpose of the nonlinear key signatures is to minimize the occurrence of accidentals throughout the score. Therefore, anyone who attempts to analyze the tablature score with standard key signatures must interpret the 7-limit ratios of the tuning according to conventional Western music theory. Given a more complex composition based, for example, on a 13-limit tuning, such attempts at ordinary analysis may prove counterproductive. Finally, ambiguities with respect to key signatures also exist in "The Letter." Notice that Measures 72–89 are not distinctly in the key of F♯-minor.

I have played the traditional score in Example 12.4 on many different conventional upright and grand pianos. With respect to tuning and timbre, none of these pianos compared favorably to Just Keys. On this instrument, the intonational clarity of the just tuning and the musical clarity of the thin strings produce a unique aural experience. I offer the traditional score only as a suggestion of how this composition should sound.

Percussion Instruments

DIAMOND MARIMBA

12.12

The Diamond Marimba in Plate 7 is based on a 13-limit tonality diamond. Max F. Meyer (1873–1967) first described the concept of a two-dimensional tonality diamond in his book *The Musician's Arithmetic*, published in 1929. On p. 22, Meyer shows the diagram of a 7-limit Tonality Diamond that includes 16 just intoned frequency ratios. (See Figure 10.57.) In 1946, Harry Partch (1901–1974) transformed and expanded Meyer's original design and built an 11-limit Diamond Marimba with 36 just intoned bars. (See Figure 10.59.) With respect to my Diamond Marimba, Figure 12.5 shows the 49 bars required by a 13-limit tonality diamond. Here the frequency ratios of the diagonals that ascend from left to right include odd numbers 1, 5, 3, 7, 9, 11, 13 — or "octave-multiples" of these numbers — in the *numerators;* conversely, the frequency ratios of the diagonals that descend from left to right include odd numbers 1, 5, 3, 7, 9, 11, 13 — or "octave-multiples" of these numbers — in the *denominators.* A careful examination of Meyer's 7-limit, Partch's 11-limit, and my 13-limit diamond reveals that the row that runs through the center of these designs represents a sequence of unisons. For this reason, I refer to the center row as the *neutral axis.* On the 11-limit and 13-limit Diamond Marimbas, the neutral axis sounds the tone of the tonic, ratio $^1/_1$, below all the bars in the *upper* halves of the diamonds. Furthermore, on the 13-limit Diamond Marimba, the neutral axis produces the tone of the "octave," ratio $^2/_1$, above the following 15 bars in the *lower* half of the diamond: $^{14}/_{13}$, $^{12}/_{11}$, $^{10}/_9$, $^8/_7$, $^{14}/_{11}$, $^4/_3$ ($^{12}/_9$), $^{18}/_{13}$, $^{10}/_7$, $^{14}/_9$, $^8/_5$, $^{18}/_{11}$, $^5/_3$, $^{22}/_{13}$, $^{12}/_7$. And it produces the tone of the "double-octave," ratio $^4/_1$, above the following 6 bars in the *lower* half of the diamond: $^{16}/_{13}$, $^{16}/_{11}$, $^{20}/_{13}$, $^{16}/_9$, $^{20}/_{11}$, $^{24}/_{13}$.

Now, a bar that sounds the fundamental frequency, ratio $^1/_1$, below the lowest bar, or below the "sharp minor third," ratio $^{16}/_{13}$, is *not* a part of the diamond. Also, a bar that sounds the "octave," ratio $^2/_1$, between the "sharp minor seventh," ratio $^{24}/_{13}$, and the "sharp minor second," ratio $^{14}/_{13}$, is *not* included. Consequently, I decided to append the basic structure of the diamond design. In the lower part of the instrument, Figure 12.5 illustrates that I added a bar for the fundamental G_3 at 196.0 cps, and a bar for the "octave" G_4 at 392.0 cps. The neutral axis now produces the interval of the "double-octave" G_5 at 784.0 cps above the fundamental. Figure 12.5 shows that I also included three more bars that produce the intervals of the "fourth," ratio $^4/_3$, the "fifth," ratio $^3/_2$, and the

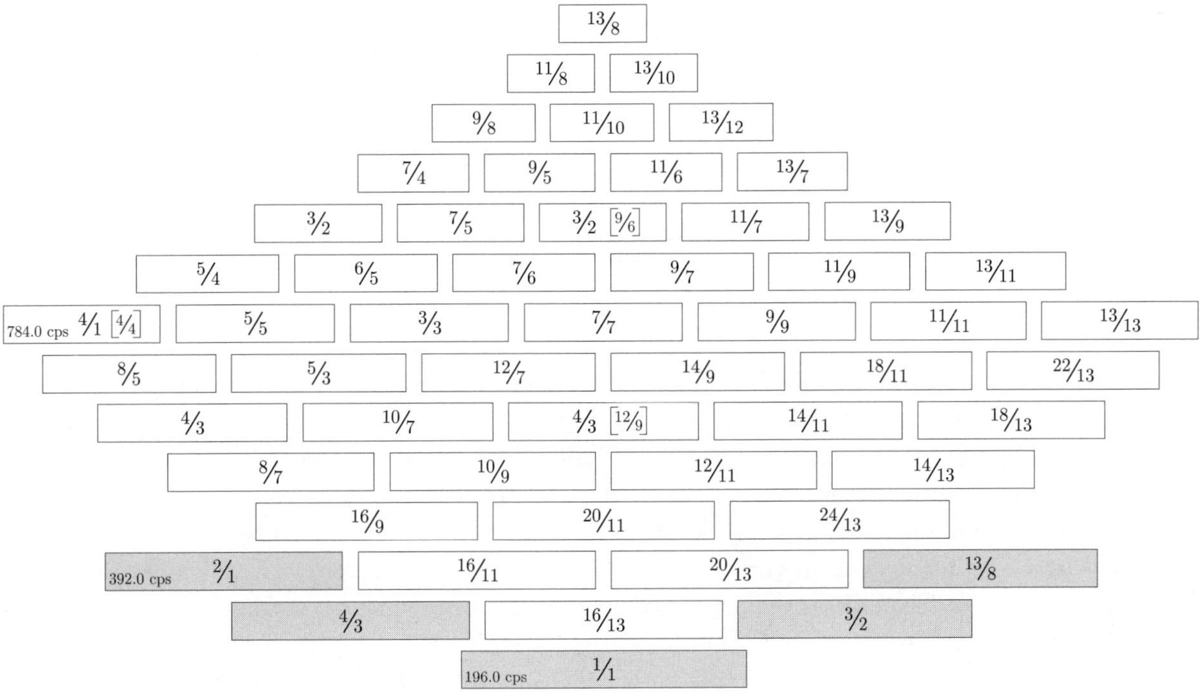

Figure 12.5 Frequency ratios of the Diamond Marimba. Forty-nine central bars represent the ratios required by a 13-limit tonality diamond. Five extra bars in the lower part of the instrument provide essential consonances not included in the basic diamond design. (Not to scale.)

"sharp minor sixth," ratio 13/8, above the fundamental. Therefore, the Diamond Marimba in Plate 7 has a total number of 49 bars + 5 bars = 54 bars.

The Diamond Marimba stand consists of six parts: a lower base, four poles, and an upper platform. The Honduras rosewood bars are mounted on a terraced platform that consists of fourteen rows of bars. Beginning with the second row, each succeeding row rises a half inch above the previous row, so that the difference in height between the first row and the last row equals 13 × ½ in. = 6½ in. Underneath the platform, I mounted a quarter-wavelength resonator for each bar.

DIAMOND MARIMBA

Built: 1978
5-Bar Extension: 1982
Rebuilt: 1989

Dimensions	
Total number of bars	54
Longest bar	16 11/16 in. × 13/16 in. × 2 1/4 in.
Shortest bar	7.0 in. × 13/16 in. × 1 13/16 in.
Length of platform	59.0 in.
Height to the first row	34.0 in.
Height to the neutral axis	37½ in.
Height to the last row	40½ in.
Width of platform	38.0 in.

(See Sections 7.10–7.11.) The resonators are made from cast acrylic tubes, and the stand poles, from cast acrylic rods. In Plate 7, note that the profile of the fundamental bar in the first row shows the triple-arch design used to tune the first *three* modes of vibration. (See Sections 6.10–6.14.) For the others, I tuned the first *two* modes of the bars in the $^{16}/_{13}$–$^{7}/_{5}$ range, and only the *first* or fundamental mode of the bars in the $^{13}/_{9}$–$^{13}/_{8}$ range. (See Section 6.15.)

BASS MARIMBA

12.13

In Plate 8, the Bass Marimba is by far the largest, most massive, and most powerful instrument I have built to date. It is over 12 feet long, and all the 24 exceptionally large bars are made of Honduras rosewood. During performances in concert halls, I am always concerned that this instrument causes air conditioning ducts and various other fixtures to buzz and rattle.

The Bass Marimba has two different kinds of resonators. Plate 8 shows 19 standard wavelength resonators and 5 cavity resonators. (See Chapter 7, Part VII.) The reason for the cavity resonators is that extremely low frequencies require extremely long tubes, which in turn require a high stand for the instrument and a high riser for musicians to stand on. For example, for the first bar, which sounds G_1 at 49.00 cps, Equation 7.30 informs us that a 4.0 in. diameter closed tube would need a cut length of

$$L_{\text{c cut}} = \frac{13{,}504 \text{ in/s}}{4(49.00 \text{ cps})} - 0.3(4.0 \text{ in}) = 67.70 \text{ in} = 5.64 \text{ ft}$$

Similarly, the third bar, which sounds C_2 at 65.33 cps, would need a tube with a length of

$$L_{\text{c cut}} = \frac{13{,}504 \text{ in/s}}{4(65.33 \text{ cps})} - 0.3(4.0 \text{ in}) = 50.48 \text{ in} = 4.21 \text{ ft}$$

However, as discussed in Sections 7.17–7.18, the C_2 cavity resonator has an *inside* height of only 32.0 in., or approximately 2.7 feet. (In Chapter 7, I refer to this cavity resonator as Resonator II.) With respect to amplitude and ring-time, there are no appreciable differences between the wavelength resonators and the cavity resonators. The principal reason for this uniformity in amplification is that I carefully tuned the frequencies of the cavity resonators to the fundamental frequencies of the bars.

Figure 12.6 gives the frequency ratios of the 24 bars of the Bass Marimba, which indicate that this instrument spans the interval of a “double-octave” plus a “small whole tone.” Observe that

BASS MARIMBA

Started: 1983
Finished: 1985–86

Dimensions	
Total number of bars	24
Longest bar	44 1/16 in. × 1.0 in. × 4 1/4 in.
Shortest bar	19 9/16 in. × 15/16 in. × 3 3/8 in.
Length of stand	145.0 in.
Height of stand	40.0 in.
Width of stand above the wheels	44 1/8 in.
Height to the top of the runners that support the bars and resonators	36 1/4 in.

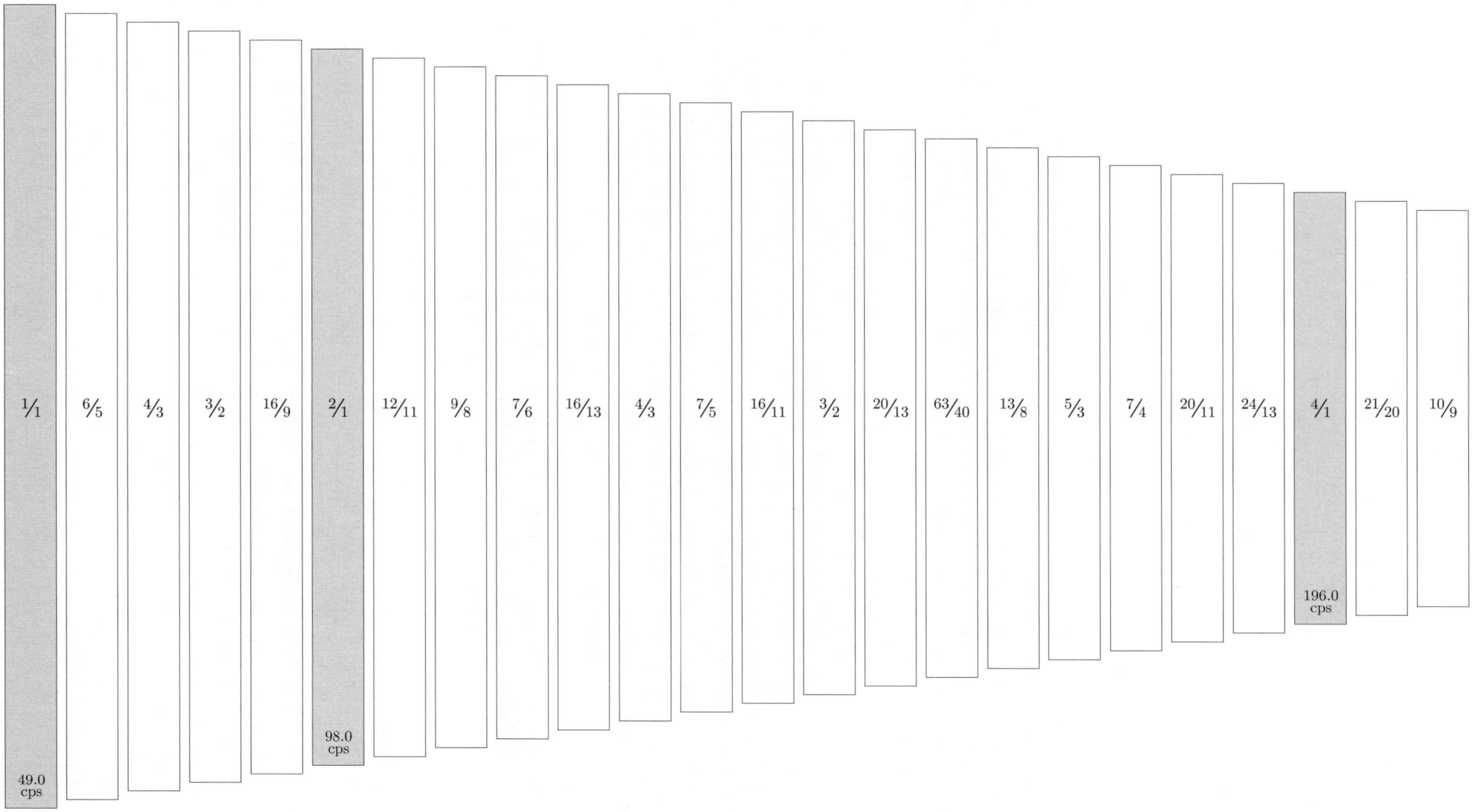

Figure 12.6 Frequency ratios of the Bass Marimba. Note that the 24 bars of this instrument span the interval of a "double-octave" plus a "small whole tone." (Not to scale.)

the frequency of the "double-octave" G_3 at 196.0 cps is identical to the frequency of the lowest bar on the Diamond Marimba. As discussed in Chapter 6, Part II, all 24 bars on the Bass Marimba have triple arches for tuning the first three modes of vibration. Also, in Plate 8, note that the cast acrylic tubes have moveable green felt-lined stoppers for adjusting the amplitude and ring-time of each resonator. Finally, despite its enormous size, this instrument requires only a screwdriver to disassemble. Notice that hand knobs hold all the large structural components together.

Friction Instrument

GLASSDANCE

12.14

Plate 9 shows the Glassdance, an instrument that consists of 48 revolving crystal glasses. With respect to parts, materials, and tooling, this is by far the most complex instrument I have built to date. Initially, I planned to build a traditional *glass armonica* based on the design by Benjamin Franklin (1706–1790). Franklin's invention requires a series of graduated glass bowls that fit closely inside each other so that only the rims of the bowls are exposed. The bowls are mounted on a horizontal metal axle that passes through holes in the center of the bowls. Musicians rotate the axle by activating a foot pedal, and play the bowls by simply touching the revolving rims. Because the bowls revolve, one may easily play two or three bowls with one hand. However, Franklin's design poses three significant problems. (1) An instrument builder not trained in glass making must depend on a specialist for the graduated bowls. (2) Since the glassmaker is also the tuner of the bowls, it would be very costly to order a non-standard series of bowls tuned to a new tuning system. Given such a tuning, and given that the graduated bowls must fit closely inside each other, the dimensions of all the bowls would have to be recalculated. (3) In the event that an old bowl breaks, or that the instrument requires a new bowl with a different tuning, the axle design is exceedingly impractical. If the old bowl is near the center of the axle, then all the other bowls from either the left or the right end of the axle must first be removed to access the old bowl.

The design of the Glassdance resolves all of these difficulties. First, all the crystal glasses on this instrument were produced by commercial manufacturers. Second, the need for a series of graduated bowls does not exist because each glass has its own center of revolution. Third, because all the glasses revolve independently of each other, it is very easy to install any number of new glasses.

Plate 10 is a detail shot of the inside of the case that houses the drive components of the glasses. Note three strips of black neoprene that divide the front of the case into four separate panels. The panels diminish the transmission of sound from the drive components because they prevent the front from vibrating like a large soundboard. Each panel includes 12 large red chain sprockets, 12 ball bearings (or one ball bearing behind each sprocket), and one red drive chain. These chains do not have individual links like conventional machine or bicycle chains. Instead, they consist of $\frac{1}{32}$ in. diameter stainless steel cables covered with polyurethane. Since the chains bend by virtue of being flexible, they are completely silent. Also, each panel includes one large red drive sprocket, one small red idler sprocket, and two more ball bearings. These sprockets are partially hidden from view by four large and four small red transmission sprockets mounted on the bottom of the case. A heavier yellow polyurethane transmission chain that drives these sprockets wraps around a raised ninth sprocket in the lower left corner of the case. This sprocket sits at the end of a drive shaft that connects to a variable speed DC motor housed inside a soundproof enclosure. A brown felt-covered table — that I bolted to the back of the Glassdance stand — supports the motor and enclosure. The blue liner on the bottom side of the case is a material called E.A.R. (See Section 12.3.) This

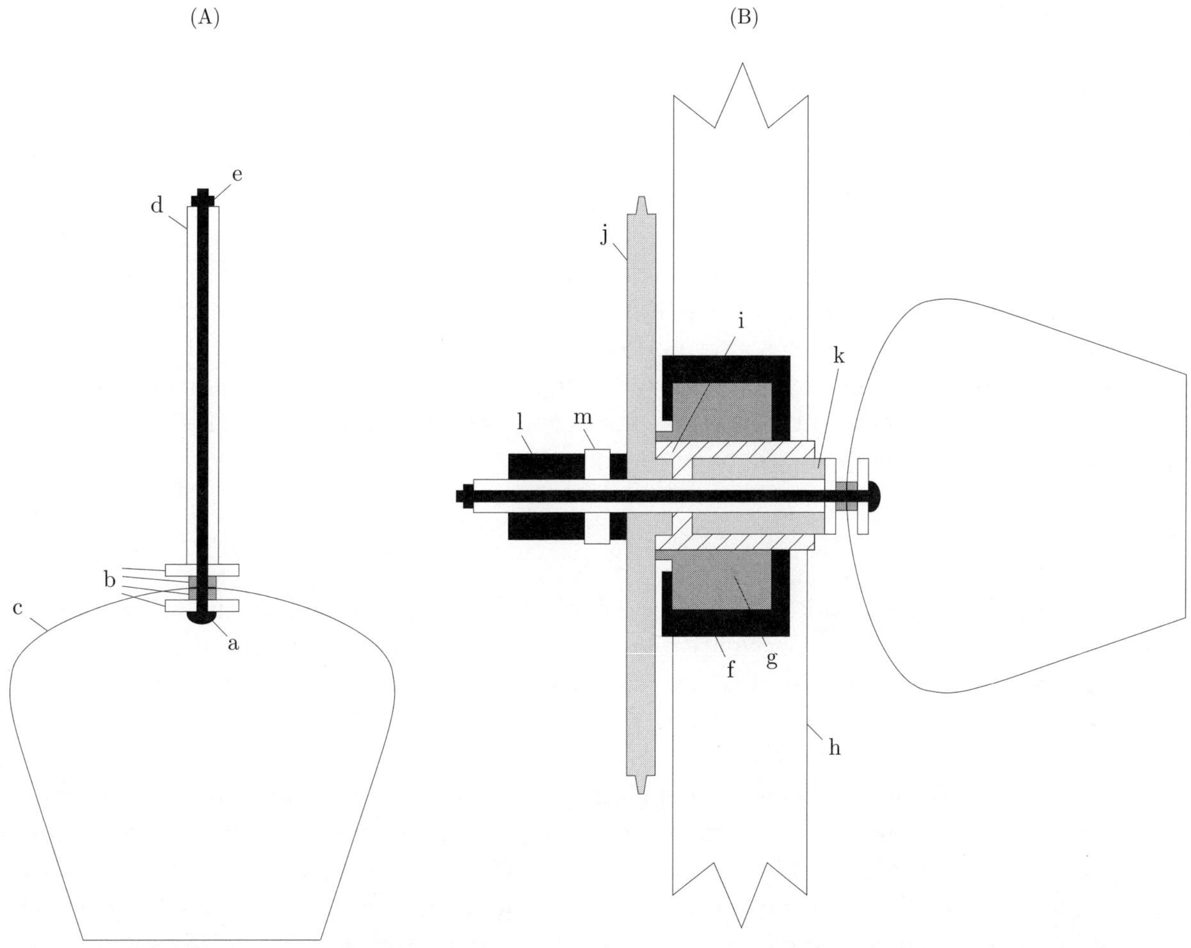

Figure 12.7 Parts and construction of the Glassdance stem and panel assemblies. (A) This transverse cross-section illustrates that a machine screw (a) passes through two standoff washers (b), a hole in the bottom of the crystal glass (c), two more standoff washers (b), and an aluminum stem (d). A nut (e) at the end of the machine screw holds these seven parts of the stem assembly together. (B) This transverse cross-section shows that I epoxied a neoprene ball bearing sleeve (f), which holds ball bearing (g), into a hole in the back of the Glassdance panel (h). I also epoxied an aluminum tube (i) into the inner race of the ball bearing. The hub of a chain sprocket (j) fastens into the inner opening of the tube, and a natural rubber liner (k) slips into the outer opening of the tube. Finally, the aluminum stem passes through the rubber liner, the sprocket hub, and a neoprene retainer (l). A hose clamp (m) tightens around the retainer, which holds the crystal glass securely in the panel assembly. (Not to scale.)

material eliminates the structure-borne sound produced by the ball bearings that support the eight transmission sprockets. A black box near the upper left corner of the case contains the DC motor controls. The left side of the box has an on/off toggle switch and an infinitely adjustable speed control switch. The performer accesses these switches through an opening in the left side of the case.

12.15

To understand the coupling between the crystal glasses and the chain sprockets, refer to Figure 12.7. Because commercially produced glasses have glass stems that are extremely fragile, I removed all the stems of the crystal glasses on the Glassdance. First, I drilled a hole dead center through the bottom of each glass with a diamond core drill bit attached to a water pump. Next, I cut off the stems with a diamond wire saw. Figure 12.7(A) shows that I passed a round head machine screw (a) through two standoff washers (b), the hole in the bottom of the crystal glass (c), two more standoff washers (b), and a new round aluminum stem (d). A nut (e) at the far end of the machine screw holds these seven parts of the stem assembly together. Figure 12.7(B) shows that I epoxied a neoprene ball bearing sleeve (f), which holds ball bearing (g), into a hole in the back of the Glassdance panel (h). The neoprene sleeve acts as a resilient mounting collar that significantly reduces the transmission of sound from the revolving bearing. I also epoxied an aluminum tube (i) into the inner race of the ball bearing. The hub of a chain sprocket (j) fastens into the inner opening of the tube, and a natural rubber liner (k) slips into the outer opening of the tube. The rubber liner provides a resilient seat for the outer portion of the aluminum stem, and for the large standoff washer outside the crystal glass. Finally, the aluminum stem passes through the rubber liner, the sprocket hub, and a neoprene retainer (l). A hose clamp (m) tightens around the retainer, which holds the crystal glass securely in the panel assembly.

12.16

With the exception of Glass #1 in the lower left-hand corner of Plate 9, all the others are large brandy glasses called snifters. The remarkable acoustic properties of these crystal snifters enabled me to tune two "octaves" from a single kind of glass. Even though the short glasses in the upper rows look completely different from the long glasses in the lower rows, they are all identical with respect to model number and manufacturer.

One of the most surprising moments in building the Glassdance occurred when I attempted to tune a snifter. Equipped with a precision diamond blade band saw, I sliced a ¾-in.-high ring from the rim of a glass. While absorbed in this delicate operation, I intended to increase the fundamental frequency of the glass. To my complete astonishment, the fundamental *decreased* by about 300 ¢. After a further removal of a 1-in.-high ring, the fundamental, as expected, *increased* by about 750 ¢. For a second glass, I sliced a 3⁄16-in.-high ring from the rim and the frequency *decreased* by about 200 ¢; and after a further removal of a ¾-in.-high ring, the fundamental decreased by only 78 ¢. All subsequent removals *increased* the fundamental.

To comprehend why the frequency of the fundamental decreased after reducing the mass of the glass, turn back to Chapter 6. Recall that stiffness acts as the only restoring force that returns a vibrating bar to its equilibrium position. This principle also applies to a vibrating glass. In Figure 12.8, observe that because the walls of a snifter constrict at the opening, the restoring force due to stiffness has an especially high value at the rim of the glass. In the upper portion indicated by three arrows, a removal of circular sections has a greater effect on the restoring force than on the mass. Removing rings of glass in this area causes the walls to become less stiff, or more flexible. Consequently, the walls vibrate less rapidly, which in turn *decreases* the fundamental frequency of the glass. However, after slicing three or four narrow rings from the top, the removal of material has a greater effect on the mass than on the restoring force. This causes the walls in the lower portion to vibrate more rapidly, which in turn *increases* the fundamental frequency of the glass. (See Section 6.9, for an analogous discussion on the effects of removing sections of materials from bars.)

I tune all the crystal glasses on the Glassdance in three steps. (1) With the diamond blade band saw, I cut rings from the glasses to bring them within about 100 ¢ of the desired tuning. (2) On a lap machine, which consists of a horizontally rotating flat cast-iron wheel, I use water and 180-, 220-, and 240-grit carborundum powder to bring them within about 25 ¢ of the desired tuning. (3) I then fine-tune the glasses with wet/dry 180-, 220-, 320-, 600-, and 1200-grit paper. Finally, I polish the rims with rouge compound on a solid wool buffing wheel. Figure 12.9 gives the frequency ratios of the Glassdance. The lowest tone is G_4 at 392.0 cps. The first "octave" up to G_5

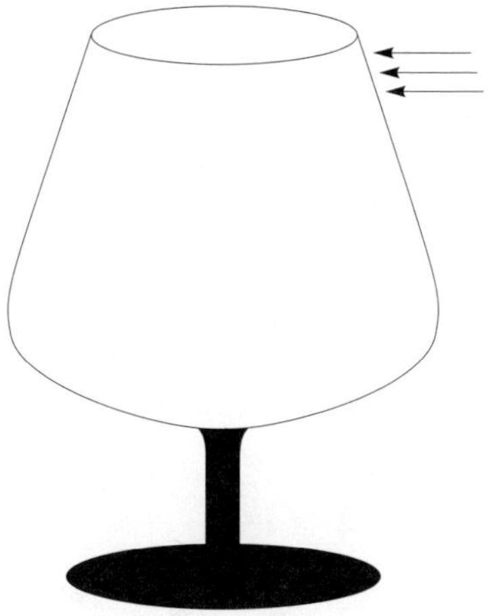

Figure 12.8 For a snifter, the restoring force due to stiffness has an especially high value at the constricted rim. In the upper portion indicated by the arrows, the removal of circular sections has a greater effect on the restoring force than on the mass. Removing rings of glass in this area causes the walls to vibrate less rapidly, which in turn *decreases* the fundamental frequency of the glass. However, after slicing three or four such rings from the top, the removal of material has a greater effect on the mass than on the restoring force. This causes the walls in the lower portion to vibrate more rapidly, which in turn *increases* the fundamental frequency of the glass.

at 784.0 cps contains 24 glasses, and the second "octave" up to G_6 at 1568.0 cps, 23 glasses. For all rows, the frequencies of the glasses increase from left to right.

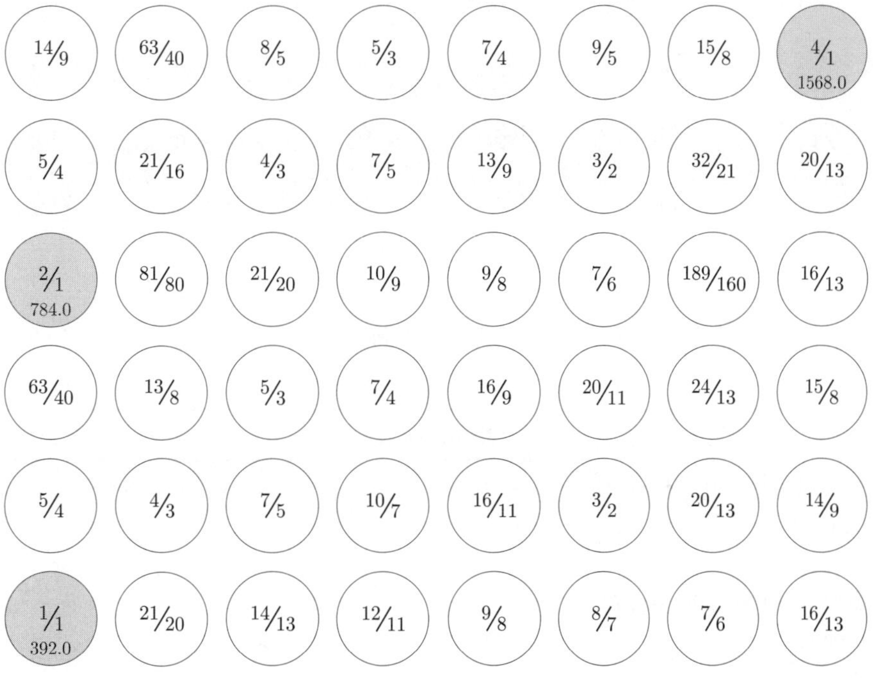

Figure 12.9 Frequency ratios of the Glassdance. Forty-eight crystal glasses span the interval of a "double-octave." The lower "octave" contains 24 glasses, and the upper "octave," 23 glasses.

12.17

In Section 10.21, I discussed the influence of the Greek theorist Claudius Ptolemy (*c.* A.D. 100 – *c.* 165) on the works of the Italian musician and theorist Gioseffo Zarlino (1517–1590). I also briefly mentioned my own fascination with Ptolemy's Soft Diatonic. Turn to Figure 12.10(a), and observe that when one plays the intervals of Ptolemy's Tense Diatonic — the Western major scale — in a descending direction, the result is a minor scale that includes four chromatic tones. Now, if we assign 7-limit ratios to these four chromatic tones, then Figure 12.10(b) indicates that one possible interpretation of this scale results in Ptolemy's Soft Diatonic in an ascending direction.

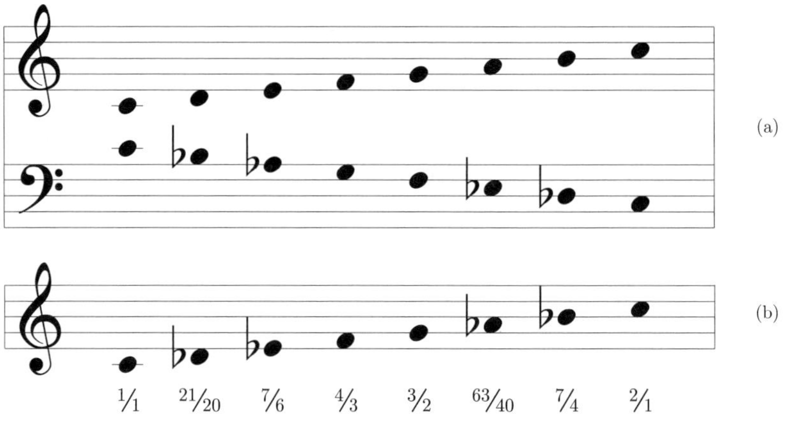

Figure 12.10 (a) The intervals of Ptolemy's Tense Diatonic in a descending direction produce his (b) Soft Diatonic in an ascending direction.

The Glassdance includes three versions of Ptolemy's Soft Diatonic, which begin on 1/1, 4/3, and 3/2:

1/1	21/20	**21/20**	10/9	**7/6**	8/7	**4/3**	9/8	**3/2**	21/20	**63/40**	10/9	**7/4**	8/7	**2/1**
4/3	21/20	**7/5**	10/9	**14/9**	8/7	**16/9**	9/8	**2/1**	21/20	**21/20**	10/9	**7/6**	8/7	**4/3**
3/2	21/20	**63/40**	10/9	**7/4**	8/7	**2/1**	9/8	**9/8**	21/20	**189/160**	10/9	**21/16**	8/7	**3/2**

GLASSDANCE

Built: 1982–83

Dimensions	
Total number of crystal glasses	48
Length of stand	55½ in.
Height of stand	42⅝ in.
Width of stand above the wheels	41⅞ in.
Length of case	51⅛ in.
Height of case	39.0 in.
Width of case	11 11/16 in.
Overall height of instrument	76⅜ in.

Wind Instruments

SIMPLE FLUTES

12.18

Plate 11 shows three Simple Flutes I made in 1995. For convenience, I will refer to the flutes on the left, in the middle, and on the right as Flute 1, Flute 2, and Flute 3, respectively. As discussed in Section 8.12, Flute 1 and Flute 3 are made from extruded acrylic tubes; and as discussed in Section 8.9, Flute 2 is made of amaranth wood. Table 8.2(b) gives the dimensions and tuning of Flute 1, and Table 8.3, the dimensions and tuning of Flute 2. For Flutes 1 and 3, the bore diameters (d_1), the tone hole diameters (d_H), the embouchure hole diameters (d_E), the wall thickness or the lengths of the tone holes (ℓ_H), and the tunings are identical. However, because the fundamental frequency of Flute 1 is G_4 at 392.0 cps, and the fundamental frequency of Flute 3 is D_4 at 294.0 cps, the lengths of the flute tubes and the distances between the embouchure holes and tone holes are different. Readers interested in the acoustics and design considerations of Flutes 1 and 2 should read, study, and absorb Chapter 8.

13 / BUILDING A LITTLE CANON

Parts, Materials, Labor, and Detailed Dimensions

The Little Canon in Plate 12 is the first musical instrument I built. Since a small canon is not too difficult to make, the following description may inspire some readers to build such an instrument, and to verify for themselves which intervals and scales sound consonant, and which sound dissonant.

The Little Canon consists of a long rectangular sound box equipped with six strings. Figure 13.1 shows a transverse cross-section of the sound box. The top or soundboard (a) and two sides (b) are redwood. Clear kiln-dried redwood is fairly resonant and, in Northern California, is easily obtained in many different dimensions. However, Sitka spruce works just as well, and produces a better tone. The base (c) is birch plywood. Plate 12 does not reveal the layers of the plywood base because I veneered the exterior edge with birch veneer. A rigid base is very important because it prevents the instrument from bending and twisting out of shape after the strings are tensioned. Also in Figure 13.1, note that the top and base overlap the side pieces. This design ensures that the top and base provide flat gluing surfaces. Now, in the corners along the entire lengths of the top and side pieces, and along the entire lengths of the base and side pieces, redwood liners (d) reinforce the sound box joints and strengthen the instrument as a whole. First, I glued the upper and lower liners to the sides. Next, I used flat head wood screws (e) and glue to secure the base to the sides. Finally, I fastened the top to the sides.

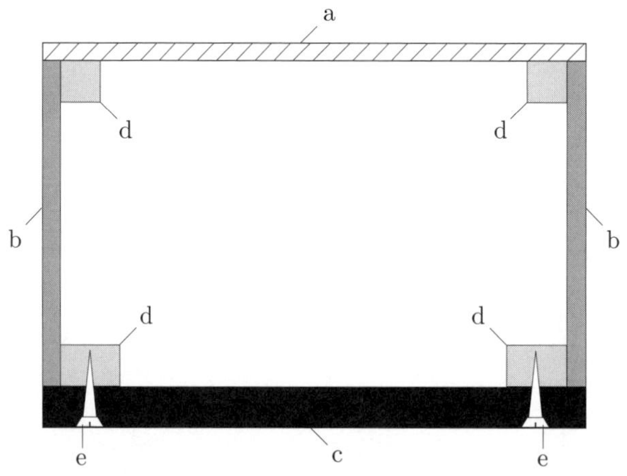

Figure 13.1 Parts and construction of the sound box of the Little Canon. This transverse cross-section shows that redwood top (a) and birch plywood base (c) overlap the redwood sides (b). Redwood liners (d), glued into the corners along the lengths of the top and side pieces, and along the lengths of the base and side pieces, reinforce the sound box joints. Flat head wood screws (e) secure the base to the sides.

Turn to Figure 13.2, which shows a longitudinal cross-section of the Little Canon. To close the structure, notice that I glued redwood end pieces (a) to the top and sides at the ends of the sound box. However, observe carefully that the plywood base (b) extends beyond the two end pieces. Flat head wood screws secure a rounded beech hitch block (c) to the base at the right end, and a short angled birch block (d) to the base at the left end of the instrument. I also glued these two blocks to the end pieces. Plate 12 shows that the hitch block on the right has six holes for threading and fastening the ends of the strings. The angled block on the left supports a birch tuning gear bracket (e). Four oval head wood screws secure the tuning gear bracket to the angled block. Also, note that I cut two long slots into the bracket. I then drilled three holes that pass through the front edge, the front slot, and into the body of the bracket; similarly, three holes pass through the back edge, the back slot, and into the body of the bracket. Next, I inserted three nylon posts of a tuning gear assembly (f) through the front holes, and three nylon posts of a tuning gear assembly through the back holes. Four screws hold each assembly in place. Three strings enter each slot and wind around the nylon posts to tension the strings.

Plate 12 and Figure 13.2 show that a birch nut (g) and a stationary maple bridge (h) support six strings (i). The nut and bridge have hard rosewood caps to prevent the strings from cutting into these parts. I glued the nut into an angled slot in the tuning gear bracket and against the left end piece; and I epoxied the bridge on the top near the hitch block. Both components have a height of ⅞ in. above the redwood top or soundboard so that the strings run parallel to the surface of the soundboard. Finally, six moveable oak bridges (j) divide the strings into different vibrating lengths.

With respect to materials, there are two basic kinds of wood: softwoods and hardwoods. Spruce and redwood are domestic softwoods; birch, beech, maple, and oak are domestic hardwoods. Rosewood is a tropical hardwood with a weight density greater than water, which means it does not float. (See Appendices E and G.) For the sound box and liners, it is important to use clear kiln-dried redwood or spruce. However, for the rest of the instrument, all domestic hardwoods work equally well. I used five different hardwoods simply because they were available to me.

I strongly recommend yellow woodworking glue called aliphatic resin glue, and two-part clear epoxy. Do not use white glue or hide glue. Also, I no longer use wood screws. The tapered shanks and shallow threads of these screws do not cut into the fibers of the wood very well. Instead, I use sheet metal screws (also called tapping screws) in wood. These screws have cylindrical shanks and extremely sharp and deep threads.

The lengths of commercial acoustic guitar strings determine the distance of the Little Canon from the farthest tuning gear posts to the hitch block. Since this instrument requires six identical strings, one must buy six identical sets of guitar strings because all the strings in a single set have different diameters. Readers interested in building large canons with long strings must make their own strings. Piano supply houses and some local piano technicians sell high-carbon spring steel music wire in 1 lb. rolls. However, piano wires do not work for making canon strings because the diameters are too thick and, therefore, require too much tension to produce a good tone. See Appendix D for ordering thin steel music wire sizes with diameters in the 0.016–0.024 in. range. Also, tuning gears equipped with long nylon posts are available from local guitar shops.

Readers who would like to own a small canon but are not inclined to build one must hire a woodworker. A professional should require approximately 10 hours to build such an instrument. The sound box is the most time-consuming task. First, thick boards must be either resawn or surface planed to make the thin top, side, and end pieces. Then the liners must be glued to the inside surfaces of the sides before the sound box can be assembled. While the glue is drying, all the other parts can be made. To minimize labor charges, the reader should have the tuning gears and strings available for measuring before the building begins.

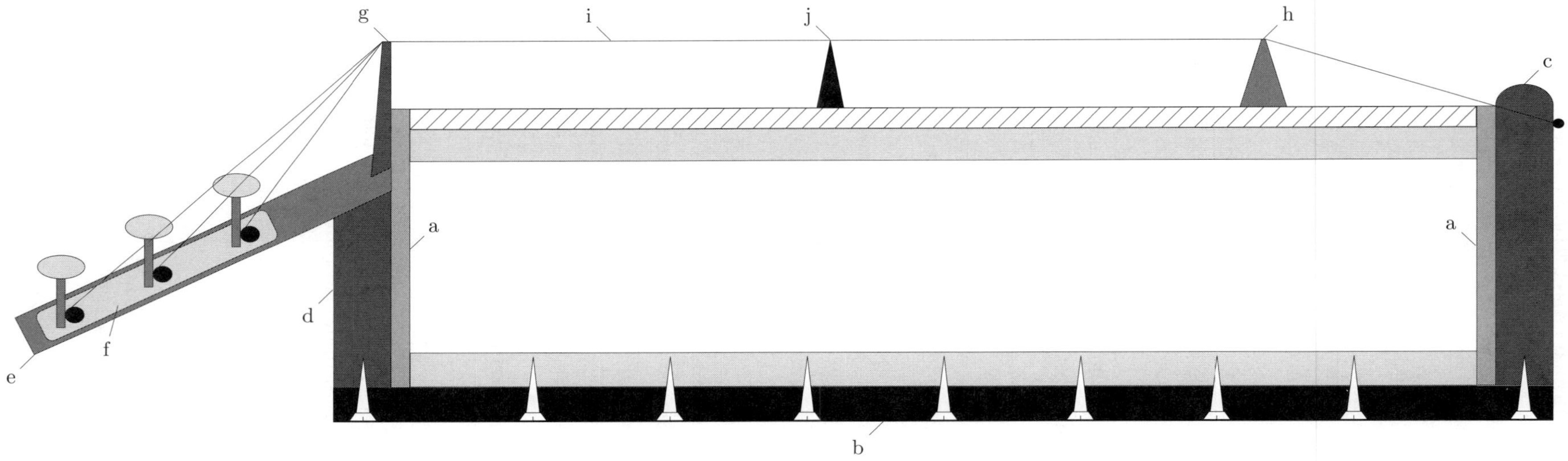

Figure 13.2 Parts and construction of the Little Canon. This longitudinal cross-section shows that redwood end pieces (a) close the sound box as described in Figure 13.1. Birch plywood base (b) extends beyond the end pieces. Flat head wood screws secure beech hitch block (c) and angled birch block (d) to the base. The hitch block anchors six strings, and the angled block supports a birch tuning gear bracket (e). The latter part holds two tuning gear assemblies (f). Birch nut (g) and stationary maple bridge (h) support six strings (i) above the redwood top or soundboard. Finally, six moveable oak bridges (j) divide the strings into different vibrating lengths. (Not to scale.)

In conclusion, according to Equation 2.10, a steel string with a fundamental frequency of middle C at 260.0 cps, a vibrating length of $24\frac{7}{8}$ in., and a diameter of 0.022 in. has a tension of 46.62 lbf; six such strings produce 279.72 lbf. This total amount of force is well within the structural limitations of the Little Canon.

LITTLE CANON

Built: 1975

Detailed Dimensions	
Total number of strings	6
Vibrating length of strings from the left nut to the stationary bridge	$24\frac{7}{8}$ in.
Length of top piece	28.0 in.
Thickness of top piece	$\frac{3}{16}$ in.
Width of top piece	$5\frac{7}{16}$ in.
Length of side pieces	28.0 in.
Thickness of side pieces	$\frac{3}{16}$ in.
Height of side pieces	$3\frac{1}{8}$ in.
Length of upper liners	28.0 in.
Width and height of upper liners	$\frac{1}{2}$ in. × $\frac{1}{2}$ in.
Length of lower liners	28.0 in.
Width and height of lower liners	$\frac{3}{4}$ in. × $\frac{1}{2}$ in.
Length of end pieces	$5\frac{7}{16}$ in.
Thickness of end pieces	$\frac{3}{16}$ in.
Height of end pieces	$3\frac{5}{16}$ in.
Length of plywood base	$29\frac{5}{8}$ in.
Thickness of base	$\frac{1}{2}$ in.
Width of base	$5\frac{7}{16}$ in.
Length of hitch block	$5\frac{7}{16}$ in.
Thickness of hitch block	$\frac{11}{16}$ in.
Height of hitch block to the top of the curve	$3\frac{1}{2}$ in.
Length of angled block	$5\frac{7}{16}$ in.
Thickness of angled block	$\frac{9}{16}$ in.
Height of angled block to the top of the angle	$2\frac{3}{16}$ in.
Height of angled block to the bottom of the angle	$2\frac{1}{16}$ in.
Overall length of tuning gear bracket	6.0 in.
Thickness of tuning gear bracket	$\frac{3}{4}$ in.
Width of tuning gear bracket at wide end	$5\frac{1}{4}$ in.
Width of tuning gear bracket at narrow end	$2\frac{7}{8}$ in.
Length of tuning gear bracket that holds the tuning gear assemblies	$4\frac{5}{8}$ in.

LITTLE CANON
(continued)

Detailed Dimensions	
Length of left nut	5¼ in.
Thickness of left nut at the bottom	¼ in.
Thickness of left nut at the top	⅛ in.
Overall height of left nut	1¾ in.
Height of left nut above the top piece	⅞ in.
Length of stationary bridge	5⅝ in.
Thickness of stationary bridge at the bottom	⅜ in.
Thickness of stationary bridge at the top	⅛ in.
Height of stationary bridge above the top piece	⅞ in.
Distance from the right bottom edge of the bridge to the hitch block	3¼ in.
Height of moveable bridges	1.0 in.
Thickness of moveable bridges at the bottom	⅜ in.
Thickness of moveable bridges at the top	1/16 in.
Width of moveable bridges	1.0 in.

Epilog

After years of reading *Musical Mathematics* through its many manifestations, I was elated when Cris completed the manuscript. As we prepared the volume for publication, though, I couldn't dispel the idea that something was still missing. It finally occurred to me that the book contained very little personal information about its author, and no explanation at all about how such a unique work had evolved. To rectify the situation, I proposed to write this epilog. I realized that my intimate perspective has given me a unique vantage point from which to tell the inside story of Cris Forster and his life's work. Because of his modesty, he rarely mentions himself directly in the book, nor does he discuss the Chrysalis Foundation, a nonprofit he established in 1982 to support his creative endeavors as builder, composer, performer, and writer. His journey has been fascinating, and the result of his dedication to the field of acoustic music now rests in your hands. In the next few pages, I hope to convey a more comprehensive overview of how this book came to be, and of the remarkable man who has given us all the gift of *Musical Mathematics*.

Cris Forster was born in Rio de Janeiro, Brazil, in 1948. He immigrated with his intrepid mother to Berlin, Germany, in 1954, and together they took the ocean voyage to New York in 1958. Having undergone two intercontinental immigrations by the age of ten, Cris was already beginning to develop his hallmark traits of independence and nonconformity. He spent his high school years in Southern California, surfing, listening to Beethoven and jazz, and attempting to assimilate. After living on both coasts of the United States and becoming a U.S. citizen in 1966, assimilation still eluded him.

In early fall of his high school senior year, Cris traveled to Santa Cruz, California, to meet the man who would change the course of his life from that day forward. Page Smith was provost of Cowell College, and one of the principal founders of the University of California at Santa Cruz. He had designed the newly established school around his philosophy of learning from original sources. Provost Smith saw great potential in the young man before him, despite the rough edges of his academic résumé, and granted him admission to the university. The same time next year, Cris was in his element, thriving in a world of redwood groves and original texts, learning from the masters of history, literature, and philosophy in their own words. In 1970, after four of the happiest years of his life, he received a B.A. in history, cum laude, from U.C. Santa Cruz.

With his first degree completed, Cris could no longer ignore his intensifying desire to study music. Although he always yearned to play the piano, the nomadic nature of his family precluded owning such a large instrument, so he had conceded to playing traditional piano repertoire on a more portable substitute, the accordion. Now, at last, he was free to pursue his passion. Opportunity came to him while sitting on the courthouse steps in Santa Cruz, fasting in protest of the Vietnam War. He struck up a conversation with the man who eventually sold him his first piano. For the next year, Cris spent mornings walking the town as a door-to-door salesman, afternoons and evenings in the blissful immersion of intense practicing. With the help of Anna Hermitage, a retired music teacher he met on his sales route one day, he learned the basic theory he craved, and subsequently made the crucial decision to study music seriously. By 1974, he had received his second degree, a B.A. in music, piano performance, from Lone Mountain College, San Francisco.

At Lone Mountain, Cris had practiced eight hours a day, studying the great works of piano literature. He had also trained to become a certified piano tuner and technician, a skill that would serve as a springboard into his future life as an instrument builder, as well as an important source of income. For the next twenty years, he would cultivate his expertise in every aspect of piano tuning, reconstruction, and maintenance.

While he was learning to tune pianos, Cris discovered that he had acutely sensitive hearing. He became intrigued by the possibility of tuning systems beyond twelve-tone equal temperament, and he began to contemplate instruments that could produce such tunings. Gradually, the interpretive life of a concert performer began to lose its appeal, while the freedom of conceptual creativity beckoned. Now the choices were becoming more critical, the stakes higher. Should he stay on his current path and accept the full scholarship offered him to pursue his master's degree in music, or leave academia behind and chart his own course? He chose the latter, and thus began his life as builder of original acoustic instruments and musical explorer.

Never one to vacillate, Cris sold his grand piano to buy a band saw and went to work. There is a picture of him holding his first instrument, a little canon, with a look of pure happiness on his face. Propelled by the exhilaration of being on the right path, Cris learned everything he could about the world of tools and materials, then launched into building his first concert-size instrument. He remembers the day the bridge he had crafted out of rosewood exploded under excessive string tension, instilling in him a healthy respect for the powerful forces of the physical world. After regaining his composure, he successfully rebuilt the bridge from aluminum. When it was finished in 1976, he named his instrument in tribute to a proverb told him by Anna Hermitage: "Never help a butterfly escape its chrysalis. It needs the struggle to gain the strength for flight."

Inspired by the Chrysalis, Cris completed his next instrument, the Harmonic/Melodic Canon, in 1976. (This instrument evolved over the next ten years, undergoing reconstruction in 1981 and 1987 until it satisfied his exacting requirements.) Soon after completing the prototype Canon, he received a Special Projects Grant from the California Arts Council to compose and perform his first major work, *Song of Myself: Intoned Poems of Walt Whitman* for voice, Chrysalis, and Harmonic/Melodic Canon. The composition, a setting of eleven poems from Whitman's original fifty-two, was completed in 1976. He initially performed his entire cycle from memory; later, he devised an ingenious notational system and transcribed the score by hand, printing the First Edition in 1980. We privately published an edited Second Edition of this score in 2000.

Ever questing for hands-on experience, Cris moved to San Diego to be near the microtonal community thriving there. His skill and dedication were quickly recognized, and he was appointed curator for the Harry Partch Foundation, a position he held from 1976 to 1980. During this time, he tuned, repaired, and rebuilt virtually all of Partch's instruments. In addition to his instrument tuning and maintenance responsibilities, Cris cataloged Partch's personal correspondences and private effects. Without his meticulous care, many important documents would have been lost forever. He acted as liaison between the Partch Foundation and prominent figures in the contemporary music community. And, he learned to play several of the percussion and stringed instruments, soon becoming a fiery performer with the Partch ensemble. Despite the many hours he spent in service to the Partch Foundation, his own work continued with the construction of the Diamond Marimba, completed in 1978. (As with the Harmonic/Melodic Canon, he would revise the Diamond in 1982 and completely rebuild it in 1989.)

In 1980, Cris coordinated a production of Partch's *The Bewitched* at the Berlin Music Festival, followed by a recording session in Cologne. For this tour, he designed huge crates to accommodate all the instruments, constructing them to meet airline forklift specifications and cargo hold dimensions. His fluent German made him an indispensable negotiator with festival directors in Germany, and later, translator to the troupe of touring musicians who relied upon him for everything from meals to medications. Still, Cris found time and energy for his own work. He performed *Song of Myself* at the Berlin festival, where it was warmly received. An eloquent review by Sybill Mahlke for *Der Tagesspiegel* describes his magical performance of the Whitman poem cycle.

Cris left the Partch Foundation after the Berlin tour. He returned to his profession of piano tuner and technician, and he gained respect as a tuner of bar percussion instruments. These pursuits made ends meet, but his imagination was filled with ideas for more instruments, and he was struggling to afford the expensive tooling, machinery, and raw materials required to build them. He realized he would need more than just determination and good luck to accomplish his goals, so, in 1982, he established the Chrysalis Foundation.

Cris used his nonprofit status in an unconventional way. Rather than to ask for donations of money, he went directly to industrial manufacturers in the United States and Japan to solicit parts, tools, and materials for the construction of his instruments. He met with resounding success. Many companies generously donated or discounted their products in return for recognition in Chrysalis Foundation publicity materials and concert program notes. Fafnir Bearing donated ball bearings for the Glassdance, then featured an article about Cris and his instrument in their trade publication, *The Precisionist.* Sasaki Crystal furnished fine crystal brandy snifters; several years later, Mr. Sasaki himself visited from Japan to see and hear the instrument that incorporated his glasses. Impressed, he invited the young builder to come work for him in Japan, an offer that Cris politely refused. The list of providers grew to impressive proportions. These companies appreciated the prospect of such novel applications for their products, and so the ensemble of instruments continued to grow. Cris constructed his most complex instrument, the Glassdance, in 1982 and 1983, then started to build the Bass Marimba in 1983, working out of a one-car garage in San Diego. During this time, his efforts attracted attention and articles appeared in numerous publications, including *Life Magazine*, *San Diego Magazine*, *Omni Magazine*, and *The New Grove Dictionary of Musical Instruments.*

In 1983, Cris decided to move back to San Francisco, and our paths converged. I had initially met him at Lone Mountain College in 1973, while living in the dorms there and attending the San Francisco Conservatory of Music. He tuned my piano, and we struck up a friendship based on our mutual love of music. When I heard him perform *Song of Myself*, I was profoundly moved. His music inspired me as none had ever done before, inviting me into a realm of subtle and intimate human expressiveness. I followed his career with fascination and our friendship continued, even after he had moved to San Diego. We reunited upon his return to San Francisco and were married in 1985.

Cris transformed our basement into a professional workshop where he proceeded to build increasingly imaginative and sophisticated musical instruments. In a remarkable burst of inspired energy from 1984 through 1990, he completed the giant and powerful Bass Marimba (1986); invented the String Winder (1987); designed and built the Bass Canon (1989); and created the Just Keys (1990). In addition, he composed, trained musicians, gave lectures in conjunction with exhibits of the instruments, and staged public performances of his works.

I was fortunate to be in the midst of such intense creativity. I marveled at Cris' boundless energy and absorbed all that I could through observing him at work. To live with these splendid instruments was a musician's dream come true, but to have their physical properties and the mathematical principals behind their tunings explained to me by their maker was even better. Cris introduced me to the thrill of having direct contact with these vibrating sources of extraordinary sound, and he gave me free access to explore all the instruments. The one that most enchanted me was the Glassdance, which I loved for its ethereal, translucent tones, and for its distinctive ability to generate flowing, sustained streams of sound. Cris patiently taught me to play the Glassdance, first using all types of handheld glasses to sensitize my fingers and ears to the medium, later, transferring this familiarity to the instrument, where he showed me how to produce the best sound by moving my body freely and efficiently. Learning to play the Glassdance will be a lifetime discipline. During our first seven years together, I played Cris' music with an ensemble of musicians under his direction that performed in San Francisco and around the Bay Area.

Simultaneously, Cris and I were developing the more conventional aspects of the Chrysalis Foundation. We established a board of trustees, then gradually began to cultivate a community of patrons who contributed time, energy, and funds to keep the work going. In return, we were motivated to reciprocate through community service projects. Cris donated his materials and labor to build musical instruments for other nonprofit organizations; the Foundation sponsored two children's musical theater productions, organized art exhibits, and funded performances by independent musicians.

Throughout these years, Cris was continually at work on a growing series of compositions destined to become part of a large work for musicians and dancers entitled *Ellis Island/Angel Island: A Vision of the American Immigrants.* Based on his own life experiences and scored for the full ensemble of instruments, this ambitious project occupied his musical imagination. His efforts to compose were seriously constrained, however, by the lack of a studio. The instruments were scattered over three floors of our home in San Francisco, from the upstairs living room to the ground floor workshop. Finally, it became impossible to continue. Despite our efforts, we were unable to attain a space large enough to house all of the instruments.

Frustrated and exhausted, Cris stopped building and performing. He withdrew into isolation to seek another pathway for his artistic energy. Although he had considered it many times before, he now decided in earnest to write a book. He wanted to create a comprehensive volume that would elucidate all he had learned and experienced during his twenty-year immersion in the study of acoustic music, and to share this with his fellow musicians. Little did he know when he began in 1990 that *Musical Mathematics* would take ten years of intensive work to write, and another nine to correct, edit, index, typeset, and prepare for publication. It was an arduous, concentrated, all-consuming labor of love. In his research for the book, Cris was grateful to be in the midst of so many fine libraries, and he frequented many university campuses throughout the Bay Area. He went online to access libraries worldwide, and through them obtained valuable books, treatises, and dissertations. Motivated by his early training at Santa Cruz, he diligently sought original texts to study. He worked tirelessly, always holding the thought of his reader foremost in his mind. His goal was to make *Musical Mathematics* accessible to anyone with a high school background in music and math, and a desire to learn. Chapter by chapter, the book took on a life of its own and inexorably pulled him deeper and deeper into its requirements: research of original sources, distillation of massive amounts of information into essential principles, and confirmation of everything via hands-on experimentation in the shop or on the instruments.

By 2000, after a ten-year hiatus from building, composing, and performing, Cris was ready to return to music making, fortified and inspired by all he had learned on his long journey into *Musical Mathematics.* He began to practice once again. I reactivated the Chrysalis Foundation and recruited a community of patrons to support our work. We renewed our efforts to find a studio large enough to house the full ensemble of instruments and, in 2002, finally succeeded in leasing a 2100-square-foot building in San Francisco. Although the space had great potential, it took seven months of strenuous work and the help of a team of generous individuals to convert an empty warehouse into the intimate rehearsal/performance space we had envisioned. In June 2003, we moved the instruments into their new home, the Chrysalis New Music Studio. Cris' persistent nightmares about finding and losing shelter for his instruments ceased at last.

With the instruments securely together under one roof, Cris returned to his musical life, practicing many hours each day and once again applying himself to the rigors of composing *Ellis Island/ Angel Island.* The Chrysalis Foundation continued its tradition of presenting groundbreaking performances by opening the doors of the Chrysalis New Music Studio to enthusiastic audiences. Cris devoted many patient hours to training young musicians who participated in an internship program sponsored by the Argosy Foundation Contemporary Music Fund. And, in 2006, with the generous collaboration of esteemed professional filmmaker Eli Noyes, I wrote and produced a documentary about Cris and the Chrysalis Foundation entitled *A Voyage in Music.* In a single hour of film, it encapsulates thirty years of development in the field of acoustic music and gives viewers a succinct yet comprehensive overview of a remarkable man's lifework.

By 2007, we had succeeded in accomplishing many significant goals; yet one aspiration remained unfulfilled. *Musical Mathematics* was gathering dust, and the burden of its unresolved publication was weighing heavy on Cris' soul. Efforts to find an academic or scientific press with the courage to espouse such a revolutionary work had proved futile. It seemed that our only remaining option was to self-publish, and that prospect grew increasingly viable as we researched sophisticated advancements in desktop publishing. Delving deeper into the requirements of preparing a 1400-page manuscript to go to press, we discovered that it must be reformatted and professionally typeset to reduce its size and bring it up to publishing standards. Once again, Cris faced the dilemma of sacrificing his musical work in service to the book. Although he was absorbed in composing and planning another internship program, he realized that he alone was qualified to successfully navigate the restructuring of his complicated network of ideas and relationships. On August 1, 2008, in what he calls a "mythological moment," he walked away from the studio and began the unenviable task of transforming *Musical Mathematics* into its present manifestation.

Farsighted patrons supported this new venture, expressing conviction in the significance of the book, and optimism toward bequeathing it to future generations. Buoyed by their encouragement, and equipped with his intimate knowledge of the manuscript and his technological competence, Cris dedicated himself completely to working on this enormous undertaking. Our kind and generous friend Douglas Monsour donated a state-of-the-art computer system to manage the complicated demands of the design software programs. Aided by this powerful machine, and with his inimitable iron discipline, Cris made excellent progress. In the same way that he makes jigs to facilitate his building process, he created more than three hundred macros to automate all the programs used in reformatting *Musical Mathematics.* Just as he fabricates parts for his instruments that don't exist commercially, he designed fonts and specialized glyphs of his own invention for the book. And, as the form of his instruments always follows their musical function, so the restructuring of the book illuminates its content and enhances its accessibility for readers. In June 2009, Cris finished redesigning and typesetting the book.

Meanwhile, in a development nothing short of miraculous, Chronicle Books stepped forward with an offer to publish *Musical Mathematics.* All the years of hard work had culminated in this astonishing decision by an established and well-respected publishing company to recognize the book's long-term potential. Their resolve has translated into this hardbound volume, now circulating in the world with the power to enlighten, influence, and invigorate the development of acoustic music.

Prospects for the future are bright. Cris continues to compose original music of profound significance. The musician recruitment and training program is carrying out the educational aims of the Foundation, and distribution of *Musical Mathematics* will reach a far larger audience of potential students. Ongoing work-in-progress performances at the Chrysalis New Music Studio will lead to collaboration with a choreographer, dancers, designers, and technicians, and to the final goal of this phase in Chrysalis Foundation history: the premiere of *Ellis Island/Angel Island* at a major San Francisco venue.

I would like to close this epilog with a few thoughts about the importance of *Musical Mathematics.* This book is an integral catalyst to the future development of acoustic music. If we are to influence the course of musical history, the full history must first be told, and that is exactly what Cris Forster has done. He has taken the complex history of Western tuning and the even more inscrutable subject of world tunings out of the realm of the elitist. He has distilled massive amounts of information into essential principles, and translated his experiences as a practicing builder, composer, and musician into language that is accessible to a wide audience. The instruments he has built are the physical embodiments of principles discussed in the book, and the music he composes for them illustrates some of the vast creative potential to be found through exploring new tunings.

This work strives to raise the standard for the study of acoustic music, and to challenge all those who care about this discipline to a more thorough and rigorous investigation into what it means to make music.

Innovators have always met with fierce resistance during their lifetimes. There is always fear that a challenge to the status quo will cause disruption of established hierarchies, and always a tendency to gravitate toward complacency, especially when the subject at hand is one so revered as music. But I am hopeful that *Musical Mathematics* will have the power to dissolve such criticism and apathy. Cris' independent spirit has cleared a path for the next generation to explore. He teaches us, by example, that the work of a musician is more complex, more demanding, more challenging, and ultimately, more rewarding than we ever dreamed. Music is, after all, a fine art, and to perpetuate only what we know is not enough. Cris Forster's visionary work elevates our awareness of what we take for granted, encourages us to question these "constants," and shows us that creativity lives within variables.

Ultimately, only history holds the power to validate. In the future, I am certain that this book will be considered a milestone in the evolution of musical thought. The sooner it enters the mainstream, the sooner it can exert its influence upon an art form in need of revitalization. Through *Musical Mathematics*, music can continue to be a vital force capable of addressing and expressing the complexities of our modern minds and spirits.

Heidi Forster
San Francisco, California
January 2010

Plate 1

CHRYSALIS

Photo by Will Gullette

Plate 2 HARMONIC/MELODIC CANON *Photo by Will Gullette*

Plate 3 BASS CANON *Photo by Will Gullette*

Plate 4 STRING WINDER (machine) *Photo by Will Gullette*

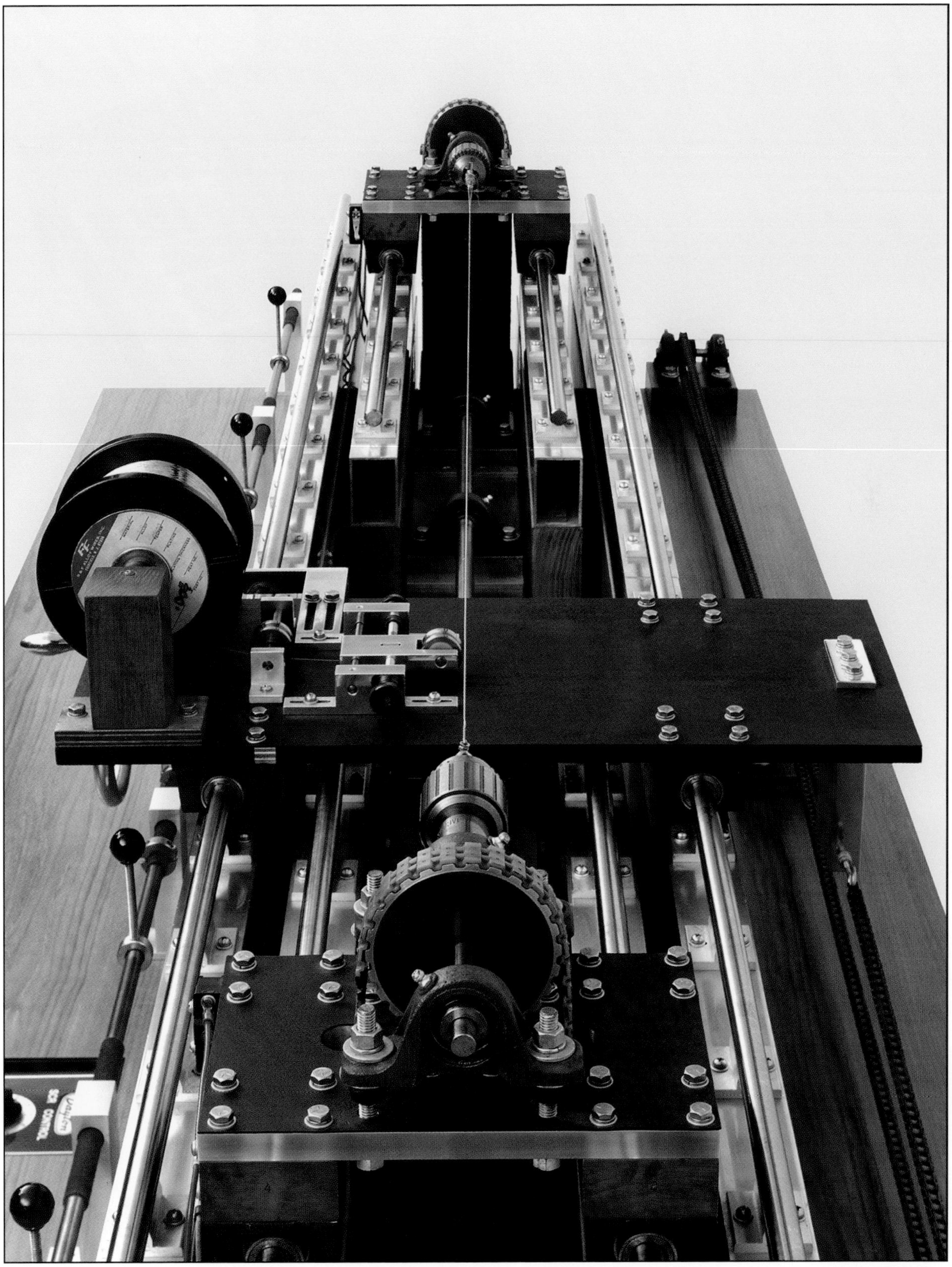

Plate 5 STRING WINDER (detail) *Photo by Will Gullette*

Plate 6 JUST KEYS *Photo by Will Gullette*

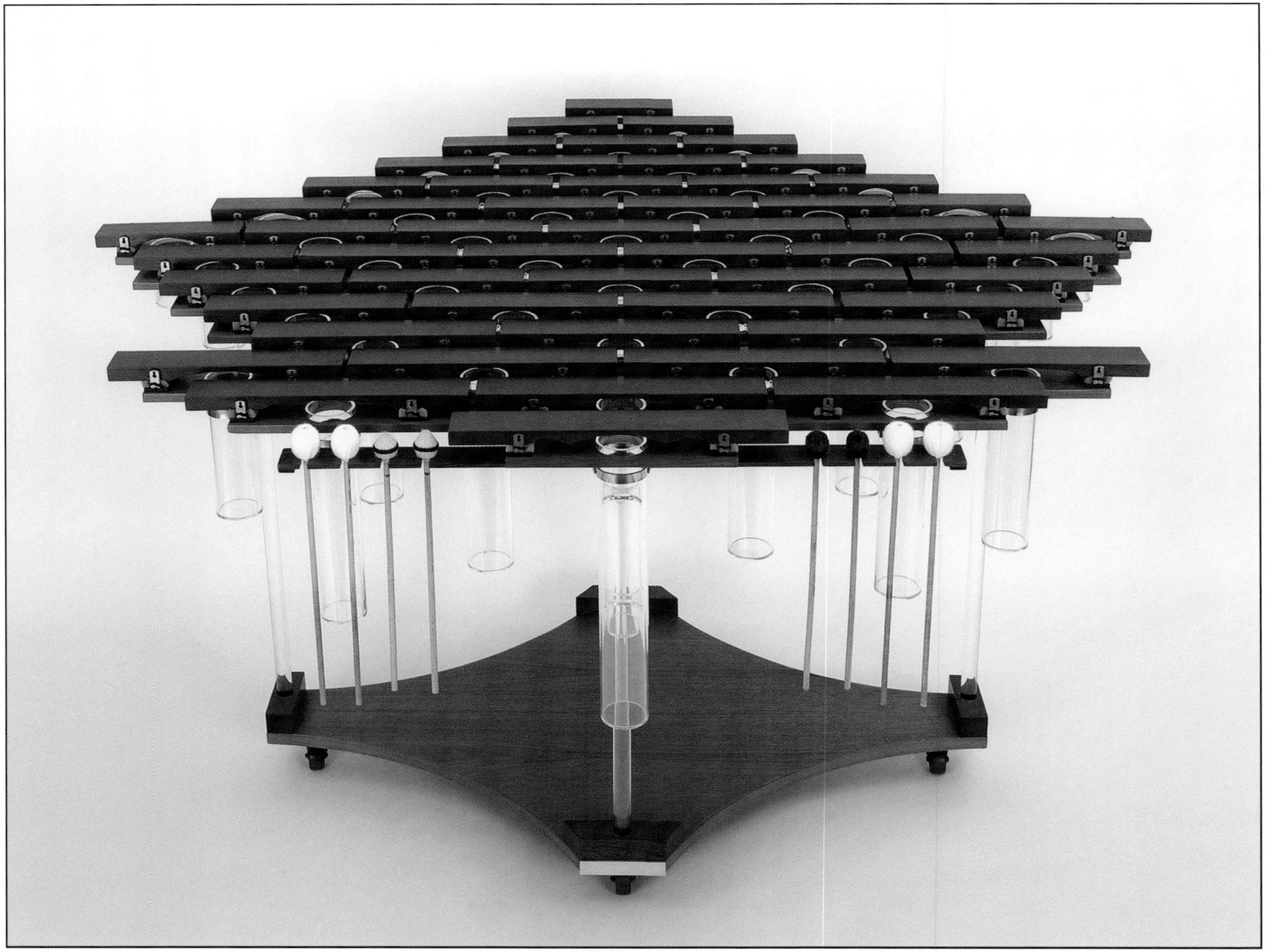

Plate 7 DIAMOND MARIMBA *Photo by Will Gullette*

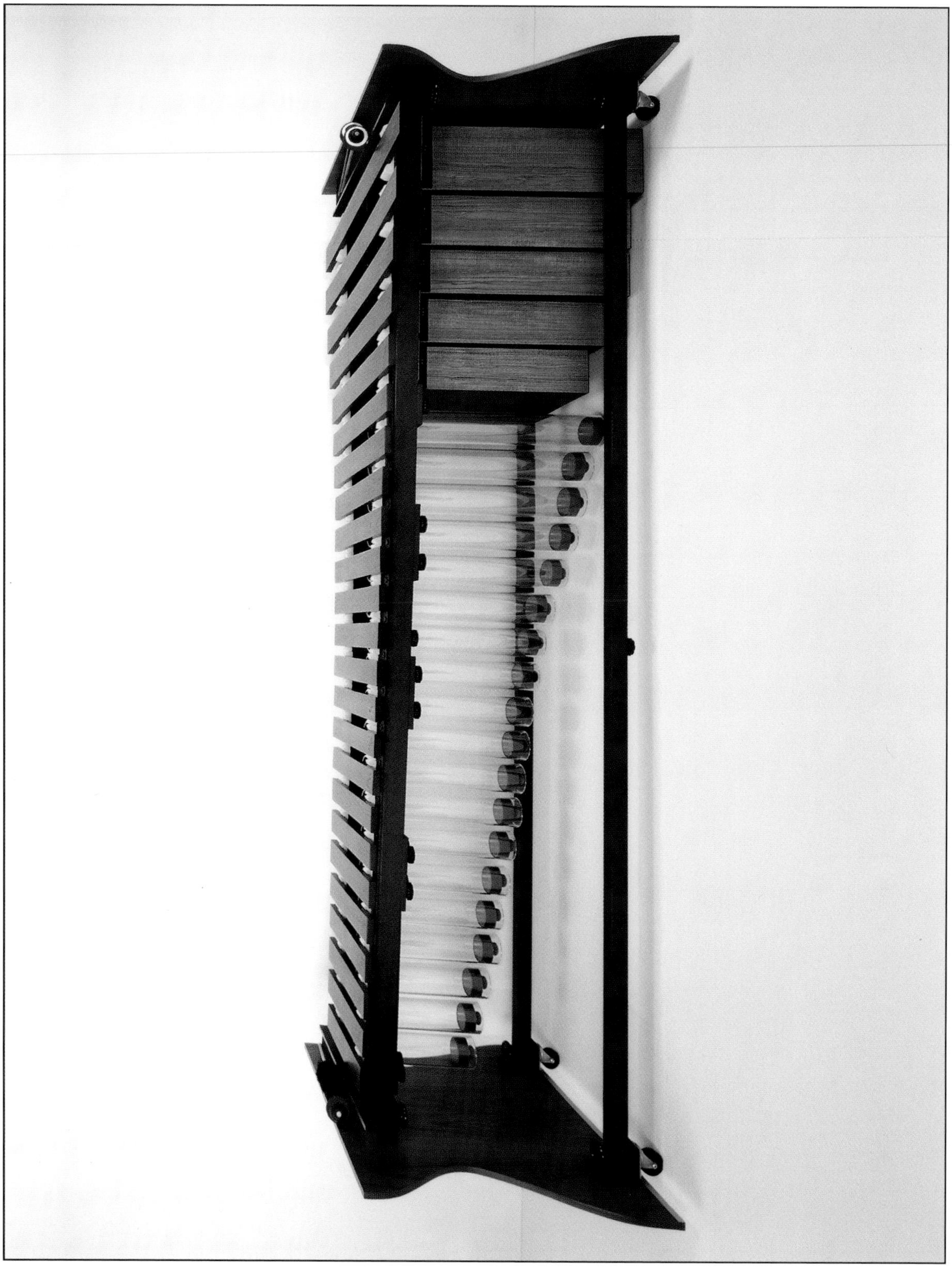

Plate 8 BASS MARIMBA *Photo by Will Gullette*

Plate 9 GLASSDANCE *Photo by Will Gullette*

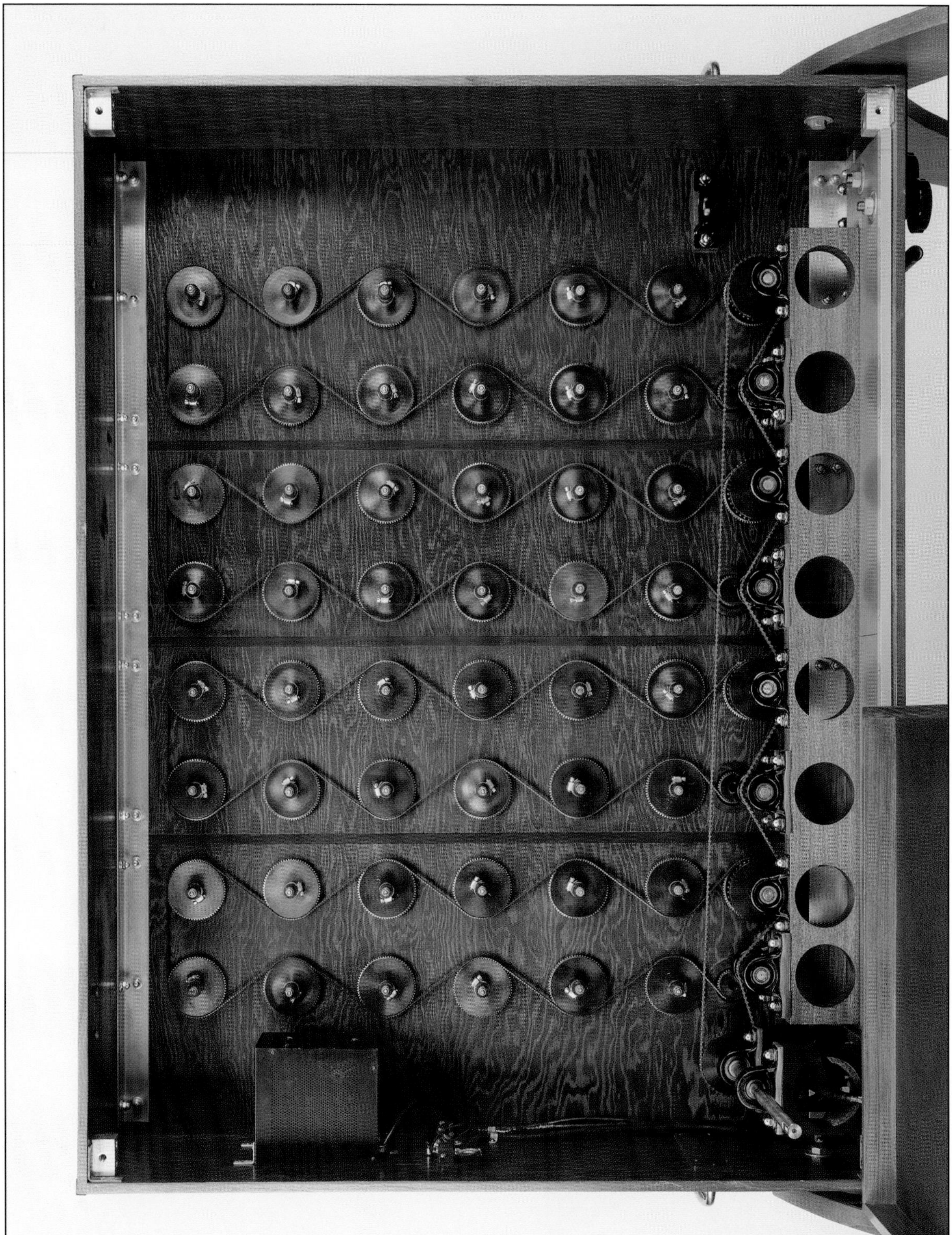

Plate 10 GLASSDANCE (back)

Photo by Will Gullette

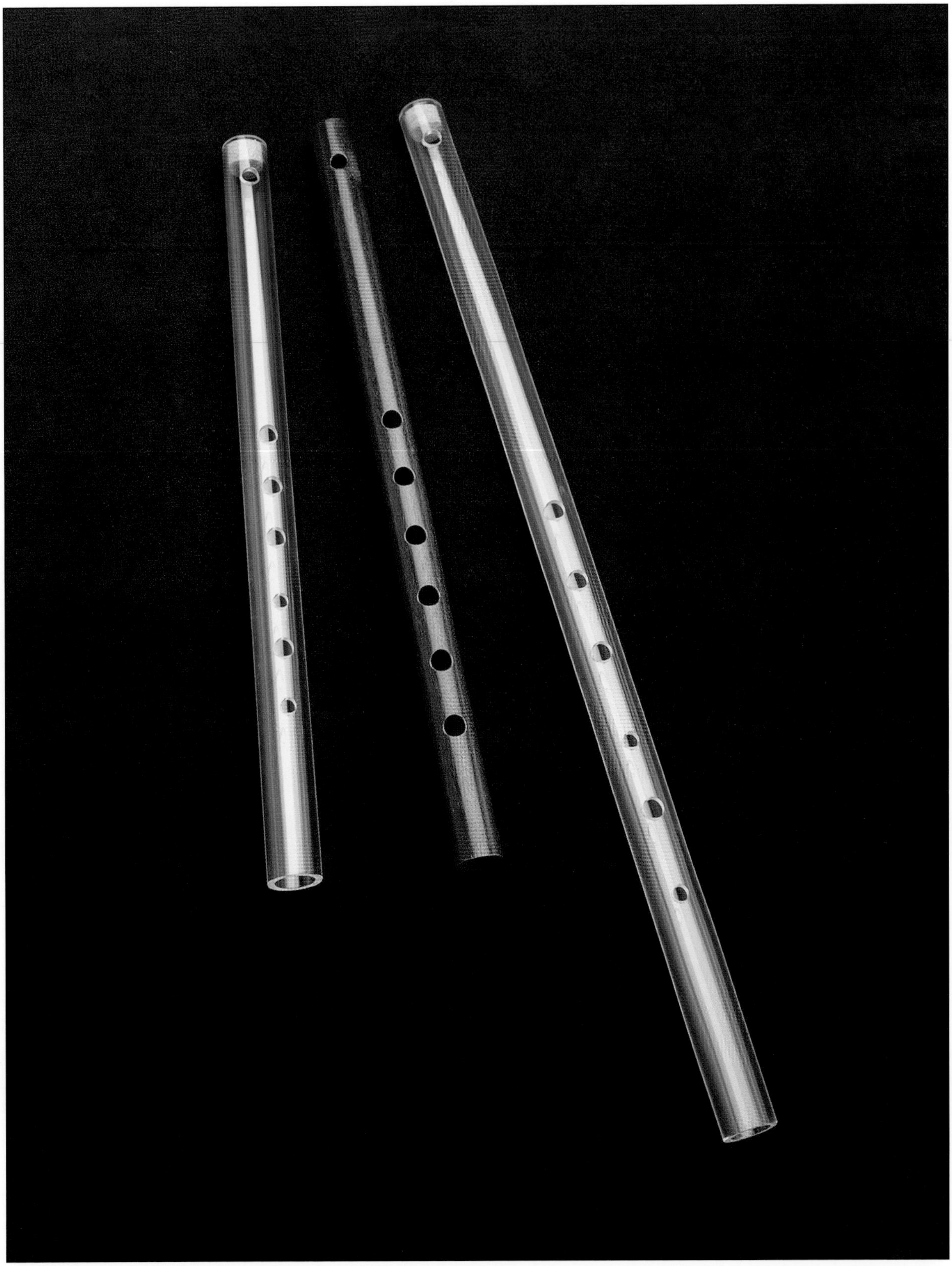

Plate 11 SIMPLE FLUTES *Photo by Will Gullette*

Plate 12 LITTLE CANON

Photo by Will Gullette

Plate 13 CRIS FORSTER with CHRYSALIS (1981) *Photo by Norman Seeff*

Plate 14 *Photo by Will Gullette*

HEIDI FORSTER playing GLASSDANCE

Plate 15 From left to right: *Photo by Will Gullette*

DAVID CANRIGHT, HEIDI FORSTER, and CRIS FORSTER

Plate 16 CHRYSALIS FOUNDATION WORKSHOP *Photo by Will Gullette*

BIBLIOGRAPHY

Chapters 1–9

Askenfelt, A., Editor (1990). *Five Lectures on The Acoustics of the Piano.* Royal Swedish Academy of Music, No. 64, Stockholm, Sweden.

Askill, J. (1979). *Physics of Musical Sound.* D. Van Nostrand Company, New York.

Baines, A. (1967). *Woodwind Instruments and Their History.* Dover Publications, Inc., New York, 1991.

Barbera, A., Translator (1991). *The Euclidean Division of the Canon: Greek and Latin Sources.* University of Nebraska Press, Lincoln, Nebraska.

Barker, A., Translator (1989). *Greek Musical Writings.* Two Volumes. Cambridge University Press, Cambridge, Massachusetts.

Bell, A.J., and Firth, I.M. (1986). The physical properties of gut musical instrument strings. *Acustica* **60**, No. 1, pp. 87–89.

Benade, A.H., and French, J.W. (1965). Analysis of the flute head joint. *Journal of the Acoustical Society of America* **37**, No. 4, pp. 679–691.

Benade, A.H. (1967). Measured end corrections for woodwind toneholes. *Journal of the Acoustical Society of America* **41**, No. 6, p. 1609.

Benade, A.H. (1976). *Fundamentals of Musical Acoustics.* Dover Publications, Inc., New York, 1990.

Berliner, P.F. (1978). *The Soul of Mbira.* University of California Press, Berkeley, California, 1981.

Blevins, R.D. (1979). *Formulas for Natural Frequency and Mode Shape*, Reprint. Krieger Publishing Company, Malabar, Florida, 1993.

Boehm, T. (1847). *On the Construction of Flutes, Über den Flötenbau.* Frits Knuf Buren, Amsterdam, Netherlands, 1982.

Boehm, T. (1871). *The Flute and Flute-Playing.* Dover Publications, Inc., New York, 1964.

Boyer, H.E., and Gall, T.L., Editors (1984). *Metals Handbook, Desk Edition.* American Society for Metals, Metals Park, Ohio, 1989.

Bray, A., Barbato, G., and Levi, R. (1990). *Theory and Practice of Force Measurement.* Academic Press, San Diego, California.

Burkert, W. (1962). *Lore and Science in Ancient Pythagoreanism.* Translated by E.L. Minar, Jr. Harvard University Press, Cambridge, Massachusetts, 1972.

Cadillac Plastic Buyer's Guide. Cadillac Plastic and Chemical Company, Troy, Michigan, 1986.

Campbell, M., and Greated, C. (1987). *The Musician's Guide to Acoustics.* Schirmer Books, New York, 1988.

Capstick, J.W. (1913). *Sound.* Cambridge University Press, London, England, 1932.

Chapman, R.E., Translator (1957). *Harmonie universelle: The Books on Instruments*, by Marin Mersenne. Martinus Nijhoff, The Hague, Netherlands.

Cohen, H.F. (1984). *Quantifying Music.* D. Reidel Publishing Company, Dordrecht, Netherlands.

Coltman, J.W. (1979). Acoustical analysis of the Boehm flute. *Journal of the Acoustical Society of America* **65**, No. 2, pp. 499–506.

Cremer, L., Heckl, M., and Ungar, E.E. (1973). *Structure-Borne Sound*, 2nd ed. Springer-Verlag, Berlin and New York, 1988.

Cremer, L. (1981). *The Physics of the Violin*, 2nd ed. The MIT Press, Cambridge, Massachusetts, 1984.

Crew, H., and De Salvio, A., Translators (1914). *Dialogues Concerning Two New Sciences*, by Galileo Galilei. Dover Publications, Inc., New York.

Den Hartog, J.P. (1934). *Mechanical Vibrations.* Dover Publications, Inc., New York, 1985.

Den Hartog, J.P. (1948). *Mechanics.* Dover Publications, Inc., New York, 1984.

D'Erlanger, R., Bakkouch, ʿA.ʿA., and Al-Sanūsī, M., Translators (Vol. 1, 1930; Vol. 2, 1935; Vol. 3, 1938; Vol. 4, 1939; Vol. 5, 1949; Vol. 6, 1959). *La Musique Arabe.* Librairie Orientaliste Paul Geuthner, Paris, France.

Diels, H. (1903). *Die Fragmente der Vorsokratiker, Griechisch und Deutsch.* Three Volumes. Weidmannsche Verlagsbuchhandlung, Berlin, Germany, 1951.

D'Ooge, M.L., Translator (1926). *Nicomachus of Gerasa: Introduction to Arithmetic.* The Macmillan Company, New York.

Dunlop, J.I. (1981). Testing of poles by using acoustic pulse method. *Wood Science and Technology* **15**, pp. 301–310.

Du Pont Bulletin: "Tynex 612 Nylon Filament." Du Pont Company, Wilmington, Delaware.

Düring, I., Translator (1934). *Ptolemaios und Porphyrios über die Musik.* Georg Olms Verlag, Hildesheim, Germany, 1987.

Einarson, B., Translator (1967). *On Music*, by Plutarch. In *Plutarch's Moralia, Volume 14.* Harvard University Press, Cambridge, Massachusetts.

Elmore, W.C., and Heald, M.A. (1969). *Physics of Waves.* Dover Publications, Inc. New York, 1985.

Fenner, K., *On the Calculation of the Tension of Wound Strings*, 2nd ed. Verlag Das Musikinstrument, Frankfurt, Germany, 1976.

Fishbane, P.M., Gasiorowicz, S., and Thornton, S.T. (1993). *Physics for Scientists and Engineers.* Prentice-Hall, Englewood Cliffs, New Jersey.

Fletcher, H., Blackham, E.D., and Stratton, R.S. (1962). Quality of piano tones. *Journal of the Acoustical Society of America* **34**, No. 6, pp. 749–761.

Fletcher, H. (1964). Normal vibration frequencies of a stiff piano string. *Journal of the Acoustical Society of America* **36,** No. 1, pp. 203–209.

Fletcher, N.H., and Rossing, T.D. (1991). *The Physics of Musical Instruments*, 2nd ed. Springer-Verlag, Berlin and New York, 1998.

Fogiel, M., Editor (1980). *The Strength of Materials & Mechanics of Solids Problem Solver.* Research and Education Association, Piscataway, New Jersey, 1990.

Goodway, M., and Odell, J.S. (1987). *The Historical Harpsichord, Volume Two: The Metallurgy of 17th– and 18th–Century Music Wire.* Pendragon Press, Stuyvesant, New York.

Gray, D.E., Editor (1957). *American Institute of Physics Handbook*, 3rd ed. McGraw-Hill Book Company, New York, 1972.

Halliday, D., and Resnick, R. (1970). *Fundamentals of Physics*, 2nd ed. John Wiley & Sons, New York, 1981.

Hamilton, E., and Cairns, H., Editors (1963). *The Collected Dialogues of Plato.* Random House, Inc., New York, 1966.

Helmholtz, H.L.F., and Ellis A.J., Translator (1885). *On the Sensations of Tone.* Dover Publications, Inc., New York, 1954.

Hoadley, R.B. (1980). *Understanding Wood.* The Taunton Press, Newtown, Connecticut, 1981.

Hubbard, F. (1965). *Three Centuries of Harpsichord Making*, 4th ed. Harvard University Press, Cambridge, Massachusetts, 1972.

Ingard, U. (1953). On the theory and design of acoustic resonators. *Journal of the Acoustical Society of America* **25**, No. 6, pp. 1037–1061.

Ingard, K.U. (1988). *Fundamentals of Waves and Oscillations.* Cambridge University Press, Cambridge, Massachusetts, 1990.

Jan, K. von, Editor (1895). *Musici Scriptores Graeci.* Lipsiae, in aedibus B.G. Teubneri.

Jerrard, H.G., and McNeill, D.B. (1963). *Dictionary of Scientific Units*, 6th ed. Chapman and Hall, London, England, 1992.

Jones, A.T. (1941). End corrections of organ pipes. *Journal of the Acoustical Society of America* **12**, pp. 387–394.

Kinsler, L.E., and Frey, A.R. (1950). *Fundamentals of Acoustics*, 2nd ed. John Wiley & Sons, Inc., New York, 1962.

Klein, H.A. (1974). *The Science of Measurement.* Dover Publications, Inc., New York, 1988.

Land, F. (1960). *The Language of Mathematics.* Doubleday & Company, Inc., Garden City, New York.

Lemon, H.B., and Ference, M., Jr. (1943). *Analytical Experimental Physics.* The University of Chicago Press, Chicago, Illinois.

Levin, F.R., Translator (1994). *The Manual of Harmonics, of Nicomachus the Pythagorean.* Phanes Press, Grand Rapids, Michigan.

Liddell, H.G., and Scott, R. (1843). *A Greek-English Lexicon.* The Clarendon Press, Oxford, England, 1992.

Lide, D.R., Editor (1918). *CRC Handbook of Chemistry and Physics*, 73rd ed. CRC Press, Boca Raton, Florida, 1992.

Lindeburg, M.R. (1988). *Engineering Unit Conversions*, 2nd ed. Professional Publications, Inc., Belmont, California, 1990.

Lindeburg, M.R. (1990). *Engineer-in-Training Reference Manual*, 8th ed. Professional Publications, Inc., Belmont, California, 1992.

Lindley, M. (1987). "Stimmung und Temperatur." In *Geschichte der Musiktheorie, Volume 6*, F. Zaminer, Editor. Wissenschaftliche Buchgesellschaft, Darmstadt, Germany.

McLeish, J. (1991). *Number.* Bloomsbury Publishing Limited, London, England.

Moore, J.L. (1971). *Acoustics of Bar Percussion Instruments.* Ph.D. dissertation printed and distributed by University Microfilms, Inc., Ann Arbor, Michigan.

Morse, P.M., and Ingard, K.U. (1968). *Theoretical Acoustics.* Princeton University Press, Princeton, New Jersey, 1986.

Nash, W.A. (1957). *Strength of Materials*, 3rd ed. Schaum's Outline Series, McGraw-Hill, Inc., New York, 1994.

Nederveen, C.J. (1969). *Acoustical Aspects of Woodwind Instruments.* Frits Knuf, Amsterdam, Netherlands.

Nederveen, C.J. (1973). Blown, passive and calculated resonance frequencies of the flute. *Acustica* **28**, pp. 12–23.

Newton, R.E.I. (1990). *Wave Physics.* Edward Arnold, a division of Hodder & Stoughton, London, England.

Norton, M.P. (1989). *Fundamentals of Noise and Vibration Analysis for Engineers.* Cambridge University Press, Cambridge, Massachusetts.

Oberg, E., Jones, F.D., Horton, H.L., and Ryffel, H.H. (1914). *Machinery's Handbook*, 24th ed. Industrial Press Inc., New York, 1992.

Olson, H.F. (1952). *Music, Physics and Engineering*, 2nd ed. Dover Publications, Inc., New York, 1967.

Pierce, A.D. (1981). *Acoustics.* Acoustical Society of America, Woodbury, New York. 1991.

Pierce, J.R. (1983). *The Science of Musical Sound.* Scientific American Books, W.H. Freeman and Company, New York.

Pikler, A.G. (1966). Logarithmic frequency systems. *Journal of the Acoustical Society of America* **39**, No. 6, pp. 1102–1110.

Rao, S.S. (1986). *Mechanical Vibrations*, 2nd ed. Addison-Wesley Publishing Company, Reading, Massachusetts, 1990.

Richardson, E.G. (1929). *The Acoustics of Orchestral Instruments and of the Organ.* Edward Arnold & Co., London, England.

Rossing, T.D. (1989). *The Science of Sound*, 2nd ed. Addison-Wesley Publishing Co., Inc., Reading, Massachusetts, 1990.

Sadie, S., Editor (1984). *The New Grove Dictionary of Musical Instruments.* Macmillan Press Limited, London, England.

Schlesinger, K. (1939). *The Greek Aulos.* Methuen & Co. Ltd., London, England.

Schuck, O.H., and Young, R.W. (1943). Observations on the vibrations of piano strings. *Journal of the Acoustical Society of America* **15**, No. 1, pp. 1–11.

Sears, F.W., Zemansky, M.W., and Young, H.D., *University Physics*, 7th ed. Addison-Wesley Publishing Company, Reading, Massachusetts, 1988.

Skudrzyk, E. (1968). *Simple and Complex Vibratory Systems.* Pennsylvania State University Press, University Park, Pennsylvania, 1981.

Smith, D.E. (1925). *History of Mathematics.* Two Volumes. Dover Publications, Inc., New York, 1958.

Standards Handbook, Part 2 — Alloy Data, Wrought Copper and Copper Alloy Mill Products, Eighth Edition, Copper Development Association, Inc., Greenwich, Connecticut, 1985.

Stauss, H.E., Martin, F.E., and Billington, D.S. (1951). A piezoelectric method for determining Young's modulus and its temperature dependence. *Journal of the Acoustical Society of America* **23**, No. 6, pp. 695–696.

Steinkopf, O. (1983). *Zur Akustik der Blasinstrumente.* Moeck Verlag, Celle, Germany.

Stiller, A. (1985). *Handbook of Instrumentation.* University of California Press, Berkeley, California.

Suzuki, H. (1986). Vibration and sound radiation of a piano soundboard. *Journal of the Acoustical Society of America* **80**, No. 6, pp. 1573–1582.

Thompson, S.P. (1910). *Calculus Made Easy*, 3rd ed. St. Martin's Press, New York, 1984.

Thomson, W.T. (1972). *Theory of Vibration with Application*, 4th ed. Prentice Hall, Englewood Cliffs, New Jersey, 1993.

Timoshenko, S., and Woinowsky-Krieger, S. (1940). *Theory of Plates and Shells*, 2nd ed., McGraw-Hill Book Company, New York, 1959.

Timoshenko, S.P. (1953). *History of Strength of Materials.* Dover Publications, Inc., New York, 1983.

Towne, D.H. (1967). *Wave Phenomena.* Dover Publications, Inc., New York, 1988.

Tropfke, J. (1921). *Geschichte der Elementar-Mathematik.* Seven Volumes. Vereinigung Wissenschaftlicher Verleger, Walter de Gruyter & Co., Berlin and Leipzig, Germany.

U.S. Business and Defense Services Administration (1956). *Materials Survey: Aluminum.* Department of Commerce, Washington, D.C.

Weaver, W., Jr., Timoshenko, S.P., and Young, D.H., *Vibration Problems in Engineering*, 5th ed. John Wiley and Sons, New York, 1990.

White, W.B. (1917). *Piano Tuning and Allied Arts*, 5th ed. Tuners Supply Company, Boston, Massachusetts, 1972.

Wogram, K. (1981). Akustische Untersuchungen an Klavieren. Teil I: Schwingungseigenschaften des Resonanzbodens. *Das Musikinstrument* **24**, pp. 694–702, 776–782, 872–879. English translation: Acoustical research on pianos. Part I: Vibrational characteristics of the soundboard. In *Musical Acoustics: Selected Reprints*, T.D. Rossing, Editor, pp. 85–98. American Association of Physics Teachers, College Park, Maryland, 1988.

Wolfenden, S. (1916). *A Treatise on the Art of Pianoforte Construction.* The British Piano Museum Charitable Trust, Brentford, Middlesex, England, 1975.

Wood, A.B. (1930). *A Textbook of Sound.* The Macmillan Company, New York, 1937.

Wood, A. (1940). *Acoustics.* Dover Publications, Inc., New York, 1966.

Young, R.W. (1952). Inharmonicity of plain wire piano strings. *Journal of the Acoustical Society of America* **24**, No. 3, pp. 267–272.

Zanoncelli, L., Translator (1990). *La Manualistica Musicale Greca.* Angelo Guerini e Associati, Milan, Italy.

Zebrowski, E., Jr. (1979). *Fundamentals of Physical Measurement.* Duxbury Press, Belmont, California.

Chapter 10

Adkins, C.D. (1963). *The Theory and Practice of the Monochord.* Ph.D. dissertation printed and distributed by University Microfilms, Inc., Ann Arbor, Michigan.

Al-Faruqi, L.I. (1974). *The Nature of the Musical Art of Islamic Culture: A Theoretical and Empirical Study of Arabian Music.* Ph.D. dissertation printed and distributed by University Microfilms, Inc., Ann Arbor, Michigan.

Asselin, P. (1985). *Musique et Tempérament.* Éditions Costallat, Paris, France.

Barbera, C.A. (1977). Arithmetic and geometric divisions of the tetrachord. *Journal of Music Theory* **21**, No. 2, pp. 294–323.

Barbera, A., Translator (1991). *The Euclidean Division of the Canon: Greek and Latin Sources.* University of Nebraska Press, Lincoln, Nebraska.

Barbour, J.M. (1933). The persistence of the Pythagorean tuning system. *Scripta Mathematica,* Vol. 1, pp. 286–304.

Barbour, J.M. (1951). *Tuning and Temperament.* Da Capo Press, New York, 1972.

Barker, A., Translator (1989). *Greek Musical Writings.* Two Volumes. Cambridge University Press, Cambridge, England.

Barnes, J. (1979). Bach's keyboard temperament. *Early Music* **7**, No. 2, pp. 236–249.

Beck, C., Translator (1868). *Flores musice omnis cantus Gregoriani,* by Hugo Spechtshart [von Reutlingen]. Bibliothek des Litterarischen Vereins, Stuttgart, Germany.

Bower, C.M., Translator (1989). *Fundamentals of Music,* by A.M.S. Boethius. Yale University Press, New Haven, Connecticut.

Briscoe, R.L., Translator (1975). *Rameau's "Démonstration du principe de l'harmonie" and "Nouvelles reflections de M. Rameau sur sa démonstration du principe de l'harmonie:" An Annotated Translation of Two Treatises by Jean-Philippe Rameau.* Ph.D. dissertation printed and distributed by University Microfilms, Inc., Ann Arbor, Michigan.

Brun, V. (1964). Euclidean algorithms and musical theory. *L'Enseignement Mathématique* **X**, pp. 125–137.

Burkert, W. (1962). *Lore and Science in Ancient Pythagoreanism.* Translated by E.L. Minar, Jr. Harvard University Press, Cambridge, Massachusetts, 1972.

Chalmers, J.H., Jr. (1993). *Divisions of the Tetrachord.* Frog Peak Music, Hanover, New Hampshire.

Chandler, B.G., Translator (1975). *Rameau's "Nouveau système de musique théorique:" An Annotated Translation with Commentary.* Ph.D. dissertation printed and distributed by University Microfilms, Inc., Ann Arbor, Michigan.

Chapman, R.E., Translator (1957). *Harmonie universelle: The Books on Instruments*, by Marin Mersenne. Martinus Nijhoff, The Hague, Netherlands.

Coelho, V., Editor (1992). *Music and Science in the Age of Galileo*. Kluwer Academic Publishers, Dordrecht, Netherlands.

Cohen, H.F. (1984). *Quantifying Music*. D. Reidel Publishing Company, Dordrecht, Netherlands.

Compact Edition of the Oxford English Dictionary. Oxford University Press, Oxford, England, 1974.

Crew, H., and De Salvio, A., Translators (1914). *Dialogues Concerning Two New Sciences*, by Galileo Galilei. Dover Publications, Inc., New York.

Crocker, R.L. (1963). Pythagorean mathematics and music. *The Journal of Aesthetics and Art Criticism* **XXII**, No. 2, Part I: pp. 189–198, and No. 3, Part II: pp. 325–335.

Crocker, R.L. (1966). "Aristoxenus and Greek Mathematics." In *Aspects of Medieval and Renaissance Music: A Birthday Offering to Gustave Reese*, J. LaRue, Editor. Pendragon Press, New York.

Crone, E., Editor; Fokker, A.D., Music Editor; Dikshoorn, C., Translator (1966). *The Principal Works of Simon Stevin*. Five Volumes. C.V. Swets & Zeitlinger, Amsterdam.

Crookes, D.Z., Translator (1986). *Syntagma musicum II: De organographia, Parts I and II*, by Michael Praetorius. The Clarendon Press, Oxford, England.

Daniels, A.M. (1962). *The De musica libri VII of Francisco de Salinas*. Ph.D. dissertation printed and distributed by University Microfilms, Inc., Ann Arbor, Michigan.

De Haan, D.B., Publisher (1884). *Vande Spiegeling der Singconst*, by Simon Stevin. Amsterdam.

D'Erlanger, R., Bakkouch, 'A.'A., and Al-Sanūsī, M., Translators (Vol. 1, 1930; Vol. 2, 1935; Vol. 3, 1938; Vol. 4, 1939; Vol. 5, 1949; Vol. 6, 1959). *La Musique Arabe*, Librairie Orientaliste Paul Geuthner, Paris, France.

Diels, H. (1903). *Die Fragmente der Vorsokratiker, Griechisch und Deutsch*. Three Volumes. Weidmannsche Verlagsbuchhandlung, Berlin, Germany, 1951.

D'Ooge, M.L., Translator (1926). *Nicomachus of Gerasa: Introduction to Arithmetic*. The Macmillan Company, New York.

Dupont, W. (1935). *Geschichte der musikalischen Temperatur*. C.H. Beck'sche Buchdruckerei, Nördlingen, Germany.

Düring, I., Editor (1930). *Die Harmonielehre des Klaudios Ptolemaios*. Original Greek text of Ptolemy's *Harmonics*. Wettergren & Kerbers Förlag, Göteborg, Sweden.

Düring, I., Translator (1934). *Ptolemaios und Porphyrios über die Musik*. Georg Olms Verlag, Hildesheim, Germany, 1987.

Farmer, H.G. (1965). *The Sources of Arabian Music*. E.J. Brill, Leiden, Netherlands.

Farmer, H.G., Translator (1965). *Al-Fārābī's Arabic-Latin Writings on Music*. Hinrichsen Edition Ltd., New York.

Fend, M., Translator (1989). *Theorie des Tonsystems:* Das erste und zweite Buch der *Istitutioni harmoniche* (1573), von Gioseffo Zarlino. Peter Lang, Frankfurt am Main, Germany.

Fernandez de la Cuesta, I., Translator (1983). *Siete libros sobre la musica*, by Francisco Salinas. Editorial Alpuerto, Madrid, Spain.

Flegg, G., Hay, C., and Moss, B., Translators (1985). *Nicolas Chuquet, Renaissance Mathematician.* D. Reidel Publishing Company, Dordrecht, Holland.

Gossett, P., Translator (1971). *Traité de l'harmonie* [Treatise on Harmony], by Jean-Philippe Rameau. Dover Publications, Inc., New York.

Green, B.L. (1969). *The Harmonic Series From Mersenne to Rameau: An Historical Study of Circumstances Leading to Its Recognition and Application to Music.* Ph.D. dissertation printed and distributed by University Microfilms, Inc., Ann Arbor, Michigan.

Guthrie, K.S., Translator (1987). *The Pythagorean Sourcebook and Library.* Phanes Press, Grand Rapids, Michigan.

Hamilton, E., and Cairns, H., Editors (1966). *The Collected Dialogues of Plato.* Random House, Inc., New York.

Hawkins, J. (1853). *A General History of the Science and Practice of Music.* Dover Publications, Inc., New York, 1963.

Hayes, D., Translator (1968). *Rameau's Theory of Harmonic Generation; An Annotated Translation and Commentary of "Génération harmonique" by Jean-Philippe Rameau.* Ph.D. dissertation printed and distributed by University Microfilms, Inc., Ann Arbor, Michigan.

Heath, T.L., Translator (1908). *Euclid's Elements.* Dover Publications, Inc., New York, 1956.

Heath, T. (1921). *A History of Greek Mathematics.* Dover Publications, Inc., New York, 1981.

Hitti, P.K. (1937). *History of the Arabs.* Macmillan and Co. Ltd., London, England, 1956.

Hubbard, F. (1965). *Three Centuries of Harpsichord Making,* 4th ed. Harvard University Press, Cambridge, Massachusetts, 1972.

Hyde, F.B. (1954). *The Position of Marin Mersenne in the History of Music.* Two Volumes. Ph.D. dissertation printed and distributed by University Microfilms, Inc., Ann Arbor, Michigan.

Ibn Sīnā (Avicenna): *Auicene perhypatetici philosophi: ac medicorum facile primi opera in luce redacta...* This Latin translation was published in 1508. Facsimile Edition: Minerva, Frankfurt am Main, Germany, 1961.

Jacobi, E.R., Editor (1968). *Jean-Philippe Rameau (1683–1764): Complete Theoretical Writings.* American Institute of Musicology, [Rome, Italy].

James, G., and James, R.C. (1976). *Mathematics Dictionary,* 4th ed. Van Nostrand Reinhold, New York.

Jorgensen, O. (1977). *Tuning the Historical Temperaments by Ear.* The Northern Michigan University Press, Marquette, Michigan.

Jorgenson, D.A. (1957). *A History of Theories of the Minor Triad.* Ph.D. dissertation printed and distributed by University Microfilms, Inc., Ann Arbor, Michigan.

Jorgenson, D.A. (1963). A résumé of harmonic dualism. *Music and Letters* **XLIV**, No. 1, pp. 31–42.

Kastner, M.S., Editor (1958). *De musica libri VII,* by Francisco Salinas. Facsimile Edition. Bärenreiter-Verlag, Kassel, Germany.

Kelleher, J.E. (1993). *Zarlino's "Dimostrationi harmoniche" and Demonstrative Methodologies in the Sixteenth Century.* Ph.D. dissertation printed and distributed by University Microfilms, Inc., Ann Arbor, Michigan.

Lawlor, R. and D., Translators (1978). *Mathematics Useful for Understanding Plato*, by Theon of Smyrna. Wizards Bookshelf, San Diego, California, 1979.

Levin, F.R., Translator (1994). *The Manual of Harmonics, of Nicomachus the Pythagorean.* Phanes Press, Grand Rapids, Michigan.

Lindley, M. (1984). *Lutes, Viols and Temperaments.* Cambridge University Press, Cambridge, England.

Litchfield, M. (1988). Aristoxenus and empiricism: A reevaluation based on his theories. *Journal of Music Theory* **32**, No. 1, pp. 51–73.

Mackenzie, D.C., Translator (1950). *Harmonic Introduction*, by Cleonides. In *Source Readings in Music History*, O. Strunk, Editor. W. W. Norton & Company, Inc., New York.

Macran, H.S., Translator (1902). *The Harmonics of Aristoxenus.* Georg Olms Verlag, Hildesheim, Germany, 1990.

Marcuse, S. (1964). *Musical Instruments: A Comprehensive Dictionary.* W. W. Norton & Company, Inc., New York, 1975.

Maxham, R.E., Translator (1976). *The Contributions of Joseph Sauveur to Acoustics.* Two Volumes. Ph.D. dissertation printed and distributed by University Microfilms, Inc., Ann Arbor, Michigan.

Mersenne, M. (1636–37). *Harmonie universelle contenant la théorie et la pratique de la musique.* Three Volumes. Facsimile Edition. Éditions du Centre National de la Recherche Scientifique, Paris, France, 1963.

Meyer, M.F. (1929). *The Musician's Arithmetic.* Oliver Ditson Company, Boston, Massachusetts.

Miller, C.A., Translator (1993). *Musica practica*, by Bartolomeo Ramis de Pareia. Hänssler-Verlag, Neuhausen-Stuttgart, Germany.

Niven, I. (1961). *Numbers: Rational and Irrational.* Random House, New York.

Palisca, C.V. (1961). "Scientific Empiricism in Musical Thought." In *Seventeenth Century Science and the Arts*, H.H. Rhys, Editor. Princeton University Press, Princeton, New Jersey.

Palisca, C.V. (1985). *Humanism in Italian Renaissance Musical Thought.* Yale University Press, New Haven, Connecticut.

Palisca, C.V., Translator (2003). *Dialogue on Ancient and Modern Music*, by Vincenzo Galilei. Yale University Press, New Haven, Connecticut.

Partch, H. (1949). *Genesis of a Music*, 2nd ed. Da Capo Press, New York, 1974.

Rameau, J.P. (1722). *Traité de l'harmonie reduite à ses principes naturels.* Facsimile Edition. Biblioteca Nacional de Madrid, Spain, 1984.

Rasch, R., Editor (1983). *Musicalische Temperatur*, by Andreas Werckmeister. The Diapason Press, Utrecht, Netherlands.

Rasch, R., Editor (1984). *Collected Writings on Musical Acoustics*, by Joseph Sauveur. The Diapason Press, Utrecht, Netherlands.

Rasch, R., Editor (1986). *Le cycle harmonique* (1691), *Novus cyclus harmonicus* (1724), by Christiaan Huygens. The Diapason Press, Utrecht, Netherlands.

Reichenbach, H. (1951). *The Rise of Scientific Philosophy.* The University of California Press, Berkeley and Los Angeles, California, 1958.

Roberts, F. (1692). A discourse concerning the musical notes of the trumpet, and the trumpet-marine, and of the defects of the same. *Philosophical Transactions of the Royal Society of London* **XVII**, pp. 559–563.

Rossing, T.D. (1989). *The Science of Sound*, 2nd ed. Addison-Wesley Publishing Co., Inc., Reading, Massachusetts, 1990.

Sadie, S., Editor (1980). *The New Grove Dictionary of Music and Musicians.* Macmillan Publishers Limited, London, England, 1995.

Shirlaw, M. (1917). *The Theory of Harmony.* Da Capo Press Reprint Edition. Da Capo Press, New York, 1969.

Solomon, J., Translator (2000). *Ptolemy Harmonics.* Brill, Leiden, Netherlands.

Soukhanov, A.H., Executive Editor (1992). *The American Heritage Dictionary of the English Language*, 3rd ed. Houghton Mifflin Company, Boston, Massachusetts.

Stephan, B. (1991). *Geometry: Plane and Practical.* Harcourt Brace Jovanovich, Publishers, San Diego, California.

Truesdell, C. (1960). *The Rational Mechanics of Flexible or Elastic Bodies: 1638–1788.* Orell Füssli, Zürich, Switzerland.

Wallis, J. (1677). Dr. Wallis' letter to the publisher, concerning a new musical discovery. *Philosophical Transactions of the Royal Society of London* **XII**, pp. 839–842.

West, M.L. (1992). *Ancient Greek Music.* The Clarendon Press, Oxford, England, 1994.

White, W.B. (1917). *Piano Tuning and Allied Arts*, 5th ed. Tuners Supply Company, Boston, Massachusetts, 1972.

Wienpahl, R.W. (1959). Zarlino, the *Senario*, and tonality. *Journal of the American Musicological Society* **XII**, No. 1, pp. 27–41.

Williams, R.F., Translator (1972). *Marin Mersenne: An Edited Translation of the Fourth Treatise of the "Harmonie universelle."* Three Volumes. Ph.D. dissertation printed and distributed by University Microfilms, Inc., Ann Arbor, Michigan.

Williamson, C. (1938). The frequency ratios of the tempered scale. *Journal of the Acoustical Society of America* **10**, pp. 135–136.

Winnington-Ingram, R.P. (1932). Aristoxenus and the intervals of Greek music. *The Classical Quarterly* **XXVI**, Nos. 3–4, pp. 195–208.

Winnington-Ingram, R.P. (1936). *Mode in Ancient Greek Music.* Cambridge University Press, London, England.

Winnington-Ingram, R.P. (1954). "Greek Music (Ancient)." In *Grove's Dictionary of Music and Musicians, Volume 3*, 5th ed., E. Blom, Editor. St. Martin's Press, Inc., New York, 1970.

Zarlino, R.M.G. (1571). *Dimostrationi harmoniche.* Facsimile Edition, The Gregg Press Incorporated, Ridgewood, New Jersey, 1966.

Zarlino, R.M.G. (1573). *Istitutioni harmoniche.* Facsimile Edition, The Gregg Press Limited, Farnborough, Hants., England, 1966.

Chapter 11

Chinese Music

Apel, W., Editor (1944). *Harvard Dictionary of Music*, 2nd ed. Harvard University Press, Cambridge, Massachusetts, 1972.

Gulik, R.H., Translator (1941). *Poetical Essay on the Lute*, by Hsi K'ang. In Gulik's *Hsi K'ang and His Poetical Essay on the Lute*, Sophia University, Tokyo, Japan.

Kaufmann, W. (1967). *Musical Notations of the Orient.* Indiana University Press, Bloomington, Indiana.

Kaufmann, W. (1976). *Musical References in the Chinese Classics.* Detroit Monographs in Musicology, Detroit, Michigan.

Kuttner, F.A. (1965). A musicological interpretation of the twelve lüs in China's traditional tone system. *Journal of the Society for Ethnomusicology* **IX**, No. 1, pp. 22–38.

Lieberman, F., Translator (1977). *The Mei-an Ch'in-p'u*, by Hsü Li-sun. In Lieberman's *The Chinese Long Zither Ch'in: A Study Based on the Mei-an Ch'in-p'u.* Ph.D. dissertation printed and distributed by University Microfilms, Inc., Ann Arbor, Michigan.

Lieberman, F., Translator (1983). *The Mei-an Ch'in-p'u*, by Hsü Li-sun. In Lieberman's *A Chinese Zither Tutor.* University of Washington Press, Seattle, Washington.

Lui, T. (1968). A short guide to *ch'in. Selected Reports* **I**, No. 2, pp. 180–201. Publication of the Institute of Ethnomusicology of the University of California at Los Angeles.

Needham, J. (1962). *Science and Civilization in China, Volume 4, Part I.* Cambridge University Press, Cambridge, England.

Reinhard, K. (1956). *Chinesische Musik*, 2nd ed. Im Erich Röth-Verlag, Kassel, Germany.

Robinson, K. (1980). *A Critical Study of Chu Tsai-yü's Contribution to the Theory of Equal Temperament in Chinese Music.* Franz Steiner Verlag GmbH, Wiesbaden, Germany.

Sachs, C. (1940). *The History of Musical Instruments.* W. W. Norton & Company, Inc., New York.

Sadie, S., Editor (1980). *The New Grove Dictionary of Music and Musicians.* Macmillan Publishers Limited, London, England, 1995.

Wang, L., and Needham, J. (1955). Horner's Method in Chinese Mathematics: Its origins in the root-extraction procedures of the Han Dynasty. *T'oung Pao Archives* **XLIII**, No. 5, pp. 345–401. Leiden, Netherlands.

Wang, K. (1956). *Chung-kuo yin yueh shih.* Taipei, Formosa: Chung hua shu chu.

Indonesian Music

Apel, W., Editor (1944). *Harvard Dictionary of Music*, 2nd ed. Harvard University Press, Cambridge, Massachusetts, 1972.

Blom, E., Editor (1954). *Grove's Dictionary of Music and Musicians*, 5th ed. St. Martin's Press, Inc., New York, 1970.

Hood, M. (1954). *The Nuclear Theme as a Determinant of Paṭet in Javanese Music.* Da Capo Press, Inc., New York, 1977.

Hood, M. (1966). *Sléndro* and *pélog* redefined. *Selected Reports* **I**, No. 1, pp. 28–48. Publication of the Institute of Ethnomusicology of the University of California at Los Angeles.

Lentz, D.A. (1965). *The Gamelan Music of Java and Bali.* University of Nebraska Press, Lincoln, Nebraska.

Martopangrawit, R.L. (1972). *Catatan-Catatan Pengetahuan Karawitan* [*Notes on Knowledge of Gamelan Music*], translated by M.F. Hatch. In *Karawitan, Volume 1*, J. Becker and A.H. Feinstein, Editors. Center for South and Southeast Asian Studies, The University of Michigan, 1984.

McDermott, V., and Sumarsam (1975). Central Javanese music: The *paṭet* of laras *sléndro* and the *gendèr barung*. *Journal of the Society for Ethnomusicology* **XIX**, No. 2, pp. 233–244.

McPhee, C. (1966). *Music in Bali: A Study in Form and Instrumental Organization in Balinese Orchestral Music.* Yale University Press, New Haven, Connecticut.

Ornstein, R.S. (1971). *Gamelan Gong Kebjar: The Development of a Balinese Musical Tradition.* Ph.D. dissertation printed and distributed by University Microfilms, Inc., Ann Arbor, Michigan.

Poerbapangrawit, R.M.K. (1955). *Gendhing Jawa* [*Javanese Gamelan Music*], translated by J. Becker. In *Karawitan, Volume 1*, J. Becker and A.H. Feinstein, Editors. Center for South and Southeast Asian Studies, The University of Michigan, 1984.

Rai, I, W. (1996). *Balinese Gamelan Semar Pagulingan Saih Pitu: The Modal System.* Ph.D. dissertation printed and distributed by University Microfilms, Inc., Ann Arbor, Michigan.

Randel, D.M., Editor (1986). *The New Harvard Dictionary of Music*, 6th ed. The Belknap Press of Harvard University Press, Cambridge, Massachusetts, 1993.

Sadie, S., Editor (1984). *The New Grove Dictionary of Musical Instruments.* Macmillan Press Limited, London, England.

Schaareman, D., Editor (1992). *Balinese Music in Context: A Sixty-fifth Birthday Tribute to Hans Oesch.* Amadeus Verlag, Winterthur, Switzerland.

Sindoesawarno, K. (1955). *Ilmu Karawitan* [*Knowledge About Gamelan Music*], translated by M.F. Hatch. In *Karawitan, Volume 2*, J. Becker and A.H. Feinstein, Editors. Center for South and Southeast Asian Studies, The University of Michigan, 1987.

Sumarsam (1975). Gendèr barung, its technique and function in the context of Javanese gamelan. *Indonesia* **20**, pp. 161–172.

Sumarsam (1992). *Gamelan: Cultural Interaction and Musical Development in Central Java.* The University of Chicago Press, Chicago, Illinois, 1995.

Surjodiningrat, W., Sudarjana, P.J., and Susanto, A. (1972). *Tone Measurements of Outstanding Javanese Gamelans in Jogjakarta and Surakarta*, 2nd ed. Gadjah Mada University Press, Jogjakarta, Indonesia.

Tenzer, M. (2000). *Gamelan Gong Kebyar: The Art of Twentieth-Century Balinese Music.* The University of Chicago Press, Chicago, Illinois.

Toth, A.F. (1975). The Gamelan Luang of Tangkas, Bali. *Selected Reports* **II**, No. 2, pp. 65–79. Publication of the Institute of Ethnomusicology of the University of California at Los Angeles.

Toth, A.F. (1993). "Selera Yang Selaras: Pepatutan Gong Ditinjau Dari Segi Akustika dan Estetika." *Mudra: Jurnal Seni Budaya*, pp. 92–117. Edisi Khusus.

Indian Music

Aiyar, M.S.R., Translator (1932). *Svaramēlakalānidhi*, by Rāmāmātya. The Annamalai University, India.

Ayyar, C.S. (1939). *The Grammar of South Indian (Karnatic) Music.* Smt. Vidya Shankar, Madras, India, 1976.

Bhandarkar, R.S.P.R. (1912). Contribution to the study of ancient Hindu music. *The Indian Antiquary* **XLI**, pp. 157–164, pp. 185–195, pp. 254–265.

Bhandarkar, R.S.P.R. (1913–1914). Kuḍimiyāmalai inscription on music. *Epigraphia Indica* **XII**, No. 28, pp. 226–237.

Bhatkhande, V.N. (1930). *A Comparative Study of Some of the Leading Music Systems of the 15th, 16th, 17th, and 18th Centuries.* Indian Musicological Society, Baroda, India, 1972.

Bhise, U.R., Translator (1986). *Nāradīyā Śikṣā*, by Nārada. Bhandarkar Institute Press, Poona, India.

Coomaraswamy, A.K. (1930). The parts of a *vīṇā*. *Journal of the American Oriental Society* **50**, No. 3, pp. 244–253.

Gangoly, O.C. (1935). *Rāgas and Rāginīs.* Nalanda Publications, Bombay, India, 1948.

Ghosh, M., Translator (Vol. 1, Ch. 1–27, 1950; Vol. 2, Ch. 28–36, 1961). *The Nāṭyaśāstra*, by Bharata. Bibliotheca Indica, The Asiatic Society, Calcutta, India.

Iyer, T.L.V. (1940). The scheme of 72 *mēḷas* in Carnatic Music. *The Journal of the Music Academy* **XI**, Parts I–IV, pp. 80–86, Madras, India.

Jairazbhoy, N.A. (1971). *The Rāgs of North Indian Music.* Wesleyan University Press, Middletown, Connecticut.

Jairazbhoy, N.A. (1975). An interpretation of the 22 *śrutis*. *Asian Music* **VI**, Nos. 1–2, pp. 38–59.

Junius, M.M. (1974). *The Sitar.* Heinrichshofen's Verlag, Wilhelmshaven, Germany.

Kaufmann, W. (1968). *The Rāgas of North India.* Indiana University Press, Bloomington, Indiana.

Kaufmann, W. (1976). *The Rāgas of South India.* Indiana University Press, Bloomington, Indiana.

Krishnaswamy, A. (1981). *Mēḷakarta and Janya Rāga Chart.* Sakthi Priya Publication, Madras, India.

Lath, M., Translator (1978). *A Study of Dattilam: A Treatise on the Sacred Music of Ancient India.* Impex India, New Delhi, India.

Marcotty, T. (1974). *Djovari: Giving Life to the Sitar.* This essay on how to make a parabolic *sitar* bridge is in *The Sitar*, by Manfred M. Junius. Heinrichshofen's Verlag, Wilhelmshaven, Germany.

Nijenhuis, E.W., Translator (1970). *Dattilam: A Compendium of Ancient Indian Music.* E. J. Brill, Leiden, Netherlands.

Powers, H.S. (1958). *The Background of the South Indian Rāga-System.* Ph.D. dissertation printed and distributed by University Microfilms, Inc., Ann Arbor, Michigan.

Ramachandran, K.V. (1938). The *mēḷakarta* — a critique. *The Journal of the Music Academy* **IX**, Parts I–IV, pp. 31–33, Madras, India.

Ramachandran, K.V. (1950). Carnatic *rāgas* from a new angle — *Śaṅkarābharaṇa*. *The Journal of the Music Academy* **XXI**, Parts I–IV, pp. 88–99, Madras, India.

Ramachandran, K.V. (1950). Carnatic *rāgas* and the textual tradition. *The Journal of the Music Academy* **XXI**, Parts I–IV, pp. 99–106, Madras, India.

Ramachandran, K.V. (1950). *Apurva rāgas* of Tyāgarāja's songs. *The Journal of the Music Academy* **XXI**, Parts I–IV, pp. 107–109, Madras, India.

Ramachandran, N.S. (1938). *The Rāgas of Karnatic Music.* University of Madras, Madras, India.

Rao, T.V.S. (1945 and 1946). The *rāgas* of the Sangita Saramrita. *The Journal of the Music Academy* **XVI**, Parts I–IV, pp. 45–64, and **XVII**, Parts I–IV, pp. 104–134, Madras, India.

Rowell, L. (1981). Early Indian musical speculation and the theory of melody. *Journal of Music Theory* **25.2**, pp. 217–244.

Roy, H.L. (1937). *Problems of Hindustani Music.* Bharati Bhavan, Calcutta, India.

Sachs, C. (1940). *The History of Musical Instruments.* W. W. Norton & Company, Inc., New York.

Sadie, S., Editor (1980). *The New Grove Dictionary of Music and Musicians.* Macmillan Publishers Limited, London, England, 1995.

Sadie, S., Editor (1984). *The New Grove Dictionary of Musical Instruments.* Macmillan Press Limited, London, England.

Sambamoorthy, P. (Vol. 1, A–F, 1952; Vol. 2, G–K, 1959; Vol. 3, L–N, 1971). *A Dictionary of South Indian Music and Musicians.* The Indian Music Publishing House, Madras, India.

Sastri, S.S. (1931). Venkaṭamakhi and his twelve notes. *The Journal of the Music Academy* **II**, No. 1, pp. 22–23, Madras, India.

Sathyanarayana, R., Editor (1957). *Kuḍimiyāmalai Inscription on Music.* Śri Varalakshmi Academies of Fine Arts, Parimala Press, Mysore, India.

Shankar, R. (1968). *My Music, My Life.* Simon and Schuster, New York, New York.

Sharma, P.L., Editor and Translator (Vol. 1, Ch. 1, 1992; Vol. 2, Ch. 2–6, 1994). *Bṛhaddeśi* of Śri Mataṅga Muni. Indira Gandhi National Centre for the Arts in association with Motilal Banarsidass Publishers, Delhi, India.

Shringy, R.K., and Sharma, P.L., Translators (Vol. 1, Ch. 1, 1978; Vol. 2, Ch. 2–4, 1989). *Saṅgītaratnākara*, by Sārṅgadeva. *Volume 1*, Motilal Banarsidass, Delhi, India; *Volume 2*, Munshiram Manoharlal, New Delhi, India.

Sorrell, N., and Narayan, R. (1980). *Indian Music in Performance.* New York University Press, New York, New York. This book comes boxed with an excellent cassette tape recording.

Widdess, R. (1995). *The Rāgas of Early Indian Music.* The Clarendon Press, Oxford, England.

Arabian, Persian, and Turkish Music

Al-Faruqi, L.I. (1974). *The Nature of the Musical Art of Islamic Culture: A Theoretical and Empirical Study of Arabian Music.* Ph.D. dissertation printed and distributed by University Microfilms, Inc., Ann Arbor, Michigan.

Al-Faruqi, L.I. (1981). *An Annotated Glossary of Arabic Musical Terms.* Greenwood Press, Westport, Connecticut.

Avenary, H., Translator (1974). The Hebrew version of Abū l-Ṣalt's treatise on music. *Yuval* **III**, pp. 7–82.

Barker, A., Translator (1989). *Greek Musical Writings.* Two Volumes. Cambridge University Press, Cambridge, England.

Cowl, C., Translator (1966). Al-Kindī's essay on the composition of melodies. *The Consort,* No. 23, pp. 129–159.

Crookes, D.Z., Translator (1986). *Syntagma musicum II: De organographia, Parts I and II,* by Michael Praetorius. The Clarendon Press, Oxford, England. The first edition of this work was published in 1618.

D'Erlanger, R., Bakkouch, 'A.'A., and Al-Sanūsī, M., Translators (Vol. 1, 1930; Vol. 2, 1935; Vol. 3, 1938; Vol. 4, 1939; Vol. 5, 1949; Vol. 6, 1959). *La Musique Arabe,* Librairie Orientaliste Paul Geuthner, Paris, France.

Dieterici, F., Translator (1858–1890; 16 Volumes). *Die Philosophie der Araber im IX. und X. Jahrhundert n. Chr. aus der Theologie des Aristoteles, den Abhandlungen Alfarabis und den Schriften der Lautern Brüder.* The quoted passage on music is in *Volume 6*, entitled: *Die Propaedeutik der Araber im zehnten Jahrhundert.* E.S. Mittler und Sohn, Berlin, Germany, 1865.

El-Hefny, M., Translator (1931). *Ibn Sīnā's Musiklehre* [Ibn Sīnā's teaching on music]. Ph.D. dissertation printed by Otto Hellwig, Berlin, Germany.

Farhat, H. (1965). *The Dastgāh Concept in Persian Music.* Ph.D. dissertation printed and distributed by University Microfilms, Inc., Ann Arbor, Michigan.

Farhat, H. (1990). *The Dastgāh Concept in Persian Music.* Cambridge University Press, Cambridge, England.

Farmer, H.G. (1925). Clues for the Arabian influence on European musical theory. *The Journal of the Royal Asiatic Society,* First Quarter, pp. 61–80.

Farmer, H.G. (1928). Ibn Khurdādhbih on musical instruments. *The Journal of the Royal Asiatic Society,* Third Quarter, pp. 509–518.

Farmer, H.G. (1929). *A History of Arabian Music.* Luzac Oriental, London, England, 1994.

Farmer, H.G. (1953–1954). The song captions in the *Kitāb al-aghānī al-kabīr. Transactions of the Glasgow University Oriental Society* **XV**, pp. 1–10.

Farmer, H.G. (1954). "'Ūd." In *Grove's Dictionary of Music and Musicians, Volume 8,* 5th ed., E. Blom, Editor. St. Martin's Press, Inc., New York, 1970.

Farmer, H.G. (1957). "The Music of Islam." In *New Oxford History of Music, Volume 1: Ancient and Oriental Music,* E. Wellesz, Editor. Oxford University Press, London, England, 1960.

Farmer, H.G. (1965). *The Sources of Arabian Music.* E.J. Brill, Leiden, Netherlands.

Farmer, H.G., Translator (1965). *Al-Fārābī's Arabic-Latin Writings on Music.* Hinrichsen Edition Ltd., New York.

Farmer, H.G. (1965). The old Arabian melodic modes. *Journal of the Royal Asiatic Society,* Parts 3 & 4, pp. 99–102.

Farmer, H.G. (1978). *Studies in Oriental Musical Instruments, First and Second Series.* Longwood Press Ltd., Tortola, British Virgin Islands.

Hitti, P.K. (1937). *History of the Arabs.* Macmillan and Co. Ltd., London, England, 1956.

Lachmann, R. and El-Hefni, M., Translators (1931). *Risāla fī hubr tā'līf al-alḥān* [Über die Komposition der Melodien], by Al-Kindī. Fr. Kistner & C.F.W. Siegel, Leipzig, Germany.

Lewis, B., Editor (1976). *Islam and the Arab World.* Alfred A. Knopf, New York.

Maas, M. and Snyder, J.M. (1989). *Stringed Instruments of Ancient Greece.* Yale University Press, New Haven, Connecticut.

Marcus, S.L. (1989). *Arab Music Theory in the Modern Period.* Ph.D. dissertation printed and distributed by University Microfilms, Inc., Ann Arbor, Michigan.

Marcus, S.L. (1992). Modulation in Arab music: Documenting oral concepts, performance rules and strategies. *Ethnomusicology* **36**, No. 2, pp. 171–195.

Racy, A.J. (1977). *Musical Change and Commercial Recording in Egypt, 1904–1932.* Ph.D. dissertation printed and distributed by University Microfilms, Inc., Ann Arbor, Michigan.

Racy, A.J. (1978). "Music." In *The Genius of Arab Civilization*, 2nd ed., J.R. Hayes, Editor. MIT Press, Cambridge, Massachusetts, 1983.

Ribera, J. (1929). *Music in Ancient Arabia and Spain.* This work was translated and abridged from the Spanish by Eleanor Hague and Marion Leffingwell. Stanford University Press, Stanford University, California.

Ronzevalle, P.L., Translator (1913). *Un Traité de Musique Arabe Moderne*, by Mīkhā'īl Mashāqah. *Mélanges de la Faculté Orientale* **VI**, pp. 1–120. Université Saint-Joseph, Beirut, Lebanon.

Sachs, C. (1940). *The History of Musical Instruments.* W. W. Norton & Company, Inc., New York.

Sadie, S., Editor (1984). *The New Grove Dictionary of Musical Instruments.* Macmillan Press Limited, London, England.

Shiloah, A. (1972). The *simsimīyya:* A stringed instrument of the Red Sea area. *Asian Music* **IV**, No. 1, pp. 15–26.

Shiloah, A., Translator (1978). *The Epistle on Music of the Ikhwān Al-Ṣafā.* Tel-Aviv University, Tel-Aviv, Israel.

Shiloah, A. (1979). *The Theory of Music in Arabic Writings (c. 900–1900).* G. Henle Verlag, München, Germany.

Shiloah, A. (1981). The Arabic concept of mode. *Journal of the American Musicological Society* **XXXIV**, No. 1, pp. 19–42.

Signell, K.L. (1973). *The Turkish 'Makam' System in Contemporary Theory and Practice.* Ph.D. dissertation printed and distributed by University Microfilms, Inc., Ann Arbor, Michigan.

Signell, K.L. (1986). *Makam: Modal Practice in Turkish Art Music.* Da Capo Press, New York, New York.

Smith, E., Translator (1847). *A Treatise on Arab Music*, by Mīkhā'īl Mashāqah. *Journal of the American Oriental Society* **I**, No. 3, pp. 173–217. Boston, Massachusetts.

Touma, H.H. (1996). *The Music of the Arabs.* Amadeus Press, Portland, Oregon.

Wright, O. (1966). Ibn al-Munajjim and the early Arabian modes. *The Galpin Society Journal* **XIX**, pp. 27–48.

Chapter 12

Writings on Cris Forster

Editors. "Cris Forster." In *Für Augen und Ohren*, Magazine of the Berlin Music Festival. January–February, 1980, pp. 16–17. Dr. Ulrich Eckhardt, Publisher. Berlin, Germany.

Mahlke, S. "Barde mit zwei Saitenspielen." *Der Tagesspiegel.* January 25, 1980. Berlin, Germany.

Garr, D. "The Endless Scale." *Omni.* March, 1981, p. 48. New York, New York.

McDonald, R. "Cris Forster: Making Music." *San Diego Magazine.* September, 1982, pp. 136–139, 198, 228. San Diego, California.

Fleischer, D. "Sounds of Infinity." *Connoisseur.* August, 1983, pp. 102, 105. New York, New York.

Levine, J. "Expanded Musical Palette Is Inventor's Note-able Goal." *The Tribune.* September 6, 1983. San Diego, California.

Brewster, T. "A Medley of New Instruments: A Wheel Like the Wind." *Life.* November, 1983, p. 142. New York, New York.

Editors. "Klingen wie der Wind." *Stern.* January, 1984, pp. 146–148. Hamburg, Germany.

Davies, H. (1984). "Microtonal Instruments," pp. 656–657. In *The New Grove Dictionary of Musical Instruments, Volume 2*, S. Sadie, Editor. Macmillan Press Limited, London, England.

Drye, S.L. (1984). *The History and Development of the Musical Glasses*, pp. 46–49. Master's thesis, North Texas State University.

Arnautoff, V. "Hill Musician Composes, Builds Own Instruments." *The Potrero View.* November, 1985, p. 5. San Francisco, California.

Editors. "This Californian and His Bearings Are Making Beautiful Music Together." *Precisionist: A Publication of the Torrington Company.* Summer, 1987, pp. 14–15. Torrington, Connecticut.

Bowen, C. "Making Music from Scratch." *Métier.* Fall, 1987, p. 7. San Francisco, California.

Snider, J. "Chrysalis: A Transformation in Music." *Magical Blend.* April, 1989, pp. 98–102. San Francisco, California.

Hopkin, B. "Review." *Experimental Musical Instruments.* April, 1990, p. 4. Nicasio, California.

Editors. "Forster, Cris." *PITCH for the International Microtonalist* **I**, No. 4, Spring 1990, p. 142. Johnny Reinhard, Editor. New York, New York.

Canright, D. "Performance: Concert in Celebration of the Chrysalis New Music Studio — Instruments and Music by Cris Forster." *1/1, the Journal of the Just Intonation Network* **11**, No. 4. Spring, 2004, pp. 19–20. San Francisco, California.

Videos on Cris Forster

Gaikowski, R., Producer and Director (1988). *Musical Wood, Steel, and Glass: A video featuring Cris Forster, composer, musician, inventor.* One Way Films/Videos, San Francisco, California.

Noyes, E., Director and Editor; Forster, H., Producer and Writer (2006). *A Voyage in Music: A retrospective of Cris Forster's work over the past thirty years.* A Chrysalis Foundation production. San Francisco, California.

Appendix A

FREQUENCIES OF EIGHT OCTAVES OF 12-TONE EQUAL TEMPERAMENT

	C_0	C_1	C_2	C_3	C_4	C_5	C_6	C_7
C	16.3516	32.7032	65.4064	130.813	261.626	523.251	1046.50	2093.00
C♯	17.3239	34.6478	69.2957	138.591	277.183	554.365	1108.73	2217.46
D	18.354	36.7081	73.4162	146.832	293.665	587.33	1174.66	2349.32
D♯	19.4454	38.8909	77.7817	155.563	311.127	622.254	1244.51	2489.02
E	20.6017	41.2034	82.4069	164.814	329.628	659.255	1318.51	2637.02
F	21.8268	43.6535	87.3071	174.614	349.228	698.456	1396.91	2793.83
F♯	23.1247	46.2493	92.4986	184.997	369.994	739.989	1479.98	2959.96
G	24.4997	48.9994	97.9989	195.998	391.995	783.991	1567.98	3135.96
G♯	25.9565	51.9131	103.826	207.652	415.305	830.609	1661.22	3322.44
A	27.5000	55.0000	110.000	220.000	440.000	880.000	1760.00	3520.00
A♯	29.1352	58.2705	116.541	233.082	466.164	932.328	1864.66	3729.31
B	30.8677	61.7354	123.471	246.942	493.883	987.767	1975.53	3951.07

Appendix B

Conversion Factors*		
MULTIPLY	**BY**	**TO OBTAIN**
LENGTH:		
Meters	39.37	Inches
Centimeters	0.3937	Inches
Millimeters	0.039 37	Inches
Feet	12.0	Inches
AREA:		
Square Meters	1,550.0	Square Inches
Square Centimeters	0.155	Square Inches
Square Millimeters	0.001 55	Square Inches
Square Feet	144.0	Square Inches
VOLUME:		
Cubic Meters	61,023.744	Cubic Inches
Cubic Centimeters	0.061 023 744	Cubic Inches
Cubic Millimeters	0.000 061 023 744	Cubic Inches
Cubic Feet	1,728.0	Cubic Inches
MASS:		
Kilograms	0.005 71	Micas
Grams	0.000 005 71	Micas
Pounds	0.002 590 08	Micas
Slugs	0.083 333 3	Micas
MASS:		
Kilograms	2.204 622 62	Pounds
Grams	0.002 204 622 62	Pounds
Micas	386.0886	Pounds
Slugs	32.174	Pounds
MASS/LENGTH:		
Kilograms/Meter	0.000 145	Micas/Inch
Kilograms/Millimeter	0.145	Micas/Inch
Grams/Centimeter	0.000 014 5	Micas/Inch
Grams/Millimeter	0.000 145	Micas/Inch
Pounds/Inch	0.002 590 08	Micas/Inch
Slugs/Foot	0.006 944	Micas/Inch

*To convert units from the third column to the first column, divide by the conversion factors.

Appendix B
(continued)

Conversion Factors*		
MULTIPLY	**BY**	**TO OBTAIN**
MASS/AREA:		
Kilograms/Square Meter	0.000 003 683 96	Micas/Square Inch
Kilograms/Square Millimeter	3.683 96	Micas/Square Inch
Grams/Square Centimeter	0.000 036 839 6	Micas/Square Inch
Grams/Square Millimeter	0.003 683 96	Micas/Square Inch
Pounds/Square Inch	0.002 590 08	Micas/Square Inch
Slugs/Square Foot	0.000 578 704	Micas/Square Inch
MASS/VOLUME:		
Kilograms/Cubic Meter	0.000 000 093 573	Micas/Cubic Inch
Grams/Cubic Meter	0.000 000 000 093 573	Micas/Cubic Inch
Grams/Cubic Centimeter	0.000 093 573	Micas/Cubic Inch
Pounds/Cubic Foot	0.000 001 499	Micas/Cubic Inch
MASS/VOLUME:		
Pounds/Cubic Inch	0.002 590 08	Micas/Cubic Inch
Slugs/Cubic Foot	0.000 048 2	Micas/Cubic Inch
Kilograms/Cubic Meter	0.062 427 96	Pounds/Cubic Foot
Kilograms/Cubic Meter	0.000 036 127 292	Pounds/Cubic Inch
Grams/Cubic Centimeter	62.427 96	Pounds/Cubic Foot
Grams/Cubic Centimeter	0.036 127 292	Pounds/Cubic Inch
FORCE:		
Newtons	0.2248	Pounds-force
Dynes	0.000 002 248	Pounds-force
PRESSURE:		
Newtons/Square Meter	0.000 145 04	Pounds-force/Sq. In.
Newtons/Square Millimeter	145.04	Pounds-force/Sq. In.
Dynes/Square Centimeter	0.000 014 504	Pounds-force/Sq. In.
Dynes/Square Millimeter	0.001 450 4	Pounds-force/Sq. In.
Atmospheres	14.696	Pounds-force/Sq. In.
TEMPERATURE:		
°Celsius	(9/5)°C + 32	°Fahrenheit
°Fahrenheit	(5/9)(°F − 32)	°Celsius
°Celsius	°C + 273.15	Kelvin
°Fahrenheit	°F + 459.67	°Rankine
°Rankine	(5/9)°R	Kelvin
Kelvin	(9/5)K	°Rankine

*To convert dimensional units from the third column to the first column, divide by the conversion factors.

Appendix C

PROPERTIES OF STRING MAKING MATERIALS

Material	Young's Modulus of Elasticity E psi	Tensile Strength psi	Weight Density W lbf/in^3	Mass Density ρ mica/in^3	Notes
	$\times 10^3$	$\times 10^3$			
Gut	300–650	35–105	0.052	0.00013468	1
Nylon 612 Monofilament, 'Tynex'	560	56	0.039	0.00010101	2
Nylon 066 Monofilament	600	61	0.041	0.00010619	2
Copper (CDA 110), Piano bass string wrap wire	17,000	35–66	0.323	0.00083660	3
Copper (CDA 162), Cadmium Copper	17,000	38–100	0.321	0.00083142	3
Bronze (CDA 220) 90/10: Copper/Zinc	17,000	40–90	0.318	0.00082365	3
Bronze (CDA 226) 88/12: Copper/Zinc	17,000	40–97	0.317	0.00082106	3
Brass (CDA 230) 85/15: Copper/Zinc	17,000	41–105	0.316	0.00081847	3
Brass (CDA 240) 80/20: Copper/Zinc	16,000	44–125	0.313	0.00081070	3
Phosphor Bronze (CDA 510) 95/5: Copper/Tin	16,000	50–140	0.320	0.00082883	3
Phosphor Bronze (CDA 521) 92/8: Copper/Tin	16,000	60–140	0.318	0.00082365	3
Music Wire, High-Carbon Spring Steel	30,000	300–400	0.283	0.00073299	4

Properties of String Making Materials

Copper, brass, bronze, and steel tensile strength values depend on the *temper* and the *diameter* of the wire. For metal wires, there are three general classifications: soft, hard, and spring temper. In general, thin diameter wires have higher tensile strength than thick wires. The drawing process through increasingly smaller dies creates a greater alignment of molecules, which results in greater elasticity and strength for thin wires. When in doubt, or for preliminary calculations, use average tensile strength values.

1. Bell, A.J., and Firth, I.M. (1986). The physical properties of gut musical instrument strings. *Acustica* **60**, No. 1, pp. 87–89.

The weight and mass density figures represent average values. Young's modulus of elasticity and tensile strength figures represent low psi values to high psi values, which were measured with gut strings that varied from a wide diameter of 0.099 in. (2.51 mm) to a narrow diameter of 0.020 in. (.52 mm), respectively. The authors add the following qualifying statement:

"It is well known that for wire and nylon strings, thinner strings tend to have higher values of tensile strength than the thicker ones. This is due to the manufacturing process, where the wire or nylon is drawn or extruded through a die, producing a stronger outer layer — or "skin" — where the material has been subjected to greater microscopic alignment. This skin represents a greater fraction of the cross-section of the area in thinner strings giving them a larger tensile strength.

"At first sight this should not be the case for gut strings as no die is used in the manufacturing process. Furthermore, one might expect the thinner gut strings to be weakened, because the effects of centerless grinding (which is used in the manufacture of these strings) would break a greater fraction of the fibers in the strings. The results do not substantiate this argument, for thinner gut strings have a higher tensile strength than the thicker strings. The reason for the enhanced tensile strength for thinner strings is not known, but it could be that the varnish that is applied to the strings during manufacture strengthens the surfaces. Further research is being conducted to investigate the effect of the varnish on the strength of the string."

Readers who wish to use these tensile strength values in the context of antique instruments should probably use relatively low values in the 20,000–90,000 psi range because (1) varnish was not used, and (2) the process of curing, selecting, and manufacturing gut strings was not controlled with sophisticated machinery.

2. Du Pont Bulletin: "Tynex 612 Nylon Filament." Du Pont Company, Wilmington, Delaware.

3. *Standards Handbook, Part 2 — Alloy Data, Wrought Copper and Copper Alloy Mill Products*, Eighth Edition, Copper Development Association, Inc., Greenwich, Connecticut, 1985.

4. (A) Blevins, R.D. (1979). *Formulas for Natural Frequency and Mode Shape*, Reprint, p. 437 Krieger Publishing Company, Malabar, Florida, 1993.

This page gives detailed values for E for five different kinds of steel.

(B) *Steel Music Wire Bulletin*, Schaff Piano Supply Company, Lake Zurich, Illinois.

These are average tensile strength values. In Appendix D, detailed tensile strength values were compiled by the Schaff Piano Supply Company, Lake Zurich, Illinois.

Appendix D

SPRING STEEL MUSIC WIRE TENSILE STRENGTH AND BREAK STRENGTH VALUES

Size/Gage	Decimal Diameters in.	Tensile Strength Range psi	Break Strength Range lbf
		$\times 10^3$	
4/0	0.006	415–455	11.7–12.9
3/0	0.007	407–447	15.7–17.2
2/0	0.008	399–434	20.1–21.8
1/0	0.009	393–428	25.0–27.2
1	0.010	387–422	30.4–33.1
2	0.011	382–417	36.3–39.6
3	0.012	377–412	42.6–46.6
4	0.013	373–408	49.5–54.2
5	0.014	369–404	57–62
6	0.016	362–392	73–79
7	0.018	356–386	91–98
8	0.020	350–380	110–119
9	0.022	345–375	131–143
10	0.024	341–371	154–168
11	0.026	337–367	179–195
12	0.029	333–363	220–240
12 ½	0.030	330–360	233–254
13	0.031	330–360	249–272
13 ½	0.032	327–357	263–287
14	0.033	327–357	280–305
14 ½	0.034	324–354	294–321
15	0.035	324–354	312–341
15 ½	0.036	321–351	327–357
16	0.037	321–351	345–377
16 ½	0.038	318–348	361–395
17	0.039	318–348	380–416
17 ½	0.040	315–345	396–434
18	0.041	315–345	416–455
18 ½	0.042	313–343	434–475
19	0.043	313–343	455–498
19 ½	0.044	313–343	476–522
20	0.045	309–339	491–539
20 ½	0.046	309–339	514–563
21	0.047	309–339	536–588
21 ½	0.048	306–336	554–608
22	0.049	306–336	577–634
23	0.051	303–333	619–680
24	0.055	300–330	713–784
25	0.059	296–326	809–891
26	0.063	293–323	913–1007

Appendix E

PROPERTIES OF BAR MAKING MATERIALS

Material	Young's Modulus of Elasticity E psi	Weight Density W lbf/ft^3	Weight Density W lbf/in^3	Mass Density ρ mica/in^3	Notes
	$\times 10^3$				
Honduras rosewood, *Dalbergia stevensonii*	2,900–3,200	66	0.0382	0.00009894	1
Brazilian tulipwood, *Dalbergia frutescens*	2,500–2,800	59	0.0341	0.00008832	2
Brazilian rosewood, *Dalbergia nigra*	2,100–2,400	52	0.0301	0.00007796	3
East Indian rosewood, *Dalbergia latifolia*	1,900–2,200	51	0.0295	0.00007641	4
Pernambuco (Brazilwood), *Caesalpinia echinata*	3,500–3,800	72	0.0417	0.00010801	5
Macawood (Hormigo), *Platymiscium pinnatum*	3,200–3,500	70	0.0405	0.00010490	6
African padauk, *Pterocarpus soyauxii*	2,000–2,300	49	0.0284	0.00007356	7
Sitka spruce, *Picea sitchensis*	1,500–1,700	26	0.0150	0.00003885	8
Osage orange, *Maclura pomifera*	1,800–2,100	55	0.0318	0.00008236	9
White oak, *Quercus alba*	1,800–2,000	42	0.0243	0.00006294	10
Aluminum 2024-T4, Vibraphone Alloy	10,600	173	0.1001	0.00025927	11
Aluminum 2024-T3, Seamless Tube Alloy	10,600	173	0.1001	0.00025927	12
Aluminum 6061, Conventional Alloy	10,000	169	0.0978	0.00025331	13
Steel SAE 1042, Orchestra Bells Alloy	30,000	489	0.2830	0.00073299	14
Glass	9,000	156	0.0903	0.00023388	15

Properties of Bar Making Materials

Wood Section

Values of Young's modulus of elasticity for wood represent average properties obtained from my own dynamic vibration tests. (See Section 6.16.) Weight densities for wood also represent average properties based on a kiln-dried moisture content between 6–8%.

1. Honduras rosewood is the finest marimba wood available. Mature stock has a deep red-brown color with black stripes.

2. Brazilian tulipwood is also very good. For marimba bars, it should have many dark red stripes. Avoid cream-colored beige stock with only a few pink stripes. In general, mature rosewood has a dark color, which signifies that the stock originates from the inner heartwood area of the tree. Light-colored rosewood comes from immature trees, or from the outer sapwood area of the log. This wood is relatively soft and wet, and lacks density and elasticity.

3. Although Brazilian rosewood is acceptable, it does not have high elastic properties, and therefore is not an ideal material for percussion instruments. It is very rare and expensive, and cherished by guitar makers for its strength and beauty.

4. East Indian rosewood has a deep purple color and is readily available. It is very unstable and produces a weak, non-resonant tone.

5. Better than Brazilian tulipwood, pernambuco is the second best wood for marimba bars. Extremely resilient, it is prized by string players as the finest wood for bows. The wood from mature trees is deep orange to deep red, and has an iridescent sheen. Avoid brown to black, or light orange colored stock. The former indicates that it is too heavy, and the latter, that it is too light, which means that the wood will not resonate very well.

6. Macawood, also known as Hormigo, Granadillo, and Quira, is one of the most popular marimba woods used throughout Mexico and Guatemala. Mature stock has a deep brown color with black stripes.

7. Padauk is classified as a medium resonant wood. It has a dark red to brown color. For marimba bars, the grain should be very close and have only a few open pores.

8. In spruce, the longitudinal speed of sound

$$c_{\text{L}} = \sqrt{\frac{E}{\rho}}$$

can exceed that of steel. Sitka spruce is greatly valued by shipbuilders for its flexibility and strength. European spruce (*Picea abies*) is the finest wood for violin and guitar tops, and is used in the construction of piano soundboards. Large spruce boards make excellent bass marimba bars.

9. Osage orange, when properly aged and kiln dried, is one of the best domestic hardwoods for xylophone bars. Although it cannot be compared to rosewood, pernambuco, or macawood, it does have a good musical tone. Unfortunately, most logs are rather small.

10. White oak and its heavier cousin, live oak, is an inexpensive and readily available domestic hardwood perfect for children's instruments. When played with hard mallets it has a very bright, clear tone.

Metal Section

11. (A) Moore, J.L. (1970). *Acoustics of Bar Percussion Instruments*, p. 19. Ph.D. dissertation printed and distributed by University Microfilms, Inc., Ann Arbor, Michigan.

According to Moore, Musser Division of Ludwig Industries uses this material for the manufacture of their vibe bars.

(B) U.S. Business and Defense Services Administration (1956). *Materials Survey: Aluminum*, pp. VI–17, VI–18, VI–19. Department of Commerce, Washington, D.C.

These three pages list Young's modulus of elasticity and weight density values for all aluminum alloys in Appendix E.

12. Erv Wilson cites this material in the construction of his Tubulong instruments. Unpublished correspondence, 1992.

13. This is the most inexpensive aluminum available for experimentation.

14. *Acoustics of Bar Percussion Instruments*, p. 20.

15. Plate glass 1/4 in. thick has very good resonance. This also applies to marble slabs. Fine tuning is difficult and may require diamond tools and a lapping machine. However, untuned plate-glass bars cut to size in a glass shop sound very pleasing when played with large, soft mallets.

Appendix F

PROPERTIES OF SOLIDS

Solid	Young's Modulus of Elasticity E psi	Weight Density W lbf/in^3	Mass Density ρ mica/in^3	Longitudinal Wave Speed c_L in/s	c_L m/s	Notes
	$\times 10^3$					
Gold	11,600	0.697	0.00180529	80,160	2036	1
Iron	28,500	0.284	0.00073558	196,837	5000	1
Lead	2,000	0.409	0.00105934	43,451	1104	1
Nickel	30,000	0.322	0.00083401	189,660	4817	1
Platinum	21,300	0.775	0.00200731	103,011	2616	1
Silver	11,000	0.379	0.00098164	105,857	2689	1
Tin	6,500	0.264	0.00068378	97,499	2476	1
Zinc	15,300	0.258	0.00066824	151,314	3843	2
Brick	3,500	0.065	0.00016836	144,183	3662	2
Concrete (porous)	250	0.022	0.00005698	66,238	1682	3
Concrete (light)	540	0.047	0.00012173	66,604	1692	3
Concrete (dense)	3,800	0.083	0.00021498	132,951	3377	3
Plaster	630	0.061	0.00015799	63,147	1604	3
Plywood	780	0.022	0.00005698	117,000	2972	3
Plexiglas, Cast Acrylic	450	0.042	0.00010878	64,318	1634	4

Properties of Solids

1. Boyer, H.E., and Gall, T.L., Editors (1984). *Metals Handbook, Desk Edition*, pp. **1**-44 – **1**-48. American Society for Metals, Metals Park, Ohio, 1989.

2. Lide, D.R., Editor (1918). *CRC Handbook of Chemistry and Physics*, 73rd ed., p. **12**-147, **14**-31. CRC Press, Boca Raton, Florida, 1992.

3. Cremer, L., Heckl, M., and Ungar, E.E. (1973). *Structure-Borne Sound*, 2nd ed., p. 242. Springer-Verlag, Berlin and New York, 1988.

4. *Cadillac Plastic Buyer's Guide*, pp. 17–18. Cadillac Plastic and Chemical Company, Troy, Michigan, 1986.

Appendix G

PROPERTIES OF LIQUIDS

Liquid	Temperature °F	Ratio of Specific Heats γ	Weight Density W lbf/in^3	Mass Density ρ mica/in^3	Longitudinal Wave Speed c_L m/s	in/s	Notes
Mercury	68	1.13	0.4913	0.00127251	1450	57,087	1
Water (fresh)	68	1.004	0.0361	0.00009350	1481	58,307	1
Water (sea)	55	1.01	0.0371	0.00009609	1500	59,055	1

Properties of Liquids

1. Kinsler, L.W., and Frey, AR. (1950). *Fundamentals of Acoustics*, 2nd ed., p. 503. John Wiley & Sons, Inc., New York, 1962.

Appendix H

PROPERTIES OF GASES

AT 1 ATMOSPHERE OF PRESSURE, OR 14.696 PSI

Gas	Temperature °F	Ratio of Specific Heats γ	Weight Density W lbf/in³	Mass Density ρ mica/in³	Longitudinal Wave Speed c_L m/s	Longitudinal Wave Speed c_L in/s	Notes
Air	32	1.402	0.0000467	0.000000121	331.6	13,055	1
Air	68	1.402	0.0000436	0.000000113	343	13,504	1
Carbon dioxide	68	1.299	0.0000660	0.000000171	268	10,551	2
Helium	68	1.666	0.0000062	0.000000016	994	39,134	2
Hydrogen	68	1.408	0.0000031	0.000000008	1292	50,866	2
Nitrogen	68	1.402	0.0000421	0.000000109	349	13,740	2
Oxygen	68	1.396	0.0000479	0.000000124	327	12,874	2
Steam	212	1.320	0.0000212	0.000000055	477	18,780	3

Properties of Gases

1. Kinsler, L.W., and Frey, A.R. (1950). *Fundamentals of Acoustics*, 2nd ed., p. 503. John Wiley & Sons, Inc., New York, 1962.

2. Lemon, H.B., and Ference, M., Jr. (1943). *Analytical Experimental Physics*, p. 191. The University of Chicago Press, Chicago, Illinois.

3. Towne, D.H. (1967). *Wave Phenomena*, p. 444. Dover Publications, Inc., New York, 1988.

Index

B

F

G

Q

R

T

U